UNIVERSITY CASEBOOK SERIES

FEDERAL PUBLIC LAND AND RESOURCES LAW

FIFTH EDITION

by

GEORGE CAMERON COGGINS
Frank Edwards Tyler Professor of Law
University of Kansas

CHARLES F. WILKINSON
Moses Lasky Professor of Law
University of Colorado

JOHN D. LESHY
Distinguished Professor of Law
University of California
Hastings College of the Law

NEW YORK, NEW YORK
FOUNDATION PRESS

2002

Mat #40020961

COPYRIGHT © 1981, 1987, 1993, 2001 FOUNDATION PRESS
COPYRIGHT © 2002 By FOUNDATION PRESS
       395 Hudson Street
       New York, NY 10014
       Phone Toll Free 1–877–888–1330
       Fax (212) 367–6799
       fdpress.com

ISBN 1–58778–391–6

TEXT IS PRINTED ON 10% POST
CONSUMER RECYCLED PAPER

TO
JEAN COGGINS
ANN AMUNDSON
HELEN M. SANDALLS

*

PREFACE

Public land and resources law has been basically reordered in modern times. Among other developments, discussed more fully in chapter one, doctrines involving resources that traditionally have been treated separately are coalescing, and a variety of concerns reflecting the public interest are being infused into the legal process.

We have attempted to synthesize these developments in this book. It has been customary to treat some public land issues in separate courses, such as water law or mining law; this volume is not an attempt to supercede any of those specialized subjects. Rather, in our view, modern public land law demands a coordinated treatment of the various legal doctrines applicable to all public resources and their interrelationships.

We believe that this book, though a considerable departure, nevertheless is the logical extension of previous casebooks on natural resources. In 1951, Clyde Martz published CASES ON NATURAL RESOURCES, the first comprehensive effort to organize and integrate teaching materials on that subject. The Martz casebook was succeeded and updated in 1965 by Professors Trelease, Bloomenthal, and Geraud in the publication of CASES AND MATERIALS ON NATURAL RESOURCES. These pioneering casebooks included some public issues, but both were largely devoted to "private law;" that is, they dealt primarily with issues relating to whether a private entity could use or acquire ownership of federal land or resources. In each, heavy emphasis was placed on the fields of water law, mining law, and oil and gas law. That neither work paid much attention to "public law" or "public interest litigation" is not a criticism because, for all practical purposes, such public law issues had not yet surfaced on the public lands. We have made a determined effort to outline the historical context of recent disputes, but the great bulk of cases reprinted in this volume were decided since 1970. The legal doctrines that they represent have supplemented or replaced prior law.

This book's approach to federal land and resources law is the product of many years' development. Each of these editors independently concluded that major public resource themes were related and could be grouped around the concept of federal land ownership. Each of us taught courses in 1975 that sought to investigate federal regulation of the federal resources. Those crude efforts gradually evolved through the development of separate classroom materials until several colleagues familiar with our efforts urged us to pool our resources, natural and otherwise. With assistance from the Rocky Mountain Mineral Law Foundation, we did so, making available the first edition of this casebook in 1980.

The more we study this field, the more it becomes apparent that public land law has been fundamentally altered and that changes are accelerating. Even so, there is a commonality in the usual issues that cuts across traditional subject matter lines. Federal vs. state regulatory power, federal reserved rights or interests, multiple use management problems, withdrawals and reservations, judicial review notions—all of these are common threads running through legal consideration of all of the major resources. Recent enactments recognize and further the unification of federal natural resources law.

The first four chapters are devoted to the historical background, the constitutional underpinnings, and the administrative systems governing public land policy. Chapter one is an overview of federal lands and resources; it concludes with several perspectives on the bases of federal land policy. The history of public land law, treated in chapter two, remains a matter of vital interest today because ancient notions, doctrines, and problems refuse to be relegated to molding archives: several sections conclude with recent Supreme Court decisions and another outlines the contemporary "Sagebrush Rebellion," a movement rooted in history whereby some states have sought to divest federal ownership of lands within their borders. The chapter is lengthy, reflecting our view that history is a fundamental component of modern public land law.

Chapter three follows by analyzing the respective constitutional powers of the federal and state governments over activities on the public lands. Although the federal government usually can preempt state authority, the more difficult question to be investigated is whether, in any particular instance, Congress intended to do so. The fourth chapter introduces the student to several basic problems that permeate all that follows: executive withdrawals and reservations; judicial review of land management agency decisions; and administrative planning mandated by novel statutes, especially the National Environmental Policy Act of 1969.

The remaining seven chapters take up the law of the seven major federal resources in this order: water, minerals, timber, range, wildlife, recreation, and preservation. Case selection and placement is necessarily arbitrary to some degree, for resource conflicts almost always involve more than one resource or value. Thus, a case in which a timber contract is enjoined because it would alter the wilderness characteristics of an area could as well go into the Timber Resource chapter as the Preservation chapter, and so forth on down the line. The second maxim of ecology, that everything is related to everything else, is both trite and true.

We have strived to make this treatment as readable and enjoyable as we think it is worthwhile. It is, of course, just a casebook and subject to all of the limitations of that art form, so complete success is virtually impossible. But the subject matter itself, from the exciting Gold Rush to the progress of settlement by homesteading, from the great railroad land grabs to the episodic range wars, from the Alaska Pipeline to the Snail Darter, cannot help but interest and delight all but the most jaded of students.

A word about the editing form and style used throughout. We have sought to be rigorous in eliminating irrelevant or tangential matters. Discussions of repetitive procedural defenses, common statements of law (particularly boilerplate recitations on NEPA), and string citations were more often than not axed. Thus, any case or article reproduced below is not necessarily complete—it probably is not—and the researching student is advised to consult the original.

Most original footnotes have also been omitted. Where footnotes are retained, they still bear the court's or author's original number. Footnotes inserted by the editors are preceded by a lower case letter instead of a number. Textual deletions are indicated by "* * *," but omissions of authorities have not been signalled.

We of course accept full responsibility for the inevitable errors, omissions, and lack of foresight commonly associated with these ventures. We would caution that some selectivity on the part of the instructor is assumed; the materials in these pages are more than is necessary for a normal one-semester course.

Expressisng gratitude to those who have assisted an endeavor such as this is a dangerous business, for often one is left out who should be included. With a blanket "thanks" to the many who have contributed, we single out first our research assistants. Debra Arnett, Michael Axline, Kurt Burkholder, Derb Carter, Susan Driver, Parthenia Blessing Evans, and Martin Miller all contributed to the first edition. At that time, we predicted that all would make their own marks on public land law and, six years later, our forecast has proved to be accurate. We give our thanks and our similar high regard to those students who worked on this edition: Alexandra Callam, Jeremy Firestone, Sandy Hoffman, Stephanie Matthews, Doris Nagel, and Matt Selby. The typing was done by Marcea Metzler, Joan Wellman, and Mary Jo Guy. Dean Mike Davis of the University of Kansas has provided us with invaluable support over the years. Dean Chapin Clark of Oregon walked the extra mile to provide us with resources for the first edition. Professor Wilkinson was a visiting professor at the University of Michigan Law School during the preparation of this second edition and both of us extend our appreciation for the inordinately generous assistance provided by Associate Dean Edward H. Cooper and Dean Terrance Sandalow. We are also grateful to the Rocky Mountain Mineral Law Foundation for its support, and the advice of its members, on both the first and second editions. Finally, we appreciate the helpful suggestions of several colleagues, including Gail L. Achterman, Harrison C. Dunning, Kent Frizzell, David H. Getches, Arthur D. Smith, Sally K. Fairfax, H. Michael Anderson, Maryanne Chambers, Cameron LaFollette, and Darius M. Adams.

GEORGE CAMERON COGGINS
CHARLES F. WILKINSON

October, 1986

*

PREFACE TO THE THIRD EDITION

With this edition, the original editors welcome a third editor, John D. Leshy, who has been involved in public lands issues for two decades; almost five years with the Natural Resources Defense Council, three-plus years with the Department of the Interior, and the last dozen with Arizona State University's College of Law. Prior users will find intact the focus and much of the organization of the first two editions. The discussion of editing form and style in the preceding preface is still pertinent. The material has been thoroughly updated and reworked to reflect emerging trends as much as possible; for example, a new section on access has been added at the end of chapter two to capture some of the burgeoning litigation in this area; and a new section on takings has been added at the end of chapter three. We have tried to keep the length manageable (only slightly longer than the second edition) and to maintain the teachable quality of the earlier editions. As always we welcome feedback from users.

Thanks in the preparation of this edition go to Dean Richard Morgan of the A.S.U. College of Law for his support; Donna Larson Bennett, Marianne Alcorn, and Susan Brodsky of the A.S.U. College of Law Library for indefatigable assistance; A.S.U. law student research assistants Michael Brown and Nancy LaPlaca; Carolyn Landry and Fran Kendall for help in preparing the manuscript; Kaid Benfield, Grove Burnett, Joe Feller, Larry McBride, Zygmunt Plater, Deborah Reames and Johanna Wald for some helpful information; and to Helen and Alec for their patience and support.

George Cameron Coggins
Charles F. Wilkinson
John D. Leshy

June 1992

*

PREFACE TO THE FIFTH EDITION

An unusually large number of important judicial opinions have made their appearance in the area of federal public land and resources law in the last couple of years. A flurry of activity at the end of the Clinton Administration produced a number of initiatives worthy of treatment, including a spate of new national monuments and new regulations on national forest roadless areas, national forest planning, hardrock mining on public lands, and the use of snowmobiles and personal watercraft in the national park system. The Park Service also adopted new policies interpreting its Organic Act. The Bush (II) Administration's reexamination of a number of these initiatives furnishes some nice opportunities for exploring transitions in federal land policymaking. All these are addressed in this new edition.

Besides being thoroughly updated, this edition reflects some substantial reorganization. A new chapter 5 pulls together material on the public trust doctrine, the National Environmental Policy Act (NEPA), and the Endangered Species Act (ESA), and also provides a new generic overview of federal land management agencies' planning processes. In earlier editions NEPA and, to a lesser extent, the ESA, were treated in cases scattered throughout the last half of the book. This consolidation has enabled the subsequent subject matter chapters, especially on minerals, timber and grazing, to be reduced somewhat in size. New sections have been added on contract rights and remedies (at the end of chapter 3); federal hydropower relicensing (in chapter 6); and the Migratory Bird Treaty Act, recently a very fertile field for litigation (in chapter 10). In addition, more materials on cultural resource preservation (addressing the increasing attention being paid to Native American concerns) have been added to chapter 12.

While modestly shorter than the previous edition, we believe the new material will provide users more flexibility regarding coverage. In particular, this edition reflects the increasingly national scope of federal lands and resources law. Footnotes inserted by the editors are indicated by an asterisk; footnotes retained from original court opinions or other excerpted material bear their original number. Textual deletions are indicated by "* * *," but omissions of authorities are not generally indicated.

Thanks in the preparation of this edition go to Kelly McDonald, a third year student at Hastings College of the Law, who provided estimable research assistance, and to a number of colleagues and friends who made good suggestions and provided some helpful information: Molly McUsic, Michael Anderson, Bob Keiter, Federico Cheever, David Watts, Bruce Kramer, Henry Smith, Joe Feller, Patty Beneke, Ken Weiner, Armin Rosencranz, Amy Kelley, Peter Appel, Bob Anderson, and Jamie Grodsky. And much appreciation to Helen for her toleration of this enterprise. Errors of course are ours (especially Leshy's). As always we welcome feedback from users (send to leshyj@uchastings.edu).

GEORGE CAMERON COGGINS
CHARLES F. WILKINSON
JOHN D. LESHY

May 2002

SUMMARY OF CONTENTS

*

TABLE OF CONTENTS

*

TABLE OF CASES

Principal cases are in bold type. Non-principal cases are in roman type. References are to Pages.

*

Federal Public Land and Resources Law

*

CHAPTER 1

PUBLIC LAND LAW: AN INTRODUCTION

A. THE FIELD OF PUBLIC LAND LAW

Many people are unaware of the full extent to which the United States government owns or controls land. Many are generally familiar with the flagship national parks, the "crown jewels" of the federal land holdings. Those who have gazed into the Grand Canyon, marveled at the natural wonders of Yellowstone, or found incomparable beauty in Yosemite Valley may have breathed a prayer of thanksgiving that some of our predecessors had the wisdom to protect those unique areas for the awe of generations then unborn. But the national parks are merely the tip of the federal iceberg: they account for only a part of the lands managed by the National Park Service, which in turn are only about 12% of the Nation's total federal land. Many people may have visited national forests without realizing that they are in a management system separate from the national parks, in the charge of a different agency (the U.S. Forest Service) in a different department (Agriculture rather than Interior). Only in the West and in Alaska are the existence and activities of the Bureau of Land Management (BLM) common knowledge, but this little-publicized agency controls more federal land than any other, nearly one-tenth of the total national land surface. Most citizens also are at least vaguely aware that a variety of federal agencies own land for some purpose, from post offices to reservoirs, from military forts to wildlife refuges, and from atomic reactor sites to office buildings. In all, the United States owns in fee about 650 million acres, or about 28% of all land in the country.

Public land law is at the core of the history of national economic development, but it encompasses far more than mundane legalities. Federal land policy impelled homesteaders to seek new lives, validated gold rush mining claims, brought about the range wars, and helped justify construction of massive water projects in the West. Even today the livelihoods of pipeline roughnecks, subsistence hunters, loggers, cattle barons, mineral prospectors, and other latterday rugged individualists remain intertwined with public land law. Contemporary concern over the uses and abuses of the public lands and natural resources goes much deeper than interest in romantic exploits. Lord Macaulay long ago noted that the true test of American institutions would come when the free public domain was exhausted and an increased population competed for ownership of the land and its depleted resources. That time has long since arrived, and the competition is intense. The controversies, large and small, that contribute

1

to growth and direction of federal land and resources law provide some of the most entertaining and informative studies in all of legal literature.

A brief introductory note on terminology [from George C. Coggins & Robert Glicksman, 1 PUBLIC NATURAL RESOURCES LAW § 1.9 (2001)]:

"Public domain" has had two traditional meanings. It referred, first, to lands acquired by the United States from other sovereigns, including Indian tribes, and still federally-owned. This meaning contrasts with "acquired lands," which were once in private or state ownership. "Public domain" also took on the connotation of "lands open to entry and settlement." This meaning is the opposite of "reserved" and "withdrawn" lands. As virtually all federal lands are now off-limits to traditional entry and settlement, this [term is an artifact]. * * *

"Acquired lands" are lands the United States acquired from private or state owners by gift, purchase, exchange, or condemnation. In most but not all cases, such lands actually have been "reacquired," because the United States previously had purchased or won them from foreign and Indian sovereigns. Distinguishing between lands because of ownership origins that go back over a century is a policy with little to recommend it, but some statutes and judicial opinions maintain the distinction. * * *

The meaning of the term "public lands" has varied greatly. In common parlance, the term simply means all lands owned by the United States. Matters are not that simple, however. At some times, the term was synonymous with both meanings of "public domain" described * * * above. Its common law definition came to be "unreserved and unappropriated public domain lands open to entry, settlement, and appropriation." But the common law meaning, never precise, has been superseded to a considerable extent by statutory definitions. In 1920, for instance, Congress defined "public lands" for purposes of federal power development to mean unreserved lands "subject to private appropriation and disposal." Congress in 1976 complicated the matter further by defining public lands as "any land and interest in land owned by the United States * * * and administered by the Bureau of Land Management, without regard to how the United States acquired ownership," except Indian and offshore lands. A 1979 statute defines public lands as all federally-owned lands for limited purposes.

The terms "public lands" and "federal lands" may also include less than full fee interests, such as severed mineral estates. They usually do not, however, refer to submerged lands off the seacoasts (over which the United States asserts jurisdiction but not title), or lands held in trust for Indians. Like so much of public land law, in other words, consistency is not a hallmark and generalization is hazardous.

This book is organized around the concepts that the public lands and the resources they contain are, indeed, public, and that public land law is an expression of and is guided by the public interest. Society through its elected representatives professes to see virtue in many things; for example, it wishes to have both energy production and wilderness preservation. Through such competing impulses must come decisions as to how individual tracts of public land will be managed. Of course as the country and its economy have changed radically over the years, the issues and particulars and forums of public land disputes have likewise changed, as has the nature of public land law. But the one enduring element is the argument over what course of action will best serve the public interest.

1.   TRADITIONAL PUBLIC LAND LAW: PRIVATE RIGHTS IN CONFLICT

It took the United States a long time to fully embrace the notion that large tracts of federal lands should be retained in federal ownership and managed by federal agencies for the general public interest. For a century and a half, public land law existed basically to facilitate the disposal of federal lands and resources into state and private hands, and several thousand separate statutes were adopted over the years concerned with disposition of the federal lands. These were, in turn, interpreted and applied in thousands of court cases and administrative rulings. It is not, then, difficult to see that the practice of public natural resources law for a long time approached the arcane. Moreover, it was common to ignore or evade public land laws in the Nation's restless expansion across the continent.

Starting a little more than a century ago, the United States began reserving ever-increasing tracts of land for permanent retention in federal ownership, and this began to change the nature of public land law. From a single-minded emphasis on disposal, it grew to mean those statutes, rules, practices, and common law doctrines which defined who has a right to own or use a parcel of federal land or its tangible resources. Contests no longer exclusively concerned individuals or entities contesting between themselves for use of federal lands, such as now-legendary contests between cattle and sheep ranchers over priority to graze the public domain, mining claim-jumping and resultant litigation, and disputes between agricultural surface owners and holders of subsurface mineral rights.

In the old days, the cast of characters was usually rather small; most involved relatively simple private property disputes. In these private fights, the government and the direct public interest became involved only indirectly. Increasingly over time, disputes came to engage the government as landowner, and the question of how to resolve collisions between private rights and public responsibilities. Resolution of these questions continues to be a main business of practicing lawyers, and this volume presents the basic legal doctrines governing private interests in the public resources.

2.   MODERN FEDERAL LAND AND RESOURCES LAW: THE SEARCH FOR THE PUBLIC INTEREST

During the last few decades, the central place of private rights, private disputes, and private law as components of overall public land law has been partly superseded by overriding public considerations. Whether viewed as a new direction in traditional public land management, or as an instance of counterproductive federal overregulation, modern federal land and resources law encompasses far more than questions of property rights. The natural resources lawyer now must be conversant with such subjects as federal land planning, environmental impact statements, competing recreational, preservation, wildlife and cultural values, and other limitations on economic activity. These, in the aggregate, have come to be as important to public land users as classic private contests. Because of this development, Professors Coggins and Glicksman argue that the phrase "public land law"—traditionally referring to laws relating to public domain disposition—is outmoded. To reflect more accurately the modern focus, they suggest the term "public natural resources law." G. Coggins & R. Glicksman, 1 PUBLIC NATURAL RESOURCES LAW § 1.6 (2001).

Modern public land law therefore has become somewhat broader in dimension and more diverse in concept. New disputants with different philosophies have entered oldtime controversies; Congress has changed the statutory framework drastically; and winds of reform periodically sweep through land management agencies. Throughout the question has always been to determine what is the public interest in handling these vast public resources. In this search for the public interest in myriad factual settings, no one simple answer can suffice. A modern public land dispute may arise in many forms, such as:

— should cattle or wild horses or elk be removed from an overgrazed tract of public land?

— what considerations govern whether to sell timber from a national forest?

— does a hunter have a right of access over an unpatented mining claim?

— should off-road vehicles be banned from certain areas?

— should creation of a wilderness area impliedly override state water laws?

— should a road to a potentially valuable mineral deposit be cut through an area used by grizzly bears for denning?

But, in every such case, the initial inquiries are the same: Where lies the public interest? Who decides where it lies in particular situations? What are the legal and practical consequences of the choice?

Preconceptions of the public interest are hazardous to mental health. To ardent wilderness advocates, wilderness preservation is one of the highest endeavors of organized society. But potential wilderness areas may have supplied the lumber that built wilderness advocates' houses, the materials with which their vehicles are built, and the fuel that makes them go. Few who complain of pollution from the local utility generating plant would readily give up air conditioning altogether. On the other hand, those who espouse production over all else have an equally narrow perspective. There are points of diminishing returns: the oil burned or old growth timber cut now will not be available ten or twenty years from now to fuel even more expansion for us and for our descendants. Further, as society grows richer, it values more than ever things that cannot be readily measured in the marketplace. Many more people now prefer to watch birds than to hunt them. Legislation has gradually come to reflect these public preferences. More and more preservation and recreation lands systems have been created in the past three decades, and more and more lands have been set aside for special, non-economic purposes.

Compared to times past, there are fewer heroes or villains in modern public land controversies, only people with differing conceptions of the public interest. Most state and local politicians now concede that not all federal environmental regulation or public interest litigation is necessarily bad. There is wide consensus that development of some federal natural resources is appropriate if done in an environmentally sound manner. Natural resource extraction industries are generally accepting of (or at least resigned to) the new fabric of legal constraint; increasingly, they seek accommodation. Government has become generally more open and participatory.

Even though the conservation movement won some notable victories in the late 19th century, it is fair to say that non-commodity-oriented interests did not achieve an equal, or even significant, voice until the last few decades. But now they have, and the principal modern controversies examined in this book tend to subordinate private rights to an initial determination of public rights in the decisional process. No longer is the question whether a ski resort should be developed on public land one solely between the developer and the federal agency. No longer is a timbercutting contract in a national forest automatically granted on the rationale that the nation needs lumber. No longer is the condition of BLM grazing lands of concern to ranchers alone. No longer can wildlife and recreation values be ignored in multiple use management. In these and many other disputes over use of public lands, a new class of disputants has successfully challenged all of the old assumptions and ushered in a new era.

This new class is not just the self-styled "public interest" organization. For example, in some cases, private landowners have risen up in litigation against new mines, energy facilities, logging operations, and the like, partly reflecting "not in my backyard" attitudes. Allied to new landowner attitudes is a new aggressiveness on the part of non-consumptive economic users of public lands. Resorts, guides, river outfitters, backpacking equipment manufacturers, and so forth have resisted development of a resource valuable to them as primitive real estate. Growing numbers of economists and political conservatives are calling into question the many federal subsidies afforded to developers of public lands and resources.

Still, many of the largest changes have come about through institutional strategies and actions by established and new environmental organizations. Among the most active and effective organizations are groups like the Sierra Club whose names adorn many of the cases in this book. These organizations alone—and there are dozens of similar if less visible groups—have wrought legislative change, pursued hundreds of successful lawsuits and mobilized considerable public support. Coalitions among otherwise divergent entities are common. In the 1980's, for instance, when a large coal slurry pipeline was proposed to send Wyoming coal to Louisiana, common cause was joined by environmentalists, ranchers (fearing the shipment of scarce western water), and railroads (fearing the loss of lucrative shipping contracts). Overlap and coalitions among organizations are common.

The emergence of so-called public interest guardians has not lessened the role of the traditional economically-oriented disputants. To the contrary, new emphases in the legal processes affecting public land use and management have caused extractive and consumptive industries to redouble their efforts in courts, Congress, and agencies. Groups like the Pacific Legal Foundation and the Mountain States Legal Foundation (where conservative Interior Secretaries James Watt and Gale Norton earned their spurs) have sprung up, financed by industries and conservative individuals to present a more conservative view of the public interest in resource litigation. Some powerful economic interests have large stakes in the direction of public land policy. Oil companies have paid billions of dollars for the privilege of drilling on offshore and other federal lands. Other energy companies have leased much federal coal and coalbed methane. Public utilities rely upon federal fossil fuels, federal dams for hydroelectric power, and federal land for siting generation and transmission facilities. Mining companies jealously guard their statutory right to extract any mineral locatable on the public domain. Timber companies still harvest hundreds of millions of board feet of timber from national forests annually, and many small communities are dependent on such harvesting. Most of the politically powerful cattle and sheep ranchers of the West use federal lands for grazing their stock.

Federal land management agencies are frequently caught in the middle of modern federal land use controversies. Historical missions and practices have been severely eroded by new statutes, and new missions have been charted, but congressional directives often have held out little concrete guidance in concrete situations, and procedural requisites have proliferated. Interests over a wide spectrum forcibly argue that their conception of the public interest should prevail in the circumstances, and all sides are willing to resort to litigation or political processes if dissatisfied with decisional results.

We believe that the student should know how legal rules are fashioned as well as what they are. In fact, the law in this area is an everchanging complex of rules derived from and altered by different sources. Although the final determination usually resides in Congress, each of the three branches of government has and uses the power to alter or upset the result reached in another branch. Throughout this volume are scattered "non-legal" or "quasi-legal" materials affording a glimpse into the interactive and interdisciplinary nature of public land law.

From about 1964 to 1980 a veritable revolution was worked in federal public land law. Hundreds of old United States Code sections were swept away at a stroke. Congress applied planning and environmental mandates to all federal land management agencies. 1964 saw enactment of the

Wilderness Act, and 1968, the Wild & Scenic Rivers Act. Thoroughgoing reform came to the Forest Service, the oldest federal land agency, in the National Forest Management Act of 1976. The Bureau of Land Management finally received a statutory mission in the sweeping Federal Land Policy and Management Act enacted the same year. The Alaska National Interest Lands Conservation Act of 1980 allocated more than 100 million federal acres in Alaska to various conservation systems.

This wave of developments led to a predictable backlash, manifested first in the "Sagebrush Rebellion" of the late 1970s and early 1980s, and later in the short-lived "County Supremacy" movement of the 1990s. In the meantime, the federal agencies plodded on, moving forward to implement these sweeping new mandates and, not surprisingly, finding themselves buffeted both from those who thought the pace was too slow and those who thought it too slow.

At the dawn of the twenty-first century, the western public lands are seeing more than ever controversies growing out of competition among different kinds of recreationists (off-road vehicles versus hikers), and conflicts between recreationists and preservationists. Still, there are throwbacks to earlier eras; a new concern with energy development is putting more pressure on federal lands in Alaska and the Rocky Mountains. There is a massive boom in coalbed methane in Wyoming and a few other parts of the West. Much of the western livestock industry faces curtailment and some of it is very marginal economically. The enormously rich history of public land law and policy leads to only two safe predictions: There will be more change, and it will be interesting.

B. THE FEDERAL LANDS AND RESOURCES

Except for the area of the original thirteen colonies, Texas, and Hawaii, the United States government once owned nearly all of the land within its present borders. The real estate comprising this original "public domain" is probably the richest in the variety and extent of its natural resources of all comparable areas in the world. The forests, farmlands, rivers, mineral wealth, and scenic wonders are of literally inestimable economic, social, and aesthetic value.

Most of the original national legacy passed out of national ownership as the public lands were opened for settlement and development. Easy availability of land was the primary incentive for pioneers, then settlers, to move west and populate the Nation. Each wave of settlers chose the available lands that were then thought to be the most economically valuable. New cities grew up around the ports and many of the strategic river junctions. The heart of public land policy was to promote the small family farm: After the best agricultural lands in the Midwest were settled, the homesteaders moved to the Willamette Valley in Oregon, the Central Valley in California, and other verdant agricultural areas. Prospectors and mining firms claimed the land over the fabulous gold, silver, iron, and copper deposits in areas such as the California Mother Lode country, the

Comstock Lode in Nevada, the Mesabi Range in Minnesota, and Butte in Montana. The timber industry obtained prime timber lands throughout the country; their relatively low-lying lands in the Pacific Northwest remain especially valuable. In this century, reclamation projects were built to irrigate otherwise arid homesteads in the Great Plains, the Great Basin between the Sierra Nevada and Rocky Mountains, and elsewhere.

In the mid–19th century, Congresses and presidents withdrew a few public land parcels from the various programs for disposition into private hands and dedicated—or "reserved"—them for some specific purpose. Reservation for other than military or Indian purposes began haltingly with establishment of Yellowstone National Park in 1872, and "conservation" momentum has grown ever since. Large-scale homesteading ended in 1934, and eventually retention supplanted disposition as official federal public land policy. In the modern era, however, land selection by the State of Alaska and Alaska Natives are taking nearly 150 million acres out of federal ownership. Furthermore, some minor sales or exchanges of lands especially suited for certain forms of non-federal ownership are still authorized. Conversely, some acquisitions of private lands by the federal government likely will continue. On balance, however, today the outlines of the federal landed estate seem reasonably stable, despite periodic proposals for renewed largescale disposition.

While it used to be said that the U.S. owned about one-third of the Nation's total land area of 2.3 billion acres, the Alaska Native and State-hood grants have reduced the proportion somewhat to about 28%, or about 650 million acres. Although federal public lands are located in all states, the highest proportion is found eleven western states (Arizona, California, Colorado, Idaho, Montana, Nevada, New Mexico, Oregon, Utah, Washington, and Wyoming) and especially in Alaska, which still has about 250 million federal acres, or about 38% of all federal lands. All told, federal lands constitute nearly half of the land in the eleven western states in the lower 48 and about two-thirds of the land in Alaska. (Because nearly all of these states have relatively small populations, they still have more non-federal land per capita than states in the east and midwest.) While federal lands are a smaller proportion of total land area in states outside the west, a number of non-western states have sizeable chunks of federal lands; e.g., 4 million acres of Michigan, 3 million acres each in Arkansas, Florida and Minnesota, almost that number in North Carolina and Texas, and more than 2 million in Virginia. Eleven other nonwestern states have more than one million acres of federal land. Federal land and resources law is increasingly national, as the principal cases in this new edition attest, being drawn from all regions of the country.

The federal government also owns major less-than-fee interests. In addition to such holdings as acquired waterfowl easements, the United States retains subsurface mineral interests under some 60 million acres in the West. The federal government asserts sovereignty over the resources of the outer continental shelf, an area of over half a billion acres extending from 3 miles offshore (3 marine leagues off the Florida and Texas coasts) seaward to the edge of the geographic shelf.

Because of the historical pattern of national disposition, the federal lands tend to be relatively more arid and infertile, higher in elevation, and remote from major transportation systems. Nevertheless, such generalizations may prove too much: in fact, immense riches of many kinds remain in federal ownership. The last of several blue-ribbon commissions to study federal land policy, the congressionally created Public Land Law Review Commission, had this to say in its 1970 Report, ONE THIRD OF THE NATION'S LAND (p. 22):

One of the most important characteristics of the public lands is their great diversity. Because of their great range—they are found from the northern tip of Alaska to the southern end of Florida—all kinds of climate conditions are found on them. Arctic cold, rain forest torrents, desert heat, mountain snows, and semitropical littoral conditions are all characteristic of public lands in one area or another.

Great differences in terrain are also typical. The tallest mountain in North America, Mount McKinley in Alaska, is on public lands, as is the tallest mountain in the 48 contiguous states, Mount Whitney in California. But the lowest point in the United States, Death Valley, is also on public lands, as are most of the highest peaks in the White Mountains of New Hampshire and the Appalachians of the southeastern states.

Not all of these lands are mountains and valleys, however. Vast areas of tundra and river deltas in Alaska are flat, marked only with an incredible number of small lakes. Other vast areas in the Great Basin area of Nevada and Oregon are not marked with lakes, but with desert shrubs. Still other areas of rolling timber-covered mountains extend for mile after mile, both in the Pacific Northwest and the Inland Empire of Idaho, eastern Washington, and western Montana, and in the Allegheny, Green, and Ouachita Mountains of Pennsylvania, Vermont, and Arkansas. And still other vast areas are rangelands used for grazing domestic livestock.

However, not all of these public lands can be characterized as vast wild or semideveloped expanses. In many instances, Federal ownership is scattered in relatively small tracts among largely privately owned lands. The condition of the land may still be undeveloped, but our consideration of how the land should be used is necessarily influenced by the scattered nature of the Federal ownership. In some cases, public lands are found almost in the midst of urban areas and here again we must view the use of the lands in relation to the surrounding lands.

The great diversity of these lands is a resource in itself. As needs of the Nation have changed, the public lands have been able to play a changing role in meeting these needs. Whether the demand is for minerals, crop production, timber, or recreation, and whether it is national or regional, the public lands are able to play a role in meeting them.

Comparison of Federal Land With Total Acreage By State as of September 30, 1999
(In Thousands of Acres)

State	Acreage owned by the Federal Government	Acreage of state[1]	Percent owned by Federal Government[2]
Alabama	1,234	32,678	3.8
Alaska	250,281	365,482	62.4
Arizona	32,389	72,688	44.6
Arkansas	3,238	33,599	9.6
California	43,713	100,207	43.6
Colorado	24,239	66,486	36.5
Connecticut	14	3,135	0.5
Delaware	8	1,266	0.6
Dist of Columbia	9	39	22.7
Florida	3,066	34,721	8.8
Georgia	1,864	37,295	5.0
Hawaii	618	4,105	15.1
Idaho	33,079	52,933	62.5
Illinois	574	35,795	1.6
Indiana	501	23,158	2.2
Iowa	195	35,860	0.5
Kansas	673	52,511	1.3
Kentucky	1,234	25,512	4.8
Louisiana	1,159	28,868	4.0
Maine	168	19,848	0.8
Maryland	167	6,319	2.6
Massachusetts	72	5,035	1.4
Michigan	4,079	36,492	11.2
Minnesota	4,206	51,206	8.2
Mississippi	1,647	30,223	5.5
Missouri	2,095	44,248	4.7
Montana	25,783	93,271	27.6
Nebraska	647	49,032	1.3
Nevada	58,226	70,264	82.9
New Hampshire	759	5,769	13.2
New Jersey	119	4,813	2.5
New Mexico	26,626	77,766	34.2
New York	106	30,681	0.3
North Carolina	2,356	31,403	7.5
North Dakota	1,771	44,452	4.0
Ohio	392	26,222	1.5
Oklahoma	1,323	44,088	3.0
Oregon	32,315	61,599	52.5
Pennsylvania	670	28,804	2.3
Rhode Island	4	677	0.6
South Carolina	1,107	19,374	5.7
South Dakota	2,662	48,882	5.4
Tennessee	1,658	26,728	6.2
Texas	2,568	168,218	1.5
Utah	34,005	52,697	64.5
Vermont	372	5,937	6.3
Virginia	2,284	25,496	9.0
Washington	12,152	42,694	28.5
West Virginia	1,178	15,411	7.6
Wisconsin	1,182	35,011	5.3
Wyoming	31,071	62,343	49.8
Total	652,550	2,271,343	27.7

1. Represents the most current data available from the General Services Administration. Does not include inland water.
2. Excludes trust properties
SOURCE: PUBLIC LAND STATISTICS 2000, TABLE 1–3, P. 7

Because the federal government's official policy is generally to retain ownership of most federal lands, the basic legal conflicts are over use, not disposition, of the public resources. In some instances, use of a parcel for development of one resource can be entirely compatible with a different use: timber harvesting can benefit some wildlife and recreation resources by creating meadows beneficial for deer habitat; a wilderness area can provide watershed protection for downstream development; a reclamation project for irrigation purposes can also produce electrical energy and recreation. But sometimes management for one type of purpose is fundamentally inconsistent with other uses. The designation of a tract of federal land as wilderness generally eliminates timber harvesting and mineral development. Developing the mineral resources of another tract may be inconsistent with recreation or timber harvesting or grazing. Logging may impair wildlife and destroy cultural resources, and so forth. Avoiding or resolving such resource conflicts is the overriding problem of modern land law. This book identifies and treats somewhat distinctly seven major resources of the federal lands—water, minerals, timber, range, wildlife, recreation, and preservation. Each deserves its own introduction.

WATER

Water tends to be in the middle of many tough resource use choices. Availability of water has always been a limiting factor for development in many Trans–Mississippi regions. Wallace Stegner, one of the most respected modern commentators on the American west, has observed that the region's aridity and large concentration of public lands are the two most distinctive features of western society. See W. Stegner, THE SOUND OF MOUNTAIN WATER 33 (1969). Justice Rehnquist, who has joined Justices Field, Van Devanter, and McKenna among the most prolific public land law opinion writers, commented in California v. United States, 438 U.S. 645, 648–50 (1978):

> * * * The final expansion of our Nation in the 19th century into the arid lands beyond the hundredth meridian of longitude, which had been shown on early maps as the "Great American Desert," brought the participants in that expansion face to face with the necessity for irrigation in a way that no previous territorial expansion had.

> * * * [During the last half of the nineteenth century] irrigation expanded throughout the arid States of the West, supported usually by private enterprise or the local community. By the turn of the century, however, most of the land which could be profitably irrigated by such small scale projects had been put to use. Pressure mounted on the Federal Government to provide the funding for the massive projects that would be needed to complete the reclamation, culminating in the Reclamation Act of 1902.

> The arid lands were not all susceptible of the same sort of reclamation. The climate and topography of the lands that constituted the "Great American Desert" were quite different than the climate and topography of the Pacific Coast States. * * * [T]he latter States not only had a more pronounced seasonal variation and precipitation than the intermountain States, but the interior portions of California had climatic advantages which many of the intermountain States did not.

Almost two-thirds of the run-off in the eleven western states, and all the great western rivers, originate on federal lands. These lands comprise most of the Continental Divide, the Sierra Nevada, the Cascade Range, and other mountainous areas in the West. Moreover, much of the federal lands in the east were purchased into federal ownership in the early twentieth century because of their value as watersheds. Although water is a renewable (as well as reusable, and storable) resource, there has never been enough in the right places at the right times to fulfill human desires, especially in the arid regions. In the twentieth century, the United States, through at least eight separate agencies, has developed water resources in an engineering effort unparalleled in history. These projects have provided irrigation water, municipal drinking supplies, electricity, and recreational opportunities, but they have also taken a heavy toll on wildlife and the amenities of free-flowing rivers. Problems of federal ownership and development of water—and particularly those concerning state-federal relationships—are examined in Chapter 6.

MINERALS

Minerals found on the public lands have played a signal role in the economic and social history of the Nation. The discovery of gold in the California foothills in 1848 prompted the true opening of the west, and later bonanzas would lead miners and then settlers to many other western states. Mining has long been subject to "boom and bust" cycles, but in spite of virtually unlimited prospecting for over a century, the present federal lands are still thought to hold large deposits of minerals. Fossil fuels like coal, oil, and gas, and fertilizer minerals like phosphate and sodium compounds, exist in large quantities on federal land. Federal coal production rose from 285 million tons annually in 1991 to nearly 400 million tons by the turn of the century, and the proportion of national coal production coming from federal lands rose from about one-quarter to one-third. As of 1998, federal lands onshore and offshore accounted for 26.5% of total domestic production of oil and gas, up from 16.3% in 1989. Much of the nation's output of precious metals and other "hardrock" minerals (gold, silver, nickel, lead, copper, zinc, molybdenum, etc.) also come from deposits found wholly or partially on federal lands. The value of cumulative federal production over the years is many billions of dollars. The legal regimes governing mineral extraction and the problems they create vis-a-vis other resources are taken up in Chapter 7.

TIMBER

The federal government owns about 18% of the nearly 500 million acres of commercial timber lands in the United States. Six-sevenths of federal commercial timber is in national forests. Before World War II, federal timber holdings managed by the Forest Service and the Bureau of Land Management were managed conservatively, producing only about five percent of the national total timber harvest. One result of that former conservatism is that the federal lands still hold a comparatively large amount of old-growth, virgin timber of great economic value, especially in the Pacific Northwest. About half of the national softwood timber inventory is located on national forests, roughly three times the amount owned by the forest industry, with small private owners and other public entities controlling the rest. Many of the lands containing timber, particularly the extraordinary stands of old-growth Douglas fir, redwood, and pine, also contain unique scenic and aesthetic values. The timber resource is explored in Chapter 8.

GRAZING

More acres of federal lands are used for domestic livestock grazing than for any other single use except recreation. The number of animals on the federal range has declined substantially, but ranchers still graze cattle and sheep on about 159 million acres of BLM lands and 85 million acres within the national forests. (Federal land forage is, however, only a tiny fraction of the total grass consumed by livestock in the country.) Historically, the public domain was a "commons" where grazing was allowed with no federal regulation whatsoever, a situation that took a great toll on the forage resource, as the following excerpt from Phillip Foss's classic study shows:

> Competition for water and the scant grass and browse of this free land was chiefly responsible for the range wars and the "romantic" legend of the guntoting cowboy. Stockmen attempted to reserve grazing rights for themselves by homesteading waterholes, by acquiring land along creeks, by checkerboard patterns of ownership, and by various other devices. These schemes all had as their objective the free and exclusive use of parts of the public domain. This kind of finagling does not necessarily imply that the early stockmen were rogues or possessed of any particularly sinister or wicked intent. Most of the land so manipulated was of such low productivity that homestead tracts were too small to provide a reasonable living. Consequently, stockmen and farmers were forced to supplement their homestead with "free land" or go bankrupt.* * *
>
> There were two general results of this "free land" situation. First, squabbles over range and water continued interminably and even the most powerful operators lived an uncertain economic existence. Second, the "free land" *had* to result in overgrazing. Cattlemen and sheepmen could not be expected to withhold stock from government range to prevent overgrazing when they knew that other stockmen would get the grass they left. Overgrazing permitted an accelerated rate of erosion by removing the forage that held moisture and soil. Erosion of soil led to still greater erosion with the result that the carrying capacity of the range decreased and floods and desert land increased.
>
> Overgrazing caused millions of acres of grassland to become desert. Lands which produced native grasses "up to your stirrups" within the lifetime of persons now living became, and remain today, virtual deserts.

P. Foss, POLITICS AND GRASS 3–4, 74, 77 (1960).

Today millions of domestic animals spend part of their lives on federal rangeland, sharing the forage with thousands of wild horses and burros and millions of antelope, deer, moose, and mountain sheep. In spite of some federal regulations since the 1930's (and earlier, in the case of national forests), the public range is largely in "fair" or "poor" condition and overgrazing by modern standards is still widespread in some areas. Regulation to reconcile the competition among those uses and to increase the productivity of grazing lands is the dominant theme of Chapter 9.

WILDLIFE

The federal lands contain some of the most valuable wildlife habitat in the world. Maintenance of wildlife in the wild is valuable to hunters, to industries that depend upon wildlife products or that support recreational pursuits, to people who only watch wildlife, and to those who simply believe that wild animals should remain free and wild. The native ranges of certain species, such as wild turkeys, moose, elk, and mountain sheep, correspond closely to public land holdings. Even in many eastern states, big game species depend heavily on habitat found on federal lands. In some instances, the public lands offer the last refuge for species in danger. Management and protection of the wildlife resource on federal lands is the subject of Chapter 10.

RECREATION

Minerals, timber, water, forage, and even wildlife are commonly considered the conventional resources on the public lands. Nothing better symbolizes the evolution of federal land policy in the last half-century than the emergence of recreation and preservation as co-equal and competing resources. As an economic matter, the recreation resource in the third millennium swamps all of the commodity resources combined. Americans with their leisure time, affluence, new philosophies, and means of transportation desire recreational opportunities in myriad forms, and they demand that such opportunities be made available on the federal lands. Congress and federal land management agencies have responded to the popular will. Every major federal land system offers something of a recreational nature to somebody, from hiking to powerboating to resorts. One can tour a national park by car, shoot the rapids on a wild river, fish, swim, and boat in federal reservoirs, ride jeeps through grazing districts, and collect rocks in national forests. These opportunities have been considered "givens," unchallenged rights available to all citizens. But, as in the case of all resources, the underlying productivity of the recreation resource can be threatened by human overuse. The novel legal questions arising from conflicts between recreational use and other resources are addressed in Chapter 11.

PRESERVATION

American society was indelibly marked in 1868 when John Muir stepped on the wharf in San Francisco, and said, "Take me anywhere that is wild." Because of the work of Muir and others, Congress was moved to set aside numerous national parks in the late 19th and early 20th centuries. National parks were and are an important part of the preservation resource, but government officials came to recognize the need to preserve truly wild areas without roads, lodges, or restaurants. Before wilderness was fashionable, Aldo Leopold, at one time a forester in the Forest Service, commented:

Like winds and sunsets, wild things were taken for granted until progress began to do away with them. Now we face the question whether a still higher "standard of living" is worth its cost in things natural, wild, and free. For us of the minority, the opportunity to see geese is more important than television, and the chance to find a pasque-flower is a right as inalienable as free speech.

These wild things, I admit, had little human value until mechanization assured us of a good breakfast, and until science disclosed the drama of where they come from and how they live. The whole conflict thus boils down to a question of degree. We of the minority see a law of diminishing returns in progress: our opponents do not.

A. Leopold, A SAND COUNTY ALMANAC vii (1949).

From obscure philosophical beginnings, the movement to preserve wild areas has succeeded in persuading Congress to create a new system of federal lands, the dominant purpose of which is preservation. One of the most articulate wilderness advocates, the late Justice William O. Douglas, made the following observations on the place of preservation in national resource priorities:

> * * * The islands of wilderness, even if they never shrink in acreage, shrink *per capita*. For the pressure of population is ever and ever greater; and the year is drawing near when one who wants to backpack or travel by pack train into the High Sierras, the Northern Cascades, the Wind River Range, or the Tetons must get a permit—just as he does today for picnicking along Rock Creek Park, Washington, D.C. * * *

William O. Douglas, A WILDERNESS BILL OF RIGHTS 61–70 (1965).*

There is no longer an open "public domain" where ranchers can graze their stock without regulation and citizens can obtain land by homesteading. But the phrase "public domain" is still commonly used, and those who know the public lands have a mental image of the public domain. It is high desert or plains country, uncluttered and quiet. The colors are not dramatic—it is a land of pastels. There is a growing awareness that this land, too, has preservation values:

> For years, the public domain—especially outside Alaska—has suffered from a bad press; even those who have fought for its preservation have frequently assumed that it consisted of little more than godforsaken wastelands, bleak alkali flats, smelly sumps, and monotonous stretches of sand and sagebrush. In fact, it is quite as varied in all its characteristics as the West itself (not too surprising, since in many respects the public domain *is* the West), and is neither bleak nor forsaken by God. If a good deal of it is desert (and it might be useful to remember that the Son of God once walked in deserts), it also includes grasslands and prairie and tundra; mountain peaks as sheer and rock-ribbed as

anything in Rocky Mountain National Park; swamps, lakes, streams, rivers, tarns, marshlands, hot springs, and geysers; forests of chaparral, oak, juniper, redwood, western red cedar, white pine, yellow pine, and bristlecone pine; flattopped mesas that float in the distance like mirages, spectacular canyons that look as if they had been sliced into the earth with a knife yesterday afternoon, and balancing rocks, toadstool rocks, caves, caverns, sandstone arches, and all the other geological formations carved by the hand of time; a zoological index of deer, antelopes, elk, caribou, moose, bears—black, brown, and grizzly—beaver, otters, coyotes, wolves, mountain lions, golden eagles and bald eagles, pelicans, peregrine falcons, and ospreys, and hundreds more, including such rare fish as the desert pupfish and the Utah cutthroat trout; and the marks of twenty thousand years of human history, from the delicate petroglyphs of prehistoric Indians to the axle-grease scrawls of wagontrain pioneers, from the cliff dwellings of the Anasazi and Moqui to the prospect holes of the new Jasons of the nineteenth century.

Thomas Watkins & Charles Watson, Jr., THE LANDS NO ONE KNOWS 138 (1975). The legal underpinnings of the preservation movement, and its implications for other federal land uses, are explored in the concluding Chapter 12.

These, then, are the primary resources of the public lands. For every proposed use there are phalanxes of disparate advocates and opponents. Some claim that if the United States were literally to "lock up" for preservation many of these resources, catastrophic social and economic consequences would follow. On the other hand, opening all federal lands for wholesale, unregulated development would irreparably wound a special part of the national spirit. Because of the compulsion to compromise inherent in our political, legal, and administrative mechanisms, resource decisions mostly fall in the middle of the two extremes. It is within this diverse and emotional context that legislators, land management officials, and judges must operate in making and reviewing decisions affecting the national resources.

It is difficult to locate a common legal denominator among the many diverse instances of present federal ownership. The federal purposes behind construction of a post office and creation of a wilderness area are so different that comparison in legal terms is nearly impossible. One writer has divided all federal holdings into three broad classifications: resource preservation lands; multiple resource use lands; and lands used for specific non-resource-oriented purposes. Jerome Muys, The Federal Lands, in FEDERAL ENVIRONMENTAL LAW 495 (1974). The "resource preservation" lands include the National Park System (which includes Monuments, Preserves, Recreation Areas, Seashores, Lakeshores, Trails, and Rivers), Wilderness Areas, and the National Wildlife Refuge System. The "multiple use" category includes National Forests (including the National Grasslands), the BLM lands (the traditional "public domain"), outer continental shelf lands, and the lands administered for power, irrigation, or flood control purposes by the Federal Energy Regulatory Commission, the Army

Corps of Engineers, and the Bureau of Reclamation. The final "non-resource-oriented" category is a catchall for all other forms of federal land ownership. That category is not necessarily negligible—the Department of Defense administers millions of acres—but the focus of this volume is on the vast bulk of the federal lands in the two "resource" categories.

A large number of books deal with public lands policy. In addition to the authorities excerpted in the following section—designed to introduce various perspectives on the field—see, e.g., RETHINKING THE FEDERAL LANDS (Sterling Brubaker, ed. 1984); Roderick Nash, WILDERNESS AND THE AMERICAN MIND (3d ed. 1983); Philip Fradkin, A RIVER NO MORE: THE COLORADO RIVER AND THE WEST (1981); William Wyant, WESTWARD IN EDEN: THE PUBLIC LANDS AND THE CONSERVATION MOVEMENT (1982); Paul Culhane, PUBLIC LANDS POLITICS: INTEREST GROUP INFLUENCE ON THE FOREST SERVICE AND THE BUREAU OF LAND MANAGEMENT (1981); WESTERN PUBLIC LANDS (J. Francis & R. Ganzel eds., 1984); Marion Clawson, THE PUBLIC LANDS REVISITED (1983); P. Truluck, PRIVATE RIGHTS AND PUBLIC LANDS (1983); James Conaway, THE KINGDOM IN THE COUNTRY (1987); S. Fairfax and C. Yale, FEDERAL LANDS (1987).

Professors George C. Coggins and Robert Glicksman's three volume treatise, PUBLIC NATURAL RESOURCES LAW (2001) is a useful complement to this casebook, covering all the topics addressed here in comprehensive fashion. Ernest Baynard's PUBLIC LAND LAW AND PROCEDURE (1986), addresses primarily the management of nonmineral resources on BLM public lands. Robert Glicksman & George C. Coggins, MODERN PUBLIC LAND LAW IN A NUTSHELL, is based on and keyed to this casebook.

C. Perspectives on Public Land and Resources Law

Garrett Hardin, The Tragedy of the Commons

162 Science 1243 (1968).

The tragedy of the commons develops in this way. Picture a pasture open to all. It is to be expected that each herdsman will try to keep as many cattle as possible on the commons. Such an arrangement may work reasonably satisfactorily for centuries because tribal wars, poaching, and disease keep the numbers of both man and beast well below the carrying capacity of the land. Finally, however, comes the day of reckoning, that is, the day when the long-desired goal of social stability becomes a reality. At this point, the inherent logic of the commons remorselessly generates tragedy.

* * *

Adding together the component partial utilities, the rational herdsman concludes that the only sensible course for him to pursue is to add another animal to his herd. And another; and another. * * * But this is the conclusion reached by each and every rational herdsman sharing a commons. Therein is the tragedy. Each man is locked into a system that compels him to increase his herd without limit—in a world that is limited. Ruin is the destination toward which all men rush, each pursuing his own best interest in a society that believes in the freedom of the commons. Freedom in a commons brings ruin to all. * * *

In an approximate way, the logic of the commons has been understood for a long time, perhaps since the discovery of agriculture or the invention of private property in real estate. But it is understood mostly only in special cases which are not sufficiently generalized. Even at this late date, cattlemen leasing national land on the western ranges demonstrate no more than an ambivalent understanding, in constantly pressuring federal authorities to increase the head count to the point where overgrazing produces erosion and weed-dominance. * * *

The National Parks present another instance of the working out of the tragedy of the commons. At present, they are open to all, without limit. The parks themselves are limited in extent—there is only one Yosemite Valley—whereas population seems to grow without limit. The values that visitors seek in the parks are steadily eroded. Plainly, we must soon cease to treat the parks as commons or they will be of no value to anyone.

What shall we do? We have several options. We might sell them off as private property. We might keep them as public property, but allocate the right to enter them. The allocation might be on the basis of wealth, by the use of an auction system. It might be on the basis of merit, as defined by some agreed upon standards. It might be by lottery. Or it might be on a first-come, first-served basis, administered to long queues. These, I think, are all the reasonable possibilities. They are all objectionable. But we must choose—or acquiesce in the destruction of the commons that we call our National Parks.

One Third of the Nation's Lands

Report to the Congress by the Public Land Law Review Commission, p. 1–7 (1970).

[The Commission's 289 page Report (exclusive of appendices and the many voluminous supporting studies) is by most accounts the most prominent, comprehensive, and successful investigation into public land law ever undertaken. It has been analyzed, discussed, dissected, criticized, and cited more than any other like document, and it is still a primary research resource for the serious student. A number of its recommendations were eventually, after considerable massaging, translated into statute; principally, in the Federal Land Policy and Management Act in 1976. The following excerpts are the main general policy recommendations from the first chapter of the Report.]

Congress should establish national policy in all public land laws by prescribing the controlling standards, guidelines, and criteria for the exercise of authority delegated to executive agencies. * * *

Congress assert its constitutional authority by enacting legislation reserving unto itself exclusive authority to withdraw or otherwise set aside public lands for specified limited-purpose uses and delineating specific delegation of authority to the Executive as to the types of withdrawals and set asides that may be effected without legislative action. * * *

Statutory goals and objectives should be established as guidelines for land-use planning under the general principle that within a specific unit, consideration should be given to all possible uses and the maximum number of compatible uses permitted. This should be subject to the qualification that where a unit, within an area managed for many uses, can contribute maximum benefit through one particular use, that use should be recognized as the dominant use, and the land should be managed to avoid interference with fulfillment of such dominant use. * * *

Statutory guidelines be established providing generally that the United States receive full value for the use of the public lands and their resources retained in Federal ownership, except that monetary payment need not represent full value, or so-called market value, in instances where there is no consumptive use of the land or its resources. * * *

Fundamental premises are beliefs set forth in the foregoing underlying principles as well as in the implementing recommendations that follow. These are:

1. *Functioning of Government in a manner that reflects the principles set forth in the Constitution.*

In adhering to this principle, we seek to give recognition particularly to these specific principles:

— Congress, elected by and responsive to the will of the people, makes policy; the executive branch administers the policy.

— Maintenance of a strong Federalism. The Federal Government not only recognizes the importance of state and local governments in the Federal system but affirmatively supports and strengthens their roles to the maximum extent possible.

— The Federal Government protects the rights of individual citizens and assures that each one is dealt with fairly and equitably.

2. *Balancing of all major interests in order to assure maximum benefit for the general public.*

— No one of the interests we have identified should benefit to the unreasonable detriment of another unless there is an overriding national interest present.

3. *Providing responsible stewardship of the public lands and their resources.* * * *

— Guidelines must be established to provide for priorities in reducing conflicts among users and resolving conflicts when they arise.

4. *In addition to serving national requirements, the public lands must serve regional and local needs.*

— In many areas, consideration must be given to dependence of regional and local social and economic growth upon public lands and land policy.

— In planning the use of public lands, the uses of nonpublic lands must be given consideration.

Richard L. Stroup & John A. Baden, Natural Resources: Bureaucratic Myths and Environmental Management*

118–27 (1983).

When well-trained economists look at the [Forest Service] planning process, they see many problems in the way values are assigned, in the way criteria are set, and in the lack of distinction between the two. These problems can be easily explained. They are caused by the lack of good data inherent in a failure to price outputs as well as inputs, in a failure to recognize the opportunity cost of capital, and to the pressures that must come to bear when decision makers are held accountable only through the political system. The wonder is that the national forests have been managed as well as they have.

Privatizing the national forests should end many of the obstacles to good management. Not only would decision makers be given larger amounts of validated and continuously updated information, but political obstacles to efficient management would largely disappear. Perhaps just as important, environmentalists, timber producers, miners, recreationists, and others who make demands on the Forest Service would quickly move away from their carping and faultfinding toward positive and constructive accommodation.

Whenever someone owns a piece of land, everyone with a potential interest in it begins to act *as if* they cared about everyone else. Each party's goals can best be reached by close, constructive, and even imaginative cooperation with all other parties. This results whenever trade occurs by the rule of willing consent, for such trade must be mutually beneficial. This process contrasts sharply with debates over public land, where the name of the game is discrediting the other side's views and rejecting compromises unless defeat appears imminent. When the price is zero, each side naturally wants it all. * * *

* * * We believe that it does not matter very much who owns a resource when it comes to determining how that resource will be used. Any owner, whatever his goals, will find those goals frequently met more fully by cooperation with others through trade. Since dollars, additional wilder-

* Reprinted with the permission of the Pacific Institute for Public Policy Research.

ness lands, buffer zones for existing wilderness, and other items attainable through trade are desired by any potential owner, it follows that even a zealot who owns the land can gain by listening carefully and discussing constructively the alternatives proposed by nonowners who desire wilderness, mineral, or other values from the landowner. Until all rights are (for the moment) optimally allocated among competing and compatible uses and users, further trade can make all parties to the trade better off in the pursuit of their various goals. * * *

The point is that if a mining company bought an entire forest, it would have every incentive to maximize the value of the 98 percent that it didn't really want by carefully considering the amenity effects of its exploration and mining operations. Similarly, if the Audubon Society submitted the high bid on ecologically critical portions of all the resold part of the forest, it would carefully consider its information and preferences. Demanding more only increases the required bid. The major reason we expect improvement in forest management is that a market system holds every private owner accountable to the rest of society by having to outbid everyone else— or reject others' bids—for every alternative forgone (or destroyed) on the land.

* * * But what about the individual who does not want to buy a part of the national forest but still wants access? Consider what people from Montana do when they want to use facilities in New York City but do not want to purchase real estate there. Just as some of the living space in New York is rented by the day or by the month, some of the private land in our country is leased by the hour, the week, or the year. Some people will pay a higher price for vacations filled with amenities, and many owners of the world's resources are happy to accommodate such vacationers. Access to a unique ecological site may be compared with access to a Rembrandt painting. In both cases, the admission fee can make it worthwhile for the owner to share the asset and, indeed, take elaborate precautions against its depreciation.

A key feature of our proposal is that the immense forest wealth of our nation would be more broadly shared among all citizens. Instead of a few favored firms and individuals enjoying the benefits of the forest, everyone would benefit from the revenues. Those revenues would capture the high bidder's estimate of the present capitalized value of all future benefits that could be derived from the land.

How large would the revenues from the sale of the national forests be? No one really knows. But it is not the *average* person's value that would determine the sale price of any tract. It is, rather, the most optimistic view, shared by the minimum number of people necessary to win the auction for a piece of land. * * *

* * * With the constructive attitudes and imaginative entrepreneurship unleashed by implementation of our proposal, the national forests could be sold for several hundred billion dollars.

* * *

Our proposal would help the American productivity problem * * *. [I]t would make better use of the mineral, timber, recreation, and amenity values found in the public forests. * * * Perhaps as important to the future of the nation would be a fundamental change in attitude. From the fierce and never-ending battles of lobbyist pressures and alarmist rhetoric would emerge a positive sum game. Rewards would be given for imaginative and constructive solutions to resource conflicts rather than for carefully articulated pleas and raw political clout. The formidable power of American entrepreneurs would be shifted from the negative sum political arena to the positive sum private arena, where every change must be mutually beneficial.

William H. Rodgers, Jr., Building Theories of Judicial Review in Natural Resource Law*

53 U.Colo.L.Rev. 213 (1982).

By necessity, legal academics are in the perpetual presence of normative values and are called upon regularly to adjudge a particular outcome "right" or "wrong." This presupposes a baseline from which we measure compliance, and this baseline is accepted as the governing ethical arrangement. It seems inescapable that we are thus forced into a consideration of ethical theories. There are many candidates, and only some of these theories are derived from human preferences expressed biologically, culturally, or economically.

Moral philosophy may offer some guidance, but hardly in the detail satisfactory for the particularized needs of the law. Philosophical theories like those of John Rawls, moreover, exude confidence in the power of human rationality to prescribe just outcomes; there is much to be said for the contrary view that many seemingly nonrational cultural practices reflect an unarticulated wisdom presumptively deserving respect. Also, moral philosophy does not purport to be an empirical science, and for this lawyer at least, that stance gives the arguments a suspiciously hypothetical character. Rawls' fairminded soul, hiding behind the veil of ignorance, resembles nobody I ever knew, and in that respect is quite like the calculating rational person of economic theory. These twin caricatures are hardly the full measure of human nature, although legal theorists sometimes act as if they were.

Let me use as an illustration the case of Mr. Bryznowski, the northern Minnesota farmer, who had the misfortune to lose one, perhaps two, head of livestock to a pack of hungry wolves.[39] Bryznowski then persuaded the Fish and Wildlife Service to assign a trapper, full time, to hang around his farm and repulse the advances of the hungry wolves. This conflict fits the classical nuisance pattern, and resource law teachers could be expected to turn to the popular economic analyses for suggested solutions. Coase points out that through exchange the parties can be expected to achieve the most

* Reprinted with permission of the University of Colorado Law Review.

39. Fund for Animals v. Andrus (Minnesota Wolf Kill), 11 ERC 2189 (1978).

efficient combination of wolf-raising and cow-rearing.[40] The idea of Bryz-nowski negotiating with a pack of wolves troubles me not at all. In fact, it might be easier to strike an understanding with wolves than the operators of the chemical plants, pulp mills, and smelters commonly invoked in Coasian analyses. Whatever may be said of wolves, they keep their word, by which I mean behavior and needs are predictable and consistent.

What is the least costly means of averting this wolf damage? Indulge me further by assuming that Bryznowski, with the aid of the Fish and Wildlife Service, can go forth and suppress or exterminate the invaders at a cost of $400 a month; he can do nothing and accept the loss, randomly inflicted against his stock, of $200 a month; or he can select his puniest cow, at a cost of $100 per month, and stake it out in the woods as a bribe to the pack. This bribe turns out to be the efficient means of loss-avoidance. After all, in the causation-neutral world of economics the loss can be attributed as much to the tastiness of cows as to the hunger of wolves.

Will Bryznowski settle for the efficient outcome? Not likely under a psychological or biological model of human behavior which accepts people as they are, not as the reasonable economic beings they are supposed to be. Bryznowski, under this view, would pursue the absolutist line of complete defense because he perceives injustice in this random misfortune, or because his genes recall the days before the technology of firearms, or because he lives in a house of straw. In the reported case, Bryznowski not only adhered to the absolutist line but the Fish and Wildlife Service agreed with him. While there may be no absolute rights to work or to eat, the right to be free of wolves is decidedly nonutilitarian.

Nor would I expect Bryznowski to be any better as a philosopher than as an economist. How far would you get persuading him to retreat behind the Rawlsian veil of ignorance with one of the wolves to talk things over on the assumption that either one might emerge as farmer or wolf?[41] It seems that any way the situation is hypothesized, Bryznowski's biological vote, and probably the cultural vote of his neighbors, is unlikely to be favorable to the wolves. In this case, I would be unwilling to accept the local biological and cultural preference, which is a reminder that the search for a governing ethic in law is ongoing and demanding. It is tempting to invoke the rights of wolves, or of people present and future who care about wolves, to condemn Bryznowski's conviction as prejudice and his neighbors' sup-port as superstition. There is nothing central to his existence as a farmer in northern Minnesota that turns on recognition of a continuing right to exterminate wolves. Professors Coggins and Wilkinson would compensate Bryznowski for loss of the right to be free of wolves, pointing out that a payoff would be a tiny fraction of the cost of trapper protection.[42] Wolf damage, in my opinion, is merely another form of just loss not unlike that inflicted by a wide variety of natural hazards.

---

40. Coase, *The Problem of Social Cost,* 3 J.Law & Econ. 1 (1960).

41. J. Rawls, A Theory of Justice (1971).

42. See G.C. Coggins & C.F. Wilkinson, Federal Public Land & Resources Law 671 (2d ed.1980).

Robert L. Glicksman, Fear and Loathing on the Federal Lands

43 Kan. L. Rev. 647 (1997).

On July 4, 1994, Dick Carver, a rancher and a Commissioner of Nye County, Nevada, climbed aboard his twenty-two-ton D-7 Caterpillar and began bulldozing open a road in the Toiyabe National Forest. The county had asked the United States Forest Service, an agency within the Agriculture Department responsible for managing the national forests, to reopen a former stagecoach trail, but the agency said an archaeological survey was needed first. Without waiting for Forest Service approval, and with the consent of his fellow Commissioners, Carver drove the bulldozer to the road and began plowing a roadbed outside the existing right-of-way. In front of him stood an armed agent of the United States Forest Service, who held a hand-lettered sign ordering Carver to halt. The agent stumbled to his hands and knees, but Carter drove on, waving his pocket-sized copy of the United States Constitution, as his son-in-law stood by and sang the national anthem. Spurred on by a local rancher who argued that the United States had been won by "fighting men and bloodshed," and that peaceful solutions were no longer sufficient, a crowd of about 200 onlookers, many waving guns, cheered. The Nye County Commission subsequently requested that criminal charges be brought against the two Forest Service employees.

This story is not unique. Similar incidents have occurred in other parts of the West in recent years. The most recent example took place on lands in Utah, which, in the fall of 1996, President Clinton included within the newly established Staircase–Escalante National Monument. Officials of the Bureau of Land Management (BLM), while conducting an inventory in October 1996 of undeveloped lands inside the national monument for possible wilderness designation, noticed that hundreds of miles of trails had been bulldozed and graded without agency approval. It turned out that the counties in which the lands are located, which asserted ownership of the graded roads, ordered the bulldozing in an attempt to disqualify the areas from further consideration as wilderness. They did so despite warnings by the BLM that they lacked the authority to engage in those acts on lands under the BLM's jurisdiction. Instead of resorting to legal means of resolving the dispute first, the counties began leveling. They stopped only when the federal government filed suit alleging trespass by the counties and a federal district court issued an injunction to stop the unauthorized work. Even after the suit was filed, Garfield County officials declared that they would "not be beholding" to the federal officials who brought suit. One Utah rancher's response to the creation of the national monument may have summarized the feelings of many when he declared that he would "like to secede from the nation. I'd like to go to war."

Recent dissatisfaction with ownership and management of the federal lands has manifested itself in more ominous forms as well. Pipe bombs have appeared in the Gila Wilderness in New Mexico. An unknown assailant shot at a Forest Service biologist in California. A bomb was thrown onto the roof of the BLM's state headquarters in Nevada on Halloween night in 1993. School children have been beaten because their parents work for the Forest Service. In August 1995, the family van of a forest ranger in Carson City, Nevada, was blown up while parked in his driveway. That episode marked the second time within a year in which violence was directed at the ranger, who previously supervised Forest Service lands in Nye County.

Incidents of civil disobedience involving the disruption of lawful activities on the federal lands have not been confined to those who oppose restrictions on development that stem from environmental and natural resource protection laws. Radical environmentalists, for example, have spiked trees and otherwise sought to disrupt logging in the national forests. The difference between those protests and the ones I have been discussing is that only the latter have occurred under the sponsorship of local governments.

Although no sweeping proposals to defuse the tinderbox of federal lands policy in the West readily suggest themselves, several steps are worth considering. The easiest to accomplish would be to tone down the inflammatory, reckless, and irresponsible rhetoric that has emanated from all levels of government, from county commissions to the halls of the United States Congress. Pandering to the basest instincts of one's constituents cannot help but encourage them to take the low road, too.

Federal employees also may be able to discourage lawless and violent behavior by resorting to the courts. In 1995, a group called the Public Employees for Environmental Responsibility sued a Catron County company that held an unpatented mining claim on property in the Gila National Forest for harassment and malicious prosecution of government workers. Those workers had been charged by the mine operator with trespassing for conducting water sampling at a mining site on federal lands, but the state court had dismissed the trespass action. Similar tactics have been used successfully against environmental extremists. In November 1996, an Idaho jury awarded $150,000 in compensatory damages and $1 million in punitive damages against twelve members of the environmental group Earth First! for damage to equipment and work delays resulting from protests against timber harvesting in the forests of that state. The imposition of punitive damages on those who participate in unlawful acts on the federal lands may provide an important deterrent to such conduct.

Richard W. Behan, RPA/NFMA—Time to Punt*

79 Journal of Forestry 802 (1981).

The controversies over the management of the national forests in the 1970s—the now historic battles on the Bitterroot and Monongahela national forests—clearly called for reforms in the ways we were doing business.

During that decade, we hammered out a piece of legislation, the Resources Planning Act of 1974 as amended by the National Forest

---

*   Reprinted with the permission of the
Journal of Forestry.

Management Act of 1976, to effect those reforms. We used the vehicle of statute to reform the management of the national forests, and I believe now, altogether after the fact, we made a serious mistake in doing so. I believe the Resources Planning Act, as amended by the National Forest Management Act, should be repealed. * * *

I offer this opinion not as flippant iconoclasm but as a sincerely sad commentary on our contemporary fixation with legislation (and the litigation that always follows) as the main approach to public problems. * * *

What do we have in general and abstract terms? A planning process as close to the classic rational and comprehensive model, and as close to perfection, as human imagination can design and implement. The legislation is long and detailed; the regulations added much specificity; the adopted procedures and * * *, the analytical model that the agency insisted upon, are rational and comprehensive and at least theoretically rigorous and invincible; and the training manual for planning teams highlights and prescribes the very latest in mathematical, conceptual, and analytical elegance.

RPA/NFMA mandates with the force of law that forest plans will be rational, comprehensive, and essentially perfect. We have adopted an idealized planning process and blessed it with all the force and power and rigor of statute that a law-based society can muster.

Superficially, I suppose that's fine. I was genuinely enthusiastic as we all worked in various ways on the legislation. But a corollary of statutory perfection has become apparent lately, and it is sobering, indeed: an imperfect plan is an illegal plan * * * [a]nd that means, ultimately, forest management by court decisions, instead of the considered judgment of professional land managers.

Without a law, you can't litigate, and that's one reason to repeal RPA/NFMA. From the land manager's point of view, repealing the law is a guaranteed way to help get forest management decisions out of the courtroom and back into the forest. * * *

[Another reason for repeal] is that the requirements of legal proceedings impose a distortion on the planning process. Documentation, consistency, and correct procedure become far more important than a land manager's solid, professional, experienced judgment—the essence of resource planning, in my view. * * * And so the viability of any plan becomes more tenuous still; not only does it need to be comprehensive and perfect, but it cannot deviate from strict legal procedure. It is jeopardized from another direction.

Another reason to repeal the law is the matter of cost-effectiveness. At enormous costs in money, manpower, political energy, and activity (and legal fees), we are achieving very, very little. * * *

And the final reason, I believe, is the most serious of all. Because it is mandated in law, the forest planning process now has the capability of paralyzing or displacing completely the management and production responsibilities of the agency. * * *

RPA/NFMA is a monster on the landscape, and I am compelled to suggest an axiom: Idealized, perfect planning that is mandated in law, and constrained only by an agency's budget, will exhaust that budget. And, given manpower ceilings, planning efforts can expand only at the expense of other activities. There will come a time when the Forest Service can do nothing but plan, and all its management, production, and protection activities will cease. * * *

RPA/FMA cannot be made to work. Its flaw is fundamental: it is a *law*, and it needs to be repealed. We failed, in our collective problem solving, by placing too much faith in planning and by placing far too much faith in statute. It is time to punt.

Sally K. Fairfax, Barbara T. Andrews & Andrew P. Buchsbaum, Federalism and the Wild and Scenic Rivers Act: Now You See It, Now You Don't*

59 Wash.L.Rev. 417 (1984).

[Acting under an obscure provision of the federal Wild & Scenic Rivers Act, California Governor Jerry Brown in July 1980 asked the Secretary of the Interior to designate 4000 miles of rivers along California's north coast as federal Wild & Scenic Rivers. The Governor's reasoning was in part to placate the environmental community in California that had been offended by some of his water resource development policies, and in part to enhance state influence over federal forest management policies on the north coast. After an accelerated review process, Secretary of the Interior Andrus, in his last act in office, eventually designated some but not all of the nominated segments for inclusion. Unsuccessful litigation was brought by water development interests and local governments challenging the process and designation.]

The details of [this] story challenge familiar notions: (1) that the federal-state conflict is the core of federalism; (2) that cooperation between governments is preferable to confrontation; and (3) that the role of the courts is to act (or to refrain from acting) as umpires in the conflict.

The traditional federal-state conflict model suggests implacable, clearly identifiable foes locked in battle over authority and control. The North Coast story is one of complex and shifting alliances that does not, except for temporary convenience, form around identifiable—let alone permanent—ties to a particular level of government or an institutional configuration. *Part* of the state—particularly the Resources Agency and the Governor—was initially at odds with *part* of the federal government—the United States Forest Service—over priorities for North Coast river management. There was, however, great cooperation between the Resources Agency and other federal entities, agencies in the Department of the Interior, in pressing for the controversial river designations. Neither the cooperation nor the conflict has been stable largely because the players are not stable.

* Reprinted with permission of the University of Washington Law Review.

Moreover, the Forest Service, target of the initial action, regularly cooperates on other issues with the Resources Agency and with many other state agencies, who frequently sue their North Coast partners in the Department of the Interior. Changing coalitions of affected groups reflect the incomplete divisions between and among timber, fisheries, mineral, water, recreation, and aesthetic interest groups and their various state and county government allies. Evolving conditions shift alliances and alter both the "state" and the "federal" positions. This volatility is enhanced by the changing of administrations in both Washington and Sacramento. The insufficiency of the traditional federal conflict model is underscored by the tension between the designation controversy, which could be forced to fit fleetingly into the format, and the larger and more durable controversy about resource management priorities which involves significantly different players, issues, and interactions.

Cooperative federalism theorists will likewise find little succor in the North Coast controversy. Cooperation in the North Coast situation * * * [was followed] only momentarily [on] a small subset of the complex pattern of interactions which comprise the policy field.

Finally, the role of the courts in this controversy is neither so pivotal nor so profound as one might anticipate on the basis of the "court as the umpire of federalism" concept. Very few instances of litigated federal-state conflict actually involve state and federal parties or major constitutional principles. The North Coast situation is not an exception. * * * The basic dispute was among competing private groups. * * * Interestingly, it was a fragile coalition of California *counties* which initially challenged Governor Brown's proposal. The legal issues [were] largely unrelated to the resource management disputes that are the heart of the conflict.

Joseph L. Sax, Mountains Without Handrails: Reflections on the National Parks*

103–09 (1980).

* * * [M]ost conflict over national park policy does not really turn on whether we ought to have nature reserves (for that is widely agreed), but on the uses that people will make of those places—which is neither a subject of general agreement nor capable of resolution by reference to ecological principles. The preservationists are really moralists at heart, and people are very much at the center of their concerns. They encourage people to immerse themselves in natural settings and to behave there in certain ways, because they believe such behavior is redeeming.

Moreover, the preservationists do not merely aspire to persuade individuals how to conduct their personal lives. With the exception of Thoreau, who predated the national park era, they have directed their prescriptions to government. The parks are, after all, public institutions which belong to everyone, not just to wilderness hikers. The weight of the preservationist view, therefore, turns not only on its persuasiveness for the individual as

* Reprinted with permission from the University of Michigan Press.

such, but also on its ability to garner the support—or at least the tolerance—of citizens in a democratic society to bring the preservationist vision into operation as official policy. It is not enough to accept the preservationists simply as a minority, speaking for a minority, however impressive. For that reason I have described them as secular prophets, preaching a message of secular salvation. I have attempted to articulate their views as a public philosophy, rather than treating them merely as spokesmen for an avocation of nature appreciation, because the claims they make on government oblige them to bear the weightier burden.

This is not to say that what they preach cannot be rejected as merely a matter of taste, of elitist sentiment or as yet another reworking of pastoral sentimentalism. It is, however, to admit that their desire to dominate a public policy for public parks cannot prevail if their message is taken in so limited a compass. If they cannot persuade a majority that the country needs national parks of the kind they propose, much as it needs public schools and libraries, then the role they have long sought to play in the governmental process cannot be sustained. The claim is bold, and it has often been concealed in a pastiche of argument for scientific protection of nature, minority rights, and sentimental rhetoric. I have tried to isolate and make explicit the political claim, as it relates to the fashioning of public policy, and leave it to sail or sink on that basis.

It may also seem curious that I have put the preservationists into the foreground, rather than the Congress or the National Park Service. Of course Congress has the power to be paternalistic if it wishes, and it often is. It thinks a lot of things are good for us, from free trade and a nuclear defense system to public statuary and space exploration. But no unkindness is intended by the observation that Congress doesn't really think at all. At best it responds to the ideas that thinkers put before it, considers the merits of those thoughts, tests them against its sense of the larger themes that give American society coherence, and asks whether the majority will find them attractive or tolerable. The fundamental question then—and the question I have tried to address here—is whether the ideas of nature preservationists meet these tests. If they do, Congress will ultimately reflect them.

The National Park Service, and other bureaucracies that manage nature reserves, are also basically reflective institutions. Strictly speaking, they enforce the rules Congress makes, doing what they are told. But no administrative agency is in fact so mechanical in its operation. It has its own sense of mission, an internal conception of what it ought to be doing, and that sense of mission also harks back to what thinkers have persuaded it, institutionally, to believe. If the Park Service is basically dominated by the ideology of the preservationists, it will act in certain ways, given the opportunity. If, on the other hand, it has come to believe in the commodity-view of the parks, it will behave quite differently. Thus, again, the capacity of the preservationist view to persuade is the essential issue.

At the same time, no bureaucracy behaves simply according to its own sense of mission. It lives in a political milieu, with constituencies of users and neighbors who impose strong, and at times irresistable, pressures on it.

What the general public believes about the appropriate mission of the national parks is also essential. If the preservationist is to prevail, he must gain at least the passive support of the public, which will indirectly be felt by the Park Service in the decisions it makes in day to day management. * * *

[T]o the preservationists themselves, in whose ranks I include myself, the message is that the parks are not self-justifying. Your vision is not necessarily one that will commend itself to the majority. It rests on a set of moral and aesthetic attitudes whose force is not strengthened either by contemptuous disdain of those who question your conception of what a national park should be, or by taking refuge in claims of ecological necessity. Tolerance is required on all sides, along with a certain modesty.

Frank J. Popper and Deborah E. Popper: The Reinvention of the American Frontier*

The Amicus Journal (Summer 1991) pp. 4–7.

In 1893 Frederick Jackson Turner declared America's frontier closed. It was a significant national moment. * * * The nation * * * essentially accepted Turner's argument, and the frontier faded from its awareness.

We would like to suggest an alternative understanding. A huge frontier survived throughout the twentieth century, but in a hidden form few Americans recognized. In the twenty-first century, an even larger frontier will appear in clear public view. The twenty-first-century American frontier, more than the nineteenth-and twentieth-century ones, will constitute a deliberate human creation, for it will spring primarily from preservation and conservation impulses. If it works, it could be environmentally magnificent. If it does not, it could be environmentally disastrous. In either case, this reinvented frontier will be impossible to ignore or overlook. * * *

During the nineteenth century, the United States acquired land on the frontier and allocated it; much of it went to the federal government, remaining in the public domain, while other portions went to settlers, railroad companies, and other interested private parties. During the twentieth century, Americans primarily extracted natural resources from both public and private land on the frontier, and—secondarily, and often reluctantly—preserved its scenic, aesthetic, and historic settings. On the twenty-first-century frontier, extraction and preservation will change places: preservation uses such as tourism, recreation, and retirement will become primary; extractive activities such as ranching, farming, logging, and mining (including for oil) will become secondary. Extraction will not disappear and in some places will flourish, but in general will contract to more economically and environmentally appropriate places. As the extraction-to-preservation shift proceeds, the western frontier will expand, reappear before American eyes, and once again fascinate them.

Across much of the rural West, extractive uses have long been in steep decline. Despite recurrent local booms such as the present one in gold, extraction accounts for an ever-smaller share of the West's total income. * * * Extraction throughout the West yields low and falling wages and is subject to wrenching boom-and-bust cycles whose bust sides are coming to predominate. Extraction frequently causes immense environmental damage and produces dwindling communities that cannot keep their young and so become disproportionately aged. Extraction requires increasingly questionable federal subsidies, and extractive industries are disproportionately dangerous for their employees.

These conditions chronically oppress large parts of the American countryside, but they have hit with special, accelerating force in the rural West: the region is already less populated, less economically diverse, more remote and arid, and often poorer and more ecologically vulnerable than the other suffering American rural places. * * *

Consider also the recent burgeoning of western environmentalism, which has combined with public and private financial concerns to favor the preservation economy over the extractive one. * * * Throughout the West, the livestock and logging industries have come under mounting attack. Environmental and economic pressures are driving the large parts of these industries that are mobile to shift their operations from public land in the West to private land in the South. * * * Preservation uses will usually be the most plausible replacements on the land extraction will abandon. * * *

Some private land will be deserted, and eventually move into public or quasi-public holdings. * * * The ecological restoration of land damaged by previous extractive uses will be a big business; so will ecological tourism.

The emergence of the twenty-first-century frontier will have important urban and political consequences as well. Ironically, by many measures the West is already America's most urban region; the bulk of the West consists of urban islands in a frontier sea. The expanding frontier will only reinforce this pattern, as western cities continue to grow in population. The urban areas will in fact provide the political impetus to protect the environment of the frontier ones. * * * The underlying political conditions are becoming continually less favorable for * * * anti-environmentalism, for the West's urban areas keep growing. * * *

The return of the American frontier will have profound cultural effects. Unlike the nineteenth-century frontier, the twenty-first-century one will not be a place to conquer. Unlike the twentieth-century frontier, it will not be a place to ignore. Unlike the nineteenth-and twentieth-century frontiers, it will be more a place of preservation than of extraction. Call it the kinder, gentler frontier.

Michael Bean and Melanie Rowland, The Evolution of National Wildlife Law*

3d ed. 1997, at 277–81.

We know far too little about ecosystems to replace decades of experience in species management with vague notions of ecosystem management.

This emerging concept, also called "landscape planning," "watershed analysis," and the like, is an elusive one. Reduced to its simplest terms, ecosystem management acknowledges the interconnectedness of seemingly isolated actions and attempts to coordinate those actions in a way that will minimize their impacts on ecosystem function. But it is a process, not a goal. Recognizing connections in nature does not, by itself, assure healthy ecosystems or viable wildlife populations; these will result only if we choose to make them overriding goals of land and water management.

Scientific complexity alone makes managing ecosystems to conserve biodiversity a daunting enterprise. In the last twenty years, we have moved from viewing ecosystems as stable, closed, and internally regulated, to a new picture of more open systems in constant flux, usually without long-term stability, and affected by a series of human and other stochastic factors. Resource conservation and ecosystem change consequently are characterized by uncertainty. Moreover, ecosystems cover large areas, their boundaries are vague and fluid, and they are infinitely complex as well as dynamic.

A further complication arises from the fact that the goals of ecosystem management must be defined from the social and economic perspective, as well as the scientific. Human social and economic systems favor predictability. Governmental units have conspicuous artificial boundaries, and there often is little communication among governing entities. Our political system and the regulatory agencies have trouble dealing with complexity and change. Nature is full of both.

Were society to overcome these obstacles and agree on conservation of biodiversity as a high priority for land and water management, the public lands would seem to be a logical starting point for land and water management. These lands are relatively undeveloped, and they are owned by all the people of the nation. In contrast to private lands, public lands are physically and politically easier to manage for biodiversity. In addition, the laws under which they are managed emphasize land use planning.

The federal public lands cover over a third of the country, concentrated in the western states; there, they comprise half the land base. They include some of the most important lands in the nation for wildlife. Almost 50% of threatened and endangered species are found on federal lands.

* * * [C]urrent laws governing most federal lands permit managers to set conserving biodiversity as an overarching goal-but with few exceptions they do not *require* managers to do so. Federal resource managers have long enjoyed a great deal of discretion in decisionmaking. But this nearly unfettered discretion is starting to be limited in significant ways. Tracing the evolution of the law affecting wildlife on federal public lands reveals a concerted effort by citizen groups to narrow agency discretion and to require better planning, more informed decisionmaking, and consideration of a broader range of goals and concerns than resource extraction and exploitation.

The record also shows that the efforts, with a few notable exceptions, have met with some success in Congress but little in the courts. In the vast majority of cases, courts are unwilling to overturn agency decisions, whether the challenge is by a conservation group or a resource user group.

To be sure, there have been some striking successes that have caused major shifts in federal wildlife management. The best known is the series of cases in the Pacific Northwest in the late 1980s and early 1990s in which a court enjoined most logging in old growth forests on the country's most productive national forests because the Forest Service had failed to manage for viable populations of the northern spotted owl. * * *

These cases resulted in perhaps the most high-profile and comprehensive federal land management plan in history: a document prepared under order from the President of the United States, drafted by six federal agencies working together, covering hundreds of old-growth associated species, in forests ranging from the Canadian border to northern California. Jack Ward Thomas, a wildlife biologist and head of the team that prepared the plan, became the first biologist appointed Chief of the Forest Service. It is noteworthy that this landmark ecosystem management plan was the result not of the Endangered Species Act, but primarily of the National Forest Management Act and the National Environmental Policy Act.

The success conservationists attained in these and some other cases in the 1980s and early 1990s has met fierce political opposition. * * * [Many bills were introduced in the 1995 and 1996 sessions of Congress to weaken or dilute conservation laws and promote more extractive uses of federal lands. A 1995 law weakened the management plan for the old growth forests in the Northwest,] leading to civil disobedience and hundreds of arrests in Oregon and Washington when the forests once again began to fall.

This past decade has been a dynamic one for wildlife conservation on federal lands. We have moved into a time of transition, one in which our knowledge of ecosystem dynamics and our concerns about species decline are growing rapidly. Wildlife concerns are receiving ever-increasing attention from land managers, begetting intense political reaction from those who have been content with past management policies. It is hard to predict when equilibrium will be restored, or where wildlife conservation federal lands will be when it is.

CHAPTER 2

HISTORY OF PUBLIC LAND LAW

The policy of the United States toward the lands it owned has changed drastically over the twenty-two decades since the Revolutionary War ended. The treaty with Britain established the western boundary of the new nation at the Mississippi River, but seven of the thirteen original states claimed land under their colonial charters to large portions of this Western wilderness. Disputes over these claims among the former colonies and with the national government occupied much time and attention in the Nation's early years.

Once these were resolved, and as the Native Americans were subdued in the Nation's relentless march to the west, the national policy for the next century or more was to sell or give away the public lands to individuals, corporations, and states in order that the Nation would be tamed, farmed, and developed. Individuals were granted land by credit or cash sale and later by the process of establishing farms, or homesteading. Newly admitted states were granted land outright for education, transportation, and other purposes. A vast amount of land was given to railroads in return for construction of the rails that opened up the West. Other laws allowed the private acquisition of timber and mineral resources essentially for free. These means cumulatively disposed of well over one billion acres of federal land.

These various granting mechanisms were often tainted by maladministration and chicanery, even while achieving the larger purpose of sustaining the westward expansion. Gradually, in reaction to a growing concern about fraud and waste, national policy began a gradual shift toward the end of the 19th century. Sometimes with and sometimes without the official imprimatur of Congress, the Executive Branch began to "withdraw" specific tracts of land from the operation of the disposition laws and to "reserve" some of them for specific national purposes. A classification process evolved by which certain federal lands were deemed chiefly valuable for one or more specific uses. Active management of the retained lands gradually replaced custodial management, and professional bureaucracies grew up to meet that need. Continuing public concern about depletion of mineral, timber, and forage resources in the early 20th century led to further restrictions on federal largess, and accelerated the trend toward national retention of ownership. Indeed, in the early 20th century the United States embarked on a major program of land acquisition for conservation purposes, which created a system of national forests in the eastern part of the country (and often involved the reacquisition of land previously sold or given away). Large scale disposition ended in 1934. Since then, the special case of Alaska aside, the national land base has remained relatively stable.

Occasionally a movement arises seeking to change that basic configuration. Some free market and private property advocates are discomfited by the national government's ownership of nearly a third of the Nation's land, and states occasionally attempt to assert title or more control over the federal lands within their borders. Nevertheless, the tradition of national ownership and control has endured and indeed been strengthened over the last century. At the dawn of the 21st century, the prospect is for continued retention of a large federal land base, and even its expansion through acquisitions primarily for purposes of environmental protection, restoration and recreation.

Most contemporary federal land controversies cannot be fully comprehended without an understanding of public land law history. Standard terms still in current use, such as "withdrawal," "entry," "location," "patent," or "in lieu selection," are foreign to those not versed in historical development. As will be apparent in the materials that follow, modern public land litigation often hinges on interpretation of century-old statutes or cases. While public land law history is a complicated and intricate mosaic, some themes constantly recur, and furnish a rich context for contemporary management challenges and legal applications. This chapter begins by sketching out how the United States first asserted ownership over these lands, resolving the controversies with the colonies, establishing a legal basis for wresting title from Native Americans, and embarking on a program of acquisition from foreign governments. It then proceeds to the ways in which the Nation disposed of two-thirds of its conquests and purchases. The disposition policies and the actions taken to further them are grouped according to the main beneficiaries: states, farmers and ranchers, miners, railroads, irrigators, and loggers. Then the rise of the conservation movement and the change in policy from disposition to retention are discussed, and the final sections introduce the developments leading to present federal land management systems.

This chapter was compiled from many sources. The primary authorities include Paul Gates, HISTORY OF PUBLIC LAND LAW DEVELOPMENT (1968); Louise Peffer, THE CLOSING OF THE PUBLIC DOMAIN (1951); Benjamin H. Hibbard, A HISTORY OF PUBLIC LAND POLICIES (1924, U.Wis. ed., 1965); Samuel T. Dana, FOREST AND RANGE POLICY (1956) (2d ed., 1980, with Sally Fairfax); and Roy Robbins, OUR LANDED HERITAGE (1942) (2d ed., 1976). Basic non-legal sources are collected in Charles Wilkinson, The Law of the American West: A Critical Bibliography of the Nonlegal Sources, 85 Mich.L.Rev. 953 (1987).

A.   ACQUISITION OF THE PUBLIC DOMAIN

All of the land the United States has acquired on the North American continent was previously "owned" both by foreign nations and by Indian tribes, and some of it was subject to claims under the charters of some of the original colonies. Federal acquisition came about by a combination of cession, purchase and conquest.

1. FROM THE ORIGINAL COLONIES

Upon ratification of the Treaty of Ghent ending the Revolutionary War, the infant United States gained dominion over lands between the Alleghenies and the Mississippi. But efforts to establish a national policy for these lands was complicated by "western land claims" of seven of the thirteen original colonies. Virginia's claim, the largest, stretched across what later became six states in the midwest. The claims were grounded in the colonial charters from the British Crown, some of which had been extravagantly interpreted to extend to the Pacific Ocean or the South Seas. See Paul Gates, HISTORY OF PUBLIC LAND LAW DEVELOPMENT, at 49. Before the American Revolution, Britain had acted to limit the scope of these grants, and in fact such limitations were among the grievances against the Crown cited by Thomas Jefferson in the Declaration of Independence. See Peter Appel, "The Power of Congress 'Without Limitation': The Property Clause and Federal Regulation of Private Property," 86 Minn. L. Rev. 1 (2001). See also Daniel Feller, THE PUBLIC LANDS IN JACKSONIAN POLITICS, pp. 3–8 (1984).

States without such western land claims, which tended to be smaller and less populous anyway, staunchly opposed the claims, fearing the larger states would become even richer and more populous through sales and settlement of the western lands. The issue (and the closely linked question of whether and how new states might be created) was a major and divisive one in the deliberations over the Articles of Confederation and eventually the Constitution. In 1780, New York promised to cede its western land claims to the national government, whose Continental Congress implored the other claimant states to follow suit. Virginia fell in line in 1784, and most of the other states followed suit within a few years, although Georgia held out till 1802. The Articles of Confederation adopted during the Revolutionary War did not expressly authorize the national Congress to govern the western lands. This did not stop the Congress from enacting three major laws—the Ordinance of 1784, the Land Act of 1785, and the Northwest Ordinance of 1787—that set a pattern of federal land policy which has in some respects endured to the present. Most important for present purposes, in these laws the national government assumed the major responsibility of owning large tracts of land and managing them to serve the ends of national policy, and cautioned the states not to interfere with U.S. policy:

> [D]uring the period of the Articles of Confederation, the question of the ownership of and governance over the western lands occupied a considerable amount of time of the Continental Congress. In that period, the country saw a complete shift from an express rejection of the notion of federal ownership of the western territories to a complete embrace of it. * * * The era of the Articles of Confederation ended with the Continental Congress legislating and creating a system of government for the western territories despite the Articles' lack of express authority for these actions. These early acts to manage the lands the federal government acquired also stipulated that the local governments would

not interfere with federal authority. Practice, if not law, established federal power over the western lands.

Appel, 86 Minn. L. Rev. at 24–25. Doubts about the congressional authority being exercised here played out in the Constitutional Convention of 1787, as described in section B.1 below.

2. FROM FOREIGN NATIONS

It had taken more than 170 years from the establishment of the first permanent European settlement at Jamestown in 1607 for settlement to begin in earnest in this New West, an area larger than the original thirteen colonies. Such a huge area might have been expected to satisfy even the most voracious land hunger of the three million citizens of the new United States for many years. In fact, however, opportunity and opportunism so coincided that, over the next ninety years, national land ownership quadrupled.

Besides the Indians, only England, Spain, and Russia had, at the time of the Revolution, claims to land in North America. Dutch and Swedish claims had long been extinguished and the French government had more recently been defeated and ejected from the continent. The British settlements in Canada attracted the continuing but unsuccessful attention of American expansionists. Other lands claimed by the English and the Spanish (and later the Mexicans) gradually succumbed to Manifest Destiny. Acquisition of the tenuous Russian claims was last and easiest.

In the 1790's, the population of the United States expanded 35%, three new states were admitted, and national economic policies brought about stability, prosperity, and new settlement. Beyond the Alleghenies, trade was funneled through New Orleans and other Spanish-held ports on the Mississippi. Ill-feeling and annoyance from trade restrictions and runaway slave havens abounded, even though the Pinckney Treaty of 1795 confirmed the right of navigation on the Mississippi. When Spain ceded its Louisiana lands to France in 1800, the greatest menace yet to the new Republic was created.

a. LOUISIANA PURCHASE

The negotiations that Jefferson began with Napoleon for the purchase of New Orleans were greatly aided by the decimation of a French expeditionary force in Santo Domingo. Although doubtful that he could accept without constitutional amendment, Jefferson decided he could not refuse Napoleon's unexpected, unparalleled offer to sell the entire Louisiana Territory. A grave danger was turned into a great political victory, and 523 million acres were added to the public domain in 1803 for three cents an acre, doubling the territory of the United States.

New England Federalists were unhappy with Western prospects, fearing the growing influence of the radical Republican representatives from the frontiers. Lewis and Clark promptly penetrated the new territory and beyond, but settlement proceeded mostly east of the Mississippi. Louisiana was admitted to statehood in 1812, but with the admission of Missouri in 1821, the slavery question began to loom larger.

b.   FLORIDA ACQUISITION AND SETTLING THE NORTHERN BORDER

Irritations on remaining borders with Spanish territory did not cease after unfettered commerce was established. Indians raided Georgia from the Spanish holdings and slaves sought freedom in them. In 1817–19, Indian conflicts became acute in Florida, whereupon Andrew Jackson crossed into Florida and defeated the Creeks. He also summarily executed their leaders and two accused British instigators, all of which Spanish officials were powerless to prevent. Spain accepted the inevitable and agreed to surrender East and West Florida and its claims to the Oregon Territory in exchange for only a guarantee of its Texas border and payment of claims by the United States. In 1818, Great Britain agreed to extend the Canadian border along the 49th parallel from Minnesota to the Rocky Mountains; the United States thus gained undisputed title to the rich Red River Valley. A similar dispute over the boundary of Maine was not settled until 1842.

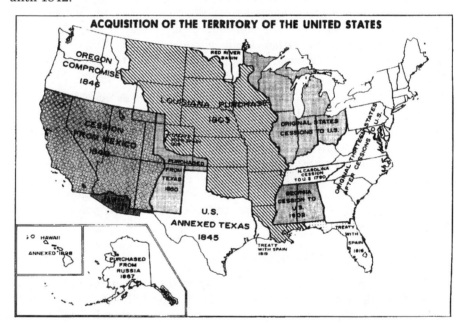

Acquisition of the Territory of the United States   *Prepared by the Bureau of Land Management*

c.   TEXAS, THE TREATY OF GUADALUPE HIDALGO, AND THE GADSDEN PURCHASE

Hundreds of millions of acres of productive land remained unsettled in the first half of the 19th century, but the insatiable American land hunger led explorers and settlers further afield. The storied Mountain Men, with the indomitable Jedediah Smith in the vanguard, explored most of the unknown West while decimating the beaver in the Rockies. Stephen Austin established colonies in Texas, Marcus Whitman led settlers to Oregon, and Brigham Young took the Mormon Saints to the inhospitable "place" that became Utah. Then, between 1845 and 1853, the United States acquired another 781 million acres, of which 613 million acres were added to the public domain.

After Mexico gained its independence from Spain, it made the mistake of contracting with promoters such as Austin to bring in American settlers. The generous grant terms offered to Texas immigrants were taken up by 20,000 Americans and their one thousand slaves by 1830. The Mexican officials quickly regretted their invitation, however, as the Americans resented Mexican efforts to outlaw slavery and to require Catholicism. The Alamo and Texas independence ensued in 1835–36.

But the newly independent "nation" was unexpectedly refused admission into the United States for another nine years because of the slavery question. Under the Missouri Compromise of 1820, northern legislators had anticipated only two more slave states; they were now unwilling to admit an area (46 times the size of Massachusetts) in which five or six additional "slavocracies" could be created. Manifest Destiny eventually won out: the 1844 election of James K. Polk was a victory for expansion, and Texas was annexed and then admitted the following year.

Admission, however, was on different terms from those worked out with other new states. During its Independence, Texas had granted away some 30 million acres but still had a huge debt, fueled by many questionable tricks of finance. The United States left the remaining lands in the possession of the new State to avoid investigating prior practices and assuming the debt. After annexation, Texas sold 79 million acres of its western lands (now parts of New Mexico, Oklahoma, Wyoming, Colorado, and Kansas) to the federal government, the only Texas acreage to enter the national "public domain."

Boundary and other disputes with Mexico continued, and negotiations failed while feeling ran high. A Mexican incursion into the disputed territory gave President Polk a pretext for declaring war, and the Mexicans were soundly defeated. In the 1848 Treaty of Guadalupe Hidalgo, Mexico ceded most of the Southwest including California to the United States for $15 million. For a pittance, the Nation gained title to spectacular scenic resources, including the Grand Canyon and other canyonlands of the Colorado Plateau, Yosemite and the rest of the Sierra Nevada range, and San Francisco Bay, as well as to vast mineral wealth. Shortly thereafter, with railroads being projected or promoted in all directions, it was seen that a New Orleans to San Diego line would require additional land for a favorable route. In 1853, James Gadsden negotiated the purchase of Arizona below the Gila River from Mexico for $10 million.

d. THE OREGON COMPROMISE

In the meantime, the United States had agreed with Great Britain on the northwest boundary. The area around the Columbia had long been used by the Hudson's Bay Company in its trapping operations, but the British were overwhelmed by the influx of American settlers in the 1840's, and the beaver had virtually disappeared. Recognizing the inevitable, England agreed to a boundary fixed at the 49th parallel, except that Vancouver Island below that line was retained for Canada. The settlement of the Oregon question added 180 million acres north of California to the public domain.

e.   THE ALASKA PURCHASE

The surprising acquisition of Alaska had not been preceded by public demand or even public discussion. The Russians were anxious to sell, however, and Secretary of State Seward wanted to buy, so the transaction was quickly consummated. For $7.2 million, the United States purchased an enormous unsurveyed area only lightly touched by human habitation.

Alaska was the last significant addition to the federal public domain. Later acquisitions of Hawaii, Puerto Rico, the Philippines, Guam, Samoa, the Virgin Islands, and smaller Pacific islands made no addition to the public lands except for buildings, parks, and minor reservations.

3.   FROM INDIAN TRIBES

Of course the lands ceded from the colonies and acquired from foreign nations between 1789 and 1867 were also subject to the claims of their inhabitants, the American Indians. The Native Americans fiercely resisted white intrusions into their ancestral tribal lands. They were eventually subdued, decimated by European diseases, defeated in conflicts and removed to "reservations" or assimilated. In the process, however, legal questions of land ownership and title had to be resolved.

The following opinion by Chief Justice John Marshall is a landmark in public land law. It reconciled the property rights of the United States, American Indian tribes, foreign nations, and the settlers anxious to obtain title to real property on the frontier. In doing so, the Court laid the legal predicates for the federal disposition program and the westward expansion.

Johnson v. M'Intosh

Supreme Court of the United States, 1823.
21 U.S. (8 Wheat.) 543.

■ MARSHALL, CH.J., delivered the opinion of the court.

[The litigation involved title to land within what is now the State of Illinois. Johnson claimed title based on grants in 1773 and 1775 from chiefs of the Illinois and Piankeshaw tribes. In 1795, these tribes entered into treaties with the United States, retaining certain lands as reservations but ceding to the federal government other land, including that earlier transferred to Johnson's predecessors. In 1818, the United States granted to defendant M'Intosh a patent to the parcels in question. Johnson then brought this quiet title action.] * * * The inquiry * * * is, in a great measure, confined to the power of Indians to give, and of private individuals to receive, a title, which can be sustained in the courts of this country. * * *

On the discovery of this immense continent, the great nations of Europe were eager to appropriate to themselves so much of it as they could respectively acquire. Its vast extent offered an ample field to the ambition and enterprise of all; and the character and religion of its inhabitants afforded an apology for considering them as a people over whom the superior genius of Europe might claim an ascendancy. The potentates of the old world found no difficulty in convincing themselves that they made ample compensation to the inhabitants of the new, by bestowing on them civilization and Christianity, in exchange for unlimited independence. But as they were all in pursuit of nearly the same object, it was necessary, in order to avoid conflicting settlements, and consequent war with each other, to establish a principle, which all should acknowledge as the law by which the right of acquisition, which they all asserted, should be regulated, as between themselves. This principle was, that discovery gave title to the government by whose subjects, or by whose authority, it was made, against all other European governments, which title might be consummated by possession.

The exclusion of all other Europeans, necessarily gave to the nation making the discovery the sole right of acquiring the soil from the natives, and establishing settlements upon it. It was a right with which no Europeans could interfere. It was a right which all asserted for themselves, and to the assertion of which, by others, all assented. * * *

In the establishment of these relations, the rights of the original inhabitants were, in no instance, entirely disregarded; but were, necessarily, to a considerable extent, impaired. They were admitted to be the rightful occupants of the soil, with a legal as well as just claim to retain possession of it, and to use it according to their own discretion; but their rights to complete sovereignty, as independent nations, were necessarily diminished, and their power to dispose of the soil, at their own will, to whomsoever they pleased, was denied by the original fundamental principle, that discovery gave exclusive title to those who made it.

While the different nations of Europe respected the right of the natives, as occupants, they asserted the ultimate dominion to be in themselves; and claimed and exercised, as a consequence of this ultimate dominion, a power to grant the soil, while yet in possession of the natives. These grants have been understood by all, to convey a title to the grantees, subject only to the Indian right of occupancy.

The history of America, from its discovery to the present day, proves, we think, the universal recognition of these principles. * * *

[The opinion then discussed various competing claims to the New World, many dating to the 15th and 16th centuries, made by Spain, Great Britain, Portugal, France, and Holland. It described the French and Indian War between France and Great Britain, at the end of which, by treaty of 1763, France ceded Canada to Great Britain and fixed the western boundary of the British colonies at the Mississippi.] This treaty expressly cedes, and has always been understood to cede, the whole country, on the English side of the dividing line, between the two nations, although a great and valuable part of it was occupied by the Indians. Great Britain, on her part, surrendered to France all her pretensions to the country west of the Mississippi. It has never been supposed that she surrendered nothing, although she was not in actual possession of a foot of land. She surrendered all right to acquire the country; and any after attempt to purchase it from the Indians, would have been considered and treated as an invasion of the territories of France.

By the 20th article of the same treaty, Spain ceded Florida, with its dependencies, and all the country she claimed east or southeast of the Mississippi, to Great Britain. Great part of this territory also was in possession of the Indians.

By a secret treaty, which was executed about the same time, France ceded Louisiana to Spain; and Spain has since retroceded the same country to France. At the time both of its cession and retrocession, it was occupied chiefly by the Indians.

Thus, all the nations of Europe, who have acquired territory on this continent, have asserted in themselves, and have recognized in others, the exclusive right of the discoverer to appropriate the lands occupied by the Indians. Have the American States rejected or adopted this principle?

By the treaty which concluded the war of our revolution, Great Britain relinquished all claim, not only to the government, but to the "propriety and territorial rights of the United States," whose boundaries were fixed in the second article. By this treaty, the powers of government, and the right to soil, which had previously been in Great Britain, passed definitively to these States. * * *

After these States became independent, a controversy subsisted between them and Spain respecting boundary [sic]. By the treaty of 1795, this controversy was adjusted, and Spain ceded to the United States the territory in question. This territory, though claimed by both nations, was chiefly in the actual occupation of Indians.

The magnificent purchase of Louisiana, was the purchase from France of a country almost entirely occupied by numerous tribes of Indians, who are in fact independent. Yet, any attempt of others to intrude into that country, would be considered as an aggression which would justify war.

Our late acquisitions from Spain [of Florida] are of the same character; and the negotiations which preceded those acquisitions, recognize and elucidate the principle which has been received as the foundation of all European title in America.

The United States, then, have unequivocally acceded to that great and broad rule by which its civilized inhabitants now hold this country. They hold, and assert in themselves, the title by which it was acquired. They maintain, as all others have maintained, that discovery gave an exclusive right to extinguish the Indian title of occupancy, either by purchase or by conquest; and gave also a right to such a degree of sovereignty, as the circumstances of the people would allow them to exercise.

* * * Conquest gives a title which the courts of the conqueror cannot deny, whatever the private and speculative opinions of individuals may be,

respecting the original justice of the claim which has been successfully asserted. The British government, which was then our government, and whose rights have passed to the United States, asserted a title to all the lands occupied by Indians, within the chartered limits of the British colonies. It asserted also a limited sovereignty over them, and the exclusive right of extinguishing the titles which occupancy gave to them. These claims have been maintained and established as far west as the river Mississippi, by the sword. The title to a vast portion of the lands we now hold, originates in them. It is not for the courts of this country to question the validity of this title, or to sustain one which is incompatible with it. * * *

[T]he tribes of Indians inhabiting this country were fierce savages, whose occupation was war, and whose subsistence was drawn chiefly from the forest. To leave them in possession of their country, was to leave the country a wilderness; to govern them as a distinct people, was impossible, because they were as brave and as high-spirited as they were fierce, and were ready to repel by arms every attempt on their independence. * * *

Frequent and bloody wars, in which the whites were not always the aggressors, unavoidably ensued. European policy, numbers and skill prevailed. As the white population advanced, that of the Indians necessarily receded. The country in the immediate neighborhood of agriculturists became unfit for them. The game fled into thicker and more unbroken forests, and the Indians followed. The soil, to which the crown originally claimed title, being no longer occupied by its ancient inhabitants, was parcelled out according to the will of the sovereign power, and taken possession of by persons who claimed immediately from the crown, or mediately, through its grantees or deputies. * * *

However extravagant the pretension of converting the discovery of an inhabited country into conquest may appear; if the principle has been asserted in the first instance, and afterwards sustained; if a country has been acquired and held under it; if the property of the great mass of the community originates in it, it becomes the law of the land, and cannot be questioned. So too, with respect to the concomitant principle, that the Indian inhabitants are to be considered merely as occupants, to be protected, indeed, while in peace, in the possession of their lands, but to be deemed incapable of transferring the absolute title to others. However this restriction may be opposed to natural right, and to the usages of civilized nations, yet, if it be indispensable to that system under which the country has been settled, and be adapted to the actual condition of the two people, it may, perhaps, be supported by reason, and certainly cannot be rejected by courts of justice. * * *

[The Court affirmed the judgment of the District Court of Illinois in favor of defendant M'Intosh.]

NOTES AND QUESTIONS

1. What kind of title to real estate did the European nations obtain by claiming lands in the New World? What kind of title did the United States

receive from these European nations when it executed treaties with them? What interest did the Indians have? What steps did the United States need to take in order to "clear" title obtained from foreign nations so that the United States could dispose of land for settlement? What, in short, is the chain of title to the public domain?

2.   Indian title (also called aboriginal title or Indian right of occupancy) was a unique property interest. It allowed Indian tribes to reside, hunt, and fish upon their aboriginal lands and to sue trespassing parties for damages. It also allowed tribes to transfer title, but only to or with the consent of the United States, a limitation that has had modern implications, explored in paragraph 5, below. Six decades after Johnson v. M'Intosh, the U.S. Supreme Court held that Indian title can be taken by the United States without payment of just compensation. Tee–Hit–Ton Indians v. United States, 348 U.S. 272 (1955). Absent U.S. consent, however, Indian title cannot be affected by the actions of states or private parties. On Indian title, see F. Cohen, HANDBOOK OF FEDERAL INDIAN LAW 486–93 (1982 ed.).

3.   Johnson v. M'Intosh acknowledged the right of the United States to obtain Indian title by "conquest" as well as by "purchase." In actual practice, the federal government usually went through the formal process of purchase, although bargaining power was hardly equal. As the Secretary of the Interior drily noted in his 1862 Annual Report: "Although the consent of the Indians [to yield their territory to advancing settlement] has been obtained in the form of treaties, it is well known that they have yielded to a necessity which they could not resist." John O'Sullivan, editor of a widely circulated magazine, nicely captured the national sentiment— and gave expression to the whole westward movement—when he criticized foreign interference with the U.S. annexation of Texas in 1845:

> Away, away with all these cobweb tissues of rights of discovery, exploration, settlement, contiguity, etc. * * * The American claim is by the right of our manifest destiny to overspread and to possess the whole of the continent which Providence has given us for the development of the great experiment of liberty and federative self-government entrusted to us. It is a right such as that of the tree to the space of air and earth suitable for the full expansion of its principle and destiny of growth.

Quoted in Richard White, IT'S YOUR MISFORTUNE AND NONE OF MY OWN: A HISTORY OF THE AMERICAN WEST 73 (1991). Arrangements with Indians were usually embodied in treaties until 1871, when the House of Representatives rebelled at being cut out of the process (treaties being subject to confirmation only by the Senate). Even after that date, the United States continued the process of clearing Indian title and establishing reservations by other means, primarily statutes and executive orders. A leading authority in Indian law estimated that the clearing of Indian title resulted, by the end of World War II, in the payment to tribes of between 500 million and one billion dollars. Felix Cohen, Original Indian Title, 32 Minn.L.Rev. 28 (1947). In 1946, Congress passed the Indian Claims Commission Act, which created a process for tribes to try to recover payments for past dealings where the U.S. had engaged in "dishonorable dealings" with tribes. 25 U.S.C. §§ 70–70v–1. On the workings of the Indian Claims Commission, see Felix S. Cohen, HANDBOOK OF FEDERAL INDIAN LAW 160–62 (1982 ed.).

4. Most tribes, by treaty or otherwise, transferred the majority of their aboriginal lands to the United States and reserved some of the remaining lands to themselves. These transactions had the effect of resolving Indian title, and converted the lands and resources the tribes reserved into "recognized" property interests which are compensable property interests protected by the Fifth Amendment. Legal title to these lands are generally held in trust by the United States, with beneficial interest in the tribes. Lands ceded by the tribes in these transactions were cleared of Indian claims. This left the United States free to open them for homesteading or other disposition, or to retain them for other purposes.

5. Indian title has continuing importance. As Johnson v. M'Intosh held, Indian land transactions are valid only if approved by the United States. This rule, codified in the Indian Trade and Intercourse Act of 1790, now found, as amended, at 25 U.S.C. § 177, regularized frontier property dealings and allowed reasonably orderly disposition of the lands by the United States through various land grants, homesteading, and other devices. But there were many transactions like those to Johnson, where tribes purported to convey title to non-federal parties but which were never sanctioned by the United States. In modern times considerable litigation has sought to declare such transactions void. In 1985, the Supreme Court held invalid a 1795 land transfer from the Oneida Nation to the State of New York, never approved by Congress, and ruled that the tribe's suit for possession was not barred by the statute of limitations or other defenses based on the passage of time. See Oneida County v. Oneida Indian Nation, 470 U.S. 226 (1985). See generally Robert Clinton & Margaret Tobey Hotopp, Judicial Enforcement of the Federal Restraints on Alienation of Indian Land: The Origins of the Eastern Land Claims, 31 Me. L. Rev. 17 (1979). Several other similar claims have been litigated or are currently in litigation. A number of such claims have been settled, with the tribes receiving title to part of their aboriginal lands. See, e.g., Maine Claims Settlement Act of 1980, 25 U.S.C. §§ 1721–1735.

6. This principle has also limited the ability of federal land agencies to dispose of or manage federal lands that have remained subject to Indian title which has not been extinguished. See, e.g., Cramer v. United States, 261 U.S. 219 (1923) (voiding a federal patent to lands to which Indian title had not been cleared); see also United States v. Santa Fe Pacific R. Co., 314 U.S. 339 (1941). In United States v. Dann, 470 U.S. 39 (1985), the Court rejected the claim of Western Shoshone Indians that grazing leases issued on federal lands were unauthorized, holding that Indian title to 13 million acres in western Nevada had been extinguished because the tribe had been compensated in a money damages case brought pursuant to the Indian Claims Commissions Act of 1946.

7. Today, some 56 million acres of Indian lands are held in trust by the United States. Even though bare legal title is in the United States, they are not properly public lands, because they are held in trust for Indian beneficiaries. Nevertheless, Indian lands are not unaffected by modern

policies regarding publicly owned resources. The Bureau of Indian Affairs, which oversees the federal government's trust management responsibility for these lands, is located in the Department of the Interior, and the laws and processes governing development of Indian resources in some cases resemble those applicable to public lands. See Del–Rio Drilling Programs, Inc. v. United States, 146 F.3d 1358 (Fed.Cir.1998). See generally Felix S. Cohen, HANDBOOK OF FEDERAL INDIAN LAW (1982 ed.).

8.   Indian treaty or other rights may limit or otherwise influence how non-Indian federal resources are managed. The most obvious example is in the water area, where federal reserved rights for Indians can have a major effect on management of other public resources, as discussed in Chapter 6. Sometimes Indians reserved hunting and fishing rights on lands ceded to the United States, and these have been recognized in modern times, and may run with the land when the United States disposes of it. The most prominent example concerns the rights of Northwest Indian tribes under the so-called "Stevens treaties" (negotiated by federal representative Isaac Stevens in the mid-nineteenth century) of "taking fish, at usual and accustomed grounds and stations [including off-reservation sites] * * * in common with all citizens of the Territory." See Washington v. Washington State Commercial Passenger Fishing Vessel Assn., 443 U.S. 658 (1979). See also Minnesota v. Mille Lacs Band of Chippewa Indians, 526 U.S. 172 (1999) (Tribe's treaty right to hunt and fish on lands it ceded to the United States was not abrogated by subsequent events, including the admission of Minnesota to the Union); Swim v. Bergland, 696 F.2d 712 (9th Cir.1983) (Tribe's right, in agreement with U.S. ratified by Congress in 1900, to cut timber, pasture livestock, and hunt and fish on federal lands justifies Forest Service cancelling non-Indian grazing permits); Kimball v. Callahan, 493 F.2d 564 (9th Cir.1974) (right of Indians to hunt on nearby national forest); State v. Coffee, 97 Idaho 905, 556 P.2d 1185 (1976) (right of Indians to hunt on "open and unclaimed" public lands). Other decisions have rejected such claims. See, e.g., South Dakota v. Bourland, 508 U.S. 679 (1993) (Tribe's reservation of right to hunt and fish on land ceded to the federal government did not give tribe the right to apply its game laws to non-Indians using these lands); United States v. Dion, 476 U.S. 734 (1986) (Indian treaty did not insulate a tribal member from prosecution under the federal Bald Eagle Protection Act); United States v. Billie, 667 F.Supp. 1485 (S.D.Fla.1987) (same result under Endangered Species Act); Crow Tribe v. Repsis, 866 F.Supp. 520 (D.Wyo.1994), *aff'd*, 73 F.3d 982 (10th Cir.1995) (treaty right to hunt on unoccupied federal lands held abrogated by at admitting Wyoming into the Union and reservation of land as national forest); United States v. Peterson, 121 F.Supp.2d 1309 (D.Mont. 2000) (Treaty right to hunt on a tract of federal land was abrogated when the United States included the land in Glacier National Park).

B.   DISPOSITION OF THE PUBLIC DOMAIN

1.   EARLY PUBLIC LAND POLICY ISSUES

The vast public domain had many suitors: states, entrepreneurs and other developers, speculators, military veterans, and settlers. Even before the Revolution, speculation in the unsettled western lands and squatting upon them before they were formally opened to settlement or surveyed were already common habits of the colonists. Other colonial practices, such as rewarding war veterans with a grant of lands, also became entrenched in public policy or tradition. Prominent from the beginning was a conflict between those who sought to use the public domain to advance the Jeffersonian ideal of an agrarian society dominated by small, independent farmers, and those to whom land was a commodity to be developed for the most valuable uses the marketplace would dictate.

As noted above, the Congress of Confederation enacted some important public land laws. The enduring contribution of the Land Ordinance of 1785 was the rectangular survey system by which the lands were divided into square townships of 36 identically-numbered sections, each section containing 640 acres or one square mile.* A drawing showing the section numbering system is found on p. 93 infra. Under the 1785 Ordinance, lands once surveyed were to be offered at auction for a minimum price of one dollar an acre, and section 16 in each township was reserved for public education. No limitations on speculation were imposed, and no provisions for the protection of squatters, already numerous, were made. Little settlement was accomplished under the Ordinance, for surveying had to be completed, Indian resistance in the Ohio Territory was strong, and large scale speculators were attempting to make private deals with the Congress of Confederation. That body viewed land sales as an important revenue source, but it forsook the profit motive when it rewarded Revolutionary War veterans and refugees with bounty warrants or scrip entitling them to select lands from the Military Reserves in Ohio.

The Congress of Confederation also enacted the Northwest Ordinance of 1787, which created a system of government for the territory north of the Ohio River to which Virginia had ceded its colonial claim in 1781. Among other things it defined a three-stage process whereby states could be carved out of this territory (following on provisions of an Ordinance enacted in 1784) and, significantly, it outlawed the practice of slavery in this region. Also significant was the provision in the 1787 Ordinance that the territorial government and "new States, shall never interfere with the primary disposal of the Soil by the United States * * *, nor with any regulations Congress may find necessary for securing the title in such soil to the bona fide purchasers."

Doubts about the constitutionality of the Northwest Ordinance were a consideration in the drafting of the United States Constitution in Philadelphia shortly thereafter. The framers responded by including three clauses of relevance. Article IV, section 3, clause 1 provides for the admission of new states. Article I, section 8, clause 17 (the "Enclave" Clause), gives Congress exclusive authority over the seat of government and "other needful Buildings." The third, Article IV, § 3, clause 2 (the Property

---

* This survey system has been followed ever since. Even though the United States Geological Survey has continued the work of its predecessors—going back at least to George Washington—many millions of acres in remote areas, principally in the West and Alaska, have yet to be officially surveyed.

Clause), is most important for our purposes, and reads, in relevant part: "The Congress shall have Power to dispose of and make all needful Rules and Regulations respecting the Territory or other Property belonging to the United States."**

The drafting of the language that would become the "Property Clause" of Article IV, § 3, did not generate much excitement. The available materials on the Convention's deliberations reflect no serious dispute over the idea that the Congress should be specifically given the power to dispose of federal lands, and when Governeur Morris moved the convention to adopt the language which (with one technical change) became that clause, only one state dissented. See Peter Appel, "The Power of Congress 'Without Limitation': The Property Clause and Federal Regulation of Private Property," 86 Minn. L. Rev. 1, 26 (2001). In the subsequent debates over ratification, including the Federalist Papers, the Property Clause did not attract much attention. Id., at 26–30. But federal lands remained an abiding concern of the national government: It has been estimated that about a quarter of all legislation enacted by Congress up to the Civil War related to public lands and land settlement. Roy Robbins, OUR LANDED HERITAGE 236.

a.   LAND GRANTS MADE BY FOREIGN GOVERNMENTS

One of the first tasks of the new national government was to determine just what lands were "Property belonging to the United States." Predecessor governments had made various grants of land over which the American government eventually gained sovereignty. In the Jay Treaty of 1794, the young Nation agreed to recognize pre-existing grants, and this practice was followed in all subsequent acquisitions. Translating this simple principle into reality proved an immense task. It took generations for the courts and Congress to decide the validity and extent of prior grants made by the governments of Great Britain, Spain, France, and Mexico. The claims ranged from the size of town lots in Detroit to a 1.5 million acre grant in Florida. The disputes were widespread and long-lasting; 126 such cases were decided by the Supreme Court before 1860, and many more thereafter. "[I]ncredible forgeries, fraud, subornation, and perjuries" were all too common. Territorial administrators as well as the likes of Johnstone Amerson (a "poor wandering wretch, equally destitute of morality or character willing to testify, on moderate terms, for any man who would pay him for it") participated in the purchase and fabrication of prior land grants. Corruption was so common that one historian felt compelled to protest that "[n]ot all public officials participated in the grab and by no means all of the claims acquired by officers were improperly obtained or tainted with fraud." Paul Gates, HISTORY OF PUBLIC LAND LAW DEVELOPMENT, at 228. Language difficulties, political patronage appointments of land officials, incomplete foreign records, abandonment of grants, and similar factors complicated the process.

** Armed with this authority, the new Congress quickly reconfirmed and extended the provisions of the Northwest Ordinance of 1787. See Act of August 7, 1789, ch. VIII, 1 Stat. 50; Paul Gates, HISTORY OF PUBLIC LAND LAW DEVELOPMENT 288 (1970).

Congress was extremely patient with dilatory claimants and generous in recognizing questionable claims, and Boards of Land Commissioners and other administrators struggled with questions of title for generations. Emotions on such questions ran high: a United States Senator killed the son of a federal judge in a Missouri duel caused by disputes over the validity of Spanish land grants, and another federal judge was later impeached (but not convicted) for incidents arising out of similar squabbles. The Presidential Proclamation of December 12, 1815 declared that "uninformed or evil-disposed persons" occupying Spanish land grants in violation of the 1807 Anti–Intrusion Act would be forcibly removed. However, the federal marshal of the same Territory responded by warning that not "five Militia men of this Territory would * * * march against the intruders on public lands."

The claimants of large tracts generally prevailed in the end because of their persistence, congressional sympathy, and superior representation before Congress, courts, and commissioners. (Daniel Webster and Thomas Hart Benton represented claimants while serving in the U.S. Senate.) But not always. In one of the most celebrated disputes, most of the claims of Swiss immigrant Johann Sutter to vast acreage in California pursuant to grants from Mexico in the early 1840s (and whose mill was the site of the discovery that triggered the fabled California Gold Rush) were in the end rejected by the courts. See, e.g., United States v. Sutter, 62 U.S. (21 How.) 170 (1858); United States v. Nye, 62 U.S. (21 How.) 408 (1858); In re Sutter, 69 U.S. (2 Wall.) 562 (1864). Ultimately, 34 million acres in 19 states were confirmed to grantees of former governments, and these lands were usually the most desirable acreage that otherwise would have been available to settlers. In the protracted disputes, one might guess that the primary beneficiaries were the lawyers.

b. EARLY STEPS TOWARD RETENTION OF FEDERAL LANDS

The biggest point of controversy about federal lands was not whether they would be retained or disposed of, for the assumption was widespread that most of these lands would eventually pass out of national ownership. Rather, the overriding issue was whether the states or the national government would supervise the process of disposal. The Property Clause squarely settled that question in favor of the national government. But it did so in terms which seemed to recognize that the United States might retain and manage some of these lands for national purposes. Early on, in fact, the U.S. created a system for leasing rather than selling certain federal lands with mineral values in the Midwest. Eventually, the constitutionality of this practice came before the U.S. Supreme Court.

United States v. Gratiot

Supreme Court of the United States, 1840.
39 U.S. (14 Peters) 526.

■ THOMPSON, J.

[The U.S. brought an action on a debt, alleging that the defendants, who had a federal license to smelt lead ore obtained from U.S. mines in

Illinois had not paid the U.S. the royalty in kind provided in the license, of six pounds of lead for every 100 pounds smelted. The defendants responded by challenging the constitutionality of the 1807 federal statute which authorized the President to contract for the development of lead on the public lands. Senator Thomas Hart Benton argued for the defendants that the only authority the Property Clause gave Congress over the public lands is "to dispose of them, and to make rules and regulations respecting the preparation of them for sale; for their preservation, and their sale." "The power to make rules and regulations, applies to the power to dispose of the lands. The rules are to carry the disposal into effect; to protect them; to explore them; to survey them." If the Property Clause were understood to have authorized federal retention and management, Benton went on, the states would have stoutly resisted, and those with western land claims would have never ceded them. The Court's unanimous response was curt:]

The term territory, as here used [in the Property Clause] is merely descriptive of one kind of property; and is equivalent to the word lands. And Congress has the same power over it as over any other property belonging to the United States; and this power is vested in Congress without limitation; and has been considered the foundation upon which the territorial governments rest. * * * [T]he words "dispose of," cannot receive the construction contended for at the bar; that they vest in Congress the power only to sell, and not to lease such lands. The disposal must be left to the discretion of Congress. And there can be no apprehensions of any encroachments upon state rights, by the creation of a numerous tenantry within their borders; as has been so strenuously urged in the argument. The law of 1807, authorizing the leasing of the lead mines, was passed before Illinois was organized as a state; and she cannot now complain of any disposition or regulation of the lead mines previously made by Congress. She surely cannot claim a right to the public lands within her limits. It has been the policy of the government, at all times in disposing of the public lands, to reserve the mines for the use of the United States. And their real value cannot be ascertained, without causing them to be explored and worked, under proper regulations. The authority given to the President to lease the lead mines, is limited * * * to a short period, so as not to interfere with the power of Congress to make other disposition of the mines, should they think proper to do so.

NOTES AND QUESTIONS

1.   The earliest Property Clause cases dealt with Congress's power to put in place the governmental machinery, such as a judicial system, to govern territories. They read the Clause broadly; indeed, they seemed to assume that Congress would have the power even if the Property Clause did not exist. See Peter Appel, "The Power of Congress 'Without Limitation': The Property Clause and Federal Regulation of Private Property," 86 Minn. L. Rev. 1, 30–33 (2001).

2. Justice Joseph Story strongly expounded the position taken in Gratiot in his influential COMMENTARIES ON THE CONSTITUTION OF THE UNITED STATES, § 1318, at 193–94 (Da Capo Press 1970) (1833). See Appel, at 33–35.

3. Does *Gratiot* resolve whether the admission of Illinois as a state in 1818 might affect Congress's power over this property? The statute authorizing lead mine development under federal control had been enacted in 1807, but the license to Gratiot was not issued until September 1834, after statehood. Does that make any difference?

4. Should the Court's reference to a power "without limitations" really be taken literally? Could Congress enact a law prohibiting political speech on federal land?

5. The most limiting (and tragic) interpretation of the Property Clause ever put forward by the U.S. Supreme Court came in its most infamous decision in history. In Dred Scott v. Sandford, 60 U.S. (19 How.) 393, 432–52 (1856), Chief Justice Taney took the view that the "territory" referred to in the Property Clause referred only to the territory that some of the original states had ceded to the United States. (See pp. 36–37, supra.) He also narrowly read Congress's power to make "needful rules and regulations" under the Property Clause. The Court's conclusion that Congress could not prohibit slavery in territories and new states made the Civil War inevitable. The Court had never before, and has never after, taken such a view of the Property Clause. Taney's reasoning is severely criticized, and the opinions of the other Justices on the Property Clause issue critically examined, in Peter Appel, "The Power of Congress 'Without Limitation': The Property Clause and Federal Regulation of Private Property," 86 Minn. L. Rev. 1, 34–51 (2001).

2. STATEHOOD AND EQUAL FOOTING

From the admission of Ohio in 1803 to that of Alaska in 1959, the state-making procedure involved Congress and the people of the territories in complicated political disputes. Territorial interests seeking statehood were brought, sometimes with some reluctance, to give up plans some entertained for either acquiring or controlling and managing the federal lands found within their borders.* By a curious legal quirk and implication, however, new states did receive some land at statehood; namely, the lands underlying navigable waters within their boundaries. The starting point was the Supreme Court's decision that title to lands underlying navigable waters in the original thirteen states had passed from the British Crown to their colonies, before the establishment of the United States. Martin v. Waddell's Lessee, 41 U.S. (16 Pet.) 367 (1842). In that case, Chief Justice Taney wrote that "when the people of New Jersey took * * * into their

---

* The thirteen original states, along with early admittees Vermont, Maine, Tennessee and Kentucky (and, later, Texas and Hawaii), have never been considered "public land" states, because the federal government never had appreciable ownership of lands within their borders. Whether or not a state is considered a public land state has no legal significance, however.

own hands the powers of sovereignty [several decades before the American Revolution], the prerogatives and regalities which before belonged either to the crown or the parliament, became immediately and rightfully vested in the state." Upon the establishment of the national government, the states held "the absolute right to all their navigable waters and the soils under them for their own common use, subject only to the rights since surrendered by the Constitution to the general government." Three years later, the next shoe dropped.

Pollard v. Hagan

Supreme Court of the United States, 1845.
44 U.S. (3 How.) 212.

[Alabama was admitted to the Union in 1819, having been carved out of territory formerly claimed by Georgia and ceded to the United States. Plaintiffs claimed title to land formerly covered by high tide under a patent from the United States confirmed by an 1836 Act of Congress. Defendants claimed title under a prior Spanish land grant recognized by Alabama in 1795. The trial court charged that if the land was below high tide when Alabama became a state, the United States could not later grant title to plaintiffs. The Supreme Court affirmed the judgment for defendant. Mr. Justice McKINLEY's majority opinion contained the following comments about state admission on an equal footing and the corresponding powers and duties of the United States.]

We think a proper examination of this subject will show, that the United States never held any municipal sovereignty, jurisdiction, or right of soil in and to the territory, of which Alabama or any of the new states were formed; except for temporary purposes, and to execute the trusts created by the acts of the Virginia and Georgia legislatures, and the deeds of cession executed by them to the United States, and the trust created by the treaty with the French republic, of the 30th of April, 1803, ceding Louisiana. * * *

* * * Taking the legislative acts of the United States, and the states of Virginia and Georgia, and their deeds of cession to the United States, and giving to each, separately, and to all jointly, a fair interpretation, we must come to the conclusion that it was the intention of the parties to invest the United States with the eminent domain of the country ceded, both national and municipal, for the purposes of temporary government, and to hold it in trust for the performance of the stipulations and conditions expressed in the deeds of cession and the legislative acts connected with them. To a correct understanding of the rights, powers, and duties of the parties to these contracts, it is necessary to enter into a more minute examination of the rights of eminent domain, and the right to the public lands. When the United States accepted the cession of the territory, they took upon themselves the trust to hold the municipal eminent domain for the new states, and to invest them with it, to the same extent, in all respects, that it was held by the states ceding the territories. * * *

When Alabama was admitted into the union, on an equal footing with the original states, she succeeded to all the rights of sovereignty, jurisdiction, and eminent domain which Georgia possessed at the date of the cession, except so far as this right was diminished by the public lands remaining in the possession and under the control of the United States, for the temporary purposes provided for in the deed of cession and the legislative acts connected with it. Nothing remained to the United States, according to the terms of the agreement, but the public lands. And, if an express stipulation had been inserted in the agreement, granting the municipal right of sovereignty and eminent domain to the United States, such stipulation would have been void and inoperative; because the United States have no constitutional capacity to exercise municipal jurisdiction, sovereignty, or eminent domain, within the limits of a state or elsewhere, except in the cases in which it is expressly granted.

By the 16th clause of the 8th section of the 1st article of the Constitution, power is given to Congress "to exercise exclusive legislation in all cases whatsoever, over such district (not exceeding ten miles square) as may by cession of particular states, and the acceptance of Congress, become the seat of government of the United States, and to exercise like authority over all places purchased, by the consent of the legislature of the state in which the same may be, for the erection of forts, magazines, arsenals, dockyards, and other needful buildings." Within the District of Columbia, and the other places purchased and used for the purposes above mentioned, the national and municipal powers of government, of every description, are united in the government of the union. And these are the only cases, within the United States, in which all the powers of government are united in a single government, except in the cases already mentioned of the temporary territorial governments, and there a local government exists. The right of Alabama and every other new state to exercise all the powers of government, which belong to and may be exercised by the original states of the union, must be admitted, and remain unquestioned, except so far as they are, temporarily, deprived of control over the public lands.

We will now inquire into the nature and extent of the right of the United States to these lands, and whether that right can in any manner affect or control the decision of the case before us. This right originated in voluntary surrenders, made by several of the old states, of their waste and unappropriated lands, to the United States, under a resolution of the old Congress, of the 6th of September, 1780, recommending such surrender and cession, to aid in paying the public debt, incurred by the war of the Revolution. The object of all the parties to these contracts of cession, was to convert the land into money for the payment of the debt, and to erect new states over the territory thus ceded; and as soon as these purposes could be accomplished, the power of the United States over these lands, as property, was to cease.

Whenever the United States shall have fully executed these trusts, the municipal sovereignty of the new states will be complete, throughout their respective borders, and they, and the original states, will be upon an equal footing, in all respects whatever. We, therefore, think the United States hold the public lands within the new states by force of the deeds of cession, and the statutes connected with them, and not by any municipal sovereignty which it may be supposed they possess, or have reserved by compact with the new states, for that particular purpose. The provision of the Constitution above referred to shows that no such power can be exercised by the United States within a state. Such a power is not only repugnant to the Constitution, but it is inconsistent with the spirit and intention of the deeds of cession. The argument so much relied on by the counsel for the plaintiffs, that the agreement of the people inhabiting the new states, "that they for ever disclaim all right and title to the waste or unappropriated lands lying within the said territory; and that the same shall be and remain at the sole and entire disposition of the United States," cannot operate as a contract between the parties, but is binding as a law. Full power is given to Congress "to make all needful rules and regulations respecting the territory or other property of the United States." This authorized the passage of all laws necessary to secure the rights of the United States to the public lands, and to provide for their sale, and to protect them from taxation. * * *

* * * This right of eminent domain over the shores and the soils under the navigable waters, for all municipal purposes, belongs exclusively to the states within their respective territorial jurisdictions, and they, and they only, have the constitutional power to exercise it. To give to the United States the right to transfer to a citizen the title to the shores and the soils under the navigable waters, would be placing in their hands a weapon which might be wielded greatly to the injury of state sovereignty, and deprive the states of the power to exercise a numerous and important class of police powers. But in the hands of the states this power can never be used so as to affect the exercise of any national right of eminent domain or jurisdiction with which the United States have been invested by the Constitution. For, although the territorial limits of Alabama have extended all her sovereign power into the sea, it is there, as on the shore, but municipal power, subject to the Constitution of the United States, "and the laws which shall be made in pursuance thereof."

By the preceding course of reasoning we have arrived at these general conclusions: First. The shores of navigable waters, and the soils under them, were not granted by the Constitution to the United States, but were reserved to the states respectively. Second. The new states have the same rights, sovereignty, and jurisdiction over this subject as the original states. Third. The right of the United States to the public lands, and the power of Congress to make all needful rules and regulations for the sale and disposition thereof, conferred no power to grant to the plaintiffs the land in controversy in this case.

The judgment of the Supreme Court of the state of Alabama is therefore affirmed.

■ MR. JUSTICE CATRON dissented. * * *

NOTES AND QUESTIONS

1. Article IV, section 3, clause 1 of the Constitution provides, in pertinent part, simply that "New States may be admitted by the Congress

into this Union." As explained in Coyle v. Smith, 221 U.S. 559, 566–67 (1911), the "equal footing doctrine" assures those new states that they will possess governmental authority equal to all other states. Coyle struck down a provision in Oklahoma's statehood admission act that prevented the new state from moving the location of its state capitol for a brief period of time. See also John Hanna, Equal Footing in the Admission of States, 3 Baylor L.Rev. 519 (1951).

2.   Although Justice McKinley used some sweeping language characterizing the expectation that the U.S. would not retain and manage lands in new states, only *Pollard*'s narrow holding has survived the test of time. More than a century after *Pollard*, the U.S. Supreme Court put it this way (Arizona v. California, 373 U.S. 546, 596–97 (1963)):

> Arizona's contention that the Federal Government had no power, after Arizona became a State, to reserve waters for the use and benefit of federally reserved lands rests largely upon statements in Pollard's Lessee v. Hagan, 3 How. 212 (1845), and Shively v. Bowlby, 152 U.S. 1 (1894). Those cases and others that followed them gave rise to the doctrine that lands underlying navigable waters within territory acquired by the Government are held in trust for future States and that title to such lands is automatically vested in the States upon admission to the Union. But those cases involved only the shores of and lands beneath navigable waters. They do not determine the problem before us and cannot be accepted as limiting the broad powers of the United States to regulate navigable waters under the Commerce Clause and to regulate government lands under Art. IV, § 3, of the Constitution.

Such statements did not prevent many in the West from insisting on the invalidity of federal land ownership in the course of the 1970s Sagebrush Rebellion and the 1990s County Supremacy Movement. See infra Ch. 3, § B.

3.   The rule in Pollard might have been limited only to those new states like Alabama which were carved out of the land claims of the original thirteen colonies. It has, however, always been read as applying to all new states:

> On the public domain within states created out of territories, the states acquired title to the beds and banks up to high-water mark of that water which was navigable under the federal test on the date of admission of each such state. In these states, the federal government continued to hold nearly all of the remaining land as public domain, the newly admitted states acquiring only thin ribbons of land comprising the beds and banks of navigable waters. That may sound ridiculous, but it is true.

R.   Clark, 1 WATERS AND WATER RIGHTS 250–51 (1967). The Supreme Court has more recently made clear that states also succeed to ownership of submerged lands subject to the ebb and flow of tides, whether the waters are navigable or not. Phillips Petroleum Co. v. Mississippi, 484 U.S. 469 (1988).

4. The states' title is not "granted" by the federal government, but rather passes automatically to the state at statehood. This seemingly simple principle can create enormous uncertainty in the real world. It may be many years before a determination of navigability-at-statehood, and therefore title, is made. In the meantime, the states hold inchoate claims to the beds of waterbodies that may have been navigable when the states were admitted to the Union. A uniform federal test is used to determine navigability:

> [S]treams or lakes which are navigable in fact must be regarded as navigable in law; that they are navigable in fact when they are used, or are susceptible of being used, in their natural and ordinary condition, as highways for commerce, over which trade and travel are or may be conducted in the customary modes of trade and travel on water; and further that navigability does not depend on the particular mode in which such use is or may be had—whether by streamboats, sailing vessels or flatboats—nor on an absence of occasional difficulties in navigation, but on the fact, if it be a fact, that the stream in its ordinary condition affords a channel for useful commerce.

United States v. Holt State Bank, 270 U.S. 49, 56 (1926).

5. "Navigability" is a confusing concept, partly because it serves federal purposes other than determining title to the beds of waterbodies. For example, "navigability" helps determine the extent of federal admiralty jurisdiction, and it was frequently used in the country's early legal history as a shorthand for "commerce" in defining the extent of Congress's power to regulate. See, e.g., Gibbons v. Ogden, 22 U.S. 1 (1824). Congress has in modern times sometimes continued the practice of using "navigable waters" as the touchstone for federal regulatory power, even when it defines those waters as "waters of the United States." See, e.g., United States v. Riverside Bayview Homes, 474 U.S. 121 (1985); Solid Waste Agency of Northern Cook County v. U.S. Army Corps of Engineers, 531 U.S. 159 (2001). Adding to the difficulty, states may apply their own definitions of navigability for state law purposes.

6. Navigability-for-title disputes still find their way to the courts whenever there is a reason to determine ownership of beds of waterbodies; e.g., for mineral development. Considerable litigation has occurred in Alaska to sort out ownership of riverbeds among the United States, Native communities, and the state, and the state has prevailed in the early rounds. See, e.g., State v. United States, 201 F.3d 1154 (9th Cir.2000); Alaska v. Ahtna, Inc., 891 F.2d 1401 (9th Cir.1989). Given the abundance of water and federal land in Alaska, and its history of state-federal animosities, it is easy to foresee many problems if the state is vested with title to threads or ribbons of submerged lands throughout the many national parks, wildlife refuges, and other federal reservations found within its borders.

7. Even if the state succeeds to ownership of the beds of waters navigable at statehood, the United States is not without legal claims to the waters or the resources they contain. In Alaska v. Babbitt, 72 F.3d 698 (9th Cir.1995), the court determined that "public lands," as defined in the Alaska National Interest Lands Act (ANILCA) for purposes of applying that

statute's preference for subsistence hunting and fishing by rural residents, include navigable waters in which the United States has reserved water rights. The Alaska Supreme Court rejected that proposition, Totemoff v. State, 905 P.2d 954 (Alaska 1995), but the Ninth Circuit later rejected a claim for en banc review of its earlier decision (three judges dissenting), Katie John v. United States, 247 F.3d 1032 (9th Cir.2001), and the State did not seek Supreme Court review.

8. The Court in Pollard v. Hagan did not resolve questions of title to submerged lands off the coasts of the United States. In United States v. California, 332 U.S. 19 (1947), the Supreme Court held that the United States, and not the coastal states, owned these submerged lands. The coastal states then sought a political remedy, and the issue became a hot one in the 1952 Presidential election. When Dwight Eisenhower won that election and helped sweep the Republicans into control of Congress, the United States gave the states title to lands underneath coastal waters up to three miles offshore (or three marine leagues, along the Gulf of Mexico) in the Submerged Lands Act of 1953, 43 U.S.C. §§ 1301–1315. The United States retained ownership and jurisdiction of lands further out. See p. 672 below.

9. The *Pollard* principle is subject to a very important exception; namely, the United States may reserve the beds of navigable waters for federal purposes prior to statehood, and the Court has held that this prevents title from passing to the new state. The Court has, however, adopted the interpretive principle that such reservations must be clearly expressed in order to be effective. See, e.g., Utah Div. of State Lands v. United States, 482 U.S. 193 (1987). Where such clarity is not found, the *Pollard* rule recognizes that states have inholdings in the submerged lands underlying waterbodies that were navigable at statehood in federal reservations such as national parks, even if they were created prior to statehood. In its most recent decision on this issue, the Court split 5–4, the slim majority holding that the U.S. had reserved part of the bed of Lake Coeur d'Alene and part of the St. Joe River to bar transfer of title to Idaho at statehood. Idaho v. United States, 533 U.S. 262 (2001).

10. Sometimes the application of these rules can have large fiscal and environmental consequences. In 1957 the Secretary of the Interior formally proposed a withdrawal of lands (including submerged lands under navigable waters) in northeast Alaska in order to create the Arctic National Wildlife Refuge. The withdrawal was not formally completed, however, until after Alaska gained statehood in 1959. The state later sued to quiet title to the submerged lands to advance its desire to exploit possible oil and gas resources in the area, which is to the east of the giant Prudhoe Bay oil field that supplies Alaska with the bulk of its state revenue. The Supreme Court ruled, 6–3, that the 1957 proposal effectively segregated the submerged lands and prevented them from passing to the State at statehood. United States v. Alaska, 521 U.S. 1 (1997). Justice O'Connor, writing for the majority, reasoned that (1) the 1957 proposal "reflected a clear intent to reserve submerged lands as well as uplands;" (2) the Interior Department's position, expressed in a regulation promulgated in 1952, was that a

proposal for a withdrawal temporarily segregated the lands in the proposal pending final action by the Secretary; and (3) the Statehood Act contained a specific provision that the State would not take title to "lands withdrawn *or otherwise set apart as* refuges or reservations for the protection of wildlife," 72 Stat. 340–41 (emphasis added), and the temporary segregation in 1957 fell within the italicized language of the Statehood Act. Therefore, federal ownership of the submerged lands in the Refuge survived statehood and the *Pollard* principle. Justice Thomas, joined by Chief Justice Rehnquist and Justice Scalia, dissented.

a.   A BRIEF DETOUR: THE PUBLIC TRUST DOCTRINE

An opinion by the Supreme Court in 1892 (which has retained some vitality in modern times, especially in state law) holds that lands underlying navigable waters are subject to a public trust.

Illinois Central Railroad Co. v. Illinois

Supreme Court of the United States, 1892.
146 U.S. 387.

■ MR. JUSTICE FIELD delivered the opinion of the court.

[The State of Illinois granted to the Illinois Central Railroad a large part of Chicago's waterfront on Lake Michigan, including the submerged lands in Chicago's harbor. The grant was made under highly dubious circumstances. The Illinois Legislature later attempted to revoke it, and the Illinois Attorney General brought suit to invalidate it. The Court first recited the *Pollard v. Hagan* rule that the State succeeded to ownership of lands beneath navigable waters and held that Illinois acquired title to the lands in dispute upon statehood.]

The question, therefore, to be considered is whether the legislature was competent to thus deprive the State of its ownership of the submerged lands in the harbor of Chicago, and of the consequent control of its waters; or, in other words, whether the railroad corporation can hold the lands and control the waters by the grant, against any future exercise of power over them by the State.

* * * [T]he State holds the title to the lands under the navigable waters of Lake Michigan, within its limits, in the same manner that the State holds title to soils under tide water, by the common law, * * * and that title necessarily carries with it control over the waters above them whenever the lands are subjected to use. But it is a title different in character from that which the State holds in lands intended for sale. It is different from the title which the United States hold in the public lands which are open to preemption and sale. It is a title held in trust for the people of the State that they may enjoy the navigation of the waters, carry on commerce over them, and have liberty of fishing therein freed from the obstruction or interference of private parties. The interest of the people in the navigation of the waters and in commerce over them may be improved in many instances by the erection of wharves, docks and piers therein, for

which purpose the State may grant parcels of the submerged lands; and, so long as their disposition is made for such purpose, no valid objections can be made to the grants. [Such] grants * * * do not substantially impair the public interest in the lands and waters remaining * * *. But that is a very different doctrine from the one which would sanction the abdication of the general control of the State over lands under the navigable waters of an entire harbor or bay, or of a sea or lake. Such abdication is not consistent with the exercise of that trust which requires the government of the State to preserve such waters for the use of the public. The trust devolving upon the State for the public, and which can only be discharged by the management and control of property in which the public has an interest, cannot be relinquished by a transfer of the property. The control of the State for the purposes of the trust can never be lost, except as to such parcels as are used in promoting the interests of the public therein, or can be disposed of without any substantial impairment of the public interest in the lands and waters remaining. * * * [T]he distinction [must be maintained] between a grant of such parcels for the improvement of the public interest, or which when occupied do not substantially impair the public interest in the lands and waters remaining, and a grant of the whole property in which the public is interested * * *. General language sometimes found in opinions of the courts, expressive of absolute ownership and control by the State of lands under navigable waters, irrespective of any trust as to their use and disposition, must be read and construed with reference to the special facts of the particular cases. A grant of all the lands under the navigable waters of a State has never been adjudged to be within the legislative power; and any attempted grant of the kind would be held, if not absolutely void on its face, as subject to revocation. The State can no more abdicate its trust over property in which the whole people are interested, like navigable waters and soils under them, so as to leave them entirely under the use and control of private parties, except in the instance of parcels mentioned for the improvement of the navigation and use of the waters, or when parcels can be disposed of without impairment of the public interest in what remains, than it can abdicate its police powers in the administration of government and the preservation of the peace. In the administration of government the use of such powers may for a limited period be delegated to a municipality or other body, but there always remains with the State the right to revoke those powers and exercise them in a more direct manner, and one more conformable to its wishes. So with trusts connected with public property, or property of a special character, like lands under navigable waters, they cannot be placed entirely beyond the direction and control of the State.

The harbor of Chicago is of immense value to the people of the State of Illinois in the facilities it affords to its vast and constantly increasing commerce; and the idea that its legislature can deprive the State of control over its bed and waters and place the same in the hands of a private corporation created for a different purpose, one limited to transportation of passengers and freight between distant points and the city, is a proposition that cannot be defended. * * *

Any grant of the kind is necessarily revocable, and the exercise of the trust by which the property was held by the State can be resumed at any time. Undoubtedly there may be expenses incurred in improvements made under such a grant which the State ought to pay; but, be that as it may, the power to resume the trust whenever the State judges best is, we think, incontrovertible. The position advanced by the railroad company in support of its claim to the ownership of the submerged lands and the right to the erection of wharves, piers and docks at its pleasure, or for its business in the harbor of Chicago, would place every harbor in the country at the mercy of a majority of the legislature of the State in which the harbor is situated.

We cannot, it is true, cite any authority where a grant of this kind has been held invalid, for we believe that no instance exists where the harbor of a great city and its commerce have been allowed to pass into the control of any private corporation. But the decisions are numerous which declare that such property is held by the State, by virtue of its sovereignty, in trust for the public. The ownership of the navigable waters of the harbor and of the lands under them is a subject of public concern to the whole people of the State. The trust with which they are held, therefore, is governmental and cannot be alienated, except in those instances mentioned of parcels used in the improvement of the interest thus held, or when parcels can be disposed of without detriment to the public interest in the lands and waters remaining. * * *

NOTES AND QUESTIONS

1. Is the Court saying that certain kinds of government-owned property are different from other kinds, and justifies a continuing servitude or limitation on their title? What kinds? What makes these lands different from other government lands?

2. Is this just a special form of eminent domain? Is that what Justice Field meant when he said grants of such land are "necessarily revocable"? Did he mean that the State can choose to take the land back at any time (in effect, exercising a right of eminent domain), not by paying the grantee fair market value, but rather simply compensating the grantee for its "expenses incurred in improvements made under such a grant"?

3. Or is the idea simply one of police power regulation; namely, that the state does not, by granting this land, "abdicate general control" over it? Is Justice Field saying that property like a harbor has such high public values that the state does not relinquish, by mere transfer of title, strong regulatory control over how such lands are used, in order to protect the public interest. (Today, of course, the notion of regulatory police power has evolved so that it is generally understood to apply to the use of practically all kinds of property.)

4. What is the source of this public trust limitation? The federal constitution? Federal common law? State law? Can it be overturned by statute?

5. The public trust doctrine is not moribund, at least in Illinois. In 1990, history seemed to repeat itself when a federal district court applied it to void the conveyance by Illinois of submerged lands under Lake Michigan to a university for expansion of its campus. Lake Michigan Federation v. U.S. Army Corps of Engineers, 742 F.Supp. 441 (N.D.Ill.1990). Further consideration is given to the public trust doctrine in Chapter 5, infra p. 382.

3. Grants to States

a. STATEHOOD GRANTS

States were primary beneficiaries of federal land disposition policy, especially through land grants made as part of the statehood process. The creation of new states on an "equal footing" with other states was first and foremost a political process, worked through the Congress. The admission of Ohio in 1803 created the basic model for later federal land grants to new states. After considerable wrangling, Congress agreed to grant the Buckeye State four percent of its land area for the benefit of its common schools, five percent of the net proceeds of federal land sales within the state for road-building fund, and other incidental interests in land.

The grants to the states took two basic forms. The first, and more important, were "in-place" grants of specified numbered sections of land. These were usually for the purpose of supporting the new state's "common schools." The actual location of these lands could not be determined until the land was surveyed and section lines established. The survey might not be completed for many decades after statehood; indeed, there is still some federal land that has never been surveyed. If, before survey, the federal government had disposed of or made other uses of these land sections by formal reservation or withdrawal, the states were given the right to make "in lieu" selections of other available federal lands as "indemnity" for the unsatisfied "in-place" school grants. Andrus v. Utah, below, involved this type of grant. The second form was "quantity" grants of a specified amount of acreage, not identified on the ground by survey, but rather to be selected by the state from available federal land, to support various public purposes, such as highways, jails, or other public purposes. Under both forms, the granted lands were not expected to be used as actual sites for schools, highways, jails, and so forth (although they could be used for such purposes). Instead, they were supposed to be sold or leased or otherwise managed to produce income to be devoted to these purposes.

As more and more states were admitted, the purposes of the grants were modified, and the quantities of the grants were gradually liberalized. Some new states were given federal lands for higher education, for jails and other public buildings, and for internal improvements other than roads. Utah (admitted in 1896) was the first to be given four sections of federal land in every township, or about 11% of the acreage in the state, for common schools. Arizona and New Mexico (admitted in 1912) each received that amount of common school lands, plus over two million acres of other federal lands for various public purposes. Appendix C to Paul Gates'

HISTORY OF PUBLIC LAND LAW DEVELOPMENT (1970), pp. 804–05, contains a convenient summary table of federal land grants to public land states. State school systems were the largest recipient of federal largess: Overall, federal land grants totaled 77 million acres for common schools and 21 million acres for higher education. As the following case shows, the terms and effect of statehood grants still provoke litigation.

Andrus v. Utah

Supreme Court of the United States, 1980.
446 U.S. 500.

■ MR. JUSTICE STEVENS delivered the opinion of the Court.

The State of Utah claims the right to select extremely valuable oil shale lands located within federal grazing districts in lieu of and as indemnification for original school land grants of significantly lesser value that were frustrated by federal preemption, or private entry, prior to survey. The question presented is whether the Secretary of the Interior is obliged to accept Utah's selections of substitute tracts of the same size as the originally designated sections even though there is a gross disparity between the value of the original grants and the selected substitutes. We hold that the Secretary's "grossly disparate value" policy is a lawful exercise of the broad discretion vested in him by § 7 of the Taylor Grazing Act of 1934, as amended in 1936, 43 U.S.C. § 315f, and is a valid ground for refusing to accept Utah's selections.

Utah became a State in 1896. In the Utah Enabling Act of 1894, Congress granted Utah, upon admission, four numbered sections in each township for the support of public schools. [Eds. note: The Act awarded Utah numbered sections 2, 16, 32 and 36 in each township; see the township chart reproduced on p. 93 below.] The statute provided that if the designated sections had already "been sold or otherwise disposed of" pursuant to another act of Congress, "other lands equivalent thereto * * * are hereby granted." The substitute grants, denominated "indemnity lands" were "to be selected within [the] State in such manner as [its] legislature may provide with the approval of the Secretary of the Interior."

Because much of the State was not surveyed until long after its admission to the Union, its indemnity or "in lieu" selections were not made promptly. On September 10, 1965, Utah filed the first of 194 selection lists with the Bureau of Land Management of the Department of the Interior covering the land in dispute in this litigation. The 194 indemnity selections include 157,255.90 acres in Uintah County, Utah, all of which are located within federal grazing districts created pursuant to the Taylor Grazing Act.

In January 1974, before Utah's selection lists had been approved or disapproved, the Governor of Utah agreed that the Secretary of the Interior could include two tracts comprising 10,240 acres of selected indemnity lands in an oil shale leasing program, on the understanding that the rental proceeds would ultimately be paid to the State if its selections were approved. The proceeds of the leases are of substantial value.[2]

---

2. The District Court found that as of May 25, 1976, $48,291,840 had been accumu-   lated. It should be noted that these proceeds were derived from only 10,240 acres out of

In February 1974, the Secretary advised the Governor that he would not approve any indemnity applications that involved "grossly disparate values."[3] He wrote:

> * * * In January 1967, the then Secretary of the Interior [Stewart Udall] adopted the policy that in the exercise of his discretion under, *inter alia*, Section 7 of the Taylor Grazing Act, he would refuse to approve indemnity applications that involve grossly disparate values. That policy remains in effect.
>
> In the present case, although the land values are not precisely determined, it appears that the selections involve lands of grossly disparate values, within the meaning of the Department's policy. While the Department is not yet prepared to adjudicate the State's applications, I feel it is appropriate at this time to advise you that we will apply the above-mentioned policy in that adjudication.

[The State promptly challenged this policy in federal court. The lower courts ruled for Utah, and the Supreme Court granted certiorari, noting that seven western states still had unsatisfied indemnity selection rights to nearly 700,000 acres.]

I

The Enabling Act of each of the public land States admitted into the Union since 1802 has included grants of designated sections of federal lands for the purpose of supporting public schools. Whether the Enabling Act contained words of present or future grant, title to the numbered sections did not vest in the State until completion of an official survey. Prior to survey, the Federal Government remained free to dispose of the designated lands "in any manner and for any purpose consistent with applicable federal statutes." In recognition of the fact that the essentially random grants in place might therefore be unavailable at the time of survey for a variety of reasons, Congress authorized grants of indemnity or "lieu" lands of equal acreage.

As Utah correctly emphasizes, the school land grant was a "solemn agreement" which in some ways may be analogized to a contract between private parties. The United States agreed to cede some of its land to the State in exchange for a commitment by the State to use the revenues derived from the land to educate the citizenry.

The State's right to select indemnity lands may be viewed as the remedy stipulated by the parties for the Federal Government's failure to perform entirely its promise to grant the specific numbered sections. The fact that the Utah Enabling Act used the phrase "lands equivalent thereto"

the total area selected comprising over 157,-000 acres.

3. Suggested guidelines of the Department of the Interior provide that the policy will not be applied unless the estimated value of the selected lands exceeds that of the base lands by more than $100 per acre or 25% whichever is greater. If the values are grossly disparate using those criteria, the case will be submitted to the Washington office for evaluation of all the circumstances.

and described the substituted land as "indemnity lands" implies that the purpose of the substitute selections was to provide the State with roughly the same resources with which to support its schools as it would have had had it actually received all of the granted sections in place.[10] Thus, as is typical of private contract remedies, the purpose of the right to make indemnity selections was to give the State the benefit of the bargain.

The history of the general statutes relating to land grants for school purposes confirms this view. Thus, for example, in 1859, when confronted with the fact that many settlers had occupied unsurveyed lands that had been included in school grants, Congress confirmed the settlers' claims and granted to the States "other lands of like quantity." 11 Stat. 385. The substitution of an equal quantity of land provided the States a rough measure of equal value.

The school land grants gave the States a random selection of public lands subject, however, to one important exception. The original school land grants in general, and Utah's in particular, did not include any numbered sections known to be mineral in character by the time of survey. United States v. Sweet, 245 U.S. 563. This Court so held even though the Utah Enabling Act "neither expressly includes mineral lands nor expressly excludes them." The Court's opinion stressed "the practice of Congress to make a distinction between mineral lands and other lands, to deal with them along different lines, and to withhold mineral lands from disposal save under laws specially including them." Mineral lands were thus excluded not only from the original grants in place but also from the indemnity selections.[11] Since mineral resources provide both the most significant potential source of value and the greatest potential for variation in value in the generally arid western lands, the total exclusion of mineral lands from the school land grants is consistent with an intent that the States' indemnity selections of equal acreage approximate the value of the numbered sections lost.

In 1927, some nine years after the decision in United States v. Sweet, supra, Congress changed its policy to allow grants of school lands to embrace numbered sections that were mineral in character. But the 1927 statute did not expand the kinds of land available for indemnity selections. Thus, after 1927 even if the lost school lands were mineral in character, a State was prohibited from selecting mineral lands as indemnity. It was not until 1958 that Congress gave the States the right to select mineral lands to replace lost school lands, and that right was expressly conditioned on a determination that the lost lands were also mineral in character. 43 U.S.C. § 852. For 30 years, then, States were not even permitted to select lands

---

10. See Heydenfeldt v. Daney Gold and Silver Mining Co., 93 U.S. 634, 639–640:

"Until the *status* of the lands was fixed by a survey, and they were capable of identification, Congress reserved absolute power over them; and if in exercising it the whole or any part of a 16th or 36th section had been disposed of, the State was to be compensated by other

lands equal in quantity, and *as near as may be in quality.*" (Emphasis added.)

11. Under the 1891 general indemnity selection statute then in effect, selections were limited to "unappropriated, surveyed public lands, not mineral in character." 26 Stat. 796–797.

roughly equivalent in value to replace lost mineral lands. The condition in the 1958 statute, that the lost lands be mineral in character before mineral lands could be selected as indemnity, rather clearly reflects an intention to restore the character of the indemnity selection as a substitute of roughly equal value.

Throughout the history of congressional consideration of school land grants and related subjects—a history discussed at great length in the voluminous briefs submitted to us—we find no evidence whatever of any congressional desire to have the right to select indemnity lands do anything more than make the States whole for the loss of value resulting from the unavailability of the originally designated cross section of lands within the State. There is certainly no suggestion of a purpose at any time, including 1958, to allow the States to obtain substantially greater values through the process of selecting indemnity land.

Thus, viewing the program in this broad historical perspective, it is difficult to identify any sensible justification for Utah's position that it is entitled to select any mineral lands it chooses regardless of the value of the school sections lost. Nevertheless, Utah is quite correct in arguing that the Secretary has no power to reject its selections unless Congress has given it to him. We have no doubt that it has.

II

Prior to the 1930's, cases in this Court had made it perfectly clear that the Federal Government retained the power to appropriate public lands embraced within school grants for other purposes if it acted in a timely fashion. On the other hand, it was equally clear that the States' title to unappropriated land in designated sections could not be defeated after survey, and that their right to indemnity selections could not be rejected if they satisfied the statutory criteria when made, and if the selections were filed before the lands were appropriated for other purposes. The authority of the Secretary of the Interior was limited to determining whether the States' indemnity selections met the relevant statutory criteria. See Wyoming v. United States, 255 U.S. 489; Payne v. New Mexico, 255 U.S. 367, 371.

In the 1930's, however, dissatisfaction with the rather loose regime governing use and disposition of unappropriated federal lands, prompted mostly by the waste caused by unregulated stock grazing, led to a series of congressional and executive actions that are critical to this case. By means of these actions, all unappropriated federal lands were withdrawn from every form of entry or selection. The withdrawal did not affect the original school land grants in place, whether or not surveyed, but did include all lands then available for school indemnity selections. The lands thus withdrawn were thereafter available for indemnity selections only as permitted by the Secretary of the Interior in the exercise of his discretion.

The sequence of events was as follows. In 1934, Congress enacted the Taylor Grazing Act "[t]o stop injury to the public grazing lands by preventing overgrazing and soil deterioration, to provide for their orderly use, improvement, and development, to stabilize the livestock industry dependent upon the public range, and for other purposes." 48 Stat. 1269. Section 1 authorized the Secretary of the Interior to establish grazing districts in up to 80 million acres of unappropriated federal lands; the establishment of such a district had the effect of withdrawing all lands within its boundaries "from all forms of entry of settlement." That section also expressly provided that "Nothing in this Act shall be construed in any way * * * to affect any land heretofore or hereafter surveyed which, except for the provisions of this Act, would be a part of any grant to any State * * *." Thus, § 1 preserved the original school land grants, whether or not the designated sections had already been identified by survey, but the statute made no provision for school indemnity selections.

Because the Taylor Grazing Act as originally passed in 1934 applied to less than half of the federal lands in need of more orderly regulation, President Roosevelt promptly issued Executive Order 6910 withdrawing all of the unappropriated and unreserved public lands in 12 western States, including Utah, from "settlement, location, sale or entry" pending a determination of the best use of the land. The withdrawal affected the land covered by the Taylor Grazing Act as well as land not covered by the statute. The President's authority to issue Executive Order 6910 was expressly conferred by the Pickett Act.

Congress responded to Executive Order No. 6910 by amending the Taylor Grazing Act in 1936 in two respects that are relevant to this case. First, it expanded the acreage subject to the Act. Second, it revised § 7 of the Act, to give the Secretary the authority, in his discretion, to classify both lands within grazing districts and lands withdrawn by the recent Executive order as proper not only for homesteading, but also, for the first time, for satisfaction of any outstanding "lieu" rights, and to open such lands to "selection." The section [43 U.S.C. § 315f], thus amended, provided in pertinent part:

> "The Secretary of the Interior is authorized, in his discretion, to examine and classify any lands withdrawn or reserved by Executive order * * * or within a grazing district, which are * * * proper for acquisition in satisfaction of any outstanding lieu, exchange or script rights or land grant, and to open such lands to entry, selection or location for disposal in accordance with * * * applicable public-land laws. * * * *Such lands shall not be subject to disposition * * * until after the same have been classified* * * *." (Emphasis added.)

The changes in this section were apparently prompted in part by the fact that while the Taylor Grazing Act withdrawal preserved the States' school grants in place, no provision had been made in the 1934 version for the States' indemnity selections from land within grazing districts even though the States had expressed the concern that "the establishment of a grazing district would restrict the State in its indemnity selections." While this omission may not have been critical in 1934 when the Act was passed—since only about half of the unappropriated federal land was then affected—by 1936, as a consequence of Executive Order No. 6910, no land at all was available in the public domain for indemnity selections. It is therefore reasonable to infer that the amendments to § 7 were at least in part a response to the complaint expressed in congressional hearings in 1935, that there was no land available under current law for indemnity selections.

The 1936 amendment to § 7 rectified that problem, but did not give the States a completely free choice in making indemnity selections. Rather, Congress decided to route the States' selections through § 7, and thereby to condition their acceptance on the Secretary's discretion. That decision was consistent with the dominant purpose of both the Act and Executive Order No. 6910, to exert firm control over the Nation's land resources through the Department of the Interior. In sum, the Taylor Grazing Act, coupled with the withdrawals by Executive order, "locked up" all of the federal lands in the western States pending further action by Congress or the President, except as otherwise permitted in the discretion of the Secretary of the Interior for the limited purposes specified in § 7.

This was Congress' understanding of the Taylor Grazing Act in 1958 when it amended the school land indemnity selection statute to permit selection of mineral lands. * * * Since Congress was specifically dealing with school indemnity selections, the reports make it perfectly clear that Congress deemed school indemnity selections to be subject to § 7 of the Taylor Grazing Act. And since the congressional decision in 1958 to allow school land indemnity selections to embrace mineral lands was expressly conditioned on a determination that the lost school lands were also mineral in character, it is manifest that Congress did not intend to grant the States any windfall. It only intended to restore to the States a rough approximation of what was lost.

We therefore hold that the 1936 amendment to the Taylor Grazing Act conferred on the Secretary the authority in his discretion to classify lands within a federal grazing district as proper for school indemnity selection. And we find no merit in the argument that the Secretary's "grossly disparate value" policy constitutes an abuse of the broad discretion thus conferred. On the contrary, that policy is wholly faithful to Congress' consistent purpose in providing for indemnity selections, to give the States a rough equivalent of the school land grants in place that were lost through pre-emption or private entry prior to survey. Accordingly, the judgment of the Court of Appeals is reversed.

■ Mr. Justice Powell, with whom The Chief Justice, Mr. Justice Blackmun, and Mr. Justice Rehnquist join, dissenting.

Since the early days of the Republic, the Federal Government's compact with each new State has granted the State land for the support of education and allowed the State to select land of equal acreage as indemnity for deficiencies in the original grant. Today, the Court holds that the Taylor Grazing Act abrogated those compacts by approving selection requirements completely at odds with the equal acreage principle. Nothing in the Court's opinion persuades me that Congress meant so lightly to breach compacts that it has respected and enforced throughout our Nation's history. * * *

Utah has selected land in satisfaction of grants made to support the public education of its citizens. Those grants are part of the bilateral compact under which Utah was admitted to the Union. They guarantee the State a specific quantity of the public lands within its borders. * * * Nothing in the Taylor Grazing Act empowers the Secretary to review Utah's selections under a comparative value standard explicitly at odds with principles consistently respected since the early days of our Republic.

NOTES AND QUESTIONS

1.   This case illustrates a number of prominent features of federal land disposal and management policy over time. For example, what was the rationale behind the "in-place" grants, giving the states isolated sections of land scattered across the entire state?

2.   How does the majority read the word "equivalent" in the statute giving the state indemnity rights? How does the dissent read it? Does the majority opinion leave it open to a future Secretary to repeal Secretary Udall's "grossly disparate value" policy? Is, in other words, the Secretary's *power* to reject an unequal value selection the same as a *duty* to reject it? (This question of executive discretion recurs throughout public natural resource law.) Does the majority opinion provide any clues to resolving it?

3.   What was the rationale behind Congress's long-standing practice of *not* disposing of lands that were deemed "mineral in character" at the time of survey under the *land* disposal laws? This practice was so entrenched that the Supreme Court had no difficulty deciding, in United States v. Sweet, 245 U.S. 563 (1918) (discussed in the principal case) that the statehood common school grant to Utah excluded federal lands "mineral in character," even though Congress had not deemed it necessary to say so specifically in the statehood enabling act. This policy of "withhold[ing] mineral lands from disposal save under laws specially including them" (*Sweet*, at 567) was followed until the second decade of the twentieth century, when Congress began to authorize federal land grants that simply reserved minerals in federal ownership. Federal mineral policy is dealt with in more detail in Chapter 7.

4.   While Utah might be said to have been looking for a windfall here, consider the flip side of the problem: California never got the opportunity to take title to several sections of "in-place" common school grants in its Central Valley because the federal government, prior to their being surveyed, included the area in the Elk Hills Naval Petroleum Reserve. Oil was later discovered on the land, and the "lost" sections are worth many millions of dollars. No federal land in California is available for indemnity selection that comes close to the value of these "lost" sections. Does California have a remedy? Does the federal government satisfy the "solemn [statehood] agreement" by offering as indemnity lands of equal acreage, but worth much less in value? See California v. Watkins, No. CV F–87–665 EDP (E.D. Cal. Feb. 12, 1990, July 29, 1991) (yes). Illustrating the political nature of the process, California then took its grievance to the Congress, which responded by giving California a share of the proceeds of Elk Hills

reserve when it was auctioned off in 1996. See 104 Pub.L.No.106, 110 Stat. 186.

5. Notice also the Court's discussion of the Taylor Grazing Act, President Franklin Roosevelt's withdrawal of essentially all the public domain lands in 1934 and 1935 and Congress's responsive amendment of the Taylor Grazing Act in 1936. How did those events in effect control the outcome of this case? Apart from their effect on state school indemnity selections, this sequence of actions effectively closed the public domain to widespread disposition.

6. Litigation over in lieu land selection was not quelled by the principal case. See, e.g., Oregon v. Bureau of Land Management, 876 F.2d 1419 (9th Cir.1989). For further discussion of the issues here (written prior to the Supreme Court's decision), see Denise Dragoo, The Impact of the Federal Land Policy and Management Act Upon Statehood Grants and Indemnity Land Selections, 21 Ariz.L.Rev. 395 (1979).

A NOTE ON STATE MANAGEMENT OF FEDERALLY GRANTED LANDS

Early statehood grants tended to be rather loosely worded in expressing the purposes of the grants, and the states exploited this by using the proceeds derived from federally granted lands for purposes other than those sought to be served. Over time, the Congress responded to these abuses by progressively tightening the language in the grants. Grants to later admitted states such as Oklahoma, New Mexico and Arizona have quite detailed terms. These states may dispose of the granted land only for "full value," and Congress also sometimes required procedural safeguards such as public notice and an auction. These various restrictions on management and disposition of federal land grants to states are often referred to as creating a "trust" to be administered for the designated beneficiaries; e.g., common schools. Federally granted lands to serve common schools are usually called "school trust lands." This "trust"—concerned primarily with the raising and expenditure of money derived from these lands—is somewhat distinct from the "public trust doctrine" applied in the *Illinois Central Railroad* decision, supra p. 58.

The U.S. Supreme Court has issued a number of decisions strictly enforcing the restrictions placed on federal land grants. In Ervien v. United States, 251 U.S. 41 (1919), for example, the Court rejected the New Mexico legislature's attempt to devote 3% of the proceeds of sales and leases of federally granted lands to advertising the virtues of living and investing in New Mexico. The Enabling Act was, in the Court's view, "special and exact," and "in prophetic realization" Congress had anticipated "that the state might be tempted to do that which it has done, lured * * * to speculative advertising in the hope of a speedy prosperity." 251 U.S. at 47–48. The Court traced the history of statehood land grants, and enforced the "full value" requirement for common school land grants, in Lassen v. Arizona, 385 U.S. 458 (1967). Other Supreme Court decisions enforcing the restrictions are Alamo Land & Cattle Co. v. Arizona, 424 U.S. 295 (1976), and ASARCO, Inc. v. Kadish, 490 U.S. 605 (1989). One lower federal court took strict enforcement to a very high level. In United States v. New Mexico, 536 F.2d 1324 (10th Cir.1976), the Court held that New Mexico could not use income from a federal land grant made for the purpose of supporting "miners' hospitals for disabled miners" to help underwrite a consolidation of state hospitals, which changed its Miners' Hospital into a more limited facility, with disabled miners eligible to receive care at other institutions. The court explained (536 F.2d at 1326–27):

> While the underlying motivation for the trust may have been a desire on the part of Congress generally to provide for the health care of miners, the specific purpose of the trust was the establishment and maintenance of a "miners' hospital." The wording of the Enabling Act evidences a determination by Congress that the health needs of New Mexico miners could best be provided by a separate hospital for miners. To imply a more expansive purpose for the trust than that stated in the Enabling Act is to indulge in a license of construction which Congress intended to prevent.

What happens to the proceeds from this federal land grant when there are no more miners in New Mexico? Is this statutory interpretation too wooden? Should the courts be more flexible? If not, what is New Mexico's remedy?

Some statehood enabling acts not only set out detailed restrictions, but went further to require the new state to put identical restrictions in its state constitution. For an illustration of the politics behind this process, see John Leshy, The Making of the Arizona Constitution, 20 Ariz.St.L.J. 1, 7–27 (1988). This has led to a series of state Supreme Court decisions also strictly enforcing the terms of the federal land grants, as a matter of federal law (the enabling acts) or of state law (similar restrictions expressed in the state constitution or statutes). See, e.g., State v. University of Alaska, 624 P.2d 807 (Alaska 1981); Oklahoma Education Ass'n, Inc. v. Nigh, 642 P.2d 230 (Okl.1982).

Some interesting issues are raised in this litigation. In many states, state school trust land has long been leased for livestock grazing for small sums of money. Often, in fact, state lands are interspersed with federal lands that are likewise leased for grazing. In some modern cases (especially in Idaho and New Mexico) environmental interests have sought to bid against ranchers for renewal of their grazing leases, not to graze the land but to retire it from grazing. If the environmentalists outbid the ranchers, must the state lease them the land? This can raise severe political problems for state land boards which have traditionally been friendly to ranching interests. To the extent the school trust is designed to produce income, and not cows, it would seem ranchers have an uphill argument. See, e.g., Idaho Watersheds Project v. State Board of Land Commissioners, 133 Idaho 64, 982 P.2d 367 (1999) (state law administered to exclude conservation interests from bidding on grazing leases on state land violated state constitution by removing potential bidders who might provide "maximum long term financial return" to the schools); Forest Guardians v. Wells, 34 P.3d 364 (Ariz.2001) (state may not reject application of high bidder for state land grazing lease just because bidder's object is restoration or preservation of grazing land, the court pointing out that 90% of the state school trust land was classified for grazing); Montanans for the Responsible Use of the School Trust v. State ex rel. Bd. of Land Comm'rs, 989 P.2d 800 (Mont.1999) (state statutes that fail in certain respects to recover full market value for school trust lands are inconsistent with the state constitution). But see Forest Guardians v. Powell, 24 P.3d 803 (N.M.Ct.App.2001) (neither environmentalists nor parents of school children have standing to sue to challenge state administration of school trust land, including leasing the land without advertisement or public auction because, among other things, plaintiffs cannot show that increased competition would result in more funds actually going to schools, because the legislature could choose to offset any increase from trust lands by reducing appropriations from the state general fund).

There also may be a question whether state school trust land can be exchanged for federal or private land elsewhere. Such exchanges are usually negotiated on an equal value basis as determined by appraisal. Where the statehood enabling act (and/or state law) requires a public auction before disposition, are such exchanges illegal? The Arizona Supreme Court said yes in Deer Valley Unified School Dist. v. Superior Court, 157 Ariz. 537, 760 P.2d 537 (1988). As will be explored in Chapter 4, land exchanges can be a progressive land management technique, allowing for reconfiguration of ownerships to better serve public and private management goals. Environmental and other interests in Arizona have tried twice to persuade Arizona voters to amend the state constitution to overrule this decision, but lost both times by very narrow margins.

A second issue is related to the first; namely, to what extent does the trust emphasis on income production prevent the state from managing some of its federally granted lands for such purposes as recreation, wildlife, and wilderness? Does the trust require income maximization over the short run, without considering the long run? Or may a state choose not to lease some of its granted land for mineral production or livestock grazing now, in the expectation that it might be more valuable for other purposes, even though those other purposes cannot, at least in the short run, produce as much income? May the grant purpose of promoting the common schools be served by setting aside a tract of state school trust land as an environmental "classroom" or laboratory where schoolchildren can observe biodiversity? See, e.g., Branson School District RE–82 v. Romer, 161 F.3d 619 (10th Cir.1998) (rejecting a facial challenge to a rewrite of the management principles underlying the state school land trust that shifted "away from its prior focus on short-term profit maximization toward a more sustainable approach focusing on the long-term yields of the trust lands"). See generally Gregory A. Hicks, Managing State Trust Lands for Ecosystem Health: The Case of Washington State's Range and Agricultural Lands, 6 Hastings W.-N.W. J.Env.L. & Pol'y 1 (1999); Melinda Bruce & Teresa Rice, Controlling the Blue Rash: Issues and Trends in the State Land Management, XXIX Land & Water L. Rev. 1 (1994); Jon A. Souder, Sally K. Fairfax and Larry Ruth, Sustainable Resources Management and State School Lands: The Quest for Guiding Principles, 34 Nat. Res. J. 271 (1994); Sally Fairfax,

Jon Souder, and Gretta Goldenman, The School Trust Lands: A Fresh Look at Conventional Wisdom, 22 Envtl.L. 797 (1992); Wayne McCormack, Land Use Planning and Management of State School Lands, 1982 Utah L.Rev. 524.

b.   OTHER GRANTS

Congress made many other grants to the states outside the statehood enabling act process. Some of these were influenced by the lively debate over much of the Nation's first century regarding whether the national government could constitutionally play a role in financing or otherwise promoting public works projects in the states—so-called "internal improvements." At one time or another, for example, such luminaries as Thomas Jefferson, James Madison and James Monroe thought the Constitution needed to be amended in order to give the national government such authority. Federal land grants offered those with a narrow view of federal authority a way to justify federal involvement, and Congress "[c]heerfully [began] exploiting this constitutional loophole" early on. See Daniel Feller, THE PUBLIC LANDS IN JACKSONIAN POLITICS 49 (1984). Six million acres of federal land grants to western states went to support canal building and river navigation improvements, and another three million acres for roads, in the first half of the nineteenth century. The canal grants started the practice of parcelling out alternate sections of land along the canal right-of-way. This practice reached stupendous proportions with the railroad land grants, discussed further below.

In an 1841 statute, Congress gave every public land state an outright grant of 500,000 acres for internal improvements (minus acreage that had already been received for those purposes). Diversion of these funds to other purposes by recipient states helped influence Congress to abandon this general grant approach in 1889 in favor of specific trust grants such as that in United States v. New Mexico, supra. Meanwhile, Congress had also determined to give states the unclaimed, seemingly useless swampland within their borders. After an experimental grant to Louisiana, the General Swamp Land Act of 1850 allowed states to select and acquire such lands under certain criteria. Administrative implementation was so lacking, however, that erroneous and fraudulent selections were common. It was intended that five or six million acres would pass by this method, but over 80 million acres of purported swamplands were ultimately selected, though not all selections were approved for fee title. With the connivance of state officials, a predecessor of the giant Kern County Land Company received over 80,000 valuable acres through this process. According to historian Paul Gates, one agent for the state of Mississippi reportedly "judged as swampland all tracts over which a boat could pass [so he] drove a work animal 'hitched to a canoe across thousands of acres' of pinelands at fairly high elevations, listed his selections and, though contested by the Federal government, they were finally patented to the state." Paul Gates, HISTORY OF PUBLIC LAND LAW DEVELOPMENT, at 328. Conflicts with other grants, notably to the railroads, abounded. See Work v. Louisiana, 269 U.S. 250 (1925); Martin v. Marks, 97 U.S. (7 Otto) 345 (1877).

Remedial legislation was passed, and contests were initiated, but many conflicts were not resolved for decades; several state patent applications were confirmed as late as 1963. "Despite Congress' unmistakable intention to benefit the states, the titles it created have proved extremely unstable." Kent Shearer, Federal Land Grants to the States: An Advocate's Dream; A Title Examiner's Nightmare, 14 Rocky Mtn. Min.L.Inst. 185, 188 (1968).

By the famous Morrill Act of 1862, each state (including the original, "non-public land" states) received the rights to 30,000 acres for each of its senators and representatives, to be used for support of an agricultural and mechanical college. These grants differed from the norm in that states could not select such lands within their boundaries but rather were given "scrip" for the acreage, entitling them to sell the rights to public lands elsewhere. There was inevitably some evasion of the conditions, and great landed estates grew out of speculation in scrip, but Morrill's purpose of providing low-cost, practical higher education has been realized in some measure by the establishment of what have become known as "land grant colleges," a number of which have evolved into major universities such as Cornell and Michigan State.

The Morrill Act was one of the few disposition laws that allowed the non-public land states to share directly in the proceeds from sale of public domain land. The controversy between East and West had raged for decades with inconclusive results. "Distribution," "deposit," and similar revenue sharing schemes from which eastern states would benefit either never passed or were short-lived due to economic exigencies. While mostly losing its battle for a direct cut in the proceeds from western lands, eastern interests have had much more success, starting shortly after the Civil War, in pressuring the national government to withdraw and reserve millions of acres of public lands in the west for conservation and preservation purposes, often in the face of western opposition.

The outright land grants to states were scarcely the only way the national government used public lands to assist the states. Beginning with the Reclamation Act of 1902, 43 U.S.C. § 371 et seq., a series of federal statutes has provided that revenues accruing from uses of the retained public lands will be shared with the states in which the lands are located. These continuing federal programs under the Reclamation Act, the Mineral Leasing Act of 1920, 30 U.S.C. § 181 et seq., the Federal Power Act of 1920, 16 U.S.C. §§ 791a–825r, and the Taylor Grazing Act of 1934, 43 U.S.C. § 315 et seq., among others, will be discussed below. We will now turn our attention to the various forms of individual homesteading by which the bulk of the country was settled.

4. GRANTS TO SETTLERS

Official national public land policy for 150 years was directed primarily at getting the lands into the hands of the pioneer, the individual farmer seeking a new life on the frontier. The official policy was undercut from many directions, it sometimes resulted in heartbreak instead of prosperity, and it both succeeded and failed. It succeeded in that millions were able to build new lives on cheap or free land, there to develop communities, commerce, and other attributes of civilization. The country was developed and unified; the lands and resources nurtured and sustained the characteristic American ingenuity and industry; and the Nation rapidly rose to pinnacles of wealth and power. But the national policy also failed in many respects. Disdain for legal requirements bred widespread lawlessness. The development of individual and corporate monopoly ownerships operated to exclude the small farmer. Many could not make a go of it; the berserk Colorado farmwife in Michener's *Centennial* and the tribulations of the homesteading couple in the 1979 movie *Heartland* had many models from real life.

The following account of how individual settlers could and did acquire title to public lands is painted with a broad brush and necessarily omits most nuances and details. As an introduction, consider these excerpts from Benjamin H. Hibbard, A HISTORY OF THE PUBLIC LAND POLICIES* 136, 138–39 (1924, U.Wis.ed. 1965):

> For a half century, or more, following 1841 the policy of using the public domain in the promotion of settlement, the very basis of national strength and security, of civilization itself, was accepted and furthered in the disposition of the western lands. It was the fruition of the work and teachings of such men as Gallatin, Jefferson and Benton. In 1826 Benton had said regarding a liberal treatment of the western pioneer: "I speak to Senators who know this to be a Republic, not a Monarchy, who know that the public lands belong to the People and not to the Federal Government." Thus debts were to be forgiven, preemption was to be granted, land was to be made easy of access and of acquisition, indeed free as soon as the East could be converted to the view.

> Every new Territory and State wanted people to take up and use the vacant lands. Immigration agents were employed by the state. Advertising campaigns were adroitly conducted by the railroads. The private land agent became an institution, offering to conduct land seekers to the best locations. All forces combined to get the land into the hands of settlers. The government helped the campaign along. With the transportation lines established, the ownership of land assumed a new aspect; values were expected to increase. In the early years of the development of farms on the frontier the settler was looking for room, for a chance to support himself and family. With a market assured, not by going around half a continent by water, taking weeks for the trip, but going with speed directly toward the eastern seaboard with its cities, meant a price for product which would soon reflect itself in land values of the West. Thus the farmer, not altogether for the first time,

but with a new emphasis, began to look upon the land as a prize in itself, easily obtained, and likely to increase rapidly in value. With this optimism permeating the imaginations of the oncoming waves of settlers it was inevitable that more enterprising adventurers should precede them and profit by the optimism by taking the first advance in price over the government minimum. The Preemption Act was designed to preclude, at least to restrict this practice.

a. PREEMPTION

Since before the Revolution, the common practice—as epitomized in the exploits of Daniel Boone—was to stake out a claim on the edge of the frontier and later, perhaps, pay whoever turned out to be the owner. Squatting has had a long if less than honorable history; in the early days of the Republic, troops were called out on several occasions to remove squatters from land owned by the government or speculators. As Jefferson noted in 1776, "they will settle the lands in spite of everybody." The United States struggled with the problem for a century, and while the right of "preemption" usually prevailed, the dilemma between the desire to accommodate the actual settlers and protection of actual or potential purchasers was never finally resolved.

Preemption was the preferential right of settler-squatters to buy their claims at modest prices without competitive bidding or, alternatively, to be paid compensation for any improvements they had made. From 1790 onward, Congress received numerous impassioned petitions and memorials asking for confirmation of title to those who had illegally braved the frontier hazards. To quiet settler resentment of prevailing policy, 24 special acts were adopted before 1820 granting preemption privileges to special groups or within certain territories and states. Payment was usually required, but liberal credit was extended—and extended again. Since the squatters had often ranged beyond the surveyors and land offices, title questions long remained unsettled. A uniform policy was hard to come by: eastern congressmen criticized the Westerners for being greedy, lawless, disloyal landgrabbers who had no respect for order, absentee owners, or Indian rights; western representatives, however, presented the squatters as loyal people who had exhausted their resources in reaching the West and who had defended the frontier against the marauding Indians.

In 1830, a retroactive, one-year general preemption measure was passed (because it was ignored in the heat of more pressing matters), but abuses by those claiming under it retarded progress toward a permanent preemption law. Nevertheless, and despite acute difficulties in administration, another series of limited preemption acts was passed up to 1840, and several million acres were eventually patented for $1.25 per acre under this method. Some thought that preemption rights had become unnecessary because "claims associations" of settlers had sprung up to keep competition out of bidding by threats of violence, as speculators had done by illegal agreement. Until 1841, all preemption statutes had been retroactive; i.e., they validated previous claims but did not authorize future squatting.

The General Preemption Act of 1841, 5 Stat. 453, finally authorized prospective preemption as part of a package of provisions engineered by Henry Clay, including such pot sweeteners as 500,000 acre grants to states. The Act abandoned the view that all settlement on unoffered public land was illegal, but it sanctioned further settlement only on public land that had been surveyed. Occupying settlers could obtain a maximum of 160 acres for $1.25 per acre, if they met a number of eligibility conditions. The Act was abused by the common sports of the day, speculation and fraud, which included the practice of squatting on timberland, stripping it bare, and then abandoning the claim for another. It was estimated in 1849 that "not three of a hundred" preemption declarations actually went to patent (documentary fee title). Prior to the Civil War, preemption tended to achieve its goals of settlement and title security in spite of its many problems, but abuses so mounted after the War that eventually, in 1891, it was repealed. In one notable case, the Supreme Court voided a preemption claim in the Yosemite Valley, finding that a narrow interpretation "is the only construction which preserves a wise control in the government over the public lands, and prevents a general spoliation of them under the pretence of intended settlement and preemption." The Yosemite Valley Case (Hutchings v. Low), 82 U.S. (15 Wall.) 77, 88 (1872). More usual homesteading methods had proceeded concurrently with preemption.

b.   GRANTS TO VETERANS

Individuals serving the armed forces in time of war were given special rights to public lands. Grants of public land to military veterans have ancient origins; they conveniently reward military adventurers by removing them from the vicinity of civilization. The practice was followed by the United States after the Revolution, and for as long thereafter as the Nation was land rich and cash poor. Because the early grants were commonly made in scrip, ownership concentration became common, and absentee ownership generated disputes with squatters and others. It is not known how many acres were granted to veterans over the past 200 years, but bounty warrants for over 60 million acres were issued between 1847 and 1906. See James Oberly, SIXTY MILLION ACRES (1990). The practice ended after the Spanish–American War, but scrip and warrants were still dribbling into government land offices in the mid–20th century. By a 1955 statute, scrip of all descriptions had to be recorded within two years, and any unsatisfied existing rights were to be extinguished by purchase thereafter.

c.   CREDIT AND CASH SALES

The young Nation had a legacy of debt and but two sources of revenue: tariffs and land sales. After some years of inconclusive debate over whether revenue-raising or settlement was the more important objective, whether sales should be for cash of on credit, and whether landholdings should be limited, Congress passed the Land Act of 1796. It continued the 36 section rectangular system of survey first adopted by the Congress of the Confederation in 1785, and provided for land auctions at minimum prices of $2.00

per acre (Hamilton had advocated 20 cents), but with only five percent of the purchase price down, the balance due in a year. The important distinction (for preemption) between offered and unoffered tracts was also created. To administer this system, the General Land Office was created in 1812. It remained in business until it was absorbed into the BLM in 1946.

The 1796 Act did not produce the revenue anticipated. Thereafter Congress progressively liberalized the credit terms and other conditions. Sales greatly increased (giving rise to the enduring phrase "doing a Land Office business"), but speculation became common and many settlers could not make payments. That led to a series of relief acts by which delinquents were relieved of prospect of forfeiture. Relief only increased speculation and indebtedness; by the end of 1819, the federal government was holding many millions of dollars of delinquent debt from purchasers. In 1820 Congress ended its experiment with credit sales, although it continued its liberality toward hard-pressed settlers for decades.

The 1820 Act required cash at the time of purchase at auction. Public lands offered but unsold at auction were opened to private entry at a lower price. Settlers detested auction sales and urged their postponement year after year to thwart cash-rich speculators. Western politicians like Senator Thomas Hart Benton of Missouri advocated more rapid divestiture. "[T]he public lands belong to the People, and not to the Federal Government," he declared in a widely circulated speech in 1826, and he endorsed either accelerated sales or the ceding of the public lands to the Western states. See Daniel Feller, THE PUBLIC LANDS IN JACKSONIAN POLITICS, p. 75 (1984). The activities of speculators' and claims' associations grew more fraudulent and more violent, and the claims clubs did not end with grant of prospective preemption in 1841. An 1830 act which prohibited combinations to prevent competition at land auctions accomplished little, even though the westerners professed themselves totally against "Monopoly." Even after the great land boom of the 1830's, less than half of the 190 million acres of surveyed, offered lands had been purchased by cash sale, preemption, or otherwise. Fraud and speculation had become so virulent, and large monopolistic land companies so prevalent, that in the Specie Circular of 1836, President Andrew Jackson (himself no mean speculator) placed severe limitations on future sales and recommended that only actual bona fide settlers be allowed to purchase and patent. The Panic of 1837 and the ensuing depression caused land sales to fall off drastically until 1845. Public policy was riven by the now traditional East–West split, and was further confused by acute ambiguity in the settlers' policy desires. But with preemption, veteran's bounties, and grants to states, a new land rush commenced that was not abated until President Pierce withdrew 31 million acres from entry in 1853. Uncertain of the constitutionality of that action, Pierce then restored the lands the following year. Railroad and canal grants opened even more land at this time.

In the great rush westward, vast acreage considered undesirable remained unsold in the older public land states. In 1854 the Graduation Act was passed, providing that the price for land long unclaimed would be reduced in proportion to the time unsold, down to $1.00 after 10 years, and down to 12½ cents an acre after 30 years ("one-bit" land). As in earlier and later legislation, a limit of 320 acres per claimant was imposed but, as in the other legislation, it was easily circumvented. The Graduation Act triggered another land rush; e.g., in Missouri, 64 percent of the 14 million acres of "graduated" land had been taken by 1862. Coupled with sales under other statutes, an unprecedented amount of land passed out of the public domain in the 1850's, causing endless confusion and antagonism. States, railroads, miners, speculators, and settlers all disputed with the federal government and each other. Ferment for land reform grew side by side with political ferment over slavery.

Although the federal policy of disposing of the public domain almost as fast as possible frequently was accomplished by dubious means, it did achieve in large measure its end of providing land for small farmers. The speculators and money lenders may have been despised, but their self-interest also contributed greatly to the development of the Trans–Appalachian West. Jefferson's goal of a dominant agrarian "yeomanry" was substantially realized although, at the same time, tenant farming was also increasing. Appendix B to Paul Gates' HISTORY OF PUBLIC LAND LAW DEVELOPMENT, pp. 802–03, contains a statistical summary of public lands sales, by year.

d. HOMESTEADING

"By 1862, the government had made such great progress in disposing of the public domain that only about one billion acres still remained the property of the United States. Perhaps two thirds of this remaining domain, however, was not arable land, and could not be parceled out so easily." Roy Robbins, OUR LANDED HERITAGE 236. The proportion of the total federal revenue that derived from land sales had declined drastically. Immigration and industrialization had created a class of landless, unemployed eastern workers. The cash requirement favored speculators and was thought to retard settlement. The government had resorted to "donation" acts, essentially giving away to actual settlers lands it wished quickly settled, such as Oregon. An Illinois Representative, arguing for free land, emoted:

> Unless the government shall grant head rights * * * prairies, with their gorgeous growth of flowers, their green carpeting, their lovely lawns and gentle slopes, will for centuries continue to be the home of the wild deer and wolf; their stillness will be undisturbed by the jocund song of the farmer, and their deep and fertile soil unbroken by the ploughshare. Something must be done to remedy this evil.*

The South had previously opposed liberalizing public land grants, correctly fearing that new antislavery states would be created. But the secession of the slaveholding states opened the way for the northern legislators to push through a program of agrarian distribution of the public lands that would, in various permutations, remain on the books for more than a century. The great Homestead Act of May 20, 1862, 43 U.S.C. § 161 et seq. (repealed

---

* Quoted in Philip Foss, POLITICS AND GRASS 20 (1960).

1976) authorized entry onto 160 acres of any public land subject to preemption. (Later, it was extended to unsurveyed lands to which Indian title had been extinguished.) To those who met the requirements, the land was free, except for filing fees. A settler was allowed six months to establish actual residence after application. Thereafter, actual settlement and cultivation were required for five years, to be supported by affidavit, at which point fee simple title would be conveyed. (In practice, however, many homesteaders chose not to wait the five years, but instead "commuted" their claim by payment.)

Other forms of disposition (preemption, cash sales, state and railroad grants) remained in effect. More specialized land grant acts, summarized below, complicated the overall picture. Indian reservations were broken up both by treaty and, starting with the Dawes Act in 1884, by allotment to individual tribal members. In either case, many of the lands soon passed into white hands. As the Nation rebuilt after the Civil War, this somewhat incongruous congregation of public land disposal laws of the United States combined to produce what one historian described as the "Great Barbecue,"** a generation's unparalleled exploitation of public natural resources.

As homesteading became a national preoccupation (by the 1880's, homesteads constituted a majority of new farms), difficulties in its administration multiplied. Perjury was practiced to surmount legal barriers such as the 160 acre limitation. A fundamental problem with the original homestead law was that the semi-arid federal lands beyond the 100th meridian were, for the most part, simply not sufficiently productive to support farming units of 160 acres or less. Surveying was limited, fragmented, incomplete, and sometimes downright fraudulent. Like preemption claims, homestead claims were sometimes used as a pretense to strip public lands of timber without any payment. The tide toward disposition at any cost flowed strongly; federal officials who tried to hew to the strict letter of the law or decried abuses put their jobs in jeopardy. Lands that remained in public ownership were considered to be a grazing commons for livestock owners, and this gave rise to a generation of "range wars" among settlers, sheepherders, and cattle ranchers. Some gained control over immense tracts of public land: one company was said to have fenced in over a million acres of public and private land. Congress responded to the practice of fencing off public land with the famous Unlawful Inclosures Act of 1885 (addressed in Camfield v. United States, infra p. 92; see also Paul Gates, HISTORY OF PUBLIC LAND LAW DEVELOPMENT 327–30, 463–94).

Notwithstanding the many difficulties and fraud, much of the West was settled under the Homestead and cognate acts—from 1868 to 1904, nearly 100 million acres were homesteaded, many if not most by the yeoman tillers of the soil that the expressed national policy was intended to benefit. A half-million farms were created between 1880 and 1900. True, some farm holdings were far larger than the legal limits, but often conditions dictated larger farming units. Hostility to large holdings was directed particularly at aliens, and in 1887 alien ownership was severely

** Vernon Parrington, THE BEGIN-NINGS OF CRITICAL REALISM IN AMER-ICA (vol. 3 of MAIN CURRENTS IN AMERICAN THOUGHT (1930)), pp. 23–26.

restricted. Many of the more abused laws were repealed in 1891, but the Homestead Act survived.

e. DESERT LANDS

Although lands east of the 100th meridian were settled quickly, arid public lands to the west often went begging because they were unsuitable to conventional farming without irrigation, which usually demanded larger blocs of land and access to substantial capital for water storage and delivery facilities. By 1877, much of the remaining unclaimed land was in the arid and semi-arid regions of the West. Although circumvention of the acreage limitations of the Homestead Act was scarcely unknown, pressure built for more specialized disposition laws under which larger tracts could pass legally. One solution, large grants to corporations, was in bad odor in the wake of the railroad land grant abuses recounted further below. Instead, Congress enacted the Desert Land Act of 1877, 43 U.S.C. §§ 321–339. It authorized entry of up to 640 acres of public land at only 25 cents an acre, with patent to follow upon proof that the land had been irrigated. (This Act also contained an important, and lasting, allocation of authority over water resources between the national government and the states, addressed in Chapter 6, below.) Although over 33 million acres would eventually be entered, and over ten million acres patented (see Paul Gates, HISTORY OF PUBLIC LAND LAW DEVELOPMENT 643), the Desert Land Act did not accomplish its purposes. Large corporations got the bulk of the available lands through dummies. Some people received patents after hauling a can of water to the claim and swearing that irrigation had been achieved. Very little land ever became irrigated; most claims were used for stock grazing.

Concern about the misuse of the Desert Land Act led Congress in 1888 to provide for reservation from entry of lands found by the Geological Survey to be necessary for reservoirs and irrigation works. Effective administration of the proviso, however, removed so much land from entry that in 1890 the withdrawn land was restored to the public domain—although new claims were limited to 320 acres. This episode, which effectively ended the public career of John Wesley Powell, is recounted at pp. 99–100, infra. The failure of private irrigation efforts led more or less directly to the Reclamation Act of 1902, infra at pp. 100–01.

f. STOCK–RAISING HOMESTEADS

With the repeal of preemption and historian Frederick Jackson Turner's famous pronouncement of the closing of the frontier by 1890, it might seem that entry for homesteading and other purposes would have declined if not ceased by 1900. That was not to be the case. Congress was still determined to create settlement opportunities through federal land disposal if it possibly could. In Nebraska, for example, Congress took note that almost nine million acres open to entry had gone unclaimed, so it responded with the Kinkaid Act of 1904, 43 U.S.C. § 224 (repealed 1976). It allowed entry of 640 acre tracts in the western part of the state for $1.25 per acre. By 1920 nearly all the land in Nebraska had been claimed. The purpose of encouraging small stock-raising homesteads was thwarted by weather and less neutral means. Nearly all of the land passed to the large ranchers; in one county in 1928, the average ranch was 6,681 acres, or more than ten times the allowable homestead size.

A more generic disposition measure was the Enlarged Homestead Act of 1909, 43 U.S.C. §§ 218–221 (repealed 1976). It allowed entry upon 320 instead of 160 acres west of the 100th meridian. The rush to take up enlarged homesteads abated with a drought, and most entries ended in failure for the same reason: in one area, 247 out of 250 claims were abandoned. Enlarged homesteads that were patented mostly ended up in the hands of large ranchers, even after later liberalization of settlement conditions. Dry farming was, and remains, an financially risky occupation. For modern accounts, see Ian Frazier, THE GREAT PLAINS (1989); Jonathan Raban, BAD LAND: AN AMERICAN ROMANCE (1996).

Congress was slow to learn the lessons of these experiences. In spite of a growing sentiment for a leasing system, even among cattlemen, the Stock–Raising Homestead Act of 1916, 43 U.S.C. §§ 291–301 (repealed 1976), authorized entry on 640 acres of land "designated" (not "classified") as chiefly valuable for grazing, on minimal conditions. In a few years over 50 million acres had been entered and more than thirty million acres patented. The 1916 Act not only caused the usual settler heartbreak, speculation, and aggrandizement, but also, in breaking up the great public domain grazing areas, contributed to the deterioration of the range. It had one feature that set it apart from practically all other disposition laws: Instead of passing fee simple title, it reserved the minerals in the United States, creating "split-estate" lands that give rise to occasional disputes and litigation, recounted in Chapter 7, section D.

The sponsor of the Stock–Raising Homestead Act was Edward Taylor of Colorado. Interestingly, he was also the sponsor of the Taylor Grazing Act of 1934, 43 U.S.C. § 315 et seq., which reversed the policies of the 1916 Act. The 1934 Act ushered in the end of the homesteading era, as recounted in Andrus v. Utah, supra p. 62. While Franklin Roosevelt's executive withdrawals in the wake of the Act effectively closed most of the public domain to disposition, the following case illustrates that homesteading remained possible, if barely so, until it was officially ended with repeal of the Homestead Act and other surviving disposition statutes in the Federal Land Policy and Management Act of 1976, 43 U.S.C. §§ 1701–1784.

Stewart v. Penny

United States District Court, District of Nevada, 1965.
238 F.Supp. 821.

■ THOMPSON, DISTRICT JUDGE.

[In 1953, Charles Stewart filed an application for entry under the Homestead Act on 120 acres of public land in Nevada classified as "open to entry." The Stewart family built a house and tried to cultivate 20 acres by irrigation. Crops failed "because of freezing, depredations by mice, rabbits, and other rodents, and invasions of ranging livestock." The BLM denied

Stewart's claim on the grounds that he had neither irrigated nor cultivated the requisite one-eighth of the entry. The agency had erred—apparently due to an administrative mistake in classification—by requiring irrigation, which was a requirement under the Desert Lands Act but not under the Homestead Act. Accordingly, the issue was reduced to whether cultivation had been achieved.] * * *

The inadequacy of our public land laws to afford reasonably workable methods, under present conditions, for the acquisition of public lands by private citizens is a matter of growing national concern. It is of particular concern to the State of Nevada inasmuch as approximately eighty-five per cent of the area of this State (the seventh largest) is still in the public domain. Much of it has a valuable potential for private use. Yet the archaic federal land laws, enacted in an era of an agrarian economy, are ill-suited to an orderly disposition of the lands into private ownership. The laws were enacted with the laudable motive of enabling the penniless pioneer to acquire a home for himself and family primarily through toil and with little capital expenditure. That purpose was long ago achieved and most of the lands of the Western States which had a valuable agricultural potential, even if only marginally so, have been patented to individuals under the beneficent laws to the exclusion of the wealthy who, under a different policy, might have acquired large blocks of public lands by purchase. The inapplicability of this policy to modern conditions has, during the past quarter-century, accomplished a virtual deep-freeze of public lands in federal ownership. * * *

The Government has filed an excellent brief in which it argues, in part, that the decision of the Secretary finding non-compliance with the statutory requirements for valid homestead entry is conclusive and binding upon the courts. We recognize the peculiar and specialized knowledge of the officials of the Department of the Interior respecting the interpretation of the multifarious laws and regulations relating to public lands, and that Congress has entrusted the guardianship of the public domain to the Department of the Interior. We have relied upon that knowledge and expertise in reaching our conclusions. We cannot, however, accept without limitation a contention that a high administrative official in Washington, D.C. is better qualified than others to analyze and draw conclusive fact inferences from a cold record produced at an evidentiary hearing three thousand miles away and relating to physical conditions with which he has questionable familiarity, conditions normally deemed to be within the realm of judicial notice. * * *

The omnipotence of the Department of the Interior as guardian of the public domain is exhibited when the Department acts affirmatively and grants patents under the public land laws. The converse is not true. An entry or application for patent which is contested or rejected by the Secretary presents issues regarding the legal rights of the entryman under the public land laws. These are rights established by Congress which the Secretary of the Interior may not arbitrarily or capriciously ignore and which must be determined within the due process safeguards of the Administrative Procedure Act. * * *

The Director of the Bureau placed his decision of April 11, 1961 upon the ground that the applicant had not shown good faith. This was not an issue presented by the contest complaint. The Secretary discarded the issue of good faith, saying:

> "Hence, I am unable to find, on the basis of the evidence adduced at the hearing, that there was a total want of the type of cultivation reasonably calculated to produce profitable results. If this were the only pertinent factor in the case, it would be necessary to remand the case for the taking of further evidence. However, I believe that this is unnecessary since, after a careful examination of the evidence, I am obliged to conclude that the entryman did not apply the processes of cultivation which he employed to the required ⅛ of the acreage of the entry so that he failed to meet the cultivation requirement of the homestead law for this reason."

The good faith requirement stems from 43 U.S.C. § 162 requiring the applicant to make oath "that such application is honestly and in good faith made for the purpose of actual settlement and cultivation, and not for the benefit of any other person, persons or corporation, and that he or she will faithfully and honestly endeavor to comply with all the requirements of law as to settlement, residence and cultivation necessary to acquire title to the land applied for." * * * An appropriate statement of the meaning of good faith in this context is found in Carr v. Fife (CC Wash.1891), 44 F. 713:

> " * * * whether he (the applicant) had actually, within the time limited by law, established his residence upon the land, with the intention of acquiring it for a home; whether he had continued to actually reside upon the land; whether he was really engaged in improving the land, or in good faith intending to do so; or whether he was only making a *colorable pretense* of residing upon and improving the land for the purpose of stripping it of its valuable timber, and acquiring it for *speculative purposes,* without complying with the terms of the homestead law." (Emphasis added)

The words "colorable pretense" and "speculative purposes" are operative and characterize the meaning of good faith in fulfilling the specific requirements of residence and cultivation under the homestead law. They refer to the intent and motive of the applicant.

In the light of what Stewart did on the land, it is inconceivable to this Court that there could be found the slightest semblance of an issue of good faith. * * * He was seventy-eight years old when final proof was filed, about four years after homestead entry was approved. There is not the least intimation that the land is valuable for anything other than grazing and agriculture, so there is no basis for speculating about "speculative purposes". * * *

That the homestead laws should be liberally applied in favor of the entryman is established by law and is not a matter of the whim or predisposition of the particular Secretary of the Interior who graces the office. The Supreme Court of the United States has established the principle. Ard v. Brandon, 1895, 156 U.S. 537:

The law deals tenderly with one who, in good faith, goes upon the public lands, with a view of making a home thereon. If he does all that the statute prescribes as the condition of acquiring rights, the law protects him in those rights, and does not make their continued existence depend alone upon the question whether or not he takes an appeal from an adverse decision of the officers charged with the duty of acting upon his application.

* * * On the issue of the acreage cultivated, the * * * correct rule is stated in Foster v. Seaton, 271 F.2d 836 (D.C.Cir.1959) involving a mining claimant. The reasoning there expressed is equally applicable to a homestead entryman. The true proponent of the rule or order is the applicant for patent or other right to public lands claiming compliance with the public land laws. The government "bears only the burden of going forward with sufficient evidence to establish a prima facie case, and the burden then shifts to the claimant to show by a preponderance of the evidence that his claim is valid." * * *

We have related the administrative history of this case at some length. The varying approaches to decision adopted in the administrative hierarchy seem to us to stem from a basic feeling that the area was not properly classified for homestead entry. This may or may not be so. Perhaps it would have been more prudent to classify less than the entire 120 acres covered by the amended application as suitable for homestead entry. Once the entry was allowed, however, all the entryman had to do was comply with the statutory requirements to be entitled to patent. The photographs, maps and testimony prove that he did [actually cultivate 15 acres], taking into consideration "the degree and condition in life" of the entryman and the obstacles of nature and environment with which he contended.

NOTES AND QUESTIONS

1. Although §§ 702–703 of the Federal Land Policy and Management Act of 1976 repealed nearly all the laws relating to homesteading and other disposals of the federal lands, it allowed them to continue to apply in Alaska until 1986. See 43 U.S.C. § 1701 note.

2. In Faulkner v. Watt, 661 F.2d 809 (9th Cir.1981), plaintiffs claimed that their request that the Secretary of the Interior open public land for entry under the Desert Lands Act, 43 U.S.C. §§ 321–323 (pursuant to the procedure in the Taylor Grazing Act, 43 U.S.C. § 315f) required the Secretary to accept the applications and to give them a preference right to enter if and when the lands were ever opened to entry. (The Department had earlier classified the land as unsuitable for agriculture and was rejecting all petitions to reclassify the land.) The court rejected plaintiffs' arguments, hold that the Secretary's refusal to accept applications to reclassify already classified land was not an abuse of discretion.

3. Paul Gates summed up the homesteading experience this way: "That 1,322,107 homesteaders carried their entries to final patent after 3 or 5 years of residence is overwhelming evidence that, despite the poorly framed legislation with its invitation to fraud, [homesteading] was the

successful route to farm ownership of the great majority of settlers moving into the newer areas of the West after 1862." HISTORY OF PUBLIC LAND LAW DEVELOPMENT 798 (1970). The same source contains useful statistical tables summarizing the homestead experience.

4. For an economist's argument that homesteading policy was appropriate to protect the property rights of the United States, see Douglas Allen, Homesteading and Property Rights, or "How the West Was Really Won," 34 J.L. & Econ. 1 (1991). Allen argues that the homestead policy was effectively a means for the U.S. to "hire" settlers to reduce the costs of enforcing fragile U.S. property rights against others, especially Indians:

> The slow, but eventual, removing of homesteading and other costly disposal devices was not, as is often stated, the result of a change in attitude toward the public domain. Rather, the more 'economical' policies of public land management are possible because of the removal of simultaneous claims made on these lands. * * * Given this, the policy of rushing settlers to limited parts of the territory to *establish* rights cannot be viewed as inefficient. That it was costly there can be no doubt, but that it was not a perfect solution is irrelevant.

5. GRANTS TO MINERS

Old public land laws like preemption, homesteading, and railroad grants have passed into the mists of history, but mining is a somewhat different story: it is still governed to some extent by a statute that was ancient before the frontier was closed. Full treatment of the Mining Law of 1872 and more modern statutes is found in Chapter 7; only a few historical developments will be touched on here.

Although the Congress of Confederation had reserved to the Nation one-third of the precious metals on public lands, that measure died with ratification of the Constitution. Twenty years later, Congress authorized leasing of public lands in Indiana, Illinois, and Missouri for lead mining purposes, to raise revenue and to insure ammunition. This experiment lasted from 1807 until 1846, when it was abandoned. It did result in two important cases in early public land law; namely, United States v. Gratiot, supra p. 49, and United States v. Gear, 44 U.S. (3 How.) 120 (1845) (unauthorized mining on the public domain is an actionable trespass).

As discussed in Andrus v. Utah, supra p. 62, federal land disposal policy had traditionally distinguished between public lands that were "mineral in character" and other lands; only the latter were generally subject to disposal under the homestead and other non-mineral disposal laws. Between the repeal of the early experiment with mineral leasing in 1846 and the adoption of the federal Mining Act of 1866, no federal law authorized entry onto or disposition of mineral lands. Nevertheless, from 1847 on, most of the mineral land east of the Mississippi, including the immensely valuable iron and copper ore in Michigan and Minnesota, went for $1.25 an acre via preemption, cash purchase, or homestead. The government was unable or unwilling to check this seeming perversion of the public land acts, and the local people found nothing strange in home-stead entries on claims virtually worthless for agriculture.

The great California Gold Rush initiated by James Marshall's gold discovery in early 1848 took place almost entirely on federal lands. Yet the only law governing the mining activity was (as explained in Morton v. Solambo Copper Mining Co., infra) the "law of the mining camps." A great deal of nonsense has been written about the customary mining camp law as a distinctive contribution to American jurisprudence. In fact, it was conceived out of necessity, it was simple, it followed a general common-sense principle of first in time, first in right, and it was sometimes enforced at the end of a rope. It contained useful specifics such as requirements for the marking of mining claims, limits on their acreage and the number that could be held, requirements to diligently develop them, and so forth. Similar customary "laws" governed mining camps that mushroomed and died all over the West in the years that followed the Gold Rush, because Congress took no action until 1866.

a.   THE CALIFORNIA GOLD RUSH

Rodman W. Paul, California Gold*

20–25 (1947).

In the history of almost any of the American states one can find a few events and trends that in significance stand out from the purely local as sharply as a single tree upon a desert plain. The Gold Rush is an instance. Within California the Gold Rush was a revolution that changed forever the character of the state. Beyond California's boundaries it was a magnetic force that sent its lines of attraction into every nation.

Within two years of Marshall's discovery every civilized country knew the name "California," although at that time few persons in Europe, or Asia, or Latin America could have identified Illinois, or Massachusetts, or Georgia. In all parts of the world men made ready to seek the Golden Fleece, or to venture their money in the expeditions organized by those more daring than themselves, or to invest in the expansion of trade and shipping to which the Gold Rush was giving rise.

Even if cautious men decided to remain at home and keep their capital with them, still they could not escape entirely the effects of the train of events set in motion [by Marshall's discovery] * * * In the United States alone, gold production multiplied seventy-three times during the six years that began in 1848, and from a position of insignificance among the gold producing nations, the United States climbed upward so rapidly that during the period from 1851 to 1855 it contributed nearly 45 per cent of the world's total output. The result was an inflation that affected all the countries on the earth's surface.

More dramatic and more immediately obvious was the functioning of the Gold Rush as a population movement. Here the first phase was confined to California itself. It consisted of a tumultuous stampede to the Sierra foothills by the people already in the province. * * *

Until midsummer, 1848, California's own population had sole possession of the mines. Then commenced the rush from outside the province. * * * Rumors of the discovery reached the Atlantic seaboard of the United States in August, but did not attract much attention until mid-September, and they were not established as fact until confirmed by the President's message to Congress on December 5. * * *

The bulk of the American immigration did not reach California until the vanguard of the Cape Horn sailing vessels had made port in June, July, and August, 1849, or until the overland caravans had begun to straggle in during August and September. Direct immigration from Europe was even later, and can hardly be placed much before the close of the year. Indirectly, a considerable number of Europeans of dubious background came to California during 1849 and 1850 from England's Australian penal colony.

How many joined in the rush of "forty-eight," "forty-nine," and the early fifties will never be known with any degree of accuracy, but it is clear that the influx of 1848 was comparatively so small that it was no more than a prelude to the stampede of 1849 and the subsequent years. * * * One may summarize these several sets of figures by saying that California's population jumped from 14,000 in 1848 to something less than 100,000 at the close of 1849, and that it then advanced to 223,000 by the latter part of 1852.

Morton v. Solambo Copper Mining Co.

Supreme Court of California, 1864.
26 Cal. 527.

[Joseph Dejon located a lode mining claim which he posted with his name and the names of plaintiffs' assignors without their knowledge. This quadrupled the permissible size of the claim under local miners' rules. A few days later Dejon tore down the original location notice and replaced it with one bearing the names of defendant's assignors. The trial court instructed that if the claim was validly located, plaintiffs' assignors acquired a right to it as tenants in common, notwithstanding their lack of knowledge or consent. After reciting these facts, the California Supreme Court, per Sanderson, C.J., discussed the law of the camps.]

The six hundred and twenty-first section of the [California] Practice Act provides that: "In actions respecting 'mining claims' proof shall be admitted of the customs, usages or regulations established and in force at the bar or diggings embracing such claims; and such customs, usages or regulations, when not in conflict with the Constitution and laws of this State, shall govern the decision of the action."

At the time the foregoing became a part of the law of the land there had sprung up throughout the mining regions of the State local customs and usages by which persons engaged in mining pursuits were governed in the acquisition, use, forfeiture or loss of mining ground. (We do not here use the word forfeiture in its common law sense, but in its mining law sense as used and understood by the miners who are the framers of our mining codes.) These customs differed in different localities and varied to a greater or less extent according to the character of the mines. They prescribed the acts by which the right to mine a particular piece of ground could be secured and its use and enjoyment continued and preserved and by what non-action on the part of the appropriator such right should become forfeited or lost and the ground become, as at first, *publici juris* and open to the appropriation of the next comer. They were few, plain and simple, and well understood by those with whom they originated. They were well adapted to secure the end designed to be accomplished, and were adequate to the judicial determination of all controversies touching mining rights. And it was a wise policy on the part of the Legislature not only not to supplant them by legislative enactments, but on the contrary to give them the additional weight of a legislative sanction. These usages and customs were the fruit of the times, and demanded by the necessities of communities who, though living under the common law, could find therein no clear and well defined rules for their guidance applicable to the new conditions by which they were surrounded, but were forced to depend upon remote analogies of doubtful application and unsatisfactory results. Having received the sanction of the Legislature, they have become as much a part of the law of the land as the common law itself, which was not adopted in a more solemn form. And it is to be regretted that the wisdom of the Legislature in thus leaving mining controversies to the arbitrament of mining laws has not always been seconded by the Courts and the legal profession, who seem to have been too long tied down to the treadmill of the common law to readily escape its thraldom while engaged in the solution of a mining controversy. These customs and usages have, in progress of time, become more general and uniform, and in their leading features are now the same throughout the mining regions of the State, and however it may have been heretofore, there is no reason why Judges or lawyers should wander, with counsel for the appellant in this case, back to the time when Abraham dug his well, or explore with them the law of agency or the Statute of Frauds in order to solve a simple question affecting a mining right, for a more convenient and equally legal solution can be found nearer home, in the "customs and usages of the bar or diggings embracing the claim" to which such right is asserted or denied.

The only question for us to determine in the present case is whether the instruction of the Court contains a correct exposition of the mining rule or custom under which the Solambo Claim was located, for that custom contains all the law applicable to the question before us, and by it the question is to be solved, whether the custom is written or unwritten, without any reference to the Statute of Frauds, or the law of agency, except as declared in the custom itself.

The custom provides that any person who has discovered a vein or lode and desires to locate a mining claim upon it for himself, or for himself and others, may do so by putting up a notice, with his own name and the names of those whom he may choose to associate with him appended thereto, to that effect, designating the extent of his claim, which may amount to three hundred feet for himself and one hundred and fifty feet for each of his associates. Thus the law itself makes the discoverer the agent of those for whom he chooses to act, and makes his act their act regardless of the fact whether they have any knowledge of it or not. * * * It follows that the instruction was correct, and the judgment must be affirmed.

NOTES AND QUESTIONS

1.   The miners were technically trespassing on federal land. When Colonel Mason of the U.S. Army outpost at Monterey, California toured the Sierra gold fields in the summer of 1848, he engaged in "serious reflection" about how the government ought to extract a fee from the miners, but prudence won out: "[U]pon considering the large extent of country, the character of the people engaged, and the small scattered force at my command [many of his soldiers had deserted to look for gold], I resolved not to interfere." His warning proved prophetic: "[S]till the Government is entitled to rents for this land, and immediate steps should be devised to collect them, for the longer it is delayed the more difficult it will become." Mason's report is reprinted in Thomas Donaldson, THE PUBLIC DO-MAIN: ITS HISTORY WITH STATISTICS 312–17 (1884).

2.   Today one might question whether the combination of congressional silence and the state of California's rather wholesale and dynamic (that is, ongoing) incorporation into its own law of the mining camp customs was an unlawful delegation of lawmaking power to private entities. Cf. Carter v. Carter Coal Co., 298 U.S. 238 (1936) (delegation of power to fix maximum hours of labor to coal producers and mineworkers "is legislative delegation in its most obnoxious form; for it is not even delegation to an official or an official body, presumptively disinterested, but to private persons whose interests may be and often are adverse to the interests of others in the same business"). But necessity can be the mother of invention in law as in other human endeavors.

3.   The California Gold Rush was more of a middle class movement than one of the dispossessed and downtrodden. It was, then, perhaps not so surprising that the miners had a penchant for creating a legal order in the mining camps. See John Leshy, THE MINING LAW: A STUDY IN PER-PETUAL MOTION 13 (1987).

b.   THE GENERAL MINING LAW OF 1872

Between 1850 and 1866, various bills to regulate mining activities were introduced in Congress, particularly when conflicts between miners and other settlers became acute, but discussion bogged down over such questions as how to exclude the Chinese from the harvest of metals. But pressure grew, and, after much legislative maneuvering by Senator William Stewart of Nevada (who would go on to make a fortune representing miners), to get around the opposition of Congressman George Julian of Indiana (who wanted the United States to reap some direct financial benefit from the minerals it owned), Congress finally produced the Mining Law of 1866 under the quaint title: "An Act granting the Right of Way to Ditch and Canal Owners over the Public Lands," with which it was scarcely concerned.

The 1866 Act legalized the minors' trespasses by declaring that "mineral lands are free and open to exploration and occupation" under local usage and custom. Lode claims, which are veins of ore, could be patented— fee title obtained—if the miner expended $500 in labor or improvements and filed a description with the local land office. Existing claims were retroactively validated. The area of the claim was limited to a maximum of 20 acres, and the cost for a patent was $5 per acre. Surface rights and extralateral rights were flexible, depending upon where the vein went. Four years later, Congress corrected an oversight in the earlier law by allowing the location of so-called "placer claims," which encompasses deposits in unconsolidated beds like gravel, defined as "all forms of deposit, excepting veins of quartz, or other rock in place." Placer locations were limited to 160 acres, and could be purchased for $2.50 an acre.

The Mining Law of 1872, 30 U.S.C. §§ 22–39, still the main statutory provision for hardrock mining, and sometimes called the "miners' Magna Carta," consolidated and modified the 1866 and 1870 laws. It qualified coverage by referring to "valuable" minerals, it required $100 worth of annual development work for either type of claim, and made other adjustments. From 1872 to the present, mining law (exclusive of fossil fuel and fertilizer minerals and a few special problems) has concerned itself primarily with interpretation of the Mining Act of 1872.

The Supreme Court described the principal interest granted by the 1872 Act—the unpatented mining claim—this way in Belk v. Meagher, 104 U.S. 279, 283–84 (1881):

> A mining claim perfected under the law is property in the highest sense of that term, which may be bought, sold, and conveyed, and will pass by descent. There is nothing in the act of Congress which makes actual possession any more necessary for the protection of the title acquired to such a claim by a valid location, than it is for any other grant from the United States. The language of the act is that the locators "shall have the exclusive right of possession and enjoyment of all the surface included within the lines of their locations," which is to continue until there shall be a failure to do the requisite amount of work within the prescribed time. Congress has seen fit to make the possession of that part of the public lands which is valuable for minerals separable from the fee, and to provide for the existence of an exclusive right to the possession, while the paramount title to the land remains in the United States. * * *

The reach of the 1872 Act has been progressively limited by various subsequent statutes. Oil and gas and other fossil fuels, along with fertilizer minerals like potash and sodium, were put into a leasing system in 1920. Common varieties of widely occurring minerals were put under a discretionary sales system in the mid-twentieth century. A growing number of environmental and other regulatory restrictions now apply to activities under the miners' Magna Carta. These are discussed in Chapter 7.

6. Grants to Railroads

By the mid–19th century, the West wanted railroads. Congress had been granting railroads rights-of-way up to 100 feet wide through the public lands since 1835. (In 1852 it adopted a general law to that effect which also authorized the use of earth, stone, and timber from adjacent public lands.) In 1850, a statute granted Illinois, Mississippi, and Alabama even-numbered sections of non-mineral public land within six miles of the proposed Chicago to Mobile rail line. The states assigned the land to the builder, and the rush was on. (Thereafter, odd-numbered sections of non-mineral public land were granted so the railroads would not lose sections 16 and 36, because by common practice these were held in reserve to support common schools in the new states.) The logic of the checkerboard is explained at p. 148, infra.

Eventually over 90 million acres of public lands were granted to the railroads directly. Another 35–40 million acres were granted to states to be used by the railroads. This was all in addition to another 200 million acres of public lands disposed of to support general "internal improvements," some of which were also granted to railroads.

This massive disposition program, like the others, was not always carried out smoothly. The first transcontinental line is the best known story, thanks to Stephen Ambrose's NOTHING LIKE IT IN THE WORLD (1999), and illustrated some of the problems. The Union Pacific and the Central Pacific were financed by the Act of July 1, 1862, ch. 120, 12 Stat. 489, (liberalized in 1864), signed into law by President Lincoln six weeks after he put his pen to the Homestead Act. It provided the railroads construction loans and a 400 foot right of way, together with their choice of 20 odd-numbered sections of public land within a 20–mile belt for every mile built. Just two years later Congress doubled the size of the grant by expanding the belt to a width of forty miles. In furtherance of homesteading, the Act required the railroads to dispose of their lands within three years at $1.25 per acre. The Supreme Court eventually upheld the device of "disposing" of the lands by mortgaging them to affiliates, Platt v. Union Pacific R. Co., 99 U.S. (9 Otto) 48 (1878), and watered down a provision for reversion to federal ownership if conditions were not met. Schulenberg v. Harriman, 88 U.S. (21 Wall.) 44 (1874).* While the roads were building, enormous quantities of land were withdrawn from settlement, and the railroads frequently delayed selection to avoid taxes. The West, which had pressed hard for railroad land grants, became hostile to the railroads as the supply of free land dried up. From 1871 on, most efforts were directed at redressing real and imagined grievances stemming from railroad ownership and practices, but few effective remedies were ever instituted.

---

* Only a few isolated forfeitures, declared by Congress, ever resulted from the widespread failures to comply. The timber-rich "O & C" lands in western Oregon (originally granted to underwrite construction of the Oregon and California Railroad) were returned to the public domain in that fashion. See Chapter 8, p. 773 infra.

The Gilded Age was one of the low points of public morality in the United States, but the changes wrought by the railroad land grants had some positive effects. Railroads encouraged and directed immigration, and were also among the first promoters of tourism centered on the wonders of the West. The Northern Pacific, for example, was one of the prime movers behind the creation of the world's first national park at Yellowstone. The West was developed, and many towns sprang up in the railroads' wake. Socially and economically, the railroad enterprise was instrumental in ending the frontier.

Prior and subsequent federal reservations of land within railroads' grant areas raised "in lieu" selection problems analogous to those faced by Utah in Andrus v. Utah, supra at p. 62. The Forest Lieu Exchange Act of 1897 allowed the railroads to exchange their inholdings in reserved lands for other lands outside the federal reservations; the Transportation Act of 1940, 49 U.S.C. § 65(b), released railroads from rate limitations in exchange for their relinquishment of in lieu rights. See Neuhoff v. Secretary of the Interior, 578 F.2d 810 (9th Cir.1978).

The railroad land grants have had one enduring legacy for modern public land management law and policy: the "checkerboard" problem. Well over 100 million acres, in alternate odd-numbered sections, were granted to the railroads, directly and indirectly, between 1850 and 1871. When the even-numbered sections the national government retained did not pass out of federal ownership by homesteading or other means, and the era of disposition faded, the checkerboard remained. The use of federal lands as a grazing commons exacerbated the awkward landownership pattern. As a leading public land historian put it:

> The methods adopted by users of the range are well known to readers of Western fiction. Great blocks of the public domain were fenced in by established ranchers for their exclusive use. * * * By 1885, illegal fencing had become so general that Congress passed a law prohibiting [enclosures of the public domain]. In 1886, President Cleveland, by proclamation, ordered removal of all fences. Secretary Lamar immediately threatened prosecution if the removals were not carried out without delay. Unfortunately, he did not have a staff in the field large enough or always willing to enforce the President's order and the new law.

Louise Peffer, THE CLOSING OF THE PUBLIC DOMAIN 80–81 (1951). But sometimes the government did attempt to enforce the law, as illustrated by the following case, involving a successor to the Union Pacific Railroad Company grant (the railroad, vitally interested in the outcome, filed an *amicus* brief).

Camfield v. United States

Supreme Court of the United States, 1897.
167 U.S. 518.

[Section 1 of the Unlawful Inclosures Act, 43 U.S.C. § 1061, provides: "All inclosures of any public lands * * * constructed by any person * * * to any of which land included within the inclosure the person * * * had no claim or color of title made or acquired in good faith * * * are hereby declared to be unlawful." Section 3, 43 U.S.C. § 1063, prohibits any person "by force, threats, intimidation, or by any fencing or inclosing, or any other unlawful means," from obstructing or preventing "free passage or transit over or through the public lands," or peaceable entries onto the public lands for purposes of establishing a settlement or residence under the public land laws. It also contains the proviso that it does not affect the "right or title of persons, who have gone upon, improved or occupied said lands under the land laws of the United States, claiming title thereto, in good faith." District courts are vested with jurisdiction to order offending fences removed.

The United States brought suit in federal district court in Colorado to compel the removal of a fence built and maintained by defendants Camfield and Drury. The following diagram of one township, from the 9th Circuit opinion, illustrates the manner in which the fence was constructed on the privately-owned odd-numbered sections so as to enclose the even-numbered sections that remained in federal ownership. The fence is indicated by the dotted lines. Defendants admitted they built the fence, but pointed out that they had installed a swinging gate to afford access to the public domain enclosed, and argued that they were installing irrigation works and developing the land which "was of great importance and utility, and would redound to the great advantage of the United States and its citizens."]

6	5	4	3	2	1
7	8	9	10	11	12
18	17	16	15	14	13
19	20	21	22	23	24
30	29	28	27	26	25
31	32	33	34	35	36

■ MR. JUSTICE BROWN delivered the opinion of the court.

* * * Defendants are certainly within the letter of this statute. They did enclose public lands of the United States to the amount of 20,000 acres, and there is nothing tending to show that they had any claim or color of title to the same, or any asserted right thereto under a claim made in good faith under the general laws of the United States. The defence is in substance that, if the act be construed so as to apply to fences upon private property, it is unconstitutional.

There is no doubt of the general proposition that a man may do what he will with his own, but this right is subordinate to another, which finds expression in the familiar maxim: *Sic utere tuo ut alienum non laedas.** His right to erect what he pleases upon his own land will not justify him in maintaining a nuisance, or in carrying on a business or trade that is offensive to his neighbors. Ever since *Aldred's case,* 9 Coke, 57, it has been the settled law, both of this country and of England, that a man has no right to maintain a structure upon his own land, which, by reason of disgusting smells, loud or unusual noises, thick smoke, noxious vapors, the jarring of machinery or the unwarrantable collection of flies, renders the occupancy of adjoining property dangerous, intolerable or even uncomfortable to its tenants. No person maintaining such a nuisance can shelter himself behind the sanctity of private property.

While the lands in question are all within the State of Colorado, the Government has, with respect to its own lands, the rights of an ordinary proprietor, to maintain its possession and to prosecute trespassers. It may deal with such lands precisely as a private individual may deal with his farming property. It may sell or withhold them from sale. It may grant them in aid of railways or other public enterprises. It may open them to preemption or homestead settlement; but it would be recreant to its duties as trustee for the people of the United States to permit any individual or private corporation to monopolize them for private gain, and thereby practically drive intending settlers from the market. It needs no argument to show that the building of fences upon public lands with intent to enclose them for private use would be a mere trespass, and that such fences might be abated by the officers of the Government or by the ordinary processes of court of justice. To this extent no legislation was necessary to vindicate the rights of the Government as a landed proprietor.

But the evil of permitting persons, who owned or controlled the alternate sections, to enclose the entire tract, and thus to exclude or frighten off intending settlers, finally became so great that Congress passed the act of February 25, 1885, forbidding all enclosures of public lands, and authorizing the abatement of the fences. If the act be construed as applying only to fences actually erected upon public lands, it was manifestly unnecessary, since the Government as an ordinary proprietor would have the right to prosecute for such a trespass. It is only by treating it as prohibiting

---

* [Eds. The translation is "so use your   BLACK'S LAW DICTIONARY (1999 ed.).] own as not to injure another's property"

all "enclosures" of public lands, by whatever means, that the act becomes of any avail. The device to which defendants resorted was certainly an ingenious one, but it is too clearly an evasion to permit our regard for the private rights of defendants as landed proprietors to stand in the way of an enforcement of the statute. So far as the fences were erected near the outside line of the odd-numbered sections, there can be no objection to them; but so far as they were erected immediately outside the even-numbered sections, they are manifestly intended to enclose the Government's lands, though, in fact, erected a few inches inside the defendants' line. Considering the obvious purposes of this structure, and the necessities of preventing the enclosure of public lands, we think the fence is clearly a nuisance, and that it is within the constitutional power of Congress to order its abatement, notwithstanding such action may involve an entry upon the lands of a private individual. The general Government doubtless has a power over its own property analogous to the police power of the several States, and the extent to which it may go in the exercise of such power is measured by the exigencies of the particular case. If it be found to be necessary for the protection of the public, or of intending settlers, to forbid all enclosures of public lands, the Government may do so, though the alternate sections of private lands are thereby rendered less available for pasturage. The inconvenience, or even damage, to the individual proprietor does not authorize an act which is in its nature a purpresture of government lands. While we do not undertake to say that Congress has the unlimited power to legislate against nuisances within a State, which it would have within a Territory, we do not think the admission of a Territory as a State deprives it of the power of legislating for the protection of the public lands, though it may thereby involve the exercise of what is ordinarily known as the police power, so long as such power is directed solely to its own protection. A different rule would place the public domain of the United States completely at the mercy of state legislation.

We are not convinced by the argument of counsel for the railway company, who was permitted to file a brief in this case, that the fact that a fence, built in the manner indicated, will operate incidentally or indirectly to enclose public lands, is a necessary result, which Congress must have foreseen when it made the grants, of the policy of granting odd sections and retaining the even ones as public lands; and that if such a result inures to the damage of the United States it must be ascribed to their improvidence and carelessness in so surveying and laying off the public lands, that the portion sold and granted by the Government cannot be enclosed by the purchasers without embracing also in such enclosure the alternate sections reserved by the United States. Carried to its logical conclusion, the inference is that, because Congress chose to aid in the construction of these railroads by donating to them all the odd-numbered sections within certain limits, it thereby intended incidentally to grant them the use for an indefinite time of all the even-numbered sections. It seems but an ill return for the generosity of the Government in granting these roads half its lands to claim that it thereby incidentally granted them the benefit of the whole. * * *

These grants were made in pursuance of the settled policy of the Government to reserve to itself the even-numbered sections for sale at an increased price; and if the defendants in this case chose to assume the risk of purchasing the odd-numbered sections of the railroad company for pasturage purposes, without also purchasing or obtaining the consent of the Government to use the even-numbered sections, and thereby failed to derive a benefit from the odd-numbered ones, they must call upon their own indiscretion to answer for their mistake. The law and practice of the Government were perfectly well settled, and if it had chosen in the past to permit by tacit acquiescence the pasturage of its public lands, it was a policy which it might change at any moment, and which became the subject of such abuses that Congress finally felt itself compelled to pass the act of February 25, 1885, and thereby put an end to them. * * * The defendants were bound to know that the sections they purchased of the railway company could only be used by them in subordination to the right of the Government to dispose of the alternate sections as it seemed best, regardless of any inconvenience or loss to them, and were bound to avoid obstructing or embarrassing it in such disposition, and were bound to avoid obstructing or embarrassing it in such disposition. If practices of this kind were tolerated, it would be but a step further to claim that the defendants, by long acquiescence of the Government in their appropriation of public lands, had acquired a title to them as against every one except the Government, and perhaps even against the Government itself.

It is no answer to say that, if such odd-numbered sections were separately fenced in, which the owner would doubtless have the right to do, the result would be the same as in this case, to practically exclude the Government from the even-numbered sections, since this was a contingency which the Government was bound to contemplate in granting away the odd-numbered sections. So long as the individual proprietor confines his enclosure to his own land, the Government has no right to complain, since he is entitled to the complete and exclusive enjoyment of it, regardless of any detriment to his neighbor; but when, under the guise of enclosing his own land, he builds a fence which is useless for that purpose, and can only have been intended to enclose the lands of the Government, he is plainly within the statute, and is guilty of an unwarrantable appropriation of that which belongs to the public at large. It may be added, however, that this is scarcely a practical question, since a separate enclosure of each section would only become desirable when the country had been settled, and roads had been built which would give access to teach section. * * *

NOTES AND QUESTIONS

1. Is the Court correct in concluding that Camfield's fence was "within the letter of" the statute?

2. Is the holding here derived more from congressional intent or from notions of "equitable considerations"? In this connection, look closely at the railroad company's argument as *amicus curiae*. Did Congress intend

this result when it created the checkerboards? What do you suppose Congress did intend?

3. The fence here was made possible by an important technological development in the late nineteenth century; namely, the invention and mass production of barbed wire. Where timber for wooden fences was scarce, "[b]arbed wire proved to be the cattle raisers' best friend." Richard White, "Animals and Enterprise," in OXFORD HISTORY OF THE AMERICAN WEST 264 (1994).

4. Does *Camfield* hold that the United States may regulate land use on private lands that affects the use or quality of the public lands? Could the United States prohibit, for instance, snowmobiles from operating on private land adjacent to a national wildlife refuge? Or unsightly curio shops or hot dog stands on private land at the entrance to a national park? Or is the United States merely in the same position as any landowner with a "nuisance" next door? (Is a fence a nuisance?) National power to protect the public lands under the Property Clause of the Constitution and the relationship between federal and state law in this context is an important and recurring issue in federal land and resources law; it is addressed in detail in Chapter 3. The questions posed in this paragraph are treated in some detail in section B of that Chapter, pp. 198–203, infra.

5. In Mackay v. Uinta Development Co., 219 Fed. 116 (8th Cir.1914), the question was whether Mackay, a nomadic sheepherder, was liable for trespass damages when he trailed his sheep across open, unfenced checkerboarded private lands while going to and from pastures on public lands. Relying on the Unlawful Enclosures Act as construed in *Camfield,* and on Buford v. Houtz, 133 U.S. 320 (1890), in which the Supreme Court held that congressional acquiescence in their trespasses gave all nomadic herders an implied license to graze their animals on the public lands, the court reversed a judgment for the private landowner, observing:

> This case illustrates the conflict between the rights of private property and the public welfare under exceptional conditions. It is difficult to say that a man may not inclose his own land, regardless of the effect upon others; but the Camfield Case, supra, has been recognized as sustaining the doctrine that "wholesome legislation" may be constitutionally enacted, though it lessens in a moderate degree what are frequently regarded as absolute rights of private property. * * * This large body of land, with the odd-numbered sections of the company and the even-numbered sections of the public domain located alternately like the squares of a checker-board, remains open as nature left it. Its appearance is that of a common, and the company is so using the contained public portions. In such use it makes no distinction between them and its own holdings. It has not attempted physically to separate the latter for exclusive private use. It admits that Mackay had the right in common with the public to pass over the public lands. But the right admitted is a theoretical one, without utility, because practically it is denied except on terms it prescribes. Contrary to the prevailing rule of construction, it seeks to cast upon the government and its licensees all the disadvantages of the interlocking arrangement of the odd and even

numbered sections because the grant in aid of the railroad took that peculiar form. It could have lawfully fenced its own without obstructing access to the public lands. That would have lessened the value of the entire tract as a great grazing pasture, but it cannot secure for itself that value, which includes as an element the exclusive use of the public lands, by warnings and actions in trespass.

A dissenting judge, noting that Mackay's 3500 sheep had stripped 90% of the forage off of a 3/4 mile swath of plaintiff's alternating sections of land, would have affirmed the trial court's award of damages for the forage consumed, even assuming Mackay had a right to cross the private lands.

6.   One way to pose the question raised in *Mackay* is to ask, who has the duty where no lands are fenced—the owners of the livestock (to fence them in or otherwise control them to avoid others' lands)? Or the other landowner (to fence her own land or shoo others' livestock away if she wants to avoid trespassing livestock)? The first is the English common law rule, generally followed in the eastern states of the United States. That is, the owner of livestock is liable for trespass if the stock strays on the lands of another. What is the western "common law" answer, according to *Mackay* (and Buford v. Houtz)? Can both answers be "common law"? Writing in an Arizona territorial water law case, Oliver Wendell Holmes once said that an Arizona statute generally adopting the common law of England "is far from meaning that patentees of a ranch on the San Pedro are to have the same rights as owners of an estate on the Thames." Boquillas Land & Cattle Co. v. Curtis, 213 U.S. 339, 345 (1909). For a modern western case holding that while a livestock owner in open range country may have an immunity under state law from trespass damages caused by wandering cows, the owner is not immune from damage claims by motorists injured by collisions with such cows on public highways, see Carrow v. Lusby, 167 Ariz. 18, 804 P.2d 747 (1990).

7.   If a landowner has a duty under state law to fence livestock in (the English and eastern states' common law rule), is the United States bound by that rule when it allows livestock to graze on federal land in that state? Some older cases suggest the answer is no; e.g., United States v. Johnston, 38 F.Supp. 4 (S.D.W.Va.1941); Shannon v. United States, 160 Fed. 870 (9th Cir.1908) (arising in Montana). Why not?

8.   Note that the United States was not a party in either *Mackay* or *Buford v. Houtz*, even though federal land was involved. For a case involving livestock and trespass where the federal government was a party, see Light v. United States, infra p. 110.

9.   The last section in this chapter addresses access questions that have arisen in the modern era as a result of the history of national policy toward federal lands.

7.   GRANTS FOR RECLAMATION

The beginnings of fundamental changes in the national policy of disposition came in the federal treatment of renewable resources, notably water and timber. The Desert Land Act of 1877 had opened the arid lands, and state water laws (the prior appropriation system) allowed the taking and use of water, but the laws did nothing to solve the physical problem of water scarcity. Many lands were still available for homesteading, but they would go unclaimed until large-scale water diversion and storage capacity was developed. Neither the states nor private entrepreneurs were able to meet this widely perceived need.

In 1878 John Wesley Powell, a Civil War veteran (who lost an arm in the battle of Shiloh) and leader of the pathbreaking trip down the Colorado River through the Grand Canyon in 1869—a trip which filled in the heart of the last white spot on the map of the lower 48 states—issued his landmark *Report on the Land of the Arid Regions* of the United States. Bernard DeVoto called it "[o]ne of the most remarkable books ever written by an American." This report, widely admired as a landmark step in characterizing the reality of western lands and settlement possibilities, was a warning of the need to adapt the public land disposition and settlement laws and policies to the realities of the arid West. It did not fall on particularly in receptive ears. As DeVoto put it, "[i]t is a scientific prophecy and it has been fulfilled—experimentally proved. Unhappily the experimental proof has consisted of human and social failure and the destruction of land."*

As it became apparent that the Desert Land Act had failed to achieve its sponsors' aim of increased productivity through private irrigation efforts,

> Congress took action by dusting off one of Powell's core ideas. In 1888 it authorized an irrigation survey * * * to identify the reservoir sites and canal rights-of-way necessary to develop irrigation in the arid lands. These lands were to be withdrawn from the public domain and reserved for the construction of an appropriate infrastructure.
>
> Speculators, however, kept a close eye on the [results]. It took no great intelligence to divine which lands the new surveys would propose to irrigate, and with water the value of those lands would rapidly appreciate. So speculators * * * hastened to file on land before it could be withdrawn. [In response the Interior Department in August 1889] invoked an obscure amendment to the Irrigation Survey's first appropriation bill, authorizing it to withdraw from entry "all lands made susceptible of irrigation." * * * The Department determined to apply [the withdrawal] to the entirety of the public domain and to close all public land to entry. Moreover it made the closure retroactive to October 2 of the previous year, throwing nearly a year's worth of claims into administrative limbo. * * *
>
> The resulting furor doomed the Irrigation Survey. Land filings in the late 1880s and early 1890s averaged 25 million acres a year. Dryland farming may have faltered on the prairies, but Americans were still hungry for land, still settling and speculating, still moving west across

---

* Foreword to Wallace Stegner's BE- (1954), a prize-winning biography of Powell.
YOND THE HUNDREDTH MERIDIAN

the plains and east from California and churning the ownership and occupancy of every state and territory in between. Nothing since the Civil War and Reconstruction had made so many Americans so mad.

William deBuys, SEEING THINGS WHOLE; THE ESSENTIAL JOHN WESLEY POWELL 213–14 (2001). Congress stepped in and rescinded the Department's power to reserve land, gutted Powell's budget, and greatly diminished his influence.

In 1894 Congress came back with the Carey Act, which offered each of the western states with "desert lands" up to a million acres of federal land if they would move out smartly to develop irrigation projects to make the lands productive within ten years. 43 U.S.C. §§ 641–48. This too failed, although a million acres were patented under it (60% of these in Idaho and 20% in Wyoming). Finally, with the Reclamation Act of 1902, 43 U.S.C. § 371 et seq., called the Newlands Act after its sponsor, Senator Francis Newlands of Nevada, the federal government embarked on a major program to irrigate western lands. The constitutionality of the Act was in doubt for some time; the issue was a reiteration of the early constitutional debates over the power of the national government to fund "internal improvements" (see p. 72, supra). See Kansas v. Colorado, 206 U.S. 46 (1907) (suggesting congressional power in this area was very limited). For a time, Congress attempted to justify reclamation projects such as Hoover Dam and the massive California Valley Project (CVP) on the dubious ground of improving navigation. The need for pretense was obviated by the decision in United States v. Gerlach Live Stock Co., 339 U.S. 725, 738 (1950), holding that "the power of Congress to promote the general welfare through large-scale projects for reclamation, irrigation, or other internal improvement, is now as clear and ample as its power to accomplish the same results indirectly through resort to strained interpretation of the power over navigation."

The Reclamation Act, which proved to be a major impetus to settlement, led to federal construction and operation of many major water projects in the West. Farmers receiving reclamation project water apply it to their private lands, and the water rights for the projects are generally perfected under state, not federal law, but reclamation law also assumes some continuing federal control over the use of the water. See generally Amy Kelley, Staging a Comeback—Section 8 of the Reclamation Act, 18 U.C.D. L.Rev.97 (1984). The original contemplation was that, while the United States would make the capital investments out of federal funds, the projects would be financed by the proceeds from federal land sales, and the water users would repay the costs of project construction and maintenance. It did not work out that way. Congress soon began to amend the law to extend repayment terms and forgive debts. The end result has been rather heavy subsidies for western agriculture. See, e.g., Joseph Sax, Selling Reclamation Water Rights: A Case Study in Federal Subsidy Policy, 64 Mich.L.Rev. 13 (1965). The reclamation program is critically examined in the late Marc Reisner's now-classic work, CADILLAC DESERT (1986).

The reclamation program eventually grew beyond the wildest hopes of its sponsors. By 1906 the Reclamation Service had commenced projects in

15 states for the irrigation of 2½ million acres. Still to come were such huge undertakings as Hoover Dam, which marked a transition in reclamation from primarily serving agriculture to multiple aims including flood control and municipal and industrial water. The course of diverted water under the Reclamation Act never did run smooth; many technical and economic problems were encountered, and the program sometimes fell short of living up to its original promise of carrying out the Jeffersonian vision of peopling the West with small family farms. The 1902 Act limited reclamation project water deliveries to a maximum of 160 acres per "any one landowner," and required the landowner to be "an actual bona fide resident on such land." Even though the Supreme Court unanimously upheld the acreage limitation in Ivanhoe Irrigation Dist. v. McCracken, 357 U.S. 275 (1958), with a ringing declaration that reclamation projects were "designed to benefit people, not land," and to distribute benefits "in accordance with the greatest good to the greatest number of individuals," enforcement of this restriction was, to put it charitably, spotty. The federal government, the states, and the project beneficiaries were more interested in building and operating projects than in social engineering. A lonely voice for carrying out the original social vision of the Act was Professor Paul Taylor, who wrote a series of law review articles decrying the lack of enforcement; e.g., 5 Ecology L.Q.1 (1975); 52 Calif.L.Rev. 978 (1964); 9 U.C.L.A. L.Rev. 1 (1962); 47 Calif.L.Rev. 499 (1959); 64 Yale L.J. 477 (1955). After the Carter Administration proposed to get tougher about enforcement, Congress enacted legislation in 1982 which significantly liberalized the acreage limitation (and repealed the residency requirement). Reclamation Reform Act of 1982, 43 U.S.C. §§ 390aa to 390zz–1. A significant part of this legislative overhaul was to require larger landowners who exceeded the new 960 acre limitation to pay "full cost" for federally-delivered water. Landowners unsuccessfully challenged this so-called "hammer clause" on constitutional grounds in Peterson v. U.S. Department of the Interior, 899 F.2d 799 (9th Cir.1990); see also Barcellos and Wolfsen, Inc. v. Westlands Water District, 899 F.2d 814 (9th Cir.1990). See generally Deborah Moore & Zack Willey, Water in the American West: Institutional Evolution and Environmental Restoration in the 21st Century, 62 U. Colo. L. Rev. 775 (1991); Hamilton Candee, The Broken Promise of Reclamation Reform, 40 Hastings L.J. 657 (1989).

8. Grants of Timber

Another fundamental shift in public land policy can be traced through successive congressional treatments of lands chiefly valuable for timber. For centuries, of course, the forest was the enemy, the wilderness standing between the pioneer and agrarian productivity. Timber was cleared from public lands to make way for agriculture. It has been conservatively estimated that by 1900, trees containing 600 billion board feet of lumber had been cut down to clear the land. On the other hand, some of the earliest examples of federal reservations and protection of lands for public purposes grew out of the national need for timber for construction of naval vessels in the early nineteenth century. See Paul Gates, HISTORY OF PUBLIC LAND LAW DEVELOPMENT 532–34 (1970).

Demand for lumber from the growing midwestern cities created vast logging industries in Michigan, Wisconsin, and other forested states. Wood-burning steamboats and railroad engines added to demand. The public lands supplied most of this seemingly insatiable market, usually by fraudulent means, including outright theft. By the use of their own "claim clubs," lumbermen seldom paid more than the minimum $1.25 per acre price, if they paid at all. Sawmills operated on federal land in Minnesota for eleven years before an acre of public land was sold. When reformer Secretary of the Interior Carl Schurz initiated some timber trespass prosecutions in the 1870's, Congress responded by refusing to appropriate funds for protecting the federal forests. Ironically, a few years before, in 1872, Congress had enacted the Timber Culture Act, which gave settlers forty acres of public lands if they would plant and cultivate trees. A few groves planted under this Act have survived on the Great Plains, but the main use of the Act was preemptive, for a settler could control the Timber Culture land claimed for 13 years without payment. Ten million acres went to patent under this Act.

In spite of the known abuses, Congress followed up with the Timber and Stone Act of 1878, which allowed persons to appropriate public lands "chiefly valuable for timber (or stone)" in several western states for $2.50 an acre. Abuses under this Act were also common. Occasionally the executive branch tried to protect federal timber lands from wholesale exploitation and privatization. The lonely efforts of General Land Commissioner W.A.J. Sparks to this end in 1885–87 was noteworthy, but had little lasting effect except to stir up western antagonism. The long history of exploitation of federal forest land eventually led to the rise of the first conservation movement toward the end of the nineteenth century.

C.   Reservation, Withdrawal, and Reacquisition

Throughout the 19th century, unprecedented population and economic growth and territorial expansion had taken place. The United States had truly become the haven for the oppressed—save Indians—and a world power. In 1893, historian Frederick Jackson Turner called attention to the fact that the Superintendent of the Census had declared end of the frontier in his bulletin on the 1890 census with these words: "Up to and including 1880 the country had a frontier of settlement, but at present the unsettled area has been so broken into by isolated bodies of settlement that there can hardly be said to be a frontier line." For Turner, the end of the frontier "closed the first period of American history," for up to then "American history has been in a large degree the history of the colonization of the Great West. The existence of an area of free land, its continuous recession, and the advance of American settlement westward, explain American development." This demographic change, along with a growing recognition of the shortcomings of public land disposal policy (and growing perception of the abuse of the public land laws), contributed to the rise to a national movement that would first significantly limit, and eventually replace, that policy. The consequence was the emergence of a policy to retain many tracts of land in federal ownership (and acquire or reacquire other tracts into federal ownership), as conservation would become a critical national concern.

Federal land policy in the first century of the Nation's existence had not be exclusively one of disposal. There were occasions when federal lands were held for the common good to serve interests of national importance. Withdrawals by the executive for military purposes and, beginning around mid-century, for Indian reservations, were not uncommon. But the purposes for which the lands were reserved would broaden substantially, and the pace of withdrawal and reservation would accelerate dramatically, as the nineteenth century drew to a close. The following case illustrated the emerging impulse to preserve some land in federal ownership to such broader cultural purposes. Today, the railroad company's legal argument seems utterly ludicrous on these particular facts. That it passed the "red-face" test in that era illustrates the boldness of those who advocated reservation of vast tracts of land permanently in public ownership, and the courage of those who were beginning to make such reservations.

United States v. Gettysburg Elec. R. Co.

Supreme Court of the United States, 1896.
160 U.S. 668.

■ Mr. Justice Peckman delivered the opinion of the court.

[The United States sought to condemn the Railroad's land for inclusion in what was to be Gettysburg National Military Park.] The really important question to be determined in these proceedings is, whether the use to which the petitioner desires to put the land described in the petitions is of that kind of public use for which the government of the United States is authorized to condemn land.

It has authority to do so whenever it is necessary or appropriate to use the land in the execution of any of the powers granted to it by the Constitution.

* * * In [the relevant acts] of Congress * * * the intended use of this land is plainly set forth. It is stated in the second volume of Judge Dillon's work on Municipal Corporations, (4th ed. § 600) that when the legislature has declared the use or purpose to be a public one, its judgment will be respected by the courts, unless the use be palpably without reasonable foundation. Many authorities are cited in the note, and, indeed, the rule commends itself as a rational and proper one.

* * * Upon the question whether the proposed use of this land is a public one, we think there can be no well founded doubt. And also, in our judgment, the government has the constitutional power to condemn the land for the proposed use. It is, of course, not necessary that the power of condemnation for such purpose be expressly given by the Constitution. The right to condemn at all is not so given. It results from the powers that are given, and it is implied because of its necessity, or because it is appropriate in exercising those powers. Congress has power to declare war and to create and equip armies and navies. It has the great power of taxation to be

exercised for the common defence and general welfare. Having such powers, it has such other and implied ones as are necessary and appropriate for the purpose of carrying the powers expressly given into effect. Any act of Congress which plainly and directly tends to enhance the respect and love of the citizen for the institutions of his country and to quicken and strengthen his motives to defend them, and which is germane to and intimately connected with and appropriate to the exercise of some one or all of the powers granted by Congress must be valid. This proposed use comes within such description. * * *

The end to be attained by this proposed use, as provided for by the act of Congress, is legitimate, and lies within the scope of the Constitution. The battle of Gettysburg was one of the great battles of the world. The numbers contained in the opposing armies were great; the sacrifice of life was dreadful; while the bravery and, indeed, heroism displayed by both the contending forces rank with the highest exhibition of those qualities ever made by man. The importance of the issue involved in the contest of which this great battle was a part cannot be overestimated. The existence of the government itself and the perpetuity of our institutions depended upon the result. Valuable lessons in the art of war can now be learned from an examination of this great battlefield in connection with the history of the events which there took place. Can it be that the government is without power to preserve the land, and properly mark out the various sites upon which this struggle took place? Can it not erect the monuments provided for by these acts of Congress, or even take possession of the field of battle in the name and for the benefit of all the citizens of the country for the present and for the future? Such a use seems necessarily not only a public use, but one so closely connected with the welfare of the republic itself as to be within the powers granted Congress by the Constitution for the purpose of protecting and preserving the whole country. * * *

No narrow view of the character of this proposed use should be taken. Its national character and importance, we think, are plain. The power to condemn for this purpose need not be plainly and unmistakably deduced from any one of the particularly specified powers. Any number of those powers may be grouped together, and an inference from them all may be drawn that the power claimed has been conferred.

* * * This, we think, completes the review of the material questions presented by the record. The first and important question in regard to whether the proposed use is public or not, having been determined in favor of the United States, we are not disposed to take any very technical view of the other questions which might be subject to amendment or to further proof upon the hearing below.

NOTES AND QUESTIONS

1. The modern U.S. Supreme Court generally does not regard the issue of whether a use is public for purposes of the fifth amendment condemnation as raising a significant judicial question. See Hawaii Housing Authority v. Midkiff, 467 U.S. 229 (1984) (the government must show only

a rational relationship to a conceivable public purpose); Berman v. Parker, 348 U.S. 26 (1954). In Buffalo River Conservation & Recreation Council v. National Park Service, 558 F.2d 1342 (8th Cir.1977), cert. denied, 435 U.S. 924 (1978), the court curtly rejected a challenge to federal condemnation of land for the Buffalo National River in Arkansas, noting that "[f]or at least eighty years the power of the United States to create parklands has been a recognized and popular function of the national government."

2. A number of federal statutes authorize the government to acquire lands for particular purposes specifically by "donation," "exchange," or "purchase with donated or appropriated funds." See, e.g., 16 U.S.C. § 460w–2 (Apostle Islands National Lakeshore Act). But such statutes do not limit the application of generic condemnation authority such as that found in the General Condemnation Act of 1888, 40 U.S.C. § 257, which provides that in "every case in which [an officer of the United States has been] authorized to procure real estate * * * for public uses, he may acquire the same for the United States by condemnation, under judicial process, whenever in his opinion it is necessary or advantageous to the Government to do so * * *." See United States v. 16.92 Acres of Land, 670 F.2d 1369 (7th Cir.1982) ("unless it desires to exclude condemnation, there is no need for Congress to specifically include 'condemnation' as a permissible method of property acquisition in a statute").

3. Federal condemnation procedures are summarized in Kirby Forest Industries, Inc. v. United States, 467 U.S. 1 (1984), involving a Park Service acquisition to expand Big Thicket National Park in Texas.

4. Other federal statutes limit the purposes for which eminent domain authority may be exercised. For example, the Federal Land Policy and Management Act gives the BLM condemnation authority only to provide access to federal lands. 43 U.S.C. § 1715(a); see United States v. 82.46 Acres of Land, 691 F.2d 474 (10th Cir.1982). Access questions are discussed in more detail in the last section of this chapter, and federal agency acquisitions are discussed in Chapter 4.

1. The Emergence of Withdrawal and Reservation

Although Congress had reserved four sections of land in Arkansas as early as 1832 because it contained hot springs thought to be of medicinal value (see 4 Stat. 405), the true origins of new federal policy can be traced to the Civil War era. The conservation-oriented writings of George Perkins Marsh in 1864 supplied a rationale for action by federal reformers such as Carl Schurz. Congress took a faltering step toward conservation when it gave Yosemite Valley to California in 1864 on the "express conditions that the premises shall be held for public use, resort and recreation [and] shall be inalienable for all time."* See 13 Stat. 325 (1864). But it was the creation of Yellowstone National Park as a "pleasuring ground" on a large

---

* The same section of the Yosemite Act continued: "but leases not exceeding ten years may be granted for portions of said premises."

and remote tract of federal lands in northeast Wyoming in 1872 which may rightly be regarded as the beginning of the modern federal lands systems.**

In sheer acreage terms, however, a more significant milestone was enactment of what Charles Wilkinson (in CROSSING THE NEXT MERIDIAN 122 (1992)) called a "little-noticed, seemingly innocuous" single sentence buried deep in an 1891 law blandly entitled the General Revision Act, 16 U.S.C. § 471, which repealed the Preemption and Timber Culture Acts, among other things. That sentence, added in conference committee with no comment in the Senate and a meager discussion in the House, authorized the President to "set apart and reserve * * * any part of the public lands wholly or in part covered with timber or undergrowth, whether of commercial value or not, as public reservations." Over the next fifteen years, a succession of Presidents (mostly Republican, as it turned out) used this authority in a series of executive orders to reserve most of the lands today embraced in the national forest system.

Although a number of tracts originally set aside as forest reservations eventually became national parks,* in 1907 an Oregon Senator, Charles Fulton, attached a rider to a vital Agriculture appropriation bill that repealed the President's authority to make new forest reserves in six northwestern states (Oregon, Washington, Idaho, Montana, Colorado, and Wyoming). When the bill reached the White House, Roosevelt responded in typical fashion. Over the next few days, a "forced draft of Administration clerks—some of them working forty-eight hour shifts—completed all the paperwork necessary for the President to proclaim twenty four new forest reserves, and eleven enlarged ones, in the six states specified." Edmund Morris, THEODORE REX 487 (2001). As the ink was drying on these new orders, Roosevelt signed the appropriations bill into law. Great controversies raged over such withdrawals, but a new age in public land law had dawned.

In the middle of this controversy over reservations, Congress paused long enough to enact, also as a rider to a general appropriation bill, what came to be known as the "organic act" for what came to be known as the national forests. It gave the Secretary of the Interior** general authority to

---

** Yellowstone was, for much of the time between 1886 and 1918, overseen by Army troops, who defended it against miners, loggers, and others bent on exploiting its resources.

* Other federal lands were designated national parks by Congress around the turn of the century without first being reserved as forests; e.g., Sequoia and Yosemite in 1890 (even though Yosemite Valley was not returned to federal ownership and added to the Park until 1906). See John Ise, OUR NATIONAL PARK POLICY 52–55 (1924).

** Congress transferred management authority over the Forest Reserves to the Secretary of Agriculture in 1905, except for functions relating to surveys and patenting and,

importantly, prospecting for minerals and locating mining claims. See 16 U.S.C. § 472. Although the transfer is usually regarded as reflecting a reaction to perceived mismanagement of the forests by the Interior Department, public land historian Louise Peffer concluded this was "not a fair criticism. It was the Department of the Interior which, from the time of Carl Schurz, Secretary from 1877 to 1881, spearheaded the movement to have forest reservations created. Year after year, through the 1890s, it was the Department of the Interior which stressed the need for protection and supervision denied by Congressional refusal to appropriate funds." THE CLOSING OF THE PUBLIC DOMAIN 177 (1951).

manage the Forest Reserves and to issue rules and regulations regarding their occupancy and use. The statute began by announcing that no national forest should be established "except to improve and protect the forest within the boundaries, or for the purpose of securing favorable conditions of water flows, and to furnish a continuous supply of timber for the use and necessities of citizens of the United States." It disclaimed any intent to "prohibit any person from entering upon such forest reservations for all proper and lawful purposes" so long as such persons "comply with the rules and regulations covering such forest reservations." It also authorized the Secretary to "make such rules and regulations * * * as will insure the objects of such reservations; namely, to regulate their occupancy and use, and to preserve the forests thereon from destruction." The statute also set out criminal penalties for violations. These provisions are now found in 16 U.S.C. §§ 475, 478, 551.

Passage of this law did not lessen the unpopularity of the forest reserves in many parts of the West, and there were genuine questions as to the constitutionality of the entire enterprise. The following two classic public land law opinions, issued the same day, crushed the hopes of opponents and laid the conservationists' fears to rest.

United States v. Grimaud

Supreme Court of the United States, 1911.
220 U.S. 506.

■ MR. JUSTICE LAMAR:

The defendants were indicted for grazing sheep on the Sierra Forest Reserve without having obtained the permission required by the regulations adopted by the Secretary of Agriculture. They demurred on the ground that the forest reserve act of 1897 was unconstitutional, in so far as it delegated to the Secretary of Agriculture power to make rules and regulations, and made a violation thereof a penal offense. [The lower court dismissed the federal prosecutions, and the government appealed.] * * *

Under these acts, therefore, any use of the reservation for grazing or other lawful purpose was required to be subject to the rules and regulations established by the Secretary of Agriculture. To pasture sheep and cattle on the reservation, at will and without restraint, might interfere seriously with the accomplishment of the purposes for which they were established. But a limited and regulated use for pasturage might not be inconsistent with the object sought to be attained by the statute. The determination of such questions, however, was a matter of administrative detail. What might be harmless in one forest might be harmful to another. What might be injurious at one stage of timber growth, or at one season of the year, might not be so at another.

In the nature of things it was impracticable for Congress to provide general regulations for these various and varying details of management. Each reservation had its peculiar and special features; and in authorizing the Secretary of Agriculture to meet these local conditions, Congress was merely conferring administrative functions upon an agent, and not delegating to him legislative power. The authority actually given was much less than what has been granted to municipalities by virtue of which they make by-laws, ordinances, and regulations for the government of towns and cities. Such ordinances do not declare general rules with reference to rights of persons and property, nor do they create or regulate obligations and liabilities, nor declare what shall be crimes, nor fix penalties therefor. * * *

It must be admitted that it is difficult to define the line which separates legislative power to make laws, from administrative authority to make regulations. This difficulty has often been recognized, and was referred to by Chief Justice Marshall in Wayman v. Southard, 10 Wheat. 1, where he was considering the authority of courts to make rules. He there said: "It will not be contended that Congress can delegate to the courts, or to any other tribunals, powers which are strictly and exclusively legislative. But Congress may certainly delegate to others powers which the legislature may rightfully exercise itself." What were these nonlegislative powers which Congress *could* exercise, but which might also be delegated to others, was not determined, for he said: "The line has not been exactly drawn which separates those important subjects which *must* be entirely regulated by the legislature itself, from those of less interest, in which a general provision may be made, and power given to those who are to act under such general provisions to fill up the details."

From the beginning of the government, various acts have been passed conferring upon executive officers power to make rules and regulations,— not for the government of their departments, but for administering the laws which did govern. None of these statutes could confer legislative power. But when Congress had legislated and indicated its will, it could give to those who were to act under such general provisions "power to fill up the details" by the establishment of administrative rules and regulations, the violation of which could be punished by fine or imprisonment fixed by Congress, or by penalties fixed by Congress, or measured by the injury done. * * *

[T]he authority to make administrative rules is not a delegation of legislative power, nor are such rules raised from an administrative to a legislative character because the violation thereof is punished as a public offense.

It is true that there is no act of Congress which, in express terms, declares that it shall be unlawful to graze sheep on a forest reserve. But the statutes from which we have quoted declare that the privilege of using reserves for "all proper and lawful purposes" is subject to the proviso that the person so using them shall comply "with the rules and regulations covering said forest reservation." The same act makes it an offense to violate those regulations; that is, to use them otherwise than in accordance with the rules established by the Secretary. Thus the implied license under which the United States has suffered its public domain to be used as a pasture for sheep and cattle, mentioned in Buford v. Houtz, 133 U.S. 320, was curtailed and qualified by Congress, to the extent that such privilege should not be exercised in contravention of the rules and regulations. Wilcox v. Jackson, 13 Pet. 498.

If, after the passage of the act and the promulgation of the rule, the defendants drove and grazed their sheep upon the reserve, in violation of the regulations, they were making an unlawful use of the government's property. In doing so they thereby made themselves liable to the penalty imposed by Congress.

It was argued that, even if the Secretary could establish regulations under which a permit was required, there was nothing in the act to indicate that Congress had intended or authorized him to charge for the privilege of grazing sheep on the reserve. These fees were fixed to prevent excessive grazing, and thereby protect the young growth and native grasses from destruction, and to make a slight income with which to meet the expenses of management. In addition to the general power in the act of 1897, already quoted, the act of February 1st, 1905 [33 Stat. 628] clearly indicates that the Secretary was authorized to make charges out of which a revenue from forest resources was expected to arise. * * *

The Secretary of Agriculture could not make rules and regulations for any and every purpose. Williamson v. United States, 207 U.S. 462. As to those here involved, they all relate to matters clearly indicated and authorized by Congress. The subjects as to which the Secretary can regulate are defined. The lands are set apart as a forest reserve. He is required to make provision to protect them from depredations and from harmful uses. He is authorized "to regulate the occupancy and use and to preserve the forests from destruction." A violation of reasonable rules regulating the use and occupancy of the property is made a crime, not by the Secretary, but by Congress. The statute, not the Secretary, fixes the penalty. * * *

NOTES AND QUESTIONS

1. *Grimaud* was a remarkable case. When it first came before the Court, the lower court opinion dismissing the prosecution was affirmed when the Justices split 4–4. A little more than a month later, however, the Court granted the government's motion for rehearing, and more than a year after that reversed the lower court without a single dissent. (In the meantime, Justices Hughes, Van Devanter and Lamar had joined the Court.)

2. *Grimaud* was a federal criminal prosecution. Did that aspect make the delegation issue harder or easier? Is the Court correct in characterizing this statute as not delegating legislative power, but merely giving the administering agency "power to fill up the details"? How much substantive guidance did Congress give the Secretary in this legislation?

3. Consider the Court's "impracticability" argument. At issue in *Grimaud* was the Forest Service's general regulation requiring a permit before grazing livestock in a Forest Reserve. Was it impracticable for Congress to make the decision that a permit ought to be required? Had Congress made such a decision?

4. In Whitman v. American Trucking Ass'n, 531 U.S. 457 (2001), the Supreme Court unanimously upheld the Clean Air Act's broad delegation of authority to the Environmental Protection Agency to set ambient air quality standards, and applied the test of whether the Congress had laid down an "intelligible principle" for the agency to conform to in exercising the authority granted. Justice Scalia's opinion pointed out that in its entire history the Court had struck down only two statutes on nondelegation grounds, "one of which provided literally no guidance for the exercise of discretion, and the other of which conferred authority to regulate the entire economy on the basis of no more precise a standard than stimulating the economy by assuring 'fair competition'." 531 U.S. at 474. Did the 1897 Act supply such an "intelligible principle"? What was it?

Light v. United States

Supreme Court of the United States, 1911.
220 U.S. 523.

■ MR. JUSTICE LAMAR:

The defendant was enjoined from pasturing his cattle on the Holy Cross Forest Reserve, because he had refused to comply with the regulations adopted by the Secretary of Agriculture, under the authority conferred by the act of June 4, 1897, (30 Stat. 35), to make rules and regulations as to the use, occupancy and preservation of forests. * * *

The bill alleged, and there was evidence to support the finding, that the defendant, with the expectation and intention that they would do so, turned his cattle out at a time and place which made it certain that they would leave the open public lands and go at once to the Reserve, where there was good water and fine pasturage. When notified to remove the cattle, he declined to do so and threatened to resist if they should be driven off by a forest officer. He justified this position on the ground that the statute of Colorado provided that a landowner could not recover damages for trespass by animals unless the property was enclosed with a fence of designated size and material. Regardless of any conflict in the testimony, the defendant claims that unless the Government put a fence around the Reserve it had no remedy, either at law or in equity, nor could he be required to prevent his cattle straying upon the Reserve from the open public land on which he had a right to turn them loose.

At common law the owner was required to confine his live stock, or else was held liable for any damage done by them upon the land of third persons. That law was not adapted to the situation of those States where there were great plains and vast tracts of unenclosed land, suitable for pasture. And so, without passing a statute, or taking any affirmative action on the subject, the United States suffered its public domain to be used for such purposes. There thus grew up a sort of implied license that these lands, thus left open, might be used so long as the Government did not cancel its tacit consent. Buford v. Houtz, 133 U.S. 326. Its failure to object, however, did not confer any vested right on the complainant, nor did it deprive the United States of the power of recalling any implied license under which the land had been used for private purposes. Steele v. United States, 113 U.S. 130; Wilcox v. Jackson, 13 Pet. 513.

It is contended, however, that Congress cannot constitutionally withdraw large bodies of land from settlement without the consent of the State where it is located; and it is then argued that the act of 1891 providing for the establishment of reservations was void, so that what is nominally a Reserve is, in law, to be treated as open and unenclosed land, as to which there still exists the implied license that it may be used for grazing purposes. * * *

The United States can prohibit absolutely or fix the terms on which its property may be used. As it can withhold or reserve the land it can do so indefinitely, Stearns v. Minnesota, 179 U.S. 243. It is true that the "United States do not and cannot hold property as a monarch may for private or personal purposes." * * *

"All the public lands of the nation are held in trust for the people of the whole country." United States v. Trinidad Coal Co., 137 U.S. 160. And it is not for the courts to say how that trust shall be administered. That is for Congress to determine. The courts cannot compel it to set aside the lands for settlement; or to suffer them to be used for agricultural or grazing purposes; nor interfere when, in the exercise of its discretion, Congress establishes a forest reserve for what it decides to be national and public purposes. In the same way and in the exercise of the same trust it may disestablish a reserve, and devote the property to some other national and public purpose. These are rights incident to proprietorship, to say nothing of the power of the United States as a sovereign over the property belonging to it. Even a private owner would be entitled to protection against willful trespasses, and statutes providing that damage done by animals cannot be recovered, unless the land had been enclosed with a fence of the size and material required, do not give permission to the owner of cattle to use his neighbor's land as a pasture. They are intended to condone trespasses by straying cattle; they have no application to cases where they are driven upon unfenced land in order that they may feed there.

Fence laws do not authorize wanton and willful trespass, nor do they afford immunity to those who, in disregard of property rights, turn loose their cattle under circumstances showing that they were intended to graze upon the lands of another. * * *

NOTES AND QUESTIONS

1. The Forest Reserves encompassed almost 100 million acres of land susceptible to grazing. Charles Wilkinson described Pinchot's 1906 grazing regulations as "incendiary to the cattle industry," with several western legislatures passing memorials denouncing it, labeling Pinchot as a dictator and carpetbagger. Fred Light, a longtime rancher in the Roaring Fork River valley in Colorado, was a widely respected figure, and his fight became a cause celebre in Colorado and in ranching circles nationally, with stock associations and the Colorado legislature contributing to the payment

of his attorneys' fees. Once he lost, he "acceded graciously and obtained federal permits for his animals [and o]ther ranchers grudgingly followed." CROSSING THE NEXT MERIDIAN 91–92 (1993).

2.   How does Light's complaint differ from Grimaud's?

3.   How does the Court characterize the powers of the federal government over the public lands? As a sovereign? As a proprietor (ordinary landowner)? Compare Pollard v. Hagan, 44 U.S. (3 How.) 212 (1845), supra at p. 52. Can the difference between the formulations in the two cases be explained by the evolution in congressional policy between 1845 and 1911?

4.   Are there intimations of a "public trust" doctrine in this decision? Is the view expressed here of the enforceability of the trust in the courts consistent with Illinois Central Railroad, supra p. 58?

As the twentieth century approached, the public land policies of the nineteenth had served their intended goals, albeit crudely. But altered circumstances and opinions began to bring about fundamental changes. Most land that could be productively farmed without irrigation had already passed out of federal ownership; private irrigation was but a drop in the bucket; western grazing lands were in poor condition; wildlife resources were at historical lows; and timber resources were severely depleted. Scandal was common, reforms had been repeatedly thwarted, and the trend toward large holdings and monopoly grew. Clear thinkers like John Wesley Powell had forcefully urged new methods of dealing with the public domain in relation to western settlement, but his career had been cut short by a hostile congressional reaction to the blanket withdrawals for the irrigation survey in 1889. A few years later, Gifford Pinchot emerged as the strongest advocate for fundamental revision in public land policy.

Stewart T. Udall, The Quiet Crisis

97–108 (1963).

Gifford Pinchot saw the climax of the Big Raids in the 1890's, and he described the scene with both candor and color:

> Out in the Great Open Spaces where Men were Men the domination of concentrated wealth over mere human beings was something to make you shudder. I saw it and fought it, and I know. * * * Big money was King in the Great Open Spaces, and no mistake. * * * The powers and principalities which controlled the politics and the people of the West began to emerge from the general landscape. Principalities like the Homestake Mine in the Black Hills, the Anaconda Mine in the Rockies, Marcus Daly's feudal overlordship of the Bitterroot Valley, and Miller and Lux's vast holdings of flocks and herds and control of grazing lands on the Pacific slope—these and others showed their hands or their teeth. So did powers like the Northern and Southern Pacific and

the Great Northern Railroads, the irrigation interests of California, and the great cattle and sheep stock growers' association. * * *

By any standards, Gifford Pinchot was a magnificent bureaucrat. In his time the Forest Service was the most exciting organization in Washington. It was more a family than a bureau. In the field, around campfires, and in his home GP discussed the next moves and gave his associates the feeling that they served on the general staff in a national crusade. A natural leader, he chose his men well, gave them authority, aroused an *esprit de corps* and sent them forth to save the forests. The rule book he wrote for his men was filled with crisp, common-sense guidelines. Typical Pinchot maxims were: "The public good comes first," and "Local questions will be decided by local officers on local grounds." In a matter of months his new "forest rangers" were winning over the West. * * *

What was needed now was a word, a name—to sum up the concept. A conversation with forester Overton Price brought up the fact that government forests in India were called "conservancies." Pinchot and Price liked the ring of the word, and thus a concept that had originated in the seminal thinking of such men as Thoreau and Marsh now had an expressive name—conservation. * * *

The conservation movement was a river of many tributaries, and if GP was not, as he liked to believe in his later years, its fountainhead, he was nevertheless one of its vital sources. He was a key man of a key decade, and his leadership was crucial in persuading the American people to turn from flagrant waste of resources to programs of wise stewardship. * * *

The classic encounter that embroiled him and other dedicated conservationists involved the first head-on collision between the Pinchot idea of conservation-for-use and the park concept of scenic preservation. The controversy was known by an improbable name: Hetch Hetchy. Pinchot's chief opponent, a friend who knew even more about the American out-of-doors than he, was an improbable person—John Muir.

While the Forest Reserves were the first great system of public lands that had been withdrawn from the public domain, the national park system was close behind. Since the withdrawal and reservation of Yellowstone 1872, Congress had created a handful of other national parks, among them Mackinac Island in Michigan in 1875, Sequoia and Yosemite in 1890, Mount Rainier in 1899, and Crater Lake in 1902. It was not until 1916, however, that the National Park Service (NPS) was chartered, with organic authority to administer this young National Park System. The quietly revolutionary statute directed NPS to "conserve the scenery and the natural and historic objects and the wild life [in national parks] and to provide for the enjoyment of the same in such manner and by such means as will leave them unimpaired for the enjoyment of future generations." 16 U.S.C. § 1. This was the third leg in what had become, by early in the twentieth century, a trichotomy of resource philosophies, described roughly as uncontrolled extraction, regulated use, and preservation.

Harold W. Wood, Jr., Pinchot and Mather: How the Forest Service and Park Service Got That Way*

Not Man Apart, December 1976.

Gifford Pinchot was the person most responsible for establishing the US Forest Service and dedicating it to utilitarian uses of natural resources. Stephen Mather was the person most responsible for organizing the National Park Service, dedicated to the preservation of natural features in the undisturbed state. The conflicts epitomized by these agencies have continued into the present day, so an understanding of the contrasting viewpoints of these two architects of policy may help us understand some of the land-use conflicts we still have to deal with. * * *

Pinchot's fundamental attitude toward the environment was utilitarian. He consistently favored resource development over mere preservation, as illustrated by two controversies of his day—issues we are still struggling with. One contest was over the Adirondack Forest Preserve in New York, where voters had passed an amendment to the state constitution that prohibited any timber from the area being sold, removed, or destroyed. Pinchot felt that the prohibition was tremendous waste and said forestry had nothing to do with decoration of public places, "that scenery is altogether outside its province." * * *

But by far the most famous episode in the utilitarian/aesthetic battle was the controversy over Hetch Hetchy Valley in Yosemite National Park. The preservationists, led by John Muir and the Sierra Club, believed that the park should not be violated. San Francisco, however, wanted to build a dam to provide a water supply for the city. Pinchot sided with the city and used his influence in Washington on its behalf.

Pinchot was adamant in his position: "I am fully persuaded that * * * the injury * * * by substituting a lake for the present swampy floor of the [Hetch Hetchy] valley. * * * is altogether unimportant compared with the benefits to be derived from its use as a reservoir." * * * Pinchot, like others, ignored the fact that alternative sites were available, if at a higher cost of construction.

John Muir's view on Hetch Hetchy was just as succinctly put: "Dam Hetch Hetchy! As well dam for water-tanks the people's cathedrals and churches, for no holier temple has ever been consecrated by the heart of man."

The Sierra Club and its allies lost Hetch Hetchy to the dam-builders in 1913. It is probable that the controversy, with all its publicity, helped generate public support in 1916 for the National Park Service Act, which would better protect National Parks from such encroachment.

Pinchot expanded his philosophy of forestry into a full-scale political ideology in 1905 when he became Chief Forester of the newly established US Forest Service, which had jurisdiction over the forest reserves. In his instructions from Agriculture Secretary James Wilson in 1905 (which

Pinchot wrote himself), he was told: "All the resources of forest reserves are for *use* * * * where conflicting interests must be reconciled, the question will always be decided from the standpoint of the greatest good for the greatest number in the long run." With this last phrase, Pinchot thought he had found an unbeatable formula for success. * * *

His utilitarian attitude led him to believe that national parks, and not just national forests, should be open to such development as grazing and lumbering. As early as 1904 he recommended to Congress that the national parks be transferred to the Forest Service for administration. He opposed bills to create a separate National Park Service by saying it was "no more needed than two tails to a cat."

The Forest Service consistently opposed bills to create new parks and reliably suggested national forest status instead. When the bill to establish Glacier National Park appeared in Congress, Pinchot objected because the only commercial use to be allowed was removal of dead, down, or decaying timber by settlers. He prepared a rival measure to permit timber cutting, water power development, and railroad construction within the park.

Stephen Mather was every bit as energetic as Pinchot and just as dedicated to his own cause. * * *

Some of Mather's biggest struggles in protecting the parks came during World War I, at the beginning of his administration. Secretary Lane was a "hawk" on the President's cabinet and favored using all resources in the war effort. It is reported that after Mather had failed to keep cattle out of Yosemite legally, he had some of the cows caught and staked near trails, hoping to incite hikers into denouncing the business to their Representatives. (Mather always denied this; he said it was too good an idea to be his own.) * * *

While the National Park Service is usually considered preservationist, Mather was not a complete purist. He believed that the national parks should be opened up to development to provide visitors' accommodations. Much of his effort went into having roads constructed and improved, having inns and hotels built, and encouraging railroads to bring people to the parks.

He did all of this, however, within certain limits. For example, he refused to allow railroad lines *within* Yellowstone Park, although he had gone out of his way to encourage railroad lines *to* the Park.

While he believed in providing inns and hotels, he wouldn't allow such concessions unwarranted power. When the Great Northern Railroad set up a sawmill to construct a hotel in Glacier National Park, Mather watched the progress carefully. When the hotel was finished, he reminded the company that the sawmill and its sawdust must go. The company asked for a little more lumber, which Mather reluctantly let it have. The stay expired on August 10, 1925, and the railroad company again asked for more time, although the hotel was already taking in tourists. Mather was in the park on business at the time, so that afternoon he rounded up the Park Service trail crews and had the sawmill blown up. * * *

It might seem that Mather's attitude was ambivalent. The parks were dedicated to preservation, but also to the people's enjoyment. Translating this dualistic approach into workable policies is much more difficult than interpreting a simple utilitarianism such as Pinchot's. Nevertheless, Stephen Mather had criteria and sound reasoning with which to provide suitable development compatible with preservation. Considering the enormous pressure to commercialize the parks, Mather did an admirable job of keeping preservation foremost.

It cannot be said that Mather objected to sustained-yield forestry, and he did not think that national park standards and management practices should be applied to national forests. In contrast, Pinchot implacably felt that national parks should be managed just as the national forests were.
* * *

It is ironic that Pinchot had such a comprehensive view of managing natural resources, even speaking of conserving human resources, and yet entirely neglected aesthetic values. Mather certainly did not attempt to enlarge his ideas on preservation into a political philosophy, as Pinchot did, but he still accepted the need for both preservation and utilitarian conservation—as long as the utilization wasn't in the national parks.

If it were not for Pinchot's recalcitrant opposition to the preservationists, the utilitarian and aesthetic schools of conservation probably would not have become so split. For many years, agency rivalry between the Forest Service and the National Park Service created ugly moods. The squabbling was often as much over jurisdiction as philosophy. But, partly in response to the Park Service's carving new parks and monuments out of national forests, the Forest Service began its own program of recreational development and safeguards for scenic resources. With the help of men such as Arthur Carhart, Robert Marshall, and Aldo Leopold of the Forest Service, a system of wilderness areas began developing in the 1930's. Without the competition, it is likely that this would not have been done for a long time.*

2.   JOHN MUIR AND THE MODERN CONSERVATION MOVEMENT

Pinchot and Mather were men of affairs, personally wealthy, influential, and highly placed in the national government. Their accomplishments were great and their philosophies were advanced. Their names will long live in public land annals. Their fame was eclipsed by John Muir. Muir never held an important position except, perhaps, President of the young Sierra Club, which he helped found in 1892. He was a philosopher, a traveler, a nature lover, and a writer. He lived in and for the mountains. His contribution to public land and resources law was spiritual, a lasting legacy of love for the land and its creatures. He was the archetypal preservationist

---

* [Eds.: For a summary of more recent scholarship on Pinchot and Mather, see Federico Cheever, The United States Forest Service and the National Park Service: Paradoxical Mandates, Powerful Founders, and the Rise and Fall of Agency Discretion, 74 Denv. U.L.Rev. 625, 630–39 (1997).]

whose ironbound, indomitable will more than matched those of the "timber barons" and other large-scale users of the land whom he so despised.

Muir inspired a new ethic that has been absorbed into the American consciousness, an ethic that is not less real for its lack of precise definition. Its most important manifestation has been the formation of groups composed of private citizens who, like Muir, are willing to devote their time and money to environmental causes. Muir's contribution to public land policy is incapable of measurement. But the esteem that he has inspired in later generations is reflected in the fact that more things in California, from Muir Woods to the John Muir Trail (not to mention the USS *John Muir*), are named after him than any other individual. In 1976, a citizen poll named Muir the "single greatest Californian" in history.

E.W. Teale, The Wilderness World of John Muir

XIV, XIX–XX (1954).

Before his first book came from the press John Muir was already famous as a writer. His sequence of "Sierra Studies" in the old *Overland Monthly* and his articles in the *Century Magazine* had had wide influence and had given him a national reputation. * * * An exactness and depth of firsthand observation characterizes all his pages. He was by turn a scientist, a poet, a mystic, a philosopher, a humorist. Because he saw everything, mountains and streams and landscapes, as evolving, unfinished, in the process of creation, there is a pervading sense of vitality in all he wrote. Even his records of scientific studies read like adventure stories. * * *

Considerable as was John Muir's contribution to science, even greater was his stature in the long fight for conservation. During those critical years around the turn of the century, his was the most eloquent and powerful voice raised in defense of nature. He was the spearhead of the western movement to preserve wild beauty, a prime mover in the national park system so valued today. Beside a campfire at Soda Springs on the Tuolumne Meadows in 1889, he and Robert Underwood Johnson mapped the seventeen-year battle that preserved Yosemite as a national park. Beside other campfires under sequoias, while on a three-day outing with Theodore Roosevelt in 1903, he presented the case for the preservation of numerous wilderness areas with moving effect. Major credit for saving the Grand Canyon and the Petrified Forest, in Arizona, is ascribed to John Muir. He was president of the Sierra Club from the formation of that militant conservation organization in 1892 until the time of his death in 1914. His last long battle to save Hetch Hetchy, the beautiful Yosemite Park valley flooded to form a reservoir for San Francisco water—water that could have been obtained elsewhere—ended only the year before he died. It represents one of the great heroic struggles of conservation, no less heroic because the cause was lost.

Near the end of his life Muir said to a close friend, "I have lived a bully life. I have done what I set out to do." Rich in time, rich in enjoyment, rich in appreciation, rich in enthusiasm, rich in understanding, rich in expression, rich in friends, rich in knowledge, John Muir lived a full and rounded life, a life unique in many ways, admirable in many ways, valuable in many ways. "A man in his books," he once wrote, "may be said to walk the earth long after he had gone." In his writings and in his conservation achievements, Muir seems especially present in a world that is better because he lived here. His finest monument is the wild beauty he called attention to and helped preserve—beauty, however, that is never entirely safe, beauty that needs as vigilant protection today and tomorrow as it needed yesterday.

––––––––––

Muir was a catalyst, but workaday legislators brought about conservationist reforms through law. Two of the most important were the Mineral Leasing Act of 1920 and the Taylor Grazing Act of 1934, discussed further below. One other important enactment of this era was the Weeks Act of 1911, 36 Stat. 961, 16 U.S.C. § 513, which authorized the purchase of timber lands in the east and added them to the national forest system. Historian Roy Robbins said this "marked the extension of the conservation movement from the Western regional focus to the nation at large." OUR LANDED HERITAGE 370. Western Senators supported the Weeks Act, leading Robbins to speculate they hoped the east would get sick of the forest reserves and help them abolish the reserves across the country. It didn't happen.

3. EXECUTIVE WITHDRAWAL AUTHORITY SETTLED

The Mining Act of 1872 was as subject to abuse as the other disposal laws, but it has survived because of the power of inertia and the idea that the Law was vital to mineral development, which in turn has been seen as a necessary requisite to national growth and development. By the turn of the 20th century, however, it was becoming apparent that the Mining Law did not serve the nation's needs for fossil fuels and fertilizer minerals. Legislation for disposition of federal coal lands was first passed in 1864, and by 1873 had evolved into a system which provided for entry and patent in a fashion similar to agricultural entry, but at a higher price. This was in sharp contrast to the free mining policy for metals. The usual abuses led President Roosevelt in 1906 to withdraw from all forms of entry 66 million acres where "workable coal is known to occur," and to call for a leasing system. Much of the land withdrawn was later returned to the public domain, but the attention created helped pass several statutes in ensuing years that severed the rights to underlying coal from the surface estate, reserving the former for the United States. The 30-odd million acres patented under the Stock–Raising Homestead Act, for instance, are said to overlay more energy in the form of coal than Saudi Arabia has as oil. (These "split-estate" lands are considered in Chapter 7, § D infra.)

In the meantime, petroleum had gone from a curiosity to a highly valuable resource. Oil strikes all over the country caused fevers reminiscent of the Gold Rush. The legal status of petroleum on federal lands was somewhat unclear until Congress, in the Oil Placer Act of 1897, confirmed that petroleum locations were to be governed by the General Mining Law of 1872. This opened the door for the industry to enter and locate mining claims on the public lands without obtaining government approval, to explore for and obtain a vested property right to any petroleum deposits they discovered, to develop the resource without paying the United States any rental or royalty payments, and to acquire fee simple title to the land and all the minerals it might contain for a mere $2.50 per acre.

Fearing that all oil lands would soon pass into private ownership, forcing the Navy to buy back the oil that was being given away, President William Howard Taft in 1909 asked Congress to put petroleum under a leasing system so the United States would have more control over the development of this strategic resource on the public lands. Then, on September 27, 1909, without advance warning, he went further, issuing an order that "withdrew" from the Mining Law and other disposition acts three million acres of federal land in Wyoming and California thought to be valuable for oil. Uncertain of the constitutional basis for his action, Taft requested congressional validation, which Congress promptly supplied in the Pickett Act of 1910, 43 U.S.C. §§ 141–143 (repealed 1976). While the Act granted the executive broad power to make "temporary" withdrawals for all "public purposes,"* it was prospective only, and expressly refused to say whether Taft's 1909 withdrawals were valid. Nevertheless, as Robert Swenson has observed:

> After several years of squabbling about the usurpation of congressional power over the public domain by Executive withdrawals, Congress did have the opportunity in 1910 to wrestle the entire conservation program from the control of the President. It showed no inclination to do so. This can only be a reflection of the general sentiment in the country which was unsympathetic to the attitude of Congress toward conservation in the previous decade.

"Legal Aspects of Mineral Resources Exploitation," in Gates, HISTORY OF PUBLIC LAND LAW DEVELOPMENT 735 (1970). In 1915, the Supreme Court reviewed the validity of Taft's prior withdrawals, giving rise to the following landmark opinion in public natural resources law.

United States v. Midwest Oil Co.

Supreme Court of the United States, 1915.
236 U.S. 459.

■ MR. JUSTICE LAMAR:

All public lands containing petroleum or other mineral oils and chiefly valuable therefor, have been declared by Congress to be "free and open to occupation, exploration and purchase by citizens of the United States * * * under regulations prescribed by law." Act of February 11, 1897, c. 216, 29 Stat. 526 [Oil Placer Act, which parroted the language of the Mining Law of 1872].

---

* The Pickett Act also stipulated that lands subsequently withdrawn would still be open to "metalliferous" mineral entry, which is treated further below at pp. 341–44.

As these regulations permitted exploration and location without the payment of any sum, and as title could be obtained for a merely nominal amount, many persons availed themselves of the provisions of the statute. Large areas in California were explored; and petroleum having been found, locations were made, not only by the discoverer but by others on adjoining land. And, as the flow through the well on one lot might exhaust the oil under the adjacent land, the interest of each operator was to extract the oil as soon as possible so as to share what would otherwise be taken by the owners of nearby wells.

The result was that oil was so rapidly extracted that on September 17, 1909, the Director of the Geological Survey made a report to the Secretary of the Interior which, with enclosures, called attention to the fact that, while there was a limited supply of coal on the Pacific coast and the value of oil as a fuel had been fully demonstrated, yet at the rate at which oil lands in California were being patented by private parties it would "be impossible for the people of the United States to continue ownership of oil lands for more than a few months. After that the Government will be obliged to repurchase the very oil that it has practically given away." * * * "In view of the increasing use of fuel by the American Navy there would appear to be an immediate necessity for assuring the conservation of a proper supply of petroleum for the Government's own use * * *" and "pending the enactment of adequate legislation on this subject, the filing of claims to oil lands in the State of California should be suspended."

This recommendation was approved by the Secretary of the Interior. Shortly afterwards he brought the matter to the attention of the President who, on September 27, 1909, issued the following Proclamation:

"Temporary Petroleum Withdrawal No. 5."

"In aid of proposed legislation affecting the use and disposition of the petroleum deposits on the public domain, all public lands in the accompanying lists are hereby temporarily withdrawn from all forms of location, settlement, selection, filing, entry, or disposal under the mineral or nonmineral public-land laws. All locations or claims existing and valid on this date may proceed to entry in the usual manner after field investigation and examination."

The list attached described an area aggregating 3,041,000 acres in California and Wyoming—though, of course, the order only applied to the public lands therein, the acreage of which is not shown.

On March 27, 1910, six months after the publication of the Proclamation, William T. Henshaw and others entered upon a quarter section of this public land in Wyoming so withdrawn. They made explorations, bored a well, discovered oil and thereafter assigned their interest to the Appellees, who took possession and extracted large quantities of oil. On May 4, 1910, they filed a location certificate.

As the explorations by the original claimants, and the subsequent operation of the well, were both long after the date of the President's Proclamation, the Government filed, in the District Court of the United States for the District of Wyoming, a Bill in Equity against the Midwest Oil

Company and the other Appellees, seeking to recover the land and to obtain an accounting for 50,000 barrels of oil alleged to have been illegally extracted. * * *

* * * On the part of the Government it is urged that the President, as Commander-in-Chief of the Army and Navy, had power to make the order for the purpose of retaining and preserving a source of supply of fuel for the Navy, instead of allowing the oil land to be taken up for a nominal sum, the Government being then obliged to purchase at a great cost what it had previously owned. It is argued that the President, charged with the care of the public domain, could, by virtue of the executive power vested in him by the Constitution (Art. 2, § 1), and also in conformity with the tacit consent of Congress, withdraw, in the public interest, any public land from entry or location by private parties.

The Appellees, on the other hand, insist that there is no dispensing power in the Executive and that he could not suspend a statute or withdraw from entry or location any land which Congress had affirmatively declared should be free and open to acquisition by citizens of the United States. They further insist that the withdrawal order is absolutely void since it appears on its face to be a mere attempt to suspend a statute— supposed to be unwise—in order to allow Congress to pass another more in accordance with what the Executive thought to be in the public interest.

1. We need not consider whether, as an original question, the President could have withdrawn from private acquisition what Congress had made free and open to occupation and purchase. The case can be determined on other grounds and in the light of the legal consequences flowing from a long continued practice to make orders like the one here involved. For the President's proclamation of September 27, 1909, is by no means the first instance in which the Executive, by a special order, has withdrawn land which Congress, by general statute, had thrown open to acquisition by citizens. [The Presidents have] during the past 80 years, without express statutory authority—but under the claim of power so to do—made a multitude of Executive Orders which operated to withdraw public land that would otherwise have been open to private acquisition. They affected every kind of land—mineral and nonmineral. The size of the tracts varied from a few square rods to many square miles and the amount withdrawn has aggregated millions of acres. The number of such instances cannot, of course, be accurately given, but the extent of the practice can best be appreciated by a consideration of what is believed to be a correct enumeration of such Executive Orders mentioned in public documents.

They show that prior to the year 1910 there had been issued

> 99 Executive Orders establishing or enlarging Indian Reservations;
>
> 109 Executive Orders establishing or enlarging Military Reservations and setting apart land for water, timber, fuel, hay, signal stations, target ranges and rights of way for use in connection with Military Reservations;
>
> 44 Executive Orders establishing Bird Reserves.

In the sense that these lands may have been intended for public use, they were reserved for a public purpose. But they were not reserved in pursuance of law or by virtue of any general or special statutory authority. For, it is to be specially noted that there was no act of Congress providing for Bird Reserves or for these Indian Reservations. There was no law for the establishment of these Military Reservations or defining their size or location. There was no statute empowering the President to withdraw any of these lands from settlement or to reserve them for any of the purposes indicated.

But when it appeared that the public interest would be served by withdrawing or reserving parts of the public domain, nothing was more natural than to retain what the Government already owned. And in making such orders, which were thus useful to the public, no private interest was injured. For prior to the initiation of some right given by law the citizen had no enforceable interest in the public statute and no private right in land which was the property of the people. The President was in a position to know when the public interest required particular portions of the people's lands to be withdrawn from entry or location; his action inflicted no wrong upon any private citizen, and being subject to disaffirmance by Congress, could occasion no harm to the interest of the public at large. Congress did not repudiate the power claimed or the withdrawal orders made. On the contrary it uniformly and repeatedly acquiesced in the practice and, as shown by these records, there had been, prior to 1910, at least 252 Executive Orders making reservations for useful, though non-statutory purposes.

This right of the President to make reservations—and thus withdraw land from private acquisition—was expressly recognized in Grisar v. McDowell, 6 Wall. 363, 381 (1867), where it was said that "from an early period in the history of the Government it has been the practice of the President to order, from time to time, as the exigencies of the public service required, parcels of land belonging to the United States to be reserved from sale and set apart for public uses." * * *

2. It may be argued that while these facts and rulings prove a usage they do not establish its validity. But government is a practical affair intended for practical men. Both officers, law-makers and citizens naturally adjust themselves to any long-continued action of the Executive Department—on the presumption that unauthorized acts would not have been allowed to be so often repeated as to crystallize into a regular practice. That presumption is not reasoning in a circle but the basis of a wise and quieting rule that in determining the meaning of a statute or the existence of a power, weight shall be given to the usage itself—even when the validity of the practice is the subject of investigation. * * *

3. These decisions do not, of course, mean that private rights could be created by an officer withdrawing for a Rail Road more than had been authorized by Congress in the land grant act. Southern Pacific R. Co. v. Bell, 183 U.S. 685 * * *. Nor do these decisions mean that the Executive can by his course of action create a power. But they do clearly indicate that the long-continued practice, known to and acquiesced in by Congress,

would raise a presumption that the withdrawals had been made in pursuance of its consent or of a recognized administrative power of the Executive in the management of the public lands. This is particularly true in view of the fact that the land is property of the United States and that the land laws are not of a legislative character in the highest sense of the term (Art. 4, § 3) "but savor somewhat of mere rules prescribed by an owner of property for its disposal." Butte City Water Co. v. Baker, 196 U.S. 126.

These rules or laws for the disposal of public land are necessarily general in their nature. Emergencies may occur, or conditions may so change as to require that the agent in charge should, in the public interest, withhold the land from sale; and while no such express authority has been granted, there is nothing in the nature of the power exercised which prevents Congress from granting it by implication just as could be done by any other owner of property under similar conditions. The power of the Executive, as agent in charge, to retain that property from sale need not necessarily be expressed in writing.

For it must be borne in mind that Congress not only has a legislative power over the public domain, but it also exercises the powers of the proprietor therein. Congress "may deal with such lands precisely as a private individual may deal with his farming property. It may sell or withhold them from sale." Camfield v. United States, 167 U.S. 524; Light v. United States, 220 U.S. 536. Like any other owner it may provide when, how and to whom its land can be sold. It can permit it to be withdrawn from sale. Like any other owner, it can waive its strict rights, as it did when the valuable privilege of grazing cattle on this public land was held to be based upon an "implied license growing out of the custom of nearly a hundred years." Buford v. Houtz, 133 U.S. 326. So too, in the early days the "Government, by its silent acquiescence, assented to the general occupation of the public lands for mining." Atchison v. Peterson, 20 Wall. 512. If private persons could acquire a privilege in public land by virtue of an implied congressional consent, then for a much stronger reason, an implied grant of power to preserve the public interest would arise out of like congressional acquiescence.

The Executive, as agent, was in charge of the public domain; by a multitude of orders extending over a long period of time and affecting vast bodies of land, in many States and Territories, he withdrew large areas in the public interest. These orders were known to Congress, as principal, and in not a single instance was the act of the agent disapproved. Its acquiescence all the more readily operated as an implied grant of power in view of the fact that its exercise was not only useful to the public but did not interfere with any vested right of the citizen.

4. The appellees, however, argue that the practice thus approved, related to Reservations—to cases where the land had been reserved for military or other special public purposes—and they contend that even if the President could reserve land for a public purpose or for naval uses, it does not follow that he can withdraw land in aid of legislation.

When analyzed, this proposition, in effect, seeks to make a distinction between a Reservation and a Withdrawal—between a Reservation for a purpose, not provided for by existing legislation, and a Withdrawal made in aid of future legislation. It would mean that a Permanent Reservation for a purpose designated by the President, but not provided for by a statute, would be valid, while a merely Temporary Withdrawal to enable Congress to legislate in the public interest would be invalid. It is only necessary to point out that, as the greater includes the less, the power to make permanent reservations includes power to make temporary withdrawals. For there is no distinction in principle between the two. The character of the power exerted is the same in both cases. In both, the order is made to serve the public interest and in both the effect on the intending settler or miner is the same. * * *

[T]hat the existence of [withdrawal] power was recognized and its exercise by the Executive assented to by Congress, is emphasized by [a] Report which the Secretary of the Interior made in 1902, in response to a resolution of the Senate calling for information "as to what, if any, of the public lands have been withdrawn from disposition under the settlement or other laws by order of the Commissioner of the General Land Office and *what, if any, authority of law exists for such order of withdrawal.*"

The answer to this specific inquiry was returned March 3, 1902, (Senate Doc. 232, 57th Cong., 1st Sess., Vol. 17). On that date the Secretary transmitted to the Senate the elaborate and detailed report of the Commissioner of the Land Office, who in response to the inquiry as to the authority by which withdrawals had been made, answered that:

> "the power of the Executive Department of the Government to make reservations of land for public use, and to temporarily withdraw lands from appropriation by individuals as exigencies might demand, to prevent fraud, to aid in proper administration and in aid of pending legislation is one that has been long recognized both in the acts of Congress and the decisions of the court; * * * that this power has been long exercised by the Commissioner of the General Land Office is shown by reference to the date of some of the withdrawals enumerated. * * * The attached list embraces only such lands as were withdrawn by this office, acting on its own motion, in cases where the emergencies appeared to demand such action in furtherance of public interest and does not include lands withdrawn under express statutes so directed." * * *

This report refers to *Withdrawals* and not to *Reservations.* It is most important in connection with the present inquiry as to whether Congress knew of the practice to make temporary withdrawals and knowingly assented thereto. It will be noted that the Resolution called on the Department to state the extent of such withdrawals and the authority by which they were made. The officer of the Land Department in his answer shows that there have been a large number of withdrawals made for good but for non-statutory reasons. He knows that these 92 orders had been made by virtue of a long-continued practice and under claim of a right to take such action in the public interest "as exigencies might demand. * * * " Congress with notice of this practice and of this claim of authority, received the Report. Neither at that session nor afterwards did it ever repudiate the action taken or the power claimed. Its silence was acquiescence. Its acquiescence was equivalent to consent to continue the practice until the power was revoked by some subsequent action by Congress. * * *

■ DAY, MCKENNA, and VAN DEVANTER, JJ., dissenting.

* * * [T]he lands here in controversy are situated in the state of Wyoming * * * [and] were withdrawn solely upon the suggestion that a better disposition of them could be made than was found in the existing acts of Congress controlling the subject. * * * [By the Property Clause of the Constitution] the power to dispose of lands belonging to the United States is broadly conferred upon Congress, and it is under the power therein given that the system of land laws for the disposition of the public domain has been enacted. * * *

It is true that many withdrawals have been made by the President and some of them have been sustained by this court, so that it may be fairly said that, within limitations to be hereinafter stated, Executive withdrawals have the sanction of judicial approval; but, as we read the cases, in no instance has this court sustained a withdrawal of public lands for which Congress has provided a system of disposition, except such withdrawal was—(a) in pursuance of a policy already declared by Congress as one for which the public lands might be used, as military and Indian reservations, for which purposes Congress has authorized the use of the public lands from an early day, or (b) in cases where grants of Congress are in such conflict that the purpose of Congress cannot be known, and therefore the Secretary of the Interior has been sustained in withdrawing the lands from entry until Congress had opportunity to relieve the ambiguity of its laws by specifically declaring its policy. * * *

The constitutional authority of the President of the United States (art. 2, §§ 1,3) includes the * * * duty to see that the laws are faithfully executed. * * * The Constitution does not confer upon him any power to enact laws or to suspend or repeal such as the Congress enacts. * * *.

* * * [A] given withdrawal must have been expressly authorized by Congress, or there must be that clear implication of congressional authority which is equivalent to express authority; and when such authority is wanting there can be no Executive withdrawal of lands from the operation of an act of Congress which would otherwise control.

In our opinion, the action of the Executive Department in this case, originating in the expressed view of * * * the desirability of a different system of public land disposal than that contained in the lawful enactments of Congress, did not justify the President in withdrawing this large body of land from the operation of the law, and virtually suspending, as he necessarily did, the operation of that law, at least until a different view expressed by him could be considered by the Congress. * * *

NOTES AND QUESTIONS

1. What was the legal effect of "withdrawing" these federal lands from the operation of the 1897 Oil Placer Act? Is the President simply, and unilaterally, nullifying the operation of that Act on these withdrawn lands?

2. The Court did not reach the question whether the President had authority to withdraw lands under his power as Commander in Chief, Article II, § 2, cl. 1, or under the basic executive authority, Article II, § 1, cl. 1 ("The executive Power shall be vested in a president * * * "). Would presidential power to make these withdrawals from mineral entry have been upheld on either of these two bases if no longstanding executive practice had existed? See generally Laurence Tribe, AMERICAN CONSTITUTIONAL LAW Vol. I, 677 (3rd ed. 2000), discussing both provisions. *Midwest Oil* continues to be cited in landmark cases construing presidential power; e.g., Youngstown Sheet & Tube Co. v. Sawyer, 343 U.S. 579, 611, 655 n. 1, 661 n. 3, 689–93, 703 (1952); Dames & Moore v. Regan, 453 U.S. 654, 686 (1981). Considering the issue here in the broader context of the Constitution's general allocation of authority between the Congress and the President, is there something special about federal real property—land and other natural resources—that warrants altering this allocation?

3. Were these withdrawals within the scope of implied authority created by the earlier kinds of withdrawals described in the majority opinion? Is this where the majority and the dissent part company in their respective views?

4. Would the President be upheld if a withdrawal were made for a new purpose, such as a wilderness area, unrelated to those kinds of withdrawals to which Congress had given its "longstanding acquiescence"? More broadly, does this case suggest that the President did not need the authority granted by Congress in the 1891 Forest Reservation provision in order to withdraw federal lands from disposal to create national forests?

5. Why does the Court say that "no private interest was injured" by the withdrawal? Is the answer found in the 1909 Executive Order?

6. In 1916, after he had left office, President Taft criticized Theodore Roosevelt's view that the President possesses broad residual power, calling it "an unsafe doctrine * * * that might lead under emergencies to results of an arbitrary character, doing irremediable injustice to private right." According to Taft, the executive

> can exercise no power which cannot be fairly and reasonably traced to some specific grant of power or justly implied and included within such express grant as proper and necessary to its exercise. Such specific grant must be either in the Federal Constitution or in an act of Congress passed in pursuance thereof. There is no undefined residuum of power which he can exercise because it seems to him to be in the general public interest.

William Howard Taft, OUR CHIEF MAGISTRATE AND HIS POWERS, quoted in John P. Roche and Leonard W. Levy, THE PRESIDENCY 23–25 (1964). Justice Jackson quipped, "It * * * seems that President Taft cancels out Professor Taft." Youngstown Sheet & Tube Co. v. Sawyer, 343 U.S. 579, 634 n. 1 (1952) (Jackson, J. concurring). See also Harold H. Bruff, Judicial Review and the President's Statutory Powers, 68 Va. L.Rev. 1, 36–39 (1982).

7. Professor Henry Monaghan has said that *Midwest Oil* is "occasionally cited as a decision—the *only* decision, I should add—in which the Supreme Court upheld presidential law-making contrary to the terms of an Act of Congress." Monaghan offered several possible explanations, including that *Midwest Oil* was confined to the exercise of power "necessarily incident to the President's role as 'chief administrator' in connection with government lands and perhaps other property." In Monaghan's view, however, the decision "has not been confined as a precedent to the notion of President as chief administrator." Instead, the Court has understood the decision "to sanction presidential conduct invading private rights if this conduct is supported by congressional acquiescence or tacit consent, and the question then becomes what congressional conduct suffices for that purpose." Mere congressional inaction is not enough, according to Monaghan; instead, " 'adjacent' congressional legislation must presume the validity of a prior presidential practice." Henry P. Monaghan, Marbury and the Administrative State, 83 Colum. L.Rev. 1, 44–47 (1983). See also Peter M Shane & Harold H. Bruff, SEPARATION OF POWERS LAW 61–63 (1996).

8. Suppose Congress enacts a statute prohibiting mining in national parks. Does *Midwest Oil* allow an exploitation-minded President nevertheless to issue an Executive Order "withdrawing" a particular national park from the operation of this statute? How does that differ from President Taft's withdrawal upheld in *Midwest Oil*?

9. The subject of withdrawals and reservations is critical to public land law; Chapter 4, § B addresses it in detail.

4. THE MINERAL LEASING ACT

It took five more years of struggle after *Midwest Oil*, but finally, in 1920, Congress enacted the minerals legislation that reformers like Taft wanted. The Mineral Leasing Act, 30 U.S.C. § 181 et seq., remains a cornerstone of natural resources law. It withdrew from location all fossil fuels (coal, oil, gas, oil shale) and specified fertilizer minerals (potash, potassium, sodium, and sulfur), and it ended the governmental policy of outright sale or grant of these particular mineral resources. It required competitive bidding for leases of lands thought to contain minerals, and authorized the issuance of exploration or prospecting permits for other lands, which could ripen into leases if valuable deposits were discovered. Royalty payments to the treasury were required under the leases, with the money going to states, the Reclamation Fund, and the federal treasury. The leasing system was later extended to the offshore lands and to geothermal resources. See Chapter 7, § B infra.

The most important thing about the Mineral Leasing Act, however, was how it addressed the issue of public versus private control over the development of these fossil fuel and fertilizer minerals found on federal land. This was made clear in the following case.

United States ex rel. McLennan v. Wilbur

Supreme Court of the United States, 1931.
283 U.S. 414.

■ MR. JUSTICE McREYNOLDS delivered the opinion of the Court.

* * * The Act of Congress approved February 25, 1920, 41 Stat. 437, intended to promote certain mining operations, contains thirty-eight sections.

> Section 1. That deposits of coal, phosphate, sodium, oil, oil shale, or gas, and lands containing such deposits owned by the United States, * * * shall be subject to disposition in the form and manner provided by this Act. * * *

> Sec. 13. That the Secretary of the Interior is hereby authorized, under such necessary and proper rules and regulations as he may prescribe, to [issue prospecting permits and leases under certain terms and conditions] * * *

Section 9 authorizes the Secretary to lease lands containing deposits of phosphates under such general regulation as he may adopt. By section 17 unappropriated deposits of oil or gas situated within the known geologic structure of a producing oil or gas field "may be leased by the Secretary of the Interior to the highest responsible bidder, * * * " such leases to be conditioned upon the payment by the lessee of such bonus as may be accepted and of such royalty as may be fixed in the lease, etc. Section 21 authorizes the Secretary to lease deposits of oil shale under such regulations as he may prescribe, for indefinite periods.

Section 2 declares that the Secretary "is authorized to, and upon the petition of any qualified applicant shall, divide any of the coal lands or the deposits of coal, classified and unclassified, owned by the United States, outside of the Territory of Alaska, into leasing tracts of forty acres each, * * * " and thereafter "shall, in his discretion, upon the request of any qualified applicant or on his own motion, from time to time, offer such lands or deposits of coal for leasing, and shall award leases thereon by competitive bidding or by such other methods as he may by general regulations adopt, to any qualified applicant. * * * "

These provisions quite plainly indicate that Congress held in mind the distinction between a positive mandate to the Secretary and permission to take certain action in his discretion. Also, the difference between applicants for mere privileges and those persons who, because of expenditures, or otherwise, deserved special consideration.

The petitioners, acting separately and as directed by the general rules and regulations, either filed or sought to file applications for permits to prospect for oil and gas under section 13. In order to effectuate the conservation policy of the President, the Secretary of the Interior by a general order either rejected or refused to receive their applications. Thereupon these proceedings were begun [seeking] * * * writs of mandamus to compel the Secretary to receive or reinstate the applications and act upon each according to its merits.

* * * The answers aver "that under the Act, (1920) the granting of a prospecting permit for oil and gas is discretionary with the Secretary of the Interior, and any application may be granted or denied, either in part or in its entirety as the facts may be deemed to warrant." Having examined the act, we cannot say that by any clear and indisputable language it refutes his position. Certainly there is ground for a plausible, if not conclusive, argument that, so far as it relates to the leasing of oil lands, it goes no further than to empower the Secretary to execute leases which, exercising a reasonable discretion, he may think would promote the public welfare.

It is unnecessary now to declare the precise meaning of the relevant provisions of the act. It was passed when according to a widely accepted view decline of petroleum production in the United States was imminent. In fact, there has been an enormous increase and a consequent troublesome surplus. Looking only at its words, one may interpret section 13 as the Secretary says he did. And this conclusion is aided by consideration of his general powers over the public lands as guardian of the people [citing, *inter alia*, United States v. Grimaud]; also the right of the President to withdraw public lands from private appropriation, United States v. Midwest Oil Co; Withdrawal Act, 1910 [the Pickett Act]. * * *

The judgments under review must be affirmed.

NOTES AND QUESTIONS:

1. Which of the following are permissible reasons for not offering public lands for lease: A desire to gain more money for the Treasury in the form of bonus bids by waiting until demand for the minerals is higher? A desire to promote more demand for minerals from private lands? A desire to protect ranchers who are using the surface of the federal lands for livestock grazing? A desire to protect environmental values?

2. Notice that a refusal to lease is closely related to a decision to withdraw particular areas of federal lands from mineral leasing—such as President Taft's order upheld in *Midwest Oil*, supra p. 119. The relationship between these two ways to say no to development of federal minerals is explored in more detail at pp. 345–48, infra.

5. The Taylor Grazing Act

The tragedy of the commons is nowhere more evident than in the history of grazing on the public domain. After the lands chiefly valuable for farming, timbering, mining, townsites, etc. had been claimed by successive waves of settlers and entrepreneurs, most of the public lands remaining were useful only for grazing. By 1930, the federal government still owned 340 million acres of federal land in the arid and semi-arid West. About 140 million acres was in national forests and parks (some 90% of this in national forests, and much of it open to livestock grazing); about 12 million acres was reserved mineral lands, and the remaining 190 million acres were unreserved and unappropriated. Naturally, it was in the economic self-interest of ranchers to take for their own herds and flocks all of the free forage available. Late in the nineteenth century, the number of livestock on the public lands exploded, particularly in the arid lands of the southwest, before a combination of drought and harsh winters decimated herds, but not before millions of acres of marginal, semi-arid lands were turned into wastelands by the resulting overgrazing. See, e.g., J.R. Hastings and R.M. Turner, THE CHANGING MILE (1965) (graphically illustrating the permanent conversion of southwestern grasslands to sagebrush-dominated deserts by side-by-side before-and-after photographs of the same areas). See also David T. Cox, Deterioration of Southern Arizona's Grasslands: Effects of New Federal Legislation Concerning Public Grazing Lands, 20 Ariz. L.Rev. 697 (1979). Disputes among homesteaders, ranchers, and sheepmen over these commons sometimes flared into violent range wars, and have ascended into the mists of legend in Western history, immortalized in such classic stories (and films) as Shane. As the following case shows, until 1934 on the public domain (i.e., outside of the national forests and the few national parks), state law—that is, almost no law—applied on the open range because of the absence of federal regulation of grazing.

Omaechevarria v. Idaho

Supreme Court of the United States, 1918.
246 U.S. 343.

■ MR. JUSTICE BRANDEIS delivered the opinion of the court.

For more than forty years the raising of cattle and sheep have been important industries in Idaho. The stock feeds in part by grazing on the public domain of the United States. This is done with the Government's acquiescence, without the payment of compensation, and without federal regulation. Buford v. Houtz, 133 U.S. 320, 326. Experience has demonstrated, says the state court, that in arid and semi-arid regions cattle will not graze, nor can they thrive, on ranges where sheep are allowed to graze extensively; that the encroachment of sheep upon ranges previously occupied by cattle results in driving out the cattle and destroying or greatly impairing the industry; and that this conflict of interests led to frequent and serious breaches of the peace and the loss of many lives. Efficient policing of the ranges is impossible; for the State is sparsely settled and the public domain is extensive, comprising still more than one-fourth of the land surface. To avert clashes between sheep herdsmen and the farmers who customarily allowed their few cattle to graze on the public domain near their dwellings, the territorial legislature passed in 1875 the so-called "Two Mile Limit Law." It was enacted first as a local statute applicable to three counties, but was extended in 1879 and again in 1883 to additional counties, and was made a general law in 1887. * * * To avert clashes between the sheep herdsmen and the cattle rangers, further legislation was found necessary; and in 1883 * * * [a state statute] was enacted which prohibits any person having charge of sheep from allowing them to graze on a range previously occupied by cattle. For violating this statute the plaintiff in error, a sheep herdsman, was convicted in the local police court and sentenced to pay a fine. The judgment was affirmed by * * * the

Supreme Court of Idaho. 27 Idaho, 797. On writ of error from this court the validity of the statute is assailed on the ground that the statute is inconsistent both with the Fourteenth Amendment and with the Act of Congress of February 25, 1885, c. 149, 23 Stat. 321, entitled, "An act to prevent unlawful occupancy of the public lands."

First: It is urged that the statute denies rights guaranteed by the Fourteenth Amendment, namely: Privileges of citizens of the United States, in so far as it prohibits the use of the public lands by sheep owners; and equal protection of the laws, in that it gives to cattle owners a preference over sheep owners. * * * The police power of the State extends over the federal public domain, at least when there is no legislation by Congress on the subject. We cannot say that the measure adopted by the State is unreasonable or arbitrary. It was found that conflicts between cattle rangers and sheep herders on the public domain could be reconciled only by segregation. In national forests, where the use of land is regulated by the Federal Government, the plan of segregation is widely adopted. And it is not an arbitrary discrimination to give preference to cattle owners in prior occupancy without providing for a like preference to sheep owners in prior occupancy. For experience shows that sheep do not require protection against encroachment by cattle, and that cattle rangers are not likely to encroach upon ranges previously occupied by sheep herders. The propriety of treating sheep differently than cattle has been generally recognized. That the interest of the sheep owners of Idaho received due consideration is indicated by the fact that in 1902 they opposed the abolition by the Government of the free ranges. * * *

Third: It is further contended that the statute is in direct conflict with the Act of Congress of February 25, 1885 [construed in Camfield v. United States, p. 92 supra]. That statute which was designed to prevent the illegal fencing of public lands, contains at the close of § 1 the following clause with which the Idaho statute is said to conflict: "and the assertion of a right to the exclusive use and occupancy of any part of the public lands of the United States in any State or any of the Territories of the United States, without claim, color of title, or asserted right as above specified as to inclosure, is likewise declared unlawful, and hereby prohibited."

An examination of the federal act in its entirety makes it clear that what the clause quoted from § 1 sought to prohibit was merely the assertion of an exclusive right to use or occupation by force or intimidation or by what would be equivalent in effect to an enclosure. That this was the intent of Congress is confirmed by the history of the act. The reports of the Secretary of the Interior upon whose recommendation the act was introduced, the reports of the committees of Congress, and the debates thereon indicate that this alone was the evil sought to be remedied, and to such action only does its prohibition appear to have been applied in practice. * * *

The Idaho statute makes no attempt to grant a right to use public lands. * * * The State, acting in the exercise of its police power, merely excludes sheep from certain ranges under certain circumstances. Like the forcible entry and detainer act of Washington, which was held in Denee v.

Ankeny [246 U.S. 208 (1918)] not to conflict with the homestead laws, the Idaho statute was enacted primarily to prevent breaches of the peace. The incidental protection which it thereby affords to cattle owners does not purport to secure to any of them, or to cattle owners collectively, "the exclusive use and occupancy of any part of the public lands." For every range from which sheep are excluded remains open not only to *all* cattle, but also to horses, of which there are many in Idaho. This exclusion of sheep owners under certain circumstances does not interfere with any rights of a citizen of the United States. Congress has not conferred upon citizens the right to graze stock upon the public lands. The Government has merely suffered the lands to be so used. Buford v. Houtz, supra. It is because the citizen possesses no such right that it was held by this court that the Secretary of Agriculture might, in the exercise of his general power to regulate forest reserves, exclude sheep and cattle therefrom. United States v. Grimaud, 220 U.S. 506; Light v. United States, 220 U.S. 523.

All the objections urged against the validity of the statute are unsound. The judgment of the Supreme Court of Idaho is

Affirmed.

■ MR. JUSTICE VAN DEVANTER and MR. JUSTICE MCREYNOLDS dissent.

NOTES AND QUESTIONS

1.   Why does the state open range law *not* apply in Light v. United States, supra p. 110, yet does apply here?

2.   Is the effect of state law here to enclose the public lands and give certain kinds of livestock preference (specifically, cattle over sheep) for their use? If so, why doesn't this violate the Unlawful Inclosures Act?

3.   Does the Idaho law give cattle ranchers a property right to graze on federal lands? Could the state do that if it wished?

4.   What principle emerges from this case about when a state may enforce its own laws on federal lands? May a state enforce its criminal and civil laws, including taxing and regulatory statutes, on such lands only where Congress has specifically allowed it, or can it do so where Congress has not specifically forbidden it? Does it depend upon the character of the state laws?

By the early 1930s, overgrazing and drought had reduced the public grazing lands, never very productive, to a state of crisis. Neither free access nor enlarged homesteads contributed to betterment of range conditions. In 1930, President Hoover revived a plan promoted by Senator John C. Calhoun a century earlier, and suggested that the United States convey all the remaining public domain to the states to be used to support public education. Congress authorized a commission to look at the idea, and Hoover named James R. Garfield, who had served for two years as Secretary of the Interior under Theodore Roosevelt, to chair it. The

Commission report, issued in 1931, generally supported Hoover's idea with some fine-tuning—most importantly, by recommending that the minerals be reserved in the U.S. for at least some time. Paul Gates, HISTORY OF PUBLIC LAND LAW DEVELOPMENT 523–29. The proposal never got traction in Congress. Some of the Western states opposed the idea, especially because of the mineral reservation. Conservationists were opposed, and ranchers were divided.

But public lands ranchers, and one of their longstanding champions in Congress, Edward Taylor of Colorado, eventually came around to the view that something had to be done because of conflicts among livestock owners and deteriorating rangelands. Shortly after FDR's inauguration in March 1933, new Secretary of the Interior Harold Ickes wrote to ask for FDR's support for pending legislation to give the Secretary "broad powers to limit and regulate the use of the public domain for grazing purposes with the view to preventing partial or total destruction of a natural resource which is essential for our future well being." FDR wrote in longhand at the bottom, "Yes, but there will be a howl," and sent it back to Ickes.* The reaction Roosevelt predicted was not strong enough to kill the idea; the next year, he signed the Taylor Grazing Act into law. 43 U.S.C. § 315 et seq.

E.L. Peffer, The Closing of the Public Domain*

214–224 (1951).

No more convincing proof of the collapse of the long stand for the transfer of the public land and its resources to the States could have been offered than that Representative Taylor sponsored this grazing bill. Almost from the day he entered Congress in 1909 his voice could be heard in condemnation of the withdrawal features advocated by the conservationists and of having anything to do with the leasing of the public domain. * * * Taylor's zeal was that of a convert. * * * [The campaign to pass the bill] was completely under his generalship. When called before Congressional committees to explain and defend his bill, he did not resemble the usual witness at such hearings. He dominated them. On the floor of the House, he parried all arguments skillfully. He knew the rocks upon which earlier attempts at regulation had foundered. * * * The usual tribute to the homesteader appeared and the lament was heard that the Taylor bill would banish him from the American scene. Mr. Taylor had an answer for that:

> The praises and eulogies upon the American homesteader will continue as long as our Republic survives. The West was built, and its present proud development rests most largely upon the courage, privations, and frightfully hard work of the pioneer homesteaders. * * * But my dear sirs, if those hardy pioneers had had to go onto the kind of land

* Copy on file with Professor Leshy.

* Excerpted from THE CLOSING OF THE PUBLIC DOMAIN by E. Louise Peffer with the permission of the publishers, Stanford University Press. Copyright 1951 by the Board of Trustees of the Leland Stanford Junior University. Copyright renewed 1979. Reprinted by Arno Press Inc., 1972.

that is contemplated within this bill, the West would still be a barren wilderness. * * *

Other factors eased the way for the passage of the bill. President Roosevelt wanted it. Secretary of the Interior Harold L. Ickes jumped into the fight, scolding the stockmen for having interposed obstacles in the way of the passage of a law which would work so materially for their benefit. When Congress did not pass the Taylor bill during the first session of the 73d Congress, Ickes inquired into his authority under the Pickett Act of 1910 to withdraw the remaining public lands, pending passage of a law for their protection. He was advised that he had the authority; nevertheless, he concluded that it would be best to postpone recourse to this action. At the same time, however, he let it be known that he had this expedient in mind should Congress delay action much longer. * * *

The debates leading to the passage of the Taylor bill in Congress differed little in content from debates on previous public land bills. The ethical claim of the Western states to the lands within their borders was reasserted. The tribute to the homesteader was heard again. There were familiar protests against turning over the large acreage involved to the big cattlemen. They were all there—all the old, familiar strains. But they were like faint echoes of all the other debates which had gone before, diluted by time and the hopelessness of the cause they represented. * * *

The Taylor Grazing Act passed the House of Representatives on April 11, 1934 and the Senate on June 12. Between these dates occurred what was later considered the most devastating of conceivable condemnations of past land policy. The dust storms of May 11 carried sands from Western deserts to the sidewalks of New York and sifted them down around the dome of the Capitol in Washington. They provided what Senator Gore of Oklahoma later called "the most tragic, the most impressive lobbyist, that have ever come to this Capital." [74th Cong., 1st Sess. Cong. Rec. LXXIX, 6013] * * *

PROVISIONS OF THE TAYLOR GRAZING ACT

The Taylor Grazing Act vests in the Secretary of the Interior authority to create grazing districts in areas "which in his opinion are chiefly valuable for grazing and raising forage crops," but not until local reactions, gained through public hearings, had been ascertained. The Secretary is empowered to make all necessary regulations to carry out the purposes of the act and to grant grazing permits for periods up to ten years, with preference to settlers and landowners within or near the respective districts. He is instructed to enter into co-operative agreements with other departments of the government, with state land officials, and users of the districts. He may accept gifts of land or make exchanges of public land outside of grazing districts for private or state-owned lands within their limits. * * * Section 15 of the bill provides that isolated or disconnected tracts or parcels of 640 acres or more of grazing land, not capable of being included within grazing districts, may be leased to owners of contiguous property. (These have come to be known as Section 15 lands.) * * *

The amendment to the Taylor Grazing Act passed Congress on June 20, 1936, and was approved by the President on June 26. It increased the area to which the law applies to 142,000,000 acres and created the post of Director of Grazing, which appointment was to be made by the Secretary of the Interior and approved by the Senate. * * * Western interests were considered in the further stipulation that "No Director of Grazing, Assistant Director, or grazier shall be appointed who at the time of appointment or selection has not been for one year a bona-fide citizen or resident of the State or of one of the States in which such Director, Assistant Director, or grazier is to serve." * * *

SUBSEQUENT WITHDRAWALS

At long last the government was able to care for its grazing lands. The Taylor Grazing Act did not itself do, however, what has been claimed for it—"close the public domain to further entry by homesteaders and [bury] a policy which had been slowly dying." That was accomplished, in effect, but with no express intention of permanence, by two executive orders of the President, those of November 26, 1934 and February 5, 1935. In November, acting under the authority of the Taylor Grazing Act, he withdrew for classification all public land in the twelve Western states. Then, in February, he withdrew all remaining parcels in all other states for use in connection with Federal Emergency Relief Administration.

The President by these withdrawals implemented the classification feature of the Taylor Grazing Act and made certain that it would apply to all remaining Western public lands. Thus it was that the classification which for more than fifty years had been urgently recommended by the land specialists of the country was finally authorized. It was not done until the results of nature's own classification had become disastrously apparent.

If the Taylor Grazing Act and supporting measures did not completely close the public domain, they at least were a signpost pointing to a radical change in direction of public land policy. They represented official admission of the exhaustion of the values which had made the public domain a dynamic force in the building of the country. There was still land in plenty, but such opportunity as it might have represented had literally "gone with the wind." Overgrazed, wind-eroded expanses, interspersed with rocky peaks and barren slopes, were all that remained of the public domain in 1934. The days of its greatness * * * had long since passed. The open public domain of the future was to be more a sentimental and political issue than an active factor in American life.

Just as the forest reservation provision in the 1891 legislation had flowered into the national forest system, the Taylor Act brought into being a new federal land system. The lands under its aegis were usually simply called the "public lands" or, since the Bureau of Land Management was created in 1946 to manage them, the "BLM lands." The Taylor Grazing Act did not bring immediate improvement to range conditions; indeed, perhaps half of BLM's rangeland acreage and riparian-wetlands areas today remain, by BLM's own estimates, impaired (PUBLIC LAND STATISTICS 2000, Tables 2–1, 2–2). The grazing lands before 1934 had not been "managed" in the modern sense, and the changeover to a new system embodying a new philosophy was not without difficulty. The following reminiscences made in 1974 by Ferry Carpenter, a Harvard-trained lawyer who was the first director of the Grazing Service, illustrate some of the practical difficulties of implementation.

[In Grand Junction I conducted] the first meeting ever held under the recently passed Taylor Grazing Act to see whether they could put the show on the road or not. I got my appointment on September 7 and on the 12th I was here, with no instructions what to do, and this is what I found: Grand Junction was packed with stockmen. The cattle boys had the LaCourt Hotel and the woolgrowers had the LaHarpe Hotel, and neither would speak to the other. There were so many of them and the next morning when we looked around for a hall, we couldn't begin to get them in any hall. We adjourned and went out on the city park here and took over the exhibition building. The cowboys sat on one side * * * and the sheepherders on the other * * * and we got ready for business like a peace talk between two nations that had been fighting—and they had been fighting and I knew they had been fighting. What were they there to talk about? Why did Congress wake up and say they should have to drag grass into the conservation program? They put water in under the Reclamation Act; put trees under the Forest Act; put minerals and oils under the Mineral Reserve Act. But not the grass. Everybody could get the grass if you knew how to get it. All of a sudden they passed the Taylor Grazing Act. The boys out here didn't know the Act existed but they were there to see that they got their share of the grass. There were two factions and they were ready to continue the war they had been having for fifty years to fight over it. That's the woolgrowers and the cowboys.

I didn't get any help from Washington on what to do. There wasn't anybody in the whole Department that knew which end of the cow got up first. I went to the Land Office. I said "You want me to straighten out this land—give me a map of it." "Oh! We haven't got any map. There is filing on it day and night all over 27 local land offices, but we haven't got any map." "Well, how in the hell can I find the land if I haven't got a map!" "That's for you." That was for me. So, when I came here, I said I'm supposed to set up grazing districts. I don't know whether you want them or not and I wouldn't know where they go and Washington doesn't know where they would go and nobody knows where they would go. But you fellows have been fighting over this thing, you know every blessed acre there is and the poorer the acre, the harder you fight for it. I found that out, too. But I had one little piece of advice that I followed—and I am going to follow it until the end of my days—and it was a little saying by Justice Cardozo on the Supreme Court. "When the task is to clean house, it is sensible and usual to first consult with the inhabitants." There I was and there were the inhabitants—cowboys ready to jump and sheepherders ready to jump—everybody at each other's throat. But they were the inhabitants.

Well, they read a message from President Roosevelt. He said it was a great day for the West. Read a message from Secretary Ickes; he said he was the Lord's anointed! And now we got down to business and they began asking me questions about the Act, like how near was near. I didn't know how near was near. I didn't know the answer to them but I did know what to do with them. So, I said, all right; you woolgrowers go out there and caucus and pick five men to speak for you. You cowboys do the same.

Quoted in Charles Conklin, PLLRC Revisited—A Potpourri of Memories, 54 Denver L.J. 445, 446–47 (1977).

D.   THE FEDERAL LANDS TODAY

In theory, the Taylor Act was an interim measure: the range management it authorized was to control "pending final disposition." In fact, the creation of grazing districts and Franklin Roosevelt's withdrawal orders marked the "closing of the public domain," even though a few small tracts were claimed as homesteads thereafter. The federal government now owns retained and acquired lands for many diverse purposes, but the focus of this volume is on the federal lands classified as national forests, BLM or public lands, national parks and monuments, national wildlife refuges, and wilderness and other protected areas.

Public land management systems are usually classified according to what uses are allowed in them. With the "use" of disposition by sale or grant now mostly a nostalgic memory, the primary or dominant public land uses are for mining, grazing, logging, recreation, wildlife, biodiversity, and preservation. The national forests and the BLM lands are commonly described as "multiple use" lands in which all of the above uses are permitted, although in practice some uses tend to predominate on some lands. Furthermore, although national park system lands and national wildlife refuges tend to have dominant uses (recreation, preservation, and wildlife), other uses may be permitted on some of these lands. All of this is by way of saying that federal land classification is not an exact science. No classification of public lands is exclusive or immutable (even classifications chosen expressly by Congress), and overlapping functions and common problems are more of a rule than an exception.

This section briefly describes the four principal federal land management agencies. It also discusses preservation lands—such as wilderness areas and wild and scenic rivers—some of which are managed by each of those four agencies. Finally, this section introduces major federal legal entities, other than courts, which contribute to public land law development.

1.   THE NATIONAL FOREST SYSTEM

The withdrawals of the Forest Reserves beginning in 1891, the creation of Pinchot's Forest Service in the Department of Agriculture, and the transfer of the Forest Reserves to Agriculture in 1905, combined to create the present National Forest System. Some of the original reservations were later returned to the public domain, and other national forest land has been transferred to the Department of the Interior, but national forests still contain about 192 million acres, the second largest system by acreage. (Proposals to transfer management of the national forests back to Interior have surfaced every decade or two, but none has yet succeeded.)

The National Forest System was also the major beneficiary of the first major program to reacquire into federal ownership, primarily for conservation purposes, lands from private owners. Between 1912 and World War II, the Forest Service purchased several million acres of agriculturally depressed or abandoned land east of the Mississippi under the so-called Weeks Act. It also acquired what came to be known as the National Grasslands by purchase from bankrupt dirt farmers in drought-ridden Depression years. These 24 million acres of acquisitions plus the forest reservations from the public domain has given the Forest Service landholdings in nearly every state.

The Forest Reserves that became the national forests were established "to improve and protect the forest * * * [and] for the purpose of securing favorable conditions of water flows, and to furnish a continuous supply of timber." 16 U.S.C. § 475. For decades, the management of the forests was primarily custodial: before World War II they supplied less than five percent of the annual timber harvests. See generally James Huffman, A History of Forest Policy in the United States, 8 Envtl.L. 239 (1978). It was not until 1940 that the annual harvest from the national forests exceeded 2 billion board feet; that figure doubled by 1951; doubled again by 1959; and reached 12 billion board feet in 1966. Bureau of the Census, HISTORICAL STATISTICS OF THE UNITED STATES (1970) 534. With the post-war housing boom and the relative depletion of privately-owned commercial forests, pressure on the national forests to produce more sawtimber led first to a refinement of Pinchot's utilitarian philosophy and then to the enactment of the multiple use mandate into law. Multiple–Use, Sustained–Yield Act of 1960, 16 U.S.C. §§ 528–531. Environmental restrictions and other factors have reduced the average annual cut today to a fraction of what it was. The management of the timber resource on the national forests is now controlled in large part by the National Forest Management Act of 1976 (NFMA), 16 U.S.C. § 1601 et seq., discussed in detail in Chapter 8.

2. THE BLM PUBLIC LANDS

The lands subject to the Taylor Grazing Act were administered by the Department of the Interior's Grazing Service until 1946, when it was merged with the General Land Office to form the Bureau of Land Management. In the lower 48 states, the BLM is responsible for the management of nearly 180 million acres of mostly arid and semi-arid land, nearly all of it in the eleven western states and Alaska. In Alaska, the BLM retains jurisdiction over about 86 million acres, a sharp reduction from three decades ago owing to statehood grants, grants to Alaskan Natives under the Native

Claims Settlement Act of 1971, and transfers to other agencies under the Alaska National Interest Lands Conservation Act of 1980, described on pp. 144–47 infra.

BLM stewardship has not, for the most part, undone the damage wrought before the agency existed. Like the Forest Service, the BLM evolved internally a multiple use philosophy over the years, but with emphasis on grazing and mining instead of logging (leading some wags to call it the "Bureau of Livestock and Mining"). BLM's "organic" management act is the Federal Land Policy and Management Act of 1976 (FLPMA), 43 U.S.C. §§ 1701–1784.* Although late to the game of managing federal lands for conservation purposes, BLM has in the last couple of decades come to administer several wilderness areas, conservation areas and national monuments, as well "areas of critical environmental concern." BLM has traditionally been given challenging management tasks with little funding compared to other federal agencies. Its transition from a custodial agency dominated by ranching and mining interests to a modern, conservation-oriented land management agency is one of the more interesting stories of public land policy in the last quarter century, and is dealt with especially in Chapters 7 (mining) and 9 (grazing).

3. THE NATIONAL WILDLIFE REFUGE SYSTEM

The present National Wildlife Refuge System began when President Roosevelt set aside Pelican Island off the Florida coast for the benefit of wildlife in 1903. The President and the Congress reserved federal lands and purchased nonfederal lands over the years under various authorities until, in conjunction with the first Endangered Species Act, the National Wildlife Refuge System was created in 1966 and provided with an organic act. National Wildlife Refuge Administration Act of 1966, 16 U.S.C. § 668dd et seq. A revised organic act was adopted three decades later. See National Wildlife Refuge System Improvement Act of 1997 (NWRSIA)., 16 U.S.C. §§ 668dd-ee. The system is administered by the U.S. Fish and Wildlife Service (FWS) in the Department of the Interior, and comprises about 93 million acres in fee ownership (75 million of which are in Alaska), together with lesser interests such as waterfowl easements in other property. Currently, the agency operates 538 national wildlife refuges, 166 waterfowl production areas, and 51 wildlife coordination areas.

The National Wildlife Refuge System is the only category of federal lands administered primarily for the conservation of wildlife, although states have wildlife areas and wildlife management is a concern on practically all federal lands. Additions to the system are funded through special segregated tax revenues derived from such sources as sale of duck stamps, but the refuges have suffered from underfunding, political neglect, and

---

* FLPMA continued Congress's longstanding lack of consistency in semantics by defining BLM lands as "public lands." 43 U.S.C. § 1702(e). In some other contexts, Congress has defined "public lands" to include the national forests; e.g., 16 U.S.C. § 1332 (Wild, Free–Roaming Horses and Burros Act of 1971). In its 1970 Report, the Public Land Law Review Commission used "public lands" to describe all federally-owned areas, which is also common, if confusing, usage.

popular overuse. Although wildlife conservation is the main criterion in refuge management under the relevant statutes, almost every other common use is allowed to some extent on some refuges. Typical legal issues growing out of FWS management are dealt with in Chapter 10.

4.   THE NATIONAL PARK SYSTEM

Among the uses allowed and encouraged on the foregoing three systems are forms of recreation such as bird watching, camping, and hunting; to that extent they can be considered "recreational lands." The various categories of lands within the National Park System are, however, devoted primarily to recreation and preservation. The System now includes nearly 80 million acres (nearly two-thirds of which are in Alaska) located in almost every state. An orientation toward preservation has characterized the Park Service since its inception in 1916, but its mission has been broadened substantially in recent years by assignment of responsibility for recreation areas, urban parks, cultural areas, and the like. The 59 National Parks, the most famous units in the System, are still managed for the "enjoyment of future generations," but more intensive recreation is typical on other land designations within the System.

The recreation opportunities inherent in the reservoir created by Hoover Dam inspired Congress in 1936 to designate the lake and surrounding shoreline as the Lake Mead National Recreation Area. The concept was popular and has since been followed at Lake Powell, Flaming Gorge, Ross Lake, and other impoundments. Congress also experimented with National Parkways such as Blue Ridge in the 1930's; concern about possible incongruence of parks and roads, however, led to the formation of the Wilderness Society in protest and the parkway system has not been expanded. Recreation continued to grow as an important facet of public land policy. Congressional desires to satisfy demand for outdoor recreation resulted in an explosion of new land categories, many under NPS jurisdiction. There are now National Seashores (e.g., Point Reyes in California), National Lakeshores (e.g., Sleeping Bear in Michigan), National Rivers (e.g., the Buffalo in Arkansas), the Boundary Water Canoe Area in Minnesota, National Wild and Scenic Rivers (e.g. the Allegash in Maine), National Trails (e.g., the Pacific Crest), National Gateway Parks, (e.g. Golden Gate in and near San Francisco), and the fourteen National Preserves. The Park Service also manages historical memorials, battlefield monuments, and many of the Washington, D.C. area parks and memorials. Chapter 11 addresses a variety of issues growing out of the popularity of recreation on federal land.

5.   THE PRESERVATION LANDS AND OTHER GENERIC CATEGORIES

The national park lands are to be managed for preservation as well as recreation, but many felt that park resources alone were too few and too vulnerable for national needs. In 1964 Congress created yet another lands category by passage of the Wilderness Act, 16 U.S.C. §§ 1131–1136, under which lands so designated are to be devoted primarily to preservation.

Some nine million acres, in roadless areas of over 5,000 acres "untrammeled by man," were set aside initially, and the National Wilderness Preservation System has continued to grow. Additions to the System, now encompassing over 100 million acres (60% of it in Alaska), have been and are being carved out of other federal lands by a lengthy process of selection, inventory, presidential recommendation, and congressional designation. A wilderness area is managed by the agency under whose jurisdiction the area fell before designation.

Another federal lands category is that of national monuments, usually created by Presidential proclamation under authority of the 1906 Antiquities Act, 16 U.S.C. §§ 431–433. This statute authorizes the President to reserve federal lands to protect "historic landmarks, historic and prehistoric structures, and other objects of historic or scientific interest." Although only the "smallest area compatible with the proper care and management of" the object(s) protected is to be so reserved, large areas such as Grand Canyon, Death Valley and Glacier Bay were first protected by Presidential proclamation under this statute. President Clinton revived the statute from nearly two decades of disuse, and used it to protect more acres of federal land than any chief executive other than Jimmy Carter, who designated more than 56 million acres of national monuments in Alaska in 1978. Many of President Clinton's monuments were made on BLM land, and BLM remains the manager. Congress has sometimes legislated national monuments, and has usually eventually confirmed Presidential monuments. Nearly all the acreage in President Carter's monuments were, for example, given legislative confirmation in the Alaska National Interest Lands Conservation Act of 1980. Many of the crown jewel national parks were first protected by Presidential action under the Antiquities Act.

In the last few decades Congress has added to the categories of land that are managed primarily for preservation purposes. The Wild and Scenic Rivers Act of 1968 and the Alaska National Interest Lands Conservation Act of 1980 were landmarks; the latter created such new designations as "park preserve." More recently, designating tracts of federal land as "national conservation areas" or "national recreation areas" (the latter expanding upon the designations given earlier to such areas as Lake Mead and Glen Canyon) has gained popularity in Congress. While neither is generally as strictly preservationist as wilderness, both are considerably less resource-exploitive than traditional multiple use designations. These and other related legal developments have led commentators to label (as a trend rather than a general truth) the era since 1964 as the "Age of Preservation." See George Cameron Coggins & Robert Glicksman, 1 PUBLIC NATURAL RESOURCES LAW, § 2.16 (2001).

6. THE LEGAL OFFICES

An agency with special pertinence to public land law is the Office of the Solicitor in the Department of the Interior. The Solicitor is general counsel to the Secretary. The Solicitor's Office houses all the lawyers who give legal advice to the Department's disparate land management agencies. Lawyers in the Solicitor's Office write opinions, draft regulations, and render legal advice to the land management agencies. The Solicitor's Office does not, however, represent the Department in court; that task is left to the Department of Justice. Although General Counsel in the Department of Agriculture serves a similar function for the Forest Service, the concentration of resource issues in Interior and the wealth of Solicitor's Opinions (collected in Interior Decisions) mean that the Interior Solicitor's Office is a primary source of law on the public lands.*

Another important entity for lawyers involved in public land law is the Interior Board of Land Appeals (IBLA), the major organ of the Interior Department's Office of Hearings and Appeals. Since 1970, several kinds of decisions of land management agencies (especially BLM) may be appealed to the IBLA, which possesses broad authority delegated by the Secretary to decide such appeals. Many of the roughly 1000 appeals filed each year with the IBLA involve mineral resources (including royalty disputes), but the agency's jurisdiction also encompasses a wide variety of subjects including grazing, special use permits, wilderness review, and wild horses and burros. The IBLA usually sits in panels of three judges each (although en banc decisions are possible). Judges are appointed by the Secretary. Their jurisdiction and processes are set out in 43 C.F.R. Part 4. The Forest Service also has quite an elaborate internal administrative appeal process, but it is not lodged in a separate division. Rather, the appellate chain leads from the Supervisors of individual forests through the Regional Foresters to the Chief of the Forest Service, and ultimately to the Secretary of Agriculture.

7.   THE UNITED STATES CONGRESS

Congress has since the nation's founding played a critical role in public land law and policy making. Through much of the nineteenth century, the importance of the federal lands—as a source of revenue, for military strategy, and as an element in the nation's "Manifest Destiny" to spread from sea to sea—ensured close legislative scrutiny. Influential congressional representatives were active on public lands issues, not only in the halls of Congress, but in the courts (representing private citizens in public lands disputes) and (ethical standards being somewhat more lax than they are today) as private investors and speculators. Daniel Webster, Thomas Hart Benton, Henry Clay and other legislative giants left their mark on public land policy in many ways. In the latter part of the century, Senator William Stewart of Nevada (the principal drafter of the Mining Law, who made a fortune in various mining ventures and as a lawyer representing claimants) and Congressman George Julian of Indiana were perhaps most influential, although a number of others, such as Senator (and later Secretary of the Interior) Henry Teller of Colorado, were also prominent.

Following completion of the task of admitting the first 48 states in 1912, the priority of public lands issues on the congressional agenda was somewhat reduced. The closing of this frontier coincided with the emergence of the United States as a world power, and other competing responsi-

---

* Coauthor John Leshy was Solicitor of the Interior Department from 1993 to 2001.

bilities captured more congressional attention. Throughout most of this century, in fact, public lands issues have been viewed on Capitol Hill as something of a sideshow, with representatives from the remainder of the nation often tending to defer to members from the western states.

The committee structure in Congress plays a crucial role in all legislation, and public land policy is no exception. Under various names and with varied jurisdictions, there were almost from the beginning specific committees in both houses of Congress with primary responsibility over public land legislation. For most of the nation's existence (from 1805 to 1951 in the House, and from 1816 to 1948 in the Senate) these were called committees on Public Lands or Public Lands & Surveys. Separate committees on mines and mining existed in each house from 1865 until 1947. Thereafter, the Public Lands and Mining Committees in each house were collapsed (in 1948 in the Senate, and in 1951 in the House) into committees on "Interior and Insular Affairs." The House Interior Committee became the House Natural Resources Committee in 1992, but the victorious Republican majority dropped "Natural" in early 1995. Its counterpart in the Senate became the Committee on Energy and Natural Resources in 1977. For much of this century, these committees (usually referred to as "resource committees" for convenience) were "stacked" with westerners for good reason: Westerners sought such committee assignments to enhance their influence over issues of concern back home, and non-westerners tended to avoid the assignments because of their lack of impact on their constituents. As a result, the chairs of these committees, commonly the two most influential legislators on public lands issues in the entire Congress, were usually (though not always) from the West. Some have had great impact, such as Senator Henry M. "Scoop" Jackson of Washington (chair of the Senate Committee from 1963 until 1981), and Congressmen Wayne Aspinall of Colorado and Morris Udall of Arizona (chairs of the House Committee from 1959 to 1973 and from 1977 to 1991, respectively).

Like the public land policy universe in general, however, the congressional committee jurisdictional allocation is quite untidy. Legislation dealing with most aspects of the Forest Service is primarily the responsibility of the agriculture committees in both houses, although jurisdiction on some issues, such as wilderness designation in the national forests, is shared with the resources committees. Wildlife issues on federal lands are partly the responsibility of committees other than the resources committees. Of course, the appropriations committees of both houses can have great say in public land policy, both through their power over the purse-strings, and through the increasingly common technique of attaching substantive legislative "riders" to appropriations bills. Significant legislative struggles in recent years—over such issues as whether to prohibit land patenting under the Mining Law, whether to increase grazing fees on public lands, and how much road-building and timber harvesting should take place in the national forests—have taken place primarily in the appropriations process.

Some public land legislation is generic, applicable to all lands in a particular management system (such as the Federal Land Policy and Management Act or the National Forest Management Act). But some, such as legislation creating a particular national park, is specific to a particular state. In recent years, something of a trend has emerged to package certain kinds of legislation (such as that designating lands of a particular agency as wilderness, or designating a cluster of wild and scenic rivers) on a state-wide basis. By a strong congressional tradition, public land legislation that primarily affects a single state is very difficult to pass without the support (or at least the acquiescence) of most if not all of the state's congressional delegation. The 1980 Alaska legislation recounted immediately below was a very rare exception; the Alaska congressional delegation stoutly resisted it but in the end was defeated by a broad national coalition spearheaded by environmental groups.

E. THE SPECIAL CASE OF ALASKA

The public land law eras that played themselves out over the course of two centuries in the Lower 48 States were recreated, compressed, and intensified in Alaska. The high-stakes events in the largest public lands state—"The Last Pork Chop," as one writer dubbed it—can only be briefly summarized here.

The word Alaska means "Great Land," but the territory was long known as "Seward's Folly" after the Secretary of State who engineered its purchase from Russia in 1867. Because of Alaska's daunting remoteness and clime, the new sovereign did little with it for many decades. Alaska became a federal judicial district in 1884 and a territory in 1912. Alaskans, like other territorial residents before them, chafed under rule from Washington, D.C. but their cries of "colonialism" were perhaps even stronger. When statehood came to Alaska in 1959, its 375 million acres of land remained almost completely in federal ownership because only a relatively negligible amount of land was suitable for homesteading or other disposition under the public land laws then existing. Meanwhile, over the years since Alaska was purchased, Congress had given almost no attention to Alaska Natives. No treaties with them had been negotiated and almost no reservations had been established by statute or executive order.

Alaskans drove the most successful statehood bargain of all. Under the Alaska Enabling Act, the new state government won the right to select 104 million acres of federal land. State officials promptly ordered surveys to determine the choicest parcels. At about the same time, rumors of extensive oil and gas deposits were bruited about as mineral companies conducted exploration programs. In the mid–1960's, Alaska Natives began to protest in earnest, taking the position that their aboriginal title had never been disturbed and that any administrative transfers of title to the state or the mining industry would violate Native property rights. (On Indian title, see supra at pp. 40–46.) Interior Secretary Stewart Udall listened and, in 1966, acted. In a bold stroke he suspended the issuance of almost all patents and mineral leases. The pressure heightened in 1968 when the discovery of massive oil deposits on state-selected lands at Prudhoe Bay on Alaska's north slope was confirmed. Udall then withdrew all unreserved lands in Alaska from all forms of entry (Public Land Order 4582, the 1968 "Superfreeze") until Congress had resolved the Native claims.

It took three more years before the Alaska Native Claims Settlement Act of 1971 (ANCSA), 43 U.S.C. §§ 1601–1624, became law. Paving the way for the Alaska Pipeline, ANCSA extinguished all Native title, granted Alaska Natives the right to select 44 million acres of federal land in the state, provided Natives nearly $1 billion in federal funds, and allowed state selections to resume. The 1971 Act also reflected the emerging power of the modern environmental movement. ANCSA's so-called "d(2)" provision, 43 U.S.C. § 1616(d)(2), authorized the Secretary of the Interior to withdraw up to 80 million acres of land that might merit inclusion in the four "national interest" systems (national parks, forests, wildlife refuges, and wild rivers). Thus, after ANCSA, four major potential sets of landowners— the state, Alaska Native corporations, the mineral companies, and the United States—were undergoing overlapping and conflicting selection processes involving hundreds of millions of acres. The d(2) "national interest" withdrawals were frustrating to those Alaskans who wanted no impediments to mineral development. See, e.g., Joseph Rudd, Who Owns Alaska?—Mineral Rights Acquisition Amid Rapidly Changing Land Ownership, 20 Rocky Mtn.Min.L.Inst. 109 (1975). On the passage of ANCSA, see Mary Clay Berry, THE ALASKA PIPELINE (1979); Barry Lopez, ARCTIC DREAMS (1986).

By the terms of ANCSA, the d(2) withdrawals expired on December 16, 1978. Although Congress had labored hard, it had failed to complete work on conservation legislation that would have protected the lands permanently. Faced with the prospect of these lands being opened back up to exploitation, President Jimmy Carter and Secretary of the Interior Cecil Andrus executed massive, overlapping withdrawals and Antiquities Act reservations that effectively extended the d(2) withdrawals and staved off mineral development and state selections of these federal lands. Congress finally finished the legislation in a lame-duck session after the 1980 elections and on December 2, 1980, President Carter signed the Alaska National Interest Lands Conservation Act (ANILCA) into law. This major and complex legislation (it encompasses 181 pages in statutes-at-large) is found at 16 U.S.C. §§ 3101–3233 and in scattered sections of titles 16 and 43.

Superseding (but confirming the effectiveness of) the Carter withdrawals, ANILCA allocated more than 103 million acres, mostly former BLM lands, to the federal conservation systems. It added 43.5 million acres to the National Park System, 53.7 million acres to the National Wildlife Refuge System, and 56.4 million acres to the National Wilderness Preservation System. Thirteen rivers were added to the National Wild and Scenic Rivers System. Congress made two special designations for BLM lands, the 1.2 million acre Steese Conservation Area, and the 1 million acre White Mountains National Recreation Area. The acres allocated to specific preservation systems far exceeded the 103 million acres actually affected because of some double classifications; for example, large amounts of the new national parks and wildlife refuges were also simultaneously designated as wilderness.

ANILCA multiplied several times over the size of the major preservation systems. In one fell swoop it doubled the size of the national park system; tripled the size of the national wildlife refuge system, and quadrupled the size of the national wilderness preservation system. Similarly, ANILCA made significant alterations in the amount of lands administered by federal agencies nationally. The following changes in total agency land holdings, according to the most recent available figures, have been wrought primarily by ANILCA and by state and Native selections of BLM lands in Alaska:

Federal Agency Land Holdings (by millions of acres) *

Agency	1978	2000
Bureau of Land Management	480.5	264.4
Forest Service	188.9	192.4
Fish and Wildlife Service	31.3	95.0
National Park Service	26.6	83.6
All other agencies	47.7	17.2
TOTAL PUBLIC LANDS	775.9	652.6

ANILCA also includes many provisions dealing with Alaska public lands generally, not just lands added to the preservation systems. It implements a preference for rural residents to engage in subsistence hunting and fishing, including traditional uses of snowmobiles and motorboats, on federal lands in Alaska. It allows many existing uses in the new wilderness areas, including cabins and access by airplanes and motorboats, to continue. Detailed provisions govern mineral development on ANILCA lands. See generally Sandy Sagalkin & Mark Panitch, Mineral Development Under the Alaska Lands Act, 10 UCLA–Alaska L.Rev. 117 (1981); Comment, Preservation and Strategic Mineral Development in Alaska: Congress Writes a New Equation, 12 Envtl.L. 137 (1981). The timber industry obtained a provision that "the Secretary of the Treasury shall make available" to the Forest Service at least $40 million annually to maintain the timber harvest for the Tongass National Forest at 4.5 billion board feet per decade, but that was substantially modified, after much criticism from environmental groups, by legislation enacted in 1990. See 16 U.S.C. § 439d; Jim Grode, The Tongass Timber Reform Act: A Step Towards Rational Management of the Forest, 62 U.Colo.L.Rev. 873 (1991).

Senator Paul Tsongas called ANILCA "perhaps the greatest conservation achievement of the century;" environmentalists harkened back to the poet Horace (ANILCA is "a monument more lasting than bronze," Sierra 5 (Jan./Dec.1981)). See generally Robert Cahn, THE FIGHT TO SAVE WILD

---

* Sources: Bureau of Land Management, U.S. Department of the Interior, PUBLIC LAND STATISTICS (1978), (2000); telephone survey of other federal agencies. Figures given in various reports for land managed by various agencies can differ, largely because some compilations include all land within, say, a national forest or park, including non-federal inholdings, while others include only acres to which the United States holds title.

ALASKA (1982); Alaska Geographic Society, ALASKA NATIONAL INTEREST LANDS (1981); Glenn E. Cravez, ANILCA, Directing the Great Land's Future, 10 UCLA–Alaska L.Rev. 33 (1980)

F. A MODERN LEGACY OF PUBLIC LAND HISTORY: ACCESS TO AND ACROSS FEDERAL LANDS

As this chapter has illustrated, federal public land policy has been gradually but thoroughly revised in the Nation's second century. The age of wholesale disposition is over; the age of retention and management is middle-aged; and the age of conservation and recreation is well underway. Preserving that old enemy of the settler, wilderness, has become a prominent goal of national policy.

The foregoing recitation of public land law history was intended for more than general information. Two centuries of legal development cannot be ignored, even as change accelerates. The rights, interests, and liabilities created over the past two hundred years are established, and modern systems must recognize them. Century-old cases still are persuasive precedent. And some century-old statutes, enacted with a view of the future that did not always prove out, continue to pose legal problems in modern public land management.

To illustrate the importance of this history, it is useful to examine a set of important modern problems in public land law that grow directly out of that historical legacy. These stem largely from the patchwork, haphazard character of federal disposal policies, and the sometimes dizzying patterns of land ownership that have resulted. It may seem surprising that for a long time court disputes over access questions involving federal lands were rare. But no longer—more such litigation has been brought in the past couple of decades than in the previous ten. Many of the issues raised, as in the following cases, result from the collision of ancient and modern law and policy. History can be determinative when the rubber meets the road, as it were, on access. The discussion that follows is divided into two parts: Access across non-federal land to federal land, and access across federal land.

1. ACCESS ACROSS NONFEDERAL LAND TO FEDERAL LAND

Leo Sheep Co. v. United States

Supreme Court of the United States, 1979.
440 U.S. 668.

■ MR. JUSTICE REHNQUIST delivered the opinion of the Court.

This is one of those rare cases evoking episodes in this country's history that, if not forgotten, are remembered as dry facts and not as adventure. Admittedly the issue is mundane: Whether the Government has an implied easement to build a road across land that was originally granted to the Union Pacific Railroad under the Union Pacific Act of 1862—a grant that was part of a governmental scheme to subsidize the construction of the transcontinental railroad. But that issue is posed against the backdrop of a fascinating chapter in our history. As this Court noted in another case involving the Union Pacific Railroad, "courts, in construing a statute, may with propriety recur to the history of the times when it was passed; and this is frequently necessary, in order to ascertain the reason as well as the meaning of particular provisions in it." United States v. Union Pacific Railroad Co., 91 U.S. 72, 79 (1875). In this spirit we relate the events underlying passage of the Union Pacific Act of 1862.

The idea of a transcontinental railroad predated the California gold rush. * * * [A]nimating it all was the desire of the Federal Government that the West be settled. This desire was intensified by the need to provide a logistical link with California in the heat of the Civil War. That the venture was much too risky and much too expensive for private capital alone was evident in the years of fruitless exhortation; private investors would not move without tangible governmental inducement.

In the mid–19th Century there was serious disagreement as to the forms that inducement could take. Justice Story, in his Commentaries on the Constitution, described one extant school of thought which argued that "internal improvements," such as railroads, were not within the enumerated constitutional powers of Congress. Under such a theory, the direct subsidy of a transcontinental railroad was constitutionally suspect—an uneasiness aggravated by President Andrew Jackson's 1830 veto of a bill appropriating funds to construct a road from Maysville to Lexington within the State of Kentucky.

The response to this constitutional "gray" area, and source of political controversy, was the "checkerboard" land grant scheme. The Union Pacific Act of 1862 granted public land to the Union Pacific Railroad for each mile of track that it laid. Land surrounding the railway right-of-way was divided into "checkerboard" blocks. Odd-numbered lots were granted to the Union Pacific; even-numbered lots were reserved by the Government. As a result, Union Pacific land in the area of the right-of-way was usually surrounded by public land, and vice versa. The historical explanation for this peculiar disposition is that it was apparently an attempt to disarm the "internal improvement" opponents by establishing a grant scheme with "demonstrable" benefits. * * *

In 1850 this technique was first explicitly employed for the subsidization of a railroad when the Illinois delegation in Congress, which included Stephen A. Douglas, secured the enactment of a bill that granted public lands to aid the construction of the Illinois Central Railroad. * * * Before this line was constructed, public lands had gone begging at the Government's minimum price; within a few years after its completion, the railroad had disposed of more than one million acres and was rapidly selling more at prices far above those at which land had been originally offered by the Government.

The "internal improvements" theory was not the only obstacle to a transcontinental railroad. In 1853 Congress had appropriated monies and authorized Secretary of War Jefferson Davis to undertake surveys of various proposed routes for a transcontinental railroad. Congress was badly split along sectional lines on the appropriate location of the route—so badly split that Stephen A. Douglas, now a Senator from Illinois, in 1854 suggested the construction of a northern, central, and southern route, each with connecting branches in the East. That proposal, however, did not break the impasse.

The necessary impetus was provided by the Civil War. Senators and Representatives from those States which seceded from the Union were no longer present in Congress, and therefore the sectional overtones of the dispute as to routes largely disappeared. * * *

* * * As is often the case, war spurs technological development, and Congress enacted the Union Pacific Act in May 1862. Perhaps not coincidentally, the Homestead Act was passed the same month. * * *

The land grants made by the 1862 Act included all the odd-numbered lots within 10 miles on either side of the track. When the Union Pacific's original subscription drive for private investment proved a failure, the land grant was doubled by extending the checkerboard grants to 20 miles on either side of the track. Private investment was still sluggish, and construction did not begin until July 1865, three months after the cessation of Civil War hostilities.[13] Thus began a race with the Central Pacific Railroad, which was laying track eastward from Sacramento, for the government land grants which went with each mile of track laid. The race culminated in the driving of the golden spike at Promontory Point, Utah, on May 10, 1869.

This case is the modern legacy of these early grants. Petitioners, the Leo Sheep Company and the Palm Livestock Company, are the Union Pacific Railroad's successors in fee to specific odd-numbered sections of land in Carbon County, Wyo. These sections lie to the east and south of the Seminoe Reservoir, an area that is used by the public for fishing and hunting. Because of the checkerboard configuration, it is physically impossible to enter the Seminoe Reservoir sector from this direction without

---

13.   Construction would not have begun then without the Credit Mobilier, a limited liability company that was essentially owned by the promoters and investors of the Union Pacific. One of these investors, Oakes Ames, a wealthy New England shovel maker, was a substantial investor in Credit Mobilier and also a Member of Congress. Credit Mobilier contracted with the Union Pacific to build portions of the road, and by 1866 several individuals were large investors in both corporations. Allegations of improper use of funds and bribery of Members of the House of Representatives led to the appointment of a special congressional investigatory committee that during 1872 and 1873 looked into the affairs of Credit Mobilier. These investigations revealed improprieties on the part of more than one Member of Congress, and the committee recommended that Ames be expelled from Congress. The investigation also touched on the career of a future President. See M. Leech & H. Brown, The Garfield Orbit (1978).

In 1872 the House of Representatives enacted a resolution condemning the policy of granting subsidies of public lands to railroads. Cong. Globe, 42d Cong., 2d Sess., 1585 (1872); see Great Northern R. Co. v. United States, 315 U.S. 262, 273–274 (1942). Of course, the reaction of the public or of Congress a decade after the enactment of the Union Pacific Act to the conduct of those associated with the Union Pacific cannot influence our interpretation of that Act today.

some minimum physical intrusion upon private land. In the years immediately preceding this litigation, the Government had received complaints that private owners were denying access over their lands to the reservoir area or requiring the payment of access fees. After negotiation with these owners failed, the Government cleared a dirt road extending from a local county road to the Reservoir across both public domain lands and fee lands of the Leo Sheep Company. It also erected signs inviting the public to use the road as a route to the Reservoir.*

Petitioners initiated this action pursuant to 28 U.S.C. § 2409a to quiet title against the United States. The District Court granted petitioners' motion for summary judgment, but was reversed on appeal by the Court of Appeals for the Tenth Circuit. The latter court concluded that when Congress granted land to the Union Pacific Railroad, it implicitly reserved an easement to pass over the odd-numbered sections in order to reach the even-numbered sections that were held by the Government. Because this holding affects property rights in 150 million acres of land in the Western United States, we granted certiorari and now reverse.

The Government does not claim that there is any express reservation of an easement in the Union Pacific Act that would authorize the construction of a public road on the Leo Sheep Company's property. Section 3 of the 1862 Act sets out a few specific reservations to the "checkerboard" grant. The grant was not to include land "sold, reserved, or otherwise disposed of by the United States," such as land to which there were homestead claims. 12 Stat., at 492. Mineral lands were also excepted from the operation of the Act. Ibid. Given the existence of such explicit exceptions, this Court has in the past refused to add to this list by divining some "implicit" congressional intent. * * * To overcome the lack of support in the Act itself, the Government here argues that the implicit reservation of the asserted easement is established by "settled principles of property law" and by the Unlawful Inclosures of Public Lands Act of 1885.

Where a private landowner conveys to another individual a portion of his lands in a certain area and retains the rest, it is presumed at common law that the grantor has reserved an easement to pass over the granted property if such passage is necessary to reach the retained property. These rights of way are referred to as "easements by necessity." There are two problems with the Government's reliance on that notion in this case. First of all, whatever right of passage a private landowner might have, it is not at all clear that it would include the right to construct a road for public access to a recreational area.[15] More importantly, the easement is not actually a matter of necessity in this case because the Government has the power of eminent domain. Jurisdictions have generally seen eminent domain and easements by necessity as alternative ways to effect the same

---

* [Eds. A map of the area, from the Tenth Circuit opinion, is found at p. 155 infra.]

15. It is very unlikely that Congress in 1862 contemplated this type of intrusion, and it could not reasonably be maintained that failure to provide access to the public at large would render the Seminoe Reservoir land useless. Yet these are precisely the considerations that define the scope of easements by necessity. * * *

result. For example, the State of Wyoming no longer recognizes the common-law easement by necessity in cases involving landlocked estates. It provides instead for a procedure whereby the landlocked owner can have an access route condemned on his behalf upon payment of the necessary compensation to the owner of the servient estate.[16] For similar reasons other state courts have held that the "easement by necessity" doctrine is not available to the sovereign.

The applicability of the doctrine of easement by necessity in this case is, therefore, somewhat trained, and ultimately of little significance. The pertinent inquiry in this case is the intent of Congress when it granted land to the Union Pacific in 1862. The 1862 Act specifically listed reservations to the grant, and we do not find the tenuous relevance of the common-law doctrine of ways of necessity sufficient to overcome the inference prompted by the omission of any reference to the reserved right asserted by the Government in this case. It is possible that Congress gave the problem of access little thought; but it is at least as likely that the thought which was given focused on negotiation, reciprocity considerations, and the power of eminent domain as obvious devices for ameliorating disputes.[18] So both as matter of common-law doctrine and as a matter of construing congressional intent, we are unwilling to imply rights of way, with the substantial impact that such implication would have on property rights granted over 100 years ago, in the absence of a stronger case for their implication than the Government makes here.

16.   Wyo.Stat.Ann. §§ 24–9–101 to 24–9–104 (1977); see Snell v. Ruppert, 541 P.2d 1042, 1046 (Wyo.1975) (statute "offers complete relief to the shut-in landowner and covers the whole subject matter") * * * In light of the history of public land grants related in Part I of this opinion, it is not surprising that "private" eminent domain statutes like that of Wyoming are most prevalent in the Western United States.

18.   The intimations that can be found in the Congressional Globe are that there was no commonly understood reservation by the Government of the right to enter upon granted lands and construct a public road. Representative Cradlebaugh of Nevada offered an amendment to what became the Union Pacific Act of 1862 that would have reserved the right to the public to enter granted land and prospect for valuable minerals upon the payment of adequate compensation to the owner. The proposed amendment was defeated. The only representative other than Cradlebaugh who spoke to it, Representative Sargent of California, stated:

> "The amendment of the gentleman proposes to allow the public to enter upon the lands of any man, whether they be mineral lands or not, and prospect for gold and silver, and as compensation proposes some loose method of payment for the injuries inflicted. Now, sir, it may turn out that the man who thus commits the injuries may be utterly insolvent, not able to pay a dollar, and how is the owner of the property to be compensated for tearing down his dwellings, rooting up his orchards, and destroying his crops?" Cong.Globe, 37th Cong., 2d Sess., 1910 (1862).

In debates on an earlier Pacific Railroad Bill it was explicitly suggested that there be "a reservation in every grant of land that [the Government] shall have a right to go through it, and take it at proper prices to be paid thereafter." The author of this proposal, Senator Simmons of Rhode Island, lamented the lack of such a reservation in the bill under consideration. Cong.Globe, 35th Cong., 2d Sess., 579 (1859). Apparently the intended purpose of this proposed reservation was to permit railroads to obtain rights of way through granted property at the Government's behest. Senator Simmons' comments are somewhat confused, but they certainly do not evince any prevailing assumption that the Government implicitly reserved a right-of-way through granted lands.

The Government would have us decide this case on the basis of the familiar canon of construction that when grants to federal lands are at issue, any doubts "are resolved for the Government not against it." Andrus v. Charlestone Stone Products Co., 436 U.S. 604, 617 (1978). But this Court long ago declined to apply this canon in its full vigor to grants under the railroad acts. In 1885 this Court observed that:

> "The solution of [ownership] questions [involving the railroad grants] depends, of course, upon the construction given to the acts making the grants; and they are to receive such a construction as will carry out the intent of Congress, however difficult it might be to give full effect to the language used if the grants were by instruments of private conveyance. To ascertain that intent we must look to the condition of the country when the acts were passed, as well as to the purpose declared on their face, and read all parts of them together." Winona and St. Peter R. Co. v. Barney, 113 U.S. 618, 625 (1885).

The Court harmonized the longstanding rule enunciated most recently in *Andrus,* supra, with the doctrine of *Winona* in United States v. Denver and Rio Grande R. Co., 150 U.S. 1, 14 (1893) when

it said:

> It is undoubtedly, as urged by the plaintiffs in error, the well-settled rule of this court that public grants are construed strictly against the grantees, but they are not to be so construed as to defeat the intent of the legislature, or to withhold what is given either expressly or by necessary or fair implication. * * *

> * * * When an act, operating as a general law, and manifesting clearly the intention of Congress to secure public advantages, or to subserve the public interests and welfare by means of benefits more or less valuable, offers individuals or to corporations as an inducement to undertake and accomplish great and expensive enterprises or works of a *quasi* public *character in or through an immense and undeveloped public domain, such legislation stands upon a somewhat different footing from merely a private grant, and should receive at the hands of the court a more liberal construction in favor of the purposes for which it was enacted.

Thus invocation of the canon reiterated in *Andrus* does little to advance the Government's position in this case.

Nor do we find the Unlawful Inclosures of Public Lands Act of 1885 of any significance in this controversy. That Act was a response to the "range wars," the legendary struggle between cattlemen and farmers during the last half of the 19th Century. Cattlemen had entered Kansas, Nebraska, and the Dakota Territory before other settlers, and they grazed their herds freely on public lands with the Federal Government's acquiescence. To maintain their dominion over the ranges, cattlemen used homestead and pre-emption laws to gain control of water sources in the range lands. With monopoly control of such sources, the cattlemen found that ownership over a relatively small area might yield effective control of thousands of acres of grassland. Another exclusionary technique was the illegal fencing of public lands which was often the product of the checkerboard pattern of railroad grants. By placing fences near the borders of their parts of the checkerboard, cattlemen could fence in thousands of acres of public lands. Reports of the Secretary of Interior indicated that vast areas of public grazing land had been preempted by such fencing patterns. In response Congress passed the Unlawful Inclosures Act of 1885.*

The Government argues that the prohibitions of this Act should somehow be read to include the Leo Sheep Company's refusal to acquiesce in a public road over its property, and that such a conclusion is supported by this Court's opinion in Camfield v. United States, 167 U.S. 518 (1897). We find, however, that *Camfield* does not afford the support that the Government seeks. That case involved a fence that was constructed on odd-numbered lots so as to enclose 20,000 acres of public land, thereby appropriating it to the exclusive use of Camfield and his associates. This Court analyzed the fence from the perspective of nuisance law, and concluded that the Unlawful Inclosures Act was an appropriate exercise of the police power.

There is nothing, however, in the *Camfield* opinion to suggest that the Government has the authority asserted here. In fact, the Court affirmed the grantee's right to fence completely his own land [quoting *Camfield*, supra p. 92]. Obviously if odd-numbered lots are individually fenced, the access to even-numbered lots is obstructed. Yet the *Camfield* Court found that this was not a violation of the Unlawful Inclosures Act. In that light we cannot see how the Leo Sheep Company's unwillingness to entertain a public road without compensation can be a violation of that Act. It is certainly true that the problem we confront today was not a matter of great concern during the time the 1862 railroad grants were made. The order of the day was the open range—barbed wire had not made its presence felt—and the type of incursions on private property necessary to reach public land was not such an interference that litigation would serve any motive other than spite. Congress obviously believed that when development came, it would occur in a parallel fashion on adjoining public and private lands and that the process of subdivision, organization of a polity and the ordinary pressures of commercial and social intercourse would work itself into a pattern of access roads.[23] The *Camfield* case expresses similar sentiments. After the passage quoted above conceding the authority of a private landowner to fence the entire perimeter of his odd-numbered lot, the Court opined that such authority was of little practical significance "since a separate enclosure of each section would only become desirable

---

* [Eds. The relevant text of the Act is quoted near the beginning of the opinion in Camfield v. United States, 167 U.S. 518 (1897) supra at p. 92.]

23. This expectation was fostered by the general land grants scheme. Each block in the checkerboard was a square mile—640 acres. The public lots were open to homesteading, with 160 acres the maximum allow-able claim under the Homestead Act. Act of May 20, 1862, ch. 75, 12 Stat. 392. The Union Pacific was required by the 1862 Act to sell or otherwise dispose of the land granted to it within three years after completion of the entire road, with lands not so disposed of within that period subject to homesteading and pre-emption. Thus in 1862 the process of subdivision was perceived, to a great degree, as inevitable.

when the country had been settled, and roads had been built which would give access to each section." Ibid. It is some testament to common sense that the present case is virtually unprecedented, and that in the 117 years since the grants were made, litigation over access questions generally has been rare.

Nonetheless, the present times are litigious ones and the 37th Congress did not anticipate our plight. Generations of land patents have issued without any express reservation of the right now claimed by the Government. Nor has a similar right been asserted before.[24] When the Secretary of Interior has discussed access rights, his discussion has been colored by the assumption that those rights had to be purchased.[25] This Court has traditionally recognized the special need for certainty and predictability where land titles are concerned, and we are unwilling to upset settled expectations to accommodate some ill-defined power to construct public thoroughfares without compensation. The judgment of the Court of Appeals of the Tenth Circuit is accordingly

Reversed.

■ MR. JUSTICE WHITE took no part in the consideration or decision of this case.

NOTES AND QUESTIONS

1. *The intent of Congress.* Did Congress deliberately set about to create this checkerboard pattern? Is that relevant to the resolution of this question of access? The Circuit Court opinion in *Leo Sheep* had relied upon *Camfield, Mackay,* and Buford v. Houtz, cited in the main opinion at note 24, in finding that "Congress, by its 1862 grant to the railroad of the odd-numbered sections, did by implication intend to reserve a right of access to the inter-locking even-numbered sections not conveyed to the railroad." "To hold to the contrary would be to ascribe to Congress a degree of carelessness or lack of foresight which in our view would be unwarranted." 570 F.2d 881, 885 (10th Cir.1977). Clyde Martz, the experienced attorney for plaintiffs, told one of these editors that this passage inspired him to

---

24. This distinguishes the instant case from Buford v. Houtz, 133 U.S. 320 (1890). The appellants there were a group of cattle ranchers seeking, *inter alia,* an injunction against sheep ranchers who moved their herds across odd-numbered lots held by the appellants in order to graze their sheep on even-numbered public lots. This Court denied the requested relief because it was contrary to a century-old grazing custom. The Court also was influenced by the sheep ranchers' lack of any alternative.

"Upon the whole, we see no equity in the relief sought by the appellants in this case, which undertakes to deprive the defendants of this recognized right to permit their cattle to run at large over the lands of the United States and feed upon the grasses found in them, while, under pretence of owning a small proportion of the land which is the subject of controversy, they themselves obtain the monopoly of this valuable privilege." Id., at 332. Here neither custom nor necessity supports the Government.

25. In 1887 the Secretary of Interior recommended that Congress enact legislation providing for a public road around each section of public land to provide access to the various public lots in the checkerboard scheme. The Secretary also recommended that to the extent building these roads required the taking of property that had passed to private individuals, "the bill should provide for necessary compensation."

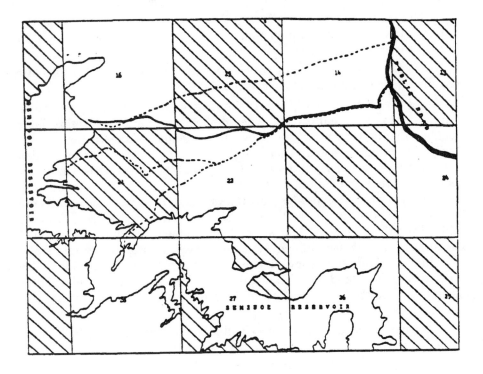

Area Near Seminoe Dam, Carbon County, Wyoming

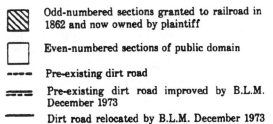

Odd-numbered sections granted to railroad in 1862 and now owned by plaintiff

Even-numbered sections of public domain

Pre-existing dirt road

Pre-existing dirt road improved by B.L.M. December 1973

Dirt road relocated by B.L.M. December 1973

seek certiorari even though only a few square feet of land were involved. For, he said, the U.S. Supreme Court sitting in Washington has a much closer and realistic view of the "carelessness" of which Congress is capable. For more on the logic of the checkerboard, see Paul W. Gates, THE ILLINOIS CENTRAL RAILROAD AND ITS COLONIZATION WORK (1934).

2.   *Canons of construction of federal grants.* In a case decided twenty-three years earlier, and involving this very same railroad land grant, Justice Douglas's majority opinion relied on the "established rule that land grants are construed favorably to the Government, that nothing passes except what is conveyed by clear language, and that if there are doubts they are resolved for the Government, not against it." United States v. Union Pacific R. Co., 353 U.S. 112, 116 (1957). The majority concluded that Union Pacific did not own the minerals under the right-of-way over which the railroad passed. *Leo Sheep* does not cite this decision. What policy underlies the idea of construing ambiguities in grants from the United States in favor

of the United States? (Does it have to do with the generousness of the grants?) How does that canon compare to canons of construction in ordinary contract or property law?

3. Is *Leo Sheep* consistent with *Camfield*? Is what Leo Sheep Co. did here any different from what the rancher did in Camfield?

4. Is the issue in *Leo Sheep* as simple and straightforward as Justice Rehnquist makes it out to be? The implied reservation of rights later thought to be necessary for the enjoyment of lands retained is not a novel concept in public land jurisprudence. See, e.g., the concept of the implied federal reserved water right discussed at pp. 513–48, infra. Does the Court mean to say that the United States (which made this grant) is in a worse position than the sheepherders in *Mackay* and *Buford*? What relevance does state property law have to the question of asserted federal property rights? Does the "necessity" for an implied easement disappear because the federal government has eminent domain power? Do railroad grants stand on a higher plane than, say, a simple 160–acre homestead claim? Are *Camfield, Buford,* and the Unlawful Inclosures Act truly irrelevant or insignificant? Is this an instance where hard and fast concepts of property ownership break down?

5. What practical consequences will follow? Obviously, the BLM must condemn and pay for the lands necessary to provide access to the Seminoe Reservoir if the facility is to be used for the purpose intended. Short of condemnation, can the local BLM manager now reach Seminoe Reservoir without paying Leo Sheep an access fee? Does it depend on whether the manager walks or drives a jeep?

6. Consider the converse of *Leo Sheep:* could the BLM close its lands to plaintiffs, cutting off their access to their property? Sauce for the goose * * *? Does Leo Sheep Co. have an implied right of access across retained U.S. lands? If you were a BLM official, would you recommend such retaliation? Why? Would it work? Is there, ultimately, any "fair" resolution to this controversy available?

7. If the United States had conveyed the cornering sections it retained to homesteader X, would Leo Sheep Co. have a right of access across X's land? Would X have a right of access across Leo Sheep Co. land? Would state or federal law control the answer to these questions? Energy Transp. Systems, Inc. v. Union Pacific R. Co., 606 F.2d 934 (10th Cir.1979) was a consolidated opinion on three cases (one from Wyoming and two from Kansas) between a railroad and a competing coal slurry pipeline company. The latter had purchased easements underneath the railroad right of way from homesteaders; the railroad challenged whether the homesteaders had anything to convey. In the Wyoming case the homesteader had taken title from the United States. The court applied federal law and held for the homesteader on the ground that the railroad did not own the land under the right of way under the principle of the 1957 *Union Pacific* decision, discussed in note 2 above. In the two Kansas cases, the homesteaders had bought their land from the railroad (which had obtained its title from the United States), with the railroad reserving a right of way across the land it conveyed. The homesteaders won here as well, the court of appeals affirm-

ing the district court determination that federal law controlled (and answered affirmatively) whether the railroad could convey the subsurface to the homesteader; but that state law controlled (and answered affirmatively) whether the railroad in fact did convey such an interest.

8.   In Granite Beach Holdings v. State ex rel. Department of Natural Resources, 11 P.3d 847 (Wash.App.2000), the plaintiff, part of a modern breed of land speculator in the West, bought an inholding in an area where the government and conservation groups were actively buying land. Plaintiff argued that it had an implied easement of necessity to cross state land to access and develop the inholding it had purchased, on the theory that the United States was the original grantor and had reserved an easement. Relying on *Leo Sheep*, the Court held that no reservation should be implied in favor of the United States.

———

Another case involving, like *Leo Sheep*, access across non-federal land for federal purposes, put a modern twist on the problem litigated in *Camfield v. United States*, supra p. 92. Rancher Lawrence constructed a fence twenty-eight miles long in a 20,000 acre area of private, state, and federal land in south central Wyoming that had been "checkerboarded" as a result of the Union Pacific Railroad grant. As in *Camfield*, the fence enclosed federal lands even though it was constructed entirely on private land. Lawrence had federal permits under the Taylor Grazing Act to graze livestock on these federal lands. In contrast to *Camfield*, however, here the federal government was seeking to open federal land to the passage of wildlife rather than human settlement. Lawrence's fence was antelope-proof, and in the severe winter of 1983 antelope collected against the fence and starved trying to reach their winter range. The federal government sued Lawrence under the Unlawful Inclosures Act. The district court ordered Lawrence to remove the fence or modify it to allow antelope to go under and over it, and the court of appeals affirmed. United States ex rel. Bergen v. Lawrence, 848 F.2d 1502 (10th Cir.1988), cert. denied, 488 U.S. 980 (1988).

The Tenth Circuit held that *Camfield* rather than *Leo Sheep* was controlling, quoting the district court's conclusion that while the former "is not applicable to a road question, * * * it clearly has much to say on the subject of defendant's fence." The court of appeals continued (848 F.2d at 1506):

> * * * [T]he UIA [Unlawful Inclosures Act] remains federal law, and was amended in 1984 when Congress modified a procedural provision. We refuse to repeal the UIA by implication, and therefore, must give effect to its provisions. The UIA declares enclosures of federal lands to be unlawful and orders that such enclosures be removed. It creates no easements or servitudes. Thus, Lawrence's central argument, that the antelope have no easement across his lands, is not relevant to our

decision.[6] We conclude with the district court that "while *Leo Sheep* has no applicability in this matter, *Camfield* is dispositive of it." *Bergen*, 620 F.Supp. at 1420.

The court of appeals then turned to Lawrence's argument that the UIA is "simply inapplicable to antelope" because there was no mention of wildlife in its legislative history. The court observed that section 1 of the UIA is "emphatic and absolute" that "all inclosures of any public lands * * * are * * * declared to be unlawful." [Eds.: 43 U.S.C. § 1061; a more complete version is found at the beginning of the *Camfield* opinion supra p. 92.] The court saw no need to look at the history because the statute was clear on its face. It also relied on early cases such as Stoddard v. United States, 214 Fed. 566 (8th Cir.1914), which applied the UIA to fences on private land that obstructed the free range of livestock to public land. *Stoddard* had concluded that the UIA "was intended to prevent the obstruction of free passage or transit for *any and all lawful purposes over public lands.*" The Tenth Circuit continued:

> Thus, the question becomes whether winter forage by antelope is a lawful purpose of public lands. Any doubt may be resolved by reference to FLPMA, where Congress directed that "the public lands be managed in a manner * * * that will provide food and habitat for fish and wildlife and domestic animals." 43 U.S.C. § 1701(a)(8).

> Lawrence objects to the reliance on FLPMA to ascertain the limits of the UIA: "It is absurd to suppose that 1976 declarations of Congress regarding public land administration could be construed to amend by implication the language and purpose of the UIA enacted in 1885." This criticism misses the point of the analysis. Neither this court nor the district court rely on FLPMA to *amend* the UIA. The UIA proscribes unlawful enclosures; enclosures are unlawful when they deny access to public lands for "lawful purposes"; Congressional guidance in FLPMA is relevant to assist the court in determining what uses of the public lands are lawful, and therefore protected under the UIA. Obviously, lawful uses of the public lands will change over time. For example, as Lawrence notes, the primary purpose of the UIA in the early part of this century was to prevent the exclusion of homesteaders from the public lands. With the repeal of the homesteading laws, that is no longer a "lawful purpose." The district court did not look to FLPMA to determine the intent of Congress in 1885, but rather, to determine what "lawful purposes" were protected by the UIA in 1985. That was both appropriate and necessary. * * *

> * * * [T]he UIA preserves access to federal lands for "lawful purposes," including forage by wildlife. Where a fence is constructed so

---

6. While we do not decide this question, we note in passing that the Wyoming and National Wildlife Federations, as intervenor-appellees, make a strong case for distinguishing the antelope's right of access from the government's case in *Leo Sheep*. Accordingly, we are not saying that wildlife have no such rights relative to federal lands; we simply do not reach that question in this case. Cf., e.g., *Leo Sheep*, 440 U.S. at 687 n. 24 (distinguishes *Leo Sheep* from Buford v. Houtz, 133 U.S. 320 (1890)).

that it does not obstruct other lawful uses of the federal lands, it is not an unlawful enclosure.

Finally, Lawrence claims that because the fence includes several unlocked gates, there is no unlawful enclosure absent evidence that the fence excludes entry by members of the public with "lawful entitlement to use of the enclosed public lands." * * * We have already held that the UIA applies to wildlife as well as people. It follows that Lawrence's antelope-proof fence is prohibited by the UIA.

The court also rejected Lawrence's argument that he fit within a defense recognized by the UIA; namely, that he had, in the court's words, a "claim or color of title to the enclosed lands that was acquired in good faith." See 43 U.S.C. §§ 1061, 1063. Prior cases had required a color of *fee* title to assert this defense, and federal grazing permits do not create any title in federal lands; see infra, Chapter 8, § A. Finally, the court rejected Lawrence's argument that the district court's ruling had unconstitutionally "taken" his property; see Chapter 3, § F infra.

NOTES AND QUESTIONS

1. Do you suppose Congress in 1885 really was interested in safeguarding access by wildlife? Wasn't it more likely to have been interested in protecting homesteaders (such as, perhaps, Lawrence's forebears)? Does the court adequately distinguish *Leo Sheep*?

2. More generally, how should a century-old statute like this be construed when public values and tastes have changed so dramatically? Probably to most people in 1885, antelope were a source of meat or a nuisance; now they are prized by many in their wild state. Should the interpretation of the statute change to accommodate that shift in public opinion? Justice Rehnquist in *Leo Sheep* noted that the access problem in that case was "certainly * * * not a matter of great concern" when Congress enacted the pertinent statute. But the federal government lost *Leo Sheep* and won *Lawrence*. Why?

3. Did the Tenth Circuit use bootstrapping to get to its conclusion? The words "lawful purposes" which are relied on here do not actually appear in the UIA; they are in an earlier court opinion interpreting the UIA. Should that make a difference?

4. The General Accounting Office surveyed the adequacy of access to BLM and Forest Service lands in 1992. The responses of agency officials indicated that permanent, legal public access to somewhat more than fifty million acres of these lands (or 14% of the total managed by these agencies) was considered inadequate, largely because adjacent private landowners had been increasingly unwilling to provide such access out of a concern about vandalism and potential liability, and their desire for privacy or exclusive personal use of the federal lands in question. The agencies reported that they had been taking steps to acquire legal access; in 1990–92 permanent legal access (through such measures as donated or acquired perpetual easements) was obtained for about 4.5 million acres of federal

land. See generally GAO, Federal Lands: Reasons for and Effects of Inadequate Public Access (April 1992).

2.   ACCESS ACROSS FEDERAL LAND

For most of the Nation's first two centuries, it was generally assumed that everyone had the ability to go upon most federal lands as they pleased. In the 1866 Mining Act, Congress had issued an open-ended invitation to construct highways on unreserved federal lands (R.S. 2477, discussed infra). In that same statute Congress had also "acknowledged and confirmed" the right of way "[f]or the construction of ditches and canals" on federal lands to promote irrigation works. See 43 U.S.C. § 1769 (also repealed 1976). Nearly two decades later, Congress had generally forbidden fencing off the federal lands in the Unlawful Inclosures Act of 1885, discussed in *Camfield*, supra. In decisions like Buford v. Houtz, 133 U.S. 320, 326 (1890), the United States Supreme Court had endorsed the idea of an "implied license, growing out the custom of nearly a hundred years, that the public lands of the United States, especially those in which the native grasses area adapted to the growth and fattening of domestic animals, shall be free to the people who seek to use them, where there are left open and uninclosed, and no act of government forbids this use."

Nevertheless, in many cases, no access "rights" of lasting value were established by such means. The access authority gained in implied licenses was revocable at will by the United States as landowner. The Forest Service could and did revoke implied grazing licenses by requiring grazing permits, and was upheld in Light v. United States, 220 U.S. 523 (1911), supra p. 110. Access to lands in the national park and national wildlife refuge system was always restricted, and the amount of lands in these systems has steadily grown over the years. Finally, in FLPMA, enacted in 1976, Congress culminated a long trend toward ending the historic practice of free and easy access by repealing most of the ancient statutes authorizing construction of highways, ditches, etc. Instead, FLPMA provided that anyone desiring to cross or use national forests or BLM lands for noncasual purposes must obtain a right-of-way from the relevant agency. 43 U.S.C. §§ 1761–65. Rights-of-way essentially are permits for limited purposes and limited durations. Holders must pay fair market value for the permits and are subject to potentially extensive regulation by the federal land manager to protect other uses and values of the lands; specifically, the permits must contain terms and conditions to "minimize damage to scenic and aesthetic values in fish and wildlife habitat and otherwise protect the environment," id. § 1765(a). The statute also expresses a preference for right-of-way "corridors" wherever practical, in order to "minimize adverse environmental impacts and the proliferation of separate rights-of-way." 43 U.S.C. § 1763.

FLPMA's new regime was, however, made subject to "valid existing rights," which means that historical origins of access claims remain of more than academic interest today. A rising tide of litigation has centered on whether the holder has preexisting rights, and, if so, whether and to what extent the agency may regulate the exercise of those rights to further other public purposes. The following case involves a quaint provision enacted along with the Mining Law of 1866 commonly called R.S. 2477 (for that was how it was codified in the "Revised Statutes"). Repealed in FLPMA, subject to valid existing rights, it said, in its entirety: "[T]he right of way for the construction of highways over public lands, not reserved for public uses, is hereby granted."

Sierra Club v. Hodel

United States Court of Appeals, Tenth Circuit, 1988.
848 F.2d 1068.

■ Logan, Circuit Judge.

The Burr Trail winds for sixty-six miles through federally owned land in the rugged, dramatic terrain of southern Utah's Garfield County. Connecting the town of Boulder with Lake Powell's Bullfrog Basin Marina, the road at various points traverses across or next to unreserved federal lands, two wilderness study areas, the Capitol Reef National Park, and the Glen Canyon National Recreation Area. The trail has hosted a variety of uses: during the late 1800s and early 1900s to drive cattle, sheep and horses to market; around 1918 to facilitate oil exploration; and since the 1930s for various transportation, emergency, mineral, agricultural, economic development, and tourist needs. Garfield County (the County) has maintained the Burr Trail since the early 1940s. The combination of public uses and county maintenance has created a right-of-way in favor of Garfield County, pursuant to Congress' grant of public land in R.S. 2477. * * *

The current controversy arises out of the County's immediate plan to improve the western twenty-eight miles of the Burr Trail from an essentially one-lane dirt road into an improved two-lane graveled road.[2]

[Concerned about the impact of the project on adjacent federal lands, including tracts being considered for possible designation as wilderness, a group of environmental organizations led by the Sierra Club sued the County and the Department of the Interior to enjoin it. The complaint alleged violations of various federal laws, including FLPMA and the National Environmental Policy Act (NEPA). The district court held for the defendants on most issues, and both sides appealed. Discussion of issues relating to NEPA and wilderness study is omitted.] * * *

[Prior to FLPMA, agency regulations provided that] a right-of-way could be obtained without application to, or approval by, the federal government. * * * Rather, "[t]he grant referred to in [R.S. 2477] [became] effective upon the construction or establishing of highways, in accordance with the State laws." 43 C.F.R. § 244.55 (1939).

FLPMA, passed in 1976, vests the Secretary of the Interior with broad authority to manage the federal government's vast land holdings. The statute departs from the federal government's earlier policy of giving away

---

2. The County plans eventually to improve the entire sixty-six mile trail, as well as to pave it. These plans are not part of the current proposal.

public lands, in favor of a philosophy of retention and management to maximize the multitudinous interests in the lands. To that end, FLPMA repeals R.S. 2477 and its open-ended grant of rights-of-way over public lands while explicitly protecting R.S. 2477 rights-of-way in existence on the date of FLPMA's passage. See FLPMA §§ 509(a), 701(a), and 701(h), codified respectively at 43 U.S.C. §§ 1769(a) and 1701, Savings Provisions (a) and (h). Any new rights-of-way must be obtained under the stricter provisions of FLPMA Subchapter V, codified at 43 U.S.C. §§ 1761–1771. * * *

A major part of this case involves the interplay between FLPMA and preexisting R.S. 2477 grants, such as the Burr Trail. Sierra Club maintained in the district court that the County's plans for the right-of-way conflict with FLPMA in two ways. Sierra Club first claimed that the plans require significant deviations from the existing right-of-way, constituting, in effect, an attempt to obtain a new right-of way, and thereby triggering the permit requirements of FLPMA Subchapter V. Sierra Club sought to enjoin the improvements on the Burr Trail until the County obtains a FLPMA permit. Second, Sierra Club contended that * * * widening the trail to a twenty-four-foot, two-lane road would exceed the scope of the right-of-way.[9] * * *

BLM and Garfield County propose a two-part standard for measuring the scope of an R.S. 2477 right-of-way:

a) the baseline is the historical extent of use, i.e., the beaten path *both* as it is now and once existed; *plus*

b) the right to deviate from the beaten path when "reasonable and necessary" to meet the exigencies of increased travel.

This right to deviate when "reasonable and necessary" is derived entirely from Utah case law.

Sierra Club, in contrast, advocates an "actual construction" standard derived from the federal R.S. 2477 statute, which granted a right-of-way for "the construction of highways." This standard would measure an R.S. 2477 right-of-way entirely by the actual construction which the right-holder has performed. "Construction" indisputably does not include the beaten path; rather there must be some evidence of maintenance, e.g., grading, drainage ditches, culverts.

The salient issue is whether the scope of R.S. 2477 rights-of-way is a question of state or federal law. The statute itself does not specify whether state or federal law should define the scope of rights-of-way granted thereunder. There is no legislative history to R.S. 2477, and the legislative context of R.S. 2477 sheds little light. R.S. 2477 was originally enacted as section 8 of the Act of July 26, 1866. Congress explicitly adopted state or local law as the rule of decision of sections 1, 2, 5 and 9 of the 1866 Act; just as explicitly, Congress asserted the applicability of federal laws or

---

9. The "scope" of a right-of-way refers to the bundle of property rights possessed by the holder of the right-of-way. This bundle is defined by the physical boundaries of the right-of-way as well as the uses to which it has been put.

regulations in sections 7, 10, and 11. The silence of section 8 reflects the probable fact that Congress simply did not decide which sovereign's law should apply. * * *

The federal regulations heavily support a state law definition. At least since 1938, the Secretary of the Interior has interpreted R.S. 2477 as effecting the grant of a right-of-way "upon the construction or establishing of highways, in accordance with State laws * * *." 43 C.F.R. § 244.55 (1939). BLM, the Secretary's designee, has followed this interpretation consistently and has incorporated it in the Bureau's manual: "State law specifying widths of public highways within the State shall be utilized by the authorized officer to determine the width of the R.S. 2477 grant." Especially when an agency has followed a notorious, consistent, and long-standing interpretation, it may be presumed that Congress' silence denotes acquiescence * * *. United States v. Midwest Oil Co., 236 U.S. 459, 472–73 (1915).

Sierra Club challenges this reliance on BLM's interpretation. First, it challenges the consistency of BLM's interpretation of R.S. 2477. It cites a 1980 opinion letter from the Solicitor of the Interior Department stating that "The question of whether a particular highway has been legally established under R.S. 2477 remains a question of federal law." While this letter admits of at least three possible interpretations, none aids Sierra Club here. One interpretation, which Sierra Club propounds, is that state law plays no role whatsoever in the determination of the existence and scope of R.S. 2477 rights-of-way. This position, however, clearly conflicts with more than four decades of agency precedent, subsequent BLM policy as expressed in the BLM Manual, and over a century of state court jurisprudence. So viewed, the opinion letter would be highly suspect and would deserve little weight. A second reading is that the Solicitor is stating that, as a matter of federal law, the use of the word "construction" in R.S. 2477 imposes actual construction as a baseline requirement for *perfection* of a right-of-way, a requirement which state law can interpret but cannot disregard or emasculate. This reading of the Solicitor's opinion does not help Sierra Club, however, as it speaks only to what is necessary to perfect an R.S. 2477 right, not the scope of such a right once perfected. Sierra Club does not dispute that an R.S. 2477 right-of-way for the Burr Trail was perfected before passage of FLPMA, even under an "actual construction" standard for perfection. The third possible reading of this letter would return us to BLM's regulations: as a matter of federal law, state law has been designated as controlling. This third reading, we think, is most consonant with reason and precedent. * * *

The next of Sierra Club's arguments is the most troubling. It contends that a "reasonable and necessary" standard violates FLPMA's policy of "freezing" rights of way at their October 21, 1976 width. See FLPMA §§ 509(a), 701(a) and 701(h), 43 U.S.C. §§ 1769(a), 1701 Savings Provisions (a) and (h).* Although these savings provisions are phrased in terms

---

* [Eds. note: These savings clauses read, respectively: "Nothing in this title shall have   the effect of terminating any right-of-way or right-to-use heretofore issued, granted, or

of protecting existing "rights" and not existing "widths," Sierra Club's point is a good one. The Bullfrog Marina could become so popular that an eight-lane superfreeway becomes "reasonable and necessary." The superfreeway would represent an expansion of the right-of-way far beyond the use and width existing at the time of FLPMA's passage, and such expansion arguably would violate the "freeze" on existing rights. This concern, however, addresses not the choice of governing law, but the construction this court will put on it, which we discuss below.

Having considered the arguments of all parties, we conclude that the weight of federal regulations, state court precedent, and tacit congressional acquiescence compels the use of state law to define the scope of an R.S. 2477 right-of-way.

Determining the scope of the Burr Trail right-of-way requires us to ascertain Utah law and to apply that law to the uses of the Burr Trail.

A Utah statute enacted in 1963 provides: "The width of rights-of-way for public highways shall be such as the highway authorities of the state, counties, cities or towns may determine for such highways under their respective jurisdiction." * * * On June 15, 1987, the Garfield County Commission acted for apparently the first time under [this section], establishing a uniform width of 100 feet for all R.S. 2477 roads in the County. This determination has no effect, however, for FLPMA preserved only preexisting rights-of-way as they existed on the date of passage, October 21, 1976. Thus, Garfield County's rights, as they existed under Utah law on that date, are the maximum rights it can exercise today. Garfield County, not having established a right-of-way width under the 1963 act before passage of FLPMA in 1976, is limited, we hold, to the width permitted by state law as of that date.

The district court held that Utah case law defined the width of an R.S. 2477 right-of-way "to be that which is reasonable and necessary for the type of use to which the road has been put." 675 F.Supp. at 607 (citing Lindsay Land & Live Stock Co. v. Churnos, 75 Utah 384, 285 P. 646, 649 (1929)). The district court noted further that the Utah Supreme Court

> "has also said that rights-of-way should not be restricted to the actual beaten path, but should be widened to meet the exigencies of increased travel. More specifically, they should be wide enough to allow travelers to pass each other. Whitesides v. Green, 13 Utah 341, 44 P. 1032, 1033 (1896)."

675 F.Supp. at 607. Thus, under Utah common law, the road could be widened as necessary to meet the exigencies of increased travel, at least to the extent of a two-lane road.

We believe the "reasonable and necessary" standard must be read in the light of traditional uses to which the right-of-way was put. Surely no Utah case would hold that a road which had always been two-lane with

permitted." (§ 509(a)). "Nothing in this Act * * * shall be construed as terminating any valid * * * right-of-way, or other land use right or authorization existing on the date of approval of this Act." (§ 701(a)) "All actions by the Secretary * * * under this Act shall be subject to valid existing rights." (§ 701(h)).]

marked and established fence lines, could be widened to accommodate eight lanes of traffic without compensating the owners of property that would be destroyed to accommodate the increased road width. Rights-of-way are a species of easements and are subject to the principles that govern the scope of easements. Utah adheres to the general rule that the owners of the dominant and servient estates "must exercise [their] rights so as not unreasonably to interfere with the other." Big Cottonwood Tanner Ditch Co. v. Moyle, 109 Utah 213, 174 P.2d 148, 158 (1946). See Nielson v. Sandberg, 105 Utah 93, 141 P.2d 696, 701 (1943) (an easement is limited to the original use for which it was acquired).

Applying the "reasonable and necessary" standard in light of traditional uses does not mean, however, that the County's right-of-way is limited to the uses to which the Burr Trail was being put when it first became an R.S. 2477 road. R.S. 2477 was an open-ended and self-executing grant. Under the BLM regulations, the right-of-way became effective upon construction or establishment by the state, see, e.g., 43 C.F.R. § 2822.2–1 (1979); and "no action on the part of the [federal] government [was] necessary." See, e.g., id. at § 2822.1–1. Because the grantor, the federal government, was never required to ratify a use on an R.S. 2477 right-of-way, each new use of the Burr Trail automatically vested as an incident of the easement. Thus, all uses before October 21, 1976, not terminated or surrendered, are part of an R.S. 2477 right-of-way. As there is no contention or evidence of termination or surrender in this case, the County's right-of-way as of the repeal of R.S. 2477 on October 21, 1976, was that which was "reasonable and necessary" for the Burr Trail's preexisting uses.

The district court opinion recited several pre-October 21, 1976, uses: driving livestock; oil, water, and mineral development; transportation by County residents between Bullfrog and other cities in Garfield County; and, at least since 1973, access for tourists to Bullfrog Marina on Lake Powell. These findings of fact are not clearly erroneous and must be affirmed. Thus, the scope of Garfield County's right-of-way is that which is reasonable and necessary to ensure safe travel for the uses above-mentioned, including improving the road to two lanes so travelers could pass each other.

We do not read the district court opinion as deciding the precise width of the easement or that it could be widened in the future to accommodate perceived needs developing after 1976. The court found only that the width was sufficient to accommodate the contemplated widening to two lanes proposed by the County. We do not have before us sufficient facts to determine whether a reasonable need existed in 1976 with respect to the Burr Trail to require some particular width beyond that needed for the presently planned improvements. See Hunsaker v. State, 29 Utah 2d 322, 509 P.2d 352 (1973). Thus, we also do not decide the precise width of this road easement held by the County. * * *

NOTES AND QUESTIONS

1. What do you suppose was Congress's purpose in enacting R.S. 2477 in 1866? How do the plaintiffs and defendants interpret it? How does the court interpret it?

2. Note that the decision appears to assume that the County has a valid existing right to the RS 2477 right-of-way, and the only question is the scope of that right and the degree to which it is subject to regulation by the holder of the dominant estate, the United States. Other cases raise questions whether such a right exists at all in particular circumstances. For example, in Southern Utah Wilderness Alliance v. BLM, 147 F.Supp.2d 1130 (D.Utah 2001) (appeal pending), the district court upheld BLM's rejection of dozens of claims of RS 2477 rights on a variety of grounds, including that the terms of statute's text had not been met; i.e., in some cases there had been no "construction" of the highways, and some of the land had been "reserved for public uses" inconsistent with the construction of highways. The court distinguished Sierra Club v. Hodel and refused to borrow and incorporate state law on the question of whether rights under the statute existed (as opposed to determining the scope of those rights). See also United States v. Gates of the Mountains Lakeshore Homes, Inc., 732 F.2d 1411, 1413 (9th Cir.1984) (no R.S. 2477 right for a utility easement); Shultz v. Department of the Army, 96 F.3d 1222 (9th Cir.1996) (withdrawing earlier opinion at 10 F.3d 649 (9th Cir.1993) and affirming lower court decision that a RS 2477 right of way had not been established), cert. denied, 523 U.S. 1072 (1998).

3. The court interprets the statute as "borrowing" or incorporating state law on some questions. Is such "borrowing" appropriate, when Congress had not plainly indicated any deference to state law? Does it downgrade the national interest in these lands? Is lack of a uniform rule across all federal lands (variety from state to state) a problem? To whom? Compare the discussion of preemption in Chapter 3, infra pp. 206–26.

4. Under the "reasonable and necessary" standard borrowed from state law to determine the scope of the right-of-way here, what were the types of use to which the road had been put prior to repeal of RS 2477? Should those be categorized broadly (e.g., industrial uses) or narrowly (to transport livestock)? How the use is categorized may affect the determination of what is "reasonable and necessary" for that type of use. Might this standard be construed as allowing Garfield County to build an eight-lane freeway over the Burr Trail?

5. Where a valid RS 2477 right was established, what happens if the United States conveys the underlying fee to a private party? Because RS 2477 was on the books for more than a century, and because during that time the United States conveyed away many millions of acres of land into state or private ownership, much of that now nonfederal acreage might be encumbered with RS 2477 rights. The more generously RS 2477 is interpreted today, then, the more it might threaten or restrict these private property rights. In some situations, the U.S. Forest Service has reportedly sought to argue that public highways have been established under RS 2477 in order to gain access over private land to national forests for timber and recreational use.

6. The Burr Trail saga is one of the longest-running controversies in public land law, and it still goes on. For more recent decisions, see Sierra Club v. Lujan, 949 F.2d 362 (10th Cir.1991); United States v. Garfield

County, 122 F.Supp.2d 1201 (D.Utah 2000). The latter case held that the County's grading and widening of an existing dirt path to make it passable by vehicles prior to reservation of the underlying land as part of the national park was sufficient "construction" to perfect the County's right of way in the road, but that the County needed permission from the National Park Service to widen and realign the roadway, and its failure to obtain permission before going forward was actionable trespass, and the proper measure of damages was the cost of revegetating the excavated area.

7. Other decisions addressing the federal land manager's authority to regulate valid RS 2477 rights-of-way include United States v. Vogler, 859 F.2d 638, 642 (9th Cir.1988) (even assuming R.S. 2477 right-of-way was established before a National Park Preserve was created, National Park Service may regulate its use by a miner through a permit requirement to "conserve the natural beauty of the Preserve"); Wilkenson v. Department of Interior, 634 F.Supp. 1265 (D.Colo.1986) (National Park Service may regulate but not prohibit access pursuant to R.S. 2477 right-of-way created before National Monument was established).

8. R.S. 2477 has emerged, especially in Utah and Alaska, as a major argument of opponents of wilderness and other conservation measures. In Utah, for example, the state and counties have asserted more than 10,000 claims of R.S. 2477 rights-of-way. Many of these are based on tracks left long ago by mining explorationists which have never been maintained by the counties. The Clinton Administration tried to promulgate regulations to govern validity determinations and the exercise of R.S. 2477 rights-of-way, see proposed regulations at 59 Fed. Reg. 39216 (1994), but the Congress prevented the implementation of new regulations without its consent in an appropriation rider. See 110 Stat. 3009, § 101(d) (1996).

9. Other ancient right of way statutes also repealed by FLPMA (subject to valid existing rights) can raise similar questions. See City & County of Denver v. Bergland, 695 F.2d 465 (10th Cir.1982); Tom Lustig, Recent Struggles for Control of the Public Lands: Shall We "Deliver It up to Wild Beasts?," 57 U.Colo.L.Rev. 593, 601–06 (1986).

In an obscure section of the Alaska National Interest Lands Conservation Act (ANILCA) of 1980, 16 U.S.C. § 3170, Congress addressed the issue of access to non-federal land across certain kinds of federal land, as follows:

> Sec. 1323. (a) Notwithstanding any other provision of law, and subject to such terms and conditions as the Secretary of Agriculture may prescribe, the Secretary shall provide such access to nonfederally owned land within the boundaries of the National Forest System as the Secretary deems adequate to secure to the owner the reasonable use and enjoyment thereof: *Provided*, That such owner comply with rules and regulations applicable to ingress and egress to or from the National Forest System.

(b) Notwithstanding any other provision of law, and subject to such terms and conditions as the Secretary of the Interior may prescribe, the Secretary shall provide such access to nonfederally owned land surrounded by public lands managed by the Secretary under the Federal Land Policy and Management Act of 1976 (43 U.S.C. 1701–82) as the Secretary deems adequate to secure to the owner the responsible use and enjoyment thereof: *Provided*, That such owner comply with rules and regulations applicable to access across public lands.

1.   This statute raises a number of interpretive questions. See generally Steven P. Quarles & Thomas Lundquist, You Can Get There From Here: The Alaska Lands Act's Innovations in the Law of Access Across Federal Lands, XXII Land & Water L.Rev. 347 (1987). First, because it was adopted as part of a major piece of federal lands legislation that otherwise applied only to Alaska, does it apply to federal lands outside of Alaska? In Montana Wilderness Association v. United States Forest Service, 655 F.2d 951 (9th Cir.1981), cert. denied, 455 U.S. 989 (1982), the court held that subsection (a) does apply to national forest lands in the lower forty-eight states. It reached this result primarily because a congressional conference committee, convened three weeks *after* final passage of ANILCA to reconcile differences between the House and Senate versions of a wilderness bill for Colorado, interpreted this section as applying to lands in Colorado. The Ninth Circuit also suggested, in *dictum,* that subsection (b) of this ANILCA section (dealing with access across "public lands") applies only in Alaska, because ANILCA specifically defines "public lands" as certain lands "situated in Alaska." See 16 U.S.C. § 3102(3). 655 F.2d at 954. The Interior Board of Land Appeals has considered but not yet rendered a definitive ruling on the question. See Alvin R. Platz, 114 IBLA 8, 11–12 n. 2 (1990). In United States v. Srnsky, 271 F.3d 595 (4th Cir.2001), the Fourth Circuit questioned the Ninth Circuit's conclusion that subsection (a) applies outside of Alaska, in part because it thought it clear that subsection (b) applied only in Alaska, but ultimately decided the matter on other grounds without rendering a definitive ruling on the issue.*

2.   *Montana Wilderness Ass'n* upheld a claim by Burlington Northern Inc. (BN), which owned timberland checkerboarded within the Gallatin National Forest near Bozeman, Montana (the legacy of the Northern Pacific Land Grant Act of 1864) that this section gave it a right of access to its land, but did not address the extent to which BN's access could be regulated by the Forest Service in order to protect other values. BN was seeking to build an access road in order to remove timber from its land. Eventually the matter was mooted when BN and the Forest Service entered into a major land exchange, ultimately approved by Congress, that removed BN's inholdings from the forest. See Gallatin Range Consolidation and

---

* Congress has sometimes addressed access in specific conservation legislation in the lower 48; e.g., major California Desert legislation enacted in 1994 directed the Secretary of the Interior to "provide adequate access to nonfederally owned land or interests in land within the boundaries of the conservation units and wilderness areas" it designated "which will provide the owner * * * the reasonable use and enjoyment thereof." 16 U.S.C. § 410aaa–78.

Protection Act of 1993, 107 Stat. 987; see also Gallatin Land Consolidation Act of 1998, 112 Stat. 2371.

3.   The ultimate issue in the *Montana Wilderness Ass'n* case was whether the areas of federal land around the Burlington Northern inholdings might be preserved unroaded as wilderness. A section of the Wilderness Act (16 U.S.C. § 1134(a)) specifically addresses access to non-federal inholdings in federal wilderness areas:

> [W]here State-owned or privately-owned land is completely surrounded by national forest [wilderness] lands * * *, such State or private owner shall be given such rights as may be necessary to assure adequate access to such State-owned or privately owned land * * * or the State-owned or privately owned land shall be exchanged for federally owned land in the same State of approximately equal value * * *.

In a footnote in its opinion, the court suggested that in cases involving statutory wilderness areas, "the Secretary has the option of exchanging land of equal value so that the wilderness area may be preserved;" and therefore the Wilderness Act access provision "could be construed to apply in the specific case of a wilderness area, and [the ANILCA access provision] could be construed to apply in all other cases." 655 F.2d at 957 n.12.

4.   Apart from its geographical applicability, what are the dimensions of the "right of access" provided by the ANILCA provision? May the Secretary require the inholder to obtain a right-of-way permit before exercising the right? May the Secretary specify the route or means of access? May, for example, the Secretary require a route that is twice as costly as the inholder's preferred route, in order to avoid important wildlife habitat? May the Secretary allow access only by four-wheel drive vehicles, as opposed to passenger cars? Or by pack mule? Or by helicopter rather than across the surface? The Forest Service has adopted regulations implementing this section. See 36 C.F.R. Parts 251(B); 293; see also 36 C.F.R. § 212.6 (generic policy on ingress and egress). The preamble to the Forest Service's "roadless rule," discussed in Chapter 8 infra, p. 757, 66 Fed. Reg. 3244, 3253 (2001), said that under the ANILCA provision

> [a]ccess does not have to be a road in all cases, nor does it have to be the most economical, direct, or convenient for the landowner, although the agency tries to be sensitive to the cost in time and money to the inholder. The cost to construct or reconstruct road access to non-Federal lands is usually the responsibility of the inholder, not the Forest Service. During the application process for such access, applicable laws, such as the National Environmental Policy Act and the Endangered Species Act, still must be considered.

5.   Suppose the inholder's land derives from a homestead patent, and she now seeks to build a resort, and to pave a road through a pristine tract of federal land to accommodate thousands of tourists. May the Secretary forbid the pavement, and limit access to a crude dirt road? Compare footnote 15 in the *Leo Sheep* opinion, and the discussion of the scope of the right-of-way in *Sierra Club v. Hodel* (Burr Trail).

6.   Jenks owned three ranches in Catron County, New Mexico, each of which required access across national forest land. The Forest Service sought to require him to apply for and obtain "special use permits" under the ANILCA access provision, but he refused, and in the spring of 1990 the Forest Service sued him to compel compliance. In United States v. Jenks, 22 F.3d 1513 (10th Cir.1994), the court held that the Forest Service could use a permit system to regulate a landowner's statutory right of access under the ANILCA section, but that the district court erred in failing to adjudicate the inholder's claim that he had a right growing out of a land patent or the common law to access greater than that granted in the ANILCA statute. On remand the district court held again for the government, finding the defendant had no prexisting patent or common law right of access. As the case was heading back to the court of appeals, the Forest Service unexpectedly granted Catron County thirty year public road easements to use the three access roads in question. Although the issues concerning the ANILCA statute were made moot because defendant could freely use the now public roads to access his ranches, the court went on to discuss defendant's counterclaim that he had a right of access over the three roads "free from government interference" under his patents or the common law. United States v. Jenks, 129 F.3d 1348 (10th Cir.1997). Regarding defendant's argument that he had a right by an easement of necessity, the court said there was no necessity because of the public road easements the County now possessed, and because defendant also had a statutory right of access under ANILCA, "albeit subject to reasonable government regulation." The court went on to say:

> If both the public road easements and statutory rights of access cease to exist, however, Defendant might successfully claim easements by necessity. *See* 4 Powell [*on Real Property* § 34.07 (rev.ed., 1997)] at 34–76 (better view is that public policy favoring land utilization applies where the original unity of ownership was in the government, as well as where such ownership was in a private individual); *but see* Rights-of-Way Across Nat'l Forests, 43 Op. Att'y Gen. 243, 255 (1980) (common law doctrine of easement by necessity does not apply to federal lands). But we need not now decide that hypothetical and unlikely situation.

The court also rejected defendant's argument that he had an easement by implication, arising from the Homestead Act of 1862, that could not be regulated by the government:

> To be sure, throughout our nation's western expansion, a right of access across government lands was implied if necessary to effectuate the purpose for which an inholding was granted. But it does not follow that the right of access accompanying the grant of an inholding was necessarily a property interest known as an implied easement. * * * Nothing in the Homestead Act of 1862 suggests that Congress intended to abrogate its right to regulate access over roads located on federal lands. * * * Thus, we reject Defendant's argument that he has implied easements for use of the access roads free from reasonable government regulation. This is not to say, however, that the government's imposition of onerous requirements on inholders seeking access rights which

are unrelated or disproportionate to any expected public benefit will never constitute arbitrary and capricious conduct in violation of law.

7. In Adams v. United States (I), 3 F.3d 1254 (9th Cir.1993) and Adams v. United States (II), 255 F.3d 787 (9th Cir. 2001), the court held that an inholder on national forest land in Nevada was required by the terms of federal laws like ANILCA to apply for a special use authorization from the Forest Service for any use of a road through forest land which exceeded use of the road for travel by the general public, or for access which would cause surface-disturbing activities. Finding these statutes preemptive of state common law claims, it rejected the inholder's argument that it had a common law easement that exempted it from the need to apply for a permit. Other cases support the idea that federal land managers have reasonably broad authority to regulate the manner and means of access, short of outright prohibition, regardless of the origin of the access right. Clouser v. Espy, 42 F.3d 1522 (9th Cir.1994); Elko County Board v. Glickman, 909 F.Supp. 759 (D.Nev.1995).

8. Compare United States v. Srnsky, 271 F.3d 595 (4th Cir.2001), where Snrsky's predecessor in interest had conveyed 742 acres to the U.S. for national forest purposes, and reserved an inholding of seven acres without expressly reserving a right of access to it. Concerned about the possible effects of road use on an endangered plant species in the area, the Forest Service demanded Srnsky apply for a special use permit to continue to use the road. The court held that Srnsky's allegation that he held a state common law implied easement could, if proved, be a good defense to the Forest Service's claim, because the court refused to construe ANILCA and other federal statutes applicable to the national forests to preempt state common law easement claims, distinguishing *Jenks* and *Adams.*

9. Lands acquired by the U.S. for conservation purposes, such as for wildlife refuges, may also raise difficult access issues. In Coupland v. Morton, 5 Envtl. L. Rptr. 20504 (E.D.Va.1975), aff'd, 526 F.2d 588 (4th Cir.1975), the U.S. Fish and Wildlife Service severely restricted access to adjacent private land along a barrier island beach in a Refuge because the increasing traffic was adversely affecting management. Plaintiff property owners challenged the restrictions on a variety of grounds, but the court denied relief. Later, however, political pressure forced the USFWS to relax the access rules, and a few years later Congress enacted a law permitting some full-time residents to commute across the refuge daily. 94 Stat. 958–59 (1980); see Michael J. Bean and Melanie J. Rowland, THE EVOLUTION OF NATIONAL WILDLIFE LAW 293–94 (3d ed. 1997).

CHAPTER 3

AUTHORITY ON THE PUBLIC LANDS: THE CONSTITUTION, THE NATIONAL GOVERNMENT AND THE STATES

Many contemporary as well as historical natural resource disputes involve the allocation of jurisdictional power between federal and state governments. The conflict among governments on the public lands has a history nearly as colorful as disputes involving miners, homesteaders, ranchers, and conservationists. Tensions among governments are inherent in our federal system, and are bound to continue, even if the rhetorical excess of the "Sagebrush Rebellion" and "County Supremacy" movements in the last quarter century is not repeated. While the federal government's ownership of federal lands and resources is seldom questioned, the question of which sovereign's law controls their management is raised every day. The answer is usually context-specific, requiring case-by-case analysis.

The starting point is, of course, the constitutional power of Congress. The commerce, treaty, and spending clauses of the U.S. Constitution have all had some relevance to the public lands. (and are discussed briefly in Section C, further below.) For the most part, however, federal-state conflicts over federal lands are governed by two constitutional provisions that deal specifically with federal lands and property: The "Enclave Clause" (Article I, § 8, cl. 17), and what has emerged as far more important, the "Property Clause," (Article IV, § 3, cl. 2). Section A of this chapter addresses the Enclave Clause; Section B, the Property Clause. Section C briefly examines other relevant constitutional powers, and Section D addresses preemption issues, where the question is whether Congress has overridden state law in particular situations. Section E explores some implications of federal sovereignty over federal lands, including regulatory and taxing immunities. Section F examines a separate constitutional limit on the power of Congress—the "takings" clause of the fifth amendment. Finally, Section G looks at a separate restriction on legislative and regulatory power, arising out of contracts the United States may enter into for the use of public resources. This restriction may not prevent the government from acting, but may result in the other party being able to rescind the contract and seek restitution of moneys paid. Although such limitations do not, strictly speaking, have a constitutional basis, they are close enough in operation to be treated along with takings in this chapter.

A. JURISDICTION WITHIN FEDERAL ENCLAVES

Article I, § 8, cl. 17 of the U.S. Constitution provides (emphasis supplied):

> Congress shall have power to exercise *exclusive Legislation* in all Cases whatsoever over such District (not exceeding ten Miles square) as may, by Cession of particular States, and the Acceptance of Congress, become the Seat of the Government of the United States, and *to exercise like Authority* over all Places *purchased* by the *Consent* of the Legislature of the State in which the Same shall be, for the Erection of Forts, Magazines, Arsenals, dock-Yards, and *other needful Buildings.*

This Clause's reference to "exclusive legislation" has always been interpreted as meaning "exclusive jurisdiction," e.g., United States v. Bevans, 16 U.S. (3 Wheat.) 336, 387 (1818). The lands to which this clause applies are commonly called "federal enclaves," and the clause has come to be known as the Enclave Clause. As described more fully in the notes following the next case, enclaves can be found sprinkled among practically all categories of federal land including some but not all military bases, post offices, and national parks. However, only about 6% of the federal lands fall wholly or partially in this category. There is, unfortunately, no systematic, unified, up-to-date catalogue of such lands readily available.

Fort Leavenworth R. Co. v. Lowe

Supreme Court of the United States, 1885.
114 U.S. 525.

■ MR. JUSTICE FIELD delivered the opinion of the court.

[Plaintiff railroad has, since 1880, owned a railroad within the federal Fort Leavenworth Military Reservation. The state levied a property tax on the railroad, which the railroad paid under protest. The railroad then brought suit, arguing that the property, being entirely within the Reservation, was exempt from state taxation.]

The land constituting the Reservation was part of the territory acquired in 1803 by cession from France, and, until the formation of the State of Kansas, and her admission into the Union, the United States possessed the rights of a proprietor, and had political dominion and sovereignty over it. For many years before that admission it had been reserved from sale by the proper authorities of the United States for military purposes, and occupied by them as a military post. The jurisdiction of the United States over it during this time was necessarily paramount. But in 1861 Kansas was admitted into the Union upon an equal footing with the original States, that is, with the same rights of political dominion and sovereignty, subject like them only to the Constitution of the United States. Congress might undoubtedly, upon such admission, have stipulated for retention of the political authority, dominion and legislative power of the United States over the Reservation, so long as it should be used for military purposes by the government; that is, it could have excepted the place from the jurisdiction of Kansas, as one needed for the uses of the general government. But from some cause, inadvertence perhaps, or over-confidence that a recession of such jurisdiction could be had whenever desired, no such stipulation or exception was made. The United States, therefore, retained, after the admission of the State, only the rights of an ordinary proprietor; except as an instrument for the execution of the powers of the general government, that part of the tract, which was actually used for a fort or military post, was beyond such control of the State, by taxation or otherwise, as would defeat its use for those purposes. So far as the land constituting the Reservation was not used for military purposes, the possession of the United States was only that of an individual proprietor. The State could have exercised, with reference to it, the same authority and jurisdiction which she could have exercised over similar property held by private parties. This defect in the jurisdiction of the United States was called to the attention of the government in 1872. * * * The Attorney General replied * * * that to restore the federal jurisdiction over the land included in the Reservation, it would be necessary to obtain from the State of Kansas a cession of jurisdiction, which he had no doubt would upon application be readily granted by the State Legislature. 14 Opin. Attorneys General, 33 [1872]. It does not appear from the record before us that such application was ever made; but, on the 22d of February, 1875, the Legislature of the State passed an act entitled "An Act to cede jurisdiction to the United States over the territory of the Fort Leavenworth Military Reservation," the first section of which is as follows:

"That exclusive jurisdiction be, and the same is hereby ceded to the United States over and within all the territory owned by the United States, and included within the limits of the United States military reservation known as the Fort Leavenworth Reservation in said State, as declared from time to time by the President of the United States, saving, however, to the said State the right to serve civil or criminal process within said Reservation, in suits or prosecutions for or on account of rights acquired, obligations incurred, or crimes committed in said State, but outside of said cession and Reservation; and saving further to said State the right to tax railroad, bridge, and other corporations, their franchises and property, on said Reservation." Laws of Kansas, 1875, p. 95.

The question as to the right of the plaintiff to recover back the taxes paid depends upon the validity and effect of the last saving clause in this act. As we have said, there is no evidence before us that any application was made by the United States for this legislation, but, as it conferred a benefit, the acceptance of the act is to be presumed in the absence of any dissent on their part. The contention of the plaintiff is that the act of cession operated under the Constitution to vest in the United States exclusive jurisdiction over the Reservation, and that the last saving clause, being inconsistent with that result, is to be rejected. [The opinion then quoted Art. 1, sec. 8, cl. 17.]

The necessity of complete jurisdiction over the place which should be selected as the seat of government was obvious to the framers of the Constitution. * * *

Upon the second part of the clause in question, giving power to "exercise like authority," that is, of exclusive legislation "over all places purchased by the consent of the Legislature of the State in which the same shall be, for the erection of forts, magazines, arsenals, dock-yards, and other needful buildings," the Federalist [No. 43] observes that the necessity of this authority is not less evident. "The public money expended on such places," it adds, "and the public property deposited in them, require that they should be exempt from the authority of the particular State. Nor would it be proper for the places on which the security of the entire Union may depend to be in any degree dependent on a particular member of it. All objections and scruples are here also obviated by requiring the concurrence of the States concerned in every such establishment." "The power," says Mr. Justice Story, repeating the substance of Mr. Madison's language, "is wholly unexceptionable, since it can only be exercised at the will of the State, and therefore it is placed beyond all reasonable scruple." [quoting Story's Constitutional Commentaries, vol. 2, § 1219] This power of exclusive legislation is to be exercised, as thus seen, over places purchased, by consent of the Legislatures of the States in which they are situated, for the specific purposes enumerated. It would seem to have been the opinion of the framers of the Constitution that, without the consent of the States, the new government would not be able to acquire lands within them. * * *.

But not only by direct purchase have the United States been able to acquire lands they needed without the consent of the States, but it has been held [in Kohl v. U.S., 91 U.S. 367 (1875)] that they possess the right of eminent domain within the States, using those terms, not as expressing the ultimate dominion or title to property, but as indicating the right to take private property for public uses when needed to execute the powers conferred by the Constitution; and that the general government is not dependent upon the caprice of individuals or the will of State Legislatures in the acquisition of such lands as may be required for the full and effective exercise of its powers. * * *

Besides these modes of acquisition, the United States possessed, on the adoption of the Constitution, an immense domain lying north and west of the Ohio River, acquired as the result of the Revolutionary War from Great Britain, or by cessions from Virginia, Massachusetts and Connecticut; and, since the adoption of the Constitution, they have by cession from foreign countries, come into the ownership of a territory still larger, lying between the Mississippi River and the Pacific Ocean, and out of these territories several States have been formed and admitted into the Union. The proprietorship of the United States in large tracts of land within these States has remained after their admission. There has been, therefore, no necessity for them to purchase or to condemn lands within those States, for forts, arsenals, and other public buildings, unless they had disposed of what they afterwards needed. Having the title, they have usually reserved certain portions of their lands from sale or other disposition, for the uses of the government.

This brief statement as to the different modes in which the United States have acquired title to lands upon which public buildings have been erected will serve to explain the nature of their jurisdiction over such places * * *. When the title is acquired by purchase by consent of the Legislatures of the States, the federal jurisdiction is exclusive of all State authority. This follows from the declaration of the Constitution that Congress shall have "like authority" over such places as it has over the district which is the seat of government; that is, the power of "exclusive legislation in all cases whatsoever." Broader or clearer language could not be used to exclude all other authority than that of Congress; and that no other authority can be exercised over them has been the uniform opinion of Federal and State tribunals, and of the Attorneys General. The reservation which has usually accompanied the consent of the States that civil and criminal process of the State courts may be served in the places purchased, is not considered as interfering in any respect with the supremacy of the United States over them; but is admitted to prevent them from becoming an asylum for fugitives from justice. * * *

* * * These authorities are sufficient to support the proposition which follows naturally from the language of the Constitution, that no other legislative power than that of Congress can be exercised over lands within a State purchased by the United States with her consent for one of the purposes designated; and that such consent under the Constitution operates to exclude all other legislative authority.

But with reference to lands owned by the United States, acquired by purchase without the consent of the State, or by cessions from other governments, the case is different. Story, in his Commentaries on the Constitution, says: "If there has been no cession by the State of the place, although it has been constantly occupied and used under purchase, or otherwise, by the United States for a fort or arsenal, or other constitutional purpose, the State jurisdiction still remains complete and perfect" * * *.

Where, therefore, lands are acquired in any other way by the United States within the limits of a State than by purchase with her consent, they will hold the lands subject to this qualification: that if upon them forts, arsenals, or other public buildings are erected for the uses of the general government, such buildings, with their appurtenances, as instrumentalities for the execution of its powers, will be free from any such interference and jurisdiction of the State as would destroy or impair their effective use for the purposes designed. Such is the law with reference to all instrumentalities created by the general government. Their exemption from State control is essential to the independence and sovereign authority of the United States within the sphere of their delegated powers. But, when not used as such instrumentalities, the legislative power of the State over the places acquired will be as full and complete as over any other places within her limits.

As already stated, the land constituting the Fort Leavenworth Military Reservation was not purchased, but was owned by the United States by cession from France many years before Kansas became a State; and whatever political sovereignty and dominion the United States had over the place comes from the cession of the State since her admission into the Union. It not being a case where exclusive legislative authority is vested by the Constitution of the United States, that cession could be accompanied with such conditions as the State might see fit to annex not inconsistent with the free and effective use of the fort as a military post. * * *

The Military Reservation of Fort Leavenworth was not, as already said, acquired by purchase with the consent of Kansas. And her cession of jurisdiction is not of exclusive legislative authority over the land, except so far as that may be necessary for its use as a military post; and it is not contended that the saving clause in the act of cession interferes with such use. There is, therefore, no constitutional prohibition against the enforcement of that clause. The right of the State to subject the railroad property to taxation exists as before the cession. The invalidity of the tax levied not being asserted on any other ground than the supposed exclusive jurisdiction of the United States over the reservation notwithstanding the saving clause, the judgment of the court below must be

Affirmed.

NOTES AND QUESTIONS

1. Was the Fort Leavenworth land "purchased?" If so, was it purchased with the "consent" of the state, under the terms of the Enclave Clause? Did Kansas cede "exclusive" jurisdiction over Fort Leavenworth to the United States?

2. To the extent any of the answers in the first paragraph is no, is Kansas's cession governed by the Enclave Clause, or something else? What else? Put another way, if the Enclave Clause were the sole basis for the adjustment of jurisdiction on public lands, would the State's cession of jurisdiction have been void?

3. What do you suppose was the intent behind the Enclave Clause? Did the Court construe the clause strictly in accordance with its intent? If the Clause were strictly or literally construed, would it prevent the United States from condemning state or private land in a state for use for federal purposes (e.g., a military base) without state consent? (In fact, it has long been held that Congress possesses an inherent power of eminent domain, acknowledged in the fifth amendment, as an attribute of its sovereignty, see, e.g., United States v. Gettysburg Elec. R. Co., 160 U.S. 668 (1896), Chapter 2, § C1, and it has long been assumed that this power can be exercised in a state without its consent.)

4. In James v. Dravo Contracting Co., 302 U.S. 134 (1937), the Court construed the Enclave Clause's reference to "other needful buildings" to include "whatever structures are found to be necessary in the performance of the functions of the Federal Government," such as federal dams and locks constructed to improve navigation. *James* also followed *Fort Leavenworth* by upholding the state's reservation of concurrent jurisdiction despite the clause's reference to "exclusive" federal jurisdiction. The next year, in Collins v. Yosemite Park & Curry Co., 304 U.S. 518 (1938), the Court reviewed the complex series of statutes creating Yosemite National Park. The Park was comprised of both federal public domain land and

acquired land (the United States had conveyed Yosemite Valley and the Mariposa Big Tree Grove of giant sequoias to California in 1864 and reacquired it in 1906). California had ceded jurisdiction to the U.S. in 1919, but had reserved the right to tax specified transactions. Noting that the Enclave Clause "has never been strictly construed," the Court upheld the arrangement and made it clear that the states and the federal government were free to adjust jurisdiction wholly outside of the strictures of the Enclave Clause:

> The United States has large bodies of public lands. These properties are used for forests, parks, ranges, wild life sanctuaries, flood control, and other purposes which are not covered by Clause 17. In Silas Mason Co. v. Tax Commission of Washington, 302 U.S. 186 [1937] we upheld in accordance with the arrangements of the State and National Governments the right of the United States to acquire private property for use in "the reclamation of arid and semiarid lands" and to hold its purchases subject to state jurisdiction. In other instances, it may be deemed important or desirable by the National Government and the State Government in which the particular property is located that exclusive jurisdiction be vested in the United States by cession or consent. No question is raised as to the authority to acquire land or provide for national parks. As the National Government may, "by virtue of its sovereignty" acquire lands within the borders of states by eminent domain and without their consent, the respective sovereignties should be in a position to adjust their jurisdictions. There is no constitutional objection to such an adjustment of rights.

5.   If it is not found in the Enclave Clause, what is the authority for the United States to enter into these consensual arrangements with states which allocate jurisdiction over federal lands? The Property Clause (considered further below)? The inherent power of the U.S. as a sovereign? Is the Court in these cases essentially saying that consensual jurisdictional arrangements over federal land which are reached through the political processes of the state and federal governments will be enforced by the courts without serious scrutiny, because the political processes of both governments provide a sensible check on their content? Is there anything objectionable about that?

6.   In fact, states have often attached conditions or retained some jurisdictional powers in ceding jurisdiction over particular tracts of federal land to the federal government. The result is that jurisdictional arrangements on enclaves may be quite complex. See generally George Coggins & Robert Glicksman, 1 PUBLIC NATURAL RESOURCES LAW (1990), § 3.03[2]. The Public Land Law Review Commission somewhat understatedly called the patchwork and haphazard character of these cessions "a jumbled condition." ONE THIRD OF THE NATION'S LAND 278 (1970). Most of the federal land subject to such formal cessions of state jurisdiction involve land managed by the military or the National Park Service.

7.   The obscurity as well as complexity of these cessions of jurisdiction can lay traps for the unwary. For example, in United States v. 319.88 Acres of Land, 498 F.Supp. 763 (D.Nev.1980), the United States condemned a

private inholding in the Nevada portion of the Lake Mead National Recreation Area, part of the National Park System and managed by the National Park Service. At issue was the fair market value of the land. The property owner claimed the value was $880,000, calculated on the assumption its highest use was for a gambling casino. The U.S. discovered just before trial that Nevada had in 1974 ceded to the U.S. jurisdiction over all land within the external boundaries of the Lake Mead National Recreation Area, including this private inholding. The state cession had reserved only the right to serve process on the land. Therefore, relying on a Park Service regulation prohibiting gambling "on privately owned lands within park areas under the legislative jurisdiction of the United States," the U.S. argued the value was only $240,000, because the highest non-gambling use of the property was for recreational homesites. The U.S. prevailed.

8.   Why would a state ever want to voluntarily relinquish a piece of its sovereignty, by ceding to the U.S. partial or exclusive jurisdiction over an area of land within its borders?

9.   Must a cession of jurisdiction be express? In United States v. Brown, 552 F.2d 817, 819 (8th Cir.), cert. denied, 431 U.S. 949 (1977), and United States v. Armstrong, 186 F.3d 1055 (8th Cir.1999), cert. denied, 529 U.S. 1033 (2000), the court of appeals held that the state of Minnesota had effectively ceded jurisdiction over the waters of Voyageurs National Park (VNP). The cession was not express. The state had participated in and supported the creation of the VNP. A few months before federal legislation creating the park was signed into law in late 1971, the state had enacted legislation donating to the United States 25,000 acres of state-owned land within the boundaries of the 219,000 acre VNP. While the state did not transfer its claim of ownership (based on the assumption that the waters were navigable at statehood) of the beds of 80,000 acres of lakes within the park to the federal government, the court of appeals held in *Brown* that the state had effectively ceded jurisdiction over the waters. This holding was reaffirmed "without reservation" in *Armstrong,* even though the state had, in 1995, enacted another statute providing that "[o]wnership of and jurisdiction over these waters and their beds has not been ceded by the state, either expressly or implicitly, to the United States." The court said this was ineffective based on prior Supreme Court decisions holding that once a state cedes jurisdiction under the Enclave Clause, it cannot unilaterally reassert it. See, e.g., Paul v. United States, 371 U.S. 245, 264 (1963).

10.   An 1841 statute, 5 Stat. 468, forbade the expenditure of public money on "any site or land hereafter purchased by the United States" for the purposes of erecting public buildings of any kind until the "consent of the legislature of the State in which the land or site may be shall be given to such purchaser." In 1940, the statute (40 U.S.C. § 255) was amended to drop the requirement of state consent to purchase and to allow agencies of the national government, "in such cases and at such times as [they] may deem desirable, accept or secure from the State in which [the lands are situated] * * * consent to or cession of such jurisdiction, exclusive or partial * * * over any such lands or interests as [they] may deem desirable * * *."

NOTE: ASSIMILATION OF STATE LAW IN FEDERAL ENCLAVES

Even where states have ceded jurisdiction over federal land and the U.S. has accepted the cession, the Congress can give some jurisdiction back to the states, by specific or generic legislation. In fact, several federal statutes address matters of state and federal jurisdiction within enclaves. The Buck Act, enacted in 1947, 4 U.S.C. §§ 104–110, allows states to collect uniform income, gasoline, sales, and use taxes within enclaves, although direct taxation of the United States and federal instrumentalities (such as officers' clubs, United States v. State Tax Comm'n, 412 U.S. 363 (1973)), is barred. Other statutes allow state unemployment and workers' compensation laws to apply to persons who live and work on federal lands, including federal enclaves. 26 U.S.C. § 3305(d); 40 U.S.C. § 290. State property taxes do not reach federal property, but federal Impact Aid payments are made to local school districts serving children of federal employees living on federal property, whether or not they are within federal enclaves. 20 U.S.C. §§ 236–244, 631–647. In the area of civil liberties, the Supreme Court, in Evans v. Cornman, 398 U.S. 419 (1970), held that the Fourteenth Amendment requires states to allow residents of federal enclaves to vote in state elections.

In 1825 Congress passed the first Assimilative Crimes Act to provide a body of criminal laws for federal enclaves. The Act, now codified at 18 U.S.C. § 13, "assimilates" criminal laws of the host state when no federal law applies, and provides for prosecution in federal court under the "borrowed" state substantive law:

> Whoever within or upon any of the places now existing or hereafter reserved or acquired as provided in section 7 of this title, is guilty of any act or omission which, although not made punishable by any enactment of Congress, would be punishable if committed or omitted within the jurisdiction of the State, Territory, Possession, or District in which such place is situated, by the laws thereof in force at the time of such act or omission, shall be guilty of a like offense and subject to a like punishment.

18 U.S.C. § 7, referred to in the Assimilative Crimes Act, defines lands covered by the Act as follows:

> Any lands reserved or acquired for the use of the United States, and under the exclusive or concurrent jurisdiction thereof, or any place purchased or otherwise acquired by the United States by consent of the legislature of the State in which the same shall be, for the erection of a fort, magazine, arsenal, dockyard, or other needful building.

The Assimilative Crimes Act was challenged on the ground that it is beyond Congress's power to incorporate state laws enacted after the Act's effective date. In United States v. Sharpnack, 355 U.S. 286 (1958), for example, the prosecution was based upon sex crimes as defined in a 1950 Texas statute, but the most recent reenactment of the Assimilative Crimes Act had been in 1948. The Court rejected the challenge, upholding dynamic, ongoing incorporation of state laws.

There is no comprehensive, ongoing incorporation of state *civil* as opposed to criminal laws in federal enclaves. This can lead to anomalous results. In Arlington Hotel Co. v. Fant, 278 U.S. 439 (1929), plaintiff hotel guests sued to recover the value of their property lost when the hotel in Hot Springs National Park burned down. In 1832, Congress had reserved four sections of federal land, including where the hotel was located, for medicinal purposes. In 1903 Arkansas ceded, and the United States in 1904 accepted, "sole and exclusive jurisdiction" over the resort. At that time Arkansas common law made the innkeeper an insurer of guests' property, but in 1913 the Arkansas law was changed to make the innkeeper liable only for negligence. There concededly being no contrary federal law, plaintiffs claimed, and the Arkansas courts held, that the cession effectively "froze" the law applicable to Hot Springs as of 1904, making the innkeeper strictly liable without proof of negligence, even though the hotel fire occurred in 1920. The Supreme Court, without discussion, agreed. The rationale is a principle borrowed from international law; namely, that "whenever political jurisdiction and legislative power over any territory are transferred from one nation or sovereign to another," those laws "intended for the protection of private rights" of the country losing jurisdiction "continue in force until abrogated or changed by the new government or sovereign." Chicago, Rock Island & Pac. R. Co. v. McGlinn, 114 U.S. 542, 546 (1885). Interestingly, the *Arlington Hotel* litigation originated in state court, even though the state had ceded "sole and exclusive jurisdiction" over the area to the federal government. Although the Supreme Court did not directly address the matter in that case, it seems that state courts may, if they choose to do so, exercise jurisdiction over causes of action arising under federal law in enclaves, even when the state does not expressly reserve such authority.

In 1928, Congress had provided a measure of assimilation of civil law by incorporating on an ongoing basis state wrongful death and personal injury laws. 16 U.S.C. § 457; Morgan v. United States, 709 F.2d 580 (9th Cir.1983). But under *Arlington Hotel*, other state civil laws in effect at the time the state cedes and the U.S. accepts jurisdiction are effectively frozen until altered by Congress. E.g., James Stewart & Co. v. Sadrakula, 309 U.S. 94 (1940); Pacific Coast Dairy v. Department of Agriculture, 318 U.S. 285 (1943). In a few instances, federal land management agencies have assimilated state civil laws selectively by administrative action. A notable example is the Park Service's incorporation of state fishing laws that do not conflict with federal laws or regulations. 36 C.F.R. § 2.3(a) (2001). Violators of the incorporated state laws are prosecuted before federal magistrates.

NOTES AND QUESTIONS ON ASSIMILATING STATE LAW IN ENCLAVES

1. Does borrowing this principle from international law make sense in this context, where the "new" sovereign, the United States, does not normally pass laws implementing the full range of police powers? Assuming no federal law exists on the subject today, what law applies to an innkeep-

er's liability for property loss that occurs in 2001 in Hot Springs National Park?

2. Should Congress pass a comprehensive "Assimilative Civil Law Act" to eliminate the problem raised by Arlington Hotel v. Fant? Congress took a preliminary step in 1976 by granting the Interior Department authority to cede back to states all or part of federal jurisdiction within units of the National Park System, 16 U.S.C. § 1a–3, but it appears the authority has been employed sparingly.

B. THE PROPERTY CLAUSE

For most practical purposes relating to federal land management, the Enclave Clause is now overshadowed by the Property Clause. That Clause, Article IV, § 3, cl. 2, provides, in pertinent part, that "[t]he Congress shall have Power to dispose of and make all needful Rules and Regulations respecting the Territory or other Property belonging to the United States * * *." Background on adoption of the Property Clause is set out in section B of Chapter 2, pp. 47–48 supra. A major early case read this clause broadly in addressing the right of the federal government to establish policies regarding management of public lands before states were created over them. See United States v. Gratiot (1840), supra p. 49.

As new states were created, other questions arose. The first was one of title: did the state obtain title to all or part of federal lands found within their borders at statehood? Pollard v. Hagan, 44 U.S. (3 How.) 212 (1845), Chapter 2, § B, supra p. 52, held that the states did, under the equal footing doctrine, come into title of lands underlying navigable waters. But the United States retained title to large amounts of other land, not under navigable waters, in new states. Except for the relatively few situations in which a state formally ceded partial or whole jurisdiction over these lands to the U.S., the question remained: Did the federal government have only the proprietary powers of an ordinary private owner of these lands, or could it assert the far more expansive power of a sovereign? Some early cases contained suggestions that federal power was limited to that of a proprietor. But after the disastrous and wholly anomalous view of the property clause embraced by the Supreme Court in the *Dred Scott* decision (see p. 51 supra), the Court began again to speak broadly of congressional power under the Property Clause. In Gibson v. Chouteau, 80 U.S. (13 Wall.) 92, 99 (1872), for example, the Court upheld the claim of the holder of a federal patent to land in the State of Missouri against a competing claim by another who was relying on state law. The Court repeated that Congress's power under the Property Clause "is subject to no limitations;" that Congress has an "absolute right" to decide upon the disposition of federal land; and that "[n]o State legislation can interfere with this right or embarrass its exercise." *Gibson* was followed by decisions in which the Supreme Court moved toward an explicit recognition of federal sovereign as well as proprietary power over federal lands. Leading cases here are Camfield v. United States, 167 U.S. 518 (1897), Chapter 2, § B6, supra pp.

92, and Light v. United States, 220 U.S. 523 (1911), Chapter 2, § C1, supra pp. 110.

In 1917 a unanimous Supreme Court, speaking through a Justice from Wyoming, Willis Van Devanter, seemed to definitively resolve the matter. Utah Power & Light Co. v. United States, 243 U.S. 389 (1917). The utility had built electric generation works on national forests in Utah without federal permission., and argued Utah law should apply, because there had been no cession of jurisdiction by the state under the Enclave Clause. The Court replied:

> To this we cannot assent. Not only does the Constitution (Art. IV, § 3, cl. 2) commit to Congress the power "to dispose of and make all needful rules and regulations respecting" the lands of the United States, but the settled course of legislation, congressional and state, and repeated decisions of this court have gone upon the theory that the power of Congress is exclusive and that only through its exercise in some form can rights in lands belonging to the United States be acquired. True, for many purposes a State has civil and criminal jurisdiction over lands within its limits belonging to the United States, but this jurisdiction does not extend to any matter that is not consistent with full power in the United States to protect its lands, to control their use and to prescribe in what manner others may acquire rights in them. Thus while the State may punish public offenses, such as murder or larceny, committed on such lands, and may tax private property, such as live stock, located thereon, it may not tax the lands themselves or invest others with any right whatever in them. United States v. McBratney, 104 U.S. 621, 624 * * * From the earliest times Congress by its legislation, applicable alike in the States and Territories, has regulated in many particulars the use by others of the lands of the United States, has prohibited and made punishable various acts calculated to be injurious to them or to prevent their use in the way intended, and has provided for and controlled the acquisition of rights of way over them for highways, railroads, canals, ditches, telegraph lines and the like. The States and the public have almost uniformly accepted this legislation as controlling, and in the instances where it has been questioned in this court its validity has been upheld and its supremacy over state enactments sustained. * * * Camfield v. United States, * * * Light v. United States. And so we are of opinion that the inclusion within a State of lands of the United States does not take from Congress the power to control their occupancy and use, to protect them from trespass and injury and to prescribe the conditions upon which others may obtain rights in them, even though this may involve the exercise in some measure of what commonly is known as the police power. "A different rule," as was said in Camfield v. United States, supra, "would place the public domain of the United States completely at the mercy of state legislation."

It results that state laws, including those relating to the exercise of the power of eminent domain, have no bearing upon a controversy such as is here presented, save as they may have been adopted or made applicable by Congress.

Only a handful of cases raising Property Clause issues were decided over the succeeding years. In McKelvey v. United States, 260 U.S. 353 (1922), three sheepherders were denied passage over public lands by defendant cattle ranchers who, after warning and threatening them, "shot and seriously injured one of [them], threatened to finish him, and did other things calculated to put all three in terror." The ranchers were convicted of violating that part of the Unlawful Inclosures Act which prohibits any person, "by force, threats, [or] intimidation" from preventing or obstructing anyone "from peaceably entering upon * * * any tract of public land." 43 U.S.C. § 1063. On appeal, defendants claimed Congress's prescription of criminal penalties was beyond its power and an encroachment on the state police power. Writing for the Court, Justice Van Devanter would have none of it: "It is firmly settled that Congress may prescribe rules respecting the use of the public lands. It may sanction some uses and prohibit others, and may forbid interference with such as are sanctioned." In Hunt v. United States, 278 U.S. 96, 100 (1928), the Court summarily brushed aside Arizona's argument that the U.S. could not kill large numbers of deer on federal lands in northern Arizona without conforming to state law.* The Court said simply that "the power of the United States to * * * protect its lands and property does not admit of doubt, * * * the game laws or any other statute of the state to the contrary notwithstanding." See also Ashwander v. Tennessee Valley Authority, 297 U.S. 288, 335–37 (1936) ("it lies in the discretion of the Congress, acting in the public interest, to determine of how much of [its] property it shall dispose"); United States v. San Francisco, 310 U.S. 16, 29 (1940) (the "power over the public land" given to Congress in the Property Clause "is without limitations").

Over the twentieth century, through world wars, a great economic depression, and then unparalleled growth and prosperity, public land policy and law changed considerably. Reservation and management for conservation as well as development replaced disposition as fundamental national public land policy. New ideas, such as protecting wild (feral) horses and burros, were incorporated into federal law.

Kleppe v. New Mexico

Supreme Court of the United States, 1976.
426 U.S. 529.

■ MR. JUSTICE MARSHALL delivered the opinion of the Court.

At issue in this case is whether Congress exceeded its powers under the Constitution in enacting the Wild Free–Roaming Horses and Burros Act.

---

* The program was conducted after elimination of the deer's chief predators—mountain lions, coyotes, wolves, bobcats and eagles—to protect local ranching operations caused the deer population to explode more than twentyfold in fewer than two decades. See Joseph Wood Krutch, THE GRAND CANYON 215 (1957).

[The Act], 16 U.S.C. §§ 1331–1340, was enacted in 1971 to protect "all unbranded and unclaimed horses and burros on public lands of the United States," § 2(b) of the Act, 16 U.S.C. § 1332(b), from "capture, branding, harassment, or death." § 1 of the Act, 16 U.S.C. § 1331. The Act provides that all such horses and burros on the public lands administered by the Secretary of the Interior through the Bureau of Land Management (BLM) or by the Secretary of Agriculture through the Forest Service are committed to the jurisdiction of the respective Secretaries, who are "directed to protect and manage [the animals] as components of the public lands * * * in a manner that is designed to achieve and maintain a thriving natural ecological balance on the public lands." § 3(a) of the Act, 16 U.S.C. § 1333(a).* If protected horses or burros "stray from public lands onto privately owned land, the owners of such land may inform the nearest Federal marshall or agent of the Secretary, who shall arrange to have the animals removed."[1] § 4 of the Act, 16 U.S.C. § 1334.

Section 6 of the Act, 16 U.S.C. § 1336, authorizes the Secretaries to promulgate regulations, see 36 CFR § 231.11 (1975) (Agriculture); 43 CFR pt. 4710 (1975) (Interior), and to enter into cooperative agreements with other landowners and with state and local governmental agencies in furtherance of the Act's purposes. On August 7, 1973, the Secretaries executed such an agreement with the New Mexico Livestock Board (the Livestock Board), the agency charged with enforcing the New Mexico Estray Law, N.Mex.Stat.Ann. § 47–14–1 et seq. (1953).[2] The agreement acknowledged the authority of the Secretaries to manage and protect the wild free-roaming horses and burros on the public lands of the United States within the State and established a procedure for evaluating the claims of private parties to ownership of such animals.

The Livestock Board terminated the agreement three months later. Asserting that the Federal Government lacked power to control wild horses and burros on the public lands of the United States unless the animals were moving in interstate commerce or damaging the public lands and that neither of these bases of regulation was available here, the Board notified the Secretaries of its intent

"to exercise all regulatory impoundment and sale powers which it derives from the New Mexico Estray Law, over all estray horses, mules

* [Eds. note: The Act defines the "public lands" to include national forests as well as BLM-managed lands.]

1. The landowner may elect to allow straying wild free-roaming horses and burros to remain on his property, in which case he must so notify the relevant Secretary. He may not destroy any such animals, however. § 4 of the Act, 16 U.S.C. § 1334.

2. Under the New Mexico law, an estray is defined as:

"Any bovine animal, horse, mule or ass, found running at large upon public or private lands, either fenced or unfenced, in the state of New Mexico, whose owner is unknown in the section where found, or which shall be fifty [50] miles or more from the limits of its usual range or pasture, or that is branded with a brand which is not on record in the office of the cattle sanitary board of New Mexico * * *." N.Mex.Stat.Ann. § 47–14–1 (Repl.1966).

It is not disputed that the animals regulated by the Wild Free–Roaming Horses and Burros Act are estrays within the meaning of this law.

or asses found running at large upon public or private lands within New Mexico * * *. This includes the right to go upon Federal or State lands to take possession of said horses or burros, should the Livestock Board so desire." App. 67, 72.

The differences between the Livestock Board and the Secretaries came to a head in February 1974. On February 1, 1974, a New Mexico rancher, Kelley Stephenson, was informed by BLM that several unbranded burros had been seen near Taylor Well, where Stephenson watered his cattle. Taylor Well is on federal property, and Stephenson had access to it and some 8,000 surrounding acres only through a grazing permit issued pursuant to the Taylor Grazing Act. After BLM made it clear to Stephenson that it would not remove the burros and after he personally inspected the Taylor Well area, Stephenson complained to the Livestock Board that the burros were interfering with his livestock operation by molesting his cattle and eating their feed.

Thereupon the Board rounded up and removed 19 unbranded and unclaimed burros pursuant to the New Mexico Estray Law. Each burro was seized on the public lands of the United States and, as the director of the Board conceded, each burro fit the definition of a wild free-roaming burro under § 2(b) of the Act. App. 43. On February 18, 1974, the Livestock Board, pursuant to its usual practice, sold the burros at a public auction. After the sale, BLM asserted jurisdiction under the Act and demanded that the Board recover the animals and return them to the public lands.

[New Mexico promptly sued the U.S. in federal district court, claiming the Wild Free–Roaming Horses and Burros Act was unconstitutional. The district court found the act unconstitutional because it] "conflicts with * * * the traditional doctrines concerning wild animals," 406 F.Supp. 1237, 1238 (1975), and is in excess of Congress' power under the Property Clause of the Constitution, Art. IV, § 3, cl. 2. That Clause, the court found, enables Congress to regulate wild animals found on the public land only for the "*protection* of the public lands from damage of some kind." 406 F.Supp., at 1239 (emphasis in original). Accordingly, this power was exceeded in this case because "[t]he statute is aimed at protecting the wild horses and burros, not at protecting the land they live on." Ibid.[6] We noted probable jurisdiction, 423 U.S. 818 (1975), and we now reverse.

* * * In passing the Wild Free–Roaming Horses and Burros Act, Congress deemed the regulated animals "an integral part of the natural system of the public lands" of the United States, § 1 of the Act, 16 U.S.C. § 1331, and found that their management was necessary "for achievement of an ecological balance on the public lands." According to Congress, these animals, if preserved in their native habitats, "contribute to the diversity of

6. The Court also held that the Act could not be sustained under the Commerce Clause because "all the evidence establishes that the wild burros in question here do not migrate across state lines" and "Congress made no findings to indicate that it was in any way relying on the Commerce Clause in enacting this statute." While the Secretary argues in this Court that the Act is sustainable under the Commerce Clause, we have no occasion to address this contention since we find the Act, as applied, to be permissible exercise of congressional power under the Property Clause.

life forms within the Nation and enrich the lives of the American people."
§ 1 of the Act, 16 U.S.C. § 1331. Indeed, Congress concluded, the wild free-
roaming horses and burros "are living symbols of the historic and pioneer
spirit of the West." § 1 of the Act, 16 U.S.C. § 1331. Despite their
importance, the Senate Committee found that these animals

> "have been cruelly captured and slain and their carcasses used in the
> production of pet food and fertilizer. They have been used for target
> practice and harassed for 'sport' and profit. In spite of public outrage,
> this bloody traffic continues unabated, and it is the firm belief of the
> committee that this senseless slaughter must be brought to an end."
> S.Rep. No. 92–242, 92d Cong., 1st Sess., 2 (1971), U.S.Code Cong. &
> Admin.News 1971, p. 2149.

For these reasons, Congress determined to preserve and protect the
wild free-roaming horses and burros on the public lands of the United
States. The question under the Property Clause is whether this determination can be sustained as a "needful" regulation "respecting" the public
lands. In answering this question, we must remain mindful that, while
courts must eventually pass upon them, determinations under the Property
Clause are entrusted primarily to the judgment of Congress. United States
v. San Francisco, 310 U.S. 16, 29–30 (1940); Light v. United States, 220
U.S. 523, 537 (1911); United States v. Gratiot, 14 Pet. 526, 537–538 (1840).

Appellees argue that the Act cannot be supported by the Property
Clause. They contend that the Clause grants Congress essentially two kinds
of power: (1) the power to dispose of and make incidental rules regarding
the use of federal property; and (2) the power to protect federal property.
According to appellees, the first power is not broad enough to support
legislation protecting wild animals that live on federal property; and the
second power is not implicated since the Act is designed to protect the
animals, which are not themselves federal property, and not the public
lands. As an initial matter, it is far from clear that the Act was not passed
in part to protect the public lands of the United States[7] or that Congress
cannot assert a property interest in the regulated horses and burros
superior to that of the State.[8] But we need not consider whether the Act
can be upheld on either of these grounds, for we reject appellees' narrow
reading of the Property Clause.

Appellees ground their argument on a number of cases that, upon
analysis, provide no support for their position. Like the District Court,
appellees cite Hunt v. United States, 278 U.S. 96 (1928), for the proposition
that the Property Clause gives Congress only the limited power to regulate
wild animals in order to protect the public lands from damage. But *Hunt*,
which upheld the Government's right to kill deer that were damaging
foliage in the national forests, only holds that damage to the land is a

---

7. Congress expressly ordered that the animals were to be managed and protected in order "to achieve and maintain a thriving natural ecological balance on the public lands." § 3(a), 16 U.S.C. § 1333(a).

8. The Secretary makes no claim here, however, that the United States owns the wild free-roaming horses and burros found on public land.

sufficient basis for regulation; it contains no suggestion that it is a necessary one.

Next appellees refer to Kansas v. Colorado, 206 U.S. 46, 89 (1907). The referenced passage in that case states that the Property Clause "clearly * * * does not grant to Congress any legislative control over the states, and must, so far as they are concerned, be limited to authority over the property belonging to the United States within their limits." But this does no more than articulate the obvious: that the Property Clause is a grant of power only over federal property. It gives no indication of the kind of "authority" the Clause gives Congress over its property.

Camfield v. United States, 167 U.S. 518 (1897), is of even less help to appellees. Appellees rely upon the following language from *Camfield:*

> "While we do not undertake to say that Congress has the unlimited power to legislate against nuisances within a state which it would have within a territory, we do not think the admission of a territory as a state deprives it of the power of legislating for the protection of the public lands, though it may thereby involve the exercise of what is ordinarily known as the 'police power,' *so long as such power is directed solely to its own protection.*" Id., at 525–526 (emphasis added).

Appellees mistakenly read this language to limit Congress' power to regulate activity on the public lands; in fact, the quoted passage refers to the scope of congressional power to regulate conduct on *private* land that affects the public lands. And *Camfield* holds that the Property Clause is broad enough to permit federal regulation of fences built on private land adjoining public land when the regulation is for the protection of the federal property. *Camfield* contains no suggestion of any limitation on Congress' power over conduct on its own property; its sole message is that the power granted by the Property Clause is broad enough to reach beyond territorial limits.

Lastly, appellees point to dicta in two cases to the effect that, unless the State has agreed to the exercise of federal jurisdiction, Congress' rights in its land are "only the rights of an ordinary proprietor * * *." Fort Leavenworth R. Co. v. Lowe, 114 U.S. 525, 527 (1885). See also Paul v. United States, 371 U.S. 245 (1963). In neither case was the power of Congress under the Property Clause at issue or considered and, as we shall see, these dicta fail to account for the raft of cases in which the Clause has been given a broader construction.[9]

In brief, beyond the *Fort Leavenworth* and *Paul* dicta, appellees have presented no support for their position that the Clause grants Congress only the power to dispose of, to make incidental rules regarding the use of, and to protect federal property. This failure is hardly surprising, for the

---

9. Indeed, Hunt v. United States, 278 U.S. 96 (1928), and Camfield v. United States, 167 U.S. 518 (1897), both relied upon by appellees, are inconsistent with the notion that the United States has only the rights of an ordinary proprietor with respect to its land. An ordinary proprietor may not, contrary to state law, kill game that is damaging his land, as the Government did in *Hunt;* nor may he prohibit the fencing in of his property without the assistance of state law, as the Government was able to do in *Camfield.*

Clause, in broad terms, gives Congress the power to determine what are "needful" rules "respecting" the public lands. And while the furthest reaches of the power granted by the Property Clause have not yet been definitively resolved, we have repeatedly observed that "[t]he power over the public land thus entrusted to Congress is without limitations." United States v. San Francisco, 310 U.S., at 29.

* * *

The decided cases have supported this expansive reading. It is the Property Clause, for instance, that provides the basis for governing the territories of the United States. And even over public land within the States, "[t]he general government doubtless has a power over its own property analogous to the police power of the several states, and the extent to which it may go in the exercise of such power is measured by the exigencies of the particular case." Camfield v. United States, 167 U.S. 518, 525 (1897). We have noted, for example, that the Property Clause gives Congress the power over the public lands "to control their occupancy and use, to protect them from trespass and injury, and to prescribe the conditions upon which others may obtain rights in them * * *." Utah Power & Light Co. v. United States, 243 U.S. 389, 405 (1917). And we have approved legislation respecting the public lands "[i]f it be found to be necessary, for the protection of the public or of intending settlers [on the public lands]." Camfield v. United States, 167 U.S., at 525. In short, Congress exercises the powers both of a proprietor and of a legislature over the public domain. Although the Property Clause does not authorize "an exercise of a general control over public policy in a State," it does permit "an exercise of the complete power which Congress has over particular public property entrusted to it." United States v. San Francisco, 310 U.S., at 30 (footnote omitted). In our view, the "complete power" that Congress has over public lands necessarily includes the power to regulate and protect the wildlife living there.[10]

Appellees argue that if we approve the Wild Free–Roaming Horses and Burros Act as a valid exercise of Congress' power under the Property Clause, then we have sanctioned an impermissible intrusion on the sovereignty, legislative authority and police power of the State and have wrongly infringed upon the State's traditional trustee powers over wild animals. The argument appears to be that Congress could obtain exclusive legislative jurisdiction over the public lands in the State only by state consent, and that in the absence of such consent Congress lacks the power to act contrary to state law. This argument is without merit.

---

10. Appellees ask us to declare that the Act is unconstitutional because the animals are not, as Congress found, "fast disappearing from the American scene." § 1 of the Act, 16 U.S.C. § 1331. At the outset, no reason suggests itself why Congress' power under the Property Clause to enact legislation to protect wild free-roaming horses and burros "from capture, branding, harassment, or death," ibid., must depend on a finding that the animals are decreasing in number. But responding directly to appellees' contention, we note that the evidence before Congress on this question was conflicting and that Congress weighed the evidence and made a judgment. What appellees ask is that we reweigh the evidence and substitute our judgment for that of Congress. This we must decline to do.

Appellees' claim confuses Congress' derivative legislative powers, which are not involved in this case, with its powers under the Property Clause. Congress may acquire derivative legislative power from a state pursuant to Art. I, § 8, cl. 17, of the Constitution by consensual acquisition of land, or by nonconsensual acquisition followed by the State's subsequent cession of legislative authority over the land. Paul v. United States, 371 U.S. 245, 264 (1963); Fort Leavenworth R. Co. v. Lowe, 114 U.S. 525, 541–542 (1885).[11] In either case, the legislative jurisdiction acquired may range from exclusive federal jurisdiction with no residual state police power, to concurrent, or partial, federal legislative jurisdiction, which may allow the State to exercise certain authority.

But while Congress can acquire exclusive or partial jurisdiction over lands within a State by the State's consent or cession, the presence or absence of such jurisdiction has nothing to do with Congress' powers under the Property Clause. Absent consent or cession a State undoubtedly retains jurisdiction over federal lands within its territory, but Congress equally surely retains the power to enact legislation respecting those lands pursuant to the Property Clause. And when Congress so acts, the federal legislation necessarily overrides conflicting state laws under the Supremacy Clause. U.S.Const., Art. VI, cl. 2. * * * As we said in Camfield v. United States, 167 U.S., at 526, in response to a somewhat different claim, "A different rule would place the public domain of the United States completely at the mercy of state legislation."

Thus, appellees' assertion that "[a]bsent state consent by complete cession of jurisdiction of lands to the United States, exclusive jurisdiction does not accrue to the federal landowner with regard to federal lands within the borders of the state," is completely beside the point; and appellees' fear that the Secretary's position is that "the Property Clause totally exempts federal lands within state borders from state legislative powers, state police powers, and all rights and powers of local sovereignty and jurisdiction of the states," is totally unfounded. The Federal Government does not assert exclusive jurisdiction over the public lands in New Mexico, and the State is free to enforce its criminal and civil laws on those lands. But where those state laws conflict with the Wild Free–Roaming Horses and Burros Act, or with other legislation passed pursuant to the Property Clause, the law is clear: the state laws must recede.

Again, none of the cases relied upon by appellees are to the contrary. * * *

In short, these cases do not support appellees' claim that upholding the Act would sanction an impermissible intrusion upon state sovereignty. The Act does not establish exclusive federal jurisdiction over the public lands in New Mexico; it merely overrides the New Mexico Estray Law insofar as it attempts to regulate federally protected animals. And that is but the necessary consequence of valid legislation under the Property Clause.

---

11. * * * The Clause has been broadly construed, and the acquisition by consent or cession of exclusive or partial jurisdiction over properties for any legitimate govern- mental purpose beyond those itemized is permissible. Collins v. Yosemite Park Co., 304 U.S. 518, 528–530 (1938).

Appellees' contention that the Act violates traditional state power over wild animals stands on no different footing. Unquestionably the States have broad trustee and police powers over wild animals within their jurisdictions. But as Geer v. Connecticut cautions, those powers exist only "in so far as [their] exercise may be not incompatible with, or restrained by, the rights conveyed to the federal government by the constitution." 161 U.S., at 528. "No doubt it is true that as between a State and its inhabitants the State may regulate the killing and sale of [wildlife], but it does not follow that its authority is exclusive of paramount powers." Missouri v. Holland, 252 U.S. 416, 434 (1920). * * * We hold today that the Property Clause also gives Congress the power to protect wildlife on the public lands, state law notwithstanding.

In this case, the New Mexico Livestock Board entered upon the public lands of the United States and removed wild burros. These actions were contrary to the provisions of the Wild Free–Roaming Horses and Burros Act. We find that, as applied to this case, the Act is a constitutional exercise of congressional power under the Property Clause. We need not, and do not, decide whether the Property Clause would sustain the Act in all of its conceivable applications.

Appellees are concerned that the Act's extension of protection to wild free-roaming horses and burros that stray from public land onto private land, § 4 of the Act, 16 U.S.C. § 1334, will be read to provide federal jurisdiction over every wild horse or burro that at any time sets foot upon federal land. While it is clear that regulations under the Property Clause may have some effect on private lands not otherwise under federal control, Camfield v. United States, 167 U.S. 518 (1897), we do not think it appropriate in this declaratory judgment proceeding to determine the extent, if any, to which the Property Clause empowers Congress to protect animals on private lands or the extent to which such regulation is attempted by the Act. * * *

NOTES AND QUESTIONS

1.   The best evidence is that today's wild horses and burros are descendants of once domesticated horses and burros first introduced into the American West by early Spanish explorers and settlers and miners. There may have been counterpart large ungulate animals in prehistoric times, perhaps driven to extinction by ancestors of Indians. See Shepard Krech III, THE ECOLOGICAL INDIAN (1999). The protection statute here was co-sponsored by Congressman Walter Baring of Nevada, in whose state many wild horses and burros roam the public lands. He credited a constituent, Velma Johnston (widely known as "Wild Horse Annie"), with awakening Americans to their drastic decline on federal lands, from an estimated 2 million to 17,000 when the Act was adopted. See generally Richard Symanski, WILD HORSES AND SACRED COWS (1985); Symanski, Dances with Horses: Lessons from the Environmental Fringe, 10 Conservation Biology 708 (1996).

2. Who owns the wild horses and burros at issue in *Kleppe*? Is ownership relevant? Geer v. Connecticut, 161 U.S. 519 (1896), cited in Justice Marshall's opinion, held that a state could forbid the export of game taken within its borders without contravening the so-called "dormant" commerce clause of the U.S. Constitution. The decision rested in part on the concept that the states "owned" the wildlife within their borders in trust for the people. The idea of state "ownership" had eroded over time, and *Geer* was overruled two years after *Kleppe*, in Hughes v. Oklahoma, 441 U.S. 322 (1979). Justice Brennan for the majority explained that abandoning the "19th century legal fiction of state ownership" left the states with "ample allowance for preserving, in ways not inconsistent with the commerce clause, the legitimate state concerns for conservation and protection of wild animals." 441 U.S. at 335–36.

3. If the Property Clause gives Congress plenary preemptive power over federal lands, where does that leave the limitations in the Enclave Clause? Does *Kleppe's* reading of the Property Clause make the Enclave Clause superfluous? Could, for example, Congress adopt legislation abrogating the right of Kansas to tax railroad property within military reservations (and thus undo the state's reservation of jurisdiction upheld in *Fort Leavenworth*)? Or consider this: Suppose New Mexico had in 1960 ceded exclusive jurisdiction to the U.S. over a tract of land in a national forest within its borders, except that the state expressly reserved the power to regulate wild horses and burros on the tract. Can the U.S. nevertheless enforce the Wild Horse and Burro Act on this tract under *Kleppe*?

4. Could Congress unilaterally (without state consent) oust all state laws and establish exclusively federal jurisdiction on all federal lands under the Property Clause? In Commonwealth of Virginia v. Reno, 955 F.Supp. 571 (E.D.Va.1997), Virginia argued that the operation of a federal correctional facility on federal land within its borders exceeded the jurisdiction over some of the property involved that Virginia had previously ceded to the national government under the Enclave Clause, and therefore the facility had to be closed. Judge Ellis, providing the most comprehensive exploration of the relationship between the two constitutional clauses in modern times, rejected the claim. He observed that judicial construction of the Enclave Clause "is both broader and narrower than its wording and history suggest," that the Property Clause provides a "separate mechanism[] by which the federal government may obtain, hold, and regulate its property," and that the Enclave Clause "in no way diminishes the government's power over federal property held pursuant to the Property Clause." Therefore any limitations in Virginia's cession of jurisdiction could not defeat Congress's power to regulate and control the correctional facility. While his decision was on appeal, Virginia's pursuit of a political remedy succeeded, with Congress enacting legislation closing the facility, mooting the issue. See 122 F.3d 1060 (4th Cir.1997).

5. Justice Marshall's opinion says that New Mexico's "fear" of losing all authority over federal lands with a broad reading of the Property Clause "is totally unfounded." Is it? As a matter of constitutional law (see paragraph 4, immediately preceding)? Or as a matter of political reality? Cf.

Herbert Weschler, The Political Safeguards of Federalism: The Role of the States in the Composition and Selection of the National Government, 54 Colum.L.Rev. 543 (1954). In this connection, can New Mexico regulate hunting (other than for wild horses and burros) on federal lands after *Kleppe*?

6.   Although *Kleppe* was unanimous, new information has come to light that suggests the Court's unanimity was in doubt for a time. When the papers of former Supreme Court Justice Thurgood Marshall were made public after his death, they were found to contain a cryptic note from Chief Justice Burger regarding *Kleppe v. New Mexico,* dated a few days before the Court issued its judgment:

> "The enthusiasm that the rancher-water Justices exhibited for my scholarly analysis of the grazing problems leads me to abandon the idea of separate writing. I assumed ranchers would want to be free to shoot trespassing burros but if Byron [White] and Bill Rehnquist want to put wild burros on a new form of 'welfare' I will submit. In short, I join you."

7.   For an argument that the decline of the Enclave Clause and the ascent of the Property Clause in the Supreme Court has moved generally in parallel with the evolution of congressional policy over federal lands from a vendor to a custodian to an active manager, see Eugene R. Gaetke, Refuting the "Classic" Property Clause Theory, 63 N.C.L.Rev. 617 (1985). For a recent comprehensive history and ringing endorsement of a broad interpretation of the Property Clause, see Peter Appel, The Power of Congress "Without Limitation": The Property Clause and Federal Regulation of Private Property, 86 Minn.L.Rev. 1 (2001). Some users of federal land continue to have a hard time accepting the notion that the U.S. has broad power over federal lands. See, e.g., United States v. Vogler, 859 F.2d 638 (9th Cir.1988), cert. denied, 488 U.S. 1006 (1989) (rejecting argument that Property Clause does not support federal legislative power over federal lands because it is not found in Article I of the Constitution).

NOTE: THE SAGEBRUSH REBELLION AND COUNTY SUPREMACY MOVEMENTS

Federal ownership of large tracts of lands within the borders of western states has always been a politically attractive whipping boy for western politicians. Some defenders of "states' rights" were outraged when Congress in 1976 made explicit what had long been implicit: the United States was going to retain most BLM-managed public lands in federal ownership. Their bitterness was not assuaged by the fact that primary shapers of this legislation, the Federal Land Policy and Management Act, were westerners in Congress.

Growing environmental restrictions on the use of these federal lands combined with a disaffection with national government in the late 1970s to create a movement to claim ownership of federal lands in the western states. Called the "Sagebrush Rebellion" by its supporters, and the "Great Terrain Robbery" by opponents, the movement was led by disgruntled ranchers whose grazing privileges on public lands were threatened with reduction. Utah Senator Orrin Hatch, succumbing to oratorical excess in his support for the rebellion, saw the local federal land manager as akin to the Sheriff of Nottingham. The Sagebrush Rebels asserted that their claim of ownership had a constitutional basis, putting forward primarily a tenth amendment and an equal footing argument (relying on *dicta* in Pollard v. Hagan, p. 52 supra). Several Western states, led by Nevada, passed laws claiming ownership of BLM-managed public land and, in a couple of cases, national forest land as well. (Shortly after the Nevada legislature enacted this statute into law, state officials hurried to Washington to make sure that their claim of ownership would not result in interruption of federal payments to the state which were based on continuing federal land ownership. The various programs authorizing these payments are described at pp. 226–31 infra.)

The Rebellion gained considerably publicity in 1980; Ronald Reagan declared himself a Sagebrush Rebel during his successful campaign for the Presidency. Litigation sought to test these claims, but the courts never reached the merits in any final judgment. See Nevada ex rel. Nevada State Bd. of Agric. v. United States, 512 F.Supp. 166 (D.Nev.1981), aff'd, 699 F.2d 486 (9th Cir.1983). On the litigation and the motivating forces behind it, see generally John Leshy, Unraveling the Sagebrush Rebellion: Law, Politics, and Federal Lands, 14 U.C.D. L.Rev. 317 (1980); Richard Clayton, The Sagebrush Rebellion: Who Should Control the Public Lands?, 1980 Utah L.Rev. 505; Constandina Titus, The Nevada "Sagebrush Rebellion" Act: A Question of Constitutionality, 23 Ariz.L.Rev. 263 (1981).

In the 1990s, conservation restrictions on the use of federal land led to another outbreak of anti-federal sentiment, again led by ranchers in the rural Rocky Mountain west. Once again continuing federal ownership and management of federal lands was claimed to be unconstitutional. This time around, however, two things were different. First, no state joined the movement, although a few counties did. Second, the courts did get to the merits of the claim, and soundly rejected it.

United States v. Gardner

United States Court of Appeals, Ninth Circuit, 1997.
107 F.3d 1314, cert. denied, 522 U.S. 907 (1997).

■ CHOY, CIRCUIT JUDGE

[The Gardners owned a ranch near the Humboldt National Forest in Nevada, and had a permit to graze some cattle on a portion of the forest. A fire burned a portion of their allotment in 1992, and the Forest Service and the State of Nevada reseeded the burned area and closed it to grazing for two years to allow it to recover. The Gardners disobeyed the closure order and were fined for trespassing. They refused to pay, and the U.S. brought a lawsuit seeking damages and an injunction.]

I.   The United States' Title to Federal Land in Nevada[1]

---

1. An Amicus Brief was filed on behalf of the states of New Mexico, Alaska, Maine, Montana, Oregon, Vermont, and, significantly, Nevada supporting the position of the

Gardners argue that grazing their livestock in the Humboldt National Forest without a permit does not constitute trespass because the federal government does not have title to the land on which the grazing took place. Gardners contend that, while the United States may have received the land in question from Mexico in the Treaty of Guadalupe Hidalgo in 1848, the United States was entitled only to hold the land in trust for the creation of future states, and was not authorized to retain the land for its own purposes. After Nevada became a state, Gardners argue, all of the public lands within the state boundaries reverted to the state of Nevada.[2] * * *

The claim by Gardners that it is the duty of the United States to hold public lands in trust for the formation of future states is founded on a case dealing with land acquired by the United States from the thirteen original states. In that case, *Pollard's Lessee v. Hagan,* 44 U.S. (3 How.) 212, the Supreme Court discussed the extent of the United States' authority over lands ceded to it from Virginia and Georgia to discharge debt incurred by those states during the Revolutionary War. The Court stated that the United States held this land in trust for the establishment of future states. Once those new states were established, the United States' authority over the land would cease. This decision was based on the terms of the cessions of the land from Virginia and Georgia to the United States. Before becoming a state, however, Nevada had no independent claim to sovereignty, unlike the original thirteen states. Therefore, the same reasoning is not applicable to this case, in which the federal government was the initial owner of the land from which the state of Nevada was later carved.

* * *

The United States, then, was not required to hold the public lands in Nevada in trust for the establishment of future states. Rather, under the Property Clause, the United States can administer its federal lands any way it chooses, including the establishment of a national forest reserve.

II. The Equal Footing Doctrine

Gardners argue that, under the Equal Footing Doctrine, a new state must possess the same powers of sovereignty and jurisdiction as did the original thirteen states upon admission to the Union. Because the federal government owns over eighty percent of the land in the state of Nevada, Gardners argue, Nevada is not on an equal footing with the original thirteen states.[3] Gardners claim that Nevada must have "paramount title

United States in this case. Additionally, a federal district court in Nevada has held that title to the public lands within Nevada's boundaries rests in the United States. *United States v. Nye County,* 920 F.Supp. 1108 (D.Nev.1996).

2. Gardners point out that [in 1979 Nevada] * * * passed a statute claiming ownership over all public lands within its boundaries, Nev.Rev.Stat. 321.5973. Gardners claim that the passage of this law further

demonstrates that title to the public lands in Nevada properly rests in the state, not the federal, government. Gardners fail to note, however, that the Nevada statute by its own terms excludes national forest lands from the public lands claimed by Nevada. *See* Nev.Rev. Stat. § 321.5963.

3. For example, in New Hampshire the federal government owns just under thirteen percent of the land. The federal government owns between two and seven percent of the

and eminent domain of *all* lands within its boundaries" to satisfy the Equal Footing Doctrine. * * *

[T]he Supreme Court has declined to extend the Equal Footing Doctrine to lands other than those underneath navigable waters or waters affected by the ebb and flow of the tides. * * * [Here the Court cited and discussed *Scott v. Lattig,* 227 U.S. 229, 244 (1913) and *Texas v. Louisiana,* 410 U.S. 702, 713 (1973), for the proposition that the Equal Footing Doctrine] does not operate to reserve title to fast dry lands to individual states.

Moreover, Supreme Court has long held that the Equal Footing Doctrine refers to "those attributes essential to [a state's] equality in dignity and power with other States." *Coyle v. Smith,* 221 U.S. 559, 568 (1911). The Court has noted that a new state enters the Union "in full equality with all the others," and that this equality may forbid a compact between a new state and the United States "limiting or qualifying political rights and obligations." *Stearns v. Minnesota,* 179 U.S. 223, 245 (1900). However, "a mere agreement in reference to property involves no question of equality of status." *Id.* The Court has observed that "[s]ome States when they entered the Union had within their boundaries tracts of land belonging to the Federal Government; others were sovereigns of their soil." *United States v. Texas,* 339 U.S. 707, 716 (1950). While these disparities may cause economic differences between the states, the purpose of the Equal Footing Doctrine is not to eradicate all diversity among states but rather to establish equality among the states with regards to political standing and sovereignty.

The Equal Footing Doctrine, then, applies to political rights and sovereignty, not to economic or physical characteristics of the states. Moreover, the Equal Footing Doctrine applies primarily to the shores of and lands beneath navigable waters, not to fast dry lands. Therefore, the Equal Footing Doctrine would not operate, as Gardners argue, to give Nevada title to the public lands within its boundaries.

III.   The Validity of Nevada's "Disclaimer Clause"

When Congress invited Nevada to join the Union in 1864, it mandated that the Nevada constitutional convention pass an act promising that Nevada would "forever disclaim all right and title to the unappropriated public lands lying within said territory, and that the same shall be and remain at the sole and entire disposition of the United States...." Nevada Statehood Act of March 21, 1864, 13 Stat. 30, 31 § 4. The state constitutional convention did so. Ordinance of the Nevada Constitution.

Gardners claim that this clause is invalid and unconstitutional as an attempt to divest Nevada of its title to the unappropriated lands within its boundaries. Gardners cite to *Van Brocklin v. Tennessee,* 117 U.S. 151, 167 (1886) for the premise that such disclaimer clauses "are but declaratory,

land within the borders of nine of the other original thirteen states. In Connecticut, New York and Rhode Island, less than one percent of the land is owned by the federal govern- ment. Bureau of Land Management, U.S. Department of the Interior, Public Land Statistics 1993, at 5, Table 3 (September 1994).

and confer no new right or power upon the United States." Therefore, Gardners argue, Nevada could not have given the United States title to the public lands within its boundaries through the disclaimer clause.

Gardners are correct in their argument that the disclaimer is declaratory. However, the United States did not need the disclaimer clause to gain title to the public lands in Nevada. The United States already had title to those lands through the Treaty of Guadalupe Hidalgo, and the disclaimer clause was merely a recognition of the preexisting United States title, as opposed to a grant of title from Nevada to the United States.

IV. The Tenth Amendment

Gardners argue that federal ownership of the public lands in Nevada is unconstitutional under the Tenth Amendment. Such ownership, they argue, invades "core state powers reserved to Nevada," such as the police power.

Federal ownership of the public lands within a state does not completely divest the state from the ability to exercise its own sovereignty over that land. The state government and the federal government exercise concurrent jurisdiction over the land. * * * *Kleppe v. New Mexico* * * * The state of Nevada, then, is not being unconstitutionally deprived of the ability to govern the land within its borders. The state may exercise its civil and criminal jurisdiction over federal lands within its borders as long as it exercises its power in a manner that does not conflict with federal law. * * *

NOTES AND QUESTIONS

1. Does Nevada own the beds of waters within its borders, including those within forest reserves, which were navigable at statehood, under the doctrine of *Pollard v. Hagan*? See Chapter 2, supra p. 52. If it does, does the court adequately explain why the equal footing doctrine draws a line between the beds of navigable waters and uplands? Is there a principled basis for that line other than that the Supreme Court applied the doctrine to the beds of navigable waters in *Pollard v. Hagan* because it then viewed the relationship between the national government and the states differently from how it viewed it in later cases? Is that explanation satisfactory?

2. Why do you suppose Nevada and other states filed an *amicus* brief in support of the United States? At this time, Nevada still had on its books the 1979 statute it had passed claiming ownership of BLM public lands. Recall also that in 1930 President Hoover supported the transfer of title to the unappropriated public lands to the states, but the states were lukewarm or hostile to the idea. See pp. 132–33 supra.

3. Why don't opponents of federal land management, and particularly of the restrictions on use that come with this management, take their case to Congress rather than to the courts? Why, in other words, do they often choose to couch their opposition in arguments that it is unconstitutional for the federal government to own these lands?

4. For background on the "county supremacy" movement, written before the *Gardner* decision, see Paul Conable, Equal Footing, County Supremacy, and the Western Public Lands, 26 Envtl. L. 1263 (1996).

NOTE: THE PROPERTY CLAUSE AND NUCLEAR WASTE

Although it has been almost fifty years since the federal government embarked on a program of promoting the use of nuclear energy for peaceful purposes, a final decision on a permanent repository for the resulting long-lived radioactive wastes has not yet been made. In 1982, Congress enacted the Nuclear Waste Policy Act, directing the Department of Energy to undertake a wide-ranging review of possible sites around the country. This effort bogged down, and in 1987 Congress amended the Act to narrow the appraisal of possible repository sites to just one: Yucca Mountain on federal land in the Nellis Air Force Range and Nuclear Testing Site northwest of Las Vegas. The state government went ballistic, as it were—filing lawsuits, enacting obstructive legislation, and otherwise attempting to assert a veto to the federal plan. One of the lawsuits raised questions about whether Congress's constitutional power over federal lands supported the 1987 amendments. State of Nevada v. Watkins, 914 F.2d 1545 (9th Cir.1990). The court, relying principally on Kleppe v. New Mexico, found that the Property Clause left the matter to Congress, and the Enclave Clause does not limit that power by requiring the consent of the State. The court went on to hold that the equal footing doctrine and Pollard v. Hagan did not restrict Congress's power over federal property, and rejected several other constitutional arguments. Litigation and legislative maneuvering continue; see Rosen, *Nevada v. Watkins*: Who Gets the Shaft?, 10 Va. Envt'l L.J. 239 (1991); State of Nevada v. U.S. Department of Energy, 993 F.2d 1442 (9th Cir.1993). In February 2002, President Bush endorsed the Yucca Mountain site.

Congress also authorized construction of a Waste Isolation Pilot Project (WIPP) on federal land in New Mexico for disposal of military radioactive waste in New Mexico. Like Nevada, New Mexico opposed the project in and out of court, with but limited success. See New Mexico v. EPA, 114 F.3d 290 (D.C.Cir.1997). The facility is now in operation.

THE PROPERTY CLAUSE AND NON–FEDERAL LAND

The Court in *Kleppe v. New Mexico* did not expressly address Congress's power, under the Property Clause, to regulate wild horses and burros when they wander off federal property. (Federal power under other constitutional provisions is addressed in the next section.) A substantial line of cases affirms that the Property Clause does give Congress authority to regulate activities occurring *off* federal lands if their effects can be felt on federal lands. The first case was Camfield v. United States, supra p. 92. It was followed by United States v. Alford, 274 U.S. 264 (1927), where the Court, speaking through Justice Holmes, rejected Alford's contention that a 1910 federal statute which prohibited leaving unextinguished a fire "in or near" any public forest could not be enforced on private lands, in typically

Holmesian fashion: "The danger depends upon the nearness of the fire, not upon the ownership of the land where it is built. * * * The statute is constitutional. Congress may prohibit the doing of acts upon privately owned lands that imperil the publicly owned forests." These cases did not indicate how far the Congress could go in regulating activities on nonfederal land, especially in the modern environmentally conscious age.

Minnesota v. Block

United States Court of Appeals, Eighth Circuit, 1981.
660 F.2d 1240, cert. denied, 455 U.S. 1007 (1982).

■ BRIGHT, CIRCUIT JUDGE.

These appeals arise from three consolidated cases involving multiple challenges to provisions of the Boundary Waters Canoe Area Wilderness Act of 1978 (BWCAW Act or the Act). * * * [Plaintiff-appellants State of Minnesota, the National Association of Property Owners (NAPO) and numerous individuals, businesses, and organizations] allege that Congress unconstitutionally applied federal controls on the use of motorboats and snowmobiles to land and waters not owned by the United States. * * *

The BWCAW, a part of the Superior National Forest, consists of approximately 1,075,000 acres of land and waterways along the Minnesota–Canadian border. * * * [The Court recounted the long efforts by the national government, starting with the first reservation of forest land in 1902, to protect the boundary waters area, including its "primitive character." This culminated in enactment of the BWCAW]. At issue here are portions of section 4 of the Act, the provision barring the use of motorized craft in all but designated portions of the wilderness. Section 4(c) limits motorboat use to designated lakes and rivers, allowing a maximum of either ten or twenty-five horsepower motors on these waters. Section 4(g) permits certain limited mechanized portages. Section 4(e) restricts the use of snowmobiles to two designated trails. With these exceptions, the Act as construed by the federal government and by the district court, prohibits all other motorized transportation on land and water falling within the external boundaries of the wilderness area.

The boundaries of the BWCAW circumscribe a total surface area of approximately 1,080,300 acres—920,000 acres of land and 160,000 of water. The United States owns approximately 792,000 acres of land surface, while the State of Minnesota owns approximately 121,000 acres of land,[12] in addition to the beds under the 160,000 acres of navigable water. Congress recognized that Minnesota would retain jurisdiction over the waters, but provided that the State could not regulate in a manner less stringent than that mandated by the Act. * * *

On appeal, Minnesota and the intervening plaintiffs [argue, among other things] * * * that Congress acted in excess of its authority under the property clause by curtailing the use of motor-powered boats and other

---

12. Private parties own approximately 7,300 acres of land.

motorized vehicles on lands and waters not owned by the United States
* * *.

* * * [W]e must decide the question left open in *Kleppe*—the scope of
Congress' property clause power as applied to activity occurring off federal
land. Without defining the limits of the power, the Court in *Kleppe,* relying
on its decision in Camfield v. United States, 167 U.S. 518 (1897), acknowledged that "it is clear the regulations under the Property Clause may have
some effect on private lands not otherwise under federal control." * * *

Under this authority to protect public land, Congress' power must
extend to regulation of conduct on or off the public land that would
threaten the designated purpose of federal lands. Congress clearly has the
power to dedicate federal land for particular purposes. As a necessary
incident of that power, Congress must have the ability to insure that these
lands be protected against interference with their intended purposes. As
the Supreme Court has stated, under the property clause "[Congress] may
sanction some uses and prohibit others, and *may forbid interference with
such as are sanctioned.*" McKelvey v. United States, 260 U.S. 353, 359
(1922) (emphasis added).

* * *

Having established that Congress may regulate conduct off federal land
that interferes with the designated purpose of that land, we must determine whether Congress acted within this power in restricting the use of
motorboats and other motor vehicles in the BWCAW. In reviewing the
appropriateness of particular regulations, "we must remain mindful that,
while courts must eventually pass upon them, determinations under the
Property Clause are entrusted primarily to the judgment of Congress."
Kleppe v. New Mexico, supra, 426 U.S. at 536. Thus, if Congress enacted
the motorized use restrictions to protect the fundamental purpose for
which the BWCAW had been reserved, and if the restrictions in section 4
reasonably relate to that end, we must conclude that Congress acted within
its constitutional prerogative.

Congress passed the BWCAW Act with the clear intent of insuring that
the area would remain as wilderness and could be enjoyed as such.
Specifically concerning the motor use regulations, Congressman Fraser, in
introducing the 1978 Act, stated:

> The bill has four major thrusts. First, and most important, it seeks to
> end those activities that threaten the integrity of the BWCA's wilder-
> ness character by expressly prohibiting the following uses: * * * Recre-
> ational uses of motorized watercraft and snowmobiles * * *.

Congress based its conclusions on certain statutory findings:

> SECTION 1. The Congress finds that it is necessary and desirable to
> provide for the protection, enhancement, and preservation of the
> natural values of the lakes, waterways, and associated forested areas
> known (before the date of enactment of this Act) as the Boundary
> Waters Canoe Area, and for the orderly management of public use and
> enjoyment of that area as wilderness, and of certain contiguous lands

and waters, while at the same time protecting the special qualities of the area as a natural forest-lakeland wilderness ecosystem of major esthetic, cultural, scientific, recreational and educational value to the Nation. [92 Stat. 1649.]

Hearings and other evidence provided ample support for Congress' finding that use of motorboats and snowmobiles must be limited in order to preserve the area as a wilderness. Testimony established that the sight, smell, and sound of motorized vehicles seriously marred the wilderness experience of canoeists, hikers, and skiers and threatened to destroy the integrity of the wilderness.

As a result of considerable testimony and debate and a series of compromises, Congress enacted section 4 in an attempt to accommodate all interests, determining the extent of motorized use the area might tolerate without serious threat to its wilderness values.[22]

The motor use restrictions form only a small part of an elaborate system of regulations considered necessary to preserve the BWCAW as a wilderness. The United States owns close to ninety percent of the land surrounding the waters at issue. Congress concluded that motorized vehicles significantly interfere with the use of the wilderness by canoeists, hikers, and skiers and that restricted motorized use would enhance and preserve the wilderness values of the area. From the evidence presented, Congress could rationally reach these conclusions. We hold, therefore, that Congress acted within its power under the Constitution to pass needful regulations respecting public lands.[24]

NOTES AND QUESTIONS

1.   Refresher question: How did the State of Minnesota come to gain title to the subsurface land (26% of the total acreage) it owned in the Boundary Waters Canoe Area? See Chapter 2, p. 52, supra.

2.   Other modern decisions reach similar results. In Free Enterprise Canoe Renters Association v. Watt, 549 F.Supp. 252 (E.D.Mo.1982), aff'd, 711 F.2d 852 (8th Cir.1983), the court relied on *Minnesota v. Block* to hold that the National Park Service could prohibit the use of state roads within the Ozark National Scenic Riverway for canoe pickups by canoe renters who lacked a Park Service permit. United States v. Lindsey, 595 F.2d 5 (9th Cir.1979) was a repeat of *Alford* (see p. 198 supra), upholding the prosecution of a person who built a campfire without permission on state land within the boundaries of Hells Canyon National Recreation Area, contrary to a Forest Service regulation. See also United States v. Arbo, 691 F.2d 862 (9th Cir.1982) (upholding the conviction of mining claimant for

---

22.   We find no merit in appellants' argument that Congress should have banned all motorized travel if it were serious about protecting the wilderness. Congress retains the freedom, as well as the obligation and ability, to balance competing interests. Courts should not lightly set aside the resulting compromises.

24.   Like the district court, we need not decide whether Congress could have enacted these regulations pursuant to its commerce clause or treaty making powers.

interfering with forest officers seeking to inspect his mining operation, the court noting that whether the actions complained of took place on federal land or not, the land adjacent to his claim was federal, and the officers were taking reasonable steps to protect the adjacent federal property from, among other things, pollution and fire); United States v. Brown, 552 F.2d 817 (8th Cir.1977), cert. denied, 431 U.S. 949 (1977) (upholding conviction of violating a federal regulation prohibiting hunting in a national park, rejecting the argument that the regulation could not apply to duck hunting from a boat on waters over state submerged lands in the park). See generally Peter Appel, The Power of Congress "Without Limitation": The Property Clause and Federal Regulation of Private Property, 86 Minn. L.Rev. 1 (2001); Eugene R. Gaetke, The Boundary Waters Canoe Area Wilderness Act of 1978: Regulating Non–Federal Property Under the Property Clause, 60 Or.L.Rev. 157 (1981); Joseph Sax, Helpless Giants: The National Parks and the Regulation of Private Lands, 75 Mich.L.Rev. 239 (1976). For a case study, see John F. Lambert, Private Landholdings in the National Parks: Examples from Yosemite National Park and Indian Dunes National Lakeshore, 6 Harv. Envtl. L. Rev. 35 (1982).

3.   Is Congress's Property Clause power to regulate activities on *state* land any greater or lesser than its power to regulate activities on *private* land? Should it be? The Supreme Court has expressed much concern in recent years with federal commerce clause regulation that directly impacts state government operations. E.g., New York v. United States, 505 U.S. 144 (1992); Printz v. United States, 521 U.S. 898 (1997). Does it make any difference that the regulation here is of activities by private persons (recreational boaters and snowmobilers) using state lands? See also the discussion of the 8th Circuit decisions concerning Voyageurs National Park in *Brown* and *Armstrong* in note 9, p. 179 supra. If the court in those cases had held that the state had not ceded jurisdiction to the U.S. over the waters of the Park, could it still have reached the same result, that federal regulation was proper?

4.   What was the injury to federal lands from the operation of motor-boats on waters over state lands? Was it physical or aesthetic? (Is there a clear line between the two?) Does the reach of Congress's power in this context turn on whether there is a physical impact on federal lands?

5.   The cases addressing the reach of Congress's Property Clause power over non-federal lands generally involve regulation of activities on inholdings (tracts of nonfederal land entirely surrounded by federal land). Should a different test be employed if the federal government seeks to regulate conduct on non-federal lands outside the boundaries of a federal reservation? Could Congress regulate signs or billboards on non-federal land leading to national parks, because of their aesthetic impact on the park experience? Could it regulate sources of noise for the same reason? Could it regulate to prevent the filling of isolated wetlands on private land near a national park on the ground that those wetlands are useful to sustain natural systems found in the park? Could Congress use the Property Clause to prohibit all hunting of migrating animals whose habitat is on the public lands only during certain seasons of the year? In at least some of

these hypotheticals, recent Supreme Court decisions suggest that Congress's power to regulate under the commerce clause is doubtful. See pp. 205–06 infra. To the extent that is true, can the Property Clause be used to fill the gap?

6.   In this case, a fairly extensive record showed that, in fashioning the BWCAW, Congress considered the need to regulate activities on non-federal land in order to protect federal land. Does Congress need to show, in statutes or legislative history, the connection between activities it regulates on non-federal lands and federal lands? What kind of connection, and how strong must it be? Or is the court here saying that there is no meaningful judicial review of Congress's exercise of its Property Clause power? Compare the Supreme Court's current view of the connection Congress must draw between the subject it is regulating and interstate commerce, when it exercises its commerce clause authority. See United States v. Lopez, 514 U.S. 549, 561, 562 (1995); United States v. Morrison, 529 U.S. 598, 612 (2000).

7.   Should there be a more searching judicial inquiry when the federal land management agency seeks to regulate activities off federal land in order to protect the federal land, but the statute giving the agency generic regulatory authority is silent on whether that authority may be extended to activities off federal land?

C.   OTHER CONSTITUTIONAL AUTHORITIES OVER FEDERAL LANDS AND NATURAL RESOURCES

Although the Property Clause would appear to provide an ample basis for a vast array of legislation relating to lands and natural resources owned by the United States, federal authority to regulate activities on or off federal lands may also be found in the Commerce, Spending, and Treaty Clauses. Sometimes the courts address these constitutional powers in contexts relevant to federal natural resources. For example, Congress's authority over interstate commerce includes federal control of navigation, which has been held sufficient to support federal hydropower licenses issued in contravention of state law. First Iowa Hydro–Elec. Coop. v. FPC, 328 U.S. 152 (1946). The spending power has been used to justify such things as federal water projects to promote the general welfare, especially in the West. United States v. Gerlach Live Stock Co., 339 U.S. 725 (1950).

The treaty power supports a general exercise of federal power off as well as on public lands, and has been repeatedly exercised in connection with wildlife and water resources. In the landmark case of Missouri v. Holland, 252 U.S. 416 (1920), the Court upheld the 1918 Migratory Bird Treaty Act, which had been adopted to implement a 1916 treaty with Great Britain (on behalf of Canada). Missouri had challenged the legislation as an interference with state authority and beyond the power of Congress to enact. Justice Holmes's characteristically terse opinion explained:

> The State * * * founds its claim of exclusive authority upon an assertion of title to migratory birds, an assertion that is embodied in

[state] statute. No doubt it is true that as between a State and its inhabitants the State may regulate the killing and sale of such birds, but it does not follow that its authority is exclusive of paramount powers. To put the claim of the State upon title is to lean upon a slender reed. Wild birds are not in the possession of anyone; and possession is the beginning of ownership. The whole foundation of the State's rights is the presence within their jurisdiction of birds that yesterday had not arrived, tomorrow may be in another State and in a week a thousand miles away. * * *

Here a national interest of very nearly the first magnitude is involved. It can be protected only by national action in concert with that of another power. The subject matter is only transitorily within the State and has no permanent habitat therein. But for the treaty and the statute there soon might be no birds for any powers to deal with. We see nothing in the Constitution that compels the Government to sit by while a food supply is cut off and the protectors of our forests and our crops are destroyed. It is not sufficient to rely upon the States. The reliance is vain, and were it otherwise, the question is whether the United States is forbidden to act.

See generally George Cameron Coggins, Wildlife and the Constitution: The Walls Come Tumbling Down, 55 Wash.L.Rev. 295 (1980).

Only eight years before *Holland*, the Court had struck down federal regulation of wildlife on the ground that it interfered with state's rights, because they were then regarded as owning the wildlife within their borders. The Abby Dodge, 223 U.S. 166 (1912). Although *Holland* upheld Congress's power to regulate wildlife under the treaty power, since 1937 the Supreme Court's broad reading of the Commerce Clause as a source of congressional power has led to more reliance upon it to uphold federal regulation of wildlife. See, e.g., Andrus v. Allard, 444 U.S. 51 (1979) (Migratory Bird Treaty Act also justified under the commerce clause); Cerritos Gun Club v. Hall, 96 F.2d 620, 624–27 (9th Cir.1938) (upholding regulation of Secretary of Agriculture prohibiting baiting to lure wild ducks and geese in their migration for hunting); United States v. Helsley, 615 F.2d 784 (9th Cir.1979) (upholding federal Airborne Hunting Act). See also State of Wyoming v. United States, 279 F.3d 1214 (10th Cir.2002)(rejecting state's argument that the Tenth Amendment "reserves to the State the right to manage wildlife on [federal lands] to protect its own wildlife and domestic livestock," the court noting that while states have historically possessed broad powers over wildlife, even on federal lands, "those powers are not constitutionally based").

In recent years the Supreme Court has begun once again to restrict the reach of the Commerce Clause in cases like United States v. Lopez, 514 U.S. 549 (1995) (Congress's Commerce Clause power exceeded when it made it a federal crime to possess a firearm within 500 feet of a school), and United States v. Morrison, 529 U.S. 598 (2000) (same result when Congress provided a federal cause of action for damages to women harmed by acts of violence directed against them because of their gender). To date these decisions have not had demonstrable impact in the wildlife context, at least yet, albeit they have produced lower court decisions where judges have rather bitterly split on the question. See National Assoc. of Home Builders v. Babbitt, 130 F.3d 1041 (D.C.Cir.1997), cert. denied, 524 U.S. 937 (1998) (Endangered Species Act's application to protect a species of fly with a small, wholly intrastate habitat was within Congress's constitutional power to regulate interstate commerce); Gibbs v. Babbitt, 214 F.3d 483 (4th Cir.2000), cert. denied *sub nom.* Gibbs v. Norton, 531 U.S. 1145 (2001) (same result with respect to prohibition of taking endangered red wolf on private land). See generally John C. Nagle, The Commerce Clause Meets the Delhi Sands Flower–Loving Fly, 97 Mich. L.Rev. 174 (1998); Eric Brignac, The Commerce Clause Justification of Federal Endangered Species Protection: Gibbs v. Babbitt, 79 N.C.L.Rev. 873 (2001).

Also in recent years the Court has invoked constitutional concerns about federalism to construe federal environmental regulatory statutes narrowly. See Solid Waste Agency of Northern Cook County v. U.S. Army Corps of Engineers, 531 U.S. 159 (2001) (rejecting a broad interpretation of Clean Water Act where it "would result in a significant impingement of the State's traditional and primary power over land and water use"). Whether this approach to statutory construction will have impact in the field of federal land and natural resources law remains to be seen.

NOTES AND QUESTIONS

1. Could Congress's power to "regulate Commerce * * * among the several States," U.S.Const., Art. I, § 8, justify the Wild Horse and Burro Act? Is it easier or harder to justify it under the Commerce as opposed to the Property Clause? Cf. Columbia River Gorge United—Protecting People and Property v. Yeutter, 960 F.2d 110, 113–14 (9th Cir.1992) (federal legislation authorizing the establishment of a bi-state commission to regulate land use along the scenic Columbia River Gorge, which includes federal, state, and private lands along the river, was upheld under the Commerce Clause, the court noting that the Property Clause might also have been used, although it did not decide that question).

2. As the Supreme Court narrows Congress's power under the Commerce Clause in decisions such as United States v. Lopez and United States v. Morrison, might the Property Clause emerge as a useful source of authority for regulatory schemes that are connected in some way to federal lands, that might be beyond Congress's authority under the Commerce Clause? See generally Peter Appel, The Power of Congress "Without Limitation": The Property Clause and Federal Regulation of Private Property, 86 Minn. L.Rev. 1, 122 (2001) ("Congress could prohibit individuals from harming endangered and threatened species off federal property if members of those species sometimes occupy federal lands and if Congress reasonably concludes that extraterritorial preservation of such species preserves the overall value of federal lands"); see also Holly Doremus, Patching the Ark: Improving Legal Protection of Biological Diversity, 18 Ecology L.Q. 265, 292 (1991) (*Kleppe*'s reasoning "could justify federal protection of virtually any biological resource"). What about using the

Property Clause to prohibit the destruction of wetlands on private lands on which migratory birds rely, if those birds also use federal lands? How strong a showing would Congress have to make of the value of the migratory birds to the federal lands and resources, and of the value of the wetlands sought to be protected to the migratory birds, in order to use the Property Clause?

3. To what extent could the Congress use its power over spending to induce the states to regulate activities outside federal lands to protect federal lands? For example, as explained further below (see pp. 226–30), there are many programs by which Congress gives state and local governments federal dollars either as a form of "revenue sharing" or "compensation" for the federal lands within their borders. Could Congress withhold such money from states which refuse to adopt legislation regulating land uses on the borders of national parks? Or which refuse to adopt legislation protecting migratory wildlife that use federal lands for part of the year? Cf. South Dakota v. Dole, 483 U.S. 203 (1987) (upholding Congress's use of the spending power to withhold a portion of federal highway funds to any state that did not raise its drinking age from 18 to 21).

4. Suppose the United States entered into a treaty with other countries in which mutual commitments were made to protect endangered species within each signatory nation's borders. Would that support enactment of the domestic Endangered Species Act to protect species that might not be protected under the Commerce Clause? Even if those species don't cross international boundaries? Is it sufficient that the treaty be aimed at the preservation of all species as a common heritage of mankind? See Gavin R. Villareal, One Leg to Stand on: The Treaty Power and Congressional Authority for the Endangered Species Act After United States v. Lopez, 76 Texas L.Rev. 1125 (1998); Omar N. White, The Endangered Species Act's Precarious Perch: A Constitutional Analysis under the Commerce Clause and the Treaty Power, 27 Ecology L.Q. 215 (2000).

D. FEDERAL PREEMPTION

The Constitution's Supremacy Clause, Article VI, clause 2, protects federal action authorized by the Constitution from interference by state law. See, e.g., Kleppe v. New Mexico, supra p. 184. (Generally, in this context, local law is regarded as standing on the same footing as state law, as local governments are subdivisions of state government, although Congress may choose to preempt one and not the other.) Sometimes Congress specifically and unequivocally addresses the extent to which state law is preempted in any given circumstance. When that happens, the result is foregone; if Congress says that state law is preempted, that ends the matter.

Much more often, however, a congressional intent regarding preemption of state law is simply not clear on the face of federal statutes or in their legislative history. In these situations, the courts tend to use one of two modes of inquiry in determining whether state laws are preempted.

One is that Congress has determined to "occupy the regulatory field," leaving no room for state law to operate. This may be found where the federal regulation is "so pervasive as make reasonable the inference that Congress left no room for the States to supplement it. Or the Act of Congress may touch a field in which the federal interest is so dominant that the federal system will be assumed to preclude enforcement of state laws on the same subject." Rice v. Santa Fe Elevator Corp., 331 U.S. 218 (1947). The other mode of inquiry is to ask whether state and federal laws are in conflict, so that compliance with both is not possible. See, e.g, Florida Lime & Avocado Growers, Inc. v. Paul, 373 U.S. 132 (1963). The classic summary of doctrine in this area was provided by Justice Black's majority opinion in Hines v. Davidowitz, 312 U.S. 52 (1941):

> This Court, in considering the validity of state laws in the light [of] federal laws touching the same subject, has made use of the following expressions: conflicting; contrary to; occupying the field; repugnance; difference; irreconcilability; inconsistency; violation; curtailment; and interference. But none of these expressions provides an infallible constitutional test or an exclusive constitutional yardstick. In the final analysis, there can be no one crystal clear distinctly marked formula. Our primary function is to determine whether, under the circumstances of [the particular case, the state] law stands as an obstacle to the accomplishment and execution of the full purposes and objectives of Congress.

In some traditionally federal areas or areas where uniform national regulation is important, such as aliens, navigation, Indian affairs, labor, and civil rights, the Supreme Court has been quick to find preemption. See generally Laurence Tribe, AMERICAN CONSTITUTIONAL LAW 1174–79, 1204–1212 (3d ed.2000). Federal lands have never been regarded as such an area. Indeed, although active, directive management of federal lands by federal land managers has greatly increased over the past century, state law continues to play an important role, applying to much private activity on federal lands.

In Kleppe v. New Mexico, the conflict between state and federal law was irreconcilable: New Mexico law provided that the burros could be rounded up, sold, and killed, while federal law prohibited harassment, sale, or killing. Seldom is the incompatibility so clear cut. In most cases, Congress has been at least somewhat solicitous of state sensibilities when enacting laws governing federal lands. Sometimes, in fact, Congress cannot reach a consensus on the extent to which state law should be preempted. In such circumstances, it often resorts to a favorite device of negotiators and drafters; namely, papering over the lack of agreement by either silence or ambiguity. This leaves the question of preemption for the courts to resolve. Moreover, as a practical matter, it is difficult for Congress to anticipate and provide clear answers on the role of state law in individual settings, particularly in complex, generic legislation. In these instances, which are probably at least as numerous as those in which Congress provides clear answers, the compatibility of federal and state law becomes more difficult to determine.

As *Kleppe* shows, there is no doubt Congress can preempt state authority on the public lands. The more frequent and vexing question is whether, in particular contexts, Congress intended to do so. The following cases explore that question.

Ventura County v. Gulf Oil Corp.

United States Court of Appeals, Ninth Circuit, 1979.
601 F.2d 1080, affirmed without opinion, 445 U.S. 947 (1980).

■ HUFSTEDLER, CIRCUIT JUDGE.

The question on appeal is whether the County of Ventura ("Ventura") can require the federal Government's lessee, Gulf Oil Corporation ("Gulf"), to obtain a permit from Ventura in compliance with Ventura's zoning ordinances governing oil exploration and extraction activities before Gulf can exercise its rights under the lease and drilling permits acquired from the Government. The district court denied Ventura's motion for a preliminary injunction, and dismissed Ventura's second amended complaint. Ventura appeals. * * *

On January 1, 1974, the Department of the Interior, Bureau of Land Management, pursuant to the Mineral Lands Leasing Act of 1920 (30 U.S.C. §§ 181 et seq.), leased 120 acres located within the Los Padres National Forest in Ventura for purposes of oil exploration and development. * * * [Gulf's proposal to drill an oil well on the lease had been approved by the Geological Survey, Department of the Interior; the Forest Service; and the Oil & Gas Division of the State of California Resources Agency. D]rilling operations were commenced on April 28, 1976 * * *.

Throughout this period the leased property has been zoned Open Space ("O–S") by Ventura. Under its zoning ordinance, oil exploration and extraction activities are prohibited on O–S property unless an Open Space Use Permit is obtained from the Ventura County Planning Commission in accordance with Articles 25 and 43 of the Ventura County Ordinance Code. The O–S Use Permits are granted for such time and upon such conditions as the Planning Commission considers in the public interest. The permits contain 11 mandatory conditions and additional conditions are committed to the Planning Board's discretion.

On May 5, 1976, Ventura advised Gulf that it must obtain an O–S Use Permit if it wished to continue its drilling operations. Gulf refused to comply, and on May 20, 1976, Ventura brought suit * * *.

Although Ventura and amicus argue extensively that congressional enactments under the Property Clause generally possess no preemptive capability, we believe that Kleppe v. New Mexico (1976) 426 U.S. 529, is dispositive. * * * In light of *Kleppe*, the renewed attempt to restrict the scope of congressional power under the Property Clause in the present case is legally frivolous.

Ventura next contends that even if Congress had the power to enact overriding legislation, there is no evidence of either a congressional intent to preempt local regulation or a conflict between local and federal law that can be resolved only by exclusion of local jurisdiction. We need not consider the extent to which local regulation of any aspect of oil exploration and extraction upon federal lands is precluded by federal legislation; the local ordinances impermissibly conflict with the Mineral Lands Leasing Act of 1920 and on this basis alone they cannot be applied to Gulf.

The extensive regulation of oil exploration and drilling under the Mineral Leasing Act is evident from the present record. The basic lease assigned to Gulf in 1974 contains approximately 45 paragraphs including requirements of diligence and protection of the environment as well as reservation of a one-eighth royalty interest in the United States. Because the lands lie within a National Forest, the lease requires Gulf's acceptance of additional Department of Agriculture conditions designed to combat the environmental hazards normally incident to mining operations. Specific drilling permits were also required from the Department of the Interior, Geological Survey, and the Department of Agriculture, Forest Service. The Geological Survey * * * approved the proposed drilling on February 25, 1976, subject to 10 conditions which assure continued and detailed supervision of Gulf's activities. And on March 8, and April 15, 1976, the Forest Service issued a drilling permit subject to conditions focusing upon protection of the National Forest. Finally, Gulf is subject to the extensive regulations governing oil and gas leasing (43 C.F.R., Part 3100) and both sub-surface and surface operations (30 C.F.R., Part 221) promulgated by the Secretary of the Interior under his authority "to prescribe necessary and proper rules and regulations to do any and all things necessary to carry out and accomplish the purposes" of the act. (30 U.S.C. § 189.) And since the lease concerns lands within a National Forest, Secretary of Agriculture regulations governing oil and gas development are also applicable. (36 C.F.R., Part 252.)

Despite this extensive federal scheme reflecting concern for the local environment as well as development of the nation's resources, Ventura demands a right of final approval. Ventura seeks to prohibit further activity by Gulf until it secures an Open Space Use Permit which may be issued on whatever conditions Ventura determines appropriate, or which may never be issued at all. The federal Government has authorized a specific use of federal lands, and Ventura cannot prohibit that use, either temporarily or permanently, in an attempt to substitute its judgment for that of Congress.

The present conflict is no less direct than that in Kleppe v. New Mexico, supra. Like *Kleppe,* our case involves a power struggle between local and federal governments concerning appropriate use of the public lands. That the New Mexico authorities wished to engage in activity that Congress prohibited, while the Ventura authorities wish to regulate conduct which Congress has authorized is a distinction without a legal difference. * * *

Ventura * * * [relies on] reservations of local jurisdiction contained in sections 30 and 32 of the Mineral Lands Leasing Act (30 U.S.C. §§ 187, 189).[4] It contends that * * * [a finding of preemption] is unwarranted

---

4. Before its 1978 amendment, section 30 provided in pertinent part:

"Each lease shall contain provisions for the purpose of insuring the exercise of

given the broad savings provisions contained in the Mineral Lands Leasing Act.

The proviso in § 187 provides that "[n]one of *such provisions* shall be in conflict with the laws of the states in which the leased property is situated." (30 U.S.C. § 187.) But, as Gulf points out, by the use of the language "such provisions," the proviso relates only to the provisions of the preceding sentence. These provisions relate to employment practices, prevention of undue waste and monopoly, and diligence requirements. There is no mention of land use planning controls. Moreover, the proviso assures only that the Secretary of the Interior shall observe state standards in drafting the lease's terms. It is not a recognition of concurrent state jurisdiction.

Nor is the savings clause in § 189 of any avail. * * * The proviso preserves to the states only "any rights which they may have." While this is an express recognition of the right of the states to tax activities of the Government's lessee pursuant to its lease and has been relied upon in part to uphold forced pooling and well spacing of federal mineral lessee operations (Texas Oil & Gas Corp. v. Phillips Petroleum Co. (W.D.Okl.1967) 277 F.Supp. 366, 371, aff'd (10th Cir.1969) 406 F.2d 1303, 1304), the proviso cannot give authority to the state which it does not already possess. Although state law may apply where it presents "no significant threat to any identifiable federal policy or interest" (Texas Oil & Gas Corp. v. Phillips Petroleum Co., supra, at 371), the states and their subdivisions have no right to apply local regulations impermissibly conflicting with achievement of a congressionally approved use of federal lands and the proviso of § 189 does not alter this principle.

Finally, we are reassured in the correctness of our decision by policy considerations implicitly reflected in the structure and operation of the Mineral Lands Leasing Act of 1920 and the National Environmental Policy Act of 1969 (42 U.S.C. §§ 4321 et seq.). As Ventura recognized in filing its second amended complaint, the National Environmental Protection [sic] Act ("NEPA") and the guidelines, regulations, and Executive Orders issued in pursuance of that act, mandate extensive federal consideration and

reasonable diligence, skill, and care in the operation of said property; * * * [provisions for worker safety and welfare, for the prevention of 'undue waste' and several other subjects] * * * and such other provisions as he may deem necessary to insure the sale of the production of such leased lands to the United States and to the public at reasonable prices, for the protection of the interests of the United States, for the prevention of monopoly, and for the safeguarding of the public welfare. None of such provisions shall be in conflict with the laws of the states in which the leased property is situated."

Section 32 provides:

"The Secretary of the Interior is authorized to prescribe necessary and proper rules and regulations and to do any and all things necessary to carry out and accomplish the purposes of this chapter * * *. Nothing in this chapter shall be construed or held to affect the rights of the States or other local authority to exercise any rights which they may have, including the right to levy and collect taxes upon improvements, output of mines, or other rights, property, or assets of any lessee of the United States."

federal-local cooperation concerning the local, environmental impact of federal action under the Mineral Lands Leasing Act. If federal officials fail to comply with these requirements, Ventura has a remedy against those officials.

Our decision does not mean that local interests will be unheard or unprotected. In rejecting a local veto power while simultaneously guarding local concerns under NEPA, local interests can be represented, the integrity of the federal leases and drilling permits reconciling national energy needs and local environmental interests can be protected, and the ultimate lessee will be responsible to a single master rather than conflicting authority.

Although we recognize that federal incursions upon the historic police power of the states are not to be found without good cause * * * we must affirm because "under the circumstances of this particular case, [the local ordinances] stand as an obstacle to the accomplishment and execution of the full purposes and objectives of Congress." (Hines v. Davidowitz (1941) 312 U.S. 52, 67 * * *). "[W]here those state laws conflict * * * with other legislation passed pursuant to the Property Clause, the law is clear: The state laws must recede." (Kleppe v. New Mexico.* * *)

AFFIRMED.

NOTES AND QUESTIONS

1. Does the Ninth Circuit here correctly construe section 30 of the Mineral Leasing Act (quoted in footnote 4 of its opinion)? Shouldn't state or local land use laws be regarded as intended to promote "safeguarding of the public welfare"? If so, does the last sentence of section 30 preserve the applicability of such laws to federal mineral leases?

2. Does section 30 authorize the Secretary to include in a mineral lease a clause expressly requiring the lessee to comply with state and local laws? Could the Secretary, in other words, reverse the outcome of this case by her choice of lease terms? Can the Secretary do this even if it makes the lessee responsible to possibly "conflicting authority" rather than a "single master," in the words of the *Ventura County* opinion?

3. Conversely, if the Mineral Leasing Act had been construed as ambiguous on the preemption issue, could the Secretary have preempted state law by including a provision in the lease that said the lessee did *not* have to comply with state or local land use laws? While federal preemption is often, as here, found in statutes themselves, the Supreme Court has recognized that "agency regulations implementing federal statutes have been held to pre-empt state law under the Supremacy Clause," Chrysler Corp. v. Brown, 441 U.S. 281, 295–296 (1979), if the agency is acting within the scope of authority delegated to it by the Congress. Should the courts give stricter scrutiny to preemption claims arising from an agency regulation rather than from a statute?

4. In Gulf Oil Corp. v. Wyoming Oil & Gas Conservation Com'n, 693 P.2d 227 (Wyo.1985), decided after *Ventura County*, the Wyoming Supreme

Court held that a decision by the state regulatory commission to issue a permit to Gulf to drill a well on national forest land Gulf had leased from the federal government, subject to the condition that Gulf refrain from using its preferred access route to the well site, was not preempted by federal law. The Commission had rejected the route—which would have extended an existing county road for about 3.8 miles over national forest land and private land—in part because of its aesthetic impacts and lack of reclaimability. Relying on the same two sections of the Mineral Leasing Act as involved in *Ventura County*, the Wyoming court distinguished the Ninth Circuit's reasoning this way: "In contrast to the zoning ordinance[] at issue in *Ventura County*, [state] mining permit requirements designed to safeguard the environment * * * constitute legitimate means of guiding mineral development [on federal lands] without prohibiting it. * * * [W]e find no intent by Congress to exclude states from regulating mining activities on federal land so as to safeguard environmental values. Neither do we find a direct conflict between [the Commission order] and federal laws or objectives."

5. Section 32 of the Mineral Leasing Act was before the U.S. Supreme Court in Commonwealth Edison Co. v. Montana, 453 U.S. 609 (1981). At issue was whether Montana's sizeable severance tax on coal production could be applied to federal coal production within the state. After rejecting the argument of the coal producers and their out-of-state utility customers that the tax placed an impermissible burden on interstate commerce, the majority held that section 32 "expressly authorized the States to impose severance taxes on federal lessees without imposing any limits on the amount of such taxes." It found "nothing in language or legislative history" of the Act to support the assertion that Congress "intended to maximize and capture *all* 'economic rents' from the mining of federal coal * * *. By definition, any state taxation of federal lessees reduces the 'economic rents' accruing to the Federal Government, and appellants' argument would preclude any such taxes despite the explicit grant of taxing authority to the States by § 32." Justice Blackmun, joined by Justices Powell and Stevens, dissented, but only on commerce clause grounds. Does section 32's specific reservation of any rights the state "may have" to tax the "output of mines" leased under the Act provide a stronger basis for finding no preemption of state taxes than section 30 provides for state environmental regulation?

6. Determining whether federal statutes preempt sometimes requires very close reading. Does Section 32, for example, answer the question what rights the states have to tax the output of federal mines, or does it just preserve whatever rights the states had before enactment of the Mineral Leasing Act (which may be none)?

7. Even where Congress seems to address preemption head-on in a statute, the results may be debatable. Remember that Congress will often have a political motive not to resolve the question clearly. Members of Congress may be split on whether preemption is a good idea. Or Congress may simply be unable or unwilling to examine all the different state laws that might be applied, and decide the extent to which they should apply.

The result might be a studied effort to leave, as Yogi Berra allegedly said, the status quo right where it is. Consider, for example: "Nothing in this Act shall be construed as limiting or restricting the power and authority of the United States or * * * as expanding or diminishing Federal or State jurisdiction, responsibility, interests, or rights in water resources development or control." FLPMA, § 701(g), 43 U.S.C. § 1702 Note. Or the following, which appears in several federal laws: "Nothing in this Act shall constitute an express or implied claim or denial on the part of the Federal Government as to exemption from State water laws." See, e.g., 16 U.S.C. § 668dd(i). What does such language say about the application of state law to water found on federal lands? In United States v. Vesterso, 828 F.2d 1234, 1240 (8th Cir.1987), the court concluded that the phrase "or denial" in this disclaimer allows a finding that state water law is preempted in a particular situation. Taken as a whole, then, the disclaimer "is not to be interpreted as changing the body of law which interprets the interaction of federal and state interests in water." Id., at note 5. (The general issue of the applicability of state water law to federal lands is explored in Chapter 6.)

The following preemption case also involved mineral activity on national forest land in California, but this time under a different statutory scheme, and with a different result.

California Coastal Commission v. Granite Rock Co.

Supreme Court of the United States, 1987.
480 U.S. 572.

■ JUSTICE O'CONNOR delivered the opinion of the Court.

This case presents the question whether Forest Service regulations, federal land use statutes and regulations, or the Coastal Zone Management Act of 1972 (CZMA), 16 U.S.C. § 1451 et seq. pre-empt the California Coastal Commission's imposition of a permit requirement on operation of an unpatented mining claim in a national forest.

Granite Rock Company is a privately owned firm that mines chemical and pharmaceutical grade white limestone. Under the Mining Act of 1872, 17 Stat. 91, as amended, 30 U.S.C. § 22 et seq., a private citizen may enter federal lands to explore for mineral deposits. If a person locates a valuable mineral deposit on federal land, and perfects the claim by properly staking it and complying with other statutory requirements, the claimant "shall have the exclusive right of possession and enjoyment of all the surface included within the lines of their locations," 30 U.S.C. § 26, although the United States retains title to the land. The holder of a perfected mining claim may secure a patent to the land by complying with the requirements of the Mining Act and regulations promulgated thereunder, see 43 CFR § 3861.1 et seq.(1986), and, upon issuance of the patent, legal title to the land passes to the patent holder. Granite Rock holds unpatented mining claims on federally owned lands on and around Mount Pico Blanco in the Big Sur region of Los Padres National Forest.

From 1959 to 1980, Granite Rock removed small samples of limestone from this area for mineral analysis. In 1980, in accordance with federal regulations, see 36 CFR § 228.1 et seq. (1986), Granite Rock submitted to the Forest Service a 5–year plan of operations for the removal of substantial amounts of limestone. The plan discussed the location and appearance of the mining operation, including the size and shape of excavations, the location of all access roads, and the storage of any overburden. The Forest Service prepared an Environmental Assessment of the plan. The Assessment recommended modifications of the plan, and the responsible Forest Service Acting District Ranger approved the plan with the recommended modifications in 1981. Shortly after Forest Service approval of the modified plan of operations, Granite Rock began to mine.

Under the California Coastal Act (CCA), Cal.Pub.Res.Code Ann. § 30000 et seq. (West 1986), any person undertaking any development, including mining, in the State's coastal zone must secure a permit from the California Coastal Commission. §§ 30106, 30600. According to the CCA, the Coastal Commission exercises the State's police power and constitutes the State's coastal zone management program for purposes of the federal CZMA. In 1983 the Coastal Commission instructed Granite Rock to apply for a coastal development permit for any mining undertaken after the date of the Commission's letter.

Granite Rock immediately filed an action in the United States District Court for the Northern District of California seeking to enjoin officials of the Coastal Commission from compelling Granite Rock to comply with the Coastal Commission permit requirement * * *.

Granite Rock does not argue that the Coastal Commission has placed any particular conditions on the issuance of a permit that conflict with federal statutes or regulations. Indeed, the record does not disclose what conditions the Coastal Commission will place on the issuance of a permit. Rather, Granite Rock argues, as it must given the posture of the case, that there is no possible set of conditions the Coastal Commission could place on its permit that would not conflict with federal law—that any state permit requirement is *per se* pre-empted. The only issue in this case is this purely facial challenge to the Coastal Commission permit requirement. * * *

Granite Rock and the Solicitor General as amicus [on behalf of the United States] have made basically three arguments in support of a finding that any possible state permit requirement would be pre-empted. First, Granite Rock alleges that the Federal Government's environmental regulation of unpatented mining claims in national forests demonstrates an intent to pre-empt any state regulation. Second, Granite Rock and the Solicitor General assert that indications that state land use planning over unpatented mining claims in national forests is pre-empted should lead to the conclusion that the Coastal Commission permit requirement is pre-empted. Finally, Granite Rock and the Solicitor General assert that the CZMA, by excluding federal lands from its definition of the coastal zone, declared a legislative intent that federal lands be excluded from all state coastal zone regulation. We conclude that these federal statutes and regulations do not, either independently or in combination, justify a facial challenge to the Coastal Commission permit requirement.

Granite Rock concedes that the Mining Act of 1872, as originally passed, expressed no legislative intent on the as yet rarely contemplated subject of environmental regulation. * * * [In an 1897 statute] Congress has delegated to the Secretary of Agriculture the authority to make "rules and regulations" to "regulate [the] occupancy and use" of national forests. 16 U.S.C. § 551. Through this delegation of authority, the Department of Agriculture's Forest Service has promulgated regulations so that "use of the surface of National Forest System lands" by those such as Granite Rock, who have unpatented mining claims authorized by the Mining Act of 1872, "shall be conducted so as to minimize adverse environmental impacts on National Forest System surface resources." 36 CFR §§ 228.1, 228.3(d) (1986). It was pursuant to these regulations that the Forest Service approved the Plan of Operations submitted by Granite Rock. If, as Granite Rock claims, it is the federal intent that Granite Rock conduct its mining unhindered by any state environmental regulation, one would expect to find the expression of this intent in these Forest Service regulations. * * *

Upon examination, however, the Forest Service regulations that Granite Rock alleges pre-empt any state permit requirement not only are devoid of any expression of intent to pre-empt state law, but rather appear to assume that those submitting plans of operations will comply with state laws. The regulations explicitly require all operators within the national forests to comply with state air quality standards, 36 CFR § 228.8(a) (1986), state water quality standards, § 228.8(b), and state standards for the disposal and treatment of solid wastes, § 228.8(c). The regulations also provide that, pending final approval of the plan of operations, the Forest Service officer with authority to approve plans of operation "will approve such operations as may be necessary for timely compliance with the requirements of Federal and *State laws* * * *." § 228.5(b) (emphasis added). Finally, the final subsection of § 228.8, "[r]equirements for environmental protection," provides:

> "(h) Certification or other approval issued by *State agencies* or other Federal agencies of compliance with laws and regulations relation to mining operations will be accepted as compliance with similar or parallel requirements of these regulations" (emphasis supplied).

It is impossible to divine from these regulations, which expressly contemplate coincident compliance with state law as well as with federal law, an intention to pre-empt all state regulation of unpatented mining claims in national forests. Neither Granite Rock nor the Solicitor General contends that these Forest Service regulations are inconsistent with their authorizing statutes.

Given these Forest Service regulations, it is unsurprising that the Forest Service team that prepared the Environmental Assessment of Granite Rock's plan of operation, as well as the Forest Service officer that approved the plan of operation, expected compliance with state as well as federal law. The Los Padres National Forest Environmental Assessment of the Granite Rock plan stated that "Granite Rock is responsible for obtaining any necessary permits which may be required by the California Coastal Commission." The Decision Notice and Finding of No Significant Impact issued by the Acting District Ranger accepted Granite Rock's plan of operation with modifications, [and stated that] * * * "[t]he claimant is further responsible for obtaining any necessary permits required by State and/or county laws, regulations and/or ordinance."

The second argument proposed by Granite Rock is that federal land management statutes demonstrate a legislative intent to limit States to a purely advisory role in federal land management decisions, and that the Coastal Commission permit requirement is therefore pre-empted as an impermissible state land use regulation.

In 1976 two pieces of legislation were passed that called for the development of federal land use management plans affecting unpatented mining claims in national forests. Under the Federal Land Policy and Management Act of 1976 (FLPMA), 43 U.S.C. § 1701 et seq., the Department of the Interior's Bureau of Land Management is responsible for managing the mineral resources on federal forest lands; under the National Forest Management Act (NFMA), 16 U.S.C. §§ 1600–1614, the Forest Service under the Secretary of Agriculture is responsible for the management of the surface impacts of mining on federal forest lands. Granite Rock, as well as the Solicitor General, point to aspects of these statutes indicating a legislative intent to limit States to an advisory role in federal land management decisions. For example, the NFMA directs the Secretary of Agriculture to "develop, maintain, and, as appropriate, revise land and resource management plans for units of the National Forest System, coordinated with the land and resource management planning processes of State and local governments and other Federal agencies," 16 U.S.C. § 1604(a). The FLPMA directs that land use plans developed by the Secretary of the Interior "shall be consistent with State and local plans to the maximum extent [the Secretary] finds consistent with Federal law," and calls for the Secretary, "to the extent he finds practical," to keep apprised of state land use plans, and to "assist in resolving, to the extent practical, inconsistencies between Federal and non-Federal Government plans." 43 U.S.C. § 1712(c)(9).

For purposes of this discussion and without deciding this issue, we may assume that the combination of the NFMA and the FLPMA pre-empts the extension of state land use plans onto unpatented mining claims in national forest lands. The Coastal Commission asserts that it will use permit conditions to impose environmental regulation. See Cal.Pub.Res.Code Ann. § 30233 (West 1986) (quality of coastal waters); § 30253(2) (erosion); § 30253(3) (air pollution); § 30240(b) (impact on environmentally sensitive habitat areas).

While the CCA gives land use as well as environmental regulatory authority to the Coastal Commission, the state statute also gives the Coastal Commission the ability to limit the requirements it will place on the permit. The CCA declares that the Coastal Commission will "provide maximum state involvement in federal activities allowable under federal law or regulations * * *." Cal.Pub.Res.Code Ann. § 30004 (West 1986). Since the state statute does not detail exactly what state standards will and will not apply in connection with various federal activities, the statute must be understood to allow the Coastal Commission to limit the regulations it will impose in those circumstances. In the present case, the Coastal Commission has consistently maintained that it does not seek to prohibit mining of the unpatented claim on national forest land. See 590 F.Supp. at 1373 ("The [Commission] seeks not to prohibit or 'veto,' but to regulate [Granite Rock's] mining activity in accordance with the detailed requirements of the CCA * * *. There is no reason to find that the [Commission] will apply the CCA's regulations so as to deprive [Granite Rock] of its rights under the Mining Act"); "[T]he question presented is merely whether the state can *regulate* uses rather than *prohibit* them. Put another way, the state is not seeking to *determine* basic uses of federal land: rather it is seeking to *regulate* a given mining use so that it is carried out in a more environmentally sensitive and resource-protective fashion".

The line between environmental regulation and land use planning will not always be bright; for example, one may hypothesize a state environmental regulation so severe that a particular land use would become commercially impracticable. However, the core activity described by each phrase is undoubtedly different. Land use planning in essence chooses particular uses for the land; environmental regulation, at its core, does not mandate particular uses of the land but requires only that, however the land is used, damage to the environment is kept within prescribed limits. Congress has indicated its understanding of land use planning and environmental regulation as distinct activities. As noted above, 43 U.S.C. § 1712(c)(9) requires that the Secretary of the Interior's land use plans be consistent with state plans only "to the extent he finds practical." The immediately preceding subsection, however, requires that the Secretary's land use plans "provide for compliance with applicable pollution control laws, including State and Federal air, water, noise, or other pollution standards or implementation plans." § 1712(c)(8). Congress has also illustrated its understanding of land use planning and environmental regulation as distinct activities by delegating the authority to regulate these activities to different agencies. The stated purpose of part 228, subpart A of the Forest Service regulations, 36 CFR § 228.1 (1986), is to "set forth rules and procedures" through which mining on unpatented claims in national forests "shall be conducted so as to minimize adverse environmental impacts on National Forest System surface resources." The next sentence of the subsection, however, declares that "[i]t is not the purpose of these regulations to provide for the management of mineral resources; the responsibility for managing such resources is in the Secretary of the Interior." Congress clearly envisioned that although environmental regulation and land use planning as distinct activities, it would be anomalous to maintain that Congress intended any state environmental regulation of unpatented mining claims in national forests to be *per se* pre-empted as an impermissible exercise of state land use planning. Congress' treatment of environmental regulation and land use planning as generally distinguishable calls for this Court to treat them as distinct, until an actual overlap between the two is demonstrated in a particular case.

Granite Rock suggests that the Coastal Commission's true purpose in enforcing a permit requirement is to prohibit Granite Rock's mining entirely. By choosing to seek injunctive and declaratory relief against the permit requirement before discovering what conditions the Coastal Commission would have placed on the permit, Granite Rock has lost the possibility of making this argument in this litigation. Granite Rock's case must stand or fall on the question whether *any possible* set of conditions attached to the Coastal Commission's permit requirement would be pre-empted. As noted in the previous section, the Forest Service regulations do not indicate a federal intent to pre-empt all state environmental regulation of unpatented mining claims in national forests. Whether or not state land use planning over unpatented mining claims in national forests is pre-empted, the Coastal Commission insists that its permit requirement is an exercise of environmental regulation rather than land use planning. In the present posture of this litigation, the Coastal Commission's identification of a possible set of permit conditions not pre-empted by federal law is sufficient to rebuff Granite Rock's facial challenge to the permit requirement. This analysis is not altered by the fact that the Coastal Commission chooses to impose its environmental regulation by means of a permit requirement. If the Federal Government occupied the field of environmental regulation of unpatented mining claims in national forests—concededly not the case—then state environmental regulation of Granite Rock's mining activity would be pre-empted, whether or not the regulation was implemented through a permit requirement. Conversely, if reasonable state environmental regulation is not pre-empted, then the use of a permit requirement to impose the state regulation does not create a conflict with federal law where none previously existed. The permit requirement itself is not talismanic. * * * [The majority's discussion of the Coastal Zone Management Act is omitted.]

Granite Rock's challenge to the California Coastal Commission's permit requirement was broad and absolute; our rejection of that challenge is correspondingly narrow. Granite Rock argued that any state permit requirement, whatever its conditions, was *per se* pre-empted by federal law. To defeat Granite Rock's facial challenge, the Coastal Commission needed merely to identify a possible set of permit conditions not in conflict with federal law. The Coastal Commission alleges that it will use its permit requirement to impose reasonable environmental regulation. Rather than evidencing an intent to pre-empt such state regulation, the Forest Service regulations appear to assume compliance with state laws. Federal land use statutes and regulations, while arguably expressing an intent to pre-empt state land use planning, distinguish environmental regulation from land use planning. Finally, the language and legislative history of the CZMA expressly disclaim an intent to pre-empt state regulation.

Following an examination of the "almost impenetrable maze of arguably relevant legislation," Justice Powell concludes that "[i]n view of the Property Clause * * *, as well as common sense, federal authority must control * * *." As noted above, the Property Clause gives Congress plenary power over the federal land at issue; however, even within the sphere of the Property Clause, state law is pre-empted only when it conflicts with the operation or objectives of federal law, or when Congress "evidences an intent to occupy a given field," Silkwood v. Kerr–McGee Corp., 464 U.S., at 248. The suggestion that traditional pre-emption analysis is inapt in this context can be justified, if at all, only by the assertion that the state regulation in this case would be "duplicative." The description of the regulation as duplicative, of course, is based on Justice Powell's conclusions that land use regulation and environmental regulation are indistinguishable, and that any state permit requirement, by virtue of being a permit requirement rather than some other form of regulation, would duplicate federal permit requirements. Because we disagree with these assertions, we apply the traditional pre-emption analysis which requires an actual conflict between state and federal law, or a congressional expression of intent to pre-empt, before we will conclude that state regulation is pre-empted.

Contrary to the assertion of Justice Powell that the Court today gives States power to impose regulations that "conflict with the views of the Forest Service," we hold only that the barren record of this facial challenge has not demonstrated any conflict. We do not, of course, approve any future application of the Coastal Commission permit requirement that in fact conflicts with federal law. Neither do we take the course of condemning the permit requirement on the basis of as yet unidentifiable conflicts with the federal scheme. * * *

■ JUSTICE POWELL, with whom JUSTICE STEVENS joins, concurring in part and dissenting in part.

* * * The most troubling feature of the Court's analysis is that it is divorced from the realities of its holding. The Court cautions that its decision allows only "reasonable" environmental regulation and that it does not give the Coastal Commission a veto over Granite Rock's mining activities. But if the Coastal Commission can require Granite Rock to secure a permit before allowing mining operations to proceed, it necessarily can forbid Granite Rock from conducting these operations. It may be that reasonable environmental regulations would not force Granite Rock to close its mine. This misses the point. The troubling fact is that the Court has given a state authority—here the Coastal Commission—the power to prohibit Granite Rock from exercising the rights granted by its Forest Service permit. This abdication of federal control over the use of federal land is unprecedented. * * *

The dangers of duplicative permit requirements are evident in this case. The federal permit system reflects a careful balance between two important federal interests: the interest in developing mineral resources on federal land, and the interest in protecting our national forests from environmental harm. The Forest Service's issuance of a permit to Granite Rock reflects its conclusion that environmental concerns associated with Granite Rock's mine do not justify restricting mineral development on this portion of a federal forest. Allowing the Coastal Commission to strike a different balance necessarily conflicts with the federal system. * * *

In summary, it is fair to say that, commencing in 1872, Congress has created an almost impenetrable maze of arguably relevant legislation in no less than a half-dozen statutes, augmented by the regulations of two Departments of the Executive. There is little cause for wonder that the language of these statutes and regulations has generated considerable confusion. There is an evident need for Congress to enact a single, comprehensive statute for the regulation of federal lands.

Having said this, it is at least clear that duplicative federal and state permit requirements create an intolerable conflict in decisionmaking. In view of the Property Clause of the Constitution, as well as common sense, federal authority must control with respect to land "belonging to the United States." Yet, the Court's opinion today approves a system of twofold authority with respect to environmental matters. The result of this holding is that state regulators, whose views on environmental and mineral policy may conflict with the views of the Forest Service, have the power, with respect to federal lands, to forbid activity expressly authorized by the Forest Service. I dissent.

Justice SCALIA, with whom Justice WHITE joins, dissenting.

* * * It seems to me ultimately irrelevant whether state environmental regulation has been pre-empted with respect to federal lands, since the exercise of state power at issue here is not environmental regulation but land use control. * * * [The California Coastal Act] is plainly a land use statute, and the permit that statute requires Granite Rock to obtain is a land use control device. Its character as such is not altered by the fact that the State may now be agreeable to issuing it as long as environmental concerns are satisfied. Since, as the Court's opinion quite correctly assumes, state exercise of land use authority over federal lands is pre-empted by federal law, California's permit requirement must be invalid. * * *

Any competent lawyer, faced with a demand from the California Coastal Commission that Granite Rock obtain a * * * coastal development permit for its Pico Blanco operations, would have responded precisely as Granite Rock's lawyers essentially did: Our use of federal land has been approved by the Federal Government, thank you, and does not require the approval of the State. We should not allow California to claim, in the teeth of the plain language of its legislation, * * * that it would use the permitting requirement to achieve, not land use management, but only environmental controls. We should particularly not give ear to that claim since it was not the representation made to Granite Rock when application for the permit was demanded. If environmental control is, as California now assures us, its limited objective in this case, then it must simply achieve that objective by means other than a land use control scheme. If and when it does so, we may have occasion to decide (as we need not today) whether state environmental controls are also pre-empted. More likely, however, the question will not arise in the future, as it has not arisen in the past, because of the Federal Government's voluntary accommodation of state environmental concerns—an accommodation that could not occur here only because California neglected to participate in the proceedings. * * *

NOTES AND QUESTIONS

1. Is *Granite Rock* consistent with *Ventura County*, decided eight years earlier? Note *Ventura* was summarily affirmed (without opinion) by the Supreme Court. In *Granite Rock*, surprisingly, only Justice Scalia's dissenting opinion even cited *Ventura County*, and that only in passing. How much of *Ventura County* survives *Granite Rock*? Preemption cases are usually specifically tied to the facts and particular laws involved, but should the Court in *Granite Rock* have addressed its recent decision in a closely related context?

2. Justice O'Connor suggests that if a state regulation is "environmental" rather than "land use" in character, it will not be preempted. Is the difference between the two clear? Suppose, for example, that on remand the state Coastal Commission issues Granite Rock a permit to mine, but requires the mined land to be restored to its approximate original contour and revegetated to preserve the aesthetics of the coastline. The company objects, arguing that restoration is so expensive that to require it makes mining uneconomic, and therefore the condition effectively prohibits mining. Is the condition an "environmental" or a "land use" regulation?

3. The same question could easily arise in other contexts; for example: (a) The state enacts a law to prevent soil erosion and protect water quality, and one of its features limits the amount of livestock grazing in riparian areas (along streams and other watercourses). Can the state apply this law to livestock grazing on federal lands? (b) The state law says no mineral development within 1000 feet of a church, school, or cemetery. Can this be applied to mineral development on federal lands?

4. Note that the majority here only *assumes without deciding* that FLPMA and the NMFA "preempts the extension of state land use plans onto unpatented mining claims in national forest lands." On the basis of the pertinent excerpts from these laws, is that assumption correct? Notice, as Justice O'Connor's opinion reflects, FLPMA requires that the Secretary of the Interior's land use plans be consistent with state land use plans "to the extent he finds practical." 43 U.S.C. § 1712(c)(8). Modern federal resource management laws often contain this notion of what has been called "cooperative federalism," requiring federal land management agencies to comply with state and local law "to the maximum extent practicable" in various contexts. See FLPMA, 43 U.S.C. §§ 1720, 1721(c), 1733(d), 1747, 1765(a); National Forest Management Act, 16 U.S.C. § 1612; Fish and Wildlife Coordination Act, 16 U.S.C. § 661. What kind of reason(s) does a federal land manager have to have to defend a decision that compliance with state land use plans is not "practical"? That it's too much trouble? That it's unwise as a matter of principle to give the state an effective veto over proposed federal land uses? That national policy promotes mining on federal lands?

5. The Forest Service here said that Granite Rock is "responsible for obtaining any necessary permits which may be required by the California Coastal Commission." Is the Forest Service saying that it doesn't regard state law as being preempted? Is that what "necessary" means? Or is it

saying Granite Rock must get a permit if (and only if) it is legally necessary? Another example of studied ambiguity on the preemption question is provided by 43 U.S.C. § 1712(c)(8), discussed in the majority opinion, which requires the Secretary's land use plans to "provide for compliance with *applicable*" state pollution standards and plans (emphasis added). What does this indicate, if anything, about which state standards and plans are "applicable"? All of them? If not all, which ones?

6. In a sense, *Granite Rock* was a narrow decision; it decided only that the miner on federal land had to apply for a state permit. As a result, the Court did not address how far the state could go in regulating the mining activity through conditions or limitations placed on the permit. Nevertheless, by giving states the opportunity to apply their permit processes (and by burdening miners with that obligation), the decision significantly shifts regulatory leverage toward the states. Suppose, after this decision, Granite Rock applies to the Commission for a permit. Two years go by and the state is still sitting on the permit application. State law says no mining without a permit. Does the company have any recourse? What? (In fact, after the decision Granite Rock abandoned its plan to open the mine.)

7. Could the Forest Service here have changed the outcome in the case by providing in its regulations for explicit preemption of state law? Or could it have explicitly preempted state law in either its land use plan for this area of the forest, or its decision approving the company's plan of operations under the regulations? Compare United States v. Brown, 552 F.2d 817, 821 (8th Cir.1977), cert. denied, 431 U.S. 949 (1977), upholding the conviction of a duck hunter for carrying firearms in a national park, even though his conduct was lawful under state law. Congress had not spoken directly to the question of hunting in this national park, but Park Service regulations prohibited possession of firearms:

> The National Park Service Act allows the Secretary of the Interior to promulgate "such rules and regulations as he may deem necessary or proper for the use and management of the parks." 16 U.S.C. § 3. The regulations prohibiting hunting and possession of a loaded firearm were promulgated pursuant to that authority, 36 C.F.R. §§ 2.11 and 2.32, and are valid prescriptions designed to promote the purposes of the federal lands within the national park. Under the Supremacy Clause the federal law overrides the conflicting state law allowing hunting within the park.

8. Would, in Justice Scalia's phrase, "[a]ny competent lawyer" have responded precisely as Granite Rock's lawyers did here, by bringing a facial challenge to the Coastal Commission's attempt to exercise jurisdiction? Were there any alternative strategies that would, at least in hindsight, have been better?

9. Surprisingly, the Supreme Court did not cite here a number of state appellate court decisions that had found state environmental laws applicable to hardrock mining operations on the federal lands. See, e.g., State ex rel. Andrus v. Click, 97 Idaho 791, 554 P.2d 969 (1976); State ex rel. Cox v. Hibbard, 31 Or.App. 269, 570 P.2d 1190 (1977). But see

Brubaker v. Board of County Commissioners, El Paso County, 652 P.2d 1050 (Colo.1982), which held that a county's denial, pursuant to its zoning ordinance, of a permit to conduct exploratory drilling on mining claims on federal land in the county was preempted by federal law. A federal court later relied primarily on *Brubaker* to find preempted a county ordinance that prohibited the issuance of all new surface mining permits in the scenic Spearfish Canyon area of the Black Hills National Forest. South Dakota Mining Assn. v. Lawrence County, 977 F.Supp. 1396 (D.S.D.1997). In 1998, Montana voters approved a state initiative, proposition 137, which banned cyanide heap-leach gold mining operations throughout the state, including on federal lands, because of water quality concerns. The mining industry promptly challenged it in state and federal courts on a variety of grounds, including preemption. As of this writing no decisions on the merits have been rendered.

10. *Granite Rock* elicited considerable commentary. See, e.g., John Leshy, Granite Rock and the States' Influence over Federal Land Use, 18 Envt'l L. 99 (1987); Eric Freyfogle, *Granite Rock,* Institutional Competence and the State Role in Federal Land Planning, 59 U.Colo.L.Rev. 475 (1988); Richard H. Cowart & Sally Fairfax, Public Lands Federalism: Judicial Theory and Administrative Reality, 15 Ecology L.Q. 375 (1988).

11. The federal government did not participate at all in *Ventura County,* and it participated only as *amicus* in *Granite Rock.* Why is the federal government frequently *not* a party to these preemption cases, even though management of its lands are directly affected? Further, in *Granite Rock,* why do you think the Reagan Administration argued in favor of preemption, given its strong rhetorical support for states' rights in many contexts?

12. Suppose that the mineral developers in both *Ventura County* and *Granite Rock* needed to locate certain processing and transportation facilities on *non-federal* land; e.g., a pipeline for oil and gas in the former, and a shipping facility for the limestone in the latter. Do the mineral developers have an argument that state or local law is preempted by the federal law? If not, does this give state or local governments an effective, if somewhat more indirect, veto over the production of oil from federal lands? In May 2001, Las Animas County, Colorado, enacted land use regulations that impose various requirements on oil and gas development facilities on private land. Oil and gas operators have challenged the regulations on various grounds, including that they are preempted by federal mineral leasing laws. The case is pending.

13. Should Congress or the courts establish general rules for the proper role for state and local governments on federal lands, which would presumably vary with the subject-matter? For example, is the national interest in timber or minerals or energy stronger or weaker than the national interest in wildlife or recreation or livestock? Or should preemption turn on the character and strength of the states' interest? Is the state (or local) interest in environmental or consumer protection stronger or weaker than its interest in taxation or health and safety or law enforcement? Should the courts *presume* preemption when the pertinent statutes

are unclear, or do the opposite? Because Congress has the ultimate power to draw lines here, should there be a bright-line judicial rule that in effect instructs Congress: "Be clear one way or we'll conclude the other"?

NOTE: A "DORMANT PROPERTY CLAUSE"?

Where title to land is concerned, a federal "common law" may override state property law in some instances, even when the U.S. acquires property whose characteristics of title was heretofore fully controlled by state property law. In United States v. Little Lake Misere Land Co., 412 U.S. 580 (1973), the United States had acquired private land in Louisiana for a bird refuge, with the seller reserving the mineral rights. Louisiana law provided that, where the federal government was the purchaser, the seller's mineral rights would never lapse, even though they would lapse from nonuse if they had been located under private lands. Noting, among other things, this discrimination against the United States, the Court held that federal common law, not state law, controlled the property right the federal government acquired. The Court did not cite the Property Clause, but Professor Peter Appel has suggested that the Court was really applying a "dormant emanation" from that Clause, analogous to the dormant commerce clause used by the Supreme Court to strike down state legislation in situations where Congress has not acted. Appel, The Power of Congress "Without Limitation": The Property Clause and Federal Regulation of Private Property, 86 Minn. L.Rev. 1, 125–27 (2001).

Little Lake Misere was extended in United States v. Albrecht, 496 F.2d 906 (8th Cir.1974). This case involved a federal program to protect the principal waterfowl breeding grounds in the continental United States, the northern Great Plains, and especially North Dakota. The focus of federal acquisition efforts has been so-called "prairie potholes," which were described by the court this way: "Each square mile * * * is dotted by approximately 70 to 80 potholes of three to four feet deep. * * * [On certain types of land] the potholes usually retain water through July or August, and therefore, provide an excellent environment for the production of aquatic invertebrates and aquatic plants, the basic foods for breeding adult ducks and their offspring. Essential to the maintenance of the land as a waterfowl production area is the availability of shallow water in these numerous potholes during the usually drier summer months."* In *Albrecht*, the defendants' assignors had sold a "waterfowl easement" to the United States, which prohibited the seller from draining potholes on the land. A "stealthy ditchdigger" caused the area to be drained, and the United States brought suit to force defendants to fill in the ditches. Defendants argued

---

* The "Prairie Pothole" region of the northern Great Plains in the U.S. and Canada has been described as "one of the most extensive and valuable freshwater resources in the world," although little appreciated. More than two-thirds of North American ducks depend upon the potholes, which is "threatened with a process of destruction by incremental acts of land drainage." See John H. Davidson and Philip P. Chandler, The Minimal Effects Exemption and the Regulation of Headwater Wetlands under Swampbuster, with a Coda on the Theme of SWANCC, 31 Env. L. Rptr. 11417 (2001).

that the easement was invalid because North Dakota law did not recognize a "waterfowl easement" property interest. The court replied:

> [U]nder the context of this case, while the determination of North Dakota law in regard to the validity of the property right conveyed to the United States would be useful, it is not controlling, particularly if viewed as aberrant or hostile to federal property rights. Assuming *arguendo* that North Dakota law would not permit the conveyance of the right to the United States in this case, the specific federal governmental interest in acquiring rights to property for waterfowl production areas is stronger than any possible "aberrant" or "hostile" North Dakota law that would preclude the conveyance granted in this case. *Little Lake*, [412 U.S.] at 595, 596. We fully recognize that laws of real property are usually governed by the particular states; yet the reasonable property right conveyed to the United States in this case effectuates an important national concern, the acquisition of necessary land for waterfowl production areas, and should not be defeated by any possible North Dakota law barring the conveyance of this property right. To hold otherwise would be to permit the possibility that states could rely on local property laws to defeat the acquisition of reasonable rights to their citizens' property pursuant to 16 U.S.C. § 718(c) and to destroy a national program of acquiring property to aid in the breeding of migratory birds. We, therefore, specifically hold that the property right conveyed to the United States in this case, whether or not deemed a valid easement or other property right under North Dakota law, was a valid conveyance under federal law and vested in the United States the rights as stated therein. Section 718d(c) specifically allows the United States to acquire wetland and pothole areas and the "interests therein."

In North Dakota v. United States, 460 U.S. 300, 317–21 (1983), the Supreme Court applied the *Little Lake Misere Land Co.* principle in the context of the same waterfowl easement acquisition program involved in *Albrecht*. The typical easement acquired by the federal government contained a legal description of a parcel of land, and imposed restrictions on all wetland areas within the parcel, including not only those already in existence or subject to recurrence but also "any enlargements of said wetlands areas resulting from normal or abnormal increased water." North Dakota enacted a state law that authorized landowners to drain any after-expanded wetland or water area, contrary to the terms of easements the U.S. had already acquired, and also limited easements to a maximum term of 99 years. The Court found the state law "hostile to federal interests" and said it could not be applied. "To respond to the inherently fluctuating nature of wetlands, the Secretary has chosen to negotiate easement agreements imposing restrictions on after-expanded wetlands as well as those described in the easement itself. As long as North Dakota landowners are willing to negotiate such agreements, the agreements may not be abrogated by state law." The same analysis was followed with regard to the state attempt to impose a term limit on the federally acquired easements.

Another situation where a federal law of property may come into play is in the area of water rights. In some circumstances, the United States may appropriate available water through state legal processes for purposes that are not recognized as "beneficial" under state water law, but which are necessary to carry out federal land programs. For a recent example of how this may work, see the Great Sand Dunes legislation enacted in 2000, 16 U.S.C. § 410hhh–7, and John Leshy, Water Rights for Federal Land Conservation Programs: A Turn-of-the-Century Evaluation, 4 Water L.Rev. 273 (2001).

E.   FEDERAL LANDS–BASED IMMUNITIES AND REVENUE SHARING

Although there are many circumstances in which states may regulate private entities conducting federally authorized activities on federal land, it is generally understood that, absent a rather clear expression by Congress, states are generally prohibited from regulating the federal government itself. This regulatory immunity arises from the sovereignty of the United States, combined with the idea behind the Supremacy Clause of the U.S. Constitution, Art. VI, § 3, cl. 2. Outside the public lands context, for example, the Supreme Court has used Supremacy Clause-based notions of federal immunity to construe ambiguous statutes as not subjecting federal agencies to state permit processes, even if they did subject federal agencies to substantive state environmental regulation. See, e.g., Hancock v. Train, 426 U.S. 167 (1976) (Clean Air Act); EPA v. California ex rel. State Water Resources Control Board, 426 U.S. 200 (1976) (Clean Water Act). Like other immunities, this regulatory immunity can be waived. In fact, Congress swiftly reversed the results in those cases by amending the statutes in question to make clear that federal agencies needed state permits. See 91 Stat. 711 (1977) (Clean Air Act); 91 Stat. 1597, 1598 (1977) (Clean Water Act).

A similar notion of federal regulatory immunity has been applied in the federal lands context. For example, BLM issued a right-of-way permit to a unit of the federal Department of Energy to construct a powerline across BLM lands. The permit was issued under the Federal Land Policy and Management Act, which requires such permits to "contain * * * terms and conditions which will * * * require compliance with State standards for [inter alia] environmental protection * * * if those standards are more stringent than applicable Federal standards." 43 U.S.C. § 1765(a)(iv). In Columbia Basin Land Protection Association v. Schlesinger, 643 F.2d 585, 602–06 (9th Cir.1981) and Citizens and Landowners Against the Miles City/New Underwood Powerline v. Secretary, U.S. Dept. of Energy, 683 F.2d 1171 (8th Cir.1982), the courts held that the Department of Energy had to conform to state powerline siting standards, but did not need to obtain a state permit. In Montana v. Johnson, 738 F.2d 1074 (9th Cir. 1984), the court held that a state requirement to achieve "minimum adverse environmental impact" was "too subjective and vague to serve as a 'standard' for purposes of [FLPMA, because it was] incapable of offering any guidance to the [relevant federal agency]." Other more specific provisions such as those dealing with erosion control and reseeding of disturbed land did qualify as "standards," even though they had not been previously promulgated and had not been generally applicable.

Federal sovereignty and the Supremacy Clause immunize federal property from state tax laws. See Van Brocklin v. Anderson, 117 U.S. 151 (1886). But the federal tax immunity does *not* generally extend to situations where the state imposes taxes not on the federal government directly, but rather on federal employees or private contractors doing business with the federal government on federal lands. Such decisions go back a long way; e.g., in Forbes v. Gracey, 94 U.S. 762 (1876), the Supreme Court held that a state has the power to tax a miner's interest in a mining claim on federal land, even though the United States retained legal title to the land and the mineral. For a time the Court took an expansive view of federal immunity, but then gradually restricted its scope. See Laurence Tribe, AMERICAN CONSTITUTIONAL LAW, vol.I, pp. 1220–37 (3d ed. 2000). In United States v. County of Fresno, 429 U.S. 452 (1977), for example, the Court upheld a county tax on the possessory interest of Forest Service employees in housing on federal land provided by the federal government. Noting that the legal incidence of the tax fell directly on private citizens (the federal employees), the Court was not moved by the fact that it might indirectly impose an economic burden on the Forest Service (by requiring it to pay its employees more). Instead, it said the tax can be invalidated "only if it discriminates against the Forest Service or other federal employees, which it does not do." This narrow view of the scope of the federal tax immunity has been applied in other cases since; e.g., United States v. New Mexico, 455 U.S. 720 (1982). Tribe, supra. See also Commonwealth Edison v. Montana, 453 U.S. 609 (1981), supra, p. 212.

Of course, such judicial decisions narrowly construing federal tax immunity do not negate the power of Congress to broaden the immunity by statute. But here the "political safeguards of federalism"—the powerful influence state governments have on national government policymaking—frequently come into play. Perhaps the most vivid illustration of this influence is in the various ways that Congress has sought to compensate for the tax exempt status of federal lands. While Congress has not waived its immunity from taxation, it has adopted many programs to provide payments in lieu of taxes so that state and local governments will realize an income stream from federal lands.

Historically, a common way to do this is to pay the states (or local governments) a percentage of proceeds from resource development. For example, counties receive 25% of cash receipts the federal government realizes from timber harvesting on national forests, 16 U.S.C. § 500, and 50% of such receipts on the timber-rich "Oregon & California" (O & C) lands administered by the BLM. See 43 U.S.C. § 1181f. The state of origin receives 50% of revenues from oil and gas leases under the provisions of the Mineral Leasing Act—except Alaska, which receives 90% of such revenues. 30 U.S.C. § 191. The Wildlife Refuge Revenue Sharing Act provides that 25% of the revenues realized from the development of refuge resources are paid to the local counties. See 16 U.S.C. § 715s; see Watt v. Alaska, 451 U.S. 259 (1981) (Alaska continues to be entitled to 90% of the revenue from federal mineral leasing in wildlife refuges, because a 1964 amendment making mineral revenues in wildlife refuges subject to the 25% revenue sharing provision did not implicitly repeal its 90% entitlement under the Mineral Leasing Act).

Not all federal-land-based payments to state and local governments are tied to federal resource development. The Payment In Lieu of Taxes Act (PILOT), 31 U.S.C. § 6901 et seq., provides a minimum federal payment of 75 cents per acre of land managed by the BLM, Forest Service and Park Service to local governments regardless of development revenues, and provides other forms of compensation. Adopted in 1976, PILOT follows on a similar program, dating back to 1935, which reimburses local governments for revenues lost because of the tax-exempt status of national wildlife refuges. See 16 U.S.C. § 715s. The PILOT formula is complicated; among other things, its payments are reduced depending on money received through timber revenue sharing. In Lawrence County v. Lead–Deadwood School Dist., 469 U.S. 256 (1985), the Court held that counties are free to spend PILOT funds for any governmental purposes, and that the states cannot place restrictions on such county expenditures:

> The Payment in Lieu of Taxes Act was passed in response to a comprehensive review of the policies applicable to the use, management, and disposition of federal lands. Public Land Law Review Commission, One Third of the Nation's Land (1970). The Federal Government had for many years been providing payments to partially compensate state and local governments for revenues lost as a result of the presence of tax-exempt federal lands within their borders. But the Public Land Law Review Commission and Congress identified a number of flaws in the existing programs. Prominent among congressional concerns was that, under systems of direct payment to the States, local governments often received funds that were insufficient to cover the full cost of maintaining the federal lands within their jurisdictions. Where these lands consisted of wilderness or park areas, they attracted thousands of visitors each year. State governments might benefit from this federally inspired tourism through the collection of income or sales taxes, but these revenues would not accrue to local governments, who were often restricted to raising revenue from property taxes. Yet it was the local governments that bore the brunt of the expenses associated with federal lands, such as law enforcement, road maintenance, and the provision of public health services.

Other forms of federal-lands-based aid to state and local governments are somewhat more obscure. The Federal Highway Act has traditionally increased the federal contributing share for construction of interstate and other federal highways in any state where the percentage of federal and Indian landholdings in that state (other than national forests, parks and monuments) exceeded 5% of the state's total land area. 23 U.S.C.A. § 120. See generally Sally Fairfax & C. Kemm Yates, THE FINANCIAL INTER-

EST OF WESTERN STATES IN NON–TAX REVENUES FROM THE PUBLIC LANDS (1985); John Leshy, Sharing the Federal Multiple–Use Lands—Historic Lessons and Speculations for the Future, in RETHINKING THE PUBLIC LANDS 235 (1984).

On the whole, there is much evidence that the states with significant amounts of public lands receive far more economic benefits from federal land ownership than detriments, and there seems to be a "pork-barrel" element in such federal revenue sharing programs. *Id.* In September 2001, for example, the Bozeman Chronicle reported that Gallatin County, Montana, received $1.13 in federal PILOT money in fiscal year 2001 for every acre of federal land, whereas private forest and grazing land was taxed between 44 and 70 cents per acre. On top of this, besides federal payments in lieu of taxes, Montana receives substantial direct revenues by taxing private development activities on federal lands. See, e.g., Commonwealth Edison Co. v. Montana, 453 U.S. 609 (1981) (upholding the application of Montana's 30% severance tax to lessees of federal coal). It also receives 50% of the federal revenues from the coal leasing. And it will receive substantial revenues from the state's large tourist industry, which is attracted by the resources located on federal lands.

While the various formulae for these state and local payments set the amounts that are to paid, in almost all cases, the funds must be appropriated out of the U.S. Treasury each year by Congress. (The congressional appropriations committees abhor true "revolving" funds where the payments are automatic, because it diminishes their power over the purse strings.) Sometimes a temptation exists to cut the payments in favor of some other competing priority for federal funds, but in practice the appropriation of money for this purpose is very popular, and payments are almost never interrupted or significantly cut.

When the amount of federal aid is tied directly to resource development (as in the timber stumpage and mineral leasing payments), the effect is to make state and local governments advocates of more federal timber sales and mineral leasing. This effect has been noted and criticized, particularly by environmental advocates. See, e.g., Dan Barney, THE LAST STAND 118–19 (1974); see also Jerome C. Muys, The Federal Lands, in FEDERAL ENVIRONMENTAL LAW 532–35 (1974). Environmentalists have long tried to persuade Congress to "uncouple" payments to state and local governments from resource development. After a long battle, they are beginning to make a little headway. In the year 2000, Congress guaranteed counties reliant upon national forest timber sale revenues a stable level of payment for the next several years, regardless of the amount of federal timber sold. In the meantime, Congress will consider whether to make this permanent or otherwise reform the payment system. See Pub.L.No. 106–393, 114 Stat. 1608–15.

This financial incentive sometimes leads state or local governments to bring lawsuits against federal land managers when they restrict resource development; see, e.g., See, e.g., Douglas County v. Babbitt, 48 F.3d 1495 (9th Cir.1995), cert. denied, 516 U.S. 1042 (1996), or to intervene as defendants in cases seeking to apply environmental laws to reduce timber harvesting, see, e.g., Forest Conservation Council v. United States Forest Serv., 66 F.3d 1489 (9th Cir.1995). Resource developers sometimes try to "partner" with the states in order to lessen their opposition to federal resource development. For example, federal law currently puts 100% of the federal revenue from the lucrative oil and gas development on the outer continental shelf in the federal treasury. 43 U.S.C. § 1338. Many, indeed nearly all, coastal states have been opposed to federal oil and gas leasing on the outer continental shelves off their shores, driven mostly by local environmental concerns. In response, the oil and gas industry and its supporters in Congress have favored giving the coastal states a share of federal offshore oil and gas lease revenues, such as happens onshore, in the hopes of inducing states to back off their opposition.

While state and local governments tend to support federal resource development to increase their revenue sharing payments, Alaska took its self-interest to new heights when, in 1993, it sued the United States for $29 billion (yes, billion), claiming it had lost this amount in foregone revenue sharing payments because the federal government had withdrawn some areas of federal land in the state from mineral leasing. Finding "two hundred years of law recognizing in the Federal Government a virtually unfettered discretion as to the management of its own lands," and also finding it undisputed that the United States had "made no promise to make federal mineral lands productive of royalty revenues for the State," the court dismissed the suit. State of Alaska v. United States, 35 Fed.Cl. 685 (1996), *aff'd w/o op.*, 119 F.3d 16 (Fed.Cir.1997), cert. denied, 522 U.S. 1108 (1998).

Alaska's revenue sharing has been an issue in the long-running national debate over whether to open the coastal plain of the federal Arctic National Wildlife Refuge to oil and gas development. As noted earlier, Alaska receives 90% rather than the usual state share of 50% of federal onshore mineral leasing revenues. Proponents of drilling the Arctic Refuge have argued that revenue from oil and gas lease sales and development would help balance the federal budget, but the argument is not very effective so long as the federal share was only 10%. In early 1996 Congress sent the President legislation that would have opened the Refuge to drilling, but cut Alaska's share from 90% to 50%. President Clinton vetoed the legislation (part of a massive "budget reconciliation" bill) on environmental grounds in January 1996. Alaska has argued that Congress has no power to change the revenue sharing formula because it was first included in the Alaska Statehood Act (72 Stat. 339 (1958)) which, Alaska maintains, is a solemn contract between sovereigns that cannot be breached.

ANOTHER ASPECT OF FEDERAL IMMUNITY: MAY THE U.S. BE ESTOPPED BY THE ACTS OF ITS AGENTS?

In Utah Power and Light Co. v. United States, 243 U.S. 389 (1917), noted at p. 183, supra, the utility company built electrical generation and distribution facilities on a national forest without explicit permission from the Forest Service. One of the utility's defenses was that when the forest reservations were created an understanding and agreement was had between the defendants, or their predecessors, and some unmentioned officers or agents of the United States to the effect that the reservations would not be an obstacle to the construction or operation of the works in question; that all rights essential thereto would be allowed and granted under the [relevant statute]; that consistently with this understanding and agreement and relying thereon the defendants, or their predecessors, completed the works and proceeded with the generation and distribution of electric energy, and that in consequence the United States is estopped to question the right of the defendants to maintain and operate the works. Of this it is enough to say that the United States is neither bound nor estopped by acts of its officers or agents in entering into an arrangement or agreement to do or cause to be done what the law does not sanction or permit.

* * * And, if it be assumed that the rule is subject to exceptions, we find nothing in the cases in hand which fairly can be said to take them out of it as heretofore understood and applied in this court. A suit by the United States to enforce and maintain its policy respecting lands which it holds in trust for all the people stands upon a different plane in this and some other respects from the ordinary private suit to regain the title to real property or to remove a cloud from it. Causey v. United States, 240 U.S. 399, 402.

NOTES AND QUESTIONS

1.   What is the legal basis for holding that adverse possession, equitable estoppel, and similar doctrines do not apply against the federal government? Does the same idea hold true for other sovereigns; e.g., state or tribal governments? Does the idea rest solely on sovereign immunity, or does separation of powers between the legislative and executive branches (a subject explored in the next chapter) have something to do with it?

2.   Is there also a practical basis for such a result? What might be the consequences if government could be bound by the acts of its agents, even if they are acting beyond the scope of their authority?

3.   Can Congress waive this principle? Should it? That is, should the federal lands be subject to adverse possession and quiet title laws in the same manner as private land? In fact, Congress has enacted some limited waivers of its sovereign immunity. The Color of Title Act, 43 U.S.C. §§ 1068–1068b, requires either (a) good faith adverse possession for more than 20 years and either cultivation or erection of valuable improvements, or (b) continuous good faith possession since January 1, 1901. Knowledge of federal ownership is a bar. See, e.g., Day v. Hickel, 481 F.2d 473 (9th Cir.1973). The Quiet Title Act of 1972, 28 U.S.C. §§ 2409a, 1346(f), 1402(d), waives immunity, on specified terms, as to those who claim title based on a valid conveyance rather than on adverse possession, but many private claims are barred by its 12–year statute of limitations, which generally begins to run on the date a plaintiff knew or should have known of the opposing claim to title by the United States. See Block v. North

Dakota, 461 U.S. 273 (1983). In United States v. Beggerly, 524 U.S. 38 (1998), the Supreme Court ruled that no equitable tolling of the QTA is permissible because the "knew or should have known" trigger incorporates the concept by itself. See also, e.g., California v. Yuba Goldfields, Inc., 752 F.2d 393 (9th Cir.1985), cert. denied, 474 U.S. 1005 (1985). The QTA was amended in 1986 to relax the limitation on state claims in certain circumstances. 100 Stat. 3351. On the title difficulties that can be created when the government carries out new surveys of public lands, see James M. Picone, Resurveys of Public Lands, 30 Rocky Mtn.Min.L.Inst. 20–1 (1985).

4.   The *Utah Power & Light* formulation continues to be the law on the application of estoppel based on the conduct of federal employees. In modern times, the Supreme Court has continued to reject arguments that the government should be estopped in particular circumstances, although it has said it is "hesitant * * * to say that there are *no cases* in which the public interest in insuring that the Government can enforce the law free from estoppel might be outweighed by the countervailing interest of citizens in some minimum standard of decency, honor and reliability in their dealings with their Government." Heckler v. Community Health Services of Crawford County, 467 U.S. 51, 58 (1984) (emphasis in original); see also Office of Personnel Management v. Richmond, 496 U.S. 414 (1990). Some lower courts have allowed estoppel against the United States in extreme cases. For example, in United States v. Wharton, 514 F.2d 406 (9th Cir.1975), the Ninth Circuit held that the BLM was estopped by its conduct to eject a family that had resided on a federal parcel since 1919. But other courts have refused; e.g., Bischoff v. Glickman, 54 F.Supp.2d 1226 (D.Wyo. 1999); City & County of Denver v. Bergland, 517 F.Supp. 155, 194–97 (D.Colo.1981), modified on other grounds, 695 F.2d 465 (10th Cir.1982).

F.   "TAKINGS" LIMITS ON THE EXERCISE OF CONGRESSIONAL POWER

One other important constitutional limit on Congress's power to regulate activities to protect federal land deserves examination. The Fifth Amendment to the U.S. Constitution bars the federal government from "taking" property for public use without payment of just compensation. Most "takings" litigation involves private property held in fee simple, in which the existence of a constitutionally protected property interest is not contested. When takings claims are made in the context of federal lands and resources, by contrast, the property interest alleged to have been taken is almost always less than a fee simple interest. Sometimes there is a question whether the private property interest claimed actually exists; if it does not, the takings limitation does not apply. Even where the plaintiff can legitimately claim a property interest, its legitimate investment-backed expectations may be reduced by the fact of public ownership of the resources in question. That, plus the public interest typically served by regulating the use of such resources, may tip the balance against the assertion that a taking has occurred.

United States v. Locke

Supreme Court of the United States, 1985.
471 U.S. 84.

■ Justice Marshall delivered the opinion of the Court.

* * * From the enactment of the general mining laws in the nineteenth century until 1976, those who sought to make their living by locating and developing minerals on federal lands were virtually unconstrained by the fetters of federal control. * * *

By the 1960s, it had become clear that this nineteenth century laissez faire regime had created virtual chaos with respect to the public lands. In 1975, it was estimated that more than six million unpatented mining claims existed on public lands other than the national forests; in addition, more than half the land in the National Forest System was thought to be covered by such claims. Many of these claims had been dormant for decades, and many were invalid for other reasons, but in the absence of a federal recording system, no simple way existed for determining which public lands were subject to mining locations, and whether those locations were valid or invalid. As a result, federal land managers had to proceed slowly and cautiously in taking any action affecting federal land lest the federal property rights of claimants be unlawfully disturbed. Each time the Bureau of Land Management (BLM) proposed a sale or other conveyance of federal land, a title search in the county recorders office was necessary; if an outstanding mining claim was found, no matter how stale or apparently abandoned, formal administrative adjudication was required to determine the validity of the claim.

After more than a decade of studying this problem in the context of a broader inquiry into the proper management of the public lands in the modern era, Congress in 1976 enacted the Federal Land Policy and Management Act. Section 314 of the Act establishes a federal recording system that is designed both to rid federal lands of stale mining claims and to provide federal land managers with up-to-date information that allows them to make informed land management decisions. For claims located before FLPMA's enactment, the federal recording system imposes two general requirements. First, the claims must initially be registered with the BLM by filing, within three years of FLPMA's enactment, a copy of the official record of the notice or certificate of location. Second, in the year of the initial recording, and "prior to December 31" of every year after that, the claimant must file with state officials and with BLM a notice of intention to hold the claim, an affidavit of assessment work performed on the claim, or a detailed reporting form. Section 314(c) of the Act provides that failure to comply with either of these requirements "shall be deemed conclusively to constitute an abandonment of the mining claim * * * by the owner."

The second of these requirements—the annual filing obligation—has created the dispute underlying this appeal. Appellees, four individuals engaged "in the business of operating mining properties in Nevada," purchased in 1960 and 1966 ten unpatented mining claims on public lands near Ely, Nevada. These claims were major sources of gravel and building material: the claims are valued at several million dollars, and, in the 1979–1980 assessment year alone, appellees' gross income totalled more than one million dollars. Throughout the period during which they owned the claims, appellees complied with annual state law filing and assessment work requirements. In addition, appellees satisfied FLPMA's initial recording requirement by properly filing with BLM a notice of location, thereby putting their claims on record for purposes of FLPMA.

At the end of 1980, however, appellees failed to meet on time their first annual obligation to file with the Federal Government. After allegedly receiving misleading information from a BLM employee, appellees waited until December 31 to submit to BLM the annual notice of intent to hold or proof of assessment work performed required under section 314(a) of FLPMA, 43 U.S.C. § 1744(a). As noted above, that section requires these documents to be filed annually "prior to December 31." Had appellees checked, they further would have discovered that BLM regulations made quite clear that claimants were required to make the annual filings in the proper BLM office "on or before December 30 of each calendar year." 43 CFR § 3833.2–1(a) (1980) (current version at 43 CFR 3833.2–1(b)(1) (1984)). Thus, appellees' filing was one day too late.

This fact was brought painfully home to appellees when they received a letter from the BLM Nevada State Office informing them that their claims had been declared abandoned and void due to their tardy filing. In many cases, loss of claim in this way would have minimal practical effect; the claimant could simply locate the same claim again and then rerecord it with BLM. In this case, however, relocation of appellees' claims, which were initially located by appellees' predecessors in 1952 and 1954, was prohibited by the Common Varieties Act of 1955, 30 U.S.C. § 611; that Act prospectively barred location of the sort of minerals yielded by appellees' claims. Appellees' mineral deposits thus escheated to the Government.

[The claimants sued, and prevailed in the lower court on a "takings" claim and on the argument that they had "substantially complied" with the FLPMA filing requirement. Justice Marshall's opinion rejected the "substantial compliance" argument, noting that while the statutory phrase "prior to December 31" may be "clumsy," its "meaning is clear." It also identified some fourteen other federal statutes that contemplated action "prior to December 31." Moreover, the statute clearly expressed congressional intent to "extinguish those claims for which timely filings were not made," regardless of the magnitude or justification for the failure. The opinion then addressed the constitutional issue.]

* * * The framework for analysis of this question, in both its substantive and procedural dimensions, is set forth by our recent decision in Texaco, Inc. v. Short, 454 U.S. 516 (1982). There we upheld a state statute pursuant to which a severed mineral interest that had not been used for a period of 20 years automatically lapsed and reverted to the current surface owner of the property, unless the mineral owner filed a statement of claim in the county recorder's office within two years of the statute's passage.

Under *Texaco*, we must first address the question of affirmative legislative power: whether Congress is authorized to "provide that property rights of this character shall be extinguished if their owners do not take the affirmative action required by the" statute. Even with respect to vested property rights, a legislature generally has the power to impose new regulatory constraints on the way in which those rights are used, or to condition their continued retention on performance of certain affirmative duties. As long as the constraint or duty imposed is a reasonable restriction designed to further legitimate legislative objectives, the legislature acts within its powers in imposing such new constraints or duties. * * *

This power to qualify existing property rights is particularly broad with respect to the "character" of the property rights at issue here. Although owners of unpatented mining claims hold fully recognized possessory interests in their claims, we have recognized that these interests are a "unique form of property." * * * The United States, as owner of the underlying fee title to the public domain, maintains broad powers over the terms and conditions upon which the public lands can be used, leased, and acquired. See, e.g., Kleppe v. New Mexico, 426 U.S. 529, 539 (1976). * * * Claimants thus take their mineral interests with the knowledge that the Government retains substantial regulatory power over those interests. * * *

Against this background, there can be no doubt that Congress could condition initial receipt of an unpatented mining claim upon an agreement to perform annual assessment work and make annual filings. That this requirement was applied to claims already located by the time FLPMA was enacted and thus applies to vested claims does not alter the analysis, for any "retroactive application of [FLPMA] is supported by a legitimate legislative purpose furthered by rational means. * * * " The purposes of applying FLPMA's filing provisions to claims located before the Act was passed—to rid federal lands of stale mining claims and to provide for centralized collection by federal land managers of comprehensive and up-to-date information on the status of recorded but unpatented mining claims—are clearly legitimate. In addition, § 314(c) is a reasonable, if severe, means of furthering these goals; sanctioning with loss of their claims those claimants who fail to file provides a powerful motivation to comply with the filing requirements, while automatic invalidation for noncompliance enables federal land managers to know with certainty and ease whether a claim is currently valid. Finally, the restriction attached to the continued retention of a mining claim imposes the most minimal of burdens on claimants; they must simply file a paper once a year indicating that the required assessment work has been performed or that they intend to hold the claim. Indeed, appellees could have fully protected their interests against the effect of the statute by taking the minimal additional step of patenting the claims. As a result, Congress was well within its affirmative powers in enacting the filing requirements, in imposing the penalty of extinguishment set forth in § 314(c), and in applying the requirements and sanction to claims located before FLPMA was passed.

We look next to the substantive effect of § 314(c) to determine whether Congress is nonetheless barred from enacting it because it works an impermissible intrusion on constitutionally protected rights. * * * Regulation of property rights does not "take" private property when an individual's reasonable, investment-backed expectations can continue to be realized as long as he complies with reasonable regulatory restrictions the legislature has imposed. * * *

Finally, the Act provides appellees with all the process that is their constitutional due. In altering substantive rights through enactment of rules of general applicability, a legislature generally provides constitutionally adequate process simply by enacting the statute, publishing it, and, to the extent the statute regulates private conduct, affording those within the statute's reach a reasonable opportunity both to familiarize themselves with the general requirements imposed and to comply with those requirements. * * * The requirement of an annual filing thus was not so unlikely to come to the attention of those in the position of appellees as to render unconstitutional the notice provided by the 3–year grace period.

Despite the fact that FLPMA meets the three standards laid down in *Texaco* for the imposition of new regulatory restraints on existing property rights, the District Court seemed to believe that individualized notice of the filing deadlines was nonetheless constitutionally required. The District Court felt that such a requirement would not be "overly burdensome" to the Government and would be of great benefit to mining claimants. The District Court may well be right that such an individualized notice scheme would be a sound means of administering the Act. But in the regulation of private property rights, the Constitution offers the courts no warrant to inquire into whether some other scheme might be more rational or desirable than the one chosen by Congress; as long as the legislative scheme is a rational way of reaching Congress' objectives, the efficacy of alternative routes is for Congress alone to consider. * * * Because we deal here with purely economic legislation, Congress was entitled to conclude that it was preferable to place a substantial portion of the burden on claimants to make the national recording system work. * * * The judgment below is reversed, and the case remanded for further proceedings consistent with this opinion. * * *

[Justice O'Connor concurred separately, agreeing with the result, but noting that the issue of whether BLM's actions had estopped it from extinguishing "a property interest that has provided a family's livelihood for decades" was still open on remand. Justice POWELL dissented, finding the statutory phrase "prior to December 31" unconstitutionally vague in light of the "natural tendency to interpret this phrase as 'by the end of the calendar year.'" Justice STEVENS, joined by Justice BRENNAN, also dissented, finding the "unique factual matrix" here—an ambiguous statute, substantially complied with, where the agency had allegedly not alerted claimholders sufficiently, and a valuable active mine was at stake— justified finding substantial compliance with the statute.]

NOTES AND QUESTIONS

1. The mining claims at issue in *Locke* were located many years prior to enactment of FLPMA and its annual filing requirement. Does the prior existence of the claims lessen the power of the government to impose an additional burden—enforceable by the penalty of loss of the property interest—on the claimant? Does it make any difference why the government was imposing the new requirement? In *Locke*, what was the government's purpose in imposing the recordation and annual filing requirements? Is the filing requirement here any different from an ordinary statute of limitations? That is, are the Lockes here in any different situation from a person injured allegedly by another's negligence, who fails to file a tort action until one day after the limitation period expires?

2. The Boundary Waters Canoe Area Wilderness Act gave the United States a right of first refusal at the sale of any nonfederal inholding in the area. In *Minnesota v. Block*, supra p. 200, the owner of an inholding argued that this provision was an unconstitutional "taking" of his property, because it created a cloud on his title, and the one hundred-day waiting period diminished the value of the land by deterring potential buyers. The State also argued that the statute effectively created an option in the property which was itself a property interest that was "taken" by the United States. The court rejected the arguments (660 F.2d at 1254–56):

> In our view, the mere conditioning of the sale of property * * * cannot rise to the level of a taking. Even if some diminution in value results * * * any effect on the landowner's aggregate property rights would be minimal. Section 5(c) does not interfere with the owner's use or enjoyment of his property; it does not compel the surrender of the land or any portion thereof; it does not affect the owner's ability to give his property or to transfer it in any manner to members of his immediate family. Section 5(c) may affect slightly an owner's ability to alienate property, but it has little effect on even that "strand" in the bundle of property rights. We hold, therefore, that section 5(c), on its face, does not unlawfully take property in violation of the fifth amendment.

See also Stevenson v. Rominger, 909 F.Supp. 779 (E.D.Wash.1995) (essentially upholding a provision of Columbia River Gorge National Scenic Area Act which gave the United States three years to determine whether to accept a nonfederal landowner's offer to sell land in a special management area, before the landowner could use the land in a way inconsistent with the regulations applicable to land in the area).

3. Upon remand, the principal case was settled on a basis that allowed the Lockes to continue to mine their claims, suggesting that the entire exercise had been a test case (on rather extreme facts) to establish the federal government's authority to apply new filing requirements to existing claimants.

4. In Swanson v. Babbitt, 3 F.3d 1348 (9th Cir.1993), the court held that legislation that eliminated the longstanding legal right of a miner on federal land to gain fee title (a "patent") to mining claims was not a taking, even as applied to a miner who had already applied for, but had not yet

gained approval of, a patent. The court said that Swanson had no vested right to a patent when the legislation was enacted, because the Department had determined to contest the application on the ground that it did not meet the requirements of existing law. It quoted Cameron v. United States, 252 U.S. 450, 460 (1920): "Of course, the land department has no power to strike down any claim arbitrarily, but so long as the legal title remains in the Government it does have power, after proper notice and upon adequate hearing, to determine whether the claim is valid and, if it be found invalid, to declare it null and void." See generally Michael Graf, Application of Takings Law to the Regulation of Unpatented Mining Claims, 24 Ecology L.Q. 57 (1997).

In FLPMA, Congress ordered the Secretary of the Interior to "take any action necessary to prevent unnecessary or undue degradation" of the public lands, including from mining operations like that of the Lockes. 43 U.S.C. § 1732(b). Would the Lockes have an argument that applying this requirement to their claims would be an unconstitutional "taking"? Does it make any difference how "reasonable" the regulation was? What impact it had on the profitability of the Lockes' mine? This raises classic questions of so-called regulatory takings, and requires some consideration of general takings law.

Regulatory takings jurisprudence began with Justice Holmes' opinion in Pennsylvania Coal Co. v. Mahon, 260 U.S. 393 (1922). Although the history of the fifth amendment strongly suggested that its framers intended to require compensation only when the government actually took title to private property (as through the exercise of condemnation authority), the Court ruled that the Constitution required compensation even when the government did not take title, but instead regulated the use of the property so severely as to effectively "take" the property. In ruling that a state law* aimed at preventing subsidence of land surface as a result of underground coal mining constituted a taking of the separately owned mineral estate, Justice Holmes declined to lay down any bright line rules, contenting himself to say that a regulation that "goes too far" will effect a taking and an obligation to compensate. Justice Brandeis registered a strong dissent, arguing that the Pennsylvania subsidence law was a safety measure designed to prevent a public nuisance, and should not be regarded as a taking.

Although the Court has attempted over the years to lay down more specific and predictable rules, regulatory takings law remains very complex and fact-specific. The following summarizes some of the more notable cases.

---

* The Constitution has been interpreted to require states as well as the federal government to compensate private property owners for regulatory takings, because the takings clause of the fifth amendment was one of the very first provisions of the Bill of Rights to be incorporated into the due process clause of the fourteenth amendment and applied to the states. See Chicago, B. & Q.R.R.Co. v. Chicago, 166 U.S. 226 (1897). Most regulatory takings cases in fact involve state regulatory programs.

In Penn Central Transp. Co. v. New York City, 438 U.S. 104 (1978), the Court (6–3) upheld New York City's landmark preservation law, which prevented the the owner of Grand Central Station from constructing a new building that would have impaired the old landmark's Beaux Arts facade. The Court summarized its prior cases as identifying several factors of particular significance, including "[t]he economic impact of the regulation on the claimant and, particularly, the extent to which the regulation has interfered with distinct investment-backed expectations;" and the "character of the governmental action;" that is, a taking "may more readily be found when the interference with property can be characterized as a physical invasion by the government * * * than when interference arises from some public program adjusting the benefits and burdens of economic life to promote the common good." Justice Brennan's opinion emphasized that resolution of takings questions involved "essentially ad hoc factual inquiries."

A unanimous ruling the following year held that a dealer in rare bird feathers did not suffer a taking when the government prohibited the sale of such artifacts, including those that had been lawfully acquired, in order to destroy a market that promoted their capture in the wild. The Court found that because the dealer could still possess, transport, and exhibit the feathers, he had not been deprived of all uses of his property. Andrus v. Allard, 444 U.S. 51 (1979). In 1987, in what was largely a replay of the 1922 *Mahon* case, the Court upheld, 5–4, a Pennsylvania law intended to prevent subsidence from underground coal mines, but did not overrule *Mahon*.

In Lucas v. South Carolina Coastal Council, 505 U.S. 1003 (1992), the Court, again by a 5–4 vote, substantially reworked the jurisprudence in this area. In 1988, the South Carolina legislature adopted a Beachfront Management Act which prevented lot owners in certain coastal zones from erecting permanent habitable structures on their property. Lucas, who had bought two lots on a barrier island in a covered zone in 1986 with the intention of building single-family homes on them, sued for compensation. The trial court found that the 1988 law made his lots "valueless" and awarded him $1.2 million. The South Carolina Supreme Court reversed, finding that the statute was a legitimate exercise of the state's police power to prevent harm to the public, and thus was governed by a line of U.S. Supreme Court decisions creating a so-called "nuisance" exception to the fifth amendment's compensation mandate. See Mugler v. Kansas, 123 U.S. 623 (1887) (law prohibiting manufacture of alcoholic beverages); Hadacheck v. Sebastian, 239 U.S. 394 (1915) (law barring operation of brick mill in residential area); Miller v. Schoene, 276 U.S. 272 (1928) (order to destroy diseased cedar trees to prevent infection of nearby orchards); Goldblatt v. Hempstead, 369 U.S. 590 (1962) (law effectively preventing continued operation of quarry in residential area).

In an opinion joined by Chief Justice Rehnquist and Justices O'Connor, Thomas, and White, Justice Scalia construed past Court decisions as having created "at least two discrete categories of regulatory action as compensable [under the fifth amendment] without case-specific inquiry into the public interest advanced in support of the restraint." The first "encompass-es regulations that compel the property owner to suffer a physical 'inva-sion' of his property. In general (at least with regard to permanent invasions), no matter how minute the intrusion, and no matter how weighty the public purpose behind it, we have required compensation."

The second "is where regulation denies all economically beneficial or productive use of land." Justice Scalia explained that "total deprivation of beneficial use is, from the landowner's point of view, the equivalent of physical appropriation," and also, when land is required to be "left sub-stantially in its natural state," it carries with it a "heightened risk that private property is being pressed into some form of public service under the guise of mitigating serious public harm."

The majority opinion then addressed the so-called "nuisance" excep-tion on which the South Carolina Supreme Court had rested its denial of compensation. That Court had relied on the legislative findings in the Beachfront Management Act to the effect that the beach/dune coastal areas were an "extremely valuable public resource"—helping to protect life and property as a storm barrier, providing habitat for numerous species of plants and animals (including rare ones), and so forth—that were subject to accelerated erosion, instability, and other hazards from unwise develop-ment. Justice Scalia held that the South Carolina Supreme Court was "too quick to conclude" that the "nuisance exception"—the power of govern-ment to proscribe "harmful or noxious uses" of property without compen-sation—decided this case. He characterized the distinction between "harm-preventing" (or nuisance-based) and "benefit-conferring" governmental regulation as

> often in the eye of the beholder. It is quite possible, for example, to describe in either fashion the ecological, economic, and aesthetic con-cerns that inspired the South Carolina legislature in the present case. One could say that imposing a servitude on Lucas's land is necessary in order to prevent his use of it from "harming" South Carolina's ecological resources; or, instead, in order to achieve the "benefits" of an ecological preserve.

Because a "harm-preventing" justification "can be formulated in every case," Justice Scalia suggested that, for the Court to hold that no compen-sation is required when the legislature has "recited a harm-preventing justification for its action" would amount to a "test of whether the legislature has a stupid staff. We think the Takings Clause requires courts to do more than insist upon artful harm-preventing characterizations."

Justice Scalia's opinion construed the Court's previous decisions apply-ing the "nuisance" exception as not really resting on a notion of the power of government to prevent all economic uses of land in order to prevent "harmful" or "noxious" uses. Instead, the "nuisance" exception is narrow:

> Where the State seeks to sustain regulation that deprives land of all economically beneficial use, we think it may resist compensation only if the logically antecedent inquiry into the nature of the owner's estate shows that the proscribed use interests were not part of his title to

begin with. * * * It seems to us that the property owner necessarily expects the uses of his property to be restricted, from time to time, by various measures newly enacted by the State in legitimate exercise of its police powers; "as long recognized, some values are enjoyed under an implied limitation and must yield to the police power." Pennsylvania Coal Co. v. Mahon, 260 U.S., at 413. * * * In the case of land, however, we think the notion pressed by the Council that title is somehow held subject to the "implied limitation" that the State may subsequently eliminate all economically valuable use is inconsistent with the historical compact recorded in the Takings Clause that has become part of our constitutional culture.

The rule that emerges from this analysis, according to Justice Scalia, is that compensation is required where governmental regulations "prohibit all economically beneficial use of land" unless the restriction or prohibition

inhere[s] in the title itself, in the restrictions that background principles of the State's law of property and nuisance already place upon land ownership. A law or decree with such an effect must, in other words, do no more than duplicate the result that could have been achieved in the courts—by adjacent landowners (or other uniquely affected persons) under the State's law of private nuisance, or by the State under its complementary power to abate nuisances that affect the public generally, or otherwise.

On this analysis, the owner of a lake bed, for example, would not be entitled to compensation when he is denied the requisite permit to engage in a landfilling operation that would have the effect of flooding others' land. Nor the corporate owner of a nuclear generating plant, when it is directed to remove all improvements from its land upon discovery that the plant sits astride an earthquake fault. Such regulatory action may well have the effect of eliminating the land's only economically productive use, but it does not proscribe a productive use that was previously permissible under relevant property and nuisance principles. The use of these properties for what are not expressly prohibited purposes was always unlawful, and (subject to other constitutional limitations) it was open to the State at any point to make the implication of those background principles of nuisance and property law explicit. * * * When * * * a regulation that declares "off-limits" all economically productive or beneficial uses of land goes beyond what the relevant background principles would dictate, compensation must be paid to sustain it.

The "total taking" inquiry we require today will ordinarily entail (as the application of state nuisance law ordinarily entails) analysis of, among other things, the degree of harm to public lands and resources, or adjacent private property, posed by the claimant's proposed activities, see, e.g., Restatement (Second) of Torts §§ 826, 827, the social value of the claimant's activities and their suitability to the locality in question, see, e.g., id., §§ 828(a) and (b), 831, and the relative ease with which the alleged harm can be avoided through measures taken by the claimant and the government (or adjacent private landowners) alike, see, e.g., id., §§ 827(e), 828(c), 830. The fact that a particular use has long been engaged in by similarly situated owners ordinarily imports a lack of any common-law prohibition (though changed circumstances or new knowledge may make what was previously permissible no longer so, see Restatement (Second) of Torts, supra, § 827, comment g). So also does the fact that other landowners, similarly situated, are permitted to continue the use denied to the claimant.

It seems unlikely that common-law principles would have prevented the erection of any habitable or productive improvements on petitioner's land * * *. The question, however, is one of state law to be dealt with on remand. We emphasize that to win its case South Carolina must do more than proffer the legislature's declaration that the uses Lucas desires are inconsistent with the public interest * * *. Instead, as it would be required to do if it sought to restrain Lucas in a common-law action for public nuisance, South Carolina must identify background principles of nuisance and property law that prohibit the uses he now intends in the circumstances in which the property is presently found. Only on this showing can the State fairly claim that, in proscribing all such beneficial uses, the Beachfront Management Act is taking nothing.

Justice Kennedy concurred in the judgment remanding the case, but disagreed with the majority's emphasis on the common law of nuisance. It was, he said, "too narrow a confine for the exercise of regulatory power in a complex and interdependent society. The State should not be prevented from enacting new regulatory initiatives in response to changing conditions, and courts must consider all reasonable expectations whatever their source." For him, for example, coastal property "may present such unique concerns for a fragile land system that the State can go further in regulating its development and use than the common law of nuisance might otherwise permit."

Justices Blackmun and Stevens wrote separate, vehement dissents. Justice Stevens said the majority offered "no basis for its assumption that the only uses of property cognizable under the Constitution are developmental uses," and its approach "effectively freezes the State's common law..." And further:

Arresting the development of the common law is not only a departure from our prior decisions; it is also profoundly unwise. The human condition is one of constant learning and evolution—both moral and practical. Legislatures implement that new learning; in doing so they must often revise the definition of property and the rights of property owners. * * * New appreciation of the significance of endangered species * * * the importance of wetlands * * * and the vulnerability of coastal lands * * * shapes our evolving understandings of property rights.

Of course, some legislative redefinitions of property will effect a taking and must be compensated—but it certainly cannot be the case that every movement away from common law does so. There is no reason, and less sense, in such an absolute rule. We live in a world in which changes in the economy and the environment occur with increasing frequency and importance. If it was wise a century ago to allow Government " 'the largest legislative discretion' " to deal with "the special exigencies of the moment," Mugler, 123 U.S., at 669, it is imperative to do so today. The rule that should govern a decision in a case of this kind should focus on the future, not the past.

In Tahoe–Sierra Preservation Council v. Tahoe Regional Planning Agency, ___ U.S. ___, 122 S.Ct. 1465 (2002), a six-Justice majority of the Supreme Court ruled that *Lucas* carved out but a "narrow exception to the rules governing regulatory takings." The exception applied only in the "extraordinary circumstance" of a "permanent deprivation of all beneficial use" of property. *Tahoe–Sierra* upheld a several-year-long governmental moratorium on development of private land in the fragile Lake Tahoe Basin astride the California–Nevada border, in order to devise and implement more effective plans to protect the Lake's famed, and threatened, water quality. The majority, speaking through Justice Stevens, firmly endorsed the propriety of land use regulations, and revived the "essentially ad hoc, factual" approach to regulatory takings espoused in the Court's 1978 decision in *Penn Central*. Justice Stevens said that a "rule that required compensation for every delay in the use of property would render routine government processes prohibitively expensive or encourage hasty decision-making." If governments abandoned moratoria on land development while they were devising regulatory plans, it would give landowners "incentives to develop their property quickly before a comprehensive plan can be enacted, thereby fostering inefficient and ill-conceived growth."

Chief Justice Rehnquist and Justices Scalia and Thomas dissented. They read the Court's prior decisions as rejecting "any distinction between temporary and permanent takings when a landowner is deprived of all economically beneficial use of his land," and said the several year ban on development was, from the property owner's perspective, the equivalent of the government leasing, or physically appropriating, the landowner's property.

NOTES AND QUESTIONS:

1. The significance of these recent decisions for federal land and resources law is not entirely clear. For one thing, private property rights obtainable in federal resources are not fee simple interests like those held in most of these cases. For another, they are based on federal, not state law. Third, they may not be directly subject to state nuisance law. How, then, does the *Lucas* focus on the "implied limitations" that state nuisance law places on the use of land held in fee simple translate into the context of less-than-fee-simple property interests that are created in federal resources under federal statutory law, through such devices as timber sale contracts, grants of rights-of-way, mining claims, mineral leases, and concession contracts? What are the "background principles" comparable to state nuisance law that may restrict or prevent the use of federal natural resources like coal or timber that is leased or sold to private interests?

Private property interests that may exist in federal land and resources, and the government's power to regulate their exercise, are both bottomed on legislative enactments rather than the common law (because of the Property Clause's grant of power to the Congress to "make all needful rules and regulations" governing federal land). Therefore, may it be said that federal statutes and administrative regulations implementing them are the real "common law" of federal land and resource use for purposes of the Takings Clause?

2. Justice Scalia's majority opinion in *Lucas* discussed a property owner's expectations in acquiring and holding property. He conceded that a landowner "necessarily expects the uses of his property to be restricted, from time to time, by various measures newly enacted by the State in legitimate exercise of its police powers." He went on to suggest that a distinction may be drawn between "land" and "personal property," because the owner of the latter "ought to be aware" of the government's "traditionally high degree of control over commercial dealings," and the "possibility that new regulation might even render his property economically worthless." Where do property interests in federal land and natural resources fit in this classification? Are they more like "personal property" or "land"? In *Locke*, the Court said that the mining claimants "took their mineral interests with the knowledge that the Government retains substantial regulatory power over those interests." In Atlas Corp. v. United States, 895 F.2d 745, 758 (Fed.Cir.1990), the court concluded that the company's expectation that "it would not have to spend its own money to remediate health and environmental hazards created by its [activities] * * * cannot be a reasonable commercial expectation" requiring governmental compensation, at least in an industry traditionally subject to regulation. Should the courts adopt at least a presumption that industries operating on federal lands should have little or no commercial expectation that they will be free from new regulatory burdens?

3. Is it important that the regulatory restrictions are in place on, say, the use of federal coal at the time the coal is leased? Does that fact mean the coal lessee has no taking claim from the application of the restriction? In Palazzolo v. Rhode Island, 533 U.S. 606 (2001), a property owner claimed that the state had taken his property by denying his requests to fill and develop wetlands. The Court held that the claim was not barred by the fact that he acquired title *after* the state wetlands protection law was enacted. Justice O'Connor, concurring (and the swing vote in the 5–4 decision) noted:

> Today's holding does not mean that the timing of the regulation's enactment relative to the acquisition of title is immaterial to the *Penn Central* analysis. Indeed, it would be just as much error to expunge this consideration from the takings inquiry as it would be to accord it exclusive significance. * * * Interference with investment-backed expectations is one of a number of factors that a court must examine. Further, the regulatory regime in place at the time the claimant acquires the property at issue helps to shape the reasonableness of those expectations.

The Court also decided that the *per se* takings test approved in *Lucas* did not apply because the state wetlands law did not eliminate all economic value and use of the property (even though it retained only $200,000 in value under the regulation, as against the owner's estimate that the value without the regulation would be nearly $3.2 million). The Court found this more than a "token interest" which did not leave the property "economically idle."

4. In one sense, the less-than-fee-simple interest non-federal parties typically obtain in federal land and natural resources could make it easier to conclude—if the *Lucas* analysis is to be applied in this context—that federal regulation deprives owners of these property interests of "all economically valuable uses" of their property. That is, whatever property interest exists in a mining claim or timber sale contract relates to the right to extracting minerals or harvest timber. Alternative uses, such as for residential development or ski areas, are simply not part of the interest. Thus while the brewery owner in *Mugler v. Kansas* could presumably use the building and the land for something else after the State adopted its law prohibiting the manufacture of alcoholic beverages, the owner of a mining claim on federal land presumably has no such option if she is forbidden from extracting minerals from it. Thus governmental denial of permission to mine may, in Justice Scalia's words, "eliminat[e] the [property interest's] only productive use." Assuming the *Lucas* analysis applies, does this by itself require compensation? If not, is it or should it be a relevant factor in deciding whether compensation is owed?

5. Many private interests in federal natural resources are created wholly or largely by bilateral contract; e.g., leases of federal minerals, contracts for the sale of federal timber, permits for development of ski areas on federal land, and contracts to operate tourist concessions in national parks and other recreation areas. If these legal instruments (contracts, leases, and permits) expressly bind the non-federal party to abide by existing and future governmental regulations designed to protect the public interest, can there ever be compensable taking of whatever property interest they otherwise convey? Conversely, if the government agency does not reserve this authority, are its hands tied? Do contract remedies like rescission for mutual mistake, or impossibility of performance, come into play here as a substitute for the fifth amendment? The issue of contractual remedies and compensation for contractual breach is closely related to takings issues. It is treated at some length in the next, concluding section of this chapter.

6. All of the cases discussed above in connection with *Lucas*, except *Allard*, involved state or local regulation. Inverse condemnation actions against the United States must be brought in the Court of Federal Claims under the Tucker Act, 28 U.S.C. § 1491. That court, and the Court of Appeals for the Federal Circuit (to which such actions may be appealed), are on the front lines of addressing these questions. A number of cases address whether the Army Corps of Engineers' denial of a permit to dredge and fill wetlands under § 404 of the Clean Water Act constitutes a taking. See Florida Rock Ind., Inc. v. United States, 18 F.3d 1560 (Fed.Cir.1994);

Loveladies Harbor, Inc. v. United States, 28 F.3d 1171 (Fed.Cir.1994); Deltona Corp. v. United States, 657 F.2d 1184 (1981).

7.   Other recent decisions raising takings issues of relevance to federal lands and resources include Del–Rio Drilling Programs, Inc. v. United States, 146 F.3d 1358 (Fed.Cir.1998) (giving a tribe a veto over access to an oil and gas lease may be a taking); M & J Coal Co. v. United States, 47 F.3d 1148 (Fed.Cir.1995) (federal requirement to leave coal in place to prevent surface damage is not a taking); Broughton Lumber Co. v. United States, 30 Fed.Cl. 239 (1994) (interest in a preliminary small hydro permit was too speculative to be taken); Rith Energy v. United States, 247 F.3d 1355 (Fed.Cir.2001) (federal Office of Surface Mining suspended a company's mining permit because the area it was mining contained high levels of potentially toxic materials that could pollute the groundwater in the area through what is known as "acid mine drainage;" no taking resulted because the coal owner had no reasonable expectation when it acquired the property that it would be permitted to mine in a way likely to produce acid mine drainage); see also 270 F.3d 1347 (Fed.Cir.2001) (denying rehearing with an opinion discussing the Supreme Court's recent decision in *Palazzolo v. Rhode Island*, and noting that because coal mining is a "highly regulated industry, the plaintiff's reasonable investment-backed expectations are an especially important consideration in the takings calculus," and the "likelihood of regulatory restraint is especially high with regard to possible adverse environmental effects, such as potentially harmful runoff from the mining operations, which have long been regarded as proper subjects for the exercise of the state's police power").

8.   Cases are now pending which raise questions whether restrictions on land and water use to comply with the Endangered Species Act require compensation. See, e.g., Tulare Lake Basin Water Storage District v. United States, 49 Fed.Cl. 313 (2001), appeal pending. See generally Mark Sagoff, "Muddle or Muddle Through?" Takings Jurisdiction Meets the Endangered Species Act, 38 Wm. & Mary L. Rev. 825 (1997).

Recall the discussion earlier about the Property Clause authority extending to reach activities on nonfederal land where such activities could affect federal property. See, e.g, *Minnesota v. Block*, supra p. 199. If the federal government takes action that, directly or indirectly, limits the use of adjacent private property, might that have takings implications? This question is addressed in the following case.

Mountain States Legal Foundation v. Hodel

United States Court of Appeals, Tenth Circuit, 1986.
799 F.2d 1423, cert. denied, 480 U.S. 951 (1987).

■ EN BANC.

■ MCKAY, CIRCUIT JUDGE.

The Mountain States Legal Foundation and the Rock Springs Grazing Association (collectively referred to hereinafter as "the Association") brought this action on behalf of their members against the Secretary of the Interior and other government officials to compel them to manage the wild horse herds that roam public and private lands in an area of southwestern Wyoming known locally as the "checkerboard." The checkerboard comprises over one million acres of generally high desert land and has been used by the Association since 1909 for the grazing of cattle. The lands involved in this case are in the Rock Springs District of the checkerboard, an area approximately 40 miles wide and 115 miles long. In this area of the checkerboard, the Association's cattle roam freely on property owned by the Association and on the alternate sections of land owned by the federal government. Thousands of wild horses also roam these lands.

The Association sought a declaratory judgment that the Secretary had mismanaged the wild horses, and that the Secretary's failure to remove wild horses from the Association's land was arbitrary and capricious. On this basis, the Association also sought a writ of mandamus to compel the Secretary to remove the wild horses from its lands and to reduce the size of the wild horse herds on adjacent public lands. The Association also sought damages under the Fifth Amendment for the alleged uncompensated taking of its lands. For this alleged taking, the Association sought to recover $500,000 from the Director of the Bureau of Land Management ("BLM") and ten dollars [sic] from the United States.

The district court granted the Association's petition for mandamus, dismissed the Association's claim against the Director of the BLM, and granted summary judgment for the government on the Association's Fifth Amendment takings claim. The Association appealed the dismissal of the claim against the Director and the grant of summary judgment. The government did not challenge the grant of mandamus on appeal. We affirmed the dismissal, but reversed and remanded the grant of summary judgment, holding that an unresolved factual issue precluded a summary determination of the takings claim. Mountain States Legal Foundation v. Clark, 740 F.2d 792 (10th Cir.1984), vacated sub nom. Mountain States Legal Foundation v. Hodel, 765 F.2d 1468 (10th Cir.1985). We granted the government's petition for rehearing en banc to consider whether the Secretary's failure to manage the wild horse herds, in accordance with the requirements of the Wild Free–Roaming Horses and Burros Act, 16 U.S.C. §§ 1331–1340 (1982), gives rise to a claim for taking of the Association's property under the Fifth Amendment. * * *

Wild horses and burros are the progeny of animals introduced to North America by early Spanish explorers. They once roamed the western rangelands in vast herds. But over time, desirable grazing land was fenced off for private use, while the animals were slaughtered for sport and profit. The herds began to dwindle, and the remaining animals were driven to marginal, inhospitable grazing areas. Alarmed at the decline of these herds, Congress in 1971 enacted the Wild Free–Roaming Horses and Burros Act, 16 U.S.C. §§ 1331–1340 (1982), to protect the wild horses and burros from "capture, branding, harassment, or death." * * *

The Association alleges that the Secretary has disregarded its repeated requests to remove wild horses from its lands, that it is prohibited by section 1338 of the Act from removing the wild horses itself, and that the wild horses grazing on its lands have eroded the topsoil and consumed vast quantities of forage and water. In support of its Fifth Amendment claim, the Association argues that "it is the panoply of management responsibilities set forth in the Act and its regulations, *including* [section 4 of the Act, which provides that, if protected horses or burros 'stray from public lands onto privately owned land, the owners of such land may inform the nearest Federal marshall or agent of the Secretary, who shall arrange to have the animals removed.'], which * * * subject the United States to liability due to its pervasive control over the horses' existence." In our prior opinion in this case, a panel of this court, with one judge dissenting, found that the government's "complete and exclusive control" over wild horses made the Wild Free–Roaming Horses and Burros Act "unique" in the field of wildlife protection legislation. 740 F.2d at 794. This degree of control, the court said, was potentially "significant" in determining the government's liability under the Fifth Amendment. With the benefit of additional briefing and oral argument, it is now apparent to us that, in the area of wildlife protection legislation, there is nothing novel about the nature and degree of the government's control over wild horses and burros.

At the outset, it is important to note that wild horses and burros are no less "wild" animals than are the grizzly bears that roam our national parks and forests. Indeed, in the definitional section of the Act, Congress has explicitly declared "all unbranded and unclaimed horses and burros on public lands" to be "*wild* horses and burros." 16 U.S.C. § 1332(b) (1982) (emphasis added).[4]

In exercising their powers "to preserve and regulate the exploitation of an important resource," both the state and federal governments have often enacted sweeping and comprehensive measures to control activities that may adversely affect wildlife. [The Court's discussion of such laws, e.g., the Marine Mammal Protection Act, 16 U.S.C. §§ 1361–1407; the Migratory Bird Treaty Act, 16 U.S.C. §§ 703–711; the Bald and Golden Eagle Protection Act, 16 U.S.C. §§ 668–668d; and the Endangered Species Act, 16 U.S.C. §§ 1531–1543, is omitted.] * * *

With respect to each of these federal wildlife protection statutes, the degree of governmental control over activities affecting the wildlife in question cannot be said to be different in character from that mandated by the Wild and Free–Roaming Horses and Burros Act. Indeed, in some of these examples, the governmental control over the wildlife is more pervasive, more sweeping, and more restrictive than that provided by the Wild Free–Roaming Horses and Burros Act.

---

4. When the United States Supreme Court considered and upheld the constitutionality of the Act in Kleppe v. New Mexico, 426 U.S. 529 (1976), it decided the scope of the federal government's authority over "wildlife" on federal lands and referred consistently throughout its opinion to "wildlife" rather than feral or domestic animals. The Court held that "the Property Clause also gives Congress the power to protect *wildlife* on the public lands, state law notwithstanding." * * *

Many state wildlife conservation laws provide similar, comprehensive control over activities affecting protected species. Most states, for example, have enacted endangered species laws containing prohibitions that parallel those contained in federal wildlife protection laws.

The foregoing discussion demonstrates the fallacy in the Association's argument that the wild horses are, in effect, instrumentalities of the federal government whose presence constitutes a permanent governmental occupation of the Association's property. In structure and purpose, the Wild Free–Roaming Horses and Burros Act is nothing more than a land-use regulation enacted by Congress to ensure the survival of a particular species of wildlife. It is not unique in its impact on private resource owners.

Of the courts that have considered whether damage to private property by protected wildlife constitutes a "taking," a clear majority have held that it does not and that the government thus does not owe compensation. The Court of Claims rejected such a claim for damage done to crops by geese protected under the Migratory Bird Treaty Act in Bishop v. United States, 126 F.Supp. 449, 452–53 (Ct.Cl.1954), cert. denied, 349 U.S. 955 (1955). * * * Several state courts have also rejected claims for damage to property by wildlife protected under state laws. See, e.g., Jordan v. State, 681 P.2d 346, 350 n. 3 (Alaska App.1984) (defendants were not deprived of their property interest in a moose carcass by regulation prohibiting the killing of a bear that attacked the carcass because "their loss was incidental to the state regulation which was enacted to protect game"). * * *

The majority view that rejects takings claims for damage caused by protected wildlife is consistent with the Supreme Court precedent that controls our decision. * * *

In an unbroken line of cases, the Supreme Court has sustained land-use regulations that are reasonably related to the promotion of the public interest, consistently rejecting the notion that diminution in property value, standing alone, constitutes a taking under the Fifth Amendment. * * * [I]n Kleppe v. New Mexico, 426 U.S. 529 (1976), the Supreme Court recognized the important governmental interest in preserving wild horses and burros in their natural habitat, citing congressional findings that their preservation would " 'contribute to the diversity of life within the Nation and enrich the lives of the American people.' " The provisions of the Wild Free–Roaming Horses and Burros Act advance this important governmental interest.

The Association has not argued, or even suggested that the Act deprives it of the "economically viable use" of its property. Rather, it contends that the consumption of forage by the wild horses, standing alone, requires the government to pay just compensation. In determining whether a particular land-use regulation deprives a property owner of the "economically viable use" of his land, the court must examine the impact of the regulation on the property as a whole. * * *

Considering the economic impact on the Association's property as a whole, the Act does not interfere with the Association's "distinct invest-ment-back expectations" of using its property for grazing cattle. Nor does it impair the Association's right to hold the property for investment purposes. Moreover, the Association has not been deprived of its "right to exclude" the wild horses and burros. Admittedly, the grazing habits of the wild horses have diminished the value of the Association's property. But "a reduction in the value of property is not necessarily equated with a taking." *Allard*, 444 U.S. at 66. In this case, the reduction in the value of the property pales in comparison to that sustained in *Village of Euclid*, 272 U.S. at 384 (75% of property value lost) and *Hadacheck*, 239 U.S. at 405 (92.5% of property value lost).

Whether a particular land-use regulation gives rise to a taking under the Fifth Amendment is essentially on *ad hoc* inquiry. Although the economic burden imposed on the Association is significant, the Association has not even contended that it has been deprived of the "economically viable use" of its lands. In view of the important governmental interest involved here, we conclude that no taking has occurred and that the district court correctly granted summary judgment for the government. * * *

■ SETH, CIRCUIT JUDGE, dissenting. * * *

■ BARRETT, CIRCUIT JUDGE, dissenting.

I must respectfully dissent. I continue to adhere to the reasoning of the prior opinion by a panel of this court reversing and remanding the grant of summary judgment on the basis that wild free-roaming horses and burros are not "wild animals." * * * Assuming, however, that the animals protected under the [Wild Horse Act] are "wild animals," I would nonetheless dissent from the majority opinion. [The Association] should not be precluded from litigating its "taking" claim as a matter of law given the Act's unique wildlife protection scheme. Summary judgment is inappropriate and this case should be remanded to the district court to determine whether the facts here, i.e., the amount of damage to [its] property and the cause of that damage, entitle [it] to relief under the Taking Clause of the Fifth Amendment. * * *

■ HOLLOWAY, CHIEF JUDGE, joins in the dissents of CIRCUIT JUDGES SETH and BARRETT.

NOTES AND QUESTIONS

1. Would there have been a taking if the United States was protecting the wild horses' freedom to roam on and off federal land in order eventually to capture and sell them to pet food manufacturers?

2. Does the U.S. owe compensation to the owner of lambs eaten on private land by eagles or other species of wildlife protected by federal law? In Christy v. Hodel, 857 F.2d 1324 (9th Cir.1988), cert. denied, 490 U.S. 1114 (1989), a rancher was fined for violating the Endangered Species Act (ESA) by killing a grizzly bear that apparently had killed his sheep. The Act allows the killing of protected species like the grizzly bear to protect himself or another person from bodily harm, 16 U.S.C. § 1504(a)(3), (b)(3),

but, by implication, not in defense of property like sheep.* The court rejected the argument that this violated the rancher's constitutional rights:

> The U.S. Constitution does not explicitly recognize a right to kill federally protected wildlife in defense of property. * * * In light of the Supreme Court's admonition [in Bowers v. Hardwick, 478 U.S. 186, 194 (1986)] that we exercise restraint in creating new definitions of substantive due process, we decline plaintiffs' invitation to [so] construe the fifth amendment. * * * [Therefore] we are not required to subject the ESA and the grizzly bear regulation to strict scrutiny. Instead, we must determine whether those enactments rationally further a legitimate governmental objective.

The court went on to find that the Act and the regulations had a rational basis; that the Act did not deny plaintiff equal protection by allowing sport hunting of a protected species in narrowly defined circumstances; and, relying in part on the *Mountain States* case, that plaintiff had not suffered an unconstitutional taking because its loss was "the incidental, and by no means inevitable, result of reasonable regulation in the public interest."

3. Is the ownership of wild horses relevant to the taking question in this context? Who does own them? See note 1 following Kleppe v. New Mexico, supra p. 184.

4. Is it relevant that when the ranchers acquired title to their property, wild horses were unprotected by federal law? Would it made a difference if wild horses had been extirpated from this area decades earlier, and the federal government had reintroduced them as part of "restoration of western heritage" program? In Moerman v. State, 21 Cal.Rptr.2d 329 (Cal.Ct.App.1993), the court rejected a takings claim brought by a landowner seeking compensation for destruction of fences and loss of forage on his property caused by elk relocated near his property under a state wildlife restoration program. The general rule that immunized the state from destruction caused by wild animals was not affected by the fact that here the state wildlife agency captured, tagged, released, and monitored the elk.

5. Wildlife takings cases go back many decades. In Bailey v. Holland, 126 F.2d 317 (4th Cir.1942), the court tersely rejected a landowner's argument that the federal government's prohibition of hunting migratory birds on his land constituted a taking. The government had purchased land nearby and established a migratory bird refuge on it. "Merely because the Government purchases certain land in order to do more than prohibit hunting, it does not follow that compensation must be made for all [nonfederal] land closed to hunting." See also Michael J. Bean and Melanie J. Rowland, THE EVOLUTION OF NATIONAL WILDLIFE LAW 90–92 (3d ed. 1997).

---

* The majority opinion in the principal case contained a footnote (#8) which pointed this out, and went on to say: "Several state courts have held that, as a matter of state constitutional law, a person may kill wildlife contrary to the state's conservation laws where such action is necessary to protect his property. See, e.g., Cross v. State, 370 P.2d 371 (Wyo.1962). No case has yet addressed whether a similar right exists under the United States Constitution, though the bodily injury defense contained in the Endangered Species Act suggests a congressional view it does not."

6. Would the result in *Mountain States* be the same if the wild horses were such voracious consumers of forage that they rendered the private land here totally unsuited for livestock grazing? But what if the land had other economically viable uses? Is the property right at stake here the grass, or is it the land as a whole? If, for example, using the grazing land as a shopping mall or a factory site were possible, would there be a taking on these facts? In *Penn Central*, Justice Brennan's majority opinion unequivocally rejected the railroad's claim that the property interest to be considered was its "air rights" to build a skyscraper over Grand Central Station: " 'Taking' jurisprudence does not divide a single parcel into discrete segments and attempt to determine whether rights in a particular segment have been entirely abrogated. In deciding whether a particular governmental action has effected a taking, this Court focuses rather both on the character of the action and on the nature and extent of the interference with rights in the parcel as a whole * * *." 438 U.S. at 131. In footnote 7 of his majority opinion in *Lucas*, Justice Scalia backed off this result (without discussing *Penn Central*), and seemed to leave open the possibility that a less than "parcel-as-a-whole" analysis might be appropriate in some circumstances. In *Tahoe–Sierra Preservation Council*, however, Justice Stevens for the 6–3 majority unequivocally reaffirmed the rule against disaggregation of property interests: "This requirement that 'the aggregate must be viewed in its entirety' explains why, for example, * * * restrictions on the use of only limited portions of the parcel, such as set-back ordinances * * * or a requirement that coal pillars be left in place to prevent mine subsidence * * * were not considered regulatory takings." He quoted *Andrus v. Allard*, 444 U.S. at 65–66 (1979): "[W]here an owner possesses a full 'bundle' of property rights, the destruction of one 'strand' of the bundle is not a taking."

7. The Wild, Free–Roaming Horses and Burros Act (relevant portion quoted in brackets in the majority opinion, and also in the second paragraph of the opinion in Kleppe v. New Mexico, p. 184 supra) *requires* the Secretary to remove wild horses and burros that stray from public lands onto privately owned land. The lower court here issued a writ of mandamus requiring such removal, and the U.S. did not appeal. Is that relevant to the "takings" issue? How? Is it an alternative remedy to compensation? But what about the damage or forage loss that occurs before the feds remove the horses?

8. Another way to think about *Mountain States* is as posing the issue: Who has the duty to fence, the U.S. or the rancher? In United States ex rel. Bergen v. Lawrence, Chapter 2, supra pp. 157–59, the Tenth Circuit rejected the rancher's argument that requiring him to remove the fence on his land (or to modify it to allow antelope to pass) was a taking requiring compensation. It noted, first, that his antelope-proof fence had effectively been declared a nuisance by the federal Unlawful Inclosures Act to the extent it enclosed federal lands. The Tenth Circuit followed the principal case here in finding that antelope foraging in the checkerboarded area was not a taking. It also noted that the evidentiary record indicated that competition for forage between antelope and cattle was "minimal," and that Lawrence retained the right to exclude antelope from his private land

so long as he could do so without "effecting an enclosure of the public lands." See 848 F.2d at 1507–08.

9. In Fallini v. United States, 56 F.3d 1378 (Fed.Cir.1995), the court found a rancher's claim for compensation for private water consumed by federally protected wild horses was untimely. Cf. Teegarden v. United States, 42 Fed.Cl. 252 (1998) (federal government's failure to prevent destruction of plaintiff's property during a forest fire was not a taking).

10. Notice that state or federal law may define the contours of the property interest alleged to have been taken. In *Locke*, the interest (a mining claim) was defined by federal law. In *Mountain States* (as well as *Lucas*), the property interest was defined by state law. In some cases it might be a mixture of the two. For example, in Leo Sheep v. United States, supra p. 147, the rancher's private property interest initially came into being through federal law (a grant of federal land to a railroad, subject some to some continuing limitations of federal law), but it became a fee interest whose attributes were presumably at least partially controlled by Wyoming law. See the note on the *ETSI* case at p. 156, supra.

Sometimes in enacting new regulatory or management regimes for federal lands, Congress seeks to deflect "takings" issues with statutory language. Typical is the disclaimer in § 701(h) of FLPMA: "All actions by the Secretary * * * under this Act shall be subject to valid existing rights." While this language has proved extremely handy, appearing in numerous pieces of legislation relating to the federal lands,* it raises questions. What are "valid existing rights"? Only property rights that are compensable under the fifth amendment? Or does the concept encompass an expectancy or other interest that does not rise to the level of compensability under the Constitution? Further, what does "subject to" mean? Does it mean that the Secretary cannot take action under the new regulatory regime that could affect in any way the exercise of such rights? Or does it mean the Secretary may apply new regulations to the exercise of the rights up to the constitutional limit; i.e., is this a shorthand for saying the Secretary can regulate the exercise of these rights up to the point of burdening their exercise so heavily as to effect a regulatory "taking"? And what is the remedy if the Secretary does not properly respect such "valid" existing rights? An injunction restraining secretarial action? Or compensation?

Perhaps the most contentious of the "valid existing rights" provisions is § 522(e) of the Surface Mining Control and Reclamation Act of 1977, 30 U.S.C. § 1272(e), which prohibits surface coal mining within national forests, parks, wildlife refuges, and other designated areas "subject to valid existing rights." The Interior Department's Office of Surface Mining attempted over a couple of decades to define that phrase. See generally

---

* One search found more than one hundred uses of variants of the phrase "valid existing rights" in the U.S. Code. James N. Barkeley & Lawrence V. Albert, A Survey of Case Law Interpreting "Valid Existing Rights"—Implications for Unpatented Mining Claims, 34 Rocky Mt. Min.L.Inst. 9–1, 9–6 n.7, 9–56 n. 301 (1988).

Symposium on Valid Existing Rights, 5 J. of Mineral Law & Policy 381–755 (1989–90); see also Appalachian Power Co. v. United States, 607 F.2d 935 (Ct.Cl.1979), cert. denied 446 U.S. 935 (1980) (company holding federal license to build hydropower project not entitled to loss of opportunity to build the project when the Congress enacted a law prohibiting construction because any property interest the company had in the license did not vest until judicial review of the license issuance had been completed). The meaning of a "valid existing rights" provision was exhaustively and inconclusively litigated in Stupak–Thrall v. United States, 89 F.3d 1269 (6th Cir.1996), cert. denied, 519 U.S. 1090 (1997). See generally Jan G. Laitos and Richard A Westfall, Government Interference with Private Interests in Public Resources, 11 Harv. Envtl. L. Rev. 1 (1997).

The political process often produces compensation in various forms for those adversely affected by governmental regulation. In the *Penn Central* case, supra p. 239, the railroad received "transferable development rights," or TDRs, which effectively entitled it to build larger buildings than otherwise would be possible on other land it owned. This fact was noted, although not heavily relied upon, by the six-Justice majority that found no taking. Dissenting Justice Rehnquist (joined by two other Justices) would have found a taking, and remanded for a determination of whether the TDRs constituted just compensation. Penn Central Transp. Co. v. New York City, 438 U.S. 104, 113–15, 137 (1978). The TDRs were later sold for a reported price of upwards of sixty million dollars. Wall Street Journal, Jan. 23, 1985, p. 37.

Similarly, when the Congress decided to expand Redwood National Park by acquiring adjacent property from private landowners, it not only paid for the property, but also established a compensation program for timber industry workers adversely affected. See 92 Stat. 173 (1978). Local sawmills which were adversely affected did not qualify for aid, however, and their claim of a taking was rejected because their loss was merely "an expectancy" that they would continue to receive raw materials from the lands involved. PVM Redwood Co., Inc. v. United States, 686 F.2d 1327 (9th Cir.1982), cert. denied, 459 U.S. 1106 (1983).

Although successful takings arguments in cases involving federal lands and resources have been rare, some observers believe that may change with the ascendancy of an increasingly property-minded U.S. Supreme Court. In other recent decisions the Court has indicated a much greater willingness to police and enforce substantive boundaries of government regulation of private property. For example, in Dolan v. City of Tigard, 512 U.S. 374 (1994), a property owner challenged the City's requirement, imposed as a condition of rezoning plaintiff's property to allow it to expand its business (which would draw more people to the area), that the plaintiff dedicate a fifteen foot strip for a public pedestrian/bicycle path across its property. Justice Rehnquist's majority opinion said that the city "must make some effort to quantify its findings in support of the dedication for the pedestrian/bicycle pathway beyond the conclusory statement that it would offset some of the traffic demand generated." Four Justices dissented; Justice Stevens charged that the Court had made "a serious error by abandoning the traditional presumption of constitutionality and imposing a novel burden of proof" on the city. A number of cases later in this book illuminate both what property interests (if any) users of the federal lands and resources have, and the extent of governmental regulatory power over the exercise of property rights.

G. Limitations Imposed by Contracts for the Use of Federal Land and Resources

Despite its placement in this chapter, this section does not involve constitutional issues. Instead, it examines contractual limitations on the power of the government to regulate the development of public resources. It is included here because it bears some similarities to "takings" issues discussed in the previous section. Like the takings clause, contractual commitments may effectively limit the ability of the government to manage natural resources.

As a general matter, much of the development of publicly owned resources like oil and gas and timber is done through government contracts with the private sector. These contracts may take many forms: Leases (such as mineral leases governed by the Mineral Leasing Act); contracts of sale (such as timber sales contracts); or other arrangements, such as concession contracts, whereby nonfederal parties contract with land managing agencies like the National Park Service to operate visitor facilities and services—hotels, restaurants, campgrounds, river running tours—on federal areas. In such contracts, the nonfederal party undertakes to do something with governmental resources for the benefit of both the government and the other party, and usually involves financial terms.

Such contracts may be said to differ from "permits," which are normally thought of as governmental exercises of regulatory authority in the form of permission to take certain actions. The line between contracts and permits may, however, be indistinct. Permits can also involve financial terms. And both permits and contracts may be governed by statutes and regulations and performance under them is subject to the government's continuing police power. Ski areas on federal land are, for example, developed by private parties under "permit," not contract.* Then Circuit Judge Stephen Breyer discussed the relationship between a term permit for a ski area and a contract in Meadow Green–Wildcat Corp. v. Hathaway, 936 F.2d 601 (1st Cir.1991), involving a dispute between the agency and the permittee over financial calculations for a permit fee:

> This case turns on the meaning of [a provision] in a land use permit that the Forest Service issued to a ski resort owner. It raises a difficult question about the standard of review that a court should apply to the Forest Service's own interpretation of such a document. * * *

---

* Ski area permitting is addressed in the context of NEPA in the *Methow Valley* case, Chapter 5, infra p. 392; and the current system for permitting ski areas is described in Chapter 11, pp. 983–85 infra.

In deciding the meaning of [the document] * * * are we to defer to the agency's interpretation of those words? In other words, are we to treat the Term Permit as if it were an agency regulation, or a statute in which Congress has delegated interpretive power to the administering body? See, e.g., Chevron v. Natural Resources Defense Council, Inc., 467 U.S. 837 (1984) (courts should defer to reasonable agency interpretations of statutes); Udall v. Tallman, 380 U.S. 1, 4 (1965) (courts should give controlling weight to reasonable agency interpretations of regulations). Or, should we treat the Permit like a contract that the government might make with a private party, giving less weight to the agency's interpretation of the document's language, the meaning of which raises a "question of law?" * * *

We believe that for several reasons we should treat the Term Permit document rather like a contract for reviewing purposes. First, the Permit document itself reads like a contract. It provides long-term authority to use land in return for the permittee's payment of a rental fee. It is twenty-two pages long and contains a highly detailed set of terms and conditions. It uses contract-like language. * * * Both the Forest Supervisor and the permittee have signed the document, the latter placing his signature under the statement that he "accepts and will abide by" the document's "terms and conditions." We think the expectation of a person signing such a document is that its terms would bind both him *and* the Service. Although the terms of the document give the Service power to change various conditions, such as rental conditions, for the future, or even to revoke the Permit on 30 days notice, nothing in the document, or regulations, or authorizing statute suggests that the Service is to have some special advantage, not shared by the permittee, in interpreting the meaning of the document's terms. Indeed, it would seem surprising and unfair if the terms of this document, without so stating, bind the permittee but leave the other party (the Service) free to interpret those same terms as it wishes (limited only by the bounds of "reasonableness").

Second, the statutes that authorize the Forest Service to issue Term Permits state that their purpose is to allow the construction and operation of "hotels, resort, and other recreational structures," 16 U.S.C. § 497, all facilities that "are * * * likely to require long-term financing." 16 U.S.C. § 497b. These phrases suggest that one function of the permit is to offer a permittee the security needed to raise many millions of dollars in investment. It is difficult to reconcile the Service's desire for "deference" to its interpretation of the Permit with this purpose. We do not see how a document, the terms of which one party remains comparatively free to interpret to its own advantage, can provide the other party (and its financial backers) the security, stability, or assurance a large and long-term investment would seem to require.

Third, the Service's official regulations treat the Term Permit as if it were a kind of contract. * * * [They] state that the Permit is "compensable according to its terms." 36 C.F.R. § 251.51. Moreover, these regulations define a Term Permit very much as they define a "lease," an instrument the terms of which bind the parties. * * * Although the regulations also state that the Government is free to "revoke" or "terminate" the Permit in the manner and for the reasons specified by the Permit, a contract that one party may terminate for specified reasons is no less a contract. * * *

* * * Thus, without holding that the Permit "is" a contract, or that courts should always consider it as such, we shall treat it like a contract for purposes of deciding how much weight to give the interpretation one party (here the agency) offers for one of its nontechnical terms.

Many legal questions can arise as to the extent of the government's authority to regulate activities carried out under these contracts (or analogous permits) without incurring liability. With the concern for the environment that characterizes the modern age, how to deal with environmental damage that may occur during the implementation of contracts or leases for the development of federal natural resources is an important question. How to deal with it at the time the contract or lease is signed may be particularly challenging, because many years may go by between the government's initial decision to contract for development of the resource and the actual on-the-ground activity. New information may become available which changes the initial assumption about the risk or magnitude of environmental impact that may be caused. In general, because public resources are involved, and because the government's police power is so broad, there is usually no question about the power of the government to nullify contract terms or require the other party to act or not act in ways inconsistent with the terms of the contract. Questions are often raised, however, about whether the government owes money for doing so. The following materials explore these issues.

Mobil Oil Exploration and Producing Southeast, Inc. v. United States

Supreme Court of the United States, 2000.
530 U.S. 604.

Justice BREYER delivered the opinion of the Court.

Two oil companies, petitioners here, seek restitution of $156 million they paid the Government in return for lease contracts giving them rights to explore for and develop oil off the North Carolina coast. The rights were not absolute, but were conditioned on the companies' obtaining a set of further governmental permissions. The companies claim that the Government repudiated the contracts when it denied them certain elements of the permission-seeking opportunities that the contracts had promised. We agree that the Government broke its promise; it repudiated the contracts; and it must give the companies their money back.

A description at the outset of the few basic contract law principles applicable to this case will help the reader understand the significance of the complex factual circumstances that follow. "When the United States enters into contract relations, its rights and duties therein are governed generally by the law applicable to contracts between private individuals." United States v. Winstar Corp., 518 U.S. 839, 895 (1996) (plurality opinion) (internal quotation marks omitted). The Restatement of Contracts reflects many of the principles of contract law that are applicable to this case. As set forth in the Restatement of Contracts, the relevant principles specify that, when one party to a contract repudiates that contract, the other party "is entitled to restitution for any benefit that he has conferred on" the repudiating party "by way of part performance or reliance." Restatement (Second) of Contracts § 373 (1979) (hereinafter Restatement). The Restatement explains that "repudiation" is a "statement by the obligor to the obligee indicating that the obligor will commit a breach that would of itself give the obligee a claim for damages for total breach." Id., § 250. And "total breach" is a breach that "so substantially impairs the value of the contract to the injured party at the time of the breach that it is just in the circumstances to allow him to recover damages based on all his remaining rights to performance." Id., § 243.

As applied to this case, these principles amount to the following: If the Government said it would break, or did break, an important contractual promise, thereby "substantially impair[ing] the value of the contract[s]" to the companies, ibid., then (unless the companies waived their rights to restitution) the Government must give the companies their money back. And it must do so whether the contracts would, or would not, ultimately have proved financially beneficial to the companies. The Restatement illustrates this point as follows:

> "A contracts to sell a tract of land to B for $100,000. After B has made a part payment of $20,000, A wrongfully refuses to transfer title. B can recover the $20,000 in restitution. The result is the same even if the market price of the land is only $70,000, so that performance would have been disadvantageous to B." Id., § 373, Comment a, Illustration 1.

In 1981, in return for up-front "bonus" payments to the United States of about $158 million (plus annual rental payments), the companies received 10–year renewable lease contracts with the United States. In these contracts, the United States promised the companies, among other things, that they could explore for oil off the North Carolina coast and develop any oil that they found (subject to further royalty payments) provided that the companies received exploration and development permissions in accordance with various statutes and regulations to which the lease contracts were made "subject."

The statutes and regulations, the terms of which in effect were incorporated into the contracts, made clear that obtaining the necessary permissions might not be an easy matter. In particular, the Outer Continental Shelf Lands Act (OCSLA) and the Coastal Zone Management Act of 1972 (CZMA) specify that leaseholding companies wishing to explore and drill must successfully complete the following four procedures.

First, a company must prepare and obtain Department of the Interior approval for a Plan of Exploration. 43 U.S.C. § 1340(c). Interior must approve a submitted Exploration Plan unless it finds, after "consider[ing] available relevant environmental information," § 1346(d), that the proposed exploration

> "would probably cause serious harm or damage to life (including fish and other aquatic life), to property, to any mineral ..., to the national security or defense, or to the marine, coastal, or human environment." § 1334(a)(2)(A)(I).

> Where approval is warranted, Interior must act quickly—within "thirty days" of the company's submission of a proposed Plan. § 1340(c)(1).

Second, the company must obtain an exploratory well drilling permit. To do so, it must certify (under CZMA) that its Exploration Plan is consistent with the coastal zone management program of each affected State. 16 U.S.C. § 1456(c)(3). If a State objects, the certification fails, unless the Secretary of Commerce overrides the State's objection. If Commerce rules against the State, then Interior may grant the permit. § 1456(c)(3)(A).

Third, where waste discharge into ocean waters is at issue, the company must obtain a National Pollutant Discharge Elimination System permit from the Environmental Protection Agency. 33 U.S.C. §§ 1311(a), 1342(a). It can obtain this permit only if affected States agree that its Exploration Plan is consistent with the state coastal zone management programs or (as just explained) the Secretary of Commerce overrides the state objections. 16 U.S.C. § 1456.

Fourth, if exploration is successful, the company must prepare, and obtain Interior approval for, a Development and Production Plan—a Plan that describes the proposed drilling and related environmental safeguards. 43 U.S.C. § 1351. Again, Interior's approval is conditioned upon certification that the Plan is consistent with state coastal zone management plans—a certification to which States can object, subject to Commerce Department override. § 1351(a)(3).

The events at issue here concern the first two steps of the process just described—Interior's consideration of a submitted Exploration Plan and the companies' submission of the CZMA "consistency certification" necessary to obtain an exploratory well drilling permit. The relevant circumstances are the following:

1. In 1981, the companies and the Government entered into the lease contracts. The companies paid the Government $158 million in upfront cash "bonus" payments.

2. In 1989, the companies, Interior, and North Carolina entered into a memorandum of understanding. In that memorandum, the companies promised that they would submit an initial draft Exploration Plan to North Carolina before they submitted their final Exploration Plan to Interior. Interior promised that it would prepare an environmental report on the initial draft. It also agreed to suspend the companies'

annual lease payments (about $250,000 per year) while the companies prepared the initial draft and while any state objections to the companies' CZMA consistency certifications were being worked out, with the life of each lease being extended accordingly.

3. In September 1989, the companies submitted their initial draft Exploration Plan to North Carolina. Ten months later, Interior issued the promised ("informal" pre-submission) environmental report * * * [which] concluded that the proposed exploration would not "significantly affec[t]" the marine environment or "the quality of the human environment."

4. On August 20, 1990, the companies submitted both their final Exploration Plan and their CZMA "consistency certification" to Interior.

5. Just two days earlier, on August 18, 1990, a new law, the Outer Banks Protection Act (OBPA), § 6003, 104 Stat. 555, had come into effect. That law prohibited the Secretary of the Interior from approving any Exploration Plan or Development and Production Plan or to award any drilling permit until (a) a new OBPA-created Environmental Sciences Review Panel had reported to the Secretary, (b) the Secretary had certified to Congress that he had sufficient information to make these OCSLA-required approval decisions, [but] * * * in no event could he issue an approval or permit for the next 13 months (until October 1991). § 6003(c)(3). OBPA also required the Secretary, in his certification, to explain and justify in detail any differences between his own certified conclusions and the new Panel's recommendations. § 6003(c)(3)(A)(ii)(II).

6. About five weeks later, and in light of the new statute, Interior wrote a letter to the Governor of North Carolina with a copy to petitioner Mobil. It said that the final submitted Exploration Plan "is deemed to be approvable in all respects." It added:

> "[W]e are required to approve an Exploration Plan unless it is inconsistent with applicable law or because it would result in serious harm to the environment. Because we have found that Mobil's Plan fully complies with the law and will have only negligible effect on the environment, we are not authorized to disapprove the Plan or require its modification."

But, it noted, the new law, the "Outer Banks Protection Act (OBPA) of 1990 ... prohibits the approval of any Exploration Plan at this time." It concluded, "because we are currently prohibited from approving it, the Plan will remain on file until the requirements of the OBPA are met." In the meantime a "suspension has been granted to all leases offshore the State of North Carolina." *Ibid.*

About 18 months later, the Secretary of the Interior, after receiving the new Panel's report, certified to Congress that he had enough information to consider the companies' Exploration Plan. He added, however, that he would not consider the Plan until he received certain further studies that the new Panel had recommended.

7. In November 1990, North Carolina objected to the companies' CZMA consistency certification on the ground that Mobil had not provided sufficient information about possible environmental impact. A month later, the companies asked the Secretary of Commerce to override North Carolina's objection.

8. In 1994, the Secretary of Commerce rejected the companies' override request, relying in large part on the fact that the new Panel had found a lack of adequate information in respect to certain environmental issues.

9. In 1996, Congress repealed OBPA. § 109, 110 Stat. 1321–177.

In October 1992, after all but the two last-mentioned events had taken place, petitioners joined a breach-of-contract lawsuit brought in the Court of Federal Claims. [The trial court held for the companies, finding the government had repudiated the contracts and were entitled to restitution of their "bonus" payments. The Federal Circuit reversed, holding that the the State's objection to the companies' CZMA consistency statement would have prevented the companies from exploring regardless of the government's action. The Supreme Court granted certiorari.]

The record makes clear (1) that OCSLA required Interior to approve "within thirty days" a submitted Exploration Plan that satisfies OCSLA's requirements, (2) that Interior told Mobil the companies' submitted Plan met those requirements, (3) that Interior told Mobil it would not approve the companies' submitted Plan for at least 13 months, and likely longer, and (4) that Interior did not approve (or disapprove) the Plan, ever. The Government does not deny that the contracts, made "pursuant to" and "subject to" OCSLA, incorporated OCSLA provisions as promises. The Government further concedes, as it must, that relevant contract law entitles a contracting party to restitution if the other party "substantially" breached a contract or communicated its intent to do so. See Restatement § 373(1). Yet the Government denies that it must refund the companies' money.

This is because, in the Government's view, it did not breach the contracts or communicate its intent to do so; any breach was not "substantial"; and the companies waived their rights to restitution regardless. We shall consider each of these arguments in turn.

The Government's "no breach" arguments depend upon the contract provisions that "subject" the contracts to various statutes and regulations. Those provisions state that the contracts are "subject to" (1) OCSLA, (2) "Sections 302 and 303 of the Department of Energy Organization Act," (3) "all regulations issued pursuant to such statutes and in existence upon the effective date of" the contracts, (4) "all regulations issued pursuant to such statutes in the future which provide for the prevention of waste and the conservation" of Outer Continental Shelf resources, and (5) "all other applicable statutes and regulations." The Government says that these provisions incorporate into the contracts, not only the OCSLA provisions we have mentioned, but also certain other statutory provisions and regulations that, in the Government's view, granted Interior the legal authority to refuse to approve the submitted Exploration Plan, while suspending the leases instead. * * *

[T]he Government refers to 30 CFR § 250.110(b)(4) (1999), a regulation stating that "[t]he Regional Supervisor may . . . direct . . . a suspension of any operation or activity . . . [when the] suspension is necessary for the implementation of the requirements of the National Environmental Policy Act or to conduct an environmental analysis." The Government says that this regulation permitted the Secretary of the Interior to suspend the companies' leases because that suspension was "necessary . . . to conduct an environmental analysis," namely, the analysis demanded by the new statute, OBPA.

The "environmental analysis" referred to, however, is an analysis the need for which was created by OBPA, a later enacted statute. The lease contracts say that they are subject to then-existing regulations and to certain future regulations, those issued pursuant to OCSLA and §§ 302 and 303 of the Department of Energy Organization Act. This explicit reference to future regulations makes it clear that the catchall provision that references "all other applicable . . . regulations," *supra,* at 2433, must include only statutes and regulations already existing at the time of the contract, see 35 Fed.Cl., at 322–323, a conclusion not questioned here by the Government. Hence, these provisions mean that the contracts are not subject to future regulations promulgated under other statutes, such as new statutes like OBPA. Without some such contractual provision limiting the Government's power to impose new and different requirements, the companies would have spent $158 million to buy next to nothing. In any event, the Court of Claims so interpreted the lease; the Federal Circuit did not disagree with that interpretation; nor does the Government here dispute it.

Instead, the Government points out that the regulation in question—the regulation authorizing a governmental suspension in order to conduct "an environmental analysis"—was not itself a *future* regulation. Rather, a similar regulation existed at the time the parties signed the contracts, 30 CFR § 250.12(a)(iv) (1981), and, in any event, it was promulgated under OCSLA, a statute exempted from the contracts' temporal restriction. But that fact, while true, is not sufficient to produce the incorporation of future statutory requirements, which is what the Government needs to prevail. If the pre-existing regulation's words, "an environmental analysis," were to apply to analyses mandated by *future* statutes, then they would make the companies subject to the same unknown future requirements that the contracts' specific temporal restrictions were intended to avoid. Consequently, whatever the regulation's words might mean in other contexts, we believe the contracts before us must be interpreted as excluding the words "environmental analysis" *insofar as* those words would incorporate the requirements of future statutes and future regulations excluded by the contracts' provisions. Hence, they would not incorporate into the contracts requirements imposed by a new statute such as OBPA.

* * * [The Government also relies on] OCSLA, 43 U.S.C. § 1334(a)(1), which, after granting Interior rulemaking authority, says that Interior's

"regulations ... shall include ... provisions ... for the suspension ... of any operation ... pursuant to any lease ... *if there is a threat of serious,* irreparable, or immediate *harm* or damage to life ..., to property, to any mineral deposits ..., or to the marine, coastal, or *human environment.*" (Emphasis added.)

The Government points to the OBPA Conference Report, which says that any OBPA-caused delay is "related to ... environmental protection" and to the need "for the collection and analysis of crucial oceanographic, ecological, and socioeconomic data," to "prevent a public harm." H.R. Conf. Rep. No. 101–653, p. 163 (1990). * * * OBPA mentions "tourism" in North Carolina as a "major industry ... which is subject to potentially significant disruption by offshore oil or gas development." § 6003(b)(3). From this, the Government infers that the pre-existing OCSLA provision authorized the suspension in light of a "threat of ... serious harm" to a "human environment."

The fatal flaw in this argument, however, arises out of the Interior Department's own statement—a statement made when citing OBPA to explain its approval delay. Interior then said that the Exploration Plan "fully complies" with current legal requirements. And the OCSLA statutory provision quoted above was the most pertinent of those current requirements. * * * Insofar as the Government means to suggest that the new statute, OBPA, *changed* the relevant OCSLA standard (or that OBPA language and history somehow constitute findings Interior must incorporate by reference), it must mean that OBPA in effect created a *new* requirement. For the reasons set out *supra,* however, any such new requirement would not be incorporated into the contracts. * * *

We conclude, for these reasons, that the Government violated the contracts. Indeed, as Interior pointed out in its letter to North Carolina, the new statute, OBPA, *required* Interior to impose the contract-violating delay. * * *

* * * OBPA changed pre-existing contract-incorporated requirements in several ways. It delayed approval, not only of an Exploration Plan but also of Development and Production Plans; and it delayed the issuance of drilling permits as well. It created a new type of Interior Department environmental review that had not previously existed, conducted by the newly created Environmental Sciences Review Panel; and, by insisting that the Secretary explain in detail any differences between the Secretary's findings and those of the Panel, it created a kind of presumption in favor of the new Panel's findings.

The dissent argues that only the statements contained in the letter from Interior to the companies may constitute a repudiation because "the enactment of legislation is not typically conceived of as a 'statement' of anything to any one party in particular," and a repudiation requires a "statement by the obligor to the obligee indicating that the obligor will commit a breach." (quoting Restatement § 250). But if legislation passed by Congress and signed by the President is not a "statement by the obligor," it is difficult to imagine what would constitute such a statement. In this case, it was the United States who was the "obligor" to the contract. * * * Although the dissent points out that legislation is "addressed to the public at large," * * * that "public" includes those to whom the United States had contractual obligations. If the dissent means to invoke a special exception such as the "sovereign acts" doctrine, which treats certain laws as if they simply created conditions of impossibility, see Winstar, 518 U.S., at 891–899, (principal opinion of Souter, J.), 923–924 (Scalia, J., concurring in judgment), it cannot do so here. The Court of Federal Claims rejected the application of that doctrine to this case, and the Government has not contested that determination here. Hence, under these circumstances, the fact that Interior's repudiation rested upon the enactment of a new statute makes no significant difference.

We do not say that the changes made by the statute were unjustified. We say only that they were changes of a kind that the contracts did not foresee. They were changes in those approval procedures and standards that the contracts had incorporated through cross-reference. The Government has not convinced us that Interior's actions were authorized by any other contractually cross-referenced provision. Hence, in communicating to the companies its intent to follow OBPA, the United States was communicating its intent to violate the contracts.

The Government next argues that any violation of the contracts' terms was not significant; hence there was no "substantial" or "material" breach that could have amounted to a "repudiation." In particular, it says that OCSLA's 30-day approval period "does not function as the 'essence' of these agreements." Brief for United States 37. The Court of Claims concluded, however, that timely and fair consideration of a submitted Exploration Plan was a "necessary reciprocal obligation," indeed, that any "contrary interpretation would render the bargain illusory." 35 Fed.Cl., at 327. We agree.

We recognize that the lease contracts gave the companies more than rights to obtain approvals. They also gave the companies rights to explore for, and to develop, oil. But the need to obtain Government approvals so qualified the likely future enjoyment of the exploration and development rights that the contract, in practice, amounted primarily to an *opportunity* to try to obtain exploration and development rights in accordance with the procedures and under the standards specified in the cross-referenced statutes and regulations. Under these circumstances, if the companies did not at least buy a promise that the Government would not deviate significantly from those procedures and standards, then what did they buy? Cf. id., at 324 (the companies bought exclusive rights to explore and develop oil "*if they met*" OCSLA requirements (emphasis added)).

The Government's modification of the contract-incorporated processes was not technical or insubstantial. It did not announce an (OBPA-required) approval delay of a few days or weeks, but of 13 months minimum, and likely much longer. The delay turned out to be at least four years. And lengthy delays matter, particularly where several successive agency approvals are at stake. Whether an applicant approaches Commerce with an Interior Department approval already in hand can make a difference (as can failure to have obtained that earlier approval). Moreover, as we have pointed out, OBPA changed the contract-referenced procedures in several other ways as well.

The upshot is that, under the contracts, the incorporated procedures and standards amounted to a gateway to the companies' enjoyment of all other rights. To significantly narrow that gateway violated material conditions in the contracts. The breach was "substantia[l]," depriving the companies of the benefit of their bargain. Restatement § 243. And the Government's communication of its intent to commit that breach amounted to a repudiation of the contracts.

The Government argues that the companies waived their rights to restitution. * * * Indeed, acceptance of performance under a once-repudiated contract can constitute a waiver of the right to restitution that repudiation would otherwise create. Restatement § 373, Comment *a;* cf. Restatement of Restitution § 68, Comment *b* (1936).

The United States points to three events that, in its view, amount to continued performance of the contracts. But it does not persuade us. First, the oil companies submitted their Exploration Plan to Interior two days *after* OBPA became law. *Supra,* at 2431. The performance question, however, is not just about what the oil companies did or requested, but also about what they actually received from the Government. And, in respect to the Exploration Plan, the companies received nothing.

Second, the companies subsequently asked the Secretary of Commerce to overturn North Carolina's objection to the companies' CZMA consistency certification. And, although the Secretary's eventual response was negative, the companies did at least receive that reply. The Secretary did not base his reply, however, upon application of the contracts' standards, but instead relied in large part on the findings of the new, OBPA-created, Environmental Sciences Review Panel. Consequently, we cannot say that the companies received from Commerce the kind of consideration for which their contracts called.

Third, the oil companies received suspensions of their leases (suspending annual rents and extending lease terms) pending the OBPA-mandated approval delays. However, a separate contract—the 1989 memorandum of understanding—entitled the companies to receive these suspensions. * * * And the Government has provided no convincing reason why we should consider the suspensions to amount to significant performance of the lease contracts in question.

We conclude that the companies did not receive significant postrepudiation performance. We consequently find that they did not waive their right to restitution.

Finally, the Government argues that repudiation could not have hurt the companies. Since the companies could not have met the CZMA consistency requirements, they could not have explored (or ultimately drilled) for oil in any event. Hence, OBPA caused them no damage. As the Government puts it, the companies have already received "such damages as were actually caused by the [Exploration Plan approval] delay," namely, none. This argument, however, misses the basic legal point. The oil companies do not seek damages for breach of contract. They seek restitution of their initial payments. Because the Government repudiated the lease contracts, the law entitles the companies to that restitution whether the contracts would, or would not, ultimately have produced a financial gain or led them to obtain a definite right to explore. If a lottery operator fails to deliver a purchased ticket, the purchaser can get his money back—whether or not he eventually would have won the lottery. And if one party to a contract, whether oil company or ordinary citizen, advances the other party money, principles of restitution normally require the latter, upon repudiation, to refund that money. Restatement § 373.

Contract law expresses no view about the wisdom of OBPA. We have examined only that statute's consistency with the promises that the earlier contracts contained. We find that the oil companies gave the United States $158 million in return for a contractual promise to follow the terms of pre-existing statutes and regulations. The new statute prevented the Government from keeping that promise. The breach "substantially impair[ed] the value of the contract[s]." *Id.*, § 243. And therefore the Government must give the companies their money back. * * *

Justice STEVENS, dissenting.

Since the 1953 passage of the Outer Continental Shelf Lands Act (OCSLA), 43 U.S.C. § 1331 *et seq.*, the United States Government has conducted more than a hundred lease sales of the type at stake today, and bidders have paid the United States more than $55 billion for the opportunity to develop the mineral resources made available under those leases. [Eds. This is the amount received in bonus bids at lease auction. Over the same time period, Justice Stevens pointed out in a footnote, the U.S. Treasury has received more than $64 billion in royalties from oil and gas production offshore.] The United States, as lessor, and petitioners, as lessees, clearly had a mutual interest in the successful exploration, development, and production of oil in the Manteo Unit pursuant to the leases executed in 1981. If production were achieved, the United States would benefit both from the substantial royalties it would receive and from the significant addition to the Nation's energy supply. Self-interest, as well as its duties under the leases, thus led the Government to expend substantial resources over the course of 19 years in the hope of seeing this project realized.

From the outset, however, it was apparent that the Outer Banks project might not succeed for a variety of reasons. Among those was the risk that the State of North Carolina would exercise its right to object to the completion of the project. That was a risk that the parties knowingly assumed. They did not, however, assume the risk that Congress would enact additional legislation that would delay the completion of what would obviously be a lengthy project in any event. I therefore agree with the Court that the Government did breach its contract with petitioners in failing to approve, within 30 days of its receipt, the plan of exploration petitioners submitted. As the Court describes, the leases incorporate the provisions of the OCSLA into their terms, and the OCSLA, correspondingly, sets down this 30–day requirement in plain language. 43 U.S.C. § 1340(c).

I do not, however, believe that the appropriate remedy for the Government's breach is for petitioners to recover their full initial investment. When the entire relationship between the parties is considered, with particular reference to the impact of North Carolina's foreseeable exercise of its right to object to the project, it is clear that the remedy ordered by the Court is excessive. I would hold that petitioners are entitled at best to damages resulting from the delay caused by the Government's failure to approve the plan within the requisite time.

* * * At the time of the Government's breach, petitioners had no reasonable expectation under the lease contract terms that the venture would come to fruition in the near future. Petitioners had known since 1988 that the State of North Carolina had substantial concerns about petitioners' proposed exploration; North Carolina had already officially objected to petitioners' NPDES submission—a required step itself dependent on the State's CZMA approval. At the same time, the Federal Government's own substantial investments of time and resources, as well as its extensive good-faith efforts both before and after the OBPA was passed to preserve the arrangement, gave petitioners the reasonable expectation that the Government would continue trying to make the contract work. And indeed, both parties continued to behave consistently with that expectation.

While apparently recognizing that the substantiality of the Government's breach is a relevant question, the Court spends almost no time at all concluding that the breach was substantial enough to award petitioners a $156 million refund. * * * In the end, the Court's central reason for finding the breach "not technical or insubstantial" is that "lengthy delays matter." I certainly agree with that statement as a general principle. But in this action, that principle does not justify petitioners' request for restitution. On its face, petitioners' contention that time was "of the essence" in this bargain is difficult to accept; petitioners themselves waited seven years into the renewable 10–year lease term before even floating the Outer Banks proposal, and waited another two years after the OBPA was passed before filing this lawsuit. After then accepting a full 10 years of the Government's above-and-beyond-the-call performance, time is now suddenly of the essence? As with any venture of this magnitude, this undertaking was rife with possibilities for "lengthy delays," indeed "inordinate delays encountered by the lessee in obtaining required permits or consents, including administrative or judicial challenges or appeals," 30 CFR § 250.10(b)(6) (1990). The OBPA was not, to be sure, a cause for delay that petitioners may have anticipated in signing onto the lease. But the State's CZMA and NPDES objections, and the subsequent "inordinate delays" for appeals, certainly were. The Secretary's approval was indeed "a gateway to the companies' enjoyment of all other rights," but the critical word here is "a"; approval was only one gateway of many that the petitioners knew they had to get through in order to reap the benefit of the OCSLA leases, and even that gate was not closed completely, but only "narrow [ed]." Any long-term venture of this complexity and significance is bound to be a gamble. The fact that North Carolina was holding all the aces should not give petitioners the right now to play with an entirely new deck of cards.

The risk that North Carolina would frustrate performance of the leases executed in 1981 was foreseeable from the date the leases were signed. It seems clear to me that the State's objections, rather than the enactment of OBPA, is the primary explanation for petitioners' decision to take steps to avoid suffering the consequences of the bargain they made. As a result of the Court's action today, petitioners will enjoy a windfall reprieve that Congress foolishly provided them in its decision to pass legislation that, while validly responding to a political constituency that opposed the development of the Outer Banks, caused the Government to breach its own contract. Viewed in the context of the entire transaction, petitioners may well be entitled to a modest damages recovery for the *two months* of delay attributable to the Government's breach. But restitution is not a default remedy; it is available only when a court deems it, in all of the circumstances, just. A breach that itself caused at most a delay of two months in a protracted enterprise of this magnitude does not justify the $156 million draconian remedy that the Court delivers.

NOTES AND QUESTIONS

1. How broad or narrow are the principles being applied here? Specifically, consider whether the outcome would have been different in the following circumstances:

A. Suppose Interior had *not* said, when it told Mobil it was not giving the OK to its exploration plan, that it was "approvable in all respects" but for the legislated moratorium in the Outer Banks Protection Act (OBPA). Suppose, in other words, Interior had told Mobil, "we have not finished our review of the plan, and now we must delay a final decision because of the moratorium in the OBPA"? Did Interior's decision to say what it did cost the federal treasury $128 million?

B. Suppose the OCS Lands Act, the statute governing offshore oil development, had not required Interior to make a decision within 30 days of the company's submission of a proposed exploration plan. 43 U.S.C. § 1340(c)(1). If the statute had contained no time frame, and Congress had passed a statute that called for more careful scrutiny, and that had delayed a decision about approval, would there have been a breach of the lease?

2. Justice Breyer acknowledged that the government did not give Mobil an absolute right to explore for and develop any oil and gas it found on its offshore lease. Indeed, he conceded that the government basically conveyed the "*opportunity* to try to obtain" the necessary permits and leases under the procedures then in place. (Emphasis in original) But he then used the limited nature of the rights conveyed by the government to justify requiring strict performance by the government. Is that appropriate?

3. Did Justice Breyer adequately respond to dissenting Justice Stevens' point that because Mobil's ability to go forward with oil and gas exploration and development was so doubtful anyway, the incremental negative effect of the OBPA does not justify complete restitution of the $156 million Mobil paid?

4. Note Justice Breyer carefully parsed Mobil's lease to determine just what risks were assumed by the parties, what authority the government reserved, and what authority it did not reserve. (For example, notice the government did reserve authority to apply regulations adopted in the future to this lease in some narrow circumstances, but this extended only to regulations adopted under existing statutes, not new statutes like the OBPA.) Suppose Mobil's lease with the government had included a term which provided that the contract was subject to "all statutes, regulations and directives now *or hereafter adopted* which seek to protect the environment." Would that have led to a different outcome in this litigation? See Amfac Resorts v. U.S. Dept. of the Interior, 142 F.Supp.2d 54, 78–80 (D.D.C.2001), aff'd on other grounds, 282 F.3d 818 (D.C.Cir.2002)(a provision in the Park Service's standard concession contract that requires the concessioner to comply with all present and future laws and regulations is not impermissibly ambiguous or illusory).

Consider, in this connection, Everett Plywood Corp. v. United States, 651 F.2d 723 (Ct.Cl.1981), where the Forest Service canceled part of a timber sale when it later discovered that roadbuilding in connection with the sale would cause unacceptable environmental damage. The timber contractor sued and won damages against the United States. The court noted that the contract "provided for termination in some instances but did not contain any provision for termination in the event that occurred." Specifically, the contract contained various provisions addressing "various supervening events and the effect such events should have upon the contract." If a catastrophic event made performance impracticable, the purchaser was granted the option of terminating the contract. If events of less than catastrophic character occurred, the contract gave the purchaser cost adjustments. No provision addressed what would happen if performance of the contract caused environmental harm. The court concluded that "the contract as fairly read allocates to defendant the risk of being in breach if it must cancel because of the risk of environmental damage." The court then distinguished

> between the power of the government to terminate the contract and the extent of its liability for the exercise of that power. Clearly, the government ought not to have stood idly by and continued with the contract if unacceptable damage to the environment were foreseen. On the other hand, whether the government can terminate the contract and escape making compensation is another issue, the issue we are concerned with. * * *
>
> * * * Where an event is reasonably foreseeable and a provision is not written into the contract to cover that event, one questions whether that event should be considered supervening, at least where the government is claiming the excuse under a standard contract in which

all the provisions are predetermined and accepted on a "take it or leave it" basis by the highest bidder. The government could have promulgated regulations if necessary or inserted a provision to terminate the contract in an event of this type, thereby escaping breach liability. For this court to rewrite the contract and, in effect, insert such a provision might be unfair to the plaintiff, since the appearance of such a provision initially might have influenced plaintiff's deciding whether to adhere to the contract terms proposed, take it or leave it, or bid a lesser amount. Defendant could have proposed a termination article to cover the case; plaintiff could not have. * * *

Even if the government's knowledge that environmental damage could occur was not dispositive and only probative, given the facts of this case and the decisions of this court in the area of impracticability of performance, the risk of the occurrence of the event is on the government. * * * It was defendant, not plaintiff, who as owner of the tracts to be harvested would be presumed to be the party informed as to soil conditions and geologic structure that might indicate that logging would endanger the environment. * * *

The government designed the logging roads in question. It thus was or should have been in the best position to evaluate the effects of road construction on soil conditions. * * * [T]he fact that the government did design the specified roads is relevant for purposes of allocating the risk of environmental damages caused by the construction of those roads.

The court accused the trial judge of

seiz[ing] on a contract doctrine evolved for quite unlike circumstances in order to further the high cause of environmentalism. It is a cause with numerous and devoted adherents, some of whom will not tolerate the balancing of environmental considerations against others perhaps equally high but of a different nature. Here the cause is deemed to override the normal obligations of a government contract, i.e., if the Secretary of Agriculture is acting on behalf of the environment he can make any contract of his Department null and void. The effort of the government which has stepped into the market place and made contracts binding on others, to void them as applied to itself on behalf of some high public policy, is an old phenomenon in the law.

5. Would you advise the Forest Service to adopt a regulation to provide for cancellation of a timber sales contract upon a determination that the operations would result in "serious environmental degradation or resource damage"? Could it apply such a regulation to existing contracts as well as new contracts? Could it do so without providing compensation? In fact, the Forest Service has a regulation that provides for cancellation of timber sale contracts when the Chief of the Forest Service determines that

operations thereunder would result in serious environmental degradation or resource damage and with reasonable compensation to the purchaser for unrecovered costs incurred under the contract and the difference between the current contract value and the average value of comparable National Forest timber sold during the preceding 6–month period.

36 C.F.R. § 223.116 (2001); see also 36 C.F.R. § 223.40 (2001). Is this a fair solution to the problem?

6.   If the government adopts a regulation or a standard contract term that reserves broad power to cancel a contract issued after competitive bidding any time it determines that unacceptable environmental damage will result, and puts the total financial risk of loss on the purchaser, what might be the effect on bidding? Would the government in effect be trading lower revenues for more protection of the environment? Is there anything unfair (or unconstitutional) about that? Is it good policy? Or is it better to give the bidders some security that if they are ultimately prevented by governmental action from carrying out the venture, they can get some or all of their money back (and presumably get higher bids)? Should the answer be controlled by the government's assessment of how likely it is that unanticipated damage will result? (But how do you measure that, if it's unanticipated?) Or is it about more than just monetary risk?

7.   If the government reserves broad power to deal with emerging knowledge or changed conditions, will it have less incentive to do a good job up front in assessing what the risks are? On the other hand, if the government knows that a decision to adopt new restrictions on an existing contract is going to cost it money, will it have the will to act, or will it be more willing to accept environmental damage rather than take a monetary hit? Actually, here the government does not have the same set of incentives as a private party. Damage claims for both contracts and constitutional takings do not come out of the responsible agency's budget, but rather comes out of something called the "claims and judgments fund" administered by the Department of Justice. See 31 U.S.C. § 1304. This fund is what is known in appropriations parlance as a "no year appropriation," which means effectively that it is something akin to a bottomless pit of money. Agency officials are not, in other words, directly constrained by concerns about their agency budgets in risking takings liability through their administration of natural resource programs. Should they be? If they were, would parochial concerns about their financial well-being make them too cautious to protect the public interest?

8.   In Scott Timber Co. v. United States, 44 Fed.Cl. 170 (1999), the plaintiff purchased timber from the Forest Service in 1990 (pursuant to a special act of Congress that sought to accelerate some timber sales in the Pacific Northwest as logging declined in the region, owing in part to endangered species concerns). Soon thereafter the Forest Service suspended performance under the contracts because of concern about protection of a small bird, the marbled murrelet, which was newly listed under the Endangered Species Act. After consultation with the Fish and Wildlife Service, the Forest Service canceled some of the sales, and the company sued for breach of contract. One of the issues was whether the Forest Service had, in the contract, assumed the duty to design the timber sales in question adequate to protect the bird, in which case it may have breached that duty when the sales as designed were found to pose threats to the bird. The pertinent contract term was clause C6.25, which provided, in pertinent

part: "Location of areas needing special measures for [among other things, listed species] are shown on Sale Area Map and identified on the ground. Measures needed to protect such areas have been included * * *." The clause went on to provide that if other areas needing special protection are discovered, the Forest Service "may either cancel * * * or unilaterally modify this contract to provide additional protection regardless of when such facts become known." The court first held that this language "warranted that the Forest Service had taken adequate measures" to protect the bird "when designing the sales," 40 Fed.Cl. 492 (1998), but upon reconsideration the court reversed itself. It said the Forest Service had reasonably concluded that the special statute enacted by Congress to authorize these particular sales had relieved the agency of a duty to identify protective areas for the bird before sale, and found that the contract language did not constitute an implied warranty by the Forest Service that no protective measures were necessary to protect the bird. Because the contract language "alludes to continued information gathering by the Forest Service and possible suspension of the sales, if necessary," the Forest Service's suspension of the contracts was not "unnecessary and unreasonable," and "Scott Timber could not have reasonably expected breach damages" as a result of that action. 44 Fed.Cl. at 181.

9.   The Forest Service has discretion to extend a timber sales contract that is about to expire. May it refuse to grant the extension unless the other party agrees to extensive contractual modifications to protect the environment? In Louisiana Pacific Corp. v. United States, 15 Cl.Ct. 413 (1988), the court said that a Forest Service custom or practice of granting timber sale contract extensions without adding extensive new obligations may in effect be so well-established as to become part of the contract. If so, a determination by the Forest Service to grant such an extension only upon extensive modification might be a breach. In that case, however, the court ultimately concluded that the actual Forest Service policy had been to allow an extension without significant changes from the terms of the original contract only upon a determination that the U.S. "would not be disadvantaged, environmentally or otherwise." It went on to hold it within the Forest Service's authority not simply to extend a contract that "would permit or perpetuate the destruction of" the various natural resources found on the national forests. For this reason, imposing new conditions on the contract extension "in response to a heightened sensitivity to environmental considerations" was not a breach. See also Peters v. United States, 694 F.2d 687 (Fed.Cir.1982) (the successful bidder on a Forest Service timber sale "took a calculated risk" in submitting a high bid, knowing that contract terms required conducting some of the logging by expensive, but environmentally preferable, helicopter, and therefore the successful bidder could not now complain that the Forest Service's refusal to allow him to use cheaper, conventional logging methods was a breach).

NOTES ON WINSTAR, THE "UNMISTAKABILITY DOCTRINE" AND THE "SOVEREIGN ACTS DOCTRINE"

In a major, albeit confusing decision, the Supreme Court held in United States v. Winstar, 518 U.S. 839 (1996), that the United States had assumed the risk of future regulatory change and therefore was liable to certain financial institutions for breach of contract when it changed the law to impose new uniform regulatory requirements on the savings and loan industry, thereby abrogating contractual promises of favorable accounting treatment it had made to these institutions in order to persuade them to take over insolvent savings and loan companies. A seven person majority produced three separate opinions which were not wholly consistent with each other, making it difficult to divine majority reasoning.

One of the defenses urged by the government against the breach of contract claim is called, somewhat misleadingly, the "unmistakability" doctrine. It rests on the idea that the government generally does not, in making contracts, relinquish its sovereign power to govern, a power which includes making new or adjusting existing laws and regulations. The doctrine holds that sovereign power "is an enduring presence that governs all contracts subject to the sovereign's jurisdiction, and will remain intact unless surrendered in unmistakable terms." Merrion v. Jicarilla Apache Tribe, 455 U.S. 130, 148 (1982). In *Winstar*, the government argued that it had not made an "unmistakable" commitment in the contracts with the financial institutions that it would not impose new regulatory restrictions on the them. Justice Souter's opinion for four Justices found the argument inapplicable because the contracts did not prevent the government from acting, but merely shifted the cost of acting to the government. This drastic narrowing of the scope of the defense may rest on the assumption that the threat of liability for breach of contract will not limit the exercise of the government's sovereign powers, an assumption which has been questioned. See generally Michael W. Graf, The Determination of Property Rights in Public Contracts after *Winstar v. United States*: Where Has the Supreme Court Left Us?, 38 Nat. Res. J. 197, 233 (1998) (*Winstar* "effectively precludes a coherent analysis of how the unmistakability doctrine applies to government contract interpretation * * * and what the substantive 'unmistakability' standard should be").

Another defense considered in *Winstar* (and one which did not, according to Justice Breyer, apply in *Mobil*) was the so-called "sovereign acts doctrine." This doctrine was conveniently summarized by the Claims Court in its first decision in Scott Timber Co. v. United States, supra, 40 Fed.Cl. at 507 (1998), as follows:

> * * * [T]he government argues that it is shielded from liability for any alleged breach of its contracts with plaintiff under the sovereign acts defense. The government argues that numerous acts—the listing of the marbled murrelet * * * and the actions of the Forest Service pursuant to the ESA and its implementing regulations—were "sovereign acts" which precluded plaintiff from harvesting timber * * * and which required that the Forest Service suspend plaintiff's contracts. Therefore, the government argues that the Forest Service cannot be held liable for breaching its contracts with plaintiff Scott Timber.

> The sovereign acts doctrine or defense has long been applied by this court, and its predecessor courts, to shield the United States from liability for breach of contract when the United States, by virtue of a

"sovereign act," impairs the performance of a contract to which the United States is a party. *See Horowitz v. United States,* 267 U.S. 458, 461, (1925). The essence of the sovereign acts defense is the notion that "the United States as contractor cannot be held liable directly or indirectly for the public acts of the United States as a sovereign." *Jones v. United States,* 1 Ct.Cl. 383, 385 (1865); *see also Horowitz,* 267 U.S. at 461 ("[T]he United States when sued as a contractor cannot be held liable for an obstruction to the performance of the particular contract resulting from its public and general acts as a sovereign.").

As the Supreme Court's recent decision in *United States v. Winstar Corp.,* 518 U.S. 839 (1996) (plurality) demonstrates, application of the sovereign acts doctrine essentially involves a two-step analysis. First, the court must ask whether the action that impedes the government's performance of the contract is in fact a "sovereign act," that is, whether the act is "public and general" and therefore attributable to the government as sovereign. *See Winstar,* 518 U.S. at 895–98. An act of government is considered public and general, in turn, so long as the impact on public contracts is "merely incidental to the accomplishment of a broader governmental objective." *Winstar,* 518 U.S. at 898; *see also O'Neill,* 231 Ct.Cl. at 826 (noting that the sovereign acts doctrine recognizes that "the Government's actions, otherwise legal, will occasionally *incidentally impair* the performance of contracts" (emphasis added)).

If the court finds that the government action which prevents performance of the contract is, in fact, attributable to the government as sovereign, then the court must determine in the second step of its analysis whether the government as contractor should be discharged from liability under the common law doctrine of impossibility. *See Winstar,* 518 U.S. at 903–05. To successfully show that the government should be shielded from liability under the impossibility defense, "the Government, like any other defending party in a contract action, must show that [the sovereign act] rendering its performance impossible was an event contrary to the basic assumption of the parties." *Id.* at 904. Put differently, to satisfy the second prong of the sovereign acts defense, the government must show that the "nonoccurrence of [the sovereign act] was a basic assumption of the[ ] contract[ ]." *Id.* (citing Restatement (Second) of Contracts § 261).

Although * * * the listing of the marbled murrelet was a sovereign act, thereby satisfying the first prong of the sovereign acts defense, the government cannot satisfy the second prong of the defense. In particular, the government cannot establish that the non-occurrence of the listing of the marbled murrelet was a basic assumption of the contract. Quite the contrary, clauses C6.01 and C6.25 of the contracts between plaintiff and the Forest Service show that the parties specifically foresaw the possibility that additional species might be added to the list of endangered or threatened species, that additional protected species might be located on the sale areas, or that performance of the contracts might threaten the existence of protected species. In addition, and as detailed above, clauses C6.01 and C6.25 specifically sets forth the rights and responsibilities of the parties, if any, if those contingencies should arise, as they did in this case. Under these circumstances, the terms of the contracts should control, and the government should not be permitted to shield itself from any potential liability under the sovereign acts defense. *See Winstar,* 518 U.S. at 906 (government not excused from liability under sovereign acts defense where contracts specifically anticipated regulatory changes that caused government to breach its contracts with financial institutions).

To explore how the "sovereign acts" doctrine might have applied in *Mobil,* suppose that in that case Congress had passed, instead of the OBPA, a more general OCS Protection Act (OCSPA). Suppose further that the OCSPA (a) was aimed at toughening environmental review processes and environmental protection standards everywhere on the outer continental shelf, in contrast to the OBPA (which was aimed at this particular geographic area and these particular leases); (b) was adopted in response to some serious pollution incidents from offshore oil and gas platforms around the world, and required the installation of expensive control equipment; (c) specifically said its new standards should apply to existing leases; and (d) its new tougher standards would in fact make oil and gas development off North Carolina unprofitable to pursue. Would the OCSPA qualify for the "sovereign acts" defense, and allow the government to avoid a finding that it had breached Mobil's lease?

Or, suppose the Endangered Species Act was adopted only after the lease to Mobil was issued. Suppose also there are endangered species in the waters off North Carolina that would be threatened by oil and gas development there, and the ESA effectively prevented Mobil from exploring. Is the government liable for restitution?

Prior to *Winstar* and *Mobil,* federal courts have generally rebuffed arguments of contractual liability or limitation on the government's power in the context of other natural resources developed under federal law, such as water in reclamation projects, see O'Neill v. United States, 50 F.3d 677 (9th Cir.1995); Madera Irr. Dist. v. Hancock, 985 F.2d 1397 (9th Cir.1993); Peterson v. U.S. Dept. of the Interior, 899 F.2d 799 (9th Cir.1990); and coal leased under the Mineral Leasing Act; see Western Energy Co. v. Department of the Interior, 932 F.2d 807 (9th Cir.1991); Trapper Mining Inc. v. Lujan, 923 F.2d 774 (10th Cir.1991); Western Fuels–Utah, Inc. v. Lujan, 895 F.2d 780 (D.C.Cir.1990); FMC Wyoming Corp. v. Hodel, 816 F.2d 496 (10th Cir.1987). How much of change the Supreme Court's more recent decisions will work in this area remains to be seen. See generally Graf, The Determination of Property Rights in Public Contracts after *Winstar v. United States*: Where Has the Supreme Court Left Us?, 38 Nat. Res. J. 197, 213, 217, 230, 239–40 (1998); Joan E. Drake, Contractual Discretion and the Endangered Species Act: Can the Bureau of Reclamation Reallocate Federal Project Water for Endangered Species in the Middle Rio Grande?, 41 Nat. Res. J. 487 (2001).

As the following case illustrates, sometimes disputes about contracts and natural resources are about simply money, and not the environment.

Prineville Sawmill Co. v. United States

United States Court of Appeals, Federal Circuit, 1988.
859 F.2d 905.

■ Michel, Circuit Judge.

[The facts are complex. The Forest Service advertised the sale of timber in the Deschutes National Forest in Oregon in the spring of 1987. The sale notice set out the Forest Service's estimate of the volume of timber, by species, in the sale area, as follows: 10,450 thousand board feet (MBF) of Ponderosa Pine, 3,650 MBF of Lodgepole Pine, and 290 MBF of White Fir and other timber. The agency estimated the total value of the timber offered at approximately $1.8 million. Prospective bidders were warned that they should not rely on the agency estimates, and that the Service "reserved the right to reject any and all bids."]

The procedure for the sale called for each bidder to submit, prior to the oral auction, a sealed bid specifying the price that the purchaser would pay per MBF of the biddable species. In accordance with standard Forest Service policy, the total value of the sealed bids would be determined by multiplying the bid rate on each species by the Forest Service's estimate of the species, and adding the total amounts bid for each species.[1] Each bidder whose total bid exceeded the Forest Service's appraised value for the timber qualified to participate in the subsequent oral auction. The total price of the oral bids would also be determined on the basis of the Forest Service's species estimates. The oral auction was to proceed at discrete bidding intervals, as long as each subsequent bid resulted in a total bid price higher than the previous bid, until no further bids were offered. Thus, the last bid properly made would also be the high bid.

Even though the Forest Service species estimates would be used in determining the total bid prices at the auction and in correspondingly determining the high bidder, the high bidder's final total bid price would not be the actual purchase price ultimately paid by that bidder (the purchaser). Rather, the purchaser would pay the Forest Service for the total amount of timber as actually measured (scaled) upon removal from the sale area, at the rates specified in the prevailing bid. Thus, the true final purchase price, and the amount that the Forest Service would receive from the sale, would not be known until the timber was removed.

Prior to the auction, Prineville obtained its own estimate of the volume of the various species at the South Crater site[, which showed] less

---

1. Specifically, the total dollar value of each prospective purchaser's bid would be determined in accordance with the following formula:

Total Bid Price = ((Bid Price for Ponderosa Pine) x 10,450) + ((Bid Price for Lodgepole Pine) x 3,650) + ((Bid Price for White Fir) x 290)

where each bid price is in dollars per MBF and the numbers represent the Forest Service estimates in MBF for the individual species.

Lodgepole Pine than the Forest Service. In reliance on its assumption that its estimate of the Lodgepole Pine volume was more accurate, Prineville prepared to follow a skewed bidding strategy at the oral auction, as permitted under Forest Service policy. Under such a bidding strategy, a bidder would submit an unusually high bid for the species which it believes to have been overestimated by the Forest Service and a correspondingly lower than usual bid on the remaining, more accurately-estimated species.[2] The skewed bidding strategy permits the bidder to offer the Forest Service an apparently higher overall price for the total timber than could be offered without skewing the bids. Since the actual purchase price is calculated from the scaled timber values as removed from the site, a skewed bidder awarded the contract would end up paying less for the salvage timber than would a bidder using its bid values against the Forest Service estimates. However, the bidder pays less only if its estimates were indeed more accurate than the Forest Service's.

At the timber sale, six bidders, including Prineville, submitted qualifying written bids. In the subsequent oral bidding, all six bidders kept their bid price for the White Fir constant. The five bidders other than Prineville altered their total bid prices by varying their bids on Ponderosa Pine, while keeping their Lodgepole Pine bid constant. Prineville alone, however, skewed its bid with respect to Lodgepole Pine.

Eventually, Prineville submitted the final bid of the auction. This bid reflected per MBF bid rates of $161.76 for Ponderosa Pine, $515.00 for Lodgepole Pine, and $11.15 for White Fir. When multiplied by the Forest Service species estimates, this bid resulted in a bid price of $3,573,375.50. DAW Forest Products had submitted the last previous (next highest) bid which contained per MBF bid rates of $339.00 for Ponderosa Pine, $7.00 on Lodgepole Pine, and $11.15 on White Fir, for a total price of $3,571,333.50. At the close of bidding, the Forest Service designated Prineville's final bid as being "responsive" to the Forest Service offering and designated Prineville as the highest bidder. On June 4, 1987, the Forest Service confirmed by letter that Prineville was the highest bidder.

Thereafter, prompted by Prineville's bidding strategy, the Forest Service checked its estimate * * * [and] determined that a variety of computational (arithmetical, transpositional, and tabular) errors had been made in estimating Lodgepole Pine. According to the Forest Service's new approximation, the sale area contained only 2,960 MBF of Lodgepole Pine, 690 less MBF than originally estimated. Assuming the revised estimate to be more accurate than the original, there was 19% less Lodgepole Pine and 5% less total timber. By letter dated July 8, 1987, the contracting officer notified Prineville that, notwithstanding the confirmed designation of Prineville as the highest bidder, the Forest Service had decided to reject all bids on the sale because of the errors in its original estimate. Specifically, the letter stated that the Forest Service errors "so flawed this sale offering that your [Prineville's] apparent high bid was not in fact the high bid."

---

2. Since the bid prices on the individual species are either higher or lower than what would ordinarily be offered, the term "skewed" is used to refer to the bids.

[Prineville promptly sued, arguing that the government could only reject the highest bid, once it was public, for a "cogent or compelling" reason which did not exist here. The government argued it had an "unlimited" right to reject all bids, and won in the trial court.]

An invitation for bids issued by the government carries, as a matter of course, an implied contractual obligation to fairly and honestly consider all responsive bids. * * * [G]overnment consideration of solicited bids is reviewed as to whether it was arbitrary and capricious, an abuse of discretion, and thus not in keeping with the government's fairness obligation.

Furthermore, although the Forest Service has been given discretionary authority to prescribe rules and regulations for the sale of timber from our national forests, see 16 U.S.C. § 472a(a) (1985), and has, under the rules that it has promulgated, the power to reject bids, 36 C.F.R. §§ 223.100–101 (1987), the Forest Service nonetheless also has an obligation to treat fairly responsive bids it receives. In fact the same statute specifically limits the Service's discretion in conducting timber sales by requiring that bidding methods used "insure open and fair competition." 16 U.S.C. § 472a(e)(1)(A).

* * * [Therefore] we simply cannot accept the government's argument that there is no limitation on the right of the Forest Service to reject responsive bids it receives whenever it pleases. To the extent such rejections are determined to be arbitrary and capricious, an aggrieved bidder is entitled to equitable relief. * * *

In Hi–Ridge Lumber Co. v. United States, 443 F.2d 452 (9th Cir.1971), the Forest Service had rejected all bids because the appellant, the high bidder, refused to perform under the announced terms of sale. The purchaser was to construct 10.7 miles of road, of which 1.8 miles were outside and north of the sale area. However, the appellant's planned method of removing the timber did not require construction of the northern road so it sought to avoid this provision of the contract. Eventually, in light of the appellant's continued refusal to build the 1.8 mile road section required by the contract, the Forest Service decided to reject all the bids and reoffer the timber. 443 F.2d at 453.

In view of Hi–Ridge Lumber's refusal to comply with the contract provision, it would seem that the Forest Service's action was well within its discretion[4] and that, therefore, the *Hi–Ridge* court need not have determined the outer limits of Forest Service discretion. Nonetheless, the court * * * stated that under the regulations then in effect, the Forest Service could reject all bids with or without reason. 443 F.2d at 455. The court further stated that there were "no standards" under which it could review the rejection of all bids by the Forest Service since it lacked the "technical expertise" necessary "to provide an informed review of executive decision-making" and concluded that Forest Service sales should be insulated from

---

4. Certainly, the Forest Service would not have been required to accept performance of a different contract than the one that the other bidders had bid on and which the government sought to have performed.

judicial review because of the Forest Service's "continuing and comprehensive managerial function."

We are unpersuaded by the suggestion that, because the Service possesses technical expertise and is entrusted with the continuing management of national timber, the Service may do as it pleases, and that its actions are not reviewable for basic fairness. If agency claims of "expertise" were to operate as an instant talisman permitting the agency to escape judicial review, then practically no agency action would be reviewable since, as a general matter, agencies exist for the very purpose of serving as experts and taking action in a given area of specialization. We specifically reject the notion that this court cannot provide an informed review of the fairness of the Forest Service's actions. * * *

With regard to legal context, it is significant in our view that * * * *Hi-Ridge Lumber* * * * [was decided before] the National Forest Service Management Act, * * * which imposed the above-discussed limitation that Forest Service bidding practices "insure open and fair competition." * * * [E]ven assuming that the statements of the Ninth Circuit in * * * *Hi-Ridge Lumber* [were] correct with respect to there being no limitation on the Service's power to reject bids at the time * * * [it was] decided, there now exists an explicit statutory obligation for open and fair competition to which a court must hold the government. * * *

* * * [W]e conclude that the Forest Service's actions in this case are subject to review and that Forest Service's power is not limitless as the government argues, but must be able to withstand Prineville's attack that the Service's actions were arbitrary, capricious, and an abuse of discretion.

The issue then is whether the Forest Service abused its discretion, as a matter of law, under the circumstances presented. * * *

In reviewing the Forest Service's exercise of discretion in this case, the Claims Court utilized the criteria set forth in Keco Industries, Inc. v. United States, 492 F.2d 1200, 203 Ct.Cl. 566 (1974), * * * as general guidelines, [the court] recognizing that "[t]here may well be no one umbrella rule or principle for all such cases." The relevant factors include: subjective bad faith on the part of the officials; the absence of a reasonable basis for the administrative decision; the amount of discretion entrusted to the procurement officials by applicable statutes and regulations; and proven violation of pertinent statutes or regulations. Application of these four criteria often depends on the type of error committed by the government and the factual setting of the bidding at issue, but there is no requirement or implication in *Keco Industries* that each of the factors must be present in order to establish arbitrary and capricious action by the government.

Applying the *Keco Industries* factors to this case leads us to conclude that the Forest Service did indeed abuse its discretion in rejecting all bids in the South Crater timber sale.

* * * Congress did not vest unlimited discretion in the Forest Service officials to reject responsive bids in timber sales. Nor do we believe that the express reservation contained in the advertisement in which the Forest Service reserved the right to reject all bids allows the Service the discretion

to be arbitrary or capricious in rejecting all bids. If the Service could free itself from statutory obligations merely by written warnings to parties with whom it deals, statutes of the kind at issue here would have no binding significance. Congress clearly limited the Forest Service's still-considerable discretion by the explicit requirement that it "insure open and fair" bidding. Thus, to the extent that the Forest Service failed to insure fair and open bidding, it was acting either outside the scope of its discretion or in violation of the statutory mandate of 16 U.S.C. § 472a(e)(1)(A).

* * * [T]he high bidder at an oral auction can be * * * disadvantaged by a sale cancellation after the end of the auction * * *. Having been alerted to possible favorable bidding opportunities, such as discrepancies in the government's estimates, by the skewed bidding strategy employed by Prineville, the nonprevailing bidders would be motivated, as was the Forest Service itself here, to conduct further investigation prior to reoffering in order to determine the basis for the skewed bidding by Prineville. As long as at least one bidder learned of the reason for Prineville's skewed bidding strategy in the original auction, then Prineville's "advantage," gained by Prineville's independent research as recommended by the Forest Service itself, would be lost.

* * *

From the outset of the bidding process at issue here, both the government and the bidders understood that the true amount of each timber species would not be ascertained until the high bidder actually removed the timber from the sale site. Any estimate, whether by the Forest Service or by a prospective purchaser, whether before bidding or after bidding, would remain simply that—an estimate which would be almost certain to be different from the actual timber removed from the site. The government admits that "the Forest Service timber auction is not a perfect system" and "does not always return perfect results." The government acknowledges that the actual timber amounts ultimately removed from the site may reveal that the government would have received more money had the bid rates of a different (lower) bidder been applied to the actual volume. The government further concedes that, should that occur, it is nevertheless bound to "award" the sale to the highest bidder as determined at the auction in keeping with the Forest Service estimate. Yet the Service nevertheless seeks to accomplish, through amending its estimate upon which the auction bidding was based, that which it would not accomplish once the actual volume of timber was ascertained, and with no assurance that its new estimate might not contain enough deviation from the actual timber volume to allow skewed bidding and justify another "20/20 hindsight" bid cancellation. In our view, this is clearly unreasonable.

Furthermore, we must disagree with the government's position that * * * its timber estimates supplied in the original bidding documents were unreasonably inaccurate or based on a gross miscalculation, clear error, or a patent mistake. Cf. Timber Investors, Inc. v. United States, 587 F.2d 472, 476 (Ct.Cl.1978) (grossly erroneous estimates can support a reformation claim). Assuming the government's second estimate to be completely accurate, the "error" of the government's initial volume estimate for Lodgepole

Pine was 10%, and the error for total timber was only 5%. Guidelines in the Forest Service Manual relating to timber estimates as were made in this case indicate that such estimates should be accurate to within 20% for every 95 of 100 "cruises" (estimates), and accurate to within 10% for every 67 of 100 estimates. Variations of plus or minus 10% are common. * * *

[T]he Claims Court accepted and relied on the government's bid "recalculation" which indicates that Prineville's bid would have been $348,478 lower than that of the "apparent second high bid" if the revised Forest Service estimate had been used in place of its original estimate. In fact, despite the government's recognition that the bid of the actual purchaser may not ultimately return the most money to the government once the actual timber volumes are determined in the field, the government asserts that its new estimate "proves" that its rejection of the bids was reasonable and proper since "Prineville was not the highest bidder." In our view, bids on the individual species made at the oral auction cannot be divorced from the volume estimates on which they were based at the time of the auction. Once the volume estimates on which the total bid is determined are changed, bids on the individual species which were based on the former volume estimates become meaningless. Rather than proving that Prineville was not the highest bidder, the government's arguments and actions come much close to "proving" that its reason for canceling the sale was not to ensure that the competition was fair and that the bidders were not prejudiced, but simply to get even more money for its timber.[7]

Our conclusion * * * does not mean that the Forest Service may never cancel an oral auction once the oral bidding has been concluded and the high bidder determined. As is to be expected when this court undertakes the narrow scope of review accorded this court of agency decision awarding contracts, a conclusion of an abuse of discretion by the agency will be made only upon a strong showing by the rejected bidder. Indeed, there are many cases which, under the reasoning here, would not result in a conclusion that the Service abused its discretion * * *. [Here, however,] the Forest Service's own estimating errors were the basis for its decision to cancel and, in fact, the Service was alerted to its own estimation errors only by Prineville's permissibly skewed bid.

* * * [T]he Forest Service at any time between its initial cruise and the oral auction could have checked its records and discovered [its] computational errors * * *. Had the Service acted sooner, this would have been a different case. All bidders would have had the corrected Service estimate and would have been able to formulate bidding strategies in accordance with that corrected estimate. As it happened, however, the Service simply waited too long. * * *

---

7. Significantly, Prineville's final bid, as well as those of the last bidders, exceeded the Forest Service's appraised value of $1.8 million for its estimated volume of timber in the south Crater sale area by more than $1.5 million. There has been no showing that the purchase price likely to be derived from using Prineville's bid and the recalculated volume estimate will not also result in a bid price substantially above the appraised value for the timber in the sale area. Thus, the Forest Service will apparently still realize a substantial "profit" on the timber sale, without having to reject the bids of those who "bared all" at oral auction.

* * * Under the circumstances of this case, the Forest Service's decision to reject all the bids can only be viewed as an abuse of discretion.

NOTES AND QUESTIONS

1.   The Forest Service's sales prospectus here expressly "reserved the right to reject any and all bids." If ordinary principles of contract law were applied to these facts, should the Forest Service win? Why is the actual outcome here different?

2.   Could the Forest Service protect itself in the future in these situations by expressly reserving "the right to reject any and all bids *for any reason whatsoever, or for no reason*"? If it could, what might be the effect on bidding behavior, and ultimate returns to the federal treasury?

3.   The court here relied to some extent on a requirement in the National Forest Management Act that the Forest Service "insure open and fair competition." The statute (16 U.S.C. 472a(e)) says, in pertinent part, that in conducting timber sales the Forest Service "shall select the bidding method or methods which ... insure open and fair competition ... [and] that the Federal Government receive not less than the appraised value [of the timber] ...." Is this statute aimed only at insuring that the government plays fair among bidders? That is, is it possible to construe the statute merely as, on these facts, forbidding the Forest Service from awarding the sale to the next highest bidder, but not forbidding the Forest Service from refusing to award the sale to anyone, and starting over? What the Forest Service did here was choose to protect the federal treasury and rebid the sale. Does the Court correctly construe the statute as insuring that the government does not favor the federal treasury over a bidder like Prineville?

4.   Should the same degree of judicial scrutiny be applied to acts of a federal land management agency when it is accused of harming the public interest, as opposed to situations where "only money" is at stake, and the agency is accused of dealing unfairly with a private party?

5.   In Amfac Resorts Inc. v. U.S. Dept. of the Interior, 142 F.Supp.2d 54 (D.D.C.2001), aff'd on other grounds, 282 F.3d 818 (D.C.Cir.2002), the court rejected a national park concessioner's argument that Park Service regulations governing selecting the winning bid for concession contracts had impermissibly altered the statutory selection formula. The statute directed the Secretary to consider four specific factors plus "such secondary factors as the Secretary deems appropriate," and left it up to the Secretary to decide how to weigh the various factor, other than directing the Secretary to weigh one of the factors (the proposed franchise fee) less than one of the others (the responsiveness of the proposal to the objectives of "protecting, conserving, and preserving resources of the unit of the National Park System and of providing necessary and appropriate facilities and services to the public at reasonable rates"). 16 U.S.C. § 5952. The regulations created a point system to weigh various factors, and allowed for consideration of such things as the bidder's interest in environmental management programs and activities such as energy conservation and waste reduction and

recycling, and employment of Indians and subcontracting with Indians or minority or women-owned businesses. The court held that the regulations were based on a permissible construction of the statute.

6.   While the government has large power over contract performance, and companies doing business with the government may operate with some disadvantages, they also enjoy some advantages when times turn sour, because the political process can be more responsive than the marketplace in making adjustments to ease financial distress. During the 1970's, for example, the federal timber bidding process was a boon to timber companies who purchased timber when the market was down, and did not get around to harvesting the timber until prices were much higher. In the early 1980's, the tables turned. The timber industry in western states went into decline as the housing industry entered a deep recession. Timber sold in federal contracts for $300 per thousand board feet in 1980 brought less than $200 per thousand in 1982. The timber companies took their dilemma to the courts and to Congress. The latter proved more pliable. In North Side Lumber Co. v. Block, 753 F.2d 1482 (9th Cir.1985), cert. denied, 474 U.S. 931 (1985), the court refused to void the contracts, finding it had no jurisdiction because the United States had not waived its sovereign immunity for purposes of declaratory relief. In the meantime, however, Congress enacted the Federal Timber Contract Payment Modification Act of 1984, 16 U.S.C. § 618, which relieved timber companies of some contractual obligations.

CHAPTER 4

AUTHORITY ON THE PUBLIC LANDS: THE EXECUTIVE AND THE COURTS

In modern public land and resources law, actions of the executive branch are subject to scrutiny by the courts on a variety of procedural and substantive grounds. Section A of this chapter introduces the general subject of judicial review of administrative agency decisions. Section B looks generally at delegations of power to make decisions about federal land management from Congress to the executive branch, and from Congress or the executive to nonfederal decisionmakers. Section C examines executive power to withdraw federal lands from the operation of otherwise applicable laws, and to reserve federal lands for particular uses. Section D covers executive power to acquire lands into federal ownership, and to dispose of federal lands by exchange or sale.

A. JUDICIAL REVIEW

Intensive judicial review of federal land and resource decisionmaking did not really become routine until the last quarter of the twentieth century. The Forest Service appeared in the Supreme Court as early as 1911 (in Light v. United States and United States v. Grimaud, supra pp. 107 and 110), but those were constitutional challenges to federal power; nothing approaching a major national forest management issue made it to the courts until around 1970. The BLM historically has had a reasonably large litigation load, but its cases almost always arose out of essentially private disputes involving such things as mining claims, mineral leases, and homestead applications. The National Park Service and the U.S. Fish & Wildlife Service were rarely in court until the last three decades.

Several things gave rise to the boom in public policy litigation involving federal lands and resources litigation in recent decades. First, the courts became more aggressive in reviewing administrative actions of all kinds. Standing, sovereign immunity, and other potential barriers to judicial review were lowered by a confluence of court decision and statutory modification. In that respect, federal land law has joined the mainstream of administrative law. The so-called "hard look" doctrine of judicial review fashioned in Citizens to Preserve Overton Park, Inc. v. Volpe, 401 U.S. 402 (1971), licensed the courts to scrutinize both the substance of federal agency decisions and the processes by which they were reached. Although the Court thereafter cautioned the lower courts to stick to "their appointed function" and not to substitute their judgments for those of the agencies, see Vermont Yankee Nuclear Power Corp. v. NRDC, 435 U.S. 519 (1978), this has still left much room for the courts to play a significant role in federal land management. See generally Richard E. Levy & Robert Glicksman, Judicial Activism and Restraint in the Supreme Court's Environmental Law Decisions, 42 Vand. L.Rev. 383 (1989). See also Richard Lazarus, Thirty Years of Environmental Protection Law in the Supreme Court, 17 Pace Envt'l L.Rev. 1 (1999); Richard Lazarus, Restoring What's Environmental About Environmental Law in the Supreme Court, 47 U.C.L.A.L.Rev. 703 (2000). For a detailed review of judicial review of federal land management agency decisions, see George Coggins & Robert Glicksman, 1 PUBLIC NATURAL RESOURCES LAW ch. 8 (2001).

Second, Congress in the modern era has enacted much more hard statutory law to govern these federal land decisions. These laws govern both the process by which agencies make decisions, (principally, the National Environmental Policy Act, or NEPA, enacted in 1969), and the substance of those decisions. It is far easier to sue over violations of specific statutory commands, such as those in the Endangered Species Act (1973) and, to a lesser extent, in the National Forest Management Act (1976), and the Federal Land Policy and Management Act (1976), than it is to challenge an action taken pursuant to vague, discretionary mandates that were characteristic of earlier eras. Administrative regulations implementing the management statutes have also become much more detailed. The result is that plaintiffs are increasingly able to challenge land agencies for alleged violations of the law where, as opposed to factual issues, oversight comes more easily to the courts

Third, judicial review has burgeoned in part simply because there are many new classes of plaintiffs and lawyers available to represent them. With the help of private foundations, several "public interest law firms" on both the left and right sides of the political spectrum have become active litigators on public lands issues. Recreational and environmentally-concerned members of the public have organized themselves to pursue judicial remedies when they find themselves aggrieved by agency action.

Most federal land law litigation involves principles of administrative law, because the typical lawsuit is brought by a private party against a federal agency. Some aspects and doctrines of administrative law figure prominently in the context of litigation over federal lands and resources questions. Before a litigant can obtain a ruling on the merits of a suit against the agency, a procedural obstacle course may have to be run.

1. STANDING

Most cases involving federal lands and natural resources are filed pursuant to the Administrative Procedure Act (APA), which authorizes suit by any person "adversely affected or aggrieved by agency action within the meaning of a relevant statute." 5 U.S.C. § 702. The groundbreaking case construing that statute in the context of federal lands is Sierra Club v. Morton, 405 U.S. 727 (1972). The Sierra Club sought to enjoin an extensive ski resort development by private interests in the Mineral King Valley, basing its standing upon an allegation that it had "a special interest in the conservation and sound maintenance of the national parks, game refuges and forests of the country." The Court held that this allegation was insufficient to establish standing, but in the process expanded traditional standing doctrine so as to turn nominal defeat into a long-term victory for environmental plaintiffs. Specifically, the Court pointedly noted that the Club had failed to allege that "its members would be affected in any of their activities or pastimes by the Disney development. Nowhere in the pleadings or affidavits did the Club state that its members use Mineral King for any purpose * * *." The Court also validated the representation by an organization of its members, and held that once standing is found, the substantive challenge to agency action is not confined to the grounds for standing. On remand, the Sierra Club amended its complaint to allege such use by its members, and the lawsuit continued to the merits. In United States v. Students Challenging Regulatory Agency Procedures, 412 U.S. 669 (1973), the Court liberalized the doctrine even further. It found plaintiff law students' allegations that they could be injured by a proposed 2.5% surcharge on railroad freight rates (because a possible result could be less recycling and increases of litter on recreational trails they used) sufficient to withstand a motion to dismiss their claim that the Interstate Commerce Commission should have prepared an environmental impact statement under NEPA in deciding whether to object to the proposed rate increase. That was the highwater mark, for the Supreme Court has since taken a more conservative view of standing, as exemplified in the following case.

Lujan v. National Wildlife Federation

Supreme Court of the United States, 1990.
497 U.S. 871.

■ JUSTICE SCALIA delivered the opinion of the Court.

[The National Wildlife Federation (hereinafter respondent) brought suit against the Interior Department in 1985, alleging violations of several federal statutes in the administration of what the complaint styled as the BLM's "land withdrawal review program." The executive's power to withdraw federal land, upheld in United States v. Midwest Oil, Chapter 2, supra p. 119, is addressed in more detail in Section C of this chapter. In the first part of its opinion, the Court recounted the history of such withdrawals, and of related "classifications" of federal land for retention or disposal, which had together created a "chaotic" situation for federal land managers and private users.]

[As a result, in the Federal Land Policy and Management Act of 1976 (FLPMA), Congress had authorized review of existing classifications of public lands in the land use planning process FLPMA created. The statute also said that] the Secretary could "modify or terminate any such classification consistent with such land use plans." [43 U.S.C.] § 1712(d). It also authorized the Secretary to "make, modify, extend or revoke" withdrawals. § 1714(a). Finally it directed the Secretary, within 15 years, to review withdrawals in existence in 1976 in 11 western States, § 1714(*l*)(1), and to "determine whether, and for how long, the continuation of the existing withdrawal of the lands would be, in his judgment, consistent with the statutory objectives of the programs for which the lands were dedicated and of the other relevant programs," § 1714(*l*)(2). The activities undertaken by the BLM to comply with these various provisions [to review and possibly revoke existing withdrawals and to reclassify public lands for disposal or various uses] constitute what respondent's amended complaint styles the BLM's "land withdrawal review program," which is the subject of the current litigation.

In its complaint, respondent averred generally that the reclassification of some withdrawn lands and the return of others to the public domain would open the lands up to mining activities, thereby destroying their natural beauty. * * * [The complaint alleged that in carrying out this program, the Department had violated FLPMA and the National Environmental Policy Act (NEPA). The district court rejected the government's motion to dismiss for lack of standing, relying on two affidavits from members of the Wildlife Federation that their use of land "in the vicinity" of federal land affected by the government's withdrawal revocations and reclassifications would be adversely affected. The court of appeals affirmed, 835 F.2d 305 (D.C.Cir.1987). Back in the district court, the government then moved for summary judgment on the standing issue. After argument of this motion, the plaintiff submitted four additional affidavits from its members on the standing issue. The district court then granted the government's motion, finding the first two affidavits legally insufficient, and rejecting the four additional affidavits as untimely. The court of appeals reversed, finding a sufficient showing of standing had been made, and the Supreme Court granted certiorari.]

We first address respondent's claim that the Peterson and Erman affidavits alone suffice to establish respondent's right to judicial review of petitioners' actions. Respondent * * * claims a right to judicial review under § 10(a) of the [Administrative Procedure Act], which provides: "A person suffering legal wrong because of agency action, or adversely affected or aggrieved by agency action within the meaning of a relevant statute, is entitled to judicial review thereof." 5 U.S.C. § 702. * * *

We assume, since it has been uncontested, that the allegedly affected interests set forth in the affidavits—"recreational use and aesthetic enjoyment"—are sufficiently related to the purposes of respondent association that respondent meets the requirements of § 702 if any of its members do.

As for the "agency action" requirement, we think that each of the affidavits can be read, as the Court of Appeals believed, to complain of a particular "agency action" as that term is defined in § 551. The parties agree that the Peterson affidavit, judging from the geographic area it describes, must refer to * * * [a BLM order] terminating the withdrawal classification of some 4500 acres of land in that area. * * *

We also think that whatever "adverse effect" or "aggrievement" is established by the affidavits was "within the meaning of the relevant statute"—i.e., met the "zone of interests" test. The relevant statute, of course, is the statute whose violation is the gravamen of the complaint—

both the FLPMA and NEPA. We have no doubt that "recreational use and aesthetic enjoyment" are among the *sorts* of interests those statutes were specifically designed to protect. The only issue, then, is whether the facts alleged in the affidavits showed that those interests of *Peterson and Erman* were actually affected.

The Peterson affidavit averred:

"My recreational use and aesthetic enjoyment of federal lands, particularly those in the vicinity of South Pass–Green Mountain, Wyoming have been and continue to be adversely affected in fact by the unlawful actions of the Bureau and the Department. In particular, the South Pass–Green Mountain area of Wyoming has been opened to the staking of mining claims and oil and gas leasing, an action which threatens the aesthetic beauty and wildlife habitat potential of these lands." App. to Pet. for Cert. 191a.

Erman's affidavit was substantially the same as Peterson's, with respect to all except the area involved.

* * * In ruling upon a Rule 56 motion, "a District Court must resolve any factual issues of controversy in favor of the non-moving party" only in the sense that, where the facts specifically averred by that party contradict facts specifically averred by the movant, the motion must be denied. That is a world apart from "assuming" that general averments embrace the "specific facts" needed to sustain the complaint. As set forth above, Rule 56(e) provides that judgment "shall be entered" against the nonmoving party unless affidavits or other evidence "set forth specific facts showing that there is a genuine issue for trial." * * *

At the margins there is some room for debate as to how "specific" must be the "specific facts" that Rule 56(e) requires in a particular case. But where the fact in question is the one put in issue by the § 702 challenge here—whether one of the respondent's members has been, or is threatened to be, "adversely affected or aggrieved" by Government action—Rule 56(e) is assuredly not satisfied by averments which state only that one of the respondent's members uses unspecified portions of an immense tract of territory, on some portions of which mining activity has occurred or probably will occur by virtue of the governmental action. It will not do to "presume" the missing facts because without them the affidavits would not establish the injury that they generally allege. * * *

Respondent places great reliance, as did the Court of Appeals, upon our decision in United States v. Students Challenging Regulatory Agency Procedures (SCRAP), 412 U.S. 669 (1973). The *SCRAP* opinion, whose expansive expression of what would suffice for § 702 review under its particular facts has never since been emulated by this Court, is of no relevance here, since it involved not a Rule 56 motion for summary judgment but a Rule 12(b) motion to dismiss on the pleadings. The latter, unlike the former, presumes that general allegations embrace those specific facts that are necessary to support the claim. * * *

[In part V of its opinion, the majority rejected the Wildlife Federation's separate argument that it has standing as an organization in its own right to complain about the defendant's failure to publish regulations, invite public participation, and assess the environmental impact of its "land withdrawal review program." The Federation had supported this argument with an affidavit from one of its vice-presidents, Lynn Greenwalt, to the effect that the Federation's purpose is to "inform its members and the general public about conservation issues;" and to advocate improvements in laws and administrative practices "pertaining to the protection and enhancement of federal lands;" which had been impaired by the government's failure "to provide adequate information and opportunities for public participation with respect to the Land Withdrawal Review Program." The majority responded:]

Even assuming that the affidavit set forth "specific facts," Fed. R.Civ.P. 56(e), adequate to show injury to respondent through the deprivation of information; and even assuming that providing information to organizations such as respondent was one of the objectives of the statutes allegedly violated, so that respondent is "aggrieved within the meaning" of those statutes; nonetheless, the Greenwalt affidavit fails to identify any particular "agency action" that was the source of these injuries. * * * As we discussed earlier, the "Land Withdrawal Review Program" is not an identifiable action or event. With regard to alleged deficiencies in providing information and permitting public participation, as with regard to the other illegalities alleged in the complaint, respondent cannot demand a general judicial review of the BLM's day-to-day operations. The Greenwalt affidavit, like the others, does not set forth the specific facts necessary to survive a Rule 56 motion. * * *

For the foregoing reasons, the judgment of the Court of Appeals is reversed.

■ [Justice Blackmun, joined by Justices Brennan, Marshall, and Stevens, dissented, arguing that the two affidavits were sufficient to establish standing, and that the district court abused its discretion by refusing to consider the four supplemental affidavits. The dissenters pointed out that the government's summary judgment motion did not require the plaintiffs to prove standing, but just to show a genuine factual issue as to their alleged injury. The two affidavits "doubtless could have been more artfully drafted, but they definitely were sufficient to withstand the Government's summary judgment motion."]

NOTES AND QUESTIONS

1. How big a setback is this for environmental protection advocates? Was the failure here simply one of inadequate homework in making detailed showings of injury; that is, is it simply an insistence that the plaintiffs' lawyers carefully dot their "i"s and cross their "t"s? Or is the conservative majority signaling a broader effort to close the doors of the federal courts to broad-based challenges to sweeping federal programs? Could the Wildlife Federation ever show injury sufficient to satisfy the Court's majority that it had the right to challenge the BLM's withdrawal review program?

2. The Court further tightened its approach to standing in Lujan v. Defenders of Wildlife, 504 U.S. 555 (1992) (*Lujan II*), by holding that environmental organizations had no standing to challenge a Department of the Interior regulation that exempted species in foreign countries from the obligation of federal agencies to consult with the Department under the Endangered Species Act (ESA) before taking actions that could threaten species protected by the Act. The plaintiffs introduced affidavits from their members attesting that they had visited, and intended to visit again, the habitats of protected species abroad which could be affected by specific federally assisted projects upon which consultation under the Act would no longer be required as a result of the regulation. The majority, speaking through Justice Scalia, conceded that "the desire to use or observe an animal species, even for purely aesthetic purposes, is undeniably a cognizable interest for purpose of standing," but held that the affidavits did not show the kind of "imminent injury" required for standing. Past visits to the area "prove[] nothing;" and a stated intent to return "without any description of concrete plans" for doing so is not enough. (One of the projects in question was in Sri Lanka, and the majority was not persuaded that the civil war then raging in that country made it difficult to specify when a return might be possible.) Cf. Bear Lodge Multiple Use Ass'n v. Babbitt, 175 F.3d 814 (10th Cir.1999) (rock climbers had no standing to challenge a Park Service policy discouraging rock climbing at Devils Tower National Monument during the month of June out of respect for American Indian use of the site; they suffered no injury in fact, because they remained free to climb during that month; and a commercial guide had no standing because he did not substantiate his claim of economic injury as a result of the plan).

3. *Lujan II* also reversed the lower court's ruling that plaintiffs had suffered a "procedural injury" by the government's alleged failure to follow the "consultation" requirement of the ESA. The ESA citizen suit provision authorized "any person" to file a civil suit "to enjoin any person," including any federal agency, "alleged to be in violation of any provision" of the ESA. The Supreme Court held that this did not authorize any person to challenge the government's failure to follow the correct procedure unless they alleged a discrete injury flowing from that failure. Justice Scalia's majority opinion acknowledged in a footnote that " 'procedural rights' are special: The person who has been accorded a procedural right to protect his concrete interests can assert that right without meeting all the normal standards for redressability and immediacy." But this could not confer standing on "persons who have no concrete interests affected" by the procedural noncompliance. 504 U.S. at 573, n.6. Justice Scalia continued: "To permit Congress to convert the undifferentiated public interest in executive officers' compliance with the law into an 'individual right' vindicable in the courts is to permit Congress to transfer from the President to the courts the Chief Executive's most important constitutional duty, to 'take Care that the Laws be faithfully executed,' Art. II, § 3."

4. Although the matter is perhaps debatable, a good argument can be made that application of *Lujan I & II* in the lower courts has not thrown out many cases on standing grounds, at least where plaintiffs have carefully

drafted complaints and supplied, if necessary, supporting affidavits. See, e.g., Desert Citizens Against Pollution v. Bisson, 231 F.3d 1172 (9th Cir.2000). See generally Katharine B. Steuer & Robin L. Juni, Court Access for Environmental Plaintiffs: Standing Doctrine in Lujan v. National Wildlife Federation, 15 Harv. Envt'l L. Rev. 187 (1991). For a comparative law view, looking at the United Kingdom and Australia, see Jon Owens, Comparative Law and Standing to Sue: A Petition for Redress for the Environment, 7 Envt'l L. 321 (2001).

5. In Friends of the Earth v. Laidlaw Environmental Services, 528 U.S. 167 (2000), the Court distinguished *Lujan* and found private plaintiffs had standing to seek civil penalties payable to the government under the Clean Water Act, even though the district court had held that the defendant's actions, while out of compliance with the Act, had not resulted in "any health risk or environmental harm." Justice Ginsburg's majority opinion found that the relevant injury "is not injury to the environment but injury to the plaintiff," and plaintiffs' "reasonable concerns" that defendant's pollution may have damaged land they otherwise would have used is sufficient injury for standing. Their affidavits and testimony sufficiently asserted that defendants' activities "directly affected [their] recreational, aesthetic, and economic interests." See Robert V. Percival and Joanna B. Goger, Escaping the Common Law's Shadow: Standing in the Light of Laidlaw, 12 Duke Envtl.L. & Policy F. 119 (2001). See also Richard J. Pierce, Jr., Is Standing Law or Politics?, 77 N.C.L.Rev. 1741, 1786 (1999) (" Modern standing law is closer to a part of the political system than to a part of the legal system. It is characterized by numerous malleable doctrines and numerous inconsistent precedents. Judges regularly manipulate the doctrines and rely on selective citation of precedents to further their own political preferences").

6. As exemplified most prominently in the APA, Congress has generally accepted the notion that judicial review of agency action is a good thing. In modern times it has sometimes attached "citizen suit" provisions to regulatory statutes. On the federal lands, the Endangered Species Act involved in *Lujan II* is the most important statute with such a provision. (Most federal lands statutes do not have special "citizen suit" provisions; instead, litigation is grounded solely on the APA.) For a discussion of the interrelation of the APA and the ESA's citizen suit provisions, see Bennett v. Spear, 520 U.S. 154 (1997). There the Court determined that ranchers and irrigation districts which might lose water as a result of an ESA biological opinion had standing to challenge that opinion, concluding that the ESA was intended to serve not only the purpose of protecting species, but also of avoiding "needless economic dislocation produced by agency officials zealously but unintelligently pursuing their environmental objectives," 520 U.S. at 176–77, and therefore plaintiffs satisfied the "zone of interests" test that the Court applies (as a matter of policy, not constitutional law) in cases when standing to challenge administrative action was questioned.

7. As noted above, in *Lujan* (and a number of other cases) the Supreme Court has rejected the notion that Congress has unlimited power

to confer standing, because actual injury is a constitutional requirement that cannot be waived by Congress. On the other hand, Congress does have the authority to waive or relax standing principles that are grounded in so-called "prudential" or judicial policy principles as opposed to constitutional requirements.

8.   Suppose Congress adopts legislation acknowledging that "all Americans have [a] property right—a tenancy in common" in federal lands, or in the continued existence of endangered species anywhere in the world. Could Congress go on to say that violation of those rights constitutes injury to all holders of those rights, and thereby accord standing to all Americans? See Cass Sunstein, What's Standing After Lujan? Of Citizen Suits, Injuries, and Article III, 91 Mich. L.Rev. 163, 234 (1992).

9.   On the "zone of interests" test, see also National Wildlife Federation v. Burford, 871 F.2d 849 (9th Cir.1989) (environmental groups had standing to challenge the federal government's alleged failure to obtain fair market value in a sale of federal coal, because the Mineral Leasing Act, the statute requiring that fair market value be obtained, reflected a "clear concern for protecting social, economic, and environmental interests from damage to mineral production"); Desert Citizens Against Pollution v. Bisson, 231 F.3d 1172 (2000) (same result in applying the requirement of the Federal Land Policy and Management Act that land exchanges be for "equal value").

10.   A plaintiff must also show a "substantial likelihood" that the relief the plaintiff seeks will "redress the injury" it claims to suffer. See, e.g., Duke Power Co. v. Carolina Envtl. Study Group, 438 U.S. 59, 75 n. 20 (1978). Several cases from the Tenth Circuit have held that plaintiffs who have objected to various governmental actions have failed to meet this requirement. For example, a coal company that sought to set aside an exchange of land and coal between the United States and a private entity was denied standing to object, because its alleged injury—the opportunity to bid on the coal should it be retained in federal ownership and put up for bid—could not be redressed by the court, because whether to offer the coal for competitive leasing was entirely within the discretion of the executive branch. Ash Creek Mining Co. v. Lujan, 969 F.2d 868 (10th Cir.1992). See also Wyoming ex re. Sullivan v. Lujan, 969 F.2d 877 (10th Cir.1992) (to the same effect; the plaintiff State alleging injury because the exchange takes federal coal off the market, and the State would get a share of the proceeds were it leased); Mount Evans Co. v. Madigan, 14 F.3d 1444 (10th Cir.1994) (private concessioner had no standing to object to government's decision not to rebuild a government structure used by concessioner which had been destroyed by fire, because whether the government awarded a concession contract to the concessioner was within its discretion, even if the structure were rebuilt); Baca v. King, 92 F.3d 1031 (10th Cir.1996) (rancher with permits to graze cattle on BLM land denied standing to object to a BLM land exchange that privatized some of the public land where his cattle grazed, resulting in cancellation of his grazing permits, because court could not order the Secretary to allow the public lands to be grazed if the

exchange were voided, since that was "completely within the Secretary of the Interior's discretion").

2. EXHAUSTION OF REMEDIES, THE FORECLOSURE RULE, LACHES, AND RIPENESS

A variety of doctrines operate to further the policy of requiring litigants to seek relief in the agencies before resorting to the courts. The federal land management agencies all have some form of internal administrative appeal process, although they vary widely. Many BLM and some FWS decisions can be appealed inside the Interior Department to a quasi-judicial body, the Interior Board of Land Appeals. Many Forest Service decisions can be appealed to higher-level agency and Departmental officials. For a summary, see Bradley C. Bobertz and Robert L. Fischman, Administrative Appeal Reform: The Case of the Forest Service, 64 U. Colo. L. Rev. 372 (1993) (Interior procedures summarized in Appendix, at 444–52); see also Carl Tobias, Fact, Fiction, and Forest Service Appeals, 32 Nat. Res.J. 649 (1993). Forest Service administrative appeals were reformed by legislation in 1994; see 106 Stat. 1419, reprinted at 16 U.S.C. § 1612, note, § A, codified at 7 U.S.C. § 6912(e), and implementing regulations, 36 C.F.R. §§ 215.20, 217.

The exhaustion doctrine is flexible, involving balancing tests in which a wide variety of equities can be considered, McKart v. United States, 395 U.S. 185 (1969). The doctrine can, however, exclude people from the courts if they have not raised issues in the administrative process despite having clear opportunity to do so. In Kleissler v. United States Forest Service, 183 F.3d 196 (3d Cir.1999), the court, relying on the 1994 Forest Service appeals reform legislation, held that plaintiffs had failed to exhaust administrative remedies by failing to bring to the attention of the Forest Service specific concerns it had with two proposed timber cutting projects. The court observed: "The policy underlying [this reform] is simple: objects and issues should first be reviewed by those with expertise in the contested subject area." It rejected plaintiffs' entreaty to take a "flexible and liberal view" of the exhaustion requirement. Among other things, the court noted that while the plaintiff was unrepresented by counsel during the administrative process, he was "not a neophyte" in these matters, being a founding member of an environmental group whose website described its "Paper Monkeywrench"* methods of encouraging writing letters and filing appeals with the Forest Service so that the agency "has more work to do." See also Shenandoah Ecosystems Defense Group v. U.S. Forest Service, 144 F.Supp.2d 542 (W.D.Va.2001); Idaho Sporting Congress, Inc. v. United States Forest Service, 843 F.Supp. 1373 (D.Idaho 1994); but see Sierra Club v. Dombeck, 161 F.Supp.2d 1052, 1066 (D.Ariz.2001) (exhaustion not required where it would be futile). An adjunct to the exhaustion doctrine is the requirement that a plaintiff must normally raise all factual and legal

---

* The reference to "monkeywrenching" is from Edward Abbey's cult novel, THE MONKEYWRENCH GANG (1975), whose protagonist engages in a variety of disruptive and illegal tactics to protect the environment in southern Utah from various kinds of development projects.

issues in the agency: otherwise, the plaintiff may be "foreclosed" from raising those issues on review. The foreclosure doctrine is also flexible and is not rigidly applied if extenuating circumstances are shown.

Some courts have disfavored laches in environmental cases to "avoid defeat of Congress' environmental policy," Coalition for Canyon Preservation v. Bowers, 632 F.2d 774, 779 (9th Cir.1980); and because the plaintiff is usually not the only victim of alleged environmental damage, Daingerfield Island Protective Society v. Lujan, 920 F.2d 32, 38 (D.C.Cir.1990) (Ruth B. Ginsburg, Circuit Judge), cert. denied, 502 U.S. 809 (1991).

Ripeness is another administrative law defense that has become more important in federal land and resources law as a result of recent Supreme Court decisions. All federal agencies prepare resource management plans for areas under their jurisdiction; the following case concerns that of the Forest Service, which is probably the most elaborate. (This case also provides a useful introduction to federal land and resources planning, a subject treated in more detail in the next chapter, section C.)

Ohio Forestry Association, Inc. v. Sierra Club

Supreme Court of the United States, 1998.
523 U.S. 726.

■ JUSTICE BREYER delivered the opinion of the Court.

The Sierra Club challenges the lawfulness of a federal land and resource management plan adopted by the United States Forest Service for Ohio's Wayne National Forest on the ground that the plan permits too much logging and too much clearcutting. We conclude that the controversy is not yet ripe for judicial review.

The National Forest Management Act of 1976 (NFMA) requires the Secretary of Agriculture to "develop, maintain, and, as appropriate, revise land and resource management plans for units of the National Forest System." 16 U.S.C. § 1604(a). The System itself is vast. It includes 155 national forests, 20 national grasslands, 8 land utilization projects, and other lands that together occupy nearly 300,000 square miles of land located in 44 States, Puerto Rico, and the Virgin Islands. The National Forest Service, which manages the System, develops land and resource management plans pursuant to NFMA, and uses these forest plans to "guide all natural resource management activities," 36 CFR § 219.1(b) (1997), including use of the land for "outdoor recreation, range, timber, watershed, wildlife and fish, and wilderness." 16 U.S.C. § 1604(e)(1). In developing the plans, the Service must take both environmental and commercial goals into account. See, e.g., § 1604(g); 36 CFR § 219.1(a) (1997).

This case focuses upon a plan that the Forest Service has developed for the Wayne National Forest located in southern Ohio. When the Service wrote the plan, the forest consisted of 178,000 federally owned acres (278 sq. mi.) in three forest units that are interspersed among privately owned lands, some of which the Forest Service plans to acquire over time. See

Land and Resource Management Plan, Wayne National Forest, United States Department of Agriculture, Forest Service, Eastern Region (1987) 1–3, 3–1, A–13 to A–17 (hereinafter Plan). The Plan permits logging to take place on 126,000 (197 sq. mi.) of the federally owned acres. At the same time, it sets a ceiling on the total amount of wood that can be cut—a ceiling that amounts to about 75 million board feet over 10 years, and which, the Plan projects, would lead to logging on about 8,000 acres (12.5 sq. mi.) during that decade. According to the Plan, logging on about 5,000 (7.8 sq. mi.) of those 8,000 acres would involve clearcutting, or other forms of what the Forest Service calls "even-aged" tree harvesting.

Although the Plan sets logging goals, selects the areas of the forest that are suited to timber production, 16 U.S.C. § 1604(k), and determines which "probable methods of timber harvest," are appropriate, § 1604(f)(2), it does not itself authorize the cutting of any trees. Before the Forest Service can permit the logging, it must: (a) propose a specific area in which logging will take place and the harvesting methods to be used, 53 Fed.Reg. 26835–26836 (1988); (b) ensure that the project is consistent with the Plan, 16 U.S.C. § 1604(i); 36 CFR § 219.10(e) (1997); (c) provide those affected by proposed logging notice and an opportunity to be heard, 106 Stat. 1419 (note following 16 U.S.C. § 1612); 36 CFR pt. 215, § 217.1(b) (1997); (d) conduct an environmental analysis pursuant to the National Environmental Policy Act of 1969 (NEPA), 42 U.S.C. § 4332 *et seq.;* to evaluate the effects of the specific project and to contemplate alternatives, 40 CFR §§ 1502.14, 1508.9(b) (1997); and (e) subsequently take a final decision to permit logging, which decision affected persons may challenge in an administrative appeals process and in court, see 106 Stat. 1419–1420 (note following 16 U.S.C. § 1612); 5 U.S.C. § 701 *et seq.* Furthermore, the statute requires the Forest Service to "revise" the Plan "as appropriate" 16 U.S.C. § 1604(a). Despite the considerable legal distance between the adoption of the Plan and the moment when a tree is cut, the Plan's promulgation nonetheless makes logging more likely in that it is a logging precondition; in its absence logging could not take place. See *ibid.* (requiring promulgation of forest plans); § 1604(i) (requiring all later forest uses to conform to forest plans).

* * * [The Sierra Club challenged the plan, alleging that the logging it countenanced violated several federal laws. The district court ruled for the Forest Service on the merits. The court of appeals found that the matter was ripe and then ruled for the plaintiff, finding that the Plan improperly favored clearcutting and therefore violated NFMA.]

* * * We find that the dispute is not justiciable, because it is not ripe for court review.

As this Court has previously pointed out, the ripeness requirement is designed

"to prevent the courts, through avoidance of premature adjudication, from entangling themselves in abstract disagreements over administrative policies, and also to protect the agencies from judicial interference until an administrative decision has been formalized and its effects felt in a concrete way by the challenging parties." *Abbott Laboratories v. Gardner,* 387 U.S. 136, 148–149 (1967).

In deciding whether an agency's decision is, or is not, ripe for judicial review, the Court has examined both the "fitness of the issues for judicial decision" and the "hardship to the parties of withholding court consideration." *Id.,* at 149. To do so in this case, we must consider: (1) whether delayed review would cause hardship to the plaintiffs; (2) whether judicial intervention would inappropriately interfere with further administrative action; and (3) whether the courts would benefit from further factual development of the issues presented. These considerations, taken together, foreclose review in the present case.

First, to "withhol[d] court consideration" at present will not cause the parties significant "hardship" as this Court has come to use that term. *Ibid.* For one thing, the provisions of the Plan that the Sierra Club challenges do not create adverse effects of a strictly legal kind, that is, effects of a sort that traditionally would have qualified as harm. To paraphrase this Court's language in *United States v. Los Angeles & Salt Lake R. Co.,* 273 U.S. 299, 309–310 (1927) (Brandeis, J.), they do not command anyone to do anything or to refrain from doing anything; they do not grant, withhold, or modify any formal legal license, power or authority; they do not subject anyone to any civil or criminal liability; they create no legal rights or obligations. Thus, for example, the Plan does not give anyone a legal right to cut trees, nor does it abolish anyone's legal authority to object to trees' being cut.

Nor have we found that the Plan now inflicts significant practical harm upon the interests that the Sierra Club advances—an important consideration in light of this Court's modern ripeness cases. See, *e.g., Abbott Laboratories, supra,* at 152–154. As we have pointed out, before the Forest Service can permit logging, it must focus upon a particular site, propose a specific harvesting method, prepare an environmental review, permit the public an opportunity to be heard, and (if challenged) justify the proposal in court. The Sierra Club thus will have ample opportunity later to bring its legal challenge at a time when harm is more imminent and more certain. Any such later challenge might also include a challenge to the lawfulness of the present Plan if (but only if) the present Plan then matters, *i.e.,* if the Plan plays a causal role with respect to the future, then-imminent, harm from logging. Hence we do not find a strong reason why the Sierra Club must bring its challenge now in order to get relief.

Nor has the Sierra Club pointed to any other way in which the Plan could now force it to modify its behavior in order to avoid future adverse consequences, as, for example, agency regulations can sometimes force immediate compliance through fear of future sanctions. * * *

The Sierra Club does say that it will be easier, and certainly cheaper, to mount one legal challenge against the Plan now, than to pursue many challenges to each site-specific logging decision to which the Plan might eventually lead. It does not explain, however, why one initial site-specific victory (if based on the Plan's unlawfulness) could not, through preclusion principles, effectively carry the day. See *Lujan v. National Wildlife Federa-*

tion, 497 U.S. 871, 894 (1990). And, in any event, the Court has not considered this kind of litigation cost-saving sufficient by itself to justify review in a case that would otherwise be unripe. The ripeness doctrine reflects a judgment that the disadvantages of a premature review that may prove too abstract or unnecessary ordinarily outweigh the additional costs of—even repetitive—post-implementation litigation. See, *e.g., ibid.* ("The case-by-case approach . . . is understandably frustrating to an organization such as respondent, which has as its objective across-the-board protection of our Nation's . . . forests. . . . But this is the traditional, and remains the normal, mode of operation of the courts").

Second, from the agency's perspective, immediate judicial review directed at the lawfulness of logging and clearcutting could hinder agency efforts to refine its policies: (a) through revision of the Plan, *e.g.,* in response to an appropriate proposed site-specific action that is inconsistent with the Plan, see 53 Fed.Reg. 23807, 26836 (1988), or (b) through application of the Plan in practice, *e.g.,* in the form of site-specific proposals, which proposals are subject to review by a court applying purely legal criteria. Hearing the Sierra Club's challenge now could thus interfere with the system that Congress specified for the agency to reach forest logging decisions.

Third, from the courts' perspective, review of the Sierra Club's claims regarding logging and clearcutting now would require time-consuming judicial consideration of the details of an elaborate, technically based plan, which predicts consequences that may affect many different parcels of land in a variety of ways, and which effects themselves may change over time. That review would have to take place without benefit of the focus that a particular logging proposal could provide. Thus, for example, the court below in evaluating the Sierra Club's claims had to focus upon whether the Plan as a whole was "improperly skewed," rather than focus upon whether the decision to allow clearcutting on a particular site was improper, say, because the site was better suited to another use or logging there would cumulatively result in too many trees' being cut. See 105 F.3d, at 250–251. And, of course, depending upon the agency's future actions to revise the Plan or modify the expected methods of implementation, review now may turn out to have been unnecessary.

This type of review threatens the kind of "abstract disagreements over administrative policies," *Abbott Laboratories*, 387 U.S., at 148, that the ripeness doctrine seeks to avoid. In this case, for example, the Court of Appeals panel disagreed about whether or not the Forest Service suffered from a kind of general "bias" in favor of timber production and clearcutting. Review where the consequences had been "reduced to more manageable proportions," and where the "factual components [were] fleshed out, by some concrete action" might have led the panel majority either to demonstrate that bias and its consequences through record citation (which it did not do) or to abandon the claim. *National Wildlife Federation*, 497 U.S., at 891. * * *

Finally, Congress has not provided for pre-implementation judicial review of forest plans. Those plans are tools for agency planning and management. The Plan is consequently unlike agency rules that Congress has specifically instructed the courts to review "pre-enforcement." Cf. *National Wildlife Federation, supra,* at 891; 15 U.S.C. § 2618 (Toxic Substances Control Act) (providing pre-enforcement review of agency action); 30 U.S.C. § 1276(a) (Surface Mining Control and Reclamation Act of 1977) (same). Nor does the Plan, which through standards guides future use of forests, resemble an environmental impact statement prepared pursuant to NEPA. That is because in this respect NEPA, unlike the NFMA, simply guarantees a particular procedure, not a particular result. Compare, 16 U.S.C. § 1604(e) (requiring that forest plans provide for multiple coordinated *use* of forests, including timber and wilderness) with 42 U.S.C. § 4332 (requiring that agencies prepare environmental impact statements where major agency action would significantly affect the environment). Hence a person with standing who is injured by a failure to comply with the NEPA procedure may complain of that failure at the time the failure takes place, for the claim can never get riper.

The Sierra Club makes one further important contrary argument. It says that the Plan will hurt it in many ways that we have not yet mentioned. Specifically, the Sierra Club says that the Plan will permit "many intrusive activities, such as opening trails to motorcycles or using heavy machinery," which activities "will go forward without any additional consideration of their impact on wilderness recreation." At the same time, in areas designated for logging, "affirmative measures to promote undisturbed backcountry recreation, such as closing roads and building additional hiking trails" will not take place. *Ibid.* These are harms, says the Sierra Club, that will not take place at a distant future time. Rather, they will take place now.

This argument suffers from the legally fatal problem that it makes its first appearance here in this Court in the briefs on the merits. The Complaint, fairly read, does not include such claims. Instead, it focuses on the amount and method of timber harvesting. The Sierra Club has not referred us to any other court documents in which it protests the Plan's approval of motorcycles or machinery, the Plan's failure to close roads or to provide for the building of trails, or other disruptions that the Plan might cause those who use the forest for hiking. As far as we can tell, prior to the argument on the merits here, the harm to which the Sierra Club objected consisted of too much, and the wrong kind of, logging.

The matter is significant because the Government concedes that if the Sierra Club had previously raised these other kinds of harm, the ripeness analysis in this case with respect to those provisions of the Plan that produce the harm would be significantly different. The Government's brief in the Court of Appeals said

> "If, for example, a plan incorporated a final decision to close a specific area to off-road vehicles, the plan itself could result in imminent concrete injury to a party with an interest in the use of off-road vehicles in that area."

And, at oral argument, the Solicitor General agreed that if the Sierra Club's claim was "that [the] plan was allowing motorcycles into a birdwatching area or something that like, that would be immediately justiciable." Thus, we believe these other claims that the Sierra Club now raises are not fairly presented here, and we cannot consider them.

For these reasons, we find the respondents' suit not ripe for review. We vacate the decision of the Court of Appeals, and we remand this case with instructions to dismiss.

NOTES AND QUESTIONS

1. The decision was unanimous. The lawyers for the Forestry Association have interpreted the decision as exemplifying "the theme expressed in *Lujan v. NWF* that many programmatic issues should not be heard by courts, and that judicial review is more manageable in site-specific controversies." See Steven P. Quarles & Thomas Lundquist, The Supreme Court Restricts the Availability of Forest–Wide Judicial Review in *Ohio Forestry Ass'n v. Sierra Club*, 28 Envtl.L.Rptr. 10 (1998). Is this a decision about the availability of review of broad issues addressed in land use plans, or is it merely about the timing of such review? More specifically, when the Forest Service gets around to conducting a timber sale under this plan, may the Sierra Club challenge not only the specific sale, but also the terms of the plan which authorizes it? See, e.g., Wilderness Society v. Bosworth, 118 F.Supp.2d 1082 (D.Mont.2000) (plaintiffs may challenge "forest-wide standards" adopted in a land use plan in the context of site-specific final agency actions).

2. Justice Breyer acknowledges that review of NEPA compliance in connection with the preparation of land use plans is immediately available. This sets up the possibility of bifurcated review of generic agency decisions reached in the planning process—NEPA review immediately upon promulgation of the plan, with review of the plan itself awaiting some later implementing action. Cf. City of Williams v. Dombeck, 151 F.Supp.2d 9 (D.D.C.2001), which involved various challenges to a Forest Service land exchange. The court held that challenges to the merits of the exchange (whether the appraisal of land value was improper, and whether the agency had properly concluded the public interest would be served) were not ripe because, after the agency approved the exchange, the local county had voted down a zoning ordinance which was necessary to allow the exchange to go forward. The court went on, however, to hold that a challenge to the adequacy of the Forest Service's NEPA compliance on the exchange was ripe. See also Kern v. Bureau of Land Management, 284 F.3d 1062 (9th Cir.2002).

3. *Ohio Forestry* has had an immediate impact on litigation challenging federal agency land and resource planning. See, e.g., Wilderness Society v. Thomas, 188 F.3d 1130 (9th Cir.1999) (rejecting a generalized claim that a forest plan violated a statutory standard regarding suitability for livestock grazing, but addressing the claim in the context of specific decisions to allow grazing in particular areas); Ecology Center v. U.S. Forest Service, 192 F.3d 922 (9th Cir.1999) (relying on *Ohio Forestry* to reject a challenge to the Forest Service's failure to conduct monitoring under a forest plan

because, "although the Forest Service's monitoring duty is mandatory under the Plan, legal consequences do not necessarily flow from that duty nor do rights or obligations arise from it"); Kentucky Heartwood, Inc. v. Worthington, 20 F.Supp.2d 1076 (E.D.Ky.1998) (holding some claims ripe and others not; some time-barred and others not, and also addressing standing and exhaustion); see also Wyoming Outdoor Council v. U.S. Forest Service, 165 F.3d 43 (D.C.Cir.1999). If the Supreme Court thought that narrowed concepts of ripeness would streamline judicial review, should it think again?

4.   In Park Lake Resources Ltd. Liab. Co. v. U.S. Dept. of Agriculture, 197 F.3d 448 (10th Cir.1999), a mining company challenged a Forest Service decision to designate an area of national forest as a Research Natural Area because it contained a unique alpine ecosystem which included ten rare plant species. Applicable regulations did not forbid mining activities on the land, and the plaintiff had not made a concrete proposal to conduct operations on mining claims it had located in the area. Finding that it would be "speculative gymnastics" to foresee what the Forest Service might do if a specific proposal were submitted to it, the court held the challenge was not ripe. Another twist on ripeness was provided in Coalition for Sustainable Resources v. U.S. Forest Service, 259 F.3d 1244 (10th Cir.2001), where plaintiffs sought to have the Forest Service implement provisions of a forest plan calling for increased timber harvesting, because the plaintiffs argued this would increase water runoff and help protect endangered species downstream from the forest. The court held the action not ripe because the Forest Service was revising its forest plan and working with other agencies to develop a conservation strategy for the downstream species.

5.   Were the questions presented in *Ohio Forestry* legal or factual or both? Is it relevant that the Administrative Procedure Act never uses the words "standing," "ripeness," "exhaustion," "primary jurisdiction," "laches," and so forth, but simply says that "the reviewing court shall decide all relevant questions of law"? 5 U.S.C. § 706.

6.   It is sometimes said that the flip side of ripeness (challenging action too early) is mootness (challenging action too late). In Fund for Animals v. Babbitt, 89 F.3d 128 (2d Cir.1996), animal rights groups challenged a U.S. Fish & Wildlife Service decision to fund a "moose investigation project" being carried out by the state of Vermont. Plaintiffs claimed the funding was being used by the state to carry out a moose hunt, and that the federal agency should have complied with NEPA before deciding whether to fund it. The district court held that the state was no longer receiving federal funds directly related to the hunt, and dismissed the case as moot. Vacating and remanding, the court of appeals found this conclusion premature, because the state was continuing to receive federal funds that could be used to facilitate future moose hunts the state might conduct.

Closely related to the question of ripeness is the issue of whether the agency has taken any reviewable "action" at all. Eight years before *Ohio Forestry*, Justice Scalia, speaking for the Supreme Court in Lujan v. National Wildlife Federation (I), went on to say—after finding that the plaintiff had made an insufficient showing of standing (see pp. 285–93 supra)—that the environmental group's challenge to Interior's alleged "land withdrawal review program" was not proper because there was no

> "agency action" within the meaning of the APA § 702, much less a "final agency action" within the meaning of § 704. The term "land withdrawal review program" * * * is simply the name by which [the Department has] occasionally referred to the continuing (and thus constantly changing) operations of the BLM in reviewing withdrawal revocation applications and the classifications of public lands and developing land use plans as required by the FLPMA. It is no more an identifiable "agency action"—much less a "final agency action"—than a "weapons procurement program" of the Department of Defense or a "drug interdiction program" of the Drug Enforcement Administration. As the District Court explained, the "land withdrawal review program" extends to, currently at least, "1250 or so individual classification terminations and withdrawal revocations." 699 F.Supp., at 332.[2]

Respondent alleges that violation of the law is rampant within this program—failure to revise land use plans in proper fashion, failure to submit certain recommendations to Congress, failure to consider multiple use, inordinate focus upon mineral exploitation, failure to provide required public notice, failure to provide adequate environmental impact statements. Perhaps so. But * * * [u]nder the terms of the APA, respondent must direct its attack against some particular "agency action" that causes it harm. Some statutes permit broad regulations to serve as the "agency action," and thus to be the object of judicial review directly, even before the concrete effects normally required for APA review are felt. Absent such a provision, however, a regulation is not ordinarily considered the type of agency action "ripe" for judicial review under the APA until the scope of the controversy has been reduced to more manageable proportions, and its factual components fleshed out, by some concrete action applying the regulation to the claimant's situation in a fashion that harms or threatens to harm him. (The major exception, of course, is a substantive rule which as a practical matter requires the plaintiff to adjust his conduct immediate-

---

2. Contrary to the apparent understanding of the dissent, we do not contend that no "land withdrawal review program" exists, any more than we would contend that no weapons procurement program exists. We merely assert that it is not an identifiable "final agency action" for purposes of the APA. If there is in fact some specific order or regulation, applying some particular measure across-the-board to all individual classification terminations and withdrawal revocations, and if that order or regulation is final, and has become ripe for review in the manner we discuss subsequently in text, it can of course be challenged under the APA by a person adversely affected—and the entire "land withdrawal review program," insofar as the content of that particular action is concerned, would thereby be affected. But that is quite different from permitting a generic challenge to all aspects of the "land withdrawal review program," as though that itself constituted a final agency action.

ly. Such agency action is "ripe" for review at once, whether or not explicit statutory review apart from the APA is provided.) * * *

The case-by-case approach that this requires is understandably frustrating to an organization such as respondent, which has as its objective across-the-board protection of our Nation's wildlife and the streams and forests that support it. But this is the traditional, and remains the normal, mode of operation of the courts. Except where Congress explicitly provides for our correction of the administrative process at a higher level of generality, we intervene in the administration of the laws only when, and to the extent that, a specific "final agency action" has an actual or immediately threatened effect. Toilet Goods Assn., 387 U.S., at 164–166. Such an intervention may ultimately have the effect of requiring a regulation, a series of regulations, or even a whole "program" to be revised by the agency in order to avoid the unlawful result that the court discerns. But it is assuredly not as swift or as immediately far-reaching a corrective process as those interested in systemic improvement would desire. Until confided to us, however, more sweeping actions are for the other Branches.

NOTES AND QUESTIONS

1.   Does the majority in *Lujan* (I) allow the government to avoid effective judicial review simply by characterizing general policy decisions as individual, site-specific, determinations? Suppose a Secretary of the Interior announces, early in her tenure, a general policy of seeking to open up as much federal land as possible to mineral development, as fast as possible. Would that policy ever be subject to judicial review on its face, or would it only be subject to review in the many circumstances in which it might be implemented; e.g., in specific decisions to revoke withdrawals, issue mineral leases, approve exploration and mining plans, etc.? Or suppose an energy company applies to the Secretary of the Interior for six different federal coal leases in six western states, and the Secretary rejects each one pursuant to individual determinations (rather than a generically stated policy) that no more coal leasing is needed to satisfy demand. May the company challenge the Department's policy in one generic lawsuit, or must it challenge each of the six determinations?

2.   In Sierra Club v. Peterson, 228 F.3d 559 (5th Cir.2000) (en banc), the majority relied heavily on *Lujan* (I) in holding that the plaintiff environmental groups' challenge to past, ongoing, and future timber sales approved by the Forest Service in four Texas national forests was not justiciable. The majority held that though the pleadings identified some specific timber sales being challenged, these sales were "merely used * * * as evidence to support their sweeping argument that the Forest Service's 'on-the-ground' management of the Texas forests over the last twenty years violates the [National Forest Management Act] * * * [and] go well beyond any challenge to discrete sales." A dissent argued that the allegations properly put general management practices at issue through focus on particular sales and particular tracts of land.

3. Both Justice Breyer in *Ohio Forestry* and Justice Scalia in *Lujan (I)* note that Congress has authority to direct, in applicable statutes, that some challenges to agency programs may occur immediately. Should Congress amend the various planning statutes to authorize immediate judicial review of all decisions in the plan? What are some arguments pro and con?

3. SOVEREIGN IMMUNITY

The common law policy that "the King can do no wrong" was turned upside down in the doctrine of sovereign immunity, which operates to shield such wrongs from judicial review. In an earlier era, the doctrine was employed with some frequency in public lands cases. See, e.g., Malone v. Bowdoin, 369 U.S. 643 (1962); Dugan v. Rank, 372 U.S. 609 (1963). See generally Antonin Scalia, (yes, *that* Scalia), Sovereign Immunity and Non-statutory Review of Federal Administrative Action: Some Conclusions from the Public–Lands Cases, 68 Mich.L.Rev. 867 (1970). In litigation challenging agency action and seeking equitable relief rather than damages (which is the vast bulk of litigation in the federal lands context), the sovereign immunity rule had long been largely swallowed by its exceptions before Congress applied the coup de grace in 1976. An amendment to the Administrative Procedure Act (APA), 5 U.S.C. § 702, abolished sovereign immunity for most purposes:

> An action in a court of the United States seeking relief other than money damages and stating a claim that an agency or an officer or employee thereof acted or failed to act in an official capacity or under color of legal authority shall not be dismissed or relief therein be denied on the ground that it is against the United States or that the United States is an indispensable party.

Because the amendment applies only to suits for "other than money damages," damage suits continue to be governed by the Federal Tort Claims Act, 28 U.S.C. §§ 1346(b), 2671 et seq. [see Chapter 10, § F infra], and the Tucker Act, 28 U.S.C. §§ 1346(a), 1391. Specific statutes limiting the waiver of sovereign immunity prevail over the more general waiver in 5 U.S.C. § 702. The most important examples of specific limited waiver in the federal lands context are the Color of Title Act and the Quiet Title Act, Chapter 3, supra p. 231; these and related statutes amount to narrow waivers of sovereign immunity when persons seek to quiet title to public lands.

A general six year statute of limitations applies to civil actions commenced against the United States. 28 U.S.C. § 2401(a). Though seemingly straightforward, it is not always easy to apply. See Ayers v. Espy, 873 F.Supp. 455, 462–63 (D.Colo.1994) (party challenging a recent application of a regulation adopted more than six years earlier, and not the regulation itself, not barred); see also United States v. Beggerly, 524 U.S. 38 (1998) (no equitable tolling of the QTA).

4. PROCEDURE; STANDARD FOR INJUNCTIVE RELIEF

Besides waiving sovereign immunity, the 1976 legislation greatly simplified the process for reaching the merits in administrative litigation. It amended 28 U.S.C. § 1331 to eliminate the $10,000 minimum amount in controversy for review of federal agency decisions. No longer is it necessary to name specific agency officials as defendants; a complaint may name as defendant the United States, the agency, or the appropriate officer. 5 U.S.C. § 703. If an injunction is issued, it may be directed to a specified officer, even if not originally named as a defendant in the action. 5 U.S.C. § 702. The APA has always allowed for injunctive or declaratory relief, 5 U.S.C.§ 703, both of which are normally requested by plaintiffs. Mandamus-style relief is authorized by 5 U.S.C. § 706, which authorizes reviewing courts to "compel agency action unlawfully withheld or unreasonably delayed." Many courts have refused to set more than a nominal security bond when issuing injunctions in environmental cases brought by nonprofit organizations; e.g. Friends of the Earth, Inc. v. Brinegar, 518 F.2d 322 (9th Cir.1975).

The Supreme Court has held that while there is no presumption of irreparable injury when an agency fails to thoroughly evaluate the environmental impact of a proposed action as required by NEPA, "[e]nvironmental injury, by its nature, can seldom be adequately remedied by money damages and is often permanent or at least of long duration, i.e., irreparable." Therefore, if such an injury is sufficiently likely, "the balance of harms will usually favor the issuance of an injunction to protect the environment." Amoco Production Co. v. Village of Gambell, 480 U.S. 531, 544–45 (1987). See also TVA v. Hill, 437 U.S. 153 (1978), Chapter 5, infra p. 435, which stands for the proposition that an injunction to restrain action taken in violation of the Endangered Species Act is virtually automatic, given the fact that "Congress has spoken in the plainest of words, making it abundantly clear that the balance has been struck in favor of affording endangered species the highest of priorities * * *." Cf. Weinberger v. Romero–Barcelo, 456 U.S. 305 (1982) (issuance of an injunction for a violation of the Clean Water Act was within the equitable discretion of the trial judge). Sometimes agencies themselves lay the basis for injunctions against them; e.g., in Sierra Club v. United States, 23 F.Supp.2d 1132 (N.D.Cal.1998), the trial judge quoted the Park Service's general management plan description of Yosemite ("a premiere masterwork of the natural world * * * of incalculable value * * * [and] superlative scenic grandeur [which offers] a constant test of our wisdom * * * to preserve [it] as a treasure for all people") in finding that an injunction should issue.

5.   COMMITTED TO AGENCY DISCRETION BY LAW

The Administrative Procedure Act, 5 U.S.C. § 701(a), contains two exceptions to the general availability of judicial review; namely, where "(1) statutes preclude judicial review; or (2) agency action is committed to agency discretion by law." The first exception has little or no application in federal land and resources law as statutes expressly precluding judicial review are rare. The applicability of the second exception is very limited, but it occasionally operates in federal land and resources law. The seminal modern case is Citizens to Preserve Overton Park, Inc. v. Volpe, 401 U.S. 402 (1971). At issue was the Secretary of Transportation's implementation of a provision of the Federal Highway Act that prohibited the Secretary from approving the use of federal funds to construct highways through public parklands unless "there is no feasible and prudent alternative * * *." The threshold question was whether by this language the Congress had, in the words of the APA, "committed" the decision to "agency discretion by law."

The Supreme Court described this as a "very narrow exception," applicable only in "those rare instances" where the statute controlling the decision was framed so broadly as to give the agency "no law to apply." There was, in other words, a "basic presumption in favor of judicial review." In part, this presumption may be said to stem from notions of separation of powers, and from the Supreme Court's willingness to approve broad delegations of power from the Congress to the Executive. See, e.g., United States v. Grimaud, Chapter 2, supra p. 107. If Congress gives an agency unbridled discretion to make decisions without specifying *any* guidelines, the delegation is unconstitutional. See, e.g, A.L.A. Schechter Poultry v. United States, 295 U.S. 495 (1935). On the other hand, if Congress supplies an "intelligible principle" for agencies to follow, see Whitman v. American Trucking Ass'n, 531 U.S. 457 (2001), it is in effect giving the agency (and reviewing courts) enough "law to apply" to allow for judicial review. The Court has occasionally referred to judicial review as helping to cure and control broad delegations of legislative power; e.g., American Power & Light Co. v. SEC, 329 U.S. 90, 106 (1946).

Since *Overton Park*, it is a rare case where judicial review in the public natural resource area has been avoided altogether, as cases in subsequent chapters will illustrate. One important exception to the general presumption of reviewability is, however, when a plaintiff seeks to require an agency to bring an action to enforce federal law. The Supreme Court has analogized this to prosecutorial discretion in criminal cases, and reversed the presumption of reviewability, e.g., Heckler v. Chaney, 470 U.S. 821 (1985).

One might argue that resource decisions are appropriate for no—or minimal—judicial review because some public land statutes by their lack of specificity confer great discretion on land management agencies, and because it is appropriate to presume that resource management requires technical expertise beyond judicial understanding. Congress, however, appears generally not only content with, but affirmatively supportive of, judicial review in the context of public natural resources. Modern statutes have in fact rather often encouraged judicial review by including such devices as authority for "citizen suits" and by authorizing the payment of attorneys' fees in appropriate cases. See, e.g., Endangered Species Act, 16 U.S.C. § 1540(g). Such citizen suit provisions do not waive constitutional requirement that plaintiffs must show actual injury as a result of the actions being challenged. See, e.g., Glover River Organization v. U.S. Department of the Interior, 675 F.2d 251 (10th Cir.1982).

6. THE RECORD ON REVIEW AND THE SCOPE OF REVIEW

Generally speaking, review of an administrative agency action under the APA is confined to the agency's own administrative record. See Camp v.

Pitts, 411 U.S. 138, 142 (1973). If the agency record is inadequate for some reason, the "proper course, except in rare circumstances, is to remand to the agency for additional investigation." Florida Power & Light Co. v. Lorion, 470 U.S. 729, 744 (1985). Judge Richard Posner summarized the approach this way in a case challenging a Forest Service timber sale:

> In such a suit the district court is a reviewing court * * * it does not take evidence. * * * Not often, anyway. An evidentiary hearing in district court may be necessary to reconstruct the agency's action or the grounds thereof, if the action and its ground were not set forth in written decision, though an even better response might be to stay the judicial review proceeding until the agency completed the record. * * * [O]nly in an emergency should a reviewing court * * * conduct its own evidentiary hearing.
>
> Confining the district court to the record compiled by the administrative agency rests on practical considerations that deserve respect. Administrative agencies deal with technical questions, and it is imprudent for the generalist judges of the [federal bench] to consider testimonial and documentary evidence bearing on those questions unless the evidence has first been presented to and considered by the agency. Trees may seem far removed from the arcana of administrative determination, but one has only to glance at the documents submitted in this case to realize that "silviculture" is in fact a technical field, and not just one with a dry and forbidding vocabulary.
>
> Therefore only if there is no record and no feasible method of requiring the agency to compile one in time to protect the objector's rights—in short, only (to repeat) if there is an emergency—should an objector be allowed to present evidence in court showing why the agency acted unlawfully.

Cronin v. U.S. Dept. of Agriculture, 919 F.2d 439, 444–45 (7th Cir.1990). These days agency decisions of any moment are usually explained in some sort of written record of decision, making review strictly confined to the administrative record more and more common.

It is sometimes said that the core of administrative law is encapsulated in the slogan: "Factual questions are for the agency and legal questions are for the court." That describes the basic positions typically taken by advocates in public land litigation. Government lawyers argue that the case turns on factual determinations with which management officials have expertise. Lawyers attacking management decisions contend that the case depends on legal analysis of statutes, regulations, or the Constitution—matters more within the special qualifications of courts. The statute that defines the scope of review in public lands cases is normally the Administrative Procedure Act, 5 U.S.C. § 706:

> To the extent necessary to decision and when presented, the reviewing court shall decide all relevant questions of law, interpret constitutional and statutory provisions, and determine the meaning or applicability of the terms of an agency action. The reviewing court shall—

(1) compel agency action unlawfully withheld or unreasonably delayed; and

(2) hold unlawful and set aside agency action, findings, and conclusions found to be—

> (A) arbitrary, capricious, an abuse of discretion, or otherwise not in accordance with law;

> (B) contrary to constitutional right, power, privilege, or immunity;

> (C) in excess of statutory jurisdiction, authority, or limitations, or short of statutory right;

> (D) without observance of procedure required by law;
  * * *.

In making the foregoing determinations, the court shall review the whole record or those parts of it cited by a party, and due account shall be taken of the rule of prejudicial error.

The courts, as well as the commentators, seldom fully agree as to the appropriate scope and depth of judicial review in any set of circumstances. In *Overton Park*, for example, the Court held that the Secretary's decision was arbitrary because the record showed that the Secretary had not thoroughly considered all relevant factors surrounding the availability of alternative routes for the highway. The Court said that though the "arbitrary, capricious, abuse of discretion" standard of review was narrow, the reviewing court's inquiry "is to be searching and careful." That has scarcely ended the matter. In a subsequent decision not involving federal lands, Motor Vehicle Mfrs. Ass'n v. State Farm Mut. Auto. Ins. Co., 463 U.S. 29, 43 (1983), the Court said that an agency's decision may be arbitrary and capricious if it

> has relied on factors which Congress had not intended it to consider, entirely failed to consider an important aspect of the problem, offered an explanation for its decision that runs counter to the evidence before the agency, or is so implausible that it could not be ascribed to a difference in view or the product of agency expertise.

Professor William Rodgers has developed an inventive typology that he terms "the central premise of judicial review." When there is a "vague mandate" from Congress, the substantive decision will often be left to the agency but the courts will scrutinize the procedures followed by the agencies, and may determine whether the agency considered all relevant factors and whether it based its decision on irrelevant factors. When the controlling legislation provides a "specific mandate," the courts will also analyze the substance of the decision by determining whether it conformed to the statutory intent. W. Rodgers, ENERGY AND NATURAL RESOURCES LAW 190–240 (2d ed. 1983).

Many decisions in this and succeeding chapters discuss and apply many of the principles of judicial review identified in this brief summary. The following opinions frame some of the general issues of judicial review.

Udall v. Tallman

Supreme Court of the United States, 1965.
380 U.S. 1.

■ MR. CHIEF JUSTICE WARREN delivered the opinion of the court.

[The facts were rather bewildering; in a nutshell: In 1941, the President by Executive Order No. 8979 created the Kenai National Moose Range in Alaska, and withdrew most of it from "settlement, location, sale, or entry or other disposition * * * under any of the public-land laws applicable to Alaska." In 1948, the Secretary of the Interior issued an order (No. 487) withdrawing lands in Alaska, including most of the Moose Range, from "settlement, location, sale or entry * * *." In 1951, the Secretary issued still other orders (Nos. 751, 778) withdrawing a small part of the lands previously withdrawn from "all forms of appropriation under the public-land laws, including the mining laws and the mineral-leasing laws."

In 1953 the BLM announced that, pending a possible revision in the general policy regarding oil and gas leasing in federal wildlife reserves like the Moose Range, action on pending oil and gas lease offers in such refuges would be "suspended." In 1954 and 1955, the Griffin group applied for oil and gas leases in the northern part of the Moose Range. Action on them was suspended in accordance with the 1953 directive. Finally, in 1958, the Secretary issued an order closing the southern half of the Moose Range to oil and gas leasing in order to protect wildlife, but making lands in the northern half available for leasing. 23 Fed. Reg. 5883 (1958). This order also said that (1) "pending" offers to lease upon which action had been suspended "will now be acted upon;" and (2) offers to lease land now open to leasing will be "accepted for filing" beginning August 14, 1958.

On August 14, the Tallman group filed applications to lease the same lands that were the subject of the earlier-filed Griffin applications. The applicable statute at the time gave preference to the "person first making application for the lease." The Secretary issued the leases to the Griffin group, and the Tallman group sued. The district court held for the Griffin group. The court of appeals reversed, holding that, because of the various orders described above, the lands had been withdrawn from mineral leasing at the time of the Griffin applications. Therefore they were "nullities," and the Tallman group was thus the first applicant to lease these lands.] * * *

When faced with a problem of statutory construction, this Court shows great deference to the interpretation given the statute by the officers or agency charged with its administration. "To sustain the Commission's application of this statutory term, we need not find that its construction is the only reasonable one, or even that it is the result we would have reached had the question arisen in the first instance in judicial proceedings." Unemployment Comm'n v. Aragon, 329 U.S. 143, 153. * * * "Particularly is this respect due when the administrative practice at stake 'involves a contemporaneous construction of a statute by the men charged with the responsibility of setting its machinery in motion, of making the parts work efficiently and smoothly while they are yet untried and new.'" Power Reactor Dev. Co. v. Electricians, 367 U.S. 396, 408. When the construction of an administrative regulation rather than a statute is in issue, deference is even more clearly in order.

"Since this involves an interpretation of an administrative regulation a court must necessarily look to the administrative construction of the regulation if the meaning of the words used is in doubt. * * * [T]he ultimate criterion is the administrative interpretation, which becomes of controlling weight unless it is plainly erroneous or inconsistent with the regulation." Bowles v. Seminole Rock Co., 325 U.S. 410, 413–414.

In the instant case, there is no statutory limitation involved. While Executive Order No. 8979 was issued by the President, he soon delegated to the Secretary full power to withdraw lands or to modify or revoke any existing withdrawals. * * * Public Land Order No. 487 was issued by the Secretary himself.

Moreover, as the discussion in Section I of this opinion demonstrates, the Secretary has consistently construed Executive Order No. 8979 and Public Land Order No. 487 not to bar oil and gas leases. * * * The Secretary's interpretation had, long prior to respondents' applications, been a matter of public record and discussion. * * * [A]lmost the entire area covered by the orders in issue has been developed, at very great expense, in reliance upon the Secretary's interpretation. In McLaren v. Fleischer, 256 U.S. 477, 480–481, it was held:

In the practical administration of the act the officers of the land department have adopted and given effect to the latter view. They adopted it before the present controversy arose or was thought of, and, except for a departure soon reconsidered and corrected, they have adhered to and followed it ever since. Many outstanding titles are based upon it and much can be said in support of it. If not the only reasonable construction of the act, it is at least an admissible one. It therefore comes within the rule that the practical construction given to an act of Congress, fairly susceptible of different constructions, by those charged with the duty of executing it is entitled to great respect and, if acted upon for a number of years, will not be disturbed except for cogent reasons.

If, therefore, the Secretary's interpretation is not unreasonable, if the language of the orders bears his construction, we must reverse the decision of the Court of Appeals.

Executive Order No. 8979, 6 Fed.Reg. 6471, provided:

None of the above-described lands excepting [a described area] shall be subject to settlement, location, sale, or entry, or other disposition (except for fish trap sites) under any of the public-land laws applicable to Alaska, or to classification and lease under the provisions of the act of July 3, 1926, entitled 'An Act to provide for the leasing of public lands in Alaska for fur farming, and for other purposes', 44 Stat. 821, U.S.C., title 48, secs. 360–361, or the act of March 4, 1927, entitled 'An Act to provide for the protection, development, and utilization of the public lands in Alaska by establishing an adequate system for grazing livestock thereon', 44 Stat. 1452, U.S.C., title 48, secs. 471–471o * * *.

"Settlement," "location," "sale" and "entry" are all terms contemplating transfer of title to the lands in question. It was therefore reasonable for the Secretary to construe "or other disposition" to encompass only dispositions which, like the four enumerated, convey or lead to the conveyance of the title of the United States—for example, "grants" and "allotments." Cf. Opinion of the Solicitor, 48 I.D. 459 (1921). An oil and gas lease does not vest title to the lands in the lessee. See Boesche v. Udall, 373 U.S. 472, 477–478. Moreover, the term "public-land laws" is ordinarily used to refer to statutes governing the alienation of public land, and generally is distinguished from both "mining laws," referring to statutes governing the mining of hard minerals on public lands, and "mineral leasing laws," a term used to designate that group of statutes governing the leasing of public lands for gas and oil. * * *

The reference in Executive Order No. 8979 to the 1926 and 1927 statutes also lends support to the Secretary's interpretation. For both statutes relate to leasing rather than alienation of title; it would be reasonable to infer from their specific addition that "disposition" was not intended to encompass leasing. The Secretary also might reasonably have been influenced by a belief that in view of his overriding discretionary authority to refuse to issue an oil and gas lease on a given tract whenever he thought that granting a lease would undercut the purposes of the withdrawal, inclusion of such leases in the withdrawal order would have been unnecessary. Cf. Haley v. Seaton, 281 F.2d 620 (1960). * * *

The placement of the fish trap exception—"(except for fish trap sites)"—a phrase admittedly not relating to alienation of title to land, does tend to cut against the Secretary's interpretation of Executive Order No. 8979. However, it appears that the exception was designed to assure the Alaskans, whose livelihood is largely dependent on the salmon catch, that they could continue—despite the order—to use fish traps. * * * Since it was a reassurance not technically necessary and therefore not functionally related to any part of the regulation, it is no surprise to find it carelessly placed. * * * We do not think the position of the fish trap exception is sufficient to justify a court's overturning the Secretary's construction as unreasonable.

Public Land Order No. 487 withdrew the lands it covered from "settlement, location, sale or entry," but contained no reference to "other disposition." Nor did it contain anything analogous to the fish trap exception. The reasonableness of the Secretary's interpretation of Public Land Order No. 487 therefore follows *a fortiori* from the reasonableness of his construction of Executive Order No. 8979.

NOTES AND QUESTIONS

1. The Court found that no "disposition" was involved and that the mining laws were not "public land laws." Does the Court draw a clear roadmap through this mess of terms and phrases? Does a land order that withdraws lands "from settlement and entry, or other form of appropriation" remove the lands from the operation of the hardrock mining laws? In

Mason v. United States, 260 U.S. 545 (1923), it was argued that "other form of appropriation" meant forms akin to "settlement" (at a time when homesteading was still active), and that mining claims were acquired by "location." The Supreme Court held against the mining claimant:

> Here the supposed specific words are sufficiently comprehensive to exhaust the genus and leave nothing essentially similar upon which the general words may operate. If the appropriation of mineral lands by location and development be not akin to settlement and entry, what other form of appropriation can be so characterized? None has been suggested, and we can think of none.

Mason was not cited in Udall v. Tallman. On whether mineral leases are "dispositions," is it relevant that the first section in the Mineral Leasing Act, 30 U.S.C. § 181, states that "deposits of * * * oil * * * shall be subject to disposition in the form and manner provided by this chapter"? Is the Mineral Leasing Act a "public land law"? The general subject of withdrawals is treated in more detail in the next section of this chapter.

2. Udall v. Tallman is often cited for the general proposition that courts should defer to administrative interpretations of regulations and statutes. Why should such administrative interpretations receive deference? Can't courts interpret statutes at least as well as agency lawyers can?

3. Here, in fact, the issue was not statutory interpretation, but rather how prior agency orders should be interpreted. Should the agency be given more, the same, or less deference in that context? Hadn't the executive branch here created the problem by its welter of confusing, seemingly inconsistent, and somewhat overlapping orders of withdrawal? Does the general idea that ambiguities in a contract or other document are ordinary construed *against* the drafter come into play here? (Is the contest here essentially between the government and a private party, or between two private parties?)

The "deference" issue is frequently raised in federal lands litigation because of the large number of administrative interpretations of statutes and orders, found especially in agency regulations and written opinions of agency lawyers. The next case addressed the issue in the context of one of the largest construction projects in history.

Wilderness Society v. Morton (the TAPS case)

United States Court of Appeals, District of Columbia Circuit, 1973 (en banc).
479 F.2d 842, cert. denied, 411 U.S. 917 (1973).

■ J. SKELLY WRIGHT, CIRCUIT JUDGE:

The question before us in these cases is whether a permanent injunction should issue barring appellee Secretary of the Interior from carrying out his stated intention of granting rights-of-way and special land use permits [SLUPs] necessary for construction by appellee Alyeska Pipeline Service Company (Alyeska), across lands owned by the United States, of a 48–inch–wide oil pipeline which would stretch some 789 miles from

Prudhoe Bay on the North Slope of the State of Alaska to the Port of Valdez on the southern Pacific coast of Alaska. * * *

[The district court issued a preliminary injunction against the project in April 1970 for failure to comply with the National Environmental Policy Act (NEPA) on the proposal, 325 F.Supp. 422, and then in August 1972, following preparation of an environmental impact statement, dissolved the injunction and dismissed the case.]

While the parties to this action have managed to produce a record and a set of briefs commensurate with the multi-billion-dollar project at stake, the basic contentions of the parties, and our views with respect thereto, may be summarized quite briefly. Appellants contend that issuance of certain rights-of-way and special land use permits by the Secretary of the Interior to Alyeska and to the State of Alaska would violate Section 28 of the Mineral Leasing Act of 1920, 30 U.S.C. § 185, by exceeding the width limitation of that section.*

[The oil companies, through their agent TAPS (Trans–Alaska Pipeline System), acknowledged a need for a 54' "primary" right-of-way (the pipe itself was 48" in diameter), an additional parallel 46' of "secondary" right-of-way for construction purposes, another 100' right-of-way for a haul road alongside the pipeline, and temporary use of an additional 200–500' on each side of all river and stream crossings and for construction camps at some other locations. The Interior Department was prepared to issue SLUPs for the area of the right-of-way outside the 50' statutory limitation.] * * *

In brief, it is our view that the legislative history clearly indicates that when Congress enacted Section 28 it intended that all construction work take place within the confines of the width limitation of the section—that is, within the area covered by the pipe itself (4 feet) and 25 feet on either side. In addition, the relevant regulations require that all special land use permits be revocable, and we hold that the permit in this case does not meet the requirement as it has previously been construed. Since all parties agree that construction of the proposed 48-inch diameter pipeline is impossible if all construction work must take place within the width limitation of Section 28, we must enjoin issuance of this special land use permit until Congress changes the applicable law, either by amending Section 28's width limitation or by exempting this project from its provisions. * * *

* * * [W]hile our maxims of statutory construction might have led us to conclude that Congress "must have intended" that those building pipelines could make use of land outside the statutory right-of-way for construction purposes, the legislative history [of the Mineral Leasing Act] simply indicates otherwise. One might have expected the Congress of the United States to exercise foresight in a situation in which it was expressly

---

* [Eds.: At the time, Section 28 authorized the Secretary of the Interior to issue rights of way across public lands and national forests for oil and gas pipelines "to the extent of the ground occupied by said pipeline and twenty-five feet on each side of the same under such regulations and conditions * * * as may be prescribed by the Secretary * * * Provided further, that no right-of-way shall hereafter be granted over said lands for the transportation of oil or natural gas except under and subject to the provisions, limitations, and conditions of this section."]

warned that the statute it was enacting was then, or might in the future become, ineffective. But such foresight was notably lacking. Foresight no doubt would have been the wisest choice in this instance, since after the passage of the Mineral Leasing Act pipeline technology developed to permit construction of larger pipelines needing greater amounts of construction space. It might fairly be said that Congress overreacted to the prior excesses of railroad rights-of-way. But it is not our function, when we pass on either the constitutionality of statutes or their interpretation, to substitute our opinion as to what is wise for that of Congress. Congress chose not to be foresightful; it chose to retain control of the width of pipeline rights-of-way over public land itself, and that decision and its consequences must stand until Congress chooses otherwise.

Appellees have placed their primary reliance on the administrative practice with respect to SLUPs. While we find it unnecessary to review the administrative history in great detail, looking at that history in the light most favorable to appellees it indicates (1) that ever since the Mineral Leasing Act was passed the informal policy of the Bureau of Land Management has been to permit those constructing pipelines to use land for construction purposes outside the statutory right-of-way; (2) that since 1960 this informal practice has begun to become formalized through the procedure of granting SLUPs for construction space to supplement the statutory right-of-way; and (3) that the Department of the Interior and other agencies have granted SLUPs for a multitude of purposes other than pipeline purposes for the last 100 years, oftentimes in situations where the SLUP "supplemented" a limited statutory right-of-way. Appellees argue that this administrative practice should be accorded great weight and deference in the interpretation of the effect of Section 28 on SLUPs for construction purposes, and should lead us to conclude that Section 28 does not affect the Secretary's authority to issue SLUPs.

* * * We do not question the settled principle that administrative interpretations of statutes are entitled to great weight. Udall v. Tallman, 380 U.S. 1 (1965). But it is our firm belief that a line must be drawn between according administrative interpretations deference and the proposition that administrative agencies are entitled to violate the law if they do it often enough. Not to draw this line is to make a mockery of the judicial function. "[T]he courts are the final authorities on issues of statutory construction * * * and 'are not obliged to stand aside and rubber-stamp their affirmance of administrative decisions that they deem inconsistent with a statutory mandate or that frustrate the congressional policy underlying a statute.' * * * 'The deference owed to an expert tribunal cannot be allowed to slip into a judicial inertia * * *.' " Volkswagenwerk Aktiengesellschaft v. F.M.C., 390 U.S. at 272. * * * An administrative practice which is plainly contrary to the legislative will may be overturned no matter how well settled and how long standing.

Balancing the maxim of deference to administrative interpretations with the principle that the courts remain the final arbiter of the meaning of the law is unquestionably a difficult process. [We must] analyze the rationales behind the doctrine of deference and * * * ask if they apply in this case. * * * [I]f they do not, the maxim of deference must inevitably bow before the principle of judicial supremacy in matters of statutory construction. Application of that methodology to the instant case leads us to conclude that "[t]hose props that serve to support a disputable administrative construction are absent here." Zuber v. Allen, supra, 396 U.S. at 193.

Perhaps the primary rationale behind the doctrine of deference is the idea of administrative expertise. * * * "Administrative construction is less potent than it otherwise would be where it does not rest upon matters peculiarly within the administrator's field of expertise." Thompson v. Clifford, 408 F.2d 154, 167 (D.C.Cir.1968).

There * * * is no need for administrative expertise in resolving the question of the meaning of Section 28. Expertise might be needed to decide what is a reasonable pipeline construction area, but it is not needed to decide whether Section 28 precludes construction outside the statutory right-of-way. * * *

The second basic rationale for the doctrine of deference is the concept of congressional acquiescence in the administrative interpretation. "Under some circumstances, Congress' failure to repeal or revise [a statute] in the face of such administrative interpretation has been held to constitute persuasive evidence that that interpretation is the one intended by Congress." Zemel v. Rusk, 381 U.S. 1, 11 (1965). Thus in actual cases courts have to analyze whether there is any reason to believe that the particular administrative interpretation in question came to the attention of Congress so that it might reasonably be said that Congress, by failing to take any action with respect thereto, approved the interpretation. As we have had occasion to note, "Legislative silence cannot mean ratification unless, as a minimum, the existence of the administrative practice is brought home to the legislature." Thompson v. Clifford, supra, 408 F.2d at 164.

Applying the rationale to the present case, there is absolutely no indication that the practice of granting SLUPs for pipeline construction purposes has ever been brought to the attention of Congress, either through testimony at a congressional hearing or by any other means. Nor is the practice of granting SLUPs for pipeline construction purposes of such public knowledge that it is reasonable to assume that congressmen, as members of the general public, knew of the practice. Indeed, it is ironic that the very oil companies which now claim that it was settled and well known administrative practice to grant pipeline construction SLUPs apparently did not know about the practice when they first made application for rights-of-way for the trans-Alaska pipeline. The first application * * * requested an additional permanent right-of-way for construction purposes. * * * Even today the Bureau's policy is not publicized through a formal rule or through any other "expressly articulated position at the administrative level." We are constrained to conclude, therefore, that the practice of granting pipeline construction SLUPs has never come to the attention of Congress, and that there can be no finding of congressional acquiescence. * * *

We need not rest our decision holding the SLUP here to be illegal on Section 28 alone, for appellants have also demonstrated that this SLUP violates the agency's own regulations governing the granting of special land use permits.

* * * 43 C.F.R. § 2920.3(a)(1) (1972) provides: "A special land-use permit will be revocable in the discretion of the authorized officer at any time, upon notice, if in his judgment the lands should be devoted to another use, or the conditions of the permit have been breached." Appellants contend * * * that the SLUP violates Section 2920.3(a)(1) because it is not "revocable in the discretion of the authorized officer at any time" as that phrase has been construed in prior cases. * * *

* * * [D]espite the fact that the application states that the SLUP is revocable and temporary, it is for all real purposes irrevocable and as permanent as the basic pipeline right-of-way. To suggest that during or after pipeline construction an administrator, or for that matter Congress, could revoke the permits and treat all entry into the SLUP land as a trespass is simply to suggest the incredible. By issuing the SLUP the United States is put in a position of suffering continued trespass on its lands or destroying a multibillion-dollar investment.

Even were continued access not vital to the maintenance and operation of the pipeline, it is obvious that the thick gravel pad to be erected on SLUP property will become a permanent feature of the arctic landscape. * * * Alyeska obviously has no intention of removing the pad and the Interior Department will never require removal. The construction pad, a gravel roadway up to five feet deep, will be built with about 34 million cubic yards of gravel, taken from 234 gravel pits located along the pipeline route. The Department clearly is not going to require Alyeska to bear the great cost of breaking up this improvement and returning the gravel to its source. * * * [O]nce the pad is constructed, it is environmentally more detrimental to remove it than to keep it in place. We cannot believe, in light of all the effort the Department has expended in developing stipulations to minimize detrimental environmental effects, that the Department will ever force Alyeska affirmatively to degrade the environment. * * *

We therefore conclude that the SLUP to be issued for pipeline construction violates the Bureau's own requirement of revocability. * * *

CONCLUSION

"[G]reat cases are called great," Mr. Justice Holmes said 70 years ago, "not by reason of their real importance in shaping the law of the future, but because of some accident of immediate overwhelming interest * * *." Northern Securities Co. v. United States, 193 U.S. 197, 400 (1904) (dissenting opinion). The same may be said about the present litigation over the Alaska pipeline. These cases are indeed "great" because of the obvious magnitude and current importance of the interest at stake: billions of gallons of oil at a time when the nation faces an energy crisis of serious proportions; hundreds of millions of dollars in revenue for the State of Alaska at a time when financial support for important social programs is badly needed; industrial development and pollution of one of the last major unblemished wilderness areas in the world, at a time when we are all becoming increasingly aware of the delicate balance between man and his natural environment.

But despite these elements of greatness, the principles of law controlling these cases are neither complex nor revolutionary. Although the first part of this opinion went to great lengths to demonstrate that special land use permits for construction purposes were illegal under the Mineral Leasing Act, at the heart of that discussion is the following very simple point. Congress, by enacting Section 28, allowed pipeline companies to use a certain amount of land to construct their pipelines. These companies have now come into court, accompanied by the executive agency authorized to administer the statute, and have said, "This is not enough land; give us more." We have no more power to grant their request, of course, than we have the power to increase congressional appropriations to needy recipients. * * *

In the last analysis, it is an abiding function of the courts, in the course of decision of cases and controversies, to require the Executive to abide by the limitations prescribed by the Legislature. The scrupulous vindication of that basic principle of law, implicit in our form of government, its three branches and its checks and balances, looms more important in the abiding public interest than the embarkation on any immediate or specific project, however desirable in and of itself, in contravention of that principle. We think it plain that the Executive Branch, when confronted with the legal problems attendant upon the Alaska pipeline, should have taken note of the limitations that had been prescribed by Congress, and should have presented to Congress the case for revision of the basic statute. * * *

NOTES AND QUESTIONS

1. What was TAPS' argument that the statutory limitation to fifty feet did not control? Is the statute clear?

2. Would the result have been the same in the TAPS case if the Department of the Interior had published a formal regulation in the Federal Register interpreting the TAPS right of way grant to apply only to the ground actually occupied by the pipeline, and reciting that a special land use permit (SLUP) would be issued for any additional land needed? The U.S. Supreme Court has generally followed the rule that an agency is bound by its own formal regulations. See, e.g., United States v. Nixon, 418 U.S. 683 (1974); Note, Violations by Agencies of Their Own Regulations, 87 Harv. L.Rev. 629 (1974). In the federal lands area, as elsewhere, the usual (although not wholly consistent) practice is for federal agencies to flesh out statutory provisions with (or create new processes through) detailed regulations. These are typically adopted after notice and opportunity for comment through the Federal Register, and compiled in the Code of Federal Regulations (CFR).

3. How much knowledge is required in the Congress in order for a court to find that Congress has acquiesced in an interpretation of a statute

made by an administrative agency? The knowledge of one member of Congress? Of one committee, in one house of Congress? Does it make any difference that the membership in Congress whose awareness of agency interpretation is in question will usually not be the same membership as that of the Congress which enacted the statute the agency is interpreting?

4. Suppose that the Mineral Leasing Act specifically provides that oil lessees shall pay "a maximum rental of five cents per acre leased." Assume that figure, never changed by Congress, has been rendered trivial by inflation. Can the Secretary of the Interior promulgate a regulation raising the rental to $5 per acre? Would oil industry arguments against that increase be any different from the environmentalist plaintiffs' argument in the *TAPS* case?

5. The consortium of oil companies building TAPS were willing to risk several billion dollars of their own money to construct the pipeline, dependent upon a right of way permit that was revocable at will. Why? Because no federal officer would have the temerity to revoke the permit once the pipeline was built and in operation? Or because, if the permit were revoked, the odds were great that Congress would reinstate it?

Seven months after the Supreme Court denied certiorari in the *TAPS* case, Congress overhauled the right-of-way portion of the Mineral Leasing Act. It authorized rights-of-way in excess of the fifty-foot limitation in certain cases, added substantial regulatory controls aimed at protecting the environment, and made other changes. 30 U.S.C. § 185. The same legislation, by a narrow margin (Vice–President Agnew casting the tie-breaking vote in the Senate) exempted TAPS from further environmental review.

The ultimate goals of the plaintiffs in the *TAPS* case were primarily to strengthen environmental regulation of the construction and operation of TAPS, and to force the Department to give more serious consideration to an alternative route for the pipeline, from the North Slope across Canada to the U.S. Midwest. Environmentalists preferred this route for two basic reasons. First, the all-land route would avoid the need to ship oil by tanker through hazardous waters south of the pipeline's terminus in Valdez, Alaska, and would connect with existing pipelines for shipment to the areas of greatest demand for imported oil in the eastern United States. Second, it was widely expected that a second pipeline, to transport natural gas off the North Slope, would also be necessary, and would likely involve a route through Canada to the Midwest. The environmentalists thought a single corridor for both pipelines was preferable.

The litigation and subsequent legislation substantially achieved the goal of tighter environmental regulation of the pipeline; practically all observers have conceded that the result was a better, environmentally safer pipeline, which currently delivers about 15% of the country's domestically produced oil. Questions still arise whether all the safeguards are being observed. See General Accounting Office, Trans–Alaska Pipeline: Regulators Have Not Ensured That Government Requirements Are Being Met,

(July 1991). The right-of-way had a thirty year term; as of this writing, the Department has begun a NEPA process looking toward its renewal.

Congress's 1973 decision to short-cut further environmental review foreclosed a closer look at the Canadian alternative. That meant that oil tanker traffic from the pipeline's southern terminus would remain a hazard, and the rest, as they say, is history—the Exxon Valdez struck Bligh Reef south of Valdez in March 1989, causing a massive oil spill that fouled waters, beaches and wildlife across Prince William Sound and beyond. (For the most recent decision on that incident, see In re the Exxon Valdez v. Hazelwood, 270 F.3d 1215 (9th Cir.2001)). Meanwhile, despite various proposals over the years, a second pipeline for natural gas has not yet been built, and the gas produced with the North Slope oil is being reinjected in the ground, awaiting a way to transport it to market.

NOTE: THE CHEVRON DOCTRINE AND DEFERENCE

In Chevron, USA, Inc. v. Natural Resources Defense Council, 467 U.S. 837, 842–45 (1984), reversing a lower court decision, the Supreme Court upheld an Environmental Protection Agency interpretation of the Clean Air Act on the basis of the following general principle:

> When a court reviews an agency's construction of the statute which it administers, it is confronted with two questions. First, always, is the question whether Congress has directly spoken to the precise question at issue. If the intent of Congress is clear, that is the end of the matter; for the court, as well as the agency, must give effect to the unambiguously expressed intent of Congress.[9] If, however, the court determines Congress has not directly addressed the precise question at issue, the court does not simply impose its own construction on the statute, as would be necessary in the absence of an administrative interpretation. Rather, if the statute is silent or ambiguous with respect to the specific issue, the question for the court is whether the agency's answer is based on a permissible construction of the statute.[11]

> "The power of an administrative agency to administer a congressionally created * * * program necessarily requires the formulation of policy and the making of rules to fill any gap left, implicitly and explicitly, by Congress." Morton v. Ruiz, 415 U.S. 199, 231 (1974). If Congress has explicitly left a gap for the agency to fill, there is an express delegation of authority to the agency to elucidate a specific provision of the statute by regulation. Such legislative regulations are given controlling weight unless they are arbitrary, capricious, or manifestly contrary to

---

9. The judiciary is the final authority on issues of statutory construction and must reject administrative constructions which are contrary to clear congressional intent. See, e.g., FEC v. Democratic Senatorial Campaign Committee, 454 U.S. 27, 32 (1981).

11. The court need not conclude that the agency construction was the only one it permissibly could have adopted to uphold the construction, or even the reading the court would have reached if the question initially had arisen in a judicial proceeding. FEC v. Democratic Senatorial Campaign Committee, 454 U.S., at 39.

the statute. Sometimes the legislative delegation to an agency on a particular question is implicit rather than explicit. In such a case, a court may not substitute its own construction of a statutory provision for a reasonable interpretation made by the administrator of an agency.

We have long recognized that considerable weight should be accorded to an executive department's construction of a statutory scheme it is entrusted to administer, and the principle of deference to administrative interpretations "has been consistently followed by this Court whenever decision as to the meaning or reach of a statute has involved reconciling conflicting policies, and a full understanding of the force of the statutory policy in the given situation has depended upon more than ordinary knowledge respecting the matters subjected to agency regulations." [citations omitted]

" * * * If this choice represents a reasonable accommodation of conflicting policies that were committed to the agency's care by the statute, we should not disturb it unless it appears from the statute or its legislative history that the accommodation is not one that Congress would have sanctioned." [citations omitted]

If *Chevron, USA* had been decided before *Udall v. Tallman* or the *TAPS* case, would the result in the latter have been different?

The Supreme Court has in recent years issued several decisions muddying up the *Chevron* doctrine. In United States v. Mead Corp., 533 U.S. 218, 226–27 (2001), the Court said: "We hold that administrative implementation of a particular statutory provision qualifies for *Chevron* deference when it appears that Congress delegated authority to the agency generally to make rules carrying the force of law, and that the agency interpretation claiming deference was promulgated in the exercise of that authority." Other recent Supreme Court guidance on when deference to administrative agencies is appropriate is found in Food and Drug Administration v. Brown & Williamson Tobacco Corp., 529 U.S. 120 (2000). See William S. Jordan III, United States v. Mead: Complicating the Delegation Dance, 31 Envtl.L.Rptr. 11425 (2001).

In Christensen v. Harris County, 529 U.S. 576 (2000), involving the Labor Department's interpretation of the federal Fair Labor Standards Act, Justice Thomas, speaking for the majority, noted that "an agency's interpretation of its own regulation is entitled to deference * * * [but] only when the language of the regulation is ambiguous." 529 U.S. at 588. He then addressed the fact that there the agency interpretation was expressed in an "opinion letter" of an agency official:

Here * * * we confront an interpretation contained in an opinion letter, not one arrived at after, for example, a formal adjudication or notice-and-comment rulemaking. Interpretations such as those in opinion letters—like interpretations contained in policy statements, agency manuals, and enforcement guidelines, all of which lack the force of law—do not warrant *Chevron*-style deference. [citations omitted.] Instead, interpretations contained in formats such as opinion letters are "entitled to respect" but only to the extent that those interpretations have the "power to persuade." [citations omitted]

529 U.S. at 587.

In Southern Ute Tribe v. Amoco, 119 F.3d 816 (10th Cir.1997), aff'd en banc, 151 F.3d 1251 (10th Cir.1998), rev'd on other grounds, 526 U.S. 865 (1999), the question was whether to construe early twentieth century statutes reserving "coal" to the United States as including a reservation of coalbed methane gas. The Solicitor of the Interior Department in a 1981 Opinion had concluded that the gas was not reserved with the coal. In rejecting this conclusion, the court of appeals concluded that the opinion did not deserve *Chevron* deference because it was not promulgated either through notice-and-comment rulemaking, nor through an adjudication. It observed in a footnote:

> A Solicitor's opinion is issued at the personal discretion of the Solicitor, without notice and comment, and can be overruled or modified at any time. The opinion at issue here, although presented as authoritative statutory construction, is nothing more than a public pronouncement that Interior will not assert the federal government's right to CBM under its reservation of coal; in that context, the opinion is a valid and useful document. As a simple policy statement, however, the Solicitor's opinion fails to provide the procedural protections required for *Chevron* deference to attach.

It concluded: "Agencies can make law only in two formats, legislative rules and adjudications; the Solicitor's opinion was not promulgated with the procedural protections attendant to either format. Accordingly, *Chevron* does not mandate that we give deference to the 1981 Solicitor's opinion."

The court then went on to consider how much consideration to give to the Opinion under the so-called *Skidmore* doctrine, after Skidmore v. Swift & Co., 323 U.S. 134, 140 (1944), where the Supreme Court said:

> We consider that the rulings, interpretations and opinions of the [agency], . . . while not controlling upon the courts by reason of their authority, do constitute a body of experience and informed judgment to which courts and litigants may properly resort for guidance. The weight of such a judgment in a particular case will depend upon the thoroughness evident in its consideration, the validity of its reasoning, its consistency with earlier and later pronouncements, and all those factors which give it power to persuade, if lacking power to control.

The Tenth Circuit in *Southern Ute* found the Solicitor's analysis faulty in several respects, and refused to follow it. This analysis and result was not disturbed upon en banc review, but the Supreme Court reversed on the merits, without discussing the Solicitor's Opinion or the deference owed it.

The federal land management agencies all have internal manuals that contained detailed guidelines for the conduct of agency business and various miscellaneous matters. Unfortunately no clear line, legal or otherwise, separates what is set forth in an agency manual and what is published as a formal regulation. Some manual provisions have been published for comment in the Federal Register or otherwise promulgated in accordance with the APA's standards for regulations, but most have not. On the latter, the question occasionally arises whether agencies are bound by such provisions in their manuals. *Christensen* addresses whether these provisions get deference, but there is also a question whether they are legally binding on the agency, so that they may be enforced by courts. The lower courts have not reached entirely consistent results on the issue. Compare Western Radio Servs. Co. v. Espy, 79 F.3d 896, 901 (9th Cir.), cert. denied, 519 U.S. 822 (1996); Hi–Ridge Lumber Co. v. United States, 443 F.2d 452, 455 (9th Cir.1971)(Forest Service Manual not binding), with Foundation for North American Wild Sheep v. U.S. Dept. of Agriculture, 681 F.2d 1172, 1182 (9th Cir.1982) (suggesting Forest Service Manual is binding); Davis v. Latschar, 202 F.3d 359, 366 n. 4 (D.C.Cir.2000) (Park Service Management Policies are binding because they are intended to be binding); McGrail & Rowley v. Babbitt, 986 F.Supp. 1386 (S.D.Fla.1997), aff'd w/o opinion, 226 F.3d 646 (8th Cir.2000) (U.S. Fish & Wildlife Service Manual not binding). See generally Robert A. Anthony, Interpretive Rules, Policy Statements, Guidances, Manuals and the Like—Should Federal Agencies Use Them to Bind the Public?, 41 Duke L.J. 1311 (1992).

NOTES AND QUESTIONS

1. The "deference" issue is an important one, frequently involved in federal land and resource law litigation because of the large number of statutes, regulations, and administrative interpretations involved. To what extent should administrative agency interpretations of statutes or regulations receive deference? Is there an argument they should receive no deference; that is, can't courts interpret statutes at least as well as agency lawyers can?

2. What difference does it make whether an agency legal opinion or policy judgment is adopted through formal rulemaking or an adjudication? Is there a notion that an adversary process, or the process of soliciting public comment, will improve the result?

3. In *Udall v. Tallman*, the executive branch had created ambiguities by using imprecise language and by promulgating several confusing, seemingly inconsistent, and somewhat overlapping orders of withdrawal. Does the general idea that ambiguities in a contract or other document are ordinary construed *against* the drafter come into play here? Or should such private contract notions be applied in the context of federal lands, where the government is a sovereign as well as a landowner?

4. What standard of judicial review should apply when an agency *changes* its mind, on a policy issue, or on a legal interpretation? In Motor Vehicle Mfrs. Ass'n v. State Farm Mut. Auto. Ins. Co., 463 U.S. 29, 42 (1983), the Court said "an agency changing its course by rescinding a rule is obligated to supply a reasoned analysis for the change beyond that which may be required when an agency does not act in the first instance."

B. DELEGATION

The Property Clause literally vests the power to manage the public lands in Congress, not the executive branch. Normally, therefore, any power exercised over federal property by the President or administrative agencies must be delegated by Congress. Broad delegations have been common, and have been upheld in such cases as United States v. Grimaud, Chapter 2, supra p. 107. Moreover, "implied" delegations by acquiescence have also been upheld in United States v. Midwest Oil, supra p. 119. As noted in the first section of this chapter, the Supreme Court has recently affirmed the propriety of broad delegations, so long as the agency is given an "intelligible principle" to apply. Whitman v. American Trucking Ass'n, 531 U.S. 457 (2001).

A general delegation of authority to a cabinet-level officer or to an agency head is normally construed to include an implied power to subdelegate authority down through the department or agency. K. Davis, ADMINISTRATIVE LAW 215–18 (1972). Subdelegations must, however, be express. In United States v. Gemmill, 535 F.2d 1145 (9th Cir.1976), for example, trespass convictions were overturned because power to close a part of a national forest had not been administratively subdelegated to the field official who had ordered the closure. Moreover, a Cabinet Secretary may not transfer jurisdiction from one agency to another inside his Department if it contradicts congressional direction. See Trustees for Alaska v. Watt, discussed in Chapter 10, p. 858, infra.

Recently interest has grown in the idea that management authority over particular tracts or areas of land ought to be devolved or delegated to local or regional collaborative bodies. In most cases proponents do not claim or seek title or ownership of federal resources; they seek only a more formal and influential role in how they are managed. Sometimes proponents look for alternatives to federal acquisition of nonfederal land whereby that land can be managed with an eye toward protecting national interests. In other situations proponents do not look to enlarge the role of state or local governments per se, but instead advocate that some management authority be taken out of the hands of established federal agencies, and given to ad hoc groups composed of a variety of interests, including private economic interests.

This section concerns two issues. The first is the extent to which subdelegations of decisionmaking authority can be made to nonfederal sources under existing, generally-worded statutes. This raises rather straightforward legal questions of statutory interpretation, as reflected in the following two cases. The second issue is whether this kind of devolution is a good idea as a matter of policy. As the notes following these two cases show, Congress increasingly has fashioned unconventional federal land management schemes in a number of geographic areas.

National Park & Conservation Association v. Stanton

United States District Court, District of Columbia, 1999.
54 F.Supp.2d 7.

■ KESSLER, DISTRICT JUDGE.

Plaintiffs National Parks and Conservation Association ("NPCA"), Barry Harper, and the American Canoe Association ("ACA") bring this suit against Robert Stanton, Director of the National Park Service ("NPS"), and Bruce Babbitt, Secretary of the Department of the Interior ("Secretary"), challenging Defendants' plan for management of the Niobrara National Scenic River ("Niobrara"), located in Nebraska. The challenged management plan, under which NPS delegates all its responsibilities for managing the Niobrara to an independent local council over which NPS has virtually no control, is the first of its kind. * * *

The Niobrara, a unique river with abundant resources that runs through north-central Nebraska, is known for its historical, paleontological, archaeological, and ecological treasures. Its forests abound with ponderosa pine, American elm, but oak, green ash, basswood, hackberry, and black walnut trees. There is striking bio-diversity among the vegetation, where 160 plant species from eastern, western, and northern forest ecosystems intermingle along the River valley. The Niobrara provides shelter and homes for bald eagles, turkeys, grouse, quails, doves, pheasants, ducks, and geese. It is also home to several threatened and endangered species, including the peregrine falcon, the interior least tern, the piping plover, and the whooping crane. Palaeontologists find a wealth of artifacts on the fossil beds along the Niobrara, including deposits from eighty species of extinct vertebrates. In one fossil excavation site, at least 146 vertebrate species were found. Of the 164 cataloged fossil excavation sites, 15 were rated as internationally significant, and 37 were rated nationally significant. The River was named one of the 10 best canoeing rivers in the nation by Backpacker magazine, and one of the eight special camping areas in the nation by Outside magazine.

One of the Niobrara's unique features is that it runs largely through private land. In 1991, Congress, despite local opposition, designated portions of the Niobrara to become components in the pre-existing national Wild and Scenic Rivers system. Niobrara Scenic River Designation Act of 1991, Pub.L. 102–50, 105 Stat. 254 (1991) ("NSRDA"); 16 U.S.C. § 1274(a)(117). Recognizing that the area along the River was largely privately-held, Congress limited the amount of land the federal government could acquire, and encouraged state and local involvement in the administration and management of the River locale. NSRDA, 105 Stat. at 255. Congress also created the eleven member Niobrara Scenic River Advisory Commission ("Advisory Commission"), an advisory group representing local interests, for the purpose of aiding NPS in developing a management plan for the area. *Id.*

As the agency responsible for overseeing the administration of the Niobrara, NPS developed, with the help of the Advisory Commission, a General Management Plan and Environmental Impact Statement ("GMP/EIS"). The GMP/EIS outlined four management alternatives for administering the Niobrara * * *. [The NPS ultimately selected] Alternative B[, which] provided for management by a local council, which would include members from various county and state agencies, as well as local landowners and business people[.] * * *

* * * In July of 1997, NPS entered into the Interlocal Cooperative Agreement ("Interlocal Agreement") with local Nebraska governmental entities. The Interlocal Agreement established the Niobrara Council ("Council"), and outlined the Council's duties, which included: enter into agreements with NPS or the U.S. Fish and Wildlife Service ("FWS"); obtain and use funds from any source to perform its functions; coordinate management of the Niobrara with the responsible agencies; assist the four cooperating counties in developing zoning and other land protection methods; review county zoning ordinances and actions for consistency with the GMP; provide a forum for landowner/government conflict; work with landowners and provide technical assistance where there is no zoning; manage law enforcement, public access sites, visitor use levels, and other operational functions; retain the services of professionals as necessary to perform its duties; retain staff members to perform its functions; and acquire and manage real and personal property for staff office purposes only. Interlocal Agreement, at ¶ 5. The Interlocal Agreement also noted that the Council should attempt to find outside sources of money, to avoid having NPS "dictate the decisions of the council." *Id.*

The Council may only be dissolved by act of the four cooperating counties, or by termination of the Interlocal Agreement by NPS. By–Laws of Niobrara Council, art. IV, ¶ 1 ("By–Laws"). Any of the four counties may withdraw from the Interlocal Agreement upon 60 days' notice, but the withdrawal of any county does not terminate the agreement. Interlocal Agreement, at ¶ 11.

The Council consists of fifteen members: four county commissioners (one from each participating county); four landowners (one from each participating county) two representatives of local Natural Resource Districts; one timber industry representative; one recreational business representative; one representative of the Nebraska Game and Parks Commission; one FWS representative; and one NPS representative. By–Laws, art. I, ¶ 4. Decisions are reached through simple majority vote. *Id.* at art. I, ¶ 10(k)(1).

On August 6, 1997, the Council entered into a Cooperative Agreement with NPS, as called for in the ROD. The Cooperative Agreement can be terminated by either party upon sixty days' notice, and can be modified by mutual written agreement. By–Laws, art. VII, ¶ A. If the Council fails to manage and protect the Niobrara as set forth in the GMP/EIS, NPS has the authority to terminate the Agreement and implement one of the other Alternatives for managing the Niobrara. Under the GMP/EIS, the Council must carry out its activities to meet standards acceptable to NPS. A.R. at 965–1175. Under the Cooperative Agreement, NPS must "consider for consistency with the GMP the advice and recommendations of the Council during and upon completion of its activities identified above." Cooperative Agreement, Art. II.B.

Plaintiffs allege that although it has been over one and a half years since the Council was established, nothing has been done to protect or manage the Niobrara's resources. Plaintiffs challenge the decision to adopt Alternative B, the duties that have been delegated to the Council, and NPS' compliance with NEPA. Plaintiffs seek an injunction requiring NPS to administer the Niobrara itself, and requiring NPS to complete a more thorough EIS under NEPA. * * *

Plaintiffs argue that NPS' decision to adopt Alternative B for management of the Niobrara was an unlawful delegation of its responsibilities and authority. The Court must first examine the extent of NPS' existing statutory obligations before reaching the delegation issue. * * *

In 1968, Congress passed the Wild and Scenic Rivers Act to "preserve [the] selected rivers or sections thereof in their free-flowing condition to protect the water quality of such rivers and to fulfill other vital national conservation purposes". 16 U.S.C. § 1271 (1999). In 16 U.S.C. § 1274, Congress enumerated the rivers that would compose the Wild and Scenic Rivers system, and further indicated which agencies would manage those rivers. The Niobrara Amendment to this statute reads:

(A) The 40–mile segment from Borman Bridge southeast of Valentine downstream to its confluence with Chimney Creek and the 30–mile segment from the river's confluence with Rock Creek downstream to the State Highway 137 bridge, both segments to be classified as scenic and *administered by the Secretary of the Interior. * * *

(B) The 25–mile segment from the western boundary of Knox County to its confluence with the Missouri River, including that segment of the Verdigre Creek from the north municipal boundary of Verdigre, Nebraska, to its confluence with the Niobrara, to be *administered by the Secretary of the Interior* as a recreational river. After consultation with State and local governments and the interested public, the Secretary shall take such action as is required under subsection (b) of this section.

16 U.S.C. § 1274(a)(117) (1999) (emphasis added). The duties of the Secretary of the Interior are further explained in 16 U.S.C. § 1281(c) (1999) (emphasis added):

The Secretary of the Interior, in his *administration* of any component of the national wild and scenic rivers system, may utilize such general statutory authorities relating to areas of the national park system and such general statutory authorities otherwise available to him for *recreation and preservation purposes and for the conservation and management of natural resources* as he deems appropriate to carry out the purposes of this chapter.

These statutes give the Secretary of the Interior sole responsibility for administering the lands included in the National Parks system and the National Wild and Scenic Rivers system. Basic rules of statutory construction provide that "absent ambiguity or unreasonable result, the literal language of the statute controls". *United States v. Lin,* 101 F.3d 760, 765 (D.C.Cir.1996). The meaning of "administer" is perfectly clear in this context: it means "to manage ... to direct or superintend the execution, use, or conduct of ... to manage or conduct affairs". Webster's Third New International Dictionary at 27 (1993). Thus, the Secretary, who is specifically charged with administering these lands and rivers, cannot wholly delegate his responsibility to a local entity which is not bound by the statutory obligations set forth above.

The creation of the Advisory Commission does not abrogate the Secretary's duties. The extensive legislative history shows that Congress was aware of the unique situation in the Niobrara (i.e., largely privately owned land), and strongly encouraged local participation in the management of the area. In recognition of this situation, Congress created the Advisory Commission to deflect local opposition to national designation and to aid NPS in developing a management plan for the area.[4] But it is clear that in creating the Advisory Commission, Congress did not intend to undermine the Secretary's duties or shift them to any other entity. * * *

In light of NPS' unambiguous statutory obligation to manage the Niobrara, it must be determined whether NPS' choice of Alternative B, allowing the Council to administer and manage the Niobrara, was permissible.

NPS cannot, under the unlawful delegation doctrine, completely shift its responsibility to administer the Niobrara to a private actor, *Perot v. Federal Election Comm'n*, 97 F.3d 553, 559 (D.C.Cir.1996), particularly a private actor whose objectivity may be questioned on grounds of conflict of interest. *Sierra Club v. Sigler*, 695 F.2d 957, 962 (5th Cir.1983). "The relevant inquiry in any delegation challenge is whether Congress intended to permit the delegatee to delegate the authority conferred by Congress." *United States v. Widdowson*, 916 F.2d 587, 592 (10th Cir.1990) (citing *United States v. Giordano*, 416 U.S. 505, 94 S.Ct. 1820, 40 L.Ed.2d 341 (1974)). There is no indication in the relevant statutes or the legislative history that Congress intended any variation on the doctrine of unlawful delegation.

Delegations by federal agencies to private parties are, however, valid so long as the federal agency or official retains final reviewing authority. *United Black Fund, Inc. v. Hampton*, 352 F.Supp. 898, 904 (D.D.C.1972) (holding that no unlawful delegation of authority had occurred because chairman of the U.S. Civil Service Commission retained authority to review policies to make sure they met federal requirements). The relevant inquiry in this case therefore becomes whether, in delegating its responsibility to the Council to administer the Niobrara, NPS retained sufficient final reviewing authority over Council actions to prevent a violation of the unlawful delegation doctrine.

---

4. Plaintiffs argue that Congress created the Advisory Commission as the "primary channel" for local input regarding the administration of the Niobrara, and that the creation of a local managing council violates the intent of Congress. Defendants point out that Plaintiffs' contention would render meaningless the statutes authorizing the creation of cooperative agreements [Eds. See 16 U.S.C. § 1281(e), quoted further below in the body of the Opinion]. While Defendants are correct that the Advisory Commission was meant to be primarily an advisory body for aiding NPS in the creation of the management plan, the Advisory Commission's recommendation for the creation of a local council can not shield NPS from the finding that by following that recommendation it may have unlawfully delegated its duties to the council.

According to the GMP, the Interlocal Agreement, and the Cooperative Agreement, Alternative B calls for management of the Niobrara by a local council, with NPS merely serving as liaison and providing technical support as needed. The Council is responsible for hiring staff, monitoring the River resources, evaluating access sites and land protection needs, providing educational and information services, providing law enforcement and emergency services, and maintaining roads, bridges, and other river access sites. These are all duties which fall squarely within the Secretary's responsibilities for managing the Niobrara. The Interlocal Agreement is, however, clear that it is the Council which shall manage the River. Moreover, the Council is encouraged to seek outside sources of funding to avoid having its decisions "dictated" by NPS. To further ensure that NPS does not "dictate" the decisions of the Council, NPS has only one voting member on the Council, and all decisions are made by majority vote. In short, it is clear that NPS retains virtually no final authority over the actions—or inaction—of the Council.

In their defense, Defendants argue that the relevant statutes encourage and authorize NPS to cooperate with local governments, and enter into cooperative agreements, in administering the Niobrara[. A generally applicable portion of the Wild & Scenic Rivers Act provides]:

> The Federal agency charged with the administration of any component of the national wild and scenic rivers system may enter into written cooperative agreements with the Governor of a State, the head of any State agency, or the appropriate official of a political subdivision of a State *for State or local governmental participation in the administration of the component*. The States and their political subdivisions shall be encouraged to cooperate in the planning and administration of components of the system which include or adjoin State-or county-owned lands.

16 U.S.C. § 1281(e) (1999) (emphasis added).

> (1) The Secretary of the Interior, the Secretary of Agriculture, or the head of any other Federal agency, shall *assist, advise, and cooperate with States or their political subdivisions, landowners, private organizations, or individuals to plan, protect, and manage river resources*. Such assistance, advice, and cooperation may be through written agreements or otherwise. This authority applies within or outside a federally administered area and applies to rivers which are components of the National Wild and Scenic Rivers System and to other rivers. Any agreement under this subsection may include provisions for limited financial or other assistance to encourage participation in the acquisition, protection, and management of river resources.

16 U.S.C. § 1282(b)(1) (1999) (emphasis added).

Although NPS is given the authority to enter into cooperative agreements with local governments, there is nothing in any of the statutes or legislative history cited by either party to suggest that Congress wished to change the traditional role of NPS in managing lands and rivers under its stewardship. Furthermore, there is no precedent for the extent to which

NPS has delegated its responsibilities to the Council. This is the first such agreement of its kind in NPS' history.

The relevant statutes and legislative history are clear that NPS retains its statutory obligation to manage and administer the Niobrara. Even though NPS is required to consider the recommendations of the Advisory Commission, and NPS may enter into cooperative agreements with local entities in carrying out its obligations, the fact remains that the administration of such areas is still the responsibility of NPS. Nothing in the statutes or legislative history gives NPS the discretion to completely abdicate its responsibilities to a local entity.

The Court concludes that Defendants' delegation of its statutory management duties to the Council violates the unlawful delegation doctrine because NPS retains no oversight over the Council, no final reviewing authority over the council's actions or inaction, and the Council's dominant private local interests are likely to conflict with the national environmental interests that NPS is statutorily mandated to represent. NPS lacks the authority to: appoint or remove members of the Council, aside from its own representative; determine which interests will be represented; select Council officers; establish Council sub-committees; determine the term limit for Council members; veto Council decisions which are contrary to the GMP; independently review Council decisions prior to implementation; and control Council funding. The delegation is also unlawful because the Council, made up almost wholly of local commercial and land-owning interests, does not share NPS' national vision and perspective. NPS controls only one of the 15 Council members, and is the only member, besides FWS, who represents national environmental concerns.

The only power NPS retains is the extreme remedy of totally terminating the Cooperative Agreement if the Council is not managing the Niobrara consistent with the GMP. Use of such a draconian weapon is highly unlikely, especially since NPS claims that without local participation, it could not effectively meet its goals and objectives because of local opposition to federal management.

Defendants argue at length that they have supervisory power over the Council, that they are not bound by Council decisions, that they retain ultimate accountability and authority over management of the Niobrara, that they can review the Council's actions for consistency with the GMP, and that they can evaluate the Council's progress. Defendants offer no specifics to support their argument, and in fact, the exact nature and scope of the relationship between the Council and NPS remains vague and unclear. * * *

The tenuous relationship between the Council and NPS raises additional questions as to how exactly NPS intends to ensure compliance with all applicable federal laws (such as the APA; NEPA; the Freedom of Information Act, 5 U.S.C. § 552; Land and Water Conservation Fund Act, 16 U.S.C. § 460*l*–4, *et seq.;* National Historical Preservation Act, 16 U.S.C. § 470, *et seq.,* etc.), considering that the Council is not a federal entity and thus not obligated to comply with these laws. Although NPS claims that it will ensure that all federal statutes are complied with, Defendants have offered no specifics, and presented no evidence, to support their argument that they would be able to ensure compliance, especially given that compliance would require extensive and *voluntary* participation by the Council.

In the end, Defendants' only authority over the Council appears to be its ability to terminate the Cooperative Agreement, a draconian remedy that NPS would be unlikely to exercise except in an extreme situation. This does not constitute the "final reviewing authority" required to prevent an unlawful delegation. Since it is clear that NPS has no "final reviewing authority" over the Council, the selection of Alternative B violates the unlawful delegation doctrine, constitutes an abuse of discretion, is not in accordance with the law, and is in excess of the Secretary's and NPS' statutory jurisdiction.

NOTES AND QUESTIONS

1. The Department did not appeal this decision. How might the Department "cure" the defects scored by the court? Would a sufficient cure be to give the head of the National Park Service, or the Secretary of the Interior, the right to overrule council decisions?

2. Did the court give too short a shrift to the 60–day termination clause, which allowed the NPS to terminate for any reason? Why doesn't that maintain sufficient NPS oversight on the management of this area?

3. Note that this stretch of the River was included in the national Wild & Scenic River System "over local opposition," as the court put it. That is, the designation of the Niobrara Scenic River thrust the NPS into a somewhat hostile world. Note also that the Congress had, in the court's words, "strongly encouraged local participation in the management of the area," and had created an Advisory Commission in the statute designating Niobrara Scenic River. The Advisory Commission, in turn, had recommended that a local council be created. See fn. 4 in the court's opinion. Why, therefore, was it illegal for the NPS to try to secure local "buy-in" by creating the Council and vesting it with some management responsibility?

4. Look closely at the makeup of the Council. Would the result have been the same if the NPS delegation had not been to an ad hoc public-private committee, but instead been to the local county, or by cooperative agreement to an ad hoc body composed exclusively of local governmental officials? See 16 U.S.C. § 1281(e), quoted in the opinion.

5. If a delegation of the kind described in paragraph 4, supra, were held proper, would that body have responsibility for complying with federal laws such as NEPA, or would the NPS retain such responsibility?

6. Did the NPS cleverly invite defeat here, playing this situation both ways? The delegation was designed to placate the locals, but the ultimate result was a court decision that ringingly endorsed NPS's management authority.

When the Reagan Administration took office in 1981, it sought ways to devolve management of federal lands long used for livestock grazing to ranchers. The following case resulted.

Natural Resources Defense Council, Inc. v. Hodel

United States District Court, Eastern District of California, 1985.
618 F.Supp. 848.

■ RAMIREZ, DISTRICT JUDGE.

* * * The case before the Court is complex and involves issues of national importance and first impression. The regulations under attack are amendments to existing Department of Interior regulations * * *. [to provide for] so-called "Cooperative Management Agreements" (CMAs) by which defendants have permitted selected ranchers to graze livestock on the public lands in the manner that those ranchers deem appropriate. * * * The regulation establishing the Cooperative Management Agreement (CMA) program authorizes the BLM to enter into special permit arrangements with selected ranchers who have demonstrated "exemplary range-land management practices." 43 C.F.R. § 4120.1(a). "Exemplary practices" are not defined in the regulation, rather, the choice of ranchers is apparently within the discretion of BLM officials.

The expressed purpose of the CMA program is to allow these ranchers the heretofore *verboten* opportunity to "manage livestock grazing on the allotment as they determine appropriate." 48 Fed.Reg. at 21823–24 (proposed 43 C.F.R. § 4120.1). The BLM is bound by the terms of a CMA for ten years. All CMAs must be "consistent with, and incorporate by reference" existing land use plans and the "terms of the authorization[s]" issued to the cooperative permittee. 43 C.F.R. § 4120.1(a).[23] The rule envisions periodic evaluations and provides for cancellation or modification only in the event of unauthorized transfers, violation of whatever terms and conditions the Secretary inserts in the CMA, or violation of regulations unrelated to overgrazing.

* * * On June 20, 1984, the Bureau issued the "BLM Manual Handbook H–4120–1," Document No. 182 (hereinafter "Handbook") which included procedural direction and standards for CMAs. Also, twenty-seven individual CMAs were entered into by the BLM prior to the filing of this lawsuit.

The Handbook defines a CMA as a "formal, written agreement between the BLM and a permittee * * * that recognizes the cooperator as the steward of the allotment" and which must "be consistent with, and incorporate by reference" relevant provisions of existing land use plans. The Handbook makes plain that CMAs are neither AMPs *nor* permits containing prescriptions for numbers of animals or seasons of use. In fact, defendants instruct BLM officers in the Handbook, that in the event an AMP is in existence when the CMA is executed: "[t]he CMA *may* incorporate the objectives of the AMP, but *must* provide the permittee * * * with

---

23. What defendants intended by the term "authorizations" is facially mysterious.

special recognition and an opportunity to exercise *additional* management flexibility." Thus, the CMA *supersedes* existing authorizations.

The Handbook also clarifies how defendants have managed to reward favored permittees with "secure tenure." The instructions indicate that CMA permittees shall not be subject to evaluation before "the end of the first 5 years" at which time a "joint evaluation" will take place. The permittee is automatically entitled to a CMA renewal (transforming it into a fifteen-year contract) if the mutual examination reveals that the agreement's objectives are being met. If the objectives have *not* been realized after five years, the permittee is nevertheless entitled to an additional five years within which to comply. The BLM, therefore, forfeits any remedy for the rancher's failure to meet objectives except that of denying renewal of the CMA after ten years of non-compliance. This is secure tenure indeed.[26]

A review of the CMAs which have been drafted and executed by defendants, confirms that the Secretary's expressed purposes for the CMA program (secure rancher tenure and self-management) have been implemented. Example agreements cited by *both* plaintiffs' and defendants' counsel indicate that CMAs need not contain specific performance standards such as numbers of animals or seasons of use. See *Spring Cove CMA*, (August, 1984, Shoshone, Idaho District, BLM); *McMullin Bros. CMA*, (August, 1983, Miles City, Montana District, BLM). These agreements list no terms or conditions whatsoever which prescribe the manner in or extent to which livestock grazing shall be managed on these allotments. The permits which accompany these agreements are brief documents containing no grazing specifications. The agreements do contain, however, the BLM's promise of non-interference and secure tenure as outlined in the Handbook.

* * * Defense counsel's chief argument to uphold the CMA Program is premised on a clever interpretation of the Experimental Stewardship Program (ESP), contained in [the Public Rangelands Improvement Act] PRIA of 1978. 43 U.S.C. § 1908. Congress by enacting ESP directed the Secretary to select areas of the rangelands of representative conditions, trends, and forages and in concentrating on these areas to "explore innovative grazing management policies and systems which might provide incentives to improve range conditions." Id. The incentive projects were to be experimental and ready for Congressional review by December of 1985 when the Secretary was directed to report the "results" of the program.

The government has maintained that even if the CMA program cannot be upheld under the Taylor Act and FLPMA, it is nevertheless fully justified by ESP. * * * [T]he Court finds this argument unsound.

This Court would ordinarily defer to the Secretary's judgment on matters such as the applicability of a particular program to a concededly

---

26. While defendants have ostensibly reserved authority to cancel, suspend, or modify CMAs for violations of the terms and conditions of the CMA, the only performance standards included in the CMA agreements are termed "objectives" rather than terms or conditions. Terms and conditions are purposefully vague. Thus, it is apparently impossible for a permittee to risk mid-term interruption of a CMA by mere overgrazing.

generous delegation of experimental authority. However, it is blatantly obvious from the record that the Secretary did not in fact rely upon ESP when he promulgated the regulation authorizing the CMA program. Not only is there no record of the Secretary ever relying on ESP for such authority, evidence in the record establishes that BLM has already completed its experimental stewardship projects. * * *

The apparent truth is that the CMA program was never intended as a stewardship experiment. The Court must therefore view counsel's ESP argument as a *post hoc* rationalization for the CMA program and, as such, deserving of none of the customary deference accorded agency interpretations.

* * * It is also manifest from the language of section 1908 that the CMA program simply does not meet the description of the projects ESP was intended to encourage. The CMA program is *not* an experiment, but is a permanent system of permit issuance aimed at a group of favored permittees. * * *

Faced with such overwhelming evidence that ESP was never intended by Congress to open up exceptions to the permit issuance requirements in FLPMA, defense counsel argued at the hearing on this motion that the Secretary's ability to experiment under ESP "is bounded only by imagination." For this proposition, counsel relied exclusively upon scholarly comments of Professor Coggins, who described ESP in one of his articles in sweeping language:

> The Experimental Stewardship Program offers the BLM an opportunity to break out of an historical rut of range management counterproductivity. The agency is required to try new approaches, and the Act holds out carrots for cooperating ranchers. *The ability of the BLM to experiment is bounded only by imagination and available funding.*

[citing The Law of Public Rangeland Management IV: FLPMA, PRIA, and the Multiple Use Mandate, 14 Envtl. L. 1, 128 (1983)] (emphasis supplied). Putting aside for present the lack of precedential value in a law review article, Professor Coggins was surely *not* to be understood to be opining that the Secretary's ability to experiment was not also bounded by existing law.[37] At any rate, it is the ruling of this Court that any experimentation with new permit issuance procedures *is* bounded by existing law, as well as by the Secretary's imagination, and the ESP does not create an exception to the FLPMA permit requirements. Therefore, in order to uphold the CMA regulation, this Court must be satisfied that the Secretary is authorized under the Taylor Act and FLPMA to enter into cooperative management agreements with selected ranchers.

---

37. A later article by Professor Coggins corrects any such misreading of his earlier statement about ESP. Coggins lambastes the proposed regulations at issue in this lawsuit. He argues that the "overall impulse in the regulations" is to "return grazing management to near-total rancher control" and that, in his view, such experimentations "have little or no warrant in the statutes." Coggins, The Law of Public Rangeland Management V: Prescriptions for Reform, 14 Envtl.L. 497, 499 n. 8 (1984).

D.   Violations of Federal Grazing Statutes

Plaintiffs' principal contention is that the CMA regulation, as finally promulgated and implemented by the Secretary and the BLM, is a naked violation of defendants' affirmative duties under the Taylor Grazing Act, FLPMA, and PRIA. The Court agrees. The CMA program disregards defendants' duty to prescribe the manner in and extent to which livestock practices will be conducted on public lands. The program also overlooks defendants' duty of expressly reserving, in all permits, sufficient authority to revise or cancel livestock grazing authorizations when necessary.

* * * [A]ny defense of the [CMA] program begins on the shakiest of legs since the dominant message and command of defendants' Congressional mandate is that *defendants* shall prescribe the extent to which livestock grazing shall be conducted on the public lands. The apparent goal and inevitable result of the CMA program is to allow ranchers, for a term of at least ten years, to rule the range as they see fit with little or no governmental interference. * * * Some or all of these knowledgeable permittees may even be *inclined* to limit their livestock grazing to levels which will guarantee the vitality of such values, even at the expense of their own private ranching interests. Had Congress left a gap in its regulatory scheme which allowed defendants to decide whether individual ranchers should be entrusted with such decisions, this Court would be in no position to second guess the *wisdom* of the CMA program. However, Congress, in directing that the Secretary prescribe the extent of livestock practices on each allotment, precluded such entrustment, apparently because after years of rancher dominance of range decisions, it found substantial evidence of rangeland deterioration.

* * * Defendants' assertion that the CMA regulation is valid because it requires specification of "performance standards" is without merit. The statute requires specification of numbers and seasons, not generalized standards or responsibilities. CMAs, by definition and in practice, fail to comply with this Congressional mandate.

* * * Defendants are also required to incorporate into each permit an express revocation or suspension clause, 43 U.S.C. § 1732(c), and must retain constant authority to "cancel, suspend, or modify" each permit "in whole or in part" for violations of permit or regulatory requirements. 43 U.S.C. § 1752(a). * * *

The CMA regulation and program falls far short of the standard set by Congress in FLPMA. * * * [F]or ten years, assuming only that the BLM complies with its CMA agreements and that certain rancher covenants which are unrelated to the condition of the public lands are fulfilled, CMA permittees are guaranteed secure tenure. This is not partial or substantial compliance with the permit issuance requirements of the grazing statutes— it is simple *non* compliance. The statutes cannot be reasonably interpreted to allow defendants to tie their own hands with respect to their authority to modify, adjust, suspend, or cancel permits. Nor is there any statutory provision creating exceptions for "exemplary" ranchers or those grazing livestock on public lands which, in defendants' view, require no improvement. Permittees must be kept under a sufficiently real threat of cancellation or modification in order to adequately protect the public lands from overgrazing or other forms of mismanagement. Any other interpretation of Congressional intent is inconsistent with the dominant purposes expressed in the Taylor Grazing Act, FLPMA, and PRIA. * * * It is for Congress and not defendants to amend the grazing statutes. In the meantime, it is the public policy of the United States that the Secretary and the BLM, not the ranchers, shall retain final control and decisionmaking authority over livestock grazing practices on the public lands. * * *

V. CONCLUSION

The problems facing defendants in managing the public lands are gigantic. While the Court has noted that livestock grazing policy and politics have often involved conflicting interests butting heads on the western range, it is obvious that no such simplistic analysis tells the whole story. It is true that private business and ranching values are sometimes in basic conflict with environmental quality and other societal values. But nothing in this opinion should be construed as a finding by this Court that defendants have consciously compromised one set of values in favor of another. Rather, the assumption throughout has been that defendants and plaintiffs merely possess opposing views as to the best way to strike a proper balance between competing interests.

Moreover, the Court recognizes that Congress has left most grazing management judgments to the discretion of defendants. Therefore, the Court has only interposed a third viewpoint in those instances where Congress has already spoken clearly on the subject over which defendants and plaintiffs debate. * * *

NOTES AND QUESTIONS

1.   Here too the government decided not to appeal. Are there any grounds on which an appeal might have been successful? Did the district court give appropriate deference to the agency interpretation of statutes it administers? After this decision, what options remain for the BLM if it persists in trying to give permittee ranchers more discretion and responsibility for range condition?

2.   Is it really necessary for the government to specify the number of cows allowable in a particular area of public lands? Is it micromanaging for Congress to require this? Why can't the agency allow some room for rancher judgment to operate in these circumstances? Is the rancher always and totally motivated by maximizing the number of cows in the short term, to the long-term detriment of the range?

3.   Are there legal or policy arguments that more delegation to non-federal entities ought to be permitted in the grazing situation than in the Niobrara Scenic River? Is the private interest stronger, and the national interest weaker, in federal grazing lands than in a scenic river corridor? Or is the interest in private lands in the scenic river corridor stronger than the interest of ranchers in federal grazing lands? How must or should these context-specific factors influence how the courts approach these issues?

The examples of Congress (rather than the Executive branch) fashioning ad hoc entities with the authority to manage federal lands seem to be growing, and the following summarizes some adopted in the last quarter century. These arrangements should be distinguished from the formation of "Advisory Councils" such as was directed in the Niobrara River legislation. Such purely advisory councils are common in federal legislation designating areas of federal lands for particular uses.

In 1977 Congress created the Pinelands National Reserve in New Jersey's Pine Barrens, one million acres of (mostly non-federal) "pine-oak forest, extensive surface and ground water resources of high quality, and a wide diversity of rare plant and animal species," which provided "significant ecological, natural, cultural, recreational, educational, agricultural, and public health benefits." A principal object of this legislation was to "protect, preserve and enhance" the resources of the area through the combined efforts of federal, state and local governments and the private sector, as "an alternative to large-scale direct federal acquisition and management" of the area. The legislation created a "planning entity" composed of fifteen persons (7 locally appointed, 7 state appointed, and one federally-appointed) and directed it to prepare a comprehensive management plan for the Reserve, to be submitted to the Secretary of the Interior for approval. In passing on the plan, the Secretary was to consider, among other things, whether it "requires the exercise of [police power regulation of land and water use] to the greatest extent practicable * * * in a manner consistent with the purposes of this section," and whether it would both "adequately protect" the resources and, "consistent with such protection, provide adequate and appropriate outdoor recreational opportunities and economic activities within the area." 16 U.S.C. § 471i(a)–(m). The Secretary's approval of the plan was upheld in Hovsons Inc. v. Secretary of the Interior, 519 F.Supp. 434 (D.N.J.1981), aff'd on basis of district court opinion, 711 F.2d 1208 (3d Cir.1983). Among the key ingredients to this legislation were: (1) the federal government put up dollars for land acquisition by the State, but the state had to pay it back if it did not follow the plan; and (2) other federal agencies (such as the Army Corps of Engineers and the Federal Highway Administration) also had to conform to the plan—a result the State strongly desired.

In 1986 Congress enacted the Columbia River Gorge National Scenic Area Act to protect scenic, recreational and other interests in a large area of federal and non-federal land along the Columbia River. 16 U.S.C. §§ 544–44p; see Bowden Blair, Jr., The Columbia River Gorge National Scenic Area: The Act, Its Genesis and Legislative History, 17 Envtl.L. 863 (1987). The statute directed the Forest Service to administer "Special Management Areas" (SMAs) consisting of mostly national forest land, and directed a regional agency known as the Columbia River Gorge Commission, created by an interstate agreement consented to by Congress, to administer "General Management Areas" (GMAs) consisting of non-federal land. See W. Birkenfeld Trust v. Bailey, 827 F.Supp. 651, modified, 837 F.Supp. 1083 (E.D.Wash.1993). Nonfederal landowners in the SMAs can "opt out" by requiring the government to pay fair market value for their land within a period of time; if the government does not, the SMA provisions lapse. See Stevenson v. Rominger, 909 F.Supp. 779 (E.D.Wash. 1995). The commission administering the GMAs is specifically not to be considered a federal agency for purposes of any federal law. It consists of 12 voting members (one appointed from each of the 3 counties on each state's side of the River, and three appointed by each state's governor) and one nonvoting federal member appointed by the Secretary of Agriculture (the Forest Service being the principal federal land manager in the area). A management plan for the scenic area was required within 3 years, and had to be approved by the Secretary. Moreover, each county (or failing that, the Commission) had to adopt land use ordinances consistent with the plan (under guidelines developed by the Secretary in consultation with the Commission), with the Secretary policing compliance. Persons who were denied permits to develop their property by the Commission brought a broad-based facial attack on the constitutionality of the arrangement, but were rebuffed. See Columbia River Gorge United—Protecting People and Property v. Yeutter, 960 F.2d 110 (9th Cir.), cert. denied, 506 U.S. 863 (1992).

In 1996 Congress created the Presidio Trust, a government corporation, to manage that part of the San Francisco Presidio (a former Army base at the south end of the Golden Gate, part of the Golden Gate National Recreation Area), which contains buildings and other structures of commercial value. The Trust is governed by a 7–member board composed of the Secretary of the Interior (or her designee) and 6 nonfederal members appointed by the President. The legislation directs the Trust to develop a comprehensive program for management of the facilities under its jurisdiction, to "reduce expenditures by the National Park Service and increase revenues to the Federal Government to the maximum extent possible." The legislation specifically provides that the Trust is the successor in interest to the Park Service so far as compliance with applicable environmental laws is concerned. See generally 110 Stat. 4097–4104 (1996), as amended; 16 U.S.C. §§ 460bb, historical and statutory notes.

In 2000 Congress authorized the acquisition of the 95,000 acre Baca Ranch, part of an old Spanish land grant in a scenic caldera west of Los Alamos, New Mexico, and upon its acquisition established the Valles Caldera National Preserve. Although part of a unit of the national forest system, the management of the Preserve was vested in a newly established government corporation known as the Valles Caldera Trust, governed by a 9–member Board consisting of the national forest supervisor, the superintendent of the adjacent Bandelier National Monument (part of the national park system), and 7 nonfederal members appointed by the President in consultation with the New Mexico congressional delegation, each having a different areas of expertise (forestry, livestock, wildlife, conservation, etc.). The purposes of the Preserve are to protect the area's scientific, scenic, geologic, watershed, fish, wildlife, historic, cultural, and recreational values, and to provide for multiple use and sustained yield of its renewable resources. The Trust is responsible for complying with federal environmental laws, and must administer the Preserve in accordance with laws pertaining to the national forest system, with a few exceptions. The Trust was directed to develop a program to provide for the operation of the

Preserve as a working ranch, with public access for recreation, and to "optimiz[e] the generation of income based on existing market conditions, to the extent that it does not unreasonably diminish the long-term scenic and natural values of the area, or the multiple use and sustained yield capability of the land." The Trust terminates after twenty years unless extended by Congress.

Two other recent unusual arrangements deserve mention. In 1996, Congress created the Tallgrass Prairie National Preserve, an 11,000 acre remnant of an ecotype that once covered 400,000 square miles in North America. A nonprofit entity had acquired the land, and the legislation set up a unique arrangement whereby title to the Preserve would remain in private hands, but be a unit of the National Park System, and the Secretary would administer it with the consent of the nonfederal landowner, consistent with the laws and regulations applicable to that System. Federal land acquisition authority in the area was limited, and the legislation not only called for preparation of a general management plan, but specified in some detail its contents on such matters as honoring existing mineral leases, grazing rights, hunting and fishing, and state law on fencing. 16 U.S.C. §§ 698u.

In 1998, Congress enacted a statute authorizing a pilot project for three national forests in the northern Sierra Nevada range in California to implement what had become known as the Quincy Library Group proposal. See 112 Stat. 2681 et ff., 16 U.S.C. 2104 Note. This group of representatives of fisheries, timber, environmental, county government, citizen groups and local communities had developed a resource management program to promote both economic and ecological health for the area. National environmental groups opposed the legislation, which directs the Forest Service, after completing an environmental impact statement, to conduct a pilot project to "implement and demonstrate the effectiveness of the resource management activities" recommended by the group, to the extent they were consistent with applicable Federal law, and to report on the results.

NOTES AND QUESTIONS

1. The emergence of public-private collaborations has scarcely been confined to federal lands and resources. Compare "negotiated rulemaking" that was somewhat in vogue in administrative law circles a few years back. There is a burgeoning general commentary on the subject; e.g., Jody Freeman, Collaborative Governance in the Administrative State, 45 U.C.L.A. L.Rev. 1 (1997) (collecting many sources).

2. Is there any doubt about Congress's ability to create these arrangements? If Congress has the power under the Property Clause to dispose of federal lands altogether, may it retain title yet vest management authority in nonfederal entities without federal supervision, or with minimal federal supervision? Are there some responsibilities which may not be delegated outside the government; i.e., that are inherently governmental? At the Niobrara Wild & Scenic River, for example, the NPS gave the Council

authority over "law enforcement." Is it problematic to have nongovernmental entities prosecute violations of federal law?

3. To some extent, these arrangements seek to provide alternative ways to balance national and local interests, a balance that is struck in somewhat different ways in the great federal land systems covered in this book (national parks, forests, wildlife refuges, BLM lands). National environmental groups, for example, are generally skeptical of such arrangements, fearing that the national interest will be sacrificed in the zeal to get buy-in by local interests. Advocates of such arrangements sometimes accuse national groups of simply fearing a loss of their own influence. Can both be right?

4. Is there a value in having some uniformity and consistency of management across an entire national system of lands (e.g., national forests, national parks) by a single institution (the U.S. Forest Service; the National Park Service)? To the extent that is true, how big a threat to that value is the fragmentation inherent in the arrangements described above?

5. Conversely, is there a value in experimenting with different management models, and in giving institutions like the U.S. Forest Service and National Park Service some competition in how units of their systems are managed?

6. Is more formally collaborative management an appropriate policy in areas where significant amounts of nonfederal lands are involved (e.g., the Niobrara River corridor; the Pine Barrens, the Columbia Gorge)? Or where peculiar local challenges exist (e.g., the management of more than one million square feet of commercial office space and rental housing in the Presidio)? Might it be less appropriate where the land is mostly or wholly federal (e.g., the Baca Ranch, after acquisition)? To a substantial extent the character of these various local arrangements reflects the attitudes of key members of the congressional delegations who as a matter of practical politics must sign off on authorizing legislation. At the Baca Ranch, for example, Senator Domenici would agree to support federal acquisition only if an alternative to conventional Forest Service management were devised. At the Tallgrass Prairie, the Kansas congressional delegation would not permit outright federal acquisition. In each case, conservation interests compromised on management arrangements in order to bring the areas under the protection of federal law.

7. Is federal policy gradually moving toward a paradigm where federal lands of high national interest (for example, "crown jewel" national parks) will be managed exclusively by the federal government, and areas of not so high national importance will be managed under more collaborative arrangements with state and local governments and private organizations?

8. How should generic federal environmental laws like the National Environmental Policy Act, the Endangered Species Act, and the Clean Water Act apply in these cases? Should the new managing entity be responsible for compliance? With or without the supervision of the federal agency involved?

C.   EXECUTIVE WITHDRAWALS AND RESERVATIONS

In federal land law history, a "withdrawal" is a generic term referring to a statute, an executive order, or an administrative order that changes the designation of a described parcel of federal land from "available" to "unavailable" for certain kinds of activities, usually involving resource extraction or use. It is a protective measure to preserve the status quo and prevent specified future uses in specified land. A withdrawal can be made by Congress or the Executive, and it can be temporary or permanent. A "reservation" means a dedication of withdrawn land to a specified purpose, more or less permanently.* Whether a particular parcel remains open to mining, mineral leasing, logging, grazing, hunting and fishing, or intensive recreation is the key to many modern disputes on the federal public lands. See generally Ernest Baynard, PUBLIC LAND LAW AND PROCEDURE ch. 5 (1986).

Executive withdrawals are now governed mostly by the provisions of the Federal Land Policy and Management Act of 1976, 43 U.S.C. § 1714, discussed in detail further below. FLPMA now defines "withdrawal" in a considerably broader sense than was previously customary, to include reservations and transfers of jurisdiction among agencies. Specifically, 43 U.S.C. § 1702(j) defines withdrawal as

> withholding an area of Federal land from settlement, sale, location, or entry, under some or all of the general land laws, for the purpose of limiting activities under those laws in order to maintain other public values in the area or reserving the area for a particular public purpose or program; or transferring jurisdiction over an area of Federal land * * * from one department, bureau or agency to another department bureau or agency.

In addition to the terms withdrawal and reservation, the term "classification" is also relevant here. It is often used to describe decisions of land management agencies, operating pursuant to broad statutory authority, to formally categorize (and recategorize) lands according to how they may be used. A rough rule of thumb is that withdrawals and reservations are usually large-scale and accomplished by Congress, the President, or the heads of agencies, while classifications tend to be administrative fine-tuning by agency managers on a parcel-by-parcel basis. Examples of classifications include the Interior Department's designations of lands available for in lieu selection by states, Andrus v. Utah, chapter 2, supra p. 62; and for various other specific uses; see Lujan v. National Wildlife Federation, supra p. 286.

---

* The word reservation is also used in federal land law in a different sense, referring to bilateral transactions. Thus, where a state cedes land or jurisdiction to the United States, it may "reserve" the right to tax activities on the granted land. See Chapter 3, § A. Or the United States may "reserve" subsurface mineral rights in a homestead patent, or a party conveying land to the U.S. may "reserve" mineral rights. See Chapter 7, § C.

Bright lines do not always separate classifications, withdrawals, and reservations. Moreover, over the long history of federal lands, the sources of legal authority for making them are diverse, and the procedures to accomplish them may also vary. A rough division of authority between Congress and the President has grown up around specific statutes and long-term understandings.

First, in some cases Congress has itself retained the sole power to withdraw and reserve certain lands. National parks, for instance, may be created only by an Act of Congress. The same is true of other—but not all—elements of the national park system such as national preserves, national seashores and lakeshores, and national recreation areas. (The exception is that national monuments may be created and put into the national park system by the executive pursuant to the Antiquities Act; see p. 353 below.) Designation of areas for inclusion in the National Wilderness Preservation System also require explicit congressional designation, but designation is ordinarily preceded by administrative studies and evaluations and Presidential recommendations, and agencies may (and sometimes must) manage lands under their jurisdiction to preserve their wilderness qualities. See Chapter 12, § E. Designation of stretches of rivers for inclusion in the national system of Wild & Scenic Rivers is handled in much the same way, although the Secretary of the Interior has been delegated limited power to include river reaches in the national system upon nomination by a State, without approval of Congress. See Chapter 12, § D. Generally speaking, Congress may itself do directly what the executive may do (e.g., it may legislate national monuments or national wildlife refuges), and it always possesses the power to undo whatever it or the President has done.

Second, the Executive, exercising power delegated to it by Congress, may and frequently has withdrawn and reserved federal lands for certain purposes. The classic example grew out of the Forest Reserve Amendment of 1891, which authorized the President to withdraw and reserve public lands covered with timber or undergrowth. The grant was repealed as to most western states, and some acreage returned to the public domain in 1907, but not before the Presidents from Cleveland through Theodore Roosevelt had set aside most of the lands that now comprise the National Forest System. See pp. 106–07 supra. Withdrawals and reservations authorized by the Antiquities Act of 1906, 16 U.S.C. §§ 431–433, and the Pickett Act of 1910, 43 U.S.C. §§ 141–142 (repealed 1976), both considered further below, are also important examples of such statutory delegations. Other less sweeping statutes have been adopted over the years to delegate withdrawal powers to the President and his subordinates for more limited purposes.

Third, a specific natural resource may simply be withdrawn from disposition (and not accompanied by a reservation). By the Mineral Leasing Act of 1920, 30 U.S.C. § 181 et seq., for example, Congress withdrew oil, gas, coal, and like minerals on all public lands from the operation of the Mining Law of 1872 and associated acts, and made them subject to disposition only by leasing. Congress did much the same thing in 1947 and

1955 for common varieties of widely occurring minerals like sand, stone, gravel, clay, pumice, pumicite and cinders, making them subject to disposition thereafter only by lease or sale. See 30 U.S.C. §§ 611–15.

All of the foregoing withdrawals and reservations have resulted from either unilateral congressional action, or from the Executive acting pursuant to congressionally-delegated authority. Despite the fact that the Constitution vests authority over public lands in Congress rather than the Executive, Presidents have long claimed and exercised an implied or inherent power to withdraw—and in some cases, to reserve—public lands in the public interest. For example, Presidents carved military reservations out of the public domain by executive order. (These actions were arguably justified by the Constitution's making the President "Commander in Chief" of the military; Article II, § 2.) Between 1855 and 1919, Presidents also set aside some 23 million acres of public lands for Indian reservations, a purpose less directly related to military exigency. Presidents also made withdrawals and reservations for other purposes; most prominently, beginning with Theodore Roosevelt's reservation of Pelican Island in 1903, for migratory bird refuges. Eventually the executive's practice of withdrawals unsupported by express legislative authority came before the U.S. Supreme Court.

United States v. Midwest Oil Co.

Supreme Court of the United States, 1915.
236 U.S. 459.

[Relevant excerpts from this decision are found in Chapter 2, supra p. 119. The Court upheld President Taft's extensive withdrawals of oil lands in 1909, made in order to prevent private companies from appropriating federally-owned oil under the Mining Law, on the ground that a longstanding pattern of congressional acquiescence to executive withdrawals amounted to an implied delegation of authority under the Property Clause.]

NOTES AND QUESTIONS

1. *Midwest Oil* also validated executive withdrawals of federal land for Indian reservations. See Arizona v. California, 373 U.S. 546, 594–601 (1963).

2. In 1910, shortly after the Taft withdrawals, but before the decision in *Midwest Oil*, Congress enacted the Pickett Act of 1910, which provided, in pertinent part:

> The President may, at any time in his discretion, temporarily withdraw from settlement, location, sale, or entry any of the public lands of the United States, including Alaska, and reserve the same for water-power sites, irrigation, classification of lands, or other public purposes to be specified in the orders of withdrawals, and such withdrawals or reservations shall remain in force until revoked by him or by an Act of Congress. [43 U.S.C. § 141]

> All lands withdrawn under the provisions of this section and section
> 141 of this title shall at all times be open to exploration, discovery,
> occupation, and purchase under the mining laws of the United States,
> so far as the same apply to metalliferous minerals * * *. [43 U.S.C.
> § 142]

This Act was prospective only, and therefore the Supreme Court could not
rely on it to uphold Taft's withdrawals. Although the Pickett Act was
repealed by FLMPA in 1976, many withdrawals made under it are still in
effect.

Notice that while the Act gave the President very broad discretion to
make withdrawals, its first sentence spoke of "temporarily" withdrawing
lands. Yet the end of that same sentence provided that such withdrawals
"shall remain in force until revoked" by the executive or Congress. As a
result, Pickett Act withdrawals nearly four decades old were upheld in
Mecham v. Udall, 369 F.2d 1, 4 (10th Cir.1966). The Pickett Act was,
however, subject to one important limitation (a testament to the political
power of the hardrock mining industry in 1910); namely, the President
could not use it to withdraw federal lands from "metalliferous minerals."
So what was the President to do when he determined to withdraw a tract of
federal lands from all mining, including for metalliferous minerals? Did
there still exist an implied power along the lines sketched out in *Midwest
Oil* to withdraw lands apart from the Pickett Act? This question was
intensively debated inside the U.S. Department of Justice in 1940–41.
Attorney General Robert Jackson (soon to become a Justice on the Supreme Court) initially came to the conclusion that the *Midwest Oil* authority no longer existed because the Pickett Act had occupied the field and
recaptured Congress's authority. After strong objections from Secretary
Harold Ickes and others, Jackson ultimately changed his mind, and issued
an opinion in 1941 that affirmed the nonstatutory authority of the President to make "permanent" withdrawals of public lands, as opposed to the
"temporary" withdrawals authorized by the Pickett Act. See Charles
Wheatley, Jr., WITHDRAWALS AND RESERVATIONS OF PUBLIC DO-
MAIN LANDS 5 (Study Report for the Public Land Law Review Commission, 1969).

Attorney General Jackson's opinion was neither approved nor rejected
by the Congress. Nearly thirty years later, Secretary of the Interior Stewart
Udall withdrew 3 million acres of federal land in Colorado, Wyoming, and
Utah from, among other things, appropriation under the mining laws
relating to "metalliferous minerals." Because of this feature, the Pickett
Act could not be used as authority for the withdrawal. Portland General
Electric Co. located mining claims for uranium (a metalliferous mineral) on
some of the land in question after Udall made his withdrawal, and challenged the Secretary's authority to make it. The Secretary relied on
Midwest Oil. In Portland Gen. Elec. Co. v. Kleppe, 441 F.Supp. 859
(D.Wyo.1977), the court, after briefly recounting the pertinent history,
upheld the withdrawal. It relied in part on the legislative history of a 1958
statute placing express limits on the executive's power to withdraw lands
for military purposes. The Senate Committee Report on this act noted that

"Congress—applying the Midwest Oil yardstick—has perhaps, since 1941 remained silent, and has therefore indulged in a practice * * * equivalent to acquiescence and consent that the practice be continued until the power exercised is revoked." The 1958 legislation, according to the committee report, was "specifically aimed at breaking that silence * * * [and] signaling an end to the implied consent by direct congressional enactment limiting the power exercised." Because the 1958 act did *not* affect the executive's power over *non-military* withdrawals, like Udall's, and because a committee of Congress had been made aware of Secretary Udall's withdrawal and done nothing in response, the court concluded that "Congress had knowledge of and acquiesced in repeated assertions of the implied authority under which [these lands] were withdrawn."

The Pickett Act, and most other claimed sources for the power to withdraw federal lands, authorize withdrawals for broadly expressed "public purposes." As *Midwest Oil* and *Portland General Electric* suggest, the most common reason for withdrawing federal lands has been to put them off limits to disposal. Especially since the decline and eventual abolition of homesteading, the Mining Law has prompted more withdrawals than any other purpose, although withdrawals can also be made to forestall mineral leasing (a subject explored further below at pp. 345–48), or other forms of exploitation. Sometimes it is not easy to discern what a particular withdrawal is withdrawing the lands in question from. Typical language of a withdrawal order is to withdraw federal lands "from settlement and entry, or other form of appropriation." On whether this removes the lands from the operation of the hardrock mining laws, see Mason v. United States, 260 U.S. 545 (1923), discussed at p. 311, supra.

Because the mining industry has been the most frequent target of executive withdrawals, that industry has been in the forefront of a continuing debate, extending back more than a century, over uses and alleged abuses of the withdrawal power. Reservation of the national forests did not *ipso facto* affect the availability of land for hardrock mineral exploration, because Congress explicitly provided in the 1897 organic act for national forests that they generally remained open to the mining laws. Most subsequent withdrawals have, however, decreased the amount of land open to the mining industry. Consequently, the establishment of parks, monuments, wilderness areas, and other special purpose categories on which mining is forbidden or restricted have not been met with universal acclaim.

Preservationists and conservationists have long supported a vigorous executive withdrawal authority. They argue that the executive branch must have the legal authority (as well as the political will) to act to preserve federal land over the long term from disposal or intensive industrial development, and also to react quickly to emergency situations when imminent development threatens important wildlife and recreation resources. The minerals industries and their allies have sought strict limitations on executive discretion to withdraw. Generally speaking, the conservationists have won, although FLPMA, enacted in 1976, did make some attempt to reconcile the competing concerns.

FLPMA's withdrawal provisions apply only prospectively, 43 U.S.C. § 1714(a). Although it repealed numerous older statutes dealing with withdrawals, including the Pickett Act (see section 704, 90 Stat. 2792), FLPMA did not disturb the many pre-FLPMA withdrawals that cover many millions of acres of federal lands. Thus issues relating to withdrawals made between the Pickett Act in 1910 and FLPMA in 1976 can remain alive, as Portland General Electric Co. v. Kleppe, supra, decided after FLPMA, demonstrates.

NOTE: MODERN WITHDRAWAL PRACTICE UNDER FLPMA

One thing Congress sought to do in FLPMA was to abolish the President's implied withdrawal power, by taking the unusual step of naming a Supreme Court decision in a statute: "Effective on and after the date of approval of this Act, the implied authority of the President to make withdrawals and reservations resulting from acquiescence of the Congress (U.S. v. Midwest Oil Co., 236 U.S. 459) * * * [is] repealed." § 704, 90 Stat. 2792.

Questions: Does this kill it? How might it be revived? Is there, after *Midwest Oil,* the legal equivalent of a wooden stake through the heart that can get rid of implied executive power forever? If the Executive continues to withdraw land without other authority, and Congress with knowledge of the Executive's action does nothing, has the "power by acquiescence" been recreated?

The answer to this question may be mostly academic, for FLPMA went beyond the Pickett Act by repealing its "metalliferous mining" exception. Withdrawals may be made under FLPMA in order to "maintain * * * public values" or reserve the area "for a particular public purpose or program." See FLPMA's definition of withdrawal quoted at p. 339, supra.

Withdrawal process and limitations: The Congress did, however, establish rather detailed procedures for the withdrawal of Interior and Forest Service lands. These may be briefly summarized as follows: The Act allows the Secretary to make withdrawals of fewer than 5000 acres for up to twenty years. 43 U.S.C. § 1714(d). Most withdrawals in excess of 5000 acres are limited to an initial term of twenty years (but can be renewed) and are subject to a "congressional veto" within 90 days under complex procedures. Proposed withdrawals must be sent to Congress with a report that must detail answers to numerous questions, including a "clear explanation" of the reason for the withdrawal; what its effects will be, economically and environmentally; whether alternatives to the withdrawal exist and were considered; the extent to which the public and other governmental agencies were consulted; and detailed information on the geology and future mineral potential of the area proposed for withdrawal. See 43 U.S.C. § 1714(c)(2). The Secretary may make "emergency" withdrawals of any size for three years, in which case the report shall be furnished within three months after the withdrawal. See 43 U.S.C. § 1714(e), discussed below at pp. 348–53.

Procedurally, a withdrawal is accomplished by the issuance of a public land order. Under FLPMA, withdrawal authority can be subdelegated within Interior only to presidential appointees in the Office of the Secretary (e.g., the Under Secretary and Assistant Secretaries). 43 U.S.C. § 1714(a). Therefore, withdrawals made by line agencies such as the BLM or by officials in field offices are void. See City of Kotzebue, 26 IBLA 264 (1976). Regulations governing withdrawals are found at 43 C.F.R. Part 2300 (2000).

Review, revocation and termination of withdrawals. Primarily for the benefit of the minerals industry, one part of FLPMA's withdrawal procedures did attempt to get at the problem of the hodge-podge of past withdrawals. Specifically, § 1714(*l*) required the Secretary of the Interior by 1991 to review most existing withdrawals of lands from the mining and mineral leasing laws in the eleven western states in the lower 48. The review was to lead to reports to the President and Congress with an eye toward lifting withdrawals for which the original purpose may long since have passed. This section forbade "termination" of any withdrawal made by Congress, and did not require the termination of other withdrawals, but did require a new determination of "whether, and for how long, the continuation of the existing withdrawal * * * would be, in [the Secretary's] judgment, consistent with the statutory objectives of the programs for which the lands were dedicated and of other relevant programs."

Perhaps to confuse future law students, however, FLPMA also speaks of the Secretary's power to "make, modify, extend, or *revoke* withdrawals." 43 U.S.C. § 1714(a). Seizing on the difference between "termination" and "revocation" of withdrawals, the Department has claimed the power to revoke withdrawals in the ordinary course of business, apart from "terminating" them pursuant to the comprehensive review in 1714(*l*). In the early 1980s, the Reagan Administration's aggressive efforts to terminate protective classifications and revoke withdrawals on many millions of acres of federal land under these authorities led to the Supreme Court's decision in Lujan v. National Wildlife Federation, 497 U.S. 871 (1990), p. 286 supra. Because the Supreme Court threw out the National Wildlife Federation's generic challenge on threshold grounds, the ultimate issue—how FLPMA, NEPA and the APA apply to withdrawal revocations and reclassifications—is still open to litigation in the context of individual revocation or reclassification decisions.

NOTE: IS A DECISION NOT TO AUTHORIZE AN ACTIVITY ON FEDERAL LAND A WITHDRAWAL?

Withdrawals are generally conceived as generic decisions to rule certain activities off limits on specific tracts of federal lands. FLPMA defines withdrawal in part as "withholding an area of Federal land from settlement, sale, location, or entry, under some or all of the general land laws * * *." 43 U.S.C. § 1702(j). There are any number of situations in which the managing agency may exercise discretion and decide not to conduct particular activities on particular tracts of federal land. For example, the

Department of the Interior may decide not to issue mineral leases or grazing permits, or the Forest Service may decide not to conduct timber sales, in a particular area, or even on a specific tract of land.

Back in the days when withdrawals were largely done informally, without public process, it did not matter whether such decisions were considered withdrawals, or simply exercises of agency discretion not to do something. Once FLPMA created a rather detailed process for making withdrawals, however, the issue has sometimes been litigated. The agency clearly has the power to decide not to go forward with leases or permits (so long as the decision is not arbitrary), whether or not the decision is considered a withdrawal. The issue is whether the somewhat cumbersome FLPMA withdrawal procedures (and possibly NEPA) must be followed when the agency says no to certain activities. The courts have not spoken consistently on the question.

Between 1977 and 1980 the Forest Service and the BLM withheld action on applications for oil and gas leases in national forest roadless areas while the lands were being studied for possible inclusion in the wilderness system. The court in Mountain States Legal Foundation v. Andrus, 499 F.Supp. 383 (D.Wyo.1980), held this inaction a "de facto withdrawal" of those lands that should have been subject to the FLPMA procedures, stating (at 391, 395, 397):

> the combined actions of the Department of the Interior and the Department of Agriculture fit squarely within the foregoing definition of withdrawal found in 43 U.S.C. § 1702(j). The combined actions of the Secretaries have (1) effectively removed large areas of federal land from oil and gas leasing and the operation of the Mineral Leasing Act of 1920, (2) in order to maintain other public values in the area, namely those of wilderness preservation. That's the plain meaning of Congress' definition of "withdrawal". * * *

> We conclude that it was the intent of Congress with the passage of FLPMA to limit the ability of the Secretary of the Interior to remove large tracts of public land from the operation of the public land laws by generalized use of his discretion authorized under such laws.

> We cannot allow the Defendants to accomplish by inaction what they could not do by formal administrative order.

A similar conclusion was reached by the same court in Mountain States Legal Foundation v. Hodel, 668 F.Supp. 1466 (D.Wyo.1987). The Department did not appeal either decision. Shortly thereafter, the Ninth Circuit refused to follow *Mountain States*. In Bob Marshall Alliance v. Hodel, 852 F.2d 1223, 1229–30 (9th Cir.1988), cert. denied, 489 U.S. 1066 (1989), one of the issues was whether the Forest Service was required by NEPA to consider the "no action" alternative of not issuing any oil and gas leases in an area of the Lewis & Clark National Forest known as Deep Creek. A defendant lessee argued that

> if the agencies had either denied or deferred action on the Deep Creek lease applications, their action would have constituted an illegal administrative "withdrawal" of Deep Creek from mineral leasing. Therefore,

he contends, further consideration of these options was not required. We reject this argument. "Withdrawal" of public lands requires a formal procedure which, for parcels exceeding 5000 acres, includes congressional approval; the land is effectively segregated from the operation of public land laws for a period of up to 20 years. Federal Land Policy and Management Act, 43 U.S.C. § 1714 (1982). We fail to see how a decision not to issue oil and gas leases on Deep Creek would be equivalent to a formal withdrawal. Kohlman cites only one case, Mountain States Legal Foundation v. Andrus, 499 F.Supp. 383 (D.Wyo. 1980), as authority for the proposition that deferring action on oil and gas lease applications can constitute an unlawful administrative withdrawal. *Mountain States* is not binding on us and we do not find its reasoning persuasive. In that case, the court concluded that the Interior and Agriculture Departments had illegally withdrawn over a million acres of land because they had failed to act on oil and gas lease applications and had thereby removed the land from the operation of the Mineral Leasing Act of 1920. Id. at 391. Yet as the court acknowledged, the Mineral Leasing Act gives the Interior Secretary discretion to determine which lands are to be leased under the statute. 30 U.S.C. § 226(a) (1982); see Mountain States, 499 F.Supp. at 391–92. We have held that the Mineral Leasing Act "allows the Secretary to lease such lands, but does not require him to do so * * *. [T]he Secretary has discretion to refuse to issue any lease at all on a given tract." Burglin v. Morton, 527 F.2d 486, 488 (9th Cir.1975) (citing Udall v. Tallman, 380 U.S. 1, 4 (1965)), cert. denied, 425 U.S. 973 (1976). Thus refusing to issue the Deep Creek leases, far from removing Deep Creek from the operation of the mineral leasing law, would constitute a legitimate exercise of the discretion granted to the Interior Secretary under that statute.

QUESTIONS

1. Is the issue the same with regard to decisions not to sell timber off federal lands, or not to issue grazing permits, or rights-of-way, if not doing all of these things were within the discretion of the federal land manager?

2. Which position is correct? Is withdrawal the only method for implementing land management decisions such as withholding leases? Did Congress really intend to require that the FLPMA reporting and other processes be followed for every single decision rejecting some proposed activity on federal land? On the other hand, did Congress intend that generic policy decisions (such as no mineral leasing on an entire national forest) to escape these processes?

3. Or can the two approaches be reconciled? Should a line be drawn somewhere between a decision rejecting a single or small number of lease applications in a relatively confined area of federal land, and a more generic policy decision putting a large area off limits? Has Congress already drawn such a line in the FLPMA definition of withdrawal? If so, where is it? Should the courts do it by interpretation?

4. The Solicitor of the Department of the Interior has opined that there are actually at least three ways to put into effect a decision not to make a particular tract of land available for mineral leasing: (1) deciding not grant any applications for leases exercising the authority recognized in United States ex rel. McLennan v. Wilbur, 283 U.S. 414 (1931) (see p. 128 supra); (2) withdrawing the area from mineral leasing in a FLPMA withdrawal order; and (3) declaring the land unavailable for leasing in the applicable land use plan for the area. Memorandum to Secretary from the Solicitor regarding Jack Morrow Hills Coordinated Activity Plan (Dec. 22, 2000). For authority that decisions in a land use plan putting some lands off limits to some actions is not a FLPMA "withdrawal," see Seattle Audubon Society v. Lyons, 871 F.Supp. 1291 (W.D.Wash.1994), aff'd on other grounds 80 F.3d 1401 (9th Cir.1996). See also Mark Squillace, The Monumental Legacy of the Antiquities Act of 1906 (2002) (forthcoming).

NOTE: FLPMA WITHDRAWAL PROCEDURES AND THE LEGISLATIVE VETO

FLPMA generally calls for consultation between the executive and the Congress in withdrawal decisions. But in three situations the statute goes beyond mere reporting and consultation. First, 43 U.S.C. § 1714(c)(1) requires the Secretary to terminate a withdrawal the executive proposes to make if, within ninety days of the day notice of such withdrawal has been submitted to each house of Congress, "the Congress has adopted a concurrent resolution stating that such House [sic] does not approve the withdrawal." Second, 43 U.S.C. § 1714(e) allows for emergency withdrawals when "extraordinary measures must be taken to preserve values that would otherwise be lost." These withdrawals may be made on the Secretary's own initiative, "or when the Committee on Interior and Insular Affairs of either the House of Representatives or the Senate notifies the Secretary" that a qualifying emergency exists. Third, as part of the withdrawal review program addressed in the *Lujan v. National Wildlife Federation* case, supra, the statute provides that the Secretary may terminate withdrawals after reporting to Congress "unless [within ninety days of notice] the Congress has adopted a concurrent resolution" of disapproval. 43 U.S.C. § 1714(l)(2).

The constitutionality of these provisions is debatable as a result of the post-FLPMA decision in Immigration and Naturalization Service v. Chadha, 462 U.S. 919 (1983), which held that somewhat similar statutory requirements requiring concurrence by less than the full Congress, and without an opportunity for the President to object, violated the constitutional requirements of bicameralism and presentment, U.S. Const. Art. I, § 7, cl. 2 (requiring that every "Bill" pass both houses and be presented to the President for veto or concurrence):

> In purely practical terms, it is obviously easier for action to be taken by one House without submission to the President; but it is crystal clear from the records of the Convention, contemporaneous writings and debates, that the Framers ranked other values higher than efficiency.

> The records of the Convention and debates in the States preceding
> ratification * * * [reflect] a determination that legislation by the
> national Congress be a step-by-step, deliberate and deliberative pro-
> cess.
>
> The choices we discern as having been made in the Constitutional
> Convention impose burdens on governmental processes that often seem
> clumsy, inefficient, even unworkable, but those hard choices were
> consciously made by men who had lived under a form of government
> that permitted arbitrary governmental acts to go unchecked. There is
> no support in the Constitution or decisions of this Court for the
> proposition that the cumbersomeness and delays often encountered in
> complying with explicit Constitutional standards may be avoided, ei-
> ther by the Congress or by the President. * * * With all the obvious
> flaws of delay, untidiness, and potential for abuse, we have not yet
> found a better way to preserve freedom than by making the exercise of
> power subject to the carefully crafted restraints spelled out in the
> Constitution.

In *dictum,* the Court approved "report and wait" provisions whereby
proposed administrative action is reported to Congress and does not take
effect until the end of a specified waiting period, 462 U.S. at 935 n. 9.

Two courts have confronted the issue whether FLPMA's provisions
giving less than the full Congress a veto over executive withdrawal actions
are constitutional. One decision came early in the Reagan Administration,
while the *Chadha* case was on its way to the Supreme Court. Interior
Secretary James Watt announced plans to issue oil and gas leases in three
wilderness areas in Montana that were legally open to mineral leasing
through December 31, 1983. Invoking its statutory "emergency withdrawal" authority under FLPMA, the House Interior Committee voted along
partisan lines to direct the Secretary to withdraw the areas from mineral
leasing. Secretary Watt expressed doubt about the constitutionality of the
Committee's action, but issued an order withdrawing the lands. Miners and
conservative legal foundations challenged his order in court.

The district court thought the issue was close, but strained to uphold
the withdrawal provisions on the seemingly artificial ground that, although
a congressional committee could order a withdrawal, the Secretary retained
power to set its duration. Pacific Legal Foundation v. Watt, 529 F.Supp.
982 (D.Mont.1981).

> Obviously, the authority vested in the Committee under even this
> limited interpretation is somewhat unique. It still requires the Execu-
> tive branch to take affirmative action at the request of a single
> congressional committee. But since the Secretary is allowed to exercise
> his discretion in implementing that request, the Committee's authority
> is sufficiently similar to traditional committee powers, and to proper
> report and wait provisions to pass constitutional muster.

This litigation, which included a brief subsequent opinion at 539
F.Supp. 1194 (D.Mont.1982), triggered a series of executive and congressional actions resulting in the withdrawal of all wilderness areas from

mineral leasing through December 31, 1983. At that point, the statutory withdrawal in the Wilderness Act took effect.

The second case was also triggered by Secretary Watt, this time in proposing to lease large tracts of federal coal in the Upper Great Plains. Once again the House Interior Committee, following on the heels of a General Accounting Office report that previous coal lease sales conducted by Secretary Watt had been $100 million below fair market value, voted to direct an emergency withdrawal of the lands under FLPMA. This time Secretary Watt, citing the Supreme Court's decision in *Chadha*, refused to make the withdrawal, and environmental groups sued, leading to the following opinion on plaintiffs' request for a preliminary injunction, addressing their likelihood of succeeding on the merits:

National Wildlife Federation v. Watt

United States District Court, District of Columbia, 1983.
571 F.Supp. 1145.

■ OBERDORFER, DISTRICT JUDGE.

* * * If Congress' authority to enact the procedure at issue here derives solely from Article I of the Constitution, or if the *Chadha* rationale applies to Article IV, Section 3, the Committee resolution will probably be held to be impermissible legislative activity. Plaintiffs' attempt to distinguish a section 204(e) withdrawal from a legislative veto on the grounds that the withdrawal is only temporary is unconvincing. A forced withdrawal, whether temporary or permanent, alters the legal rights and duties of the Secretary of the Interior, and this cannot be done, according to *Chadha*, without bicameral passage and presidential presentment. The holding in *Pacific Legal Foundation* [supra] which plaintiffs cite as support, seems susceptible to similar criticism. If section 204(e) is read to give the Secretary total discretion over the duration of the withdrawal, then the section would lose all force. Yet once the section is interpreted to mandate withdrawal for any length of time, it alters the Secretary's legal rights and duties.

Finally, section 204(e) does not seem analogous, as plaintiffs claim, to the "report and wait" provisions that passed constitutional muster in *Chadha*. * * * This grace period, uniformly applied to every new rule, allows Congress time to amend or reject the rule if it desires. There is no similar rule of postponement universally applied to coal leases so that each lease can be reviewed by Congress as a whole. Rather, the House Committee may pick and choose to delay leases that may or may not become the subject of action by Congress. *Chadha* will probably be interpreted as holding that this sort of selective review of executive action by less than the full Congress is not a permissible exercise of its legislative power under Article I.

[The Interior Department had adopted the following regulation in order to implement section 1714(e) of FLPMA:

When the Secretary determines, or when either one of the two Committees of the Congress that are specified in section 204(e) of the act (43 U.S.C. 1714(e)) notifies the Secretary, that an emergency exists * * * the Secretary shall immediately make a withdrawal which shall be limited in its scope and duration to the emergency. 43 CFR § 2310.5(a).]

Defendant's failure to follow his own regulation, or to rescind it after notice, comment, and reasoned determination, raises a more serious question. * * * [I]t will probably be held that defendant's decision not to follow his regulation, on the basis of informal, *ex parte*, unpublished legal opinions that the parallel provision of section 204(e) was void, violated those notice requirements. Reliance on such *ex parte* opinions without minimal testing by other interested persons does not satisfy the notice and comment requirements of APA. * * *

Neither the material furnished by the parties nor that otherwise available to the Court in this brief time establishes with the certainty perceived by the defendant's legal advisers that section 204(e) of the 1976 Act, the Committee resolution, and the regulation are, as defendant asserts, "patently unconstitutional." * * *

It may well be that when this Court, the Court of Appeals, or the Supreme Court has had comprehensive briefs and an adequate opportunity to consider all the relevant historical evidence about the drafting and context of Article IV, Section 3, as well as its application over the years, they will reach a conclusion contrary to the opinions relied upon by the defendant here. The Supreme Court has stated that Congress' proprietary interest in public lands gives it constitutional prerogatives which transcend those which it enjoys in its purely legislative role in respect of immigration. See, e.g., United States v. California, 332 U.S. 19, 27 (1947). Moreover, it is common historical knowledge that in the years before the Constitution was adopted (and for many years thereafter) Congress was in session for only brief periods and in recess for many months at a time. Public lands were matters of even greater public and political interest than they are now. It is not inconceivable that courts will decide from the text and context of Article IV, Section 3, that its Framers contemplated that Congress' proprietary power to "dispose of" public lands included the power to delegate power to dispose of public land to the Executive as a trustee. The Framers may well have contemplated that such an Article IV delegation might be subject to an express and narrow condition that a specified Committee of Congress could, during or in anticipation of a congressional recess, temporarily suspend that delegation in the manner now provided for in section 204(e) of the 1976 Act. Such a condition would be analogous to limitations traditionally imposed by settlors under familiar principles of trust law. * * *

[The court, reasoning that there was a probability that the plaintiffs would prevail on the merits, issued a preliminary injunction. Later, the court granted plaintiffs' motion for summary judgment. 577 F.Supp. 825 (D.D.C.1984).]

NOTES AND QUESTIONS

1.   This case illustrates how shoes may end up on different feet: In *Midwest Oil*, the executive sought to put the brakes on congressionally-directed exploitation of federal natural resources. Here, a committee of Congress sought to forestall an exploitation-minded Secretary. Where did Secretary Watt go wrong, procedurally, in his zeal to issue these coal leases?

2.   Are there grounds for distinguishing the public lands arena, and the FLPMA provisions, from the *Chadha* teachings? Should the Constitution be construed to permit Congress and/or one of its houses or committees to play an active, continuing role in setting federal natural resource policy through such devices as FLPMA creates in the withdrawal area, even when such a role is constitutionally inappropriate in other contexts? (*Chadha* involved deportation of aliens.)

3.   Does or should it make any difference in analyzing this constitutional question that the United States is a landowner here as well as a sovereign regulator? That Congress is given explicit constitutional power to make "needful Rules and Regulations" respecting federal property? That, as illustrated by *Midwest Oil*, there is a long tradition of legislative-executive dialogue and cooperation on withdrawal questions? That withdrawal questions in and of themselves (unlike *Chadha*) do not involve questions of human rights nor resolve questions of property rights, but rather only determine what legal regime will apply to specific tracts of federal lands? Does the Court's reading of the Property Clause in this case mean that FLPMA can be distinguished from the statute at issue in *Chadha* ? Can the analysis of section 1714(e) in *Pacific Legal Foundation*, giving the Secretary discretion over the duration of the withdrawal, be squared with the Supreme Court's decision in *Chadha* ?

4.   Can the emergency provision in section 1714(e) be distinguished from the two other legislative vetoes in the FLPMA withdrawal provisions? Is there a reason to defer to a congressional committee's declaration of an emergency requiring prompt action, when the executive can take that action much more promptly than the Congress can?

5.   Most of the commentators conclude that all three provisions probably violate the *Chadha* rationale. See, e.g., Robert Glicksman, Severability and the Realignment of the Balance of Power Over the Public Lands: The Federal Land Policy and Management Act of 1976 After the Legislative Veto Decisions, 36 Hast.L.J. 1, 33–51 (1984). But see Roger M. Sullivan, The Power of Congress Under the Property Clause: A Potential Check on the Effect of the *Chadha* Decision on Public Land Legislation, 6 Pub.Land L.Rev. 65, 98–102 (1985), who argues that § 1714(e) may survive *Chadha*.

6.   Even if the provisions are unconstitutional, there will remain the question whether they are severable from the rest of the statute. In *Chadha* itself, in part because the statute there at issue had a severability clause, the Court found the veto severable, allowing the rest of the Act to remain in force. Should, for example, the executive authority to make withdrawals in excess of 5000 acres be struck down, or should instead

section 1714(c) be construed so that only the veto is severed, leaving in place the duty to report large withdrawals to Congress? See Glicksman, 36 Hast.L.J. at 65–90. If the veto provision is deemed not severable, then the executive would surely be tempted to revive claims of *Midwest Oil* implied executive authority to make withdrawals.

NOTE: WITHDRAWALS AND RESERVATIONS UNDER THE ANTIQUITIES ACT

The Antiquities Act was enacted in 1906 primarily out of federal concern for protecting archeological resources of the southwest, although it was carefully drafted* so as to provide the opportunity for protection of other "objects of historic scientific interest." Its core provision is as follows (16 U.S.C. § 431):

> The President of the United States is authorized, in his discretion, to declare by public proclamation historic landmarks, historic and prehistoric structures, and other objects of historic or scientific interest that are situated upon the lands owned or controlled by the Government of the United States to be national monuments, and may reserve as a part thereof parcels of land, the limits of which in all cases shall be confined to the smallest area compatible with the proper care and management of the objects to be protected.

From the beginning, nearly all Presidents in the twentieth century used this authority rather aggressively to protect many areas of federal land. Teddy Roosevelt kicked it off when the ink was barely dry by proclaiming Devil's Tower in Wyoming as the nation's first national monument. He followed this up with well over a dozen other proclamations, including one setting aside some 270,000 acres of the Grand Canyon as a National Monument. This one eventually furnished the courts with their first opportunity to interpret the Act.

In Cameron v. United States, 252 U.S. 450 (1920), Cameron resisted federal efforts to evict him from mining claims he located along popular tourist sites around the south rim of the Grand Canyon. Among his defenses was that Roosevelt's 1908 Order exceeded his authority under the Antiquities Act. The Court, speaking through Justice Van Devanter, would have none of it:

> To this we cannot assent. The act under which the President proceeded empowered him to establish reserves embracing "objects of historic or scientific interest." The Grand Canyon, as stated in his proclamation, "is an object of unusual scientific interest." It is the greatest eroded canyon in the United States, if not in the world, is over a mile in depth, has attracted wide attention among explorers and scientists, affords an unexampled field for geologic study, is regarded as one of the great

---

* The final version was crafted by Dr. Edgar Lee Hewett, a private citizen who was asked by Commissioner Richards of the General Land Office to craft a compromise among competing bills pending in Congress. See generally Ronald F. Lee, The Antiquities Act of 1906, 42 J. of the Southwest 247 (2000); Hal Rothman, PRESERVING DIFFERENT PASTS: THE AMERICAN NATIONAL MONUMENTS (1989).

natural wonders, and annually draws to its border thousands of visitors.

Twenty-three years later, the second President Roosevelt invoked the Antiquities Act to create the Jackson Hole National Monument, composed of some 220,000 acres in northwest Wyoming. The State of Wyoming challenged the action, arguing that the area included within the Monument was "barren" of any of the features listed in the statute. State of Wyoming v. Franke, 58 F.Supp. 890 (D.Wyo.1945):

> [The United States introduced evidence of] trails and historic spots in connection with the early trapping and hunting of animals formulating the early fur industry of the West, structures of glacial formation and peculiar mineral deposits and plant life indigenous to the particular area, a biological field for research of wild life in its particular habitat within the area, involving the study of the origin, life, habits and perpetuation of the different species of wild animals, all of which it is claimed constitute matters of scientific interest within the scope and contemplation of the Antiquities Act.

The court concluded:

> If there be evidence in the case of a substantial character upon which the President may have acted in declaring that there were objects of historic or scientific interest included within the area, it is sufficient upon which he may have based a discretion. For example, if a monument were to be created on a bare stretch of sage-brush prairie in regard to which there was no substantial evidence that it contained objects of historic or scientific interest, the action * * * would undoubtedly be arbitrary and capricious and clearly outside the scope and purpose of the Monument Act.

> * * * [I]f the Congress presumes to delegate its inherent authority to Executive Departments which exercise acquisitive proclivities not actually intended, the burden is on the Congress to pass such remedial legislation as may obviate any injustice brought about as the power and control over and disposition of government lands inherently rests in its Legislative branch. What has been said with reference to the objects of historic and scientific interest applies equally to the discretion of the Executive in defining the area compatible with the proper care and management of the objects to be protected.

The Antiquities Act has been used several dozen times by nearly every President. Many of the crown jewels of the national park system were first protected by executive action under the Act, when Congress dragged its feet on legislative proposals to protect the areas. Besides the Grand Canyon and Jackson Hole (now mostly part of Grand Teton National Park), Death Valley, Glacier Bay in Alaska, Zion, Bryce Canyon, Capitol Reef, and several other large withdrawals were first made this way. Congress has not only not interfered with these actions; in thirty cases it has later converted the monuments into national parks. In recognition of the value of executive action, Congress in FLPMA expressly forbade the Secretary of the Interior from "modify[ing] or revok[ing] any withdrawal creating national monuments" under the Antiquities Act. 43 U.S.C. § 1714(j). Of course, Congress can create national monuments itself; see, e.g., 114 Stat. 1362 (2000) (Santa Rosa and San Jacinto Mountains National Monument); 96 Stat. 301 (1982) (Mount St. Helens National Volcanic Monument).

The most prominent exercise of Antiquities Act power was made by President Jimmy Carter. The background on this imbroglio is recounted briefly in Chapter 2, supra pp. 144–46. In late 1978, Congress was seeming to put the finishing touches on a massive bill to protect upwards of one hundred million acres of federal land in Alaska. Some of it would become units of the national park system, some would become wildlife refuges, some would become units of the national wilderness preservation system, and so forth. A deadline was looming, because the temporary, seven-year withdrawal Congress had made in the Alaska Native Claims Settlement Act of 1971 of 80 million acres of these lands was about to expire. Unyielding opposition to the legislation by the government of the state of Alaska and its congressional delegation stalled passage, and the state prematurely filed statehood land selections on lands the bill would protect, just before the expiration of the ANCSA withdrawal.

In a dramatic stroke on December 1, 1978, President Carter set aside 56 million acres of this Alaskan land as national monuments under the Antiquities Act, and affirmed Secretary of the Interior Cecil Andrus's temporary withdrawal, made two weeks earlier, of 105 million acres from state selection and resource exploitation. Taken together, these actions maintained the status quo of protection for these lands until Congress could finish its work on the legislation. It took two more years, but as a lame duck President Carter signed the Alaska National Interest Lands Conservation Act (ANILCA) in December 1980. The Act rescinded the Carter withdrawals but included almost all the affected lands within various preservation systems.

The State of Alaska and several resource companies challenged the executive action on various grounds, including alleged lack of compliance with NEPA, FLPMA, and the propriety of applying the Antiquities Act to such large tracts. All were rejected by the Alaska district court, and not appealed. State of Alaska v. Carter, 462 F.Supp. 1155 (D.Alaska 1978); Anaconda Copper Co. v. Andrus, 14 ERC 1853 (D.Alaska 1980). The Department had done its homework. It made a detailed record, with separate proclamations, each going to great pains to describe the areas and the facts justifying each withdrawal on the basis of "historic or scientific interest." For the texts of the proclamations, which make surprisingly good reading, see 43 Fed.Reg. 57009–57131 (Dec. 1, 1978). Maps of the withdrawals are included.

After nearly two decades of disuse, the Antiquities Act took a dramatic turn on center stage in September 1996. President Clinton used the Act to proclaim the 1.7 million acre Grand Staircase–Escalante National Monument in Southern Utah. (The GSENM has since been expanded to 1.9

million acres through land exchanges with Utah for its inholdings, a transaction discussed infra at pp. 378–79.) The new monument includes some of the most remote and unpopulated areas in the lower 48 states: Car and Driver magazine reported that one spot is more than 50 miles in any direction from the nearest paved road. The area long had been the target of proposals for developments such as coal mines and power plants, but its remoteness had left it largely unspoiled. The monument proclamation (which two of these editors helped craft) carefully described many "objects of historic and scientific interest" in the monument area, including "archaeological, geological, historical, paleontological, and botanical resources." See VISIONS OF THE GRAND STAIRCASE-ESCALANTE (R.B. Keiter, S.B. George, J. Walker, ed., 1998). Mark Squillace, The Monumental Legacy of the Antiquities Act of 1906 (2002) (forthcoming); Christine A. Klein, Preserving Monumental Landscapes under the Antiquities Act (2002) (forthcoming); James Rasband, Utah's Grand Staircase: The Right Path to Wilderness Preservation?, 70 U. Colo. L. Rev. 483 (1999).

The GESNM was just warmup for President Clinton. In the last year of his term he proclaimed nineteen new and expanded three existing national monuments, covering nearly six million acres in total. See generally, John Leshy, Shaping the Modern West: The Role of the Executive Branch, 72 U.Colo. L.Rev. 287, (2001); John Leshy, The Babbitt Legacy at the Department of the Interior: A Preliminary View, 31 Envtl.L. 199, 216–18 (2001); Sanjay Ranchod, The Clinton National Monuments: Protecting Ecosystems with The Antiquities Act, 25 Harv. Envtl.L.Rev. 535 (2001). All told, well over one hundred monument proclamations have been issued by 17 Presidents since 1906, protecting some 80 million acres of federal land.

Tulare County v. George W. Bush

United States District Court for the District of Columbia, 2001.
185 F.Supp.2d 18.

■ URBINA, DISTRICT JUDGE. * * * On April 15, 2000, President Clinton issued a proclamation establishing the Giant Sequoia National Monument pursuant to the Antiquities Act of 1906. The Proclamation states that the Monument encompasses "the smallest area compatible with the proper care and management of the objects to be protected," 327,769 acres of land located within the Sequoia National Forest in southern central California. See 65 Fed. Reg. at 24097. The Proclamation reserves this land for the purpose of protecting a variety of objects of historic and scientific interest such as: "rich and varied landscape," "magnificent groves of towering giant sequoias," "gigantic domes," and "archeological sites recording Native American occupation and adaptations." According to the Proclamation, "the monument is rich in rare plants and is home to more than 200 plant species endemic to the southern Sierra Nevada mountain range. * * *."

Regarding the use of land included in the Monument, the Proclamation provides for "continued public and recreational access and use consistent with the purposes of the monument." The Proclamation states that "[t]he establishment of this monument is subject to valid existing rights." The

Proclamation also provides for the continuing existence of timber sales under contract on the date of the Proclamation and states that the Proclamation will not affect existing special use authorizations. As to the management of the Monument, the Forest Service shall manage the Monument, "pursuant to applicable legal authorities, to implement the purposes and provisions of this proclamation." Finally, the Proclamation gives the Secretary of Agriculture three years from the date of the Proclamation to develop an official management plan for the Monument.

Tulare County, one of the plaintiffs, is a county in the State of California that holds land near and within the Monument. * * * [Other] plaintiffs use the Monument area for business and recreational purposes. * * * [Plaintiffs challenged the monument on a variety of grounds.]

The plaintiffs allege that the Monument is physically over-inclusive. According to the plaintiffs, the "Giant Sequoia groves constitute only about 20,000 acres or 6% of the Monument area." * * *

Reviewing the Proclamation on its face, this court determines that there is no set of facts on which the plaintiffs could demonstrate that the Proclamation violates the Antiquities Act. * * * [Discussion of prior court decisions on the Antiquities Act omitted.]

* * * [P]residential decisions, made pursuant to a statute that provides the President with discretion, are * * * not reviewable. In [United States v. George S. Bush & Co., 310 U.S. 371 (1940)] the Supreme Court reviewed the President's 1934 proclamation increasing the duty on canned clams imported from Japan pursuant to the Tariff Act of 1930. The Court explained that probing the reasoning of the President in issuing this proclamation would be an invasion of the legislative and executive domains.

While this court can evaluate whether President Clinton exercised his discretion in accordance with the standards of the Antiquities Act, this court cannot review the President's determinations and factual findings, as the plaintiffs suggest. To do so would invade the legislative and executive domains because Congress has directed that the President, "in his discretion," make these findings. See George Bush & Co., at 380, 16 U.S.C. § 431. Accordingly, this court limits its examination to the face of the Proclamation.

Counts One and Two assert that President Clinton violated the Antiquities Act by not reasonably identifying objects of historic and scientific interest and by designating non-qualifying objects as the basis for the Monument. In contrast, the Proclamation begins by stating, "[t]he rich and varied landscape of the Giant Sequoia National Monument holds a diverse array of scientific and historic resources." The Proclamation specifies, "[o]nly one other North American tree species * * * holds such lengthy and detailed chronologies of past changes and events." In addition, "the monument is rich in rare plants," "rare amphibians," and "[a]rchaeological sites * * * are found in the monument." In sum, the Proclamation, on its face, describes with specificity the objects of historic and scientific interest to be included in the Monument and does not designate "non-qualifying objects."

Count Three alleges that the Proclamation violates the Antiquities Act because the size of the Monument is not confined to the smallest area compatible with the proper care and management of the objects to be protected. On a similar note, Count Four asserts that the Proclamation increases the likelihood of harm to objects of historic and scientific interest within the Monument. In contrast, however, the Proclamation addresses the reason for the size of the Monument, the risk of wildfire, and the need to protect the objects of historic and scientific interest. * * *

* * * [P]laintiffs claim that "Congress has ceded its Constitutional power [under the Property Clause] by delegating unlimited discretion to the President." The plaintiffs allege that the Proclamation violates the non-delegation doctrine and the Property Clause because it is "without meaningful limitation."

On the contrary, the Antiquities Act establishes clear standards and limitations. The Antiquities Act details the types of objects that can be included in monuments and a method for determining the size of monuments. Even if standards and limitations are somewhat broad, "Congress does not violate the Constitution merely because it legislates in broad terms, leaving a certain degree of discretion to executive or judicial actors." Touby v. United states, 500 U.S. 160, 165 (1991). Therefore, the Antiquities Act represents a proper delegation of congressional authority to the President under the Property Clause.* * *

In Count Six, the plaintiffs allege that the Proclamation violates the [National Forest Management Act] by wrongfully withdrawing land from the National Forest System. * * * In creating the Giant Sequoia National Monument, President Clinton did not withdraw land from the national forest system, though he did withdraw land from disposition under public land laws, such as the sale and leasing of the land. The Proclamation establishes that the Monument land will have dual status as a monument and a part of the Sequoia National Forest. In addition, the Proclamation explicitly states that the Secretary of Agriculture, through the Forest Service, shall manage the Monument and the underlying forest pursuant to applicable legal authorities.

Enacted by Congress 70 years after the Antiquities Act, NFMA does not limit the President's authority under the Antiquities Act by prohibiting proclamations that reserve land in national forests as monuments. * * *

The Court dismisses Counts Seven and Eight for lack of subject-matter jurisdiction because the Counts wrongly allege a right to judicial review pursuant to the APA and the NEPA. * * *

A court has subject-matter jurisdiction to review an agency action under the APA only when a final agency action exists. Because the President is not a federal agency within the meaning of the APA, presidential actions are not subject to review pursuant to the APA. See Dalton v. Specter, 511 U.S. 462, 470 (1994). * * * Applying similar logic, the President is not a federal agency for the purposes of NEPA. See Alaska [v. Carter, 462 F. Supp. 1155, 1159–60 (D.Alaska 1978).]

* * * [T]he Forest Service is merely carrying out the directives of the President, and the APA does not apply to presidential action. Any argument suggesting that this action is agency action would suggest the absurd notion that all presidential actions must be carried out by the President him or herself in order to receive the deference Congress has chosen to give to presidential action. The court refuses to give the term "presidential action" such a confusing and illogical interpretation. Using this same logic, Count Eight also fails in its claim pursuant to NEPA because NEPA requires agency action, and the action in question is an extension of the President's action.

On its face, the Proclamation preserves existing rights by broadly asserting that the establishment of this monument is subject to valid exiting rights. More specifically, the Proclamation provides for the continuing existence of uses such as timber sales, water rights, and grazing permits under contract or reserved as of the date of the Proclamation. The Proclamation also states that it will not affect existing special use authorizations. * * *

The plaintiffs cannot demonstrate ripeness with respect to their claim that the current management of the Monument violates their rights because the Secretary of Agriculture has not yet implemented the final management plan called for in the Proclamation. See *Ohio Forestry*. * * *In addition, the plaintiffs have not pled in their complaint that any interim plan is causing them specific, imminent and certain harm.

NOTES AND QUESTIONS

1.   Many national monuments were controversial when first declared. Quite a few were proclaimed by lame duck Presidents. The use of the Act has been distinctly bipartisan, with some of the most vigorous uses of the act coming from Republicans like Teddy Roosevelt, Taft, and Hoover. With one exception, Congress has never altered the Act, even though there have been numerous proposals to do so. (In 1950 Congress exempted Wyoming from the Act's ambit in reaction to President Franklin Roosevelt's designation of the Jackson Hole National Monument, see 16 U.S.C. § 431a.) (A section of the Alaska National Interest Lands Conservation Act of 1980, 16 U.S.C. § 3213, limited new withdrawals of more than 5000 acres of public land in that state, which restricts the use of the Antiquities Act there.)

2.   What kinds of "objects of historic or scientific interest" can justify the designation of millions of acres of federal lands as national monuments? An entire functioning ecosystem? A prominent or unusual geological formation? An unusual biotic community? A collection of archeological sites which illustrate connections among prehistoric communities? Historic trails that may be visible over many miles? In fact, both President Carter's and President Clinton's national monument proclamations identified all of these things and more, and explained their significance and why it was important to protect them. Are there any limits? Do all federal lands have some scientific or historic value?

3. What about the statutory caution to preserve the "smallest area compatible with the proper care and management of the objects to be protected"? Although some argue the statutory text contemplates postage-stamp sized monuments around an archeological site or a particular scientific feature, from the beginning the Act has been applied to justify expansive protections. How much deference should the executive get from the courts in making these judgment calls about what area is required for "proper care and management of the objects to be protected"?

4. President Clinton did not attempt to use the procedures of the National Environmental Policy Act in designating monuments. His lawyers maintained that NEPA applies only to federal agencies, and not to the President himself. Although the Department of the Interior and some other federal agencies were heavily involved in the drafting of the proclamations and assembling the record in support of them, they were acting at the President's explicit request. The CEQ regulations acknowledge that the term "federal agency" in NEPA does not include the President. See 40 C.F.R. § 1508.12.

5. Although many of the early proclamations were quite terse and did not contain much if any guidance on how the monuments were to be managed, the Carter and especially the Clinton proclamations contained quite a bit of detail on area management; e.g., defining the extent to which water was reserved as a matter of federal law, and the extent to which grazing, off-road vehicle travel; hunting and fishing and other activities might be allowed. With only a couple of exceptions, all areas were withdrawn from mining and mineral leasing.

6. Can a Monument Proclamation be revoked? No President has ever done so, so there is no law on this subject. The Attorney General has opined that proclamations cannot be revoked, because the Antiquities Act only authorizes the President to proclaim monuments, not "unproclaim" them. 39 Op. Atty. Gen. 185 (1938).

7. Can a President shrink the boundaries of a national monument? Many national monuments have been expanded by subsequent proclamations, and a few proclamations have taken acres out monument status. See Professor Squillace's article, supra. What does a President need to show, if anything, to cut acreage out of a monument? Must he make a showing that the earlier proclamation's judgment about the area reserved being the "smallest area compatible with the proper care and management of the objects to be protected" was erroneous?

8. Most of the early national monuments were managed by the U.S. Forest Service or the National Park Service; in the 1930s, all of the Forest Service monuments were transferred to the National Park Service's care. The Antiquities Act does not require any particular agency to manage monuments, and President Clinton broke new ground by putting most of the monuments he created under the care of the Bureau of Land Management.

NOTE: THE PRESIDENT'S POWER TO GUIDE AGENCIES BY EXECUTIVE ORDER

Several times over the history of federal land and resources law, Presidents have issued executive orders to shape public land policy. Sometimes, as in the Antiquities Act, they act with clear statutory authority. At other times, however, as in Taft's withdrawal order upheld in *Midwest Oil*, they had no clear statutory mandate. There are several other examples of the latter, and some judicial discussion of the practice. For example, in National Wildlife Federation v. Babbitt, 24 E.L.R. 20200 (D.D.C.1993), the court had this to say:

> Executive Order 11,990, issued by President Carter on May 24, 1977, requires that, "in carrying out the agency's responsibility for * * * land resources planning," each agency "shall take action to minimize the destruction, loss, or degradation of wetlands." Executive Order 11,990 at § 1(a). Furthermore, agencies are required to avoid assisting construction in areas containing wetlands (permitting "construction" would include coal leasing) "unless the head of the agency finds (1) that there is no practicable alternative to such construction, and (2) that the proposed action includes all practicable measures to minimize harm to wetlands which may result from such use." Id. at § 2(a). * * * [Plaintiffs challenged the Interior Department's failure to conform to this Executive Order in adopting planning criteria for decisions on whether and how to lease federal coal.]
>
> * * * It is now fairly well established that administrative action taken pursuant to an executive order is "agency action" within the meaning of APA § 706(2), so long as the executive order has the force of law and places substantive limits on agency discretion.
>
> The court considers whether Executive Order 11,990 meets these two requirements. First, an executive order is to be "accorded the force and effect of a statute" when it has a "distinct statutory foundation." The President's proclamations and orders have the force and effect of laws when issued pursuant to a statutory mandate or delegation of authority from Congress. The President promulgated Executive Order 11,990, based on authority derived from the Constitution and unspecified statutes, "in furtherance of" NEPA, and in particular NEPA § 101(b)(3), *codified at* 42 U.S.C. § 4331(b)(3). The court is not faced with a situation where the President has acted in contradiction to a statute, or in the absence of legislative action. Rather, 42 U.S.C. § 4331(b) mandates ongoing executive action to promote the broad policies of NEPA. Congressional authorization for executive orders can be either "express or implied." United States v. New Orleans Public Service, Inc., 553 F.2d 459, 465 (5th Cir.1977). The President acted under NEPA's implied authorization when he issued Executive Order 11,990. Consequently, the court finds that Executive Order 11,990 should be accorded "the force and effect of a statute."[43]

43. Some courts have followed the same line of reasoning as this court, holding that NEPA makes an "implied authorization" for executive orders in furtherance of

* * * Executive Order 11,990 imposes a nondiscretionary duty on the heads of agencies to "take action to minimize the destruction, loss, or degradation of wetlands." EO 11,990 at § 1(a). In addition, the head of an agency may permit such damage or loss only after making a finding that "the proposed action includes all practicable measures to minimize harm to wetlands." Id. at § 2(a).

The Executive Order allows for some flexibility. In making this finding, "the head of the agency may take into account economic, environmental, and other pertinent factors." Id. In other words, measures to mitigate harm need only be "capable of attainment within relevant, existing constraints" to satisfy Executive Order 11,990. National Wildlife Federation v. Adams, 629 F.2d at 592.

However, the agency head is not free to do *nothing* to minimize harm to wetlands; nor free to permit damage to wetlands without having taken at least those mitigatory actions that are "capable of attainment within relevant, existing constraints"; nor free to permit damage to wetlands without making a finding that "all practicable measures to mitigate harm" have in fact been taken. These duties clearly place "substantive limits on agency action" as those terms are used in Chrysler v. Brown, 441 U.S. at 318, and constitute "law to apply" within the meaning of Overton Park, 401 U.S. at 410. Consequently, agency action pursuant to Executive Order 11,990 is subject to judicial review under the standards of 5 U.S.C. § 706(2).

Recently, in Minnesota v. Mille Lacs Band of Chippewa Indians, 526 U.S. 172 (1999), the Court held that an Executive Order issued by President Taylor in 1850, which terminated the Tribe's hunting, fishing and gathering rights secured by an 1837 Treaty, was ineffective because it had "no colorable source of authority" in either the Treaty or statutes or the Constitution itself. On Presidential power to issue executive orders, see Peter M. Shane and Harold H. Bruff, SEPARATION OF POWERS LAW 130–31 (1996); Joel Fleishman and Arthur Aufses, Law and Orders: The Problem of Presidential Legislation, 40 Law & Contemp. Probs. 1 (1976);

the Act, rendering those orders fully enforceable under the APA. See, e.g., City of Waltham v. U.S. Postal Service, 786 F.Supp. at 130–31 (Executive Orders 11,990 and 11,-988); Conservation Law Foundation v. Clark, 590 F.Supp. at 1477 (Executive Orders 11,-644 and 11,989).

Some courts have found executive orders issued pursuant to NEPA to be subject to APA review, but without explicitly finding that the orders were issued pursuant to a statutory mandate or delegation of authority from Congress. See, e.g., Daingerfield Island Protective Society v. Babbitt, 823 F.Supp. 950 (D.D.C.1993) (Executive Order 11,988 provides basis for APA review, given that "prevailing trend on the issue of APA review of executive orders pursuant to NEPA seems

to be in favor of granting such review"); National Wildlife Federation v. Adams, 629 F.2d 587, 591–92 (9th Cir.1980) (assuming Executive Order 11,990 provides basis for APA review); No Oilport! v. Carter, 520 F.Supp. 334, 368 (W.D.Wash.1981) (assuming Executive Order 11,988 provides basis for APA review).

One court flatly rejected the "implied authorization" approach, holding that Executive Order 11,988 lacks the force and effect of law because it is not based on a "clear statutory mandate or delegation of authority from Congress." Watershed Associates Rescue v. Alexander, 586 F.Supp. at 987. Obviously, the law on this issue remains somewhat unsettled.

AFL–CIO v. Kahn, 618 F.2d 784 (D.C.Cir.) (en banc), cert. denied, 443 U.S. 915 (1979).

An important modern example of guiding public land policy through Executive Order involved regulating off-road vehicles (ORVs) on federal lands. In February 1972, President Richard Nixon issued Executive Order No. 11644, which directed the federal land management agencies effectively to "zone" the federal lands with respect to ORV travel. See 43 U.S.C. § 4321 note. Each agency head was to create a regulatory structure that would designate "specific areas and trails on public lands on which the use of off-road vehicles may be permitted, and areas in which the use of off-road vehicles may not be permitted," within a date certain. The Order contained general environmental criteria to be used in zoning the lands for ORV use, and required the agencies to carry out this task with full public participation. It recited that it was issued "by virtue of the authority vested in me as President of the United States by the Constitution of the United States and in furtherance of the purpose and policy of [NEPA]." 43 U.S.C. § 4321 note.

BLM regulations implementing the 1972 Executive Order were promptly challenged by environmental groups. In National Wildlife Federation v. Morton, 393 F.Supp. 1286 (D.D.C.1975), the court found that the BLM had "significantly diluted the standards emphatically set forth in" the Order and not followed it in several other respects. For example, the court scored BLM's adding a new substantive criterion ("[t]he need for public use areas for recreation use") that was not specified, and implicitly not allowed, in the Executive Order; and also criticized BLM for engaging in "wholesale, blanket designation of 'open' lands" instead of evaluating "specific areas and trails to determine whether the use of ORV's should be permitted" with regard to the environmental criteria mandated by Executive Order 11644, and thus "violated the express requirements of" the Order. Tepid implementation of the Nixon Order led President Carter to issue another Executive Order early in his administration (No. 11989 (1977)) that required the federal land management agencies to ban ORVs from areas where the agency determines that continued use "will cause or is causing considerable adverse effects." For another case considering that these executive Orders have the force and effect of law and are enforceable by the courts, see Conservation Law Foundation v. Secretary of the Interior, 590 F.Supp. 1467, 1478 (D.Mass.1984), aff'd 864 F.2d 954 (1st Cir.1989). Further consideration of off-road vehicle regulation and compliance with these Orders is found in Chapter 11, infra pp. 988–1013.

NOTES AND QUESTIONS

1. Should courts tend to defer to these exercises of supervisory authority by Presidents over public land decisionmaking, given the long history of executive action on federal lands without or with the most tenuous of statutory authority? That history is briefly reviewed in John Leshy, Shaping the Modern West: The Role of the Executive Branch, 72 U.Colo.L.Rev. 287 (2001).

2. Another kind of executive order seeks to guide agency action but expressly disclaims any toehold for judicial enforcement or review. These disclaimers are taken at face value by the courts. For example, in McKinley v. United States, 828 F.Supp. 888 (D.N.M.1993), the plaintiff cattle rancher sought to invoke an Executive Order to set aside a Forest Service decision reducing the amount of cattle he could graze on a national forest:

> Appellant also contends that the decision should be set aside because the Forest Service failed to comply with Presidential Executive order 12630, 53 Fed.Reg. 8859 (March 15, 1988), which requires federal agencies, in their predecisional analyses, to assess the impact of proposed actions on private property rights. Section 6 of E.O. 12630 expressly addresses judicial review and provides that "this order is intended only to improve the internal management of the Executive branch and is not intended to create any right or benefit, substantive or procedural, enforceable at law by a party against the United States, its agencies, its officers or any person." Section VIII of the Attorney General's Guidelines for the Evaluation of Risk and Avoidance of Unanticipated Takings (June 30, 1988) implementing E.O. 12630 also reiterates that intent and additionally provides that:
>
>> Neither these Guidelines, the Appendix, nor the deliberative processes or products resulting from their implementation by agencies shall be treated as establishing criteria or standards that constitute any basis for judicial review of agency actions. Thus, the extent or quality of an agency's compliance with the Executive Order or these Guidelines shall not be justiciable in any proceedings for judicial review of agency action.
>
> The appellant, therefore, has no basis to assert a claim against the Forest Service concerning compliance with E.O. 12630.

Another example of this kind of Executive Order is one issued in 1996 by President Clinton, which directed federal land managing agencies to protect, within certain limitations, Indian sacred sites. See E.O. No. 13007, discussed in Chapter 12, infra p. 1049.

D. LAND EXCHANGES, SALES, AND OTHER TRANSFERS

As Chapter 2 illustrates, the freewheeling era of federal land disposal led to a hodge-podge of land ownership patterns, particularly in the west. One product of such patterns is burgeoning litigation over access questions, as recounted in Chapter 2, § F, above. Another product has been difficulty in managing certain resources such as vegetation and wildlife that tend to follow ecosystem rather than ownership lines. Finally, states and railroad successors who find themselves checkerboarded or surrounded by federal lands often desire to block up their holdings to facilitate development of the resources they contain. These forces have gradually combined to produce a noticeable movement toward realigning landholdings in many parts of the west along more rational lines. To some extent, ownership adjustment can be done by purchase and sale, although limitations on federal and state governmental budgets limit this option in many circumstances. Frequently a more attractive alternative is land exchanges.

Furthermore, there are some situations in which disposal or acquisition of federal land is desirable for other purposes. While the general federal policy now is to retain federal lands in federal ownership, Congress has seen fit to keep in place a number of mechanisms allowing disposal of federal lands in particular circumstances. Finally, the federal agencies retain power to acquire lands by the exercise of the power of eminent domain in many circumstances. This section will briefly cover these subjects, focusing for the most part on exchanges. For a more detailed look at federal land acquisition and disposition, see Frederick Anderson, Public Land Exchanges, Sales, and Purchases Under the Federal Land Policy and Management Act of 1976, 1979 Utah L.Rev. 657, 661–69; George Coggins & Robert Glicksman, 1 PUBLIC NATURAL RESOURCES LAW, ch. 6 (2001).

LAND ACQUISITIONS

Congress has not enacted any single statute laying out an overall land acquisition program. Instead, acquisitions by the federal land management agencies typically follow one of three patterns. First, Congress sometimes designates a special management area and authorizes the agency to acquire land within the boundaries. Second, the legislation may state a goal, such as preservation of waterfowl populations, and give the agency general authority to acquire land or interests in land to achieve that goal. Third, Congress has generally encouraged miscellaneous acquisitions for purposes of access or consolidation of existing holdings. Most federal land management agencies have generic acquisition authority by purchase, exchange, donation or eminent domain; e.g., 43 U.S.C. § 1715 (Forest Service and BLM). Statutes applicable to specific geographic areas may limit that authority.

Aside from ad hoc designations of new or expanded park and refuge system units, federal acquisition at present is mostly directed at enhancement of wildlife habitat and recreational opportunities. In the past, major federal land acquisition programs have resulted in the creation of the national forest system in the East and Midwest (under the Weeks Act) and in the national grasslands in the northern great plains. See pp. 118, 138 supra. A few national parks consist almost exclusively of acquired lands; e.g., Redwood National Park along the northern California coast, considered at pp. 1056–67 infra.

Most federal land acquisitions are now financed by the Land and Water Conservation Fund (LWCF), established in 1965 and funded primarily by federal offshore oil and gas leasing revenues. The LWCF has underwritten acquisition of nearly five million acres of land (and interests in land, such as water rights and conservation easements) by federal, state and local governments for outdoor recreation and wildlife purposes. More than half of that acreage has been included in federal conservation systems. It is treated in more detail in Chapter 11, § A, infra p. 936.

LAND SALES

Federal law sharply circumscribes the sale of national park, national forest, and national wildlife refuge system lands. Disposition laws affecting the national forests include 16 U.S.C. § 519 (sale of "small areas of land chiefly valuable for agriculture"), and 16 U.S.C. § 478a (sales of no more than 640 acres for townsites). For national parks, see 16 U.S.C. § 430g–5(b); § 4601–22(a).

Sales of BLM public lands are governed by FLPMA, which repealed various statutes authorizing sales of federal lands and substituted a single provision, 43 U.S.C. § 1713. All sales must be for fair market value. 43 U.S.C. § 1713(d).* Other substantive provisions for land sales are set out in § 1713(a):

(a) A tract of the public lands (except land in units of the National Wilderness Preservation System, National Wild and Scenic Rivers Systems, and National System of Trails) may be sold under this Act where, as a result of land use planning required under section 1712 of this title, the Secretary determines that the sale of such tract meets the following disposal criteria:

(1) such tract because of its location or other characteristics is difficult and uneconomic to manage as part of the public lands, and is not suitable for management by another Federal department or agency; or

(2) such tract was acquired for a specific purpose and the tract is no longer required for that or any other Federal purpose; or

(3) disposal of such tract will serve important public objectives, including but not limited to, expansion of communities and economic development, which cannot be achieved prudently or feasibly on land other than public land and which outweigh other public objectives and values, including, but not limited to, recreation and scenic values, which would be served by maintaining such tract in Federal ownership.

* * *

(e) The Secretary shall determine and establish the size of tracts of public lands to be sold on the basis of the land use capabilities and development requirements of the lands; and, where any such tract which is judged by the Secretary to be chiefly valuable for agriculture is sold, its size shall be no larger than necessary to support a family-sized farm.

Any lands *sold* under that provision must retain the minerals in federal ownership; 43 U.S.C. § 1719. The reservation of minerals does not

* No sale of more than 2500 acres can be made for 90 days, during which time either House may veto such a sale. 43 U.S.C. § 1713(c). This legislative veto provision may well violate *Chadha*, and the severability issues are similar to those involving withdrawals. See supra pp. 348–53.

apply to lands *exchanged* under FLPMA. Id. In FY 2000, BLM sold about 2600 acres under this provision.

Occasionally since the end of the disposal era in the 1930s proposals are made to conduct major sales of federal lands. The latest was in the early 1980s, when President Reagan issued Executive Order No. 12348, 47 Fed.Reg. 8547 (1982). It established a Property Review Board to "review real property holdings of the federal government, * * * expedite the sale of unneeded property so that it can be put to more productive use, [and] use the proceeds from property sales to begin retiring the national debt." At one point, Secretary of the Interior James Watt pushed for selling some 35 million acres of federally owned land (mostly BLM land), an area the size of Iowa. The Administration projected land sales returning $4 billion annually over a five-year period. The idea provoked controversy on many fronts, and the program never got off the ground; the Property Review Board was formally disbanded in 1984. See also Conservation Law Foundation v. Harper, 587 F.Supp. 357 (D.Mass.1984), discussing the sale program and dismissing most of the legal challenges made against it.

FLPMA authorizes limited transfers of lands to state and local governments. 43 U.S.C. § 1720. The Recreation and Public Purposes Act, 43 U.S.C. § 869 (a separate act not repealed by FLPMA), allows the Secretary to give public land to local governments in certain circumstances. The federal government retains a reversionary interest in the event such lands are no longer used for the purposes for which they are granted. Local parks, school sites and landfills seem to be the most common purposes underlying such grants. Concerned about possible BLM liability for improper waste disposal on such lands, Congress amended the Act in 1988 to grant immunity to the federal government in such circumstances. See 102 Stat. 3813.

Under the Federal Property and Administrative Services Act of 1949, 40 U.S.C. § 471 et seq., as amended (FPAS), the General Services Administration (GSA) may dispose of excess or surplus government real estate to federal agencies, other public bodies, or private enterprises, in that order, for various purposes, but public domain and national forest and national park lands are expressly excluded from disposition under the FPAS. 40 U.S.C. § 472(d)(1).

MOVING FEDERAL LANDS AROUND THE FEDERAL FAMILY

Federal land management agencies can take advantage of the FPAS to acquire land from other agencies for conservation purposes. The FPAS idea has been used to create urban "gateway" parks. In and around San Francisco, for instance, a variety of surplus military forts and reservations were turned over to the National Park Service for management as the Golden Gate National Recreation Area; see 16 U.S.C. § 460cc. The same thing happened in the New York City area with the Gateway National Recreation Area. 16 U.S.C. § 460bb.

A somewhat similar process in recent years has added significantly to the federal conservation lands base. This is the Base Realignment and Closure (BRAC) process which has governed the downsizing of military bases in the post-Cold War era. There are several statutes involved; see, e.g., 104 Stat. 1808–10 (1990). Several dozen military bases have been closed. The process gives interested federal nonmilitary agencies an opportunity to apply for transfer of all or some of the land if it fits with their existing statutory mandate and is in the best interests of the government. In some instances, the land has been transferred to the federal land management agencies, primarily for wildlife conservation and parks purposes.

The Reagan Administration proposed a broad interagency land exchange between the Forest Service and the BLM. In January, 1985, it requested Congress to authorize a trade involving some 35 million acres. The plan was to consolidate large blocks of land under each agency in order to eliminate the costs resulting from virtually side-by-side BLM and Forest Service offices found in many regions. Also, the exchange would transfer most timber lands to the Forest Service and most grazing lands to the BLM to allow for greater specialization. In Washington state, for example, all BLM lands would be transferred to the Forest Service, while in Nevada nearly all Forest Service lands would go to the BLM. The maps describing the proposal thus portrayed neat, consolidated agency ownerships. There was one exception: a long, narrow tongue of Forest Service land extended down through BLM land in western New Mexico. The reason? Forest Service Chief Max Peterson, sensitive to hallowed agency traditions, was unyielding in his refusal to relinquish the place in Lincoln National Forest where Smokey the Bear was found clinging to a charred tree in 1947. This interchange idea never gained much traction; the only significant implementation was in Nevada, where Congress approved a transfer of jurisdiction over several hundred thousand acres of land between the two agencies. The Forest Service was the big winner; it gained 662,000 acres of BLM land, while the BLM picked up only 23,000 acres of former national forest land. See 102 Stat. 2749 (1988).

LAND EXCHANGES

All the major federal land management agencies have traditionally been delegated power to exchange lands under their control for private lands; each empowering statute contains various conditions such as an "equal value" standard to prevent profiteering. Most such exchanges are undertaken to consolidate federal land holdings or acquire into federal ownership lands of high conservation value. Because livestock graziers, recreationists or other users of the public lands that go out of federal ownership in an exchange may be displaced, exchanges may provoke opposition. The BLM, given the checkerboard character of many of its lands, is perhaps the most active agency in promoting land exchanges.

Before the passage of FLPMA, Forest Service exchange authority was primarily found in the General Exchange Act of 1922, 16 U.S.C. § 485, see National Forest Preservation Group v. Butz, 485 F.2d 408 (9th Cir.1973). While FLPMA did not repeal that statute, FLPMA did include a general exchange section governing both BLM and Forest Service lands. See 43 U.S.C. § 1716. One commentator predicted that the FLPMA authority would allow BLM to "rid itself of difficult-to-manage parcels, consolidate the checkerboard of public land holdings into more efficient units, and accommodate private desires for land transactions with the BLM." Anderson, supra, 1979 Utah L.Rev. at 658. To some extent this has been the case, but exchanges can be very difficult, as discussed further below. In Fiscal Year 2000, 110 land exchanges were carried out under FLPMA, with the BLM and the Forest Service receiving a cumulative total of 51,000 acres in exchange for 44,000 acres. In addition, the Forest Service entered into 39 exchanges under the 1922 Act, receiving 53,000 acres in exchange for about 13,000 acres. Partly because of its growing recognition of the advantages of carefully done land exchanges, Congress in 1988 enacted the Federal Land Exchange Facilitation Act, or FLEFA, 102 Stat. 1086, which amended FLPMA in several respects. Generally, it streamlined the exchange process at several points, including appraising lands and providing for arbitration of valuation disputes.

FLPMA includes an "equal value" requirement and a mandate that exchange transactions be in the public interest, explained in the statute (43 U.S.C. § 1716(a)) as follows:

> when considering public interest the Secretary concerned shall give full consideration to better Federal land management and the needs of State and local people, including needs for lands for the economy, community expansion, recreation areas, food, fiber, minerals, and fish and wildlife and the Secretary concerned [must find] that the values and the objectives which Federal lands or interests to be conveyed may serve if retained in Federal ownership are not more than the values of the non-Federal lands or interests and the public objectives they could serve if acquired.

Does this definition of the public interest allow, or call for, stringent judicial review? That question, arising out of a slightly different statutory provision (contained in the Alaska National Interest Lands Conservation Act, or ANILCA), came before the court in the following case.

National Audubon Society v. Hodel

United States District Court, District of Alaska, 1984.
606 F.Supp. 825.

■ Fitzgerald, District Judge.

On August 10, 1983, Deputy Under–Secretary of the Interior, William P. Horn, acting on behalf of then Secretary of the Interior James G. Watt (the Secretary), entered into a land exchange agreement with representatives of three Alaska Native Corporations * * * referred to collectively as the CIRI Group. The Secretary transferred to the Natives a portion of St. Matthew Island, a wilderness area in the Alaska Maritime National Wildlife Refuge, in exchange for various land interests in the Kenai and Yukon Delta National Wildlife Refuges. The driving force behind the land exchange was to enable the CIRI Group to lease the St. Matthew Island parcel to private companies for construction and operation of support facilities for oil exploration and potential oil development in the Navarin Basin in the Bering Sea.

In making the exchange, the Secretary relied upon authorization granted in § 1302(h) [of ANILCA, 43 U.S.C. § 3192(h)]. The conveyance is for fifty years, or so long as commercial oil production activities occur in the Navarin Basin. * * *

[St. Matthew Island was established as a Wildlife Refuge in 1909, designated a Wilderness Area in 1970, and was made part of the Alaska Maritime National Wildlife Refuge in ANILCA.] Many factors contribute to the island's value as a wilderness area, including its isolation, remoteness, distance from shipping lanes and aircraft routes, rugged and varied terrain, and unique bird and mammal populations. Aside from minor evidence of past human presence on the island, St. Matthew remains essentially natural in appearance.

[The Department of the Interior prepared a environmental impact statement (EIS) on its proposal to issue oil and gas leases on the Outer Continental Shelf in the Navarin Basin near St. Matthew Island. Two of the three scenarios outlined in the EIS for lease exploration and development involve locating support facilities on the Island. The preferred or primary scenario would involve using the Island for air support during the exploration phase. Then, if exploration identified oil and gas deposits in commercial quantities, a major storage, loading and processing terminal would be built on the Island to allow the resource to be shipped to its consumers.]

The exchange provision in § 1302(h) of ANILCA imposes two requirements before a land exchange may be approved. First, the Secretary must determine that the exchange will result in "acquiring lands for the purposes of [ANILCA]." Second, the exchange must further the "public interest" if the lands exchanged are of unequal value.

There are two principal documents in the record which explain the considerations and the rationale upon which the Secretary rested his decision to proceed with the challenged land exchange. These include (1) the Department of the Interior Record of Decision, and (2) the Public Interest Determination for the Proposed Acquisition of Inholdings in Kenai and Yukon Delta National Wildlife Refuges by Exchange for Lands on St. Matthew Island, Alaska.

According to these documents, the Secretary concluded that both requirements were met by the terms of the St. Matthew exchange. [Discussion of first requirement omitted.] * * *

Concerning the second requirement, the Secretary's Determination concludes that the St. Matthew Island exchange would * * * further the public interest. The Secretary offered seven major reasons for his conclusion:

(1) The exchange advances longterm CSU [eds: conservation system units, referring to federal lands put into protective status by ANILCA] and general wildlife conservation and management objectives by (a) preventing the creation of over 100 Native inholdings within CSUs without permanent

loss of a single CSU acre, (b) providing federal management and public enjoyment benefits which comport with congressional intent that CSU inholdings be eliminated primarily through land exchanges, and (c) improving the protection provided [to CSU lands by means of a] nondevelopment easement and permanent federal management * * *.

(2) The exchange as a whole also advances the public interest in CSU objectives during the short term because the United States will (a) secure land interests in over three times the CSU acreage it will be conveying, (b) obtain clear title to and interest in more biologically and recreationally significant lands in terms of wildlife habitat quality than would be temporarily conveyed out of federal ownership, and (c) secure greater environmental protection by reason of the nondevelopment easement acquired in one of the most important waterfowl nesting habitats at Kokechik Bay, more than outweighing the temporary wildlife disruption authorized on St. Matthew Island. * * *

(6) * * * [The] use of the strategically located St. Matthew Island realty for a staging area for Navarin Basin energy development offers substantial environmental, human safety and economic public interest benefits because (a) the island's close location to the Navarin Basin provides critical time advantages in responding to environmental dangers and human safety emergencies when compared to other potential staging areas, and (b) the increased economic efficiency in offshore energy exploration and development allowed by St. Matthew Island's use may result in higher bidding revenues received on the lease sale and additional domestic oil and gas production. * * *

[The court rejected the argument of the CIRI Group that the Secretary's public interest determination is "committed to agency discretion by law" and therefore not judicially reviewable under the Administrative Procedure Act. The court concluded that the arbitrary and capricious standard applies.] * * *

In authorizing the Secretary to make land exchanges of unequal value when in the "public interest," Congress did not impart what factors it intended the Secretary to consider in analyzing whether such an exchange is in the public interest. In his Public Interest Determination for the St. Matthew exchange, the Secretary * * * viewed this standard broadly, considering possible benefits to the nation's economic vitality and oil production capabilities as well as to its wilderness values.* * *

I conclude the Secretary's broad view of the public interest in the context of land exchanges is a reasonable and permissible construction of ANILCA § 1302(h)'s statutory language. "Public interest" exchanges under ANILCA are exceptions to the general congressional requirement that the Secretary only enter into exchanges of equal monetary value. It therefore was reasonable for the Secretary to conclude that Congress intended that he take non-monetary benefits into account in determining whether the overall public interest would be furthered by a given exchange.* * *

In broad terms, the Secretary has stated that his Public Interest Determination is based on "a qualitative comparison of the temporary short-term loss of approximately 4,110 acres of wildlife and wilderness habitat on St. Matthew Island with the permanent addition of over 14,000 acres of wildlife habitat to the NWR System." * * *

[The Secretary has] broad discretion * * *. [T]he court may not attempt to substitute its judgment for that of the Secretary. Rather, review of the Secretary's determination must focus on whether the decision rests on an adequate record and was reached after consideration of all relevant facts. * * *

A.   Prospective Benefits to Wildlife Conservation and Public Recreation

The Secretary declared in his document of decision that the Administrative Record demonstrated that the St. Matthew land exchange would clearly result in a "net benefit" to national wildlife and conservation values. * * *

In terms of acreage, the largest acquisition by the Secretary in the exchange amounts to approximately 8000 surface acres of waterfowl nesting habitat within the Yukon Delta NWR. Recognizing the importance of this nesting region in Alaska, Congress declared a primary purpose of the Yukon Delta NWR to be "to conserve fish and wildlife populations and habitats in their natural diversity including, but not limited to, shorebirds, seabirds, whistling swans, emperor, white-fronted and Canada geese, black brant and other migratory birds."

The site of the nondevelopment easement is in Kokechik Bay and the land is owned by Sea Lion Corp. [one of the CIRI Group]. The nondevelopment easement conveyed by Sea Lion Corp. to the Secretary under the exchange [gave the Secretary the power in perpetuity to prohibit Sea Lion Corp.] from developing *docking facilities, roads, canals, airstrips, utilities, transmissions lines, pipelines, tank facilities, structures not used for subsistence purposes, or excavations* or other topographical changes: *Provided,* that development on the Real Estate may be permitted with the prior written consent of the Secretary of the Interior or his designee. * * *

The lands subject to the nondevelopment easement contain excellent waterfowl nesting and brood rearing habitat. The most dense nesting concentrations of emperor geese [in the world] are found in this area. In addition, the Kokechik Bay region is the breeding ground for half the world's population of black brant. Cackling Canada geese also breed chiefly in the areas surrounding the Kokechik Bay.

There can be absolutely no doubt that the lands subject to the nondevelopment easement are important to conservation and management objectives in protecting the black brant and the Cackling Canada and emperor geese. My inquiry does not stop here, however. The Secretary's determination that the St. Matthew exchange is in the national interest rests in substantial part upon his conclusion that the nondevelopment easement acquired in Kokechik Bay added significant environmental protections in this region.

My review of the environmental protections already in place prior to the St. Matthew exchange has revealed that the lands subject to the nondevelopment easement are for the most part located within the Yukon Delta NWR. As such, they are governed by the requirements of § 22(g) of ANCSA. [Eds. ANCSA, the Alaska Native Claims Settlement Act of 1971, gave Alaska Natives the right to select up to forty-four million acres of land in Alaska, subject to a variety of conditions; for basic background, see Chapter 2, pp. 144–47 supra.] This provision provides, in pertinent part, that:

> Notwithstanding any other provision of this chapter, *every patent* issued by the Secretary pursuant to this chapter—which covers lands lying within the boundaries of a National Wildlife Refuge on December 18, 1971—*shall contain a provision that such lands remain subject to the laws and regulations governing use and development of such Refuge.*[54]

When the Secretary conveyed these lands to the CIRI Group, he imposed covenants, pursuant to § 22(g)'s requirements, that subjected almost all of the lands to the laws and regulations of the National Wildlife Refuge System. The laws and regulations governing use and development of wildlife refuges provide that only activities which are "compatible" with the major purposes for which a particular refuge was established may be permitted by the Secretary. Although compatibility is not expressly defined in either the National Wildlife Refuge System Administration Act or ANILCA, implementing regulations for the administration of § 22(g) covenants state that compatibility means that proposed uses must not "*materially impair* the values for which the refuge was established."[55]

My reading of the language of § 22(g), which the Secretary properly inserted into the Kokechik Bay conveyances to the CIRI Group, suggests to me that these lands were already protected from incompatible uses even without the nondevelopment easement obtained by the Secretary. To this extent, I agree with Audubon's claim that the protections acquired under the easement were largely "redundant" of the environmental safeguards obtained through the § 22(g) covenants.

* * * Given the purpose for which the Yukon Delta NWR was established, there would seem to be considerable doubt as to whether docking facilities, roads, canals, airstrips, utilities, pipelines and the like would be compatible uses of the Kokechik Bay lands. Apart from that, the easement lands * * * are very important for subsistence uses by Native peoples. Certainly the sort of development precluded by the nondevelopment easement, if not so precluded, would have to be considered under [specific provisions in ANILCA expressly protecting subsistence uses against interference]. * * *

Finally, there is nothing that I have discovered in the Final Ascertainment Report that suggests the existence of any probable or potential threat

---

54. 43 U.S.C. § 1621(g) (emphasis added).

55. 43 CFR § 2650.4–6(b) (emphasis added).

of the kind of development prohibited by the nondevelopment easement obtained by the United States under the exchange. * * *

Thus it would be hard to find a more striking comparison between the potential or probable use of Kokechik Bay lowlands with the proposed use of CIRI's inholdings on St. Matthew Island. On St. Matthew Island construction of the type of facilities that would be barred by the nondevelopment easement in the Kokechik Bay lowlands is both certain and immediate. * * *

In sum, I have concluded that contrary to the Secretary's statement in his Public Interest Determination, the nondevelopment easement obtained under the exchange adds little to the environmental protections already in place for Kokechik Bay. Hence, the Secretary's conclusion that the acquisition of the nondevelopment easement significantly advances long term CSU and general wildlife conservation and management objectives is not borne out when the land status and legal restrictions otherwise applicable are examined. * * *

B.   Potential Dangers to St. Matthew Island's Wilderness Values

In concluding that relinquishing lands on St. Matthew Island to the CIRI Group for use as an oil support facility was in the public interest, the Secretary assumed that there was little possibility of long term environmental danger to the island's unique wilderness values. Being mindful of the narrow confines of the standard of review in this case, I nevertheless have found this determination fails to consider the relevant facts in the Secretary's own administrative record. My review of the record has also led me to conclude that the Secretary's determination that the placement of an oil support facility within the Alaska Maritime NWR would be compatible with this refuge's strict environmental objectives was a clear error of judgment.

* * * [C]ontrary to the Secretary's repeated descriptions of the potential environmental damage to St. Matthew's unique wilderness values as "temporary" and "remote," the administrative record reveals there is a substantial risk of significant short and long term injury to the island's wilderness qualities. Such prospective environmental degradation would conflict with the express goal of the Alaska Maritime NWR * * *.

The most ominous potential environmental destruction that might accompany development of St. Matthew will affect wildlife * * *. By FWS estimates, hundreds of thousands of seabirds nest in colonies on or immediately adjacent to the lands conveyed to the CIRI Group. * * * FWS * * * has estimated that the project will adversely affect nearly half a million nesting seabirds for a period of 80 to 100 years.

Of particular concern, the FWS report and the DEIS point to the frequent air traffic that will feed the support facility as especially dangerous to St. Matthew's seabird nesting colonies. Near flying aircraft inhibit breeding and initiate panic flights, potentially causing entire colonies to take to the air, knocking eggs and chicks into the ocean or leaving them vulnerable to predators. Continued disruption may cause reproduction failure, and, "in the worse case, colonies may be totally abandoned." * * *

In addition to a potential for serious long-term degradation to the seabird population of St. Matthew, the DEIS reveals that any major oil spill near the island is likely to cause substantial harm to the many whales that inhabit the island's waters. And by the FWS's own estimates, a major oil spill near the island is probable if pipelines eventually are used to transport oil to St. Matthew.

Although all of these facts appear on the face of the administrative record, the Secretary paid scant heed. Rather, he suggests in his Public Interest Determination that the St.Matthew Island stipulations for restoration and reconveyance assure that the land will be restored and returned to the National Wildlife and Wilderness System when use of the land as a support base for oil exploration or development comes to an end. He refers to the land transaction as a "temporarily conveyed use of federal ownership" and to the "temporary wildlife disruption authorized on St. Matthew Island" under the land use stipulations. * * *

The word "temporary" standing alone has little meaning. * * * The exchange provides by its terms that the conveyance to the CIRI Group is for 50 years, or if oil and gas have been produced in the Navarin Basin and the land has been used in connection therewith, then so long as may be necessary for completion of production. What is important are the consequences upon wildlife and wilderness habitats by the activity associated with the use of the land, and not whether that use may be characterized as "temporary." * * *

It is correct that the stipulations are useful to minimize harm to the wildlife and wilderness habitat on St. Matthew Island, but the stipulations cannot otherwise justify the Secretary's Public Interest Determination. That is, the Secretary cannot avoid consideration of potential environmental impacts * * * by suggesting that the stipulations will serve to mitigate the extent of the injury brought about by environmental impact.

My review of the underlying record has convinced me that the Secretary, by failing to consider the protections otherwise provided by law and by failing to consider relevant facts appearing of record, seriously overestimated the benefits to CSU and general wildlife conservation and management objectives advanced by this exchange. Additionally, by characterizing the effects on St. Matthew Island as temporary and by erroneously assuming that the land use stipulations would provide sufficient protection to wildlife and wilderness habitats, the Secretary failed to adequately consider the likely negative effects on St. Matthew Island. Finally, the Secretary's determination under ANCSA § 22(g) that a support base located within the Alaska Maritime NWR would be compatible with the environmental protection purposes of this refuge is contrary to the underlying record. The Secretary's Public Interest Determination thus constitutes a clear error of judgment. * * *

NOTES AND QUESTIONS

1. The "public interest" standard is frequently found, in one form or another, in modern statutes governing administrative agency decisions in a

wide variety of contexts. See, e.g., Udall v. Federal Power Comm'n, 387 U.S. 428, 450 (1967) (an early landmark decision in modern environmental law, holding that the Federal Power Commission construed the public interest standard in the Federal Power Act too narrowly in connection with a proposed hydropower license, to exclude consideration of the, among other things, "the public interest in preserving reaches of wild rivers and wilderness areas, the preservation of anadromous fish for commercial and recreational purposes, and the protection of wildlife"). Will judicial reviewability of an agency's application of such a standard vary from statute to statute, even if the statutes have identical texts? Could, in fact, a "public interest" determination in another statute be held entirely unreviewable by a court?

2.   Must an agency prepare written findings and conclusions in making a decision as to what is in the "public interest" under the statute involved here? Even if not required, would an agency be advised to document its determination to better withstand judicial scrutiny? But here the Secretary did prepare such findings, which wasn't enough to ward off an adverse judicial decision. Cf. Lodge Tower Condominium Ass'n v. Lodge Properties Inc., 880 F.Supp. 1370 (D.Colo.1995), aff'd 85 F.3d 476 (10th Cir.1996), where the court upheld a Forest Service exchange, relying heavily on the Forest Service's finding that "better land management" would result from exchanging two acres of federal land on a slope among condominiums at the Vail resort for 385 acres of private inholding (including wetlands, streams, and an endangered species of fish) in a nearby wilderness area. See generally John W. Ragsdale, Jr., National Forest Land Exchanges and the Growth of Vail and Other Gateway Communities, 31 Urb. Law. 1 (1999).

3.   Is the court here deferential enough to the Secretary? Does the Secretary have expertise that a federal district judge ought to respect, even if the Secretary is sitting in far-off Washington D.C. and the judge is sitting in Alaska, the site of the lands involved? Based upon the evidence set forth in the excerpted portions of the opinion, could the court have reached the opposite conclusion; namely, that the Secretary did not act arbitrarily and capriciously in approving the exchange? Upon review, could a court of appeals uphold either conclusion? (The decision here was not appealed.)

4.   A key question here was the meaning of the "compatibility" test for measuring proposed developments both at St. Matthew Island, and on the Alaskan Native inholdings sought to be removed from the Wildlife Refuge by the exchange. How does the Secretary interpret "compatibility"? How does the court? Is "compatibility" a question of fact, law, or is it mixed? A further discussion of compatibility is found in Chapter 10, infra pp. 873–87.

5.   What if the Secretary had been more candid in his appraisal, admitting that the harm is substantial, and the value gained through acquiring the inholding is relatively small, but going on to argue that there is a strong national interest in developing all sources of domestic oil rather than rely on imports from unstable areas of the world. If the court were

applying the FLPMA statutory standard of "public interest," quoted supra at p. 369, would that approach survive judicial review?

6. By a seemingly odd quirk, ANILCA does *not* require a "public interest" determination for exchanges where the lands are of *equal* value. See 16 U.S.C. § 3192(h). Does this bear on the proper interpretation of "public interest" that must be determined when the lands are *unequal*? Does the latter require, in effect, some sort of quantification of difficult-to-quantify values (protecting the environment, Native culture, subsistence values, the strategic value of domestic oil production) and balancing these against monetary differences in value?

7. Could the Secretary moot this case by restructuring the exchange to make it an "equal value" one? How would "equal value" be determined? By the marketplace? Is there a real market for this land? Cf. Committee of 100 on Federal City v. Hodel, 777 F.2d 711, 720 n. 3 (D.C.Cir.1985) (upholding a proposed exchange of land involving the Park Service against an "equal value" challenge, and giving the agency "[g]reat deference * * * because the matter is one largely within the technical expertise of the agency"). Is it? Appraisals are hardly an exact science, and concern that the government has failed to obtain equal value in exchanges is periodically rehearsed in the press and elsewhere. See, e.g., a series of articles in the Seattle Times, Sept. 27 to Oct. 2, 1998. See Tim Fitzgerald, Federal Land Exchanges: Let's End the Barter, PERC Policy Series No. PS–18, at 8 (June 2000):

> Land exchanges are essentially barter-trade without a medium of exchange such as money. Those who engage in land exchanges therefore face the problem of finding some way to measure the value of different goods. Without the benefit of prices or some other standard, people with different products have a difficult time determining whether a trade makes sense for each person engaged in it—that is, whether it is fair.

8. In Desert Citizens Against Pollution v. Bisson, 231 F.3d 1172 (9th Cir.2000), the plaintiffs challenged BLM's conveyance of 1745 acres of public land as part of an exchange with the private Gold Fields Co. The purpose was to allow the latter to put a landfill in Imperial County in southern California. The thrust of plaintiffs' complaint was that the exchange did not meet FLPMA's "equal value" standard because BLM had used an outdated appraisal. BLM defended the appraisal, which had concluded that the highest and best use of the federal land was either open space, or mine support, or wildlife habitat, at a value of $350 per acre, because there was no general market for use of the land as a landfill. In part this was because the parcels to be exchanged were surrounded by or adjacent to land already owned by Gold Fields, and were not large enough by themselves to support a landfill. Plaintiffs disputed this assumption (putting forward evidence that a landfill site would be worth several thousand dollars per acre) and the court agreed. Reversing the district court, it held that the "BLM appraisal should have considered the landfill use as a possible highest and best use. Information available at the time of the appraisal made it reasonably probable that the property's potential use

as a landfill was physically possible, legally permissible, and financially feasible." 231 F.3d at 1184. Although the parties had consummated the exchange the day after the district court had dismissed the case, the court ordered the exchange set aside.

9. As exchanges have become more common, so has litigation. See, e.g., National Coal Ass'n v. Hodel, 825 F.2d 523 (D.C.Cir.1987) (upholding a complex three-way exchange among the National Park Service, Princeton University and other non-profit institutions, and Rocky Mountain Energy Company); Northern Plains Resource Council v. Lujan, 874 F.2d 661 (9th Cir.1989) (upholding a straight-up exchange of coal lands); Lockhart v. Kenops, 927 F.2d 1028 (8th Cir.1991), cert. denied, 502 U.S. 863 (1991) (upholding Forest Service exchange of an isolated tract of 100 acres for a 160–acre inholding of important wildlife habitat, plus an additional 80 acres, against a variety of challenges); Muckleshoot Indian Tribe v. U.S. Forest Service, 177 F.3d 800 (9th Cir.1999) (setting aside an exchange between the Forest Service and Weyerhaeuser Co. because the agency failed to meet the requirements of NEPA and the National Historic Preservation Act). Standing has proved to be a problem with several challenges to land exchanges; see supra p. 292, ¶10.

10. Should courts scrutinize federal-*private* exchanges more closely than federal-*state* exchanges? Is there more opportunity for abuse when private interests are involved than when all the land involved stays in some form of public ownership? If your answer is yes, into which category do federal-Alaskan Native (or Indian) exchanges such as that involved in *National Audubon Society v. Hodel* fit?

NOTE: FEDERAL–STATE LAND EXCHANGES

One consequence of the scattered, "in-place" character of grants of federal land to states is that some of them become inholdings within federal conservation areas which are later created. These inholdings create management problems of various kinds. If the inholdings are developed (especially with road access), management of the surrounding federal lands for conservation or wilderness purposes may be compromised. But restricting access to or activities on inholdings to keep with the character of surrounding federal lands could thwart the purpose of the grant of lands to the state (usually, to produce income for the common schools or other purposes). An obvious solution to this dilemma, with "win-win" potential, is a land exchange—the state conveys its inholdings to the federal government in return for federal land elsewhere. Because of the equal value requirement, such exchanges raise the important question of how to value the state inholdings, which are usually isolated, scattered, and without existing road access.

State inholding issues were most acute in Utah, where the state's four sections of inholdings in each township created what some called a "blue rash" (because typical land status maps show state sections in blue). In the mid–1980s the State proposed what it dubbed "Project Bold," an ambitious effort to achieve a comprehensive land exchange. See Scott Matheson &

Ralph Becker, Improving Public Land Management Through Land Exchange: Opportunities and Pitfalls of the Utah Experience, 33 Rocky Mtn.Min.L.Inst. 4–1 (1987). While it foundered from opposition by a variety of disparate interests, it helped pave the way toward ultimate success. In 1993 Congress enacted a Utah-specific law (Pub. L. 103–93), which encouraged and created the framework for exchanging state inholdings out of national forests, national park system lands, and Indian reservations in the state. Implementation of this law had bogged down in what looked like interminable litigation over value when, in 1996, President Clinton created the Grand Staircase–Escalante National Monument (see pp. 355–56 supra). That 1.7 million acre federal monument on BLM land included within its outer boundaries nearly 180,000 acres of scattered state school sections, and in proclaiming the Monument, President Clinton committed his Administration to work to trade out these inholdings.

Delivering on the President's promise, in May 1998 Secretary Babbitt and Governor Leavitt announced a massive land exchange, billed as the largest single state-federal land exchange ever in the lower 48 states, in which the state relinquished all of its inholdings in the Grand Staircase–Escalante and all Utah units of the National Park System, and almost all of its inholdings in the Utah national forests and the Goshute and Navajo Indian reservations. All told, the exchange included 377,000 acres of state inholdings, plus an additional 66,000 acres in state mineral rights, in exchange for approximately 139,000 acres of federal land, mineral rights and money. Valuation issues were difficult, but resolution was, ironically, aided by the sweep of the effort, which allowed tradeoffs and compromises among various kinds of properties to arrive at a single deal, which was ratified by Congress without modification, in legislation signed into law in October 1998. See Utah Schools and Land Exchange Act of 1998, 16 U.S.C. 431 note.

NOTE: A NEW PARADIGM FOR FEDERAL LAND RECONFIGURATION?

An important reason why BLM has not been very interested in simply selling land under the FLPMA land sales provisions discussed earlier is because the revenue generated by the sale goes directly to the federal treasury and is not available for use by the BLM unless and until it is appropriated by Congress. If, however, BLM exchanges rather than sells land, it directly benefits by acquiring property it can manage (such as endangered species habitat) in return. As a result, informal agency practice tended to favor exchanges over sales. But exchanges are difficult, time-consuming, and can be political hot potatoes. As one practitioner has noted, "every parcel of public land has its own constituency that will urge retention of that parcel in public ownership * * * [and m]any interests are aligned to oppose any sale or other disposition of resources from the public domain." Murray D. Feldman, The New Public Land Exchanges: Trading Development Rights in One Area for Public Resources in Another, 44 Rocky Mt. Min.L.Inst. 2–1, 2–38 (1998). Inevitably, questions about valuation are raised (appraisals hardly being an exact science), especially when

BLM is disposing of land in a volatile economic climate, such as a fast-growing urban area where land values may change dramatically.

To address such concerns, Congress in 1998 enacted the Southern Nevada Public Land Management Act, P.L. 105–263, 112 Stat. 2343. Its aim is to provide for a more orderly method of disposing of surplus federal land for development purposes in the burgeoning Las Vegas, Nevada area (for the last several years, the fastest growing urban area in the Nation). The Act authorizes BLM to auction off tracts of public lands available for disposal in the Las Vegas area, with the proceeds being retained by the BLM (rather than going into the Treasury, where congressional appropriations would be required to spend it). The law gives 10% of the proceeds to the Southern Nevada Water Authority for infrastructure needs, and 5% to the State for education purposes. The remaining 85% may be spent by the BLM to acquire "environmentally sensitive land" or interests in land in the state (with priority to the Las Vegas area). In addition, the State and local governments may elect to obtain any lands BLM would otherwise put up for sale for governmental purposes under the Recreation and Public Purposes Act, supra p. 367.

About 27,000 acres of federal land, with a value roughly estimated at over $500 million, may eventually be disposed of under this statute. The competitive auction process, furnishing the truest test of market value, should reduce concerns about whether the federal government is receiving fair return for the land sold. And the revolving fund concept provides BLM and the local governments with incentives to put disposable land on the market. Debates leading to enactment centered on the percentage of the local financial share, whether BLM land sales should be subject to local government veto and to local planning and zoning (the Act says yes), and whether to create such a "revolving fund," bypassing the appropriations process. Congressional appropriations committees (very powerful because they hold the purse strings) have traditionally fiercely resisted such revolving funds, because they remove dollars from their purview and correspondingly diminish their power.

Ironically, while making more urban development possible in Las Vegas, the Act is likely to increase substantially the total federal landholdings in Nevada, at 83% already the highest in the Nation. In Fiscal Year 2000, about 8000 acres were acquired (usually inholdings in national wildlife refuges or national recreation areas or for endangered species habitat) for about $24 million the Act had generated in sales. See PUBLIC LAND STATISTICS 2000, pp. 174–80, 219–23.

It did not take Congress long to expand this basic idea across the West, for several other fast-growing Western cities still have substantial amounts of BLM land in the path of development. In 2000, Congress enacted the Federal Land Transaction Facilitation Act, 43 U.S.C. §§ 2301–2306 for the purpose, among others, of promoting "the reconfiguration of land ownership patterns to better facilitate resource management." It carries forward, with some modification, the model embodied in the Nevada Act for the eleven contiguous Western states plus Alaska, for a ten year period. It authorizes competitive sale of BLM lands "identified for disposal under approved land use plans (as in effect on July 25, 2000)''. The gross proceeds of these sales are deposited in a "Federal Land Disposal Account" and are made available, "without further Act of appropriation," to buy, from willing sellers, at a price not to exceed fair market value: (a) nonfederal inholdings in a wide but defined variety of federal lands managed primarily for conservation purposes; and (b) lands adjacent to such areas that contain "exceptional resources" where there is a "compelling need for conservation and protection under the jurisdiction of a Federal agency in order to maintain the resource for the benefit of the public." Not less than 80% of the funds are to be used in the state in which the funds were generated, and 80% shall be used to acquire inholdings (as opposed to adjacent lands). The Act declares that the funds made available under the process are to be "supplemental to any funds appropriated under the Land And Water Conservation Fund Act", but of course this does not legally bind future Congresses, who may choose to reduce LWCF appropriations by appropriate amounts if they wish.

Because BLM land use plans in effect on July 25, 2000 may not precisely indicate how much land is "available for disposal," there are no firm figures on how much BLM land might be disposed of under this Act. Still, the core idea is an interesting one—to create a revolving fund, bypassing the ordinary appropriations process, to use sales and purchases to better rationalize federal land holdings, primarily for the purpose of advancing conservation management. It is important to note that the proceeds of BLM land sales may be used to acquire inholdings or other lands for the benefit of the National Park Service, the Forest Service, and the Fish & Wildlife Service, as well as for the BLM. The legislation requires the Secretaries of Agriculture and the Interior to develop a procedure "prioritizing the acquisitions" considering, among other things, the date the inholding was established and the extent to which the acquisition will "facilitate management efficiency." It remains to be seen how much BLM's ardor to sell its land to fund acquisitions will be dampened by the fact that some benefits will inure to other agencies.

CHAPTER 5

OVERARCHING LEGAL DOCTRINES: THE PUBLIC TRUST, NEPA, PLANNING STATUTES, AND THE ENDANGERED SPECIES ACT

This chapter examines statutes and processes of generic applicability to federal lands and natural resources decisionmaking. Section A explores the public trust doctrine, whose application to federal lands and resources has been the subject of considerable commentary but very little judicial attention. Section B examines the National Environmental Policy Act, or NEPA as it is universally known, a pervasive influence in this field (as well as much other federal decisionmaking) since it was enacted more than three decades ago. Section C takes a general look at the processes by which all federal land management agencies plan or zone the federal lands under their jurisdiction for various uses and management objectives. Section D takes up the Endangered Species Act, or ESA, which in the last two decades has emerged not only as a much-used litigation lever, but more generally as a major if not dominant force across federal land management.

A. THE PUBLIC TRUST DOCTRINE IN PUBLIC NATURAL RESOURCES LAW

The public trust doctrine, which has ancient roots in Roman and English law, was the basis for the Supreme Court decision in Illinois Central Railroad Co. v. Illinois, 146 U.S. 387 (1892), Chapter 2, supra p. 58, where the Court held it forbade the State from alienating the submerged lands in the Chicago harbor that it acquired under the statehood equal footing principle. This doctrine lay largely dormant until the 1960's, when some state courts began to revive it. In 1970, Professor Joseph Sax published an influential article, The Public Trust Doctrine in Natural Resources Law: Effective Judicial Intervention, 68 Mich.L.Rev. 471 (1970), which traced its origins and explicated bases for its contemporary application. Sax emphasized its utility as a mechanism for the courts to limit the discretion of executive branch agencies.

State courts have used it to uphold public access to dry sand beaches (Van Ness v. Bay Head Improvement Ass'n, 95 N.J. 306, 471 A.2d 355 (1984)); to require strict judicial review when state parklands are leased for private use (Gould v. Greylock Reservation Com'n, 350 Mass. 410, 215

N.E.2d 114 (1966)); to demand payment of full market value when state lands are leased (Jerke v. State Dept. of Lands, 182 Mont. 294, 597 P.2d 49 (1979)); to prevent a state from relinquishing its claims to ownership of beds of waterbodies that were possibly navigable at statehood (Arizona Center for Law in the Public Interest v. Hassell, 172 Ariz. 356, 837 P.2d 158 (App.1991)); Defenders of Wildlife v. Governor Jane Dee Hull, 199 Ariz. 411, 18 P.3d 722 (App.2001); to confer standing on an environmental group to challenge a timber sale on state forest lands because of its allegation that harm to a stream and its fish will result (Selkirk–Priest Basin Ass'n v. Idaho ex rel. Andrus, 899 P.2d 949, 953–55 (Idaho 1995)); and to guide water management in Hawaii, In re Water Use Applications (Waiahole Ditch), 94 Haw. 97, 9 P.3d 409 (2000).

California has taken it the furthest. In 1940 the City of Los Angeles had established appropriative rights under state law to the waters of four tributaries to Mono Lake below the eastern escarpment of the Sierra Nevada range. Over time the City's diversions brought down the lake level with serious environmental effects. In National Audubon Society v. Superior Court, 33 Cal.3d 419, 189 Cal.Rptr. 346, 658 P.2d 709 (1983), cert. denied, 464 U.S. 977 (1983), the Court held that the City's vested water rights were subject to reexamination by the State Water Board in order to protect the public trust: "The human and environmental uses of Mono Lake—uses protected by the public trust doctrine—deserve to be taken into account. Such uses should not be destroyed because the state mistakenly thought itself powerless to protect them." 658 P.2d at 732. See also United Plainsmen Ass'n v. North Dakota State Water Conservation Com'n, 247 N.W.2d 457 (N.D.1976); Kootenai Environmental Alliance, Inc. v. State Bd. of Land Com'rs, 105 Idaho 622, 671 P.2d 1085 (1983). Commentaries include Hap Dunning, The Public Trust Doctrine and Western Water Law: Discord or Harmony?, 30 Rocky Mtn.Min.L.Inst. 17 (1985); and symposia at 14 U.C.D.L.Rev. 180 (1980);19 Envt'l L. 425–735 (1989).

The considerable scholarly debate about whether and how the doctrine should apply to federal land and natural resource management is captured in the following two excerpts.

Charles F. Wilkinson, The Public Trust Doctrine in Public Land Law*

14 U.C.D.L.Rev. 269 (1980).

* * * The federal public lands are at the outer reaches of the public trust doctrine. * * * [I]nland federal lands are not "trust resources" according to the classic formulation of the doctrine. * * * In addition to the lack of direct support in either common law or Indian law, there are a number of compelling policy reasons supporting the conclusion that the public trust doctrine, at least in its classic form, does not apply to the public lands. First, the history of public land policy denies the existence of any prohibition against disposition of federal lands. * * * No serious

* Reprinted with permission of the University of California–Davis Law Review.

suggestion could be made that private title to some 1.4 billion acres is clouded due to the United States' inability to convey clear title. Second, public land law is a heavily statutory field. The legislative matrix is sufficiently comprehensive that doubts can fairly be raised as to whether there is room for a broad, common law doctrine to operate.

Another basis for objection arises from the diversity of the public lands. * * * For example, it is one thing to refer to the dominant-use National Park Service as a trustee; it is a far different matter to place traditional trust obligations on the BLM, which must reconcile the congressionally sanctioned multiple-use tug and pull among economic and non-economic uses. This range of geographic and legal diversity makes it difficult to apply a single, unitary doctrine to all of the public lands.

Finally, while there may be majesty aplenty on the public lands, there are many, even in these land-appreciative days, who would say that most of the public land holdings are common, even mundane. * * *

[Wilkinson then argued that many modern court decisions have, implicitly or explicitly, applied public trust notions, and he advocates reading them more explicitly into the interpretation and application of statutes.] * * * The modern [public lands and natural resources] statutes are premised on the high station that today's society accords to the economic and environmental values of the federal lands and resources. They are rigorous laws designed to protect the public's interest in the public's resources. The legislation requires that public lands and resources not be sold, except in limited and exceptional circumstances; that the public resources are to be nurtured and preserved; that the public is to play a measured but significant role in decision-making; and that the lands and resources are to be managed on a sustained-yield basis for future generations.

The whole of these laws is greater than the sum of its parts. The modern statutes set a tone, a context, a milieu. When read together they require a trustee's care. Thus we can expect courts today, like courts in earlier eras, to characterize Congress' modern legislative scheme as imposing a public trust on the public resources. * * * The trust concept has been properly invoked as the best available formulation of the central doctrinal forces in public land law—that increasingly tough strictures are required, and have been imposed, on land management officials; that land management is not a private business; that ultimate accountability is to the public; and that over time the public and Congress have come to place ever greater importance on the nation's public natural resources.

The trust notion, as a generic concept, is an appropriate description of the federal role in public land law. It is a common-sense description that has evolved in regard to the inland public lands just as it has developed in closely related subject areas. The more difficult issue * * * is determining the scope and content of the trust. [After concluding that it cannot be enforced against the Congress, he sketches out some possible applications.]

[It could] operate as a limitation on the discretion of administrative agencies. First, it might be used, as it has been in several states, to require express legislative authority when public resources are being unreasonably used by administrative agencies to promote private gain. Second, it would provide the basis for an ultimate "hard look" doctrine for reviewing administrative action. As such, it would be a doctrine advanced by environmentalists and by industry and would have no ideological content. The doctrine could be invoked by industry, for example, to emphasize the high standard of care incumbent on the Forest Service if it mishandled a timber sale, or on the BLM if it unreasonably delayed the processing of competitive bidding on a mineral lease.

* * * [It could] affect the interpretation of a number of statutes. For example, the question of impliedly reserved water rights has been largely resolved on National Forest lands, but the extent of protection afforded to wildlife and public recreational and aesthetic opportunities by other land-management systems has not been determined. * * * The answers to all of these questions would be affected if the courts construed the acts to effectuate Congress' intent to act as a trustee charged with the duty of protecting and preserving the public resources.

* * * Another use of the public trust doctrine in regard to public lands is what might be called the action-forcing cases. * * * The questions arise whether public land managers can be compelled to take affirmative action, including litigation, to protect federal lands, and whether the public trust doctrine can play a part in such determinations.

Richard J. Lazarus, Changing Conceptions of Property and Sovereignty in Natural Resources: Questioning the Public Trust Doctrine*

71 Iowa L.Rev. 631, 633, 710, 715–16 (1986).

* * * [T]he historical function of the public trust doctrine has been to provide a public property basis for resisting the exercise of private property rights in natural resources deemed contrary to the public interest. In recent decades, however, especially during the last ten years, modern trends in natural resources law increasingly have eroded traditional concepts of private property rights in natural resources and substituted new notions of sovereign power over those resources. These trends, reflected in a wide variety of legal contexts ranging from federal environmental protection statutes and new state resource allocation laws to evolving common-law principles of tort law, are currently weaving a new fabric for natural resources law that is more responsive to current social values and the physical characteristics of the resources. By continuing to resist a legal system that is otherwise being abandoned, the public trust doctrine obscures analysis and renders more difficult the important process of reworking natural resources law. Of even broader concern, the doctrine threatens to fuel a developing clash in liberal ideology between furthering individual rights of security and dignity, bound up in notions of private property protection, and supporting environmental protection and resource preser-

* Reprinted with permission of the Iowa Law Review.

vation goals, inevitably dependent on intrusive governmental programs designed to achieve longer-term collectivist goals.

* * * [A]part from its failure to provide needed candor, and its inflexibility in the face of changing values and knowledge, reliance on the doctrine should be abandoned because it offers too tenuous a basis for protecting important environmental protection and resource conservation objectives. Three separate factors * * * favor such a strategic retreat. First, trust values will never adequately reflect modern environmental concerns. Second, the doctrine unjustifiably relies on the judiciary to further its environmental goals and, consequently, ultimately depends on a proenvironment judicial bias that is not enduring. Third, recent judicial decisions, in particular those of the Supreme Court, make it clear that any special legal status the trust rationale has enjoyed in the past is waning. * * *

Simply put, the public trust doctrine, even if aimed at promoting needed resource conservation and environmental protection goals, is a step in the wrong direction. The doctrine amounts to a romantic step backward toward a bygone era at a time when we face modern problems that demand candid and honest debate on the merits, including consideration of current social values and the latest scientific information. The complex and pressing resource allocation and environmental protection issues we currently face will continue to tax severely the most concerted societal efforts and the best legal and scientific minds. Dramatic shifts in legal rules, primarily in traditional notions of private property, will continue to be necessary, challenging the patience and understanding of the public, to whom the law must ultimately justify its legitimacy. Although perhaps unfortunate, short of a major redirection of this nation's social and economic infrastructure, little, if any, room is left in these tasks ahead for the mythopoeism of the public trust doctrine.

NOTES AND QUESTIONS

1. For other commentary, see Joseph L. Sax, Liberating the Public Trust Doctrine From Its Historical Shackles, 14 U.C. Davis L.Rev. 185 (1980); Charles Wilkinson, The Headwaters of the Public Trust: Some Thoughts on the Source and Scope of the Traditional Doctrine, 19 Envt.L. 425 (1989); James L. Huffman, A Fish Out of Water: The Public Trust Doctrine in a Constitutional Democracy, 19 Envtl.L. 527 (1989); Douglas L. Grant, Underpinnings of the Public Trust Doctrine: Lessons from *Illinois Central Railroad*, 33 Ariz. St.L.J. 849 (2001); Erin Ryan, Public Trust and Distrust: The Theoretical Implications of the Public Trust Doctrine for Natural Resource Management, 31 Envtl.L. 477 (2001). Even the doctrine's strongest modern advocates do not think it applies to the Congress. Given Congress's broad power over federal lands under the Property Clause, can one make a serious argument that the public trust doctrine may be judicially enforced to prevent Congress from, say, selling Yosemite Valley to private parties, or authorizing it to be leased and strip-mined?

2. In connection with Professor Wilkinson's suggestion that there is room for the courts to apply the public trust doctrine in this heavily

statutory field, consider the following: In 1978, Congress amended the National Park Organic Act to add, inter alia, the following provision (16 U.S.C. § 1):

> Congress further reaffirms, declares and directs that the protection, management and administration of [the various areas of the National Park System] shall be conducted in light of the high public value and integrity of the National Park System and shall not be exercised in derogation of the values and purposes for which these areas have been established, except as may have been or shall be directly and specifically provided by Congress.

In Sierra Club v. Andrus, 487 F.Supp. 443, 449 (D.D.C.1980), *aff'd on other grounds sub nom.* Sierra Club v. Watt, 659 F.2d 203 (D.C.Cir.1981), environmentalists argued that non-statutory trust duties of the National Park Service and the BLM required those agencies to take affirmative steps to protect water resources on the lands under their management from depletion. The Court disagreed:

> To the extent that plaintiff's argument advances the proposition that defendants are charged with "trust" duties distinguishable from their statutory duties, the Court disagrees. Rather, the Court views the statutory duties previously discussed as comprising *all* the responsibilities which defendants must faithfully discharge.

> The legislative history of the 1978 amendment to 16 U.S.C. § 1a–1 makes clear that any distinction between "trust" and "statutory" responsibilities in the management of the National Park System is unfounded. Moreover, Congress specifically addressed the authority upon which plaintiff relies to support its "trust theory":

>> The committee has been concerned that * * * [a federal court] may have *blurred the responsibilities* articulated by the 1916 Act creating the National Park Service * * *.

>> [T]he committee strongly endorses the Administration's proposed amendment to the Act of August 18, 1970, concerning the management of the National Park System *to refocus and insure the basis for decisionmaking concerning the system continues to be the criteria provided by 16 U.S.C.A. § 1 * * *. This restatement of these highest principles of management is also intended to serve as the basis for any judicial resolution of competing private and public values and interest in * * * areas of the National Park System.*

> Senate Report 95–528, supra, at 14, 7–8 (emphasis added). By asserting an explicit statutory standard "as the basis of any judicial resolution" of Park management issues, Congress eliminated "trust" notions in National Park System management. The Court also concludes that §§ 1701 and 1782(c) of title 43 United States Code embody the entire duty and responsibility to manage and protect Bureau of Land Management lands generally with which the Secretary is charged.

3. Did the Court err in giving conclusive weight to what a congressional committee in 1976 thought was the proper interpretation of the 1916 National Park Service organic act? In fact, the same Senate Committee

Report contained the following statement (at p. 9): "The Secretary has an absolute duty, which is not to be compromised, to fulfill the mandate of the 1916 Act to take whatever actions and seek whatever relief as will safeguard the units of the National Park System." Further discussion of the statutory duties of the National Park Service is found in Chapter 11, pp. 946–58.

4. If the public trust doctrine is a rationale for exercising closer judicial review of actions by federal land management agencies, does or should it apply to all such actions, or only certain kinds? For example, suppose Congress authorizes the BLM to lease federal lands for grazing at an "appropriate" fee, and fair market value is one dollar per acre. May the BLM set the fee at a nickel per acre without violating the public trust?

5. Another way to think about the doctrine is this: If it bears some analogy to private trust principles, who are the beneficiaries of the trust? The general public? Taxpayers? Do the beneficiaries include extractors of resources of the federal lands (miners, graziers, loggers)? Those who consume those extracted resources? Future generations? Suppose Congress has authorized the Secretary of the Interior to lease federal lands for energy development upon a determination that it would "serve the public interest." If foreign supplies of oil are cut off, and an energy shortage grips the country, and the Secretary refuses to lease certain lands for oil development, could a court use the public trust doctrine to order the Secretary to issue the leases?

6. In Summa Corp. v. California ex rel. State Lands Comm'n, 466 U.S. 198 (1984), the Court held that California could not assert a public trust easement over property (a) granted to a private citizen by the Mexican government, (b) safeguarded by the Treaty of Guadalupe Hidalgo, and (c) confirmed in proceedings under federal law to implement that treaty, where the patent issued as a result of those proceedings contained no recognition of the easement. Justice Rehnquist's opinion for the unanimous Court mentioned *Illinois Central Railroad* in a footnote, characterizing it as standing for the proposition that "alienation of the beds of navigable waters will not be lightly inferred." 466 U.S. at 207, n. 4.

7. Professors Coggins & Glicksman offer this summing up, in 1 PUBLIC NATURAL RESOURCES LAW § 6.05[4]:

> In sum, the much-debated public trust doctrine in federal natural resources law has had very little practical impact to date. * * * But it seems premature to conclude it is irrelevant. * * * [T]he case for public trust review of administrative decisions in public natural resources law is not negligible. In some cases, courts seem to have adopted the idea without the label. Some statutes as well could be construed to impose quasi-fiduciary duties on federal land managers.

8. Whatever the direction of the doctrine in the future, public trust implications for this field continue to be discovered in unexpected quarters, e.g., Twining v. New Jersey, 211 U.S. 78, 97 (1908) ("among the rights and privileges of National citizenship recognized by this court are * * * the right to enter the public lands * * *"). Still further research has revealed

that public trust limitations on the use of public lands are old—very, very old:

> After his father's death Beowulf king of the Danes governed his stronghold and was for a long time famous among nations. Then the great Healfdene was born. Healfdene, a fierce old veteran, ruled the Danes all his life. To him four children in all were born—Heorogar, Hrothgar, Halga the Good, and a daughter who, we are told, became the consort of Onela, the Swedish king.
>
> Such success in arms and so great a fame attended Hrothgar that his kinsmen were eager to serve under him, and in this way the number of his young retainers increased until he had a formidable army. It came into his mind to command the erection of a building that should be the greatest banqueting hall ever known, in which he could apportion to young and old everything that God had entrusted to him, with the exception of public lands and human life.

BEOWULF 28 (orig. ed. 8th cent.) (D. Wright trans., 1957).

B. THE NATIONAL ENVIRONMENTAL POLICY ACT (NEPA)

A procedural element common to almost all federal land and resource management decisionmaking is the National Environmental Policy Act of 1969 (NEPA), 42 U.S.C. § 4321 et seq. While all federal land management agencies now engage in land use planning under specific statutes (a subject explored in the next section), NEPA is a precursor for these planning systems, and the land management agencies must observe NEPA procedures while promulgating land use plans. But NEPA is not limited to formal planning (nor is it limited to decisions about federally owned lands and resources). It comes into play whenever "major federal actions that could significantly affect the quality of the human environment" are contemplated. It helps force every federal agency to put its reasons, reasoning, and conclusions regarding such actions into writing and make them subject to judicial review. Many of the cases in this book which were commenced after its enactment have been premised at least in part on it.

Some claim that NEPA is merely another layer of bureaucratic red tape or a mechanism allowing willful zealots to delay worthy developments, while some ardent environmentalists express disappointment with NEPA's limitations and lack of substantive impact. All will agree, however, that the statute has played a major role in modernizing the management of the federal lands.

NEPA's legislative history does little to illuminate its intended meaning and effect. Few legislators (other than Senator Henry Jackson, its principal sponsor) appreciated the potential sweep of the statute. President Nixon proclaimed the statute the herald of a new environmental era while believing it to be little more than an innocuous statement of policy. It turned out to be a good deal more; the federal courts (particularly the lower courts) quickly began developing a "common law" surrounding the statute's application, and applied it vigorously across a wide range of actions.

Although the Supreme Court has not shown the same enthusiasm for the statute, NEPA has been ingrained into the fabric of administrative decisionmaking and the culture of bureaucracy. It has also become perhaps the most prominent icon of environmental policy, and the Congress has never shown serious interest in repealing or significantly amending it.

Section 101 sets forth a series of somewhat imprecise, if not ambiguous, environmental quality goals for the government and the Nation. 42 U.S.C. § 4331. This section tends to be ignored by reviewing courts, which is somewhat odd because these goals are expressly incorporated into the meat of the Act, the "action-forcing" mechanism of section 102 (43 U.S.C. § 4332). It provides, in pertinent part:

> The Congress authorizes and directs that, to the fullest extent possible: (1) the policies, regulations, and public laws of the United State shall be interpreted and administered in accordance with the policies set forth in this chapter, and (2) all agencies of the Federal Government shall—
>
> (A) utilize a systematic, interdisciplinary approach which will insure the integrated use of the natural and social sciences and the environmental design arts in planning and in decisionmaking which may have an impact on man's environment;
>
> (B) identify and develop methods and procedures, in consultation with the Council on Environmental Quality established by subchapter II of this chapter, which will insure that presently unqualified environmental amenities and values may be given appropriate consideration in decisionmaking along with economic and technical considerations;
>
> (C) include in every recommendation or report on proposals for legislation and other major Federal actions significantly affecting the quality of the human environment, a detailed statement by the responsible official on—
>
> (i) the environmental impact of the proposed action,
>
> (ii) any adverse environmental effects which cannot be avoided should the proposal be implemented,
>
> (iii) alternatives to the proposed action,
>
> (iv) the relationship between local short-term uses of man's environment and the maintenance and enhancement of long-term productivity, and
>
> (v) any irreversible and irretrievable commitments of resources which would be involved in the proposed action should it be implemented.
>
> Prior to making any detailed statement, the responsible Federal official shall consult with and obtain the comments of any Federal agency which has jurisdiction by law or special expertise with respect to any environmental impact involved. Copies of such statement and the comments and views of the appropriate Federal, State, and local agencies, which are authorized to develop and enforce environmental standards, shall be made available to the President, the Council on

Environmental Quality and to the public as provided by section 552 of Title 5, and shall accompany the proposal through the existing agency review processes; * * *

(E) study, develop, and describe appropriate alternatives to recommended courses of action in any proposal which involves unresolved conflicts concerning alternative uses of available resources; * * *.

42 U.S.C. § 4335 provides that "[t]he policies and goals set forth in this chapter are supplementary to those set forth in existing authorizations of Federal agencies." The "detailed statement" referred to in section 102(2)(c) has come to be known as an environmental impact statement, or EIS.

Finally, NEPA creates the President's Council on Environmental Quality. Originally envisioned as a counterpart to the advisory Council on Economic Advisors, the importance of the CEQ has waxed and waned over the years. One important step it took fairly early on was to prepare "guidelines" for the environmental impact statement process. These "guidelines" functioned somewhat like Restatements of the Law, in that they attempted to capture the best of the agency experience and judicial guidance concerning NEPA's implementation. During the Carter Administration, these guidelines were rewritten and given the force and effect of law by Executive Order. Although some Presidents have not been so warmly disposed toward CEQ or NEPA as Carter, CEQ's NEPA regulations (found at 40 C.F.R. Part 1500) had proved so useful to the agencies and the courts that they have not been seriously tinkered with, and remain valuable sources of insight into NEPA processes and requirements. In addition, nearly every federal land management agency has its own counterpart NEPA regulations.

NEPA litigation ordinarily raises one of two questions: (1) Must the agency prepare a full EIS on some action that is before it? (2) If an EIS is prepared, is it adequate; i.e., does it meet the terms of the statute? Answering the first question involves determining whether there is being proposed a "major Federal action significantly affecting the quality of the human environment" (MFASAQHE, unpronounceable in polite company). To determine whether the action will have a significant environmental effect, the CEQ regulations usually require the agency to prepare a "mini-EIS," called an environmental assessment (EA). 40 C.F.R. § 1501.4 (1991). If the conclusion is negative, the agency makes a finding of no significant impact (FONSI). Judge Richard Posner has described the EA as a "rough-cut, low-budget environmental impact statement designed to show whether a full-fledged environmental impact statement—which is very costly and time-consuming to prepare and has been the kiss of death to many a federal project—is necessary." He went on to say that " 'rough-cut' and 'low-budget' are relative terms" for in that case the EA on a timber sale to harvest trees on 26 acres was 112 pages long, or 4.3 pages per acre. Cronin v. U.S. Department of Agriculture, 919 F.2d 439, 443 (7th Cir.1990).

Only if there is no proposed federal action, or if the action will not significantly affect the environment, can the EIS requirement be escaped. (The adjective "major" before "federal action" has never been regarded as adding much of anything to the requirement that the action "significantly affect" the environment; that is, it has no meaning independent of "significantly." See 40 C.F.R. § 1508.18.) Determining whether there is a "federal action" may sometimes be difficult, as discussed further below.

If the agency has promulgated an EIS, the adequacy issues that are frequently litigated include the following: Were the likely environmental impacts sufficiently identified and discussed? Were reasonable alternatives to the proposed action (and their environmental impacts) identified and addressed? Were adverse opinions and comments included and discussed? Was the statement sufficiently detailed? As agencies have incorporated NEPA processes into their routine decisionmaking, the focus of litigation has inevitably shifted from the failure to prepare an EIS to the adequacy of the EIS.

The reported NEPA decisions and commentary on them are voluminous. For general reference, see Daniel Mandelker, NEPA LAW AND LITIGATION (1984); Sheldon Novick, et al., eds., LAW OF ENVIRONMENTAL PROTECTION, vol. 2, ch. 9 (2001). A growing number of states have adopted "little NEPAs," patterned after the federal law. Such SEPAs (state environmental policy acts) can come into play in federal land management to the extent state law applies on federal lands. See generally Daniel P. Selmi and Kenneth A. Manaster, STATE ENVIRONMENTAL LAWS ch. 10 (1989).

Robertson v. Methow Valley Citizens Council

Supreme Court of the United States, 1989.
490 U.S. 332.

■ JUSTICE STEVENS delivered the opinion of the Court.

We granted certiorari to decide two questions of law. As framed by petitioners, they are:

> "1. Whether the National Environmental Policy Act requires federal agencies to include in each environmental impact statement: (a) a fully developed plan to mitigate environmental harm; and (b) a 'worst case' analysis of potential environmental harm if relevant information concerning significant environmental effects is unavailable or too costly to obtain."

> "2. Whether the Forest Service may issue a special use permit for recreational use of national forest land in the absence of a fully developed plan to mitigate environmental harm."

Concluding that the Court of Appeals for the Ninth Circuit misapplied * * * NEPA, and gave inadequate deference to the Forest Service's interpretation of its own regulations, we reverse and remand for further proceedings.

The Forest Service is authorized by statute to manage the national forests for "outdoor recreation, range, timber, watershed, and wildlife and fish purposes." 16 U.S.C. § 528. Pursuant to that authorization, the Forest

Service has issued "special use" permits for the operation of approximately 170 alpine and nordic ski areas on federal lands.

The Forest Service permit process involves three separate stages. The Forest Service first examines the general environmental and financial feasibility of a proposed project and decides whether to issue a special use permit. See 36 CFR § 251.54(f) (1988). Because that decision is a "major Federal action" within the meaning of NEPA, it must be preceded by the preparation of an Environmental Impact Statement (EIS). 42 U.S.C. § 4332. If the Service decides to issue a permit, it then proceeds to select a developer, formulate the basic terms of the arrangement with the selected party, and issue the permit. The special use permit does not, however, give the developer the right to begin construction. See 36 CFR § 251.56(c) (1988). In a final stage of review, the Service evaluates the permittee's "master plan" for development, construction, and operation of the project. Construction may begin only after an additional environmental analysis (although it is not clear that a second EIS need always be prepared) and final approval of the developer's master plan. This case arises out of the Forest Service's decision to issue a special use permit authorizing the development of a major destination alpine ski resort at Sandy Butte in the North Cascades mountains.

Sandy Butte is a 6,000–foot mountain located in the Okanogan National Forest in Okanogan County, Washington. At present Sandy Butte, like the Methow Valley it overlooks, is an unspoiled, sparsely populated area that the district court characterized as "pristine." In 1968, Congress established the North Cascades National Park and directed the Secretaries of Interior and Agriculture to agree on the designation of areas within and adjacent to the park for public uses, including ski areas. 16 U.S.C. §§ 90, 90d–3. A 1970 study conducted by the Forest Service pursuant to this congressional directive identified Sandy Butte as having the highest potential of any site in the State of Washington for development as a major downhill ski resort.

In 1978, Methow Recreation, Inc. (MRI) applied for a special use permit to develop and operate its proposed "Early Winters Ski Resort" on Sandy Butte and an 1,165 acre parcel of land it had acquired adjacent to the National Forest. The proposed development would make use of approximately 3,900 acres of Sandy Butte; would entice visitors to travel long distances to stay at the resort for several days at a time; and would stimulate extensive commercial and residential growth in the vicinity to accommodate both vacationers and staff.

In response to MRI's application, the Forest Service, in cooperation with state and county officials, prepared an EIS known as the Early Winters Alpine Winter Sports Study (Early Winters Study or Study). The stated purpose of the EIS was "to provide the information required to evaluate the potential for skiing at Early Winters" and "to assist in making a decision whether to issue a Special Use Permit for downhill skiing on all or a portion of approximately 3900 acres of National Forest System land." Early Winters Study 1. A draft of the Study was completed and circulated in 1982, but release of the final EIS was delayed as Congress considered including Sandy Butte in a proposed wilderness area. When the Washington State Wilderness Act of 1984 was passed, however, Sandy Butte was excluded from the wilderness designation,[4] and the EIS was released.

The Early Winters Study is a printed document containing almost 150 pages of text and 12 appendices. It evaluated five alternative levels of development of Sandy Butte that might be authorized, the lowest being a "no action" alternative and the highest being development of a 16–lift ski area able to accommodate 10,500 skiers at one time. The Study considered the effect of each level of development on water resources, soil, wildlife, air quality, vegetation and visual quality, as well as land use and transportation in the Methow Valley, probable demographic shifts, the economic market for skiing and other summer and winter recreational activities in the Valley, and the energy requirements for the ski area and related developments. The Study's discussion of possible impacts was not limited to on-site effects, but also, as required by Council on Environmental Quality (CEQ) regulations, see 40 CFR § 1502.16(b) (1987), addressed "off-site impacts that each alternative might have on community facilities, socio-economic and other environmental conditions in the Upper Methow Valley." Early Winters Study 1. As to off-site effects, the Study explained that "due to the uncertainty of where other public and private lands may become developed," it is difficult to evaluate off-site impacts, and thus the document's analysis is necessarily "not site-specific." Finally, the Study outlined certain steps that might be taken to mitigate adverse effects, both on Sandy Butte and in the neighboring Methow Valley, but indicated that these proposed steps are merely conceptual and "will be made more specific as part of the design and implementation stages of the planning process."

The effects of the proposed development on air quality and wildlife received particular attention in the Study. [Discussion of the air quality issues is deleted.]

In its discussion of adverse effects on area wildlife, the EIS concluded that no endangered or threatened species would be affected by the proposed development and that the only impact on sensitive species was the probable loss of a pair of spotted owls and their progeny. With regard to other wildlife, the Study considered the impact on 75 different indigenous species and predicted that within a decade after development vegetational change and increased human activity would lead to a decrease in population for 31 species, while causing an increase in population for another 24 species on Sandy Butte. Two species, the pine marten and nesting goshawk, would be eliminated altogether from the area of development.

In a comment in response to the draft EIS, the Washington Department of Game voiced a special concern about potential losses to the State's largest migratory deer herd, which uses the Methow Valley as a critical winter range and as its migration route. The state agency estimated that

---

4. See 98 Stat. 299. * * * [T]he Senate Committee Report explaining the decision to exclude Sandy Butte from the wilderness designation in the bill * * * [stated]: "The Forest Service and the Department of Agri-culture are directed to allow the evaluation process for the Sandy Butte development to proceed without additional delay * * *" S. Rep. No. 98–461, p. 11 (1984).

the total population of mule deer in the area most likely to be affected was "better than 30,000 animals" and that "the ultimate impact on the Methow deer herd could exceed a 50 percent reduction in numbers." The agency asserted that "Okanogan County residents place a great deal of importance on the area's deer herd." In addition, it explained that hunters had "harvested" 3,247 deer in the Methow Valley area in 1981, and that, since in 1980 hunters on average spent $1,980 for each deer killed in Washington, they had contributed over $6 million to the State's economy in 1981. Because the deer harvest is apparently proportional to the size of the herd, the state agency predicted that "Washington business can expect to lose over $3 million annually from reduced recreational opportunity." The Forest Service's own analysis of the impact on the deer herd was more modest. It first concluded that the actual operation of the ski hill would have only a "minor" direct impact on the herd, but then recognized that the off-site effect of the development "would noticeably reduce numbers of deer in the Methow [Valley] with any alternative." Although its estimate indicated a possible 15 percent decrease in the size of the herd, it summarized the State's contrary view in the text of the EIS, and stressed that off-site effects are difficult to estimate due to uncertainty concerning private development.

* * * [T]he EIS also described both on-site and off-site mitigation measures. Among possible on-site mitigation possibilities, the Study recommended locating runs, ski lifts, and roads so as to minimize interference with wildlife, restricting access to selected roads during fawning season and further examination of the effect of the development on mule deer migration routes. Off-site options discussed in the Study included the use of zoning and tax incentives to limit development on deer winter range and migration routes, encouragement of conservation easements, and acquisition and management by local government of critical tracts of land. * * * [T]he proposed options were primarily directed to steps that might be taken by state and local government.

Ultimately, the Early Winters Study recommended the issuance of a permit for development at the second highest level considered—a 16-lift ski area able to accommodate 8,200 skiers at one time. On July 5, 1984, the Regional Forester decided to issue a special use permit as recommended by the Study.[10] In his decision, the Regional Forester found that no major adverse effects would result directly from the federal action, but that secondary effects could include a degradation of existing air quality and a reduction of mule deer winter range. He therefore directed the supervisor of the Okanogan National Forest, both independently and in cooperation with local officials, to identify and implement certain mitigating measures.

[Following exhaustion of administrative remedies, four environmental groups sued to challenge the adequacy of NEPA compliance. They lost in the district court and won in the court of appeals, which found that the

---

10. His decision did not identify a particular developer, but rather simply authorized the taking of competitive bids. It was not until July 21, 1986, almost one month after the District Court affirmed the Forester's decision, that a special use permit was issued to MRI.

Forest Service should have included a "worst-case analysis" in the EIS and also should have developed measures to mitigate the environmental impact of the proposed action.] * * *

Section 101 of NEPA declares a broad national commitment to protecting and promoting environmental quality. 42 U.S.C. § 4331. To ensure that this commitment is "infused into the ongoing programs and actions of the Federal Government, the act also establishes some important 'action-forcing' procedures." 115 Cong.Rec.40416 (remarks of Sen. Jackson). * * *

The statutory requirement that a federal agency contemplating a major action prepare such an environmental impact statement serves NEPA's "action-forcing" purpose in two important respects. It ensures that the agency, in reaching its decision, will have available and will carefully consider detailed information concerning significant environmental impacts; it also guarantees that the relevant information will be made available to the larger audience that may also play a role in both the decisionmaking process and the implementation of that decision.

Simply by focusing the agency's attention on the environmental consequences of a proposed project, NEPA ensures that important effects will not be overlooked or underestimated only to be discovered after resources have been committed or the die otherwise cast. Moreover, the strong precatory language of § 101 of the Act and the requirement that agencies prepare detailed impact statements inevitably bring pressure to bear on agencies "to respond to the needs of environmental quality." 115 Cong.Rec. 40425 (1969) (remarks of Sen. Muskie).

Publication of an EIS, both in draft and final form, also serves a larger informational role. It gives the public the assurance that the agency "has indeed considered environmental concerns in its decision-making process," and, perhaps more significantly, provides a spring-board for public comment, see L. Caldwell, Science and the National Environmental Policy Act 72 (1982). Thus, in this case the final draft of the Early Winters Study reflects not only the work of the Forest Service itself, but also the critical views of the Washington State Department of Game, the Methow Valley Citizens Council, and Friends of the Earth, as well as many others, to whom copies of the draft Study were circulated.[13] Moreover, with respect to a development such as Sandy Butte, where the adverse effects on air quality and the mule deer herd are primarily attributable to predicted off-site development that will be subject to regulation by other governmental bodies, the EIS serves the function of offering those bodies adequate notice of the expected consequences and the opportunity to plan and implement corrective measures in a timely manner.

---

13. The CEQ regulations require that, after preparing a draft EIS, the agency request comments from other federal agencies, appropriate state and local agencies, affected Indian tribes, any relevant applicant, the public generally, and, in particular, interested or affected persons or organizations. 40 CFR § 1503.1 (1987). In preparing the final EIS, the agency must "discuss at appropriate points * * * any responsible opposing view which was not adequately discussed in the draft statement and [must] indicate the agency's response to the issue raised." § 1502.9. See also § 1503.4.

The sweeping policy goals announced in § 101 of NEPA are thus realized through a set of "action-forcing" procedures that require that agencies take a " 'hard look' at environmental consequences," and that provide for broad dissemination of relevant environmental information. Although these procedures are almost certain to affect the agency's substantive decision, it is now well settled that NEPA itself does not mandate particular results, but simply prescribes the necessary process. See Strycker's Bay Neighborhood Council, Inc. v. Karlen, 444 U.S. 223, 227–228 (1980) (per curiam); Vermont Yankee Nuclear Power Corp. v. Natural Resources Defense Council, Inc. 435 U.S. 519, 558 (1978). If the adverse environmental effects of the proposed action are adequately identified and evaluated, the agency is not constrained by NEPA from deciding that other values outweigh the environmental costs. In this case, for example, it would not have violated NEPA if the Forest Service, complying with the Act's procedural prerequisites, had decided that the benefits to be derived from downhill skiing at Sandy Butte justified the issuance of a special use permit, notwithstanding the loss of 15 percent, 50 percent, or even 100 percent of the mule deer herd. Other statutes may impose substantive environmental obligations on federal agencies,[14] but NEPA merely prohibits uninformed—rather than unwise—agency action.

To be sure, one important ingredient of an EIS is the discussion of steps that can be taken to mitigate adverse environmental consequences.[15] The requirement that an EIS contain a detailed discussion of possible mitigation measures flows from both the language of the Act and, more expressly, from CEQ's implementing regulations. Implicit in NEPA's demand that an agency prepare a detailed statement on "any adverse environmental effects which cannot be avoided should the proposal be implemented," 42 U.S.C. § 4332(C)(ii), is an understanding that the EIS will discuss the extent to which adverse effects can be avoided. See D. Mandelker, NEPA Law and Litigation § 10:38 (1984). More generally, omission of a reasonably complete discussion of possible mitigation mea-

---

14. See e.g., the Endangered Species Act of 1973, 87 Stat. 892, 16 U.S.C. § 1536(a)(2) (requiring that every federal agency "insure that any action authorized, funded, or carried out by such agency * * * is not likely to jeopardize the continued existence of any endangered species or threatened species"); the Department of Transportation Act of 1966, 49 U.S.C. § 303 (Secretary of Transportation may approve "use of publicly owned land of a public park, recreation area, or wildlife and waterfowl refuge * * * or land of an historic site * * * only if * * * there is no prudent and feasible alternative to using that land; and * * * the program or project includes all possible planning to minimize harm to the [area] resulting from the use").

15. CEQ regulations define "mitigation" to include:

"(a) Avoiding the impact altogether by not taking a certain action or parts of an action.

"(b) Minimizing impacts by limiting the degree or magnitude of the action and its implementation.

"(c) Rectifying the impact by repairing, rehabilitating, or restoring the affected environment.

"(d) Reducing or eliminating the impact over time by preservation and maintenance operations during the life of the action.

"(e) Compensating for the impact by replacing or providing substitute resources or environments." 40 CFR § 1508.20 (1987).

sures would undermine the "action-forcing" function of NEPA. Without such a discussion, neither the agency nor other interested groups and individuals can properly evaluate the severity of the adverse effects. An adverse effect that can be fully remedied by, for example, an inconsequential public expenditure is certainly not as serious as a similar effect that can only be modestly ameliorated through the commitment of vast public and private resources. Recognizing the importance of such a discussion in guaranteeing that the agency has taken a "hard look" at the environmental consequences of proposed federal action, CEQ regulations require that the agency discuss possible mitigation measures in defining the scope of the EIS, 40 CFR § 1508.25(b) (1987), in discussing alternatives to the proposed action, § 1502.14(f), and consequences of that action, § 1502.16(h), and in explaining its ultimate decision, § 1505.2(c).

There is a fundamental distinction, however, between a requirement that mitigation be discussed in sufficient detail to ensure that environmental consequences have been fairly evaluated, on the one hand, and a substantive requirement that a complete mitigation plan be actually formulated and adopted, on the other. In this case, the off-site effects on air quality and on the mule deer herd cannot be mitigated unless nonfederal government agencies take appropriate action. Since it is those state and local governmental bodies that have jurisdiction over the area in which the adverse effects need be addressed and since they have the authority to mitigate them, it would be incongruous to conclude that the Forest Service has no power to act until the local agencies have reached a final conclusion on what mitigating measures they consider necessary. Even more significantly, it would be inconsistent with NEPA's reliance on procedural mechanisms—as opposed to substantive, result-based standards—to demand the presence of a fully developed plan that will mitigate environmental harm before an agency can act. Cf. Baltimore Gas & Electric Co., 462 U.S., at 100 ("NEPA does not require agencies to adopt any particular internal decisionmaking structure").

We thus conclude that the Court of Appeals erred, first, in assuming that "NEPA requires that 'action be taken to mitigate the adverse effects of major federal actions,'" and, second, in finding that this substantive requirement entails the further duty to include in every EIS "a detailed explanation of specific measures which *will* be employed to mitigate the adverse impacts of a proposed action."

The Court of Appeals also concluded that the Forest Service had an obligation to make a "worst case analysis" if it could not make a reasoned assessment of the impact of the Early Winters project on the mule deer herd. [The analysis was, according to the 9th Circuit, to be "formulated on the basis of available information, using reasonable projections of the worst possible consequences of a proposed action."] Such a "worst case analysis" was required at one time by CEQ regulations, but those regulations have since been amended. Moreover, although the prior regulations may well have expressed a permissible application of NEPA, the Act itself does not mandate that uncertainty in predicting environmental harms be addressed exclusively in this manner. Accordingly, we conclude that the Court of Appeals also erred in requiring the "worst case" study.

In 1977, President Carter directed that CEQ promulgate binding regulations implementing the procedural provisions of NEPA. Exec. Order No. 11991. Pursuant to this presidential order, CEQ promulgated implementing regulations. Under § 1502.22 of these regulations—a provision which became known as the "worst case requirement"—CEQ provided that if certain information relevant to the agency's evaluation of the proposed action is either unavailable or too costly to obtain, the agency must include in the EIS a "worst case analysis and an indication of the probability or improbability of its occurrence." 40 CFR § 1502.22 (1985). In 1986, however, CEQ replaced the "worst case" requirement with a requirement that federal agencies, in the face of unavailable information concerning a reasonably foreseeable significant environmental consequence, prepare a "summary of existing credible scientific evidence which is relevant to evaluating the * * * adverse impacts" and prepare an "evaluation of such impacts based upon theoretical approaches or research methods generally accepted in the scientific community." 40 CFR § 1502.22(b) (1987). The amended regulation thus "retains the duty to describe the consequences of a remote, but potentially severe impact, but grounds the duty in evaluation of scientific opinion rather that in the framework of a conjectural 'worst case analysis.' " 50 Fed.Reg. 32237 (1985).

The Court of Appeals recognized that the "worst case analysis" regulation has been superseded, yet held that "[t]his rescission * * * does not nullify the requirement * * * since the regulation was merely a codification of prior NEPA case law." 833 F.2d, at 817, n. 11. This conclusion, however, is erroneous[.] * * * As CEQ recognized at the time it superseded the regulation, case law prior to the adoption of the "worst case analysis" provision did require agencies to describe environmental impacts even in the face of substantial uncertainty, but did not require that this obligation necessarily be met through the mechanism of a "worst case analysis." See 51 Fed.Reg. 15625 (1986). CEQ's abandonment of the "worst case analysis" provision, therefore, is not inconsistent with any previously established judicial interpretation of the statute.

Nor are we convinced that the new CEQ regulation is not controlling simply because it was preceded by a rule that was in some respects more demanding. In Andrus v. Sierra Club, 442 U.S., at 358, we held that CEQ regulations are entitled to substantial deference. In that case we recognized that although less deference may be in order in some cases in which the " 'administrative guidelines' " conflict " 'with earlier pronouncements of the agency,' " substantial deference is nonetheless appropriate if there appears to have been good reason for the change. Here, the amendment only came after the prior regulation had been subjected to considerable criticism.[17] Moreover, the amendment was designed to better serve the twin

---

17. As CEQ explained: * * * "[I]n the institutional context of litigation over EIS(s) the 'worst case' rule has proved counterpro- ductive, because it has led to agencies being required to devote substantial time and resources to preparation of analyses which are

functions of an EIS—requiring agencies to take a "hard look" at the consequences of the proposed action and providing important information to other groups and individuals. CEQ explained that by requiring that an EIS focus on reasonably foreseeable impacts, the new regulation "will generate information and discussion on those consequences of greatest concern to the public and of greatest relevance to the agency's decision," 50 Fed.Reg. 32237 (1985), rather than distorting the decision making process by overemphasizing highly speculative harms, 51 Fed.Reg. 15624–15625 (1986); 50 Fed.Reg. 32236 (1985). In light of this well-considered basis for the change, the new regulation is entitled to substantial deference. Accordingly, the Court of Appeals erred in concluding that the Early Winters Study is inadequate because it failed to include a "worst case analysis."
* * *

NOTES AND QUESTIONS

1.   In a companion decision involving the adequacy of an EIS prepared by the Corps of Engineers on a dam project in Oregon's Rogue River basin, Marsh v. Oregon Natural Resources Council, 490 U.S. 360 (1989), the Court applied *Methow Valley* and reversed the Ninth Circuit's decision that the EIS was inadequate. "[A]s long as the Corps' decision not to supplement the [EIS in light of new information about possible environmental impacts] was not 'arbitrary or capricious,' it should not be set aside." 490 U.S. at 377.

2.   What does it mean to say that NEPA is purely procedural, and "merely prohibits uninformed—rather than unwise—agency action"? Does it mean that even if an EIS reveals that the proposed action could be disastrous environmentally, the statute imposes no obligation on the agency to act differently—or at least no obligation that a court will enforce? Can this be all Congress had in mind in enacting the statute? Or does its ventilation function ensure that no agency would go forward with an environmentally disastrous decision, knowing the consequences?

3.   On the mitigation issue, what actually was threatening the adverse effects on the deer herd? The ski runs or other activities on federal land? Or the condominiums on private land? Who is responsible for the latter? Does NEPA require the Forest Service to seek to mitigate the adverse environmental effects of the ski area proposal? Did the agency assume a responsibility to mitigate adverse effects? (Notice the possible interplay here of federal law with state and local law on such things as land use planning on nonfederal lands.) What does NEPA require regarding disclosure of those mitigating steps; e.g., must they be described in the EIS?

4.   If the Forest Service had said in the EIS that it would require the developer to build an access road according to certain environmentally protective standards, and then later failed to include this requirement in the permit it issued the developer, would the plaintiffs have a cause of

not considered useful to decisionmakers and divert the EIS process from its intended pur-   pose." 50 Fed. Reg. 32236 (1985).

action to enforce the promise in the EIS? That is, are agency promises or commitments in the EIS enforceable? See, e.g., Note, NEPA: Theories for Challenging Agency Action, 1982 Ariz.St.L.J. 665–690.

5.   On the "worst-case analysis" issue (sometimes called "putting your worst foot forward"), why do you suppose agencies resist doing such analyses? Shouldn't it be a standard part of any rational decisionmaking, whether in the public or private sectors? Does a worst-case analysis supply project opponents with fodder for attacking the project (no matter how unlikely the worst case is to occur)? Was the question of the impact of the project on the mule deer herd really speculative—so close to the frontiers of human knowledge that the agency could not have attempted to forecast what the worst-case impacts might have been?

6.   Why do you suppose the CEQ reversed course on this issue in 1986? Or did the CEQ really reverse course? Did the revised CEQ regulation really say that such an analysis of possible "bad outcomes" was *not* required? Examine the amended regulation (quoted in the Court's opinion on p. 400) closely. What is the difference between what it requires and a worst-case analysis?

7.   A frequent focus of NEPA litigation challenging the adequacy of an EIS (rather than simply a failure to prepare one) turns on the question of "alternatives to the proposed action." Must all alternatives be discussed? What were the alternatives to the ski area proposal here? Alternative designs? Alternative locations (on federal land, and on private land)? Alternative forms of outdoor recreation? Alternative ways to spend discretionary income? Doing nothing? Does NEPA require that each of these, and their environmental impacts, be discussed in the EIS?

8.   Does an agency have to discuss alternatives that are beyond its legal authority to implement? Suppose, for example, that the best alternative location for a ski area here was on nearby private land, over which the Forest Service had no jurisdiction. Must that alternative be discussed in the EIS?

9.   What about alternative uses of the federal land involved here? For example, is a reasonable alternative use of the federal land here as wilderness, and to include the area in the National Wilderness Preservation System? That takes an act of Congress, and note (see text accompanying footnote 4 of the Court's opinion) that Congress in 1984 excluded the area from a wilderness bill it enacted. Must this alternative nevertheless be discussed?

10.   The proposed downhill ski resort was never built. A developer pursued a master planned resort without the downhill component, but opponents successfully challenged some of the water rights the developer proposed to use, and recently a conservation group acquired most of the property.

Notice that the Forest Service decisionmaking process for ski areas proceeds from the generic to the specific through several layers, from (1) a generic feasibility study through (2) a decision to issue a permit to a specific developer (and to formulate the terms of the permit) down to (3) the approval of a final master plan. *Methow Valley* involved NEPA compliance on stage 1, but stages 2–3 may also require some form of NEPA documentation. Many federal agency decisionmaking processes involve such multiple layers. Consider the Forest Service's process for moving from forest-wide planning down to individual timber sales or road permits, as outlined in *Ohio Forestry*, Chapter 4, supra p. 294.

The general issue of determining where and how NEPA fits in a staged decisionmaking process is characterized as "tiering" in the CEQ regulations. Specifically, "[a]gencies are encouraged to tier their environmental impact statements to eliminate repetitive discussions * * * and to focus on the actual issues ripe for decision at each level of environmental review." 40 C.F.R. § 1502.20; see also § 1508.28 (2001). The next case focuses on integrating NEPA into a complex series of federal actions dealing with coal development on federal lands.

Kleppe v. Sierra Club

Supreme Court of the United States, 1976.
427 U.S. 390.

■ Mr. Justice Powell delivered the opinion of the Court.

* * * [Respondent environmental groups sued federal agencies] responsible for issuing coal leases, approving mining plans, granting rights-of-way, and taking the other actions necessary to enable private companies and public utilities to develop coal reserves on land owned or controlled by the Federal Government. Citing widespread interest in the reserves of a region identified as the "Northern Great Plains region," and an alleged threat from coal-related operations to their members' enjoyment of the region's environment, respondents claimed that the federal officials could not allow further development without preparing a "comprehensive environmental impact statement" under § 102(2)(C) on the entire region. * * *

The District Court * * * granted the petitioners' motions for summary judgment. Respondents appealed. Shortly after oral argument but before issuing an opinion on the merits, the Court of Appeals in January 1975 issued an injunction—over a dissent—against the Department's approval of four mining plans in the Powder River Coal Basin, which is one small but coal-rich section of the region that concerns respondents. 509 F.2d 533. An impact statement had been prepared on these plans, but it had not been before the District Court and was not before the Court of Appeals. In June 1975 the Court of Appeals ruled on the merits and, for reasons discussed below, reversed the District Court and remanded for further proceedings. 514 F.2d 856. The court continued its injunction in force. * * *

The Northern Great Plains region identified in respondents' complaint encompasses portions of four States—northeastern Wyoming, eastern Montana, western North Dakota, and western South Dakota. There is no dispute about its richness in coal, nor about the waxing interest in developing that coal, nor about the crucial role the federal petitioners will play due to the significant percentage of the coal to which they control access. The Department has initiated, in this decade, three studies in areas either inclusive of or included within this region. The North Central Power Study was addressed to the potential for coordinated development of electric power in an area encompassing all or part of 15 States in the North Central United States. It aborted in 1972 for lack of interest on the part of electric utilities. The Montana–Wyoming Aqueducts Study, intended to recommend the best use of water resources for coal development in southeastern Montana and northeastern Wyoming, was suspended in 1972 with the initiation of the third study, the Northern Great Plains Resources Program (NGPRP).

While the record does not reveal the degree of concern with environmental matters in the first two studies, it is clear that the NGPRP was devoted entirely to the environment. It was carried out by an interagency, federal-state task force with public participation, and was designed "to assess the potential social, economic and environmental impacts" from resource development in five States—Montana, Wyoming, South Dakota, North Dakota, and Nebraska. Its primary objective was "to provide an analytical and informational framework for policy and planning decisions at all levels of government" by formulating several "scenarios" showing the probable consequences for the area's environment and culture from the various possible techniques and levels of resource development. The final interim report of the NGPRP was issued August 1, 1975, shortly after the decision of the Court of Appeals in this case.

In addition, since 1973 the Department has engaged in a complete review of its coal-leasing program for the entire Nation. * * * The purpose of the program review was to study the environmental impact of the Department's entire range of coal-related activities and to develop a planning system to guide the national leasing program. The impact statement, known as the "Coal Programmatic EIS," went through several drafts before issuing in final form on September 19, 1975—shortly before the petitions for certiorari were filed in this case. The Coal Programmatic EIS proposed a new leasing program based on a complex planning system called the Energy Minerals Activity Recommendation System (EMARS), and assessed the prospective environmental impact of the new program as well as the alternatives to it. We have been informed by the parties to this litigation that the Secretary is in the process of implementing the new program. * * *

The major issue remains the one with which the suit began: whether NEPA requires petitioners to prepare an environmental impact statement on the entire Northern Great Plains region. Petitioners, arguing the negative, rely squarely upon the facts of the case and the language of § 102(2)(C) of NEPA. We find their reliance well placed.

* * * § 102(2)(C) requires an impact statement "in every recommendation or report on proposals for legislation and other major Federal

actions significantly affecting the quality of the human environment." Since no one has suggested that petitioners have proposed legislation on respondents' region, the controlling phrase in this section of the Act, for this case, is "major Federal actions." Respondents can prevail only if there has been a report or recommendation on a proposal for major federal action with respect to the Northern Great Plains region. Our statement of the relevant facts shows there has been none; instead, all proposals are for actions of either local or national scope.

The local actions are the decisions by the various petitioners to issue a lease, approve a mining plan, issue a right-of-way permit, or take other action to allow private activity at some point within the region identified by respondents. * * * The petitioners * * * have prepared impact statements on several proposed actions of this type in the Northern Great Plains during the course of this litigation. Similarly, the federal petitioners agreed at oral argument that § 102(2)(C) required the Coal Programmatic EIS that was prepared in tandem with the new national coal-leasing program and included as part of the final report on the proposal for adoption of that program. Their admission is well made, for the new leasing program is a coherent plan of national scope, and its adoption surely has significant environmental consequences.

But there is no evidence in the record of an action or a proposal for an action of regional scope. The District Court, in fact, expressly found that there was no existing or proposed plan or program on the part of the Federal Government for the regional development of the area described in respondents' complaint. It found also that the three studies initiated by the Department in areas either included within or inclusive of respondents' region—that is, the Montana–Wyoming Aqueducts Study, the North Central Power Study, and the NGPRP—were not parts of any plan or program to develop or encourage development of the Northern Great Plains. That court found no evidence that the individual coal development projects undertaken or proposed by private industry and public utilities in that part of the country are integrated into a plan or otherwise interrelated. These findings were not disturbed by the Court of Appeals, and they remain fully supported by the record in this Court.

Quite apart from the fact that the statutory language requires an impact statement only in the event of a proposed action, respondents' desire for a regional environmental impact statement cannot be met for practical reasons. In the absence of a proposal for a regional plan of development, there is nothing that could be the subject of the analysis envisioned by the statute for an impact statement. Section 102(2)(C) requires that an impact statement contain, in essence, a detailed statement of the expected adverse environmental consequences of an action, the resource commitments involved in it, and the alternatives to it. Absent an overall plan for regional development, it is impossible to predict the level of coal-related activity that will occur in the region identified by respondents, and thus impossible to analyze the environmental consequences and the resource commitments involved in, and the alternatives to, such activity. A regional plan would define fairly precisely the scope and limits of the proposed development of the region. Where no such plan exists, any attempt to produce an impact statement would be little more than a study along the lines of the NGPRP, containing estimates of potential development and attendant environmental consequences. There would be no factual predicate for the production of an environmental impact statement of the type envisioned by NEPA.[14]

The Court of Appeals * * * did not find that there was a regional plan or program for development of the Northern Great Plains region * * * but concluded nevertheless that the petitioners "contemplated" a regional plan or program. * * *

We conclude that the Court of Appeals erred in both its factual assumptions and its interpretation of NEPA. We think the court was mistaken in concluding, on the record before it, that the petitioners were "contemplating" a regional development plan or program. It considered the several studies undertaken by the petitioners to represent attempts to control development on a regional scale. * * * But [the district court characterized those studies only as] efforts to gain background environmental information for subsequent application in the decisionmaking with respect to individual coal-related projects * * * [rather than] part of a plan or program to develop or encourage development. * * * All parties agreed in this Court that there still exists no proposal for a regional plan or program of development.

Even had the record justified a finding that a regional program was contemplated by the petitioners, the legal conclusion drawn by the Court of Appeals cannot be squared with the Act. The court recognized that the mere "contemplation" of certain action is not sufficient to require an impact statement. But it believed the statute nevertheless empowers a court to require the preparation of an impact statement to begin at some point prior to the formal recommendation or report on a proposal. The Court of Appeals accordingly devised its own four-part "balancing" test for determining when, during the contemplation of a plan or other type of federal action, an agency must begin a statement. * * *

The Court's reasoning and action find no support in the language or legislative history of NEPA. The statute clearly states when an impact statement is required, and mentions nothing about a balancing of factors. Rather, as we noted last Term, under the first sentence of § 102(2)(C) the moment at which an agency must have a final statement ready "is the time at which it makes a recommendation or report on a *proposal* for federal action." Aberdeen & Rockfish R. Co. v. SCRAP, 422 U.S. 289, 320 (1975)

---

14. In contrast, with both an individual coal-related action and the new national coal-leasing program, an agency deals with specific action of known dimensions. With appropriate allowances for the inexactness of all predictive ventures, the agency can analyze the environmental consequences and describe alternatives as envisioned by § 102(2)(C). Of course, since the kind of impact statement required depends upon the kind of " 'federal action' being taken," Aberdeen & Rockfish R. Co. v. SCRAP, 422 U.S. 289, 322 (1975), the statement on a proposed mining plan or a lease application may bear little resemblance to the statement on the national coal-leasing program. Nevertheless, in each case the bounds of the analysis are defined, which is not the case with coal development in general in the region identified by respondents.

(*SCRAP II*) (emphasis in original). The procedural duty imposed upon agencies by this section is quite precise, and the role of the courts in enforcing that duty is similarly precise. A court has no authority to depart from the statutory language and, by a balancing of court-devised factors, determine a point during the germination process of a potential proposal at which an impact statement *should be prepared.* Such an assertion of judicial authority would leave the agencies uncertain as to their procedural duties under NEPA, would invite judicial involvement in the day-to-day decisionmaking process of the agencies, and would invite litigation. As the contemplation of a project and the accompanying study thereof do not necessarily result in a proposal for major federal action, it may be assumed that the balancing process devised by the Court of Appeals also would result in the preparation of a good many unnecessary impact statements.[15]

[The Court held that the injunction issued by the court of appeals against the Secretary's approval of four mining plans was in error in part because] there had been filed a comprehensive impact statement on the proposed Powder River Basin mining plans themselves, and its adequacy had not been challenged either before the District Court or the Court of Appeals in this case, or anywhere else.[16] Thus, in simple equitable terms there were no grounds for the injunction: the District Court's finding of irreparable injury to the intervenors and to the public still stood, and there were—on the Court of Appeals' own terms—no countervailing equities.

* * * Respondents insist that, even without a comprehensive federal plan for the development of the Northern Great Plains, a ''regional'' impact statement nevertheless is required on all coal-related projects in the region because they are intimately related.

There are two ways to view this contention. First, it amounts to an attack on the sufficiency of the impact statements already prepared by the petitioners on the coal-related projects that they have approved or stand ready to approve. As such, we cannot consider it in this proceeding, for the

---

15. This is not to say that § 102(2)(C) imposes no duties upon an agency prior to its making a report or recommendation on a proposal for action. The section states that prior to preparing the impact statement the responsible official "shall consult with and obtain the comments of any Federal agency which has jurisdiction by law or special expertise with respect to any environmental impact involved." Thus, the section contemplates a consideration of environmental factors by agencies during the evolution of a report or recommendation on a proposal. But the time at which a court enters the process is when the report or recommendation on the proposal is made, and someone protests either the absence or the adequacy of the final impact statement. This is the point at which an agency's action has reached sufficient maturity to assure that judicial intervention will not hazard unnecessary disruption.

16. Even had the Court of Appeals determined that a regional impact statement was due at that moment, it still would have erred in enjoining approval of the four mining plans unless it had made a finding that the impact statement covering them inadequately analyzed the environmental impacts of, and the alternatives to, their approval. So long as the statement covering them was adequate, there would have been no reason to enjoin their approval pending preparation of a broader regional statement; that broader statement, when prepared, simply would have taken into consideration the regional environmental effects of the four mining plans once they were in operation, in determining the permissibility of further coal-related operations in the region. See Part V, infra.

case was not brought as a challenge to a particular impact statement and there is no impact statement in the record. It also is possible to view the respondents' argument as an attack upon the decision of the petitioners not to prepare one comprehensive impact statement on all proposed projects in the region. This contention properly is before us, for the petitioners have made it clear they do not intend to prepare such a statement.

We begin by stating our general agreement with respondents' basic premise that § 102(2)(C) may require a comprehensive impact statement in certain situations where several proposed actions are pending at the same time. NEPA announced a national policy of environmental protection and placed a responsibility upon the Federal Government to further specific environmental goals by "all practicable means, consistent with other essential considerations of national policy." § 101(b), 42 U.S.C.A. § 4331(b). Section 102(2)(C) is one of the "action-forcing" provisions intended as a directive to "all agencies to assure consideration of the environmental impact of their actions in decisionmaking." Conference Report on NEPA, 115 Cong.Rec. 40416 (1969). By requiring an impact statement Congress intended to assure such consideration during the development of a proposal or—as in this case—during the formulation of a position on a proposal submitted by private parties. A comprehensive impact statement may be necessary in some cases for an agency to meet this duty. Thus, when several proposals for coal-related actions that will have cumulative or synergistic environmental impact upon a region are pending concurrently before an agency, their environmental consequences must be considered together. Only through comprehensive consideration of pending proposals can the agency evaluate different courses of action.[21]

Agreement to this extent with respondents' premise, however, does not require acceptance of their conclusion that all proposed coal-related actions in the Northern Great Plains region are so "related" as to require their analysis in a single comprehensive impact statement. Respondents informed us that the Secretary recently adopted an approach to impact statements on coal-related actions that provides:

> "A. As a general proposition, and as determined by the Secretary, when action is proposed involving coal development such as issuing several coal leases or approving mining plans in the same region, such actions will be covered by a single EIS rather than by multiple statements. In such cases, the region covered will be determined by basin boundaries, drainage areas, areas of common reclamation problems, administrative boundaries, areas of economic interdependence, and other relevant factors."

At another point, the document containing the Secretary's approach states that a "regional EIS" will be prepared "if a series of proposed actions with

---

21. Neither the statute nor its legislative history contemplates that a court should substitute its judgment for that of the agency as to the environmental consequences of its actions. * * * The only role for a court is to insure that the agency has taken a "hard look" at environmental consequences; it cannot "interject itself within the area of discretion of the executive as to the choice of the action to be taken." Natural Resources Defense Council v. Morton, 458 F.2d 827, 838 (1972).

interrelated impacts are involved * * * unless a previous EIS has sufficiently analyzed the impacts of the proposed action(s)." Thus, the Department has decided to prepare comprehensive impact statements of the type
contemplated by § 102(2)(C), although it has not deemed it appropriate to
prepare such a statement on all proposed actions in the region identified by
respondents.

Respondents conceded at oral argument that to prevail they must show
that petitioners have acted arbitrarily in refusing to prepare one comprehensive statement on this entire region, and we agree. The determination
of the region, if any, with respect to which a comprehensive statement is
necessary requires the weighing of a number of relevant factors, including
the extent of the interrelationship among proposed actions and practical
considerations of feasibility. Resolving these issues requires a high level of
technical expertise and is properly left to the informed discretion of the
responsible federal agencies. Absent a showing of arbitrary action, we must
assume that the agencies have exercised this discretion appropriately.
Respondents have made no showing to the contrary.

Respondents' basic argument is that one comprehensive statement on
the Northern Great Plains is required because all coal-related activity in
that region is "programmatically," "geographically," and "environmentally" related [and because] * * * the petitioners themselves have approached
environmental study in this area on a regional basis. Respondents point
primarily to the NGPRP * * *. [The Court held that "studies" like the
NGPRP are, as characterized by the Secretary of the Interior, "simply [to]
provide an educational backdrop" and a "data base" for the preparation of
environmental impact statements on whatever "specific proposals for federal action" may thereafter be made.] As for the alleged "environmental"
relationship, respondents contend that the coal-related projects "will produce a wide variety of cumulative environmental impacts" throughout the
Northern Great Plains region * * * [including d]iminished availability of
water, air and water pollution, increases in population and industrial
densities, and perhaps even climatic changes. Cumulative environmental
impacts are, indeed, what require a comprehensive impact statement. But
determination of the extent and effect of these factors, and particularly
identification of the geographic area within which they may occur, is a task
assigned to the special competency of the appropriate agencies. * * * We
cannot say that petitioners' choices are arbitrary. Even if environmental
interrelationships could be shown conclusively to extend across basins and
drainage areas, practical considerations of feasibility might well necessitate
restricting the scope of comprehensive statements.

In sum, respondents' contention as to the relationships between all
proposed coal-related projects in the Northern Great Plains region does not
require that petitioners prepare one comprehensive impact statement covering all before proceeding to approve specific pending applications.[26] As we

26. Nor is it necessary that petitioners
always complete a comprehensive impact
statement on all proposed actions in an ap-

propriate region before approving any of the
projects. As petitioners have emphasized, and
respondents have not disputed, approval of

already have determined that there exists no proposal for regionwide action that could require a regional impact statement, the judgment of the Court of Appeals must be reversed, and the judgment of the District Court reinstated and affirmed. The case is remanded for proceedings consistent with this opinion.

NOTES AND QUESTIONS

1. Is the dispute here basically over *whether* NEPA requires the environmental impacts of interrelated federal actions to be assessed in a cumulative way? Or is it instead over *how* such a cumulative assessment will be "packaged" in EISs? Under the Court's interpretation of NEPA, will EISs on site-specific federal coal development actions in the region (such as an EIS on issuance of an individual coal lease, or on approval of a individual mine plan, or on a right-of-way for an individual rail line for coal transportation) have to consider the cumulative environmental impacts of the specific actions with all the other actions it has already taken or are now pending before it that relate to coal development in the region? If so, how does that differ from what the Sierra Club sought here? That is, are the Court's and the Club's vision of NEPA's application here all that different?

2. Is the Court in effect saying it will always accept at face value an agency denial that it has a particular "program", such as here, a regional coal development program? If the agency is not contemplating coal development in the Northern Great Plains on a regional scale, why did it undertake to do studies like the NGPRP? Why didn't Interior simply call the NGPRP an EIS, or convert it into one? If Interior had decided to do a "programmatic" EIS on its interrelated decisions having to do with regional coal development, and the coal/utility industry sued to stop its preparation, could a court enjoin it? On what grounds?

3. Is the Court's interpretation of NEPA, focusing literally on its text (such as "proposal"), too wooden? Because the statute is a generic one, applying to all federal decisionmaking processes, does it in effect invite the federal courts to create a "common law" of environmental impact assessment that justifies court intervention to ensure that it is applied meaningfully, instead of just literally?

4. In Thomas v. Peterson, 753 F.2d 754 (9th Cir.1985), one question was whether a proposed road on national forest land was "sufficiently related" to timber sales the Forest Service was considering "so as to require combined treatment in a single EIS that covers the cumulative effects of the road and the sales." Relying on CEQ regulations, the court concluded they were:

one lease or mining plan does not commit the Secretary to approval of any others * * *. Thus, an agency could approve one pending project that is fully covered by an impact statement, then take into consideration the environmental effects of that existing project when preparing the comprehensive statement on the cumulative impact of the remaining proposals.

It is clear that the timber sales cannot proceed without the road, and the road would not be built but for the contemplated timber sales. * * * [Among other evidence, the] Forest Service's cost-benefit analysis of the road considered the timber to be the benefit of the road, and while the Service has stated that the road will yield other benefits, it does not claim that such other benefits would justify the road in the absence of the timber sales. * * * We conclude, therefore, that the road construction and the contemplated timber sales are inextricably intertwined, and that they are "connected actions" within the meaning of the CEQ regulations.

The CEQ regulations also require that "cumulative actions" be considered together in a single EIS. * * * The record in this case contains considerable evidence to suggest that the road and the timber sales will have cumulatively significant impacts. * * * The primary cumulative effects, according to [comments submitted by the U.S. Fish & Wildlife Service, the Environmental Protection Agency, and the Idaho Department of Fish & Game] are the deposit of sediments in the Salmon River to the detriment of that river's population of salmon and steelhead trout, and the destruction of critical habitat for the endangered Rocky Mountain Gray Wolf.

* * * [S]ubsequent phases of development must be covered in an environmental impact statement on the first phase * * * [when, as here] it would be irrational to build the road then not sell the timber to which the road was built to provide access. [Furthermore, t]he Forest Service has not alleged that the Jersey Jack road has sufficient utility independent from the timber sales to justify its construction. Severence [sic] of the road from the timber sales for purposes of NEPA * * * is not permissible.

5.   Thomas v. Peterson also considered the Forest Service's argument that it was sufficient to consider the cumulative environmental effects in NEPA documentation it would do in connection with the timber sales, <u>after</u> the road was built. The court would have none of it:

A central purpose of an EIS is to force the consideration of environmental impacts in the decisionmaking process. That purpose requires that the NEPA process be integrated with agency planning "at the earliest possible time," 40 C.F.R. § 1501.2, and the purpose cannot be fully served if consideration of the cumulative effects of successive, interdependent steps is delayed until the first step has already been taken.

The location, the timing, or other aspects of the timber sales, or even the decision whether to sell any timber at all affects the location, routing, construction techniques, and other aspects of the road, or even the need for its construction. But the consideration of cumulative impacts will serve little purpose if the road has already been built. Building the road swings the balance decidedly in favor of timber sales even if such sales would have been disfavored had road and sales been considered together before the road was built. Only by selling the timber can the bulk of the expense of building the road be recovered. * * *

The Forest Service argues that the sales are too uncertain and too far in the future for their impacts to be analyzed along with that of the road. This comes close to saying that building the road now is itself irrational. We decline to accept that conclusion. Rather, we believe that if the sales are sufficiently certain to justify construction of the road, then they are sufficiently certain for their environmental impacts to be analyzed along with those of the road. * * * Where agency actions are sufficiently related so as to be "connected" within the meaning of the CEQ regulations, the agency may not escape compliance with the regulations by proceeding with one action while characterizing the others as remote or speculative.

NEPA's ubiquitousness, cutting across the grain of federal decision-making writ large, raises many interesting questions, and the courts have answered many of them. The following notes explore some of those issues most pertinent to federal land and natural resources decisionmaking.

NEPA AND FEDERAL "INACTION"

In many situations the federal land managers have authority to take action, such as issuing mineral leases or executing contracts to sell timber, but no mandate to do so. In *Kleppe v. Sierra Club*, supra, the Interior Department could have undertaken a regional coal development program, but chose not to do so. In some situations, the federal land manager could object to others (such as state governments) taking actions on federal lands, but choose not to do so. How does NEPA fit into these decisions not to take action? In Defenders of Wildlife v. Andrus, 627 F.2d 1238 (D.C.Cir. 1980), the court addressed whether the Secretary of the Interior had to comply with NEPA when he does not act to prevent the State of Alaska from conducting a program to exterminate wolves on an area of federal land as part of a wildlife management program. (The authority of Alaska to conduct the hunt, and the authority of the Secretary to object, are both considered in Chapter Ten, pp. 895–900 infra.) The court had this to say:

> Our discussion of that question must center around the fact that, while the plain language of the statute calls for an impact statement when there is "major Federal action," here it is the Secretary's *inaction* which is complained of. Appellees, as we understand them, respond that (1) the environmental consequences of inaction may be greater than the consequences of action, and (2) the purpose of the statute is to ensure that environmentally informed decisions are made, not simply that the environmental consequences of all federal programs are considered. We acknowledge the truth of the first response, but we do not understand it to change the language of the statute.
>
> As to the second response, we agree that a purpose of the statute is to ensure that environmentally informed decisions are made. Neverthe-

less, as it is written, NEPA only refers to decisions which the agency anticipates will lead to actions. This common-sense reading of the statute is confirmed by the statutory directive that the impact statement is to be part of a "recommendation or report" on a "proposal" for action. That is, only when an agency reaches the point in its deliberations when it is ready to propose a course of action need it be ready to produce an impact statement. Logically, then, if the agency decides not to act, and thus not to present a proposal to act, the agency never reaches a point at which it need prepare an impact statement. * * *

Appellees argue that, by not inhibiting an action of a private party or a state or local government, the federal government makes that action its own within the meaning of NEPA. * * * [But no court has] held that there is "federal action" where an agency has done nothing more than fail to prevent the other party's action from occurring. * * * To borrow from the language of the criminal law of conspiracy, we may say that federal "approval" of another party's action does not make that action federal unless the federal government undertakes some "overt act" in furtherance of that other party's project. * * *

Our somewhat exact reading of section 102(2)(C) [of NEPA] and our insistence on an "overt act" may seem literal and formalistic. But our approach is not only consonant with, but is commanded by, the principles and spirit of NEPA. This court has had occasion before to rule on requests that environmental impact statements be required beyond the bounds of the possible. In Sierra Club v. Andrus, 581 F.2d 895 (1978), we were asked to require the Department of the Interior to prepare statements to accompany appropriation requests for all programs having significant environmental consequences. We declined to do so except "when the request for budget approval and appropriations is one that ushers in a considered programmatic course following a programmatic review." Id. at 903. What we said then bears repeating in some detail now:

> Plaintiffs' logic-based contention * * * leads logically to the conclusion that an EIS would have to accompany every budget request for the annual operation of an environmental-conservation program, or indeed of an agency whose activities may have significant environmental impact. The principle of reductio ad absurdum is part of the landscape of logic. Plaintiffs have not suggested a limiting principle to their logic.

> * * * There is a danger of overburdening NEPA by spreading its mandate too widely. The environmental analysis required by NEPA is governed by the rule of reason, as we have held in determining the scope of realistic alternatives to the proposed action and the intensity of the required analysis. A rule requiring preparation of an EIS on the annual budget request for virtually every ongoing program would trivialize NEPA * * *.

* * * NEPA would be impaired in the manner of which we warned in Sierra Club v. Andrus were we now to decide for appellees. No agency

could meet its NEPA obligations if it had to prepare an environmental impact statement every time the agency had power to act but did not do so. Nor does it suffice to say that an agency's burden would be kept to a reasonable level by the fact that no impact statement is needed when the inaction could have no significant environmental results, for we have held that an agency which decides not to issue an impact statement must provide a written explanation of its reasons for that decision. This requirement is necessary to ensure that the agency's decision is well-considered and to provide a basis for the judicial review of the agency's decision. It would be an imaginative and vigorous agency indeed which could identify and prepare all the statements and explanations appellees' reading of NEPA would have the statute demand.

Questions: 1. Is the line between action and inaction as precise as the Court seems to assume? Suppose, for example, the Secretary's wildlife experts had proposed that he issue an order closing the lands to the state kill program? Would an EIS have to be prepared on that recommendation, or before the Secretary makes a decision on whether to accept or reject the recommendation?

2.   If the Secretary, faced with Alaska's proposal to kill wolves on BLM land, had decided to close the lands to the state program, would she have first prepare an EIS on that decision? Or could she close the lands first, and then prepare the EIS?

3.   If an oil company makes a proposal to the Secretary that she issue leases on a particular area of federal lands is open to leasing, can she take the "action" of rejecting the proposal without complying with NEPA?

4.   The State of Tennessee owns Reelfoot Lake, and leases it to the U.S. Fish and Wildlife Service for use as a national wildlife refuge. The lease does not expressly reserve any authority in the State to manipulate the Lake's water level. The State nevertheless proposes to draw down the water level for several months in an attempt to improve sport fishing spawning habitat. No federal funds are involved, and the federal agency stands aside to allow the state agency to operate the spillway to release the water to accomplish the drawdown. Opponents of the drawdown sue to enjoin it, arguing the federal agency should have first prepared an EIS. What result? See Bunch v. Hodel, 793 F.2d 129 (6th Cir.1986) (distinguishing *Defenders of Wildlife* on the grounds that here, federal agency approval for the state action was necessary under the terms of the lease, and therefore "abdication of the Service's responsibilities under the terms of the lease" does not "transform the drawdown into state action" exempt from NEPA).

5.   Some cases apply the idea that if the agency's action does not cause any change in the physical environment, NEPA is not triggered. See, e.g., Sabine River Authority v. U.S. Department of the Interior, 951 F.2d 669 (5th Cir.1992), cert. denied sub nom Texas Water Conservation Ass'n v. Department of the Interior, 506 U.S. 823 (1992) (no requirement to do EIS when the U.S. Fish & Wildlife Service accepts the donation of a non-development easement on 3800 acres of high-quality wetlands and migrato-

ry waterfowl habitat). The Ninth Circuit has taken this idea somewhat further to hold that NEPA does not apply to the designation of "critical habitat" under the Endangered Species Act (ESA) because (1) Congress intended that the ESA critical habitat procedures displace the NEPA requirements, (2) NEPA does not apply to actions that do not change the physical environment, and (3) to apply NEPA to the ESA would "further the purposes of neither statute." Douglas County v. Babbitt, 48 F.3d 1495 (9th Cir.1995).

Another kind of agency "inaction"—where the agency distanced itself from the need to approve individual private actions on federal lands it managed—was involved in Sierra Club v. Penfold, 857 F.2d 1307 (9th Cir.1988). BLM adopted rules governing hardrock mining on federal land to carry out a provision of the Federal Land Policy and Management Act that obligated the Department to "prevent unnecessary or undue degradation" from activities on the federal lands. The BLM rules created a category of mine called a "Notice" mine, described by the court as one which

> causes a cumulative surface disturbance of five acres or less per year. 43 C.F.R. § 3809.1–3(a). A Notice mining operation does not require approval by BLM before a miner can commence developing the mine. 43 C.F.R. § 3809.1–3(b). However, at least 15 days before beginning to mine, the Notice mine operator must give notice or a letter to BLM informing it of the address of the mine operator, identifying the mining claim and describing the activities proposed and the proposed start-up date. 43 C.F.R. § 3809.1–3(c). Additionally, the notice must include a statement that reclamation of disturbed areas will be completed and that reasonable measures will be taken to prevent unnecessary or undue degradation of the lands during operations. 43 C.F.R. § 3809.1–3(d). After BLM has reviewed the notice, it sends the operator a return letter indicating either: (a) the information in the notice is complete and meets federal mining regulations contained in 43 C.F.R. § 3809.1–3(c); or that (b) the notice is incomplete and mining operations may not begin until 15 days after completed notice is received. *BLM Manual: H–3809–1–Surface Management.* If an operator fails to file a notice he can be subject to, at the discretion of the BLM, being served with a notice of noncompliance or being enjoined from operating and held liable for damages for the unlawful acts until a notice is filed. 43 C.F.R. § 3809.3–2. Notice mine operations are subject to monitoring by BLM to ensure operators are not causing unnecessary or undue degradation. 43 C.F.R. § 3809.1–3(e). Periodic inspections to ensure compliance are permitted. 43 C.F.R. § 3809.3–6. Failure to prevent degradation may cause the operator to be subject to a notice of noncompliance. 43 C.F.R. § 3809.1–3(f). * * *

Sierra Club argues that BLM's processing of Notice mines pursuant to the five-acre rule in 43 C.F.R. § 3809.1–3 amounts to major federal action triggering NEPA * * * compliance in the form of EA's * * * for each proposed mine. As indicia of major Federal action, Sierra Club points to BLM's extensive review involvement of Notice mines, BLM's policies and practices in implementing Notice regulations, the compliance inspections which BLM conducts, the approval BLM grants and its letter to the operator to this effect, NEPA's broad mandate obligating compliance to the fullest extent possible and the Federal Land Policy and Management Act's, 43 U.S.C. § 1732(b), charge to take any action necessary to prevent unnecessary or undue degradation.[12]

We believe BLM does not sufficiently involve itself in the approval process to render Notice mine review a major Federal action requiring NEPA compliance. Without NEPA's applicability, an EA on each Notice mine is not required. * * * [W]e believe BLM's review of Notice mines is only a marginal federal action rather than a major action. There is no allegation that Notice mine operators receive federal funding. BLM's "systematic approval" of Notice mines is discretionary. BLM cannot require approval before an operation can commence developing the mine. 43 C.F.R § 3809.1–3(b). BLM's obligation to monitor compliance with statutory and regulatory requirements to deter undue degradation is insufficient. The right of BLM to issue notices of noncompliance is also insufficient action. While BLM does possess the authority to commence enforcement proceedings, see 43 C.F.R. § 3809.3–2, the CEQ has established that actions *"do not include* bringing judicial or administrative civil or criminal enforcement actions." 40 C.F.R. § 1508.18(a) (emphasis added).

Questions: 1. Might a mine that disturbs four acres per year significantly affect the environment? Does *Penfold* allow a federal agency to escape the requirements of NEPA by categorically excluding certain actions from it by regulation (as here, with the less-than-five-acres exemption)? BLM adopted the "notice" mine approach largely because of the paperwork involved in applying NEPA to hundreds of small-scale, "mom and pop" mining operations scattered across Alaska. New BLM rules on this subject, and the general subject of hardrock mining regulation, is found in Chapter 7, infra pp. 636–39.

2. Suppose BLM's EIS on its overall regulatory program (see footnote 12 in *Penfold*) showed that mines which disturbed fewer than five acres of federal land per year cause a lot of environmental damage. May the BLM nevertheless create an exclusion for them in the regulations, and allow them to escape NEPA analysis? Is that consistent with NEPA?

12. In promulgating the placer mining regulations, BLM did prepare an EIS before adopting the regulatory scheme. In challenging the Notice mine regulations, Sierra Club does not contest the sufficiency of this EIS as used to make the distinction between Plan, Notice and Casual mines. The district court found that BLM did not act arbitrarily and capriciously in making these distinctions based upon the EIS filed. Sierra Club does not argue on appeal that the district court erred in finding the regulations were not arbitrary and capricious. We therefore find Sierra Club's argument incongruous in this regard—for it is inconsistent to allege Notice mines require an EA when what constitutes a Notice mine was determined by an EIS, the sufficiency of which was not challenged.

3.   The CEQ regulations authorize federal agencies to adopt "categorical exclusions" of actions that do not require NEPA analysis. See 40 C.F.R. § 1508.41. For a considered discussion of how that process works, in connection with rejecting a challenge to a National Park Service determination that regulations putting restrictions on bicycle use off-road in the Golden Gate National Recreation Area were categorically excluded from NEPA analysis, see Bicycle Trails Council of Marin v. Babbitt, 82 F.3d 1445, 1456–57 (9th Cir.1996).

4.   In National Parks & Conservation Ass'n v. Babbitt, 241 F.3d 722 (9th Cir.2001), the court rejected the National Park Service's FONSI on its adoption of a vessel management plan for Glacier Bay National Park and Preserve which would increase large cruise ship visits to Glacier Bay by up to 72%, finding, among other things, its description of proposed mitigating measures and their possible effectiveness insufficient.

NEPA's APPLICATION TO NON–DISCRETIONARY FEDERAL ACTIONS

In South Dakota v. Andrus, 614 F.2d 1190 (8th Cir.) cert. denied, 449 U.S. 822 (1980), the question was whether the Department of the Interior had to prepare an EIS on a decision to issue a mineral patent to Pittsburgh, a mining company, for 240 acres of federal land. The patent conveyed fee simple title to the land, which was covered by a mining claim Pittsburgh had located under the Mining Law of 1872. Under the law then in effect, the claimant became entitled to a patent once it showed the "discovery" of a "valuable mineral deposit" on the claim, but a claimant did not need a patent in order to extract minerals from the claim. The court had this to say:

> We turn first to the question whether the granting of a mineral patent constitutes an "action" within the meaning of NEPA. As the district court noted, it is well established that the issuance of a mineral patent is a ministerial act. * * * Ministerial acts * * * have generally been held outside the ambit of NEPA's EIS requirement. Reasoning that the primary purpose of the impact statement is to aid agency decision making, courts have indicated that nondiscretionary acts should be exempt from the requirement. * * * In light of these decisions, it is at least doubtful that the Secretary's nondiscretionary approval of a mineral patent constitutes an "action" under § 102(2)(C).

> But even if a ministerial act may in some circumstances fall within § 102(2)(C), we still cannot say that the issuance of a mineral patent is a "major" federal action under the statute. * * * [T]he granting of a mineral patent does not enable the private party * * * to do anything. Unlike the case where a lease, permit or license is required before the particular project can begin, the issuance of a mineral patent is not a precondition which enables a party to begin mining operations. 30 U.S.C. § 26. * * * In light of the fact that a mineral patent in actuality is not a federal determination which enables the party to mine, we

conclude in present context that the granting of such a patent is not a "major" federal action within the meaning of § 102(2)(C).

In reaching this conclusion, we do not decide the question whether an EIS should be required at some point after the mineral patent has issued. * * * We note that Pittsburgh's proposed mining project is substantial and that if Pittsburgh decides to build the mine many actions may be necessary. For example, the claims at issue will presumably need permits from the Forest Service for roads, water pipelines and railroad rights of way. 43 U.S.C. § 1761(a)(1) and (a)(6). Moreover, the company may possibly seek to make land exchanges with the Forest Service. We leave to another day the question whether an EIS would be required in connection with any one or more such actions.

Question: 1. Although the court was correct in holding that Pittsburgh did not need a patent in order to extract minerals, the patent did free the company from federal land regulation that would otherwise would apply. After getting the patent, in other words, it might have been able to put a ski area or condominium development on the land without further federal approval. Does that suggest the court is wrong on the application of NEPA?

CAN A FEDERAL AGENCY AVOID AN EIS BY REGULATING THE PROPOSED ACTIVITY TO RESTRICT ITS IMPACT?

In Cabinet Mountains Wilderness v. Peterson, 685 F.2d 678 (D.C.Cir. 1982), environmental advocates challenged a Forest Service decision not to prepare an EIS on a proposal by ASARCO mining company to engage in minerals exploration in a wilderness area in northwestern Montana. Of particular concern were the impacts on the area's high quality grizzly bear habitat. Excerpts from the NEPA discussion follow (the Endangered Species Act issues raised are considered further below).

Both the Forest Service and the FWS concluded that the ASARCO proposal could have an adverse impact upon the grizzly bears, particularly when other concurrent activities in the Cabinet Mountains area were taken into account. Numerous specific recommendations were made to avoid this impact and mitigation measures to protect the grizzly bears were imposed upon the proposal. * * * [T]hese measures were designed to "completely compensate" both the adverse effects of the ASARCO proposal and the cumulative effects of other activities on the bears and their habitat. In light of the imposition of these measures, the Forest Service concluded that implementation of the ASARCO proposal would not result in "any significant effects upon the quality of the human environment." Therefore an EIS was found to be unnecessary.

This court has established four criteria for reviewing an agency's decision to forego preparation of an EIS: (1) whether the agency took a "hard look" at the problem; (2) whether the agency identified the relevant areas of environmental concern; (3) as to the problems studied and identified, whether the agency made a convincing case that the impact was insignificant; and (4) if there was impact of true significance, whether the agency convincingly established that changes in the project sufficiently reduced it to a minimum. The fourth criterion permits consideration of any mitigation measures that the agency imposed on the proposal. As this court noted, "changes in the project are not legally adequate to avoid an impact statement *unless they permit a determination that such impact as remains, after the change, is not 'significant.'* " [Maryland–National Capital Park and Planning Comm'n v. U.S. Postal Service, 487 F.2d 1029, 1040 (D.C.Cir.1973) (emphasis supplied)] Other courts have also permitted the effect of mitigation measures to be considered in determining whether preparation of an EIS is necessary. * * * Logic also supports this result. NEPA's EIS requirement is governed by the rule of reason, * * * and an EIS must be prepared only when significant environmental impacts will occur as a result of the proposed action. If, however, the proposal is modified prior to implementation by adding specific mitigation measures which completely compensate for any possible adverse environmental impacts stemming from the original proposal, the statutory threshold of significant environmental effects is not crossed and an EIS is not required. To require an EIS in such circumstances would trivialize NEPA and would "diminish its utility in providing useful environmental analysis for major federal actions that truly affect the environment."

Because the mitigation measures were properly taken into consideration by the agency, we have no difficulty in concluding that the Forest Service's decision that an EIS was unnecessary was not arbitrary or capricious. The record indicates that the Forest Service carefully considered the ASARCO proposal, was well informed on the problems presented, identified the relevant areas of environmental concern, and weighed the likely impacts.* * *

Finally, we perceive no difficulty in reading the project modifications as requiring compliance by ASARCO. The Forest Service approved the proposal subject to the restrictions and mitigation measures which had been devised during the review process. Failure to abide by the modifications would be contrary to terms of the approval. If necessary, the agency can redress any violations by revoking or suspending its permission to conduct the drilling program.

We conclude that the agency's decision not to prepare an EIS was reasonable and adequately supported. * * * [T]he decision as to whether an EIS should be prepared is left to the agency's informed discretion. * * * For us to overturn it under these circumstances would require an unjustifiable intrusion into the administrative process. We refuse to intrude.

The opposite result was reached by another circuit court the same year in another case involving hardrock mining activity on national forest land.

In Foundation for North American Wild Sheep v. United States Dept. of Agriculture, 681 F.2d 1172 (9th Cir.1982), the Forest Service had decided not to prepare an EIS on its decision to issue a permit to a mining company allowing the reconstruction of a road to reach its mine. The primary issue was the impact of the mine on a resident Desert Bighorn Sheep herd. Excerpts follow:

> The Service vigorously asserts that the mitigation measures incorporated into the chosen alternative (Alternative *B*) reduce the potential impact upon the Bighorn to insignificant levels. We cannot agree.

> Alternative *B* * * * provides for the closure of Road 2N06 from April 1 until June 30 in order to avoid undue disturbance of the sheep during the "lambing" season. Second, Alternative *B* requires the maintenance of a secure, locked gate and a 24–hour guard at the entrance to Road 2N06. Third, a monitoring system is to be undertaken and Road 2N06 is to be closed in the event of a forty percent reduction in the use of the area by the sheep. Finally, the Service contends that the area can be repopulated with Bighorn sheep from other areas if necessary. The efficacy of these mitigation measures was severely attacked by numerous responses to the original draft of the EA. * * *

> * * * [I]t appears that the continued use of the lambing area through which Road 2N06 passes is essential to the continued productivity of the herd at issue here. Respondents to the draft EA strongly attacked the Service's assumption that the sheep would return to the area to perform their most sensitive function after that area had been invaded by man for nine months. The Service provided no basis for its assumption in the EA. Evaluation of the reasonableness of this assumption is doubly difficult because of the Service's failure to provide data regarding the quantity of traffic expected to flow through the area. The absence of this crucial information renders a decision regarding the sheep's reaction to the traffic on Road 2N06 necessarily uninformed. Without some sort of informed idea of how the sheep will react to Road 2N06 while it is open, it is impossible to determine whether they will return to the area to "lamb" once the road has been closed. Certainly substantial questions are raised whether the closure of Road 2N06 for three months will serve to mitigate the potential harm to the sheep. Where such substantial questions are raised, an EIS must be prepared.

> We also find the provision for a locked gate and a guard at the entrance to Road 2N06 insufficient to reduce the environmental impact of the proposed reopening of the road to less than significant levels. Initially, it is noteworthy that one of the assumptions expressly set forth in the EA is that increased unauthorized traffic on Road 2N06 will result from the reopening of the road regardless of the precautions taken to prevent such traffic. Thus the efficacy of this measure is, under the Service's own assumptions, doubtful. Further this mitigation provision will only affect the quantum of harm resulting from unauthorized traffic. Consequently, it is manifestly insufficient to mitigate the harm to the sheep emanating from the authorized use of Road 2N06 by

Curtis ore trucks and is inadequate to remedy the flaws contained in the Service's analysis of that harm.

We also find the monitoring and repopulation provisions contained in Alternative *B* insufficient to support a reasonable conclusion that the reopening of Road 2N06 will have no significant impact upon the quality of the human environment. NEPA expresses a Congressional determination that procrastination on environmental concerns is no longer acceptable. Yet the provision requiring closure of Road 2N06 in the event of a forty percent reduction in the use of the area by the sheep is just this type of procrastination. It represents an agency decision to act now and deal with the environmental consequences later. Such conduct is plainly inconsistent with the broad mandate of NEPA. Moreover, the provision implicitly treats a forty percent reduction in the sheep's use of the area surrounding Road 2N06 as insignificant. No support for such a conclusion is found in the record.

Reliance on the repopulation scheme * * * [ignores the fact that for repopulation] to be required, there must necessarily be an initial reduction in the population of the herd as well as a corresponding reduction in the sheep population as a whole. This overall population reduction was ignored by the Service. * * * Moreover, the transplant of sheep from another area to the area at issue here would necessarily result in a reduction in sheep population in the area from which the transplanted sheep were removed. This factor was also ignored by the Service. * * *

We are mindful that it is not the province of this Court to substitute its judgment for that of the Service. Yet it must also be remembered that "[t]he spirit of the [NEPA] would die aborning if the facile, ex parte decision that the project was minor or did not significantly affect the environment were too well shielded from impartial review." Save Our Ten Acres v. Kreger, 472 F.2d 463, 466 (5th Cir.1973).

In the present case, the Service failed * * * to consider numerous issues obviously relevant to a determination of the likely effect of reopening Road 2N06 on the environment. Under these circumstances, we conclude that the Service's determination that no EIS was required was plainly unreasonable. * * *.

Questions: 1. The Supreme Court's subsequent decision in *Methow Valley,* supra p. 392, held that NEPA does not require adoption or even a detailed discussion of mitigation measures. Does *Methow Valley* suggest the discussion of mitigation measures in *Cabinet Mountains* was unnecessary? Or does the fact that the former involved the adequacy of an EIS once prepared, and the latter involved whether an EIS was necessary, mean that the two decisions are consistent with each other?

2. What explains the difference in result in *Cabinet Mountains* and *Foundation for North American Wild Sheep*? The facts in the record? The degree of deference accorded to the agency? Differences in perception of the importance of the EIS to decisionmaking?

3.   Some courts have held that a mitigation plan "need not be legally enforceable, funded, or even in final form to comply with NEPA's procedural requirements." National Parks & Conservation Ass'n v. U.S. Dept. of Transp., 222 F.3d 677, 681 n. 4 (9th Cir.2000). A court "need only be satisfied that the agency took the requisite 'hard look' at possible mitigation measures; but, on the other hand, a 'perfunctory description' is not adequate," and the court acknowledged that the line between the two "is not well defined." Okanogan Highlands Alliance v. Williams, 236 F.3d 468, 473, 477 (9th Cir.2000)

TO WHAT EXTENT CAN AN AGENCY "SEGMENT" OR "STAGE" ITS DECISONMAKING TO AVOID ANALYZING THE CONSEQUENCES OF LATER ACTIONS EARLIER?

Thomas v. Peterson, supra pp. 409–11, read NEPA to require the agency to assess, in connection with a particular action, the environmental impacts of later actions that were dependent on that action—there, timber sales that would be facilitated by the road building action before the agency. The issue of cumulative impact and addressing interdependent actions together sometimes arises in a different way. There has been a good deal of litigation, with varying results, over how to integrate NEPA requirements into the process for leasing oil and gas on federal lands. In Sierra Club v. Peterson, 717 F.2d 1409 (D.C.Cir.1983), plaintiff had challenged a Forest Service decision not to prepare an EIS on a decision to issue oil and gas leases on an area of federal lands, when the lease would contain a lease term (a so-called "no surface occupancy" or NSO stipulation) precluding the lessee from engaging in any activities on the lease surface without specific approval of the federal agency. The Forest Service said it would comply with NEPA later, when the lessee came to it with a proposal to drill the leasehold or otherwise occupy the surface. The district court ruled for the Forest Service because the stipulation "will effectively insure that the environment will not be significantly affected" until there is further NEPA analysis, and the Sierra Club did not appeal.

But the Club has also challenged a Forest Service decision not to do an EIS on other leases, where the lease stipulations retained only authority to "condition" surface disturbing activities to "mitigate" any environmental harm which might result. The court of appeals ruled for the Club:

> [O]nce the land is leased [with this stipulation] the Department no longer has the authority to *preclude* surface disturbing activities even if the environmental impact of such activity is significant. The Department can only impose "mitigation" measures upon a lessee who pursues surface disturbing exploration and/or drilling activities. None of the stipulations expressly provides that the Department or the Forest Service can *prevent* a lessee from conducting surface disturbing activities.[7] Thus, with respect to the smaller area with which we are

7.   * * *   In response to the court's question as to whether the agency could re- fuse to approve a lessee's plan to build an access road (a surface disturbing activity)

here concerned, the decision to allow surface disturbing activities has been made at the *leasing stage* and, under NEPA, this is the point at which the environmental impacts of such activities must be evaluated.

NEPA requires an agency to evaluate the environmental effects of its action at the point of commitment. The purpose of an EIS is to insure that the agency considers all possible courses of action and assesses the environmental consequences of each proposed action. The EIS is a decision-making tool intended to "insure that * * * environmental amenities and values may be given appropriate consideration in decision making * * *." 42 U.S.C. § 4332(2)(B). Therefore, the appropriate time for preparing an EIS is *prior* to a decision, when the decision maker retains a maximum range of options. * * * On the facts of this case, that "critical time," insofar as lands leased without a NSO Stipulation are concerned, occurred at the point of leasing.

Notwithstanding the assurance that a later site-specific environmental analysis will be made, in issuing these leases the Department made an irrevocable commitment to allow *some* surface disturbing activities, including drilling and road building. While theoretically the proposed two-stage environmental analysis may be acceptable, in this situation the Department has not complied with NEPA because it has sanctioned activities which have the potential for disturbing the environment without fully assessing the possible environmental consequences.

The Department asserts that it cannot accurately evaluate the consequences of drilling and other surface disturbing activities until site-specific plans are submitted. If, however, the Department is in fact concerned that it cannot foresee and evaluate the environmental consequences of leasing without site-specific proposals, then it may delay preparation of an EIS provided that it reserves both the authority to *preclude* all activities pending submission of site-specific proposals and the authority to *prevent* proposed activities if the environmental consequences are unacceptable. If the Department chooses not to retain the authority to *preclude* all surface disturbing activities, then an EIS assessing the full environmental consequences of leasing must be prepared at the point of commitment—when the leases are issued. The Department can decide, in the first instance, by which route it will proceed.

Notes and Questions. 1. For non-NEPA discussion of restrictive stipulations in leases and contracts, see Chapter 3G, supra p. 255, and Chapter 7, pp. 652–67 infra.

during exploration, counsel for the government stated:

> There's a very fine line between preclusion and strict control. The agency has retained strict control. They have the authority. They have the right to put certain conditions on road building.

[The government has] never contended that we could preclude all exploration and all development in these non-highly sensitive areas. * * *

2. The Ninth Circuit reached a result similar to *Peterson* in Conner v. Burford, 848 F.2d 1441 (9th Cir.1988), and Bob Marshall Alliance v. Hodel, 852 F.2d 1223 (9th Cir.1988), cert. denied *sub nom.* Kohlman v. Bob Marshall Alliance, 489 U.S. 1066 (1989). In the latter case, the court went further, holding that NEPA requires consideration of the alternative of "no–action" (in this context, not leasing at all), before issuing oil and gas leases, even ones that contain an NSO stipulation. The court explained that "consideration of alternatives is critical to the goals of NEPA even where a proposed action does not trigger the EIS process. * * * An EIS is required where there has been an irretrievable commitment of resources; but unresolved conflicts as to the proper use of available resources may exist well before that point. Thus the consideration of alternatives requirement is both independent of, and broader than, the EIS requirement." The court went on to say that because the lease sale "opens the door to potentially harmful post–leasing activity, * * * NEPA therefore requires that alternatives—including the no–leasing option—be given full and meaningful consideration." 852 F.2d at 1229. The court enjoined new leasing, and all activities on existing leases in the area, "until all statutory requirements are met." Id. at 1230.

3. On the other hand, in Park County Resource Council v. U.S. Department of Agriculture, 817 F.2d 609 (10th Cir.1987), the court, without closely analyzing the stipulations in the lease to see how much authority the federal agency retained, held that the federal agency was not required to prepare an EIS prior to issuing oil and gas leases on national forest land. The agency had done an environmental assessment exceeding 100 pages in length which concluded that an EIS was not required. The court summed up this way:

> [I]n light of the substantial EA, of the mitigating lease restrictions requiring further environmental appraisal before any surface disturbing activities commence, of the nebulousness of future drilling activity at the time of leasing, and of the continuing supervision of the federal agencies involved over future activities, the agency's decision in this case that the lease issuance itself was not a major federal action significantly affecting the quality of the human environment was not unreasonable. Furthermore, there clearly was a rational basis to defer preparation of an EIS until a more concrete proposal was submitted to BLM.

4. There has been much commentary on the issues raised by these cases. See e.g., Marla Mansfield, Through the Forest of the Onshore Oil and Gas Leasing Controversy Toward a Paradigm of Meaningful NEPA Compliance, XXIV Land & Water L.Rev. 85 (1989); Jan Laitos, Paralysis by Analysis in the Forest Service Oil and Gas Leasing Program, XXVI Land & Water L.Rev. 105 (1991); John F. Shepherd, Key NEPA Issues Affecting Oil and Gas Development on Federal Lands, 37 Rocky Mtn.Min.L.Inst. 15–1 (1991). In Sierra Club v. Hathaway, 579 F.2d 1162 (9th Cir.1978), staged NEPA compliance was upheld for federal geothermal leasing.

5. In City of Williams v. Dombeck, 151 F.Supp.2d 9 (D.D.C.2001), the court held that the U.S. Forest Service had violated NEPA when it

approved a land exchange with a private developer that made possible a proposed mixed use commercial development outside the south border of Grand Canyon National Park. (Some but not all environmentalists supported the development because it involved removing facilities from the park; the legal challenge was spearheaded by area businesses who did not want competition.) The EIS on the land exchange briefly considered a couple of options for how water would be supplied to the development, but deferred further consideration until after further NEPA analysis. The court found the water delivery system was such an "interdependent part" of the "larger action," the meaning of the CEQ regulations, 40 C.F.R. § 1508.25(a)(1)(iii), that this deferral was improper. For another NEPA decision by a different court on the same proposal, this one finding, among other things, that the Forest Service had improperly "tiered" its EIS to the Grand Canyon National Park's general management plan, see Sierra Club v. Dombeck, 161 F.Supp.2d 1052 (D.Ariz.2001).

RELIEF FOR NEPA VIOLATIONS

If a court finds a violation of NEPA, should it *automatically* enjoin agency action until full compliance with NEPA is achieved? Or should it instead first balance the equities, consider the harm to the government, and weigh the public interest? In Save the Yaak Committee v. Block, 840 F.2d 714, 722 (9th Cir.1988), the court said:

"The basis for injunctive relief is irreparable injury and inadequacy of legal remedies." Amoco Production Co. v. Village of Gambell, 480 U.S. 531, 542 (1987). [Eds. *Amoco* did not involve NEPA.] "In each case, a court must balance the competing claims of injury and must consider the effect on each party of granting or withholding of the requested relief." Id. Additionally, a Congressional grant of jurisdiction to insure compliance with a statute will not ordinarily limit the court's discretion to issue or deny injunctions unless that statute "in so many words, or by a necessary and inescapable inference, restricts the court's jurisdiction in equity." Id. There is nothing in NEPA to indicate that Congress intended to limit this court's equitable jurisdiction. Northern Cheyenne Tribe v. Hodel, 842 F.2d 224 (9th Cir.1988). Therefore, we must follow the above well-established principles governing an award of injunctive relief.

Although the Supreme Court has rejected a *Presumption* [sic] of irreparable injury when an agency fails to thoroughly evaluate the environmental impact of a proposed action, the Court has noted that "[e]nvironmental injury, by its nature, can seldom be adequately remedied by money damages and is often permanent or at least of long duration, i.e., irreparable." Amoco Production Co. v. Village of Gambell, at 545. Therefore, when environmental injury is "sufficiently likely, the balance of harms will usually favor the issuance of an injunction to protect the environment." Id.

We conclude that the risk of environmental injury is sufficiently likely to authorize enjoining further reconstruction and timber sales. Scientific evidence indicates that the reconstruction activities and related timber sales would have a severe impact on the Cabinet–Yaak Grizzly Bear populations. There is also evidence of the project's adverse effect on the caribou habitat. On the other side of the balance, this court has not been apprised of any counterveiling [sic] equities that would suggest that an injunction is inappropriate, or even counterproductive. * * * Nor is the court presently aware of any irreparable injury to third parties that would be caused by entry of an injunction against further reconstruction activities and timber sales. Accordingly, we enjoin the defendants from conducting further reconstruction and timber sales until the district court resolves these issues consistent with this opinion.

Notes and questions: 1. Is *Save the Yaak* 's approach to the relief question consistent with NEPA and its purposes? Compare the treatment of injunctive relief under the Endangered Species Act; see infra p. 459.

2. Another question involving relief for NEPA violations is raised when the government has already executed some sort of legal document, like a lease or a timber sale contract, on a decision a court later rules NEPA compliance has been lacking. May the court void and set aside the lease or contract altogether, or may it leave the lease or contract in place, and simply enjoin implementation until NEPA compliance is achieved? In Bob Marshall Alliance v. Lujan, 804 F.Supp. 1292 (D.Mont.1992), the court took up this question, left after the court of appeals had held that NEPA compliance on the decision to lease was inadequate, and concluded:

> The court finds the remedy properly imposed for the substantial procedural violations of NEPA * * * occasioned by the federal defendants' issuance of the Deep Creek leases is a cancellation of those leases. Cancellation of the leases is, in this court's opinion, the only remedy which will effectively foster NEPA's mandate requiring informed and meaningful consideration of alternatives to leasing the Deep Creek area, including the no-leasing option. Cancellation of the leases is the only remedy which will effectively ensure the goal envisioned by NEPA, particularly 42 U.S.C. § 4332(2)(E) (1982), by guaranteeing, to the fullest extent possible, that the defendant agencies have studied, developed and described alternatives, including the no-action alternative.

> [One of the lessees requested the opportunity to seek restitution of rental payments he had made to the federal government under one of the leases being voided, but the court said no, finding that he had] paid the rentals on the subject leases despite the knowledge of plaintiffs' environmental challenge to the leases' validity [and thus] * * * knowingly assumed the business risk of an injunction * * *.

Compare Northern Cheyenne Tribe v. Lujan, 804 F.Supp. 1281 (D.Mont. 1991), in which the court ruled in similar circumstances that the coal leases were void and the lessees entitled to full reimbursement.

WHEN ARE NEPA CHALLENGES "RIPE"?

Recall that in *Ohio Forestry*, Chapter 4, supra p. 294, the Court specifically held that a challenge to NEPA compliance with respect to a forest plan is ripe once the plan is published, even though challenges to the substantive provisions in the plan itself may be postponed until the provisions complained of actually move toward implementation. "[A] person with standing who is injured by a failure to comply with the NEPA procedure may complain of that failure at the time the failure takes place, for the claim can never get riper." 523 U.S. at 737, p. 298 supra.

NEPA AND PROPOSALS FOR LEGISLATION

NEPA expressly applies to "every [executive branch] recommendation or report on proposals for legislation * * * significantly affecting the quality of the human environment." In practice, however, NEPA documentation is rarely done on proposals for legislation. Relying in part on the CEQ regulations, the Supreme Court early on held, in Andrus v. Sierra Club, 442 U.S. 347 (1979), that agency requests for congressional appropriations are not proposals requiring EISs within the meaning of NEPA. Many non-appropriations legislative proposals originate in Congress (and NEPA does not apply to Congress) or outside the government rather than in the executive branch agencies. NEPA also does not apply to the President, according to the CEQ regulations (see 40 C.F.R. 1500.12) and some case law; see, e.g., State of Alaska v. Carter, 462 F.Supp. 1155 (D.Alaska 1978). Furthermore, even where legislative proposals are made by executive branch agencies, the requirement is difficult to enforce. The executive may simply serve as a "drafting service" to craft a bill for a legislator to introduce as his or her own. Even if an executive branch agency decided to prepare an EIS on one of its own proposals, Congress need not wait for the process to finish in order to take up the idea and act on it. Also, the legislative process itself may ventilate the proposal in much the same way that NEPA is designed to do. Finally, separation of powers concerns inhibit the courts from readily finding violations, or granting effective relief if they do. For these and other reasons, very few cases are brought seeking NEPA compliance on legislative proposals, and few courts have addressed how NEPA should be integrated into the legislative process. See Trustees for Alaska v. Hodel, 806 F.2d 1378 (9th Cir.1986); NRDC v. Lujan, 768 F.Supp. 870 (D.D.C.1991) (both involving legislative proposals concerning the Arctic National Wildlife Refuge); Wingfield v. Office of Management and Budget, 9 Env't Rep. Cas. 1961 (D.D.C.1977); Chamber of Commerce v. Department of the Interior, 439 F.Supp. 762 (D.D.C.1977).

THE PLACE OF NEPA IN PUBLIC NATURAL RESOURCES LAW

Preparation of environmental impact statements has become a significant industry in itself, financially benefiting biologists, hydrologists, sociologists, consultants, the paper industry, and many others, including lawyers. The process is time-consuming and can be expensive.

Is it worth it? Is NEPA just an example of proliferating paperwork and red tape that contributes to governmental inefficiency and frustration of citizens' legitimate aims? See, e.g., Joseph L. Sax, The (Unhappy) Truth About NEPA, 26 Okla. L.Rev. 239, 239 (1973) ("I know of no solid evidence to support the belief that requiring articulation, detailed findings or reasoned opinions enhances the integrity or propriety of the administrative decisions. I think the emphasis on the redemptive quality of procedural reform is about nine parts myth and one part coconut oil"). Or is NEPA a necessary device to ensure that bureaucrats engage in a minimum of thought before taking irreversible actions that may be very unwise—looking before they leap? Can that question really be answered without knowing what would have occurred without NEPA? Should the federal government be efficient? At least sufficiently so that its trains run on time?

The Supreme Court has taken the narrow view of every NEPA question it has chosen to decide. Besides the decisions already cited, see, e.g., Baltimore Gas & Elec. Co. v. NRDC, 462 U.S. 87 (1983); Weinberger v. Catholic Action of Hawaii, 454 U.S. 139 (1981); Strycker's Bay Neighborhood Council, Inc. v. Karlen, 444 U.S. 223 (1980). In spite of the Court's reluctance to allow the tail of environmental evaluation to wag the dog of normal government operations, NEPA remains an important element in federal land and resources management. To some extent it has been merged into somewhat more precise planning statutes, such as FLPMA and the National Forest Management Act of 1976, but it remains in force even as to such planning processes. The importance of NEPA as leading to change in federal land and resources law and administration has declined in inverse proportion to the growth of substantive statutory law governing public land management, agencies' increasing familiarity with NEPA requisites, and heightened congressional oversight of public land decisions. But the statute remains a major focus of federal resources litigation. Moreover, there are numerous examples where NEPA was influential in leading an agency to think more broadly and deeply about the consequences of its decision for other resources and values. For a useful set of commentaries, see Symposium on NEPA at Twenty: The Past, Present and Future of the National Environmental Policy Act, 20 Envt'l L. 447–810 (1990).

C. PLANNING PROCESSES FOR FEDERAL LANDS AND RESOURCES

Detailed, systematic planning to guide uses of the federal lands and resources, and to define the restrictions on their use, took hold in the last quarter of the twentieth century. After NEPA was enacted, Congress mandated formal planning procedures for all four of the federal land management agencies. In addition, some specific resource disposition statutes also ordain planning-type procedures; e.g., the Outer Continental Shelf Lands Act and the Federal Coal Leasing Amendments. Each of these systems shares certain characteristics and features, although they vary in the details. This section provides a brief, general overview of planning systems and requirements. Some more detail on the planning systems of some of the individual agencies are provided in the chapters covering specific natural resources and uses.

The planning processes overlap substantially with the NEPA processes. Indeed, resource management plans typically are either accompanied by EISs or actually take the form of an EIS. (The National Park Service early on experimented with preparing environmental assessments rather than full-blown environmental impact statements on plans, but abandoned the practice after protests and threatened litigation.) Lawsuits that challenge compliance with statutes governing planning also typically challenge the agency's NEPA compliance as well. This was illustrated by the Supreme Court's decision in *Ohio Forestry*, Chapter 4, supra p. 294, which was decided on ripeness grounds. (Justice Breyer's opinion contained a succinct summary of the national forest planning process.)

Planning may take place at a national, system-wide level, or by region, but usually it occurs at the level of a specific geographic unit such as a particular national park, wildlife refuge, national forest, or BLM planning area. Only the national forests have a statutory requirement for certain kinds of system-wide planning. The Forest and Rangeland Renewable Resources Planning Act of 1974 (usually called the Resources Planning Act or RPA), 88 Stat. 476, requires the Forest Service to prepare system-wide five year program documents, based on decennial assessments of conditions in the system. See 16 U.S.C. § 1602. These documents have generally been regarded as too general to be of much use, and recently Congress put a moratorium on further five year plans. See Pub.L.No. 106–291, § 321. Even where not mandated to do so by statute, agencies may prepare "vision documents" looking at their entire systems, and the Government Performance and Results Act (GPRA), 31 U.S.C. § 1101, enacted in 1993, requires all federal agencies to develop strategic plans that contain specific benchmarks for measuring progress toward long-term, programmatic goals.

A NOTE ON AGENCY "ORGANIC ACTS"

Planning systems are usually contained in a land management agency's "organic act." A few words of explanation are in order here. Each of the four major land management agencies has a statute (or interrelated set of statutes) that comprise its organic act. There is, however, no universally accepted definition for what an "organic act" actually is in the context of federal land management. See generally Robert Fischman, The National Wildlife Refuge System and the Hallmarks of Modern Organic Legislation, 29 Ecology L.Q. __ (forthcoming 2002). Historically, the term referred to a statute defining and establishing an organization of government; e.g., a municipality or territory. In public land law, the term has come to mean a charter for a particular land management agency and for the network of public lands under its care. Thus the National Park Service Organic Act of 1916 not only created the National Park Service, but also provided a structure to organize the somewhat disparate park units into a national park system. See 16 U.S.C. §§ 1–3. Amendments to that act in 1978 provided a framework for planning in that system. The Bureau of Land

Management's Organic Act is considered to be the Federal Land Policy and Management Act of 1976, 43 U.S.C. §§ 1701–82. It contains BLM's planning mandate. The U.S. Fish & Wildlife Service's Organic Act consists of legislation adopted in 1966 and overhauled in 1997, 16 U.S.C. §§ 668dd & ee. The National Forest Organic Act was first adopted in 1897, and then updated with the Multiple Use/Sustained Yield Act in 1960, and the National Forest Management Act of 1976. See 16 U.S.C. §§ 472–82, 528–31, 551.

The term "organic act" has no particular legal importance. The judiciary does not appear to attach special significance to whether statutory guidance appears in an agency's organic act instead of in other legislation. Many areas of the public lands (such as individual national parks) have specific statutes that apply only to them, and such specific statutory guidance controls over the terms of the organic act when the two differ. See, e.g., Robert L. Fischman, The Problem of Statutory Detail in National Park Establishment Legislation and its Relationship to Pollution Control Law, 74 Denv. U. L.Rev. 779 (1997). While "organic act" is widely used, it seems to be more a convenient description of a core body of authorities than anything else.

Charles F. Wilkinson & H. Michael Anderson, Land and Resource Planning in the National Forests*

64 Or.L.Rev. 1, 10–12, 69–70, 74 (1985).

For many reasons, planning on the public lands is inevitably imprecise. The plans must cover large areas of land and there is usually uncertainty over location of some resources, especially minerals and wildlife. Valuation of some resources, such as recreation and preservation, is difficult. Barriers to development, such as fragile soil conditions, may not be apparent until the implementation stage of the plan. Changing demands for various resources and the occurrence of natural phenomena such as insect infestation, droughts, and forest fires, add to the difficulty. For these and other reasons, planning on the federal lands has properly been called "an inexact art." * * *

The Forest Service planning statutes * * * require planning on several tiers, although the national forests are the basic functional unit at which plans are made and carried out. * * *

At the national forest level, land management plans (alluded to in the RPA** but elaborated upon in the NFMA) guide activities for ten to fifteen years and make projections for up to fifty years. These individual forest plans are the engines that drive the management process. Finally, the forest plans are implemented, usually at the ranger district or national

---

* Reprinted with permission of the Oregon Law Review.

** [Eds. This is the Forest and Rangeland Renewable Resources Planning Act of 1974, 88 Stat. 476, which was amended by (and subsumed in) the National Forest Management Act of 1976, and which together comprise the statutory base for planning on the national forests. 16 U.S.C. §§ 1600–1614.]

forest level, by permits, contracts, and other instruments; examples are timber contracts, camping permits, grazing leases, rights-of-way, and special land use permits. * * *

In Sierra Club v. Marita, 46 F.3d 606 (7th Cir.1995), the court summarized the national forest planning process as follows:

> The National Forest Management Act ("NFMA") requires the Secretary of Agriculture, who is responsible for the Forest Service, to develop "land and resource management plans" to guide the maintenance and use of resources within national forests. 16 U.S.C. §§ 1601–1604. In developing these plans the Secretary must determine the environmental impact these plans will have and discuss alternative plans, pursuant to the National Environmental Policy Act ("NEPA"), 42 U.S.C. § 4321 et seq. The Secretary must also consider the "multiple use and sustained yield of the several products and services obtained" from the forests, pursuant to the Multiple–Use Sustained–Yield Act ("MUSYA"), 16 U.S.C. §§ 528–531.

> The process for developing plans is quite elaborate. The Service must develop its management plans in conjunction with coordinated planning by a specially-designated interdisciplinary team, extensive public participation and comment, and related efforts of other federal agencies, state and local governments, and Indian tribes. 36 C.F.R. §§ 219.4–219.7. Directors at all levels of the Service participate in the planning process for a given national forest. The Forest Supervisor, who is responsible for one particular forest, initially appoints and then supervises the interdisciplinary team in order to help develop a plan and coordinate public participation. The Supervisor and team then develop a draft plan and draft environmental impact statement ("EIS"), which is presented to the public for comment. 36 C.F.R. §§ 219.10(a), 219.10(b). After a period of comment and revision, a final plan and final EIS are sent to the Regional Forester, who directs one of four national forest regions, for review. If the Regional Forester approves them, she issues both along with a Record of Decision ("ROD") explaining her reasoning. 36 C.F.R. § 219.10(c). An approved plan and final EIS may be appealed to the Forest Service Chief ("Chief") as a final administrative decision. 36 C.F.R. §§ 219.10(d), 211.18.

> The final plan is a large document, complete with glossary and appendices, dividing a forest into "management areas" and stipulating how resources in each of these areas will be administered. The plans are ordinarily to be revised on a ten-year cycle, or at least once every fifteen years. 36 C.F.R. § 219.10(g).

BLM planning has had a more checkered history. Professor Coggins has written: "Very little that could be dignified with the label of 'planning' for resource use took place" on the BLM-managed public lands until the last quarter century. The Law of Public Rangeland Management IV: FLPMA, PRIA, and the Multiple Use Mandate, 14 Envtl. L. 1, 80 (1983). Growing interest in outdoor recreation and concern about preservation of the resources of BLM lands eventually led to much more conflict among user interests on these lands, however, and eventually Congress was persuaded to create a comprehensive administrative process for addressing and hopefully resolving such disagreements. The Federal Land Policy and Management Act (FLPMA) of 1976 mandated a comprehensive planning system. It directed the Secretary of the Interior, in developing and revising BLM land use plans, to, *inter alia*:

(1) use and observe the principles of multiple use and sustained yield set forth in this and other applicable law;

(2) use a systematic interdisciplinary approach to achieve integrated consideration of physical, biological, economic, and other sciences;

(3) give priority to the designation and protection of areas of critical environmental concern;

(4) rely, to the extent it is available, on the inventory of the public lands, their resources, and other values;

(5) consider present and potential uses of the public lands;

(6) consider the relative scarcity of the values involved and the availability of alternative means (including recycling) and sites for realization of those values;

(7) weigh long-term benefits to the public against short-term benefits; * * *

43 U.S.C. § 1712(c). "Areas of critical environmental concern," or ACECs, are defined in § 1702(a). An ACEC designation is quite open-ended and flexible in both the purpose of the designation (encompassing public safety as well as historic, cultural, and ecosystem values), and the management restrictions that might flow from such a designation (the definition referring only to "special management attention"). There is a great deal of variation from plan to plan and state to state in the number and size of ACEC designations, and in the kinds of management restrictions that are imposed as a result. As of September 30, 2000, some 838 ACECs had been designated, encompassing some 14 million acres. PUBLIC LANDS STATISTICS 2000, Table 5–15.

Implementation of planning by BLM and the U.S. Forest Service has triggered much litigation (especially challenging the latter agency's plans), some of which is addressed in the subject matter chapters further below in this textbook.

Planning on National Wildlife Refuges managed by the U.S. Fish & Wildlife Service got a big boost with the 1997 enactment of the National Wildlife Refuge System Improvement Act, 16 U.S.C. §§ 668dd-ee(1). The Alaska National Interest Lands Conservation Act of 1980, which more than doubled the overall size of the national wildlife refuge system by adding nine new and expanding six existing refuges in Alaska, had required that plans be developed for each of the Alaska refuges. 94 Stat. 2394 (1980) (§ 304(g)(1)). In 1997, this mandate was applied across the system; each refuge must adopt a "comprehensive conservation plan" by 2012. 16 U.S.C. § 668dd(e)(1). Their content as specified by statute generally follows that of other federal land management agencies, except they must identify and describe areas "suitable for use as administrative sites or visitor facilities," and "opportunities for compatible wildlife-dependent recreational uses." 16 U.S.C. § 668dd(e)(2)(D), (F).

In the national park system, the National Park Service has for several decades developed "master plans" for many of its park units pursuant to its general management mandate. In modern times, these are called "general management plans," a label Congress used in 1978 when it directed the Park Service to prepare and revise "in a timely manner" such plans "for the preservation and use of each unit of the National Park System * * *." 16 U.S.C. § 1a–7(b). The statute requires such plans to include, at minimum:

(1) measures for the preservation of the area's resources;

(2) indications of types and general intensities of development (including visitor circulation and transportation patterns, systems and modes) associated with public enjoyment and use of the area, including general locations, timing of implementation, and anticipated costs;

(3) identification of and implementation commitments for visitor carrying capacities for all areas of the unit; and

(4) indications of potential modifications to the external boundaries of the unit, and the reasons therefor.

The National Park Service has likewise not escaped litigation over its planning processes. See, e.g., Isle Royale Boaters Ass'n v. Norton, 154 F.Supp.2d 1098 (W.D.Mich.2001). Park Service planning is considered further in Chapter 11, § B, infra.

Public participation. An important feature of all modern resource planning systems is that they provide opportunity for affected interests and the general public to participate in federal land planning. For example, FLPMA (43 U.S.C. § 1712(f)) provides:

The Secretary shall allow an opportunity for public involvement and by regulation shall establish procedures, including public hearings where appropriate, to give Federal, State, and local governments and the

public, adequate notice and opportunity to comment upon and participate in the formulation of plans and programs relating to the management of the public lands.

Binding Nature of Plans. Regardless of which agency is doing the
planning, the plans have legal effect, governing future management decisions to the extent they contain guidance relevant to that decision.* For
example, the National Forest Management Act requires that all "permits,
contracts [including timber sale contracts], and other instruments for the
use and occupancy of National Forest System lands shall be consistent with
the land management plans." 16 U.S.C. § 1604(i). The same subsection
also provides that as plans are revised, the permits, contracts and other
instruments, "when necessary, shall be revised as soon as practicable * * *
subject to valid existing rights." See also 36 C.F.R. § 219.10(e) (2001);
Sierra Club v. Martin, 168 F.3d 1, 4 (11th Cir.1999).

FLPMA provides that BLM must prepare land use plans for all areas
(43 U.S.C. § 1712); and manage the public lands "in accordance with"
those plans "when they are available, except that where a tract of such
public land has been dedicated to specific uses according to any other
provisions of law it shall be managed in accordance with such law."
(§ 1732(a)). BLM's implementing regulations provide that "[a]ll future
resource management authorizations and actions * * * shall conform to
the approved plan." 43 C.F.R. § 1610.5–3(a) (1991). Notice the slight
differences in wording in these statutes and regulations ("consistent with,"
"in accordance with," and "conform to"). Are the differences legally
significant?

The U.S. Fish & Wildlife Service must manage refuges "in a manner
consistent with the plan and shall revise the plan at any time if the
Secretary determines the conditions that affect the refuge or planning unit
have changed significantly." (16 U.S.C. § 668dd(e)(1)(E)).

Plans remain binding until changed. Even though an agency may have
initiated a process to amend land management plans, it need not impose a
moratorium on actions in the planning area that are consistent with the
existing plan, until the amending process is completed. See, e.g., ONRC
Action v. Bureau of Land Management, 150 F.3d 1132 (9th Cir.1998). Of
course, where other laws (such as the Endangered Species Act) restrict
actions that could be taken under an existing plan, those other laws must
be complied with; that is, the fact that the plan authorizes the action does
not render it immune from the other laws. See, e.g, Pacific Rivers Council
v. Thomas, 30 F.3d 1050 (9th Cir.1994), discussed infra at p. 466.

The national forest and national wildlife refuge planning statutes
require periodic revision of plans. See 16 U.S.C. § 1604(f)(5) (national
forests); § 668dd(e)(1)(A)(iv) and (E) (national wildlife refuges). In the fall
of 2001, however, Congress included a rider on the Interior Appropriations
bill essentially removing the fifteen year deadline for revising forest plans,
by providing that the Secretary of Agriculture "shall not be considered in

---

* The cryptic National Park System plan-
ing statute does not expressly make plans
legally binding. 16 U.S.C. § 1a-7.

violation of" the planning statutes "solely because more than 15 years has passed without revision of the plan for a unit of the National Forest System." Interior Department and Related Agencies Appropriation Bill for Fiscal Year 2002, § 327, 115 Stat. 414. The BLM and national park planning statutes do not contain a schedule for periodic revision.

A question to ponder, as planning in specific contexts is considered in the chapters that follow, is whether this emphasis on planning in the management of federal resources is a good thing, whether it promotes rational, participatory decisionmaking, or whether it essentially wastes paper (trees), time and energy, and foments litigation and divisiveness, all the while diverting attention from (or not really solving) pressing problems of federal land management. The ranks of critics of the federal land planning process, at least as currently implemented, seem to be growing. See, e.g., Richard Behan, RPA/NFMA–Time to Punt, Chapter 1, supra p. 25. Former BLM Director Frank Gregg once noted the irony of our "child-like faith in planning" for federal lands, at a time when centralized planning in formerly communist countries has been so discredited. (Remarks to Congressional Research Service Symposium on the Future of Multiple–Use Sustained–Yield, Washington D.C., March 6, 1992). See also Kelly Nolen, Residents at Risk: Wildlife and the Bureau of Land Management's Planning Process, 27 Envtl. L. 771 (1996) (questioning whether the planning process works to protect such resources as wildlife). Does the emphasis on planning simply reflect the lack of a societal consensus on how these lands and associated resources should be managed, and thus constitutes the second-or third-best alternative of all the major interests involved in federal land management?

The Forest Service completed, in the last year of the Clinton Administration, a major overhaul of its planning regulations, to give higher priority to ecological sustainability. See 65 Fed. Reg. 67514 (Nov. 9, 2000) (codified at 36 C.F.R. § 219.2(a) and 219.19 (2001)). The extraction industries, led by the American Forest and Paper Association, stoutly opposed the reforms, accusing the agency of using the planning process to abandon multiple use and essentially oust them from the forests. See, e.g., testimony of Steven P. Quarles on the Forest Service's Proposed Planning Rules, Subcommittee on Forests of Senate Energy and Natural Resources Committee, May 10, 2000. Industry groups filed lawsuits challenging the new regulations on a variety of grounds, and the Bush Administration has delayed implementation of these rules for one year pending further study. See 66 Fed. Reg. 27,552 (May 17, 2001).

D.   ENDANGERED SPECIES PROTECTION

1.   INTRODUCTION AND OVERVIEW—TVA v. HILL

The federal Endangered Species Act, 16 U.S.C. §§ 1531–1543—sometimes called the "pit bull" of environmental statutes—can be a formidable constraint on a wide variety of federal land uses in certain situations. Helped along by many court decisions, the Act arguably has become the most important national land use law. In general, the Act commands all agencies to "conserve" listed species, and "conservation" is defined very broadly. 16 U.S.C. § 1531(5). Section 7, 16 U.S.C. § 1536, applies specifically to federal departments and agencies, and is explored immediately below. Section 9, 16 U.S.C. § 1538, prohibits "taking" of a listed species by anyone, whether the government is involved or not, and that too is broadly defined. It is considered further below in this section.

There is a huge volume of commentary on the Act. Useful discussions can be found in Michael Bean and Melanie Rowland, THE EVOLUTION OF NATIONAL WILDLIFE LAW 192–276 (3d ed. 1997); Oliver A. Houck, The Endangered Species Act and its Implementation by the U.S. Departments of Interior and Commerce, 64 U.Colo. L.Rev. 278 (1993); ENDANGERED SPECIES ACT: LAW, POLICY, AND PERSPECTIVES (Donald Baus & Robert Irvin, eds. 2002). Other articles are cited in the materials below.* The ESA's substantive bite was forcefully underscored by the U.S. Supreme Court in the following case, one of the leading decisions in natural resources law.

Tennessee Valley Authority v. Hill

Supreme Court of the United States, 1978.
437 U.S. 153.

■ MR. CHIEF JUSTICE BURGER delivered the opinion of the Court.

The questions presented in this case are (a) whether the Endangered Species Act of 1973 requires a court to enjoin the operation of a virtually completed federal dam—which had been authorized prior to 1973—when, pursuant to authority vested in him by Congress, the Secretary of the Interior has determined that operation of the dam would eradicate an endangered species; and (b) whether continued congressional appropriations for the dam after 1973 constituted an implied repeal of the Endangered Species Act, at least as to the particular dam.

[In 1967 the Tennessee Valley Authority, a federal agency, began constructing the Tellico Dam on the Little Tennessee River near Knoxville, after Congress appropriated initial funds for it. The Dam was a multipur-

---

* An annoying quirk complicates the Act's administration: The Secretary of the Interior (through the U.S. Fish & Wildlife Service) has responsibility for terrestrial species, freshwater species, and some marine species (sea otter and marine birds), while the Secretary of Commerce (through the National Marine Fisheries Service, NMFS, part of the National Oceanic at Atmospheric Administration, or NOAA) has responsibility for most marine species and most anadromous fish. The two agencies share jurisdiction over some species, such as sea turtles and the Atlantic salmon. See Bean and Rowland, pp. 203–04; Hawksbill Sea Turtle v. Federal Emergency Mgt. Agency, 126 F.3d 461, 470 (3d Cir.1997) ("When the turtles are swimming * * * Commerce bears regulatory responsibility, and when the turtles return to the beach, the regulatory baton passes to Interior"). To simplify the text, references to the U.S. Fish & Wildlife Service in connection with administration of the Act should be taken as including NMFS unless the context indicates otherwise.

pose project designed for flood control, hydroelectric power production, and flatwater recreation. It would inundate 30 miles of the river and some 16,500 acres of land, much of it productive farmland. Shortly after NEPA took effect in 1970, dam construction was enjoined until an EIS was prepared. Following preparation of an EIS and a finding that it complied with NEPA, the district court dissolved the injunction. EDF v. TVA, 371 F.Supp. 1004 (E.D.Tenn.1973), aff'd, 492 F.2d 466 (6th Cir.1974).]

[During that litigation] a discovery was made in the waters of the Little Tennessee which would profoundly affect the Tellico Project. * * * [A] University of Tennessee ichthyologist, Dr. David A. Etnier, found a previously unknown species of perch, the snail darter, * * * [a] three-inch, tannish-colored fish, whose numbers are estimated to be in the range of 10,000 to 15,000 * * *.

Until recently the finding of a new species of animal life would hardly generate a cause célèbre. This is particularly so in the case of darters, of which there are approximately 130 known species, 8 to 10 of these having been identified only in the last five years. The moving force behind the snail darter's sudden fame came some four months after its discovery, when the Congress passed the Endangered Species Act of 1973. This legislation, among other things, authorizes the Secretary of the Interior to declare species of animal life "endangered" and to identify the "critical habitat" of these creatures. When a species or its habitat is so listed, [section 7 of the Act] becomes effective:

> " * * * All * * * Federal departments and agencies shall, in consultation with and with the assistance of the Secretary [of the Interior], utilize their authorities in furtherance of the purposes of this chapter * * * *by taking such action necessary to insure that actions authorized, funded, or carried out by them do not jeopardize the continued existence of such endangered species and threatened species or result in the destruction or modification of habitat of such species* which is determined by the Secretary, after consultation as appropriate with the affected States, to be critical." 16 U.S.C. § 1536 (emphasis added).

[In 1975, in response to plaintiff's petition, the Interior Secretary listed the snail darter as endangered, declared the area to be inundated as "critical habitat," and announced that impoundment of the river "would result in total destruction of the snail darter's habitat." The TVA insisted that the only remedy was to attempt to transplant the fish to another river.]

Meanwhile, Congress had also become involved in the fate of the snail darter. Appearing before a Subcommittee of the House Committee on Appropriations in April 1975—some seven months before the snail darter was listed as endangered—TVA representatives described the discovery of the fish and the relevance of the Endangered Species Act to the Tellico Project. At that time TVA presented a position which it would advance in successive forums thereafter, namely, that the Act did not prohibit the completion of a project authorized, funded, and substantially constructed before the act was passed. TVA also described its efforts to transplant the snail darter, but contended that the dam should be finished regardless of the experiment's success. Thereafter, the House Committee on Appropriations, in its June 20, 1975, Report, stated the following in the course of recommending that an additional $29 million be appropriated for Tellico:

> "The *Committee* directs that the project, for which an environmental impact statement has been completed and provided the Committee, should be completed as promptly as possible * * *." H.R.Rep. No. 94–319, p. 76 (1975). (Emphasis added.)

Congress then approved the TVA general budget, which contained funds for continued construction of the Tellico Project. In December 1975, one month after the snail darter was declared an endangered species, the President signed the bill into law.

[The district court refused relief, calling it "absurd" to think that Congress intended the Act to apply this way, but the court of appeals entered a permanent injunction against closure of the dam until Congress decided otherwise.] * * *

Following the issuance of the permanent injunction, members of TVA's Board of Directors appeared before Subcommittees of the House and Senate Appropriations Committees to testify in support of continued appropriations for Tellico. The Subcommittees were apprised of all aspects of Tellico's status, including the Court of Appeals' decision. TVA reported that the dam stood "ready for the gates to be closed and the reservoir filled," and requested funds for completion of certain ancillary parts of the project, such as public use areas, roads, and bridges. As to the snail darter itself, TVA commented optimistically on its transplantation efforts, expressing the opinion that the relocated fish were "doing well and ha[d] reproduced."

Both Appropriations Committees subsequently recommended the full amount requested for completion of the Tellico Project. In its June 2, 1977, Report, the House Appropriations Committee stated:

> "It is *the Committee's view* that the Endangered Species Act was not intended to halt projects such as these in their advanced stage of completion, and [the Committee] strongly recommends that these projects not be stopped because of misuse of the Act." H.R.Rep. No. 95–379, p. 104. (Emphasis added.)

As a solution to the problem, the House Committee * * * recommended a special appropriation of $2 million to facilitate relocation of the snail darter and other endangered species which threatened to delay or stop TVA projects. Much the same occurred on the Senate side, with its Appropriations Committee recommending both the amount requested to complete Tellico and the special appropriation for transplantation of endangered species. Reporting to the Senate on these measures, the Appropriations Committee took a particularly strong stand on the snail darter issue:

> "This *committee has not viewed* the Endangered Species Act as preventing the completion and use of these projects which were well under way at the time the affected species were listed as endangered. If the act has such an effect, which is contrary to *the Committee's understanding* of the intent of Congress in enacting the Endangered Species

Act, funds should be appropriated to allow these projects to be completed and their benefits realized in the public interest, the Endangered Species Act notwithstanding." S.Rep. No. 95–301, p. 99 (1977). (Emphasis added.)

TVA's budget, including funds for completion of Tellico and relocation of the snail darter, passed both Houses of Congress and was signed into law on August 7, 1977. * * *

We begin with the premise that operation of the Tellico Dam will either eradicate the known population of snail darters or destroy their critical habitat. Petitioner does not now seriously dispute this fact. * * *

Starting from the above premise, two questions are presented: (a) would TVA be in violation of the Act if it completed and operated the Tellico Dam as planned? (b) if TVA's actions would offend the Act, is an injunction the appropriate remedy for the violation? For the reasons stated hereinafter, we hold that both questions must be answered in the affirmative.

It may seem curious to some that the survival of a relatively small number of three-inch fish among all the countless millions of species extant would require the permanent halting of a virtually completed dam for which Congress has expended more than $100 million. The paradox is not minimized by the fact that Congress continued to appropriate large sums of public money for the project, even after congressional Appropriations Committees were apprised of its apparent impact upon the survival of the snail darter. We conclude, however, that the explicit provisions of the Endangered Species Act require precisely that result.

One would be hard pressed to find a statutory provision whose terms were any plainer than those in § 7 of the Endangered Species Act. Its very words affirmatively command all federal agencies "to *insure* that actions *authorized, funded,* or *carried out* by them do not *jeopardize* the continued existence" of an endangered species or "*result* in the destruction or modification of habitat of such species * * *." 16 U.S.C. § 1536. (Emphasis added.) This language admits of no exception. Nonetheless, petitioner urges, as do the dissenters, that the Act cannot reasonably be interpreted as applying to a federal project which was well under way when Congress passed the Endangered Species Act of 1973. To sustain that position, however, we would be forced to ignore the ordinary meaning of plain language. It has not been shown, for example, how TVA can close the gates of the Tellico Dam without "carrying out" an action that has been "authorized" and "funded" by a federal agency. Nor can we understand how such action will "*insure*" that the snail darter's habitat is not disrupted.[18] Accepting the Secretary's determinations, as we must, it is

---

18. In dissent, Mr. Justice Powell argues that the meaning of "actions" in § 7 is "far from 'plain,'" and that "it seems evident that the 'actions' referred to are not all actions that an agency can ever take, but rather actions that the agency is *deciding whether* to authorize, to fund, or to carry out." Aside from this bare assertion, however, no explanation is given to support the proffered interpretation. This recalls Lewis Carroll's classic advice on the construction of language:

clear that TVA's proposed operation of the dam will have precisely the opposite effect, namely the *eradication* of an endangered species.

Concededly, this view of the Act will produce results requiring the sacrifice of the anticipated benefits of the project and of many millions of dollars in public funds. But examination of the language, history, and structure of the legislation under review here indicates beyond doubt that Congress intended endangered species to be afforded the highest of priorities.

When Congress passed the Act in 1973, it was not legislating on a clean slate. [The Court recounted enactment of earlier endangered species legislation.] * * *

Despite the fact that the 1966 and 1969 legislation represented "the most comprehensive of its type to be enacted by any nation" up to that time, Congress was soon persuaded that a more expansive approach was needed if the newly declared national policy of preserving endangered species was to be realized. By 1973, when Congress held hearings on what would later become the Endangered Species Act of 1973, it was informed that species were still being lost at the rate of about one per year * * * and "the pace of disappearance of species" appeared to be "accelerating." * * * Moreover, Congress was also told that the primary cause of this trend was something other than the normal process of natural selection:

> [M]an and his technology has [sic] continued at an ever-increasing rate to disrupt the natural ecosystem. This has resulted in a dramatic rise in the number and severity of the threats faced by the world's wildlife. * * * [H]alf of the recorded extinctions of mammals over the past 2,000 years have occurred in the most recent 50–year period. * * *

That Congress did not view these developments lightly was stressed by one commentator:

> "The dominant theme pervading all Congressional discussion of the proposed [Endangered Species Act of 1973] was the overriding need *to devote whatever effort and resources were necessary* to avoid further diminution of national and worldwide wildlife resources. Much of the testimony at the hearings and much debate was devoted to the biological problem of extinction. Senators and Congressmen uniformly deplored the irreplaceable loss to aesthetics, science, ecology, and the national heritage should more species disappear." Coggins, Conserving Wildlife Resources: An Overview of the Endangered Species Act of 1973, 51 N.D.L.Rev. 315, 321 (1975). (Emphasis added.)

"When *I* use a word," Humpty Dumpty said, in rather a scornful tone, "it means just what *I* choose it to mean—neither more nor less." Through the Looking Glass, in The Complete Works of Lewis Carroll 196 (1939).

Aside from being unexplicated, the dissent's reading of § 7 is flawed on several counts. First, under its view, the words "or carry out" in § 7 would be superfluous since all prospective actions of an agency remain to be "authorized" or "funded." Second, the dissent's position logically means that an agency would be obligated to comply with § 7 only when a project is in the planning stage. But if Congress had meant to so limit the Act, it surely would have used words to that effect, as it did in the National Environmental Policy Act, 42 U.S.C. §§ 4332(2)(A), (C).

The legislative proceedings in 1973 are, in fact, replete with expressions of concern over the risk that might lie in the loss of *any* endangered species. Typifying these sentiments is the Report of the House Committee on Merchant Marine and Fisheries on H.R. 37, a bill which contained the essential features of the subsequently enacted Act of 1973; in explaining the need for the legislation, the Report stated:

"As we homogenize the habitats in which these plants and animals evolved, and as we increase the pressure for products that they are in a position to supply (usually unwillingly) we threaten their—and our own—genetic heritage.

"The value of this genetic heritage is, quite literally, incalculable."

* * *

As the examples cited here demonstrate, Congress was concerned about the *unknown* uses that endangered species might have and about the *unforeseeable* place such creatures may have in the chain of life on this planet.

In shaping legislation to deal with the problem thus presented, Congress started from the finding that "[t]he two major causes of extinction are hunting and destruction of natural habitat." S.Rep. No. 93, 307, p. 2 (1973). Of these twin threats, Congress was informed that the greatest [sic] was destruction of natural habitats * * *.

As it was finally passed, the Endangered Species Act of 1973 represented the most comprehensive legislation for the preservation of endangered species ever enacted by any nation. Its stated purposes were "to provide a means whereby the ecosystems upon which endangered species and threatened species depend may be conserved," and "to provide a program for the conservation of such * * * species * * *." 16 U.S.C. § 1531(b). In furtherance of these goals, Congress expressly stated in § 2(c) that "all Federal departments and agencies *shall* seek *to conserve endangered species* and threatened species * * *." 16 U.S.C. § 1531(c). (Emphasis added.) Lest there be any ambiguity as to the meaning of this statutory directive, the Act specifically defined "conserve" as meaning "to use and the use of *all methods and procedures which are necessary* to bring *any endangered species* or threatened species to the point at which the measures provided pursuant to this chapter are no longer necessary." § 1532(2). (Emphasis added.) Aside from § 7, other provisions indicated the seriousness with which Congress viewed this issue * * *.

Section 7 of the Act, which of course is relied upon by respondents in this case, provides a particularly good gauge of congressional intent. * * * [T]his provision had its genesis in the Endangered Species Act of 1966, but that legislation qualified the obligation of federal agencies by stating that they should seek to preserve endangered species only *"insofar as is practicable and consistent with the*[ir] *primary purposes* * * *." Likewise, every bill introduced in 1973 contained a qualification similar to that found in the earlier statutes. * * *

What is very significant in this sequence is that the final version of the 1973 Act carefully omitted all of the reservations described above. * * *

* * * The Conference Report, H.R.Conf.Rep. No. 93–740 (1973), basically adopted the Senate bill, S. 1983; but the conferees rejected the Senate version of § 7 and adopted the stringent, mandatory language in H.R. 37. While the Conference Report made no specific reference to this choice of provisions, the House manager of the bill, Representative Dingell, provided an interpretation of what the Conference bill would require, making it clear that the mandatory provisions of § 7 were not casually or inadvertently included: * * *

> "Another example * * * [has] to do with the continental population of grizzly bears which may or may not be endangered, but which is surely threatened. * * * Once this bill is enacted, the appropriate Secretary, whether of Interior, Agriculture or whatever, *will have to take action* to see that this situation is not permitted to worsen, and that these bears are not driven to extinction. The purposes of the bill included the conservation of the species and of the ecosystems upon which they depend, and *every agency of government is committed* to see that those purposes are carried out. * * * [T]he agencies of Government can no longer plead that they can do nothing about it. *They can, and they must. The law is clear.*" 119 Cong.Rec. 42913 (1973). (Emphasis added.)

* * * [T]he totality of congressional action makes it abundantly clear that the result we reach today is wholly in accord with both the words of the statute and the intent of Congress. The plain intent of Congress in enacting this statute was to halt and reverse the trend toward species extinction, whatever the cost. This is reflected not only in the stated policies of the Act, but in literally every section of the statute. * * * In addition, the legislative history undergirding § 7 reveals an explicit congressional decision to require agencies to afford first priority to the declared national policy of saving endangered species. The pointed omission of the type of qualifying language previously included in endangered species legislation reveals a conscious decision by Congress to give endangered species priority over the "primary missions" of federal agencies. * * *

Furthermore, it is clear Congress foresaw that § 7 would, on occasion, require agencies to alter ongoing projects in order to fulfill the goals of the Act. * * * [An] example is provided by the House Committee Report:

> "Under the authority of [§ 7], the Director of the Park Service would be required *to conform the practices of his agency* to the need for protecting the rapidly dwindling stock of grizzly bears within Yellowstone Park. These bears, which may be endangered, and are undeniably threatened, should at least be protected * * * *by curtailing the destruction of habitat by clearcutting National Forests surrounding the Park,* and by preventing hunting until their numbers have recovered sufficiently to withstand these pressures." H.R.Rep. No. 93–412, p. 14 (1973). (Emphasis added.)

One might dispute the applicability of these examples to the Tellico Dam by saying that in this case the burden on the public through the loss of millions of unrecoverable dollars would greatly outweigh the loss of the snail darter. But neither the Endangered Species Act nor Art. III of the

Constitution provides federal courts with authority to make such fine utilitarian calculations. On the contrary, the plain language of the Act, buttressed by its legislative history, shows clearly that Congress viewed the value of endangered species as "incalculable." Quite obviously, it would be difficult for a court to balance the loss of a sum certain—even $100 million—against a congressionally declared "incalculable" value, even assuming we had the power to engage in such a weighing process, which we emphatically do not.

* * * Congress was * * * aware of certain instances in which exceptions to the statute's broad sweep would be necessary. Thus, § 10, 16 U.S.C. § 1539, creates a number of limited "hardship exemptions," none of which would even remotely apply to the Tellico Project. In fact, there are no exemptions in the Endangered Species Act for federal agencies, meaning that under the maxim *expressio unius est exclusio alterius* we must presume that these were the only "hardship cases" Congress intended to exempt.[34]

Notwithstanding Congress' expression of intent in 1973, we are urged to find that the continuing appropriations for Tellico Dam constitute an implied repeal of the 1973 Act, at least insofar as it applies to the Tellico Project. * * * TVA points to the statements found in various House and Senate Appropriations Committees' Reports * * * [which] generally reflected the attitude of the *Committees* either that the Act did not apply to Tellico or that the dam should be completed regardless of the provisions of the Act. * * *

There is nothing in the appropriations measures, as passed, which states that the Tellico Project was to be completed irrespective of the requirements of the Endangered Species Act. These appropriations, in fact, represented relatively minor components of the lump-sum amounts for the *entire* TVA budget. To find a repeal of the Endangered Species Act under these circumstances would surely do violence to the " 'cardinal rule * * * that repeals by implication are not favored.' " Morton v. Mancari, 417 U.S. 535, 549 (1974) * * *.

---

34. Mr. Justice Powell's dissent relies on cases decided under the National Environmental Policy Act to support its position that the 1973 Act should only apply to prospective actions of an agency. The NEPA decisions, however, are completely inapposite. First, the two statutes serve different purposes. NEPA essentially imposes a procedural requirement on agencies, requiring them to engage in an extensive *inquiry* as to the effect of federal actions on the environment; by way of contrast, the [Endangered Species] Act is substantive in effect, designed to *prevent* the loss of any endangered species, regardless of the cost. Thus, it would make sense to hold NEPA inapplicable at some point in the life of a project, because the agency would no longer have a meaningful opportunity to *weigh* the benefits of the project versus the detrimental effects on the environment. Section 7, on the other hand, compels agencies not only to *consider* the effect of their projects on endangered species, but to take such actions as are necessary to *insure* that species are not extirpated as a result of federal activities. Second, even the NEPA cases have generally required agencies to file environmental impact statements when the remaining governmental action would be environmentally "significant." Under § 7, the loss of *any* endangered species has been determined by Congress to be environmentally "significant."

The doctrine disfavoring repeals by implication "applies with full vigor when * * * the subsequent legislation is an *appropriations* measure." * * * We recognize that both substantive enactments and appropriations measures are "Acts of Congress," but the latter have the limited and specific purpose of providing funds for authorized programs. When voting on appropriations measures, legislators are entitled to operate under the assumption that the funds will be devoted to purposes which are lawful and not for any purpose forbidden. Without such an assurance, every appropriations measure would be pregnant with prospects of altering substantive legislation, repealing by implication any prior statute which might prohibit the expenditure. Not only would this lead to the absurd result of requiring Members to review exhaustively the background of every authorization before voting on an appropriation, but it would flout the very rules the Congress carefully adopted to avoid this need. House Rule XXI(2), for instance, specifically provides [that no provision in an appropriations bill] "*changing existing law [shall] be in order.*" (Emphasis added.) See also Standing Rules of the Senate, Rule 16.4. Thus, to sustain petitioner's position, we would be obliged to assume that Congress meant to repeal pro tanto § 7 of the Act by means of a procedure expressly prohibited under the rules of Congress.

Perhaps mindful of the fact that it is "swimming upstream" against a strong current of well-established precedent, TVA argues for an exception to the rule against implied repealers * * * where, as here, Appropriations Committees have expressly stated their "understanding" that the earlier legislation would not prohibit the proposed expenditure. We cannot accept such a proposition. Expressions of committees * * * cannot be equated with statutes enacted by Congress, particularly not in the circumstances presented by this case. First, the Appropriations Committees had no jurisdiction over the subject of endangered species, much less did they conduct the type of extensive hearings which preceded passage of the earlier Endangered Species Acts, especially the 1973 Act. We venture to suggest that the House Committee on Merchant Marine and Fisheries and the Senate Committee on Commerce would be somewhat surprised to learn that their careful work on the substantive legislation had been undone by the simple—and brief—insertion of some inconsistent language in Appropriation Committees' Reports.

Second, there is no indication that Congress as a whole was aware of TVA's position * * *.

Having determined that there is an irreconcilable conflict between operation of the Tellico Dam and the explicit provisions of § 7 of the Endangered Species Act, we must now consider what remedy, if any, is appropriate. It is correct, of course, that a federal judge sitting as a chancellor is not mechanically obligated to grant an injunction for every violation of law. * * *

But these principles take a court only so far. Our system of government is, after all, a tripartite one, with each branch having certain defined functions delegated to it by the Constitution. While "[i]t is emphatically the province and duty of the judicial department to say what the law is,"

Marbury v. Madison, 1 Cranch 137, 177 (1803), it is equally—and emphati-cally—the exclusive province of the Congress not only to formulate legisla-tive policies and mandate programs and projects, but also to establish their relative priority for the Nation. Once Congress, exercising its delegated powers, has decided the order of priorities in a given area, it is for the Executive to administer the laws and for the courts to enforce them when enforcement is sought.

Here we are urged to view the Endangered Species Act "reasonably," and hence shape a remedy "that accords with some modicum of common sense and the public weal." But is that our function? We have no expert knowledge on the subject of endangered species, much less do we have a mandate from the people to strike a balance of equities on the side of the Tellico Dam. Congress has spoken in the plainest of words, making it abundantly clear that the balance has been struck in favor of affording endangered species the highest of priorities, thereby adopting a policy which it described as "institutionalized caution."

Our individual appraisal of the wisdom or unwisdom of a particular course consciously selected by the Congress is to be put aside in the process of interpreting a statute. Once the meaning of an enactment is discerned and its constitutionality determined, the judicial process comes to an end. * * *

We agree with the Court of Appeals that in our constitutional system the commitment to the separation of powers is too fundamental for us to pre-empt congressional action by judicially decreeing what accords with "common sense and the public weal." Our Constitution vests such respon-sibilities in the political branches.

■ MR. JUSTICE POWELL, with whom MR. JUSTICE BLACKMUN joins, dissenting.

* * * This decision casts a long shadow over the operation of even the most important projects, serving vital needs of society and national defense, whenever it is determined that continued operation would threaten extinc-tion of an endangered species or its habitat.

* * * If it were clear from the language of the Act and its legislative history that Congress intended to authorize this result, this Court would be compelled to enforce it. It is not our province to rectify policy or political judgments by the Legislative Branch, however egregiously they may dis-serve the public interest. But where the statutory language and legislative history, as in this case, need not be construed to reach such a result, I view it as the duty of this Court to adopt a permissible construction that accords with some modicum of common sense and the public weal.

* * * [The majority's interpretation of section 7] gives it a retroactive effect and disregards 12 years of consistently expressed congressional intent to complete the Tellico Project. With all due respect, I view this result as an extreme example of a literalist construction, not required by the language of the Act and adopted without regard to its manifest purpose.

* * * Under the Court's reasoning, the Act covers every existing federal installation, including great hydroelectric projects and reservoirs, every river and harbor project, and every national defense installation—

however essential to the Nation's economic health and safety. The "actions" that an agency would be prohibited from "carrying out" would
include the continued operation of such projects or any change necessary to
preserve their continued usefulness. The only precondition, according to
respondents, to thus destroying the usefulness of even the most important
federal project in our country would be a finding by the Secretary of the
Interior that a continuation of the project would threaten the survival or
critical habitat of a newly discovered species of water spider or amoeba.[13]
* * *

I have little doubt that Congress will amend the Endangered Species
Act to prevent the grave consequences made possible by today's decision.
Few, if any, Members of that body will wish to defend an interpretation of
the Act that requires the waste of at least $53 million, and denies the
people of the Tennessee Valley area the benefits of the reservoir that
Congress intended to confer. There will be little sentiment to leave this
dam standing before an empty reservoir, serving no purpose other than a
conversation piece for incredulous tourists.

But more far reaching than the adverse effect on the people of this
economically depressed area is the continuing threat to the operation of
every federal project, no matter how important to the Nation. If Congress
acts expeditiously, as may be anticipated, the Court's decision probably will
have no lasting adverse consequences. But I had not thought it to be the
province of this Court to force Congress into otherwise unnecessary action
by interpreting a statute to produce a result no one intended.

■ MR. JUSTICE REHNQUIST, dissenting. * * *

NOTES AND QUESTIONS

1.   TVA v. Hill was a notable case in a number of respects. For one
thing, the Department of the Interior (whose Fish & Wildlife Service plays
a key role in implementing the Act) was permitted by the Department of
Justice to file an "appendix" to the government's brief on behalf of the
TVA which took precisely the opposite position from TVA. This is very
rare; generally the Solicitor General takes the view that the executive has
to have a single legal position before the Court. The TVA position was
argued to the Court by Attorney General (and former Fifth Circuit Judge)
Griffin Bell, who began his argument by brandishing a jar containing a
single (dead) snail darter in formaldehyde, to illustrate (to no avail, as it
turned out) the ridiculousness of a tiny "worthless" fish stopping a big

---

13.   Under the Court's interpretation,
the prospects for such disasters are breath-
taking indeed, since there are hundreds of
thousands of candidates for the endangered
list:

  " 'The act covers every animal and plant
  species, subspecies, and population in the
  world needing protection. There are approximately 1.4 million full species of
  animals and 600,000 full species of plants

in the world. Various authorities calculate as many as 10% of them—some 200,-
000—may need to be listed as Endangered or Threatened. When one counts in
subspecies, not to mention individual
populations, the total could increase to
three to five times that number.' " [Eds.:
Quoting a Fish & Wildlife Service official.] * * *

dam. (Professor Zygmunt Plater, attorney for the plaintiffs, later remarked: "It's the only fish story I know where the fish gets smaller and smaller.") The ESA is, regrettably, susceptible to sensationalism; there are many stories of "urban legend" quality (that is, of no or little validity) where some worthy project was stopped by some ridiculous creature or a person victimized by some overzealous bureaucrat.

2.   Does anything *require* Congress to protect endangered forms of life? What are the rationales for protecting endangered species? On the utilitarian side, Aldo Leopold once wrote that "[t]o keep every cog and wheel is the first precaution of intelligent tinkering." The Round River, in A SAND COUNTY ALMANAC 175 (enlarged edition,1966). It has been estimated that perhaps half of all medical prescriptions contain substances first found in a living organism. Or does the ESA rest more on moral principle, evoking Noah and the Flood and the creation myths that all cultures seem to have produced?

3.   *Valuing natural resources.* Chief Justice Burger found that Congress thought the value of endangered species was "incalculable." Is that good policy? Should we value species protection in the abstract, or only insofar as it directly relates to human quality of life? See Barton H. Thompson Jr., People or Prairie Chickens: The Uncertain Search for Optimal Biodiversity, 51 Stan. L. Rev. 1127 (1999). Lately a good deal of attention has been devoted to the idea of putting a value on what has come to be known as "ecosystem services." See James Salzman, Barton Thompson, Gretchen Daily, Protecting Ecosystem Services: Science, Economics, and Law, 20 Stanford Envtl. L. J.309, 310–11 (2001):

> Largely taken for granted, healthy ecosystems provide a variety of critical services. Created by the interactions of living organisms with their environment, these "ecosystem services" provide both the conditions and processes that sustain human life—purifying air and water, detoxifying and decomposing waste, renewing soil fertility, regulating climate, mitigating droughts and floods, controlling pests, and pollinating plants. * * * [R]ecent research has demonstrated the extremely high costs to replace many of these services if they were to fail, on the order of many billions of dollars in the United States for water purification alone. * * * Despite their obvious importance to our well being, ecosystem services have largely been ignored in environmental law and policy.

See generally Symposium, 20 Stanford Envtl. L.J. 309–536 (2001); NATURE'S SERVICES: SOCIETAL DEPENDENCE ON NATURAL ECOSYSTEMS (Gretchen Daily ed., 1997). As Professor Salzman has noted, "a focus on ecosystem services has the potential to unify disparate parts of environmental law, linking the conservation goals in laws such as the Endangered Species Act and National Forest Management Act more closely with the human health goals in seemingly unconnected laws such as the Clean Air Act and Safe Drinking Water Act." James Salzman, The Ecosystem Approach: New Departures for Land and Water: Valuing Ecosystem Services, 24 Ecology L.Q. 887, 888–89 (1997).

In some modern environmental statutes, Congress has effectively required that dollar values be placed upon certain natural resources like wildlife. Most prominently, the Comprehensive Environmental Response, Compensation, and Liability Act (CERCLA) of 1980, makes persons responsible for releases of hazardous substances subject to suits for "damages for injury to, destruction of, or loss of natural resources" resulting from such releases. 42 U.S.C. § 9607(a)(4)(C). The Oil Pollution Act of 1990, enacted in the wake of the Exxon Valdez oil spill in Alaska, created a similar liability for loss of or injury to "natural resources." 33 U.S.C. § 2702(b)(2)(A). (The 1977 amendments to the Clean Water Act had contained a somewhat narrower provision along the same lines; see 33 U.S.C. § 1321(f)(4).) CERCLA also directed the preparation of regulations to govern "natural resource damage assessments" under the Clean Water Act and CERCLA. These regulations have been much litigated and commented upon; e.g, Kennecott Utah Copper Corp. v. U.S. Dept. of the Interior, 88 F.3d 1191 (D.C.Cir.1996); Miriam Montesinos, It May Be Silly, But It's An Answer: The Need to Accept Contingent Valuation Methodology in Natural Resource Damage Assessments, 26 Ecology L.Q. 48 (1999); James Peck, Measuring Justice for Nature: Issues in Evaluating and Litigating Natural Resources Damages, 14 J.Land Use & Envtl. Law 275 (1999); James L. Nicoll, Environmental Restoration: Challenges for the New Millennium: The Irrationality of Economic Rationality in the Restoration of Natural Resources, 42 Ariz. L.Rev. 463 (2000). A seminal work is John Krutilla & Anthony Fisher, THE ECONOMICS OF NATURAL ENVIRONMENTS: STUDIES IN THE VALUATION OF COMMODITY AND AMENITY RESOURCES (1975).

4. *Legislative history as a guide to statutory construction.* Compare the majority opinion and Justice Powell's dissent on the legislative history of the ESA and of the Tellico appropriations bills. How reliable an indicator of congressional intent and statutory construction is legislative history such as committee reports, testimony, and floor debates? In more recent years, the Supreme Court, led by Justice Scalia, has expressed more skepticism about legislative history, and focused more on the statutory text. For a debate on the reliability of legislative history, see Wisconsin Public Intervenor v. Mortier, 501 U.S. 597 (1991), where Justice Scalia said that Committee reports are not a "genuine indicator of congressional intent;" they do not necessarily indicate "what Congress as a whole thought" because the committee members are a small minority of the membership in each house and most members probably do not read the reports before voting. Justice White, writing for the majority, responded by saying that "common sense" as well as a long practice justifies resort to legislative history materials because they "are not generally so misleading that jurists should never employ them in a good faith effort to discern legislative intent." Who wins this debate? If much of the legislative history of a statute, such as committee reports, are actually written by (unelected) staff members in Congress, is that a sufficient justification for (unelected) judges to ignore it? Would Justice Scalia's position in effect enlarge the power of the judiciary and diminish the power of the people, acting through their elected representatives? (Congressional staff are, after all, hired by and subject to the

control of members of Congress.) For another judicial journey through tangled legislative history, see Defenders of Wildlife v. Andrus, Chapter 10, infra, pp. 892–900. See generally Charles Tiefer, The Reconceptualization of Legislative History in the Supreme Court, 2000 Wis. L.Rev. 206.

5. *"Appropriation Riders"—Amending substantive legislation through the appropriations process.* The Supreme Court has on occasion relied on appropriation acts to reject arguments that federal land management agencies were acting unlawfully. At issue in Brooks v. Dewar, 313 U.S. 354, 361 (1941), was a system of temporary grazing permits and fees created by the Secretary of the Interior as a transitional phase in implementing the Taylor Grazing Act. A rancher's contention that the Secretary lacked authority to do this was rejected because the Secretary's system had been disclosed to the Congress, which had appropriated a portion of the money received for range improvements. "The repeated appropriations * * * not only confirms the departmental construction of the statute, but constitutes a ratification of the action of the Secretary as the agent of Congress in the administration of the act." Why didn't that argument work in *TVA v. Hill*? Would the result in *TVA v. Hill* have been different if the language in the committee reports quoted in the majority opinion had been *in the statute itself* rather than in the reports (substituting "the Congress" for "the Committee" in the quoted excerpts)? In Lincoln v. Vigil, 508 U.S. 182 (1993), the Court expressly reaffirmed that legislative history in appropriations statutes lacks the force of law.

The rules of Congress quoted in the majority opinion in *TVA v. Hill* do not absolutely forbid substantive legislation in "riders" on appropriations acts. They merely say that such changes shall not be "in order," meaning they are subject to a "point of order," but if no member objects, they may be included. In actual legislative practice, the use of such riders has not been uncommon. Appropriations acts are one of the few kinds of legislation that Congress *must*, as a practical matter, enact each year if the government is to continue to function. For that reason, they are convenient vehicles for changing substantive law and can attract riders like honey attracts flies. For a more detailed description of the differences between appropriations acts and authorizing acts, see Andrus v. Sierra Club, 442 U.S. 347, 359–64 (1979) (request for appropriation of funds to operate the National Wildlife Refuge System was not a "proposal for legislation" requiring an EIS under NEPA). See also Jacques B. Le Boeuf, Limitations on the Use of Appropriations Riders By Congress to Effectuate Substantive Policy Changes, 19 Hast.Const.L.Q. 457 (1992).

In fact, some landmark pieces of substantive federal natural resources legislation have come in the form of appropriations riders. What came to be known as the first "organic act" for national forests was an appropriation rider. See 30 Stat. 34–36 (1897). The 1907 bill repealing the President's authority to create national forests in six northwestern states was an appropriation rider. 34 Stat. 1271 (1907). See Paul Gates, HISTORY OF PUBLIC LAND LAW DEVELOPMENT 569–70, 582. The "McCarran Amendment," which waived the sovereign immunity of the United States in general stream adjudications in state courts, was a rider on the 1952

Department of Justice appropriations bill. 43 U.S.C. § 666; see Chapter 6, infra pp. 540–48.

Appropriations acts generally make money available for designated programs for a single fiscal year. It is therefore generally presumed that an appropriation rider is effective only for that fiscal year, and sometimes the text clearly reflects that fact. In recent years, for example, Congress has included in the annual Interior appropriation bill a rider that says "[n]one of the funds *appropriated or otherwise made available pursuant to this Act* [that is, for a single fiscal year] shall be obligated or expended to accept or process applications for a patent for any mining or mill site claim located under the general mining laws," with certain exceptions. 113 Stat. 1501A–191 (Interior Department and Related Agencies FY 1998 Appropriation Bill), § 312 (emphasis added). This "patent moratorium" must be renewed each year or it expires.* On the other hand, if the rider text is written clearly to apply beyond the one year life of the bill, it will be given that effect. Thus, for example, the McCarran Amendment was drafted in open-ended terms ("consent is hereby given" to join the U.S. in state court general adjudications of water rights) and it is codified as a permanent law.

6. *Enjoining statutory violations.* Compare the Supreme Court's holding in *TVA v. Hill* on the discretion of the federal court to refuse to grant an injunction with the view of the federal courts regarding their discretion to withhold injunctive relief for NEPA violations; e.g., *Save the Yaak Committee,* supra this chapter, p. 424. Are these consistent? How does the thrust of NEPA differ from the thrust of the ESA, as bearing on the question of discretion regarding relief? Cf. footnote 34 in the majority opinion in *TVA v. Hill* and see *Thomas v. Peterson,* infra p. 459. In Weinberger v. Romero–Barcelo, 456 U.S. 305 (1982), the Supreme Court distinguished *TVA v. Hill* and held that federal courts should exercise equitable discretion rather than automatically enjoining a discharge of pollutants into waters in violation of the Clean Water Act's permit requirements. In Water Keeper Alliance v. U.S. Dept. of Defense, 271 F.3d 21, 34 (1st Cir.2001), the court upheld a denial of a preliminary injunction in an ESA case seeking to stop Naval training exercises, finding that *TVA v. Hill* does not "blindly compel our decision in this case because the harm asserted by the Navy implicates national security and therefore deserves greater weight than * * * economic harm."

7. *The Aftermath of TVA v. Hill—The "God Squad" and Statutory Exemptions.* Despite Justice Powell's confident prediction that Congress would put an end to what he regarded as the foolishness of the Court's construction of the Act, Congress reauthorized the Act in 1978, 1982, and 1988, and each time contented itself with fine-tuning the Act and its processes; weakening or qualifying a few provisions, strengthening others,

---

* Riders can cover all kinds of issues. One routinely inserted in the Interior appropriation bill in recent years effectively prohibits the National Park Service from taking any steps to remove the underground lunchroom at Carlsbad Caverns National Park. See 113 Stat. 1501A–191 (1997). NPS has expressed concern the lunchroom contaminates the fragile cave environment; Cong. Skeen, who is now chair of the House Interior Appropriations subcommittee, and who represents the area, will have none of it.

and adding some new protections. The Act has, in other words, proved to be quite popular and durable. Why? For a partial explanation, see Donald Barry, Amending the Endangered Species Act, The Ransom of the Red Chief, and Other Related Topics, 21 Envt'l L. 587 (1991).

One of the provisions Congress added in 1978 was what Michael Bean and Melanie Rowland have called an "elaborate and stringent process for exempting federal actions from the section 7 prohibitions * * * [as] a last-resort option, available only after all other avenues for avoiding conflicts have been exhausted." THE EVOLUTION OF NATIONAL WILDLIFE LAW 263 (3d ed. 1997). Ultimately, a seven member cabinet-level committee has responsibility for granting or denying an exemption. Usually known as the "God Squad," it was convened for the first time in connection with the snail darter and in 1979, after reviewing all the evidence on the conflict, concluded that the continued existence of the snail darter did indeed outweigh the completion and closing of the Tellico Dam, in substantial part because the dam's alleged benefits were dubious. Nevertheless, thanks to some adroit maneuvering by Tennessee Senator Howard Baker, Congress exempted Tellico from the ESA in a rider on an appropriation bill that the President reluctantly signed, 93 Stat. 437, 449–50 (1979), and the dam's gates were closed. As it turned out, however, so many snail darter populations were soon discovered at other locations that the little fish eventually was removed from the list of endangered species. See Nathaniel Reed & Dennis Drabelle, THE UNITED STATES FISH AND WILDLIFE SERVICE 91–92 (1984).

The exemption process has rarely been initiated and as of this writing only twice have exemptions been granted. One was the result of a settlement which the God Squad endorsed (and which allowed the species to survive). In the other, after plaintiffs in a suit to overturn the exemption won an order to have the Committee disclose all ex parte communications with the (Bush) Administration, see Portland Audubon Soc'y v. Endangered Species Comm., 984 F.2d 1534 (9th Cir.1993), the Clinton Administration withdrew the exemption request. Bean and Rowland suggest the disuse of the God Squad is because alternatives to exemption are usually available, the process for getting one is complex and difficult, and potential applicants fear bad publicity. THE EVOLUTION OF NATIONAL WILD-LIFE LAW at 263–65.

Congress has a few times (besides with the snail darter) passed special legislation to short-circuit the Endangered Species Act's review processes. For example, in 1988 it legislated a go-ahead to phase I of a telescope construction project on Mt. Graham in the Coronado National Forest in Arizona by deeming § 7 of the Act to be satisfied despite concerns about the impact of the project on the endangered Mt. Graham red squirrel. See 102 Stat. 4597 (1988). The statute was not successful. Inartfully drafted, hastily pushed through Congress without the benefit of committee hearings or reports (eventually causing some of its sponsors to seek to reinterpret its effect), it failed to end the controversy. See Mount Graham Coalition v. Thomas, 53 F.3d 970 (9th Cir.1995). Another congressional rider followed, see 110 Stat. 1321 (1996); this one worked, and the judiciary is showing signs of running out of patience with project opponents. See Apache Survival Coalition v. United States, 118 F.3d 663 (9th Cir.1997). At last report, the red squirrel was surviving.

2.   THE LISTING DECISION

Generally speaking, a species does not become subject to protection under the Act unless it is formally "listed" as threatened or endangered by the federal Fish & Wildlife Service by means of a rule published in the Federal Register. The following case effectively triggered the controversy over the spotted owl in the Pacific Northwest.

Northern Spotted Owl v. Hodel

United States District Court, Western District of Washington, 1988.
716 F.Supp. 479.

■ ZILLY, DISTRICT JUDGE.

A number of environmental organizations bring this action against the United States Fish & Wildlife Service ("Service") and others, alleging that the Service's decision not to list the northern spotted owl as endangered or threatened under the [ESA] * * * was arbitrary and capricious or contrary to law.

Since the 1970s the northern spotted owl has received much scientific attention, beginning with comprehensive studies of its natural history by Dr. Eric Forsman, whose most significant discovery was the close association between spotted owls and old-growth forests. This discovery raised concerns because the majority of remaining old-growth owl habitat is on public land available for harvest.

In January 1987, plaintiff Greenworld, pursuant to Sec. 4(b)(3) of the ESA, 16 U.S.C. § 1533(b)(3), petitioned the Service to list the northern spotted owl as endangered. * * *

The ESA directs the Secretary of the Interior to determine whether any species have become endangered or threatened[1] due to habitat destruction, overutilization, disease or predation, or other natural or manmade factors. 16 U.S.C. § 1533(a)(1). The Act was amended in 1982 to ensure that the decision whether to list a species as endangered or threatened was based solely on an evaluation of the biological risks faced by the species, to the exclusion of all other factors. * * *

The Service's role in deciding whether to list the northern spotted owl as endangered or threatened is to assess the technical and scientific data in the administrative record against the relevant listing criteria in section

---

1. The ESA defines an "endangered species" as "any species which is in danger of extinction throughout all or a significant portion of its range * * *." 16 U.S.C. § 1532(6). A "threatened species" is "any species which is likely to become an endangered species within the foreseeable future throughout all or a significant portion of its range." 16 U.S.C. § 1532(20).

4(a)(1) and then to exercise its own expert discretion in reaching its decision.

In July 1987, the Service announced that it would initiate a status review of the spotted owl and requested public comment. * * * The Service assembled a group of Service biologists, including Dr. Mark Shaffer, its staff expert on population viability, to conduct the review. The Service charged Dr. Shaffer with analyzing current scientific information on the owl. Dr. Shaffer concluded that:

> the most reasonable interpretation of current data and knowledge indicate [sic] continued old growth harvesting is likely to lead to the extinction of the subspecies in the foreseeable future which argues strongly for listing the subspecies as threatened or endangered at this time. * * *

The Service invited a peer review of Dr. Shaffer's analysis by a number of U.S. experts on population viability, all of whom agreed with Dr. Shaffer's prognosis for the owl, although each had some criticisms of his work. * * * On December 17 the Service announced that listing the owl as endangered under the Act was not warranted at this time.[5] 52 Fed.Reg. 48552, 48554 (Dec. 23, 1987). This suit followed. Both sides now move for summary judgment on the administrative record before the Court. * * *

The Status Review and the Finding to the listing petition offer little insight into how the Service found that the owl currently has a viable population. Although the Status Review cites extensive empirical data and lists various conclusions, it fails to provide any analysis. The Service asserts that it is entitled to make its own decision, yet it provides no explanation for its finding. An agency must set forth clearly the grounds on which it acted. * * * Judicial deference to agency expertise is proper, but the Court will not do so blindly. The Court finds that the Service has not set forth the grounds for its decision against listing the owl.

The Service's documents also lack any expert analysis supporting its conclusion. Rather, the expert opinion is entirely to the contrary. The only reference in the Status Review to an actual opinion that the owl does not face a significant likelihood of extinction is a mischaracterization of a conclusion of Dr. Mark Boyce: "Boyce (1987) * * * concluded that there is a low probability that the spotted owls will go extinct. He does point out that population fragmentation appears to impose the greatest risks to extinction." Status Review at 24 (footnote added). Dr. Boyce responded to the Service: "I did not conclude that the Spotted Owl enjoys a low probability of extinction, and I would be very disappointed if efforts to preserve the Spotted Owl were in any way thwarted by a misinterpretation of something I wrote."

Numerous other experts on population viability contributed to or reviewed drafts of the Status Review, or otherwise assessed spotted owl

---

5. The Service's Finding * * * [was that] "a proposed listing of the northern spotted owl is not warranted at this time. Due to the need for population trend information and other biological data, priority given by the Service to this species for further research and monitoring will continue to be high. * * *"

viability. Some were employed by the Service; others were independent. None concluded that the northern spotted owl is not at risk of extinction. * * *

The Service invited a peer review of Dr. Shaffer's analysis. Drs. Michael Soule, Bruce Wilcox, and Daniel Goodman, three leading U.S. experts on population viability, reviewed and agreed completely with Dr. Shaffer's prognosis for the owl.

For example, Dr. Soule, the acknowledged founder of the discipline of "conservation biology" (the study of species extinction), concluded:

> I completely concur with your conclusions, and the methods by which you reached them. The more one hears about *Strix occidentalis caurina*, the more concern one feels. Problems with the data base and in the models notwithstanding, and politics notwithstanding, I just can't see how a responsible biologist could reach any other conclusion than yours.

The Court will reject conclusory assertions of agency "expertise" where the agency spurns unrebutted expert opinions without itself offering a credible alternative explanation. * * * Here, the Service disregarded all the expert opinion on population viability, including that of its own expert, that the owl is facing extinction, and instead merely asserted its expertise in support of its conclusion.

The Service has failed to provide its own or other expert analysis supporting its conclusions. Such analysis is necessary to establish a rational connection between the evidence presented and the Service's decision. Accordingly, the United States Fish and Wildlife Service's decision not to list at this time the northern spotted owl as endangered or threatened under the Endangered Species Act was arbitrary and capricious and contrary to law. * * *

In deference to the Service's expertise and its role under the Endangered Species Act, the Court remands this matter to the Service, which has 90 days from the date of this order to provide an analysis for its decision that listing the northern spotted owl as threatened or endangered is not currently warranted. Further, the Service is ordered to supplement its Status Review and petition Finding consistent with this Court's ruling.

NOTES AND QUESTIONS

1.   If, upon remand, the agency found one acknowledged expert in the field who would testify that the owl was not currently endangered or threatened, would its decision not to list the species be upheld upon judicial review? Even if the plaintiffs produced nineteen experts who were of the contrary opinion, would the agency's decision not to list be arbitrary and capricious? (On remand, the agency listed the spotted owl as "threatened." 55 Fed. Reg. 26,114 (1990).)

2.   As the court here noted, Congress amended the ESA in 1982 to require the Secretary to make the listing decision "*solely* on the basis of the best scientific and commercial data available." 16 U.S.C. § 1533(b)(1)(A)

(emphasis added). Does this foreclose the U.S. Fish & Wildlife Service from considering the economic hardship that might result from listing a species? In a string of cases, courts have concluded that the statute focuses solely on biology, and economic considerations must be excluded. See generally Holly Doremus, Listing Decisions Under the ESA: Why Better Science Isn't Always Better Policy, 75 Wash. U.L.Q. 1029, 1055–56 (1997). See also Federico Cheever, Butterflies, Cave Spiders, Milk–Vetch, Bunchgrass, Sedges, Lilies, Checker–Mallows and Why the Prohibition Against Judicial Balancing of Harm under the Endangered Species Act is a Good Idea, 22 Wm & Mary Envtl. L. & Pol'y Rev. 313 (1998). On the other hand, the court held in Southwest Center for Biological Diversity v. Babbitt, 215 F.3d 58, 60 (D.C.Cir.2000), that the government is not required to conduct an actual population count before making a decision about whether to list a species, because the " 'best available data' requirement makes it clear the Secretary has no obligation to conduct independent studies."

3.   Is the agency decision on listing subject to NEPA? Pacific Legal Foundation v. Andrus, 657 F.2d 829 (6th Cir.1981) answered this question in the negative. The court said that an EIS "does not and cannot serve the purposes of" the ESA; the statutory criteria for listing species do not leave the Secretary with "discretion to consider the five factors required to be considered" in an EIS; the act of listing species itself "furthers the purpose of NEPA;" and an EIS in this context would not "serve the functions it was designed to serve." 657 F.2d at 833–41.

4.   In City of Las Vegas v. Lujan, 891 F.2d 927, 932 (D.C.Cir.1989), the plaintiffs sought to overturn an emergency decision by the Fish & Wildlife Service to list the desert tortoise north and west of the Colorado River as endangered. The court refused, finding that the Secretary had complied with the Act by setting forth "detailed reasons" justifying the listing. It also indicated it was willing to cut the agency some slack if necessary: "[W]hat might constitute arbitrary and capricious action or an unacceptable explanation for a regulation in the normal course of events might well pass muster under the emergency [listing] provisions of 16 U.S.C. § 1533(b)(7)."

5.   In United States v. Guthrie, 50 F.3d 936 (11th Cir.1995), the court refused to allow the defendant, being prosecuted for buying endangered turtles, to challenge the listing on the ground that new evidence showed the species in question was not a separate species. The court reasoned that the defendant could have, but did not, use this evidence to petition the Service to delist the species, a course of action which would have allowed the expert agency to pass on the question, rather than have it resolved in a collateral attack in the criminal case. Given the precautionary, protectionist thrust of the Act, even when a court finds a procedural irregularity in a listing, it has not set aside the listing (thus keeping the Act's the protections in place) while the government is fixing the problem. See, e.g, Idaho Farm Bureau Federation v. Babbitt, 58 F.3d 1392 (9th Cir.1995).

6.   As footnote 1 in the principal case indicates, species may be listed as either "threatened" or "endangered." The statute and its implementing regulations do not distinguish very often between the two categories. See,

e.g., footnote 5 in the *Sweet Home* decision, infra p. 477. Generally regulation may be somewhat more flexible where the species in question is listed as "threatened" rather than "endangered," but in most areas limitations on conduct are the same. Section 4(d) of the Act, 16 U.S.C. § 1533(d), directs the Secretary to "issue such regulations as he deems necessary and advisable to provide for the conservation of" threatened species. See, e.g., Louisiana ex rel. Guste v. Verity, 853 F.2d 322, 333 (5th Cir.1988) (upholding 4(d) regulations requiring shrimp nets to be equipped with special gear to reduce the capture and drowning of sea turtles, the court noting that the Secretary did not have to show that they would halt the decline of sea turtles because the Act "simply presumes that prohibited takings will deplete the species"). In Sierra Club v. Clark, 755 F.2d 608 (8th Cir.1985), however, the court struck down § 4(d) regulations that allowed sport trapping of threatened gray wolves, holding that such regulations were not for the "conservation" of the species, because the ESA defines conservation to include "regulated taking" only "in the extraordinary case where population pressures within a given ecosystem cannot be otherwise relieved," 16 U.S.C. § 1532(3), and the Secretary had not made such a finding.

7.   The ESA defines the "species" that may be listed as including "any subspecies of fish or wildlife or plants, and any *distinct population segment* of any species of vertebrate fish or wildlife which interbreeds when mature." 16 U.S.C. § 1532(16) (emphasis added). While the underscored phrase conceivably might be interpreted to protect "peripheral populations of otherwise abundant species," it has been used "sparingly in practice," mainly to "protect United States populations of species that are more common and unlisted in other countries." Michael Bean and Melanie Rowland, THE EVOLUTION OF NATIONAL WILDLIFE LAW 200 (3d ed. 1997). In Alsea Valley Alliance v. Evans, 161 F.Supp.2d 1154 (D.Or.2001), the court overturned a National Marine Fisheries Service decision to list the "Oregon Coast Evolutionary Significant Unit (ESU) coho salmon" as threatened under the ESA. The listing was based on a NMFS policy that excluded consideration of coho salmon reared in hatcheries unless they are "considered to be essential for recovery." The policy was based in part on a concern that the loss of genetic diversity in hatchery populations could lead to more risk of devastating disease or the inability of natural populations to survive relative to hatchery populations. Because hatchery coho interbreed with non-hatchery coho, and thus were part of the same "distinct population segment" as defined by the Act, the court held that it was impermissible for NMFS to make a further distinction and exclude them from consideration in the listing decision. "The NMFS listing decision creates [an arbitrary distinction between] two genetically identical coho salmon swimming side-by-side in the same stream, but only one receives ESA protection * * *."

8.   Closely related to the "distinct population segment" idea is the statutory provision that a species may be listed if it is "in danger of extinction throughout all *or a significant portion of* its range." 16 U.S.C. § 1532(6), (20) (emphasis added). This concept is not explained in the implementing regulations, and ambiguities in its meaning were explored in

Defenders of Wildlife v. Norton, 258 F.3d 1136 (9th Cir.2001), which vacated a Secretarial decision not to list the flat-tailed horned lizard under the Act for failing to give sufficient consideration to this issue, and particularly whether the lizard might "require different degrees of protection" in different places.

9.   Domestic and foreign species of fish, wildlife and plants may be listed, although the Act's protection of plants is somewhat limited. See George Coggins & Anne Fleishel Harris, The Greening of American Law? The Recent Evolution of Federal Law for Preserving Floral Diversity, 27 Nat. Res.J. 247 (1987).

10.   The net effect of the provisions discussed in paragraphs 6–8, supra, is that a single species may be listed as endangered in one geographic area, threatened in another, and not protected at all in another area. The gray wolf provides such a case. See Bean & Rowland, at 202.

11.   The ESA refers to "inadequacy of existing regulatory mechanism" [sic] as a cause of endangerment, see 16 U.S.C. § 1533(a)(1)(D), and also directs the listing agency to take into "account those efforts, if any, being made" by any State or local government "to protect such species." Id. § 1533(b)(1)(A). Sometimes efforts are made to avoid listing by securing what are called "candidate conservation agreements," whereby commitments are made to take steps to protect populations. Such an agreement was reached between NMFS and the State of Oregon in an attempt to head off the listing of the Oregon coastal coho, but a reviewing court set aside the agreement because its regulatory commitments were too vague and dependent upon future actions that might not be taken. See Oregon Natural Resources Council v. Daley, 6 F.Supp.2d 1139 (D.Or.1998). Other courts have also rejected such agreements when they rely on the promise of taking future measures or measures of uncertain effectiveness. See, e.g., Defenders of Wildlife v. Norton, 258 F.3d 1136 (9th Cir.2001); Federation of Fly Fishers v. Daley, 131 F.Supp.2d 1158 (N.D.Cal.2000); Save Our Springs v. Babbitt, 27 F.Supp.2d 739 (W.D.Tex.1997); Biodiversity Legal Found. v. Babbitt, 943 F.Supp. 23 (D.D.C.1996). A draft Policy for Evaluation of Conservation Efforts When Making Listing Decisions was published for comment at 65 Fed. Reg. 37102 (June 13, 2000). Regulations governing candidate conservation agreements are found at 50 C.F.R.17.22(d); 17.32(d) (2001).

12.   The number of potential endangered species cited in note 13 of Justice Powell's dissent in *TVA v. Hill* is probably conservative. Depending on whether the counter is a "splitter" or a "lumper," there may be upwards of five million species in the world and an incalculable number of subspecies and populations. See Norman Myers, THE SINKING ARK (1979). The complete list of officially imperilled species is found at 50 C.F.R. §§ 17.11 (wildlife) and 17.12 (plants). It includes, as of December 31, 2001, 1244 domestic and 558 foreign species. About 80% of the domestic species were listed as endangered; the remainder, as threatened. Worldwide, mammals account for 340 listed species; birds 274, reptiles 115, and fish 125. Many of these species are found on federal lands, including mammals (ranging from the grizzly bear to the black-footed ferret); birds

(ranging from the California condor to the light-footed clapper rail); reptiles; fish; crustaceans; insects; and assorted plants. New species are being added on a fairly regular basis. Perhaps few have heard of the Columbian white-tailed deer, the San Joaquin kit fox, the Attwater's greater prairie chicken, the Santa Cruz long-toed salamander, the Pahranaget Bonytail, the Pahrump Killifish, or the unarmored three spine stickleback, but the remaining few of those little devils are under Uncle Sam's own wing just as much as the more glamorous species. And these are only the species on the federal list: states are free to make their own lists, and quite a few have done so. State programs more protective than federal law are expressly preserved. 16 U.S.C. § 1535(f).

3.   CRITICAL HABITAT

The concept of critical habitat is "one of the Act's most contentious, ambiguous, and confusing concepts * * * [with] no clear, consistent, and shared understanding of what it means or what role it is to play." Bean and Rowland, at 251. As defined by a 1978 amendment, 16 U.S.C. § 1532(5)(A), critical habitat is not just the habitat in the existing range of the species, nor even the habitat upon which the species depends. See Katherine S. Yagerman, Protecting the Critical Habitat Under the Federal Endangered Species Act, 20 Envt'l L. 811 (1990). Another spotted owl decision put it this way:

> * * * [E]ven though more extensive habitat may be essential to maintain the species over the long term, critical habitat only includes the minimum amount of habitat needed to avoid short-term jeopardy or habitat in need of immediate intervention. Habitat not currently occupied by the spotted owl may be designated as critical only upon a determination by the Secretary of the Interior that such areas are essential to ensure the conservation of the species.

Northern Spotted Owl v. Lujan, 758 F.Supp. 621, 623 (W.D.Wash.1991). The Act defines "conservation" to mean bringing listed species "to the point at which the measures provided pursuant to this chapter are no longer necessary;" i.e., the species is recovered. See 16 U.S.C. § 1532(2).

Critical habitat designation guides federal agencies in fulfilling their obligations under Section 7 of the ESA, the provision in applied in *TVA v. Hill*. That is, federal agencies must not take or authorize actions that are either "likely to jeopardize the continued existence of" a listed species, *or* which would "result in the destruction or adverse modification of [designated critical] habitat * * *." 16 U.S.C. § 1536(a)(2). Critical habitat designation therefore adds protection to the species mostly to the extent that the consultation process would not otherwise find that destruction or adverse modification of critical habitat leads to jeopardy. Many biologists in the U.S. Fish & Wildlife Service believe that, in almost all cases, jeopardy will in fact be found if key habitat is modified, whether or not it is formally designated as "critical." To the extent that is true, formal designation of critical habitat adds little protection to listed species. For that and other reasons discussed in the next paragraph, only about 10% of the listed species have designated critical habitat.

The designation of critical habitat can be laborious and expensive, because the designation process is one of the few places where the Secretary must consider the probable economic or other impacts on human activities resulting from the critical habitat designation. See 16 U.S.C. § 1533(b)(2) (designation of critical habitat is on the basis of the best available scientific data "and after taking into consideration the economic impact, and any other relevant impact" of such designation, and the Secretary may exclude an area from critical habitat if she determines that the benefits of exclusion outweigh the benefits of inclusion, unless she determines that failure to designate would result in extinction). The judgment and discretion involved led the Tenth Circuit to find that NEPA applied this determination, see Catron County Board of Commissioners v. U.S. Fish & Wildlife Service, 75 F.3d 1429 (10th Cir.1996), while the Ninth Circuit has held otherwise, see Douglas County v. Babbitt, 48 F.3d 1495 (9th Cir.1995). Contributing to the Service's lack of enthusiasm for critical habitat designation is the fact that the money for critical habitat designation comes out of the same pot as money for listing, so from the Service's perspective every dollar spent on critical habitat protection is one that cannot be spent on listing, where the protection "bang for the buck" is much greater. Misunderstanding about the role of critical habitat contributes to the confusion and controversy. Many environmentalists like critical habitat designations because it's the only reference in the Act to habitat (which everyone understands is the key to long-term survival of species in peril) and it provides the only explicit tool to protect habitat which is currently unoccupied by a listed species. Many in the regulated community like the fact that designation of critical habitat is the only place in the Act that explicitly allows economic impacts to be taken into account.

The Act requires the Secretary to designate critical habitat at the time the species is listed "to the maximum extent prudent and determinable." 16 U.S.C. §§ 1533 (a)(3); see also § 1533(b)(6)(C). There has been much litigation about the designation of critical habitat. The courts have repeatedly sided with the plaintiffs. See, e.g., Sierra Club v. U.S. Fish & Wildlife Service, 245 F.3d 434 (5th Cir.2001) (rejecting the Service's arguments that critical habitat does not provide much additional protection because, it said, critical habitat should focus on "recovery" rather than just "survival" of a species, and the designation "provides informational benefits to the public, state and local governments, and scientific organizations"); see also New Mexico Cattle Growers Ass'n v. U.S. Fish & Wildlife Service, 248 F.3d 1277 (10th Cir.2001) (same view of critical habitat, although the court, in a suit by livestock operators restricted by the Act, held that the Service's critical habitat determination for the southwestern willow flycatcher did not pay sufficient attention to economic impacts). See also NRDC v. U.S. Dept. of the Interior, 113 F.3d 1121 (9th Cir.1997), where the court, over a dissent, rejected the Service's arguments that it was not prudent to designate critical habitat for the coastal California gnatcatcher, finding that not designating should be a rare exception, not the rule.

Some environmental groups have pushed critical habitat designations hard in litigation, apparently with the belief, or hope, that as court orders to designate critical habitat pile up, Congress will appropriate more money for the task, but experience suggests otherwise. In the meantime, the Service is caught in the middle, being forced to do more critical habitat designations while undertaking more thorough economic analyses, and siphoning resources from the process of deciding whether to add candidate species to the list. Commentary on critical habitat is extensive; e.g., Jason M. Patlis, Paying Tribute to Joseph Heller with the Endangered Species Act: When Critical Habitat Isn't, 20 Stan.Envtl. L.J. 133 (2001); Thomas F. Darin, Designating Critical Habitat under the Endangered Species Act: Habitat Protection Versus Agency Discretion, 24 Harv.Envtl.L.Rev. 209 (2000).

4.   THE APPLICATION OF ESA'S SECTION 7(a)(2) CONSULTATION REQUIREMENT

The "consultation" requirement of section 7 is not limited to federal lands and resources; it has government-wide and nationwide applicability. A good deal of the judicial application of this section has, however, come in the context of integrating § 7 with federal resource management decisions, as in the following opinion.

Thomas v. Peterson

United States Court of Appeals, Ninth Circuit, 1985.
753 F.2d 754.

■ SNEED, CIRCUIT JUDGE:

* * * This is another environmental case pitting groups concerned with preserving a specific undeveloped area against an agency of the United States attempting to obey the commands given it by a Congress which is mindful of both environmentalists and those who seek to develop the nation's resources. Our task is to discern as best we can what Congress intended to be done under the facts before us.

Plaintiffs—landowners, ranchers, outfitters, miners, hunters, fishermen, recreational users, and conservation and recreation organizations—challenge actions of the United States Forest Service in planning and approving a timber road in the Jersey Jack area of the Nezperce National Forest in Idaho. The area is adjacent to the Salmon River, a congressionally-designated Wild and Scenic River, and is bounded on the west by the designated Gospel Hump Wilderness and on the east by the River of No Return Wilderness. The area lies in a "recovery corridor" identified by the U.S. Fish & Wildlife Service for the Rocky Mountain Gray Wolf, an endangered species. * * *

After [neighboring lands were designated as wilderness by Congress] the Forest Service * * * proceeded to plan timber development in the Jersey Jack area. In November, 1980, the Forest Service solicited public comments and held a public hearing on a proposed gravel road that would provide access to timber to be sold. The Forest Service prepared an environmental assessment (EA), see 40 C.F.R. § 1508.9 (1984), to determine whether an EIS would be required for the road. Based on the EA, the Forest Service concluded that no EIS was required, and issued a Finding of No Significant Impact (FONSI), see 40 C.F.R. § 1508.13. The FONSI and the notice of the Forest Supervisor's decision to go ahead with the road were issued in a single document on February 9, 1981. The decision notice stated that "no known threatened or endangered plant or animal species have been found" within the area, but the EA contained no discussion of endangered species. * * * [The plaintiffs filed this lawsuit after exhausting administrative remedies and one of their principal allegations was that the] road is likely to affect the Rocky Mountain Gray Wolf * * * and the Forest Service has failed to follow procedures mandated by the Endangered Species Act. * * *

The ESA contains both substantive and procedural provisions. Substantively, [§ 9 of] the Act prohibits the taking or importation of endangered species, see 16 U.S.C. § 1538, and [§ 7] requires federal agencies to ensure that their actions are not "likely to jeopardize the continued existence of any endangered species or threatened species or result in the destruction or adverse modification" of critical habitat of such species, see 16 U.S.C. § 1536(a)(2).

The Act prescribes a three-step process to ensure compliance with its substantive provisions by federal agencies. Each of the first two steps serves a screening function to determine if the successive steps are required. The steps are:

(1) An agency proposing to take an action must inquire of the Fish & Wildlife Service (F & WS) whether any threatened or endangered species "may be present" in the area of the proposed action. See 16 U.S.C. § 1536(c)(1).

(2) If the answer is affirmative, the agency must prepare a "biological assessment" to determine whether such species "is likely to be affected" by the action. Id. The biological assessment may be part of an environmental impact statement or environmental assessment. Id.

(3) If the assessment determines that a threatened or endangered species "is likely to be affected," the agency must formally consult with the F & WS. Id. § 1536(a)(2). The formal consultation results in a "biological opinion" issued by the F & WS. See id. § 1536(b). If the biological opinion concludes that the proposed action would jeopardize the species or destroy or adversely modify critical habitat, see id. § 1536(a)(2), then the action may not go forward unless the F & WS can suggest an alternative that avoids such jeopardization, destruction, or adverse modification. Id. § 1536(b)(3)(A). If the opinion concludes that the action will not violate the Act, the F & WS may still require measures to minimize its impact. Id. § 1536(b)(4)(ii)–(iii).

Plaintiffs first allege that, with respect to the Jersey Jack road, the Forest Service did not undertake step (1), a formal request to the F & WS. The district court found that to be the case, but concluded that the procedural violation was insignificant because the Forest Service was already aware that wolves may be present in the area. The court therefore refused to enjoin the construction of the road. Plaintiffs insist, based on TVA v. Hill, 437 U.S. 153 (1978), that an injunction is mandatory once any ESA violation is found. Defendants respond, citing Village of False Pass v. Clark, 733 F.2d 605 (9th Cir.1984), that *TVA* applies only to substantive violations of the ESA, and that a court has discretion to deny an injunction when it finds a procedural violation to be *de minimis*.

We need not reach this issue. The Forest Service's failure goes beyond the technical violation cited by the district court, and is not *de minimis*.

Once an agency is aware that an endangered species may be present in the area of its proposed action, the ESA requires it to prepare a biological assessment to determine whether the proposed action "is likely to affect" the species and therefore requires formal consultation with the F & WS. The Forest Service did not prepare such an assessment prior to its decision to build the Jersey Jack road. Without a biological assessment, it cannot be determined whether the proposed project will result in a violation of the ESA's substantive provisions. A failure to prepare a biological assessment for a project in an area in which it has been determined that an endangered species may be present cannot be considered a *de minimis* violation of the ESA.

The district court found that the Forest Service had "undertaken sufficient study and action to further the purposes of the ESA." Its finding was based on affidavits submitted by the Forest Service for the litigation.[7] These do not constitute a substitute for the preparation of the biological assessment required by the ESA.

Given a substantial procedural violation of the ESA in connection with a federal project, the remedy must be an injunction of the project pending compliance with the ESA. The procedural requirements of the ESA are analogous to those of NEPA * * *; under the ESA, agencies are required to assess the effect on endangered species of projects in areas where such species may be present. 16 U.S.C. § 1536(c). A failure to prepare a biological assessment is comparable to a failure to prepare an environmental impact statement. * * *

Our cases repeatedly have held that, absent "unusual circumstances," an injunction is the appropriate remedy for a violation of NEPA's procedural requirements. [citations omitted] Irreparable damage is presumed to flow from a failure properly to evaluate the environmental impact of a major federal action. We see no reason that the same principle should not apply to procedural violations of the ESA.

The Forest Service argues that the procedural requirements of the ESA should be enforced less stringently than those of NEPA because, unlike NEPA, the ESA also contains substantive provisions. We acknowledge that the ESA's substantive provisions distinguish it from NEPA, but

---

7. The district court relied on the Forest Service's assertion that it had worked in "close cooperation" with the F & WS, but that assertion is undermined by letters in the record from the F & WS indicating that the Forest Service had not consulted with the F & WS on the impact of the road and the timber sales on the gray wolf, and that the F & WS felt that the Forest Service was not giving the wolf adequate consideration.

the distinction acts the other way. If anything, the strict substantive provisions of the ESA justify *more* stringent enforcement of its procedural requirements, because the procedural requirements are designed to ensure compliance with the substantive provisions. The ESA's procedural requirements call for a systematic determination of the effects of a federal project on endangered species. If a project is allowed to proceed without substantial compliance with those procedural requirements, there can be no assurance that a violation of the ESA's substantive provisions will not result. The latter, of course, is impermissible.

The district court, citing Palila v. Hawaii Dept. of Land and Natural Resources, 639 F.2d 495 (9th Cir.1981), held that "[a] party asserting a violation of the Endangered Species Act has the burden of showing the proposed action would have some prohibited effect on an endangered species or its critical habitat," and found that the plaintiffs in this case had not met that burden. This is a misapplication of *Palila*. That case concerned the ESA's prohibition of the "taking" of an endangered species, 16 U.S.C. § 1538(a)(1)(B), not the ESA's procedural requirements. Quite naturally, the court in *Palila* found that a plaintiff, in order to establish a violation of the "taking" provision, must show that such a "taking" has occurred. See 639 F.2d at 497. The holding does not apply to violations of the ESA's procedural requirements. A plaintiffs' burden in establishing a procedural violation is to show that the circumstances triggering the procedural requirement exist, and that the required procedures have not been followed. The plaintiffs in this case have clearly met that burden.

The Forest Service would require the district court, absent proof by the plaintiffs to the contrary, to make a finding that the Jersey Jack road is not likely to effect [sic] the Rocky Mountain Gray Wolf, and that therefore any failure to comply with ESA procedures is harmless. This is not a finding appropriate to the district court at the present time. Congress has assigned to the agencies and to the Fish & Wildlife Service the responsibility for evaluation of the impact of agency actions on endangered species, and has prescribed procedures for such evaluation. Only by following the procedures can proper evaluations be made. It is not the responsibility of the plaintiffs to prove, nor the function of the courts to judge, the effect of a proposed action on an endangered species when proper procedures have not been followed.

We therefore hold that the district court erred in declining to enjoin construction of the Jersey Jack road pending compliance with the ESA.
* * *

NOTES AND QUESTIONS

1. The joint regulations of the wildlife agencies set up a three-tiered consultation process: No consultation is required if the action agency determines its action will have no impact on listed species or critical habitat. If the action "may affect" a listed species or critical habitat, "informal consultation" or ultimately "formal consultation" may occur, as explained below. In the latter two stages, the action agency prepares a

biological assessment (BA), and the wildlife agency may prepare a biological opinion (BO). See 50 C.F.R. §§ 402.13, 402.14. *Thomas* involved the first, "may affect," stage. There was no proof that wolves actually inhabited the Jersey Jack area—only that there "may" have been wolves there. Should sightings of the species in the affected area be required before an injunction issues? May the wildlife agency's opinion on the "may be present" determination be questioned by the action agency? Reviewable by a court?

2. How does the ESA process compare with the NEPA process? Compare the steps involved in each. For example, is the BA requirement of the ESA comparable to the "environmental impact statement" process of NEPA? Note that the statute expressly provides that the action agency (here, the Forest Service) may use the NEPA process as the vehicle for complying with BA requirement of the ESA. 16 U.S.C. § 1536(c)(1). The BA is to identify any endangered or threatened species "which is likely to be affected by the [proposed] action" and it examines the probable impact of the proposed action.

3. If, on the basis of the BA, the action agency concludes that the contemplated action is "not likely to adversely affect" a listed species, the regulations authorize it to engage in *informal* consultation with the wildlife agency. The latter may either (1) issue a written concurrence in the determination; or (2) suggest modifications that the action agency could take to avoid the likelihood of adverse effects to the listed species. See 50 C.F.R. § 402.13(b). If no concurrence is reached, the regulations require *formal* consultation between the two agencies. *Id.*, § 402.14.

4. If the action agency's biological assessment shows likely affect, it must undertake *formal* consultation with the wildlife agency. The product of that consultation is the BO, which assesses whether the action would likely result in jeopardy to the species (or destruction or adverse modification of critical habitat). The ESA does not define "jeopardy." The FWS regulations define it to mean "to engage in an action that reasonably would be expected, directly or indirectly, to reduce appreciably the likelihood of both the survival and recovery of a listed species in the wild by reducing the reproduction, numbers, or distribution of that species." 50 C.F.R. § 402.02 (2001). The statute contemplates that the consultation process will be completed within 90 days of initiation, and while extensions of time are possible by agreement of the agencies, if the action is issuance of a permit or license, the extension can be no longer than 60 days without the applicant's consent. See 16 U.S.C. § 1536(b)(1)(A) and (B).

5. If the BO shows that jeopardy is likely, it must "include reasonable and prudent alternatives, if any, to avoid these effects." 16 U.S.C, § 1536(b)(3)(A). Thus a BO may have one of three conclusions: no jeopardy; jeopardy with reasonable and prudent alternatives; or jeopardy without such alternatives. A 1992 study by the General Accounting Office showed that more than 90% of formal consultations concluded "no jeopardy;" and that almost all of the "jeopardy" opinions were accompanied by reasonable and prudent alternatives. Of 100,000 consultations over a five year period, only 27 had BOs of the third category. GAO, ENDANGERED SPECIES ACT; TYPES AND NUMBER OF IMPLEMENTING ACTIONS 26 (1992).

6. In *TVA v. Hill*, there was no controversy about whether the closing of the dam would jeopardize the snail darter. In more typical situations, there may be a substantial dispute over the action's effect on the species. The BO will give the views of the wildlife consulting agency on the issue. Is the action agency free to ignore the advice? What is a reviewing court to do in the face of such an interagency disagreement? The U.S. Supreme Court has said that biological opinions have a "virtually determinative effect" on the action agency's decision. Bennett v. Spear, 520 U.S. 154 (1997). In that case the question was whether the plaintiff water users had standing to contest a biological opinion, and one of the issues was whether the threatened reduction in their water diversion (in order to meet the needs of listed species) was, under applicable standing test, "fairly traceable" to the BO, and likely to be redressed if the BO were set aside. The Court explained:

> [W]hile the Service's Biological Opinion theoretically serves an "advisory function," 51 Fed. Reg. 19928 (1986), in reality it has a powerful coercive effect on the action agency. [The government's brief explained that an action agency] "that chooses to deviate from the recommendations contained in a biological opinion bears the burden of 'articulat[ing] in its administrative record its reasons for disagreeing with the conclusions of a biological opinion.' 51 Fed. Reg. 19, 956 (1986). In the government's experience, action agencies very rarely choose to engage in conduct that the Service has concluded is likely to jeopardize the continued existence of a listed species."

> [T]he action agency must not only articulate its reasons for disagreement (which ordinarily requires species and habitat investigations that are not within the action agency's expertise), but * * * [it also] runs a substantial risk if its (inexpert) reasons turn out to be wrong. A Biological Opinion * * * alters the legal regime to which the action agency is subject. When it "offers reasonable and prudent alternatives" to the proposed action, a Biological Opinion must include a so-called "Incidental Take Statement"—a written statement specifying, among other things, those "measures that the [Service] considers necessary or appropriate to minimize [the action's impact on the affected species]" and the "terms and conditions . . . that must be complied with by the Federal agency . . . to implement [such] measures." 16 U.S.C. § 1536(b)(4). Any taking that is in compliance with these terms and conditions "shall not be considered to be a prohibited taking of the species concerned." § 1536(*o*)(2). Thus, the Biological Opinion's Incidental Take Statement constitutes a permit authorizing the action agency to "take" the endangered or threatened species so long as it respects the Service's "terms and conditions." The action agency is technically free to disregard the Biological Opinion and proceed with its proposed action, but it does so at its own peril (and that of its employees), for "any person" who knowingly "takes" an endangered or threatened species is subject to substantial civil and criminal penalties, including imprisonment. * * *

See also National Wildlife Federation v. Coleman, 529 F.2d 359 (5th Cir.), cert. denied sub nom. Boteler v. National Wildlife Federation, 429 U.S. 979 (1976) (while section 7 does not give the wildlife agency a "veto" over the action agency, on the facts there, proceeding against its advice was a "clear error of judgment"); Roosevelt Campobello International Park Commission v. EPA, 684 F.2d 1041 (1st Cir.1982) (substantially the same). Thus action agencies have ultimate authority, but proceed at a substantial risk if they fly in the face of the advice of the BO. The Incidental Take Statement (ITS) process referred to in the excerpt from *Bennett v. Spear* is an exemption from the prohibition on "taking" species found in section 9, considered further below.

7. With the decision in *Bennett v. Spear*, supra, clarifying that biological opinions were subject to judicial review when rendered, court decisions reviewing the merits of biological opinions are beginning to emerge. In Pacific Coast Federation of Fishermen's Ass'ns v. National Marine Fisheries Service, 265 F.3d 1028 (9th Cir.2001), for example, the court set aside NMFS' biological opinions that national forest timber sales along certain waterways were unlikely to jeopardize populations of listed fish, because scientific evidence was insufficient to support NMFS' conclusion that natural vegetation regrowth would adequately mitigate degradation caused by timber harvesting. In Southwest Ctr. for Biological Diversity v. U.S. Bureau of Reclamation, 143 F.3d 515 (9th Cir.1998), the court held that the USFWS need not select a "reasonable and prudent alternative" that provided the highest degree of protection if another less protective alternative nevertheless avoided jeopardizing the listed species. And compare Fund for Animals v. Rice, 85 F.3d 535 (11th Cir.1996) (upholding a "no jeopardy" opinion for a landfill in an area identified in the species recovery plan as important for protection, drawing a distinction between the avoidance of jeopardy and recovery) with Aluminum Co. of Am. v. Administrator, Bonneville Power Admin., 175 F.3d 1156 (9th Cir.1999) (upholding the application of a jeopardy standard that factored in recovery needs of the listed species).

8. Does section 7 apply to federal actions where the federal agency has no discretion? In Sierra Club v. Babbitt, 65 F.3d 1502, 1509 (9th Cir.1995), the court held that the BLM was not required to consult with the USFWS about the effect of a proposed logging road on the northern spotted owl. The road was to be built partly on BLM-managed land by a private timber company which owned lands in a checkboard with BLM, under a right of way agreement with the BLM. The agreement, which provided reciprocal rights of way to BLM and the timber company, sharply limited BLM's authority to control the project. Therefore, the court said, BLM had no duty to consult because it would be "a meaningless exercise; the agency simply does not possess the ability to implement measures that inure to the benefit of the protected species." See also Environmental Protection Information Center v. Simpson Timber Co., 255 F.3d 1073 (9th Cir.2001). If the law requires the Secretary of the Interior to issue a patent (deed) for federal property upon a showing by a mining claimant that it has made a discovery of a valuable mineral deposit on the land, must there be an ESA consultation? Compare discussion of South Dakota v. Andrus under NEPA,

supra p. 416; Constance Lundberg, Birds, Bunnies, and the Furbish Louse-wort—Wildlife and Mining on the Public Lands, 24 Rocky Mt.Min.L.Inst. 93, 114 (1978).

9. Many of the actions federal land managers take with respect to the resources under their control are plainly discretionary, and the section 7 process may apply. These include, for example, a decision to issue a mineral lease or allow livestock to graze on a particular tract of federal land known to be possible habitat for a listed species, or a decision to issue a right-of-way permit for a road across public lands to a private inholding, where the federal government has authority to select the route, and one possible access route traverses an area inhabited by a listed endangered species, and another much more costly route avoids the problem. In Natural Resources Defense Council v. Houston, 146 F.3d 1118 (9th Cir.1998), for example, the court found a duty to consult on renewal of contracts to deliver water from a federal project, because the federal agency had authority over the amount of water that could be delivered, which could affect listed species.

Many federal "actions" to which section 7 applies are relatively straightforward—issuing a permit or lease, or constructing a dam or a road. But more abstract actions, such as planning, may also be subject to consultation. This can raise a host of questions, some of them analogous to the "tiering" issues discussed in connection with NEPA. See *Kleppe v. Sierra Club*, supra p. 402. For example, there may be many layers of federal decision between a broad national or regional or area plan and an individual, on-the-ground permit. At what levels is consultation useful and legally required? What can a later consultation on a narrower decision, like issuing a timber sale contract, borrow or assume from an earlier consultation on a broader level, such as issuing a forest plan? Further, especially with respect to decisions that may be implemented over many years (such as a land use plan), or decisionmaking layers that may take years to work through, what is the consequence of listing a new species while implementation is ongoing? The complications arising from the marriage of the ESA and the planning processes are addressed in the following case.

Pacific Rivers Council v. Thomas

United States Court of Appeals, Ninth Circuit, 1994.
30 F.3d 1050, cert. denied sub nom Thomas v. Pacific Rivers Council, 514 U.S. 1082 (1995).

■ REINHARDT, CIRCUIT JUDGE:

Plaintiffs-appellants Pacific Rivers Council, et al. (PRC) appeal the district court's grant of a partial injunction. This injunction bars the United States Forest Service (Forest Service) from announcing, awarding or conducting any additional timber sales, range activities, or road building projects in the Wallowa–Whitman and Umatilla National Forests until it commences consultation procedures as required by the Endangered Species Act § 7(a)(2), 16 U.S.C. § 1536(a)(2) (ESA). The basis for the injunction was that the Forest Service had failed to consult with the National Marine Fisheries Service (NMFS) regarding the effects of certain Land and Resource Management Plans (LRMPs) on the Snake River chinook salmon, a species recently listed as "threatened" under the ESA. PRC argued that the district court should enjoin ongoing or announced timber, range, and road projects that the Forest Service had determined were not likely to affect the chinook. The district court accepted the Forest Service's determination that these projects were not irreversible or irretrievable commitments of resources in violation of ESA § 7(d), 16 U.S.C. § 1536(d).

The Forest Service also appeals the district court's order. It argues that because the LRMPs were adopted before the chinook were listed as a "threatened" species, the LRMPs are not agency actions requiring consultation under § 7(a)(2) of the ESA, 16 U.S.C. § 1536(a)(2). It also argues that even if the LRMPs are deemed agency actions, the Forest Service has already begun informal consideration of potential amendments to the LRMPs to address the listed chinook, making reinitiation of consultation superfluous.

We affirm the district court's judgment granting an injunction against the Forest Service pending compliance with the ESA. The LRMPs are important programmatic documents that set out guidelines for resource management in the forests involved in this case. As such, the LRMPs constitute continuing agency action requiring consultation under § 7(a)(2) of the ESA. We reverse, however, the district court's judgment denying an injunction against all ongoing and announced timber, range, and road projects. The district court erred in interpreting § 7(d) of the ESA to allow the ongoing activities to continue when the Forest Service had failed to enter into consultation as required by § 7(a)(2) of that statute. Accordingly, we remand to the district court with instructions to reconsider whether the ongoing and announced timber, range and road projects are irreversible and irretrievable commitments of resources which must be enjoined during consultation on the LRMPs between the Forest Service and NMFS.

In 1990, the Forest Service promulgated and approved both the Wallowa–Whitman and the Umatilla Forest LRMPs. These LRMPs establish forest-wide and area-specific standards and guidelines to which all projects must adhere for up to 15 years. The LRMPs identify lands suitable for timber production and other uses, and establish an allowable sale quantity of timber and production targets and schedules for forage, road construction, and other economic commodities. The LRMPs also seek to provide adequate fish and wildlife habitat to maintain viable populations of existing native species, and "include measures for preventing the destruction or adverse modification of critical habitat for threatened and endangered species." 36 C.F.R. § 219.1(a); 219.27(6) & (8). Every resource plan, permit, contract, or any other document pertaining to the use of the forest must be consistent with the LRMP. 16 U.S.C. § 1604(i).

Anticipating the listing of the Snake River chinook salmon as a threatened species, the Forest Service and the NMFS entered into an "Inter-agency Agreement for Fulfilling Section 7 Interagency Coordination Responsibilities under the Endangered Species Act, Snake River Basin

Salmonid Habitats." They agreed to cooperate in developing and implementing conservation strategies for the listed salmon and to consider amending LRMPs that were inconsistent with these strategies. In addition, the Forest Service agreed to conduct a biological evaluation of all proposed and ongoing activities in the Wallowa–Whitman and Umatilla Forests.

On April 22, 1992, the NMFS listed the Snake River chinook as a threatened species. See 57 Fed.Reg. 14,653. After the salmon were listed, 755 ongoing projects for the Umatilla Forest and 2,806 for the Wallowa–Whitman Forest were subjected to a biological evaluation to determine whether particular activities might affect the salmon. Over 700 projects were found "likely to adversely affect" the salmon. All of these were suspended pending completion of formal consultation with the NMFS. Just under 1,200 of the projects were found not to affect the salmon. Another 1,700 projects were found "not likely to adversely affect" the salmon. All of the "not likely to adversely affect" projects were submitted to the NMFS for informal consultation by the end of August 1992. However, the Forest Service decided to allow on-going projects to continue during the duration of the informal consultation where it previously determined that the project was not likely to adversely affect the salmon. It determined that projects it deems are "not likely to adversely affect" a species will not constitute "irreversible or irretrievable commitments of resources and can be continued." * * *

The Forest Service first argues that the district court erred in concluding that the LRMPs are agency actions under § 7(a)(2) of the ESA, 16 U.S.C. § 1536(a)(2). Specifically, the Forest Service argues that the LRMPs are not ongoing agency action throughout their duration, but only when they were adopted in 1990 or if they are revised or amended in the future. The Forest Service maintains that the district court erred in determining that the LRMPs represent ongoing agency action throughout their duration. * * *

The Forest Service contends that the courts should defer to its administration of an ambiguous statute. It argues that the LRMPs in this case are not agency action and that its interpretation of the ESA is reasonable. * * * [It argues that] only the specific activities authorized by the LRMPs are agency actions within the meaning of the ESA. The LRMPs themselves, the Service argues, do not mandate any action and are "merely" programmatic documents.

However, the Forest Service can cite no precedent of this or any other court which lends support to such a reading of the statute. And as shown above, TVA weighs heavily against the Forest Service on this point, as is evident from the TVA Court's observation that "Congress foresaw that § 7 would, on occasion, require agencies to alter ongoing projects in order to fulfill the goals of the Act." Id. at 186.

Following the Supreme Court's lead in TVA, we have also construed "agency action" broadly. More importantly, we have recognized that forest management plans have ongoing effects extending beyond their mere approval. In Lane County [Audubon Society v. Jamison, 958 F.2d 290 (9th Cir.1992)], we found that a forest management plan implemented without consultation violated the ESA. Although the management plan in that case was implemented after the listing of the threatened species, our reasoning is relevant. We stated that the "[forest management plan] is action that 'may affect' the spotted owl, since it sets forth criteria for harvesting owl habitat." 958 F.2d at 294. Thus, we implicitly recognized that forest management plans can be actions even after their implementation.

Similarly, the LRMPs are actions that "may affect" the protected salmon because the plans set forth criteria for harvesting resources within the salmon's habitat. Among its zoning decisions, the Wallowa–Whitman LRMP allocates approximately 60,000 acres to the "management area" that surrounds the spawning grounds of the Snake River chinook. This allocation, established before the Snake River chinook were listed as threatened, sets guidelines for logging, grazing and road-building activities within its boundaries. Furthermore, the plans establish the allowable sale quantity of timber as well as production targets and schedules for forage, road construction, and other economic commodities.

Perhaps most telling, the Forest Service and the NMFS are amending the LRMPs, admitting that they are inadequate because they do not address the newly listed species.[12] These amendments belie the Forest Service's claim that the LRMPs do not constitute continuing agency action. They expressly acknowledge the need to revisit the LRMPs in light of the salmon's listing as a threatened species.

Given the importance of the LRMPs in establishing resource and land use policies for the forests in question there is little doubt that they are continuing agency action under § 7(a)(2) of the ESA. The fact that the Forest Service adopted these LRMPs before the listing of the Snake River chinook is, therefore, irrelevant. We affirm the district court's order requiring the Forest Service to reinitiate consultation under § 7(a)(2).

The district court accepted the Forest Service's conclusion that ongoing and announced timber, range, and road projects that may affect the Snake River chinook were not irreversible or irretrievable commitments of resources under § 7(d) of the ESA. 16 U.S.C. § 1536(d). It refused to enjoin these activities while the Forest Service consulted with NMFS on the individual projects in the LRMPs. However, the district court erred in applying § 7(d) to the instant case. As the ESA's plain language makes clear, § 7(d) applies only after an agency has initiated consultation under § 7(a)(2).[13] As detailed above, the Forest Service has, as yet, failed to enter

---

12. The Forest Service claims that reinitiation of consultation would be superfluous and unnecessary because it is in consultation regarding the proposed amendments currently under consideration. However, consultation on the entirety of both LRMPs is required, not just [on] an amendment to the LMRPs. *Cf.* Conner v. Burford, 848 F.2d at 1453 (9th Cir. 1988) ("The ESA requires the [agency's] biological opinion to analyze the effect of the *entire* agency action.") Requir-

ing the Forest Service to reinitiate consultation is not superfluous.

13. Section 7(d) states:

After initiation of consultation required under [§ 7(a)(2)], the Federal agency and the permit or license applicant shall not make any irreversible or irretrievable commitment of resources with respect to the agency action which has the effect of foreclosing the formulation or implementation of any reasonable or prudent al-

into consultation on the LRMPs themselves, despite the fact that the LRMPs constitute continuing agency action under § 7(a)(2). Accordingly, we reverse the district court's judgment denying an injunction barring ongoing and announced projects that may affect the Snake River chinook. * * *

The Forest Service has not reinitiated consultation as required under § 7(a)(2). Thus, its determination that the timber, road, and range projects are not irreversible or irretrievable commitments of resources is of no moment. Section 7(a)(2) mandates that the Forest Service enter into consultation on the LRMPs. Its conclusion that these activities "may affect" the protected salmon is sufficient reason to enjoin these projects. Only after the Forest Service complies with § 7(a)(2) can any activity that may affect the protected salmon go forward. Accordingly, we reverse the district court's denial of an injunction barring all ongoing and announced activities that may affect the Snake River chinook from going forward. The Forest Service cannot go forward with these activities without first complying with the consultation requirements of the ESA.

Because § 7(d) could not serve as the basis for permitting any agency action at the time of the hearing, we need not address the district court's rulings on whether the various commitments of resources were irreversible and irretrievable. If the Forest Service initiates consultation on the LRMPs, the court must decide if the ongoing or announced activities can proceed during the consultation period. It may find guidance in Lane County, where we held that the Bureau of Land Management could not go forward with any new sales of timber until consultation on a forest management plan and its effect on the threatened species was completed. Most importantly, we held that timber sales constitute per se irreversible and irretrievable commitments of resources under § 7(d) and thus could not go forward during the consultation period. Lane County, 958 F.2d at 295. * * *

NOTES AND QUESTIONS

1. After the National Marine Fisheries Service issued its formal BO, which identified certain jeopardizing activities permitted under the current plans, the injunction was lifted. Pacific Rivers Council v. Thomas, 897 F.Supp. 454 (D.Idaho 1995).

2. Suppose specific activities (such as timber sales and road permits) being carried out under the forest plan had themselves undergone specific consultation under the ESA, and the determination had been made that the sales or permits were not likely to jeopardize the salmon (or reasonable and prudent alternatives existed). If that were the case, should they be enjoined while consultation is being completed on the plan itself? Is the Ninth Circuit saying here that all federal activity in a national forest that may affect a newly listed species must be halted until consultation is completed

ternative measures which would not vio-   16 U.S.C. § 1536(d) (emphasis added).
late [§ 7(a)(2)].

on the overarching forest plan, no matter whether consultation on individual actions has been completed, and these consultations disclose no jeopardy?

3.   In Conner v. Burford, 848 F.2d 1441 (9th Cir.1988), relied upon in *Pacific Rivers*, consultation on the issuance of federal oil and gas leases resulted in a BO concluding that leasing itself was not likely to jeopardize the species. The BO proposed later consultations on federal actions subsequent to lease issuance that authorized on-the-ground activity on the lease. The Ninth Circuit rejected this approach, holding that the BO at the lease issuance stage should address post-leasing activities, even though forecasting what those activities might be was difficult. The U.S. Fish & Wildlife Service must, the court said, determine at the point of leasing whether "post-leasing activities in particular areas were fundamentally incompatible with the continued existence of the species." Compare the analogous situation under NEPA, where federal agencies have been able to postpone full NEPA compliance past the lease issuance stage by including in the lease a stipulation that reserves to the government full authority to prohibit all on-the-ground environmental impacts. See, e.g., Sierra Club v. Peterson, supra p. 421. Some of these NEPA cases also addressed the ESA and reached a similar conclusion. Should the approaches to this question of segmenting decisions be identical under NEPA and the ESA? Does the more substantive and protective thrust of the ESA justify a more stringent rule? Or does the "full disclosure" policy of NEPA counsel for a more stringent approach in the NEPA context?

5.   ESA Section 7(a)(1)—A Sleeper Provision?

This brief subsection contains two general directives. The first requires the Secretaries of Commerce and the Interior (supervisors of the wildlife agencies with major responsibility for implementing the act—the U.S. Fish & Wildlife Service at Interior and the National Marine Fisheries Service at Commerce) to "review ... programs [they administer] and utilize such programs in furtherance of the purposes of [the ESA]." The second is to "[a]ll other Federal agencies," and requires them, "in consultation with and with the assistance of the [two Secretaries, to] *utilize their authorities in furtherance of the purposes of [the ESA] by carrying out programs for the conservation of [listed] species....*" 16 U.S.C. § 1536(a) (emphasis added).

Sierra Club v. Glickman

United States Court of Appeals for the Fifth Circuit, 1998.
156 F.3d 606.

■ BENAVIDES, Circuit Judge:

This is the latest in a series of cases brought by Sierra Club and others concerned about endangered species that depend on water from the Edwards Aquifer for their survival. * * * The Edwards Aquifer is a 175–mile long underground aquifer that stretches through eight counties in central Texas. The Edwards Aquifer is recharged primarily from surface waters and rainfall seeping through porous earth along its path. Unless removed by human pumping, water in the Edwards Aquifer flows west to east, before turning northeast, where it is discharged through a series of springs on the eastern edge of the aquifer, the two largest of which are the San Marcos Springs in San Marcos and the Comal Springs in New Braunfels. The San Marcos and Comal Springs are the only habitat of five federally endangered and threatened species: the fountain darter, the San Marcos gambusia (which may now be extinct), the San Marcos salamander, the Texas blind salamander, and Texas wild rice (hereinafter collectively referred to as the "Edwards-dependent species"). *See* 50 C.F.R. §§ 17.11, 17.12.

The Edwards Aquifer is of great economic significance to the State of Texas. Water from the Edwards Aquifer is used by thousands of farmers to irrigate millions of dollars worth of crops, by over two million people as their primary source of water, and by thousands of businesses upon which the entire central Texas economy depends.

Pumping from the Edwards Aquifer, however, can have significant ecological consequences to the Edwards-dependent species. In times of even mild drought, the springflow at both the San Marcos and Comal Springs can decrease enough to threaten the survival of the Edwards-dependent species. Not surprisingly, given these often competing interests, the Edwards Aquifer has been the focus of extensive efforts to conserve its limited water resources. * * *

[In 1995 plaintiffs brought suit against the U.S. Department of Agriculture (USDA), claiming, among other things, that it had violated § 7(a)(1).] * * * [T]he district court held that the USDA "has not utilized its authority to carry out programs for the conservation of previously listed Edwards-dependent species as ESA § 7(a)(1) requires" and that it had not consulted with FWS concerning utilizing its authorities to carry out such programs. The court then ordered the USDA to develop, in consultation with FWS, "an organized program for utilizing USDA's authorities for the conservation of the Edwards-dependent endangered and threatened species as contemplated by the ESA." * * *

[The Court addressed the government's argument that the plaintiffs had no standing to raise the issue because, a]ccording to the USDA, the injury suffered by Sierra Club is caused by the independent actions (*i.e.,* pumping decisions) of third party farmers, over whom the USDA has no coercive control. * * * [T]he relevant inquiry in this case is whether the USDA has the ability through various programs to affect the pumping decisions of those third party farmers to such an extent that the plaintiff's injury could be relieved. In this respect, the USDA argues that "the most [that it] could do vis-a-vis farmers would be to encourage them to use water conservation methods by offering incentives under the discretionary programs described.... However, there is no evidence that, if additional incentives were offered, there is a 'substantial likelihood' that injury at the springs would be relieved." As Sierra Club points out, however, this claim is directly contradicted by the summary judgment evidence.

Three pieces of evidence are significant to a finding of causation in this case. The first document is *Cooperative Solutions,* a 1995 study (updated in

1996) conducted by the USDA in conjunction with Texas A & M University and the Texas State Soil and Water Conservation Board. One of the programs proposed in that study—providing financial assistance to farmers for the installation of water conservation measures—would save an estimated 38,000 acre-feet of Edwards irrigation water in an average year. The savings would be even greater in a dry year. Not only does the USDA have the authority to carry out such a program, but the USDA itself has described the proposal as cost-effective.

The second key document is the 1996 Biological Evaluation ("BE"), submitted by USDA to FWS during a § 7(a)(2) consultation concerning crop subsidy payments under the 1990 farm bill. According to the USDA's irrigation pumping estimates in that BE, 38,000 acre-feet represent 20% of the total Edwards irrigation pumping in dry years, when the threat to the Edwards-dependent species is greatest, and a much greater percentage in an average year.

The final link in this causal chain is FWS's response to the 1996 BE. In its response, FWS concluded that the springflow effects of a 20% reduction in Edwards irrigation pumping would have a significant impact on the Edwards-dependent species. In fact, FWS "categorically" disagreed with the USDA's statement that a 20% decrease in Edwards irrigation pumping would have no significant effect on the Edwards-dependent species. Moreover, the USDA itself acknowledges that "FWS's expertise extends to essentially factual issues regarding how particular actions affect listed species."

Given this evidence, we find the USDA's claim that it has no effect on the irrigation decisions of the farmers to be unpersuasive. To the contrary, the evidence introduced clearly shows that the USDA's failure to adopt any of the above programs is fairly traceable to the injury to the Edwards-dependent species. * * *

[The court then turned to whether § 7(a)(1) was] "designed to protect some threatened concrete interest of [Sierra Club's] that is the ultimate basis of [its] standing." Defenders of Wildlife, 504 U.S. at 573 n.8. In order to make this determination, we necessarily turn to the language of the statute. As noted above, § 7(a)(1) provides, in pertinent part, that "[a]ll other federal agencies shall, in consultation with and with the assistance of the Secretary, utilize their authorities in furtherance of the purposes of this chapter by carrying out programs for the *conservation* of endangered species and threatened species listed pursuant to section 1533 of this title." 16 U.S.C. § 1536(a)(1) (emphasis added). At first blush, this section appears to suggest that federal agencies have only a generalized duty to confer and develop programs for the benefit of endangered and threatened species—*i.e.,* not with respect to any particular species. If this reading were correct, we would be hard pressed to find standing in this case.[4]

---

4. If the statute created only a generalized duty rather than a duty with respect to each endangered and threatened species, it would be pure speculation that an order from this court would remedy the particularized injury alleged by the plaintiff. Unlike other procedural rights cases in which the consultation ordered would necessarily take into ac-

When read in the context of the ESA as a whole, however, we find that the agencies' duties under § 7(a)(1) are much more specific and particular. * * * We find the Supreme Court's examination of the meaning of "conserve" [in TVA v. Hill] to be instructive as to the meaning of "conservation" under § 7(a)(1). By imposing a duty on all federal agencies to use "all methods and procedures which are necessary to bring *any* endangered species or threatened species to the point at which the measures provided pursuant to this chapter are no longer necessary," 16 U.S.C. § 1532(2) (emphasis added), Congress was clearly concerned with the conservation of each endangered and threatened species. To read the command of § 7(a)(1) to mean that the agencies have only a generalized duty would ignore the plain language of the statute. * * *

Given the plain language of the statute and its legislative history, we conclude that Congress intended to impose an affirmative duty on each federal agency to conserve each of the species listed pursuant to § 1533. In order to achieve this objective, the agencies must consult with FWS as to each of the listed species, not just undertake a generalized consultation.[5] Consequently, we conclude that the procedures in question were designed to protect Sierra Club's threatened concrete interest in this case. Accordingly, we conclude that Sierra Club has standing to pursue this action. * * *

[The court then turned to the government's argument that no judicial review could be obtained under the ESA citizen suit provision or the APA for various reasons, among them that the USDA's] duties under § 7(a)(1) are not judicially reviewable because there is "no law to apply." In general, there is no law to apply if the statute is drawn in such broad terms that in a given case there would be nothing against which a court could measure agency compliance with the statute. See Citizens to Preserve Overton Park v. Volpe, 401 U.S. 402, 410–11 (1971). The USDA's argument in this respect, however, relies, in large part, on its argument that § 7(a)(1) does not impose a duty on the federal agencies to consult with FWS and develop programs for the conservation of each of the endangered and threatened species. As noted above in our standing discussion, however, we find that § 7(a)(1) contains a clear statutory directive (it uses the word "shall") requiring the federal agencies to consult and develop programs for the conservation of each of the endangered and threatened species listed pursuant to the statute. That Congress has passed a statute that is

---

count the plaintiff's particularized injury, a duty to consult as to endangered and threatened species in a general sense would not necessarily address the specific injury alleged by the plaintiff. On the other hand, to the extent that the plaintiff alleged an interest in all endangered and threatened species based upon a systematic failure by a federal agency to consult as to endangered and threatened species in general, we note that such an injury would likely constitute a generalized grievance.

5. Of course, this duty to consult and duty to conserve is tempered by the actual authorities of each agency. See Platte River Whooping Crane Critical Habitat Maintenance Trust v. FERC, 962 F.2d 27, 34 (D.C.Cir.1992) (holding that § 7(a)(1) does not expand an agency's existing authorities to conserve endangered species). Whether a particular agency has the authority and/or ability to adopt programs for the benefit of a particular species, however, is a question on the merits, not relevant to a standing inquiry.

exceptionally broad in its effect, in the sense that it imposes a tremendous burden on the federal agencies to comply with its mandate, however, does not mean that it is written in such broad terms that in a given case there is no law to apply. On the contrary, given the specific requirements of § 7(a)(1), in any given case there is more than enough law against which a court can measure agency compliance.

The USDA next argues that its duties under § 7(a)(1) are not judicially reviewable because it has a substantial amount of discretion in developing programs for the benefit of the Edwards-dependent species. According to the USDA, because it enjoys a substantial amount of discretion as to ultimate program decisions, it has unreviewable discretion to ignore § 7(a)(1) altogether. This argument is entirely without merit. A mission agency's discretion to make the final substantive decision under its program authorities does not mean that the agency has unlimited, unreviewable discretion. Instead, it means that the court conducting judicial review must require the agency to show that it has considered the relevant factors and followed the required procedures, but that, if the agency has done so, the court may not substitute its judgment on the merits for the agency's judgment. * * *

We turn next to the government's argument that it has complied with the requirements of § 7(a)(1) because the Edwards-dependent species have experienced incidental benefits from national USDA programs designed and carried out for other purposes. As Sierra Club points out, however, the USDA's position directly conflicts with the plain language of § 7(a)(1), which requires each federal agency "in consultation with and with the assistance of [FWS]" to adopt programs "for the conservation of endangered species." The USDA simply cannot read out of existence § 7(a)(1)'s requirement that the USDA's substantive conservation programs for the Edwards-dependent species be carried out "in consultation with and with the assistance of [FWS]." In this case, there is no real dispute that the USDA has never fulfilled its obligations under § 7(a)(1) with respect to the Edwards-dependent species. Accordingly, we find the USDA's argument unavailing.

As a final matter, we note that the USDA has not challenged the scope of the district court's injunction with respect to § 7(a)(1). Thus, we need not address whether the district court properly ordered the USDA to develop, in consultation with FWS, "an organized program for utilizing USDA's authorities for the conservation of the Edwards-dependent endangered and threatened species as contemplated by the ESA." * * *

NOTES AND QUESTIONS

1. How much substance is there in this generally expressed duty to "utilize [the agency's] authorities in furtherance of" the ESA's purposes? If, as here, the species require water conservation by farmers in a drought, must the USDA administer its programs in such as way as to encourage such conservation? Require it? If the statutes under which the USDA

furnishes aid to farmers are silent on its authority to administer them to require conservation, does § 7(a)(1) supply such authority?

2.   A respected commentator on the ESA has called this subsection "the monumental underachiever of the ESA family;" a "sleeping giant" with the "potential to eclipse all other ESA programs." J.B. Ruhl, Section 7(a)(1) of the "New" Endangered Species Act: Rediscovering and Redefining the Untapped Power of Federal Agencies' Duty to Conserve Species, 25 Envtl. L. 1107, 1109, 1110, 1128 (1995). Professor Ruhl reminds us that the Supreme Court addressed § 7(a)(1) at length in TVA v. Hill, supra p. 435, Chief Justice Burger's opinion describing it "stringent, mandatory language" that "reveals an explicit congressional decision to require agencies to afford first priority to the declared national policy of saving endangered species." 437 U.S. at 183, 185. The subsection then rather curiously fell into curious desuetude in both the courts and the agencies; § 7(a)(1) is the only important part of the ESA that is not the subject of implementing regulations.

4.   Professor Ruhl argues that 7(a)(1) has great promise as "a shield, a sword, or a prod to help federal agencies fulfill [Congress's] vision" in enacting the ESA. He points out, among other things, that § 7(a)(1) applies to "programs" and not just "actions" by federal agencies. Does that mean the wildlife agencies can outline species conservation measures for other agencies to take outside the consultation process of § 7(a)(2)? Does 7(a)(1) impose a duty on the other agencies to take these measures, even if there is no "action," no "take," and no finding of likelihood of "jeopardy"? How are the wildlife agencies supposed to interact with the other agencies under 7(a)(1)?

5.   From the standpoint of federal land management agencies, is the authority in 7(a)(1) a blessing by providing flexibility to be proactive in protecting endangered species, without waiting for the formal processes of other parts of the act to kick in? Are its vague promises as susceptible of judicial enforcement as the more specific commands of sections 7 and 9?

6.   In Pyramid Lake Paiute Tribe of Indians v. U.S. Department of the Navy, 898 F.2d 1410 (9th Cir.1990), the court refused to find that the agency's "duty to conserve" meant that an agency had to choose a more conservation-minded alternative to its proposed action, if the alternative would as effective at serving the government's interest. See generally Ruhl, supra, and Bean and Rowland, pp. 236–39.

7.   The Tenth Circuit recently took a pass on an attempt by logging interests to use § 7(a)(1) as a tool to promote more aggressive timber harvesting practices in the Medicine Bow National Forest in the Platte River watershed in Wyoming as a way to produce more water to meet the needs of endangered species downstream. Coalition for Sustainable Resources v. U.S. Forest Service, 259 F.3d 1244 (10th Cir.2001). The court found that judicial review was not warranted at this time because the Forest Service was involved in a large interagency effort to develop a conservation strategy for the Platte River species and was also revising its forest plan.

6. SECTION 9 OF THE ESA—THE "TAKE" PROHIBITION

Section 9 has been called "perhaps * * * the most powerful piece of wildlife legislation in the world." Federico Cheever, An Introduction to the Prohibition Against Takings in Section 9 of the Endangered Species Act of 1973: Learning to Live with a Powerful Species Preservation Law, 62 U.Colo.L.Rev. 109, 111 (1991). Most of the early litigation under the ESA (such as TVA v. Hill) focused on § 7, but gradually § 9 "began to dig its way out of anonymity." Cheever, at 143. The first major decision to apply it was Palila v. Hawaii Dept. of Land and Natural Resources, discussed in *Sweet Home*, the next principal case. In response to that decision, Congress revisited the section in 1982 amendments, creating limited "incidental take" exceptions described in *Sweet Home*. As with the legislative reaction to TVA v. Hill, however, Congress only fine-tuned the Act. "Once again, Congress, faced with clear evidence that the [ESA] could and would have a significant impact, reaffirmed its commitment to protect species threatened with extinction." Cheever, supra, at 146–47, 164–67.

Babbitt v. Sweet Home Chapter

Supreme Court of the United States, 1995.
515 U.S. 687.

■ JUSTICE STEVENS delivered the opinion of the Court.

The Endangered Species Act of 1973 contains a variety of protections designed to save from extinction species that the Secretary of the Interior designates as endangered or threatened. Section 9 of the Act makes it unlawful for any person to "take" any endangered or threatened species. The Secretary has promulgated a regulation that defines the statute's prohibition on takings to include "significant habitat modification or degradation where it actually kills or injures wildlife." This case presents the question whether the Secretary exceeded his authority under the Act by promulgating that regulation.

* * * Section 3(19) of the Act defines the statutory term "take": "The term 'take' means to harass, harm, pursue, hunt, shoot, wound, kill, trap, capture, or collect, or to attempt to engage in any such conduct." 16 U.S.C. § 1532(19).

The Act does not further define the terms it uses to define "take." The Interior Department regulations that implement the statute, however, define the statutory term "harm":

> "*Harm* in the definition of 'take' in the Act means an act which actually kills or injures wildlife. Such act may include significant habitat modification or degradation where it actually kills or injures wildlife by significantly impairing essential behavioral patterns, including breeding, feeding, or sheltering." 50 CFR § 17.3 (1994).

This regulation has been in place since 1975.

A limitation on the § 9 "take" prohibition appears in § 10(a)(1)(B) of the Act, which Congress added by amendment in 1982. That section authorizes the Secretary to grant a permit for any taking otherwise prohibited by § 9(a)(1)(B) "if such taking is incidental to, and not the purpose of, the carrying out of an otherwise lawful activity." 16 U.S.C. § 1539(a)(1)(B).

* * *

Respondents in this action are small landowners, logging companies, and families dependent on the forest products industries in the Pacific Northwest and in the Southeast, and organizations that represent their interests. They * * * challenge the statutory validity of the Secretary's regulation defining "harm," particularly the inclusion of habitat modification and degradation in the definition * * * on its face. Their complaint alleged that application of the "harm" regulation to the red-cockaded woodpecker, an endangered species, and the northern spotted owl, a threatened species,[5] had injured them economically.

Respondents advanced three arguments to support their submission that Congress did not intend the word "take" in § 9 to include habitat modification, as the Secretary's "harm" regulation provides. First, they correctly noted that language in the Senate's original version of the ESA would have defined "take" to include "destruction, modification, or curtailment of [the] habitat or range" of fish or wildlife, but the Senate deleted that language from the bill before enacting it. Second, respondents argued that Congress intended the Act's express authorization for the Federal Government to buy private land in order to prevent habitat degradation in § 5 to be the exclusive check against habitat modification on private property. Third, because the Senate added the term "harm" to the definition of "take" in a floor amendment without debate, respondents argued that the court should not interpret the term so expansively as to include habitat modification.

Because this case was decided on motions for summary judgment, we may appropriately make certain factual assumptions in order to frame the legal issue. First, we assume respondents have no desire to harm either the red-cockaded woodpecker or the spotted owl; they merely wish to continue logging activities that would be entirely proper if not prohibited by the ESA. On the other hand, we must assume, *arguendo,* that those activities will have the effect, even though unintended, of detrimentally changing the natural habitat of both listed species and that, as a consequence, members of those species will be killed or injured. Under respondents' view of the law, the Secretary's only means of forestalling that grave result—even when the actor knows it is certain to occur[9]—is to use his § 5 authority to

---

5. Another regulation promulgated by the Secretary extends to threatened species, defined in the ESA as "any species which is likely to become an endangered species within the foreseeable future throughout all or a significant portion of its range," 16 U.S.C. § 1532(20), some but not all of the protections endangered species enjoy. See 50 CFR § 17.31(a) (1994). In the District Court respondents unsuccessfully challenged that regulation's extension of § 9 to threatened species, but they do not press the challenge here.

9. As discussed above, the Secretary's definition of "harm" is limited to "acts which actually kill or injure wildlife." 50 CFR § 17.3 (1994). In addition, in order to be subject to the Act's criminal penalties or the

purchase the lands on which the survival of the species depends. The Secretary, on the other hand, submits that the § 9 prohibition on takings, which Congress defined to include "harm," places on respondents a duty to avoid harm that habitat alteration will cause the birds unless respondents first obtain a permit pursuant to § 10.

The text of the Act provides three reasons for concluding that the Secretary's interpretation is reasonable. First, an ordinary understanding of the word "harm" supports it. The dictionary definition of the verb form of "harm" is "to cause hurt or damage to: injure." Webster's Third New International Dictionary 1034 (1966). In the context of the ESA, that definition naturally encompasses habitat modification that results in actual injury or death to members of an endangered or threatened species.

Respondents argue that the Secretary should have limited the purview of "harm" to direct applications of force against protected species, but the dictionary definition does not include the word "directly" or suggest in any way that only direct or willful action that leads to injury constitutes "harm."[10] Moreover, unless the statutory term "harm" encompasses indirect as well as direct injuries, the word has no meaning that does not duplicate the meaning of other words that § 3 uses to define "take." A

more severe of its civil penalties, one must "knowingly violate" the Act or its implementing regulations. 16 U.S.C. § § 1540(a)(1), (b)(1). Congress added "knowingly" in place of "willfully" in 1978 to make "criminal violations of the act a general rather than a specific intent crime." H. R. Conf. Rep. No. 95–1804, p. 26 (1978). The Act does authorize up to a $500 civil fine for "any person who otherwise violates" the Act or its implementing regulations. 16 U.S.C. § 1540(a)(1). That provision is potentially sweeping, but it would be so with or without the Secretary's "harm" regulation, making it unhelpful in assessing the reasonableness of the regulation. We have imputed scienter requirements to criminal statutes that impose sanctions without expressly requiring scienter, see, e. g., Staples v. United States, 511 U.S. 600, 128 L. Ed. 2d 608, 114 S. Ct. 1793 (1994), but the proper case in which we might consider whether to do so in the § 9 provision for a $500 civil penalty would be a challenge to enforcement of that provision itself, not a challenge to a regulation that merely defines a statutory term. We do not agree with the dissent that the regulation covers results that are not "even foreseeable . . . no matter how long the chain of causality between modification and injury." Post, at 715. Respondents have suggested no reason why either the "knowingly violates" or the "otherwise violates" provision of the stat-

ute—or the "harm" regulation itself—should not be read to incorporate ordinary requirements of proximate causation and foreseeability. In any event, neither respondents nor their amici have suggested that the Secretary employs the "otherwise violates" provision with any frequency.

10. Respondents and the dissent emphasize what they portray as the "established meaning" of "take" in the sense of a "wildlife take," a meaning respondents argue extends only to "the effort to exercise dominion over some creature, and the concrete effect of [sic] that creature." This limitation ill serves the statutory text, which forbids not taking "some creature" but "tak[ing] any [endangered] species"—a formidable task for even the most rapacious feudal lord. More importantly, Congress explicitly defined the operative term "take" in the ESA, no matter how much the dissent wishes otherwise, thereby obviating the need for us to probe its meaning as we must probe the meaning of the undefined subsidiary term "harm." Finally, Congress' definition of "take" includes several words—most obviously "harass," "pursue," and "wound," in addition to "harm" itself—that fit respondents' and the dissent's definition of "take" no better than does "significant habitat modification or degradation."

reluctance to treat statutory terms as surplusage supports the reasonableness of the Secretary's interpretation.[11]

Second, the broad purpose of the ESA supports the Secretary's decision to extend protection against activities that cause the precise harms Congress enacted the statute to avoid. * * *

Respondents advance strong arguments that activities that cause minimal or unforeseeable harm will not violate the Act as construed in the "harm" regulation. Respondents, however, present a facial challenge to the regulation. Thus, they ask us to invalidate the Secretary's understanding of "harm" in every circumstance, even when an actor knows that an activity, such as draining a pond, would actually result in the extinction of a listed species by destroying its habitat. Given Congress' clear expression of the ESA's broad purpose to protect endangered and threatened wildlife, the Secretary's definition of "harm" is reasonable.[13]

Third, the fact that Congress in 1982 authorized the Secretary to issue permits for takings that § 9(a)(1)(B) would otherwise prohibit, "if such taking is incidental to, and not the purpose of, the carrying out of an otherwise lawful activity," 16 U.S.C. § 1539(a)(1)(B), strongly suggests that Congress understood § 9(a)(1)(B) to prohibit indirect as well as deliberate takings. The permit process requires the applicant to prepare a "conservation plan" that specifies how he intends to "minimize and mitigate" the "impact" of his activity on endangered and threatened species, 16 U.S.C. § 1539(a)(2)(A), making clear that Congress had in mind foreseeable rather than merely accidental effects on listed species. No one could seriously request an "incidental" take permit to avert § 9 liability for direct, deliberate action against a member of an endangered or threatened species, but respondents would read "harm" so narrowly that the permit procedure would have little more than that absurd purpose. * * * Congress' addition

11. In contrast, if the statutory term "harm" encompasses such indirect means of killing and injuring wildlife as habitat modification, the other terms listed in § 3—"harass," "pursue," "hunt," "shoot," "wound," "kill," "trap," "capture," and "collect"—generally retain independent meanings. Most of those terms refer to deliberate actions more frequently than does "harm," and they therefore do not duplicate the sense of indirect causation that "harm" adds to the statute. In addition, most of the other words in the definition describe either actions from which habitat modification does not usually result (*e.g.,* "pursue," "harass") or effects to which activities that modify habitat do not usually lead (*e.g.,* "trap," "collect"). To the extent the Secretary's definition of "harm" may have applications that overlap with other words in the definition, that overlap reflects the broad purpose of the Act. See *infra* this page and 699–700.

13. The dissent incorrectly asserts that the Secretary's regulation (1) "dispenses with the foreseeability of harm" and (2) "fail[s] to require injury to particular animals," post, at 19. As to the first assertion, the regulation merely implements the statute, and it is therefore subject to the statute's "knowingly violates" language, see 16 U.S.C. §§ 1540(a)(1), (b)(1), and ordinary requirements of proximate causation and foreseeability. Nothing in the regulation purports to weaken those requirements. To the contrary, the word "actually" in the regulation should be construed to limit the liability about which the dissent appears most concerned, liability under the statute's "otherwise violates" provision. See n. 9, supra; post, at 8–9, 19–20. The Secretary did not need to include "actually" to connote "but for" causation, which the other words in the definition obviously require. As to the dissent's second assertion, every term in the regulation's definition of "harm" is subservient to the phrase "an act which actually kills or injures wildlife."

of the § 10 permit provision supports the Secretary's conclusion that activities not intended to harm an endangered species, such as habitat modification, may constitute unlawful takings under the ESA unless the Secretary permits them.

The Court of Appeals made three errors in asserting that "harm" must refer to a direct application of force because the words around it do.[15] First, the court's premise was flawed. Several of the words that accompany "harm" in the § 3 definition of "take," especially "harass," "pursue," "wound," and "kill," refer to actions or effects that do not require direct applications of force. Second, to the extent the court read a requirement of intent or purpose into the words used to define "take," it ignored § 11's express provision that a "knowing" action is enough to violate the Act. Third, the court employed *noscitur a sociis* to give "harm" essentially the same function as other words in the definition, thereby denying it independent meaning. The canon, to the contrary, counsels that a word "gathers meaning from the words around it." Jarecki v. G. D. Searle & Co., 367 U.S. 303, 307 (1961). The statutory context of "harm" suggests that Congress meant that term to serve a particular function in the ESA, consistent with, but distinct from, the functions of the other verbs used to define "take." The Secretary's interpretation of "harm" to include indirectly injuring endangered animals through habitat modification permissibly interprets "harm" to have "a character of its own not to be submerged by its association." Russell Motor Car Co. v. United States, 261 U.S. 514, 519 (1923).

Nor does the Act's inclusion of the § 5 land acquisition authority and the § 7 directive to federal agencies to avoid destruction or adverse modification of critical habitat alter our conclusion. Respondents' argument that the Government lacks any incentive to purchase land under § 5 when it can simply prohibit takings under § 9 ignores the practical considerations that attend enforcement of the ESA. Purchasing habitat lands may well cost the Government less in many circumstances than pursuing civil or criminal penalties. In addition, the § 5 procedure allows for protection of habitat before the seller's activity has harmed any endangered animal, whereas the Government cannot enforce the § 9 prohibition until an animal has actually been killed or injured. The Secretary may also find the § 5 authority useful for preventing modification of land that is not yet but may in the future become habitat for an endangered or threatened species. The § 7 directive applies only to the Federal Government, whereas the § 9

---

15. The dissent makes no effort to defend the Court of Appeals' reading of the statutory definition as requiring a direct application of force. Instead, it tries to impose on § 9 a limitation of liability to "affirmative conduct intentionally directed against a particular animal or animals." *Post,* at 720. Under the dissent's interpretation of the Act, a developer could drain a pond, knowing that the act would extinguish an endangered species of turtles, without even proposing a conservation plan or applying for a permit under § 10(a)(1)(B); unless the developer was motivated by a desire "to get at a turtle," *post,* at 721, no statutory taking could occur. Because such conduct would not constitute a taking at common law, the dissent would shield it from § 9 liability, even though the words "kill" and "harm" in the statutory definition could apply to such deliberate conduct. We cannot accept that limitation. In any event, our reasons for rejecting the Court of Appeals' interpretation apply as well to the dissent's novel construction.

prohibition applies to "any person." Section 7 imposes a broad, affirmative duty to avoid adverse habitat modifications that § 9 does not replicate, and § 7 does not limit its admonition to habitat modification that "actually kills or injures wildlife." Conversely, § 7 contains limitations that § 9 does not, applying only to actions "likely to jeopardize the continued existence of any endangered species or threatened species," 16 U.S.C. § 1536(a)(2), and to modifications of habitat that has been designated "critical" pursuant to § 4, 16 U.S.C. § 1533(b)(2). Any overlap that § 5 or § 7 may have with § 9 in particular cases is unexceptional, see, *e. g.*, Russello v. United States, 464 U.S. 16, and n. 2, 24 (1983), and simply reflects the broad purpose of the Act set out in § 2 and acknowledged in TVA v. Hill.

We need not decide whether the statutory definition of "take" compels the Secretary's interpretation of "harm," because our conclusions that Congress did not unambiguously manifest its intent to adopt respondents' view and that the Secretary's interpretation is reasonable suffice to decide this case. See generally Chevron U.S.A. Inc. *v.* Natural Resources Defense Council, Inc., 467 U.S. 837 (1984). The latitude the ESA gives the Secretary in enforcing the statute, together with the degree of regulatory expertise necessary to its enforcement, establishes that we owe some degree of deference to the Secretary's reasonable interpretation. * * *

The history of the 1982 amendment that gave the Secretary authority to grant permits for "incidental" takings provides further support for his reading of the Act. The House Report expressly states that "by use of the word 'incidental' the Committee intends to cover situations in which it is known that a taking will occur if the other activity is engaged in but such taking is incidental to, and not the purpose of, the activity." H.R. Rep. No. 97–567, p. 31 (1982). This reference to the foreseeability of incidental takings undermines respondents' argument that the 1982 amendment covered only accidental killings of endangered and threatened animals that might occur in the course of hunting or trapping other animals. Indeed, Congress had habitat modification directly in mind: Both the Senate Report and the House Conference Report identified as the model for the permit process a cooperative state-federal response to a case in California where a development project threatened incidental harm to a species of endangered butterfly by modification of its habitat. See S. Rep. No. 97–418, p. 10 (1982); H. R. Conf. Rep. No. 97–835, pp. 30–32 (1982). Thus, Congress in 1982 focused squarely on the aspect of the "harm" regulation at issue in this litigation. Congress' implementation of a permit program is consistent with the Secretary's interpretation of the term "harm."

When it enacted the ESA, Congress delegated broad administrative and interpretive power to the Secretary. See 16 U.S.C. § § 1533, 1540(f). The task of defining and listing endangered and threatened species requires an expertise and attention to detail that exceeds the normal province of Congress. Fashioning appropriate standards for issuing permits under § 10 for takings that would otherwise violate § 9 necessarily requires the exercise of broad discretion. The proper interpretation of a term such as "harm" involves a complex policy choice. When Congress has entrusted the Secretary with broad discretion, we are especially reluctant to substitute our views of wise policy for his. See *Chevron,* 467 U.S. at 865–866. In this case, that reluctance accords with our conclusion, based on the text, structure, and legislative history of the ESA, that the Secretary reasonably construed the intent of Congress when he defined "harm" to include "significant habitat modification or degradation that actually kills or injures wildlife."

In the elaboration and enforcement of the ESA, the Secretary and all persons who must comply with the law will confront difficult questions of proximity and degree; for, as all recognize, the Act encompasses a vast range of economic and social enterprises and endeavors. These questions must be addressed in the usual course of the law, through case-by-case resolution and adjudication.

■ Justice O'Connor, concurring.

My agreement with the Court is founded on two understandings. First, the challenged regulation is limited to significant habitat modification that causes actual, as opposed to hypothetical or speculative, death or injury to identifiable protected animals. Second, even setting aside difficult questions of scienter, the regulation's application is limited by ordinary principles of proximate causation, which introduce notions of foreseeability. These limitations, in my view, call into question Palila v. Hawaii Dept. of Land and Natural Resources, 852 F.2d 1106 (C.A.9 1988) *(Palila II),* and with it, many of the applications derided by the dissent. Because there is no need to strike a regulation on a facial challenge out of concern that it is susceptible of erroneous application, however, and because there are many habitat-related circumstances in which the regulation might validly apply, I join the opinion of the Court.

* * * The regulation has clear application, for example, to significant habitat modification that kills or physically injures animals which, because they are in a vulnerable breeding state, do not or cannot flee or defend themselves, or to environmental pollutants that cause an animal to suffer physical complications during gestation. Breeding, feeding, and sheltering are what animals do. If significant habitat modification, by interfering with these essential behaviors, actually kills or injures an animal protected by the Act, it causes "harm" within the meaning of the regulation. In contrast to Justice Scalia, I do not read the regulation's "breeding" reference to vitiate or somehow to qualify the clear actual death or injury requirement, or to suggest that the regulation contemplates extension to nonexistent animals. * * *

By the dissent's reckoning, the regulation at issue here, in conjunction with 16 U.S.C. § 1540(a)(1), imposes liability for any habitat-modifying conduct that ultimately results in the death of a protected animal, "regardless of whether that result is intended or even foreseeable, and no matter how long the chain of causality between modification and injury." *Post,* at 715; see also *post,* at 719. Even if § 1540(a)(1) does create a strict liability regime (a question we need not decide at this juncture), I see no indication that Congress, in enacting that section, intended to dispense with ordinary principles of proximate causation. Strict liability means liability without regard to fault; it does not normally mean liability for every consequence, however remote, of one's conduct. See generally W. Keeton, D. Dobbs, R. Keeton, & D. Owen, Prosser and Keeton on Law of Torts 559–560 (5th ed. 1984) (describing "practical necessity for the restriction of liability within some reasonable bounds" in the strict liability context). I would not lightly assume that Congress, in enacting a strict liability statute that is silent on the causation question, has dispensed with this well-entrenched principle. In the absence of congressional abrogation of traditional principles of causation, then, private parties should be held liable under § 1540(a)(1) only if their habitat-modifying actions proximately cause death or injury to protected animals. * * * The regulation, of course, does not contradict the presumption or notion that ordinary principles of causation apply here. Indeed, by use of the word "actually," the regulation clearly rejects speculative or conjectural effects, and thus itself *invokes* principles of proximate causation.

Proximate causation is not a concept susceptible of precise definition. See Keeton, *supra,* at 280–281. It is easy enough, of course, to identify the extremes. The farmer whose fertilizer is lifted by a tornado from tilled fields and deposited miles away in a wildlife refuge cannot, by any stretch of the term, be considered the proximate cause of death or injury to protected species occasioned thereby. At the same time, the landowner who drains a pond on his property, killing endangered fish in the process, would likely satisfy any formulation of the principle. We have recently said that proximate causation "normally eliminates the bizarre," Jerome B. Grubart, Inc. v. Great Lakes Dredge & Dock Co., 513 U.S. 527, 536 (1995), and have noted its "functionally equivalent" alternative characterizations in terms of foreseeability * * *. Proximate causation depends to a great extent on considerations of the fairness of imposing liability for remote consequences. The task of determining whether proximate causation exists in the limitless fact patterns sure to arise is best left to lower courts. But I note, at the least, that proximate cause principles inject a foreseeability element into the statute, and hence, the regulation, that would appear to alleviate some of the problems noted by the dissent. See, *e. g., post,* at 719 (describing "a farmer who tills his field and causes erosion that makes silt run into a nearby river which depletes oxygen and thereby [injures] protected fish").

In my view, then, the "harm" regulation applies where significant habitat modification, by impairing essential behaviors, proximately (foreseeably) causes actual death or injury to identifiable animals that are protected under the Endangered Species Act. Pursuant to my interpretation, *Palila II*—under which the Court of Appeals held that a state agency committed a "taking" by permitting mouflon sheep to eat mamane-naio seedlings that, when full grown, might have fed and sheltered endangered palila—was wrongly decided according to the regulation's own terms. Destruction of the seedlings did not proximately cause actual death or injury to identifiable birds; it merely prevented the regeneration of forest land not currently sustaining actual birds.

This case, of course, comes to us as a facial challenge. We are charged with deciding whether the regulation on its face exceeds the agency's statutory mandate. I have identified at least one application of the regulation *(Palila II)* that is, in my view, inconsistent with the regulation's *own* limitations. That misapplication does not, however, call into question the validity of the regulation itself. One can doubtless imagine questionable applications of the regulation that test the limits of the agency's authority. However, it seems to me clear that the regulation does not on its terms exceed the agency's mandate, and that the regulation has innumerable valid habitat-related applications. Congress may, of course, see fit to revisit this issue. And nothing the Court says today prevents the agency itself from narrowing the scope of its regulation at a later date.

■ JUSTICE SCALIA, with whom THE CHIEF JUSTICE and JUSTICE THOMAS join, dissenting.

* * * The Court's holding that the [ESA's] hunting and killing prohibition incidentally preserves habitat on private lands imposes unfairness to the point of financial ruin—not just upon the rich, but upon the simplest farmer who finds his land conscripted to national zoological use. I respectfully dissent. * * *

The regulation has three features which * * * do not comport with the statute. First, it interprets the statute to prohibit habitat modification that is no more than the cause-in-fact of death or injury to wildlife. *Any* "significant habitat modification" that in fact produces that result by "impairing essential behavioral patterns" is made unlawful, regardless of whether that result is intended or even foreseeable, and no matter how long the chain of causality between modification and injury. See, *e.g.,* Palila v. Hawaii Dept. of Land and Natural Resources, 852 F.2d 1106, 1108–1109 (C.A.9 1988) *(Palila II)* (sheep grazing constituted "taking" of palila birds, since although sheep do not destroy full-grown mamane trees, they do destroy mamane seedlings, which will not grow to full-grown trees, on which the palila feeds and nests).

Second, the regulation does not require an "act": The Secretary's officially stated position is that an *omission* will do. The previous version of the regulation made this explicit. * * *

The third and most important unlawful feature of the regulation is that it encompasses injury inflicted, not only upon individual animals, but upon populations of the protected species. "Injury" in the regulation includes "significantly impairing essential behavioral patterns, including *breeding*," 50 CFR § 17.3 (1994) (emphasis added). Impairment of breeding does not "injure" living creatures; it prevents them from propagating, thus "injuring" *a population* of animals which would otherwise have maintained or increased its numbers.

None of these three features of the regulation can be found in the statutory provisions supposed to authorize it. * * *

* * * To define "harm" as an act or omission that, however remotely, "actually kills or injures" a population of wildlife through habitat modification is to choose a meaning that makes nonsense of the word that "harm" defines—requiring us to accept that a farmer who tills his field and causes erosion that makes silt run into a nearby river which depletes oxygen and thereby "impairs [the] breeding" of protected fish has "taken" or "at-

tempted to take" the fish. It should take the strongest evidence to make us believe that Congress has defined a term in a manner repugnant to its ordinary and traditional sense.

Here the evidence shows the opposite. "Harm" is merely one of 10 prohibitory words in § 1532(19), and the other 9 fit the ordinary meaning of "take" perfectly. To "harass, pursue, hunt, shoot, wound, kill, trap, capture, or collect" are all affirmative acts (the provision itself describes them as "conduct," see § 1532(19)) which are directed immediately and intentionally against a particular animal—not acts or omissions that indirectly and accidentally cause injury to a population of animals. * * * What the nine other words in § 1532(19) have in common—and share with the narrower meaning of "harm" described above, but not with the Secretary's ruthless dilation of the word—is the sense of affirmative conduct intentionally directed against a particular animal or animals.

The penalty provisions of the Act counsel this interpretation as well. * * * [They produce] a result that no legislature could reasonably be thought to have intended: A large number of routine private activities—for example, farming, ranching, roadbuilding, construction and logging—are subjected to strict-liability penalties when they fortuitously injure protected wildlife, no matter how remote the chain of causation and no matter how difficult to foresee (or to disprove) the "injury" may be (e.g., an "impairment" of breeding). * * * Without the regulation, the routine "habitat modifying" activities that people conduct to make a daily living would not carry exposure to strict penalties; only acts directed at animals, like those described by the other words in § 1532(19), would risk liability.

The Court says that "[to] read a requirement of intent or purpose into the words used to define 'take' ... ignore[s] [§ 1540's] express provision that a 'knowing' action is enough to violate the Act." *Ante,* at 701–702. This presumably means that because the reading of § 1532(19) advanced here ascribes an element of purposeful injury to the prohibited acts, it makes superfluous (or inexplicable) the more severe penalties provided for a "knowing" violation. That conclusion does not follow, for it is quite possible to take protected wildlife purposefully without doing so knowingly. A requirement that a violation be "knowing" means that the defendant must "know the facts that make his conduct illegal," Staples v. United States, 511 U.S. 600, 606 (1994). The hunter who shoots an elk in the mistaken belief that it is a mule deer has not knowingly violated § 1538(a)(1)(B)—not because he does not know that elk are legally protected (that would be knowledge of the law, which is not a requirement, see *ante,* at 696–697, n. 9), but because he does not know what sort of animal he is shooting. The hunter has nonetheless committed a purposeful taking of protected wildlife, and would therefore be subject to the (lower) strict-liability penalties for violation.

The broader structure of the Act confirms the unreasonableness of the regulation. [Justice Scalia then discussed § 7's requirement to avoid "destruction or adverse modification of habitat" determined to be "critical;" that is, "essential to the conservation of the species."] * * * These provisions have a double significance. Even if [§§ 7 and 9] were totally independent prohibitions—the former applying only to federal agencies and their licensees, the latter only to private parties—Congress's explicit prohibition of habitat modification in the one section would bar the inference of an implicit prohibition of habitat modification in the other section. * * * [I]t would be passing strange for Congress carefully to define "critical habitat" as used in § 1536(a)(2), but leave it to the Secretary to evaluate, willy-nilly, impermissible "habitat modification" (under the guise of "harm") in § 1538(a)(1)(B). * * *

NOTES AND QUESTIONS

1. Section 9 somewhat ambiguously prohibits "take" of "species," but it has always been understood to apply to individual specimens rather than entire populations or the species itself. This is clear from the fact that the same section of the Act also prohibits possessing, selling, transporting, etc. "species," which only makes sense when applied to individual specimens.

2. Look at the last line quoted in Justice O'Connor's concurring opinion. If the Executive branch took up that invitation and repealed the regulation, would its action be sustained on judicial review?

3. Does the majority say Section 9 may be violated even if the actor has no intent to harm a species? What are O'Connor's and Scalia's views on that issue? Is Scalia correct that the various verbs in the "take" definition all require an intentional act against the critter in question?

4. How direct does the connection have to be between habitat destruction and the injury or death of the endangered species, according to the majority opinion? To Justice O'Connor? Should the concept of proximate cause and foreseeability in tort law be applied here? Foreseeable to the average person? Or to the trained biologist? As Michael Bean and Melanie Rowland have pointed out, it is common knowledge that draining a pond may kill the fish in it (to use Justice O'Connor's example), but it may not be so obvious that it would kill a turtle in it (to use Justice Scalia's example), because turtles can survive out of water. Yet to a biologist the death of the turtle may be "a highly likely and predictable result," THE EVOLUTION OF NATIONAL WILDLIFE LAW 216.

5. What kind of proof of death or injury must there be to make out a section 9 violation? A dead carcass? Is it enough to show "significant impairment of essential behavioral patterns," without more?

6. Here and in *TVA v. Hill*, the U.S. Supreme Court adopted a strong pre-environment interpretation of the ESA. In its NEPA decisions, by contrast, the Court has been much more niggardly in its approach to the statute. See p. 427 supra. What account for the difference?

7. For lower court applications of the "take" prohibition, see, e.g., Defenders of Wildlife v. Bernal, 204 F.3d 920 (9th Cir.2000) (upholding district court's well-supported factual finding that high school construction in pygmy owl critical habitat would not cause take); Marbled Murrelet v. Babbitt, 83 F.3d 1060 (9th Cir.1996) (upholding injunction against logging

project because of reasonable certainty of imminent harm to listed birds who were nesting in the area; among other things, rejecting the timber company's argument that impaired breeding is not "take" under the ESA because, while it harms the species' population, it does not harm an actual bird); National Wildlife Federation v. Burlington Northern Railroad, 23 F.3d 1508, 1513 (9th Cir.1994) (mere habitat degradation may not constitute harm, for the latter requires a showing of "significant impairment of the species' breeding or feeding habits and [proof] that the habitat degradation prevents, or possibly, retards, recovery of the species"); United States v. Glenn–Colusa Irr. Dist., 788 F.Supp. 1126 (E.D.Cal.1992) (defendants' operation of irrigation pumps "take" salmon trapped against screens through which water was pumped); Greenpeace v. National Marine Fisheries Serv., 106 F.Supp.2d 1066 (W.D.Wash.2000) (Alaskan fisheries' operations may constitute a taking of the Stellar sea lion because the fisheries are catching fish normally eaten by the sea lion); Bensman v. U.S. Forest Serv., 984 F.Supp. 1242 (W.D.Mo.1997) (removal of dead trees used by the Indiana bat for habitat and hibernation may constitute a taking).

8.   There are often, of course, multiple causes for a species decline, some traceable to specific actions by individuals or institutions, and some not. A culprit may be, for example, global climate change or the invasion of exotic species, which usually cannot meaningfully be ascribed to discrete individual actions. How should that be accounted for in Section 9? Must a specific action be the primary cause, or is a merely contributing cause sufficient to make out a § 9 violation? Are tort notions of causation and allocation of responsibility relevant here?

9.   Can inaction ever amount to a take in violation of Section 9? Suppose a federal land management agency has zoned an area of federal land as suitable for off-road vehicle travel, and has declined to impose speed limits or other controls on off-road vehicles, even though endangered species are known to exist there and are susceptible of take by the ORVs. Individual ORV operators may be liable for a "take" in that circumstance, but prosecuting them may be difficult as a practical matter. A more effective solution would be to persuade the land manager to adopt regulations. May section 9 be used as a hammer to that end? Can a regulatory agency's conscious failure to take protective action that is within its discretion violate Section 9? See, e.g., Loggerhead Turtle v. County Council of Volusia County, Florida, 896 F.Supp. 1170 (M.D.Fla.1995) (county's failure to control beach driving during nesting season of endangered turtles could be "take" under § 9). In a later proceeding of the same case, reported at 148 F.3d 1231 (11th Cir.1998), cert. denied, 526 U.S. 1081 (1999), the court of appeals addressed another concern, that artificial lighting inland of beaches disrupts behavior of endangered turtles and result in their deaths. In the context of ruling that plaintiffs had standing, it held that, under *Sweet Home*, the county may be responsible for taking in these circumstances because of its indirect control over lighting even though it does not operate every beachfront lighting source. Where a federal agency is involved, may § 7(a)(1) provide the hammer to regulate in these circumstances? See p. 474 supra.

10.   Other courts have also held that government acting as a regulator can cause takes of protected wildlife. In Strahan v. Coxe, 127 F.3d 155 (1st Cir.1997), cert. denied, 525 U.S. 830 (1998), the court held that Massachusett's state commercial fishing regulators had violated § 9 by causing takings of endangered whales when it licensed commercial fishing operations to use gillnets and lobster pots in a manner that was likely to cause whale entanglement, which had been recognized as a major source of human-caused injury or death of whales. The state argued that holding it responsible for take because it licensed fishing gear was the equivalent of holding it responsible for bank robberies because it licensed automobiles that are used in robberies. The court rejected the analogy: A person may operate an automobile licensed by Massachusetts without risking violations of law, but

> it is not possible for a licensed commercial fishing operation to use its gillnets or lobster pots in the manner permitted by the Commonwealth without risk of violating the ESA by exacting a taking. Thus, the state's licensure * * * does not involve the intervening independent actor that is a necessary component of the other licensure schemes which it argues are comparable. * * * In this instance, the state has licensed commercial fishing operations to use gillnets and lobster pots in specifically the manner that is likely to result in a violation of federal law. The causation here, while indirect, is not so removed that it extends outside the realm of causation as it is understood in the common law.

127 F.3d at 164. See also Defenders of Wildlife v. Administrator, Environmental Protection Agency, 882 F.2d 1294, 1300–01 (8th Cir.1989) (EPA's registration of pesticide strychnine for small animal control could "take" endangered species that fed on carcasses of poisoned animals, even though other persons distributed and actually used the pesticides); United States v. Town of Plymouth, Mass., 6 F.Supp.2d 81 (D.Mass.1998) (preliminary injunction issued against town from failing to regulate ORVs driving on the town beach, 70% of which is owned by the town, in order to protect piping plovers, shorebird birds listed as threatened under the ESA which breed and nest in habitat where ORVs operate).

11.   Section 9 can be enforced by the federal government or by means of citizen civil suits; successful citizen plaintiffs can recover attorneys fees. 16 U.S.C. § 1540(e), (g). "Knowing" violations are punishable criminally (but only the United States, and not citizens, can bring criminal actions). Id. § 1540(b)(1). Several cases hold this is a "general intent" crime. See, e.g., United States v. Nguyen, 916 F.2d 1016, 1019 (5th Cir.1990) ("it is sufficient that Nguyen was in possession of a turtle. The government was not required to prove that Nguyen knew that this turtle is a threatened species or that it is illegal to transport or import it"); see also United States v. McKittrick, 142 F.3d 1170, 1176–77 (9th Cir.1998).

12.   After exploring many of the issues raised by Section 9, Professor Federico Cheever concludes (62 U.Colo.L.Rev. at 177–99):

> The taking prohibition * * * is simple and sweeping. Compared to other federal environmental laws, it reads like one of the Ten Com-

mandments. Like the Commandments, it has never been fully enforced. Also, like * * * the Commandments the taking prohibition is a moral challenge. Our ability to enforce this simple prohibition in a complex world to the end of effectively protecting species threatened with extinction and the ecosystems on which they depend is a test of our ability to curb our own destructive impulses. * * *

HABITAT CONSERVATION PLANS (HCPs) AND "NO SURPRISES"

Section 9 takings may be avoided by receiving an "incidental take" permit under section 10, as discussed in *Sweet Home*. This provision was added by Congress in 1982, and has emerged as a major feature of ESA compliance. Michael Bean and Melanie Rowland have noted that while the provision for incidental take permits "seems to ease the Act's restrictions because it permits what was previously prohibited," in fact it "likely increased" the leverage of the wildlife agencies over activities that incidentally take listed species "because it substituted a flexible regulatory authority for a threat of prosecution [under § 9] that few found credible." THE EVOLUTION OF NATIONAL WILDLIFE LAW 234. Incidental take permits are issued upon Secretarial approval of a "conservation plan" (which has come to be known as a "habitat conservation plan," or HCP, even though the word "habitat" is not found in the statutory provision). 16 U.S.C. § 1539(a)(2)(A). Once approved, a plan shields the land embraced within it from some or all section 9 liability. The Secretary must find that the plan includes "steps that the applicant will take to minimize and mitigate the impacts" of the incidental take "to the maximum extent practicable," that the applicant "will ensure that adequate funding for the plan will be provided," and the incidental take "will not appreciably reduce the likelihood of the survival and recovery of the species in the wild," 16 U.S.C. § 1539(a)(2)(B), the latter being the same standard the Secretary applies to find "no jeopardy" under § 7.

A common situation for an HCP is where a landowner seeks to develop property on which endangered species are found. The landowner will negotiate with the wildlife agency over steps to be taken to protect the species and still allow some development to proceed. The landowner may agree to protect some habitat, and to stage or otherwise carry out the development in a way that provides protection for the species. If the wildlife agency agrees that the measures will meet the terms of the statute, it may approve the plan and issue an incidental take statement. HCPs may cover a few acres, or hundreds of thousands of acres. They may have terms as long as a century. They may cover a single species or several species. Increasingly, they may focus on unlisted as well as listed species, as landowners seek longer term shelter from new regulation, if they agree to take steps to protect against known risks to species from contemplated development.

In the Clinton Administration, under Secretary Babbitt, the USFWS developed a "no surprises" policy to encourage landowners to enter into HCPs. The policy provides that, under certain circumstances, the government would not ask more from the landowner over the term of the plan if unanticipated problems occur. See "Habitat Conservation Plans ('No Surprises') Rule", 63 Fed. Reg. 8859 (1998). The policy has engendered some controversy but has led to many millions of acres being brought into HCPs. The only reported decision addressing the policy to date has held a challenge to it unripe. See National Wildlife Federation v. Babbitt, 128 F.Supp.2d 1274 (E.D.Cal 2000). Commentary on the subject is burgeoning. See, e.g., John Kostyack, NWF v. Babbitt: Victory for Smart Growth and Imperiled Wildlife, 31 Envtl.L.Rev. 10712 (2001); Karin P. Sheldon, Habitat Conservation Planning: Addressing the Achilles Heel of the Endangered Species Act, 6 N.Y.U.Envtl.L.J. 279 (1998); Donald C. Baur & Karen L. Donovan, The No Surprises Policy: Contracts 101 Meets the Endangered Species Act, 27 Envtl.L. 769 (1997); Albert Lin, Participants' Experiences with Habitat Conservation Plans and Suggestions for Streamlining the Process, 23 Ecology L.Q. 369 (1996); Eric Fisher, Habitat Conservation Planning under the Endangered Species Act: No Surprises and the Quest for Certainty, 67 Colo. L.Rev. 371 (1996); J.B. Ruhl, Regional Habitat Conservation Planning under the Endangered Species Act: Pushing the Legal and Practical Limits, 44 Sw.L.J. 1393 (1991).

7.   The Relationship of Section 9 and Section 7

HCPs are not used on federal land, but federal agencies may receive an equivalent kind of protection from liability under section 9 through "incidental take statements" included in biological opinions prepared as part of the formal section 7 consultation process, if the USFWS concludes that any "taking" of a listed species "incidental to the agency action" being consulted on is not likely to jeopardize the listed species or result in destruction or adverse modification of critical habitat. See 16 U.S.C. § 1536(b)(4)(B), (o).

In this connection, notice how the Court in *Sweet Home* interprets Section 9 in relation to Section 7. Section 9 is considerably more sweeping than section 7, for the latter applies only to federal agency actions, and asks whether the action poses "jeopardy" to the species, rather than focusing on individual "takes". Federal agencies must comply with both, of course, and compliance with section 9 may be achieved through the consultation process called for by Section 7. In the federal land manager/ORV hypothetical in paragraph 9, supra p. 488, consider that if a federal agency decides to zone federal land open to off-road vehicle travel, it probably must consult under § 7 of the ESA on that decision. The following case constitutes perhaps the most searching analysis to date of how the two sections fit together.

Arizona Cattle Growers' Ass'n v. U.S. Fish & Wildlife Service

United States Court of Appeals for the Ninth Circuit, 2001.
273 F.3d 1229.

■ Before: Noonan, McKeow, and Wardlaw, Circuit Judges.

■ WARDLAW, CIRCUIT JUDGE:

At issue in these consolidated cross-appeals is whether the United States Fish and Wildlife Service's provision of Incidental Take Statements pursuant to the Endangered Species Act was arbitrary and capricious under Section 706 of the Administrative Procedure Act. * * *

[The first case involved grazing permits issued by BLM for public land in southeastern Arizona.] The Bureau of Land Management's livestock grazing program for this area affects 288 separate grazing allotments that in total comprise nearly 1.6 million acres of land. The Fish and Wildlife Service's Biological Opinion, issued on September 26, 1997, analyzes twenty species of plants and animals and concludes that the livestock grazing program was not likely to jeopardize the continued existence of the species affected nor was likely to result in destruction or adverse modification of the designated or proposed critical habitat. The Fish and Wildlife Service did, however, issue Incidental Take Statements for various species of fish and wildlife listed or proposed as endangered. * * * ACGA's summary judgment motion focused on two of the ten Incidental Take Statements, those for the razorback sucker and the cactus ferruginous pygmy-owl. * * *

[The second case] challenged Incidental Take Statements set forth in a second Biological Opinion issued by the Fish and Wildlife Service that concerns livestock grazing on public lands administered by the United States Forest Service. * * * The Fish and Wildlife Service examined 962 allotments, determining that grazing would have no effect on listed species for 619 of those allotments and cause no adverse effects for 321 of the remaining allotments, leaving 22 allotments. These allotments were each roughly 30,000 acres, but several of the allotments were significantly larger. In its Biological Opinion, the Fish and Wildlife Service concluded that ongoing grazing activities on 21 out of the 22 allotments at issue would not jeopardize the continued existence of any protected species or result in the destruction or adverse modification of any critical habitat. It determined, however, that ongoing grazing activities would incidentally take members of one or more protected species in each of the 22 allotments, and it issued Incidental Take Statements for each of those allotments. ACGA contested the issuance of Incidental Take Statements for six of the allotments * * *.

The issuance of a Biological Opinion as well as an accompanying Incidental Take Statement are considered final agency actions. Bennett v. Spear, 520 U.S. 154, 178. * * *

Judicial review of administrative decisions involving the ESA is governed by section 706 of the APA. 5 U.S.C. § 706 * * *.

We are deferential to the agency's expertise in situations, like that here, where "resolution of this dispute involves primarily issues of fact." Marsh v. Or. Natural Res. Council, 490 U.S. 360, 377 (1989). * * * Deference is particularly important "when the agency is 'making predictions, within its area of special expertise, at the frontiers of science.' " Central Ariz. Water Conservation Dist. v. EPA, 990 F.2d 1531, 1539–40

(9th Cir.1993) (quoting Balt. Gas & Elec. Co. v. Natural Res. Def. Council, Inc., 462 U.S. 87, 103 (1983)). * * *

Judicial review is meaningless, however, unless we carefully review the record to "ensure that agency decisions are founded on a reasoned evaluation of the relevant factors." Marsh, 490 U.S. at 378. Accordingly, while reviewing courts should uphold reasonable and defensible constructions of an agency's enabling act, * * * they must not "rubber-stamp ... administrative decisions that they deem inconsistent with a statutory mandate or that frustrate the congressional policy underlying a statute." NLRB v. Brown, 380 U.S. 278, 291–92 (1965).* * *

In the district court, the Fish and Wildlife Service argued that the word "taking" as used in ESA Section 7(b)(4) should be interpreted more broadly than in the context of Section 9 of the ESA, relying upon the different purposes, i.e., protective (Section 7) as opposed to punitive (Section 9), served by each Section.

Specifically, it argued that a taking as construed in Section 7 should encompass those situations in which harm to a listed species was "possible" or "likely" in the future due to the proposed action. The district court rejected this contention, and although the Fish and Wildlife Service states that it has abandoned this argument on appeal, it nevertheless maintains that the Section 7 incidental take definition should be interpreted more broadly than the definition of a take under Section 9.* * * We believe that Congress has spoken to the precise question at issue and agree with the district court that the definition of "taking" in Sections 7 and 9 of the ESA are identical in meaning and application.

[The court took up the section 9 take prohibition, starting with the statute, the regulations, and *Sweet Home*, noting that h]arming a species may be indirect, in that the harm may be caused by habitat modification, but habitat modification does not constitute harm unless it "actually kills or injures wildlife." * * * Defenders of Wildlife v. Bernal, 204 F.3d 920, 924–25 (9th Cir.1999) [quoting *Sweet Home*].

Violators of the ESA, including agencies and their employees, are subject to substantial civil and criminal penalties, including imprisonment, under Section 9 of the Act. Private citizens, as well as government entities, may bring suit to enjoin such violations. 16 U.S.C. § 1540(a), (b), (e), (g).

Section 7 of the Act imposes an affirmative duty to prevent violations of Section 9 upon federal agencies, such as the Bureau of Land Management and the U.S. Forest Service. 16 U.S.C. § 1536(a)(2). This affirmative duty extends to "any action authorized, funded, or carried out by such agency," including authorizing grazing permits on land owned by the federal government. Id.

[The court then described the § 7 consultation process, and noted that the USFWS's biological opinion] must specify whether any "incidental taking" of protected species will occur, specifically "any taking otherwise prohibited, if such taking is incidental to, and not the purpose of, the carrying out of an otherwise lawful activity." 16 U.S.C. § 1536(b)(4); 50 C.F.R. § 17.3. Its determination that an incidental taking will result leads to the publication of the "Incidental Take Statement," identifying areas where members of the particular species are at risk. Contained in the Incidental Take Statement is an advisory opinion which:

(i) specifies the impact of such incidental taking on the species,

(ii) specifies those reasonable and prudent measures that the Secretary considers necessary or appropriate to minimize such impact [and] . . .

(iv) sets forth the terms and conditions . . . that must be complied with by the Federal agency or applicant . . . or both, to implement the measures specified under clause (ii). 16 U.S.C. § 1536(b)(4) (subsection (iii) omitted).

Significantly, the Incidental Take Statement functions as a safe harbor provision immunizing persons from Section 9 liability and penalties for takings committed during activities that are otherwise lawful and in compliance with its terms and conditions. 16 U.S.C. § 1536(o). Any such incidental taking "shall not be considered to be a prohibited taking of the species concerned." Id. Although the action agency is "technically free to disregard the Biological Opinion and proceed with its proposed action . . . it does so at its own peril." Bennett, 520 U.S. at 170.

Consequently, if the terms and conditions of the Incidental Take Statement are disregarded and a taking does occur, the action agency or the applicant may be subject to potentially severe civil and criminal penalties under Section 9.

C.   Reconciling "Taking" as used in Section 9 with Section 7

The structure of the ESA and the legislative history clearly show Congress's intent to enact one standard for "taking" within both Section 7(b)(4), governing the creation of Incidental Take Statements, and Section 9, imposing civil and criminal penalties for violation of the ESA. In 1982, Congress amended the ESA to include Section 7(b)(4) to resolve the conflict between Sections 7 and 9. See H.R.Rep. No.97–567, at 15 (1982). As noted in the legislative reports, the purpose of Section 7(b)(4) and the amendment to Section 7(o) is to resolve the situation in which a Federal agency or a permit or license applicant has been advised that the proposed action will not violate Section 7(a)(2) of the Act but the proposed action will result in the taking of some species incidental to that action—a clear violation of Section 9 of the Act which prohibits any taking of a species. H.R.Rep. No. 97–567, at 26 (1982), reprinted in 1982 U.S.C.C.A.N. 2807, 2826. Absent an actual or prospective taking under Section 9, there is no "situation" that requires a Section 7 safe harbor provision.

We reject the argument that "taking" should be applied differently because the two sections serve different purposes. Interpreting the statutes in the manner urged by the Fish and Wildlife Service could effectively stop the proposed cattle grazing entirely. Such a broad interpretation would allow the Fish and Wildlife Service to engage in widespread land regulation even where no Section 9 liability could be imposed. This interpretation would turn the purpose behind the 1982 Amendment on its head.

This conclusion follows as a practical matter from the statutory scheme. Because of the potential liability imposed on federal agencies whose actions do not comply with conditions in the Incidental Take Statement, agencies regulating land are unlikely to permit nonconforming uses of their land. For this reason, as the Supreme Court has recognized, Biological Opinions exert a "powerful coercive effect" in shaping The policies of the federal agencies whose actions are at issue. Bennett, 520 U.S. at 169 (citations omitted). Here, for example, although ACGA theoretically could choose to disregard the Incidental Take Statements without explanation, the Bureau of Land Management and the Forest Service, as the action agencies, "must not only articulate [their] reasons for disagreement (which ordinarily requires species and habitat investigations that are not within the action agency's expertise), but ... [they run] a substantial risk if [their] (inexpert) reasons turn out to be wrong." Id. As the Bennett Court noted, the action agency rarely, if ever, chooses to disregard the terms and conditions of an Incidental Take Statement. In fact, the Incidental Take Statement challenged in ACGA I began by stating, "[t]he measures described below are non-discretionary, and must be implemented by the agency so that they become binding conditions of any grant or permit issued to the applicant...." As a practical matter, if ACGA's members wish to receive grazing permits, they must comply with the terms and conditions of the Incidental Take Statements. As the district court held in ACGA II, "[i]f Fish and Wildlife Service could issue an Incidental Take Statement even when a taking in violation of Section 9 was not present, those engaging in legal activities would be subjected to the terms and conditions of such statements." The court finds no authority for this result nor do we.

V. Determining When the Fish and Wildlife Service Must Issue an Incidental Take Statement

[The court then rejected the contention of the USFWS that the ESA requires it to issue an ITS in every section 7 consultation. Instead, it agreed with the district court that] issuing an Incidental Take Statement is "appropriate only when a take has occurred or is reasonably certain to occur." The Fish and Wildlife Service argues that * * * it should be permitted to issue an Incidental Take Statement whenever there is any possibility, no matter how small, that a listed species will be taken. As we believe that Congress has spoken to the precise question at issue, we must reject the agency's interpretation of the ESA as contrary to clear congressional intent. * * * Section 7(b)(4) of the ESA provides:

If after consultation under subsection (a)(2) of this section, the Secretary concludes that—

(A) the agency action will not violate such subsection, or offers reasonable and prudent alternatives which the Secretary believes would not violate such subsection;

(B) the taking of an endangered species or a threatened species incidental to the agency action will not violate such subsection; and

(C) if an endangered species or threatened species of a marine mammal is involved, the taking is authorized pursuant to section 1371(a)(5) of this title;

the Secretary shall provide the Federal agency and the applicant concerned, if any, with a written statement that—

(i) specifies the impact of such incidental taking on the species, ...

16 U.S.C. § 1536(b)(4). The Fish and Wildlife Service relies on the statutory provision directing the Secretary to provide "a written statement that . . . specifies the impact of such incidental taking on the species." Id. * * *

When read in context, it is clear that the issuance of the Incidental Take Statement is subject to the finding of the factors enumerated in the ESA. The statute explicitly provides that the written statement is subject to the consultation and the Secretary's conclusions. A contrary interpretation would render meaningless the clause stating that the Incidental Take Statement will specify "the impact of such incidental taking." 16 U.S.C. § 1536(b)(4)(i) (emphasis added). We therefore agree with ACGA that the plain language of the ESA does not dictate that the Fish and Wildlife Service must issue an Incidental Take Statement irrespective of whether any incidental takings will occur. * * *

The plain language of the implementing regulations also supports ACGA's argument. * * *

The Fish and Wildlife Service's internal handbook does not alter our conclusion. * * *. The Fish and Wildlife Service's handbook instruction to issue an Incidental Take Statement when no take will occur as a result of permitted activity is contrary to the plain meaning of the statute as well as the agency's own regulations. Accordingly, we hold that absent rare circumstances such as those involving migratory species, it is arbitrary and capricious to issue an Incidental Take Statement when the Fish and Wildlife Service has no rational basis to conclude that a take will occur incident to the otherwise lawful activity.

[The court then turned to the individual ITSs.] As a preliminary matter, however, we must address the ACGA II court's application of a "reasonable certainty" standard, about which the Fish and Wildlife Service has made much ado. It argues that "the predicate for issuing an ITS should not be a particular level of certainty that a take will occur, the ITS itself must only not be arbitrary and capricious." This argument misapprehends the ACGA II court's application of the arbitrary and capricious standard to the requirement that the Fish and Wildlife Service must find a take incidental to the otherwise lawful use before it may condition issuance of a permit on enumerated "reasonable and prudent" measures. ACGA II held merely that if the Fish and Wildlife Service cannot satisfy the court to a reasonable certainty that a take will occur, then it is arbitrary and capricious for it to issue an Incidental Take Statement imposing conditions on the use of the land. This is actually a more lenient standard than if the record were required to include evidence of an actual taking incident to the proposed use. Given that the Fish and Wildlife Service must have a reasonable basis to conclude that a take will occur as a result of the anticipated lawful activity, benchmarking such findings against a standard of reasonable certainty puts it to a lesser burden. Moreover, it would be unreasonable for the Fish and Wildlife Service to impose conditions on otherwise lawful land use if a take were not reasonably certain to occur as a result of that activity. * * *

We need not definitively resolve this question, however, because regardless of the dispute over the ACGA II court's application of the arbitrary and capricious standard, we must review de novo the actions of the Fish and Wildlife Service under the arbitrary and capricious standard mandated by the statute. Therefore, pursuant to Section 706 of the APA, we proceed to determine whether the Incidental Take Statements are founded on a rational connection between the facts found and the choices made by the Fish and Wildlife Service and whether it has committed a clear error of judgment. See Motor Vehicle Manuf. Assoc. v. State Farm Mutual Auto., 463 U.S. 29, 43 (1983).

In the Biological Opinion issued in response to ACGA's first request for land use permits, the Fish and Wildlife Service concluded that the direct effects of cattle grazing are infrequent to the razorback sucker, a moderately sized fish listed as endangered in November 1991. Although once abundant in the project area, the Fish and Wildlife Service admitted that there have been no reported sightings of the razorback sucker in the area since 1991 and that "effects of the livestock grazing program on individual fish or fish populations probably occur infrequently." Nevertheless, the Fish and Wildlife Service issued an Incidental Take Statement for the fish, anticipating take as a result of the direct effects of grazing in the project area, the construction of fences, the construction and existence of stock tanks for non-native fish, as well as other "activities in the watershed." Because the Fish and Wildlife Service could not directly quantify the level of incidental take, it determined that authorized take would be exceeded if range conditions in the allotment deteriorated and cattle grazing could not be ruled out as a cause of the deterioration.

Despite the lack of evidence that the razorback sucker exists on the allotment in question, the Fish and Wildlife Service argues that it should be able to issue an Incidental Take Statement based upon prospective harm. While we recognize the importance of a prospective orientation, the regulations mandate a separate procedure for reinitiating consultation if different evidence is later developed:

> Reinitiation of formal consultation is required and shall be requested by the Federal agency or by the Service, where discretionary Federal involvement or control over the action has been retained or is authorized by law and:
>
> (a) If the amount or extent of taking specified in the incidental take statement is exceeded;
>
> (b) If new information reveals effects of the action that may affect listed species or critical habitat in a manner or to an extent not previously considered;

(c) If the identified action is subsequently modified in a manner that causes an effect to the listed species or critical habitat that was not considered in the biological opinion; or

(d) If a new species is listed or critical habitat designated that may be affected by the identified action.

50 C.F.R. § 402.16. * * * Absent this procedure, however, there is no evidence that Congress intended to allow the Fish and Wildlife Service to regulate any parcel of land that is merely capable of supporting a protected species.

The only additional evidence that the Fish and Wildlife Service offers to justify its decision is that "small numbers of the juvenile fish . . . likely survived" in an unsuccessful attempt to repopulate the project area between 1981–1987. This speculative evidence, without more, is woefully insufficient to meet the standards imposed by the governing statute. See 50 C.F.R. § 402.14(g)(8) ("In formulating its biological opinion . . . the Service will use the best scientific and commercial data available. . . ."). Likewise, the Fish and Wildlife Service failed to present evidence that an indirect taking would occur absent the existence of the species on the property. Although habitat modification resulting in actual killing or injury may constitute a taking, the Fish and Wildlife Service has presented only speculative evidence that habitat modification, brought about by livestock grazing, may impact the razorback sucker. The agency has a very low bar to meet, but it must at least attain it. It would be improper to force ACGA to prove that the species does not exist on the permitted area, as the Fish and Wildlife Service urges, both because it would require ACGA to meet the burden statutorily imposed on the agency, and because it would be requiring it to prove a negative.

Based on a careful review of the record, we find that it is arbitrary and capricious to issue an Incidental Take Statement for the razorback sucker when the Fish and Wildlife Service's speculation that the species exists on the property is not supported by the record. We agree with the district court's ruling that the Fish and Wildlife Service failed to establish an incidental taking because it did not have evidence that the razorback sucker even exists anywhere in the area. Where the agency purports to impose conditions on the lawful use of that land without showing that the species exists on it, it acts beyond its authority in violation of 5 U.S.C.§ 706.

* * * [The court reached a similar conclusion with respect to several other ITSs, and then turned to an ITS issued on the Cow Flat Allotment, which was considered occupied loach minnow habitat.] Having determined that loach minnow exist on the allotment, Fish and Wildlife Service determined that the loach minnow are vulnerable to direct harms resulting from cattle crossings, such as trampling. Moreover, because the fish use the spaces between large substrates for resting and spawning, sedimentation resulting from grazing in pastures that settles in these spaces can adversely affect loach minnow habitat. The Biological Opinion determines that this indirect effect, along with the direct crushing of loach minnow eggs and the reduction in food availability, will result in take of the loach minnow. The

Incidental Take Statement, however, does not directly quantify the incidental takings of loach minnow and determines that such takings "will be difficult to detect." Defining the incidental take in terms of habitat characteristics, the Fish and Wildlife Service found that take will be exceeded if several conditions are not met. One such condition was if "[e]cological conditions do not improve under the proposed livestock management" plan.

We agree with the district court that the issuance of the Cow Flat Incidental Take Statement was not arbitrary and capricious. Unlike the other allotments in question, the Fish and Wildlife Service provided evidence that the listed species exist on the land in question and that the cattle have access to the endangered species' habitat. Accordingly, the Fish and Wildlife Service could reasonably conclude that the loach minnow could be harmed when the livestock entered the river. Additionally, the Fish and Wildlife Service provided extensive site-specific information that discussed not only the topography of the relevant allotment, but the indirect effects of grazing on the species due to the topography. The specificity of the Service's data, as well as the articulated causal connections between the activity and the "actual killing or injury" of a protected species distinguishes the Fish and Wildlife Service's treatment of this allotment from the other allotments at issue in the two consultations. Thus, we hold that because the Fish and Wildlife Service articulated a rational connection between harm to the species and the land grazing activities at issue, the issuance of the Incidental Take Statements for the Cow Flat Allotment was not arbitrary and capricious.

We now turn to the question whether the Service acted arbitrarily and capriciously by failing to properly specify the amount of anticipated take in the Incidental Take Statement for the Cow Flat Allotment and by failing to provide a clear standard for determining when the authorized level of take has been exceeded.

In general, Incidental Take Statements set forth a "trigger" that, when reached, results in an unacceptable level of incidental take, invalidating the safe harbor provision, and requiring the parties to re-initiate consultation. Ideally, this "trigger" should be a specific number. See, e.g., Mausolf v. Babbitt, 125 F.3d 661 (8th Cir.1997) (snowmobiling activity may take no more than two wolves); Fund for Animals v. Rice, 85 F.3d 535 (11th Cir.1996) (municipal landfill may take fifty-two snakes during construction and an additional two snakes per year thereafter); Mt. Graham Red Squirrel v. Madigan, 954 F.2d 1441 (9th Cir.1992) (telescope construction may take six red squirrels per year); Ctr. for Marine Conservation v. Brown, 917 F.Supp. 1128 (S.D.Tex.1996) (shrimping operation may take four hawksbill turtles, four leatherback turtles, ten Kemp's ridley turtles, ten green turtles, or 370 loggerhead turtles). Here, however, the "trigger" took the form of several conditions. We must therefore determine whether the linking of the level of permissible take to the conditions set forth in the various Incidental Take Statements was arbitrary and capricious.

ACGA argues that the Incidental Take Statements fail to specify the amount or extent of authorized take with the required degree of exactness. Specifically, ACGA objected to the first condition:

The [S]ervice concludes that incidental take of loach minnow from the proposed action will be considered to be exceeded if any of the following conditions are met:

[Condition 1] Ecological conditions do not improve under the proposed livestock management. Improving conditions can be defined through improvements in watershed, soil condition, trend and condition of rangelands (e.g., vegetative litter, plant vigor, and native species diversity), riparian conditions (e.g., vegetative and geomorphologic: bank, terrace, and flood plain conditions), and stream channel conditions (e.g., channel profile, embeddedness, water temperature, and base flow) within the natural capabilities of the landscape in all pastures on the allotment within the Blue River watershed.

We have never held that a numerical limit is required. Indeed, we have upheld Incidental Take Statements that used a combination of numbers and estimates. See Ramsey v. Kantor, 96 F.3d 434, 441 n. 12 (9th Cir.1996) (utilizing both harvesting rates and estimated numbers of fish to reach a permitted take); Southwest Ctr. for Biological Diversity v. U.S. Bureau of Reclamation, 6 F.Supp.2d 1119 (D.Ariz.1997) (concluding that an Incidental Take Statement that indexes the permissible take to successful completion of the reasonable and prudent measures as well as the terms and conditions is valid); Pac. Northwest Generating Coop. v. Brown, 822 F.Supp.1479, 1510 (D.Or.1993) (ruling that an Incidental Take Statement that defines the allotted take in percentage terms is valid). * * *

We agree with the ACGA II court's conclusion that, "the use of ecological conditions as a surrogate for defining the amount or extent of incidental take is reasonable so long as these conditions are linked to the take of the protected species." * * *

ACGA argues that it is entitled to more certainty than "vague and undetectable criteria such as changes in a 22,000 acre allotment's 'ecological condition.'" In response, the Fish and Wildlife Service argues that "the [Incidental Take Statement] provides for those studies necessary to provide the quantification of impacts which the Cattle Growers claim is lacking."

We disagree with the government's position. The Incidental Take Statements at issue here do not sufficiently discuss the causal connection between Condition 1 and the taking of the species at issue. Based on the Incidental Take Statement, if "[e]cological conditions do not improve," takings will occur. This vague analysis, however, cannot be what Congress contemplated when it anticipated that surrogate indices might be used in place of specific numbers. Moreover, whether there has been compliance with this vague directive is within the unfettered discretion of the Fish and Wildlife Service, leaving no method by which the applicant or the action agency can gauge their performance. Finally, Condition 1 leaves ACGA and the United States Forest Service responsible for the general ecological improvement of the approximately 22,000 acres that comprise the Cow Flat Allotment. * * *

NOTES AND QUESTIONS

1. How exactly does § 9 fit together with § 7 where, as here, a federal agency is authorizing private action that could modify habitat so as to result in the take of an endangered species? Are certain acts taken by federal agencies forbidden by one of these sections, and not the other? If the action the agency is authorizing would violate Section 9, must it also have violated Section 7? Here the USFWS found that the federal land managers' authorization of livestock grazing did not cause "jeopardy" and did not adversely modify critical habitat of listed species. Note that the concept of the "incidental take statement" was added to the ESA in 1982 to "resolve the conflict between Sections 7 and 9." How did it do that?

2. Is the court here not sensitive enough to what it calls the "importance of protective orientation"? Here the USFWS uses the ITS process to advocate management of livestock grazing on federal lands that pays close attention to the needs of listed species. While the agency cannot provide details on the number of endangered critters the actions it recommends might save (or the amount of possible "take" such actions would avoid), is the court correct in saying such details are required, given the precautionary approach to ESA enforcement the Supreme Court seemed to approve in *TVA v. Hill*?

3. What was the purpose of the conditions the USFWS imposed in the ITSs here? To avoid jeopardy? Or to help the species recover so that they might be taken off the endangered species list? The court seems to say the former is permissible and the latter is not. Why? That is, what's wrong with the USFWS engaging in what the court called "widespread land regulation even where no § 9 liability could be imposed" in these circumstances? If cattle grazing on public land has been a significant factor in the decline of the species that are now on the endangered list, why shouldn't more species-sensitive management be addressed in the section 7 process through the formation of terms and conditions in the ITS? (See also the discussion of recovery planning under the ESA in the next subsection, infra.)

4. Is the court of appeals agreeing with the district court that USFS must find, to a "reasonable certainty," that "take" will occur before it can issue an ITS imposing conditions on the use of the land?

5. Why was the Cow Flat Allotment different; i.e., what made an ITS appropriate there? But note the court went on to set aside the ITS even there. Why? Is the court creating an impossible standard for the USFWS to meet by requiring specificity in linkage between management practices and species protection?

6. Or is the court merely saying in this case that the ESA is not a license for the wildlife agencies to use the ITS process of § 7 to roam around requiring promotion of species-sensitive management practices by federal land agencies; and that instead it must pay attention to the facts on the ground?

7. In some of its possible applications, the ESA might collide with claimed property rights of a user of federal lands, such as in a mining

claim, a mineral lease or timber sale or concession contract, or in a claimed property right of access to a private inholding. Might the restrictions of the Act require the government to pay compensation if the property right is extinguished or deprived of all or most of its economic value? So far, surprisingly, very few cases have raised this kind of property rights "takings" issue—to be distinguished from species "takings" issues under section 9 of the ESA. Compare the discussion of property rights "takings" in Chapter 3, supra p. 232, and especially Christy v. Hodel, noted *id.* p. 250, where a rancher's property rights "taking" argument was rejected, and he was sanctioned for shooting a grizzly bear that had apparently killed his sheep. But see Tulare Lake Basin Water Storage District v. United States, 49 Fed.Cl. 313 (2001) (appeal pending) (finding a physical taking requiring compensation when ESA compliance reduced water deliveries under contracts that gave plaintiffs "a right to the exclusive use of prescribed quantities of water"); cf. O'Neill v. United States, 50 F.3d 677 (9th Cir.1995) (U.S. not liable for ESA-induced water delivery shortages because the contract between the United States and the irrigators allowed interruption of delivery for any reason). See Barton H. Thompson, Jr., The Endangered Species Act: A Case Study in Takings and Incentives, 49 Stan.L.Rev. 305 (1997); Oliver A. Houck, Why Do We Protect Endangered Species, and What Does That Say About Whether Restrictions on Private Property to Protect Them Constitute "Takings"?, 80 Iowa L.Rev. 297 (1995); Mark Sagoff, Muddle or Muddle Through? Takings Jurisprudence Meets the Endangered Species Act, 38 Wm. & Mary L.Rev.825 (1997).

TWO ENDANGERED SPECIES SAGAS IN A NUTSHELL

The Northern Spotted Owl. Efforts to protect the northern spotted owl gave rise to perhaps the most prominent controversy ever to emerge under the ESA. It had the broadest impact on public land management, the most significant regional economic impact, and left a tangled skein of litigation, executive and congressional action. Not bad for a bird that stands about 18″ tall, with a 40″ wingspan. Largely because of its secretive, nocturnal nature, not much was known about it before the late 1980s. Something over a thousand breeding pairs occupy several million acres of old growth Douglas Fir forests in the Pacific Northwest, about two-thirds of which is national forests, another 25% other federal land, and about 10% state, tribal, or privately-owned land.

Although controversy began before the owl was listed as a result of litigation; see p. 451 supra, the listing gave owl advocates a powerful tool, and they used it. But the ESA was not the sole ground for the several injunctions that followed; a number were based on violations of the National Forest Management Act, the Federal Land Policy & Management Act, and NEPA. The timber industry also initiated some lawsuits of its own. In 1990 Congress stepped in by enacting an appropriations rider that allowed some timber sales to go forward in spite of pending judicial proceedings. The rider was eventually upheld by the Supreme Court, see Robertson v. Seattle Audubon Soc'y, 503 U.S. 429 (1992), but eventually expired of its own terms. See generally Victor Sher & Carol Hunting,

Eroding the Landscape, Eroding the Laws: Congressional Exemptions From Judicial Review of Environmental Laws, 15 Harv.Envt'l L.Rev. 435 (1991). In 1992 new federal court decisions virtually halted timber sales in the region. One enjoined Forest Service timber sales after finding inadequate the agency's EIS on its spotted owl policy. (One of the flaws, ironically, was the EIS's failure to consider the impact on the owl of the BLM timber sales the God Squad had exempted from the Act a few weeks earlier.) Another enjoined BLM timber sales in spotted owl country, not strictly on the basis of the ESA, but because the BLM's resource management plans gave inadequate consideration to the owl.

After a regional "timber summit" conducted by President Clinton in April 1993, the President established a Forest Ecosystem Management Assessment Team to develop a comprehensive new plan for forest management across the region from northern California to the Canadian border. Centerpieces of that plan were a comprehensive approach to forest management throughout the region, regardless of ownership; a focus on maintaining diversity across many species, and not just the owl or other listed endangered species; putting the burden of protection of species on the federal lands where at all possible (to limit restrictions on private, state and tribal land); using "adaptive management" techniques (adjusting based on experience) where possible; and cushioning impact on displaced timber industry workers through a "jobs in the woods" program. The plan (which drastically reduced timber harvesting from levels most observers thought were unsustainable anyway) and its accompanying EIS were upheld in Seattle Audubon Soc'y v. Moseley, 80 F.3d 1401 (9th Cir.1996), against challenges by both environmentalists and the timber industry. See generally Steven L. Yaffee, THE WISDOM OF THE SPOTTED OWL: POLICY LESSONS FOR A NEW CENTURY (1994). Some controversy still lingers, but the owl and the ESA emerged from the long struggle relatively intact, although the economies of several rural counties in the Northwest changed forever.

Salmon. Most ESA litigation has focused on single causes of endangerment, but in the early 1990s, federal agencies listed several stocks or runs of salmon as endangered or threatened, thereby highlighting the multiple and interactive causes of salmon decline. Professor Coggins, in An Ivory Tower Perspective on Endangered Species Law, 8 Nat.Res. & Envt. No. 1, at 3 (1993), put it this way:

> Even though much of the ESA seems targeted narrowly at particular identified species, its scope is necessarily and inherently wide. Listing of a species as endangered or threatened, if at all reasonable, is more than a judgment about that species' population status; it is also a finding that one or more things are seriously wrong with that animal's environment. Bald eagles were not just being shot by disgruntled sheepherders, their entire milieu was poisoned by DDT. The recently listed salmon runs were not just being overfished, their riverine (and marine) habitat was in wretched condition from multiple causes. Few want to shoot red-cockaded woodpeckers for sport; their decline is attributable to the conversion of climax forests into monoculture tree

farms. When the Fish and Wildlife Service (FWS) lists a species, therefore, an inevitable consequence is that the species not only requires direct protective measures (e.g., a ban on taking), but radical or fundamental improvements in its habitat as well if the Act's purpose is to be achieved. Such improvements must necessarily come from land use controls.

Assume, for instance, that the agency lists as endangered a run of salmon that spawn in Idaho. First, controls on commercial, sport, and Indian fishing would be mandatory. Thereafter, * * * the regulatory focus will fall on water quantity: The responsible agencies and diverters would have to devise means to ensure that sufficient water for passage and spawning remained in the hundreds of miles of river flowing to the ocean. In the next regulatory phase, barriers to passage (e.g., dams, weirs) would come under expansive scrutiny, and retrofitting would be an obvious solution. If these measures did not markedly improve the species' survival rate, agencies or citizens would be forced to look at other causes of decline. When they did so, they would confront a wide spectrum of human activity: timber cutting; agricultural and industrial poisons; livestock grazing; irrigation; mining; recreation; and so on. The causation equation usually is many-factored. All interests that contribute to the problem of endangerment, even if their activities are legal, should bear an equitable share of the recovery costs. If comprehensive approaches are adopted, not only will the species rebound, but the entire environment it inhabits will be healthier.

Protecting listed salmon runs has given rise to much complicated litigation. A great many interests are affected, and there is much finger pointing as to who is most responsible among the four major culprits (known as the four "H's"): hatcheries (which produce a fish monoculture that can outcompete "wild" fish but increases risk of decimation by disease); hydropower (whose turbines grind up fish and whose reservoirs greatly lengthen and make more arduous the passage of young salmon to the ocean); harvest (primarily commercial harvest, particularly in the oceans); and habitat (spawning sites degraded by timber harvesting, cattle grazing, road construction and a variety of other developments). There have been many court opinions and orders, and yet many runs continue to decline. A sampling of recent cases includes Klamath Water Users Protective Ass'n. v. Patterson, 204 F.3d 1206 (9th Cir.1999); American Rivers v. National Marine Fisheries Serv., 109 F.3d 1484 (9th Cir.1997); Parravano v. Masten, 70 F.3d 539 (9th Cir.1995) (affirming reductions ordered by the National Marine Fisheries Service in ocean harvesting of Klamath River chinook salmon); Pacific Northwest Generating Co-op. v. Brown, 38 F.3d 1058 (9th Cir.1994); Northwest Resource Information Center, Inc. v. Northwest Power Planning Council, 35 F.3d 1371 (9th Cir.1994). Judge Marsh may have put his finger on a key part of the problem in Idaho Dept. of Fish and Game v. NMFS, 850 F.Supp. 886 (D.Or.1994), remanded, 56 F.3d 1071 (9th Cir.1995):

NMFS has clearly made an effort to create a rational, reasoned process for determining how the action agencies are doing in their efforts to save the listed salmon species. But the process is seriously * * * flawed because it is too heavily geared towards a status quo that has allowed all forms of river activity to proceed in a deficit situation—that is, relatively small steps, minor improvements and adjustments—when the situation literally cries out for a major overhaul. Instead of looking for what *can* be done to protect the species from jeopardy, NMFS and the action agencies have narrowly focused their attention on what the establishment is capable of handling with minimal disruption.

See generally Michael C. Blumm & Greg D. Corbin, Salmon and the Endangered Species Act: Lessons from the Columbia Basin, 74 Wash.L.Rev. 519 (1999); John M. Volkman, How Do You Learn From a River? Managing Uncertainty in Species Conservation Policy, 74 Wash. L.Rev. 719 (1999).

8. RECOVERY PLANS FOR LISTED SPECIES

The 1978 amendments added a provision to § 4 of the ESA requiring the Secretary of the Interior to "develop and implement plans (* * * 'recovery plans') for the conservation and survival of [listed species] * * * unless he finds that such a plan will not promote the conservation of the species." 16 U.S.C. § 1533(f)(1). The Secretary is to give priority to those species "most likely to benefit from such plans." Id. Recovery plans must, "to the maximum extent practicable," incorporate "a description of such site-specific management actions as may be necessary to achieve the plan's goals for the conservation and survival of the species;" "contain 'objective, measurable criteria'" for determining when the species can be removed from the list; and estimate the time and cost of the measures needed to achieve the goal and intermediate steps for that goal. Id.

While the Act contains some hopeful generalities on this score, recovery planning lacks much specificity of process or standards to measure the sufficiency of plans. As a consequence, what little litigation that has addressed this feature of the Act has regarded the content of the plans as discretionary. See, e.g., Fund for Animals v. Rice, 85 F.3d 535, 547 (11th Cir.1996) (recovery plans do not have the "force of law" but "are for guidance only," and therefore do not furnish a basis for enjoining construction of a municipal landfill on a wetlands site that is habitat to listed species); Strahan v. Linnon, 967 F.Supp. 581 (D.Mass.1997); Morrill v. Lujan, 802 F.Supp. 424, 433 (S.D.Ala.1992); National Wildlife Federation v. National Park Service, 669 F.Supp. 384 (D.Wyo.1987).

Perhaps the most extensive judicial treatment came in Fund for Animals v. Babbitt, 903 F.Supp. 96 (D.D.C.1995), and involved the recovery plan for the grizzly bear, listed as "threatened" in 1975 when its numbers in the lower 48 states shrank to below 1000 from an estimated 50,000 in 1800. In upholding the plan, the court noted that the Act "suggests" a variety of methods and procedures that may be necessary to conserve species, such as research, census, law enforcement, habitat acquisition and maintenance, propagation, live trapping, and transplantation. 16 U.S.C. § 1532(3). But "none of these methods or procedures is mandated by the

Act," which "does not detail specific methods or procedures that are necessary to achieve conservation and survival." Therefore, the ESA gives the U.S. Fish & Wildlife Service "flexibility" to "recommend a wide range of 'management actions' on a site-specific basis."

See generally Federico Cheever, The Road to Recovery: A New Way of Thinking About the Endangered Species Act, 23 Ecology Q. 1 (1996); Jason Patlis, Recovery, Conservation, and Survival Under the Endangered Species Act: Recovering Species, Conserving Resources, and Saving the Law, 17 Pub.L. & Resources L. Rev. 55 (1996). About half of listed species have recovery plans, although only about one-third of the animals do (and only about 15% of the mammals).

9.   REINTRODUCTION OF SPECIES

Full recovery of some listed species may require their reintroduction into areas from which they have been extirpated. One of the most celebrated efforts at reintroduction—to put the gray wolf back into Yellowstone National Park, where it was the only large mammal that had been extinguished from that celebrated ecoregion several decades earlier—became mired in controversy and litigation. Ultimately, however, the effort was successful, some would say fabulously so, from about every perspective.

The ESA authorizes designation of "experimental populations" of a listed species for reintroduction "outside the current range" of the species, if the Secretary determines that the release "will further the conservation of the species." § 10(j); 16 U.S.C. § 1539(j)(2)(A). The Park Service used gray wolves from Canada (where they are abundant) for reintroduction at Yellowstone. The regulation under which the experimental population was reintroduced provided specifically that the reintroduced wolves could be "taken" under certain circumstances (such as when a reintroduced wolf was preying on livestock in the reintroduced area) without violating the Act. The legal issue was created by the fact that wolves were already naturally migrating into Montana from Canada, and a handful had been seen in the general area of release.

The statute requires that the experimental population must be "wholly separate geographically from nonexperimental populations of the same species." Id. § 1539(j)(1). The purpose of this requirement is to maintain protection for indigenous populations while allowing, where separation existed, the U.S. Fish & Wildlife Service some flexibility in setting the terms of reintroduction in order to encourage and provide incentives for acceptance of reintroduction. At Yellowstone reintroduction opponents (ranchers concerned about wolf depredation on their livestock, and not assuaged by the offer of private nonprofit groups to compensate them for proven losses) were, ironically, joined by some reintroduction supporters (such as the National Audubon Society) in the argument that this separation in populations was lacking. The ranchers argued this made the release illegal. Audubon argued that the lack of separation meant that the rule allowing "take" of reintroduced wolves under certain circumstances was illegal. The USFWS argued that the presence of an occasional outlier wolf in the area (there was no evidence of breeding pairs) did not constitute a separate "population."

A Wyoming district court bought the ranchers' argument and ruled the reintroduction illegal, but was reversed on appeal. Wyoming Farm Bureau Federation v. Babbitt, 987 F.Supp. 1349 (D.Wyo.1997), rev'd, 199 F.3d 1224 (10th Cir.2000). The Ninth Circuit in the meantime had upheld the reintroduction, and affirmed the conviction on appeal of a person who shot a reintroduced wolf in circumstances unconnected to livestock depredation. United States v. McKittrick, 142 F.3d 1170 (9th Cir.1998). "We must defer to FWS's reasonable interpretation of section 10(j), particularly where the interpretation involves agency expertise * * *." FWS has interpreted the "wholly separate geographically requirement only to apply to populations; this interpretation is reasonable and we decline to disturb it." McKittrick also challenged the Service's decision to make reintroduction and recovery of the gray wolf a priority, because they were so plentiful in Canada and Alaska. The court responded: "The Secretary has broad discretion to determine what methods to use in species conservation, * * * adoption of recovery plans is discretionary, 16 U.S.C. § 1533(f); and the presence of healthy wolf populations in Canada and Alaska does not, in any event, make the recovery of U.S. populations any less crucial."

THE FUTURE—ESA AND PROTECTION OF BIODIVERSITY

There is no doubt that the ESA is working a substantial revolution in the way we manage federal lands and associated waters. Some say it's because other environmental laws (like the Clean Water Act) and laws calling for "sustained yield" management of federal renewable resources (covered in succeeding chapters) have failed to deliver on their promise. And some say it's because the ESA merely provides the excuse—the final prod or inducement—to move toward more sensible, sustainable management of natural resources that many have long known must come. But the ESA is not perfect, and it's been subject to trenchant criticism on a variety of grounds. For example, its focus on single species in what some have called an "emergency room" atmosphere has been criticized as inadequate to the task of preserving significant ecosystems. Some have called for more focus on biological hotspots; see e.g., John C. Kunich, Preserving the Womb of the Unknown Species with Hotspots Legislation, 52 Hastings L.J. 1149 (2001).

The last decade of the twentieth century saw considerable innovation and ferment in the administration of the ESA, as the federal government sought, with some success, to build support for and defuse opposition to the ESA. See generally John Leshy, The Babbitt Legacy at the Interior Department: A Preliminary View, 31 Envtl. L. 199, 212–14 (2001); J.B. Ruhl, Who Needs Congress? An Agenda for Administration Reform of the Endangered Species Act, 6 N.Y.U. Envtl.L.J. 367 (1998); Patrick Parenteau, Rearranging the Deck Chairs: Endangered Species Act Reforms in an Era of Mass Extinction, 22 Wm & Mary Envtl.L. & Pol'y Rev. 227 (1998); Zygmunt J.B. Plater, The Embattled Social Utilities of the Endangered Species Act—A Noah Presumption and Caution Against Putting Gasmasks on the Canaries in the Coalmine, 27 Envtl.L. 845 (1997); Oliver Houck, On the Law of Biodiversity and Ecosystem Management, 81 Minn.L.Rev. 869 (1997). But Congress has remained sorely divided on the ESA's future, with sentiment in that body divided across the spectrum, embracing those who want to make it essentially voluntary, those who want to broaden and strengthen its regulatory reach, and every stripe in between. Its future in its current form is, in other words, not secure.

CHAPTER 6

THE WATER RESOURCE*

The water resource is the appropriate starting place for studying specific federal public resources, for all other resource uses are dependent upon the availability of water. Mineral extraction and processing often require significant quantities. Water itself, in the form of geothermal steam or as hydropower, is an energy resource. Western farmers rely on expansive irrigation systems—as much as 80% of all developed water supplies in the eleven western states is used for irrigation. Grass and trees and fish and wildlife all need water. And so do rafters and kayakers and other recreationists. Finally, water is an essential part of ecosystems that society wishes preserved for future generations.

Acquisition of water rights has traditionally been principally a matter of state law, but this is largely due to federal restraint. As a constitutional matter, valid federal water laws are supreme: The Property, Commerce, Spending and Treaty Clauses give Congress ample authority to legislate on issues relating to water. Large scale water resources development is mainly a creature of federal money, if not federal law. While Congress has not generally legislated a federal water law, federal land management agencies frequently hold water rights bottomed on federal law. Congress can also affect state water law and water rights perfected under such law when it acts to regulate navigation, to prevent floods, to control water pollution, or to protect endangered species.

Water policy on the federal lands involves more than the distribution of water among competing users. Land management practices often determine the character of the streams and lakes within a watershed. Timber harvesting can cause stream blockages and erosion and affect the temperature, quantity, and quality of run-off. Overgrazing destroys groundcover and causes soil compaction; rainfall, instead of being absorbed and cooled by spongy soils, runs off in sheets, carrying soil with it and carving out gulleys and arroyos. Mineral development can drastically affect hydrologic conditions; large open-pit gold mines in Nevada pump large volumes of groundwater to dewater the pits and allow mining to continue. This can dry up some surface streams and greatly increase the supply in others. Development projects of all sorts usually require road systems, which can cause severe erosion. Land and resource planners therefore must give prime consideration to protection of watercourses if downstream consump-

* Portions of the discussion in this chapter are drawn, with permission, from Chapter 9 of Joseph L. Sax, Barton Thompson, John D. Leshy, and Robert Abrams, LEGAL CONTROL OF WATER RESOURCES (West. Pub. Co., 3d ed. 2000).

tive users, wildlife, and recreationists are to have adequate supplies of water.

The federal government influences national water policy in numerous ways that do not necessarily involve federal land law, but which often complicate resource decisions on the federal lands. Space and relevancy considerations prevent discussion of most of the legal issues that can arise; in particular, this chapter does not attempt to duplicate a course in water law. It is limited to aspects of water allocation that are intimately tied to the protection and development of the federal lands. Section A examines the law governing water rights for purposes related to federal lands. It focuses mostly on the doctrine of federal reserved water rights, and how such rights are established, adjudicated and protected. It also examines other means for the federal government to secure water rights and otherwise protect its interests in water in relation to federal lands. Section B contains materials on a subject of growing importance, the federal hydropower licensing process, which has special provisions to protect areas of federal lands.

A.   THE ACQUISITION OF WATER RIGHTS ON FEDERAL LANDS

1.   THE ORIGINS OF WATER LAW ON FEDERAL LANDS

Water law defines legal rights to a limited, fluid, and largely renewable resource. Geographic variations in the quantity of water available, competition among the many various uses, and differing political and social contexts have resulted in two basic types of state water rights systems. Under English common law, the owner of land adjacent to a watercourse (a "riparian" owner) acquired water rights in the stream as part of the estate in real property. Each riparian owner was entitled to the "natural flow" of the stream. None could use the water for consumptive purposes other than such modest "natural uses" as household or stockwatering, nor could they use the water off the riparian land. Instream, nonconsumptive uses (e.g., for mills) were permitted since the natural flow would be preserved. The English Rule of riparian rights came to be regarded as unsuited to the demands of industry, commerce, and agriculture where water is relatively scarce.

In the United States, the so-called "natural flow" doctrine, or English rule, came in most places to be modified to soften its hard edges. Consumptive uses were permitted if they were reasonable and did not damage other riparian owners (although such uses could not ripen into absolute rights), as were, in some jurisdictions, "reasonable" uses on nonriparian land. A very broad, "totality of the circumstances" set of criteria was applied to determine reasonableness. See, e.g., Restatement, Second, Torts §§ 850–59 (1979); A. Dan Tarlock, LAW OF WATER RIGHTS AND RESOURCES, ch. 3 (2001).

Another system of water rights—the prior appropriation doctrine— emerged out of the gold fields of California in the mid-nineteenth century. This doctrine was thought better suited not only for mining but also for those lands, (most of those west of the 100th meridian) which receive fewer than 20 inches of precipitation per year, and which therefore cannot sustain crops without artificial irrigation. Under this system an appropriator—whether or not the owner of riparian land—could obtain a vested property right superior to all later users by diverting water out of the stream and putting it to a beneficial use, a term that generally includes domestic uses and others such as agriculture and industry. The catchphrases of this legal system are "first in time, first in right" and "use it or lose it." On paper, the prior appropriation doctrine is a usufructuary system, requiring application of water to beneficial use in order to protect and maintain the right. Also, again on paper, the doctrine calls for no balancing of equities or proration among various users in times of shortage—the senior rightholder must be fully satisfied before any junior users get water. (Both of these hard-edged concepts have been softened considerably in practice.) Use in the appropriation doctrine is not limited to riparian land, not even to the watershed of origin, because miners and farmers often needed to transport water far away from the stream.

Most of the inland Rocky Mountain states have always been pure "Colorado doctrine" states, recognizing only water rights established by prior appropriation. A number of other western states (California, Kansas, Nebraska, North Dakota, Oklahoma, Oregon, South Dakota, Texas, and Washington) originally adopted what came to be known as the "California doctrine," which recognizes both riparian and appropriative rights. But all of the states in this latter group have, with very limited exceptions (mostly in California), since moved to a pure appropriation system. The result is that, generally speaking, the prior appropriation doctrine now holds sway in all states west of the 100th Meridian.

The western states have, on paper, fairly elaborate systems for adjudicating and supervising water rights. Beginning with Wyoming in 1890, most of them established administrative agencies to issue and oversee water rights. Fairly early on, states provided for general stream adjudications in which courts could determine all rights, by priority, within entire watersheds. The reality of water rights administration in the states fell far short of the promise, however, because in many states even today water rights are unsettled and uncertain.

The traditional prior appropriation doctrine, which allocated water on a laissez-faire basis to the first consumptive user, has been modified in various respects. Most states now allow new appropriations only upon a governmental agency finding that they are in the "public interest." Similarly, just about all states have abandoned the old idea that one could not legally protect a streamflow (as opposed to a water right based on diversion of water from the stream). Today it is more and more common for minimum stream flows to be legally established, by a variety of means, for protection of fish, wildlife, recreation, and the aesthetic qualities of streams and lakes. Water allocation is, however, still heavily influenced by deeply-entrenched state laws that have distributed most western water on a first-come, first-served basis to users who have actually diverted water from a watercourse and applied it to specified beneficial uses.

The following opinion provides some history of federal policy toward water allocation in the Western states.

California v. United States

Supreme Court of the United States, 1978.
438 U.S. 645.

■ MR. JUSTICE REHNQUIST delivered the opinion of the Court.

* * * [R]eclamation of the arid lands began almost immediately upon the arrival of pioneers to the Western States. Huge sums of private money were invested in systems to transport water vast distances for mining, agriculture, and ordinary consumption. Because a very high percentage of land in the West belonged to the Federal Government, the canals and ditches that carried this water frequently crossed federal land. In 1862, Congress opened the public domain to homesteading. Homestead Act of 1862, 12 Stat. 392. And in 1866, Congress for the first time expressly opened the mineral lands of the public domain to exploration and occupation by miners. Mining Act of 1866, ch. 262, 14 Stat. 251. Because of the fear that these Acts might in some way interfere with the water rights and systems that had grown up under state and local law, Congress explicitly recognized and acknowledged the local law:

> "[W]henever, by priority of possession, rights to the use of water for mining, agricultural, manufacturing, or other purposes, have vested and accrued, and the same are recognized and acknowledged by the local customs, laws, and the decisions of courts the possessors and owners of such vested rights shall be maintained and protected in the same." § 9, 14 Stat. 253.

The Mining Act of 1866 was not itself a grant of water rights pursuant to federal law. Instead, as this Court observed, the Act was " 'a voluntary recognition of a preexisting right of possession, constituting a valid claim to its continued use.' " United States v. Rio Grande Dam & Irrig. Co., supra, at 705. Congress intended "to recognize as valid the customary law with respect to the use of water which had grown up among the occupants of the public land under the peculiar necessities of their condition."[10] Basey v. Gallagher, 87 U.S. (20 Wall.) 670, 684, (1874). See Broder v. Water Co., supra, 101 U.S. at 276; Jennison v. Kirk, 98 U.S. 453, 459–461 (1878).[11]

10. Senator Stewart, the most vocal of the 1866 Act's supporters, noted during debate that § 9 "*confirms* the rights to use of the water * * * as established by local law and the decisions of the courts. In short, it proposes no new system, but *sanctions, regulates, and confirms a system to which the people are devotedly attached.*" Cong. Globe, 39th Cong., 1st Sess., 3227 (1866) (emphasis added).

11. Four years later, in the Act of July 9, 1870, 16 Stat. 218, Congress reaffirmed

that occupants of federal public land would be bound by state water law, by providing that "all patents granted, or preemption or homesteads allowed, shall be subject to any vested and accrued water rights." The effect of the 1866 and 1870 Acts was not limited to rights previously acquired. "They reach[ed] into the future as well, and approv[ed] and confirm[ed] the policy of appropriation for a beneficial use, as recognized by local rules and customs, and the legislation and judicial decisions of the arid-land states, as the test

In 1877, Congress took its first step toward encouraging the reclamation and settlement of the public desert lands in the West and made it clear that such reclamation would generally follow state water law. In the Desert Land Act of 1877, Congress provided for the homesteading of arid public lands in larger tracts

> "by [the homesteader's] conducting water upon the same, within the period of three years [after filing a declaration to do so], *Provided however* that the right to the use of water by the person so conducting the same * * * shall not exceed the amount of water actually appropriated, and necessarily used for the purpose of irrigation and reclamation: *and all surplus water over and above such actual appropriation and use, together with the water of all, lakes, rivers and other sources of water supply upon the public lands and not navigable, shall remain and be held free for the appropriation and use of the public for irrigation, mining and manufacturing purposes subject to existing rights.*" Ch. 107, 19 Stat. 377 (emphasis added).

This Court has had an opportunity to construe the 1877 Desert Land Act before. In California Oregon Power Co. v. Beaver Portland Cement Co., 295 U.S. 142 (1935), Mr. Justice Sutherland explained that, through this language, Congress "effected a severance of all waters upon the public domain, not theretofore appropriated, from the land itself." Id., at 158. The non-navigable waters thereby severed were "reserved for the use of the public under the laws of the states and territories." Id., at 162. Congress' purpose was not to federalize the prior-appropriation doctrine already evolving under local law. Quite the opposite: [id. at 163–64]

> "What we hold is that following the act of 1877, if not before, all non-navigable waters then a part of the public domain became *publici juris*, subject to the plenary control of the designated states, including those since created out of the territories named, with the right in each to determine for itself to what extent the rule of appropriation or the common-law rule in respect of riparian rights should obtain. For since 'Congress cannot enforce either rule upon any state,' Kansas v. Colorado, 206 U.S. 46, 94, the full power of choice must remain with the state. The Desert Land Act does not bind or purport to bind the states to any policy. It simply recognizes and gives sanction, in so far as the United States and its future grantees are concerned, to the state and local doctrine of appropriation, and seeks to remove what otherwise might be an impediment to its full and successful operation. See Wyoming v. Colorado, 259 U.S. 419, 465."

2. AN OVERVIEW OF FEDERAL RESERVED WATER RIGHTS

While the majority in California v. United States found a "consistent thread of purposeful and continued deference to state water law by Congress," a separate doctrine evolved around the turn of the twentieth century. In United States v. Rio Grande Dam & Irrigation Co., 174 U.S.

---

and measure of private rights in and to the non-navigable waters on the public domain." California Oregon Power Co. v. Beaver Portland Cement Co., 295 U.S. 142, 155 (1935).

690 (1899), the federal government sued to stop construction of a private dam across the Rio Grande River in the territory of New Mexico. Reversing the lower court's decision dismissing the suit, a unanimous Supreme Court acknowledged that local law generally controls, but said (174 U.S. at 703):

> [Y]et two limitations [on state power] must be recognized: First, that, in the absence of specific authority from Congress, a state cannot by its legislation destroy the right of the United States, as the owner of lands bordering on a stream, to the continued flow of its waters; so far at least as may be necessary for the beneficial uses of the government property. Second, that it is limited by the superior power of the General Government to secure the uninterrupted navigability of all navigable streams within the limits of the United States.

Nine years later, the Supreme Court built the first-mentioned limitation into the doctrine of federal reserved water rights in Winters v. United States, 207 U.S. 564 (1908). In *Winters,* the United States, as trustee for the Indian tribes occupying the Fort Belknap reservation in Montana, sought to enjoin upstream defendants on the Milk River from withdrawing water that was required for an irrigation project on the reservation. The defendants had appropriated water under Montana law after the reservation was established in 1888 but before 1898, when the Indian irrigation project was constructed. The Court tersely held that the creation of the Fort Belknap reservation not only set aside land but also impliedly reserved a sufficient quantity of water, as of the date of the reservation, to fulfill the purposes of the reservation (207 U.S. at 577): "The power of the Government to reserve the waters and exempt them from appropriation under the state laws is not denied, and could not be. United States v. Rio Grande Ditch [sic] & Irrig. Co. That the Government did reserve them we have decided * * *. This was done May 1, 1888 * * *."

Winters superimposed an implied federal water right based on setting aside federal land on a state system that based water rights on prior appropriation. The two rights do not mesh easily; the federal right is established without application of water to a beneficial use—a hallmark of prior appropriation law. Until the 1950s, *Winters* was thought to be a doctrine of Indian water rights only.* In 1955, however, the Supreme Court suggested that it could apply to other federal lands that were reserved for particular purposes. Federal Power Comm'n v. Oregon, 349 U.S. 435 (1955). This suggestion ripened into a holding eight years later.

Arizona v. California

Supreme Court of the United States, 1963.
373 U.S. 546.

[The Colorado River and its tributaries are a principal source of water for seven states in the arid Southwest. Arizona invoked the original

---

* Much of the jurisprudence that has developed around the *Winters* doctrine has come in the context of Indian water rights. In this section, however, we will consider the doctrine only as it relates to non-Indian federal land interests.

jurisdiction of the Supreme Court by filing an action against the State of California to determine each state's right to the water allocated to the lower Colorado River basin by the Colorado River Compact of 1922. The case was referred to a special master to take evidence and recommend a decree. Although the primary controversy concerned the amount of water each state had a legal right to use, the United States as intervenor asserted federal reserved rights for both Indian and non-Indian federal lands along the lower Colorado River. Near the end of its lengthy opinion largely affirming the recommendations of the special master, the Court held, per Justice Black (373 U.S. at 595, 597–98, 601)]:

In these proceedings, the United States has asserted claims to waters in the main river and in some of the tributaries for use on Indian Reservations, National Forests, Recreational and Wildlife Areas and other government lands and works. * * *

Arizona's contention that the Federal Government had no power, after Arizona became a State, to reserve waters for the use and benefit of federally reserved lands rests largely upon statements in Pollard's Lessee v. Hagan, 3 How. 212 (1845) * * *. But those cases involved only the shores of and lands beneath navigable waters. They do not determine the problem before us and cannot be accepted as limiting the broad powers of the United States to regulate navigable waters under the Commerce Clause and to regulate government lands under Art. IV, § 3, of the Constitution. We have no doubt about the power of the United States under these clauses to reserve water rights for its reservations and its property.

Arizona also argues that, in any event, water rights cannot be reserved by Executive Order. Some of the reservations of Indian lands here involved were made almost 100 years ago * * *. In our view, these reservations, like those created directly by Congress, were not limited to land, but included waters as well. * * * We can give but short shrift at this late date to the argument that the reservations either of land or water are invalid because they were originally set apart by the Executive.[102]

The Master ruled that the principle underlying the reservation of water rights for Indian Reservations was equally applicable to other federal establishments such as National Recreation Areas and National Forests. We agree with the conclusions of the Master that the United States intended to reserve water sufficient for the future requirements of the Lake Mead National Recreation Area, the Havasu Lake National Wildlife Refuge, the Imperial National Wildlife Refuge and the Gila National Forest.

The holding that the reserved rights doctrine extends to non-Indian federal land, including that withdrawn or reserved by Executive Order, gives nearly all categories of federal land some claim to water rights based

---

102. See United States v. Midwest Oil Co., 236 U.S. 459, 469–75 (1915); Winters v. United States.

on federal law. A survey of these federal water rights is set out further below. In the following case, a unanimous Supreme Court provided additional guidance on the dimensions of the *Winters* doctrine outside the Indian context.

Cappaert v. United States

Supreme Court of the United States, 1976.
426 U.S. 128.

■ MR. CHIEF JUSTICE BURGER delivered the opinion of the Court.

The question presented in this litigation is whether the reservation of Devil's Hole as a national monument reserved federal water rights in unappropriated water.

Devil's Hole is a deep limestone cavern in Nevada. Approximately 50 feet below the opening of the cavern is a pool of 65 feet long, 10 feet wide, and at least 200 feet deep, although its actual depth is unknown. The pool is a remnant of the prehistoric Death Valley Lake System and is situated on land owned by the United States since the Treaty of Guadalupe Hidalgo in 1848, 9 Stat. 922. By the Proclamation of January 17, 1952, President Truman withdrew from the public domain a 40–acre tract of land surrounding Devil's Hole, making it a detached component of the Death Valley National Monument. The Proclamation was issued under the American Antiquities Preservation Act, 16 U.S.C. § 431, which authorizes the President to declare as national monuments "objects of historic or scientific interest that are situated upon the lands owned or controlled by the Government of the United States * * *."

The 1952 Proclamation notes that Death Valley was set aside as a national monument "for the preservation of the unusual features of scenic, scientific, and educational interest therein contained." The Proclamation also notes that Devil's Hole is near Death Valley and contains a "remarkable underground pool." Additional preambulary statements in the Proclamation explain why Devil's Hole was being added to the Death Valley National Monument:

> * * * "WHEREAS the geologic evidence that this subterranean pool is an integral part of the hydrographic history of the Death Valley region is further confirmed by the presence in this pool of a peculiar race of desert fish, and zoologists have demonstrated that this race of fish, which is found nowhere else in the world, evolved only after the gradual drying up of the Death Valley Lake System isolated this fish population from the original ancestral stock that in Pleistocene times was common to the entire region; and
>
> "WHEREAS the said pool is of such outstanding scientific importance that it should be given special protection, and such protection can be best afforded by making the said forty-acre tract containing the pool a part of the said monument * * *."

The Cappaert petitioners own a 12,000 acre ranch near Devil's Hole, 4,000 acres of which are used for growing Bermuda grass, alfalfa, wheat, and barley; 1,700 to 1,800 head of cattle are grazed. The ranch represents an investment of more than $7 million; it employs more than 80 people with an annual payroll of more than $340,000.

In 1968 the Cappaerts began pumping groundwater on their ranch on land 2-1/2 miles from Devil's Hole; they were the first to appropriate groundwater. The groundwater comes from an underground basin or aquifer which is also the source of the water in Devil's Hole. After the Cappaerts began pumping from the wells near Devil's Hole, which they do from March to October, the summer water level of the pool in Devil's Hole began to decrease. * * *

[In 1970, when the Cappaerts sought permission from the Nevada State Engineer to change the use of water from several of their wells, the United States protested on the basis that continued pumping could injure the desert pupfish. The State Engineer rejected the protest. The United States filed suit in federal court to limit the Cappaerts' pumping. The lower courts issued the injunction sought by the United States, and the Supreme Court granted certiorari.] * * *

This Court has long held that when the Federal Government withdraws its land from the public domain and reserves it for a federal purpose, the Government, by implication, reserves appurtenant water then unappropriated to the extent needed to accomplish the purpose of the reservation. In so doing the United States acquires a reserved right in unappropriated water which vests on the date of the reservation and is superior to the rights of future appropriators. Reservation of water rights is empowered by the Commerce Clause, Art. I, § 8, which permits federal regulation of navigable streams, and the Property Clause, Art. IV, § 3, which permits federal regulation of federal lands. The doctrine applies to Indian reservations and other federal enclaves, encompassing water rights in navigable and nonnavigable streams. * * *

Nevada argues that the cases establishing the doctrine of federally reserved water rights articulate an equitable doctrine calling for a balancing of competing interests. However, an examination of those cases shows they do not analyze the doctrine in terms of a balancing test. For example, in Winters v. United States, supra, the Court did not mention the use made of the water by the upstream landowners in sustaining an injunction barring their diversions of the water. The "Statement of the Case" in *Winters* notes that the upstream users were homesteaders who had invested heavily in dams to divert the water to irrigate their land, not an unimportant interest. The Court held that when the Federal Government reserves land, by implication it reserves water rights sufficient to accomplish the purposes of the reservation.

In determining whether there is a federally reserved water right implicit in a federal reservation of public land, the issue is whether the Government intended to reserve unappropriated and thus available water. Intent is inferred if the previously unappropriated waters are necessary to accomplish the purposes for which the reservation was created. See, e.g., Arizona v. California; Winters v. United States. Both the District Court and the Court of Appeals held that the 1952 Proclamation expressed an intention to reserve unappropriated water, and we agree.[5] The Proclamation discussed the pool in Devil's Hole in four of the five preambles and recited that the "pool * * * should be given special protection." Since a pool is a body of water, the protection contemplated is meaningful only if the water remains; the water right reserved by the 1952 Proclamation was thus explicit, not implied.

Also explicit in the 1952 Proclamation is the authority of the Director of the Park Service to manage the lands of Devil's Hole Monument "as provided in the act of Congress entitled 'An Act to establish a National Park Service, and for other purposes,' approved August 25, 1916 (16 U.S.C. § 1–3) * * *." The National Park Service Act provides that the "fundamental purpose of the said parks, monuments, and reservations" is "to conserve the scenery and the natural and historic objects and the wild life therein and to provide for the enjoyment of the same in such manner and by such means as will leave them unimpaired for the enjoyment of future generations." 16 U.S.C. § 1.

The implied-reservation-of-water-rights-doctrine, however, reserves only that amount of water necessary to fulfill the purpose of the reservation, no more. Arizona v. California. Here the purpose of reserving Devil's Hole Monument is preservation of the pool. Devil's Hole was reserved "for the preservation of the unusual features of scenic, scientific, and educational interest." The Proclamation notes that the pool contains a "a peculiar race of desert fish * * * which is found nowhere else in the world" and that the "pool is of * * * outstanding scientific importance * * *." The pool need only be preserved, consistent with the intention expressed in the Proclamation, to the extent necessary to preserve its scientific interest. The fish are one of the features of scientific interest. The preamble noting the scientific interest of the pool follows the preamble describing the fish as unique; the Proclamation must be read in its entirety. Thus, as the District Court has correctly determined, the level of the pool may be permitted to drop to the extent that the drop does not impair the scientific value of the pool as the natural habitat of the species sought to be preserved. The District Court thus tailored its injunction, very appropriately, to minimal need, curtailing pumping only to the extent necessary to preserve an adequate water level at Devil's Hole, thus implementing the stated objectives of the Proclamation.

No cases of this court have applied the doctrine of implied reservation of water rights to groundwater. Nevada argues that the implied-reservation doctrine is limited to surface water. Here, however, the water in the pool is surface water. The federal water rights were being depleted because, as the evidence showed, the "[g]roundwater and surface water are physically

---

5. The [lower courts] correctly held that neither the Cappaerts nor their predecessors in interest had acquired any water rights as of 1952 when the United States' water rights vested. Part of the land now comprising the Cappaerts' ranch was patented by the United States to the Cappaerts' predecessors as early as 1890. None of the patents conveyed water rights because the Desert Land Act of 1877, 43 U.S.C. § 321, provided that such patents pass title only to land, not water. Patentees acquire water rights by "bona fide prior appropriation," as determined by state law. * * * Neither the Cappaerts nor their predecessors in interest appropriated any water until after 1952.

interrelated as integral parts of the hydrologic cycle." C. Corker, Groundwater Law, Management and Administration, National Water Commission Legal Study No. 6, p. xxiv (1971). Here the Cappaerts are causing the water level in Devil's Hole to drop by their heavy pumping. See Corker, supra; see also WATER POLICIES FOR THE FUTURE—Final Report to the President and to the Congress of the United States by the National Water Commission 233 (1973). It appears that Nevada itself may recognize the potential interrelationship between surface and groundwater since Nevada applies the law of prior appropriation to both. Nev. Rev. Stat. § 533.010 et seq., 534.020, 534,080, 534.090 (1973). * * * Thus, since the implied-reservation-of-water-rights doctrine is based on the necessity of water for the purpose of the federal reservation, we hold that the United States can protect its water from subsequent diversion, whether the diversion is of surface or groundwater.[7]

Petitioners in both cases argue that the Federal Government must perfect its implied water rights according to state law. They contend that the Desert Land Act of 1877, 43 U.S.C.§ 321, and its predecessors severed nonnavigable water from public land, subjecting it to state law. That Act, however, provides that patentees of public land acquire only title to land through the patent and must acquire water rights in nonnavigable water in accordance with state law. California Oregon Power Co. v. Beaver Portland Cement Co. 295 U.S. 142, 162 (1935). * * *

We hold, therefore, that as of 1952 when the United States reserved Devil's Hole, it acquired by reservation water rights in unappropriated appurtenant water sufficient to maintain the level of the pool to preserve its scientific value and thereby implement Proclamation No. 2961. Accordingly, the judgment of the Court of Appeals is affirmed.

NOTES AND QUESTIONS

1. In most situations, the statute, executive order, or other document effecting a federal land reservation is silent on water. Therefore, as in *Winters* itself, the federal reservation of water is implied. How strong was the implication that water was reserved in the order reserving the Devil's Hole? Same result if the underground pool and the pupfish had not been mentioned in the Proclamation reserving Devil's Hole?

2. By characterizing the underground pool as surface water, the Supreme Court avoided the question whether the *Winters* doctrine applies to groundwater. (The Ninth Circuit had held that the pool was groundwa-

---

7. Petitioners in both cases argue that the effect of applying the implied reservation doctrine to diversions of groundwater is to prohibit pumping from the entire 4,500 square miles above the aquifer that supplies water to Devil's Hole. First, it must be emphasized that the injunction limits but does not prohibit pumping. Second, the findings of fact in this case relate only to wells within 2–1/2 miles of Devil's Hole. No proof was intro-

duced in the district Court that pumping from the same aquifer that supplies Devil's Hole, would significantly lower the level in Devil's Hole. Nevada notes that such pumping "will in time affect the water level in Devil's Hole." Brief for Nevada 25. There was testimony from a research hydrologist that substantial pumping 40 miles away "[o]ver a period of perhaps decades [would have] a small effect." App., 79.

ter, and was reserved. See 508 F.2d 313, 317 (1974).) The question is of considerable moment because groundwater is heavily used in many parts of the country, and state law often makes it subject to a different water law doctrine from surface water. A number of western states, such as Nevada, apply the prior appropriation doctrine to groundwater. But other western states, and most non-western states, apply other doctrines that base the right to extract groundwater upon ownership of the land surface.

The old English common law rule applicable to groundwater was one of "absolute ownership." This doctrine, still followed now only in parts of Texas, is really a rule of capture, allowing all landowners to extract groundwater from beneath their land without restriction, except for malicious purposes. The "American rule" followed in many states modifies the English doctrine, and allows landowners to extract groundwater for "reasonable uses," with reasonableness being primarily determined by whether the water is being used on the land from which it is pumped. If it is conveyed off the land to the injury of others who are extracting water from the same underground source, it is *per se* unreasonable. A few states follow a version of "correlative rights," which favors on-land use like the American rule, but which apportions the water in the aquifer among overlying landowners in "fair and just proportion," usually based upon the amount of acreage owned. See generally Earl Finbar Murphy, "Quantitative Groundwater Law," chapters 18–24 in Robert Beck et al., eds., WATERS AND WATER RIGHTS, vol. 3 (1991); A.Dan Tarlock, LAW OF WATER RIGHTS AND RESOURCES ch. 4 (2001).

3.   Does the principle behind the federal reserved water rights doctrine support its application to groundwater? State courts addressing the question in the context of Indian water rights have split on the question. See In re General Adjudication of All Rights to Use Water in the Big Horn River System, 753 P.2d 76 (Wyo.1988), aff'd on other grounds by an equally divided court sub nom. Wyoming v. United States, 492 U.S. 406 (1989); *In re* Gila River System, 989 P.2d 739 (Ariz.1999), cert. denied, 530 U.S. 1250 (2000). See E. Brendan Shane, Water Rights and Gila River III: The Winters Doctrine Goes Underground, 4 U. Denv. Water L. Rev. 397 (2001).

4.   Groundwater aquifers have widely varying rates of replenishment, or "recharge." Suppose that the recharge rate here is very low, such that pumping *any* water from the aquifer that supports the pool at Devil's Hole would lower the level of the water in the pool and threaten the pupfish. Suppose also that the aquifer is very large, extending under several hundred square miles of surface, much of it privately owned. Does *Cappaert* mean that no groundwater pumping can occur? See footnote 7 in the Court's opinion.

5.   What result if the Cappaerts had begun pumping in 1950?

6.   Assuming the pupfish is listed as an endangered species, may the Endangered Species Act come into play here, totally apart from the water rights context? That is, would the Cappaerts be liable for a "take" under section 9 of the Act if they continued to pump and dried up the pool?

7. A *Cappaert*-type problem may be raised in connection with geothermal (hot water or steam) resources. For example, proposed geothermal development in a national forest adjacent to Yellowstone has been opposed by Park Service officials because of concern that geothermal wells would adversely affect Yellowstone's "fragile plumbing." Does the United States have a reserved right to the geothermal resource, with a priority date of 1872, when Yellowstone National Park was established? What do you need to know to answer that question? Reconsider it after reading the next case.

————————

Classic prior appropriation doctrine had little room for instream uses. Even where states move to establish minimum streamflow levels, such protections are usually accorded junior priority and must give way to senior rights in years of low flows. On many streams, such junior priorities may be of little use where most flows have been appropriated by senior consumptive users. The following case reflected the Forest Service's attempts to obtain federal instream water rights with senior priority dates.

United States v. New Mexico

Supreme Court of the United States, 1978.
438 U.S. 696.

■ Mr. Justice Rehnquist delivered the opinion of the Court.

[The state of New Mexico initiated in state court a general adjudication of water rights on the Rio Mimbres in the southwestern part of the state. The United States participated and claimed reserved water rights for use in the Gila National Forest.]

The question posed in this case—what quantity of water, if any, the United States reserved out of the Rio Mimbres when it set aside the Gila National Forest in 1899—is a question of implied intent and not power. * * * The Court has previously concluded that whatever powers the States acquired over their waters as a result of congressional Acts and admission into the Union, however, Congress did not intend thereby to relinquish its authority to reserve unappropriated water in the future for use on appurtenant lands withdrawn from the public domain for specific federal purposes.

Recognition of Congress' power to reserve water for land which is itself set apart from the public domain, however, does not answer the question of the amount of water which has been reserved or the purposes for which the water may be used. Substantial portions of the public domain *have* been withdrawn and reserved by the United States for use as Indian reservations, forest reserves, national parks, and national monuments. And water is frequently necessary to achieve the purposes for which these reservations are made. But Congress has seldom expressly reserved water for use on these withdrawn lands. If water were abundant, Congress' silence would pose no problem. In the arid parts of the West, however, claims to water for use on federal reservations inescapably vie with other public and private claims for the limited quantities to be found in the rivers and streams. This competition is compounded by the sheer quantity of reserved lands in the Western States, which lands form brightly colored swaths across the maps of these States.[3]

The Court has previously concluded that Congress, in giving the President the power to reserve portions of the federal domain for specific federal purposes, *impliedly* authorized him to reserve "appurtenant water then unappropriated *to the extent needed to accomplish the purpose of the reservation." Cappaert* (emphasis added) * * * While many of the contours of what has come to be called the "implied-reservation-of-water doctrine" remain unspecified, the Court has repeatedly emphasized that Congress reserved "only that amount of water necessary to fulfill the purpose of the reservation, no more." *Cappaert.* Each time this Court has applied the "implied-reservation-of-water doctrine," it has carefully examined both the asserted water right and the specific purposes for which the land was reserved, and concluded that without the water the purposes of the reservation would be entirely defeated.

This careful examination is required both because the reservation is implied, rather than expressed, and because of the history of congressional intent in the field of federal-state jurisdiction with respect to allocation of water. Where Congress has expressly addressed the question of whether federal entities must abide by state water law, it has almost invariably deferred to the state law. * * * Where water is necessary to fulfill the very purposes for which a federal reservation was created, it is reasonable to conclude, even in the face of Congress' express deference to state water law in other areas, that the United States intended to reserve the necessary water. Where water is only valuable for a secondary use of the reservation, however, there arises the contrary inference that Congress intended, consistent with its other views, that the United States would acquire water in the same manner as any other public or private appropriator. * * *

[The state courts held that the United States had no federal reserved right to an instream flow on the national forest for "aesthetic, environmental, recreational, or 'fish' purposes." They also held that no water had been reserved for stockwatering on the national forest.] * * *

The United States contends that Congress intended to reserve minimum instream flows for aesthetic, recreational, and fish-preservation purposes. An examination of the limited purposes for which Congress authorized the creation of national forests, however, provides no support for this claim. In the mid and late 1800's, many of the forests on the public domain

---

3. The percentage of federally owned land (*excluding* Indian reservations and other trust properties) in the Western States ranges from 29.5% of the land in the State of Washington to 86.5% of the land in the State of Nevada, an average of about 46%. Of the land in the State of New Mexico, 33.6% is federally owned. Because federal reservations are normally found in the uplands of the Western States rather than the flatlands, the percentage of water flow originating in or flowing through the reservations is even more impressive. More than 60% of the average annual water yield in the 11 Western States is from federal reservations. The percentage of average annual water yield range from a low of 56% in the Columbia–North Pacific water-resource region to a high of 96% in the Upper Colorado region. In the Rio Grande water-resource region, where the Rio Mimbres lies, 77% of the average runoff originates on federal reservations.

were ravaged and the fear arose that the forest lands might soon disappear, leaving the United States with a shortage both of timber and of watersheds with which to encourage stream flows while preventing floods. It was in answer to these fears that in 1891 Congress authorized the President to "set apart and reserve, in any State or Territory having public land bearing forests, in any part of the public lands wholly or in part covered with timber or undergrowth, whether of commercial value or not, as public reservations." Creative Act of March 3, 1891, § 24, 16 U.S.C. § 471 (repealed 1976).

The Creative Act of 1891 unfortunately did not solve the forest problems of the expanding Nation. To the dismay of the conservationists, the new national forests were not adequately attended and regulated; fires and indiscriminate timber cutting continued their toll. To the anguish of Western settlers, reservations were frequently made indiscriminately. President Cleveland, in particular, responded to pleas of conservationists for greater protective measures by reserving some 21 million acres of "generally settled" forest land on February 22, 1897. President Cleveland's action drew immediate and strong protest from Western Congressmen who felt that the "hasty and ill considered" reservation might prove disastrous to the settlers living on or near these lands.

Congress' answer to these continuing problems was three-fold. It suspended the President's Executive Order of February 22, 1897; it carefully defined the purposes for which national forests could in the future be reserved; and it provided a charter for forest management and economic uses within the forests. Organic Administration Act of June 4, 1897, 16 U.S.C. § 473 et seq. In particular, Congress provided:

> *No national forest shall be established, except to improve and protect the forest within the boundaries, or for the purpose of securing favorable conditions of water flows, and to furnish a continuous supply of timber for the use and necessities of citizens of the United States; * * * [16 U.S.C. § 475] (emphasis added).*

The legislative debates surrounding the Organic Administration Act of 1897 and its predecessor bills demonstrate that Congress intended national forests to be reserved for only two purposes—"[t]o conserve the water flows, and to furnish a continuous supply of timber for the people."[14] 30

---

14. The Government notes that the Act forbids the establishment of national forests except *"to improve and protect the forest within the boundaries,* or for the purpose of securing favorable conditions of water flows, and to furnish a continuous supply of timber," and argues from this wording that "improvement" and "protection" of the forests form a third and separate purpose of the national forest system. A close examination of the language of the Act, however, reveals that Congress only intended national forests to be established for two purposes. Forests would be created only "to improve and pro-tect the forest within the boundaries," or, *in other words,* "for the purpose of securing favorable conditions of water flows, and to furnish a continuous supply of timber."

This reading of the Act is confirmed by its legislative history. Nothing in the legislative history suggests that Congress intended national forests to be established for three purposes, one of which would be extremely broad. Indeed, it is inconceivable that a Congress which was primarily concerned with limiting the President's power to reserve the forest lands of the West would provide for the creation of forests merely "to improve and

Cong.Rec. 967 (1897) (Cong. McRae). See United States v. Grimaud, 220 U.S. 506, 515 (1911). National forests were not to be reserved for aesthetic, environmental, recreational, or wildlife-preservation purposes.

"The objects for which the forest reservations should be made are the protection of the forest growth against destruction by fire and ax, and preservation of forest conditions upon which water conditions and water flow are dependent. The purpose, therefore, of this bill is to maintain favorable forest conditions, without excluding the use of these reservations for other purposes. They are not parks set aside for nonuse, but have been established for economic reasons." 30 Cong.Rec. 966 (1897) (Cong. McRae).

Administrative regulations at the turn of the century confirmed that national forests were to be reserved for only these two limited purposes.

Any doubt as to the relatively narrow purposes for which national forests were to be reserved is removed by comparing the broader language Congress used to authorize the establishment of national parks. In 1916, Congress created the National Park Service and provided that the

"fundamental purpose of the said parks, monuments, and reservations * * * is to conserve the scenery and the natural and historic objects and the wild life therein and to provide for the enjoyment of the same * * * unimpaired for the enjoyment of future generations." 16 U.S.C. § 1. * * *

National park legislation is not the only instructive comparison. In the Act of Mar. 10, 1934, 16 U.S.C. § 694, Congress authorized the establishment within individual national forests of fish and game sanctuaries, *but only with the consent of the state legislatures.* * * * If, as the dissent contends, * * * Congress in the Organic Administration Act of 1897 authorized the reservation of forests to "improve and protect" fish and wildlife, the 1934 Act would have been unnecessary. Nor is the dissent's position consistent with Congress' concern in 1934 that fish and wildlife preserves only be created "with the approval of the State legislatures."

As the dissent notes, in creating what would ultimately become Yosemite National Park, Congress in 1890 explicitly instructed the Secretary of the Interior to provide against the wanton destruction of fish and game inside the forest and against their taking "for the purposes of merchandise or profit." * * * By comparison, Congress in the 1897 Organic Act expressed no concern for the preservation of fish and wildlife within national forests generally. * * *

Not only is the Government's claim that Congress intended to reserve water for recreation and wildlife preservation inconsistent with Congress' failure to recognize these goals as purposes of the national forests, it would defeat the very purpose for which Congress did create the national forest system. * * * The water that would be "insured" by preservation of the

protect the forest within the boundaries"; forests would be reserved for their improvement and protection, but only to serve the purposes of timber protection and favorable water supply. * * *

forest was to "be used for domestic, mining, milling, or irrigation purposes, under the laws of the State wherein such national forests are situated, or under the laws of the United States and the rules and regulations established thereunder." Organic Administration Act of 1897, 16 U.S.C. § 481. As this provision and its legislative history evidence, Congress authorized the national forest system principally as a means of enhancing the quantity of water that would be available to the settlers of the arid West. The Government, however, would have us now believe that Congress intended to partially defeat this goal by reserving significant amounts of water for purposes quite inconsistent with this goal.

In 1960, Congress passed the Multiple–Use Sustained–Yield Act of 1960, 16 U.S.C. § 528 et seq., which provides:

> It is the policy of Congress that the national forests are established and shall be administered for outdoor recreation, range, timber, watershed, and wildlife and fish purposes. The purposes of sections 528 to 531 of this title are declared to be supplemental to, but not in derogation of, the purposes for which the national forests were established as set forth in the [Organic Administration Act of 1897.]

The Supreme Court of New Mexico concluded that this Act did not give rise to any reserved rights not previously authorized in the Organic Administration Act of 1897. * * * While we conclude that the Multiple–Use Sustained–Yield Act of 1960 was intended to broaden the purposes for which national forests had previously been administered, we agree that Congress did not intend to thereby expand the reserved rights of the United States.[21]

* * * As discussed earlier, the "reserved rights doctrine" is a doctrine built on implication and is an exception to Congress' explicit deference to state water law in other areas. Without legislative history to the contrary, we are led to conclude that Congress did not intend in enacting the Multiple–Use Sustained–Yield Act of 1960 to reserve water for the *secondary* purposes there established.[22] A reservation of additional water could mean a substantial loss in the amount of water available for irrigation and domestic use, thereby defeating Congress' principal purpose of securing favorable conditions of water flow. Congress intended the national forests to be administered for broader purposes after 1960 but there is no indica-

---

21. The United States does not argue that the Multiple–Use Sustained–Yield Act of 1960 reserved additional water for use on the national forests. Instead, the Government argues that the Act confirms that Congress *always* foresaw broad purposes for the national forests and authorized the Secretary of the Interior as early as 1897 to reserve water for recreational, aesthetic, and wildlife-preservation uses. As the legislative history of the 1960 Act, demonstrates, however, Congress believed that the 1897 Organic Administration Act only authorized the creation of national forests for two purposes—timber preservation and enhancement of water supply— and intended, through the 1960 Act, to *ex-*

pand the purposes for which the national forests should be administered. See, e.g., H.R.Rep. No. 1551, 86th Cong., 2d Sess., 4 (1960).

Even if the 1960 Act expanded the reserved water rights of the United States, of course, the rights would be subordinate to any appropriation of water under state law dating to before 1960.

22. We intimate no view as to whether Congress, in the 1960 Act, authorized the subsequent reservation of national forests out of public lands to which a broader doctrine of reserved water rights might apply.

tion that it believed the new purposes to be so crucial as to require a reservation of additional water. By reaffirming the primacy of a favorable water flow, it indicated the opposite intent.

What we have said also answers the Government's contention that Congress intended to reserve water from the Rio Mimbres for stockwatering purposes. The United States issues permits to private cattle owners to graze their stock on the Gila National Forest and provides for stockwatering at various locations along the Rio Mimbres. The United States contends that, since Congress clearly foresaw stockwatering on national forests, reserved rights must be recognized for this purpose. The New Mexico courts disagreed and held that any stockwatering rights must be allocated under state law to individual stockwaterers. We agree.

While Congress intended the national forests to be put to a variety of uses, including stockwatering, not inconsistent with the two principal purposes of the forests, stockwatering was not itself a direct purpose of reserving the land.[23] * * *

Congress intended that water would be reserved only where necessary to preserve the timber or to secure favorable water flows for private and public uses under state law. This intent is revealed in the purposes for which the national forest system was created and Congress' principled deference to state water law in the Organic Administration Act of 1897 and other legislation. The decision of the Supreme Court of New Mexico is faithful to this congressional intent and is therefore

Affirmed.

■ MR. JUSTICE POWELL, with whom MR. JUSTICE BRENNAN, MR. JUSTICE WHITE, and MR. JUSTICE MARSHALL JOIN, dissenting in part.

I agree with the Court that the implied-reservation doctrine should be applied with sensitivity to its impact upon those who have obtained water rights under state law and to Congress' general policy of deference to state water law. I also agree that the Organic Administration Act of 1897 cannot fairly be read as evidencing an intent to reserve water for recreational or stockwatering purposes in the national forests.[1]

---

23. As discussed earlier, the national forests were not to be "set aside for non-use," 30 Cong.Rec. 966 (1897) (Cong. McRae), but instead to be opened up for any economic use not inconsistent with the forests' primary purposes. Ibid. One use that Congress foresaw was "pasturage." Ibid. See also id., at 1006 (Cong. Ellis); id., at 1011 (Cong. De Vries). As this Court has previously recognized, however, grazing was merely one use to which the national forests could possibly be put and would not be permitted where it might interfere with the specific purposes of the national forests including the securing of favorable conditions of water flow. Under the 1891 and 1897 forest Acts, "any use of the reservation for grazing or

other lawful purpose was required to be subject to the rules and regulations established by the Secretary of Agriculture. To pasture sheep and cattle on the reservation, at will and without restraint, might interfere seriously with the accomplishment of the purposes for which they were established. But a limited and regulated use for pasturage might not be inconsistent with the object sought to be attained by the statute." United States v. Grimaud, 220 U.S. 506, 515–516 (1911). See also Light v. United States, 220 U.S. 523 (1911).

1. I express no view as to the effect of the Multiple–Use Sustained–Yield Act of 1960 * * * on the United States' reserved water

I do not agree, however, that the forests which Congress intended to "improve and protect" are the still, silent, lifeless places envisioned by the Court. In my view, the forests consist of the birds, animals, and fish—the wildlife—that inhabit them, as well as the trees, flowers, shrubs, and grasses. I therefore would hold that the United States is entitled to so much water as is necessary to sustain the wildlife of the forests, as well as the plants. * * *

* * * Although the language of the statute is not artful, a natural reading would attribute to Congress an intent to authorize the establishment of national forests for three purposes, not the two discerned by the Court. The New Mexico Supreme Court gave the statute its natural reading in this case when it wrote:

> "The Act limits the purposes for which national forests are authorized to: 1) improving and protecting the forest, 2) securing favorable conditions of water flows, and 3) furnishing a continuous supply of timber."

Congress has given the statute the same reading, stating that under the Organic Administration Act of 1897 national forests may be established for "the purposes of improving and protecting the forest or for securing favorable conditions of water flows, and to furnish a continuous supply of timber * * *."

* * * [The Court] decides that the Act should be read as if it said national forests may "be created only 'to improve and protect the forest within the boundaries,' or, *in other words,* 'for the purpose of securing favorable conditions of water flows, and to furnish a continuous supply of timber.' " (emphasis in original). The Court then concludes that Congress did not mean to "improve and protect" any part of the forest except the usable timber and whatever other flora is necessary to maintain the watershed. This, however, is not what Congress said.

The Court believes that its "reading of the Act is confirmed by its legislative history." The matter is not so clear to me. From early times in English law, the forest has included the creatures that live there. J. Manwood, A Treatise and Discourse of the Laws of the Forrest 1–7 (1598);

rights in national forests that were established either before or after that Act's passage. Although the Court purports to hold that passage of the 1960 Act did not have the effect of reserving any additional water in then-existing forests, this portion of its opinion appears to be dicta. As the Court concedes, "The United States does not argue that the Multiple–Use Sustained–Yield Act of 1960 reserved additional water for use on the national forests." Likewise, the State argues only that "[n]o reserved rights for fish or wildlife can be implied in the Gila National Forest *prior to the enactment of the Multiple– Use Sustained–Yield Act of June 12, 1960.* * * * "(emphasis supplied). Indeed, the State has gone so far as to suggest that passage of the 1960 Act may well have expanded the United States' reserved water rights in the national forests, presumably with a priority date for the additional reserved rights of 1960. Read in context, the New Mexico Supreme Court's statement that the 1960 Act "does not have a retroactive effect nor can it broaden the purposes for which the Gila National Forest was established under the Organic Act of 1897," appears to mean nothing more than that the 1960 Act did not give the United States additional reserved water rights *with a priority date of before 1960*—a proposition with which I think we all would agree. But there never has been a question in this case as to whether the 1960 Act gave rise to additional reserved water rights with a priority date of 1960 or later in the Gila National Forest.

1 W. Blackstone, Commentaries 289. Although the English forest laws themselves were not transplanted to the shores of the new continent, see generally Lund, Early American Wildlife Law, 51 N.Y.U.L.Rev. 703 (1976), the understanding that the forest includes its wildlife has remained in the American mind. In establishing the first forest reservations, the year before passage of the Organic Act of 1891, Congress exhibited this understanding by directing the Secretary of the Interior to "provide against the wanton destruction of the fish * * * and game found within said reservation, and against their capture or destruction, for the purposes of merchandise or profit." Act of Oct. 1, 1890, § 2, 26 Stat. 651. * * *

One may agree with the Court that Congress did not, by enactment of the Organic Administration Act of 1897, intend to authorize the creation of national forests simply to serve as wildlife preserves. But it does not follow from this that Congress did not consider wildlife to be part of the forest that it wished to "improve and protect" for future generations. It is inconceivable that Congress envisioned the forests it sought to preserve as including only inanimate components such as the timber and flora. Insofar as the Court holds otherwise, the 55th Congress is maligned and the Nation is the poorer, and I dissent.[5] * * *

Contrary to the Court's intimations, I see no inconsistency between holding that the United States impliedly reserved the right to instream flows, and what the Court views as the underlying purposes of the 1897 Act. The national forests can regulate the flow of water—which the Court views as "the very purpose for which Congress did create the national forest system," only for the benefit of appropriators who are downstream from the reservation. The reservation of an instream flow is not a consumptive use; it does not subtract from the amount of water that is available to downstream appropriators. Reservation of an instream flow therefore would be perfectly consistent with the purposes of the 1897 Act as construed by the Court.[6]

I do not dwell on this point, however, for the Court's opinion cannot be read as holding that the United States never reserved instream flows when it set aside national forests under the 1897 Act. The State concedes, quite correctly on the Court's own theory, that even in this case "the United States is not barred from asserting that rights to minimum instream flows might be necessary for erosion control or fire protection on the basis of the recognized purposes of watershed management and the maintenance of

---

5. No doubt it will be said that the waterflow necessary to maintain the watershed including the forest will be sufficient for the wildlife. This well may be true in most national forests and most situations. But the Court's opinion, as I read it, recognizes no reserved authority in the Federal Government to protect wildlife itself as a part of the forest, and therefore if and when the need for increased waterflow for this purpose arises the Federal Government would be powerless to act. Indeed, upstream appropriators could be allowed to divert so much water that survival of forest wildlife—including even the fish and other life in the streams—would be endangered.

6. It is true that reservation of an instream flow might in some circumstances adversely affect appropriators upstream from the forest. There would be no inconsistency with the 1897 Act, however, for that Act manifestly was not intended to benefit upstream appropriators.

timber." Thus, if the United States proves, in this case or others, that the reservation of instream flows is necessary to fulfill the purposes discerned by the Court, I find nothing in the Court's opinion that bars it from asserting this right.

NOTES AND QUESTIONS

1. Examine the 1897 statute governing forest reservations closely. How does Justice Rehnquist interpret the phrase "improve and protect the forest within the boundaries"? Justice Powell? Does the former lose sight of the forest for the trees, as it were, or did Congress do so in 1897?

2. In *Cappaert* the water reserved was described as the amount of water necessary to serve the purposes for which the land was reserved. In *New Mexico*, the adjective "primary" is added as a modifier of "purposes." Is this significant?

3. Note that the Court was unanimous in holding that the 1897 Act did not reserve water for stockwatering and recreational uses, even though both are common uses of the national forests. In the absence of congressional action, what options are open to the Forest Service if it wishes to secure water for wildlife, grazing and recreation? Besides condemnation of water rights obtained under state law, the Forest Service can seek to become a state law appropriator, if unappropriated water is available. That and other strategies are considered further at pages 548–60 infra. Also considered below are the application of *Winters* and *New Mexico* to a variety of other federal reservations, including national parks, wildlife refuges, wild and scenic rivers, and wilderness.

4. *New Mexico* has emerged as the leading modern federal reserved rights case and sparked a generous commentary. Consider the opposing views of the decision in Sally Fairfax & A. Dan Tarlock, No Water for the Woods: A Critical Analysis of United States v. New Mexico, 15 Idaho L. Rev. 509 (1979) and Alan Boles & Charles Elliott, United States v. New Mexico and the Course of Federal Reserved Water Rights, 51 U. Colo. L. Rev. 209 (1980). Fairfax and Tarlock maintain that the Supreme Court's reading of the 1891 and 1897 Acts, "is arguably wrong because the reservation of water for instream uses is consistent with the original purpose of the reservations." Boles and Elliott applaud the decision and the protection it affords to existing state law appropriators whose uses might have been displaced by a grant of reserved rights for instream flows. The federal interest, they contend, can be adequately protected by the federal government through condemnation of water rights if reduced flows threaten to harm the forests. Frank Trelease, Uneasy Federalism—State Water Laws and National Water Uses, 55 U. Wash. L. Rev. 751 (1980), agrees with Boles and Elliott.

THE LEGAL BASIS FOR FEDERAL RESERVED WATER RIGHTS

The Supreme Court's discussion of the constitutional basis for federal reservations of water consists of a couple of sentences by Justice Black in

Arizona v. California, page 514 supra (expressing "no doubt" about the constitutional basis to reserve water) and equally terse sentences in Chief Justice Burger's unanimous opinion in *Cappaert*. The most complete explication of the basis for federal water rights was a lengthy opinion by the Department of Justice's Office of Legal Counsel, Federal "Non–Reserved" Water Rights, 6 Op. Off. Legal Counsel 328 (1982).* This Opinion took the view that Congress had broad authority under a number of constitutional provisions to preempt state water law, and may delegate this power to the executive branch:

> [F]ederal reserved rights are not a unique species of federal rights that arise directly out of the reservation of federal lands, so that, absent a reservation of land, no federal water rights can exist. * * * The reserved right doctrine does not rest on any unique constitutional basis.

Id. at 363. "Therefore, this power may extend to acquired lands as well as public domain." Id. at 381. "[F]ederal water rights may be asserted without regard to state law to [satisfy] specific congressional directives or authorizations that override inconsistent state law * * * [or to fulfill] primary purposes for the management of federal lands * * * that would be frustrated by the application of state law." Id. The question of "non-reserved" federal water rights is pursued further below, at pp. 557–60.

The issues most litigated and discussed are whether, in any particular situation, Congress or the Executive has reserved water under federal law independent of state law, and if so, how much. Those issues will be pursued below.

FEDERAL RESERVED WATER RIGHTS IN RIPARIAN JURISDICTIONS

The application of the *Winters* doctrine in eastern riparian jurisdictions has not been developed in any reported cases (nor, for that matter, has any case we know of squarely addressed the interface between the doctrine and riparian rights recognized in California). Indeed, an informal survey in the Department of the Interior did not uncover a single instance in which the National Park Service has ever asserted a federal reserved water right in the East. Most federal lands now found in riparian jurisdictions have been acquired into federal ownership for particular purposes; e.g., national forests, parks, or wildlife refuges. A number of segments of eastern rivers have been designated under the federal Wild & Scenic Rivers Act, which carry water rights with them, as discussed infra, page 536.

In pure riparian jurisdictions, the extent to which federal reserved water rights may be superior to state law riparian rights (to which federal riparian lands are presumably entitled) is not clear. Conceptually, there are some similarities between riparian rights and federal reserved rights. Neither is dependent upon putting water to actual use; both are related to land ownership. But there are some differences. Federal reserved water

---

* The Opinion was signed by Theodore Olson, appointed Solicitor General of the United States in 2001 by President George W. Bush.

rights come into being at some fixed date (when land is reserved or withdrawn for particular purposes), and can be quantified on the basis of the amount of water necessary to carry out those purposes. Riparian rights are more indefinite and inchoate in quantity, being dependent upon reasonableness of uses along the stream at any one point in time. Academic commentary on the subject is limited. See, e.g., Charles Meyers, The Colorado River, 19 Stan. L. Rev. 1, 68–69 (1966); Eva Hanks, Peace West of the 98th Meridian—Solution to Federal–State Conflicts over Western Waters, 23 Rutgers L. Rev. 33, 39–40 n. 25 (1968); Walter Kiechel & Martin Green, Riparian Rights Revisited: Legal Basis For Federal Instream Flow Rights, 16 Nat. Resources J. 969 (1976); Anita Robb, Applying the Reserved Rights Doctrine in Riparian States, 14 N.C. Cent. L.J. 98 (1983).

3. RESERVED WATER RIGHTS BY FEDERAL LAND CATEGORY

This subsection briefly explores some kinds of reserved rights claims connected with non-Indian federal lands and programs, building on the teachings of *Arizona v. California, Cappaert*, and *United States v. New Mexico*. As you might suspect, the array of management categories and purposes of federal reservations are quite broad.*

NATIONAL FORESTS

As Justice Rehnquist suggested at the beginning of his opinion in *New Mexico*, the most hotly contested federal non-Indian reserved rights have been in the national forests. This is probably because the national forest system is extensive (comprising nearly two hundred million acres of land) and dominates the headwaters of most important western rivers. *New Mexico* settled some basic questions about national forest reserved water rights, but left a number of other questions open.

For example, what is the precise holding of *New Mexico* regarding the effect of the Multiple Use–Sustained Yield Act of 1960 ("MUSYA")? Footnote 21 of the Court's opinion reveals that the United States did not argue that MUSYA created a 1960 reservation of water, but rather that it simply confirmed the 1897 Organic Act's reservation of water for broad purposes. Compare the first footnote in Powell's dissent. Can the United States still argue for reserved rights based on MUSYA alone? For a negative answer, see United States v. City and County of Denver, 656 P.2d 1, 24–27 (Colo.1982); United States v. City of Challis, 988 P.2d 1199 (Idaho 1999).

* In the wake of *New Mexico*, the Solicitor of the Department of the Interior issued a comprehensive Opinion that addressed the reserved rights and other water rights claims of the Interior Department's land managing agencies. 86 Interior Dec. 553 (1979). Some of the material in this note is drawn from that Opinion. For a useful collection of western state perspectives on the scope and nature of non-Indian federal reserved rights claims, both generally and through a state-by-state survey, see D. Craig Bell and James Alder, Federal Non–Indian Claims To Water (Western States Water Council, 1999). Military reservations generally fall within the principles of *Winters*, but there is little reported litigation and commentary on their claims. See William Wilcox, Maintaining Federal Water Rights in the Western United States, Army Lawyer, Oct. 1996, at 3, 10.

Many of the national parks were created by Congress in areas that had earlier been reserved from the public domain as national forests. If a national forest had been created in 1898, and the area had been designated a national park in 1930, what is the scope and priority date of the park's water right? See United States v. City and County of Denver, 656 P.2d 1, 30 (Colo.1982) (holding that the park water right has the date of the forest reservation "to the extent that the purposes of the national forests and national parks overlap," but that "[r]eservation of water for other purposes * * * will have a priority date from the time the national park was established"). See generally Eric Freyfogle, Repairing the Waters of the National Parks: Notes on a Long–Term Strategy, 74 Denv. U. L. Rev. 815 (1997).

Does the Forest Service have federal reserved rights for water flows to maintain stream channels and associated riparian areas? Note that securing "favorable conditions of water flows" was one of the two 1897 Organic Act purposes *New Mexico* had recognized for the national forest system. The Forest Service has argued that

> recent advances in the science of 'fluvial geomorphology' have shown that strong, recurring instream water flows are necessary to maintain efficient stream channels and to secure favorable conditions of water flows, and that diversions of water within the national forests by private appropriators reduce stream flows and threaten the equilibrium that preserves natural stream channels.

United States v. Jesse, 744 P.2d 491, 498 (Colo.1987) (paraphrasing the brief for the United States). In the *Jesse* case, the Colorado Supreme Court remanded for a factual trial on such claims. After a lengthy hearing involving many expert witnesses and more than a thousand exhibits, the Colorado trial court ruled that the Forest Service had failed to show that the water rights claimed were necessary to secure favorable water flows. The Forest Service did not appeal, but similar claims have been filed in other Colorado Water Divisions. See generally Wendy Weiss, The Federal Government's Pursuit of Instream Flow Water Rights, 1 U. Den. Water L. Rev. 151, 157–60 (1998).

Is the existence or scope of the reserved water right here determined by what modern science shows about the need for scouring flows to maintain healthy river channels, improve the reliability of flows and reduce downstream flooding? Or is it determined by what Congress intended when it authorized the reservation of national forests in part to maintain "favorable conditions of water flows"?

What would be the effect on water management if the Forest Service were to be awarded reserved water rights for channel maintenance? Would it have any adverse effects on downstream junior appropriators? Upstream appropriators? Inholders in the national forests, or those who divert from streams on the national forests?

NATIONAL PARKS

Recall that the Supreme Court's opinion in United States v. New Mexico in 1978 compared and contrasted the 1897 Organic Act applying to the national forest system with the counterpart 1916 Organic Act applying to the national park system. See page 524 supra. What water does the 1916 Act implicitly reserve, for what purposes? Instream flows for ecosystem maintenance? Water to sustain natural features like geysers in Yellowstone or Yosemite Falls? What about water for national park employees' residences? Water for campgrounds or service stations for park visitors? Water to grow hay for feeding the horses and mules maintained by national park concessioners? See Solicitor's Opinion, 86 Interior Dec. at 595–96 (1979); A. Dan Tarlock, Protection of Water Flows for National Parks, XXII Land & Water L.Rev. 29 (1986).

National Park water rights tend not to be so controversial because (1) parks are popular cultural icons; (2) parks are often important contributors to local economies; (3) most park water uses are either nonconsumptive (instream flows for environmental health) or do not consume much (campgrounds, hotels); and (4) many parks are in headwaters or mountainous areas and thus preserve flows for uses downstream.

NATIONAL MONUMENTS

About one hundred National Monuments (nearly all managed by the National Park Service) have been created by the President exercising delegated authority from the Congress in the Antiquities Act of 1906 to protect "objects of historic or scientific interest" on federal lands. See 16 U.S.C. § 431; Cappaert v. United States, supra page 516. If the President creates a national monument encompassing dinosaur remains or an archeological site for scientific study, and the proclamation is silent on water, does it carry with it a reserved water right? For what purpose(s)? Compare Solicitor's Opinion, 86 I.D. at 599–601, with United States v. City and County of Denver, 656 P.2d 1, 27–29 (Colo.1982); see also Wendy Weiss, The Federal Government's Pursuit of Instream Flow Water Rights, 1 U. Den. Water L. Rev. 151, 161 & nn. 87–88 (1998). In the *Denver* case, the Colorado Supreme Court rejected the claim of the United States that the enlargement of Dinosaur National Monument by President Roosevelt in 1938 reserved water for recreational flows. It noted that the monument "is located at the lowest reaches of the Yampa River in Colorado * * * [and t]o find a reserved right to instream flow that far downstream would have a significant impact on numerous upstream users." It concluded that "[r]ecreational boating is not a purpose for which the 1938 acreage was implicitly or explicitly reserved."

NATIONAL RECREATION AND NATIONAL CONSERVATION AREAS

The exact purposes of these areas vary with the statutes creating them. For example, Congress established the Sawtooth National Recreation Area in Idaho in 1973 to "assure the preservation and protection of the natural, scenic, historic, pastoral, and fish and wildlife values and to provide for the enhancement of the recreational values associated therewith." 16 U.S.C. § 460aa(a). Does this Act reserve an instream flow for salmon fishery purposes? Cf. Potlatch Corp. v. United States, 134 Idaho 912, 12 P.3d 1256 (2000).

Statutes may require close reading to determine whether water is reserved. The Hells Canyon National Recreation Area (HCNRA), 16 U.S.C. § 460gg(b), includes "waters" in the area designated, but goes on to say that the Act does not authorize any limitation on "present and future use of the waters of the Snake River and its tributaries upstream from the boundaries of" the HCNRA (16 U.S.C. § 460gg–3(a)), and that "[n]o flow requirement of any kind may be imposed on the waters of the Snake River below" the area (16 U.S.C. § 460gg–3(b)). Does the Act reserve any water under federal law? The Idaho Supreme Court has said that, taken together, these provisions constitute an express reservation of all water "originating in tributaries to the Snake River which are located within the HCNRA." Potlatch Corp. v. United States, 134 Idaho 916, 12 P.3d 1260 (2000).

NATIONAL WILDLIFE REFUGES

The national wildlife refuge system consists of not only refuges but wildlife ranges, game ranges, wildlife management areas, and waterfowl production areas managed by the Fish & Wildlife Service. Many of these areas were originally established by individual Presidential or Secretarial Orders.* For example, the Deer Flat National Wildlife Refuge was created by Executive Order in 1937 encompassing some 94 islands along 110 miles of the Snake River. An important component of the Pacific Flyway, more than 100 species of land and water birds, migratory and non-migratory, make use of the islands. The Order withdrew "all islands [in the designated area] as a refuge and breeding ground for migratory birds and other wildlife." Otherwise the Order, which also speaks of the islands as a "sanctuary for migratory birds," is silent on water. Does the Order reserve enough water, expressly or impliedly, in order to keep the islands as islands, and thus help forestall predation against birds by coyotes and other predators? United States v. Idaho, 135 Idaho 655, 23 P. 3d 117, 126 (2001), answered the question in the negative, finding that "an expectation that the islands would remain surrounded by water * * * does not equate to an intent to reserve a federal water right to accomplish that purpose." The court went on to find it "inconceivable that President Roosevelt in 1937, in the context of the dust bowl years, intended to give preference to waterfowl * * * over people." Why would a nonconsumptive use of water for instream flows necessarily prefer birds over people? The United States did not seek review in the United States Supreme Court.

In the National Wildlife Refuge System Improvement Act of 1997, Congress provided that, "[i]n administering the System, the Secretary shall * * * acquire, under State law, water rights that are needed for refuge purposes." 16 U.S.C. § 668dd(a)(4)(G). The same section goes on to provide that nothing in the Act shall "create a reserved water right, express or

---

* For general background on water for wildlife refuges, see Western Water Policy Review Advisory Commission, Water in the West: Challenge for the Next Century 5–34 (1998). Recall that Arizona v. California recognized reserved water rights for wildlife refuges along the lower Colorado River.

implied, in the United States for any purpose," nor shall it "affect any water right in existence on October 9, 1997 [the date of enactment]." 16 U.S.C. § 668dd(n). The net effect seems to be that state law may govern water rights for refuges created in the future, but that any reserved right created prior to enactment is still valid. Is that 1997 action by Congress relevant to the issue in the Deer Flat case? (The Idaho Supreme Court did not refer to it.) Which way does it cut?

WILDERNESS AREAS

Like most other statutes undergirding federal land reservations, the Wilderness Act of 1964 says very little about water,* other than a general disclaimer (found in other federal statutes as well) that nothing in it "shall constitute an express or implied claim or denial on the part of the Federal Government as to exemption from State water laws." 16 U.S.C. § 1133(d)(6).

The extent to which designation of wilderness areas reserves water has been embroiled in sometimes bitter controversy for two decades.** The reasons for all this fuss are not immediately apparent. Wilderness areas by definition are to be left alone for the forces of nature to operate in them unimpaired. Any water rights they have are to maintain natural flows, i.e., involve no artificial diversion or consumption. These areas are, moreover, usually at high altitudes, at or near the tops of watersheds, where instream flows pose no threat to other, more conventional uses. Finally, since the Wilderness Act did not pass until 1964, and most wilderness areas were designated by Congress even later, wilderness water rights have a relatively late priority date. The controversy seems more about theology than anything else.

---

* It contains a provision authorizing the President to approve water projects in wilderness areas—areas which are otherwise off limits to development, including roads or other obvious imprints of human activity. See 16 U.S.C. § 1133(d)(4). The legislative history suggests this was to allow "minor" projects, but the provision has never been used even for that purpose. See John Leshy, Water & Wilderness/Law & Politics, 23 Land & Water L. Rev. 389, 402 (1988).

** In 1979, the Solicitor of the Department of the Interior concluded that designation of wilderness areas reserves water rights necessary to carry out the preservation-oriented purposes of the Act, including science, education, inspiration and recreation. 86 Interior Dec. at 609–10. After President Reagan took office in 1981, the Forest Service failed to file claims for water rights in twenty-four national forest wilderness areas in an ongoing Colorado adjudication. This led to protracted but ultimately inconclusive litigation

brought by environmentalists. See Sierra Club v. Block, 622 F.Supp. 842, 850–51, 862 (D.Colo.1985), 661 F.Supp. 1490 (D.Colo. 1987), vacated sub nom. Sierra Club v. Yeutter, 911 F.2d 1405 (10th Cir.1990). In the midst of the litigation, a new Interior Solicitor issued a new opinion, approved by the Justice Department, which reversed the 1979 Opinion. See 96 Interior Dec. 211 (1988). That did not end things. Early in the Clinton Administration, the Attorney General, on advice of the Solicitor and the General Counsel of Agriculture (where the Forest Service is housed), vacated both the 1989 Opinion and the wilderness portion of the 1979 Opinion.

See generally Robert Abrams, Water in the Western Wilderness: The Duty to Assert Reserved Water Rights, 1986 U. Ill. L. Rev. 387; John Leshy, Water and Wilderness/Law and Politics, 23 Land & Water L. Rev. 398 (1988); Karin Sheldon, Water for Wilderness, 76 Denver U. L. Rev. 555 (1999).

In the most definitive judicial ruling to date, the Idaho Supreme Court in 1999 held, three to two, that wilderness designation did not reserve unappropriated water within wilderness areas. Potlatch Corp. v. United States, 134 Idaho 916, 12 P.3d 1260 (2000). Like practically everything else connected with this issue, this decision had a tangled and contentious history. The same court had earlier held (also by a three-to-two vote) the opposite—that water was reserved by wilderness designation. This led to a spirited, and ultimately successful, electoral campaign to throw the author of that opinion off the bench, in a campaign in which a principal issue was her opinion in that case. After she was defeated, but before she left the bench, another member of the court, the Chief Justice, switched her vote in the matter and the court reversed its decision. See Rocky Barker, Water Ruling Reversed, Idaho Statesman, Oct. 28, 2000 (available at 2000 WL 28731552).

WILD & SCENIC RIVERS

The Wild and Scenic Rivers Act contains an express, though negatively phrased, assertion of federal reserved water rights:

> *Designation* of any stream or portion thereof as a national wild, scenic or recreational river area *shall* not *be construed as a reservation of the waters of such streams for purposes* other than those specified in this chapter, or *in quantities* greater than *necessary to accomplish these purposes.**

The Act's announced policy was to preserve "certain selected rivers" which "possess outstandingly remarkable scenic, recreational, geologic, fish and wildlife, historic, cultural, or other similar values" in their "free-flowing condition," and protect the rivers "and their immediate environments" for the "benefit and enjoyment of present and future generations." 16 U.S.C. § 1271.

How much water is reserved by this Act? All the natural flows in the designated rivers? If something less than all the flows, how much less? See Solicitor's Opinion, 86 Interior Dec. at 607–09 (1979); Brian Gray, No Holier Temples, Protecting the National Parks Through Wild and Scenic River Designation, 58 U. Colo. L. Rev. 551 (1988); Potlatch Corp. v. United States, 134 Idaho 912, 12 P.3d 1256 (2000) (rejecting the argument of forest products and mining companies that the Act does not reserve water, the court finding it would be "anomalous" to conclude that an act "expressly created to preserve free-flowing rivers failed to provide for the reservation of water in the rivers").

BUREAU OF LAND MANAGEMENT (BLM) PUBLIC LANDS

The BLM-managed federal lands are, with some exceptions, the residual public domain left after disposition into non-federal ownership, or after reservation for specific purposes and transfer for management by other federal agencies like the Forest Service, Park Service, and Fish & Wildlife

---

* 16 U.S.C. § 1284(c) (emphasis added).

Service. For that reason, they are generally regarded as having no federally reserved water rights. In 1976, Congress for the first time gave BLM an organic management statute, the Federal Land Policy and Management Act (FLPMA), 43 U.S.C. §§ 1701 et seq. While this Act set forth broad purposes for which these lands were to be managed, it did not in and of itself reserve water. Sierra Club v. Watt, 659 F.2d 203, 206 (D.C.Cir.1981). The court there expressed "substantial agreement" with the government's argument in its brief:

> Under the controlling decisions of the Supreme Court, the distinction between reservation[s] and unreserved public lands is fundamental. Reserved rights attach only to the former, and then only when water is necessary to fulfill the primary purpose of the reservation. No water is reserved for uses that are merely permissive upon a reservation. *A fortiori*, then, no reserved rights arise under [FLPMA], for no reservation of land is effected.

Id. The court also focused on one of FLPMA's savings clauses, which reads that nothing in FLPMA "shall be construed as * * * *expanding* or diminishing *Federal* or State jurisdiction, responsibility, interests, or *rights in water resources development or control* * * *." FLPMA § 701(g), 90 Stat. 2786 (1976) (emphasis added). The court interpreted the italicized provisions as meaning that no federal water rights were reserved in the statute.

FLPMA essentially calls for BLM public lands to be managed for the same purposes as the national forests: multiple uses including mining, grazing, recreation, timber, and watershed protection, among others. Does it make sense that BLM has no reserved rights for these uses, and the Forest Service does for some of them? Does Congress have to act consistently in directing management of federal lands and associated water?*

BLM has one recognized category of reserved rights, growing out of a 1926 Executive Order (commonly called Public Water Reserve No. 107) that reserved lands around every "spring or waterhole" on public lands "for public use." 43 U.S.C. § 300 (repealed prospectively by FLPMA, leaving existing withdrawals intact). The idea behind the Executive Order was to prevent private monopolization of scarce water sources on the arid western public lands. There has been some debate about how broad "public use" ought to be defined—e.g., whether it includes fish propagation or fire control as well as stockwatering and human consumption. See, e.g., United States v. City and County of Denver, 656 P.2d 1, 31–32 (Colo.1982); 90 Interior Dec. 81 (1983); In re Snake River Basin Adjudication, 131 Idaho 468, 959 P.2d 449 (1998), cert. denied, 526 U.S. 1012 (1999); Angela Liston,

---

* The inconsistency was dramatized in a 1988 statute approving a Forest Service–BLM exchange of management jurisdiction over nearly 700,000 acres of land in Nevada. BLM picked up 23,000 acres of former national forest land, and lost about 662,000 acres to the Forest Service. See Pub. L. 100–550, 102 Stat. 2749 (1988). On the new national forest land, Congress "expressly reserve[d] the minimum quantity of water necessary to achieve the primary purposes" for which national forests were established, with a priority date as of the date of transfer. On the new BLM land, Congress "expressly relinquishe[d] all Federal reserved water rights created by the initial withdrawal from the public domain * * *." Id. § 8.

Reevaluating the Applicability of the Reservation Doctrine to Public Water Reserve No. 107, 26 Ariz. L. Rev. 127 (1984).

4. MODERN CONGRESSIONAL AND EXECUTIVE PRACTICE IN FEDERAL LAND RESERVATIONS

Recall that in United States v. New Mexico, supra page 521, the Court justified giving reserved rights claims careful scrutiny because they were for the most part implied from congressional enactments: "Where Congress has expressly addressed the question of whether federal entities must abide by state water law, it has almost invariably deferred to the state law." 438 U.S. at 696.

Is this accurate? Sometimes Congress has expressly addressed water rights in various federal resource management statutes. Sometimes it has, to be sure, expressly deferred to state water law. But it also has crafted disclaimers, such as the one used in the Wilderness Act of 1964 and several other statutes: "Nothing in this [Act] shall constitute an express or implied claim or denial on the part of the Federal Government as to exemption from State water laws." 16 U.S.C. § 1133(d)(6); see also Wild & Scenic Rivers Act, 16 U.S.C. § 1284(b); and FLPMA § 701(g), quoted above. What does this language mean? It asserts no claim of exemption, yet also asserts no denial of a claim of exemption. Is it calculated, as Yogi Berra supposedly said, to "leave the status quo right where it is"—a status quo that includes the implied reservation of water doctrine?

Since United States v. New Mexico was decided, an even more variegated picture has emerged. Responding to the criticism that it ought to specifically address water in making changes to the statutory management direction for particular public lands and resources, Congress has in the last two decades usually done just that. The result has not, however, been "almost invariabl[e]" deference to state water law. Consider a 1987 statute establishing a national monument, national conservation area, and wilderness on federal lands in New Mexico:

> Congress expressly reserves to the United States the minimum amount of water required to carry out the purposes [of this Act]. * * * Nothing in this section shall be construed as establishing a precedent with regard to future designations, nor shall it affect the interpretation of any other Act or any designation made pursuant thereto.

101 Stat. 1539, 1549. How should a court go about determining how much water is reserved by this statute? Why do you suppose Congress included the second sentence? Was it to make sure that no negative inference is drawn from the express reservation of water here when construing whether water is implicitly reserved in another statute that is silent on water?

Consider this 1988 statute designating wilderness areas in national park units in the State of Washington:

> Subject to valid existing rights, within the areas designated as wilderness by this Act, Congress hereby expressly reserves such water rights as necessary, for the purposes for which such areas are so designated.

The priority date of such rights shall be the date of enactment of this Act.

102 Stat. 3961, 3968. How much water is reserved? Is groundwater as well as surface water reserved? Because this statute does not use the "minimum amount necessary" language found in the New Mexico statute of a year earlier (quoted in the preceding paragraph), does this statute reserve more than the minimum? Does the absence of "no precedent" language (such as was included in the New Mexico statute) allow a court to infer that silence in similar statutes does not imply a reservation of water? See also 16 U.S.C. § 410aaa–76 (designation of California desert areas as wilderness reserved "a quantity of water sufficient to fulfill the purposes" of wilderness designation, and included "no precedent" language). For other examples, see John Leshy, Water Rights for New Federal Land Conservation Programs: A Turn-of-the-Century Evaluation, 4 Water L.Rev. 271, 277 (2001).

In its modern practice of avoiding silence on water issues, Congress has not always reserved water, but when it has not, it has often gone to some lengths to justify its action. Consider the law creating the Hagerman Fossil Beds National Monument in Idaho in 1988 (102 Stat. 4571, 4576, § 304):

> Congress finds that there are unique circumstances with respect to the water or water-related resources within the Monument designated by this title. The Congress recognizes that there is little or no water or water-related resources that require the protection of a federal reserve [sic] water right. Nothing in this title, nor any action taken pursuant thereto, shall constitute either an expressed or implied reservation of water or water right for any purpose.

Congress has not always in recent years been able to fashion agreement on specific language that addresses water (other than a disclaimer) in legislating on federal land management issues. Where agreement cannot be reached, enactment of legislation may be delayed even if there is consensus on other parts of it. This was the case in Colorado, where for about a decade Congress could not resolve how to address water in designating new wilderness areas in the State, despite broad agreement over the other features. So long as litigation raged inconclusively over whether already designated wilderness areas in Colorado carried with them reserved water rights (see page 535 supra), silence or a disclaimer was not an acceptable option to either wilderness advocates or water developers. The stalemate was finally broken with an agreement enacted into law in the Colorado Wilderness Act of 1993. The compromise expressly rejected the reservation of water in the newly designated areas, but provided an alternative mechanism to protect the water at stake—control of land access to those areas by the federal land managers. See 107 Stat. 756, 762–63. Control of water through control of access to federal lands is discussed later in this chapter at pages 549–52.

The Executive Branch has also caught the fever of expressly addressing water in new land reservations. All of President Carter's seventeen Alaska national monuments (covering fifty-six million acres of federal land) expressly reserved water. See, e.g., 43 Fed. Reg. 57,035, 57,036 (Dec. 5, 1978) (Denali National Monument) ("There is also reserved all water necessary to the proper care and management of those objects protected by this monument and for the proper administration of the monument in accordance with applicable laws"). Almost all of President Clinton's nearly two dozen national monument proclamations addressed water, though not in a uniform way. For a summary, see Leshy, supra, 4 Water L.Rev. at 278–79. Clinton's 1996 Proclamation creating the nearly two million acre Grand Staircase–Escalante National Monument in southern Utah (the largest in the lower 48 states) says this about water:

> This proclamation does not reserve water as a matter of Federal law. I direct the Secretary to address in the management plan [for the new monument that the proclamation directed be prepared within three years] the extent to which water is necessary for the proper care and management of * * * this monument and the extent to which further action may be necessary pursuant to Federal or State law to assure the availability of water.

Proc. No. 6920, 61 Fed. Reg. 50223 (1996). What result if the proclamation—which carefully describes the geologic, archeological, and biological "objects of historic or scientific interest" that qualified the area for safeguarding under the Antiquities Act—had been silent on water?

While there is no uniformity in the results, express reservations of water are becoming common. In effect, water is being considered along with boundaries, management, and other policies as part of the political process. In many situations, the actual, on-the-ground impact of reservations on other water users may be minimal. There are several reasons for this: The priority date for the reservation is recent and junior to other established uses. Second, most federal reserved water rights involve so-called "in-situ" or instream uses of water. Being non-consumptive, such uses do not foreclose, and indeed protect, opportunities for diversion and consumptive uses of water downstream. Third, while the quantity of reserved water for such purposes as wilderness would seem to be very great—possibly the entire flow of water in the streams—the real impact on existing uses is usually small or nonexistent. Most wilderness areas and many other federal land reservations are at high elevations in unpopulated areas, and there are usually few practicable future diversion opportunities upstream to be restricted. Admittedly, some federal reservations may pose more serious problems. For example, many wetlands providing bird habitat were established relatively early in the 20th century for the primary purpose of wildlife protection, and they often are located in low-lying areas below irrigated farmland using water from creeks feeding into the refuges.

5.   ADJUDICATING FEDERAL WATER RIGHTS: THE MCCARRAN AMENDMENT, STATE WATER ADJUDICATIONS AND RELATED ISSUES

Many federal reserved water rights have not yet been formally claimed or adjudicated. Often federal reserved water is being put to use, but there has been no need or occasion to adjudicate or otherwise officially establish the right. For example, the United States is often using instream flows for various purposes, but there are no competing claims for such flows, and/or no adjudication has ever required such claims to be made. Many federal reservations (such as of some national parks and many national forests) include the headwaters of watersheds, where federally reserved instream flows have only positive effects on downstream diversions (by preserving the water flows). Many other federally reserved uses (for campgrounds, for example) are for relatively small amounts of water that do not threaten uses under state law. Only when such uses are threatened by various developments (such as by Cappaert's pumping) does the United States usually take steps to protect them.

Whether they are being exercised or not, however, federal reserved rights claims can put a cloud on state water management and administration. Some state law appropriations involve storage or diversions on or above federal reservations, such as those on national forest lands in the Colorado Rockies that feed the growth of crops and people along Colorado's Front Range. See United States v. City and County of Denver, 656 P.2d 1 (Colo.1982).

The so-called McCarran Amendment, 43 U.S.C. § 666(a), enacted in 1952 as a rider on a Department of Justice appropriation act, provides a limited waiver of sovereign immunity by the United States in water rights litigation in state courts:

> Consent is given to join the United States as a defendant in any suit (1) for the adjudication of rights to the use of water of a river system or other source, or (2) for the administration of such rights, where it appears that the United States is the owner of or is in the process of acquiring water rights by appropriation under State law, by purchase, by exchange, or otherwise, and the United States is a necessary party to such suit. * * *

These deceptively simple words have provoked several U.S. Supreme Court decisions. In United States v. District Court In and For Eagle County, 401 U.S. 520 (1971), the Court held that the "or otherwise" language meant that federal reserved rights are subject to adjudication in state courts. The McCarran Amendment does not, however, divest the federal courts of federal question jurisdiction over federal water rights claims; thus, the state and federal courts have concurrent jurisdiction over these claims. Federal courts can still entertain suits involving federal water rights. See, e.g., Kittitas Reclamation Dist. v. Sunnyside Valley Irrig. Dist., 763 F.2d 1032 (9th Cir.1985); United States v. Alpine Land & Reservoir Co., 174 F.3d 1007 (9th Cir.1999) (federal court properly enjoined, at the request of the Nevada State Engineer, a state court proceeding initiated by a county seeking to overturn the State Engineer's decision on a water rights transfer involving the federal Fish & Wildlife Service, because under the applicable decree the federal district court exercises appellate jurisdiction over decisions of the State Engineer involving federally decreed water rights); and see Hage v. United States, 51 Fed.Cl. 570 (2002), where Judge Loren Smith, known for his expansive view of property rights, rejected arguments by both the State and the BLM that he should refrain from deciding a rancher's claim of taking a water right until the State had completed the general stream adjudication it had commenced.

Nevertheless, the Supreme Court has made it clear in numerous decisions that, other factors being roughly equal, state court jurisdiction is preferred. The Court has explained that state courts may be better equipped than the federal courts to exercise jurisdiction over all water rights, state and federal. See, e.g., Colorado River Water Conservation Dist. v. United States, 424 U.S. 800 (1976); Arizona v. San Carlos Apache Tribe of Arizona, 463 U.S. 545 (1983). In the one victory the federal government has had in recent decades under the McCarran Amendment, the Court ruled that the waiver of federal sovereign immunity is not broad enough to subject the United States to pay filing fees for its claims. United States v. Idaho, 508 U.S. 1 (1993).

The Amendment has been interpreted to extend only to *general* stream adjudications; that is, only to comprehensive proceedings in which the state joins all potential water rights claimants in a watershed, and not to actions that might be filed against the United States by individual water users. See, e.g., Dugan v. Rank, 372 U.S. 609 (1963). The central idea behind the provision is that the U.S. will not be an obstacle to a State's desire to adjudicate comprehensively all the water rights in a particular stream or watershed. Further, because the McCarran Amendment waives sovereign immunity only in a "suit," it is generally understood not to allow states to join the United States in state administrative proceedings concerning water rights, even ones that adjudicate rights and are subject to judicial review.

Nevertheless, the line between a general adjudication and one that singles out the federal claims can be blurry, as is the line between judicial proceedings and administrative proceedings. For example, the Ninth Circuit rejected a vigorous challenge by the United States that the Oregon general stream adjudication system was neither comprehensive nor judicial enough to meet McCarran's terms. Under that system, the Oregon state water rights agency would actually be conducting the litigation under minimal judicial supervision, and would be adjudicating primarily federal water rights, because under the Oregon stream adjudication statute, all other water users merely had to register their water rights, which the court would accept at face value, unless successfully challenged by the United States. Finally, hydrologically related groundwater was not included in the adjudication. The court brushed aside the federal objections, essentially reading the McCarran Amendment as creating a strong presumption in favor of state court adjudications, and because the features of the Oregon system to which the U.S. objected were all in place when Congress adopted the Amendment in 1952, Congress must have contemplated that the Oregon system met its terms. See United States v. Oregon, 44 F.3d 758 (9th Cir.1994). Mindful of its dismal track record in the Supreme Court, the United States did not seek certiorari. See also In re Rights to Use Water in Gila River, 857 P.2d 1236, 1247–48 (Ariz.1993) (rejecting a similar U.S. argument that failure to include all hydrologically related groundwater disqualifies an adjudication from the McCarran Amendment waiver).

How big is a "river system or other source" embraced within the McCarran Amendment? In United States v. District Court for Eagle County, 401 U.S. 520 (1971), the Court firmly rejected the United States' argument that Colorado could not join it under the McCarran Amendment in a proceeding to adjudicate only a tributary of the Colorado River. See also Elephant Butte Irrig. Dist. v. United States, 849 P.2d 372 (N.M.Ct. App.1993) (upholding joinder of U.S. in a suit to adjudicate only a portion of the Rio Grande River within New Mexico). On the other hand, the Idaho Supreme Court ruled that a McCarran Amendment adjudication in that state had to include the Snake River and all of its tributaries within Idaho. See In re General Adjudication of Snake River Basin Water System, 764 P.2d 78 (Idaho 1988).

To what extent is the McCarran Amendment retroactive? Suppose early in the twentieth century a state court (or even a state administrative agency) purported to adjudicate a federal water right, with the participation of the United States. Is that decree binding on the United States? Case law on the subject is surprisingly sparse. See, e.g., Mannatt v. United States, 951 F.Supp. 172 (E.D.Cal.1996); United States v. Hennen, 300 F.Supp. 256 (D.Nev.1968); In re Bear River Drainage Area, 2 Utah 2d 208, 271 P.2d 846 (1954).

WHEN DOES THE EXECUTIVE BRANCH HAVE A DUTY TO FILE RESERVED RIGHTS CLAIMS IN ADJUDICATIONS?

If Congress intended to create reserved rights and the Executive fails to assert them in a general stream adjudication, is a judicial remedy available? The federal Administrative Procedure Act has been interpreted to create a strong presumption of reviewability of agency action, but one of its exceptions involves matters in which "agency action is committed to agency discretion by law." See 5 U.S.C. § 702(a)(2). The Supreme Court has said that if the statute under which the agency is acting "is drawn so that a court would have no meaningful standard against which to judge the agency's exercise of discretion," the matter is committed to the agency's discretion and not subject to judicial review. Heckler v. Chaney, 470 U.S. 821 (1985).

Like most other statutes, treaties or executive orders under which *Winters* claims might be made, the Wilderness Act says nothing about asserting federal reserved water rights. In defending its failure to file water rights claims for wilderness areas against a Sierra Club lawsuit, the federal government argued, among other things, that its action was unreviewable under Heckler v. Chaney. Although the Tenth Circuit ultimately dismissed the Sierra Club's case as not ripe, Sierra Club v. Yeutter, 911 F.2d 1405 (10th Cir.1990), it seemed to suggest that judicial review was available under certain circumstances because the Wilderness Act

> does provide guidelines the agency must follow: the agency cannot abandon, by action or inaction, the statutory mandate to preserve the wilderness characteristics of the wilderness areas. To the extent the Forest Service's inaction implicates this command of the Wilderness Act, the *Chaney* presumption of unreviewability is rebutted and we may review the agency's action.

911 F.2d at 1414 n.5. The court concluded that judicial intervention was not warranted on the facts before it because the Sierra Club had not drawn a sufficient connection between the failure to file a claim for a federal reserved right for wilderness areas and harm to "wilderness water values." The court elaborated by noting, first, that "federal reserved water rights, as creatures of federal law, are protected from extinguishment under state law by the Supremacy Clause." Second, even if federal reserved water rights lost their early priority date because they were not timely filed under the rules of the Colorado adjudication, there may be no appropriations under state law that would or even could create adverse impacts on wilderness water values that a federal reserved right for wilderness would prevent. The court also acknowledged the Forest Service's argument that "there are either adequate administrative controls in place that will prevent diversions above or within wilderness area or that geographical features render such diversions or projects impractical in areas within or above the wilderness areas." These multiple "contingencies * * * underscore[] the speculative and hypothetical nature of this issue." The court left open the possibility of revisiting the matter in the future:

> When and if a water development claim that may threaten wilderness water values is filed, and the Forest Service does not assert a federal reserved water right based on the Wilderness Act, and furthermore such failure to assert the reserved water right is irreconcilable with the Forest Service's duty to protect wilderness characteristics, then the Sierra Club may either intervene in the state water proceeding as appropriate under state law or may seek judicial review of the Forest Service's failure to act in federal court. At that time the record will be more fully developed and the courts can better determine whether the Forest Service's proposed alternatives to the use of wilderness water rights are adequate to reconcile its actions with its obligations under the Act. If the proposed alternatives are not adequate, appropriate corrective orders can be issued. * * *

911 F.2d at 1418–19.

Suppose the federal government does not file a claim for a reserved right, and a new appropriation is approved under state law that allows a major diversion upstream from the federally reserved area, and the federal agency is otherwise powerless to prevent it. If the Sierra Club renews its suit against the federal agency, what "appropriate corrective orders" can the court issue? Does the Tenth Circuit require too much vigilance on the part of friends of federal reserved water rights outside the federal agencies?

For another case inconclusively addressing whether federal agencies have a duty to pursue reserved rights claims in litigation, see Sierra Club v. Andrus, 487 F.Supp. 443, 448–49 (D.D.C.1980), aff'd sub nom Sierra Club v. Watt, 659 F.2d 203 (D.C.Cir.1981). For an illustration of the courts' reluctance to interfere with the judgment of the United States in litigation over federal reserved rights, see Shoshone–Bannock Tribes v. Reno, 56 F.3d 1476 (D.C.Cir.1995).

Congress has sometimes directly addressed the problem of federal agency reluctance to make reserved water rights claims. A 1990 statute designating wilderness areas in Arizona not only expressly reserved water, but directed the Secretary of the Interior "and all other officers of the United States" to "take steps necessary to protect" the federally reserved water rights, including "filing * * * a claim for the quantification of such rights in any present or future appropriate stream adjudication * * *." 104 Stat. 4469, 4473, § 101(g)(2); see also California Desert Protection Act of 1994, 108 Stat. at 4498; San Pedro Riparian National Conservation Area Act of 1988, 102 Stat. 4571, § 102(d).

FEDERAL PARTICIPATION IN STATE ADMINISTRATIVE PROCEEDINGS

Recall that in *Cappaert*, supra page 516, the National Park Service had appeared before the State Engineer to protest Cappaert's application to change the use of water from its wells. The State Engineer rejected the protest, and the State later sought to dismiss the federal court litigation on res judicata or collateral estoppel grounds, because the United States had failed to appeal the rejection through the state court system. The Court would have none of it:

> [T]he United States was not made a party to the state administrative proceeding; * * * it did not assert any federal water-rights claims, nor did it seek to adjudicate any claims until the hydrologic studies * * * had been completed. * * * The State Water Engineer's decree explicitly stated it was "subject to existing rights."

426 U.S. at 146–47. This leaves open a number of questions. Can a federal official waive the sovereign immunity of the United States in proceedings that don't conform to the McCarran Amendment simply by making a general appearance before a State Engineer? Could the Nevada State Engineer have demanded that the National Park Service become a formal "party" to the proceeding in order to protest the Cappaert application? Could it have required the Park Service to put on proof of its water rights as a precondition to protest? Could the State Engineer have, in the course of deciding whether the Cappaert application would adversely affect the federal water right, determine the scope and quantity of the federal water right? If so, is the federal government bound by that determination unless it appeals up through the state court system?

To the extent that a federal appearance before a state agency may bind the United States, would you advise federal agencies *not* to participate in such proceedings? If the federal agencies don't participate, however, state water administrators may not gain notice that their decisions could conflict with federal water rights claims. It is possible that, with notice, the state could avoid the conflict. Does this suggest that states should allow the federal agencies to make a special appearance without waiving federal immunity?

THE CONDUCT OF STATE COURT LITIGATION INVOLVING FEDERAL RESERVED RIGHTS

State courts are bound to follow federal substantive law (such as statutes and court decisions on the federal reserved rights doctrine) in adjudicating federal water rights claims. State court decisions are subject to review in the United States Supreme Court, in exercise of its discretionary certiorari jurisdiction. See Arizona v. San Carlos Apache Tribe of Arizona, 463 U.S. 545, 571 (1983) (cautioning that "[s]tate courts, as much as federal courts, have a solemn obligation to follow federal law" in McCarran Amendment water rights adjudications). Still, the interface between federal and state law in the conduct of general stream adjudications under the McCarran Amendment gives rise to a number of questions. For example, who has the burden of proof where federal water rights are contested in a state court adjudication? Is that a matter for state or federal law? See In re General Adjudication of the Big Horn River System, 753 P.2d 76, 90 (Wyo.1988) (applying state law and holding that the burden is on the United States).

To what extent can state courts extinguish federal claims for reserved rights for failure to meet filing deadlines and other procedural require- ments of state law? Cf. United States v. Idaho, 508 U.S. 1, 7 (1993) (McCarran Amendment makes the federal government subject to "estab- lished state-law rules governing pleading, discovery, and the admissibility of evidence at trial"); see also United States v. Bell, 724 P.2d 631 (Colo. 1986), where the Colorado Supreme Court upheld a water court decision denying the United States the right to relate an amended water rights claim back to the date the original claim was filed, thereby costing the claim several decades of priority.

Is there anything anomalous about allowing a state procedural error to thwart federal substantive rights, or is that simply the logical and proper consequence of the McCarran Amendment—the presumed purpose of which was to force the United States to litigate and quantify its claims just like those of anyone else? On the other hand, what if the Colorado courts would not have enforced the procedural rule involved in *Bell* with equal vigor against a state law appropriator? (How might the United States go about proving that?) Are these issues—when can a state court rule defeat a federal right—simply a mirror image of the problems created in diversity jurisdiction cases in federal court, where federal courts apply state substan- tive law, but follow federal procedures? See Erie R.R. v. Tompkins, 304 U.S. 64 (1938) and its progeny.

THE FUTURE OF GENERAL STREAM ADJUDICATIONS INVOLVING FEDERAL WATER RIGHTS

The courts continue to make clear that, though some federal water rights disputes may be handled in federal courts, western states may adjudicate federal water rights in their own courts if they choose to do so. But funny things have happened on the way to state court quantification, bringing to mind the old story of the dog that madly chased after cars until one day it caught one. These adjudications can be lengthy and very expensive, for both the state and the participants. State efforts to have the United States help shoulder their cost were dealt a blow when, in the first McCarran Amendment victory for the United States since Dugan v. Rank, the Supreme Court ruled that its waiver of sovereign immunity is not broad enough to subject the United States to paying filing fees for its claims. See United States v. Idaho, 508 U.S. 1 (1993).

Even more important, and surprising some observers, state law appropriators have not always come out ahead in state court adjudications, because state judges have for the most part appeared to make a conscientious effort to apply the principles of federal law that govern the *Winters* doctrine.* Thus recognition of important federal reserved rights is a possible, perhaps likely, outcome of state court adjudications. Might it be preferable to live with the uncertainty of unquantified federal claims rather than adjudicate and settle them? Have the states believed too much their own rhetoric about the "need" to adjudicate these rights?

THE ADMINISTRATION OF ADJUDICATED FEDERAL RESERVED WATER RIGHTS IN STATE SYSTEMS

Subsection (2) of the McCarran Amendment specifically waives the sovereign immunity of the United States for the "administration" of water rights. In South Delta Water Agency v. United States, 767 F.2d 531, 541 (9th Cir.1985), the court held that this waiver applies only after rights have first been adjudicated under subsection (1). As state courts complete adjudications of federal reserved rights, more occasions arise for post-decree administration of the federal reserved rights by state water officials. Federal reserved rights, once adjudicated and quantified, take their place in the state's priority rolls through judicial decree. A federal reserved right holder is entitled to all of the protections of a normal state law appropriator. Most fundamentally, the reserved rights holder would be able to call the river in order to assert the rights against juniors, if necessary to vindicate the right. The call would be enforced by state officials acting pursuant to state authority.

Federal reserved rights are not, however, stripped of their federal character as a result of quantification and becoming part of the state priority system. Because federal reserved rights are not lost by non-use, for example, state forfeiture laws may not apply to them under the Supremacy Clause.** See United States v. City and County of Denver, 656 P.2d 1 (Colo.1982); see also Sierra Club v. Yeutter, supra. Between the two poles of enforcement and forfeiture—where reserved rights are most like and unlike state created rights—lies a broad range of state water rights administration issues where the precise treatment accorded to federal reserved rights remains uncertain. Consider, for example, the role of state courts when the United States proposes to modify the use of a decreed federal

---

* This is not to say they've not been asked to do otherwise. The Colorado Supreme Court in the early 1980s rejected an argument by the City of Denver that captured the theological overtones of these state-federal disputes over water: Denver argued that the Colorado Supreme Court was "not bound to abide by the relevant [*Winters* rights] decisions of the United States Supreme Court because, in Denver's view, they were 'heresy'." United States v. City and County of Denver, 656 P.2d 1, 16 n. 25 (1982).

** Abandonment may present a closer question, because the federal government conceivably could form an intention to abandon a reserved right if it were no longer needed for a federal purpose.

reserved water right. Does it have to follow state procedures and satisfy state law in making the change of use?

SETTLING FEDERAL RESERVED RIGHTS CLAIMS ASSOCIATED WITH FEDERAL LANDS

Although litigation goes forward on many fronts, a trend toward settlement of non-Indian federal reserved rights claims is emerging. An innovative resolution of the water rights claims of Zion National Park in southwestern Utah was executed in December 1996 after five years of negotiation. The Park is on the Virgin River downstream from some water development, and nearby St. George, Utah, is one of the fastest growing areas in the United States. The settlement recognizes a federal reserved water right to nearly all unappropriated flows in and above the Park. A small amount is reserved for future development upstream, but major upstream reservoirs, which had been contemplated, are prohibited. The settlement also includes a groundwater protection zone, restricting large wells along the Park's boundaries, and a transfer of federal land to allow construction of a reservoir downstream from the Park. For more detail, see Western Water Policy Review Advisory Commission, Water in the West: Challenge for the Next Century 4–13 (1998). A brief discussion of successful resolution of national park claims in Colorado is found in Wendy Weiss, The Federal Government's Pursuit of Instream Flow Water Rights, 1 U. Den. Water L. Rev. 151, 160–62 (1998).

In the 1990s in Montana, water rights for five National Park Service units (including Yellowstone and Glacier), three National Wildlife Refuges, and a BLM wilderness and Wild & Scenic River unit were all settled amicably by negotiation. Other innovative settlements are in the works regarding Cedar Breaks and Hovenweep National Monuments in Utah. A number of these these settlements involve variations on the following theme: The United States agrees to subordinate its federal reserved rights to at least some appropriations initiated after the federal reservation, in return for which the state agrees to cap further appropriations and to manage groundwater outside the boundaries of the federal reservation to protect wetlands and other water-dependent resources inside the reservation. In essence, the United States gives up some priority in return for state cooperation, rather than leaving matters to litigation under the *Cappaert* decision.

As court decisions provide a better fix on the contours of these rights, federal agencies assemble the information necessary to quantify them, states discover what little threat many of these rights pose to state water right holders, and all continue to suffer from the expense and length of adjudications, the settlement fever is likely to spread.

B.   BEYOND THE RESERVED RIGHTS DOCTRINE: OTHER MEANS OF PROTECTING FEDERAL INTERESTS IN WATER

Many of the uses of federal lands that might involve the consumption of significant amounts of water are generally understood not to be covered by the federal reserved rights doctrine. The long-time practice is for mineral developers on federal land to obtain any needed water rights under state law. See Owen Olpin, A. Dan Tarlock & Carl F. Austin, Geothermal Development and Western Water Law, 1979 Utah L.Rev. 773, 807–10, arguing that federal lessees of geothermal resources should not be able to claim federal reserved water rights (even though a 1930 executive order withdrawing hot springs from development, a 1967 withdrawal from mining of all lands valuable for geothermal steam development, and the Geothermal Act of 1970 all might arguably create a federal reserved water right in the geothermal resource). In United States v. City and County of Denver, 656 P.2d 1, 33–34 (Colo.1982), held that reservation as a hot spring did not reserve the water for geothermal energy production. Ski areas located on federal land also obtain any water needed for snow-making or domestic and sanitation uses under state law. Cf. United States v. City and County of Denver, 656 P.2d 1, 34 (Colo.1982) (holding that federal reserved rights may be used by "any permittee, licensee, or concessionaire of the federal government"). Water rights for livestock grazing is somewhat of a special case, dealt with further below.

What may the federal government do when it wants or needs water in order to carry out federal programs, such as those for conservation or recreation, where protection of streamflows is required? The following explores alternative methods for federal agencies to protect water found on federal lands, other than asserting reserved rights.

1.   CONTROLLING WATER BY REGULATING ACCESS TO FEDERAL LAND

The federal government sometimes can protect water resources found on federal land by controlling access to the land rather than by claiming water rights. This was the approach used in § 8 of the 1993 Colorado Wilderness Act, 107 Stat. 756, 762. The national forest lands it designated as wilderness were located in headwaters areas with "few, if any, opportunities for diversion, storage, or other uses of water occurring outside such lands that would adversely affect the wilderness values of such lands." Id. § 8(a)(1)(A). Therefore Congress chose to "protect the wilderness values of the lands designated * * * by means other than those based on a Federal reserved water right." Id. § 8(a)(2). The Act said the executive shall not "fund, assist, authorize, or [otherwise permit] * * * the development * * * or enlargement of any water resource facility within the [wilderness] areas" designated by the Act. Id. § 8(c). It protected, within carefully defined limits, access to maintain existing water resource facilities in the areas. Id. § 8(d)-(f).

Federal law generally gives federal land managing agencies broad power to permit or deny the use of federal lands for water development purposes. The right-of-way provisions of the Federal Land Policy and Management Act, for example, fairly bristle with environmental regulatory power, giving both the BLM and the Forest Service wide power to grant, deny, or condition access to federal lands for various purposes, including water development. 43 U.S.C. §§ 1761–71. It is not very controversial to exercise this regulatory authority to prevent new non-federal water developments (involving new or transfers of existing state law appropriations). But it is another matter where federal land managing agencies regulate land access in such a way as to limit existing, often longstanding, uses supported by state water rights.

The most prominent modern instance of this has been the so-called "bypass flows" controversy in Colorado. Many years ago non-federal water developers had built, under term-limited Forest Service permits, dams and diversion facilities on national forest land in Colorado's Front Range to supply downstream towns and farms. The developers obtained permanent water appropriations under state law (subject to maintaining beneficial use). When the federal permits expired in the 1970s, the Forest Service, responding to changing public values and a more sophisticated knowledge of environmental health, announced it would renew them only if some flows were restored to the natural stream below the diversion facilities. It based this decision on numeric aquatic protection standards in its forest plan. Providing such "bypass flows" meant reducing the amount of the diversion (by as much as 50–80% in dry years, according to the permittees), which meant, in turn, reducing the quantity secured by the state law water right. To the Forest Service, this was environmentally sound land management, and well within its legal authority. To the federal permittees (and holders of state law appropriations), it was confiscation of state water rights without compensation.

On the law, the Forest Service seemed to have the better of it. See Wyoming Wildlife Federation v. U.S. Forest Service, 792 F.2d 981 (10th Cir.1986); Nevada Land Action Ass'n v. U.S. Forest Service, 8 F.3d 713, 719 (9th Cir.1993) (upholding federal authority to consider water flows in making land use decisions). The Colorado Supreme Court said, in rejecting a claim for a federal reserved right for geothermal production, that the federal government "has complete control over access to federally held geothermal resources and can therefore fully regulate water appropriation." United States v. City and County of Denver, 656 P.2d 1, 34 (Colo.1982). Had bypass flows been required to meet the standards of the Clean Water Act or the Endangered Species Act, the federal land manager's case would have been even stronger. See Chapter 5 at pages 501–02.

After much political brouhaha Congress created a seven-member commission to examine the problem. The Republican leadership in Congress named four members; the Democratic minority and Clinton Administration named three. The commission split along party (and developer versus environmentalist) lines, with the majority contesting both the lawfulness and the wisdom of using federal land management authority to protect streamflow on federal lands. Report of the Federal Water Rights Task Force Created Pursuant to Section 389(d)(3) of Pub. L. 104–127 (1997). Meanwhile, state and local water interests insisted that any new settlements of Forest Service reserved water rights claims contain a "poison pill" that would rescind the settlement if the Forest Service requires additional bypass flows on any national forest covered by the agreement. The Forest Service responded by adopting a national policy in the spring of 1999 that sharply distinguished land use permitting affecting bypass flows from water rights proceedings, and provided that the Forest Service ability to "fully exercise discretionary regulatory authority * * * during future permitting procedures for private water diversion and storage facilities on National Forest System lands, must not be constrained, foregone, impeded, or prohibited." Despite the war of words and policies, negotiations have led to some compromise over bypass flows in particular situations. See generally Janet Neuman and Michael Blumm, Water for National Forests: The Bypass Flow Report and the Great Divide in Western Water Law, 18 Stan. Envtl. L.J. 3 (1999); David Gillian, Will There Be Water for the National Forests?, 69 U. Colo. L. Rev. 533 (1998); Thomas Snodgrass, Bypass Flow Requirements and the Question of Forest Service Authority, 70 U. Colo. L. Rev. 641 (1999).

What is the right answer here? State law appropriations usually do not insulate appropriators from the need to comply with other laws, such as zoning and environmental statutes. Moreover, state law water rights are typically not an obstacle to the implementation of new zoning or environmental quality standards that have the effect of reducing water diversions. Should federal land permitting requirements be regarded as any different? If federal permission to use federal land is granted for a specific term, but for a use that allows the permittee to perfect a state law water right without a term limit, should the state law water right in effect make that use of federal land permanent?

Collisions between federal land use controls and state law water rights can be found in many contexts. In the Northern Great Plains, for example, the federal Fish & Wildlife Service has acquired easements from farmers to preserve so-called "prairie potholes," wetland areas vital for migratory birds. See p. 224 supra. The easements typically contain a commitment that the farmer agrees to maintain the lands as a waterfowl production area "by not draining or permitting the draining of any surface water by ditching or any other means." Assuming these acquired easements do not create federal reserved rights, and assuming that state law does not acknowledge *in situ* water rights for such purposes, and/or does not coordinate groundwater and surface water doctrines, how can the United States protect itself if the farmer subject to such an easement begins pumping groundwater pursuant to a state permit, with the effect of drying up the wetlands? Cf. United States v. Vesterso, 828 F.2d 1234 (8th Cir.1987) (federal law made unlawful the construction of ditches that drained wetlands protected by federal easements, rejecting the argument that state water law—pursuant to which the State Water Commission had permitted the construction to proceed—should control).

If a state law appropriation can no longer be exercised as it traditionally has because of a new but otherwise lawful federal land use restriction, does the appropriator have a remedy? The United States brought suit to enjoin Hunter from grazing and watering his cattle within the boundaries of Death Valley, a unit of the National Park System, without a permit from the National Park Service, which managed the area. One of Hunter's defenses was that, prior to the area being made part of the National Park

System, he had perfected a valid state law water right at springs and a stream, and these water rights entitled him to continue to graze cattle there. The Ninth Circuit acknowledged he had valid water rights, but rejected the defense. It did say, however, that he "should be allowed a right of way over [Monument] lands to divert the water * * * elsewhere if he is able;" otherwise, his water right would simply lapse for non-use. Hunter v. United States, 388 F.2d 148, 154–55 n. 4 (9th Cir.1967). See also W. Douglas Kari, Groundwater Rights on Public Land in California, 35 Hastings L.J. 1007, 1034–36 (1984).

In Nevada Land Action Ass'n v. U.S. Forest Service, 8 F.3d 713, 719–20 (9th Cir.1993), ranchers argued that they had acquired vested water rights as a result of using water on federal grazing land and therefore the Forest Service had to consider these rights in adopting its land use plan for the forests. The court curtly rejected the claim:

> [T]he Service clearly has the right under NFMA to limit the use of water resources in national forests, since the statute directs the Service to manage conflicting uses of forest resources. See, e.g., 16 U.S.C. §§ 1600, 1604 (g)(3). We are unable to find any authority, and [plaintiff] cites none, suggesting that the Service must consider vested water rights in its planning process. * * * Even if the implementation of the [plan] did effect a taking under the Fifth Amendment, [plaintiff's] remedy would be to file a suit seeking compensation.

Ranchers with state law water rights to support livestock grazing on federal land still occasionally argue that their water rights give them authority over federal land uses, but these claims do not get sympathetic treatment in the courts. See, e.g., Diamond Bar Cattle Co. v. United States, 168 F.3d 1209 (10th Cir.1999); Gardner v. Stager, 103 F.3d 886 (9th Cir.1996). A few questions about whether a state law water right has been taken by the denial of a permit to graze are still in litigation. See Hage v. United States, 51 Fed.Cl. 570 (2002); Store Safe Redlands Assocs. v. United States, 35 Fed.Cl. 726 (1996); Mitchell v. United States, 41 Fed.Cl. 617 (1998).

2. CLAIMING WATER RIGHTS UNDER STATE LAW

The Supreme Court said in United States v. New Mexico, supra, that when no federal reserved water right exists to support a desired federal use (such as where water is "only valuable for a secondary use of [a] federal reservation" rather than "necessary to fulfill the very purposes for which a federal reservation was created"), the inference is that "the United States would acquire water in the same manner as any other public or private appropriator." 438 U.S. at 702 (1978). This section will explore what that means. At first blush, the matter seems straightforward: The United States would look exclusively to state law for water rights. Federal lands in a riparian jurisdiction would enjoy riparian rights like those of any of its riparian neighbors. In prior appropriation jurisdictions, the United States could appropriate water just like all other users. Federal rights to groundwater would also be governed by state law. (Of course, the United States government could also, like other governmental entities, acquire needed water rights by condemnation or eminent domain.)

There are, however, complications. While the states wield considerable influence in the federal legislature, see, e.g, Herbert Wechsler, The Political Safeguards of Federalism—The Role of the States in Composition and Selection of the National Government, 54 Colum. L. Rev. 543 (1954), the converse is not so true. In the politically delicate area of water rights, states may feel, and respond to, pressure to discriminate against federal agencies, especially if doing so would advantage state water users. The United States may also have different water needs that are not as readily recognized under state law as more conventional uses. These things may compromise the ability of the United States to obtain rights to water it needs under state law. Further, many federal water needs for federal lands involve protection of instream flows for conservation and recreation. Historically, state prior appropriation systems did not grant instream flow water rights for these purposes, but almost all states' laws now recognize some form of water right or other legal protection for instream flows. Even where a state recognizes some form of instream flow protection, it is a separate question whether the United States may make instream flow appropriations on federal land. The following unanimous opinion explores these questions:

State v. Morros

Supreme Court of Nevada, 1988.
104 Nev. 709, 766 P.2d 263.

■ PER CURIAM:

[The BLM applied for and received from the State Engineer a water right under state law for Blue Lake for public recreation and fishery purposes. The Forest Service applied for and received water rights under state law for recreation, stockwatering, and wildlife purposes. Various protestants, including the State Board of Agriculture, appealed.] * * *

The Blue Lake application is for a water right to the waters of Blue Lake *in situ*, in place as a natural body of water. The BLM manages the land surrounding the lake and desires this water right to assure maintenance of the pool of Blue Lake for public recreation and fishery purposes. The Board of Agriculture contends that Nevada water law absolutely requires a physical diversion of water to obtain a water right, and that the district court therefore erred in affirming the state engineer's grant of a right to the water of Blue Lake *in situ*.

[After analyzing Nevada statutes, the court concluded that state law no longer requires a physical diversion in order to appropriate water.] * * * The Board of Agriculture also contends that the grant of a water right for Blue Lake to a United States agency is against the public interest in Nevada and that pursuant to NRS 533.370(3) the state engineer should have denied the application on that basis.[3] We see no threat to the public

---

3. NRS 533.370(3) provides, in pertinent part, that where a proposed appropriation "threatens to prove detrimental to the public interest, the state engineer shall reject the application and refuse to issue the permit asked for."

interest, however, in the grant of a water right to Blue Lake for public recreation purposes to a public agency such as the BLM. The BLM manages the land surrounding the lake for recreation and seeks a non-consumptive water right that will not reduce the amount of water presently available for other uses. Livestock and wildlife retain access to the water of Blue Lake under the district court's order. * * *

The district court relied on this court's holding in Prosole v. Steamboat Canal Co., 37 Nev. 154, 140 P. 720 (1914), as authority for reversing the state engineer's grant of permits to the BLM and United States Forest Service to develop the new water sources for stock and wildlife watering. In *Prosole*, this court held that the person who "applies the water to the soil, for a beneficial purpose," is the actual appropriator and the owner of the water right, even if someone else, such as a canal company, diverts the water from its natural course.

The BLM and Forest Service intend to provide the water requested in the applications to the livestock of grazing permit holders on federal range lands. Wildlife would also have access to the water. The district court reasoned that since the federal agencies owned no livestock, the United States could not put the water to beneficial use. Rather, the court stated, owners of livestock actually put water appropriated for stockwatering to beneficial use. The district court concluded that therefore under *Prosole* the United States could not appropriate water for stockwatering. The district court applied the same reasoning to wildlife watering. The court noted that the United States does not own the wildlife which is to receive water, because no one "owns" animals in the wild.

We conclude that the district court applied *Prosole* in an excessively rigid fashion. The proposed new water sources are dedicated to providing water to livestock and wildlife. These are beneficial uses of water. Nevada law and longstanding custom recognize stockwatering as a beneficial use of water. * * *

Wildlife watering is encompassed in the NRS 533.030(2) definition of recreation as a beneficial use of water. Nevada law recognizes the recreational value of wildlife, NRS 501.100(2),[4] and the need to provide wildlife with water. Sport hunting, a common use of wildlife, is a form of recreation. The legislative history of NRS 533.030(2) indicates that the legislature intended the provision to include watering under the rubric of recreation as a beneficial use of water. * * * It follows that providing water to wildlife is a beneficial use of water.

In managing federal grazing lands, the United States acts in a proprietary capacity. The new water sources covered by the applications at issue will permit better use of areas of the public range where grazing is limited by the lack of watering places, a problem recognized by this court. Congress

---

4. NRS 501.100(2) provides: "The preservation, protection, management and restoration of wildlife within the state contribute immeasurably to the aesthetic, recreational and economic aspects of these natural resources."

has mandated development of water sources for livestock and wildlife as a component of the federal land management program. See 43 U.S.C. §§ 1751(b) and 1901 to 1904. Thus, the United States acts in its proprietary capacity as a landowner when federal agencies seek to appropriate water under state law for livestock and wildlife watering. Although the United States does not own the livestock and wildlife, it owns the land on which the water is to be put to beneficial use. In addition, the United States benefits as a landowner from the development of new water sources on federal land.

The United States is recognized as a "person" for the purpose of water appropriation in Nevada. NRS 533.010. The district court correctly stated that the United States "is to be treated as a person * * * it is not to be feared, given preferential treatment and certainly not discriminated against." Recently, the California Supreme Court held that the United States could not be denied the same riparian water rights for national forest lands that private riparian landowners enjoy under California water law. In re Water of Hallett Creek Stream Sys., 44 Cal.3d 448, 243 Cal.Rptr. 887, 749 P.2d 324, cert. denied sub nom. California v. United States, 488 U.S. 824 (1988). *Hallett Creek* supports the principle that the United States is entitled to equal treatment under state water law.

The Board of Agriculture argues that * * * ownership of * * * water rights by the United States is against the public interest. The Board of Agriculture states that once the water is subject to federal control it will not be available for other uses at a later date. While this may be true, it is inherent in the prior appropriation system of water rights, and we cannot discriminate against the United States on that basis.

Under NRS 533.010, therefore, applications by United States agencies to appropriate water for application to beneficial uses pursuant to their land management functions must be treated on an equal basis with applications by private landowners. Although the United States owns no livestock and does not "own" wildlife, it owns land and may appropriate water for application to beneficial uses on its land. The district court erred in deciding that the United States could not obtain water rights for stockwatering and wildlife watering, and the portion of its order denying those applications is vacated. * * *

NOTES AND QUESTIONS

1. For a similar result, see In re Water Right Claim No. 1927–2, 524 N.W.2d 855 (S.D.1994) (federal Fish and Wildlife Service may appropriate natural springflow under state law to maintain marshes and other waterfowl habitat); but see State of Idaho v. United States, 134 Idaho 106, 996 P.2d 806, 811–12 (2000) (United States not entitled to a water right for wildlife under a state constitutional method because it had not diverted the water; Idaho recognized nondiversionary rights under that method only for stockwatering, and only by state entities pursuant to state statute where it was for the "beneficial use of Idaho citizens").

2. The Nevada Supreme Court adopts the idea that the state cannot discriminate against the United States in administering its prior appropriation system. Is that based on federal law; if so, what? Although there is constitutional authority for limiting the ability of the states to discriminate against the United States in certain matters (see, e.g., Lawrence Tribe, AMERICAN CONSTITUTIONAL LAW 1225 (3d. ed. 2000)), it seems that neither the United States nor its agencies are "persons" protected against state discrimination by the equal protection clause. Would the result in *Morros* have been the same if the Nevada statute had not defined the U.S. as a "person" for purposes of the state prior appropriation system? Suppose the Nevada state legislature responded to this decision by enacting a statute that only a state agency can appropriate instream flows under state law, even on federal lands. Some states have such laws. See generally Lori Potter, The Public's Role in the Acquisition and Enforcement of Instream Flows, 23 Land & Water L. Rev. 419 (1988). Or suppose the state legislature simply did not recognize instream flow appropriations under state law, by anyone. What can BLM do in those states if it wants to protect instream flows or lake levels for recreational and fishery purposes?

3. A 1995 Nevada statute, enacted in response to new federal rules governing livestock grazing on federal lands, provides that permits to appropriate water for livestock purposes on public lands can only be issued to those "legally entitled to place livestock on the public lands." Nev. Rev. Stat. § 533.503. (This law applies only to BLM public lands, and not to national forest, state or private lands.) The Nevada Attorney General advised the State Engineer that this law prohibited the issuance of new water appropriations for livestock watering to BLM, because BLM did not own livestock. Following this advice, the State Engineer denied nine pending BLM applications in 1997, even though there was unappropriated water available. The United States challenged this decision on a variety of grounds, and in United States v. State Engineer, 27 P.3d 51 (2001), the Nevada Supreme Court ruled for the BLM. It found the quoted provision of the statute unambiguous, and because the United States, as landowner, was entitled to authorize grazing of livestock on the public lands, BLM therefore was a qualified applicant for the permit to appropriate under the state law.

4. Also in 1995, the Arizona legislature enacted legislation allowing only ranchers, and not federal land managing agencies like the BLM or the Forest Service, to hold livestock water appropriations on federal land. Moreover, Arizona sought to apply it retroactively—to strip the BLM and the Forest Service of livestock watering appropriations they had previously perfected when state law did not discriminate against the federal government. (The Arizona law protected the state's ability to perfect livestock water rights on state lands.) The Arizona Supreme Court struck down this feature of the law as a violation of the state constitution's due process clause. San Carlos Apache Tribe v. Superior Court, 972 P.2d 179, 189 (Ariz.1999) ("[l]egislation may not disturb vested substantive rights by retroactively changing the law that applies to completed events").

5. BLM grazing regulations provide that rights to use water for livestock watering on public land "shall be acquired, perfected, maintained and administered under the substantive and procedural laws of the State within which such land is located." 43 C.F.R. § 4120.3–9. They go on to say that, "[t]o the extent allowed by the law of the State within which the land is located, any such water right shall be acquired, perfected, maintained and administered in the name of the United States." Id. In a lengthy separate opinion in United States v. State Engineer, supra note 3, Justice Becker of the Nevada Supreme Court dissented from the holding that the 1995 Nevada statute authorized issuing water rights to BLM. She went on, however, to find the state law preempted by federal law to the extent it prohibited the BLM from applying for livestock water rights jointly with rancher/permittee:

> If the BLM is effectively prohibited from filing a joint application for stockwater, then the decisions on how, when and where to develop water for livestock purposes would be shifted entirely into the hands of third parties. This would be a significant interference with the BLM's control and management of its rangelands. Such interference would constitute discriminatory regulation in violation of the Supremacy Clause.

27 P.3d at 54, 65. Justice Becker cited North Dakota v. United States, 495 U.S. 423, 452 (1990) (a state law may violate the Supremacy Clause if it "actually and substantially interferes with specific federal programs"); see also Chapter 3, supra pp. 224–26. Cf. the discussion of the "federal non-reserved water right," discussed immediately below.

6. The California Supreme Court has held that the United States as riparian landowner may assert riparian water rights the same as any other riparian landowner. In re Water of Hallett Creek Stream System, 44 Cal.3d 448, 243 Cal.Rptr. 887, 749 P.2d 324, cert. denied, 488 U.S. 824 (1988).

3. Federal Non-Reserved Water Rights

Beyond federal reserved water rights or water rights under state law, is there any other way the federal government can satisfy its water needs? For example, if it has no claim to a federal reserved water right, may a federal land management agency appropriate unappropriated water (thus not disturbing any existing rights) if the kind of water right claimed by the United States is not recognized by state law? In 1979 the Interior Department Solicitor, Leo Krulitz, issued an opinion which claimed the existence of "federal non-reserved water rights." 86 I.D. 553 (1979). As its label suggested, this new federal right did not arise from a reservation of water, but rather from the actual use of water to carry out a federal program or purpose. In that respect, the right mimicked state law appropriative rights, for its foundation was the application of water to a beneficial use. But the Opinion argued that the right was not constrained by state law definitions of beneficial use. Thus, it could be used to protect an instream flow even if there were no federal reservation, and even in a state that did not recognize appropriations of instream flows. The federal non-reserved right concept provided a rationale to claim instream flows in support of national forest habitat, for example, where the *New Mexico* test for a federal reserved right could not be satisfied.

The basic legal argument to support federal non-reserved rights went like this: First, Congress has delegated its broad power to manage federal lands under the Property Clause to federal land managing agencies like the BLM. Second, when these agencies act to fulfill their statutorily prescribed federal land management responsibilities, they have, unless Congress provides otherwise, sufficient authority to meet these responsibilities. Therefore, if the requirements of state water law are an obstacle to effective exercise of the federal power, the supremacy clause empowers the federal agencies to override state water law.

Needless to say, the Krulitz opinion was not warmly received by the Western states, nor by commentators. See, e.g., Richard Simms, National Water Policy in the Wake of United States v. New Mexico, 20 Nat. Resources J. 1 (1980); Barry Vaughan, Federal Nonreserved Water Rights, 48 U. Chi. L. Rev. 758 (1981); A. Dan Tarlock & Sally Fairfax, Federal Proprietary Rights For Western Energy Development: An Analysis of a Red Herring, 3 J. Energy L. & Pol'y 1 (1982). The most trenchant objection to the Krulitz opinion was not the power it claimed, but that it did not satisfactorily demonstrate that Congress had actually delegated this power to federal land managing agencies in particular statutes, rather than deferring to state water law where no federal reserved right existed. A key issue was how to construe the water disclaimer in the Federal Land Policy and Management Act, which authorizes a wide variety of uses of the federal lands (such as livestock grazing, fish and wildlife, and recreation). That disclaimer (§ 701(g)–(h); 90 Stat. 2744) is quoted in the earlier discussion of reserved rights of the BLM at page 537.

The Krulitz non-reserved right claim was not long-lived.* A new Solicitor of the Interior rejected it in what came to be known as the Coldiron opinion. See 88 Interior Dec. 1055 (1981). Shortly thereafter the Department of Justice's Office of Legal Counsel issued a lengthy opinion affirming the Coldiron result. The Office of Legal Counsel left no doubt that federal power to preempt state water law was very broad, but said the key question was "not generally whether Congress has the power to establish federal rights to unappropriated water, but whether it has exercised that power." See Federal "Non–Reserved" Water Rights, 6 Op. Off. Legal Counsel 328, 362 (1982).

NOTES AND QUESTIONS

1. No federal statute expressly delegates to any land management agency the authority to establish water rights unilaterally as a matter of federal law. On the other hand, the organic statutes of the principal agencies all require, in varying language, that the agencies protect fish and wildlife, encourage outdoor recreation, and preserve watershed values.

---

* The same Solicitor's Opinion also dealt at length with federal reserved water rights of various Interior Department agencies; that portion of the Opinion, discussed earlier in this chapter, has had much longer staying power.

Given the traditional primacy of state control over water, does the BLM have delegated authority to set instream flows with a modern priority date? Does the Forest Service or the Park Service? Does the result change, for each of those agencies, when it is managing a wilderness area under the Wilderness Act? When it is managing a segment of a river under the Wild and Scenic Rivers Act?

2. A number of federal regulatory statutes such as the Endangered Species Act do not expressly create federal water rights, but the constraints they place on natural resources management and development can have the effect of "reserving" water for federally-mandated uses, apart from state law. See, e.g., Riverside Irr. Dist. v. Andrews, 758 F.2d 508 (10th Cir.1985); Carson–Truckee Water Conservancy Dist. v. Clark, 741 F.2d 257 (9th Cir.1984), cert. denied, 470 U.S. 1083 (1985) (Interior Department, in operating dam, may devote to endangered species protection all water not contracted for); Platte River Whooping Crane Critical Habitat Maintenance Trust v. FERC, 876 F.2d 109 (D.C.Cir.1989). See generally A. Dan Tarlock, LAW OF WATER RIGHTS AND RESOURCES § 9.23–9.36 (2001).

3. Other federal laws can implicate water use involving federal property, without giving rise to federal water rights claims. For example, in United States v. Vesterso, 828 F.2d 1234 (8th Cir.1987), the court upheld the conviction of local governmental officials for damaging federal property in waterfowl production easements by authorizing the draining of wetlands. The court held that a provision in the National Wildlife Refuge System Administration Act, 16 U.S.C. § 668dd(i) ("[n]othing in this Act shall constitute an express or implied claim or denial on the part of the Federal Government as to exemption from State water laws") did not protect the defendants, even if such draining was consistent with state water law. In Bijou Irr. Dist. v. Empire Club, 804 P.2d 175 (Colo.1991), the Colorado Supreme Court rejected the effort by the District to add recreation as a beneficial use for water stored in its reservoir, on the ground that such use was beyond the scope of the federal right of way granted to the District for the reservoir site.

4. Congress adopted a "federal non-reserved right" approach in legislation adopted in 2000 to expand the Great Sand Dunes National Monument in Colorado and convert it to a national park. Advancing scientific knowledge had demonstrated that the sand dunes ecosystem depended upon protecting the surface and groundwater resources, and water became an important issue as the proposal was being considered in Congress. In the end, Congress authorized the United States to secure a water right to protect the dunes that will be appropriated, not reserved, through the processes of state law and in accordance with the state law priority system. But the right will be defined according to the standard set in the federal statute—namely, whatever unappropriated surface and groundwater is shown necessary for protection of the dunes ecosystem. And, it will be held in the name of the National Park Service, even though state law requires a state agency to hold an instream flow water right. See 16 U.S.C. § 410hhh–7(b)(2). For a fuller description and discussion, and an argument that this approach to water rights has great potential for addressing the legitimate

needs of both the states and the federal land management agencies in future federal land conservation designations, see Leshy, supra, 4 Water L.Rev. 271, 288 (2001).

5.   For other examples of how federal agencies might protect water resources beyond asserting reserved rights, see Teresa Rice, Beyond Reserved Rights: Water Resource Protection for the Public Lands, 28 Idaho L. Rev. 715 (1992).

NOTE: THE FEDERAL RECLAMATION PROGRAM

Nineteenth century homestead policy initially dovetailed with the twentieth century reclamation policy, because more federal acreage was patented under the homestead laws after the Reclamation Act of 1902 took effect. The face of the West has been fundamentally reshaped by the large reclamation dams that supply subsidized federal water to western irrigators, large and small. See Chapter 2, supra pp. 98–101. Generally speaking, water rights for federal reclamation projects are obtained under state law, pursuant to section 8 of the Reclamation Act, 43 U.S.C. § 383, although exceptions to this deference may be created by "clear congressional directives." California v. United States, 438 U.S. 645 (1978), supra p. 512. A major exception is along the lower Colorado River, where federal statutes have been construed to give the Secretary of the Interior sweeping authority to allocate water to states and private users. See 438 U.S. at 674; Arizona v. California, 373 U.S. 546 (1963). Many federal reclamation projects have been at least partially located on federal land, and some major National Recreation Areas created by Congress have reclamation project reservoirs as their centerpiece; e.g., Lake Mead National Recreation Area and Glen Canyon National Recreation Area (Lake Powell). The federal reclamation program is treated in Amy Kelley–Pittman, Federal Reclamation Law, in Vol. 4 of Robert Beck, ed., WATERS AND WATER RIGHTS, pp. 375–419 (1991); see also Richard Wahl, MARKETS FOR FEDERAL WATER: SUBSIDIES, PROPERTY RIGHTS, AND THE BUREAU OF RECLAMATION (1989). Space and relevancy considerations prevent more extended treatment here.

C.   FEDERAL HYDROPOWER LICENSING AND FEDERAL LANDS

The federal government has had navigation-related responsibilities since the beginning of the Republic. The federal power over navigation is very broad and has been exercised almost from the Nation's founding. Gibbons v. Ogden, 22 U.S. (9 Wheat.) 1 (1824). The narrow authority to prevent obstructions to navigation in the Rivers and Harbors Act of 1899, 33 U.S.C. §§ 403–407, has grown into a large-scale series of programs for water resources regulation and flood control administered by several federal agencies.

The Federal Power Act, the last great Progressive Era piece of natural resources legislation, created the Federal Power Commission (now the

Federal Energy Regulatory Commission (FERC)) and gave it authority to license hydropower developments on navigable waters and tributaries thereto throughout the country. Such licenses were good for up to fifty years. Many of these licenses are for projects found wholly or partially on federal land, and from the beginning the Act has had special provisions to protect federal lands and other resources. The next case discusses one key provision, the so-called "mandatory conditioning" authority given to federal land management agencies in section 4(e) of the Act, 16 U.S.C. § 797(e).

Escondido Mutual Water Co. v. La Jolla Band of Mission Indians

Supreme Court of the United States, 1984.
466 U.S. 765.

■ JUSTICE WHITE delivered the opinion of the Court.

[FERC issued a new license to an existing hydropower facility located on or near several Indian reservations in southern California, but did not include in the license several conditions offered by the Secretary of the Interior. Section 4(e) of the Act authorizes the Commission

> To issue licenses ... for the purpose of constructing ... dams ... or other project works ... upon any part of the public lands and reservations of the United States ... Provided, That licenses shall be issued within any reservation only after a finding by the Commission that the license will not interfere or be inconsistent with the purpose for which such reservation was created or acquired, and shall be subject to and contain such conditions as the Secretary of the department under whose supervision such reservation falls shall deem necessary for the adequate protection and utilization of such reservations....

Another section of the Act defines "reservations" to mean "national forests, tribal lands embraced within Indian reservations, military reservations, and other lands and interests in lands owned by the United States, and withdrawn, reserved, or withheld from private appropriation and disposal under the public land laws...." 16 U.S.C. § 796(2). Thus, while the case concerned Indian reservations, the Court's opinion applies to non-Indian federal reservations as defined in the Act.] * * *

* * * [T]he Commission ruled that § 4(e) of the FPA did not require it to accept without modification conditions which the Secretary deemed necessary for the adequate protection and utilization of the reservations.[8] Accordingly, despite the Secretary's insistence, the Commission refused to prohibit the licensees from interfering with the Bands' use of a specified quantity of water, * * * [and o]ther conditions proposed by the Secretary were similarly rejected or modified. Second, [the Commission also ruled]

---

8. The Commission concluded that § 4(e) required it "to give great weight to the judgments and proposals of the Secretaries of the Interior and Agriculture" but that under § 10(a) it retained ultimate authority for determining "the extent to which such conditions will in fact be included in particular licenses." 6 FERC, at 61,414.

that its § 4(e) obligation in that respect applies only to reservations that are physically occupied by project facilities. * * *

* * * The mandatory nature of the language chosen by Congress appears to require that the Commission include the Secretary's conditions in the license even if it disagrees with them. Nonetheless, petitioners argue that an examination of the statutory scheme and legislative history of the Act shows that Congress could not have meant what it said. We disagree.

We first note the difficult nature of the task facing petitioners. Since it should be generally assumed that Congress expresses its purposes through the ordinary meaning of the words it uses, we have often stated that " '[a]bsent a clearly expressed legislative intention to the contrary, [statutory] language must ordinarily be regarded as conclusive.' " [citations omitted] Congress' apparent desire that the Secretary's conditions "shall" be included in the license must therefore be given effect unless there are clear expressions of legislative intent to the contrary.

Petitioners initially focus on the purpose of the legislation that became the relevant portion of the FPA. In 1920, Congress passed the Federal Water Power Act in order to eliminate the inefficiency and confusion caused by the "piecemeal, restrictive, negative approach" to licensing prevailing under prior law. * * * Prior to passage of the Act, the Secretaries of the Interior, War, and Agriculture each had authority to issue licenses for hydroelectric projects on lands under his respective jurisdiction. The Act centralized that authority by creating a Commission, consisting of the three Secretaries,[14] vested with exclusive authority to issue licenses. Petitioners contend that Congress could not have intended to empower the Secretary to require that conditions be included in the license over the objection of the Commission because that would frustrate the purpose of centralizing licensing procedures.

Congress was no doubt interested in centralizing federal licensing authority into one agency, but it is clear that it did not intend to relieve the Secretaries of all responsibility for ensuring that reservations under their respective supervision were adequately protected. In a memorandum explaining the administration bill, the relevant portion of which was enacted without substantive change,[15] O.C. Merrill, one of the chief draftsmen of the Act and later the first Commission Secretary, explained that creation of the Commission "will not interfere with the special responsibilities which the several Departments have over the National Forests, public lands and navigable rivers." Memorandum on Water Power Legislation from O.C.

---

14. In 1930, the Commission was reorganized as a five-person body, independent from the Secretaries. Act of June 23, 1930, ch. 572, 46 Stat. 797.

15. Between 1914 and 1917, four bills dealing with the licensing of hydroelectric projects were introduced into Congress, none successfully. In 1918, a bill prepared by the Secretaries of War, the Interior, and Agriculture, at the direction of President Wilson, was introduced. H.R.8716, 65th Cong., 2d Sess. (1918). It contained the language of the § 4(e) proviso basically as it is now framed. Because of the press of World War I and other concerns, the legislation was not enacted until 1920. See J. Kerwin, Federal Water–Power Legislation 217–263 (1926).

Merrill, Chief Engineer, Forest Service, dated October 31, 1917, App. 371. With regard to what became § 4(e), he wrote:

"4. Licenses for power sites within the National Forests to be subject to such provisions for the protection of the Forests as the Secretary of Agriculture may deem necessary. Similarly, for parks and other reservations under the control of the Departments of the Interior and of War. Plans of structures involving navigable streams to be subject to the approval of the Secretary of War.

"This provision is for the purpose of preserving the administrative responsibility of each of the three Departments over lands and other matters within their exclusive jurisdiction." Id., at 373–374.

* * * It is thus clear enough that while Congress intended that the Commission would have exclusive authority to issue all licenses, it wanted the individual Secretaries to continue to play the major role in determining what conditions would be included in the license in order to protect the resources under their respective jurisdictions. The legislative history concerning § 4(e) plainly supports the conclusion that Congress meant what it said when it stated that the license "shall ... contain such conditions as the Secretary ... shall deem necessary for the adequate protection and utilization of such reservations." * * *

Petitioners next argue that a literal reading of the conditioning proviso of § 4(e) cannot be squared with other portions of the statutory scheme. In particular, they note that the same proviso that grants the Secretary the authority to qualify the license with the conditions he deems necessary also provides that the Commission must determine that "the license will not interfere or be inconsistent with the purpose for which such reservation was created or acquired." 16 U.S.C. § 797(e). Requiring the Commission to include the Secretary's conditions in the license over its objection, petitioners maintain, is inconsistent with granting the Commission the power to determine that no interference or inconsistency will result from issuance of the license because it will allow the Secretary to "veto" the decision reached by the Commission. * * *

This argument is unpersuasive because it assumes the very question to be decided. All parties agree that there are limits on the types of conditions that the Secretary can require to be included in the license:[17] the Secretary has no power to veto the Commission's decision to issue a license and hence the conditions he insists upon must be reasonably related to the protection of the reservation and its people. The real question is whether the Commission is empowered to decide when the Secretary's conditions exceed the permissible limits. Petitioners' argument assumes that the Commission has the authority to make that decision. However, the statutory language and legislative history conclusively indicate that it does not; the Commission "shall" include in the license the conditions the Secretary deems necessary. It is then up to the courts of appeals to determine whether the conditions are valid.

---

17. Even the Secretary concedes that the conditions must be "reasonable and sup- ported by evidence in the record." Brief for Secretary of the Interior 37.

Petitioners contend that such a scheme of review is inconsistent with traditional principles of judicial review of administrative action. If the Commission is required to include the conditions in the license even though it does not agree with them, petitioners argue, the courts of appeals will not be in a position to grant deference to the Commission's findings and conclusions because those findings and conclusions will not be included in the license. However, that is apparently exactly what Congress intended. If the Secretary concludes that the conditions are necessary to protect the reservation, the Commission is required to adopt them as its own, and the court is obligated to sustain them if they are reasonably related to that goal, otherwise consistent with the FPA, and supported by substantial evidence.[20] The fact that in reality it is the Secretary's, and not the Commission's, judgment to which the court is giving deference is not surprising since the statute directs the Secretary, and not the Commission, to decide what conditions are necessary for the adequate protection of the reservation.[21] There is nothing in the statute or the review scheme to indicate that Congress wanted the Commission to second-guess the Secretary on this matter.[22]

---

20. Of course, the Commission is not required to argue in support of the conditions if it objects to them. Indeed, it is free to express its disagreement with them, not only in connection with the issuance of the license but also on review. Similarly, the Commission can refuse to issue a license if it concludes that, as conditioned, the license should not issue. In either event, the license applicant can seek review of the conditions in the court of appeals [bypassing the federal district courts], but the court is to sustain the conditions if they are consistent with law and supported by the evidence presented to the Commission, either by the Secretary or other interested parties. 16 U.S.C. § 825l(b).

We note that in the unlikely event that none of the parties to the licensing proceeding seeks review, the conditions will go into effect notwithstanding the Commission's objection to them since the Commission is not authorized to seek review of its own decisions. The possibility that this might occur does not, however, dissuade us from interpreting the statute in accordance with its plain meaning. Congress apparently decided that if no party was interested in the differences between the Commission and the Secretary, the dispute would best be resolved in a nonjudicial forum.

21. Petitioners also contend that the Secretary's authority to impose conditions on the license is inconsistent with the Commission's authority and responsibility under § 10(a) to determine that "the project adopted ... will be best adapted to a compre-

hensive plan ... for the improvement and utilization of water-power development, and for other beneficial public uses." 16 U.S.C. § 803(a). Our discussion of the alleged conflict between the Commission's authority to make its "no interference or inconsistency" determination and the Secretary's conditioning authority applies with equal force to this contention. The ultimate decision whether to issue the license belongs to the Commission, but the Secretary's proposed conditions must be included if the license issues. Any conflict between the Commission and the Secretary with respect to whether the conditions are consistent with the statute must be resolved initially by the courts of appeals, not the Commission.

Petitioners' assertion that the conditions proposed by the Secretary in this case were outside the Commission's authority to adopt goes to the validity of the conditions, an issue not before this Court. It may well be that the conditions imposed by the Secretary are inconsistent with the provisions of the FPA and that they are therefore invalid (something we do not decide), but that issue is not for the Commission to decide in the first instance but is reserved for the court of appeals at the instance of the licensees and with the participation of the Commission if it is inclined to present its views.

22. Petitioners also contend that the Commission's longstanding interpretation of § 4(e) is entitled to deference, citing language from its early decisions. E.g., *Pigeon River*

In short, nothing in the legislative history or statutory scheme is inconsistent with the plain command of the statute that licenses issued within a reservation by the Commission pursuant to § 4(e) "shall be subject to and contain such conditions as the Secretary . . . shall deem necessary for the adequate protection and utilization of such reservations." Since the Commission failed to comply with this statutory command when it issued the license in this case, the Court of Appeals correctly reversed its decision in this respect.

The Court of Appeals also concluded that the Commission's § 4(e) obligations to accept the Secretary's proposed conditions and to make findings as to whether the license is consistent with the reservation's purpose applied to the Pala, Yuima, and Pauma Reservations even though no licensed facilities were located on these reservations. Petitioners contend that this conclusion is erroneous. We agree.

Again, the statutory language is informative and largely dispositive. * * * If a project is licensed "within" any reservation, the Commission must make a "no interference or inconsistency" finding with respect to "such" reservation, and the Secretary may impose conditions for the protection of "such" reservation. Nothing in the section requires the Commission to make findings about, or the Secretary to impose conditions to protect, any reservation other than the one within which project works are located. The section imposes no obligation on the Commission or power on the Secretary with respect to reservations that may somehow be affected by, but will contain no part of, the licensed project works.

The Court of Appeals, however, purported to discover an ambiguity in the term "within." Positing that the term "reservations" includes not only tribal lands but also tribal water rights, the Court of Appeals reasoned that since a project could not be "within" a water right, the term must have a meaning other than its literal one. This effort to circumvent the plain meaning of the statute by creating an ambiguity where none exists is unpersuasive.

There is no doubt that "reservations" include "interests in lands owned by the United States" [quoting 16 U.S.C. § 796(2)] and that for many purposes water rights are considered to be interests in lands. See 1 R. Clark, Waters and Water Rights § 53.1 p. 345 (1967). But it does not follow that Congress intended the "reservations" spoken of in § 4(e) to include water rights. The section deals with project works to be located "upon" and "within" a reservation. As the Court of Appeals itself indicated, the section does tend to "paint a geographical picture in the mind of the reader," 692 F.2d, at 1236, and we find the Court of Appeals' and respondents' construc-

---

Lumber Co., 1 F.P.C. 206, 209 (1935); Southern California Edison Co., 8 F.P.C. 364, 386 (1949). Petitioners concede, however, that the Commission never actually rejected any of the Secretary's conditions until 1975. Pacific Gas & Electric Co., 53 F.P.C. 523, 526 (1975). Even then, the issue was not squarely presented because there was some question whether § 4(e) even applied in that proceeding. Ibid. It is therefore far from clear that the Commission's interpretation is a longstanding one. More importantly, an agency's interpretation, even if well established, cannot be sustained if, as in this case, it conflicts with the clear language and legislative history of the statute.

tion of the section to be quite untenable. Congress intended the obligation of the Commission and the conditioning power of the Secretary to apply only with respect to the specific reservation upon which any project works were to be located and not to other reservations that might be affected by the project.

The Court of Appeals sought to bolster its conclusion by noting that a literal reading of the term "within" would leave a gap in the protection afforded the Bands by the FPA because "a project may turn a potentially useful reservation into a barren waste without ever crossing it in the geographical sense—e.g., by diverting the waters which would otherwise flow through or percolate under it." Ibid. This is an unlikely event, for in this respect the Bands are adequately protected by other provisions of the statutory scheme. First, the Bands cannot be deprived of any water to which they have a legal right. The Commission is expressly forbidden to adjudicate water rights, 16 U.S.C. § 821, and the license applicant must submit satisfactory evidence that he has obtained sufficient water rights to operate the project authorized in the license, 16 U.S.C. § 802(b). Second, if the Bands are using water, the rights to which are owned by the license applicant, the Commission is empowered to require that the license applicant continue to let the Bands use this water as a condition of the license if the Commission determines that the Bands' use of the water constitutes an overriding beneficial public use. 16 U.S.C. § 803(a). * * * The Bands' interest in the continued use of the water will accordingly be adequately protected without requiring the Commission to comply with § 4(e) every time one of the reservations might be affected by a proposed project.** *

The scheme crafted by Congress in this respect is sufficiently clear to require us to hold that the Commission must make its "no inconsistency or interference" determination and include the Secretary's conditions in the license only with respect to projects located "within" the geographical boundaries of a federal reservation. * * *

NOTES AND QUESTIONS

1. What are the substantive limits on the Secretary's authority to prescribe conditions and insist that they be included in the license? Suppose a hydro facility located on federal land diverts water out of a river, dewatering it. The water is returned to the river downstream from the federal reservation. Could the Secretary impose a condition that requires the licensee to limit the amount of water diverted, in order to maintain a minimum level of streamflow to protect the environment of the federal reservation?

2. May the Secretary impose such a condition if the diversion limitation so interferes with the economics of the project that it makes it unprofitable? Does the licensee have any recourse? Where? With the Commission? The Court of Appeals? The Congress? Who ultimately decides whether such conditions are within the Secretary's statutory authority?

3. What are the geographic limits on the Secretary's conditioning authority? When is a project license issued "within any reservation," in

terms of the statute? Consider these variations on the example in paragraph 1: (a) The diversion facility is located upstream from the boundary of the federal reservation, but the diverted water is transported across the federal reservation in a pipe. (b) All the project facilities are located downstream from federally reserved land, but the reservoir behind the dam backs up occasionally into a federal reservation. (c) All project facilities are located upstream of federally reserved land, but the operation of the facility occasionally releases high volumes of water that inundate a downstream federal reservation. (d) The project facilities are all located in a national forest, but a downstream national park, which contains no project facilities, is adversely affected by project diversions. (With respect to this last variation, see the third paragraph from the end of the excerpted opinion.)

4.   The Court made clear that the Secretary's conditioning authority does not extend to protect streamflow where the project is not within a federal reservation, and offered reasons why the downstream reservations may be "adequately protected by other provisions of the statutory scheme." If a downstream national park (which does not contain any project facilities) is threatened by hydropower project diversions upstream, what other means does it have to protect itself? Might a federal reserved water right protect it? How, and under what conditions?

5.   Can the agency administering the reservation craft its § 4(e) conditions for mandatory inclusion in the license without any process? Does NEPA apply to its decisions on these conditions? (NEPA clearly applies to FERC, which routinely complies with it in licensing proceedings.) Does the agency have any obligation to consult with the FERC, the license applicant, or the public in formulating the conditions? Should it as a matter of policy?

6.   The Federal Energy Regulatory Commission is an independent regulatory agency, part of the so-called fourth branch of government. It has authority to represent itself in court, but when matters in which it is involved get to the Supreme Court, if its recommended position is in conflict with those of other parts of the Executive Branch, the Solicitor General of the United States decides what the position of the U.S. will be before the court. In *Escondido*, however, the Solicitor General permitted both the Commission and Interior to appear before the court, arguing inconsistent positions.

7.   Look closely at the definition of "reservation" in the Act, quoted in the bracketed introduction to the opinion. As discussed on p. 536 supra, most federal land managed by the Bureau of Land Management is not considered "reserved" for purposes of the federal reserved water rights doctrine. But might it be considered "reserved" under this definition? The Solicitor of the Department of the Interior concluded, in an opinion issued in January 2001, that the answer was yes, because once BLM land was withdrawn generally from disposal (as President Roosevelt did in the mid–1930s), it qualified for "reservation" status under he Federal Power Act, even if it didn't for purposes of the federal reserved water rights doctrine.

Two other parts of the Federal Power Act give federal fish agencies an important role in federal hydropower licensing, on and off federal lands. They are explored in the following case.

American Rivers, et al. v. Federal Energy Regulatory Commission

United States Court of Appeals for the Ninth Circuit, 1999.
201 F.3d 1186.

■ Before: LEAVY, MCKEOWN, and WARDLAW, CIRCUIT JUDGES.

■ WARDLAW, CIRCUIT JUDGE:

At stake in these consolidated petitions is the continued operation of two hydroelectric power facilities located in Lane County, Oregon along a twenty-five mile stretch of the McKenzie River. The petitioners, a coalition of conservation/environmental organizations and the Oregon Department of Fish and Wildlife, challenge the decision of the Federal Energy Regulatory Commission ("FERC" or the "Commission") to reissue a hydropower license to the incumbent licensee, the Eugene Water and Electric Board ("EWEB"). Specifically, the petitioners contend that the Commission granted the disputed license * * * in violation of sections 10(j) and 18 of the FPA.

The license under review authorizes the continued operation of the 14.5–megawatt Leaburg Hydroelectric Project and the 8–megawatt Walterville Hydroelectric Project for a duration of 40 years. * * * The Leaburg and Walterville facilities have operated since 1930 and 1911, respectively. * * * After the licenses expired, EWEB managed both developments under separate annual licenses by operation of FPA section 15(a) [which directs the Commission to issue annual licenses to the existing licensee on the same terms as the original license while the renewal application is pending].

The Leaburg development, the project's upstream facility, consists of a dam, canal, powerhouse facilities, a tailrace, and a power substation. The dam creates a fifty-seven acre backwater called Leaburg Lake which extends approximately 1.5 miles upstream. On each side of the dam are fish ladders, only one of which is operational. On the upstream side of the dam, intake gates divert water through a downstream migrant fish screen into the five-mile Leaburg power canal. The diverted water passes through the power plant forebay into the two-turbine Leaburg powerhouse. The water returns to the McKenzie River through a 1,100–foot tailrace. The bypassed reach of the McKenzie between the entrance to the Leaburg canal and the point where the diverted water rejoins the river is 5.8 miles long.

Six miles downstream, headworks divert water from the McKenzie into the unscreened, four-mile Walterville power canal. The Walterville canal feeds into a single-turbine powerhouse from which water returns to the McKenzie through a two-mile tailrace. The Walterville canal bypasses a 7.3 mile stretch of the McKenzie.

The Director issued the disputed license on March 24, 1997, pursuant to the FPA * * * [which] authorizes the Commission to issue such licenses subject to conditions that the Commission finds best suited for power development and other public uses of the nation's waters. In the mid–1980's, Congress amended these provisions to realize an increased sensitivity to environmental concerns, directing the Commission to devote greater consideration to a project's overall effect on fish and wildlife. *See* Electric Consumers Protection Act of 1986 ("ECPA"). * * * The new license reflects many of these concerns and would require EWEB to construct several new facilities and provide other measures for the benefit and protection of the fish populations that pass through and reside in the project area.[7] From a power standpoint, the new license authorizes EWEB to increase the project's generation capacity from 22.5 megawatts to 23.2 megawatts. Under the terms of the license, EWEB would achieve this increased generation capacity by raising the water level at Leaburg Lake by 18 inches, constructing fixed sill dams or other diversion structures at the head of the Walterville power canal, replacing the turbine runners at both powerhouses, and excavating the Walterville tailrace. The license also would increase the minimum flows[8] in the bypassed reaches below the diversions of both developments to 1,000 cubic feet per second.

* * * The Commission's staff * * * examined the conditions submitted by the state and federal fish and wildlife agencies under color of FPA sections 10(j) and 18.[10] The staff adopted many of the fifty-six recommendations designated pursuant to section 10(j). The final environmental impact statement, however, stated that twenty-one of the fifty-six recommendations were outside the scope of section 10(j). The Commission's staff concluded that these recommendations either did not serve to protect fish and wildlife resources or conferred final authority over the level of enhancement and project operations upon the agencies rather than the Commission. The final environmental impact statement nevertheless considered and adopted many of these submissions under FPA sections 10(a) and 4(e) which grant the Commission broader latitude to balance environ-

---

7. For instance, the license orders EWEB to install a new fish screen at the Walterville power canal intake to enhance the passage of downstream migrating fish. EWEB also must construct a tailrace barrier at the Leaburg development, replace the tailrace barrier at Walterville, and modify the left-bank fish ladder and reconstruct a newly designed right-bank ladder at the Leaburg dam. The license also requires EWEB to operate the project according to scheduled ramping rates designed to prevent the stranding of fish. In addition, EWEB is to augment spawning gravel downstream of Leaburg dam to enhance salmonid spawning gravel and monitor the success of fish habitat enhancement measures.

8. Minimum instream flow represents the amount "of water that must remain in the bypassed section of the stream and that thus remains unavailable to drive the generators." California v. Federal Energy Regulatory Comm'n, 495 U.S. 490, 494 (1990).

10. Under section 10(j) of the FPA, the Commission may impose conditions on licensees "based on recommendations received pursuant to the Fish and Wildlife Coordination Act (16 U.S.C. § 661 et seq.) from the National Marine Fisheries Service, the United States Fish and Wildlife Service, and State fish and wildlife agencies." 16 U.S.C. § 803(j)(1) (1994). Section 18 of the FPA requires the Commission to include in a license "fishways" prescribed by the Secretaries of Interior or Commerce. *See* 16 U.S.C. § 811 (1994).

mental and development interests. The Commission's staff also recommended the outright adoption of the federal agencies' section 18 conditions which required implementation of fish ladders and fish screens but determined that the remaining conditions lodged under color of section 18 did not constitute "fishway prescriptions." Again, the Commission analyzed and adopted many of these measures under sections 10(a) and 4(e).[11] * * *

Two months after the section 10(j) dispute resolution meeting between the resource agencies and Commission staff, the Secretary of Interior filed modifications to its section 18 prescriptions for the Director's consideration. These modified prescriptions met with substantially the same results as the resource agencies' earlier submissions. Like the Commission staff before him, the Director found that the Secretary's prescriptions relating to fish ladders and fish screens constituted section 18 fishways but nevertheless did not incorporate the submissions as prescribed, electing instead to establish a plan under which EWEB would "consult with the agencies in developing final designs and monitoring plans for Commission approval." As to the remaining prescriptions, the Director held that the submissions, even as modified, were beyond the scope of section 18. The Director explicitly stated for the record the basis for the rejection or reclassification of most of the submissions. * * *

* * * [P]etitioners challenge the Commission's construction of the FPA, raising two questions under related, but markedly different, statutory sections. These challenges again engender *de novo* review and require two distinct iterations of the *Chevron* standard. First, we consider whether the FPA authorizes the Commission to decide that a fish and wildlife agency recommendation submitted pursuant to section 10(j) does not qualify for treatment under that section. Second, we examine whether the Commission may reject a "fishway prescription" proposed by the Secretary of Commerce or the Secretary of Interior under FPA section 18. These are not inconsequential questions. Both questions present this Court with issues of first impression in our Circuit, and both beget answers bearing significantly on the hydropower relicensing process.

As previously explained, the FPA establishes an elaborate regulatory regime which charges the Commission with responsibility to balance the interests of hydropower licensees and other participants in the licensing process. The processes required by section 10(j) represent a vital part of that regime. Subsection 10(j)(1), as amended by the ECPA, instructs:

(1) That in order to adequately and equitably protect, mitigate damages to, and enhance, fish and wildlife (including related spawning

11. These measures included conditions that recommended: imposition of fish mortality standards at the fish screens of Leaburg and Walterville and at the Leaburg rollgates; construction of tailrace barriers; delays in raising the Leaburg Lake water level; delays in the construction of diversion structures at Walterville; the salvage of fish prior to any new construction at Walterville's tailrace; annual inspection of the Walterville tailrace; agency control over final design and monitoring of fishways; and agency enforcement of the licensee's duty to maintain fishways in efficient operating condition. The Director eventually adopted many of the reclassified recommendations or ordered EWEB to conduct studies regarding their feasibility.

grounds and habitat) affected by the development, operation, and management of the project, each license issued under this subchapter shall include conditions for such protection, mitigation, and enhancement. Subject to paragraph (2), such conditions shall be based on recommendations received pursuant to the Fish and Wildlife Coordination Act (16 U.S.C. 661 et seq.) from the National Marine Fisheries Service, the United States Fish and Wildlife Service, and State fish and wildlife agencies.

16 U.S.C. § 803(j)(1). Subsection 10(j)(2), however, specifies that the Commission should attempt to reconcile agency recommendations with the requirements of the FPA. *See* 16 U.S.C. § 803(j)(2). If, after giving due weight to these recommendations, the Commission does not adopt them, in whole or in part, the statute requires the Commission to publish the following findings (with a basis for each of the findings):

(A) A finding that adoption of such recommendation is inconsistent with the purposes and requirements of this subchapter or with other applicable provisions of law.

(B) A finding that the conditions selected by the Commission [protect and mitigate damage to fish and wildlife].

Id.

Here, our *Chevron* analysis begins and ends with the statute itself. We detect in section 10(j) the type of clear congressional mandate that suffices to curtail a *Chevron* query at step one. We are not the first court to do so. In *National Wildlife Federation v. Federal Energy Regulatory Commission,* 912 F.2d 1471 (D.C.Cir.1990), the District of Columbia Circuit affirmed a Commission order which had rejected agency recommendations submitted as section 10(j) conditions. Although these recommendations concerned a proposal not properly before the Commission, the court nonetheless concluded that:

[W]hile the Commission must pay due regard to such recommendations, [section 10(j)] cannot be read to force upon the Commission the burden of strict acceptance of each and every proper recommendation. While the Commission must address each recommendation, the discretion ultimately vests in the Commission as to how to incorporate each recommendation.

Id. at 1480; *see also California ex rel. State Water Resources Control Bd. v. Federal Energy Regulatory Comm'n,* 966 F.2d 1541, 1550 (9th Cir.1992) (noting that the ECPA amendments require the Commission "to demonstrate why conditions proposed by fish and wildlife agencies should not be included in a license"). * * *

* * * Section 10(j) and section 4(e), the provision at issue in *Escondido,* set forth very different roles for the Commission to play in the hydropower licensing process. Congress provided in subsection 10(j)(2) a mechanism for the Commission to employ when it disagrees with a submitted agency condition, unlike the pre-license certification scheme Congress set forth in FPA section 4(e). That mechanism, the publication of findings, clearly qualifies the mandatory clause of subsection 10(j)(1) and is expressly

contemplated in the phrase "[s]ubject to paragraph (2)" that prefaces the mandatory language. The ordinary meaning of "subject to" includes "governed or affected by." *Black's Law Dictionary* 1425 (6th ed.1990) * * *. We therefore interpret "subject to paragraph (2)" to mean precisely what it says: subsection 10(j)(1) is governed or affected by subsection 10(j)(2). Moreover, were we to read subsection 10(j)(1) as conferring final authority over the section 10(j) process upon the resource agencies, we impermissibly would be making surplusage of subsection 10(j)(2). * * * In sum, the divergent structures of § 10(j) and § 4(e), the plain meaning of the prefatory phrase "subject to," and the abecedarian principle of giving effect to every subsection convince us that *Escondido* is inapposite here.

* * * In denying the petitions insofar as they challenge the Commission's understanding of its statutory mandate under section 10(j), our holding is narrow. We conclude that section 10(j) clearly vests in the Commission the discretion as to how or whether it will incorporate a section 10(j) recommendation received from a listed agency. As noted above, we express no opinion on the merits of the Commission's environmental findings. Moreover, we stress that nothing we have said should be construed as eviscerating the pro-environmental object beneath the ECPA amendments. The Commission must afford "*significant* deference to recommendations made by state (and federal) fish and wildlife agencies for the 'protection, mitigation, and enhancement' of fish and wildlife." *Kelley* [v. FERC], 96 F.3d at 1486 (emphasis added). Nevertheless, Congress clearly has ordained that this deference must yield to the Commission's reasoned judgment in those instances where the parties cannot agree. Under *Chevron*, "that is the end of the matter." 467 U.S. at 842. * * *

Section 18 directs that the Commission "shall require the construction, maintenance, and operation by a licensee at its own expense of . . . such fishways as may be prescribed by the Secretary of the Interior or the Secretary of Commerce, as appropriate."* 16 U.S.C. § 811. Conspicuously absent from this provision is a qualifying clause, such as the one in FPA subsection 10(j)(2), which expressly enables the Commission to reject a recommendation submitted under color of section 10(j). Ignoring this structural distinction, the Commission argues that we must not disturb its section 18 "findings" because the Commission fully explained on the record its reasons for rejecting the fishway prescriptions. This argument misses the mark. Section 18 on its face simply does not contemplate the two-pronged approach set forth in subsection 10(j)(2). Although the presence of a qualifying clause in subsection 10(j)(2) does not foreclose the Commission's professed authority to reject fishways prescribed by either the Secretary of Interior or Secretary of Commerce, the absence of a similar provision in section 18 suggests more than mere legislative oversight. Clearly, if Congress had wanted findings under section 18, it knew how to ask for them. * * *

Taking a different tack, the Commission cautions that its statutory mission would be compromised if it were left without authority to deter-

---

* [Eds. Interior and Commerce divide jurisdiction over various kinds of fish, which is why the statute refers to them both in § 18]

mine whether a submission prescribes a fishway or instead constitutes a recommendation more appropriately evaluated under FPA sections 10(j) or 10(a). * * * [T]he Commission attempts to distinguish *Escondido,* insisting that its reasoning does not apply when what the Secretaries prescribe does not constitute a fishway.

The Commission's efforts to distinguish *Escondido* cannot withstand scrutiny. * * * [Among other things, t]he Commission * * * relies upon a strained reading of a post-ECPA congressional clarification of the Commission's authority regarding fishways contained in the Energy Policy Act of 1992 (the "Energy Act"), 106 Stat. 2776 (1992). In the Energy Act, Congress explicitly considered and rejected amendments to section 18 that would have limited the Department of the Interior's authority to prescribe fishways. The Commission had asked Congress for a statutory grant of authority to consider and balance the Department of Interior's recommendations for fishways with other values. * * * Congress rejected this approach. More significantly, Congress overturned the Commission's own rulemaking efforts to define fishway prescriptions. *See* 106 Stat. 3008 (" § 1701(b)"). The Commission initially had adopted a restrictive definition of fishways that included only facilities "used for the upstream passage of fish" through a hydropower project. 56 Fed.Reg. 23,108, 23,146 (May 20, 1991). In response to public outcry over this definition, the Commission subsequently amended its rule on rehearing to embrace both upstream and downstream passage. *See* 56 Fed.Reg. 61,137, 61,140–45 (Dec. 2, 1991). Congress promptly rejected and overturned the amended regulatory definition as still too narrow, providing:

> The definition of the term "fishway" contained in 18 C.F.R. 4.30(b)(9)(iii), as in effect on the date of enactment of this Act [Oct. 24, 1992], is vacated without prejudice to any definition or interpretation by rule of the term 'fishway' by the Federal Energy Regulatory Commission for purposes of implementing section 18 of the Federal Power Act. Provided, that any future *definition* promulgated by regulatory rulemaking shall have no force or effect unless concurred in by the Secretary of the Interior and the Secretary of Commerce: Provided further, That the items which may constitute a 'fishway' under section 18 for the safe and timely upstream and downstream passage of fish shall be limited to physical structures, facilities, or devices necessary to maintain all life stages of such fish, and project operations and measures related to such structures, facilities, or devices which are necessary to ensure the effectiveness of such structures, facilities, or devices for such fish.

§ 1701(b) (emphasis in original).

Despite this explicit rejection of the Commission's proposed fishways definitions, the Commission seizes upon a perceived ambiguity in the limiting clause at the end of § 1701(b) which sets forth the items which may constitute a fishway. The Commission argues that this final clause does not specify which agency is to determine whether a given prescription "constitutes a fishway under section 18." In light of this omission, the Commission, EWEB, and industry amici extensively cite the legislative history, attempting to educe from the record some indicia of support for their position. * * * The Commission has gone too far. The Energy Act conference report * * * clearly stated that the roles of the Commission and the Secretaries of Interior and Commerce "would continue to be as [they were] prior to [the passage of § 1701]. Nothing in this amendment is intended to limit the roles or authorities of either the Secretaries or the Commission." H.R. Conf. Rep. No. 102–1018, at 393. As noted above, prior to the passage of § 1701(b), *Escondido* delineated the respective roles of the Secretaries and the Commission under the statute. In other words, no matter how selectively the Commission quotes the legislative record and no matter how many inferential deductions it makes, there is no escaping the simple fact that *Escondido* has set forth the analytic framework which authoritatively animates the statutory scheme, both then and now.

* * * We, too, find *Escondido* controlling in the section 18 context and therefore hold that the Commission may not modify, reject, or reclassify any prescriptions submitted by the Secretaries under color of section 18. Where the Commission disagrees with the scope of a fishway prescription, it may withhold a license altogether or voice its concerns in the court of appeals, but at the administrative stages, "it is not the Commission's role to judge the validity of [the Secretary's] position-substantially or procedurally."

We note the Commission's argument that an unqualified reservation of prescription authority for the Secretaries invites a unilateral fishways determination by two agencies which do not concern themselves with the delicate economic versus environmental balancing required in every licensing. We acknowledge, as pointed out by the Commission, that the prescribing federal agencies have not promulgated regulations to guide license applicants and others in utilizing this section of the law. *See Hydroelectric Relicensing Procedures: Oversight Hearing Before the Subcomm. on Water and Power of the Senate Comm. on Energy and Natural Resources,* 105th Cong. 8 (1997) (testimony of Jerry L. Sabattis, Hydro Licensing Coordinator, Niagara Mohawk Power Corp.) ("Interior has never developed any regulations, procedures or standards for implementing Section 18 and has no internal appeal procedures for dealing with disputes which may arise."); 138 Cong. Rec. H11427–01 (daily ed. Oct. 5, 1992) (statement of Rep. Dingell) ("[I]t is somewhat disturbing that after so many years that [sic] the fishery agencies themselves have not prescribed regulations on their own initiative."). Nevertheless, Congress was acutely aware of the Secretaries' omission when it passed § 1701 and * * * [even if] we might disagree with Congressional failure to require such regulations, * * * [that] does not authorize us to rewrite section 18.

* * * We deny the petitions insofar as they challenge * * * FERC's authority to reclassify, reject, or modify section 10(j) recommendations. Nevertheless, in light of the statutory scheme, its legislative history, and the precedent which binds this Court, we grant the petitions to the extent they challenge the Commission's construction of section 18.

NOTES AND QUESTIONS

1. Note the specific measures recommended by the fish agencies that it characterized as "fishways." See footnote 11 in the court's opinion. Do all of these fit the definition of "fishway" enacted by Congress in the 1992 Energy Policy Act, quoted in the court's opinion? Are they related to "structures, facilities, or devices" for fish? Who makes this determination? The fish agencies? FERC? The court of appeals?

2. What does the Commission need to show in order to reject Interior Department recommendations under section 10(j)? Is it enough that the recommended conditions are expensive to implement? That their costs outweigh their benefits? That they will reduce licensee profits?

3. Notice that the fish agencies have never adopted regulations, standards or procedures for implementing § 18, which has been criticized, as recounted in the penultimate paragraph of the court's opinion. The same is true regarding Interior Department process for formulating § 4(e) conditions; that is, it is entirely informal. There are no formal procedures for consultation and no opportunities for administrative appeals. Do licensees have a due process argument that they must be consulted in the formulation of such conditions?

4. Is all this complexity in the licensing scheme good policy? The Commission cannot fail to include license conditions the Interior Secretary* recommends under § 4(e), or fishways recommended by fish agencies under § 18, and yet the Commission must make its own determination as to whether licensing the project is a good idea, environmentally or otherwise. Arguing that it, and not the Secretary of the Interior, should have ultimate authority over these projects, the Commission has repeatedly tried, so far without success, to persuade Congress to overturn this aspect of *Escondido*. Environmentalists, tribes and others have resisted cutting back on the Interior Department's role.

5. The Federal Power Act also poses interesting issues of state versus federal authority. Most prominently, the always delicate interplay of federal authority and state water rights is handled quite differently in the context of hydropower licensing from how it is handled in federal reclamation law. This is so even though section 27 of the Federal Power Act, 16 U.S.C. § 821, is textually very similar to section 8 of the Reclamation Act. Distinguishing California v. United States, supra, the Supreme Court has reaffirmed that FERC need not follow or give deference to state water law in licensing hydroelectric power projects. California v. FERC, 495 U.S. 490 (1990). See, e.g., Michael Blumm, Federalism, Hydroelectric Licensing and the Future of Minimum Streamflows after California v. Federal Energy Regulatory Commission, 21 Envt'l L. 113 (1991). On the other hand, a federal hydropower licensee must obtain a state certification under § 401 of the Clean Water Act before FERC can issue a hydropower license. See PUD No. 1 v. Washington Dept. of Ecology, 511 U.S. 700 (1994).

* If the reservation involved is national forest land, the Secretary of Agriculture has authority to formulate conditions under section 4(e).

"REOPENER" CLAUSES, PROFITABILITY, AND RELATED ISSUES

At issue in Wisconsin Public Service Corp. v. Federal Energy Regulatory Commission, 32 F.3d 1165 (7th Cir.1994), was whether FERC could include "reopener" clauses in licenses it issued, providing that "[a]uthority is reserved to the Commission to require the licensee to construct, operate, and maintain, or provide for the construction, operation, and maintenance of such fishways as may be prescribed by the Secretary of the Interior pursuant to Section 18 of the Federal Power Act." FERC (by a vote of 3–2) included such clauses in two licenses, and the licensees sought review in the court of appeals. Excerpts follow:

A fundamental objection of the petitioners to the Commission's reservation of fishways under the authority of Section 18 is that this invites a unilateral determination by another agency, the Department of the Interior, based upon its view of some future conservation or wildlife need, which is not balanced against the allegedly delicate economics of these water power projects. For example, the Commission staff estimated that the cost of energy from the Otter Rapids Project would be only two-tenths of a mill ($.0002) per kilowatt hour (or about $1,000 a year) less than alternative electric energy available in the region. Therefore, there would be no reasonable basis upon which the putative project licensee could estimate the future impact of a requirement to install fishways on the economics of the project. Hence, there was no rational basis on which the putative licensee could determine whether to accept the license with a fishway reservation.

This is certainly not an inconsequential issue. But * * * there can be no guarantee of profitability of water power projects under the Federal Power Act; profitability is at risk from a number of variable factors, and values other than profitability require appropriate consideration.

* * * The petitioners here contend that the Commission's reservation with respect to fishways to be exercised (or not) at some unspecified date in the future and to provide for the installation of a fishway of presently unknown design, cost and potential impact on other aspects of the project * * * provides the licensee with no reasonable or rational basis for evaluating the potential effect of a prescription. But this argument was made and rejected in State of California v. FPC, 345 F.2d 917 (9th Cir.), cert. denied, 382 U.S. 941 (1965) * * * [where] the Commission, acting under Section 10 of the Act, included a reopener clause in its license allowing it to re-evaluate after twenty years the minimum flow requirements that it had imposed on the licensee. * * *

The petitioners attempt to distinguish California v. FPC on a number of grounds. First, they point out that the Commission in that case was reserving its own authority and discretion as opposed to discretion vested in the Secretary of the Interior. But Congress, in its concern for environmental and conservation values, specifically elected to vest this authority in the Secretary of the Interior, perhaps in the belief that he would give the values in question a stronger priority than FERC, which might be more interested in energy economics. Second, petitioners claim that the reservation in *California v. FPC* was intended to address reasonably foreseeable circumstances. But here the reservation was intended to address circumstances, perhaps less foreseeable but nonetheless specifically contemplated by Congress. Third, they point out that in *California v. FPC* future action would be tested for consistency with the FPA, including its effect on project economics. This may be the case but again Congress addressed the situation here specifically with the provisions contained in Section 18. Fourth, the petitioners argue that in *California v. FPC*, as opposed to the present case, there would ultimately be a showing based on substantial evidence that the action was necessary and desirable. In the case before us, the Commission has given strong assurances to the petitioners that there would be a hearing at the time that Interior requested fishway installation. But, in any event, the need for fishways, here under Section 18, was a matter delegated to the Secretary of the Interior by the Congress. Fifth, the petitioners argue that in *California v. FPC* the licensee retained a right to challenge the validity of the action taken by the Commission. Here the petitioners can certainly raise the issue whether an ordered fishway accords with the sort of improvement contemplated by Congress.

The heart of the petitioners' argument is essentially that it is unfair to require them to decide whether or not to proceed with their water power projects when this license provision prevents them from knowing, before they undertake the activity, what their costs will be and therefore whether the activity will be commercially viable. But they ground their argument entirely on the statute; they do not raise a due process objection, and we can see nothing in the statutory scheme to distinguish this case from *California v. FPC*. The FPA cannot be read to require the Commission to protect the economic viability of all hydroelectric projects. Moreover, Section 18 specifically, and by its very terms provides for a reservation condition such as the one applied in this case. Therefore, we believe that *California v. FPC* and cases which follow it are controlling.

* * * The Commission should not be left with the untenable choice of either requiring petitioners to construct potentially needless fishways at the time of licensing or effectively eliminating the possibility of restoring migratory fish runs to the Wisconsin River. Therefore, the reservation of authority to impose a future requirement seems an appropriate measure for the protection of the public interest.

As we have noted, we think that the potential impact of the cost of the fishway on the economics of a relatively marginal power generating project may be a significant issue. However, there is no indication from this record that this is a generally applicable problem and it is certainly one that Congress can deal with within rather broad limits. In addition, we would emphasize that the Commission has committed itself to conduct hearings at such future time as fishways may have to be ordered. What precisely will be the scope of these hearings we cannot address at this point. However, we emphasize that our approval of the Commission's construction of the statute here is significantly dependent upon its commitment to conduct such hearings.

Petitioners also challenge the Commission's interpretation of Section 18 on the ground that it conflicts with the requirement for "reasonable" terms of licenses contained in Section 15. Section 15 provides that a new license be issued to an original licensee at the end of the original license term on "reasonable" terms. Petitioners argue that the possibility that the Commission's prescription of a fishway may make the project uneconomic at some future date renders the reservation an unreasonable term. Petitioners emphasize in this branch of their argument that the case for unreasonableness rests in considerable measure with the Commission's interpretation that it may not question Interior's determination of need nor may it weigh the need for a fishway against economic viability. If however, there is unreasonableness in this provision, it is the unreasonableness of Congress in enacting Section 18 rather than that of the Commission in interpreting the section. The purported "unreasonableness" springs from congressional emphasis on the priority to be given conservation considerations. There are a variety of unknown future contingencies under which the petitioners accept a license. One of the more notable of these presumably is the level of flow in the Wisconsin River in future years. By adding to the natural contingencies which must attach to any project envisioning operation over a long period of years a requirement for the construction of a fishway we do not believe that either Congress or the Commission has acted unreasonably. Reasonableness is a term of notable flexibility in both the legislative and the administrative lexicon and we do not believe that the present requirements exceed the usual and normal limits of the term.

The petitioners also challenge the Commission's construction of the FPA as being in conflict with certain requirements of the Administrative Procedure Act. They claim that there is no evidence in the record that at any time in the future a fishway will be necessary in connection with either of the two projects. We think that Congress in enacting Section 18, or its equivalent over the years has already made a finding, in effect, that a fishway may become necessary with respect to any water power project affecting fish migration in a river. Congress has delegated to the Secretary of the Interior the authority to make a determination when and if a fishway may become necessary. We can hardly expect the Commission at the present time to make a finding which would be meaningful with respect to an uncertain future event.

Also the petitioners complain that the reservation of Section 18 prescriptive authority is not necessary in light of the Commission's general authority to insert a standard reopener clause permitting it to consider and resolve fishway issues at an appropriate time and in an appropriate way.[2] We think again that Congress has already decided this in the

---

2. The standard reopener article contained in the license of both Petitions states that:

The License shall, for the conservation and development of fish and wildlife requite special case of a fishway prescription. In so doing, Congress has apparently given great weight to conservation objectives in the preservation of means for fish to pursue their migratory inclinations.

In addition, we believe that the Commission has proffered adequate reasons for the inclusion of the Section 18 reservation. As noted, Congress since 1906 had enacted provisions for fishway prescriptions similar to the present provisions of Section 18. This presumably indicates a longstanding congressional concern with conservation considerations involving fish migration. The Commission seems to us to have given a reasonable construction to these longstanding provisions. If there are complaints as to their economic impact they must be addressed to the Congress.

NOTES AND QUESTIONS

1. How awkward is the "reopener" provision for the licensee? Is the reservation of authority to prescribe a "fishway" at some point over the 30–50 year term of the license a sword of Damocles that could spell the end of a profitable facility? Should the "fish agencies" be required to decide at the time of the licensing (or relicensing) whether a fishway is a good idea, and to make a definitive decision whether to require it, rather than leave the matter open? Elsewhere these materials address other situations where agencies reserve the authority to make further decisions about natural resource development "downstream" from the initial decision. Consider, for example, the offshore oil and gas leasing situation and the *Mobil Exploration* case, Chapter 3, supra p. 257; and the "no surface occupancy" leasing stipulation discussed in the NEPA materials, Chapter 5, supra p. 421.

2. Note that the court says the issue of a future fishway prescription on profitability is not "inconsequential." But is it legally relevant to Interior's authority to prescribe it? What is the court's answer to the licensee's concern?

3. The court points out that the licensee does not argue that this uncertainty deprives it of "due process," only that the "reopener" is not authorized by statute. Could the licensee frame a credible due process argument here? Does the court here provide clues as to whether the fish agencies have any statutory or constitutional obligation to consult with FERC, the license applicant or the public in formulating fishway prescriptions?

sources, construct, maintain, and operate, or arrange for the construction, maintenance, and operation of such reasonable facilities, and comply with such reasonable modifications of the project structures and operation, as may be ordered by the Commission upon its own motion or upon the recommendation of the Secretary of the Interior or the fish and wildlife agency or agencies of any State in which the project or a part thereof is located, after notice and opportunity for hearing.

4. Suppose there are 2 different FERC-licensed hydro facilities on a particular river, both built without fish passage facilities, and effectively blocking all areas upstream to anadromous fish passage. The license for the one closest to the mouth of the river comes up for renewal in 2015. The other facility further upstream is before FERC now for relicensing. The long term goal of the fish agencies is to restore anadromous fish runs in the watershed, but it may not make sense to require fishways now for the upstream facility because until the downstream facility has fish passage facilities they are worthless. On the other hand, if the upstream facilities are given 30–50 year licenses now without fishway prescriptions, it could seriously delay implementation of the restoration goal. A possible solution might be to include a fishway prescription in the license for the upstream facility, but delay implementation for many years until fishways are installed on the downstream facility. But from the standpoint of the licensee's security, how different is that from the "reopener" clause? Furthermore, might conditions change between now and then, and more information and understanding might be gained over the interim which could change the perception of what kinds of fishways are needed at the upstream facility?

NOTE: DECOMMISSIONING AND DAM REMOVAL

Many dams constructed in the twentieth century under FERC licenses drastically diminished fish populations, despite the installation of fish ladders and other mitigating devices. By the time many licenses came up for renewal in the latter part of the century, hydropower had become a much less important source of electricity in much of the country. (Because the "fuel"—falling water—is "free," and because such facilities can be turned on and off with a push of the button, hydropower remains a valuable source of "peaking" power to meet periods of high demand.) In an environmentally conscious era what had once seemed unthinkable became a subject of serious debate: Dam removal as an element of fish-friendly river restoration. Interior Secretary Babbitt began raising the issue in public speeches, saying that dams are not like the pyramids of Egypt:

> We have plenty of powerful stakeholders willing to reassert the known, traditional benefits of dams—irrigation, hydropower [and] urban water authorities [and] engineers. But the process of putting a value on the native life intrinsic to watersheds and ecosystems is something new * * *. My parents' generation gloried in the construction of dams across America's rivers. My generation saw how those rivers were changed, deformed, killed by dams. [The next] generation must help decide if, how and where those dams stand or fall.

"Dams Are Not Forever," Address to Ecological Society of America, August 4, 1998. Most serious attention focused on smaller, obsolete dams that had little economic value but were significant obstructions to fish, many of which were FERC-licensed. (There was also talk of removing even huge dams like Glen Canyon, which were built by the federal government and do not operate under FERC license.)

In 1997, FERC broke new ground by issuing an order denying a new license and ordering the Edwards Dam on the Kennebec River in Maine removed. See Edwards Mfg. Co., 81 F.E.R.C. ¶ 61,255 (Nov. 25, 1997). Although the licensee challenged the FERC's authority to require dam removal, ultimately the case was settled when several industries along the river agreed to contribute to the costs of removal and related costs as elements of mitigation for other developments of their own on the Kennebec. This resolution has left open a number of legal issues regarding FERC's authority to take such a step.*

In the next couple of decades, several hundred FERC licenses will expire, so the issues will almost certainly arise again. Among the questions raised are whether, if FERC denies a license, it retains any regulatory authority at the site, and whether it has authority to order removal of the dam, and to require the licensee to pay the costs. FERC has adopted a lengthy policy statement addressing these questions; see 69 F.E.R.C. ¶ 61,-336. The issues basically involve statutory construction. The Federal Power Act seems clearly to contemplate that license renewals may be denied, but it is silent on what happens in that eventuality. Furthermore, the Act contains other provisions that muddy the waters somewhat.

In Wisconsin v. FERC, 104 F.3d 462 (D.C.Cir.1997), the States of Wisconsin and Michigan, intervenors in the proceeding before FERC to transfer a hydropower license from one entity to another, argued that the Commission should have inquired into the financial capability of the transferee to operate the dams, "particularly in light of the expected cost of future environmental measures likely to be required for the dams' continued operation." The states were concerned because an existing fisheries restoration plan could require the installation of costly fish passage facilities in the future, and that might make the dams "economically unviable," which could lead the licensee to abandon the facilities, and which could put the cost burden on state taxpayers. The court refused, finding it within FERC's discretion not to make the financial inquiry. It said, among other things:

> At this point, neither FERC nor Wisconsin or Michigan can predict with any certainty whether, and in what form, such requirements may eventually be imposed. Moreover, as FERC noted, the transferee has agreed to comply with all the terms and conditions of the licenses, which would include any environmental measures that may become necessary, and neither Wisconsin nor Michigan has presented any evidence that calls into question [the licensee's] commitment or ability to do so. * * * In the absence of any evidence to suggest that the projects were likely to become marginal or to be abandoned by the transferee, FERC could reasonably conclude that consideration of the

---

* Dam removal can pose complications other than legal, and the engineering and environmental costs associated with dam removal might sometimes be significant. For example, a dam captures sediment behind it, which over decades can mount up to a large volume of material. These sediments may harbor heavy metals or other noxious substances. If a dam is removed, sediments might have to be removed too (an expensive process) or otherwise isolated or managed.

impact of future environmental controls on the projects' economic viability was better deferred until such measures were actually imposed at the time of relicensing, and that the possibility that the projects might be decommissioned due to their economic unviability was too speculative to warrant requiring [the applicant] to submit additional financial documentation.

One way to think about these issues is to compare a hydro facility to, say, a coal-fired power plant or a nuclear plant. When these other generating facilities reach the end of their useful life, it seems to be taken for granted that regulatory authorities can require that they be dismantled, the sites reclaimed, and any waste and other materials properly stored or disposed of at the operator's expense. Should hydro facilities be treated any differently, as a matter of policy? Should the Commission require operators to pay an annual surcharge to be put in a fund to provide for dam removal costs when the time comes? Is the Court in the *Wisconsin* case engaged in head-in-the-sand reasoning? If the FERC concludes, 15 years from now, that the projects ought to be decommissioned, and the new owners argue they cannot afford to bear the costs of decommissioning, can FERC require them to bear it anyway?

For a general review of hydropower licensing, see Michael C. Blumm, Hydroelectric Regulation under the Federal Power Act, Chapter 40, pp. 333–74, in Vol. 4, Robert Beck, ed., WATERS AND WATER RIGHTS (1996).

CHAPTER 7

THE MINERAL RESOURCE

Historically, mining was the most lucrative and therefore the most preferred use of the federal lands. Federal mineral development also furnished the context for some of the most colorful and famous (or infamous) episodes in federal land history: the California gold rush, the Teapot Dome scandal of the 1920s, the uranium boom on the Colorado Plateau in the 1950s, the gold boom in northern Nevada in the 1980s, and, currently, the coalbed methane boom in Wyoming's Powder River basin.

Earlier chapters have highlighted some of the legal issues involved in federal mineral development. After an early attempt at leasing federal minerals (see United States v. Gratiot, Chapter 2, supra p. 49) was abandoned, miners' customs developed in the California gold rush were incorporated into state law (Morton v. Solambo Copper Mining Co., Chapter 2, supra p. 87), and eventually absorbed into federal law. The next several decades reflected a tension between the goal of all-out privatization of federal mineral resources and the goal of reserving them in public ownership for development under governmental supervision. This led to controversies over withdrawal policies culminating in United States v. Midwest Oil Co., Chapter 2, supra p. 119, and in the Mineral Leasing Act of 1920, which put the important fossil fuels and fertilizer minerals firmly under governmental control (United States ex rel. McLennan v. Wilbur, Chapter 2, supra p. 128). Withdrawal issues continue to be important (see Chapter 4, § C, supra p. 339), as do questions about the extent to which state law has been preempted (covered in Chapter 3, § D, supra p. 206). There are also questions about the extent to which governmental regulation may take private property rights perfected in federally-owned minerals (see, e.g., United States v. Locke, Chapter 3, § F supra p. 233), and questions about when evolving governmental regulatory policies may give private contractors, such as mineral lessees, contract remedies against the government (e.g., Mobil Exploration Co. v. United States, Chapter 3, § G, supra p. 257). Today, with minerals a product of a global economy, debate about mining on federal lands mostly concerns its regulation to prevent or diminish its adverse effects on the environment or other resources and amenities, and this emphasis is reflected in this chapter.

The chapter sets out the general framework for how decisions are made to move forward with development of federal minerals. Section A deals with the Mining Law of 1872. A potent political symbol as well as the legal means for obtaining public hardrock minerals, it remains by far the most prominent of the great nineteenth century disposal laws still on the books; the embodiment of frontier free enterprise. Section B examines the separate and contrasting system of mineral leasing, used today for the disposition of fossil fuels and fertilizer minerals, onshore and on the Outer Continental Shelf. Since 1920, federal statutes governing coal, oil and gas, oil shale, potash, potassium, sodium, sulfur and (since 1970) geothermal energy have retained federal ownership and control of the land overlying those resources. Section C looks briefly at the third system of federal mineral disposition—by competitive sale—which is used for common minerals such as sand, gravel, and building stone. The final section addresses legal issues growing out of so-called "split estates," where minerals and the surface estate are owned separately, one or the other being in federal ownership.

A. HARDROCK MINERALS: THE GENERAL MINING LAW OF 1872

The Mining Law contains this clarion call of entrepreneurship (30 U.S.C. § 22):

> Except as otherwise provided, all valuable mineral deposits in lands belonging to the United States, both surveyed and unsurveyed, shall be free and open to exploration and purchase, and the lands in which they are found to occupation and purchase, by citizens of the United States and those who have declared their intention to become such, under regulations prescribed by law, and according to the local customs or rules of miners in the several mining districts, so far as the same are applicable and not inconsistent with the laws of the United States.

As originally enacted, the Mining Law offered would-be mineral developers generous terms: Whoever discovers and develops a valuable mineral deposit on federal lands may mine that deposit virtually free of charge and competition, and may receive fee simple title (a "patent" purchased at $2.50 or $5 per acre) to the land containing the deposit. The system is based on self-initiation; historically the miner needed no federal permission to prospect and locate mining claims on federal lands and extract minerals from those claims.

Over the years, other concerns have been brought to bear that have destroyed this original somewhat elegant simplicity. Many public lands and many different kinds of minerals are no longer subject to the Mining Law. Even where it still applies, the right accorded the discoverer of the mineral has become less absolute; access and development are conditioned and controlled by newer statutes and regulations. As explained further below, the patent provision appears to be on its way out. Nevertheless, while the Mining Law has been limited and amended in many ways, its basic architecture has stubbornly survived a century of attempts to repeal it.

The Mining Law contains a wealth of arcana and complexity. It may have been the subject of more U.S. Supreme Court decisions (mostly from the late nineteenth century) than any single federal statute other than the Internal Revenue Code. Accordingly, there is an enormous literature on the Mining Law. The most comprehensive is a six-volume treatise produced by the Rocky Mountain Mineral Law Foundation, AMERICAN LAW OF

MINING 2d (2000). John Leshy's book, THE MINING LAW: A STUDY IN PERPETUAL MOTION (1987), deals with an array of Mining Law issues from both an historical and contemporary reform perspective. The annual proceedings of the Rocky Mountain Mineral Law Institute, collected annually in separate volumes, generate a sizeable portion of the legal literature on hardrock mining. This chapter will touch on only the highlights.

1. WHAT MINERALS ARE LOCATABLE UNDER THE MINING LAW?

The statutory reference in 30 U.S.C. § 22 to "all valuable mineral deposits in lands belonging to the United States" has been limited by Congress and the courts in several ways. When the Mining Law was adopted, it applied to all minerals except coal, which had already been made subject to sale at public auction by the Coal Act of 1864, 13 Stat. 205 (later modified by the Coal Lands Act of 1873, 17 Stat. 607). Coal was made a leasable mineral under the Mineral Leasing Act of 1920.

Oil and gas have posed special problems. In 1897, Congress passed the Oil Placer Act, 29 Stat. 526, confirming the status of oil, gas, and oil shale as locatable minerals under the Mining Law. The executive withdrawals of millions of acres of federal lands from petroleum location led to the famous decision in United States v. Midwest Oil Co., Chapter 2, supra p. 120, and eventually to passage of the Mineral Leasing Act of 1920, 30 U.S.C. §§ 181 et seq. That landmark statute removed all the major fuel and fertilizer minerals from the scope of the General Mining Law. The Geothermal Steam Act of 1970, 30 U.S.C. §§ 1001–1025, makes federal geothermal resources leasable. Other minerals have been placed in the leasable category by special statutes; see 1 AMERICAN LAW OF MINING 2d §§ 6.04–6.05 (2000). Leasable minerals are discussed in § B of this chapter.

Besides locatable and leasable minerals, there is a third category—minerals (usually very common, widely occurring minerals) available only by competitive sale. The Materials Disposal Act of 1947, 30 U.S.C. §§ 601–602, as amended by the Common Varieties Act of 1955, 30 U.S.C. § 611, provides for sale of sand, stone, gravel, pumice, cinders, and other designated "common" minerals, unless the deposit "has some property giving it distinct and special value," id. § 601, in which case it may still be located under the Mining Law. The sales system is discussed at pp. 677–79 infra.

But apart from the minerals specifically dealt with by Congress, and in light of the truism that everything that is not animal or vegetable is mineral, there sometimes remains, even in modern times, a question as to what is a mineral for purposes of the 1872 Act.

Andrus v. Charlestone Stone Products Co.

Supreme Court of the United States, 1978.
436 U.S. 604.

■ MR. JUSTICE MARSHALL delivered the opinion of the Court.

The question presented is whether water is a "valuable mineral" as those words are used in the mining law. * * * The claim at issue in this case, known as Claim 22, is one of a group of 23 claims near Las Vegas, Nev., that were located in 1942. In 1962, after respondent had purchased these claims, it discovered water on Claim 22 by drilling a well thereon. This water was used to prepare for commercial sale the sand and gravel removed from some of the 23 claims. [In what was a garden variety challenge brought by the federal government to the validity of claim 22, the Ninth Circuit inexplicably held, *sua sponte*, that Claim 22 was valid because water is a valuable mineral under the 1872 Act. 553 F.2d 1209 (9th Cir.1977). The Supreme Court granted certiorari.] * * *

We may assume for purposes of this decision that the Court of Appeals was correct in concluding that water is a "mineral," in the broadest sense of that word, and that it is "valuable." * * *

This Court long ago recognized that the word "mineral," when used in an Act of Congress, cannot be given its broadest definition. * * * As one court observed, if the term "mineral" in the statute were construed to encompass all substances that are conceivably mineral, "there would be justification for making mine locations on virtually every part of the earth's surface," since "a very high proportion of the substances of the earth are in that sense 'mineral.'" Rummell v. Bailey, 320 P.2d 653, 655 (1958). See also Robert L. Beery, 25 I.B.L.A. 287, 294–296 (1976) (noting that "common dirt," while literally a mineral, cannot be considered locatable under the mining law) * * *.

The fact that water may be valuable or marketable similarly is not enough to support a mining claim's validity based on the presence of water. Many substances present on the land may be of value, and indeed it seems likely that land itself—especially land located just 15 miles from downtown Las Vegas—has, in the Court of Appeals' words, "an intrinsic value," id., at 1216. Yet the federal mining law surely was not intended to be a general real estate law; as one commentator has written, "the Congressional mandate did not sanction the disposal of federal lands under the mining laws for purposes unrelated to mining." 1 American Law of Mining, supra, § 1.18, at 56.

In order for a claim to be valid, the substance discovered must not only be a "valuable mineral" within the dictionary definition of those words, but must also be the type of valuable mineral that the 1872 Congress intended to make the basis of a valid claim. * * *

Our opinions thus recognize that, although mining law and water law developed together in the West prior to 1866, with respect to federal lands Congress chose to subject only mining to comprehensive federal regulation. When it passed the 1866 and 1870 mining laws, Congress clearly intended to preserve "pre-existing [water] right[s]." * * *

* * * [W]ithout benefit of briefing, the court below decided that "it would be incongruous * * * to hazard that Congress was not aware of the necessary glove of water for the hand of mining." Congress was indeed aware of this, so much aware that it expressly provided a water rights policy in the mining laws. But the policy adopted is a "passive" one, 2 Waters and Water Rights § 102.1, at 53 (R. Clark ed. 1967); Congress three

times (in 1866, 1870, and 1872) affirmed the view that private water rights on federal lands were to be governed by state and local law and custom. It defies common sense to assume that Congress, when it adopted this policy, meant at the same time to establish a parallel federal system for acquiring private water rights, and that it did so *sub silentio* through laws designed to regulate mining. In light of the 1866 and 1870 provisions, the history out of which they arose, and the decisions construing them in the context of the 1872 law, the notion that water is a "valuable mineral" under that law is simply untenable.

The conclusion that Congress did not intend water to be locatable under the federal mining law is reinforced by consideration of the practical consequences that could be expected to flow from a holding to the contrary.

Many problems would undoubtedly arise simply from the fact of having two overlapping systems for acquisition of private water rights. Under the appropriation doctrine prevailing in most of the Western States, the mere fact that a person controls land adjacent to a body of water means relatively little; instead, water rights belong to "[t]he first appropriator of water for a beneficial use," but only "to the extent of his actual use." * * *

With regard to minerals located under federal law, an entirely different theory prevails. The holder of a federal mining claim, by investing $100 annually in the claim, becomes entitled to possession of the land and may make any use, or no use, of the minerals involved. See 30 U.S.C. § 28. Once fee title by patent is obtained, even the $100 requirement is eliminated.

One can readily imagine the legal conflicts that might arise from these differing approaches if ordinary water were treated as a federally cognizable "mineral." A federal claimant could, for example, utilize all of the water extracted from a well like respondent's, without regard for the settled prior appropriation rights of another user of the same water. Or he might not use the water at all and yet prevent another from using it, thereby defeating the necessary Western policy in favor of "actual use" of scarce water resources. As one respected commentator [Professor Frank Trelease] has written, allowing water to be the basis of a valid mining claim "could revive long abandoned common law rules of ground water ownership and capture, and * * * could raise horrendous problems of priority and extralateral rights." We decline to effect so major an alteration in established legal relationships based on nothing more than an overly literal reading of a statute, without any regard for its context or history.

A final indication that water should not be held to be a locatable mineral derives from Congress' 1955 decision to remove "common varieties" of certain minerals from the coverage of the mining law. 30 U.S.C. § 611. This decision was made in large part because of "abuses under the general mining laws by * * * persons who locate[d] mining claims on public lands for purposes other than that of legitimate mining activity." * * * Apparently, locating a claim and obtaining a patent to federal land was so inexpensive that many "use[d] the guise of mining locations for nonmining purposes," including the establishment of "filling stations, curio shops, cafes, * * * residence[s][and] summer camp[s]."

It has long been established that, when grants to federal land are at issue, any doubts "are resolved for the Government, not against it." United States v. Union Pacific R. Co., 353 U.S. 112, 116 (1957). *A fortiori,* the Government must prevail in a case such as this, when the relevant statutory provisions, their historical context, consistent administrative and judicial decisions, and the practical problems with a contrary holding all weigh in its favor. * * *

NOTES AND QUESTIONS

1.   For further consideration of the ways in which the Ninth Circuit's opinion might have revolutionized water law in the West, see Chapter 6, supra pp. 509–12. Interestingly, nothing in the Mining Law requires the locator to identify, at the time the claim is located, the mineral or minerals which are the object of the enterprise. Typically, a claimant has to identify the mineral or minerals only when someone (the government, or a rival locator) challenges the validity of the claim.

2.   Professor Michael Braunstein has written:

[T]he question of what constitutes a mineral for purposes of the mining law retains great vitality. This is because the mining law is more generous to private claimants of publicly owned minerals than alternative schemes of disposition. If the claimant is able to obtain title to the minerals under the mining law, he does so without charge by or permit from the government. If the minerals are obtained pursuant to one of the alternative schemes of disposition, however, the claimant must first obtain permission from the government to mine, for these other schemes all vest substantial discretion in the government concerning whether mining will be permitted. Moreover, under these schemes, the miner is required to pay a royalty or rent to the government for the privilege of mining government owned minerals. If the minerals are obtained under the mining law, however, no rent or royalty is due. For these reasons, miners and the Interior Department often find themselves in a Procrustean struggle over the meaning of the terms "minerals." Miners and their lawyers try to stretch the term to cover as many substances as possible; the Interior Department and its advocates try to shrink it, so that it just covers the core substances to which the mining law was most clearly intended to apply. * * *

The determination of whether a substance is a mineral is not a question of fact, but a conclusion of law. Consequently, whether something is properly classified as a mineral depends on the purpose of the intended classification. In the context of the mining law, calling something a mineral means that it is subject to being located under that law. For a court to make this determination, it must first decide that the transfer of the substance and the lands containing it from public to private ownership under the mining law is appropriate in light of contemporary concerns and policies. Indeed, the question of whether a substance is a mineral is almost entirely a question of policy and only incidentally a question of chemistry.

Michael Braunstein, All That Glitters: Discovering the Meaning of Mineral in the Mining Law of 1872, XXI Land & Water L.Rev. 293, 301 (1986).*

3. It is not always apparent that the Department of the Interior or the courts apply the test advocated by Professor Braunstein. Here are some examples from what is a very lengthy list of cases on the subject of what is and is not a qualifying mineral: United States v. Toole, 224 F.Supp. 440 (D.Mont.1963) (peat and organic soil not a mineral); Richter v. Utah, 27 L.D. 95 (1898) (guano is a mineral). See also Dunluce Placer Mine, 30 L.D. 357 (1900) (stalactites, stalagmites, and other "natural curiosities" not minerals); Hughes v. Florida, 42 L.D. 401 (1913) (shell rock not a mineral); Earl Douglass, 44 L.D. 325 (1915) (fossil remains of prehistoric animals not minerals); United States v. Elkhorn Min. Co., 2 IBLA 383 (1971) (radon gas not a mineral); United States v. Barngrover, 57 I.D. 533 (1941) ("drilling mud" is a mineral). See also 76 Stat. 652 (1962) (petrified wood shall not be deemed a valuable mineral deposit under the Mining Law, but the Secretary "shall provide by regulation that limited quantities of petrified wood may be removed without charge from those public lands which he shall specify").

4. Section D of this chapter shows that the question of what is a mineral may be answered in different ways in different contexts. See, e.g., Watt v. Western Nuclear, Inc., infra p. 681, holding that gravel is a mineral for purposes of the Stock–Raising Homestead Act of 1916. Cf. United States v. Union Oil Co. of California, infra p. 687, holding that geothermal energy, of which water is a main component, *is* a mineral for the purposes of the same statute.

2. What "Lands Belonging to the United States" Are Open to Claim Location Under the Mining Law?

Despite the sweep of the statutory language, hardrock mineral activity is prohibited on a large proportion of the "lands belonging to the United States." The most severe limitation on mining locations is by legislative or executive withdrawals of federal land from the Mining Law. (Withdrawals are discussed at pp. 339–64 supra.) Legislative withdrawals are found in many statutes enacted for many purposes, but the executive branch has also made equally effective withdrawals, with or without express statutory authority. See *Midwest Oil,* supra p. 119.

Even without a formal withdrawal, many federal lands are not open to Mining Law activities. In Oklahoma v. Texas, 258 U.S. 574 (1922), the two states and the federal government all disputed ownership of the bed of the Red River forming part of the states' common boundary. The Court first ruled that part of the riverbed belonged to the United States, because the river was not navigable when Oklahoma became a state. The Court then turned to whether this federally owned land was "belonging to the United States" within the meaning of the Mining Law. Speaking unanimously through Justice Van Devanter, it said no, explaining:

---

* Reprinted by permission of Land and Water Law Review.

[30 U.S.C. § 22] is not as comprehensive as its words separately considered suggest. It is part of a chapter relating to mineral lands which in turn is part of a title dealing with the survey and disposal of "The Public Lands." To be rightly understood it must be read with due regard for the entire statute of which it is but a part, and when this is done it is apparent that, while embracing only lands owned by the United States, it does not embrace all that are so owned. Of course, it has no application to the grounds about the Capitol in Washington or to the lands in the National Cemetery at Arlington, no matter what their mineral value; and yet both belong to the United States. And so of the lands in the Yosemite National Park, the Yellowstone National Park, and the military reservations throughout the Western States. Only where the United States has indicated that the lands are held for disposal under the land laws does the section apply; and it never applies where the United States directs that the disposal be only under other laws.

This decision reflects the seemingly sensible policy that if federal lands are not generally open to disposal, the Mining Law—which can lead to such disposal through the process of patenting mining claims—should not apply unless an explicit decision is made to have it apply. *Oklahoma v. Texas* creates, in other words, a basic presumption that the Mining Law is inapplicable to federal lands not otherwise available for disposal of fee title. This meant that, as the disposal era drew to a close, lands remained open to the Mining Law only if Congress explicitly mandated that result. Congress has provided that perhaps 400 million acres of federal land (mostly those managed by the BLM and the Forest Service) are still open to the Mining Law, unless otherwise withdrawn by executive or legislative action.

The legal principle announced in *Oklahoma v. Texas* has continued vitality. As Department of the Interior Instructions put it in 1941 (57 Interior Decisions 365, 372–73), "public lands reserved or withdrawn for sundry public uses and purposes * * * which do not in terms expressly include mineral lands * * * are not subject to the operation of the mineral land laws." See, e.g., Brown v. United States Dep't of the Interior, 679 F.2d 747 (8th Cir.1982) (relying on *Oklahoma v. Texas* to hold the Mining Law inapplicable in units of National Park System absent an express authorization from Congress); Pathfinder Mines Corp. v. Hodel, 811 F.2d 1288, 1291 (9th Cir.1987) (holding that a federal "Game Preserve" was not open to mining claim location even though the proclamation that designated it was silent on the subject, because "the express purposes of the Game Preserve are incompatible with entry under the [Mining Law]"). It means also that acquired lands (about 10% of all federal lands, the most important single category being eastern national forests acquired under the Weeks Act) are generally off limits to the Mining Law, because these lands are not available for disposal.*

---

* Somewhat oddly, there is no generic law which authorizes the development of hardrock minerals on federal acquired lands, although a few special statutes authorize leasing of such minerals in particular areas. The 1947 Mineral Leasing Act for Acquired

Finally, because of the *pedis possessio* doctrine (discussed infra pp. 596–603), mining claims may not, in some situations, be validly located on federal lands which are already subject to mining claims. For all these reasons, and especially because there is no central repository of withdrawals, it can be difficult to determine whether a particular tract of federal land remains open to the Mining Law. Miners have often regretted their failure to consult the record systems in BLM state offices before expending their efforts. See Verl C. Ritchie, Title Aspects of Mineral Development on Public Lands, 18 Rocky Mtn.Min.L.Inst. 471 (1973). As a general rule, to determine whether an acre of federal land is open to mining claim location, a multi-layered analysis is required: (A) Is the federal land generally available for disposal? (Today, only a relatively small amount of land is.) (B) If not, has Congress said that this category of lands is open to operation of the Mining Law? (The two general categories of federal land that are open are national forests reserved from the public domain, and BLM managed public lands.) (C) Has the land in question been withdrawn by (i) Congress (e.g., wilderness areas); or (ii) the Executive (by express or implied statutory authority)?

3. How Is a Mining Claim Located?

One of the many quaint features of the Mining Law (and one of the many that have been much litigated) is that several different types of mining claims may be located. There are two types of mineral claims—lode and placer—and there are nonmineral mining claims as well—millsites and tunnel sites. State law also plays a prominent role in the location process, for it controls locations to the extent it is not inconsistent with federal law. Butte City Water Co. v. Baker, 196 U.S. 119, 126 (1905). A starting point is 30 U.S.C. § 28:

> The miners of each mining district may make regulations not in conflict with the laws of the United States, or with the laws of the State or Territory in which the district is situated, governing the location, manner of recording, amount of work necessary to hold possession of a mining claim, subject to the following requirements: The location must be distinctly marked on the ground so that its boundaries can be readily traced. All records of mining claims * * * shall contain the name or names of the locators, the date of the location, and such a description of the claim or claims located by reference to some natural object or permanent monument as will identify the claim. * * *

Typically, state statutes require: (1) a valuable discovery; (2) prompt posting at or near the place of discovery to give notice; (3) development work to determine the character and extent of the deposit; (4) marking on the ground to establish the boundaries of the claim; and (5) recording of a notice or certificate, usually with the county clerk or recorder. See AMERI-CAN LAW OF MINING 2d at chs. 33, 35 (2000). State laws are compiled in

Lands, 30 U.S.C. §§ 351–359, provides that minerals subject to leasing on ordinary feder- al lands are also subject to lease on acquired lands.

Rocky Mountain Mineral Law Foundation, DIGEST OF MINING CLAIM LAWS (R. Pruitt ed., 4th ed., 1990). For a long time, most states' laws required actual excavation of a pit on the claim. In the *Lucky Mc* case in the next subsection, for example, Arizona state law required the claimant to drill a ten-foot hole on each claim, even though the holes had absolutely nothing to do with the exploration, which was being carried out at much greater depths. All these silly, environmentally damaging state laws seem now to have been repealed.

The two kinds of mineral claims are lode claims and placer claims. The original Mining Law of 1866 authorized only lode claims, while an 1870 amendment authorized placer claims. Classically, "lodes" referred to aggregations or veins of mineral embedded in rock, while "placer" referred to mineral deposits in gravels or other loose sediments. See, e.g., United States v. Ohio Oil Co., 240 Fed. 996 (D.Wyo.1916). Nature does not always draw such neat lines, of course, so there are ambiguous situations and the judicial results are not always predictable. See Globe Mining Co. v. Anderson, 78 Wyo. 17, 318 P.2d 373 (1957) (widespread horizontal deposit containing scattered mineralized zones deemed a lode). Don Sherwood & Gary Greer, Mining Law in a Nuclear Age: The Wyoming Example, III Land & Water L.Rev. 1, 26 (1968). The leading Mining Law treatise calls the legal distinction between lode and placer claims an "historical accident." AMERICAN LAW OF MINING, vol. 1, § 32.02[1] (2000).

The distinction is nevertheless important, because the Mining Law carefully specifies different criteria for the boundaries of lode and placer claims. *Lode* claims may not exceed 1500 feet in length or 300 feet on each side of the middle of the vein, and the end lines of the claim must be parallel. 30 U.S.C. § 23. There is no requirement that lode claims conform to survey lines, and lode claims are often irregular in shape. *Placer* claims must conform "as near as practicable" to survey lines where the area has been surveyed, 30 U.S.C. § 35. Otherwise no provisions govern the shape of the exterior boundaries of placer claims. A single claimant cannot locate a placer claim of more than 20 acres, 30 U.S.C. § 35, but associations of persons may locate placer claims of 20 acres per person, not to exceed a claim of 160 acres for an association of eight or more people. 30 U.S.C. § 36. Misidentification of a lode as a placer, or vice versa, is a ground for invalidating the claim. Cole v. Ralph, 252 U.S. 286, 295 (1920) ("A placer discovery will not sustain a lode location, nor a lode discovery a placer location"):

> The result is, for the unwary, a classic trap. For the prudent sophisticate, the result is often an additional expense for locating both types of claims on the same ground to avoid pitfalls. But the Law sets a trap for the prudent but unsophisticated, for the placer claim must be filed first; otherwise, filing it might be construed as an abandonment of the lode claim. These contortions serve absolutely no useful purpose.

John Leshy, THE MINING LAW, at 94. See also Richard Harris, Location of Lode Claims over Placer Claims, 34 Rocky Mtn.Min.L.Inst. 12–1 (1988).

Before 1976, recordation of mining claims was governed solely by state laws, which typically require recording with the county clerk or recorder, but contain no mechanism to determine whether a claim had been abandoned. By 1970, an estimated six to ten million inactive claims existed on the public lands. David H. Anderson, Federal Mineral Policy: The General Mining Law of 1872, 16 Nat.Res.J. 601, 603 (1976). In 1970 the Public Land Law Review Commission recommended federal recordation, and Congress finally included a requirement in the Federal Land Policy and Management Act (FLPMA) in 1976 that all claims be recorded with the Bureau of Land Management, or "conclusively" be deemed abandoned. 43 U.S.C. § 1744(c). Staying true to the maxim that nothing regarding the Mining Law ever follows the simplest path, this requirement apparently does not displace state recordation laws. See 43 U.S.C. § 1744(d). FLPMA also requires that every mining claimant annually file a statement of an intention to hold the claim upon penalty of losing the claim. These requirements were upheld against a constitutional challenge in United States v. Locke, Chapter 3, supra p. 233.

The federal recordation requirement has weeded out a large number of stale or abandoned mining claims. As of September 2000, about 235,000 unpatented mining claims were properly recorded with BLM. See PUBLIC LAND STATISTICS 2000, Table 3–22, p. 141. The Mining Law contains no express limit on the number of mining claims that a person can locate, even though a limit could fairly be implied, and the process by which the courts eventually came to bless the practice of multiple claim-holding (nearly a half-century after the statute was enacted) was tortuous. See John Leshy, THE MINING LAW: A STUDY IN PERPETUAL MOTION, at 169–81.

Millsites are non-mineral claims, located for the purpose of accommodating mineral processing and ancillary facilities on federal lands. Millsites are limited to five acres each, must be *noncontiguous* to mining claims, and must be located on *nonmineral* federal land open to the Mining Law. This puts an awkward burden on a millsite locator, who must show, if challenged, that the land located for a millsite does *not* contain minerals. The need for large acreages to locate processing facilities and tailings and waste rock piles has created a problem for the modern mining industry. With development of the ability to extract fine particles of widely disseminated gold deposits from rock through cyanide heap-leaching, it is now standard practice to move hundreds of tons of material to produce ounces of gold. Where to put those tons of waste rock and overburden is a problem.

The Mining Law has long been interpreted to limit millsites to one per each mineral claim. In 1997, the Solicitor of the Department of the Interior opined that this limitation was still valid (having, among other things, been reaffirmed by the Congress as recently as 1960). See M–36988, Limitations on Patenting Millsites under the Mining Law of 1872 (Nov. 7, 1997). This means that mining companies may acquire larger acreages of federal land for millsite purposes only by exchange, or by other means.

This Opinion was promptly attacked by the mining industry and its supporters in Congress. In 1999 the Congress included a rider on the Interior Department Appropriations Act, 113 Stat. 1501, 1501A–199, § 337 (1999), which effectively exempted from this Opinion "any operation for which a plan of operations has been approved" or for which a plan of operations had been submitted to the BLM or the U.S. Forest Service prior to the date of the Opinion. (Plans of operations approvals are discussed further below, at pp. 628–38.) The rider also provided that it should not "be construed as an explicit or tacit adoption, ratification, endorsement, approval, rejection or disapproval of" the Solicitor's Opinion. Interestingly, as of this writing no company had challenged the Solicitor's view in court.

Some mining companies have used mining claims for millsite purposes, and in January 2001, the Solicitor addressed the legality of this practice. (M–37004, January 18, 2001, "Use of Mining Claims for Purposes Ancillary to Mineral Extraction.") The Opinion concluded that mining claims may be used for purposes ancillary to mining as well as for mineral extraction, but that such uses may cast doubt on the validity of the mining claims, allowing an inference that they contain no discovery of a valuable mineral deposit (see discussion of "discovery" further below). Other companies have tried to circumvent the millsite limitation by "slicing and dicing" their mineral claims (e.g., dividing a formerly 20–acre mineral claim into 20 one-acre claims), and arguing that they are meeting the one millsite per mineral claim standard. The legality of this approach is challenged in Roger Flynn, The 1872 Mining Law as an Impediment to Mineral Development on the Public Lands: A 19th Century Law Meets the Realities of Modern Mining, 34 Land & Water L.Rev. 301 (1999). The Solicitor later capsulized the debate over these claim limits this way:

> The mill site imbroglio is emblematic of a larger issue: namely, how to interpret this old Mining Law. Some members of the mineral law community see the Mining Law as almost infinitely flexible, so long as the flexibility runs in one direction—to serve the interests and needs of the domestic mining industry. Our perspective has been different. Doubtless a basic purpose of the Mining Law was to promote the development of federal minerals, but if the enacting Congress had wanted the Executive Branch to bend every effort toward that end, it needed to say nothing more than that. As we all know, however, Congress instead chose to include exquisite (or mind-numbing, depending upon your perspective) details in the law. We concluded that Congress did not intend the statutory mill site acreage limitation to be ignored to give miners a right to claim (and patent) an unlimited amount of public land acreage for waste dumps and spoil piles.

John Leshy, Public Lands at the Millennium, 46 Rocky Mt. Min.L.Inst. 1, 1–13–1–14 (2000).

It often happens that after a mining claim is located, its boundaries need to be adjusted to reflect further identification and definition of an ore body. A complicated mixture of state and federal rules govern the process of changing claim boundaries, and a crucial question is often whether the claim is being "relocated" or "amended." Such issues were examined at length as a result of a challenge by environmentalists to a proposed major mining operation in the Cabinet Mountains Wilderness in northwestern Montana. Wilderness Society v. Dombeck, 168 F.3d 367 (9th Cir.1999).

Yet another complication comes from the doctrine of "extralateral rights." These rights attach to properly located unpatented mining claims, and allow the miner of a lode (but not a placer) claim to follow a vein or lode beyond the sidelines of the claim in some but not all circumstances. Extralateral rights were first recognized by custom in the mining camps and then expressly incorporated in the Mining Law in murky language:

> The locators of all mining locations made on any mineral vein, lode, or ledge, * * * shall have the exclusive right of possession and enjoyment of all the surface included within the lines of their locations, *and of all veins, lodes, and ledges throughout their entire depth, the top or apex of which lies inside of such surface lines extended downward vertically*, although such veins, lodes, or ledges may so far depart from a perpendicular in their course downward as to extend *outside the vertical side lines of such surface locations.* But their right of possession to such outside parts of such veins or ledges *shall be confined to such portions thereof as lie between vertical planes drawn downward as above described, through the end lines of their locations,* so continued in their own direction that such planes will intersect such exterior parts of such veins or ledges. Nothing in this section shall authorize the locator or possessor of a vein or lode which extends in its downward course beyond the vertical lines of his claim to enter upon the surface of a claim owned or possessed by another. (Emphasis added.)

30 U.S.C. § 26 (emphasis added). A schematic translation of extralateral rights is found in an illustration from Rocky Mountain Mineral Law Foundation, DIGEST OF MINING CLAIM LAWS 13 (4th ed., R. Pruitt, ed., 1990):

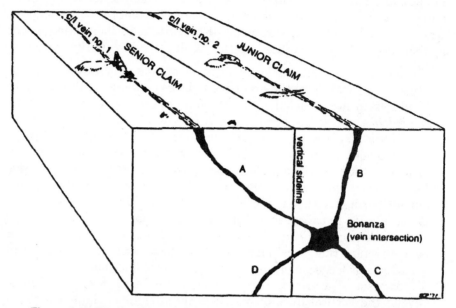

Figure 6. EXTRALATERAL RIGHTS ILLUSTRATED. Senior Claim, located along vein no. 1, may follow the dipping vein outside the sidelines projected vertically downward and mine parts A and C. Junior Claim, located along vein no. 2, may likewise follow the dipping vein outside the sidelines and mine parts B and D. The area of vein intersection, where rich orebodies usually form, belongs to the Senior Claim, even though it lies within the vertical boundaries of the Junior Claim.

[G10492]

A problem stems from the fact that lode claims are not always neat rectangles, see Iron Silver Mining Co. v. Elgin Mining & Smelting Co., 118 U.S. 196, 199 (1886) (appending a diagram of several highly irregular claims), which can complicate determinations of the existence and location of extralateral rights. Extralateral rights allow the patentee to mine out a vein beneath the land of another without liability, and they can be patented (privatized). Historically, this feature of the Mining Law was one of the most fiercely litigated. See generally 2 AMERICAN LAW OF MINING 2d at ch. 37 (1984). For a modern extralateral rights dispute, see Swoboda v. Pala Mining, Inc., 844 F.2d 654 (9th Cir.1988).

4. WHAT ARE A MINING CLAIMANT'S RIGHTS BEFORE DISCOVERY? THE PEDIS POSSESSIO DOCTRINE

A mining claimant does not have a valid unpatented claim until the physical steps of location have been completed *and* a valuable mineral deposit has been discovered. "Location is the act or series of acts whereby the boundaries of the claim are marked, etc., but it confers no right in the absence of discovery, both being essential to a valid claim." Cole v. Ralph,

252 U.S. 286, 296 (1920). The statute itself expressly requires that discovery precede claim location. See 30 U.S.C. § 23: "[N]o location of a mining claim shall be made until the discovery of a vein or lode within the limits of the claim located." Prior to discovery, courts have devised some limited protections for claim locators who are exploring in good faith, against others who try to "jump" their claims. The following case, which addresses mining claims located for petroleum, was decided a year before Congress removed fossil fuels from the ambit of the Mining Law and made them subject to leasing.

Union Oil Co. v. Smith

Supreme Court of the United States, 1919.
249 U.S. 337.

■ Mr. Justice Pitney delivered the opinion of the Court.

[Two rival groups of oil prospectors filed separate claims on the same ground. The defendant Union Oil argued it had located the ground first, many years before the plaintiff came on the scene.] * * * No discovery of oil or other minerals had ever been made upon the ground by either of the claimants or by any other person. But at the time plaintiff and his associates located [their claim on the ground,] defendant, although not then actually occupying this ground, was in actual occupation of a contiguous claim of 160 acres known as the "Sampson claim," upon which it then was drilling and afterwards continued to drill a well for the discovery of oil, the well being 1,000 feet distant from the boundary line of the disputed claim. Defendant claimed the right of possession of five contiguous claims, including [the one also claimed by the plaintiff] under locations regularly made in all respects save discovery. * * *

[I]t is clear that in order to create valid rights or initiate a title as against the United States a discovery of mineral is essential. * * * Nevertheless, [30 U.S.C. § 22] extends an express invitation to all qualified persons to explore the lands of the United States for valuable mineral deposits, and this and the following sections hold out to one who succeeds in making discovery the promise of a full reward. Those who, being qualified, proceed in good faith to make such explorations and enter peaceably upon vacant lands of the United States for that purpose are not treated as mere trespassers, but as licensees or tenants at will. For since, as a practical matter, exploration must precede the discovery of minerals, and some occupation of the land ordinarily is necessary for adequate and systematic exploration, legal recognition of the pedis possessio of a bona fide and qualified prospector is universally regarded as a necessity. It is held [by state and lower federal courts] that upon the public domain a miner may hold the place in which he may be working against all others having no better right, and while he remains in possession, diligently working towards discovery, is entitled—at least for a reasonable time—to be protected against forcible, fraudulent, and clandestine intrusions upon his possession. * * *

And it has come to be generally recognized that while discovery is the indispensable fact and the marking and recording of the claim dependent upon it, yet the order of time in which these acts occur is not essential to the acquisition from the United States of the exclusive right of possession of the discovered minerals or the obtaining of a patent therefor, but that discovery may follow after location and give validity to the claim as of the time of discovery, provided no rights of third parties have intervened. * * *

To what extent the possessory right of an explorer before discovery is to be deduced from the invitation extended in [30 U.S.C. § 22], to what extent it is to be regarded as a local regulation of the kind recognized by that section and the following ones, and to what extent it derives force from the authority of the mining states to regulate the possession of the public lands in the interest of peace and good order, are questions with which we are not now concerned. Nor need we stop to inquire whether the right is limited to the ground actually occupied in the process of exploration, or extends to the limits of the claim. These questions and others that suggest themselves are not raised by the present record * * *. Whatever the nature and extent of a possessory right before discovery, all authorities agree that such possession may be maintained only by continued actual occupancy by a qualified locator or his representatives engaged in persistent and diligent prosecution of work looking to the discovery of mineral. * * * [The Court concluded that Union Oil had no rights in the disputed claim because it was not in actual occupancy of it, even though it was engaged in exploratory drilling on the contiguous "Sampson" claim.]

NOTES AND QUESTIONS

1. Given the clarity of the Mining Law that discovery must precede claim location, how could the Court conclude here that "the order of time in which these acts occur is not essential"? Is the result consistent with the intent of the enacting Congress? By what reasoning? The year after *Union Oil*, the Supreme Court explained it this way: "In practice discovery usually precedes location, and the statute treats it as the initial act. But in the absence of an intervening right it is no objection that the usual and statutory order is reversed. In such a case the location becomes effective from the date of discovery; but in the presence of an intervening right it must remain of no effect." Cole v. Ralph, 252 U.S. 286, 296 (1920).

2. Notice the possible sources of the *pedis possessio* doctrine: (1) implied from federal law, or federal common law filling in the Mining Law's interstices; (2) the customs of miners, incorporated into the federal statute; or (3) state police power to help keep the peace in mining country (cf. Omaechevarria v. State of Idaho, supra p. 130).

3. What rights, if any, does *pedis possessio* give the claimant against the United States? For example, what would be the effect on a prospector if the United States were to withdraw the area from mining prior to discovery? See, e.g., United States v. Carlile, 67 I.D. 417 (1960) (no vested rights).

4. *Union Oil Co. v. Smith* gave the Supreme Court's imprimatur to the *pedis possessio* doctrine, but it did not provide much guidance on its

contours. The following decision by a state supreme court addressed the scope of the doctrine in the context of a modern exploration project covering a wide area.

Geomet Exploration, Limited v. Lucky Mc Uranium Corp.

Supreme Court of Arizona, 1979.
124 Ariz. 55, 601 P.2d 1339, cert. dismissed, 448 U.S. 917 (1980).

■ HAYS, JUSTICE.

* * * By use of modern scintillation equipment in September of 1976, plaintiff/appellee, Lucky Mc Uranium Corporation, detected "anomalies" (discontinuities in geologic formations) indicative of possible uranium deposits in * * * land in the federal public domain. In November, 1976, Lucky proceeded to monument and post 200 claims (4,000 acres), drill a 10–foot hole on each claim, and record notices pursuant to [state law].

Subsequently, defendant/appellant, Geomet, peaceably entered some of the areas claimed by Lucky and began drilling operations. Employees of Geomet were aware of Lucky's claims but considered them invalid because there had been no discovery of minerals in place and Lucky was not in actual occupancy of the areas Geomet entered.

Lucky instituted a possessory action seeking damages, exclusive possession and a permanent injunction against trespass by Geomet or its employees. There was insufficient evidence to establish a valid discovery, but the trial court found that Lucky was entitled to exclusive possession and a permanent injunction. * * *

Additionally, the court found that Geomet had entered the land in bad faith, knowing that Lucky was claiming it.

We must decide a single issue: Should the actual occupancy requirement of *pedis possessio* be discarded in favor of constructive possession to afford a potential locator protection of contiguous, unoccupied claims as against one who enters peaceably, openly, and remains in possession searching for minerals?

PEDIS POSSESSIO

Mineral deposits in the public domain of the United States are open to all citizens (or those who have expressed an intent to become citizens) who wish to occupy and explore them "under regulations prescribed by law, and according to the local customs or rules of miners in the several mining districts, so far as the same are applicable and not inconsistent with the laws of the United States." 30 U.S.C. § 22.

The doctrine of *pedis possessio* evolved from customs and usages of miners * * *. Regardless of compliance with statutory requisites such as monumenting and notice, one cannot perfect a location, under either federal or state law, without actual discovery of minerals in place. Best v.

Humboldt Placer Mining Co., 371 U.S. 334 (1963). Until discovery, the law of possession determines who has the better right to possession. * * *

If the first possessor should relax his occupancy or cease working toward discovery, and another enters peaceably, openly, and diligently searches for mineral, the first party forfeits the right to exclusive possession under the requirements of *pedis possessio*. Cole v. Ralph, 252 U.S. 286, 295 (1920); Davis v. Nelson, 329 F.2d 840 (9th Cir.1964). * * *

Conceding that actual occupancy is necessary under *pedis possessio,* Lucky urges that the requirement be relaxed in deference to the time and expense that would be involved in actually occupying and drilling on each claim until discovery. Moreover, Lucky points out that the total area claimed—4,000 acres—is reasonable in size, similar in geological formation, and that an overall work program for the entire area had been developed. Under these circumstances, Lucky contends, actual drilling on some of the claims should suffice to afford protection as to all contiguous claims. Great reliance is placed on MacGuire v. Sturgis, 347 F.Supp. 580 (D.Wyo.1971), in which the federal court accepted arguments similar to those advanced here and extended protection on a group or area basis. Geomet counters that *MacGuire,* supra, is an aberration and contrary to three Wyoming Supreme Court cases upholding the requisite of actual occupancy.

To adopt the premise urged by Lucky eviscerates the actual occupancy requirement of *pedis possessio* and substitutes for it the theory of constructive possession even though there is no color of title. We are persuaded that the sounder approach is to maintain the doctrine intact. * * *

We have canvassed the Western mining jurisdictions and found the requirement of actual occupancy to be the majority view. Davis v. Nelson, supra; United Western Minerals Co. v. Hannsen, 147 Colo. 272, 363 P.2d 677 (1961); Adams v. Benedict, 64 N.M. 234, 327 P.2d 308 (1958); McLemore v. Express Oil Co., 158 Cal. 559, 112 P. 59 (1910).

There are always inherent risks in prospecting. The development of *pedis possessio* from the customs of miners argues forcefully against the proposition that exclusive right to possession should encompass claims neither actually occupied nor being explored. We note that the doctrine does not protect on the basis of occupancy alone; the additional requirement of diligent search for minerals must also be satisfied. The reason for these dual elements—and for the policy of the United States in making public domain available for exploration and mining—is to encourage those prepared to demonstrate their sincerity and tenacity in the pursuit of valuable minerals. If one may, by complying with preliminary formalities of posting and recording notices, secure for himself the exclusive possession of a large area upon only a small portion of which he is actually working, then he may, at his leisure, explore the entire area and exclude all others who stand ready to peaceably and openly enter unoccupied sections for the purpose of discovering minerals. Such a premise is laden with extreme difficulties of determining over how large an area and for how long one might be permitted to exclude others.

We hold that *pedis possessio* protects only those claims actually occupied (provided also that work toward discovery is in progress) and does not extend to contiguous, unoccupied claims on a group or area basis. * * *

Finally, Lucky asserts that Geomet cannot invoke *pedis possessio* because Geomet, knowing that Lucky claimed the area, entered in bad faith. Lucky relies principally on Bagg v. New Jersey Loan Co. [88 Ariz. 182, 354 P.2d 40 (1960)] and Woolsey v. Lassen, 91 Ariz. 229, 371 P.2d 587 (1962). It is true that a potential locator must enter in good faith.

There is language in our decisions that appears to indicate that mere knowledge of a prior claim constitutes bad faith. Although we are sure that our holdings were sound in the cases Lucky cites, certain statements may have been an inadvertent oversimplification of the issue of good faith and we take this opportunity to clarify the point.

In general terms, good faith may be defined as honesty of purpose and absence of intent to defraud. * * *

Both *Bagg* and *Woolsey,* supra, dealt with those who had discovered minerals in place and were in actual occupancy when others attempted to usurp their claims. These facts immediately distinguish them from the instant case, in which Lucky had neither made discovery nor was in actual occupancy of the areas Geomet entered. * * *

In summary, both cases differ significantly from this case in their factual framework and did not depend for their resolution solely upon the element of knowledge. We stand by our conclusions in those cases but wish to emphasize that mere knowledge of a previous claim, in and of itself, does not constitute bad faith.

Since Geomet's entry concededly was open and peaceable, we hold that the entry was in good faith. * * *

NOTES AND QUESTIONS

1.   The Supreme Court granted Lucky Mc's petition for a writ of certiorari to review the Arizona Supreme Court's decision. Immediately thereafter, industry representatives urged Lucky Mc to dismiss its petition because of fears about how the Court might dispose of the case; e.g., it might extend the strict *pedis possessio* rule to all states. Eventually Lucky Mc dismissed its already-granted petition voluntarily. See John Leshy, THE MINING LAW: A STUDY IN PERPETUAL MOTION, at 106–07, 414 n. 66. It was not clear whether the Court would have had jurisdiction to decide the case in any event. Specifically, is the *pedis possessio* doctrine one of federal or state law? If no rights of the U.S. are implicated absent a discovery on a claim, are such disputes between rival claimants governed by federal law, or only by state common law rules of "possession"? If it is a rule of state law, does the U.S. Supreme Court have jurisdiction to review it? Is the Arizona Supreme Court bound by decisions of other courts, including the United States Supreme Court, on this issue? Note that the Arizona court found the view of other state courts persuasive, and rejected a contrary federal district court decision in Wyoming.

2. What if Geomet had done no more than post an armed guard on each claim? Note that in the Arizona Supreme Court's view, "occupancy alone" is not enough to gain protection of the *pedis possessio* doctrine.

3. Is *pedis possessio* the kind of open-ended doctrine that should expand its coverage to meet the needs of new technologies and changing times? Should courts adopt the more liberal rule of MacGuire v. Sturgis (the Wyoming decision discussed by the Arizona Supreme Court)? How does one "occupy" 4000 acres? See generally Kent R. Olson, New Frontiers in Pedis Possessio: MacGuire v. Sturgis, VII Land & Water L.Rev. 367 (1972).

4. What does *Lucky Mc* say about a prospector's security of possession over a large area that is typical of a modern exploration project? An experienced mining lawyer has suggested that legislative reform may be necessary:

> The complete exploration necessary to make an actual discovery of such a mineral as uranium at great depth requires a rather extensive accumulation of capital, engineering, and technological experience and expertise, and a substantial organization. Once such a deposit is found, it requires even greater capital, engineering skill, and technological resources to develop and produce it, process it, and ultimately to market it. Unless a party is able to perform all of these functions himself, he is not likely to be in a position to fail to adhere to the current customs because at some stage of the sequence of location, exploration, discovery, production, processing, and marketing, he invariably will have to enter into an arrangement or accommodation with some other member of the industry who has elected to abide by those customs. * * *

> Protection of possessory interests prior to discovery * * * is needed, but it probably is not afforded by the traditional application of pedis possessio. With the location of the claims and the existence of a proper plan for their exploration, the courts might liberalize the doctrine to grant that protection. However, the court decisions to date have not indicated the judiciary feels such a change would be proper. Therefore, operators at this time are in continuous jeopardy of loss of claims, but they really have little choice until the laws have been altered or broadened by legislation or judicial application.

Terry Fiske, Pedis Possessio: Modern Use of an Old Concept, 15 Rocky Mtn.Min.L.Inst. 181, 215–16 (1969). See also Terry Fiske, Pedis Possessio— New Dimensions or Back to Basics?, 34 Rocky Mtn.Min.L.Inst. 8–1 (1988).

5. Why doesn't Congress fix the problem? What should a legislative fix look like? If Congress did away with the occupancy requirement altogether, would this result in a few aggressive companies indefinitely tying up very large tracts of federal lands with mining claims? Who might object to such an approach? "Mom-and-pop" explorationists? Those with a penchant for claim-jumping? Environmentalists?

6. As *Union Oil Co. v. Smith* shows, the courts have sometimes been willing to adjust their interpretations of the Mining Law to accommodate

what they perceive to be the needs of the mining industry. As *Lucky Mc* shows, however, there are limits on judicial willingness to be creative in accommodating an ancient statute to changed conditions. But even when the rules in the law books do not keep pace with mining technology, mining companies can reach informal (albeit legally unenforceable) accommodations in the field to minimize conflict. See William Marsh & James M. King, Staking Mining Claims on Revoked Public Land Withdrawals: Issues and Alternative Strategies, 30 Rocky Mtn.Min.L.Inst. 9–1, 9–29 to 9–30 (1985):

> Widely publicized mining claim staking rushes in areas of high mineral potential are usually closely monitored by local law enforcement agencies. Law enforcement personnel will prevent (and rightfully so) any affirmative efforts to exclude rival claimants except perhaps verbal and written admonitions to "stay off my claim." Experience has shown that such admonitions are totally ignored. Even in the absence of law enforcement agencies, an aura of conviviality rather than hostility seems to develop. Physical violence between rival claimants is eschewed, and would certainly be viewed with a jaundiced eye in the courts.

> It is not only possible but almost universally the case that multiple rivals are "occupying" the same parcel of land while diligently (feverishly might be a more accurate description) seeking a discovery. Under these circumstances, it would seem that no such diligent occupant is entitled to any rights under the doctrine of *pedis possessio* as against another such diligent occupant, recognizing that both of them might gain *pedis possessio* rights as against a less enthusiastic participant.

> As between two or more such diligent occupants, utilizing the traditional analytical framework, correlative rights should be determined on the basis of the first rival to couple the notice posting and discovery requirements in states where applicable law permits the locator a specified period within which to mark the boundaries of his claim and record a certificate of location.

5. Gaining Rights Against the United States: Discovery of a Valuable Mineral Deposit

Castle v. Womble

Opinion of the Secretary of the Interior, 1894.
19 L.D. 455.

[On July 2, 1889, Martin Womble filed a patent application to gain title to federal land under the homestead/preemption laws. These laws did not apply to federal lands that are mineral in character. Womble's application was opposed by Walter Castle who, along with others, had located the Empire Quartz mining claim on some of the same land in 1890. Lower-ranking officials in the Interior Department concluded that Castle and his colleagues had made a valuable discovery, and denied Womble's application, and he appealed to the Secretary.]

The law is emphatic in declaring that "no location of a mining claim shall be made until the discovery of the vein or lode within the limits of the claim located." * * * And this Department [has previously said that discovery] * * * "is a prerequisite to the location, and, of course, entry of any mining claim. Without compliance with this essential requirement of the law no location will be recognized, no entry allowed.["] Has such discovery been made in this case?

In the case of Sullivan [v.] Iron Silver Mining Co. (143 U.S. 431) [1892], it was commonly believed that underlying all the country in the immediate vicinity of land in controversy was a horizontal vein or deposit, called a blanket vein, and that the patent issued was obtained with a view to thereafter develop such underlying vein. The supreme court, however, said * * * that this was mere speculation and belief, not based on any discoveries or tracings, and did not meet the requirements of the statute, citing Iron Silver Mining Co. v. Reynolds (124 U.S. 374) [1888].

In the last cited case the court, on page 384, says that the necessary knowledge of the existence of minerals may be obtained from the outcrop of the lode or vein, or from developments of a placer claim, previous to the application for patent, or perhaps in other ways; but hopes and beliefs cannot be accepted as the equivalent of such proper knowledge. In other words, it may be said that the requirement relating to discovery refers to present facts, and not to the probabilities of the future.

In this case the presence of mineral is not based upon probabilities, belief and speculation alone, but upon facts, which * * * show that with further work, a paying and valuable mine, so far as human foresight can determine, will be developed.

After a careful consideration of the subject, it is my opinion that where minerals have been found and the evidence is of such a character that a person of ordinary prudence would be justified in the further expenditure of his labor and means, with a reasonable prospect of success, in developing a valuable mine, the requirements of the statute have been met. To hold otherwise would tend to make of little avail, if not entirely nugatory, that provision of the law whereby "all valuable mineral deposits in lands belonging to the United States * * * are * * * declared to be free and open to exploration and purchase." For, if as soon as minerals are shown to exist, and at any time during exploration, before the returns become remunerative, the lands are to be subject to other disposition, few would be found willing to risk time and capital in the attempt to bring to light and make available the mineral wealth, which lies concealed in the bowels of the earth, as Congress obviously must have intended the explorers should have proper opportunity to do.

Entertaining these views, your judgment is affirmed.

QUESTIONS

1. Is the Secretary here trying to expand or relax the concept of "discovery" as a substitute for the *pedis possessio* doctrine? That is, is he

trying to protect explorers so as to encourage exploration? What is the difference between *pedis possessio* and discovery, so far as a claimant's rights against the United States are concerned? See John Leshy, THE MINING LAW: A STUDY IN PERPETUAL MOTION 135–40.

2.   "While the two kinds of location—lode and placer—differ in some respects, a discovery within the limits of the claim is essential to both." Cole v. Ralph, 252 U.S. 286, 295 (1920) (footnote omitted).

United States v. Coleman

Supreme Court of the United States, 1968.
390 U.S. 599.

■ MR. JUSTICE BLACK delivered the opinion of the Court.

In 1956 respondent Coleman applied to the Department of the Interior for a patent [fee simple title] to certain public lands based on his entry onto and exploration of these lands and his discovery there of a variety of stone called quartzite, one of the most common of all solid materials. It was, and still is, respondent Coleman's contention that the quartzite deposits qualify as "valuable mineral deposits" under 30 U.S.C. § 22 * * *. The Secretary of the Interior held that to qualify as "valuable mineral deposits" under 30 U.S.C. § 22 it must be shown that the mineral can be "extracted, removed and marketed at a profit"—the so-called "marketability test." Based on the largely undisputed evidence in the record, the Secretary concluded that the deposits claimed by respondent Coleman did not meet that criterion. * * * The Secretary denied the patent application, but respondent Coleman remained on the land, forcing the Government to bring this present action in ejectment in the District Court against respondent Coleman and his lessee, respondent McClennan. The respondents filed a counterclaim seeking to have the District Court direct the Secretary to issue a patent to them. The District Court, agreeing with the Secretary, rendered summary judgment for the Government. On appeal the Court of Appeals for the Ninth Circuit reversed, holding specifically that the test of profitable marketability was not a proper standard for determining whether a discovery of "valuable mineral deposits" under 30 U.S.C. § 22 had been made * * *. We granted the Government's petition for certiorari because of the importance of the decision to the utilization of the public lands.

We cannot agree with the Court of Appeals and believe that the rulings of the Secretary of the Interior were proper. The Secretary's determination that the quartzite deposits did not qualify as valuable mineral deposits because the stone could not be marketed at a profit does no violence to the statute. Indeed, the marketability test is an admirable effort to identify with greater precision and objectivity the factors relevant to a determination that a mineral deposit is "valuable." It is a logical complement to the "prudent-man test" which the Secretary has been using to interpret the mining laws since 1894. Under this "prudent-man test" in order to qualify as "valuable mineral deposits," the discovered deposits must be of such a character that "a person of ordinary prudence would be justified in the further expenditure of his labor and means, with a reasonable prospect of success, in developing a valuable mine * * *." Castle v. Womble, 19 L.D. 455, 457 (1894). This Court has approved the prudent-man formulation and interpretation on numerous occasions. See, for example, Chrisman v. Miller, 197 U.S. 313, 322; Cameron v. United States, 252 U.S. 450, 459; Best v. Humboldt Placer Mining Co., 371 U.S. 334, 335–336. Under the mining laws Congress has made public lands available to people for the purpose of mining valuable mineral deposits and not for other purposes. The obvious intent was to reward and encourage the discovery of minerals that are valuable in an economic sense. Minerals which no prudent man will extract because there is no demand for them at a price higher than the cost of extraction and transportation are hardly economically valuable. Thus, profitability is an important consideration in applying the prudent-man test, and the marketability test which the Secretary has used here merely recognizes this fact.

The marketability test also has the advantage of throwing light on a claimant's intention, a matter which is inextricably bound together with valuableness. For evidence that a mineral deposit is not of economic value and cannot in all likelihood be operated at a profit may well suggest that a claimant seeks the land for other purposes. Indeed, as the Government points out, the facts of this case—the thousands of dollars and hours spent building a home on 720 acres in a highly scenic national forest located two hours from Los Angeles, the lack of an economically feasible market for the stone, and the immense quantities of identical stone found in the area outside the claims—might well be thought to raise a substantial question as to respondent Coleman's real intention.

Finally, we think that the Court of Appeals' objection to the marketability test on the ground that it involves the imposition of a different and more onerous standard on claims for minerals of widespread occurrence than for rarer minerals which have generally been dealt with under the prudent-man test is unwarranted. As we have pointed out above, the prudent-man test and the marketability test are not distinct standards, but are complementary in that the latter is a refinement of the former. While it is true that the marketability test is usually the critical factor in cases involving nonmetallic minerals of widespread occurrence, this is accounted for by the perfectly natural reason that precious metals which are in small supply and for which there is a great demand, sell at a price so high as to leave little room for doubt that they can be extracted and marketed at a profit. * * *

NOTES AND QUESTIONS

1. Discovery was important in *Coleman* because he sought a patent, to gain fee title to the land (as well as the mineral). Patenting seems to be on its way out (see pp. 616–18 infra), but discovery is still important in many modern contexts. Consider this: Tex located a mining claim on federal land in 1880, and scratched out a marginal living by mining gold from it until 1900, when he died. His descendants have held onto the claim, and recorded it with the BLM pursuant to FLPMA, but have not done any

further mining. In 1990 the Secretary of the Interior withdrew the land in question from the Mining Law in order to protect wildlife habitat, subject to valid existing rights. Is Tex's mining claim a valid existing right? What information do you need to answer the question?

2. Does *Coleman* necessarily follow from Castle v. Womble? Is it "imprudent" to stake a claim to a low grade deposit that might increase in value as higher grade ores are depleted, or as mineral processing technology develops to make it profitable to mine? See, e.g., Hallenbeck v. Kleppe, 590 F.2d 852, 859 (10th Cir.1979) ("A private litigant cannot locate claims upon public lands and then simply wait until the minerals are in sufficient demand to be marketed at a profit") (quoting with approval the district court's conclusion); see also Foster v. Seaton, 271 F.2d 836, 838 (D.C.Cir. 1959) ("To allow such land [subject to mining claims] to be removed from the public domain because unforeseeable developments might some day make the deposit commercially feasible can hardly implement the congressional purpose in encouraging mineral development"). Is profitability relevant because it makes it more likely a deposit will in fact be developed? Is it a way to test the good faith of the mining claimant, as a way to determine whether the claimant really has mineral development, versus some other use, in mind for the land?

3. The price of many hardrock minerals has fluctuated rather dramatically through history. If Helen locates a claim on a copper deposit that could be profitably mined if copper sold for 80 cents per pound, and the current market price is 60 cents, has Helen made a discovery? What if the price is $1.00 when Helen locates the claim, but the average price over the last ten years was 60 cents? See, e.g., In re Pacific Coast Molybdenum, 90 I.D. 352 (1983) (historic and reasonably anticipated price ranges may be relevant).

4. What factors are *not* relevant to "marketability" or "profitability"? Distance to mills or markets? Alternative capital investment opportunities? Is any profit sufficient, or should the locator have to demonstrate a rate of profit equivalent to that experienced by other industries? As explained in more detail below, the BLM, the Forest Service, the Environmental Protection Agency and the states have been regulating hardrock mining operations on unpatented claims with increasing stringency (until recently, see pp. 637–38 infra). Requirements to reclaim land and to protect against impairment of water quality are now fairly common. Must the costs of complying with these environmental regulatory requirements be included in the discovery determination? See United States v. Kosanke Sand Corp., 80 I.D. 538, 546 (1973) ("To the extent federal, state, or local law requires that anti-pollution devices or other environmental safeguards be installed and maintained * * * [such expenditures] may properly be considered * * * with the issue of marketability * * *."). See also In re Pacific Coast Molybdenum Co., 90 I.D. 352, 361 (1983), discussed infra.

5. Should other values of the land, such as wildlife habitat or recreational use, be accounted for in the discovery determination? See note p. 609 infra, concerning the comparative value test.

6.   What about the problem of "excess reserves"? Baker applied for a patent of five mining claims he located on a volcanic cinder deposit. Each claim contained enough cinders to satisfy the entire known market (for landscaping, primarily) for 60 years; together, the five would satisfy all the market for 300 years. The Interior Department issued Baker patents on two claims and denied discovery on three, on the ground he had "too much" of the mineral to show a discovery on all five claims. Baker sued and won. Baker v. United States, 613 F.2d 224 (9th Cir.1980), cert. denied, 449 U.S. 932 (1980). In 1996, the Interior Solicitor issued a legal opinion (M–36984, "Excess Reserves under the Mining Law"), which opined that this decision had been limited by a subsequent 9th Circuit decision, and concluded that BLM could contest the validity of mining claims for industrial minerals for lacking a discovery when the mineral deposits within the claim exceed the market demand for the mineral for the reasonably foreseeable future, taking into account other resources in the mining area held by the claimant. BLM followed this with an directive that defined "reasonably foreseeable future" as forty years. BLM Instruction Memorandum No. 98–167 (1998).

7.   What about proving discovery on a mineral deposit that spans multiple claims? The Mining Law requires a discovery "within the limits of the claim located." 30 U.S.C. § 23. The courts have often stated that a discovery must be shown on each claim—that claims cannot be aggregated to show a single discovery. See, e.g., Cole v. Ralph, 252 U.S. 286, 295 (1920); Lombardo Turquoise Milling & Mining Co. v. Hemanes, 430 F.Supp. 429 (D.Nev.1977), aff'd mem., 605 F.2d 562 (9th Cir.1979). John Leshy has noted that

> * * * this rule runs head on into the modern imperative that many individual claims be grouped in order to justify a single mining operation. A prudent person would not endeavor to extract copper or uranium from a low-grade deposit if only 20 acres could be mined; in fact, an aggregated group of twenty or more claims is usually necessary to provide the economics of scale required to operate a mine involving a low-grade deposit successfully. * * * [However] no one has ever squarely raised the issue in the context of a large, low-grade mineral deposit.

THE MINING LAW: A STUDY IN PERPETUAL MOTION at 175.

8.   The *Coleman* test is applied less strictly when the contest is between rival claimants, and the government is not a party. The reasoning seems to be that, because no disposition of federal lands is involved, such private disputes do not implicate the broader public concerns that are at stake when a claimant is seeking to gain rights against the United States to public lands and minerals. See, e.g., Boscarino v. Gibson, 207 Mont. 112, 672 P.2d 1119, 1122–24 (1983). In a dispute between two rival claimants, where the U.S. is not involved, discovery serves the same function as the *pedis possessio* doctrine. This was illustrated in a case that reached a Mining Law nadir of sorts. Amax Exploration, Inc. v. Mosher, Civ. R–86–162 BRT (D.Nev.1987) (unreported). Various locators of the same ground sued each other to quiet title and to get "punitive damages for bad faith

claim jumping." After a long trial, the court ruled, among other things, that no party had made an actual discovery of a valuable mineral deposit, and no party's occupation of the ground was sufficient to establish pedis possessio protection. The court's melancholy conclusion: "The best the court can do for the parties in this case is to declare * * * that the land remains in the public domain open to peaceable exploration by the parties or by any other citizen."

9. An extended treatment of the evolving law of discovery and its modern applications is found in John Leshy, THE MINING LAW: A STUDY IN PERPETUAL MOTION, at 119–67, 175–77.

NOTE: A COMPARATIVE VALUE TEST?

Some cases have held claimants to a higher discovery standard on some categories of federal lands. See, e.g., Converse v. Udall, 399 F.2d 616, 622 (9th Cir.1968), cert. denied, 393 U.S. 1025 (1969) ("The prudent man test has long been strictly applied against one who asserts discovery on national forest lands, when the contest is between him and the government."). Conservation organizations raised the issue in In re Pacific Coast Molybdenum Co., 90 I.D. 352, 361–63 (1983), involving Misty Fjords National Monument, set aside by ANILCA in 1980. The Act withdrew the area from mining but recognized valid existing claims. In ruling on whether certain claims within the Monument were valid, the Interior Board of Land Appeals rejected the conservationists' argument:

> Appellants * * * suggest "a stronger showing of marketability is required for important recreation areas, such as Misty Fjords, than for other public lands." It is true that a number of cases in the past have indicated that a higher standard of proof is required for claims located in national forests than for other public lands. In actual practice, the Board has long since abandoned this position. We take this opportunity to expressly repudiate it. * * *
>
> As a conceptual matter, the theory that the situs of the land alters the nature of the test applied is untenable. Where the mining laws apply, they necessarily apply with equal force and effect, regardless of the characteristics of the land involved. The test of discovery is the same whether the land be unreserved public domain, land in a national forest, or even land in a national park.[11]

This has not ended the matter, however. Some federal mineral legislation permits the location of mining claims only on land that is "chiefly valuable" for certain minerals. See, e.g., 30 U.S.C. § 161, enacted in 1892, which provides that "any person authorized to enter lands under the mining laws of the United States may enter lands that are chiefly valuable for building stone under the provisions of the law in relation to placer mineral claims * * *." In 1998, in a case involving the validity of mining

---

11. This discussion assumes the validity of the location. Thus, where land is closed to mineral entry, a subsequent discovery is irrelevant as the mining laws no longer apply so as to permit a discovery.

claims located for an allegedly unique kind of building stone, Secretary of the Interior Babbitt ruled that whether a discovery existed depended in part on an analysis of the comparative value of the land for building stone as opposed to other uses. (The mining claims were in and along a stream that had high scenic and recreational value.) See United States v. United Mining Corp., 142 IBLA 339 (1998). The Secretary rested the need for comparative value on the statutory limitation to lands "chiefly valuable," and left open whether the test might apply elsewhere as well. (Because the authority of the Interior Board of Land Appeals derives exclusively from the Secretary, Secretarial decisions are binding on the IBLA; see 43 C.F.R. Part 9.)

NOTE: THE PROBLEM OF "COMMON VARIETIES"

In the *Coleman* case, the government also argued that Coleman's quartzite deposits were a "common variety" of stone within the meaning of 30 U.S.C. § 611, and thus could not furnish the basis for a valid mining claim under the mining laws. The Court agreed (390 U.S. at 603–04):

We believe that the Secretary of the Interior was also correct in ruling that "[i]n view of the immense quantities of identical stone found in the area outside the claims, the stone must be considered a 'common variety' " and thus must fall within the exclusionary language of § 3 of the 1955 Act, 30 U.S.C. § 611, which declares that "[a] deposit of common varieties of * * * stone * * * shall not be deemed a valuable mineral deposit within the meaning of the mining laws * * *." Respondents rely on the earlier 1892 Act, 30 U.S.C. § 161, which makes the mining laws applicable to "lands that are chiefly valuable for building stone" and contend that the 1955 Act has no application to building stone, since, according to respondents, "[s]tone which is chiefly valuable as building stone is, by that very fact, not a common variety of stone." This was also the reasoning of the Court of Appeals. But this argument completely fails to take into account the reason why Congress felt compelled to pass the 1955 Act with its modification of the mining laws. The legislative history makes clear that this Act (30 U.S.C. § 611) was intended to remove common types of sand, gravel, and stone from the coverage of the mining laws, under which they served as a basis for claims to land patents, and to place the disposition of such materials under the Materials Act of 1947, 61 Stat. 681, 30 U.S.C. § 601, which provides for the sale of such materials without disposing of the land on which they are found.

The status of common minerals under the Mining Law, and under the laws which provided that lands "mineral in character" were not available for homesteading or other land disposal laws, long was a problem. It was easy to show a "discovery" of a valuable deposit of sand, gravel, building stone, clay and other widely occurring substances. Could the same law that applied to these substances simultaneously work effectively for precious metals and other substances? The Department of the Interior and the courts tried various stratagems over the years to make them both work.

The history is covered in John Leshy, THE MINING LAW: A STUDY IN PERPETUAL MOTION, 130–35; see also Watt v. Western Nuclear, infra pp. 681. Remnants of the problem still exist today, but as the Court pointed out in *Coleman*, Congress solved most of it by legislating that only "uncommon varieties" of such substances (those with a "distinct and special value") may be located under the Mining Law. "Common varieties" could only be disposed of by competitive sale (see p. 677–79 infra).

The advantage of free minerals provides a powerful incentive to argue that one's claim contains "uncommon varieties;" hence, there has been considerable litigation over whether a substance has "distinct and special value." See, e.g., Boyle v. Morton, 519 F.2d 551 (9th Cir.1975), cert. denied 423 U.S. 1033 (1975) (red, gold and pink decomposed granite a "common variety"); Brubaker v. Morton, 500 F.2d 200 (9th Cir.1974) (ditto for brightly colored stone). The government and the courts seem to be losing patience with such arguments; see, e.g., United States v. McPhilomy, 270 F.3d 1302 (10th Cir.2001) (upholding conviction of theft of government property where defendants were found not to be acting in good faith, even though they were acting on an attorney's advice, when they located a mining claim and then removed common varieties of stone). The Forest Service has recently adopted regulations to tighten the test for "uncommon varieties." See 36 C.F.R. § 228.41(d) (2000) (containing a detailed set of definitions, such as "any mineral used in manufacturing, industrial processing, or chemical operations for which no other mineral can be substituted due to unique properties giving the particular mineral a distinct and special value;" "clays having exceptional qualities suitable and used for production of aluminum, ceramics, drilling mud, taconite binder, foundry castings, and other purposes for which common clays cannot be used;" and "[s]tone recognized through marketing factors for its special and distinct properties of strength and durability [but not appearance] making it suitable for structural support and used for that purpose").

SPECIAL PROBLEMS OF DISCOVERY: URANIUM AND OIL SHALE

Uranium. Although its radioactivity sets it apart from most other minerals, uranium is a metalliferous mineral subject to location under the Mining Law. It sparked a great rush in the 1950's, with old-time prospectors, weekend explorers, and large mining companies all competing for discoveries in several regions of the West, most notably the Colorado Plateau. Reminiscent of the California Gold Rush and succeeding strikes in the 19th century, enthusiasm was rampant. A popular treatment is Raye Ringholz, URANIUM FRENZY (1989). The Colorado Supreme Court captured the prevailing ethos in Smaller v. Leach, 136 Colo. 297, 316 P.2d 1030 (1957), cert. denied, 356 U.S. 936 (1958):

> Since Hiroshima was leveled in World War II the world has seen the rise of the atomic era. The active search for the wonder elements uranium and thorium has thrilled as well as disturbed mankind. It has already wrought wondrous economic changes in many sectors of our state as well as other parts of the west and has brought the hope and

partial realization of medical relief, scientific advances and cheap power to the world along with the threat of destruction by atom and H bombs. It has in the instant case turned brother against brother in a bitter quest for riches by one and the hope of sustaining integrity as well as securing wealth in the other. Our mining laws were developed years ago, first out of customs and laws of the miners and their courts, later out of Acts of the Congress and the State Legislature. Since their adoption we have had the uranium rush which, because this mineral is not usually located like other minerals have been in the past, presents difficulties. True it is that lodes of primary uranium ores have been found and may be noted by outcrops as well as radio activity; yet many secondary ores of this metal have been created by deposits of thermal waters or other means spreading the element in not only cracks, fissures, faults and fossilized trees, but also along stream and river channels and in old lake beds where no outcrops may exist. One of the most successful ways of discovering uranium, therefore, has been by means of radio detecting instruments and other modern scientific means such as fluorescent lights, photographic film, electroscope tests and even surface growing plant life. The scintillator and Geiger Counter allowing gamma ray measurements have become as familiar in the west today as the gold pan and pick and shovel were in an earlier period. The old form of grubstake agreement whereby the man who had no time or aptitude for prospecting could furnish the burro, beans and bacon to another for a half share of any discoveries made, has its modern day version in the loaning to a friend, for the weekend, of one's scintillator or counter on shares of whatever is found. And, weekend instrument prospectors have made some of our largest and best discoveries. * * *

The technology of exploration has caused courts some difficulties in determining when discovery had occurred. In Globe Mining Co. v. Anderson, 78 Wyo. 17, 318 P.2d 373, 380 (1957), an action to quiet title to lode mining claims, the Wyoming Supreme Court refused to "recognize the readings of electrical instruments such as scintillation and Geiger counters as sufficient to support discovery. * * * [S]uch counters while helpful in prospecting for uranium cannot be relied upon as the *only* test." In several disputes between rival claimants (where the U.S. was not a party), some courts retreated somewhat from this view. See, e.g., Rummell v. Bailey, 7 Utah 2d 137, 320 P.2d 653 (1958), (valid discovery could be based on radiometric detection plus geological analysis of the immediate vicinity, particularly when there are known, physically discovered deposits nearby); Dallas v. Fitzsimmons, 137 Colo. 196, 323 P.2d 274 (1958) (radiometric results, in combination with other evidence of assaying and the type of rock in place, satisfy the definitional requirements of discovery); Berto v. Wilson, 74 Nev. 128, 324 P.2d 843 (1958); Western Standard Uranium Co. v. Thurston, 355 P.2d 377 (Wyo.1960). See generally 1 AMERICAN LAW OF MINING 2d § 35.14[2][a][iv] (2000).

Oil shale. For much of the twentieth century, the immense deposits of oil shale in western Colorado, eastern Utah, and southern Wyoming captured the imagination of energy planners, the mining industry, the federal and state governments, and many others. Hundreds of billions of barrels of petroleum are locked in the rocks of the Green River Formation laid down in lake beds in an earlier age. The problem has always been that extracting the oil from the rock is difficult, and itself takes considerable amounts of energy. (The known technologies for doing so require mining the shale, crushing it, and heating it to 900 degrees Fahrenheit in a retort.) Despite these obstacles, the lure of the "rock that burns" has led to predictions, tirelessly offered for many decades, that oil shale development was right around the corner. The cruel fact remains, however, that the cost of developing oil shale has remained prohibitive, absent large government subsidies.

Until 1920, oil shale was subject to the Mining Law of 1872. In that year, the Mineral Leasing Act made it leasable, but contained a savings clause that preserved "valid claims existent on February 25, 1920, and thereafter maintained in compliance with the laws under which initiated, which claims may be perfected under such laws, including discovery." 30 U.S.C. § 193. Several thousand previously-located oil shale mining claims, mostly in Western Colorado, fell under that awkwardly worded clause. Because oil shale had never (and still has not) been commercially produced in significant quantities, it would seem to have been easy to conclude that a "prudent person" would find unjustified, in the words of Castle v. Womble, supra, the "further expenditure of * * * labor and means, with a reasonable prospect of success, in developing a valuable mine." Nevertheless, the Secretary of the Interior in 1927 succumbed to the naive belief that "there is no possible doubt of its value and of the fact that it constitutes an enormously valuable resource for future use by the American people." Therefore, he ruled, oil shale claims could be patented in the "present situation" despite the fact that there "has been no considerable production." Freeman v. Summers, 52 L.D. 201, 206 (1927). Patents were issued in the following three decades for oil shale claims covering some 350,000 acres of federal land. Committees of Congress held hearings in 1930 and 1931 on the patentability of oil shale, but no legislation was enacted to disturb the Secretary's practice.

In the early 1960s, Secretary of the Interior Stewart Udall, mindful that commercial production of oil shale had still not occurred, determined to end the practice of patenting, and the Department of the Interior began a major effort to challenge the validity of the remaining oil shale claims. Eventually the Interior Board of Land Appeals overruled Freeman v. Summers, finding that it was inconsistent with the Mining Law because there did not appear "as a *present* fact * * * a reasonable prospect of success in developing an operating mine that would yield a reasonable profit." Eventually this ruling came before the U.S. Supreme Court, in Andrus v. Shell Oil Corp., 446 U.S. 657 (1980). In a 6–3 decision (with a vigorous dissent), the Court concluded that the legislative history of the savings clause in the 1920 Mineral Leasing Act and subsequent developments prevented the Department from "imposing a present marketability requirement on oil shale claims." 446 U.S. at 672–73. The Court dropped a footnote to this statement which said that "[t]his history indicates only that a present marketability standard does not apply to oil shale. It does not affect our conclusion in United States v. Coleman that for other minerals the Interior Department's profitability test is a permissible interpretation of the 'valuable mineral' requirement." 446 U.S. at 673 n.11. Consequently, this decision has had no demonstrable impact on the discovery test applied to other minerals. See, e.g., Watt v. Western Nuclear, Inc., 462 U.S. 36, 58–59 n. 18 (1983) (other portions of this opinion are reproduced below, at pp. 681).

It speaks volumes about the Mining Law—ironically, a law designed in large part to foster more security for miners—that the validity of oil shale claims were still being litigated more than 70 years after they were located. In 1985 a federal district court issued a ninety page opinion rejecting numerous government challenges to the validity of some claims. 611 F.Supp. 1130 (D.Colo.1985). The government appealed but then settled the case before an appellate decision, by agreeing to issue patents to the claims in litigation, while reserving certain rights. The Tenth Circuit then vacated the district court decision. 826 F.2d 948 (10th Cir.1987). In Marathon Oil Co. v. Lujan, 937 F.2d 498 (10th Cir.1991), the court upheld the issuance of a writ of mandamus to compel the Department to take action on other pending patent applications for oil shale claims. And still more oil shale claims were at issue in Cliffs Synfuel Corp. v. Babbitt, 147 F.Supp.2d 1118 (D.Utah 2001), discussed immediately below. Plainly the Mining Law has generated many more dollars in attorneys fees than barrels of shale oil.

6.   HOLDING AND PRIVATIZING MINING CLAIMS

Holding claims: The assessment work requirement. Miners' local rules invariably required a miner to continue to develop his claim after he made a discovery, in order to assure maximum development of the resource, and protect against "speculators." The Mining Law codified this practice by providing that an unpatented claim will be forfeited unless "not less than $100 worth of labor shall be performed or improvements be made during each year." 30 U.S.C. § 28. Assessment work was not required during the exploration phase, before discovery, Union Oil Co. v. Smith, 249 U.S. 337, 352–53 (1919), but cautious claimants tended to do it on all claims, so as not to have to admit they did not have a discovery. The consequences for failing to do assessment work are not completely clear. 30 U.S.C. § 28 enunciates a "resumption" doctrine, providing that if the claimant fails to do the required assessment work, the land claimed "shall be open to relocation in the same manner as if no location of the same had ever been made, *provided that the original locators*, their heirs, assigns, or legal representatives, *have not resumed work upon the claim after failure and before such location*." (Emphasis added) The assessment work requirement was widely ignored, even though the required dollar amount of work, unchanged since 1872, was rendered increasingly inconsequential by inflation. The Department of the Interior had authority to raise the amount ("not less than"), but never tried to do so.

Until 1976 assessment work did not have to be reported to the federal government. FLPMA, enacted that year, requires an annual filing of an "affidavit of assessment work performed" on all claims, and provides that the failure to make such filing "shall be deemed conclusively to constitute an abandonment of the mining claim." 43 U.S.C. § 1744. This annual filing requirement also apparently does not supersede existing law that claims may be abandoned for failure to do assessment work. Thus, a mining claimant may seek to prove that a rival claimant has actually abandoned her claim, even though she has filed the annual statement pursuant to FLPMA.

Even more murky is the question of whether the federal government, as landowner, can challenge the validity of mining claims for failure to do assessment work. In Hickel v. Oil Shale Corp., 400 U.S. 48 (1970), a case growing out of Secretary Udall's challenge to pre–1920 oil shale claims, the Court, distinguishing and narrowly construing two of its prior decisions in the 1930s, ruled that the United States should, as owner of the land on which the claim is located, effectively be treated as a rival locator, and therefore allowed to challenge claims for lack of "substantial compliance" with the assessment work requirement. The Court left some ambiguity as to whether this rule applied to all mining claims, or just to those where a subsequent withdrawal made it impossible for other rival claimants to locate claims on the same ground. (In the oil shale context, Congress had withdrawn oil shale from the Mining Law by the Mineral Leasing Act in 1920.) The Department took the broader view, adopting a regulation asserting authority to cancel *any* claim, whether in a withdrawn area or not, for substantial failure to perform assessment work. 43 C.F.R. § 3851.3; see 37 Fed. Reg. 17836 (1972). Some industry lawyers roundly criticized this view; e.g., Don Sherwood, Mining—Claim Recordation and Prospecting Under the Federal Land Policy and Management Act of 1976, 23 Rocky Mtn.Min.L.Inst. 23 (1977). So far this has proved a tempest in a teapot, because except for the oil shale claims, the Department has not challenged claims for lack of assessment work, although it does routinely void claims that fail to comply with the filing requirements of FLPMA.

In Cliffs Synfuel Corp. v. Babbitt, 147 F.Supp.2d 1118 (D.Utah 2001), plaintiffs in 1989 applied for a patent on four oil shale claims originally located in 1917. Apparently no assessment work was done on the claims between 1930 and 1978. The Interior Department rejected the patent application because it construed the Supreme Court's 1970 decision in *Hickel v. Oil Shale Corp.* to mean that the "resumption" doctrine does not protect the claims against challenge by the United States. The district court rejected this position, finding that the United States "must take some affirmative action towards invalidating the claim before assessment work has resumed."

In 1992, by a rider on an appropriation bill, the Congress instituted a $100 "claim maintenance fee" for holders of unpatented claims, in lieu of assessment work. 30 U.S.C. §§ 28f–28k. Failure to pay "shall conclusively constitute a forfeiture of the * * * claim [and it] shall be deemed null and void by operation of law." *Id.* at 28i. Miners holding ten or fewer claims have the option of doing the assessment work and so certifying. Faced for the first time with the need to pay money to hold claims, many claimants abandoned ship, and the number of active mining claims almost immediately dropped by more than half. Challenges to the new fee on various constitutional grounds all failed. See, e.g., *Kunkes v. United States*, 78 F.3d 1549 (Fed.Cir.1996). The IBLA reports in recent years have been stuffed with decisions concerning the presumption of claim abandonment and the intricacies of the "small miner" exception. See, e.g. Daniel B. Koby, 139 IBLA 131 (1997). The fee was originally imposed only for six years, but in 1998 Congress renewed it for another three years. 112 Stat. 2681–235 (1998).

PRIVATIZING: PATENTING CLAIMS

From 1872 until 1994, a holder of an unpatented claim could seek fee title (a "patent") to the federal land (as well as minerals) embraced in the claim. In 1994 Congress called a halt to the practice, by including a rider on the Interior Department's annual appropriation bill that prevented the acceptance of new patent applications. Congress could restart the issuance of patents by simply failing to include the rider in any year's appropriation bill, but in recent years its inclusion has been rather automatic. Some patents may still be issued, however, because the rider allows continued processing (and if appropriate, patenting) of some 300 pending applications. For these reasons, a brief examination of patenting is still relevant.

Lode claims were patentable for $5.00 per acre, 30 U.S.C. § 29, while placer claim patents cost $2.50 per acre, id. § 37. Also, claimants could patent parcels of federal lands (maximum five acres per mineral claim) for use as a millsite. See 30 U.S.C. § 42. The applicant for the patent has the burden of proof as the "proponent of an order" under the Administrative Procedure Act. 5 U.S.C. § 556(d). The *Coleman* test for value is applied as of the date of the application for patent (or the date an unpatented claim is contested), not the date that discovery was originally made. Best v. Humboldt Placer Mining Co., 371 U.S. 334 (1963). If the land had been withdrawn after the claim had been located, the claimant must also show a discovery as of the date of the withdrawal. Thus, "even if at one time there was a valid mineral prospect on claimed land, changed economic conditions can destroy" the original discovery. Bales v. Ruch, 522 F.Supp. 150, 153 (E.D.Cal.1981).

The patent ordinarily grants a fee simple, except that patents for claims located in some special areas (for example, designated wilderness areas, see 16 U.S.C. § 1133(d)(3)) include only the minerals, not the surface estate. Applying this restriction to existing claims is not a taking. Swanson v. Babbitt, 3 F.3d 1348 (9th Cir.1993).

The highwater mark for the issuance of patents under the Mining Law was 1892, when 3,242 patents were issued. Patent issuance steadily dwindled after World War II because, with the end of the disposition era and the advent of the *Coleman* test, the Department of Interior developed "a grudging and somewhat tightfisted approach toward claims under the mining laws." Peter Strauss, Mining Claims on Public Lands: A Study of Interior Department Procedures, 1974 Utah L.Rev. 185, 187. Starting about 1950 the Department granted fewer than 200 patents per year on average. In all, approximately 65,000 mineral patents, totaling about three million acres of land, have been issued. See generally Current Mineral Laws of the United States, House Comm. on Interior and Insular Affairs, 94th Cong., 1st Sess. (Comm. Print No. 13) (1976).

Patenting has never been necessary in order to extract minerals from mining claims. In fact, the Supreme Court long ago said: "The patent adds little to the security of the party in continuous possession of a mine he has discovered or bought." Chambers v. Harrington, 111 U.S. 350, 353 (1884). Many large mines are found on mining claims that have never been patented; it is not unusual for a mine to include a combination of state, private (patented mining claims), and federal (unpatented mining claims) land. A patented claim becomes private property fully subject to the laws of the state on such subjects as land use regulation and taxation. But the U.S. Supreme Court long ago recognized that a state also has the power to tax a miner's interest in an *unpatented* claim on federal lands. Forbes v. Gracey, 94 U.S. 762 (1876).

The courts have generally held that a decision to grant a patent does not involve discretion, if the claimant can show the requirements of the law (primarily, proper location and maintenance of the claim, and a discovery of a valuable mineral deposit) have been met. In the only court decision to address the question, the Eighth Circuit held that NEPA does not apply to the decision whether to grant a patent. See South Dakota v. Andrus, 614 F.2d 1190 (8th Cir.), cert. denied, 449 U.S. 822 (1980), Chapter 5, supra p. 416. This decision might be questioned because even though a patent was not necessary for the miner to extract minerals from the claims, securing a patent does enable a patentee to do things other than extract minerals; e.g., with fee simple title, the claimant could build a ski area or a power plant on the land. For examples where the Department has granted patents and the patented land is now occupied by resorts, ski area condominiums, and the like (and not mines), see General Accounting Office, THE MINING LAW OF 1872 NEEDS REVISION (1989).

In recent decades, criticism mounted that the patenting feature of the law was out of step with modern federal land policy. While serious consideration was being given in Congress to reforming the Mining Law (and eliminating the patent opportunity), Secretary of the Interior Bruce Babbitt created a new process for examining patent applications almost immediately upon taking office in 1993. Previously, the patenting decision had been handled almost entirely at the field level, usually without careful legal review. Moreover, the BLM had in 1992 instituted a pilot project that allowed applicants to pay for third parties to prepare mineral reports that determined whether a discovery had been made. Recognizing that these decisions could have multi-billion dollar consequences, the Secretary revoked the pilot project and put in place a new process requiring detailed, multi-layered review to ensure that uniform decisions were made, and that patents were issued only when the requirements of the law had been clearly met. Mining companies whose patent applications were delayed by this new process brought suit to challenge the Secretary's authority. These lawsuits were generally unsuccessful. The lead case was Independence Mining Co. v. Babbitt, 105 F.3d 502 (9th Cir.1997). See generally Peter

Schaumberg and Karen Hawbecker, Patent Pending: Department of the Interior Administration of the Mining Laws, 46 Rocky Mt.Min.L.Inst. 16–1 (1999).

In May 1994, what may have been the most valuable patent application in history ended up on Secretary Babbitt's desk, a consolidated application from American Barrick involving dozens of mining claims covering a huge deposit in Nevada containing an estimated $10 billion dollars worth of gold in place. After a careful examination determined that all the requirements of law had been met (and after the company paid the $9000 the Mining Law required it to pay the U.S. Treasury), the Secretary signed the patent, but chose not to do it in the privacy of his office. Instead, he held a press conference where the backdrop was a gigantic check made out to the mining company in the amount of $10 billion and signed "the American taxpayer," and he took the opportunity to roundly criticize the Mining Law and the failure of Congress to reform it. A few months later, Congress began the practice of including annual moratoria on new patent applications in the Interior Appropriation bill. As noted earlier, the moratorium allowed a few hundred applications that were well along in the pipeline to continue to be processed and, if the Department determined that all the legal requirements had been met, to have patents issued.

The first few years there was a political skirmish over renewing the moratorium, but in recent years, including the first two of the new Bush Administration, the provision has been included without fuss. It therefore appears, barring some major change in sentiment, that the era of patenting is finally over; to borrow from T.S. Eliot, not with a bang but with a whimper. The Barrick episode is discussed in Scott W. Meier, Note, Mining Law—Approval of the Patent—A Command Performance, XXX Land & Water L.Rev. 109 (1995). In 1996, Congress included a rider in the Interior Appropriation Act which directed the Secretary to make final decisions on most pending mineral patent applications within five years. Pub. L. No. 104–134 § 322(c). 110 Stat. 1321 (1996). In *Independence Mining*, supra, the Ninth Circuit relied in part on this congressional time frame in refusing to mandate the Secretary to speed up the patent issuance process (105 F.3d at 510):

> We question whether the Secretary is free to make otherwise allowable administrative changes with the intent to defeat the mandate of the law by making the process so slow and for cumbersome as to ensure that no patents would issue. But, in this case, even if we were to credit IMC's allegations, IMC cannot show that it is entitled to mandamus type for relief when Congress has stepped in and formulated a specific timeframe for completion of the Secretary's review process.

7.   INROADS ON THE FREEDOM OF THE MINING CLAIMANT— MODERN ENVIRONMENTAL REGULATION

For a long time hardrock miners hastened to assume (and some unreconstructed mining claimants still fervently believe) that the Mining Law creates an absolute immunity from regulation. They pointed to the provision in the Mining Law that offered mining claimants, upon locating a valuable lode or placer claim (that is, after discovery), "the exclusive right of possession and enjoyment of all the surface included within the lines of their locations." 30 U.S.C. § 26. They urged that this provision gave the miner absolute control over the federal land embraced within the claim, with no "balancing" of relative values, indeed, with no acknowledgment of other possible uses, and with no attempt to control or mitigate effects on the environment. This extreme view, along with the many abuses of, and other defects in, the Law, long fueled efforts (so far unsuccessful) to replace the Mining Law with a leasing system like the Mineral Leasing Act, applicable to fossil fuels and fertilizer minerals.

But claimants' rights were never so absolute. The 1872 Act itself (which said claimants were subject to "regulations prescribed by law," 30 U.S.C. § 22) recognized the possibility of regulation of activities on mining claims, and the courts long implied limitations on the rights of mining claimants. Subsequent statutes like the Forest Service Organic Act of 1897, 16 U.S.C. §§ 478, 551, and Federal Land Policy and Management Act of 1976, 43 U.S.C. § 1732(b), give federal land management agencies express regulatory power over activities on mining claims (beyond the power to withdraw federal lands from the operation of the Mining Law) to protect the environment and other resources. This subsection examines the breadth of that regulatory power and the processes for challenging unpatented mining claims.

United States v. Rizzinelli

United States District Court, District of Idaho, 1910.
182 Fed. 675.

■ Dietrich, District Judge. The defendants are charged with the maintenance of saloons upon mining claims within the limits of the Coeur d'Alene National Forest without a permit * * * in violation of the rules and regulations of the Secretary of Agriculture. The claims were duly located, subsequent to the creation of the forest reserve, and they are possessory only, no application for patent ever having been made. * * *

[T]he Secretary of Agriculture, * * * formulated an elaborate set of regulations, published in what is known as the "Use Book". The particular rules alleged to have been ignored by the defendants are as follows:

"Reg. 6. Permits are necessary for all occupancy, uses, operations or enterprises of any kind within national forests, whether begun before or after the national forest was established, except: (a) Upon patented lands; (b) upon valid claims for purposes necessary to their actual development and consistent with their character; (c) upon rights of way amounting to easements for the purposes named in the grants; (d) prospecting for minerals, transient camping, hunting, fishing, and surveying for lawful projects."

"Reg. 19. The following acts within national forests are hereby forbidden: * * * (c) Erecting or conducting telephone, telegraph, or power lines, hotels, stores, sawmills, power plants, or other structures, or manufacturing or business enterprises, or carrying on any kind of work, except as allowed by law and national forest regulations, and except upon patented lands or upon a valid claim for the actual development of such claim, consistent with the purposes for which it was initiated."

* * * The defendants here have the possessory title only. They have a distinct but qualified property right, and, even if we assume that their interest is vested, it is one which may be abandoned at any moment, or forfeited. The primary title, the paramount ownership, is in the government, and upon abandonment by the locator, or his failure to comply with the conditions upon which his continuing right of possession depends, the entire estate reverts to the government; all the time, it retains the title, with a valuable residuary and reversionary interest. * * * [W]hatever [this interest] may be, [the United States] has the right to protect and obviously the interest which it retains is the entire estate, less that which is granted by the terms of [30 U.S.C. § 22], providing that locators shall have "the exclusive right of possession and enjoyment of all the surface of their locations." * * * The inquiry is substantially limited to the meaning of the phrase "exclusive enjoyment," for, notwithstanding the existence of the Coeur d'Alene forest reserve, it is conceded that the defendants are entitled to the exclusive possession of their claim not only as against third persons, but as against the United States. * * * The government inserts, after the word "enjoyment," the phrase "for mining purposes," and the defendants the phrase "for all purposes." No other language is suggested, and, indeed, no middle ground appears to be possible; the "enjoyment" is either for mining purposes alone, or for all purposes without qualification or restriction. Under a familiar rule of statutory construction, the necessity of reading into the statute one or the other of these two phrases to make it complete, and its adaptability to either of them, of itself operates strongly to determine the question in favor of the government, for it is well settled that in public grants nothing passes except that which is clearly and specifically granted, and all doubts are to be resolved in favor of the government. But, independent of this rule, considerations pertinent to the construction of private grants and contracts clearly lead to the conclusion that the right of enjoyment which Congress intended to grant extends only to mining uses. The general purpose of the mineral laws is well understood; it was to encourage citizens to assume the hazards of searching for and extracting the valuable minerals deposited in our public lands. In form the grant is a mere gratuity; but, in considering the propriety of such legislation, it may well have been thought that by reason of the stimulus thus given to the production of mineral wealth, and rendering the same available for commerce and the arts, the public would indirectly receive a consideration commensurate with the value of the grant. In that view doubtless the legislation has for a generation been generally approved as embodying a wise public policy. But under what theory should the public gratuitously bestow upon the individual the right to devote mineral lands any more than any other public lands to valuable uses having no relation to

mining, and for what reason should we read into the statute such a surprising and unexpressed legislative intent?

With much earnestness the consideration is urged that it has become more or less customary to erect valuable buildings upon lands embraced in mineral claims to be used for purposes having no necessary relation to mining operations, and that great hardship would ensue and important property rights would be confiscated if the locator's "enjoyment" of the surface be limited to uses incident to mining. But even if it be true, as suggested, that in many localities sites for dwelling houses and business structures could not be conveniently obtained except upon lands containing valuable mineral deposits and embraced in located claims, the fact is without significance and lends no support to the defendants' contention. * * *

Holding, therefore, that the right of a locator of a mining claim to the "enjoyment" of the surface thereof is limited to uses incident to mining operations, no serious difficulty is encountered in reaching the further conclusion that forest reserve lands embraced in a mining claim continue to constitute a part of the reserve, notwithstanding the mineral location, subject, of course, to all the legal rights and privileges of the locator. The paramount ownership being in the government, and it also having a reversionary interest in the possessory right of the locator, clearly it has a valuable estate which it is entitled to protect against waste and unlawful use. It is scarcely necessary to say that it is the substantial property right of the government, and not the extent to which such right may be infringed in the present case, that challenges our consideration. The burden imposed upon the principal estate by the construction and maintenance of a little saloon building may be trivial, and the damage wholly unappreciable. But that is not to the point. If a worthless shrub may as a matter of legal right be destroyed in the location of a saloon, the entire claim may be stripped of its timber, however valuable, to give place for other saloons and other structures having no connection with the operation of the mine. To concede any such right at all is necessarily to concede a right without limit; there is no middle ground. It is therefore repeated that, subject to the locator's legitimate use for mining purposes, the government continues to be the owner of the land, and is interested in conserving its value and preventing injury and waste. * * * [The convictions for maintaining saloons on mining claims were affirmed.]

NOTES AND QUESTIONS

1. Note Rizzinelli's argument, urged "[w]ith much earnestness," that what he did was "more or less customary." What does that suggest about the uses to which many mining claims are actually put?

2. If Rizzinelli had obtained a patent on the claim, could he have operated a saloon on the land?

3. If the only thing Rizzinelli was doing on the claim was operating a saloon, could the government have challenged the validity of his claim for lack of discovery? Why do you suppose it did not?

4. Could another person have "jumped" Rizzinelli's claim; i.e., was Rizzinelli protected by the *pedis possessio* doctrine?

United States v. Curtis–Nevada Mines, Inc.

United States Court of Appeals, Ninth Circuit, 1980.
611 F.2d 1277.

■ Hug, Circuit Judge:

* * * Curtis states that he located and filed [203 mining claims on federal land managed by the BLM and the Forest Service, covering some thirteen square miles] after stumbling upon an outcropping of valuable minerals while on a deer hunting trip. He states that, within this 13–mile area, he has located gold, platinum, copper, silver, tungsten, pitchblende, palladium, triduim, asmium, rhodium, ruthenium, scandium, vanadium, ytterbium, yttrium, europium, and "all the rare earths." These minerals he maintains have a value in the trillions. The mining activity of the appellees was very limited. At the time this litigation was instituted there was only one employee, who performed chiefly caretaking duties such as watching after equipment and preventing the public from entering the claims.

Hunters, hikers, campers and other persons who had customarily used the area for recreation were excluded by * * * Curtis [, who had] posted "no trespassing" signs on the claims and constructed barricades on the Blackwell Canyon Road and the Rickey Canyon Road, which lead up into the mountains and provide access to the Toiyabe National Forest. After receiving numerous complaints, the United States filed this action asserting the rights of the general public to the use of the surface of the mining claims. * * *

Section 4(b) of the [Surface Resources Act of 1955] provides in pertinent part:

Rights under any mining claim hereafter located under the mining laws of the United States shall be subject, prior to issuance of patent therefor, to the right of the United States to manage and dispose of the vegetative surface resources thereof and to manage other surface resources thereof (except mineral deposits subject to location under the mining laws of the United States). Any such mining claim shall also be subject, prior to issuance of patent therefor, to the right of the United States, its permittees, and licensees, to use so much of the surface thereof as may be necessary for such purposes or for access to adjacent land: *Provided, however,* That any use of the surface of any such mining claim by the United States, its permittees or licensees, shall be such as not to endanger or materially interfere with prospecting, mining or processing operations or uses reasonably incident thereto * * *.

30 U.S.C. § 612(b).

As noted by the district court, the meaning of "other surface resources" and of "permittees and licensees" is somewhat ambiguous. The principal issues in this case are whether recreational use is embodied within the meaning of "other surface resources" and whether the phrase "permittees and licensees" includes only those members of the public who have specific written permits or licenses. * * *

[The 1955] Act was corrective legislation, which attempted to clarify the law and to alleviate abuses that had occurred under the mining laws [citing the House Committee Report on the 1955 Act]. * * *

* * * As a practical matter, mining claimants could remain in exclusive possession of [their claims] without ever proving a valid discovery or actually conducting mining operations. This led to abuses of the mining laws when mining claims were located with no real intent to prospect or mine but rather to gain possession of the surface resources. Furthermore, even persons who did have the legitimate intent to utilize the claim for the development of the mineral content at the time of the location often did not proceed to do so, and thus large areas of the public domain were withdrawn, and as a result these surface resources could not be utilized by the general public for other purposes.

It was to correct this deficiency in the mining law that Congress in 1955 enacted the Multiple Use Act. Some of the abuses and problems that the legislation was designed to correct are detailed in House Report 730:

The mining laws are sometimes used to obtain claim or title to valuable timber actually located within the claim boundaries. Frequently, whether or not the locator so intends, such claims have the effect of blocking access-road development to adjacent tracts of merchantable Federal timber, or to generally increase costs of administration and management of adjacent lands. The fraudulent locator in national forests, in addition to obstructing orderly management and the competitive sale of timber, obtains for himself high-value, publicly owned, surface resources bearing no relationship to legitimate mining activity.

Mining locations made under existing law may, and do, whether by accident or design, frequently block access: to water needed in grazing use of the national forests or other public lands; to valuable recreational areas; to agents of the Federal Government desiring to reach adjacent lands for purposes of managing wild-game habitat or improving fishing streams so as to thwart the public harvest and proper management of fish and game resources on the public lands generally, both on the located lands and on adjacent lands.

Under existing law, fishing and mining have sometimes been combined in another form of nonconforming use of the public lands: a group of fisherman-prospectors will locate a good stream, stake out successive mining claims flanking the stream, post their mining claims with "No trespassing" signs, and proceed to enjoy their own private fishing camp. So too, with hunter-prospectors, except that their blocked-out "mining claims" embrace wildlife habitats; posted, they constitute excellent hunting camps.

The effect of nonmining activity under color of existing mining law should be clear to all: a waste of valuable resources of the surface on

lands embraced within claims which might satisfy the basic requirement of mineral discovery, but which were, in fact, made for a purpose
other than mining; for lands adjacent to such locations, timber, water,
forage, fish and wildlife, and recreational values wasted or destroyed
because of increased cost of management, difficulty of administration,
or inaccessibility; the activities of a relatively few pseudominers reflecting unfairly on the legitimate mining industry.

H.R.Rep. No. 730 at 6, U.S.Code Cong. & Admin.News, pp. 2478–79. * * *

* * * Curtis assert[s] that recreational uses are not encompassed
within the meaning of "other surface resources" in § 612(b). However, as
the district court properly held, the phrase "other surface resources" was
clearly intended to include recreational uses. It is apparent from the
[legislative history] that recreation was one of the "other surface resources" to which 30 U.S.C. § 612(b) refers. * * * It is therefore a surface
resource that the United States has a right to manage and that the United
States and its permittees and licensees have a right to use so long as the
use does not "endanger or materially interfere with prospecting, mining or
processing operations or uses reasonably incident thereto." 30 U.S.C.
§ 612(b).

The remaining question * * * concerns the identification of the "permittees and licensees" of the United States entitled to use the surface
resources. The district court held that the "permittees and licensees" are
only those who have specific written permits or licenses from any state or
federal agency allowing those persons to engage in any form of recreation
on public land. * * *

* * * [I]n the management of public lands, the United States has
historically allowed the general public to use the public domain for recreation and other purposes, and often without a specific, formal permit. Such
access has been described as an implied license.

Originally, grazing of livestock was such a use that was allowed
without a formal permit. [citing Buford v. Houtz, supra p. 98, and Light v.
United States, supra p. 110] In McKee v. Gratz, 260 U.S. 127 (1922), the
Court applied this concept of an implied license to include a license to use
large tracts of uncultivated lands for recreational uses. Mr. Justice Holmes
in the opinion of the Court stated:

> The strict rule of the English common law as to entry upon a close
> must be taken to be mitigated by common understanding with regard
> to the large expanses of unenclosed and uncultivated land in many
> parts at least of this country. Over these it is customary to wander,
> shoot and fish at will until the owner sees fit to prohibit it. A license
> may be implied from the habits of the country.

Id. at 136. * * *

[U.S. Forest Service and BLM] regulations confirm a traditional policy
for the use of public lands allowing the public to use lands within the public
domain for general recreational purposes without holding a written, formal
permit, except as to activities which have been specifically regulated.

The Multiple Use Act was designed to open up the public domain to greater, more varied uses. To require that anyone desiring to use claimed lands for recreation must obtain a formal, written license would greatly restrict and inhibit the use of a major portion of the public domain. [In a footnote, the court cited a Department of Agriculture report that several million acres were covered by mining claims but few were producing minerals.] It is doubtful that Congress would intend that such use be dependent upon a formal permit, because the federal agencies do not generally issue or require permits for recreational use of public lands. To require a formal written permit would either put the public in a position of having to obtain permits but having no place from which to obtain them, or it would require the government to institute procedures to issue permits, a process which the government argues is burdensome and unnecessary.

One of the clear purposes of the 1955 legislation was to prevent the withdrawal of surface resources from other public use merely by locating a mining claim. * * *

Consequently, in light of the historical background of the use of the public domain for many purposes without express written permits or licenses we do not find in the legislative history of the 1955 act an intent to so limit the meaning of "permittees and licensees." Most assuredly, the B.L.M. or the Forest Service can require permits for public use of federal lands in their management of federal lands; however, they need not do so as a prerequisite to public use of surface resources of unpatented mining claims.

It should be noted that mining claimants have at least two remedies in the event that public use interferes with prospecting or mining activities. Section 612(b) provides that "any use of the surface * * * shall be such as not to endanger or materially interfere with prospecting, mining or processing operations or uses reasonably incident thereto." The mining claimant can protest to the managing federal agency about public use which results in material interference and, if unsatisfied, can bring suit to enjoin the activity. Secondly, a claimant with a valid claim can apply for a patent which, when granted, would convey fee title to the property.

In the present case, appellees have not presented any evidence that the public use of land included within their unpatented mining claim has "materially interfered" with any mining activity. Absent such evidence, section 612(b) applies in this case to afford the general public a right of free access to the land on which the mining claims have been located for recreational use of the surface resources and for access to adjoining property. Therefore, we reverse the portion of the judgment that requires specific written permits or licenses for entry onto the mining claims, and we remand this case to the district court for entry of an injunction consistent with the views expressed in this opinion.

NOTES AND QUESTIONS

1. What is the legal status of a casual recreational hiker on federal land managed by the Forest Service or the BLM?

2.   Could the U.S. have contested the validity of these claims for lack of discovery? Why do you suppose it did not do so? Was a possible explanation for the claimant's motivation to keep the public off his claims suggested by the fact that he was on a deer hunting trip when he allegedly discovered minerals valued in the trillions of dollars (and subsequently put little effort into extracting this fabulous treasure)?

3.   Why was the 1955 Act even necessary? Did the federal government already have the power to prevent miners from using their claims for purposes other than mining, in ways that interfered with other uses of the federal lands? Compare United States v. Rizzinelli, supra. The Senate Committee Report on the 1955 Act had this to say: "Strict Federal enforcement of existing laws * * * could, in theory at least, have eliminated many of the abuses * * *. But the existing legal and administrative machinery has been slow and cumbersome, and personnel for adequate enforcement insufficient." S.Rept. 554, 84th Cong. 1st Sess. (1955), p. 5.

4.   What surface uses are "reasonably incident to mining" under the 1955 Act? A residential structure may qualify in some circumstances; see United States v. Langley, 587 F.Supp. 1258 (E.D.Cal.1984). But what about "a mobile home, several vehicles—both operable and inoperable—assorted animals including a bull, cows, chickens and several dogs, a sweat lodge, a chicken coop or enclosure, and a garden"? See Bales v. Ruch, 522 F.Supp. 150 (E.D.Cal.1981) (no). In 1996, the Department of the Interior adopted new regulations to detail what claimants could and could not do on their mining claims. These regulations also increased penalties for violators and streamlined enforcement mechanisms. These "use and occupancy" rules are found at 43 C.F.R. 3715 (2000).

5.   Just exactly what does "manage the vegetative resources" mean, and what is the scope of the authority it confers? For example, can a mining claimant clearcut an area of national forest, if removing the timber is reasonably incident to mining? Can the holder of an unpatented claim cut timber for sale to a third party? cf. Shiver v. United States, 159 U.S. 491 (1895). Can the claimant lease part of the claim for grazing? See United States v. Etcheverry, 230 F.2d 193 (10th Cir.1956). Can the holder cut timber for construction of a residence or graze stock for the miner's own domestic purposes? Cf. Teller v. United States, 113 Fed. 273, 282–84 (8th Cir.1901). See also People v. Wilmarth, 132 Cal.App.3d 383, 183 Cal.Rptr. 176, 179 (1982), upholding a warrantless search:

> Vegetation consists of "plant life" (Webster's New Internat.Dict. (3d ed. 1971) p. 2537). Marijuana is a plant (Health & Saf.Code, § 11018). Entry by Agent Dimmick, a federal officer, on land the site of an unpatented mining claim to search for, remove or otherwise deal with illegally cultivated marijuana is squarely within the authority reserved by Congress to the federal government to "manage and dispose of the vegetative surface resources" on such land. Arguably, illegally grown marijuana is not a "resource" within the meaning of the act; nevertheless, its discovery and removal is directly related to management of other vegetation indisputably within that classification.

A NOTE ON PROCESSES FOR CHALLENGING THE VALIDITY OF UNPATENTED MINING CLAIMS

The hundreds of thousands of unpatented mining claims on federal land are a cloud on government title, and can create serious land management problems for land managers. Moreover, because mining claims are still relatively easy to locate and maintain (if you're willing to pay $100 per year), they are, as the facts of many reported cases suggest, a tempting lure to those who seek ends other than mining. One of the more colorful episodes in Mining Law history was the saga of Ralph Cameron, who located mining claims in popular tourist areas on the southern flank of the Grand Canyon before it was withdrawn from the Mining Law, in order to mine gold from the tourists' pockets, as Professor David Getches once put it. It was only after decades of litigation that challenges to his claims eventually succeeded. See John Leshy, THE MINING LAW: A STUDY IN PERPETUAL MOTION, at 57–60.

The Mining Law is silent on the authority of the federal government to contest the validity of mining claims other than through its review of a claimant's application for a patent, or fee title. In Cameron v. United States, 252 U.S. 450 (1920), Cameron (by then a U.S. Senator from Arizona) argued that the Department of the Interior had no authority to bring an administrative contest against his claims. The Court (speaking through Justice Van Devanter) found support for the Department's right to challenge claims in statutes giving the Department general supervisory power over the federal lands, noting that holding to the contrary "would encourage the use of merely colorable mining locations in the wrongful private appropriation of lands belonging to the public." 252 U.S. at 463.

Another time-honored Mining Law tactic is that practiced by so-called "nuisance" or "strike" claimants, who locate claims mostly in the hope of being bought out by legitimate miners who otherwise would face costly litigation to oust them:

> The master of this gambit, a figure properly placed alongside Ralph Cameron in the first rank of Mining Law manipulators, was Merle Zweifel. Until his flamboyance, greed, and disarming candor about the game he was playing attracted so much attention that he could no longer be tolerated, the "old Prospector," as he styled himself, filed several million mining claims on federal land all over the west. (He himself put the figure at 30 million acres, which included an unspecified amount of land claimed on the outer continental shelf.) When Congress authorized the Central Arizona Project, part of which required construction of an aqueduct from the Colorado River to Phoenix and Tucson, the old prospector was there, filing claims on 600,000 acres along the aqueduct route. When interest in oil shale development began to revive on Colorado's west slope after 1960, Zweifel surfaced with 465,000 acres of mining claims in the Piceance Basin. Acknowledging that he would never actively explore the land (because that would damage the scenery, he said) he exploited the Law's offer of free access to the federal lands with a vengeance, though the character of his claims reflected the German meaning of his name—doubt. His

"real goal in life," he was reported as saying, was to "discredit bureaucrats and their hypocritical ways," though he also admitted that fighting large companies "is an enjoyment I can't pass up," and that, finally, "I do have a lust for money."

John Leshy, THE MINING LAW: A STUDY IN PERPETUAL MOTION, at 79. His tactics were so outrageous that the Department of the Interior was moved to bypass its own administrative contest procedures and instead to bring wholesale challenges against Zweifel's claims directly in federal court, in a quiet title action. Zweifel challenged this tactic, arguing that the Department had to use its complicated and lengthy administrative contest procedures instead (making essentially the opposite argument from the one Ralph Cameron had urged several decades earlier). The Tenth Circuit rejected his claims in United States v. Zweifel, 508 F.2d 1150 (10th Cir.), cert. denied, 423 U.S. 1008 (1975). It held that the United States could elect to proceed administratively or judicially, that primary jurisdiction did not require a remand because the question was legal and the Department had already made up its mind, and that the government had met its burden of establishing prima facie the invalidity of the claims. Zweifel has now passed on, but one of his colleagues sued the Secretary of Interior for damages resulting from the invalidation of large numbers of claims. Among other things, the complaint requested damages of "$1,346,390,400.00 due to breach of contract" and "three hundred billion dollars in damages due to breach of fiduciary duty, bad faith and unfair dealing." Relief was denied. Roberts v. Clark, 615 F.Supp. 1554 (D.Colo.1985).

Although the attempts at under-the-table appropriation are seldom as blatant or baseless as Zweifel's, abuses of the Mining Law have been common since its inception, see generally Leshy, supra, at 55–83, and continue. An adroit mining claimant took advantage of federal laxity in failing to make a timely withdrawal and located mining claims at Yucca Mountain, the site of the federal government's high-level nuclear waste repository in Nevada. It reportedly cost the Department of Energy upwards of $100,000 to buy out the claimant rather than suffer delay while litigating him out. In a study of 240 western mining claims, selected at random, the GAO found in 1974 that only one was being mined and only three had ever been mined. Comptroller General, Modernization of 1872 Mining Law Needed to Encourage Domestic Mineral Production, Protect the Environment, and Improve Public Land Management 8 (1974). BLM and Forest Service employees still must evict occasional "snowbirds" who like to winter on their mining claims on federal lands in the southwest, and continue the seemingly never-ending process of rooting out thousands of "miners" from prime recreation spots, survivalist enclaves, and hippie communes in remote areas all over the West.

Another quirk of the Mining Law as written and administered is that there is no statutory period for seeking judicial review of a Department of the Interior decision voiding a claim or denying a patent application. The claimant who loses may either relocate the claim (if the land has not been subsequently withdrawn) or simply remain in occupancy. For example, in United States v. Webb, 655 F.2d 977 (9th Cir.1981), the court held that a claimant may allege a valid claim and seek judicial review by means of a counterclaim to an ejectment proceeding nine years after the final agency decision. See also United States v. Smith Christian Mining Enterprises, Inc., 537 F.Supp. 57 (D.Or.1981). The general federal civil statute of limitations of six years has, however, been held applicable to challenges to some government decisions that adversely affect mining claims. Wind River Mining Corp. v. United States, 946 F.2d 710 (9th Cir.1991) (designation of wilderness study areas).

The Department of the Interior has taken the position that only a person with "title to or an interest in land" may contest a mining claim. See, e.g., In re Pacific Coast Molybdenum Co., 68 IBLA 325 (1982). Besides the United States, this includes a rancher who has grazing privileges on the land, but does not include a hiker or camper or other recreational user of the land. The distinction is criticized in Leshy, supra, at 257–60. The Department does, however, allow recreational users and others some rights to "protest" and appeal denials of their protests in some circumstances. See, e.g., Scott Burnham, 94 I.D. 429, 442–43 (1987). In Wilderness Soc'y v. Dombeck, 168 F.3d 367 (9th Cir.1999), the court ruled that an organization representing recreational users had standing to challenge the determination to grant mineral patents in a wilderness area.

MODERN ENVIRONMENTAL REGULATION OF OPERATIONS ON UNPATENTED MINING CLAIMS

More than a century after enactment of the Mining Law of 1872, the two principal agencies that manage federal lands on which hardrock mining activities occur finally adopted regulations providing for environmental regulation of those activities. Because their statutory authority and their regulations are somewhat different, these materials consider them separately, starting with the U.S. Forest Service. In the late 1960's and early 1970's, two conservation battles over mining—an ASARCO proposal to build an access road to a molybdenum claim deep in the White Cloud Mountains in Idaho, and a dispute over development in the Stillwater minerals complex in the Custer and Gallatin National Forests in Montana—drew the Forest Service into the business of regulating the environmental impact of hardrock mining on the national forests.* In 1974 the agency promulgated regulations under the aegis of two sections of its 1897 Organic Act. First, 16 U.S.C. § 478:

> Nor shall anything herein prohibit any person from entering upon such national forests for all proper and lawful purposes, including that of prospecting, locating, and developing the mineral resources thereof.

* Authority for administering the Mining Law has always been lodged in the BLM, even on lands managed by other federal agencies, such as the national forests. When Congress transferred most management authority over the national forests to the Secretary of Agriculture in 1905, it left the Department of the Interior with some authority over mineral activity, although the boundaries between Interior and Agriculture's authority were never sharply drawn. See 16 U.S.C. § 472. See the discussion in *Clouser v. Espy*, further below in this subsection.

Such persons must comply with the rules and regulations covering such national forests.

Second, 16 U.S.C. § 551:

The Secretary of Agriculture shall make provisions for the protection against destruction by fire and depredations upon the * * * national forests * * * and he may make such rules and regulations * * * as will insure the objects of such reservations, namely, to regulate their occupancy and use and to preserve the forests thereon from destruction * * *

The stated purpose of these regulations, now found at 36 C.F.R. Part 228, is to ensure that hardrock mining activities are "conducted so as to minimize adverse environmental impacts on National Forest System surface resources." 36 C.F.R. § 228.1 (1991). They require claimants to file a notice of intent with the local district ranger before commencing any operation that might cause surface disturbance. If the district ranger determines that such operations will "likely cause significant disturbance of surface resources," the miner must then file a plan of operations. Id. § 228.4(a). The ranger reviews and revises the submitted plan with the operator until both agree upon an acceptable plan. The regulations direct the ranger to make an initial response within 30 days if possible, and not later than 90 days. The final operating plan must include surface environmental protection and reclamation requirements, as well as a bond requirement to cover the costs of damage or unfinished reclamation. Pending final approval of the plan, the district ranger may allow mineral activities to proceed so long as it is conducted to minimize environmental impacts. The regulations also provide for access restrictions, operations in wilderness areas, periodic inspection by the Forest Service, and remedies for noncompliance with the regulations. See 36 C.F.R. §§ 228.1–228.15 (1991).

The authority for and extent of these regulations was questioned from the outset.

United States v. Weiss

United States Court of Appeals, Ninth Circuit, 1981.
642 F.2d 296.

■ J. BLAINE ANDERSON, CIRCUIT JUDGE:

* * * The appellants are owners of unpatented placer mining claims located within the St. Joe National Forest in Idaho. [They proceeded with mining operations without complying with the Forest Service regulations requiring an approved operating plan. The United States sued to require their compliance.] * * * Appellants' contention on appeal is that the regulations have not been promulgated pursuant to adequate statutory authority. * * *

* * * Under §§ 478 and 551, the Secretary may make rules and regulations for the protection and preservation of the national forests, and persons entering upon national forest land must comply with those rules and regulations. The authority of the Secretary to regulate activity on

national forest land pursuant to these sections has been upheld in a variety of non-mining instances. See United States v. Grimaud, 220 U.S. 506 (1911) (regulations concerning sheep grazing in national forests); McMichael v. United States, 355 F.2d 283 (9th Cir.1965) (regulations prohibiting motorized vehicles in certain areas of national forest); Mountain States Telephone & Telegraph Co. v. United States, 499 F.2d 611 (1974) (regulations requiring special use permit and payment of fees for a microwave relay facility within a national forest); Sabin v. Butz, 515 F.2d 1061 (10th Cir.1975) (regulations setting up a permit system for ski operations and instructions on national forest land). That authority has also been sustained to prohibit non-mining activity upon unpatented mining claims. United States v. Rizzinelli, 182 F. 675 (D.Idaho 1910). However, the precise issue of whether these statutory provisions empower the Secretary to regulate mining operations on national forest land does not appear to have been decided before. * * *

We believe that the Act of 1897, 16 U.S.C. §§ 478 and 551, granted to the Secretary the power to adopt reasonable rules and regulations regarding mining operations within the national forests.

* * * The fact that these regulations have been promulgated many years after the enactment of their statutory authority does not destroy the Congressional authorization given. The failure of an executive agency to act does not forfeit or surrender governmental property or rights. United States v. California, 332 U.S. 19, 39–40 (1947); United States v. Southern Pacific Transp. Co., 543 F.2d 676, 697 (9th Cir.1976). In this situation, a mining claimant may not claim any sort of prescriptive right which would prevent the government from protecting its superior vested property rights.

In analyzing the issue before us, we are keenly aware of the important and competing interests involved. Mining has been accorded a special place in our laws relating to public lands. The basic mining law of 1872 encouraged the prospecting, exploring, and development of mineral resources on public lands. * * *

On the other hand, our national forests have also been a fundamental part of the use of our public lands. National forests were established to improve and protect our forest land, to secure "favorable conditions of water flows, and to furnish a continuous supply of timber for the use and necessities of citizens of the United States; * * * " 16 U.S.C. § 475. The object of the Organic Administration Act of 1897 was "to maintain favorable forest conditions, without excluding the use of reservations for other purposes. They are not parks set aside for nonuse, but have been established for economic reasons. 30 Cong.Rec. 966 (1897) (Cong. McRae)." United States v. New Mexico, 438 U.S. 696, 708 (1978).

Moreover, while locators were accorded the right of possession and enjoyment of all the surface resources within their claim, the "primary title, the paramount ownership is in the government * * * it retains the title, with a valuable residuary and reversionary interest." United States v. Rizzinelli, 182 F. at 681 (D.Idaho, 1910). "The paramount ownership being in the government, and it also having a reversionary interest in the possessory right of the locator, clearly it has a valuable estate which it is entitled to protect against waste and unlawful use." Id. at 684.

We believe that the important interests involved here were intended to and can coexist. The Secretary of Agriculture has been given the responsibility and the power to maintain and protect our national forests and the lands therein. While prospecting, locating, and developing of mineral resources in the national forests may not be prohibited nor so unreasonably circumscribed as to amount to a prohibition, the Secretary may adopt reasonable rules and regulations which do not impermissibly encroach upon the right to the use and enjoyment of placer claims for mining purposes.[5]

NOTES AND QUESTIONS

1. In Okanogan Highlands Alliance v. Williams, 236 F.3d 468 (9th Cir.2000), environmentalist plaintiffs and a nearby Indian tribe challenged a Forest Service decision to approve an open pit gold mine on national forest land in northern Washington. One contention was that the Organic Act and 36 C.F.R. § 228.1 required the Forest Service to select the most environmentally preferable, but still profitable, project alternative identified in the EIS prepared on the proposal. The court said no. It noted that although the regulation required mining activities to be conducted "so as to *minimize adverse environmental impacts* on National Forest System surface resources," (emphasis added), 16 U.S.C. § 478 provides that 16 U.S.C. § 551 shall not be construed to "prohibit any person from entering upon such national forests for all proper and lawful purposes, including that of prospecting, locating, and developing the mineral resources thereof." The court continued:

> This circuit recognizes that 16 U.S.C. §§ 478 and 551 together evidence the "important and competing interests" of preserving forests and protecting mining rights. *United States v. Weiss.* * * * The statutory text, therefore, does not support Plaintiffs' assertion that, when the Forest Service is forced to choose between project alternatives, environmental interests always trump mining interests.
>
> Neither does 36 C.F.R. § 228.1 require the result Plaintiffs seek. To be sure, the regulation states that the purpose of the "rule and procedures" promulgated to govern mining operations in National Forest lands is to ensure that mining operations "minimize adverse environmental impacts." The regulation, however, sets no substantive standards that Defendants could violate. Rather, it merely explains the purpose of the *remaining* regulations, which do set substantive standards. And Plaintiffs do not claim that Defendants have violated any of those substantive standards.

---

5. We emphasize that the reasonableness of the regulations has not been put into issue. Although authority exists for the promulgation of regulations, those regulations may, nevertheless, be struck down when they do not operate to accomplish the statutory purpose or where they encroach upon other statutory rights. Appellants have not attempted to comply with the regulations; therefore, those issues are not before us on this appeal.

For those reasons, we hold that the Forest Service's selection of Alternative B did not violate the Organic Act or 36 C.F.R. § 228.1.[4]

Look closely at 16 U.S.C. §§ 478 and 551, quoted before the *Weiss* case, above. Do they really require balancing mineral and environmental values? Could they be fairly be interpreted in the way the *Okanogan* plaintiffs advocated? Could the Forest Service now adopt regulations requiring the selection of the most environmentally preferable alternative? Could a court require such a result in an appropriate case? Cf. footnote 4 in the *Okanogan* excerpt above.

2. In Clouser v. Espy, 42 F.3d 1522 (9th Cir.1994), the court rejected a miner's argument that the Forest Service lacked authority to regulate the means of transportation that plaintiffs may use to cross national forest lands in order to gain access to the claims:

> Plaintiffs assert—no doubt correctly—that the means of access permitted materially affects the commercial viability of mining claims. Under the legal standard applied by the Department of the Interior to determine whether a putative claim is "valid," validity depends in part on commercial viability. On this basis, plaintiffs argue that adjudication of questions concerning access materially affects claim validity. They therefore contend that adjudication of such issues is committed to the exclusive jurisdiction of the Department of the Interior since, the parties agree, Interior is the agency authorized to adjudicate the validity of mining claims.

> * * * In light of the broad language of [16 U.S.C.] § 551's grant of authority, [16 U.S.C.] § 478's clarification that activities of miners on national forest lands are subject to regulation under the statute, and [a] substantial body of case law, there can be no doubt that the Department of Agriculture possesses statutory authority to regulate activities related to mining * * * in order to preserve the national forests.

> As noted above, plaintiffs argue that because the permissibility of motor-vehicle access may affect whether a claim is deemed to be "valid," the issue of access is different from other matters that the Forest Service may permissibly regulate. Plaintiffs contend that means of access go to the validity of the claim and, as such, are committed to the jurisdiction of Interior. Rejecting this argument, the district court wrote:

>> I find that it is the nature of the issue presented (i.e. mode of access), not the *effect* of the determination which determines the appropriate agency forum. Thus, the fact that the Forest Service's rejection of a particular method of access may have a "material impact" on the mining claim activity does not *transform* the determination from one within the province of the Forest Service

---

4. Plaintiffs argue, in their reply brief, that the Forest Service violated the Organic Act by failing to promulgate regulations that establish criteria for choosing between project alternatives. We do not address this argument, because it was raised for the first time in Plaintiffs' reply brief.

to one within the exclusive province of the Interior Department. (emphasis in original). We concur in this conclusion. Virtually all forms of Forest Service regulation of mining claims—for instance, limiting the permissible methods of mining and prospecting in order to reduce incidental environmental damage—will result in increased operating costs, and thereby will affect claim validity, for the reasons explained above. However, the above case law makes clear that such matters may be regulated by the Forest Service, and plaintiffs have offered no compelling reason for distinguishing means of access issues from other such forms of regulation.[*]

Assuming the U.S. Forest Service (or the BLM) may impose reasonable environmental mitigation measures as part of the plan approval process, what if the cost of complying with such measures makes a marginal mining operation (as on an low-grade deposit in difficult, remote terrain) uneconomic to pursue? May the requirement be imposed anyway, if it means no mining will occur? Does that result square with *Weiss* or *Okanogan Highlands Alliance*?

3. In United States v. Shumway, 199 F.3d 1093 (9th Cir.1999), Judge Kleinfeld wrote a paean to the Mining Law, calling it a "powerful engine driving exploration and extraction of valuable minerals," and noting with satisfaction that "[d]espite much contemporary hostility to [it] * * * and high level political pressure by influential individuals and organizations for its repeal, * * * it remains the law." The Shumways had located millsites in the Tonto National Forest. The Forest Service had for many years approved plans of operations for their small scale mining operation, but friction developed between the claimants and the Forest Service in the late 1980s. The Shumways did not post a larger performance bond the agency demanded, and were ordered to cease operations, and in 1995, the United States sued to evict them from the millsites. The district court had granted summary judgment to the government. In the meantime, the Shumways' application to patent the millsites was pending before the Interior Department. Finding that the "owner of a mining claim owns property, and is not a mere social guest * * * to be shooed out the door when the [government] chooses," the court held that the district court erred in granting summary judgment because it found several genuine issues of fact in the record, including "whether the government improperly increased the bond amount to an arbitrary figure," and whether their "equipment and materials were 'junk.'" Describing the claimants' interest in the millsites as "property," the opinion concluded: "Like someone who proposes to operate a nursing home in an area zoned for single family residential and light retail, regulations may prohibit [the Shumways'] proposed use, but it does not follow that they forfeit their interests in the real estate." Is the analogy apt? Is it clear their interest in their claims is property?

4. In United States v. Doremus, 888 F.2d 630 (9th Cir.1989), cert. denied, 498 U.S. 1046 (1991), the court rejected a mining claimant's

---

* The court's discussion of the claims located in statutorily designated wilderness areas is omitted; the issues raised are dis-cussed in the materials on wilderness, Chapter 12, § E, infra.

argument that the Forest Service must prove that the claimant's activities were not "reasonably incident" to mining under 30 U.S.C. § 612(c) in order to prohibit them, even though the activities did not fall within the operating plan the Forest Service approved. It agreed with the district court that "the operating plan itself becomes the definition of what is reasonable and significant conduct under the circumstances," and held that "therefore any violation of the operating plan was *per se* unreasonable under the statute." The court also rejected the miner's argument that it could cut down trees on the claim even though this was not called for under the approved plan:

> [A]lthough appellants have a right [under 30 U.S.C. § 612(c)] to dispose of vegetative resources where such disposal is "reasonably incident" to their mining operation, they may not exercise that right without first obtaining approval of their operation in the manner specified in 36 C.F.R. Part 228. If appellants believed that their operation required the removal of trees and that the plan failed to accommodate that need, their remedy was to appeal the plan prior to commencing operations. Appellants may not blithely ignore Forest Service regulations and argue afterward that their conduct was "reasonable."

5.   Other cases have upheld and enforced the Forest Service regulations. See United States v. Goldfield Deep Mines Co. of Nevada, 644 F.2d 1307 (9th Cir.1981), cert. denied, 455 U.S. 907 (1982); United States v. Brunskill, 792 F.2d 938 (9th Cir.1986); United States v. Nordwick, 673 F.Supp. 397 (D.Mont.1987). See generally Eric Twelker, Defending Mining Claims and Mineral Leases in Environmental Lawsuits Against Federal Land Managers, 66 Denver L.J. 205 (1989); George Cameron Coggins and Robert Glicksman, 3 PUBLIC NATURAL RESOURCES LAW § 25.32 (2001).

6.   The Forest Service regulations skirt the issue whether the agency can forbid mining altogether by refusing to approve otherwise suitable plans of operations. 36 C.F.R. § 228.5(a). Do any of the above cases shed any light on this issue? In United States v. Brunskill, 792 F.2d 938, 941 (9th Cir.1986), the court declined to decide whether the Forest Service was entitled to disapprove outright a proposed mining plan, explaining that the claimant there had not appealed the agency's rejection of its proposed operating plan. The BLM has addressed this issue (see p. 636 infra).

7.   Numerous environmental statutes affect mineral development on unpatented claims, including most prominently the Clean Air Act, e.g., Robert T. Connery, The Effects of the Clean Air Act Amendments of 1977 on Mining and Energy Developments and Operations, 24 Rocky Mtn. Min.L.Inst. 1 (1978); and the Clean Water Act, e.g., United States v. Earth Sciences, Inc., 599 F.2d 368 (10th Cir.1979) (gold leaching operation is a point source subject to regulation). See generally Morris B. Hecox & Jeffrey H. Desautels, Federal Environmental Regulations Applicable to Exploration, Mining and Milling, 25 Rocky Mtn.Min.L.Inst. 9–1 (1979). The Comprehensive Environmental Response, Compensation, and Liability Act (CERCLA, or Superfund), 42 U.S.C. §§ 9601–9657, can expose the hardrock

mining industry to substantial liability for cleanup of mine wastes. See, e.g., Idaho v. Hanna Mining Co., 882 F.2d 392 (9th Cir.1989). See generally George Cameron Coggins & Robert Glicksman, PUBLIC NATURAL RE-SOURCES LAW chs. 11–11D (2001).

The BLM's principal statutory authority to regulate hardrock mining operations on the federal lands it manages is found in FLPMA, 43 U.S.C. § 1732(b) (emphasis added):

> * * * *Except as provided in* section 314, [43 U.S.C.A. § 1744, dealing with recordation of mining claims] section 603, [43 U.S.C.A. § 1782, dealing with the BLM wilderness study] and subsection (f) of section 601 of this Act [43 U.S.C.A. § 1781(f), dealing specially with the California Desert Conservation Area] and in *the last sentence of this paragraph,* no provision of this section or any other section of this Act shall in any way amend the Mining Law of 1872 or impair the rights of any locators or claims under that Act, including, but not limited to, rights of ingress and egress. *In managing the public lands the Secretary shall,* by regulation or otherwise, *take any action necessary to prevent unnecessary or undue degradation of the lands.**

How broad is this authority to regulate hardrock mining activities on unpatented claims? Is the BLM statutory authority stronger, weaker, or about the same as that of the Forest Service? Although the ("except as provided in the.... last sentence") phrasing is somewhat tortuous, putting the two quoted sentences together means that the second sentence expressly, if backhandedly, "amend[s] the Mining Law of 1872 [and] impair[s] the rights of any locators or claims under that Act."

What is "unnecessary or undue degradation"? Does it include, for example, the failure to reclaim a large open pit? Even if the cost of backfilling it is prohibitive? Does this statutory standard in effect mandate the application of something like "best available control technologies," a familiar standard under environmental regulatory laws like the Clean Air and Clean Water Acts?

The BLM's implementation of this authority has hardly followed a straight line. BLM first promulgated regulations to govern hardrock mining activities in late 1980. Found at 43 C.F.R. Part 3809, and therefore known as the "3809 regulations," they generally tracked the Forest Service's regulations, although significantly, unlike the latter, they (a) did not require plans of operations to be submitted for approval for mines that disturb fewer than five acres of ground per year; and (b) did not require the filing of reclamation bonds for all operations. Both of these exceptions were roundly criticized by environmentalists, the General Accounting Office, and

---

* [Eds. Note that the last sentence of this section applies generally to the Secretary of the Interior's management of the public lands (defined by FLPMA as lands managed by the Bureau of Land Management) in all settings, and not just in the context of the Mining Law. Other chapters explore its implications in such contexts as grazing, off-road vehicles, and wilderness.]

representatives in Congress. The sub-five-acre cut-off exempted as many as 2000 mining operations each year; such mines needed only provide a simple notice to the BLM. See Sierra Club v. Penfold, pp. 415–17, supra. Between 150–300 operations submitted plans of operations each year. See PUBLIC LAND STATISTICS 2000, Table 3–23, p. 144.

The initial rules also interpreted the "unnecessary or undue degradation" standard essentially to mean that environmental degradation caused by practices acceptable to the mainstream industry was "necessary" and "due" degradation. It defined it, in pertinent part, as

> surface disturbance greater than what would normally result when an activity is being accomplished by a prudent operator in usual, customary, and proficient operations of similar character and taking into consideration the effects of operations on other resources and land uses, including those resources and uses outside the area of operations. Failure to intitiate and complete reasonable mitigation measures, including reclamation of disturbed areas or creation of a nuisance may constitute unnecessary or undue degradation. Failure to comply with applicable environmental protection statutes and regulations thereunder will constitute unnecessary or undue degradation.

43 C.F.R. § 3809.0–5(k) (1999).

After several reports of lax enforcement and environmental problems cause by loosely regulated hardrock mining operations, in 1991 the Bush Administration embarked on a rulemaking to upgrade BLM's 3809 regulations. The rulemaking was put on hold in 1993–96 while Congress actively considered reforming the Mining Law. Once the effort was restarted by Secretary Babbitt in early 1997, it was several times interrupted by congressional riders which, among other things, called for a report by the National Research Council (*Hardrock Mining on Federal Lands*, 1999), and then required that the final rules be "not inconsistent with" the "recommendations" made in this report. Pub.L. No. 106–1134, § 357, 113 Stat. 1501 (1999). The rulemaking was completed November 21, 2000 (65 Fed. Reg. 65,998).

As the rulemaking was going forward, the Interior Solicitor issued an Opinion (#M–36999, December 27, 1999, "Regulation of Hardrock Mining") which concluded that the Secretary of the Interior had a right to reject plans of operations for proposed mines which would cause substantial and irreparable harm to significant scientific or cultural resource values of the public lands that could not be effectively mitigated. The Opinion rested on the Secretary's duty under FLPMA to prevent "undue" impairment or degradation of the public lands from, among other things, activities under the Mining Law of 1872. This so-called "right to say no" was subsequently incorporated into the 3809 regulations adopted in late 2000, which contained the following regulatory definition:

Unnecessary or undue degradation means conditions, activities, or practices that:

(a) Fail to comply with one or more of the following: The performance standards [set out in other parts of the regulation], the terms and conditions of an approved plan of operations, operations described in a complete notice, and other Federal and State laws related to environmental protection and protection of cultural resources;

(2) Are not "reasonably incident" to prospecting, mining, or processing operations as defined in [another regulation];

(3) Fail to attain a stated level of protection or reclamation required by specific laws in areas such as the California Desert Conservation Area, Wild & Scenic Rivers, BLM-administered portions of the National Wilderness System, and BLM-administered National Monuments and National Conservation Areas; or

(4) Occur on mining claims or millsites located after [enactment of FLPMA] (or on unclaimed lands) and result in substantial irreparable harm to significant scientific, cultural, or environmental resource values of the public lands that cannot be effectively mitigated.

65 Fed. Reg. 69,998 at 70,113 (Nov. 21, 2000). In January 2001 the Department decided, applying the Solicitor's Opinion, to reject a proposed mine plan of operations for the Glamis Gold Mine in the California Desert in Imperial County, California, because of an unmitigable conflict with an important Quechan Tribal cultural resource.

The Bush (II) Administration has marched to a different drummer on hardrock mining. Shortly after taking office, Secretary of the Interior Gale Norton announced that she would review the Clinton Administration's regulations with the "fundamental goal" of "enhanc[ing] the BLM's ability to protect public health, public land resources, and the nation's taxpayers," and not to "jeopardize[] the environment." Nevertheless, the Administration has deleted or greatly weakened certain key portions of Clinton Administration rules. See 66 Fed. Reg. 54834–54862 (October 30, 2001). The most important deletion was of authority to reject proposed plans of operations that cause substantial and irreparable harm. Other rollbacks in the new rule eliminate or water down key performance standards (such as those that protect water quality), greatly limit joint and several liability for proposed joint ventures, and eliminate the agency's right to impose administrative penalties for violations. (The House of Representatives earlier had voted 216–194 to add a rider to the FY 2002 Interior Appropriation bill to prohibit a rollback, but the provision was opposed by the Senate and not included in the final bill.) Although the Department's press release emphasized that it was retaining a "key" provision of the Clinton rules—the financial assurance (bonding) provision—in reality it had no choice, because improved bonding was a specific recommendation of the National Research Council, and (as noted above) the Congress had required the Department's rules not to be inconsistent with those recommendations.

Virtually simultaneously with the publication of the final rule, the Administration released a new Solicitor's Opinion (M #37007, dated October 23, 2001, "Surface Management Provisions for Hardrock Mining") which overruled the Clinton Administration's Opinion, and concluded that the statutory mandate to prevent "undue" degradation of the public lands does not add anything to the mandate to prevent "unnecessary" degradation. To interpret it otherwise, as the Clinton Administration Opinion did, would "inappropriately amend the Mining Law and impair the rights of the locator," according to the new Opinion. Both the rollback and the new Solicitor's Opinion have been challenged by environmental interests. Mineral Policy Center v. Babbitt, No. 01–73 (RBW). A month after the new Solicitor's Opinion was issued, the Administration announced it would rescind the decision to reject the Glamis Mine and reconsider the application.

NOTES AND QUESTIONS

1. Who is right on this reading of the seemingly simple phrase "unnecessary or undue degradation"? Does "or" mean "and"? Does the duty to prevent "undue degradation" mean that the Secretary may say no to requests to approve mines that involve serious environmental harm? If the Secretary says no, is that a taking of property requiring compensation?

2. In general, who has stronger statutory authority to regulate hardrock mining activities, the U.S. Forest Service or the BLM?

3. For a thorough review of current legal issues in implementing the Mining Law, see Roger Flynn, The 1872 Mining Law as an Impediment to Mineral Development on the Public Lands: A 19th Century Law Meets the Realities of Modern Mining, 34 Land & Water L.Rev. 301 (1999); see also Flynn, The Right to Say No: Federal Authority Over Hardrock Mining on Public Lands, 16 J. of Envtl. L. & Litig. 249 (2002) (forthcoming).

NOTE: REGULATING HARDROCK MINING IN NATIONAL PARKS

In 1976, in response to controversies over ongoing mining activities in Death Valley and what was then Mt. McKinley (since changed to Denali) National Parks, Congress enacted the Mining in the Parks Act, 16 U.S.C. §§ 1901 et seq. (MPA). Hardrock mining occurred in a few parks because mining claims had been located on the lands when they were open to the Mining Law, and some of these had gone to patent. The Act governed activities "resulting from the exercise of valid existing mineral rights on patented or unpatented mining claims within any area of the National Park System," and made such activities "subject to such regulations prescribed by the Secretary of the Interior as he deems necessary or desirable for the preservation and management of those areas." 16 U.S.C. § 1902. Except for valid existing rights, exploration, mining and patenting of hardrock minerals within the national park system was prohibited. The Park Service's regulations are quite detailed and stringent. 36 C.F.R. Part 9 (2000).

The Park Service has used its authority under the MPA to prevent miners from operating on mining claims, some of them patented, that were included with a national park system unit without first obtaining approval of an operations plan. United States v. Vogler, 859 F.2d 638 (9th Cir.1988). Among the arguments the court rejected were that (1) Congress lacked authority to enact such regulatory statutes because Chief Justice Taney's analysis of the property clause in Dred Scott v. Sandford (see Chapter 2, supra pp. 51–52) was still good law; and (2) the Park Service regulations violated Article 73 of the United Nations Charter, which speaks of "territories whose peoples have not yet attained a full measure of self-government."

The Ninth Circuit has also held that the Secretary has discretion under the Act to decide when and under what conditions to conduct a field inspection and mineral examination to determine the value of a discovery prior to approving plans of operations. See Northern Alaska Environmental Center v. Lujan, 872 F.2d 901 (9th Cir.1989) ("The MPA leaves it to the Secretary to determine the appropriate manner off determining whether an existing mineral right is valid," and therefore the Secretary may, considering the relatively extreme climatic conditions in Alaska, "channel his limited resources to on-site mineral examinations of isolated claims or to areas previously not subjected to mining operations").

NOTE: REFORMING THE MINING LAW

Calls for reform of the Mining Law date back over a century. Factions inside the mining industry have long advocated legislation to mitigate pedis possessio uncertainties and provide more security of tenure during the exploration phase. Proposals have long been offered to eliminate such litigation-prone features as the distinction between lode and placer claims and extralateral rights, and to substitute uniform location procedures for the patchwork of state laws. Until the 1960s, Mining Law reform was an internecine struggle within the industry, and proponents of major reform (usually the larger mining companies) could never muster enough political support to overcome the resistance of "mom & pop" prospectors and miners.

In the modern era, reformers are led by environmental groups and fiscal conservatives, who emphasize the relative lack of environmental safeguards on hardrock mining, the fact that hardrock miners pay no rental or royalty, the Law's opportunity for privatization of federal lands for a nominal fee, its numerous opportunities for abuse for purposes that have nothing to do with mining, and the inability of the federal agencies to rid their lands of stale or nuisance claims. Until the late 1980s, most reformers supported total abolition of the location system, substituting a fully discretionary leasing system modeled on the Mineral Leasing Act. Leasing proposals received serious attention in Congress in the mid–1970s, attracting the support of Presidents Nixon and Carter and key congressmen. But they were never enacted. A history of reform efforts is found in John Leshy, THE MINING LAW: A STUDY IN PERPETUAL MOTION 287–312 (1987); see also Leshy, Reforming the Mining Law: Problems and Prospects, 9 Pub.L.L.Rev. 1 (1988).

For the last quarter of a century, reform efforts have never found a political formula to overcome substantial divisions in the Congress. The House has generally favored tough reform by a substantial margin, but the power of western Senators has kept the Senate from finding sixty votes (necessary to overcome a filibuster which diehard Mining Law supporters would mount if necessary) to pass meaningful reform. Defenders of the system continue to emphasize the need they perceive for the federal government to maintain incentives for hardrock mineral development. They especially oppose a discretionary leasing system, which they argue would destroy the opportunity for initiative built into the location system. Hardrock minerals, they maintain, are more elusive to find than the more widely occurring bedded minerals like coal and phosphate that are subject to the federal Mineral Leasing Act.

In the late 1980s, the reform effort—moribund for a decade—was resuscitated. The Reagan Administration's issuance of patents for several thousand acres of old oil shale claims in western Colorado combined with several General Accounting Office and newspaper reports of environmental and patenting abuses to put the issue back before Congress. This time a number of environmental groups indicated a willingness to support major reform within the confines of the location system, rather than support all-out leasing. In 1993–94 it seemed that reform was at last at hand. For the first time in history, reform bills passed both Houses of Congress, but the two chambers could not resolve their differences and the effort died in the waning days of the 104th Congress. The next year, the Republicans took over both Houses, and eventually included a pale version of Mining Law reform (which did almost nothing to address the basic issues, and was opposed as "sham reform" by environmentalists and the Administration) in a massive omnibus "budget reconciliation bill" that was vetoed by President Clinton.

The Bush (II) Administration recently suggested that Congress ought to reform the Mining Law, but provided little detail on what it would support. In a letter of October 25, 2001 from Secretary Gale Norton to key members of Congress, the Administration identified the following issues:

—a permanent authorization of a mining claim holding fee (the current $100 fee is "temporary" although it has been in the law since 1992).

—"revision of the patent system." The Administration's intent here is ambiguous, and it provided no detail. As noted earlier, every year since 1994 Congress has included in the annual Interior Appropriations bill a moratorium on accepting new patent applications.

—"authorization of a production payment system." This presumably means some sort of royalty, though no detail was provided here either. Hardrock miners are just about the only user of the public lands left (other than some recreational uses) who provide no rental, royalty, or other fee for the privilege of using public resources (and in the case of mining, extracting and depleting them). In fact, the federal lands may be the only place left on the planet where hardrock miners can mine without paying the owners of the resource anything. On private and state lands, and in foreign countries, hardrock miners routinely pay a royalty to the mineral owner.

—authorization for administrative penalties. This was a feature of the Clinton Administration 3809 rules, which the Bush Administration concluded requires legislation.

—an expanded role for the States in managing the mining program.*

The Administration has said, however, that it does not intend to propose legislation, but merely tossed the ball to Congress. Considering that Congress hasn't successfully moved generic mining law reform for 129 years, one might be forgiven for not holding one's breath. Nevertheless, while the Mining Law has survived into the third millennium, it has been grudgingly reformed by a variety of means and measures. See generally John Leshy, Public Lands at the Millennium, 46 Rocky Mt.Min.L.Inst. 1, 1–9 through 1–21 (2000); see also Patrick Garver & Mark Squillace, Mining Law Reform—Administrative Style, 45 Rocky Mt. Min.L.Inst. 14–1 (1999).

B.   MINERAL LEASING

A leasing disposition system for some non-metalliferous minerals developed separately from the location system for hardrock minerals as much because of history as geology. Coal was made subject to a sale system in 1864, before the first Mining Law was enacted. The age of petroleum dawned a few years before the Mining Law was enacted; that Law's application to petroleum was, as illustrated in Union Oil v. Smith, supra p. 596, fraught with problems. Moreover, as demonstrated in *Midwest Oil*, Chapter 2, supra p. 119, the federal government realized by 1909 there was little sense in giving away oil reserves one day and buying them back for the Navy the next.

Leasing was not an innovation. It had been the practice of the young United States with lead mines in what is now the Midwest for several decades in the early 1800's, and had been upheld by the U.S. Supreme Court in United States v. Gratiot, Chapter 2, supra p. 49. But the modern watershed is the Mineral Leasing Act of 1920, as amended, 30 U.S.C. § 181 et seq., enacted after a several year struggle recounted in Robert W. Swenson, Legal Aspects of Mineral Resources Exploitation, in Paul Gates, HISTORY OF PUBLIC LAND LAW DEVELOPMENT (1970). The Mineral Leasing Act became the basic model for the Outer Continental Shelf Lands Act of 1953, 43 U.S.C. §§ 1331–1343, and the Geothermal Steam Act of 1970, 30 U.S.C. §§ 1001–1025. The Mineral Leasing Act's sections on coal leasing were tightened by the Federal Coal Leasing Amendments of 1976, 30 U.S.C. §§ 201 et seq.

Today, the leasable minerals include the fossil fuel minerals (oil, gas, oil shale, coal, native asphalt, bituminous rock, and solid and semi-solid bitumen); the fertilizer and chemical minerals (phosphate, potash, sodium, and, in a few states, sulphur); all minerals (but in practice, principally oil and gas) on the outer continental shelf; and geothermal resources. The Mineral Leasing Act for Acquired Lands applies to the same minerals as the Mineral Leasing Act and simply extends its principles to acquired federal lands. Hardrock minerals are leasable by regulation on acquired

---

* For a review of state regulation in this area, see James M. McElfish, Tobie Bernstein, Susan P. Bass, and Elizabeth Sheldon, Hardrock Mining: State Approaches to Environmental Protection (1998).

national forest lands and on the outer continental shelf. Minor acts cover a variety of special situations. See 1 AMERICAN LAW OF MINING 2d § 20.05 (2000).

1. Mineral Leasing Systems in a Nutshell

Generalization about mineral leasing can be somewhat hazardous because the major acts are not identical, and special provisions abound. But certain common features distinguish leasing from location systems:

a. There is no right of self-initiation. Permission must be obtained from the federal government to prospect, develop, or produce leasable minerals.

b. The United States has broad discretion whether to offer lands for lease, see United States ex rel. McLennan v. Wilbur, Chapter 2, supra p. 128; see also Ash Creek Mining Co. v. Lujan, 969 F.2d 868 (10th Cir.1992) (Wyoming had no standing to complain of Secretary's decision to exchange federal coal rather than lease it, because leasing is a decision within the discretion of the executive and federal courts lack authority to order federal lands to be leased). The government may make determinations not to lease through the land and resource planning process, and may also determine to put federal minerals off limits to leasing through the withdrawal process. As noted in Chapter 4, supra p. 345–48, the relationship between (a) an exercise of executive discretion not to lease and (b) a withdrawal of federal lands from leasing is not crystal clear, but they and the planning process are distinct ways not to develop federal mineral resources.

c. The United States also has broad power to control mineral development through lease terms and stipulations, and leases typically contain provisions to protect other competing resources and the environment.

d. The United States can require diligent development of the resource leased, on pain of forfeiture of the lease.

e. The United States typically must put mineral resources up for competitive bid, and may not accept less than fair market value for the resource. The lease offer specifies the royalty rate the lessee will pay on the unit of production; e.g., 12% of the value of resource produced. A minimum royalty rate is set by statute, and varies somewhat from mineral to mineral. Bidders compete against each other in the amount of "bonus" or cash payment they are willing to offer the government to secure the lease. In addition to the bonus bid and the royalty, lessees must pay an annual rental on a per acre basis. (The financial aspects of leasing are managed by a separate agency housed in the Interior Department, the Minerals Management Service, or MMS.)

2. Exploration Versus Development—Competition in Federal Mineral Development

Originally, most federal lands leasing systems distinguished between areas where a good deal of information existed about likely mineral occurrence, and areas of unknown potential. In the former areas, no exploration permits were thought necessary. Leases were obtained only through competitive bidding. Where knowledge was lacking, the applicable statutes authorized the federal government to issue "prospecting permits" that authorized exploration for a period of time. If the permittee discovered a "valuable deposit" or "commercial quantities" of the mineral, it would become entitled to a so-called "preference right lease," without competitive bidding. (The showing required bears a strong resemblance to the "discovery" requirement under the Mining Law.) Because there was no competition, the return to the government from noncompetitive leases was significantly less than when leases were put up for bid. The justification for this lower return was to provide an incentive for exploration.

Congress has abandoned that distinction for the most important minerals, oil, gas and coal. All offshore oil and gas leasing is by competitive bidding, although the form and contents of the bidding process can vary dramatically. See Watt v. Energy Action Ed. Found., 454 U.S. 151 (1981). In 1987, Congress reformed the onshore oil and gas leasing system to require all areas to be offered for competitive bidding. Only if an offered tract draws no bids can it thereafter be leased non-competitively with a statutory minimum royalty. Congress abandoned prospecting permits and moved to competitive leasing for coal in 1975. The issuance of prospecting permits followed by the opportunity to obtain a preference right lease still exists in geothermal leasing and in the fertilizer minerals. How this works is illustrated further below in the *Kerr-McGee* case, in the section on environmental regulation of lease activities.

Where competitive bidding is followed, the BLM, at the request of a private party or on its own initiative, publishes a notice to offer specific lands for lease. Persons may then submit bids in accordance with highly detailed requirements. Leases are issued to the qualified bidder with the highest bonus bid, but the United States may reject all bids, the most common basis being the inadequacy of the bid. The royalty is fixed by the BLM in advance; typical royalties are 12 1/2% to 25% for oil and gas, depending upon the amount of production; at least 12 1/2% for surface-mined coal; and 10 to 15% for geothermal steam. Royalty collection and administration is administered by the Minerals Management Service (MMS), a separate agency in the Department of the Interior. Royalty standards and processes for oil and gas (by far the largest category) was overhauled by the Federal Oil and Gas Royalty Management Act in 1982, see 30 U.S.C. §§ 1701–57, and then significantly amended in the Federal Oil and Gas Royalty Simplification and Fairness Act of 1996, 110 Stat. 1700–17 (1996). Consideration of the complexities of royalty management is beyond the scope of these materials.

The term of the mineral lease varies according to the mineral. Coal leases have an initial term of 20 years, 30 U.S.C. § 207(a). Oil and gas leases have primary terms of ten years. In most situations, a lease term is automatically extended beyond the primary term by production in "paying quantities," which also bears more than passing resemblance to the Mining Law's concept of discovery.

The various mineral leasing statutes generally contain limitations on the size of individual mineral leases, which vary according to the mineral. For example, a 2,560–acre limit applies to geothermal leases, while oil shale leases may encompass 5,120 acres. Oil and gas leases may not exceed 10,240 acres outside of Alaska, while competitive leases are limited to units of 2560 acres. There are no limits on the size of individual coal leases, but they cannot be combined into a logical mining unit of more than 25,000 acres. The total acres that a lessee can maintain under all leases is also restricted. See 30 U.S.C. § 184. Congress recently raised the total for coal lease acreage per owner from 46,080 to 75,000, and total nationwide cap from 100,000 to 150,000. 114 Stat. 2010 (2000). Leases must include provisions for rents and royalties, and they also require diligent development of the resource, with statutory and administrative requirements varying by mineral.

3.   WHAT IS "FAIR MARKET VALUE"?

National Wildlife Federation v. Burford

United States Court of Appeals, Ninth Circuit, 1989.
871 F.2d 849.

■ HUG, CIRCUIT JUDGE:

The National Wildlife Federation ("NWF"), Montana Wildlife Federation, Northern Plains Resource Council, and the Powder River Basin Resource Council appeal the district court's entry of summary judgment on count 1 of their amended complaint. Count 1 alleged that the Secretary of the Interior violated 30 U.S.C. § 201(a)(1) by accepting coal lease bids that fell below fair market value ("FMV"). The district court properly held that NWF had standing to bring its suit and properly concluded that the Secretary and acted within the law in selling the leases. We affirm the summary judgment.

In 1982, NWF initiated this action challenging the Department of Interior's ("DOI") sale of coal leases in the Powder River Basin area of Montana and Wyoming. The sale involved approximately 1.6 billion tons of coal distributed over 23,000 acres of public land. * * *

* * * 30 U.S.C. § 201(a)(1) provides that no bid on land offered for leasing "shall be accepted which is less than the fair market value, *as determined by the Secretary*, of the coal subject to the lease" (emphasis added). The Secretary "shall award leases * * * by competitive bidding." Id. Defined in 43 C.F.R. § 3400.0–5(n) (1981), fair market value is "that amount in cash, or on terms reasonably equivalent to cash, for which in all probability the coal deposit would be sold or leased by a knowledgeable owner willing but not obligated to sell or lease to a knowledgeable purchaser who desires but is not obligated to buy or lease."

In light of the language contained in section 201(a)(1) and the interpretative regulation, NWF's task is to show that DOI did not receive FMV for its leases in the Powder River Basin area. Since agency action is presumed to be justified, and the Secretary need present only a reasonable explanation for his actions, NWF's burden of proof is considerable.

The district court, after a careful review of the administrative record, concluded that the Secretary acted reasonably, although possibly not supremely wisely, in accepting the Powder River lease bids. He found specifically that the shift to an entry level bid ("ELB") system which allowed lower initial bids than the prior minimum acceptable bid ("MAB") system*, was satisfactorily explained in the record by information attesting to declining coal prices; that FMV refers to receipt of a fair return, and not to the procedures used; * * * that nine of the eleven tracts up for lease received high bids that met or exceeded the pre-sale estimates of FMV[3]; and that the process used to calculate the pre-sale FMV figures, which involved approximately 4,000 hours of work, was not unsound.

NWF raises two major attacks on the district court's finding of reasonableness. First, it contends that the shift to the ELB system was irrational and insufficiently explained in the record. The ELB procedure guaranteed, according to NWF, the receipt of less than FMV. Second, NWF argues that the MABs used in the sales were skewed by the DOI's reliance on a prior coal lease sale not comparable to the Powder River Basin sale. Use of these MABs as benchmarks of FMV, consequently, was improper.

The claim based on deficiencies in the ELB system is unpersuasive. First, the ELB system is not in itself arbitrary or capricious. The basis for the bidding procedure, as NWF repeatedly points out, is the presumption of competitive bidding. As section 201(a)(1) makes clear, leases shall be sold by the Secretary "by competitive bidding." The Secretary contends the ELB system stimulates competitive bidding. The Secretary can hardly be faulted for using a sales system whose purpose is to implement the statute's mandate. Second, the shift from the MAB to ELB procedure did not constitute an abrupt or unexplained departure from settled policy. As the administrative record shows, DOI had begun to consider use of the ELB system in coal lease sales in 1981. The decision to implement this system in the Powder River lease sale occurred as a result of studies suggesting a

---

* [Eds. Under the ELB system, the Department accepted all bids for consideration no matter how low. Under the MAB system the Department established a threshold amount, with all bids below that amount rejected.]

3. The Secretary accepted bids on ten of the eleven tracts. One bid was rejected. The single accepted bid that fell below the pre-sale FMV estimate involved the Little Rawhide Creek tract. The Secretary accepted this bid on the grounds that the Little Rawhide Creek tract constituted a potential by-pass tract. A bypass tract consists of "an isolated coal deposit that cannot * * * be mined economically and in an environmentally sound manner either separately or as part of any logical mining unit other than that of

the applicant." 43 C.F.R. § 3400.0–5(d) (1981). This type of tract appeals, in other words, only to a single bidder who owns an adjacent tract. The one bidder on the Little Rawhide Creek tract, Meadowlark Farms, Inc., owns the land to the north and east of the tract. The Secretary determined that, even if adjacent unleased federal coal were included with the tract, the Little Rawhide Creek tract could not, standing alone, offer the possibility of a profitable return to a potential buyer. In light of this fact, and the fact that NWF has not shown that any mining unit other than Meadowlark Farms could economically mine the tract, the Secretary reasonably decided to accept the tendered bid as a special circumstance.

decline in the western coal market. The use of the ELB to stimulate competitive bidding at the time of a softening market cannot be said to be arbitrary and capricious. Finally, despite whatever flaws may have existed in the ELB system, actual high bids on nine out of the eleven available tracts met or exceeded the presale estimate of FMV. It is the result of the bidding procedure that is important: whether the high bid represented fair market value.

NWF's second contention is that the MABs used in the pre-sale estimates were defective, and did not represent fair market value. NWF claims that in calculating presale FMV, DOI used data from one prior sale, the "AB" sale, that was not comparable while ignoring data from a comparable sale, the "CD" sale. Choice of comparable sales figures and the calculation of MABs is a technical issue subject to analysis by trained specialists. The reviewing court's task is not to resolve disagreements between differing technical perspectives. Instead, its duty "is the limited one of ascertaining that the choices made by the [Secretary] were reasonable and supported by the record * * *. That the evidence in the record may support other conclusions, even those that are inconsistent with the [Secretary's], does not prevent us from concluding that his decisions were rational and supported by the record." Lead Indus. Ass'n, Inc. v. EPA, 647 F.2d 1130, 1160 (D.C.Cir.), cert. denied, 449 U.S. 1042 (1980). The administrative record suggests that the Economic Evaluation Committee's appraisal of the AB sales led to the conclusion that the AB figures best suited the type of the leases available in the Powder River Basin. DOI had a reasonable basis for its Powder River MABs and for its conclusion that the lease price for the tracts which equaled or exceeded the pre-sale MABs represented fair market value.

Finally, NWF contends that a variety of procedural irregularities corrupted the bid process. NWF states that pre-bid pricing leaks to industry representatives, the Secretary's quick announcement that the sale was successful, and other events of a similar nature irretrievably corrupted the sale. Although these irregularities may have occurred, NWF has not met its burden of showing that the leases did not sell for a fair return as a result of these problems. Given that the pre-sale FMV figures were reasonable and that nine out of the ten leases went to bidders who met or exceeded those figures, NWF's procedural argument is unpersuasive.

NWF has not demonstrated that DOI received less than FMV for its Powder River leases and that the Secretary's decision to accept the leases was arbitrary or capricious. The district court's summary judgment ruling, consequently, is AFFIRMED.

NOTES AND QUESTIONS

1. "Fair market value" (FMV) is a rather common statutory mandate to govern sales or grants of federally–owned natural resources. Sometimes, as here, procedures like competitive bidding are required to help ensure its receipt. In such cases, is FMV determined solely by the level of bidding? At least if there is fair competition, bidding determines "market" value, but is

"market" value always "fair"? If, as the court indicated here, the market for coal in the region was "soft" or "softening," does offering leases for sale in such a market achieve FMV? Is the key decision *when* to hold the sale (in a booming or depressed market), rather than what kinds of bids to accept? Is there a difference between achieving FMV and maximizing returns to the federal treasury? Are there any grounds on which a court might second–guess the Secretary on FMV, given the text of the Mineral Leasing Act, which refers to "fair market value, *as determined by the Secretary* "(emphasis added)?

2.   Neither the rest of the Act nor the legislative history sheds much light on how FMV should be determined. A large body of case law exists to define FMV in both the taxation and eminent domain areas, and the U.S. Supreme Court has said that the same standards apply in both. Great Northern R. Co. v. Weeks, 297 U.S. 135, 139 (1936). A standard definition is contained in a manual prepared to guide federal land acquisition:

> "Fair market value" is defined as the amount in cash, or on terms reasonably equivalent to cash, for which in all probability the property would be sold by a knowledgeable owner willing but not obligated to sell to a knowledgeable purchaser who desired but is not obligated to buy. In ascertaining that figure, consideration should be given to all matters that might be brought forward and reasonably be given substantial weight in bargaining by persons of ordinary prudence, but no consideration whatever should be given to matters not affecting market value.

UNIFORM APPRAISAL STANDARDS FOR FEDERAL LAND ACQUISITIONS (Interagency Land Acquisition Conference, Gov't Printing Office, 1973), pp. 3–4 (footnotes omitted). See also Olson v. United States, 292 U.S. 246 (1934). Does this help provide a basis for judicial review of Secretarial determinations of FMV in coal lease sales? On another occasion, the Supreme Court described the application of such a test as "at best, a guess by informed persons." United States v. Miller, 317 U.S. 369, 374–75 (1943). (For an application of *Miller* in the context of determining FMV of private land that serves as "base property" for federal grazing permits, see United States v. Fuller, Chapter 9, infra p. 787.)

3.   In another case raising separate legal issues about this same coal lease sale, the court provided some useful background on the matter:

> In April and October 1982, the Department held coal lease sales in the Powder River Basin in Southeast Montana and Northeast Wyoming that were widely criticized for allegedly obtaining far less than fair market value. Department rules previously required bids to be evaluated against an independent assessment of the fair market value of a given lease prepared by the U.S. Geological Survey. The Department formally deleted this requirement the day before the first sale. A report by House Appropriations Committee staff estimated that the Department sold the leases for $60 million less than fair market value, while a General Accounting Office ("GAO") study calculated the underpayment at $100 million. * * * This scandal led to the suspension of nearly all federal coal lease sales for almost four years. In July 1983,

Congress established the Commission on Fair Market Value Policy for Federal Coal Leasing (the "Linowes Commission") to review the Department's coal valuation procedures and make recommendations for improvements.

National Wildlife Federation v. Babbitt, 24 ELR 20200, 20201 (D.D.C. 1993). The "Linowes Commission" (named after its chair) issued a 500-page report, containing 36 recommendations for improvement, in 1984. FAIR MARKET VALUE POLICY FOR FEDERAL COAL LEASING. The report contained the following conclusions, among many others:

"[F]lexibility in lease sale scheduling is desirable. The Government should seek to sell more coal when price signals indicate a greater need for Federal coal and seek to sell less when lower prices indicate less demand." [Id. at 492]

[L]easing level decisions should be made in a broader context than the effect on Federal revenues alone. The purpose of the Federal coal leasing program is to make the maximum contribution of Federal coal to the Nation's welfare. Besides earning revenues, this purpose includes providing coal to consumers at low prices, protecting the environment, furthering national security goals of reducing energy imports, conserving the Nation's coal resources, and treating residents of coal-producing areas fairly. The Federal Government's management of its coal resource differs from private resource management in that a much wider range of objectives is sought and must be reconciled. [Id. at 486]

[C]ompetition [has been] the exception rather than the rule in Federal coal leasing. * * * In some ways, current sale procedures of the Interior Department resemble negotiations, especially for maintenance and bypass tracts.[4] * * * Despite Government efforts, a substantial number of tracts are still not likely to attract competitive bidding. For these tracts, there may be no alternative to negotiation, whether it is done informally within existing sale procedures or formally through new statutory authority to negotiate. Negotiated coal lease sales require strong public confidence in the negotiators. Interior Department officials expressed concern that unreasonable public expectations might put them in a difficult position as negotiators. * * * [Id. at 507–08]

* * * Because many Federal leases will not attract competition, the appraisal process plays a critical role in helping the Government receive fair market value. The two most widely used methods of appraisal are comparable sales analysis and capitalization of projected income—also known as discounted cash flow (DCF) analysis. Both the DCF and comparable sales methods have been used * * *. At one time or another, each has been considered the preferable approach by the Department. * * * [U]navoidably, there will be circumstances where

---

4. [Eds.: The Report earlier explained that "maintenance" tracts are those that by themselves do not contain enough coal to operate a profitable mine; they must be combined with other tracts not offered in the lease sale. "Bypass" tracts are those that are encompassed within an existing mine, and are of interest only to the company operating the mine. Id. at 503–04.]

neither comparable sales methods nor DCF methods can be expected to work well. * * * [T]he inexact character of coal lease appraisals makes it all the more imperative that a set of procedures be established to ensure the unbiased nature and professional independence of the appraisal effort. [Id. at 510–11]

On the Powder River lease sale that triggered the controversy, the Commission concluded:

[T]he Interior Department probably did not receive fair market value, [but] the Commission did not attempt to quantify the amount that should have been obtained. However, the Commission concluded that the Interior Depertment [sic] probably offered excessive amounts of Federal coal reserves in a declining market and that this, in turn, probably lessened the prospect of receiving fair market value. At the very least, the Interior Department made serious errors in judgment in its procedures for conducting the 1982 Powder River lease sale and failed to provide a sound rationale for many of its actions. [Id. at 536]

Neither the district court nor the court of appeals in the principal case addressed this finding in upholding the Department of the Interior. Does this episode, with its rich, expert documentation of the failure of the Department to receive FMV, suggest that the courts cannot, or lack the appetite to, play a meaningful role in these economic matters?

4. Notice another legacy of the checkerboard pattern of federal land grants, in the "bypass" tract problem discussed in footnote 3 of the court's opinion and in the excerpts from the Linowes Commission report. How can the Secretary meet the FMV requirement in that context, where the universe of potential bidders is practicably limited to one? Where the "market" value of the coal on such a tract may be sharply limited, how does the Secretary determine what is "fair"? By appraisal only? Would the Secretary be justified in raising the royalty rate on the coal in the bypass situation, in part because of lack of competition, and in part because the existing operator already has infrastructure in place, and therefore would have a higher profit margin on the bypass tract? For example, if the standard coal lease provided for a 12 1/2% royalty, could the Secretary charge 20% for a bypass coal tract?

5. For a consideration of different kinds of bidding systems for minerals (looked at in the context of offshore oil and gas leasing), see James C. Cox, R. Mark Isaac, and Vernon L. Smith, OCS Leasing and Auctions: Incentives and the Performance of Alternative Bidding Institutions, 2 Sup. Ct. Econ.Rev. 43 (1983).

6. Leasing federal minerals has had an occasionally colorful history. Leasing under the 1920 Mineral Leasing Act got off to a particularly rocky start. See John Ise, THE UNITED STATES OIL POLICY 352–54 (1926). Naval Petroleum Reserves had been established in California and Wyoming in the previous decade (the first having led to the landmark *Midwest Oil* decision in 1915, Chapter 2, supra p. 120). Shortly after passage of the Mineral Leasing Act, Congress gave the Secretary of the Navy extensive jurisdiction over the reserves. Soon after taking office in 1921, President

Warren Harding issued a secret executive order transferring jurisdiction over the reserves to Secretary of the Interior Albert B. Fall, a former Senator from New Mexico. Later investigation revealed that Fall then secretly, without competitive bidding, leased all of the Wyoming reserve (known as "Teapot Dome," after a rock formation in the vicinity) and much of the California reserve to his friends in the oil industry. Fall received large amounts of cash from these friends at the same time, and contended they were loans. A jury disbelieved him, and he became the first American cabinet officer to serve a prison term for crimes committed in office. Fall v. United States, 49 F.2d 506 (D.C.App.1931), cert. denied, 283 U.S. 867 (1931). Interestingly, the oil company executives who bribed him (or, if Fall was to be believe, made innocent loans to him) were acquitted of bribery. The Wyoming leases were eventually canceled on fraud grounds by the Supreme Court, Mammoth Oil Co. v. United States, 275 U.S. 13 (1927). The trials are recounted in C.G. Haglund, The Naval Reserves, 20 Geo.L.J. 293 (1932). See generally Burl Noggle, TEAPOT DOME: OIL AND POLITICS IN THE 1920's (1962).

7. Oil and gas leasing again became enmeshed in controversy a few decades later. The problem was caused when Congress narrowed the circumstances in which the Department could issue competitive oil and gas leases. In the 1950s, competition grew dramatically for areas put up for lease which under the statute could only be issued to "the person first making application." The Department's solution to this dilemma, in the face of congressional refusal to change the system, was to adopt a lottery. It collected all the applications that poured in on the date the Department said it was going to receive applications for particular tracts and pulled one out of a drum to receive the noncompetitive lease. The D.C.Circuit court upheld the practice in an opinion by Skelly Wright that concluded this way:

> The history of the administration of the statute furnishes compelling proof, familiar to the membership of Congress, that the human animal has not changed, that when you determine to give something away, you are going to draw a crowd. It is the Secretary's job to manage the crowd while complying with the requirement of the Act. * * * We cannot say that [the lottery] is an impermissible implementation of the statutory purpose.

Thor–Westcliffe Development, Inc. v. Udall, 314 F.2d 257 (D.C.Cir.1963). Eventually Congress was moved to reform the system. The 1987 Reform Act led to adoption of an all-competitive bidding system for onshore oil and gas. The Act provided that the Secretary must accept the highest bid for each parcel so long as it is not less than the national minimum acceptable bid. See generally Thomas L. Sansonetti and William R. Murray, A Primer on the Federal Onshore Oil and Gas leasing Reform Act of 1987 and its Regulations, XXV Land & Water L. Rev. 375 (1990).

4.   MINERAL LEASING AND ENVIRONMENTAL REGULATION

Generally, the Department of the Interior's Bureau of Land Management is responsible for issuing and supervising activities on mineral leases, even on lands managed by other agencies (the U.S. Forest Service being the principal one affected). In some cases, such as in mineral leases on acquired lands or oil and gas leases on national forests, the BLM is required by statute to obtain the consent of the surface managing agency (usually, the U.S. Forest Service) before issuing a lease. Even where the surface managing agency does not have a statutory veto, BLM's custom has long been not to issue leases over its objection.

The various mineral leasing acts generally give the Secretary ample authority to include lease provisions to protect the environment. Recall the discussion of this issue in Ventura County v. Gulf Oil Corp., Chapter 3, supra p. 208. Although lease terms and regulations dealing with environmental matters were once vague and difficult to enforce, that picture has changed dramatically in the last few decades. The United States has authority to cancel leases for violations of lease terms or regulations. See generally Boesche v. Udall, 373 U.S. 472 (1963). A special, comprehensive statute, the Surface Mining Control and Reclamation Act of 1977, contains relatively strict reclamation requirements for surface coal mining everywhere in the U.S., requiring protection of non-mineral resources and values "to the extent possible using the best technology currently available * * *." 30 U.S.C. § 1265(b)(24). It contains special provisions dealing with coal mining on federal lands. 30 U.S.C. §§ 1265(b), 1272. See pp. 671–72 infra.

Kerr-McGee Corp. v. Hodel

U.S. District Court, District of Columbia, 1986.
630 F.Supp. 621.

■ BARRINGTON D. PARKER, DISTRICT JUDGE:

* * * Plaintiffs contend that on January 10, 1983, the Secretary of Interior wrongfully denied their applications for phosphate leases thus depriving them of vested rights to engage in phosphate mining. In response to those allegations, the federal defendants and the intervenors contend that the applications were denied because the reclamation technologies relied upon and proferred by the plaintiffs were inadequate to ensure restoration of the mined portions of the Osceola Forest to the purposes for which they were acquired and the historical uses to which they had been put, as required by the Mineral Leasing Act for Acquired Lands, 30 U.S.C. §§ 351 et seq. (1982). Specifically, the Secretary found that plaintiffs had not discovered "valuable deposits" of phosphate as required under the Act, because the costs of reclamation would be prohibitively high. * * *

The Osceola National Forest was established in 1931 by President Herbert Hoover pursuant to the Creative Act of 1891, 26 Stat. 1103, Mar. 3, 1891. The vast majority of the Forest was acquired under the authority of the Weeks Act of 1911. The primary purposes behind the acquisition and development were timber production, water shed protection, fish and wildlife protection, and preservation and maintenance of recreational opportunities. National Forest Preservation Comm'n., Sen. Doc. No. 44, 71st Cong., 2d Sess. 6 (1929). Osceola Forest consists of nearly 158 thousand acres located in North–Central Florida. Included within that acreage are cypress swamps, pine lands, unique hardwood wetlands, and upland hardwood forests. Highly diverse creek and river systems, within the area serve as a source of high quality surface and ground water, and provides an important water shed for North–Central Florida. The Forest also provides a home for important varieties of fish and wildlife species and for a number of valued and certain limited [sic] and endangered species.

The authority for phosphate leasing on federal land and the limits on the Interior Secretary's ability to lease, depends upon whether the lands are classified as "public domain" or "acquired" lands. Public domain lands are lands that have never left the control of the United States. The Mineral Leasing Act, 30 U.S.C. §§ 181, 211(b) *et seq.,* authorizes the Secretary to lease phosphate deposits on those lands. Public domain lands comprise a very limited portion of the Osceola National Forest.

For acquired lands, lands that have been either granted or sold to the United States, the source of mineral leasing authority stems from the Mineral Leasing Act for Acquired Lands, 30 U.S.C. § 352. That section provides in relevant part:

> No mineral deposit covered by this section shall be leased except with the consent of the head of the executive department ... having jurisdiction over the lands containing such deposit ... and subject to such conditions as that official may prescribe to insure the adequate utilization of the lands for the primary purposes for which they have been acquired or are being administered....

The Act also establishes the authority and conditions under which the Interior Secretary may issue phosphate leases. And, as is the case here, the Secretary must secure the consent of other departments or agencies which, because of concurrent jurisdiction over the lands, may impose requirements or stipulations. The Forest includes a significantly larger proportion of acquired lands as compared with public domain lands.

During the mid-to-late 1960s, the plaintiffs applied to the Interior Department for permits to prospect for phosphate deposits on acquired lands. The permits were issued by the Department's Bureau of Land Management pursuant to the Mineral Leasing Act for Acquired Lands and were made expressly subject to all regulations, then existing or subsequently enacted, including Special Stipulations required by the Forest Service, Department of Agriculture. * * *

Subsequently, between 1969–1972, the plaintiffs applied to Interior for preference right leases to mine phosphate on the lands embraced by their prospecting permits alleging discovery of "valuable deposits" within the meaning of section 211(b) of the Mineral Leasing Act. Thereafter, the United States Geological Survey certified that valuable deposits had been discovered and recommended that leases be issued. The certifications were based on quality and quantity standards that had been applied by the Interior Department for some time * * * [which were exclusively on the] basis of physical characteristics, namely, the quality, quantity, thickness and extent of a deposit. This approach was used without regard for mining and marketing costs or other factors bearing upon the economic feasibility of mine development. During this period, there was no regulation, decision, opinion or instruction reflecting a departmental interpretation of the term as used in the Act, or purporting to recognize the propriety of the practice.

[After the applications for preference right leases were filed, the Department undertook additional studies on the impact of phosphate mining in the area on the environment, including an EIS under NEPA, followed by a Supplement to the EIS. The Department also promulgated new regulations in 1976 which provided that an application for a preference right lease must, in order to satisfy the "valuable deposit" test, "show that there is a reasonable expectation that ... revenues from the sale of the mineral will exceed ... costs of developing the mine, and extracting, removing and marketing the mineral."] * * *

On February 4, 1982, the Forest Service of the Agriculture Department submitted to the Bureau of Land Management the [stipulations that would be attached to the preference right lease, should one be issued. The key one,] Stipulation No. 4, specified that:

> The lessee shall, except for permanent lakes created by mining, reestablish watercourses, soil stability and productivity, approximate landforms and elevations, and wetland and upland of similar vegetative communities and species diversity in approximate proportions as those existing prior to mining. *The purpose of reclamation is to reestablish plant and aquatic communities with similar interspersion of community types, i.e., pine flatwoods, cypress swamps, creek swamps and lakes.* The soil medium shall be *reestablished* to support forest tree growth by: (a) providing a ratio of clay to sand in a mixture that will retain sufficient moisture and nutrients in the root zones of forest trees making up the vegetative community; (b) by returning overburden, including topsoil, over the clay and sand mixture. (emphasis added).

* * * [The Interior Department's 1974 EIS] was pessimistic on the possibility of reclamation of native species following phosphate mining, particularly with reference to swamp hardwood plant communities. * * * [The Supplement to the EIS prepared in 1979 expressed] doubt about the success of reclamation efforts based on the then present state of technological knowledge. * * * It also concluded that research was needed to provide techniques for reestablishing the plant species and vegetative community types then found. Otherwise, it reaffirmed the pessimism on revegetation of native species as was noted in the 1974 Final Environmental Statement. * * *

[In 1982 the Interior Secretary established an interagency task force to once again assess reclamation technology. This group] concluded that no new technology had been developed since the 1979 Supplemental ES and that technology capabilities were insufficient to ensure a reasonable likelihood of the successful reclamation of mined areas consistent with the requirements established for mining in Osceola. * * * [Its report recommended] that all pending lease applications in Osceola National be rejected. [In January 1983 Secretary Watt rejected the lease applications based on his] determination that:

* * * [A] mineral deposit discovered under a prospecting permit must be of "such a character and quantity that a prudent person would be justified in the further expenditure of his labor and means with a reasonable prospect of success in developing a valuable mine." The Forest Service, as prescribed by law, has established reclamation stipulations which were used in processing [plaintiffs'] preference right lease applications. The Department of the Interior has performed studies which indicate current technology is not capable of meeting the prescribed reclamation standards. The fact that no reclamation technology exists which can reclaim these lands precludes the possibility that this phosphate deposit could meet the valuable deposit test.

* * * Although Kerr–McGee and Global dispute the Environmental Assessment team's conclusion as to the feasibility of reclamation of Osceola lands following phosphate mining, they have not identified or referred to any significant and factual data which were not considered in the preparation of the 1983 Environmental Assessment report. * * *

* * * [I]t appears that mineral development is incompatible with the primary purposes and uses of the forest and has a great potential of destroying the natural resources of the Forest. Strip mining, the technique used to secure the phosphates, [is] highly destructive of natural resources. In the process, the forest area to be mined is leveled, cleared of all vegetation and trees, and wetland areas are drained. The overburden has a depth of 20 to 60 feet. Electrical powered walking draglines, resembling giant scoops, strip the overburden and dig the mining cuts to remove the phosphate matrix averaging 8 to 10 feet thick from the earth. The mining cuts formed by these draglines average 150–200 feet wide and several thousand feet in length.

The acquired lands of the United States which are included in the Osceola Forest may be leased for mineral development only upon conditions imposed by the Mineral Leasing Act for Acquired Lands, 30 U.S.C. § 351 *et seq.* Section 3 of the Act, vests in the Interior Secretary the authority to issue a mineral lease with the consent of the head of the executive department having jurisdiction over the lands where the mineral deposits are located. The latter may prescribe such conditions as necessary "to insure the adequate utilization of the lands for the primary purposes for which they have been acquired or are being administered." 30 U.S.C. § 352. The determination of what conditions should be imposed if a mineral lease is issued on national forest land is thus committed by law to the Secretary of Agriculture.

Applicants such as Kerr–McGee and Global, to ensure their entitlement to phosphate leases, are required to demonstrate the discovery of "valuable deposits" of phosphates on the lands covered by their prospecting permits 30 U.S.C. § 211(b). * * * In determining whether a prospecting permittee has discovered a "valuable deposit" of phosphate, the cost of compliance with lease terms is an important element which must be considered, and if the applicant lacks the technological capability to comply with prescribed lease terms, he cannot satisfy the test and is not entitled to a lease. Natural Resource Defense Council, Inc. v. Berklund, 458 F.Supp.

925, 936–37 (D.D.C.1978), *aff'd,* 609 F.2d 553 (D.C.Cir.1979). The restoration technologies necessary to insure the adequate utilization of the Osceola Forest for its primary purposes did not exist in January 1983 or in 1984, and did not exist at any earlier time. To demonstrate the discovery of "valuable deposits" of phosphates, Kerr–McGee and Global must comply with the terms and conditions imposed by the Forest Service and are required to show the economic and technological feasibility of reclaiming the lands covered by the lease applications.

Until February 1982, when the Forest Service submitted to the Bureau of Land Management the final stipulations to be attached to any leases which might be issued to phosphate lease applicants in the Forest, the Interior Secretary could not determine whether the plaintiffs had satisfied the "valuable deposit" test, and no lease entitlement was vested in the plaintiffs. The earlier practices of the Department of Interior in issuing phosphate preference right leases before 1970 did not alter or change the statutory requirements and did not establish a legal standard which the Interior Secretary was bound to recognize in determining plaintiffs' lease entitlement. Chevron, Inc. v. [Natural Resources Defense] Council, Inc., 467 U.S. 837 (1984). Nor did the prior determination of the Geological Survey * * * in 1969 and 1970, that Kerr–McGee had discovered valuable phosphate deposits on lands covered by its prospecting permits, vest any right to receive leases for which it made application. The same is true for any subsequent determination of the Geological Survey * * * or any other departmental finding made between 1969 and 1983. None of those determinations precluded the Interior Secretary from subsequently finding that the requisite discovery had not been shown.

The January 10, 1983, decision of the Secretary of Interior was not arbitrary and capricious but, rather, was justified and supported by substantial and credible evidence.

NOTES AND QUESTIONS

1. If this case had come along after the Supreme Court's decision in the *Mobil* case, Chapter 4, p. 257 supra, could Kerr–McGee have made out a case for rescission and restitution? A big difference here, however, is that Kerr–McGee had not given the U.S. any significant money for the prospecting permit, which was issued to it without competition.

2. Does Kerr–McGee have an equitable argument that it is being jerked around by the government? Notice that the Forest Service did not formulate the reclamation standard for inclusion in the lease until 1982, well over a decade after the prospecting permits were issued. Should the BLM or the Forest Service have thought about whether or not phosphate-mined areas could be reclaimed *before* the prospecting permit was issued? (This situation shows the value of the idea behind NEPA. Had that statute been in effect when the federal government was considering issuing the prospecting permits, it might have forced the government to address the problem of reclamation then.)

3.   Or did Kerr–McGee assume the risk of being subject to unachievable reclamation standards when it took the prospecting permit not knowing what reclamation standard was going to be applied to it?

4.   The district court here rejected the argument that the "earlier practices of the Department * * * establish[ed] a legal standard which the Interior Secretary was bound to recognize in determining plaintiffs' lease entitlement." It also found that determinations made by the U.S. Geological Survey that Kerr–McGee had discovered valuable phosphate deposits did not preclude the Secretary, before the leases were actually issued, "from subsequently finding that the requisite discovery had not been shown." Does the court too lightly dismiss the fact that the government appeared to change its interpretation of the "valuable deposit" test after the prospecting permits had been issued, and before the decision was made on the preference right lease? When Kerr–McGee took the permit, did it have a legitimate expectation that it need only show that the phosphate it discovered was of mineable quality and quantity in order to get a preference right lease? If the Department does change its mind, should it be held to a stricter standard of review, especially if its changes undercut the reasonable expectations of those doing business with the government?

5.   In Utah International, Inc. v. Andrus, 488 F.Supp. 976 (D.Colo. 1980), the court held that the plaintiff had a right to obtain a preference right coal lease because the Department of the Interior had made an official determination that the permittee was entitled to a preference right lease several years before the Department had revised the regulations on how "commercial quantities" of coal would be determined. In Utah International, Inc. v. Andrus, 488 F.Supp. 962 (D.Utah 1979), involving almost identical facts, there was one crucial difference: The Department had not made a final determination that the applicant was entitled to a preference right coal lease before the new rules were promulgated; therefore, the applicant was subject to the new rules.

6.   Even if Kerr–McGee could have avoided the new standard for determining "valuable deposit," would it still have had a problem with the lease stipulation that required it to reclaim the land, when that seems impossible or at least very difficult? Was its ultimate, inescapable problem that the statute, 30 U.S.C. § 352, made the prospecting permit and the lease subject to "such conditions as that [agency] may prescribe to insure the adequate utilization of the lands for the primary purposes for which they have been acquired or are being administered"?

7.   A few days after Secretary Watt rejected the lease applications in January 1983, President Reagan vetoed a bill that would have (a) prohibited mining in the Osceola National Forest, (b) required the Secretary to make the "valuable deposit" determination without taking into account the cost of compliance with environmental statutes and regulations, and (c) required compensation to the plaintiffs for any deposits deemed "valuable." In September 1984, the President signed the Florida Wilderness Act of 1983, which effectively prohibited mining in the area absent a Presidential recommendation and congressional concurrence; see 98 Stat. 1665 (1984). Judge Parker's decision, issued in February 1986, did not address that Act.

The D.C. Circuit subsequently vacated Judge Parker's decision and dismissed the case as moot because of the wilderness legislation. The court said that Kerr–McGee could seek a remedy for an alleged taking of property in the U.S. Claims Court, but it "intimate[d] no views" on any taking questions. 840 F.2d 68 (D.C.Cir.1988). Kerr–McGee filed suit in the Court of Federal Claims, which issued a preliminary ruling that the government should have allowed Kerr McGee to offer evidence that it could meet the reclamation stipulations mandated by the Forest Service. 32 Fed.Cl. 43 (1994). After more inconclusive litigation, the parties reached a settlement that packaged resolution of this dispute with an unrelated Superfund case involving the same parties, and the matter was brought to an end more than thirty years after the initial applications for phosphate prospecting permits were filed.

Natural Resources Defense Council, Inc. v. Berklund, 609 F.2d 553 (D.C.Cir.1979), involved a situation somewhat similar to the *Kerr-McGee* case. The mineral was coal, however, and the federal lands involved were not acquired, so the governing statute was the coal section of the Mineral Leasing Act. It did not contain a provision equivalent to that centrally involved in *Kerr-McGee*, namely, that gave the surface managing agency the right to prescribe conditions in the lease "to insure the adequate utilization of the lands for the primary purposes for which they have been acquired." The applicable statute provided that the Department had to determine whether the prospecting permittee had discovered "commercial quantities" of coal; if so, the statute provided that it "shall be entitled to a lease." The same regulations that reformed the "valuable deposit" test for phosphate addressed in *Kerr-McGee* also applied to the "commercial quantities" test for coal. Specifically, they required a permittee to show a reasonable expectation that its revenues will exceed development and operating costs, and defined the latter to include the cost of "complying with existing governmental regulations, reclamation and environmental standards, and proposed lease terms." 43 C.F.R. § 3521.1–1(c)(2)(vi)(1978).

Plaintiff environmental groups argued that the Secretary had authority to reject lease applications by prospecting permittees. The court said no, finding "the plain meaning of the statute as well as undisturbed administrative practice for nearly 60 years leaves the Secretary no discretion to deny a [preference right] lease to a qualified applicant." It went on, however, to give the plaintiffs at least some of what they sought, by a more indirect means:

> [Under its new regulations Interior now] requires a demonstration that the estimated revenues can reasonably be expected to exceed estimated costs. Those costs can include the costs of complying with lease terms demanding complete reclamation and safeguards against environmental harm. Even after a lease is granted the awardee may be precluded from harming the environment if the agency disapproves his mining plan. Petitioners claim that these measures * * * do not account for

"societal costs" of environmental harm. We find, to the contrary, that these costs can be figured into the assessment of commercial quantities, covered in stringent lease provisions, or adopted as criteria for measuring proposed mining plans. * * * [The court will not] rewrite [the statute] to undermine the property rights of prospecting permittee lease applicants. * * * [Although Congress has changed the law so that no more prospecting permits for coal will be issued, f]or the some 183 lease applications outstanding under the former version of the provision, the property rights anticipated by permittee applicants cannot be diminished.

NOTES AND QUESTIONS

1. In *Berklund*, even accepting the court's conclusion that the Secretary has no discretion to deny a preference right lease once commercial quantities of coal are shown, could the Secretary exercise his broad authority over lease terms to include such stringent conditions to protect the environment that the permittee would flunk the "commercial quantities" test?

2. Could the Secretary, as an alternative, simply include a sufficiently high rental or royalty rate in the preference right lease to discourage the prospecting permittee from taking the lease? The leasing statutes typically require a rental and a royalty at "not less than" a specified statutory minimum, but do not contain a maximum, and leave the rate-setting to the discretion of the Secretary; e.g., 30 U.S.C. § 212 (phosphate). But is it arbitrary or an abuse of discretion for the Secretary to set a higher rental or royalty rate for preference right leases than for other leases, if the only reason to do so is avoid issuing the lease non-competitively?

3. The issue of determining economically valuable mineral deposits can also arise in another context. That is, federal leasing statutes (and many leases of minerals in private contexts) have a fixed (primary) term and extend beyond the primary term for so long thereafter as the leased mineral is produced in "paying" or "commercial" quantities. See, e.g., 30 U.S.C. § 207(a) (coal). Such a lease is generally regarded as conveying a determinable fee—an estate that terminates upon the occurrence of a possible event. Does "paying quantities" mean that the expenses of production are weighed against the value of the minerals produced? What expenses? The cost of exploration as well as the cost of production? What about overhead and management costs? Environmental costs? See, e.g., Richard D. Koljack, Jr., Determination of Paying Quantities: An Accounting Perspective, 18 Tulsa L.J. 475 (1983). Obviously, lessees may have a strong interest in holding on to a marginal lease, anticipating higher mineral prices, while lessors may have a strong competing interest in recapturing the lease for re-leasing to someone else, or using the land for other purposes.

4. What did the D.C. Circuit mean in *Berklund* when it cautioned that the "property rights anticipated by permittee applicants cannot be diminished"? Notice that the Court did not say that the permittees *had* property

rights, only that they were "anticipated." Is that a distinction without a difference?

5. Review question: Consider whether and how the discretion of the Secretary differs in each of these decisions: whether to issue preference right coal or phosphate leases; what kinds of stipulations or terms to include in mineral leases; whether to offer federal lands for competitive oil and gas leasing; whether to withdraw lands from mineral leasing or from the Mining Law; whether to approve proposed plans of operations under the Mining Law, and whether to issue patents under the Mining Law.

Copper Valley Machine Works, Inc. v. Andrus

United States Court of Appeals, District of Columbia Circuit, 1981.
653 F.2d 595.

■ MacKINNON, CIRCUIT JUDGE.

The principal issue in this appeal is whether a restriction in a drilling permit prohibiting summer drilling in the interest of conservation worked a "suspension of operations and production" that would extend the life of an oil and gas lease under section 39 of the Mineral Leasing Act of 1920, as amended, 30 U.S.C. § 209.

Effective February 1, 1966, the Secretary of Interior issued oil and gas lease A–063937 to run for an initial "period of ten years and so long thereafter as oil or gas is produced in paying quantities."

Near the end of the primary lease term, Copper Valley Machine Works, Inc. (Copper Valley), the designated operator of the lease * * * [filed with the United States Geological Survey, an agency of the Department of the Interior that then regulated operations on federal oil and gas leases,] an application for a permit to drill. On January 30, 1976 [the day before the lease was to expire] the drilling permit application was approved, "subject to conditions attached to the permit and conditions and requirements described below: * * * 10. The approved application and development plan provides for operation *during the winter season only,* as approved by the appropriate surface managing agency." (emphasis added). This "winter season only" restriction was considered "necessary because the lease itself was issued without any stipulations for protection of the tundra/permafrost environment during the months of summer thaw."

The events that then led to this dispute are described in a memorandum from the Acting Director of the Geological Survey to the Secretary of Interior:

> The well was commenced on January 31, 1976 (the expiration date of the primary term), and reached a depth of 100 feet before having to shutdown for the 1976 summer season. Following the summer shutdown from May to November 1976, operations were recommenced on February 5, 1977, and after reaching a depth of 1,070 feet on March 20, 1977, electric logs were run in the well. After evaluating the electric logs and examining the samples, the Supervisor concluded that the operator had satisfied the "diligent drilling" requirements of 43

CFR 3107.2–3,[3] and recommended to BLM that the lease be extended to January 31, 1978.

After the 1977 summer shutdown, the Supervisor advised the operator and the lessee that the lease would expire January 31, 1978, absent a well physically and mechanically capable of production in paying quantities by that date.

On January 20, 1978, the operator wrote the Supervisor and requested that the lease be extended for twelve (12) months to compensate for the two periods of summer shutdown in 1976 and 1977. The Supervisor considered this letter to be *an application to the Secretary* for an extension of [the] lease * * * pursuant to 43 CFR 3103.3–8[4] [Emphasis added.]

Although acknowledging that Copper Valley had been "unable to conduct operations on a full-time basis since January of 1976 by the imposition of the requirement that operations would be permitted only during the winter months," the Acting Director recommended that no extension of the lease be granted or recognized.

On May 22, 1978, the Secretary of Interior followed the Acting Director's recommendation, ruling that

the lease is considered to have expired by operation of law as of midnight, January 31, 1978, absent the existence of a well on that date which had been determined by the Supervisor as capable of producing in paying quantities. The reasons for the denial [of extension] are that (1) the lessee accepted the imposed restriction that drilling could be conducted only during the winter season without complaint until 11 days preceding the lease expiration date and (2) the 2–year lease extension earned by drilling across the end of the primary term of January 31, 1976, afforded sufficient additional time, despite the restriction, in which to have completed a well that was physically capable of production in paying quantities. * * *

[Copper Valley then sued, but the district court rejected its argument] that the Secretary's refusal to permit another 12 months of operations was

---

3. 43 C.F.R. § 3107.2–3. *Period of extension.*

Any lease on which actual drilling operations, or for which under an approved cooperative or unit plan of development or operation, actual drilling operations were commenced prior to the end of its primary term and are being diligently prosecuted at that time, *shall be extended for 2 years* and so long thereafter as oil or gas is produced in paying quantities.

(Emphasis added.)

4. 43 C.F.R. § 3103.3–8 provides:

Suspension of operations and production.

(a) * * * As to oil and gas leases, no suspension of operations and production will be granted on any lease in the absence of a well capable of production on the leasehold, except where the Secretary directs a suspension in the interest of conservation. * * *

(b) The term of any lease will be extended by adding thereto any period of suspension of all operations and production during such term pursuant to any direction or assent of the Secretary.

(c) A suspension shall take effect as of the time specified in the direction or assent of the Secretary. Rental and minimum royalty payments will be suspended during any period of suspension of all operations and production directed or assented to by the Secretary * * *.

unlawful. Copper Valley relied on section 39 of the Mineral Leasing Act of 1920, as amended, which provides in part:

> In the event the Secretary of Interior *in the interest of conservation,* shall direct * * * *the suspension of operations and production* under any lease granted under the terms of this Act, any payment of acreage rental or of minimum royalty prescribed by such lease likewise shall be suspended during such period of suspension or operations and productions; *and the term of such lease shall be extended by adding any such suspension * * * thereto.*

30 U.S.C. § 209 (emphasis added). * * *

Copper Valley's principal contention on appeal is that the drilling permit's "winter season only" restriction, by preventing drilling operations for 6 summer months a year, worked a "suspension of operations and production" "in the interest of conservation" and therefore, under § 209, mandated an automatic extension of the lease for a period equal to the length of the suspension. The Government responds that the drilling restrictions did not create suspensions within the meaning of § 209.

A. "In the Interest of Conservation"

* * * The parties agree that carrying on drilling operations during the summer months would have substantially damaged the permafrost character of the leasehold area. Preventing such damage is obviously in the interest of conservation if that term is to receive its ordinary meaning. While the prevention of environmental damage may not have been the "conservation" that Congress principally had in mind in 1933 when it passed § 209,[6] suspending operations to avoid environmental harm is definitely a suspension in the interest of conservation in the ordinary sense of the word. And there was no indication that Congress intended that "conservation" be given any interpretation other than its ordinary meaning.[8] * * *

The Secretary asserts that § 209 "was designed by Congress to cover only unanticipated interruptions of drilling." Under this view, whether a § 209 suspension has occurred depends on whether the "winter season only" restriction was a surprise to Copper Valley. It is in this context that the Secretary emphasizes that the lease gave "notice that drilling activities

---

6. A congressional report accompanying the bill that became § 209 stated:

> [I]t is * * * a matter of public knowledge that there has existed for some time past, and still exists, a condition of over-production [of petroleum and natural gas]. This condition has resulted in the adoption by the Interior Department of an administrative policy of conservation of oil and gas.

H.R.Rep. No. 1737, 72nd Cong., 1st Sess. 3 (1932).

8. This conclusion is consistent with *Gulf Oil Corp. v. Morton,* 493 F.2d 141 (9th Cir.1973). The court in *Morton* interpreted § 5(a)(1) of the Outer Continental Shelf (OCS) Lands Act, 43 U.S.C. § 1334(a)(1), a provision similar to 30 U.S.C. § 209. Section 5(a)(1) authorizes the Secretary of Interior to provide, "in the interest of conservation," for the "suspension of operations or production." The court rejected the oil company's argument that "interest of conservation" is confined to conservation of oil and gas, id. at 145, and concluded the Secretary was empowered to suspend drilling operations to prevent undue harm to the marine environment.

would be subject to restriction," that Copper Valley "did not protest against the restriction until two years after the permit was issued," and that Copper Valley "continued to pay rent during the thaw months without attempting to assert that the drilling permit condition was a surprise." We find it unnecessary to consider whether summary judgment was appropriate on the question whether Copper Valley could foresee the suspension of drilling, for we reject as unpersuasive the Secretary's attempt to narrow the scope of the plain terms of § 209.

As indicated in note 6 supra, § 209 was enacted in a period when the Secretary was suspending the drilling operations of oil and gas lessees in order to alleviate the problem of excess petroleum production. The congressional report explained that the bill

> relieve[s] lessees of coal and oil lands from the necessity of paying prescribed annual acreage rental, during periods when operations or production is suspended, in the interest of conservation, either by direction or assent of the Secretary of the Interior, and [provides] that the period of such suspension shall be added to the term of the lease.
> * * *

H.R.Rep. No. 1737, 72nd Cong., 1st Sess. 2–3 (1932).

Because some of the oil and gas lessees who benefitted from the lease extensions and rent moratoriums of § 209 might have been surprised by the petroleum glut and the Secretary's ensuing suspensions, the Government contends that the section, which by its terms applies to any Secretary-imposed "suspension of operations and production," actually applies only to those suspensions that are the product of unanticipated events. To state this contention is to suggest its refutation. The plain meaning of a statute cannot be overcome by speculation as to some unstated purpose. Nothing in the legislative history of § 209 suggests, much less establishes, the narrow interpretation the Secretary would have us adopt. * * * The Secretary's speculation, suspect on its own terms, has no support in the legislative history and cannot modify the statute's plain terms.

We thus find it irrelevant, insofar as extension of the lease is concerned, that Copper Valley paid rent without protest during the two year extension of the ten year primary term. By paying rent Copper Valley protected its rights by eliminating the basis for any contention by the Secretary that it was in default. Whether the lease was extended or not, rent would eventually be due for the full two year period. Now Copper Valley has fully satisfied its rent obligation through the extension period it will receive by virtue of the suspension.

The Secretary also contends that Copper Valley's interpretation of § 209 could double the term of all leases on Alaskan tundra, contrary to the congressional intent that the term of a non-producing non-competitive lease be limited to 10 years, with the possibility of a single 2–year extension. 30 U.S.C. § 226(e). Contrary to the Secretary, we perceive no conflict between Copper Valley's reading of § 209 and a sensible reading of § 226(e). Without undertaking to decide that issue, which is not before us, we note that § 226(e) gives the lessee a minimum number of years in which to develop the resources subject to his lease. Section 209, consistent with this policy, extends the life of the lease to the extent that the lessee is deprived of his full term by the Secretary's suspension of drilling operations in the interest of conservation. Far from undermining § 226(e), § 209 effectuates the policy it reflects. The law was intended to apply uniformly throughout the United States and give lessees in Alaska the same full term of enjoyment as lessees in the lower 48 states. If climatic conditions in Alaska cause the Secretary to order a suspension in the interest of conservation it is not to be considered as being any the less a suspension because the reason that prompted its imposition was foreseeable. * * *

* * * The Secretary * * * has arbitrarily ignored the language of § 209. Ordinarily this agency conduct would call for a remand for proper application of the appropriate legal standards, if the agency under the law could reasonably adhere to the result its challenged decision has reached. On the undisputed facts here, however, we conclude that no reasonable interpretation of § 209 can deny Copper Valley the extension it claims. Accordingly, the judgment of the district court granting summary judgment for the Secretary should be vacated and the district court in accordance with the foregoing opinion should grant the motion of Copper Valley for summary judgment in its favor.[12]

■ JOHN H. PRATT, DISTRICT JUDGE, concurring in the remand:

* * * Congress intended the term "conservation" in § 209 to refer to the conservation of mineral resources, and not to more general environmental protection measures which may restrict production. The history of the 1933 statute shows that the concept of mineral conservation was advanced repeatedly by the bill's sponsors and managers, and was agreed to by opponents. * * * The majority reads "conservation" in its modern sense, and inadequately weighs the special meaning of the term "conservation" intended by Congress.

The Interior Department, which had authored and advocated the 1933 and 1946 statutes, interpreted § 209 to apply only to mineral conservation. This example of contemporaneous construction by the responsible cabinet officer is strong evidence of the original meaning, especially where Congress reenacts the statute consistently with that construction. The Department acted consistently with this interpretation in subsequent administrative adjudication and rulemaking. * * *

---

12. We cannot join the speculation [in the concurring opinion] that ordering a lease extension in this case will "create significant new land title difficulties in areas which have been subject to leasing, make new investment in oil exploration substantially more risky and expensive, and shortchange the United States as lessor, by conferring an unbargained-for windfall on the holders of existing leases." The Secretary has not acquainted us with these asserted problems. If conditions in Alaska require a special exception from § 209's plain meaning and policy then Congress is free to create one. In any event, were speculation within our province, we would venture that assuring oil and gas lessees, through lease extensions, the full exploration period that Congress has given them would *promote* new investment in oil exploration and benefit the United States. The United States is not shortchanged in the process; it is merely held to the lease terms specified in its statutory bargain.

I think a remand appropriate however, for the Secretary * * * to decide explicitly whether winter-only drilling restrictions are "suspensions" under § 209, and to state the policy and legal reasons for his choice among plausible interpretations of § 209.

There are sound practical and legal reasons for this approach. We know little more about Alaskan drilling than the fact that it is expensive and difficult. By pronouncing a rule at sharp variance with present practice in Alaska, we may create significant new land title difficulties in areas which have been subject to leasing, make new investment in oil exploration substantially more risky and expensive, and shortchange the United States as lessor, by conferring an unbargained-for windfall on the holders of existing leases. These are cogent reasons for seeking a careful exercise of the Secretary's expert judgment before deciding the interpretive issue presented here. Udall v. Tallman, 380 U.S. 1, 16–18 (1965). By pronouncing a flat rule before the Secretary has acted, we may significantly impede Alaskan oil development vital to meeting the Nation's current and future energy needs. I doubt Congress intended that result.

NOTES AND QUESTIONS

1.   The "winter-only" restriction responds to climatic conditions in northern Alaska. The oil industry has made great strides in the last few decades reducing the impact of its operations on the fragile Arctic environment. Operating in the winter allows access and other activities to take place on ice, which is much less damaging that operating on the tundra, where scars in the permafrost may never heal.

2.   Note carefully the mechanism by which the "winter–only" restriction was imposed on the lessee by the Secretary. If the restriction had been *in the lease itself*, would that change the result? Would it then have been a "suspension of operations" in the "interest of conservation" that would have extended the lease term? If, in other words, the lessee had entered the lease with full knowledge of the restriction, is it unfair to the lessee to enforce it?

3.   Does the Secretary have authority to put such a restriction in the lease itself? Section 30 of the Mineral Leasing Act (discussed in *Ventura County*, supra, pp. 209) provides, in part, that "[e]ach lease shall contain * * * such other provisions as [the Secretary] may deem necessary * * * for the protection of the interests of the United States * * * and for the safeguarding of the public welfare." 30 U.S.C. § 187. Is that sufficient authority to support such a restriction in the lease? See, e.g., George Pring, "Power to Spare": Conditioning Federal Resource Leases to Protect Social, Economic, and Environmental Values, 14 Nat. Resources Law. 305 (1981).

4.   The statute provided that the lease was to be for a primary term of ten years, and extended so long thereafter as oil or gas is produced in paying quantities. 30 U.S.C. § 226(e). If the seasonal restriction means that the lease can be explored only six months a year, does that effectively mean that the primary term is only five years, and thus inconsistent with the statute?

5.   Judge Pratt, concurring, seems to conclude that the "winter-only" restriction was not "in the interest of conservation" according to what Congress intended by "conservation" in 1933. If so, then why should the issue be remanded to the Secretary? Does the Secretary have any authority to extend the lease term under his view of the statute?

6.   The lease in *Copper Valley* was issued without competition, under a provision of the Mineral Leasing Act since repealed. The lessee paid no bonus up front to secure the lease. If the lease had been subject to competitive bidding, and bidders have been given adequate notice that activities on the lease would be limited to six months per year, might the bidders adjust their bids accordingly? In effect, would the government be trading protection of the tundra for lower revenues from the lease? Is that appropriate? Lawful?

7.   In Getty Oil v. Clark, 614 F.Supp. 904 (D.Wyo.1985), aff'd sub nom. Texaco Producing, Inc. v. Hodel, 840 F.2d 776 (10th Cir.1988), the court upheld a decision by Interior's Board of Land Appeals vacating the BLM's approval of an application for a permit to drill (APD) on a lease issued prior to 1970. Distinguishing *Copper Valley*, the court held that the Secretary could reserve, in a suspension order issued at *lessee*'s request, authority to reject future requests for APDs upon a finding of unacceptable environmental impacts, without automatically extending the lease term. The court left open the question whether the lessee had a "valid existing right" to drill on the lease.

These cases hint at a common problem touched on elsewhere in these materials, made particularly acute by the emergence of the modern environmental movement; namely, do rights of users of federal lands ever vest to the extent that newer, tougher environmental standards may not be imposed on them? This problem, inherent in making a transition from one policy or set of management standards to another, can arise in any number of different situations, from timber sale contracts to grazing permits, from mineral leases to rights-of-way. It can occur either when Congress legislates a new set of statutory standards, or when the executive branch itself determines that new policies are appropriate and that it has authority in existing law to implement them.

The legal issues can be analyzed from a number of different perspectives. For example, the government's role as resource owner can be considered a proprietary one, in which case statutes and/or leases/permits/contracts can be analyzed to determine what rights are conveyed, and a similar analysis can be employed to determine when rights "vest" so as to be immune from subsequent regulatory change. Cf. *Mobil Oil Exploration*, Chapter 3, supra pp. 257. But the federal government is also a sovereign entity with police power. Thus a "takings" analysis might be employed to determine the extent of governmental regulatory power over private property interests in federal resources. Furthermore, questions about the degree of deference to be given to an agency in interpreting a statute it is charged with the responsibility of administering may also come into play. Finally, notions of estoppel and fair play, whether articulated or not, can be brought to bear. Consider, for example, the Interior Department's successful effort to inject "marketability" notions into the "prudent person" Mining Law discovery test for minerals other than oil shale (United States v. Coleman, supra p. 605), with its failed attempt to overrule its previously generous concept of "discovery" under the Mining Law in the context of oil shale (Andrus v. Shell Oil Corp., supra p. 613).

NOTE: ONSHORE OIL AND GAS LEASING, RESOURCE PLANNING AND THE ENVIRONMENT

Most of the impetus for reforming the onshore oil and gas leasing system in the 1980s came from the perception that the federal government was giving away valuable leases without competition, and from the problems of fraud and abuse growing out of the unwieldy lottery. As the bill traveled through the congressional thicket, however, environmentally-minded representatives weighed in with proposals to require decisions on oil and gas leasing in particular areas to consider more closely impacts on the environment and other values served by the federal lands. The House-passed bill included several such provisions, but the Senate bill did not. The Administration and the oil industry opposed them, and most were dropped in the conference committee convened to reconcile the two versions, with the proviso that the General Accounting Office and the National Academy of Sciences study the integration of oil and gas leasing and federal land planning and environmental protection and report back to Congress.

The Reform Act did give the Forest Service a statutory veto over BLM's issuance of oil and gas leases on national forest land, and required both agencies to "regulate all surface–disturbing activities" conducted under oil and gas leases and to "determine reclamation and other actions as required in the interests of conservation of surface resources." No permit to drill may be granted "without the analysis and approval by the [appropriate agency] of a plan of operations covering proposed surface–disturbing activities within the leased area." Bonding is required to "ensure the complete and timely reclamation of the lease tract, and the restoration of any lands or surface waters adversely affected by lease operations * * *." 30 U.S.C. § 226(g).

The most controversial litigation over the federal onshore oil and gas leasing program has concerned how to integrate the requirements of NEPA and the federal land planning statutes with the oil and gas leasing program. A panel of the National Academy of Sciences/National Research Council, which was convened at the direction of Congress in the 1987 Reform Act, provided an overview of the issues as follows:

Land Use Planning and Oil and Gas Leasing on Onshore Federal Lands

Committee on Onshore Oil and Gas Leasing, National Research Council, 1989. Pages 10–13.

Oil and gas activities on the federal lands proceed through four stages of federal authorizations—land use planning, leasing, exploration (* * *

[including] permits to drill exploration wells), and development (permits to drill production wells, pipeline rights-of-way, and facility use permits). By statutes and judicial decisions, and agency directives implementing the requirements of both, the BLM and Forest Service are asked to consider the activities and environmental impacts associated with the leasing, exploration, and development stages during the initial planning stage when all potential uses of the federal lands are addressed. Unlike most other uses that involve the consumption or enjoyment of readily discernible surface resources, however, oil and gas activities are concerned with subsurface resources about which available information may be minimal. Although the potential for oil and gas is recognized during land use planning, the volume, extent, and specific location of the resources, and the consequent surface impacts from their exploration and development, are commonly unknown.

This informational problem poses the question of whether the surface impacts of oil and gas exploration and development can be fairly and adequately identified during planning to ensure that those activities are afforded equitable consideration with other federal land uses and values—that those activities are neither prematurely excluded from, or indiscriminately included on, federal lands by inadequately informed planning decisions. To the extent that such impacts cannot be properly identified during planning, the question becomes how the congeries of values served by the public lands can be identified and protected when the relevant information becomes available during the subsequent leasing, exploration, and development stages, particularly in those circumstances where the information discloses that prospective oil and gas activities will have unacceptable impacts on other uses and values.

Originally through their own initiative, and now in response to statutory mandates, the BLM and the Forest Service prepare land use plans for the lands they manage. Under the multiple-use management requirements of the FLPMA and the NFMA, these plans address the full panoply of federal land uses, including both economic uses (e.g., mineral development, timber production, livestock grazing, and ski resorts and other recreational facilities) and noneconomic uses (e.g., hiking and camping). The plans contain the decisions of the agencies as to which uses can be accommodated where and at what times in the planned area.

Absent dramatic changes in conditions in the planned area, the life of a land use plan may span 15 years (the prescribed maximum period in NFMA (16 USC 1604(f)(5)), [and] the projected standard period for BLM plans). Most of the surface uses authorized in a plan occur, and thus impact the environment, during the plan's term, and their levels of intensity and environmental impacts can be estimated with some degree of accuracy.

The effects of oil and gas exploration and development are not necessarily as contemporaneous or predictable. Oil and gas activities are likely to occur well after the plan's term. * * * The resources may not be leased until the last year of the plan: the fifteenth year. The great majority of leases that result in any activity have the first significant ground-disturbing actions—the drilling of an exploratory well after the approval by the agencies of an Application for Permit to Drill (APD)—in the last year of the lease term: the fifth year for competitive leases [eds. note: this has since been extended to ten years by legislation adopted in 1992, 30 U.S.C. § 226(e)] and the tenth year for noncompetitive leases. If the well identifies oil or gas in commercial quantities, additional APDs for development wells are submitted, and the field is developed after other permits and rights-of-way are issued by the agency over another generally lengthy span of time: perhaps a decade. Therefore the most significant impacts—those associated with full field development—may occur 30 to 35 years or more after issuance of the land use plan, 15 to 20 years or more after the plan's expiration.

An equally significant distinction between the planning for oil and gas exploration and development and the planning for most other federal land uses is the problem encountered in projecting the level of the use's activities and thus the magnitude of the use's impacts. Unlike most surface uses and even some mineral development such as coal mining, the volume and quality of the oil or gas resource are seldom known at the time land use planning is conducted, making projections of exploration and development activity levels and environmental impacts more difficult and less reliable. Even if all the land that might be identified for leasing in the planning process is leased during the plan's life, to attempt to identify during planning where on the leased land surface-impacting activities may occur is problematic.

Although statistics to make precise calculations are not available, the committee was generally informed by the federal agencies that, as a rough rule of thumb, approximately 10 percent of all oil and gas leases are ever subject to well drilling, and only about 10 percent of the leases upon which drilling occurs ultimately produce oil and gas in commercial quantities. The committee has not attempted independent verification of this 10/10 percent rule of thumb. While * * * most leases are never drilled, and few exploration wells result in discovery, it is important to note that a single tract of land may have been leased, and then re-leased upon expiration of the old lease, several times since enactment of the Mineral Leasing Act of 1920. The rule of thumb does not, in other words, suggest that only 10 percent of the land that is leased is ever subject to exploratory drilling. Furthermore, approximately one-quarter of the total leases currently in effect (and one-fifth of the acreage currently under federal lease) are in a producing status. * * *

Finally, even if the assumption is made that exploration and development will ensue, the type and level of impacts from production are not known when planning occurs. Producing fields vary wildly in size—from a few hundred acres and a handful of wells (e.g., North Pineview, Wyoming) to more than 75,000 acres and 21 wells (e.g., Riley Ridge, Wyoming). Within the field, impacts will correspond to such factors as whether the terrain is flat or hilly (whether drill pads and roads may be prepared with minimal earth disturbance or with excavation of cut and fill slopes), what the wellhead density and concomitant number of connecting service roads and gathering lines will be (oil wells typically are spaced every 40 acres, gas wells every 640 acres, based on the wells' drainage capacity and the area's geology), and what additional facilities may be needed (e.g., dehydration plants, injection wells for disposal of produced water or reinjection for pressure maintenance, or preparation plants to remove hydrogen sulfide from sour gas).

NOTES AND QUESTIONS

1. The litigation over how much forecasting has to be done at the lease issuance stage under NEPA, and the interaction between NEPA and reserving governmental authority over future activities in the lease terms, was summarized in the NEPA discussion in Chapter 5, supra pp. 422–25.

2. What is the right approach here, as a matter of policy? Is the question finding a proper balance between giving the lessee some certainty and reserving authority in the government to say no somewhere down the line if facts emerge or values change so that what now looks like a good idea turns out not to be so?

3. Which is more defensible, for the government to reserve in the lease the right to say no if (a) the facts turn out to be different than expected (e.g., if unknown environmental hazards are encountered in the exploration process), or (b) if public opinion changes about the wisdom of the activity in that particular area?

4. If you think a line ought to be properly drawn between those two situations, might there be situations where distinguishing between the two will be difficult? After all, won't the facts usually change over the next 30 years, in terms of our understanding and appreciation of environmental hazards? And won't public opinion inevitably change as well? We might, then, develop a greater sensitivity toward environmental concerns at the same time we gain more knowledge about them.

5. Note that both might change in a way that favors mineral development rather than restricts it, although generally speaking, the long-term trend has been against all-out mineral development. For an illustration of that point, consider the history of the Mining Law. It was enacted in a climate when the consensus was that mineral development would almost always be the highest and best, and therefore was the most favored, use of practically all federal land. Over the years that consensus has virtually disappeared, and perhaps half of the federal estate is no longer open to the Mining Law, and where it does apply it is accompanied by substantial environmental regulation.

6. In Wyoming Outdoor Council v. U.S. Forest Service, 165 F.3d 43 (D.C.Cir.1999), environmentalists unsuccessfully challenged the Forest Service's interpretation of its own regulations in a way that allowed it to push toward issuing oil and gas leases without, at an early stage, determining whether leasing was adequately addressed in a NEPA document and was consistent with the applicable forest plan. The Forest Service would make such determinations prior to actual lease issuance. The court concluded that while the environmentalists' position might be the "most natural"

way to read the regulations, the regulations were ambiguous and the Forest Service reading was not plainly erroneous.

NOTE: THE SURFACE MINING CONTROL AND RECLAMATION ACT

The Surface Mining Control and Reclamation Act of 1977 (SMCRA, pronounced "smack-ra"), 30 U.S.C. §§ 1201–1328, was signed by President Carter after President Ford had earlier vetoed similar legislation. SMCRA applies almost exclusively to coal, and applies to all surface coal mining operations in the country (not just those on federal lands) that remove more than 250 tons per year. Among other things, the lengthy Act sets very specific environmental protection performance standards for such mining operations and establishes requirements for reclamation. It has been called "by far the most detailed and complex U.S. legislation established to regulate a single industry." Carl Zipper and Richard Roth, Book Review, 31 Nat.Res.J. 707 (1991). For example, all strip-mined land must be restored to its "approximate original contour" with some exceptions (30 U.S.C. § 1265(b)(3)), and reclamation plans must be approved prior to the starting up of new mines. A new federal agency, the Office of Surface Mining (OSM), was established in the Department of the Interior to oversee implementation of the Act. The extensive permanent regulations, first adopted in 1979 (and modified several times since), are located at 30 C.F.R. Parts 700–707, 730–845 (1991). Federal District Judge Thomas Flannery in Washington D.C. practically made a career out of ruling on a continuing series of challenges to the regulations. See, e.g., National Wildlife Federation v. Lujan, 733 F.Supp. 419 (D.D.C.1990), rev'd, 928 F.2d 453 (D.C.Cir. 1991).

SMCRA withstood constitutional challenges in two companion cases involving private lands. Hodel v. Virginia Surface Mining & Reclamation Association, Inc., 452 U.S. 264 (1981); Hodel v. Indiana, 452 U.S. 314 (1981). The Court upheld congressional Commerce Clause authority to regulate surface mining, finding that the Act did not usurp state sovereignty in violation of the Tenth Amendment, and also held that the Act on its face did not effect a taking of property.

SMCRA requires the Secretary of the Interior to promulgate and implement a regulatory program for coal mining on federal lands that incorporates the general standards of the Act and considers any unique characteristics of particular federal lands. 30 U.S.C. § 1273(a). Cases involving SMCRA disputes on federal lands have rarely made it to court in comparison to private land litigation. Geographical and political differences account for much of this disparity. Most western public land states had relatively complete state reclamation standards prior to SMCRA, and those states generally supported passage of the Act. Additionally, most coal production in the western United States comes from large mines primarily located in the plains region, where huge coal seams are relatively close to the surface. In contrast, smaller, more numerous mines are much more common in the East, and eastern operators are subjected to more OSM inspections and enforcement actions than western operators. See generally Hamlet J. Barry III, The Surface Mining Control and Reclamation Act of 1977 and the Office of Surface Mining: Moving Targets or Immovable Objects?, 27A Rocky Mtn.Min.L.Inst. 169, 204 (1982).

Regulation of mining operations under SMCRA can occur in a variety of ways. Surface coal mining on private lands within a state is controlled either by a state program approved by the Secretary of the Interior, 30 U.S.C. § 1253, or by the federal program in instances where a state fails to submit an adequate surface coal mining program, id. § 1254. States with approved programs may enter into cooperative agreements with the Secretary of the Interior providing for state regulation of surface coal mining operations on public lands within the state. Id. § 1273(c). The Secretary has approved the state programs of all major western coal producing states; see 30 C.F.R. Parts 906 (Colo.), 926 (Mont.), 931 (New Mexico), 944 (Utah), and 950 (Wyo.) (2002).

SMCRA declares that after 1977 no coal surface mining is allowed within the boundaries of several different federal lands systems, including national parks, wildlife refuges, wilderness, and wild and scenic rivers. 30 U.S.C. § 1272. The same section also establishes a procedure to designate lands (federal or non-federal) unsuitable for all or certain kinds of surface mining operations. It instructs the Secretary to "conduct a review of Federal lands" to determine unsuitability of surface coal mining on lands otherwise available for such mining, and allows citizens to petition the Secretary for such a determination. An area "may" be designated unsuitable if mining operations would be incompatible with state or local land use plans, could result in significant damage to the environment or other values, or could endanger life or property. Id. (In one of the few instances where SMCRA applies to other minerals, 30 U.S.C. § 1281 allows the Secretary, after review, to declare federal lands unsuitable for mining minerals *other* than coal.) Through most of the 1980s, national coal surface-mining regulation was in shambles. Interior Secretary Watt's attempts to water down the statutory requirements generally failed in litigation, but OSM's effectiveness was seriously hampered. See generally James McElfish & Ann Beier, ENVIRONMENTAL REGULATION OF COAL MINING, SMCRA'S SECOND DECADE (1990). A measure of stability was restored thereafter.

NOTE: OIL AND GAS LEASING ON THE OFFSHORE LANDS

Decisions such as Pollard v. Hagan, 44 U.S. (3 How.) 212 (1845), Chapter 2, supra p. 52, had left open the question whether states owned the submerged lands offshore, beyond the tide lines. Few cared before the advent of offshore drilling technology, but as it emerged, the matter became worth litigating. In 1947, the Supreme Court ruled that the offshore lands were and always had been owned by the United States as a feature of national sovereignty. United States v. California, 332 U.S. 19 (1947). In United States v. Maine, 420 U.S. 515 (1975), the Court confirmed that its ruling applied to all coastal states, including the original thirteen.

In the meantime, after the coastal states had succeeded in making ownership of these submerged lands a significant political issue in the 1952 presidential election, Congress in 1953 ceded to the coastal states ownership of the seabed and resources in the three-mile belt seaward of the coast. Submerged Lands Act of 1953, 43 U.S.C. §§ 1301–1315. A few months later, Congress asserted federal "jurisdiction, control, and power of disposition" over the "subsoil and seabed of the outer Continental Shelf" beyond the three-mile limit. Outer Continental Shelf Lands Act of 1953 (OCSLA), as amended, 43 U.S.C. §§ 1331–1343, at § 1332(a).

A different kind of jurisdiction was asserted by the United States in the Fishery Conservation and Management Act of 1976 (FCMA), 16 U.S.C. §§ 1801–1882. While not claiming ownership per se, Congress decreed that all living resources between three and 200 miles offshore, with a few exceptions, could be harvested or exploited only in accordance with a new federal-regional regulatory scheme. Congress has also cooperated with and financed states in imposing controls over developments in and around the tidal margins by means of the Coastal Zone Management Act (CZMA), 16 U.S.C. §§ 1451–1464. The Marine Sanctuaries Act (MSA), 16 U.S.C. §§ 1431–1434, and other more limited and specialized legislation, such as the Marine Mammal Protection Act of 1972 (MMPA), 16 U.S.C. § 1361 et seq., also aim at more protection of the coastal and marine environments.

The various forms of jurisdiction and sovereignty that the United States has asserted over offshore areas do not amount to a claim of fee ownership of the underlying lands, nor to an assumption of complete, exclusive jurisdiction over the waters. See, for example, Treasure Salvors, Inc. v. Unidentified Wrecked and Abandoned Sailing Vessel, 569 F.2d 330 (5th Cir.1978), a contest between the government and treasure seekers who had located an ancient Spanish galleon off Florida. The United States claimed that both OCSLA and the 1906 Antiquities Act, 16 U.S.C. §§ 431–433, vested ownership of the sunken ship in it. The court held that the former asserted jurisdiction for purposes of controlling exploitation of the natural resources of the OCS, which did not include wrecked ships; and the latter was inapplicable because, the court said, the seabed was not owned or controlled by the United States.

There is no single management system for the federal offshore lands. Navigation is subject to Coast Guard regulations, and obstructions to navigable capacity must be cleared by the Army Corps of Engineers. Offshore oil and gas and other subsea mineral deposits can be leased by Interior's BLM, and supervised by Interior's Minerals Management Service (MMS), an agency created in the 1980s in part to exercise regulatory supervision (formerly exercised by the United States Geological Survey) over offshore mineral leases. Fisheries resources are largely within the ambit of the National Oceanic and Atmospheric Administration, currently located in the Department of Commerce, but inshore fisheries of the same fish plus other species are subject to regulation by the Fish and Wildlife

Service. Offshore regulation may also be affected by international treaty obligations.

Deep-water off-shore drilling is a comparatively new phenomenon. Platforms had been constructed in shallow water off Santa Barbara as early as 1897, but it was not until the middle of the twentieth century that any platform was constructed out of sight of land. Since then, rapid technological advances have enabled drillers to prospect and produce in ever-deeper waters and more forbidding conditions like the North Sea. But advanced technology can also produce new risks; more difficult operations raise the possibility of major blowouts and oil spills threatening ecologically fragile coastal areas and other offshore resources. Nevertheless, the offshore industry in the U.S. has had a remarkable environmental record, with very little problem since the Santa Barbara blow-out in 1969. That widely-publicized incident led to a skein of litigation. See Gulf Oil Corp. v. Morton, 493 F.2d 141 (9th Cir.1973); Union Oil Co. v. Morton, 512 F.2d 743 (9th Cir.1975); Sun Oil Co. v. United States, 572 F.2d 786 (Ct.Cl.1978), collectively holding, in essence, that the Secretary could suspend operations in the interest of conservation, broadly defined, but only for a limited time; otherwise, the lessee's interest would be "taken."

More enduringly, the Santa Barbara incident helped give birth to NEPA, which has since become the main ground of litigation for plaintiffs opposed to further lease sales. See, e.g., NRDC v. Morton, 458 F.2d 827 (D.C.Cir.1972); Suffolk County v. Secretary of Interior, 562 F.2d 1368 (2d Cir.1977); Village of False Pass v. Clark, 733 F.2d 605 (9th Cir.1984). Resource conflicts on the frontier of the public lands raise issues conceptually similar to those common on the onshore lands. The St. Georges Bank lease sale off Massachusetts posed the specter of oil spills harming the fishery in the area, once said to be one of the world's most productive. See Commonwealth of Massachusetts v. Andrus, 594 F.2d 872 (1st Cir.1979); Massachusetts v. Watt, 716 F.2d 946 (1st Cir.1983). Leasing in the area was stopped by environmental concerns; ironically, the fishing industry then so over-exploited the fishery that it collapsed. Several lease sales allegedly threatened to harm endangered species of whales and other wildlife. See, e.g., North Slope Borough v. Andrus, 642 F.2d 589 (D.C.Cir.1980). A potential conflict between oil and gas drilling and subsistence hunting and fishing rights was the focus of conflict in Amoco Prod. Co. v. Village of Gambell, 480 U.S. 531 (1987).

The OCS Lands Act was significantly amended in 1978, primarily to strengthen environmental regulation. A leading decision construing the Act, as amended, is Secretary of the Interior v. California, 464 U.S. 312 (1984). It concerned a new twist on the age-old problem of state vs. federal law. The Supreme Court held that the contested lease sales did not "directly affect" California's coastal zone and thus, under the Coastal Zone Management Act, 16 U.S.C. § 1456(c), the Secretary did not have to find the lease sales (as opposed to approval of subsequent plans to explore for or develop petroleum resources) "consistent" with California's coastal zone plan.

The National Academy of Sciences Committee studying onshore oil and gas leasing conveniently summarized some key provisions of the offshore statutory scheme (LAND USE PLANNING AND OIL AND GAS LEASING ON ONSHORE FEDERAL LANDS (1989), at 129):

> * * * [I]n its 1978 overhaul of the 1953 Outer Continental Shelf Lands Act (43 U.S.C. § 1338), Congress explicitly made offshore leases somewhat contingent upon environmental acceptability, at the same time providing a measure of reimbursement to a lessee who is denied the right to develop a lease under certain circumstances. The act authorizes the Secretary of the Interior to cancel a lease for environmental reasons upon a determination that "(i) continued activity * * * would probably cause serious harm to * * * [the] environment; (ii) the threat of harm or damage will not disappear or decrease to an acceptable extent within a reasonable period of time; and (iii) the advantages of cancellation outweigh the advantages of continuing such lease or permit in force."
>
> Congress also required payment of compensation to the lessee if the lease is canceled under certain circumstances (43 U.S.C. § 1334(a)(2)(C)). Specifically, the lessee is entitled to receive the lesser of (1) the fair value of the canceled rights as of the date of cancellation, taking account of both anticipated revenues from the lease and anticipated costs, including costs of compliance with all applicable regulations and operating orders, liability for cleanup costs or damages, or both, in the case of an oil spill, and all other costs reasonable anticipated on the lease, or (2) the excess, if any, over the lessee's revenues, from the lease (plus interest) of all consideration paid for the lease and all direct expenditures made by the lessee after the date of issuance of such lease and in connection with exploration or development, or both, pursuant to the lease (plus interest). For leases issued prior to the 1978 amendments, the standard of compensation is (1), the fair value of the canceled rights.

This compensation feature has not been invoked to date. See General Accounting Office, Mineral Revenues: Potential Cost to Repurchase Offshore Oil and Gas Leases, No. B–242732 (1991). The Comptroller General of the United States has opined that the Secretary has broad discretion in selecting an interest rate to use in calculating any compensation due. See 72 Comp. Gen. 122 (1993).

Other parts of the offshore oil and gas leasing program have been subject to judicial review. In Watt v. Energy Action Educational Foundation, 454 U.S. 151 (1981), the Court upheld secretarial discretion to determine the form and requirements of systems for bidding on offshore leases. Secretary Watt early in 1981 announced his intention to vastly expand OCS leasing, about the same time the D.C.Circuit sent back for reevaluation a much more modest leasing program of his predecessor. California v. Watt, 668 F.2d 1290 (D.C.Cir.1981). In the years that followed, environmental concern and "not in my backyard" concerns about coastal protection led Congress to legislate moratoria on OCS leasing in many coastal areas of the United States. Today, in fact, the central Gulf of

Mexico coast (the location of nearly all the current offshore oil industry) and most of the Alaskan coast are the only large OCS areas open to new federal oil and gas leasing. See Kevin Jones, Understanding the Debate Over Congressionally Imposed Moratoria on Outer Continental Shelf Oil and Gas Leasing, 9 Temple Env.L. & Tech.J. 117 (1990).

A BRIEF NOTE ON GEOTHERMAL RESOURCES

Various elements cooperate to produce geothermal power accessible for use on the surface of the earth. Magma or molten rock from the core of the earth intrudes into the earth's crust. The magma heats porous rock containing water. The water in turn is heated to temperatures as high as 500 degrees Fahrenheit. As the heated water rises to the surface through a natural vent, or well, it flashes into steam.

Geothermal steam is used to produce electricity by turning generators. In recommending passage of the Geothermal Steam Act of 1970, the Interior and Insular Affairs Committee of the House reported: "[G]eothermal power stands out as a potentially invaluable untapped natural resource. It becomes particularly attractive in this age of growing consciousness of environmental hazards and increasing awareness of the necessity to develop new resources to help meet the Nation's future energy requirements. The Nation's geothermal resources promise to be a relatively pollution-free source of energy, and their development should be encouraged." H.R.Rep. No. 91–1544, 91st Cong., 2d Sess., reprinted at 3 U.S.Code Cong. & Admin.News 5113, 5115 (1970).

United States v. Union Oil Co. of California, 549 F.2d 1271 (9th Cir.1977), cert. denied sub nom Ottoboni v. United States, 435 U.S. 911 (1978) (discussed on p. 686 infra). Areas of the western United States with high concentrations of federally owned lands often have geological conditions favorable to the existence of developable geothermal resources, such as comparatively recent volcanism and a relatively shallow mantle. Some of the areas with potential are protected in national parks; e.g., Yellowstone and Mount Lassen. The Geothermal Steam Act of 1970, 30 U.S.C. §§ 1101–1126, defines the geothermal resource as:

(i) all products of geothermal processes, embracing indigenous steam, hot water and hot brines; (ii) steam and other gases, hot water and hot brines resulting from water, gas, or other fluids artificially introduced into geothermal formations; (iii) heat or other associated energy found in geothermal formations; and (iv) any by-product derived from them.

"Byproduct" means any minerals (exclusive of oil, hydrocarbon gas, and helium) which are found in solution or in association with geothermal steam and which have a value of less than 75 per centum of the value of the geothermal steam or are not, because of quantity, quality, or technical difficulties in extraction and production, of sufficient value to warrant extraction and production by themselves.

30 U.S.C. §§ 1001(a) and (b). In some ways, exploitation of the geothermal resource more resembles the development of hydroelectric generating facilities than mineral development. The object is direct production of energy,

not fuel or mineral extraction, and the medium is water convection. The federal mode of allocation and regulation under the 1970 Act, however, allocates and regulates geothermal production under a system comparable to that used for leasable minerals, as opposed to that used for hydroelectric licensing. For materials on the latter, see Chapter 6, pp. 560.

Interest in geothermal development peaked during the "energy crisis" of the 1970s following the first Arab oil embargo, and produced a spate of articles on various legal issues posed. See, e.g, Owen Olpin, A. Dan Tarlock & Carl F. Austin, Geothermal Development and Western Water Law, 1979 Utah L.Rev. 773, 781–83; Owen Olpin & A. Dan Tarlock, Water That Is Not Water, XIII Land & Water L.Rev. 391 (1978); Sho Sato & Thomas Crocker, Property Rights to Geothermal Resources, 6 Ecology L.Q. 250 (1977); Symposium, XIII Land & Water L.Rev. (1977) (15 articles); Raymond J. Werner, Geothermal Leasing, 54 Ore.L.Rev. 623 (1975).

Perhaps the most interesting and important set of issues involves federalism, and the extent to which state or federal law allocates rights to this fugacious resource, which can be found in common pools underlying both federal and state/private lands. The question can be further complicated depending upon whether state law treats the geothermal resource as a mineral resource, or as a water resource. How state and federal laws interact may depend upon the answer. Furthermore, geothermal resources may be hydrologically interconnected with other water systems. Questions about the interaction of state and federal law where groundwater or geothermal development off federal lands threatens to interfere with geothermal resources on federal land are explored in Chapter 12, p. 1070. While all these questions are very interesting, there is more literature than litigation providing answers to them.

C. FEDERAL MINERALS THAT ARE SUBJECT TO SALE

As noted earlier, there is a third category and system for disposing of federal minerals—very common, widely occurring minerals are available for disposition only by competitive sale. The Materials Disposal Act of 1947, 30 U.S.C. §§ 601–604, as amended by the Common Varieties Act of 1955, 30 U.S.C. § 611, provides for sale of sand, stone, gravel, pumice, cinders, and other designated "common" minerals, at the discretion of the Secretary of the Interior, unless the deposit "has some property giving it distinct and special value," id. § 601, in which case it may still be located under the Mining Law. ("Vegetative materials" found on the public lands and not subject to disposal under other laws, such as those governing commercial timber, are also subject to sale under these provisions.)

The Materials Disposal Act requires that such sales must usually be made to the highest responsible qualified bidder after advertising, with certain exceptions (such as where it is "impracticable to obtain competition"). Sales must not be "detrimental to the public interest," and must be for "adequate compensation therefor, to be determined by the Secretary."

Regulations governing these sales are found at 43 C.F.R. Parts 3600, 3610 (2000).

WHAT HAPPENS WHEN DIFFERENT MINERALS ARE TARGETS OF DEVELOPMENT ON THE SAME FEDERAL LANDS?

The same federal land may be valuable for different minerals; e.g., some strata may contain gold; others coal or oil. The same mineral deposit may contain both coal and methane gas. Common minerals like gravel or stone may be found in lands where other minerals are found. Interesting legal questions can sometimes be raised in these situations, especially to the extent different legal regimes apply to different minerals. For example, there had long been uncertainty, and conflicting legal opinion, about whether the Department of the Interior could sell common variety mineral materials (such as sand and gravel) from federal land that had been claimed under the Mining Law. The mining claimant has no right under the Mining Law to sell these materials, which are sometimes a main component of the overburden removed in order to develop locatable minerals. A 1999 Solicitor's Opinion resolved the past inconsistencies by concluding that the Secretary has authority under the Materials Act of 1947 to dispose of these materials where it can be done without endangering or materially interfering with prospecting, mining, ore reasonably related uses. Disposal of Mineral Materials from Unpatented Mining Claims, M–36998 (1999).

Where the different minerals are subject to the same law, the matter is usually straightforward. Precious metals like lead, zinc and silver are often found in association with each other. All are subject to the Mining Law of 1872, and a claim under that law embraces all the valuable minerals subject to that law found within the claim. But federal land may be claimed under the Mining Law, but also contain coal, oil or gas or another leasable mineral. Here a special federal statute, the Multiple Mineral Development Act of 1954, 30 U.S.C. §§ 521–531, establishes an uneasy compromise that is aimed at promoting compatible dual development. See Osborne v. Hammit, 377 F.Supp. 977 (D.Nev.1964); cf. Kanab Uranium Corp. v. Consolidated Uranium Mines, 227 F.2d 434 (10th Cir.1955). Special rules are provided for geothermal areas; see, e.g., 30 U.S.C. § 1003(a); Getty Oil Co. v. Andrus, 607 F.2d 253 (9th Cir.1979); Crownite Corp. v. Watt, 752 F.2d 1500 (9th Cir.1985). These matters are addressed in detail in AMERICAN LAW OF MINING (2d ed. 2000), §§ 6.05, 200.05.

Complications are possible when both minerals are subject to leasing, but under different sections of the Mineral Leasing Act. This kind of issue has occurred in spades in the Powder River Basin in Wyoming as a result of a boom in coalbed methane activity in the late 1990s. The problem came about this way. The federal government issued many oil and gas leases on minerals it owned in the Basin in the 1960s and 1970s. The expectation at the time was that there would be wildcat exploration for any deep oil and gas deposits that might exist; no one at the time the leases were issued anticipated that the gas found in shallow coal beds might be exploitable. The leases themselves simply leased "gas," without regard to the depth or formation where it might be found. Sometime thereafter, the federal government issued separate coal leases to exploit the large and shallow coal deposits. Still later, the technology was developed to extract gas from the coalbeds. If the coal is mined first, the gas is lost to the atmosphere. If the gas is extracted first, the coal can later be mined. The problem becomes, then, a problem of timing of development. The different holders of the different mineral leases may not always see eye to eye on the matter. Holders of gas leases argue that they have priority because their leases were issued first. Therefore, if they are not willing or able to extract gas before the coal lessee was ready to mine the coal, they claim a right by their lease priority either to stop the coal mining or extract compensation from the coal owner for the lost gas. The coal lessee wants to avoid that situation, of course, and wants the federal government, as owner of both resources, to step in to force the gas lessee to develop the gas in a manner compatible with the coal lessee's schedule for mining the coal. The Department's authority in this matter turns on the terms of both leases, and the Department's regulations. See Kurt M. Petersen, Coalbed Gas Development in the Western United States: Legal Issues and Operational Concerns, 37 Rocky Mt.Min.L.Inst. 13–1, 13–47 (1991); Phillip W. Lear, Multiple Mineral Development Conflicts: An Armageddon in Simultaneous Mineral Operations, 28 Rocky Mt.Min.L.Inst. 79, 89–95 (1983). Legislation has been introduced to create an improved framework for resolving these conflicts. See also IMC Kalium Carlsbad, Inc. v. IBLA, 206 F.3d 1003 (10th Cir.2000) (reversing BLM decision rejecting an oil and gas company's high bid for a potash lease; BLM thought the company was really seeking the lease simply to avoid restrictions on its oil and gas activities in the area; the court agreed with the Interior Board of Land Appeals that the evidence did not support BLM's determination that the company had acted in bad faith, and found that potential conflicts between potash and oil and gas could be addressed when permits to drill or mine are sought).

D. SPLIT ESTATES: ISSUES WHERE MINERAL INTERESTS ARE SEPARATED FROM SURFACE INTERESTS

1. FEDERAL MINERALS UNDER PRIVATE SURFACE

For most of the disposition era, the railroad, statehood, homestead and other statutes that authorized disposition of federal land were usually not applicable to federal "mineral lands," or federal lands that were "mineral in character." Such lands were not, in other words, available for selection or disposition under those statutes; instead, they were subject to the Mining Law of 1872.

Of course, it was not always easy to tell whether lands that homesteaders wanted to settle upon, or that were within the in-place grants to the states or railroads, were "mineral in character." The rule that emerged was simple: The critical determination was usually made at the point in time that the land was surveyed, which was necessary before the land could be actually conveyed. If the land was deemed mineral in character then, the homesteader could not gain title. If land subject to an in-place grant was determined to be mineral in character at the time the lands were surveyed, in lieu selection rights were provided instead. See Andrus v. Utah, Chapter 2, supra p. 62. In either case, if the land was deemed not to be mineral in character, and was then conveyed out of federal ownership, and it turned out later the land contained minerals, the grant was not affected and the grantee took the minerals. Burke v. Southern Pac. R. Co., 234 U.S. 669 (1914).

In 1957 a divided U.S. Supreme Court belatedly recognized an exception to that general notion. It held that a grant of a right of way to a railroad to build the first transcontinental railroad did not include the rights to minerals underneath the right of way. United States v. Union Pacific R. Co., 353 U.S. 112 (1957), noted in Chapter 2, supra p. 156. This decision left undisturbed the holding in *Burke* in other contexts. Justice Douglas for the majority in *Union Pacific* explained that the process for determining "mineral in character" before issuance of patent was "obviously inappropriate" for the right of way for the railroad roadbed itself, because "the route of the railroad had to be determined by engineering considerations which could not allow for the extensive detours that avoidance of land containing minerals would make necessary." Therefore the result most faithful to the intent of the Congress was to deny the railroad the minerals underneath the right of way. 353 U.S. at 116–17. There was a vigorous dissent.

Shortly after the turn of the twentieth century, this policy of separating mineral lands from other lands began to change. Starting in 1909, some statutes authorized disposition of federal land without regard to whether it was mineral in character, and instead reserved to the United States all or some minerals in that land. This is the primary reason that, in addition to the minerals underlying the federal lands and the continental shelf, the United States also owns or controls the rights to minerals under more than 60 million acres of land surface it does not own, mostly in eleven western states. While it is convenient to refer to the "surface" and "subsurface estates" in this split estate context, in reality the surface owner has title to the subsurface as well, except for whatever minerals are reserved.

This movement to reserve <u>minerals</u> instead of <u>mineral lands</u> from disposition responded to a number of concerns. It sought to satisfy the pressure to make more western federal lands available for settlement and other disposition, while also responding to a growing dependence of the country upon fossil fuels, and a growing conviction that the government should retain ownership of those fossil fuel minerals it already owned, to better control their management and disposition. That is, the increasing number of withdrawals of federal lands from disposition (President Taft's withdrawal leading to the *Midwest Oil* decision came the same year as the first statutory federal mineral reservation), and the determination that a significant amount of federal land was mineral in character, were both seen as obstacles to disposition for non-mineral purposes. At the same time, the government retained its historic reluctance to dispose of land that contained minerals to agricultural settlers. The compromise was to make the land, except for some or all of the minerals, available for disposition. See generally John C. Lacy, Conflicting Surface Interests: Shotgun Diplomacy Revisited, 22 Rocky Mt. Min.L.Inst. 731, 755–57 (1976).

The first important express general reservation of minerals in a public land disposition statute was in the Coal Lands Act of 1909, 30 U.S.C. § 81. It required that coal would be reserved in subsequent agricultural patents. It was quickly followed by the Agricultural Entry Act of 1914, 30 U.S.C. §§ 121–123 (reserving oil, gas, and other specified minerals) and the most important one, the Stock–Raising Homestead Act of 1916, 43 U.S.C. §§ 291–301 (reservation of "coal and other minerals"). Over 33 million acres were patented under the 1916 Act. Some of these acts allowed issuance of a patent without the mineral reservation if the recipient could show the land to non-mineral in character; that kind of provision was of limited assistance to patentees because of the difficulty of proof. The Stock–Raising Homestead Act did not include such an option. The individual statutes are discussed in Willis Carpenter, Severed Minerals as a Deterrent to Land Development, 51 Den.L.J. 1 (1974); Howard A. Twitty, Law of Subjacent Support and the Right to Totally Destroy Surface in Mining Operations, 6 Rocky Mt.Min.L.Inst. 497, 513–14 (1961). An estimated 60 million acres of nonfederal land contain federal mineral reservations. See Public Land Law Review Commission, ONE THIRD OF THE NATION'S LAND 137 (1970).

The issues that arise under these reservations tend to divide into two categories: First, what substances are actually reserved? And second, what are the rights of the two estate owners vis-a-vis each other, when the mineral owner seeks to develop the reserved mineral estate?

a. WHAT MINERALS ARE RESERVED?

Watt v. Western Nuclear, Inc.

Supreme Court of the United States, 1983.
462 U.S. 36.

■ JUSTICE MARSHALL delivered the opinion of the Court.

The Stock–Raising Homestead Act of 1916, the last of the great homestead acts, provided for the settlement of homesteads on lands the surface of which was "chiefly valuable for grazing and raising crops" and "not susceptible of irrigation from any known source of water supply." 43 U.S.C. § 292. Congress reserved to the United States title to "all the coal and other minerals" in lands patented under the Act. 43 U.S.C. § 299. The question presented by this case is whether gravel found on lands patented under the Act is a mineral reserved to the United States. * * *

In March 1975 respondent Western Nuclear, Inc. (Western Nuclear), acquired a fee interest in a portion of the land covered by [a 1926 Stock–Raising Homestead Act patent]. Western Nuclear is a mining company that has been involved in the mining and milling of uranium ore in and around Jeffrey City since the early 1950's. In its commercial operations Western

Nuclear uses gravel for such purposes as paving and surfacing roads and shoring the shaft of its uranium mine. In view of the expense of having gravel hauled in from other towns, the company decided that it would be economical to obtain a local source of the material, and it acquired the land in question so that it could extract gravel from an open pit on the premises.

After acquiring the land, respondent obtained * * * a [state] permit authorizing it to extract gravel from the pit located on the land. Respondent proceeded to remove some 43,000 cubic yards of gravel. * * *

On November 3, 1975, the Wyoming State Office of the BLM served Western Nuclear with a notice that the extraction and removal of the gravel constituted a trespass against the United States[.] * * *

After a hearing, the BLM determined that Western Nuclear had committed an unintentional trespass. Using a royalty rate of 30 cents per cubic yard, the BLM ruled that Western Nuclear was liable to the United States for $13,000 in damages for the gravel removed from the site. [The IBLA and then the federal district court affirmed, but the court of appeals reversed, holding that the gravel extracted by Western Nuclear was not a mineral reserved to the United States by the Act.]

In view of the importance of the case to the administration of the more than 33 million acres of land patented under the SRHA, we granted certiorari. We now reverse.

As this Court observed in a case decided before the SRHA was enacted, the word "minerals" is "used in so many senses, dependent upon the context, that the ordinary definitions of the dictionary throw but little light upon its signification in a given case." Northern Pacific R. Co. v. Soderberg, 188 U.S. 526, 530 (1903). In the broad sense of the word, there is no doubt that gravel is a mineral, for it is plainly not animal or vegetable. But "the scientific division of all matter into the animal, vegetable or mineral kingdom would be absurd as applied to a grant of lands, since all lands belong to the mineral kingdom." While it may be necessary that a substance be inorganic to qualify as a mineral under the SRHA, it cannot be sufficient. If all lands were considered "minerals" under the SRHA, the owner of the surface estate would be left with nothing.

Although the word "minerals" in the SRHA therefore cannot be understood to include all inorganic substances, gravel would also be included under certain narrower definitions of the word. For example, if the term "minerals" were understood in "its ordinary and common meaning [as] a comprehensive term including every description of stone and rock deposit, whether containing metallic or non-metallic substances," gravel would be included. If, however, the word "minerals" were understood to include only inorganic substances having a definite chemical composition, gravel would not be included.

The various definitions of the term "minerals" serve only to exclude substances that are not minerals under any common definition of that word. Cf. United States v. Toole, 224 F.Supp. 440 (D.Mont.1963) (deposits of peat and peat moss, substances which are high in organic content, do not constitute mineral deposits for purposes of the general mining laws). For a substance to be a mineral reserved under the SRHA, it must not only be a mineral within one or more familiar definitions of that term, as is gravel, but also the type of mineral that Congress intended to reserve to the United States in lands patented under the SRHA. Cf. Andrus v. Charlestone Stone Products Co., 436 U.S. 604 (1978) [eds. supra, p. 585].[5]

The legal understanding of the term "minerals" prevailing in 1916 does not indicate whether Congress intended the mineral reservation in the SRHA to encompass gravel. On the one hand, in Northern Pacific R. Co. v. Soderberg, supra, this Court had quoted with approval a statement in an English case that "everything except the mere surface, which is used for agricultural purposes; anything beyond that which is useful for any purpose whatever, whether it is *gravel,* marble, fire clay, or the like, comes within the word 'mineral' when there is a reservation of the mines and minerals from a grant of land." 188 U.S., at 536 (emphasis added). * * *

On the other hand, in 1910 the Secretary of the Interior [held that land alleged to be chiefly valuable for sand and gravel was not "mineral in character" which would have excluded it from homestead entry.] Zimmerman v. Brunson, 39 Pub.Lands Dec. 310, overruled, Layman v. Ellis, 52 Pub.Lands Dec. 714 (1929). Zimmerman claimed that gravel and sand found on the property could be used for building purposes and that the property therefore constituted mineral land, not homestead land. In refusing to cancel Brunson's homestead entry, the Secretary explained that "deposits of sand and gravel occur with considerable frequency in the public domain." He concluded that land containing deposits of gravel and sand useful for building purposes was not mineral land beyond the reach of the homestead laws, except in cases in which the deposits "possess a peculiar property or characteristic giving them a special value."

Respondent errs in relying on *Zimmerman* as evidence that Congress could not have intended the term "minerals" to encompass gravel. Although the legal understanding of a word prevailing at the time it is included in a statute is a relevant factor to consider in determining the meaning that the legislature ascribed to the word, we do not see how any inference can be drawn that the 64th Congress understood the term "minerals" to exclude gravel. It is most unlikely that many members of Congress were aware of the ruling in *Zimmerman,* which was never tested in the courts and was not mentioned in the reports or debates on the SRHA. Even if Congress had been aware of *Zimmerman,* there would be no reason to conclude that it approved of the Secretary's ruling in that case rather than this Court's opinion in *Soderberg,* which adopted a broad definition of the term "mineral" and quoted with approval a statement that gravel is a mineral.

Although neither the dictionary nor the legal understanding of the term "minerals" that prevailed in 1916 sheds much light on the question before us, the purposes of the SRHA strongly support the Government's contention that the mineral reservation in the Act includes gravel. * * *

5. The specific listing of coal in the reservation clause of the SRHA sheds no light on what Congress meant by the term "minerals." * * *

Congress' underlying purpose in severing the surface estate from the mineral estate was to facilitate the concurrent development of both surface and subsurface resources. While Congress expected that homesteaders would use the surface of SRHA lands for stock-raising and raising crops, it sought to ensure that valuable subsurface resources would remain subject to disposition by the United States, under the general mining laws or otherwise, to persons interested in exploiting them. It did not wish to entrust the development of subsurface resources to ranchers and farmers. Since Congress could not have expected that stock-raising and raising crops would entail the extraction of gravel deposits from the land, the congressional purpose of facilitating the concurrent development of both surface and subsurface resources is best served by construing the mineral reservation to encompass gravel. * * *

Given Congress' understanding that the surface of SRHA lands would be used for ranching and farming, we interpret the mineral reservation in the Act to include substances that are mineral in character (i.e., that are inorganic), that can be removed from the soil, that can be used for commercial purposes, and that there is no reason to suppose were intended to be included in the surface estate. This interpretation of the mineral reservation best serves the congressional purpose of encouraging the concurrent development of both surface and subsurface resources, for ranching and farming do not ordinarily entail the extraction of mineral substances that can be taken from the soil and that have separate value.[14]

Whatever the precise scope of the mineral reservation may be, we are convinced that it includes gravel. * * * Insofar as the purposes of the SRHA are concerned, it is irrelevant that gravel is not metalliferous and does not have a definite chemical composition. What is significant is that gravel can be taken from the soil and used for commercial purposes. * * *

It is also highly pertinent that federal administrative and judicial decisions over the past half-century have consistently recognized that gravel deposits could be located under the general mining laws until common varieties of gravel were prospectively removed from the purview of those laws by the Surface Resources Act of 1955, 30 U.S.C. § 611. While this Court has never had occasion to decide the appropriate treatment of gravel under the mining laws, the Court did note in United States v. Coleman, 390 U.S. 599, 604 (1968), that gravel deposits had "served as a

---

14. * * * We note that this case does not raise the question whether the owner of the surface estate may use a reserved mineral to the extent necessary to carry out ranching and farming activities successfully. Although a literal reading of the SRHA would suggest that any use of a reserved mineral is a trespass against the United States, one of the overriding purposes of the Act was to permit settlers to establish and maintain successful homesteads. There is force to the argument that this purpose would be defeated if the owner of the surface estate were unable to use reserved minerals even where such use was essential for stock-raising and raising crops.

In this case, however, respondent cannot rely on any right it may have to use reserved minerals to the extent necessary for ranching and farming purposes, since it plainly did not use the gravel it extracted for any such purpose. The gravel was used for commercial operations that were in no way connected with any ranching or farming activity.

basis for claims to land patents" under the mining laws prior to the enactment of the Surface Resources Act of 1955.

The treatment of gravel as a mineral under the general mining laws suggests that gravel should be similarly treated under the SRHA, for Congress clearly contemplated that mineral deposits in SRHA lands would be subject to location under the mining laws, and the applicable regulations have consistently permitted such location. * * *

Finally, the conclusion that gravel is a mineral reserved to the United States in lands patented under the SRHA is buttressed by "the established rule that land grants are construed favorably to the Government, that nothing passes except what is conveyed in clear language, and that if there are doubts they are resolved for the Government, not against it." United States v. Union Pacific R. Co., 353 U.S. 112, 116 (1957). In the present case this principle applies with particular force, because the legislative history of the SRHA reveals Congress' understanding that the mineral reservation would "limit the operation of this bill *strictly to the surface of the lands*." H.R.Rep. No. 35, supra, at 18 (emphasis added). In view of the purposes of the SRHA and the treatment of gravel under other federal statutes concerning minerals, we would have to turn the principle of construction in favor of the sovereign on its head to conclude that gravel is not a mineral within the meaning of the Act.

For the foregoing reasons, we hold that gravel is a mineral reserved to the United States in lands patented under the SRHA. * * *

■ JUSTICE POWELL, with whom JUSTICE REHNQUIST, JUSTICE STEVENS, and JUSTICE O'CONNOR join, dissenting.

The Court's opinion may have a far-reaching effect on patentees of, and particularly successors in title to, the 33,000,000 acres of land patented under the Stock–Raising Homestead Act of 1916 (SRHA). * * * [T]he Court adopts a new definition of the statutory term: "[T]he Act [includes] substances that are mineral in character (i.e., that are inorganic), that can be removed from the soil, that can be used for commercial purposes, and that there is no reason to suppose were intended to be included in the surface estate."

This definition compounds, rather than clarifies, the ambiguity inherent in the term "minerals." It raises more questions than it answers. Under the Court's definition, it is arguable that all gravel falls within the mineral reservation. This goes beyond the Government's position that gravel *deposits* become reserved only when susceptible to commercial exploitation. And what about sand, clay, and peat? As I read the Court's opinion it could leave Western homesteaders with the dubious assurance that only the dirt itself could not be claimed by the Government. It is not easy to believe that Congress intended this result. * * *

The first attempt by the Department of the Interior to acquire ownership of gravel on SRHA lands did not occur until this case began in 1975. One would think it is now too late, after a half-century of inaction, for the Department to take action that raises serious questions as to the nature and extent of titles to lands granted under SRHA.[20] Owners of patented land are entitled to expect fairer treatment from their Government. In my view, the Department should be required to adhere to the clear intent of Congress at the time this legislation was adopted. I would affirm the judgment of the Court of Appeals.

NOTES AND QUESTIONS

1.   Who is right here, the majority or the dissent? Can Congress use the same word ("mineral") to mean different things in different statutes? Is the pivotal issue whether the Congress that enacted the Stock–Raising Homestead Act in 1916 was *aware* of the 1910 Departmental decision in Zimmerman v. Brunson holding that ordinary gravel was not a mineral for purposes of the Mining Law?

2.   Is the dissent saying that the government ought to be estopped from changing its mind? Do you agree that it is "not easy" to believe that the Congress intended to leave Western homesteaders without title to the sand and gravel underneath their property?

3.   Congress reserved the minerals in part because it did not, in Justice Marshall's words, "wish to entrust the development of subsurface resources to ranchers and farmers." Is it ironic that in this case the patentee's successor wants to develop the minerals, but is found not to have the legal authority to do so?

4.   The gravel deemed reserved to the U.S. in the principal case is subject to competitive sale rather than leasing under the Mineral Leasing Act or to claim location under the Mining Law. See Section C, supra p. 677.

5.   Relying on *Western Nuclear*, the court in Hughes v. MWCA, 12 Fed.Appx. 875 (10th Cir.2001), held that "scoria," a form of volcanic cinder which became valuable in the 1970s for use in landscaping and as gas barbecue briquets, was a mineral reserved by the United States in the Stock–Raising Homestead Act. It went on to hold that the deposit of scoria at issue was a common variety subject to sale by the United States, rejecting the argument of the surface owner that it was entitled to mine and sell it because it had located mining claims on the deposit.

---

20.   The Department is in no position to adopt a new policy for land patents long granted. See Andrus v. Shell Oil Co., 446 U.S. 657 (1980). Its prior actions have caused the population generally, including respondent, to understand that gravel was not a reserved mineral. [As the district court observed:] "Until [1975], it was the practice of the Wyoming Highway Department, construction companies, and the ranchers owning the surface estate to treat the gravel as part of the surface estate, the gravel being sold or used by the rancher with the approval of the [Bu-reau of Land Management]." As Justice Rehnquist stated for the Court in Leo Sheep Co., supra:

"Generations of land patents have issued without any express reservation of the right now claimed by the Government. Nor has a similar right been asserted before. * * * This Court has traditionally recognized the special need for certainty and predictability where land titles are concerned, and we are unwilling to upset settled expectations. * * *"

6. Gravel may not be a "mineral" in other mineral reservations, especially those not made under a specific statute whose legislative history and context help in construing the term. See, e.g., United States v. Hess, 194 F.3d 1164 (10th Cir.1999).

In United States v. Union Oil Co. of California, 549 F.2d 1271 (9th Cir.1977), cert. denied sub nom Ottoboni v. United States, 435 U.S. 911 (1978), the question was whether geothermal resources were reserved to the United States in the Stock–Raising Homestead Act. The court noted that

[t]here is no specific reference to geothermal steam and associated resources in the language of the Act or in its legislative history. The reason is evident. Although steam from underground sources was used to generate electricity at the Larderello Field in Italy as early as 1904, the commercial potential of this resource was not generally appreciated in this country for another half century. No geothermal power plants went into production in the United States until 1960. Congress was not aware of geothermal power when it enacted the Stock–Raising Homestead Act in 1916; it had no specific intention either to reserve geothermal resources or to pass title to them.

* * * The Act reserves to the United States "all the coal and other minerals." All of the elements of a geothermal system—magma, porous rock strata, even water itself[5]—may be classified as "minerals." When Congress decided in 1970 to remove the issue from controversy as to future grants of public lands, it found it unnecessary to alter the language of existing statutory "mineral" reservations. It simply provided that such reservations "shall hereafter be deemed to embrace geothermal steam and associated geothermal resources." Geothermal Steam Act of 1970, 30 U.S.C. § 1024.[6] Thus, the words of the mineral reservation in the Stock–Raising Homestead Act clearly are capable of bearing a meaning that encompasses geothermal resources.

The substantial question is whether it would further Congress's purposes to interpret the words as carrying this meaning. * * * [The opinion recounted the campaign in the early 20th century to conserve

5. * * * No one contends that water cannot be classified as mineral. Appellees argue only that the water should not be included in the term "minerals" in this statutory setting. This is basically a question of legislative intent, dealt with in detail later in the text. To the extent that the argument rests on the meaning of the word itself, however, the government is entitled to have the ambiguity resolved in its favor under "the established rule that land grants are construed favorably to the Government, that nothing passes except what is conveyed in clear language, and that if there are doubts they are resolved for the Government, not against it." United States v. Union Pac. R.R., 353 U.S. 112, 116 (1957). * * *

6. Members of the Subcommittee on Mines and Mining of the House Committee on Interior and Insular Affairs went to some lengths to make it clear that whether the term "minerals" as used in prior legislation included geothermal resources was a question for the courts, on which the official position of the 89th Congress was one of neutrality. * * *

mineral resources, and the evolution of statutory reservations of minerals, beginning with the Coal Lands Act of 1909.]

* * * The title of the Act—"The Stock–Raising Homestead Act"—reflects the nature of the intended grant. * * * [The legislative history] demonstrates that the purposes of the Act were to provide homesteaders with a portion of the public domain sufficient to enable them to support their families by raising livestock, and to reserve unrelated subsurface resources, particularly energy sources, for separate disposition. This is not to say that patentees under the Act were granted no more than a permit to graze livestock, as under the Taylor–Grazing Act, 43 U.S.C. §§ 315 et seq. To the contrary, a patentee under the Stock–Raising Homestead Act receives title to all rights in the land not reserved. It does mean, however, that the mineral reservation is to be read broadly in light of the agricultural purpose of the grant itself, and in light of Congress's equally clear purpose to retain subsurface resources, particularly sources of energy, for separate disposition and development in the public interest. Geothermal resources contribute nothing to the capacity of the surface estate to sustain livestock. They are depletable subsurface reservoirs of energy, akin to deposits of coal and oil, which it was the particular objective of the reservation clause to retain in public ownership. The purposes of the Act will be served by including geothermal resources in the statute's reservation of "all the coal and other minerals." Since the words employed are broad enough to encompass this result, the Act should be so interpreted.

NOTES AND QUESTIONS

1. The court identifies the key question as "whether it would further Congress's purposes" to interpret the statute as reserving geothermal resources as a mineral. Would the *Leo Sheep* Court, Chapter 2, supra 147, have defined the issue in that manner? Is the question what was Congress's overall purpose, or what was Congress's intent regarding geothermal resources? If the latter, what is the answer?

2. Is the court here saying that the geothermal resource is a mineral? Compare Andrus v. Charlestone Stone Products Co., 436 U.S. 604 (1978), supra p. 585 (reversing a 9th Circuit decision rendered a few months after this case, and holding water is not a mineral under the Mining Law of 1872). Might the meaning of "mineral" change appreciably between 1872 and 1916? The court in Rosette Inc. v. United States, 277 F.3d 1222 (10th Cir.2002), reached the same result as the Ninth Circuit in *Union Oil* and distinguished *Charlestone* because different statutes were involved.

3. If the Stock–Raising Homestead patentee had a water right from the state to extract hot water from underneath her land, would that defeat a federal claim to ownership of the resource? The court said no in *Rosette Inc.*, supra.

4. What is really at stake in these cases; i.e., what difference does the result make in terms of future geothermal resource development? In *Rosette*, the holder of the Stock–Raising Homestead patent was extracting

hot water from a well and using it to heat greenhouses where it grew roses for commercial distribution. (It irrigated the roses with cooler water drawn from another well.) The United States sought to collect royalties and damages based on its claim it owned the geothermal resource. The court said that while Rosette might, consistent with the patent, be able to use the heated water from geothermal resources to water livestock or irrigate forage crops, it could not use it for "the commercial activity of heating greenhouses to produce roses for sale."

5. Note that the Geothermal Steam Act of 1970 provided that mineral reservations "shall hereafter be deemed to include" geothermal resources. Could Congress have made, in 1970, that pronouncement applicable to all patents previously issued under the 1916 Act? What if it did so by saying, in effect, "we are simply clarifying what we meant in 1916"? Would that control the outcome?

6. In Amoco Production Co. v. Southern Ute Indian Tribe, 526 U.S. 865 (1999), the Supreme Court held that the reservation of "coal" to the United States in the Coal Lands Acts of 1909 and 1910 did not reserve coalbed methane (CBM) gas within the coal formations. (In 1938, the United States had conveyed all the interests in land it owned in the area to the tribe; therefore, if the U.S. had reserved the coalbed methane, the tribe succeeded to that ownership.) The majority opinion said

> "[The question] is not whether, given what scientists know today, it makes sense to regard CBM gas as a constituent of coal but whether Congress so regarded it in 1909 and 1910. * * * We are persuaded that the common conception of coal at the time Congress passed [those statutes] was the solid rock substance that was [then] the country's primary energy resource. * * * Congress [then] viewed CBM gas not as part of the solid fuel resource it was attempting to conserve and manage but as a dangerous waste product, which escaped from coal as the coal was mined. * * * [While t]here is some evidence of limited and sporadic exploitation of CBM gas as a fuel prior to passage of the 1909 and 1910 Acts * * * there is every reason to think [Congress] viewed the extraction of CBM gas as drilling for natural gas, not mining coal. The distinction is significant because the question before us is not whether Congress would have thought that CBM gas had some fuel value, but whether Congress considered it part of the coal fuel. * * * Because we conclude that the most natural interpretation of 'coal' as used in the 1909 and 1910 Acts does not encompass CBM gas, we need not consider the applicability of the canon that ambiguities in land grants are construed in favor of the sovereign or the competing canons relied on by petitioners."

526 U.S. at 873–74. (In 1981 the Interior Solicitor had opined that the coal reservation did not include CBM, but that opinion was withdrawn in 1999, and the United States supported the Tribe's position in the Supreme Court; the Court did not rely on or defer to the 1981 Opinion in reaching the same result.) If *Amoco Production Co.* had been decided before the Ninth Circuit had taken up the geothermal steam reservation question in *Union Oil*, would it have made the outcome different? The statutory interpretation

issues raised are discussed by Professor Bruce M. Kramer in Amoco Production Co. v. Southern Ute Indian Tribe: Restatement or Revolution?, 45 Rocky Mt. Min.L.Inst. 7–1 (1999). The Supreme Court's decision does not apply to private mineral interests, where matters remain unsettled in many jurisdictions; see Jeff L. Lewin, Coalbed Methane: Recent Court Decisions Leave Ownership "Up in the Air," But New Federal and State Legislation Should Facilitate Production, 96 W.Va.L.Rev. 631 (1994).

7.   In Aulston v. United States, 915 F.2d 584 (10th Cir.1990), cert. denied, 500 U.S. 916 (1991), the court upheld the Department of the Interior's interpretation that the reservation of "oil and gas" in the 1914 Agricultural Entry Act included carbon dioxide.

b. PROTECTING THE ENVIRONMENT AND SURFACE VALUES IN DEVELOPING FEDERALLY RESERVED MINERALS

Statutes reserving minerals in federal ownership typically made the mineral estate dominant and the surface estate servient. Thus the Stock–Raising Homestead Act of 1916 reserved not only the minerals but also "the right to prospect for, mine, and remove the same," and "to reenter and occupy so much of the surface * * * as may be required for all purposes reasonably incident to the mining or removal of the * * * minerals." 43 U.S.C. § 299. When these statutes reserving minerals were enacted early in this century, all the reserved minerals (except coal) were subject to the Mining Law of 1872. Many of the minerals were later made subject to leasing under the Mineral Leasing Act of 1920; common varieties of widely occurring minerals like sand and gravel were made subject to sale in 1947. In both situations the government retains considerable control over whether the reserved mineral shall be available for development, and the terms (including environmental restrictions) upon which development shall proceed.

Some of the minerals the U.S. reserved (such as gold and silver reserved under the broad "minerals" reservation of the 1916 Act) are, however, still subject to the self–initiation feature of the Mining Law. This means that the initial decision to locate claims and start mineral activity lies with mining claimants rather than the government, and the government's power to control whether and how the reserved federal minerals will be developed is somewhat more ambiguous, as recounted on pp. 628–38 supra.

Even though the federal reserved mineral estate includes a right to develop the minerals, Congress never freed mining activity from all restraint in split estate situations. The Stock–Raising Homestead Act, for example, required the mineral developer to compensate the surface owner for "crops" and other "improvements" damaged by mining operations. The Supreme Court held that this provision did not require compensation for any impairment of surface resources that did not strictly qualify as a growing crop or a permanent, agriculturally–related improvement. Kinney–Coastal Oil Co. v. Kieffer, 277 U.S. 488 (1928); see also Holbrook v. Continental Oil Co., 73 Wyo. 321, 278 P.2d 798 (1955); John C. Stocker,

Protection For Surface Owners of Federally Reserved Mineral Lands, 2
UCLA–Alas.L.Rev. 171 (1973).

The mineral reservation could create serious problems for farmers,
ranchers, and even suburbanites in areas that were once privatized under
laws like the Stock–Raising Homestead Act.

> * * * [O]ne can envisage an entire residential subdivision on Stock–
> Raising Homestead Act lands. There are many such developments
> today, and more are being built. In come the prospectors, bearing not
> only their 1916 picks and shovels, but their modern day bulldozers and
> draglines. They may not harm the permanent improvements; that
> much is clear. And they must make restitution for damages to "crops."
> So they set to work in the lawn areas of the suburb, and perhaps also
> in the parks, greenbelts, and other "unimproved" areas. On at least
> one occasion such activity, or the threat of it, has prompted Congress
> to take the unusual step of specific legislation withdrawing the subject
> minerals from location and leasing.

Willis V. Carpenter, Severed Minerals as a Deterrent to Land Development,
51 Den.L.J. 1, 24–25 (1974). See also Clarence Brimmer, The Rancher's
Subservient Surface Estate, V Land & Water L.Rev. 49, 50 (1970).

Of course, the degree of disruption depends upon the mineral involved
and the method used to extract it. Oil and gas activity may involve only
limited, tolerable intrusions on the surface estate. Surface mining of coal
and other accessible deposits may virtually destroy the surface. As that
technique gained favor because of its cost and safety advantages, Congress
moved in 1949 to enlarge the liability of the developer of federally-reserved
minerals by requiring payment for damage to the value of the land for
grazing caused by "strip" or "open–pit" mining. 30 U.S.C. § 54.

Modern environmental concern for protection of surface values has
combined with rancher concern for their way of life to lead to increasing
legislative solicitude for the surface estate. The Federal Land Policy and
Management Act, for example, not only codified a sweeping power of
withdrawal, but also subjected reserved federal mineral interests to the
planning dictates of the act (by defining public lands subject to FLPMA as
including "any * * * interest in land" owned by the United States and
managed by the BLM). 43 U.S.C. § 1732(b). FLPMA also allows future
patents to be issued without reservations of minerals. And it permits
present surface owners to apply for title to the reserved minerals, but they
must pay fair market value for them. 43 U.S.C. § 1719(b)(2). In both cases,
if mineral deposits are unknown, minerals will remain with the United
States unless the BLM finds that the federal reservation "is interfering
with or precluding appropriate non-mineral development of the land and
that such development is a more beneficial use of the land than mineral
development." 43 U.S.C. § 1719(b)(1).

The most notable example of extending protection to surface owners
overlying federally reserved coal is found in the Surface Mining Control
and Reclamation Act of 1977. There Congress decided that the surface
owner must give written consent before the federal government can enter

into a coal lease "to be mined by methods other than underground mining techniques." 30 U.S.C. § 1304. "Surface owner" is defined as a person who for at least three years has held title to the surface, and who either lives on the land, personally conducts farming or ranching operations on it, or derives a significant portion of her income from such operations. Id.

Because the consent of the surface owner can be purchased by one desiring to obtain a federal coal lease, this provision in effect can operate to transfer a portion of the value of the coal underneath the land from the federal government (which presumably will receive lower bids for the coal) to the surface owner. This may especially be true in cases where the surface owner gives a non-transferable consent to a particular company, because that effectively discourages others from bidding on the coal lease. As a result, the provision may be the most significant or valuable privatization of interests in federal land in a half–century.

In 1993, Congress once again returned to the matter of protecting the surface owner, this time amending the Stock–Raising Homestead Act to require the mineral developer, among other things, to gain approval in advance from the Secretary of the Interior of a surface use plan, and to post a bond. 107 Stat. 60, 43 U.S.C. § 299(b)-(p). John C. Welborn, New Rights of Surface Owners: Changes in the Dominant/Servient Relationship Between the Mineral and Surface Estates, 40 Rocky Mt.Min.L.Inst. 22–1 (1994).

In a context where both the surface estate and the mineral estate are privately owned, such legislative readjustments of the initial allocation of rights may raise constitutional questions. Recall that two of the classic takings cases in American constitutional law arose in a split-estate context, testing (with opposite results) the authority of the state legislature to adjust the rights of the coal owner and the surface owner. Pennsylvania Coal v. Mahon, 260 U.S. 393 (1922); Keystone Bituminous Coal Ass'n v. DeBenedictis, 480 U.S. 470 (1987) (discussed at pp. 239–40 supra). Where the federal government has retained title to the reserved minerals, however, it can of course limit or otherwise impose restrictions on its own interests without raising constitutional questions. But if it has already disposed of the reserved mineral by lease or other means, any new restrictions imposed after the fact may raise either takings questions or questions of contract law such as were discussed in Chapter 4, § G, p. 256 supra.

Other interesting questions may be raised about the scope of the mineral reservation. For example, if the United States issues an oil and gas lease on the mineral estate it reserved, may it include in the lease permission to construct an oil refinery on the land surface, without compensating the surface owner? That is, under the Stock–Raising Homestead Act mineral reservation, is an oil refinery "reasonably incident" to mining or removal of the mineral? What about a geothermal power plant? In Occidental Geothermal, Inc. v. Simmons, 543 F.Supp. 870 (N.D.Cal.1982), the court found that patents issued under the 1916 Act included a reservation of geothermal plant siting rights. The court laid some emphasis on the unique nature of the energy source, where "removal" and "utilization" are inextricably linked; when geothermal steam is transported long distances, it loses its heat and pressure. "In this respect geothermal energy differs from other mineral sources of energy reserved to the United States by the 1916 Act, such as coal or oil, which can feasibly be mined and removed for subsequent utilization * * * in far-distant locales." 543 F.Supp. at 874.

Cases like *Occidental Geothermal* are actually quite rare. In practice, federal reserved mineral rights have caused less of a furor than might be expected. Private surface owners initially may not be pleased to find that their lands are the target of mineral activity, but if development looks promising, mining companies typically choose to pay substantial sums to purchase the surface owner's consent, or her land outright, rather than litigate.

Although the federal reservations include hardrock deposits as well, valuable hardrock deposits are less likely to occur on the less mountainous agricultural and grazing land typically subject to the mineral reservations. There are exceptions, however—stock-raising land in Wyoming has seen substantial uranium activity, and copper deposits have been located on some rangelands in the southwest.

Finally, a refresher question on the various systems for extracting federal minerals: Underneath Rancher Thompson's Stock–Raising Homestead Act land is a deposit of ordinary sand, and underneath that is a deposit of uranium, underneath that a deposit of coal, and still deeper a deposit of natural gas. How may rights to extract each of these substances be obtained? May the federal government prevent exploitation of any or all of them? How? May it regulate their extraction? How much? Does Rancher Thompson have any say about whether and how each is developed?

NOTE: DETERMINING WHETHER FEDERAL RIGHTS ARE RESERVED IN DISPOSITIONS

In a broad sense, the federal mineral reservations addressed here are a species of federal reserved rights akin to federal reserved water rights usually associated with federal land withdrawals; see Chapter 6, supra p. 514. In other contexts, however, claims of federal reservations have been rejected; e.g., Leo Sheep v. United States, Chapter 2, supra p. 147 (easement for public access for recreation purposes held not reserved). Can these differing outcomes be reconciled? Is there a single rule or canon of construction that can, or should, be applied to all claims of federal reserved rights? Or must each be examined on an ad hoc basis, controlled by its specific statute or order? Should the courts adopt a presumption that Congress intended, in privatizing federally owned resources, to reserve such rights as are appropriate for the reasonable, long term protection and preservation of resources on the public lands? Should wildlife, recreation, and preservation be considered as resources under such a formulation? See generally Charles Wilkinson, The Field of Public Land Law: Some Connecting Threads and Future Directions, 1 Pub.Land L.Rev. 1, 29–38 (1980).

2.   PRIVATE MINERALS UNDER FEDERAL SURFACE

This category of split estates may be found in a variety of situations. In the West, federal land purchases or exchanges, done for such purposes as consolidating former checkerboard patterns of ownership or acquiring land with high public values into federal ownership, have sometimes resulted in the federal government acquiring only surface ownership. For example, the holder of a railroad land grant or its successor may reserve the minerals while conveying the surface to the federal government. In the eastern part of the country, when the federal government embarked on a major program of acquiring lands for national forests under the Weeks Act of 1911, 16 U.S.C. §§ 513–518, 521, the private sellers often reserved mineral rights, sometimes in perpetuity and sometimes for a period of years. The same thing happened with many federal acquisitions under the Bankhead–Jones Farm Tenant Act of 1937, involved in the next principal case. Reserved private mineral interests can be found under lands managed by the National Park Service and the U.S. Fish & Wildlife Service as well. The Forest Service estimates that approximately six million acres in the national forest system has reserved nonfederal mineral rights. The National Park Service estimates that some five million acres of land it manages (and about two thirds of the individual units) contain private mineral rights, either in fee simple inholdings or reserved mineral interests. See generally Andrew C. Mergen, Surface Tension: The Problem of Federal/Private Split Estate Lands, 33 Land & Water L.Rev. 419 (1998).

a.   WHAT MINERALS ARE RESERVED?

In this context too, questions sometimes arise about what minerals are reserved and the scope of the mineral reservation. The first question is resolved by the terms of the deed or conveyance that reserved the minerals (unlike the situation of reserved federal minerals explored above, where the issue is usually one of statutory interpretation). Interestingly, at least one modern court has answered the question of what minerals are reserved in a particular deed by looking to the amount of destruction that would be caused by mineral extraction. In Downstate Stone Co. v. United States, 712 F.2d 1215 (7th Cir.1983), the question was whether the privately-owned mineral estate of "all minerals" included the right to extract limestone, a common mineral, the quarrying of which often involves destruction of the surface. The court determined that, under either federal or state law, the parties to the deed creating the estate did not intend to allow surface destruction so that limestone was not included in the grant.

In United States v. Stearns Coal & Lumber Co., 816 F.2d 279 (6th Cir.1987), the parties agreed that Kentucky law controlled construction of a deed conveying land to the Forest Service and reserving minerals to the seller. On the merits, the court held that the deed did not reserve to the mineral owner the right to strip mine coal without permission of the Forest Service, explaining in part that under the provisions of the deed, "strip mining would not be a reasonable use of the surface because * * * the parties did not contemplate that [the mineral rights holder] could totally destroy the surface." 816 F.2d at 283. See also United States v. Stearns Co., 949 F.2d 223 (6th Cir.1991) (reaffirming the earlier result, rejecting Stearns' argument that it should be reversed because of a recent Kentucky Supreme Court decision striking down a state statute prohibiting strip mining of minerals reserved by so-called "broad-form" deeds; see Akers v. Baldwin, 736 S.W.2d 294 (Ky.1987)). For later decisions from the Kentucky Supreme Court on the broad question, and the Court of Claims in the *Stearns* litigation, see Ward v. Harding, 860 S.W.2d 280 (Ky.1993); The Stearns Co. v. United States, 34 Fed.Cl. 264 (1995).

The Interior Department's Office of Surface Mining sometimes finds itself on the front lines of making these determinations. This is because the Surface Mining Control and Reclamation Act (SMCRA) provides, with certain exceptions, subject to "valid existing rights," that no coal mining which disturbs the surface "shall be permitted * * * on any federal lands within the boundaries of any national forest." 30 U.S.C. § 1272(e)(2). In Belville Mining Co. v. United States, 763 F.Supp. 1411 (S.D.Ohio 1991), the court engaged in a detailed review of the mineral reservations contained in deeds to four different tracts of land acquired by the Forest Service under the Weeks Act. It concluded that on three of the tracts, the reservations allowed strip mining. It also found that, because the OSM had concluded in 1988 that the mineral rights holder possessed "valid existing rights" under SMCRA for all four tracts, and the holder had relied on that determination by "devoting considerable resources" to securing a permit to mine from the state, OSM had no power to revoke that determination. On appeal, the Sixth Circuit affirmed the rulings as to the first three tracts but reversed as to the fourth, finding that OSM had adequate inherent, statutory, and regulatory authority to reverse its policies. 999 F.2d 989 (6th Cir.1993).

b.   AUTHORITY OF THE UNITED STATES TO CONTROL DEVELOPMENT OF RESERVED MINERAL RIGHTS

The materials that follow focus on the authority of the federal government to regulate development of reserved minerals in nonfederal ownership, especially where such development threatens surface values. As the following case indicates, sometimes a key question is whether state or federal law applies.

Duncan Energy Company v. United States Forest Service

United States Court of Appeals, Eighth Circuit, 1995.
50 F.3d 584.

■ John R. Gibson, Senior Circuit Judge.

* * * Meridian owns mineral rights on land within the Little Missouri National Grasslands area, which is part of the Custer National Forest in North Dakota. The United States owns the surface estate.[1] Duncan has an exploration agreement with Meridian.

1. The United States originally patented the land in question to Northern Pacific Railroad Company as a part of a railroad land grant. In 1916, the railroad deeded the land to various farmers, reserving "all minerals of any nature whatsoever * * * together with the use of such of the surface as may be necessary for exploring for and mining or otherwise extracting and carrying away the same." In 1937, the United States acquired

Since 1984, Meridian and its predecessor, Milestone Petroleum, have explored for oil and gas within the Custer National Forest without incident. Meridian submitted surface use plans to the Forest Service for review and obtained special use letters of authorization before developing its mineral estates. The Forest Service Regional Office reviews surface use plans by applying the standards and guidelines set forth in the Custer National Forest Land and Resource Management Plan. The Forest Service surveys resources in the area of proposed operations, analyzes potential effects, and determines whether there may be reasonable alternatives and mitigation measures. Following this review, the Forest Service issues a letter of authorization which establishes conditions and protective measures for surface use.

In 1984, the United States Forest Service and Meridian's predecessor, Milestone Petroleum, entered into a Memorandum of Understanding, which provided that the Forest Service would process a surface use plan within ten working days of the receipt of the complete surface use plan. Since 1984, Meridian has submitted fifteen surface plans to the Forest Service before drilling; the Forest Service has processed only two of the plans in fewer than ten days.

On October 15, 1992, the Forest Service and Duncan met to discuss well location, access, and road specifications for Duncan's anticipated drilling. The Forest Service suggested a different access route from that proposed by Duncan, and the access road was staked as the Forest Service suggested. On October 22, the Forest Service and several of Duncan's contractors met for an on-site surface inspection of the well location and staked access route. On December 7, 1992, Duncan submitted a surface use plan for a well site. The Forest Service advised Duncan's contractor that the surface use plan contained an inaccurate map of the proposed access route based on the October 22 meeting, and Duncan submitted a corrected map on December 24, 1992. The Forest Service then conducted an environmental analysis of the well and access route, consisting of a review of reports submitted by Duncan's contractors and consultation with the United States Fish and Wildlife Service and the North Dakota Department of Fish and Game. The Forest Service began to prepare an analysis document, which sets forth terms and conditions for the use of the federal surface.

Over the next two months, Duncan contacted the Forest Service to check the status of the Forest Service's authorization. Duncan wanted to begin drilling, as its contract with Meridian required it to drill seven wells within one year or incur liquidated damages. During this time, Duncan learned that the Forest Service believed that the Memorandum of Understanding did not apply and that the Forest Service was considering whether the more extensive National Environmental Policy Act procedures applied. Under NEPA, Duncan could not drill until the Forest Service completed an

the surface estate pursuant to the Bankhead–Jones Farm Tenant Act, subject to the mineral reservation in the 1916 deed. Meridian eventually acquired the mineral rights and

Meridian executed an oil and gas exploration agreement with Duncan on September 30, 1992.

area-wide environmental impact study and a site-specific environmental impact statement, which might take two to three years. See 42 U.S.C. § 4332(2)(C) (1988).

On March 4, 1993, Duncan sent a letter to the Forest Service stating that it had an absolute right to access and drill the site. Duncan requested that the Forest Service immediately issue a special use permit and comply with the 1984 Memorandum of Understanding. Duncan threatened to access the well as originally proposed if the Forest Service did not immediately approve the staked route. On March 16, 1993, Duncan submitted a revised map for the access route to the Forest Service. Because the new route varied two-tenths of a mile from the staked route, the Forest Service informed Duncan that it must complete the necessary environmental surveys for the new road, but that it would complete its analysis of the original route by the following week.

On Friday, March 19, 1993, at 4 o'clock p.m. Duncan telephoned the Forest Service to say that it would begin constructing the new road the next morning. The Forest Service visited the site the next morning and found that Duncan had begun constructing the road. Duncan completed all road construction by March 27. On April 6, 1993, Duncan placed the drill rig on the site, over the Forest Service's written objection. After Duncan asserted that the Forest Service was bound by the ten-day period stated in the Memorandum of Understanding, the Forest Service formally terminated the Memorandum on April 15, 1993.

Meanwhile, on March 29, 1993, Duncan filed suit against the Forest Service seeking a declaratory judgment that the Service could not prohibit access to or regulate the exploration and development of the privately owned oil and gas estate. The Forest Service filed an answer and a counterclaim asserting that Duncan had improperly used federal surface without obtaining the necessary authorization. The Forest Service requested a permanent injunction barring Duncan from further ground disturbing activity at the well site and on other National Forest System lands without the Forest Service's express written authorization.

* * * [The district court found for Duncan, reasoning] that the mineral estate is the dominant estate and that the surface estate was therefore subservient to the development, mining, and extraction of the minerals. The court held that when the United States owns only the surface estate, it does not have the authority to regulate mineral estate exploration, development, mining or extraction different from or greater than state law. The court stated that the surface owner "cannot prevent the exploration, mining or extraction of the underlying minerals even if that development will completely destroy the value of the surface estate or render it unsuitable for public usage." The court determined that if the mineral estate holder causes damage to the surface estate, the mineral estate holder is liable in damages to the surface owner, and, if this remedy is "illusory," then the damage can only be righted by condemnation and purchase of the mineral estate. After considering North Dakota law, the court concluded that an attempt to prohibit the development of mineral interests would constitute an inverse condemnation of the mineral estate. The court

rejected the Forest Service's argument that the Forest Service, as owner of the surface estate, had the power to adopt rules, regulations and permit requirements before allowing ground disturbing activity.

The Forest Service appeals, arguing that the district court's decision is incorrect because the Forest Service has authority under North Dakota law and federal law to regulate federally-owned surface lands. The Forest Service acknowledges that the mineral estate is dominant, but points out that it is not seeking to deny access to the underlying non-federal lands, but only to protect federal lands during their use by the mineral holder. * * *

Under North Dakota law, the mineral estate is dominant, carrying "inherent surface rights to find and develop the minerals." Hunt Oil Co. v. Kerbaugh, 283 N.W.2d 131, 135 (N.D.1979). The mineral developer's rights, however, are not unrestricted. The mineral developer's rights "are limited to so much of the surface and such use thereof as are *reasonably necessary* to explore, develop, and transport the minerals." Id. Thus, North Dakota law does not preclude the Forest Service from requiring that only reasonable use be made of the federal surface lands. *Hunt Oil* established that the mineral developer's right of access is subject to a standard of reasonableness:

> [I]f the manner of use selected by the dominant mineral lessee is the only reasonable, usual and customary method that is available for developing and producing the minerals on the particular land then the owner of the servient estate must yield. However, if there are other usual, customary and reasonable methods practiced in the industry on similar lands put to similar uses which would not interfere with the existing uses being made by the servient surface owner, it could be unreasonable for the lessee to employ an interfering method or manner of use.

Id. at 136–37 (quoting Getty Oil Co. v. Jones, 470 S.W.2d 618, 627–28 (Tex.1971)).

Although North Dakota law protects the surface owner's property rights by limiting the mineral holder to the "reasonable use" of the surface, North Dakota law does not * * * cloak the Forest Service with the specific authority to approve surface use plans. Indeed, there is not even specific authority to allow a surface owner to enjoin the unreasonable use of the surface. *Hunt Oil* does not discuss injunctive relief. North Dakota's Oil and Gas Production Compensation Act requires only that the mineral developer "give the surface owner written notice of the drilling operations contemplated at least twenty days prior to the commencement of the operations," and provides a damages remedy. N.D.Cent.Code § 38–11.1–05 (1987).

Nevertheless, the Forest Service contends that federal law gives it the authority to approve surface use plans. Duncan responds * * * that Congress has not given the Forest Service the authority to regulate outstanding mineral rights, as it has given the National Park Service. See 16 U.S.C. § 1902 (1988); 36 C.F.R. § 9.30(a) (1994).

Congress has the power under the property clause to regulate federal land. * * * Under the Bankhead–Jones Farm Tenant Act, Congress directed the Secretary of Agriculture "to develop a program of land conservation and land utilization." 7 U.S.C. § 1010 (1988). The Act directs the Secretary to make rules as necessary to "regulate the use and occupancy" of acquired lands and "to conserve and utilize" such lands. 7 U.S.C. § 1011(f) (Supp. V. 1993). The Forest Service, acting under the Secretary's direction, manages the surface lands here as part of the National Grasslands, which are part of the National Forest System. See 16 U.S.C. § 1609(a) (1988). Congress has given the Forest Service broad power to regulate Forest System land. See, e.g., 7 U.S.C. § 1011 (1988 & Supp. V. 1993); 16 U.S.C. § 551 (Supp. V. 1993).

The Forest Service finds its authority to regulate surface access to outstanding mineral rights in the "special use" regulations. The special use regulations provide that "[a]ll uses of National Forest System land * * * are designated 'special uses' and must be approved by an authorized officer." 36 C.F.R. § 251.50(a). * * *

* * * The only issue before us is the Forest Service's ability to regulate surface access to outstanding mineral rights. The Forest Service recognizes that it cannot prevent Duncan, as the owner of the dominant mineral estate, from exploring for or developing its minerals. * * *

[The court then considered and rejected several specific arguments by Duncan that the special use regulations and other sources show that the Forest Service has no regulatory authority here. The court then addressed the Forest Service Manual.] Although the Forest Service Manual does not cite the special use regulations, the substance of the manual is consistent with the regulations. For example, the Manual requires the mineral estate owner to submit "an operating plan for the exercise of outstanding mineral rights," including methods for controlling environmental degradation. The Manual authorizes the Forest Service to send a letter of authorization after reviewing the plan to determine whether it "[u]ses only so much of the surface as is prudently necessary for the proposed operations." Although the Manual says that the Forest Service should meet with the mineral owner to negotiate modifications, it provides for "appropriate legal action" if the mineral owner deviates from the operating plan. * * *

* * * For these reasons, we are convinced that the Forest Service has the limited authority it seeks here; that is, the authority to determine the reasonable use of the federal surface.[8]

8. Duncan explains that it resorted to proceeding without Forest Service authorization because of the Forest Service's delay in processing its surface use plan. Implicit in our conclusion that the Forest Service is authorized to determine the reasonable use of the federal surface is our assumption that the Forest Service's inquiry must be reasonable, and thus, expeditious. Otherwise, the Forest Service's authority could expand to "veto authority" over mineral development. The Forest Service concedes that it cannot prohibit mineral development and recognizes the mineral holder's absolute right to develop its mineral estate. Counsel at oral argument represented that the Forest Service approval of a surface use plan usually takes about two months. We believe such a timeframe is consistent with the Forest Service's authority to determine the reasonable use of the federal

If North Dakota law is read to allow developers unrestricted access after twenty days' notice and no injunctive relief for the surface owner, North Dakota law is inconsistent with the special use regulations. State law may be pre-empted in two ways:

> If Congress evidences an intent to occupy a given field, any state law falling within that field is pre-empted. If Congress has not entirely displaced state regulation over the matter in question, state law is still pre-empted to the extent it actually conflicts with federal law, that is, when it is impossible to comply with both state and federal law, or where the state law stands as an obstacle to the accomplishments of the full purposes and objectives of Congress.

Silkwood v. Kerr–McGee Corp., 464 U.S. 238, 248 (1984).

In addition, under choice-of-law principles, when determining whether to apply federal or state law, federal courts will apply federal law "when the case arises from or bears heavily upon a federal regulatory program." United States v. Albrecht, 496 F.2d 906, 910 (8th Cir.1974).

Allowing unrestricted access after twenty days' notice would impede Congress' objective of protecting federal lands and abrogate a congressionally-declared program of national scope. If North Dakota law is read to allow a developer unrestricted access after twenty days' notice, North Dakota law is preempted or falls under choice-of-law principles.

Accordingly, the judgment of the district court is reversed, and the case is remanded to the district court with instructions to enter summary judgment for the United States and an order declaring that Duncan violated Forest Service regulations by proceeding with mineral development absent Forest Service authorization of the surface use plan. The Forest Service's request for a permanent injunction is best considered by the district court on remand. * * *

NOTES AND QUESTIONS

1.   Duncan Energy is between a rock and a hard place: Forest Service delays may cause breach and termination of its contract with Meridian, but some "reasonable" delay is inevitable if the agency can regulate and condition Duncan's surface entry. Is this dilemma the fault of the Forest Service or of Duncan?

2.   Is there an argument that the NEPA process does not apply here, if it would result in delaying the Forest Service consideration of Duncan's plans "unreasonably"? Could the court, in other words, hold that the Forest Service has authority to regulate Duncan's activities to some extent in order to protect the surface estate, but cannot use regulatory processes such as a full-blown EIS process if it would greatly delay the exercise of that regulatory authority?

surface and does not violate the mineral holder's dominant right to access and develop its   mineral estate.

3. What about the relation between federal and state law here? The split estate here was not created under federal law; the federal government originally issued a fee simple deed for this land. The estate was later split by the Northern Pacific Railroad, under state law. That being the case, why doesn't state law control the definition of the respective rights of the mineral owner and the surface owner? Before the Forest Service acquired the surface, state law governed that issue. Why does the Forest Service have more authority than its predecessor in title to the surface could convey? Has the Court in *Duncan* effectively used federal law to make the surface estate dominant in contravention of North Dakota law?

4. Notice that the court here cites United States v. Albrecht as authority for applying federal law. That case was discussed in Chapter 3, supra p. 224. One might also consider the application of federal law here to limit the right of the surface owner as an exercise of Congress's power under the Property Clause to regulate nonfederal property in order to protect federal property. See Chapter 3, supra, pp. 198–203; see also Marla E. Mansfield, A Primer of Public Land Law, 68 Wash. L.Rev. 801 (1993).

5. While states for a long time generally applied the principle that the reserved mineral estate was dominant and the surface estate was servient, in more recent years a number of states, like the Congress, have moved to provide more protection for the surface owner. North Dakota itself, the scene of *Duncan Energy*, has enacted a statute that requires the mineral developer to pay the surface owner for all value lost as a result of the mineral development, N.D.Cent.Code § 38–11.1–01. Its constitutionality was upheld in Murphy v. Amoco Prod. Co., 729 F.2d 552 (8th Cir.1984). Other states (led, somewhat surprisingly, by wild and woolly Texas, Getty Oil v. Jones, 470 S.W.2d 618 (1971)) have judicially developed an "accommodation doctrine." As described by Andrew Mergen, it "requires the mineral owner to act with prudence and to have due regard for the interests of the surface owner in exercising its right to use the surface to explore for and extract minerals." Mergen, Surface Tension: The Problem of Federal/Private Split Estate Lands, 33 Land & Water L.Rev. 419, 433 (1998); see, e.g., Flying Diamond Corp. v. Rust, 551 P.2d 509, 511 (Utah 1976) ("wherever there exists separate ownerships of interest in the same land, each should have the right to the use and enjoyment of his interest in the property to the highest degree possible, not inconsistent with the rights of others"). In states following this idea, the conflict with the federal interest in protecting the surface may be narrowed or disappear entirely.

AGENCY SPLIT ESTATE REGULATIONS AND APPLICATION

1. *National Forest System*. Somewhat curiously, the Forest Service has bifurcated its regulatory approach to privately reserved mineral interests. One set of regulations applies to "reserved" mineral rights, which are defined as those reserved by the seller in the conveyance of the surface to the United States. 36 C.F.R. § 251.15 (2000). The Forest Service regulates "outstanding" mineral rights, which were severed from the surface *before* the United States acquired the property, under its generic "special use"

regulations. 36 C.F.R. § 251.110. The mineral rights involved in *Duncan Energy* were "outstanding," having been severed before the U.S. acquired the property. The court rejected plaintiff's argument that the Forest Service's lack of specific regulations for the exercise of such rights means state law ought to apply. See 50 F.3d at 590.

The Forest Service regulations applicable to "reserved" mineral interests require, among other things (and with some exceptions): (a) prior written notice to the agency, including submission of "satisfactory evidence of authority to exercise such rights;" (b) limitation of surface occupancy and disturbance to that "necessary in bona fide [mineral activities]"; (c) obtaining a permit, posting a bond, repairing or replacing any improvements damaged or destroyed, and "restor[ing] the land to a condition safe and reasonably serviceable for authorized programs of the Forest Service;" and (d) making "reasonable provisions * * * for the disposal of * * * deleterious materials * * * in such manner as to prevent obstruction, pollution, or deterioration of water resources."

2. *National Park System.* As noted earlier, the Park Service has comprehensive regulations that govern mining in the parks, to implement the Mining in the Parks Act of 1976, 16 U.S.C. §§ 1901–12, but the statute and the regulations apply only to patented and unpatented federal mining claims. A number of individual park enabling acts contain specific provisions relating to the regulation of private mineral rights. See Mergen, supra, 33 Land & Water L.Rev. 429, 442. In 1978, the Park Service adopted regulations that govern the development of nonfederal oil and gas rights throughout the national park system. 36 C.F.R. § 9(B) (2000). These take the same basic approach as the Forest Service regulations, requiring advance approval of a plan of operations and a bond, but are far more detailed. Many oil and gas operations in park units are grandfathered or otherwise largely exempt from these regulations, however. See Mergen, supra, at p. 466. For minerals other than oil and gas, the Park Service attempts to use special use permits or other means to protect the parks. *Id.* at 453.

In Dunn McCampbell Royalty Interest, Inc. v. National Park Service, 964 F.Supp. 1125 (S.D.Tex.1995), aff'd 112 F.3d 1283 (5th Cir.1997), the owner of a severed mineral estate within the Padre Island National Seashore challenged these regulations, claiming an "unfettered right" to "destroy," if necessary, the surface lands to develop the minerals. It argued for application of state law and claimed a taking of its property interest if the federal regulations were deemed applicable. The district court held the challenge to the regulations on their face was time-barred by the generic six year statute of limitations on civil actions against the United States. In the alternative it held the regulations a valid exercise of Park Service authority, and preempted any inconsistent state law. The takings claim was transferred to the court of claims. Over a dissent, the Fifth Circuit affirmed, without reaching the question of the validity of the regulations because the Park Service had not taken any action against plaintiff.

3. *National Wildlife Refuges.* The U.S. Fish & Service has brief and rather modest regulations on the exercise of reserved mineral rights on

refuge system lands, even though oil and gas operations are fairly common and refuge managers cite them as a frequent cause of adverse impact on refuge objectives. 50 C.F.R. § 29.32 (2002). See Mergen, supra, at 442.

4. *BLM-managed public lands.* BLM does not have regulations specifically addressing the exercise of reserved mineral rights on BLM lands. For a discussion of BLM's authority to regulate private reserved mineral interests on public lands, focusing on FLPMA's command to prevent "unnecessary or undue degradation," 43 U.S.C. § 1732(b), see Marla Mansfield, On the Cusp of Property Rights: Lessons From Public Land Law, 18 Ecology L.Q. 43 (1991).

CHAPTER 8

THE TIMBER RESOURCE

Federal policy toward wood production from federal lands is primarily implemented through the U.S. Forest Service's management of the national forest system. In the last three decades, that policy has undergone profound change. For the first seven decades of the national forests' existence, congressional directives were generally understood to mean that the Forest Service was to harvest timber on the national forests where, when and how it thought best. The principal governing law was the Organic Act of 1897, 16 U.S.C. §§ 475–482 (§ 476 repealed 1976), setting general guidelines for administering the forests; and later the Multiple–Use, Sustained–Yield Act of 1960, 16 U.S.C. §§ 528–531. Each was deemed a grant of unfettered authority, and the courts did not much intrude: Forest Service powers and discretion were routinely upheld in the few cases challenging them; e.g., Light v. United States and United States v. Grimaud , Chapter 2, supra pp. 107–11. Timber litigation mostly was a miscellany of timber theft convictions and private contract disputes until the rise of the modern environmental movement, beginning about 1970.

This historical autonomy was due in large part to the rich tradition nurtured in the Forest Service by Gifford Pinchot from the time he became the head of the Forestry Division in the Department of Agriculture in 1898. Though he originally had no trees to manage, Pinchot's brand of conservation and silviculture (the growing and tending of trees as a branch of forestry) effectively became official federal policy in 1905, when Congress transferred the forest reserves from the Interior to the Agriculture Department, and the U.S. Forest Service was formally created to manage them. Even today, Pinchot's name is commonly invoked within the Forest Service and in congressional hearings.

The Forest Service gained its share of detractors over the years, especially as annual harvests from the national forests shot up with the demands of World War II and the postwar construction boom. In the last decade, however, in one of the most sweeping changes in modern federal land law and policy, the annual timber cut has declined sharply as a result of several factors. They include: (a) limitations brought about by endangered species concerns; (b) the maturation of the Forest Service planning process under the National Forest Management Act of 1976; (c) a near-halt in the building of new roads on national forest lands in order to protect land in a roadless condition; (d) growing public opposition to clearcutting as a timber management tool; and (e) a migration of the core of the domestic timber industry from the public lands of the northwest to private tree farms in the southeast. This evolution is illustrated by statistics showing annual timber production from the national forests in selected years over the twentieth century: From Pinchot's day in the first decade of the twentieth century, the cut remained relatively consistent at about 1 billion board feet annually for a few decades, climbing to 2 billion board feet in 1940. During World War II, the harvest rose to about 4 billion board feet. In the postwar boom years, the cut shot up, reaching 12 billion board feet by the mid–1960s, where it remained until about 1990. Then, as a result of the forces just mentioned, the annual harvest steadily fell to about 3 billion board feet in 2002. Through all this, although the Forest Service concedes that its track record includes some serious professional and political misjudgments, most knowledgeable critics (from any direction) recognize that the agency's history and heritage have given it a professional tradition uncommonly respected among governmental institutions.

From the days of near-complete deference and autonomy, federal timber policy is now governed by some detailed legal standards, defined by legislation, further elaborated on by administrative rules, and enforced by the courts. A recent Chief of the Forest Service has noted that "[a]gency decisionmakers spend as much or more time with lawyers as with natural resource management personnel." Jack Ward Thomas, Stability and Predictability in Federal Forest Management: Some Thoughts from the Chief, 17 Pub.L. and Resources L. Rev. 9, 19 (1996). Elsewhere in this book some of the pertinent issues have been explored, including NEPA, the planning process, and limitations imposed in contracts, such as timber sales contracts (see Chapter 5, pp. 255–83 supra). This chapter looks at others in some detail. Section A of this chapter analyzes forest practices under the rubric of multiple use, sustained yield, a longstanding touchstone of federal forest management. Section B deals with modern national forest law stemming from stricter judicial review, focusing on the National Forest Management Act of 1976. Section C takes a brief look at the legal standards applicable to management of the timber-rich public lands managed by the BLM, the so-called O & C lands in Oregon.

For the history of the Forest Service and its practices, see Harold Steen, THE UNITED STATES FOREST SERVICE: A HISTORY (1976); Glen O. Robinson, THE FOREST SERVICE (1975); Samuel Trask Dana & Sally Fairfax, FOREST AND RANGE POLICY (2d ed. 1980); James L. Huffman, A History of Forest Policy in the United States, 8 Envt'l L. 239 (1978); Charles Wilkinson, The National Forest Management Act: The Twenty Years Behind, the Twenty Years Ahead, 68 Colo. L. Rev. 659 (1997); Kathie Durbin, TREE HUGGERS: VICTORY, DEFEAT, AND RENEWAL IN THE NORTHWEST ANCIENT FOREST CAMPAIGN (1996); Richard W. Behan, PLUNDERED PROMISE: CAPITALISM, POLITICS, AND THE PUBLIC LANDS (2001); Paul W. Hirt, A CONSPIRACY OF OPTIMISM: MANAGEMENT OF THE NATIONAL FORESTS SINCE WORLD WAR II (1996). National forest issues in the eastern United States are treated in William E. Shands & Robert G. Healy, THE LANDS NOBODY WANTED (1977).

A. TRADITIONAL FOREST SERVICE MANAGEMENT

1. THE MULTIPLE-USE, SUSTAINED-YIELD ACT

Although the 1897 Forest Service Organic Act referred primarily to management for timber, water, and protection of the forests, 16 U.S.C. § 476,* the Forest Service in fact managed its lands to serve a broader number of uses from its inception. Grazing interests had been an important presence on national forest land from the beginning; see Light v. United States, supra p. 110. Visionaries like Aldo Leopold and Bob Marshall labored from within to expand recreational opportunities in national forests, and to promote the protection of wildlife. By the 1950's, the wilderness movement had begun to make its presence felt. At the same time, the traditional users—timber operators and reclamation interests—argued for greater protection for their particular needs. As these cross-currents swirled about the agency in the middle of the twentieth century, it decided to go to Congress for ratification, delicately arguing both that new legislation was desirable to clarify the agency's mission, and that it had possessed such broad authority all along. See, e.g., Samuel Trask Dana & Sally Fairfax, FOREST AND RANGE POLICY 200–05 (2d ed. 1980).

The result was the Multiple–Use, Sustained–Yield Act of 1960 (MUSY Act), 16 U.S.C. § 528–31, the key provision of which listed five uses alphabetically. In a classic case of political optics elevating form over substance, the Forest Service's draft of the statute (accepted by Congress) took pains to show its sensitivity to recreation by modifying the word with the adjective "outdoor," in order to allow it to be listed first:

> It is the policy of the Congress that the national forests are established and shall be administered for outdoor recreation, range, timber, watershed, and wildlife and fish purposes. The purposes of this Act are declared to be supplemental to, but not in derogation of, the purposes for which the national forests were established as set forth in the Act of June 4, 1897. * * * [16 U.S.C. § 528]

> The Secretary of Agriculture is authorized and directed to develop and administer the renewable surface resources of the national forests for multiple use and sustained yield of the several products and services obtained therefrom. In the administration of the national forests due consideration shall be given to the relative values of the various resources in particular areas. * * * [16 U.S.C. § 529]

> As used in this Act, the following terms shall have the following meanings:

> (a) "Multiple use" means: The management of all the various renewable surface resources of the national forests so that they are utilized in the combination that will best meet the needs of the American people; making the most judicious use of the land for some or all these

---

* Cf. United States v. New Mexico, 438 U.S. 696 (1978), Chapter 6, supra p. 521.

resources or related services over areas large enough to provide sufficient latitude for periodic adjustments in use to conform to changing needs and conditions; that some land will be used for less than all of the resources; and harmonious and coordinated management of the various resources, each with the other, without impairment of the productivity of the land, with consideration being given to the relative values of the various resources, and not necessarily the combination of uses that will give the greatest dollar return or the greatest unit output.

(b) "Sustained yield of the several products and services" means the achievement and maintenance in perpetuity of a high-level annual or regular periodic output of the various renewable resources of the national forests without impairment of the productivity of the land. [16 U.S.C. § 531]

The BLM formally received its multiple use mandate in the Federal Land Policy and Management Act in 1976. FLPMA's definitions of these two concepts generally track those quoted above, although there are some interesting differences in the definition of "multiple use." See 43 U.S.C. § 1702(c), (h). FLPMA lists not five but an open-ended number of uses; i.e., "including, but not limited to, recreation, range, timber, minerals[*], watershed, wildlife and fish, and natural scenic, scientific and historical values * * *." It also speaks of meeting "the present *and future* needs of the American people," and of coordinating management of the various resources "without *permanent* impairment of the productivity of the land *and the quality of the environment* * * *." (differences from the MUSY Act italicized).

QUESTIONS

1. How much management discretion do these definitions leave to the managing agencies? Do they provide enough "law to apply" for the courts to engage in meaningful review of agency decisions implementing them?

2. Does the definition of "multiple use" *require* the agency to make a cost/benefit analysis in determining which uses will be allowed on specific acres? Does it *allow* the agency to use such an analysis in its discretion?

3. Might nearly every kind of resource management serve more than one use? For example, wildlife protection might also serve the needs of recreation; clearcutting of timber might improve habitat for certain kinds of wildlife; livestock grazing might accelerate water runoff; roads built for logging might promote motorized recreation, or be used for cross-country skiing in the winter, etc. Does that make meaningful judicial review for multiple use decisions more difficult?

---

* Minerals were included in the BLM definition, but not the Forest Service's, because under the terms of the 1905 Act transferring the Forest Service to the Department of Agriculture, 16 U.S.C. § 472, the BLM oversees the development of minerals on the national forests. As illustrated by various materials in Chapter 6, however, the Forest Service regulates mining activities in order to protect the other resources of the forests.

4. Look closely at the differences between the MUSY and FLPMA definitions of "multiple use." Does the listing of "natural scenic, scientific and historical values" as "multiple uses" in FLPMA suggest, by negative implication, that the U.S. Forest Service cannot manage for such uses under MUSY? Do the italicized additions in FLPMA, quoted above, call for a management standard for BLM lands meaningfully different from that applied on the national forest lands under MUSY? For example, does the statutory direction to the BLM to coordinate its management of the various resources without "permanent" impairment of the productivity of the lands mean that the Forest Service is supposed to manage its lands to prevent *any* impairment of the productivity of its lands, even a temporary impairment? Or are these questions presuming that these statutes should be read technically, when in fact they should be read as stating broad principles?

5. How does "sustained yield" differ from "multiple use"? Is the former primarily a scientific judgment, and the latter primarily a political one? If so, does that give the courts a greater or lesser basis to review sustained yield decisions?

Although "multiple use" and "sustained yield" have come to be thought of as the guiding principles for managing nearly a half a billion acres of land under the purview of the BLM and the Forest Service, they have tended to mean "all things to all people." See Charles Conklin, PLLRC Revisited: A Potpourri of Memories, 54 Denver L.J. 445, 448 (1977). "Multiple use" is difficult if not impossible to define concretely: The usual formulations are so abstract that they cannot be applied with predictability, rationality, or uniformity to actual land management problems. A widely used definition of the multiple use concept, that it is "a practice in which a given land area functions in two or more compatible ways," merely illustrates its abstractness. For example, what is a "given land area"? If the area considered is an entire forest, then multiple use may be achieved by dividing the forest into sections and allocating a different use to each section. This, however, restricts the area in which a given activity may occur, and is to that extent considered undesirable. If, on the other hand, the "land area" is a relatively small plot, mutually exclusive uses such as timber harvesting and recreation may not be able to occur simultaneously.

The Forest Service has treated this problem as if it is at least partially artificial because, no matter what use is made of the land, some other use will surely be compatible with it. Thus, clearcutting is deemed compatible with selected wildlife habitat enhancement (it increases forage for deer), and wildlife enhancement is compatible with recreation (although it does not necessarily follow that clearcutting is compatible with recreation).

Few judicial decisions have addressed agency implementation of these concepts. An early one came in connection with the largest single timber sale ever entered into by the Forest Service. In 1968, it sold 8.7 billion board feet of timber from the Tongass National Forest in southeast Alaska to U.S. Plywood–Champion Papers, Inc. The transaction encompassed more than 99% of the commercial forest lands (more than 4.5 million acres of the 16 million acre national forest), and called for harvest over a period of 50 years. It was challenged in court on several grounds, one of which was the MUSY Act. In Sierra Club v. Hardin, 325 F.Supp. 99, 122–24 (D.Alaska 1971), the court denied relief:

> Plaintiffs introduced substantial testimony as well as documentary evidence, much of it in the form of offers of proof, to show that the Tongass National Forest is being administered predominantly for timber production. While the material undoubtedly shows the overwhelming commitment of the Tongass National Forest to timber harvest objectives in preference to other multiple use values, Congress has given no indication as to the weight to be assigned each value and it must be assumed that the decision as to the proper mix of uses within any particular area is left to the sound discretion and expertise of the Forest Service. Accordingly, evidence was admitted only for the purpose of showing that the Forest Service failed to give ["due consideration" under 16 U.S.C. § 529] to any of the competing uses or that it took into consideration irrelevant matters which it should not have considered. The court must presume * * * that the Forest Service did give due consideration to the various values specified in the Multiple Use–Sustained Yield Act.

The district court's decision was vacated and remanded by the court of appeals. Sierra Club v. Butz, 3 Envtl. L. Rprtr. 20292 (9th Cir. 1973). The court explained:

> [A] report by A. Starker Leopold and Reginald H. Barrett to U.S. Plywood–Champion Papers, Inc., * * * [analyzed] the manner in which the sales contract should be carried out, with due consideration given to social values other than the economic yield of pulp or lumber. It was the view of this team of experts that "the basic precepts on which the original timber sale contract were based are not today acceptable." It recommended "that the company explore with the Forest Service the possibility of revising the cutting plan to provide more adequate protection for the wide spectrum of ecologic values that is characteristic of Southeastern Alaska." * * *

> The [lower] court, at 325 F.Supp. 123 n. 48, discussed what should be regarded as "due" consideration under the Act and concluded that what was intended was that the Forest Service should "apply their expertise to the problem after consideration of all relevant values." It concluded that "some" consideration was sufficient. (For the purposes of this order we accept this interpretation, with the caution that "due consideration" to us requires that the values in question be informedly and rationally taken into balance. The requirement can hardly be satisfied by a showing of knowledge of the consequences and a decision to ignore them.) * * *

> In our judgment the [Starker–Leopold] report tendered upon this motion may be found to bear upon the stated issues: Whether the Forest Service in truth had knowledge of the ecological consequences of

the contract and cutting plan to which it agreed; whether in reaching its decision it failed to consider the available material (the report appends a 10–page list of material cited in the report in existence at the time the contract was entered into); further, a relevant question may be whether consideration was given to alternatives (such as those recommended by the report), which, while giving prime consideration to timber values, would still afford protection to the other values to which due consideration must be given.

NOTES AND QUESTIONS

1. How can a concededly "overwhelming commitment" to timber production on the Tongass National Forest be consistent with "multiple use"? Could the Service legally decide to cut every tree in the Tongass National Forest? Could it also decree that no trees at all will be cut? As the district court observed, only a little more than one quarter of the Tongass National Forest contained commercial stands of timber. Even though the Forest Service sold practically all this timber in this sale, nearly three-quarters of the land area in the Tongass National Forest was arguably left for other uses. Is that relevant to the issue here? How useful is "due consideration" as a standard of judicial review?

2. Timber harvesting in the Tongass National Forest has been the source of continual judicial and congressional attention ever since 1973, under statutes more specific than MUSY, such as the Tongass Timber Reform Act, 16 U.S.C. § 539d. See, e.g., Hoonah Indian Assn. v. Morrison, 170 F.3d 1223 (9th Cir.1999); Friends of Southeast's Future v. Morrison, 153 F.3d 1059 (9th Cir.1998); Alaska Wilderness Recreation & Tourism Ass'n v. Morrison, 67 F.3d 723 (9th Cir.1995). See Steven A. Daugherty, The Unfulfilled Promise of an End to Timber Dominance on the Tongass: Forest Service Implementation of the Tongass Timber Reform Act, 24 Envtl. L. 1573 (1994).

3. More recent cases discussing MUSY include Perkins v. Bergland, 608 F.2d 803, 806 (9th Cir.1979), dealing with regulation of livestock grazing on federal lands, where the court described the "so-called standards" in the MUSY Act as "contain[ing] the most general clauses and phrases * * * [which] can hardly be considered concrete limits upon agency discretion. Rather it is language which 'breathe[s] discretion at every pore.'" (citation omitted); Wind River Multiple–Use Advocates v. Espy, 835 F.Supp. 1362, 1372 (D.Wyo.1993), aff'd 85 F.3d 6341 (table) (10th Cir. 1996); Big Hole Ranchers Assn. v. U.S. Forest Service, 686 F.Supp. 256, 264 (D.Mont.1988) (multiple use gives agency "wide discretion to weigh and decide the proper uses within any area"). See George Cameron Coggins, Of Succotash Syndromes and Vacuous Platitudes: The Meaning of "Multiple Use, Sustained Yield" for Public Land Management (Part I), 53 U.Colo.L.Rev. 229, 279–80 (1982); Michael Blumm, Public Choice Theory and the Public Lands: Why "Multiple Use" Failed, 18 Harv.Envtl.L.Rev. 405 (1994).

4. "Multiple use" has a powerful emotional and political content in federal land management as a shorthand for emphasizing the traditional

uses—mining, livestock grazing, and timber harvesting. As controlling law, however, it is far less significant today than before enactment of many modern statutes. NEPA and the Forest Service and BLM planning mandates together ushered in a new management era for these agencies, ending the near-plenary discretion they assumed and enjoyed in making MUSY decisions. While the modern statutes may be more procedural than substantive (and while the courts may give a higher level of scrutiny to agency process than agency outcomes), the fact remains that the "multiple use" federal lands are gradually being more or less formally zoned, with particular areas being managed for some dominant uses. Congress has directly played a role in this zoning process, by designating large tracts of Forest Service (and, increasingly, BLM) lands as Wilderness, Wild & Scenic Rivers, National Recreation Areas, National Conservation Areas, and the like. See generally Chapters 11–12, infra. There have also been numerous executive actions with similar effect, such as designations of national monuments, critical habitat, and areas of critical environmental concern, withdrawals, and zoning through the federal land planning process.

5.   Even on lands nominally still subject to "multiple use" management, laws like the National Forest Management Act, explored in the next section, provide much more specific guidance for taking account of differing resources and values. Furthermore, in recent years, partially in response to the need to comply with the Endangered Species Act, all of the federal land management agencies have begun to move toward something that has come to be known by many as "ecosystem management." Recall the cautionary comments on this idea in the excerpt from Michael Bean and Melanie Rowland's THE EVOLUTION OF NATIONAL WILDLIFE LAW, Chapter 1, supra p. 31. For the Forest Service and BLM, ecosystem management evidently is a variant of, or gloss upon, multiple use management. See Robert Keiter, Beyond the Boundary Line: Constructing a Law of Ecosystem Management, 65 U.Colo.L.Rev. 293 (1994). See also Oliver A. Houck, On the Law of Biodiversity and Ecosystem Management, 81 Minn.L.Rev. 869 (1997) (after studying the experience of the Forest Service and the BLM, among others, Professor Houck concludes that "however high we raise our sights towards managing the whole, the requirement of individual species will remain the bottom line, or we will have no bottom line, and the entire effort will fail"); Rebecca W. Thomson, Ecosystem Management: Great Idea, But What Is It, Will It Work and Who Will Pay for It, 19 Nat.Res. & Envt. No. 3 at 42 (1995).

6.   All this raises the question whether multiple-use/sustained yield—in its classic formulation as allowing consideration of a wide variety of uses, without any one having priority—has any meaning anymore, or any future. See, e.g., Wilkinson, The End of Multiple Use, High Country News, Mar. 30, 1987, at 15. In the spring of 1992 the Congressional Research Service convened a conference of experts to explore whether Congress ought to move away from MUSY as the abiding principle of national forest and public land management. See Multiple Use and Sustained Yield: Changing Philosophies for Federal Land Management? House Committee on Interior and Insular Affairs Print No. 11, 102d Cong. 2d Sess. (1992). Among the questions raised were: How is sustainability to be defined? What is to be

sustained, and how is it to be demonstrated and evaluated by land managers? How great a commitment should be made to commodity users who depend on federal resources, and how can these local needs be balanced with broader national interests? What pricing system for resource uses and outputs is fair and of greatest national benefit? Is legislative reform needed? Not surprisingly, no consensus emerged on the answers.

NOTE: THE RESOURCES PLANNING ACT OF 1974

With a few exceptions, Congress has generally refused, here and in most other areas of public natural resource law, to create "revolving funds" whereby financial receipts from federal resource programs are returned directly to the federal land management agency for its use. See, e.g., ONE THIRD OF THE NATION'S LAND 286–87 (1970); see also Chapter 4, pp. 380–81 supra. Instead, the federal land management agencies, like most other federal agencies, receive their operating funds through the annual congressional appropriations process. The Forest Service has long regarded itself as disadvantaged by the ups-and-downs of that annual exercise. In the Forest and Rangeland Renewable Resources Planning Act of 1974 (RPA), as amended, 16 U.S.C. §§ 1601–1613, Congress embarked on what proved to be a hopelessly idealistic effort to bring more rationality to the process. It acknowledged that forest lands are capital assets and that the agency requires reliable estimates of future funding to plan for timber management practices such as reforestation.

The RPA directs the Forest Service periodically to prepare three planning documents: (1) an Assessment describing the renewable resources of all the nation's forest and range lands (every ten years); (2) a Program, with a planning horizon of at least forty-five years, proposing long-range objectives and setting out the specific costs for all Forest Service activities (every five years); and (3) an Annual Report evaluating Forest Service activities in comparison with the objectives proposed in the Program. In addition, the RPA requires the President to submit two documents to Congress: (1) a Statement of Policy, which is based upon the Program and which can be modified by Congress, to be used in framing future budget requests for Forest Service activities (every five years); and (2) a Statement of Reasons, an explanation accompanying any annual proposed budget which does not request funds necessary to achieve the objectives of the Statement of Policy.

This was the triumph of the rationality of planning over political imperatives. Despite high expectations, the RPA has not fundamentally altered the Forest Service budget or budgetary politics in the White House or Congress. Budget proposals and appropriations almost immediately dropped below the amounts recommended in the 1975 Program and the resulting 1976 Statement of Policy. When President Carter's proposed 1979 budget fell well short of the funding envisioned by the Statement of Policy (intended to guide future budget requests), the National Wildlife Federation sued, taking the position that the President's Statement of Reasons did not explain the shortfall to the extent required by the RPA. In particular, the Federation objected to low budget levels for programs such as recreation and reforestation. The Court of Appeals held that the action was properly dismissed:

> Sometimes the great public importance of an issue militates in favor of its prompt resolution. * * * At other times, however, the public interest dictates that courts exercise restraint in passing upon crucial issues. We think such restraint is necessary where, as here, appellants ask us to intervene in wrangling over the federal budget and budget procedures. Such matters are the archetype of those best resolved through bargaining and accommodation between the legislative and executive branches. We are reluctant to afford discretionary relief when to do so would intrude on the responsibilities—including the shared responsibilities—of the coordinate branches.

National Wildlife Federation v. United States, 626 F.2d 917 (D.C.Cir.1980). (The opinion includes a useful description of the RPA's provisions.) Other courts have since held that RPA goals are not binding on national forest planners. See Wind River Multiple Use Advocates v. Espy, 835 F.Supp. 1362 (D.Wyo.1993), aff'd 85 F.3d 641 (table) (10th Cir.1996) (upholding a forest plan setting 12 million board feet as the timber harvesting objective instead of the RPA-derived goal of 46 million board feet, finding that, in accordance with Forest Service regulations, the incorporation of the RPA objectives in the forest plan is "anything but mandatory"). The Forest Service continues to issue periodic Assessments under the RPA, but it has stopped producing a Program, as congressional appropriations riders have blocked work on it. Instead, the Forest Service has produced a Strategic Plan pursuant to the Government Performance and Results Act (GPRA), 5 U.S.C. § 306.

Although Congress and the Executive have never met the financial targets the Forest Service defined in its five-year Programs, it is possible, but difficult to demonstrate, that the Act's national planning process may have caused the Forest Service to improve its long-range planning. Overall, though, the RPA may be best understood as the last gasp of the era of unfettered Forest Service discretion. The following material shows that, even before the RPA was enacted, events were moving quickly toward greater congressional and judicial involvement in the management of the national forests.

2.   ENACTMENT OF THE NATIONAL FOREST MANAGEMENT ACT

Federal timber policy, and the perception of the Forest Service by Congress, the courts, and the public, were reshaped by a major controversy over the practice of "clearcutting" in the late 1960's and early 1970's. Clearcutting means the complete removal of timber from an area, somewhat like shaving the land. It is an economically efficient method of providing a large flow of timber from the national forests. Some claim it is an indispensable option if high harvest levels are to be maintained.

After World War II, increased demand for timber brought more intensive management to the national forest system. Clearcutting was accelerated in forests where it was already an existing practice. In some forests it was employed for the first time. Heavy management expenditures associated with accelerated timber management, especially in areas where tree densities and growth rates were limited, meant that the Forest Service's costs of administering its management and sales program and associated roadbuilding exceeded timber sale revenues in some areas. Furthermore, local resentment grew, especially in areas near the Bitterroot National Forest in Montana and the Monongahela National Forest in West Virginia. Lengthy hearings before a subcommittee of the U.S. Senate in the spring of 1972 culminated in a report setting out broad rules for timber harvesting in general and clearcutting in particular. These "Church guidelines," named after subcommittee chairman Sen. Frank Church of Idaho, were not legally binding,* and did not dissuade environmental interests from challenging the practice in court.

The setting for this carefully targeted test case was the acquired national forest lands in the east, where many argued clearcutting was especially inappropriate in mixed hardwood stands, where they tended to be replaced with pines, reducing the overall diversity of species. In West Virginia Div. of Izaak Walton League of America, Inc. v. Butz, 522 F.2d 945 (4th Cir.1975) (sometimes known as the *Monongahela* case, after the national forest where it was brought), the court held that the practice of clearcutting violated the Forest Service's Organic Act of 1897. That statute, written when the technology and practice of logging were far different, allowed only "dead, matured, or large growth of trees" on the national forests to be sold, and before being sold, required that they be "marked and designated." 16 U.S.C. § 476. Clearcutting by definition harvests every tree of any size or degree of maturity, and while trees may be "designated" for harvest, they are not typically "marked." Citing, among other things, the Trans–Alaska Pipeline case (Wilderness Society v. Morton, Chapter 4, supra p. 311), the court read the statute literally, and held that by including it in the 1897 Act, Congress had essentially forbade the practice of clearcutting. While it based its decision "primarily upon a literal reading of the statute," the court found "convincing support" in the background and legislative history of the 1897 Act:

> This legislative history demonstrates that the primary concern of Congress in passing the Organic Act was the preservation of the national forests. While the Act as finally passed rejected the position of the extremists who wished to forbid all cutting in the forests, it specifically limited the authority of the Secretary in his selection of timber which could be sold. He could select the timber to be cut only from those trees which were dead, physiologically mature or large, and then only when such cutting would preserve the young and growing timber which remained. Following the addition of "large growth of trees" to the bill, the sponsors repeatedly made it clear that the Act would permit the sale only of the individual trees which met its specific

---

* The Church guidelines were, however, ultimately incorporated, with some modifications, into the NFMA of 1976, 16 U.S.C. §§ 1604(g)(3)(E), (F), discussed further below.

requirements which, in the words of Senator Pettigrew, were "the large trees, the dying trees and trees that will grow no better in time * * *."

The court also rejected the argument that Congress had ratified the practice of clearcutting in subsequent legislation. It noted that the MUSY Act adopted in 1960 had specifically provided that its "purposes * * * are declared to be supplemental to, but not in derogation of, the purposes for which the national forests were established as set forth in the Act of June 4, 1897." 16 U.S.C. § 528. It concluded that the MUSY Act "did not constitute a ratification of the relatively new policy of the Forest Service which applied the principles of even-aged management and clearcutting in all of the national forests." It concluded with a passage reminiscent of Judge Skelly Wright's conclusion in the Trans–Alaska Pipeline case:

> It is apparent that the heart of this controversy is the change in the role of the Forest Service which has taken place over the past thirty years. For nearly half a century following its creation in 1905, the National Forest System provided only a fraction of the national timber supply with almost ninety-five per cent coming from privately owned forests. During this period the Forest Service regarded itself as a custodian and protector of the forests rather than a prime producer, and consistent with this role the Service faithfully carried out the provisions of the Organic Act with respect to selective timber cutting. In 1940, however, with private timber reserves badly depleted, World War II created an enormous demand for lumber and this was followed by the post-war building boom. As a result the posture of the Forest Service quickly changed from custodian to a production agency. It was in this new role that the Service initiated the policy of even-aged management in the national forests, first in the West and ultimately in the Eastern forests, including the Monongahela. The appellants urge that this change of policy was in the public interest and that the courts should not permit a literal reading of the 1897 Act to frustrate the modern science of silviculture and forest management presently practiced by the Forest Service to meet the nation's current timber demands. Economic exigencies, however, do not grant the courts a license to rewrite a statute no matter how desirable the purpose or result might be. * * *

> We are not insensitive to the fact that our reading of the Organic Act will have serious and far-reaching consequences, and it may well be that this legislation enacted over seventy-five years ago is an anachronism which no longer serves the public interest. However, the appropriate forum to resolve this complex and controversial issue is not the courts but the Congress. * * *

Almost immediately a district judge in Alaska followed the Fourth Circuit decision. Zieske v. Butz, 406 F.Supp. 258 (D.Alaska 1975) (enjoining clearcutting by Ketchikan Pulp Company under a Forest Service contract), and several other cases sought to apply it to other forests. Seeing the handwriting on the wall, the Forest Service and the forest products industry turned to Congress for a repeal of the offending provision in the

1897 Organic Act. Environmentalists used the clearcutting issue as a lever to open a broad-ranging congressional debate on all forest management practices. Legislation introduced by Senator Jennings Randolph of West Virginia, chair of one of the key committees of jurisdiction, would have severely restricted Forest Service timber operations, while other bills supported by industry would have done little more than remove the strictures of the 1897 Act. The legislation that finally emerged from Congress 14 months after the Fourth Circuit decision was, like all major legislation, a compromise, but it was one so comprehensive as to amount to a new organic act for the Forest Service.

The National Forest Management Act of 1976 repealed the 1897 provisions at issue in the Fourth Circuit, and is laced with qualifying language, but it addressed on-the-ground forestry issues with a specificity unthinkable in earlier times. Before we turn to the details of that statute, it is useful to set out some general background on the place of the national forests in American forest policy.

TIMBER AREA AND VOLUME STATISTICS BY OWNERSHIP CLASSES
In billion cubic feet

Ownership classes	Commercial area held million acres	Total softwood growing stock volume			Total hardwood growing stock volume		
		Inventory (volume)	Growth	Removals	Inventory (volume)	Growth	Removals
National Forests	96	222	3.4	0.6	27	0.7	0.2
Other Public	49	51	1.4	0.6	37	1.0	0.4
Forest Industry	67	66	3.4	3.7	36	1.0	1.1
Other Private	291	144	5.4	5.2	252	7.6	4.3
National Total	503	484	13.4	10.1	352	10.2	6.0

Source: Department of Agriculture, Forest Service, W. Brad Smith, John S. Vissage, David R. Darr, and Raymond M. Sheffield, "Forest Resources of the United States, 1997," Tables 11, 18, 23, 34, and 25 (2001).

Commercial forest land traditionally has been defined as land capable of producing at least 20 cubic feet of timber per acre per year. The "other public" lands category in the table includes state, county, and municipal lands, and about eight million acres of BLM lands.*

1. *Timber Inventory and Timber Types.* As the left column on the table shows, national forests account for about 19% of the Nation's commercial timber land, but that figure is misleading because it does not measure the amount of inventory, or volume of wood, on those acres. Although the inventory of hardwood timber on national forest lands is not a significant part of the nation's total standing hardwood timber, the Forest Service presides over almost half of the Nation's inventory of softwood timber. Softwood timber, which is in greater demand than hardwood, is the primary source of construction lumber and is thus essential to the housing industry.

* Most of the issues raised here in regard to the Forest Service apply also to the smaller BLM holdings, the most important of which are dealt with briefly in a note at the end of this Chapter, infra p. 773.

2. *Old Growth Forests.* As the two columns on the left show, the forest industry owns 66 billion cubic feet of softwood timber on 67 million acres, or about 1000 cubic feet per acre. But, on national forest lands, the softwood inventory per acre is well over twice that found on private industry lands: the inventory of 222 billion cubic feet of timber on 96 million acres averages out to 2,312 cubic feet per acre. The disparity is even greater for "other private" lands (miscellaneous private holdings of 20 acres or more), which hold an average of only 500 cubic feet per acre.

These disparities exist largely because most private lands have been cut over and no large old-growth trees remain. Some private lands have been harvested by "cut and run" or "highgrading" practices, in which the best timber was cleared and no reforesting undertaken. In contrast, many of the federal lands have never been cut at all, leaving massive stands of old-growth timber intact. These valuable stands, especially in the national forests of the Pacific Northwest, include magnificent virgin fir, redwood, cedar, and pine forests. These trees are straight, large, and provide the highest quality lumber. Harvesting them is said by some to be the solution for meeting the Nation's growing demand for timber. Others argue that such stands are unique ecological resources that cannot be replaced for generations, if ever, and should be preserved.

3. *Intensive Management.* The second and third columns from the left on the table show that the annual growth rate for softwood industry lands is about 5.1% (amounting to 3.4 billion cubic feet from an inventory of 66 billion cubic feet) while the growth rate for national forest lands is about 1.5% (3.4 billion cubic feet on an inventory of 222 billion cubic feet). Industry lands produce more growth because more intensive management practices are employed. High yield management is based on growing "thrifty, young trees," starting with the prompt planting of seedlings, sometimes genetically improved. Years later, precommercial and commercial thinning removes some trees to provide more light and soil to those remaining; fertilizers and other enhancement methods are also commonly employed. A short "rotation" period (the time over which an area of forest is harvested) is used so that the intensive management cycle can be repeated. (When Weyerhauser Company called itself—correctly—"The Tree Growing Company," a Sierra Club representative replied—correctly—"Yes. They grow small trees.")

The federal old-growth forests have low growth rates because they have attained an age when annual growth tapers off. Indeed, some old growth forests actually have a negative growth rate: the slow growth of the live trees does not equal the annual mortality rate of wood fiber through rot and disease. Environmental aesthetics and silviculture collide over whether and at what rate these ancient stands should be liquidated:

> * * * [T]he legal profession has a similar kind of responsibility in its own canons of ethics as the members of the medical and forestry professions have with respect to the public health. This responsibility includes ensuring not only that laws are not permitted that allow

forests to be wasted, but that the forests be adequately protected so that man may always enjoy all their qualities. One must question the views of many lawyers who believe that more old growth forests should be put into withdrawals or reserves by laws attempting to preserve them forever in their untouched state. Such a goal is patently ridiculous and indicates that law schools need to teach prospective members of the legal profession a few facts of life about the ecology of plants. All trees have a date certain with death, just like every person. Trees were placed here by higher laws than man's for serving the human race, and they must continue to do so through protection, management and renewal, the principal purposes of the forestry profession.

When there are homeless people in the world, there is no more of a right to waste wood than there is a right to waste food when there are hungry people. Whether people like it or not, the old forest must make way for the new.

Perry Hagenstein, The Old Forest Maketh Way for the New, 8 Envt'l L. 479, 494–95 (1978). For an argument that old growth is necessary for the stability of forest ecosystems as a whole, see Glenn Patrick Juday, Old Growth Forests: A Necessary Element of Multiple Use and Sustained Yield National Forest Management, 8 Envt'l L. 497 (1978).

4. *Rate of Removal.* Although old-growth removal is itself a subject of controversy, some critics in the timber industry believe that Forest Service harvesting schedules are too conservative on all lands. The rate at which the softwood inventory is removed annually can be obtained by dividing the fourth column on the table by the second column. The rate of removal on Forest Service lands (just one-fifth of one percent) is much less than that on industry lands (5.2%) for a variety of reasons. (Even before the recent drop in the national forest timber cut, the industry's rate of removal was many times higher than the Forest Service's.) One factor is the Forest Service's use of a long rotation period; for example, the rotation period for Douglas fir is 100 years in many national forests compared with periods of 60, 50 or even 40 years on intensively managed private Douglas fir forests. In addition, Forest Service long-range projections sometimes build in conservative assumptions; for example, computer analyses may assume less than maximum returns from practices such as thinning and genetic improvement. Since the present harvest cannot exceed future growth potential, these conservative projections tend to keep annual removal lower than it otherwise might have been.

The use of economics as a means of making policy decisions is increasingly relied upon in modern forestry. The Forest Service uses computer modeling in making a number of management decisions. Economists disagree, however, on the proper application of economic theory to public timberlands. Compare John V. Krutilla & John A. Haigh, An Integrated Approach to National Forest Management, 8 Envt'l L. 373 (1978) with Richard Stroup & John Baden, NATURAL RESOURCES: BUREAUCRATIC MYTHS AND ENVIRONMENTAL MANAGEMENT (1983).; Randal

O'Toole, REFORMING THE FOREST SERVICE (1988); Thomas Michael Power, LOST LANDSCAPES AND FAILED ECONOMICS (1996).

5. *"Other Private" Forests.* The table also indicates that almost 60% of commercial forest land is located in non-industry private holdings. Most studies conclude that improving management practices on those lands is one way to help meet market demands and lessen the pressure on federal lands in the future. Coordinating silvicultural practices on these small, widely-dispersed holdings is, however, no easy matter. See William E. Towell, Managing Private Nonindustrial Forestlands: A Perennial Issue, 26 J. of Forest Hist. 192 (1982).

6. *Timber–Dependent Communities.* About one-fifth of federal commercial timberlands are located in the Great Lakes Area, New England, and the South. In those areas, as well as in many regions in the west, the economies of numerous small communities are partially or heavily dependent on jobs created by timber harvesting on federal lands. Accelerated cutting of old growth can result in a drastic decline in harvest when the last old growth is cut, severely harming local economies, because timber harvesting must cease or decrease when the large stands are gone. This has led to the Forest Service's policy of non-declining even flow, a conservative version of sustained yield management that requires a relatively level annual cut to avoid the "boom and bust" cycle that would occur if old-growth timber is harvested on an accelerated basis. See Con H. Schallau & Richard M. Alston, The Commitment to Community Stability: Policy or Shibboleth?, 17 Envt'l L. 429 (1987).

7. *Wilderness and Endangered Species.* The question of how much timber supply to put out of reach by putting land off limits to timber harvesting in order to serve other values is, of course, subject to continuing and often acrimonious debate. Endangered species issues were covered in Chapter 5, pp. 434–508; wilderness issues are addressed in Chapter 12, pp. pp. 1104–62 infra.

8. *Timber Management Practices.* How to harvest is as divisive an issue as whether to harvest. Modern forestry tries to see that streams are protected from fallen timber; that yarding (physically removing the cut timber from the logging site) is carried on with minimum erosion or damage to the remaining stand; that slash (residue such as limbs and stumps) is properly disposed of; and that restocking occurs promptly and efficiently. Many argue that such practices do not go far enough; clearcutting in particular continues to stir their ire. Another delicate issue is road building, which can cause as much or more erosion damage as timber harvesting. See generally W. Hugh O'Riordan & Scott W. Horngran, The Minimum Management Requirements of Forest Planning, 17 Envt'l L. 643 (1987).

9. *Miscellaneous Issues.* Other policy questions, which will be treated only tangentially here, include log exports to foreign countries, the application of economic theory, and bidding practices. An excellent work for the uninitiated is Marion Clawson, FORESTS: FOR WHOM AND FOR WHAT? (1975).

B. MODERN NATIONAL FOREST MANAGEMENT

Charles F. Wilkinson & H. Michael Anderson, Land and Resource Planning in the National Forests*

64 Or.L.Rev. 1, 10–12, 69–70, 74 (1985).

* * * By 1976 the mood of Congress had shifted dramatically in the wake of the clearcutting controversy. Upon introducing his bill, [Minnesota Senator Hubert] Humphrey observed that the MUSY Act had not succeeded and that a "fundamental reform" was needed. Humphrey stated: "We have had 15 years since the 1960 Multiple Use and Sustained Yield Act was passed. Much has happened, and as we look at what has transpired, the need for improvement is evident." He identified the central problem as the predominance of timber production over protection of other resources. Humphrey declared: "The days have ended when the forest may be viewed only as trees and trees viewed only as timber. The soil and the water, the grasses and the shrubs, the fish and the wildlife, and the beauty that is the forest must become integral parts of resource managers' thinking and actions." During the Senate hearings Humphrey observed that the Forest Service's record had brought into question the extent to which the agency could be trusted to guard and manage public resources. He proposed that the NFMA legislation be shaped to prevent the Forest Service from "turning the national forests into tree production programs which override other values." Senator Randolph and other members of Congress shared Humphrey's views. * * *

The NFMA will require courts to scrutinize forest plans, and activities based on those plans, on both procedural and substantive grounds. The 1976 Act contains several substantive guidelines that are markedly more specific than the broad multiple-use language [of the MUSY Act], although less absolute than the Organic Act provision in *Monongahela*. In addition, the NFMA requires forest plans to be developed in accordance with NEPA's procedural requirements. The Forest Service has correctly stated the controlling law in advising its planners that reviewing courts are likely to conduct a "searching inquiry" into the procedural adequacy of forest plans and to require "full, fair, and bona fide compliance" with the NFMA. Once the plans become final and are determined to be valid, they themselves become law. Much like zoning requirements or administrative regulations, the plans are controlling and judicially enforceable until properly revised.

TIMBER PLANNING UNDER THE NATIONAL FOREST MANAGEMENT ACT*

In broad and somewhat oversimplified terms, timber harvests for a national forest are calculated in this manner. First, planners determine

---

* Reprinted with permission of the Oregon Law Review.

* An overview of planning on the national forests, as well as on other federal lands, was set out in Chapter 5, supra pp. 427–34.

what land is suitable for timber management. They must exclude, for example: (a) land allocated to other uses (such as wilderness); (b) noncommercial timberland (traditionally defined as land growing less than twenty cubic feet of wood per acre annually) and (c) land not suitable for harvesting due to inaccessibility or to fragile slope or soil conditions. The land left available for harvest after such exclusions is the suitable land base, or inventory.

Second, the Forest Service must calculate the amount of timber that may be harvested from the inventory. This is the "allowable cut," usually expressed as an annual volume harvesting target. The two primary factors used to calculate the allowable cut are (a) the volume of timber available in the inventory, and (b) the rotation period, i.e., the time over which a stand will be harvested before a second harvesting schedule can begin. If, for example, estimated volume is 500 million board feet (mmbf) and a conservative rotation period of 100 years is used, the annual allowable cut will be 5 mmbf. The volume and rotation period calculations both depend in part upon the estimated rate of growth in the future. If optimistic projections for stand management (e.g., thinning, fertilization, reforestation, and use of genetically superior stocks) are used, the volume will be higher, and so will be the resulting harvest level. Thus, if substantial stand improvement measures are assumed, this might lead to a timber volume estimate of 750 mmbf, which means that the annual cut can be set at 7.5 mmbf, still using the same rotation period of 100 years. In the same way, if a broader definition of suitability is used, more timber may be included in the inventory, which will make the volume higher, and the annual allowable cut higher. Shortening the rotation period has the same effect; i.e., the allowable cut increases.

After the allowable cut is set, planners must determine harvesting methods (clearcutting or selective cutting; timber removal by tractor, cable, balloon, or helicopter) and the process for regenerating the stand.

It should not be surprising that the calculation of the allowable cut is an issue often contested in the planning process. The allowable cut has historically tended to be a central premise for managing national forests, and the central organizing principle for many Forest Service field offices. Acre for acre, commercial timber is the most valuable commodity resource in the National Forest System. Even as emphasis on the wildlife, recreation, and preservation resources was growing, the operative slogan of many forest rangers was still GOTAC ("get out the allowable cut"). This attitude has been changing considerably, from within and without the agency, as the materials that follow reflect.

Very few lawsuits have involved direct challenges to allowable cut determinations. These matters are inordinately complex due to the quantity of data, the imprecision of projections of future timber growth, the necessity for numerous professional judgments on economic and silvicultural issues, and the intricacies of computer programs. Lawyers must develop legal arguments and marshall the evidence, but the work of foresters and economists is more likely to determine the outcome of litigation. NFMA planning does not displace NEPA; the NFMA requires forest plans to be prepared "in accordance with" NEPA, 16 U.S.C. § 1604(g)(1); and Forest Service regulations provide that, "[t]o the extent feasible, a single process shall be used to meet planning and NEPA requirements." 36 C.F.R. § 219.12(a) (1991).

What follows is a brief examination of the NFMA provisions relating to these three central elements of timber planning: determining the suitable land base, or inventory; calculating the allowable cut; and deciding upon the appropriate methods for harvesting and regenerating the timber. In examining the sometimes remarkable specificity in the statute, a central question is whether—underneath this bristling detail—genuine standards exist to control the Forest Service's discretion, and to provide a basis for meaningful judicial review. For example, a number of the seemingly "bright-line" rules in the statute have exceptions, and the exceptions might operate in practice to swallow the rules. The discussion below raises a number of interpretive questions about the meaning of these provisions, and examines how the courts so far have dealt with them. For additional general analysis of the issues raised here, see generally Wilkinson & Anderson, supra.

The first step towards fully implementing NFMA was for the Forest Service to prepare detailed regulations. The statute created a Committee of Scientists to play a significant role in that process, and final regulations were promulgated in 1979. During much of the 1980s, the Forest Service was engaged in preparing the first generation of forest plans for most of the National Forest System. These plans involved extensive public participation, and many of them were subject to appeals on various issues by various interests up through the agency's administrative appeals system. A number of these plans were challenged in federal court, usually (but not always) by environmental protection advocates. These challenges typically alleged violations of the NFMA, NEPA, the Administrative Procedure Act and the Endangered Species Act.

The Supreme Court, in Ohio Forestry Ass'n v. Sierra Club, 523 U.S. 726 (1998), supra at Chapter 4, p. 294, put a stop to most but not all "pre-implementation" challenges to Forest Service land use plans by ruling them unripe for review. Some of the pre-*Ohio Forestry* cases discussed further below in this section might well have been dismissed on ripeness grounds if they had been brought later. Although their precedential value is thereby somewhat weakened, they still contain valuable indicia of judicial attitudes toward forest planning.

In the late 1990s, the Forest Service undertook a major overhaul of its planning process to give ecological sustainability a higher priority. See 65 Fed. Reg. 67514 (Nov. 9, 2000). The Bush Administration has delayed implementation of these rules pending further study. See 66 Fed. Reg. 27,552 (May 17, 2001). See generally Chapter 5, supra pp. 427–34.

1. PHYSICAL SUITABILITY

The NFMA gives special attention to the kinds of lands on which timber may be harvested, including especially impacts on watersheds. The "physical suitability" provision, 16 U.S.C. § 1604(g)(3)(E), requires that the regulations and the forest plans shall:

> insure that timber will be harvested from National Forest System lands only where—
>
> (i) soil, slope, or other watershed conditions will not be irreversibly damaged;
>
> (ii) there is assurance that such lands can be adequately restocked within five years after harvest; [and]
>
> (iii) protection is provided for streams, streambanks, shorelines, lakes, wetlands, and other bodies of water from detrimental changes in water temperatures, blockages of water courses, and deposits of sediment, where harvests are likely to seriously and adversely affect water conditions or fish habitat * * *

Land that does not meet these standards must be classified as unsuitable and excluded from the inventory. The provision extends to logging road construction, a major cause of erosion.

Does this provision provide a basis for searching judicial review? Is it significant that each criterion must be met separately? For example, what might "irreversible" damage [subsection i] be? Can subsection (iii) be read literally to prohibit all logging that results in "detrimental" sediment deposits in streams? What does "assurance" that the lands "can be adequately restocked within five years" mean? The Knutson–Vandenberg Act of 1930, 16 U.S.C. §§ 576a–c, authorizes the Forest Service to require deposits from timber operators to cover reforestation costs. That program has been less than entirely successful: For a long time there has been a backlog of millions of national forest acres that have not been restocked. Although the NFMA authorized an expenditure of $200 million per year to eliminate the backlog, in subsequent years Congress has not appropriated sufficient funds to do this. If Congress fails to make funds available for this purpose, could a court use this section to enjoin further timber sales until the backlog has been eliminated?

Matters of physical suitability (and many other forestry issues under the NFMA) almost always involve extensive factual records and silvicultural expertise, so that agency discretion is a formidable obstacle to parties challenging Forest Service decisions on judicial review. See generally Federico Cheever, Four Failed Forest Standards: What We Can Learn from the History of the National Forest Management Act's Substantive Timber Management Provisions, 77 Ore. L. Rev. 601 (1998). In Sierra Club v. Peterson, 185 F.3d 349 (5th Cir.1999), the circuit court affirmed a sweeping lower court injunction against a Forest Service logging program, finding, among other things, that the NFMA physical suitability provisions were substantive and that the agency-sponsored logging practices were causing substantial and permanent soil damage. Later, in en banc review, the court vacated the decision on the ground that no final agency action existed. Sierra Club v. Peterson, 228 F.3d 559 (5th Cir.2000). One procedural judicial check on physical suitability issues is to remand for further Forest Service analysis and explanation. See Citizens for Environmental Quality v.

United States, 731 F.Supp. 970 (D.Colo.1989). On the five-year restocking provision of § 1604(g)(3)(E)(ii), the decision in Big Hole Ranchers Ass'n v. U.S. Forest Service, 686 F.Supp. 256 (D.Mont.1988), gave the agency broad discretion, finding that the issue was not whether restocking "would" occur within five years but rather whether it "could" occur, while Ayers v. Espy, 873 F.Supp. 455 (D.Colo.1994), found that a Forest Service harvesting program violated the five-year restocking requirement.

2.   ECONOMIC SUITABILITY: THE "BELOW-COST TIMBER SALES" ISSUE

Considered as a whole, annual timber sale revenues from the national forest system usually exceed the costs of managing the system. Most of the profitable sales, however, take place in the humid, timber-rich Pacific Northwest. Sales in other regions, especially in the Rocky Mountains, are often below-cost—the government's costs of growing and selling trees exceed revenues from timber sales—due to a more arid climate and lower-quality commercial timber land. Roadbuilding is a large cost constituent. But roads can be used for nontimber purposes such as recreation and wildlife management as well. Many studies have found, however, that even when appropriate portions of road costs are allocated to nontimber benefits, many timber sales still fail to pay their way. See, e.g., General Accounting Office, Congress Needs Better Information on Forest Service's Below-Cost Timber Sales (GAO/RCD–84–96, 1984) (costs exceeded revenues in 27% of all sales in 1981 and in 42% of all sales in 1982). Fiscal conservatives, who dislike subsidies, and environmentalists, who oppose extending road systems into roadless areas where many of the proposed below-cost sales are proposed, join in objecting to the practice. Industry argues that below-cost sales are necessary to support local communities dependent on a continuing flow of timber from national forests. See James F. Morrison, The NFMA and Below–Cost Sales: Determining the Economic Suitability of Land for Timber Production, 17 Envt'l L. 591 (1987).

During the congressional hearings leading to the NFMA, eminent economist Dr. Marion Clawson and others objected to uneconomical sales. The Senate bill included a reasonably strict cost-benefit analysis, the House version did not directly deal with the issue, and the conference of the two chambers mediated the differences by drafting an "economic suitability," or "marginal lands" provision, which became 16 U.S.C. § 1604(k):

> In developing land management plans pursuant to this [Act], the Secretary shall identify lands within the management area which are not suited for timber production, considering physical, economic, and other pertinent factors to the extent feasible, as determined by the Secretary, and shall assure that, except for salvage sales or sales necessitated to protect other multiple-use values, no timber harvesting shall occur on such lands for a period of 10 years. Lands once identified as unsuitable for timber production shall continue to be treated for reforestation purposes, particularly with regard to the protection of other multiple-use values. The Secretary shall review his decision to classify these lands as not suited for timber production at least every

10 years and shall return these lands to timber production whenever he determines that conditions have changed so that they have become suitable for timber production.

Section 1604(*l*) directs the Forest Service to establish a process for comparing costs and receipts for timber sales and to report annually to Congress on below-cost sales—but sets no substantive standards. Following enactment, the Committee of Scientists, a group of leading experts designated by Congress to propose NFMA rules to the Forest Service, concluded that below-cost sales must be limited by some "rules of reason." See generally Denny LeMaster, DECADE OF CHANGE: THE REMAKING OF FOREST SERVICE STATUTORY AUTHORITY DURING THE 1970's, at 77 (1984). The Forest Service has continued making below-cost sales in areas of marginally productive timber, although it has taken steps to reduce the practice, which remains a point of significant controversy. In its 1998 report to Congress, the Forest Service calculated that timber sales lost $88.6 million during 1997. About 60% of this loss was the result of road construction, as this was the first year the Forest Service included the costs of building logging roads in calculating losses from timber sales. But there was more:

> House Republicans also cited Forest Service mismanagement as a reason for the huge loss reported in 1997. In fact, from 1989 to 1996, Forest Service overhead increased by 46 percent, while revenues decreased by 59 percent. But, in a statement accompanying the Forest Service report, Forest Service Chief Mike Dombeck explained that the remaining loss, which was not accounted for by road construction, was the result of transforming forest practices to improve the overall health of U.S. national forests. He stated that the Forest Service has reduced timber harvest levels by 8 billion board feet since the 1980s. According to Dombeck, the long-term benefits of clean water, plentiful fish and wildlife habitats, and increased recreational opportunities "will far outweigh any short-term losses in financial profitability."

28 Envtl. L. Rptr. 10466C (1998).

Questions: Section 1604(k) requires the Secretary to consider "economic * * * factors to the extent feasible" in determining what national forest lands are unsuitable for timber production. Does it require a cost-benefit analysis? Does it prohibit making lands available for timber harvest where the cost of preparing for the sale and extracting the timber exceed the value of the timber? Does it contain enough "meat" to provide for meaningful judicial review, or is the matter left to the discretion of the U.S. Forest Service?

In Thomas v. Peterson, 753 F.2d 754 (9th Cir.1985), the court rejected the argument that federal law prohibited timber harvesting and associated road construction where the value of the timber to be harvested is less than the cost of the road construction. The court did not address § 1604(k), but examined a provision of the RPA of 1974, which contained a congressional declaration that the national forest transportation system should "meet anticipated needs on an economical and environmentally sound basis." 16 U.S.C. § 1608(a). The court said:

Plaintiffs * * * cite Forest Service regulations, Congressional committee reports, Congressional testimony, unenacted bills, and Forest Service practices, all of which evince a concern for economically efficient management of the National Forests, for avoiding costs not justified by benefits, for obtaining fair market value in the sale of National Forest resources, and for recovery of the costs of National Forest roads and other management expenses. These sources merely counsel economic prudence. They do not evidence a statutory requirement that timber roads be built only when the proceeds of the timber sales will defray construction costs.

The Forest Service interprets "economical" to permit consideration of benefits other than timber access, such as motorized recreation, firewood gathering, and access to the area by local residents. An agency's interpretation of the statute that it is charged with administering is entitled to substantial deference, see Udall v. Tallman, 380 U.S. 1, 16 (1965), and will be upheld unless unreasonable, see id. at 18. Here it is clearly reasonable.

This ruling was followed in Big Hole Ranchers Ass'n v. U.S. Forest Service, 686 F.Supp. 256 (D.Mont.1988). In Citizens for Envt'l Quality v. United States, 731 F.Supp. 970 (D.Colo.1989), the court remanded a plan to the Forest Service to explain more fully why it allowed timber production goals to play a heavy role in determining the suitability of lands for timber production. The court said that § 1604(k) "provides the Forest Service with ample discretion to consider both economic and other pertinent factors in identifying land suitable for timber production. * * * However, * * * if production goals are to be given greater weight in the suitability analysis, then adequate reasons must be set forth for so doing. * * * In the instant case, no such justification has been set forth." Cf. Sierra Club v. Robertson, 845 F.Supp. 485 (S.D.Ohio 1994) (the lower court decision that was vacated by the Supreme Court on ripeness grounds sub nom.) Ohio Forestry Ass'n v. Sierra Club, Chapter 4, supra p. 294, where the court said that "Section 1604(k) does not impose a strict economic test for the suitability of timbering [but] vests the Secretary with broad discretion to consider a variety of possibly conflicting factors in determining whether an area is suitable for timber production."

Should § 1604(k) be construed to reach a result different from this one? Might some timber sales be so uneconomic that the courts are justified in stepping in?

As a matter of policy, should Congress prohibit or more directly limit below-cost timber sales on the national forests? Should an exception be made for timber-dependent communities, where local mills need a relatively continuous supply of timber or they will shut down?

3. DIVERSITY

This is one of the most hotly contested provisions of the NFMA. To some extent its thrust is similar to, and overlaps with, the objectives of the

Endangered Species Act. Section 1604(g)(3)(B) requires that Forest Service land management plans shall

> provide for diversity of plant and animal communities based on the suitability and capability of the specific land area in order to meet overall multiple-use objectives, and within the multiple-use objectives of a land management plan adopted pursuant to this section, provide, where appropriate, to the degree practicable, for steps to be taken to preserve the diversity of tree species similar to that existing in the region controlled by the plan. * * *

The Act does not define diversity, but the regulations define it as "the distribution and abundance of different plant and animal communities and species within the area covered by a land and resource management plan." 36 C.F.R. § 219.3 (1991). Does this faithfully carry out the statute?

To preserve diversity of species, the Forest Service has designated "indicator species" that serve as proxies for large numbers of species; in other words, rather than inventorying all species—which would be impossible—planners attempt to assure suitable habitat for the indicator species. Especially controversial was the designation of the northern spotted owl, which uses old-growth Douglas fir as a preferred habitat, as an indicator species in the Pacific Northwest. The timber industry argued that proposed forest plans may remove too much valuable timber land from the inventories in order to protect the spotted owl; environmentalists believed that more land should be set aside. This has led to much litigation, proposals for legislative "fixes," and public controversy. Although the dispute was enmeshed in the Endangered Species Act once the owl was listed as endangered, a good deal of the litigation actually centered on the "diversity" requirement of the NFMA more than the ESA. The northern spotted owl saga is discussed in Chapter 5, supra pp. 502–03.

Sierra Club v. Marita

United States Court of Appeals, Seventh Circuit, 1995.
46 F.3d 606.

■ FLAUM, CIRCUIT JUDGE.

* * * The present case concerns management plans developed for two forests: Nicolet National Forest ("Nicolet") and Chequamegon (She–WA–me–gon) National Forest ("Chequamegon"). Nicolet spreads over 973,000 acres, of which 655,000 acres are National Forest Land, in northeastern Wisconsin, while Chequamegon encompasses 845,000 publicly-owned acres in northwestern and north-central Wisconsin.[1] Collectively, the Nicolet and the Chequamegon contain hundreds of lakes and streams, thousands of

---

1. Until the mid–1800s, both the Nicolet and Chequamegon were old-growth forests consisting primarily of northern hardwoods. Pine logging around 1900, hardwood logging in the 1920s, and forest fires (caused by clear cutting) significantly affected the landscape. Government replanting and for-est-fire control efforts beginning in the 1930s have reclaimed much of the land as forest. The forests now contain a mixture of trees that markedly differs from the forests' pre–1800 "natural" conditions but is also more diverse in terms of tree type and age.

miles of roads and trails, and serve a wide variety of uses, including hiking, skiing, snowmobiling, logging, fishing, hunting, sightseeing, and scientific research. The forests are important for both the tourism and the forest product industries in northern Wisconsin.

In the late 1970s and early 1980s, the Nicolet and Chequamegon Forest Supervisors and interdisciplinary teams each began drafting a forest management plan for their respective forests. These plans were expected to guide forest management for ten to fifteen years beginning in 1986. Drafts of the Nicolet plan and an EIS comparing the proposed plan to several alternatives were issued on November 9, 1984, while similar drafts of the Chequamegon plan were issued on March 29, 1985. Both plans were followed by a period of public comment, pursuant to 16 U.S.C. § 1604(d), which resulted in a number of changes to both plans.

The Regional Forester issued final drafts of both plans on August 11, 1986, as well as final environmental impact statements ("FEIS") and RODs ["records of decision"] explaining the final planning decisions. [Following exhaustion of administrative remedies, plaintiffs sued.] The Sierra Club's primary contention concerned the Service's failure to employ the science of conservation biology, which failure led it to violate a number of statutes and regulations regarding diversity in national forests. Conservation biology, the Sierra Club asserted, predicts that biological diversity can only be maintained if a given habitat is sufficiently large so that populations within that habitat will remain viable in the event of disturbances. Accordingly, dividing up large tracts of forest into a patchwork of different habitats, as the Nicolet and Chequamegon plans did, would not sustain the diversity within these patches unless each patch were sufficiently large so as to extend across an entire landscape or regional ecosystem. See, generally, Reed F. Noss, Some Principles of Conservation Biology, As They Apply to Environmental Law, 69 Chi.–Kent L.Rev. 893 (1994). Hence, the Sierra Club reasoned, the Service did not fulfil its mandates under the NFMA, NEPA and MUYSA to consider and promote biological diversity within the Nicolet and the Chequamegon.

[The court of appeals found the claim ripe, an outcome that now likely would be different in *Ohio Forestry*, supra p. 294.] * * *

The Sierra Club claims that the Service violated the NFMA and NEPA by using scientifically unsupported techniques to address diversity concerns in its management plans and by arbitrarily disregarding certain principles of conservation biology in developing those plans. The Sierra Club asserts that the Service abdicated its duty to take a "hard look" at the environmental impact of its decisions on biological diversity in the forests on the erroneous contentions that the Sierra Club's proposed theories and predictions were "uncertain" in application and that the Service's own methodology was more than adequate to meet all statutory requirements. According to the Sierra Club, the Service, rather than address the important ecological issues the plaintiffs raised, stuck its head in the sand. The result, the Sierra Club argues, was a plan with "predictions about diversity directly at odds with the prevailing scientific literature."

Several statutes and regulations mandate consideration of diversity in preparing forest management plans. Section 6(g) of the NFMA, the primary statute at issue, directs the Secretary of Agriculture in preparing a forest management plan to, among other things,

> provide for diversity of plant and animal communities based on the suitability and capability of the specific land area in order to meet overall multiple-use objectives, and within the multiple-use objectives of a land management plan adopted pursuant to this section, provide, where appropriate, to the degree practicable, for steps to be taken to preserve the diversity of tree species similar to that existing in the region controlled by the plan[.]

16 U.S.C. § 1604(g)(3)(B).

A number of regulations guide the application of this statute. The most general one stipulates that:

> Forest planning shall provide for diversity of plant and animal communities and tree species consistent with the overall multiple-use objectives of the planning area. Such diversity shall be considered throughout the planning process. Inventories shall include quantitative data making possible the evaluation of diversity in terms of its prior and present condition. For each planning alternative, the interdisciplinary team shall consider how diversity will be affected by various mixes of resource outputs and uses, including proposed management practices.

36 C.F.R. § 219.26. Another regulation addresses the substantive goals of the plan:

> Management prescriptions, where appropriate and to the extent practicable, shall preserve and enhance the diversity of plant and animal communities, including endemic and desirable naturalized plant and animal species, so that it is at least as great as that which would be expected in a natural forest and the diversity of tree species similar to that existing in the planning area. Reductions in diversity of plant and animal communities and tree species from that which would be expected in a natural forest, or from that similar to the existing diversity in the planning area, may be prescribed only where needed to meet overall multiple-use objectives * * *.

36 C.F.R. § 219.27(g); see also 36 C.F.R. § 219.27(a)(5) (requiring that all management prescriptions "provide for and maintain diversity of plant and animal communities to meet overall multiple-use objectives"). Diversity is defined for the purposes of these regulations as "[t]he distribution and abundance of different plant and animal communities and species within the area covered by a land and resource management plan." 36 C.F.R. § 219.3.

Regulations implementing the NFMA with regard to the management of fish and wildlife resources are more specific still. First,

> [f]ish and wildlife habitat shall be managed to maintain viable populations of existing native and desired non-native vertebrate species in the planning area * * *. In order to ensure that viable populations will be

maintained, habitat must be provided to support, at least, a minimum number of reproductive individuals and that habitat must be well distributed so that those individuals can interact with others in the planning area.

36 C.F.R. § 219.19. In order to perceive the effects of management on these species, the Service must monitor the populations of specially selected "management indicator species" ("MIS"). 36 C.F.R. § 219.19(a)(1). The selection of MIS must include, where appropriate, "endangered and threatened plant and animal species" identified on state and federal lists for the area; species with "special habitat needs that may be influenced significantly by planned management programs; species commonly hunted, fished or trapped, non-game species of special interest; and additional * * * species selected because their population changes are believed to indicate the effects of management activities on other species * * * or on water quality." Id.

The NFMA diversity statute does not provide much guidance as to its execution; "it is difficult to discern any concrete legal standards on the face of the provision." Wilkinson and Anderson, supra at 296. However, "when the section is read in light of the historical context and overall purposes of the NFMA, as well as the legislative history of the section, it is evident that section 6(g)(3)(B) requires Forest Service planners to treat the wildlife resource as a controlling, co-equal factor in forest management and, in particular, as a substantive limitation on timber production." Id. * * *

The Service addressed diversity concerns in the Nicolet and Chequamegon in largely similar ways * * *. The Service defined diversity as "[t]he distribution and abundance of different plant and animal communities and species within the area covered by the Land and Resource Management Plan." The Service assumed that "an increase in the diversity of habitats increases the potential livelihood of diverse kinds of organisms."

The Service focused its attention first on vegetative diversity. Diversity of vegetation was measured within tree stands as well as throughout the forest, noting that such diversity is "desirable for diverse wildlife habitat, visual variety, and as an aid to protecting the area from wildfire, insects, and disease." The Service assessed vegetative diversity based on vegetative types, age class structure of timber types, within-stand diversity of tree species, and the spacial distribution pattern of all these elements across the particular forest. The Service also factored in other considerations, including the desirability of "large areas of low human disturbance" and amount of "old-growth" forest, into its evaluations. Using these guidelines, the Service gathered and analyzed data on the current and historical composition of the forests to project an optimal vegetative diversity.

The Service assessed animal diversity primarily on the basis of vegetative diversity. Pursuant to the regulations, the Service identified all rare and uncommon vertebrate wildlife species as well as those species identified with a particular habitat and subject to significant change through planning alternatives. The Service grouped these species with a particular habitat type, identifying 14 categories in the Nicolet and 25 (reduced to 10 similar types) in the Chequamegon. For each of these habitat types, the

Service selected MIS (33 in the Nicolet and 18 in the Chequamegon) to determine the impact of management practices on these species in particular and, by proxy, on other species in general.[8] For each MIS, the Service calculated the minimum viable population necessary in order to ensure the continued reproductive vitality of the species. Factors involved in this calculation included a determination of population size, the spatial distribution across the forest needed to ensure fitness and resilience, and the kinds, amounts and pattern of habitats needed to support the population.

Taking its diversity analysis into consideration, along with its numerous other mandates, the Service developed a number of plan alternatives for each of the forests (eight in the Nicolet and nine in the Chequamegon). Each alternative emphasized a different aspect of forest management, including cost efficiency, wildlife habitat, recreation, and hunting, although all were considered to be "environmentally, technically, and legally feasible." In the Nicolet, the Service selected the alternative emphasizing resource outputs associated with large diameter hardwood and softwood vegetation; in the Chequamegon an alternative emphasizing recreational opportunities, quality saw-timber, and aspen management was chosen.

The Sierra Club argues that the diversity statute and regulations * * * required the Service to consider and apply certain principles of conservation biology in developing the forest plan. These principles, the Sierra Club asserts, dictate that diversity is not comprehensible solely through analysis of the numbers of plants and animals and the variety of species in a given area. Rather, diversity also requires an understanding of the relationships between differing landscape patterns and among various habitats. That understanding, the Sierra Club says, has led to the prediction that the size of a habitat—the "patch size"—tends to affect directly the survival of the habitat and the diversity of plant and animal species within that habitat.

A basic generalization of conservation biology is that smaller patches of habitat will not support life as well as one larger patch of that habitat, even if the total area of the smaller patches equals the total area of the large patch. This generalization derives from a number of observations and predictions. First, whereas a large-scale disturbance will wipe out many populations in a smaller patch, those in a larger patch have a better chance of survival. Second, smaller patches are subject to destruction through "edge effects." Edge effects occur when one habitat's environment suffers because it is surrounded by different type of habitat. Given basic geometry, among other factors, the smaller the patch size of the surrounded habitat, the greater the chance that a surrounding habitat will invade and devastate the surrounded habitat. Third, the more isolated similar habitats are from one another, the less chance organisms can migrate from one habitat to another in the event of a local disturbance. Consequently, fewer organisms will survive such a disturbance and diversity will decline. This third factor is known as the theory of "island biogeography." Thus, the mere fact that a given area contains diverse habitats does not ensure diversity at all; a

---

8. A number of the MIS selected were also chosen because their endangered status required the Service to monitor them directly.

"fragmented forest" is a recipe for ecological trouble. On the basis of these submissions, the Sierra Club desires us to rule that

> [t]o perform a legally adequate hard look at the environmental consequences of landscape manipulation across the hundreds of thousands of hectares of a National Forest, a federal agency must apply in some reasonable fashion the ecological principles identified by well accepted conservation biology. Species-by-species techniques are simply no longer enough. Ecology must be applied in the analysis, and it will be used as a criterion for the substantive results. (Nicolet Appellant's Br. at 7)

As a way of putting conservation biology into practice, the Sierra Club suggested that large blocks of land (at least 30,000 to 50,000 acres per block), so-called "Diversity Maintenance Areas" ("DMAs"), be set aside in each of the forests. The Sierra Club proposed and mapped three DMAs for the Nicolet and two for the Chequamegon. In these areas, which would have included about 25% of each forest, habitats were to be undisturbed by new roads, timber sales, or wildlife openings. Neither forest plan, however, ultimately contained a DMA; the Chequamegon Forest Supervisor initially did include two DMAs, but the Regional Forester removed them from the final Chequamegon plan.

The Sierra Club contends that the Service ignored its submissions, noting that the FEISs and RODs for both the Nicolet and the Chequamegon are devoid of reference to population dynamics, species turnover, patch size, recolonization problems, fragmentation problems, edge effects, and island biogeography. According to the Sierra Club, the Service simply disregarded extensive documentary and expert testimony, including over 100 articles and 13 affidavits, supporting the Sierra Club's assertions and thereby shirked its legal duties.

The Service replies that it correctly considered the implications of conservation biology for both the Nicolet and Chequamegon and appropriately declined to apply the science. The Service asserts that it duly noted the "concern [of the Sierra Club and others] that fragmentation of the * * * forest canopy through timber harvesting and road building is detrimental to certain plant and animal species." The Service decided that the theory had "not been applied to forest management in the Lake States" and that the subject was worthy of further study. However, the Service found in both cases that while the theories of conservation biology in general and of island biogeography in particular were "of interest, * * * there is not sufficient justification at this time to make research of the theory a Forest Service priority." Given its otherwise extensive analysis of diversity, as well as the deference owed its interpretation of applicable statutory and regulatory requirements, the Service contends that it clearly met all the "diversity" obligations imposed on it. * * *

The Sierra Club's arguments regarding the inadequacy of the Service's plans and FEISs can be distilled into five basic allegations, each of which we address in turn. First, the Sierra Club asserts that the law "treats ecosystems and ecological relationships as a separately cognizable issue from the species by species concepts driving game and timber issues." The Sierra Club relies on the NFMA's diversity language to argue that the

NFMA treats diversity in two distinct respects: diversity of plant and animal communities and diversity of tree species. See 16 U.S.C. § 1604(g)(3)(B). * * * The Sierra Club concludes from these statutes and regulations that the Service was obligated to apply an ecological approach to forest management and failed to do so. In the Sierra Club's view, MISs and population viability analyses present only half the picture, a picture that the addition of conservation biology would make complete.

The Sierra Club errs in these assertions because it sees requirements in the NFMA * * * that simply do not exist. The drafters of the NFMA diversity regulations themselves recognized that diversity was a complex term and declined to adopt any particular means or methodology of providing for diversity. Report of the Committee of Scientists to the Secretary of Agriculture Regarding Regulations Proposed by the United States Forest Service to Implement Section 6 of the National Forest Management Act of 1976, 44 Fed.Reg. 26,599, 26,609 (1979). We agree with the district court that "[i]n view of the committee's decision not to prescribe a particular methodology and its failure to mention the principles that plaintiffs claims were by then well established, the court cannot fairly read those principles into the NFMA * * *." Nicolet, 843 F.Supp. at 1542; Chequamegon, 845 F.Supp. at 1330. Thus, conservation biology is not a necessary element of diversity analysis insofar as the regulations do not dictate that the service analyze diversity in any specific way.

Furthermore, the Sierra Club has overstated its case by claiming that MIS and population viability analyses do not gauge the diversity of ecological communities as required by the regulations. Except for those species to be monitored because they themselves are in danger, species are chosen to be on an MIS list precisely because they will indicate the effects management practices are having on a broader ecological community. Indeed, even if all that the Sierra Club has asserted about forest fragmentation and patch size and edge effects is true, an MIS should to some degree indicate their impact on diversity. See Report of the Committee of Scientists, 44 Fed.Reg. at 26,627 (noting that MIS are chosen "because they indicate the consequences of management on other species whose populations fluctuate in some measurable manner with the indicator species"); Judy L. Meyer, The Dance of Nature: New Concepts in Ecology, 69 Chi.–Kent L.Rev. 875, 885 (1994) (noting that the most sensitive indicator of environmental stress is the population level). While the NFMA would not permit the Service to limit its choices to either enhancing diversity or protecting a particular species, see Seattle Audubon Society v. Evans, 952 F.2d 297, 301–02 (9th Cir.1991)* such is not the case here. The Sierra Club may have wished the Service to analyze diversity in a different way, but we cannot conclude on the basis of the records before us that the Service's methodology arbitrarily or capriciously neglected the diversity of ecological communities in the two forests.

---

* [Eds. *Seattle Audubon* held that the Forest Service's duty under 36 C.F.R. § 219.19 to maintain a viable population of northern spotted owls did not cease when the owl was listed under the Endangered Species Act.]

In a second and related argument, the Sierra Club submits that the substantive law of diversity necessitated the set-aside of large, unfragmented habitats to protect at least some old-growth forest communities. The Sierra Club points out that 36 C.F.R. § 219.27(g) requires that "where appropriate and to the extent practicable" the Service "shall preserve and enhance the diversity of plant and animal communities * * * so that it is at least as great as that which would be expected in a natural forest * * *." Furthermore, "[r]eductions in diversity of plant and animal communities and tree species from that which would be expected in a natural forest or from that similar to the existing diversity in the planning area[ ] may be prescribed only where needed to meet overall multiple-use objectives." Id. Diversity, the Sierra Club asserts, requires the Service to maintain a range of different, ecologically viable communities. Because it is simply not possible to ensure the survival of any old-growth forest communities without these large, undisturbed patches of land, the Service has therefore reduced diversity. The Service was thus bound to protect and enhance the natural forest or explain why other forest uses prevented the Service from doing so. The Sierra Club believes the Service did neither.

The Sierra Club asserts that the diversity regulations require a certain procedure and that because the substantive result of the Service's choices will produce, in the Sierra Club's view, results adverse to "natural forest" diversity, the Service has violated its mandate. However, as the Service points out, the regulations do not actually require the promotion of "natural forest" diversity but rather the promotion of diversity at least as great as that found in a natural forest. The Service maintains that it did provide for such diversity in the ways discussed above. Additionally, the Service did consider the maintenance of some old-growth forest, even though the Sierra Club disputes that the Service's efforts will have any positive effects. And to the extent the Service's final choice did not promote "natural diversity" above all else, the Service acted well within its regulatory discretion. See Sierra Club v. Espy, 38 F.3d 792, 800 (5th Cir.1994) ("That [NFMA diversity] protection means something less than the preservation of the status quo but something more than eradication of species suggests that this is just the type of policy-oriented decision Congress wisely left to the discretion of the experts—here, the Forest Service.").
* * *

Fourth, the Sierra Club contends that the rejection of its "high quality" science argument on the basis of "uncertainty" in the application of conservation biology was unscrupulous. The Sierra Club asserts that conservation biology represented well-accepted and well-respected science even at the time the Service developed its management plans in the mid–1980s and that this evidence was before the Service when it drafted the forest plans. Thus, if the Service's only argument against applying the "high quality" science of conservation biology was its uncertainty, the Service has utterly failed to respond to the challenge of conservation biology.

A brief look at available evidence suggests that the district court's understanding of uncertainty was correct and the Service's explanation principled. The Service, in looking at island biogeography, noted that it had been developed as a result of research on actual islands or in the predominantly old-growth forests of the Pacific Northwest and therefore did not necessarily lend itself to application in the forests of Wisconsin. Literature submitted by the Sierra Club to the Service was not unequivocal in stipulating how to apply conservation biology principles in the Nicolet and Chequamegon. Likewise, a Sierra Club group member suggested during meetings regarding the Chequamegon that "the Forest Service should be a leader and incorporate this concept into the Plan. He indicated that it would set a precedent for other Forests and Regions." The Chequamegon Forest Supervisor also originally decided to include the DMAs in his forest plan not because science so compelled but as a way to research an as yet untested theory. Even recent literature has recognized that "new legislation may be necessary" in order to force the Service to adopt conservation biology. Robert B. Keiter, Conservation Biology and the Law: Assessing the Challenges Ahead, 69 Chi.Kent L.Rev. 911, 916 (1994). Perhaps the Service "ha[s] the ability to reinterpret [its] own governing mandates to give species protection priority over visitor services and other concerns," id. at 921, but that is not and was not required.

The amici scientific societies suggest that the district court misunderstood the nature of scientific uncertainty. Their argument on this point boils down to the assertion that all scientific propositions are inherently unverifiable and at most falsifiable. Hence, amici argue, allowing the Service to ignore the theories of conservation biology because they are "uncertain" would, on the same logic, allow the Service to ignore the theory of gravity.

Amici, like the Sierra Club, misapprehend the "uncertainty" of which the Service and the district court spoke. We agree that an agency decision to avoid a science should not escape review merely because a theory is not certain. But, however valid a general theory may be, it does not translate into a management tool unless one can apply it to a concrete situation. The Service acknowledged the developments in conservation biology but did not think that they had been shown definitively applicable to forests like the Nicolet or the Chequamegon. Thus, circumstances did not warrant setting aside a large portion of these forests to study island biogeography and related theories at the expense of other forest-plan objectives. Given that uncertainty, we appropriately defer to the agency's method of measuring and maintaining diversity. * * *

The creation of a forest plan requires the Forest Service to make trade-offs among competing interests. See Sierra Club v. Espy, 38 F.3d at 802. The NFMA's diversity provisions do substantively limit the Forest Service's ability to sacrifice diversity in those trades * * *.

Affirmed.

NOTES AND QUESTIONS

1. The large record on the science of conservation biology compiled by the plaintiffs and the participation of scientific societies as *amici* give this

the feel of a test case where plaintiffs sought to reorient national forest management. Was it a good litigation strategy to ask the courts in effect to bless a specific scientific school of thought and mandate its use in managing national forests? Was the court being asked to act as a "science court," and decide among differing scientific theories? Can courts do that easily? Should they? Should the courts have applied the standard test for determining the admissibility of scientific evidence? See Daubert v. Merrell Dow Pharmaceuticals, Inc., 509 U.S. 579, 592–95 (1993); see Patricia Smith King, Applying Daubert to the "Hard Look" Requirement of NEPA: Scientific Evidence Before the Forest Service in Sierra Club v. Marita, 2 Wis.Envtl.L.J. 147 (1995).

2.   Or did the plaintiffs pick the wrong place to litigate this? Regardless of the acceptance and credibility of conservation biology as a general school of thought, what does the court's opinion indicate about the state of knowledge and analysis of that school of thought as applied to the forests of the upper Midwest?

3.   What are the legal footholds for incorporating the science of conservation biology into national forest management? Look first at the "diversity" provision of the NFMA, 16 U.S.C. § 1604(g)(3)(B). Does it require that the U.S. Forest Service should obey, or try to mimic, the laws of nature in managing the forests? Or does management mean, inevitably, some manipulation of the natural world that will change the mix and diversity of species found there?

4.   Now look at the various regulations quoted by the court. How much flesh do they put on the bones of the statute? Do they embrace the principles of conservation biology? To the extent plaintiffs seek to enforce the regulation, as opposed to the statute, the Forest Service retains the authority to change the regulation if it doesn't like the way the courts interpret it.

5.   Was this really a dispute about two competing scientific theories? What scientific school of thought did the Forest Service follow, if any? Was the Forest Service position that it rejected the teachings of conservation biology, or was it that it wanted to apply those teachings in a way the plaintiffs disagreed with? From the standpoint of legal strategy, which would be the best course?

6.   Does the Forest Service ever have a legal (and judicially enforceable) obligation to conduct experiments on alternative management strategies to help advance science?

7.   For more commentary, see Julie A. Weis, Eliminating the National Forest Management Act's Diversity Requirement as a Substantive Standard, 27 Envtl.L. 641 (1997); Greg D. Corbin, The United States Forest Service's Response to Biodiversity Science, 29 Envtl.L. 377 (1999).

4.   DIVERSITY II: MUST POPULATION DATA BE GATHERED?

Beyond the large question about the acceptability of conservation biology addressed in *Marita*, the methodology the Forest Service has used to assess and conserve biodiversity has been much litigated, as illustrated the following materials.

Inland Empire Public Lands Council v. U.S. Forest Service

United States Court of Appeals, Ninth Circuit, 1996.
88 F.3d 754.

■ Before: WRIGHT, HALL and TROTT, CIRCUIT JUDGES.

■ CYNTHIA HOLCOMB HALL, CIRCUIT JUDGE:

The United States Forest Service proposed eight timber sales in the Upper Sunday Creek Watershed region of the Kootenai National Forest in northwest Montana. * * * Plaintiffs, a number of environmental groups, challenged the sale first in administrative hearings and ultimately in district court, claiming that the Service's analysis of the sale's impact on seven species—the lynx, boreal owl, flammulated owl, black-backed wood-pecker, fisher, bull charr, and wet-sloped cutthroat trout—was inadequate under both the National Forest Management Act, 16 U.S.C. §§ 1600, et seq., and the National Environmental Policy Act of 1969, 42 U.S.C. §§ 4321 et seq. The district court concluded that the Service's analysis was sufficient and thereafter granted summary judgment for the Service and refused to enjoin the sales. In this expedited appeal, Plaintiffs now argue [that NEPA was violated and that] the Service failed to comply with 36 C.F.R. § 219.19, which requires a minimum level of population viability analysis * * *. [The court's discussion of NEPA is omitted.]

* * * Plaintiffs claimed that the Service fell short of what the NFMA required because it never examined the species' population size, their population trends, or their ability to interact with other groups of the species living in neighboring patches of forest. The district court rejected this argument on summary judgment, reasoning that Plaintiffs were quibbling over the choice of scientific methodologies, a decision to which a reviewing court should defer.

* * * As noted above, the NFMA imposes substantive duties on the Forest Service, one of which is the duty to "provide for diversity of plant and animal communities." 16 U.S.C. § 1604(g)(3)(B). Regulation 219.19, one of the many regulations promulgated to ensure such diversity, states in relevant part that:

> Fish and wildlife habitat shall be managed to maintain viable populations of existing native and desired non-native vertebrate species in the planning area. For planning purposes, a viable population shall be regarded as one which has the estimated numbers and distribution of reproductive individuals to insure its continued existence is well distributed in the planning area. In order to insure that viable populations will be maintained, habitat must be provided to support, at least, a minimum number of reproductive individuals and that habitat must be well distributed so that those individuals can interact with others in the planning area.

36 C.F.R. § 219.19.[2] This duty to ensure viable, or self-sustaining, populations, applies with special force to "sensitive" species. [citations omitted] Because neither party disputes the Service's ultimate obligation to ensure viable populations, the key to this appeal is deciding what type of population viability analysis the Service must perform in order to comply with Regulation 219.19.

Each party suggests its own answer. The Forest Service proposes that its "habitat viability analyses" were sufficient. For four of the species (the black-backed woodpecker, lynx, fisher, and boreal owl), the Service did the following: It consulted field studies that disclosed how many acres of territory an individual of each species needed to survive and the percentage of that acreage that was used for nesting, feeding, denning, etc. (e.g. a lynx needs a 200 acre territory, 20 acres—or 10%—of which must be suitable for denning). The Service then assumed that these percentages would hold true regardless of the size of the individual's territory (e.g. that a lynx would need 10% of whatever acreage of territory it inhabited to be denning habitat). The Service examined each proposed alternative to see how many acres of each type of relevant habitat would remain after the timber was harvested (e.g. Alternative 1 would leave 2,000 acres of denning habitat). It next determined what percentage of the decision area that the remaining types of habitat constituted (e.g. decision area was 10,000 acres so that remaining denning habitat is 20% of the decision area). The Service concluded a species would remain viable as long as the threshold percentage of each type of habitat remaining in the chosen alternative was greater than the percentage required for that species to survive (e.g. the lynx population would remain viable because Alternative 1 left 20% denning habitat and a lynx needs only 10% of its territory to be suitable for denning).

Plaintiffs contend that the Service's manifold "habitat viability analyses" are insufficient. They argue that Regulation 219.19 also requires the Service to examine: (1) the population of each species; (2) the population dynamics (trends, etc.) of each species; and (3) whether the species could travel between different patches of forest ("linkages"). Mills Decl.[5] Plaintiffs claim that their form of analysis is the minimum required by law.

---

2. 36 C.F.R. § 219.27(a)(6) also requires: "All management prescriptions shall ... [p]rovide for adequate fish and wildlife habitat to maintain viable populations of existing native vertebrate species and provide that habitat for species chosen under § 219.19 is maintained and improved to the degree consistent with multiple-use objectives established in the plan." Because this section refers to § 219.19, our Regulation 219.19 analysis applies with equal force to this section.

5. The Service argues that we cannot consider Mills' declaration, because it was submitted with Plaintiffs' district court motion for summary judgment and was never part of the *administrative* record. Although the general rule prevents consideration of evidence outside the administrative record, "the court may consider, particularly in highly technical areas, substantive evidence going to the merits of the agency's action where such evidence is necessary as background to determine the sufficiency of the agency's consideration." *Love v. Thomas,* 858 F.2d 1347, 1356 (9th Cir.1988), *cert. denied sub nom. AFL–CIO v. Love,* 490 U.S. 1035, 109 S.Ct. 1932, 104 L.Ed.2d 403 (1989) (citation omitted). This is because "[i]t will often be impossible, especially when highly technical matters are involved, for the court to determine whether the agency took into consideration

In deference to an agency's expertise, we review its interpretation of its own regulations solely to see whether that interpretation is arbitrary and capricious. 5 U.S.C. § 706(2)(A); *Oregon Natural Resources Council v. Marsh,* 52 F.3d 1485, 1488 (9th Cir.1995). This is especially true when questions of scientific methodology are involved. *Inland Empire Public Lands Council v. Schultz,* 992 F.2d 977, 981 (9th Cir.1993) ("We defer to agency expertise on questions of methodology unless the agency has completely failed to address some factor, 'consideration of which was essential to a truly informed decision whether or not to prepare an EIS.'") * * *. Thus, we will uphold the Forest Service's interpretation "unless it is plainly erroneous or inconsistent with the regulation." *Nevada Land Action Ass'n,* 8 F.3d at 717 (citations and internal quotations omitted).[6]

We start, as we must, with the plain language of the Regulation. *Idaho First Nat'l Bank v. Commissioner of Internal Revenue,* 997 F.2d 1285, 1289 (9th Cir.1993) ("If the [statutory] language ... is unambiguous, and its literal application does not conflict with the intentions of its drafters, the plain meaning should prevail."). The Regulation specifically provides that the Forest Service may discharge its duties though habitat management as long as "habitat [is] provided to support, *at least,* a minimum number of reproductive individuals and that habitat [is] well distributed so that those individuals can interact with others in the planning area." 36 C.F.R. § 219.19 (emphasis added).[7]

We do not believe that the habitat management analysis conducted in this case for the black-backed woodpecker, lynx, fisher, and boreal owl was in any way "plainly erroneous" or "inconsistent" with this regulatory duty. Regulation 219.19 ultimately requires the Forest Service to maintain viable

all relevant factors unless it looks outside the record to determine what matters the agency should have considered but did not." *Asarco, Inc. v. EPA,* 616 F.2d 1153, 1160 (9th Cir. 1980). To the extent Mills' declaration is submitted to show that the Service overlooked factors relevant to a proper population viability analysis, we will consider it.

6. As a preliminary matter, the Service argues that Plaintiffs' claim is procedurally barred. The Service cites *Environment Now! v. Espy,* 877 F.Supp. 1397, 1420 (E.D.Cal. 1994), for the proposition that Regulation 219.19 "appl[ies] solely to the promulgation and management of forest plans, not individual timber sales" so as to ban a challenge to the site-specific Upper Sunday plan. *Environment Now!* adopted the rationale of an Eighth Circuit case, *Sharps v. United States Forest Serv.,* 28 F.3d 851, 855 (8th Cir.1994), and held that "only challenges to regional guides or forest plans may be brought under [these] provisions." *Environment Now!,* 77 F.Supp. at 1420. The *Sharps* court relied on the analysis of its district court, which had

noted that Regulation 219.19 limited the management of habitat to the "planning area" and that Regulation 219.3 defined "planning area" as "the area of the Forest System covered by a *regional guide or forest plan* "—which, according to the district court, would exclude district-level, site-specific plans. *Sharps v. United States Forest Serv.,* 823 F.Supp. 668, 679 (D.S.D.1993), *aff'd,* 28 F.3d 851 (8th Cir.1994).

We are not persuaded. We believe that the *Sharps* court's reading of Regulations 219.19 and 219.3 is incorrect. Regulation 219.3 defines the "planning area" as "the area ... *covered by* a regional guide or forest plan." 36 C.F.R. § 219.3 (emphasis added). Because any district contained within the boundaries of a forest having a plan would be an "area ... covered by a ... forest plan," it would be also be a planning area governed by Regulation 219.19.

7. The Forest Service's manual provides no clear guidance on whether a population viability analysis presupposes data on actual populations. * * *

populations. In this case, the Service's methodology reasonably ensures such populations by requiring that the decision area contain enough of the types of habitat essential for survival. In applying this methodology, the Service recognizes that decision areas are artificial boundaries that change depending on the project at issue, and that the species inhabiting these areas pay no attention to such boundaries.

We recognize that the Service's methodology necessarily assumes that maintaining the acreage of habitat necessary for survival would in fact assure a species' survival. The Service is entitled to rely on reasonable assumptions in its environmental analyses. *See, e.g., Sierra Club v. Marita ("Marita I"),* 845 F.Supp. 1317, 1331 (E.D.Wis.1994) (finding it permissible to assume that population trends affecting one species in a particular habitat will similarly affect other species in the same habitat), *aff'd,* 46 F.3d 606 (7th Cir.1995); *Greenpeace Action v. Franklin,* 14 F.3d 1324, 1335–36 (9th Cir.1992) (finding it permissible for Service to assume that declines in the Stellar sea lion population would be the same for the harbor seal population, given their similarities). We find the above-stated assumption eminently reasonable and therefore do not find that the Forest Service's habitat analyses for the black-backed woodpecker, lynx, fisher, and boreal owl were arbitrary or capricious.[8]

* * * The Service's treatment of the flammulated owl is also reasonable. In its EIS, the Service determined that the Upper Sunday decision area contained habitat to support three potential flammulated owl territories and concluded that Alternative E–Modified would shrink the size of the smallest of these territories from 40 to 35 acres. Biological Assessment at 29–30. The Service did not engage in a more extended analysis of the owl's nesting and feeding habitat requirements because such data were unavailable. *See* Richard T. Reynolds & Brian D. Linkhart, "The Nesting Biology of Flammulated Owls in Colorado," *Biology & Conservation of Northern Forest Owls* 259 (1987) ("It spite of its wide distribution, little is known of the flammulated owl's nesting biology and population status."). We believe that an analysis that uses all the scientific data currently available is a sound one. *See Seattle Audubon Soc'y v. Moseley,* 80 F.3d 1401, 1404 (9th Cir.1996) (upholding a viability analysis that was "based on the current state of scientific knowledge"). We therefore find no fault with the Service's analysis of the flammulated owl.

Plaintiffs contend that we must still reverse because the Service did not comply with its duties regarding the "management indicator species." Regulation 219.19 provides that the Service may select "certain vertebrate and/or invertebrate species present in the area" to be "management indicator species" when those species' "population changes are believed to indicate the effects of management activities." 36 C.F.R. § 219.19.[11] Once

---

8. We therefore reject Plaintiffs' argument that the Service must assess population viability in terms of actual population size, population trends, or the population dynamics of other species. We do not mean to suggest, however, that Plaintiffs' suggestions are in any way improper. Indeed, we would encourage such analyses and hold only that they are not required.

11. A species chosen as a management indicator species is used as a bellwether—a class representative, if you will—for the other

an indicator species is selected, the Service is obligated to evaluate planning alternatives for projects that affect that species "in terms of both amount and quality of habitat and of animal population trends of the management indicator species." 36 C.F.R. § 219.19(a)(2).

We believe that the Service has satisfied this obligation. In this case, the Service selected the pileated woodpecker as the indicator species for the old growth habitat. *See* Final EIS at III:42. The old growth areas provide special feeding and nesting conditions, upon which several species are dependent. The Service evaluated the various planning alternatives for the Upper Sunday timber sales in terms of how they would affect the old growth forest and the number of pileated woodpecker nesting and feeding territories therein. *See* Final EIS at IV:88–89. Specifically, the Service found that the chosen alternative would reduce the pileated woodpecker's old growth nesting habitat by 11–12% and the feeding habitat by 11–15%. Final EIS at II:33. Such reduction would "eliminate one nesting block . . . and reduce the number of home ranges that support good amount and distribution of nesting and feeding habitat from 10 to 9." Final EIS at IV:88. Because the number of remaining nesting and feeding territories has a direct impact on the population of the species, the EIS effectively predicts a slight downward population trend in pileated woodpeckers as a result of the timber sales. We therefore do not believe that the Service acted arbitrarily or capriciously when it estimated the effects of the alternatives on the population of the management indicator species by analyzing the amount of the species' habitat that would be reduced by each alternative. In short, the Service complied with Section 219.19(a)(2).[12]

We therefore affirm the district court's conclusion that the Service's population viability analysis was not "arbitrary and capricious."

NOTES AND QUESTIONS

1. In Sierra Club v. Martin, 168 F.3d 1 (11th Cir.1999), the court reached the opposite result.

species that have the same special habitat needs or population characteristics. The Service must choose management indicator species "where appropriate" to represent certain classes of species in order to estimate the effects of proposed management activities on fish and wildlife populations. In this case, the Service chose the pileated woodpecker as the management indicator species for old growth dependent species. Old growth forest comprises 20% of the Upper Sunday decision area, and provides special feeding and nesting conditions for several species. The use of management indicator species is intended to allow the Service to thoroughly evaluate the effects of the alternatives on fish and wildlife populations by using a "class representative," without having to evaluate each species individually.

12. For the reasons stated above, we believe that the Service satisfied its obligations under § 219.19(a)(6). *See* 36 C.F.R. § 219.19(a)(6) ("Population trends of the management indicator species will be monitored and relationships to habitat determined."). The Service specifically found that for the smaller, more reclusive species, such as the pileated woodpecker, there is no technically reliable and cost-effective method of counting individual members of the species. In light of the Service's alternative method of population trend analysis, its failure to monitor the actual population of the pileated woodpecker is not dispositive or unreasonable. *See* Forest Monitoring Report for Fiscal Year 1992, at 27.

We do agree with the Forest Service that the combination of §§ 219.26 and 219.19 require it only to collect inventory data on MIS rather than on all species in the Forest. To read § 219.26 to require inventory data on *all* species obviates the need for MIS and reduces § 219.19 to nonsense. On the other hand, the Forest Service and Timber Intervenors' interpretation of § 219.26—that they need not collect data on MIS either—would consign that regulation to a similar fate. By their reading, § 219.26 would have no meaning despite its explicit requirement that quantitative inventory data be used to measure forest diversity. Interpreting a regulation in a manner that robs it of all meaning is unacceptable. * * *

We believe that the regulations are harmonious when read together. MIS are proxies used to measure the effects of management strategies on Forest diversity; Section 219.19 requires that the Forest Service monitor their relationship to habitat changes. Section 219.26 requires the Forest Service to use quantitative inventory data to assess the Forest Plan's effects on diversity. If § 219.19 mandates that MIS serve as the means through which to measure the Forest Plan's impact on diversity and § 219.26 dictates that quantitative data be used to measure the Plan's impact on diversity, then, taken together, the two regulations require the Forest Service to gather quantitative data on MIS and use it to measure the impact of habitat changes on the Forest's diversity. To read the regulations otherwise would be to render one or the other meaningless as well as to disregard the regulations' directive that population trends of the MIS be monitored and that inventory data be gathered in order to monitor the effects of the Forest Plan. * * *.[13]

Turning now to the instant case, it becomes clear that the Forest Service's approval of the timber sales without gathering and considering data on the MIS is arbitrary and capricious. The regulations require that MIS be monitored to determine the effects of habitat changes. The timber projects proposed for the Chattahoochee and Oconee National Forests amount to 2,000 acres of habitat change. Yet, despite this extensive habitat change and the fact that the some MIS populations in the Forest are actually declining, the Forest Service has no population data for half of the MIS in the Forest and thus cannot reliably gauge the impact of the timber projects on these species.

See also Forest Guardians v. U.S. Forest Service, 180 F.Supp.2d 1273 (D.N.M.2001) (NFMA regulations requires the agency to "acquire and analyze hard population data of its management indicator species").

---

13. In so finding, we respectfully differ with the Ninth Circuit's conclusion in *Inland Empire*, 88 F.3d at 761, that habitat analyses suffice to satisfy the requirements of 36 C.F.R. § 219.19. We believe that this finding does not conform with the clear language of the regulations, which requires evaluation of "both amount and quality of habitat *and of animal population trends* of the management indicator species." 36 C.F.R. § 219.19(a)(2) (emphasis added). It bears noting, however, that the *Inland* court reached its conclusion based on a very different set of facts. In that case, the Forest Service had conducted a site-specific EIS and detailed field studies before concluding that the MIS would not be significantly harmed. *Id.* at 758, 761.

2. Environmentalist opponents of a 2000 acre expansion of the Vail ski resort in the White River National Forest in Colorado argued that the NFMA planning regulations required the Forest Service to compile hard population data on the lynx, and not just manage habitat for a hypothetical population. The Forest Service (and Vail) disagreed. In Colorado Environmental Coalition v. Dombeck, 185 F.3d 1162 (10th Cir.1999), the court sided with the agency. Excerpts follow:

To determine what type of data or analysis is necessary to satisfy 36 C.F.R. § 219.19, we, too, begin with the plain language, which unmistakably focuses on the provision and distribution of *habitat* in order to *maintain existing* viable *populations*. To the extent the regulation discusses, and therefore arguably requires, specific analysis of the estimated numbers and distribution of individual members of a species, it does so only in the narrow context of defining what constitutes a "viable population." A "viable population" exists when enough reproductive individuals of a given species are distributed throughout a given area to insure the continued existence of that species in that area. The regulatory language clearly presupposes the ascertainable presence of a species' population within a given planning area.

The administrative record before us indicates there is no existing lynx population in Category III or the White River National Forest from which to gather census or distribution data.[7] Indeed, the Colorado Division of Wildlife believes "*if* any lynx remain in Colorado their numbers are so small that they do not represent a viable population, and are not detectable by known census methods." The United States Fish and Wildlife Service similarly "concludes that a self-sustaining resident [lynx] population does not exist in Colorado, but individual animals may be present." Because no ascertainable lynx population exists within Category III or the White River National Forest,we do not read 36 C.F.R. § 219.19 to require the Forest Service to collect or evaluate hard lynx population data prior to making its decision in this case.

A review of the plain language of 36 C.F.R. § 219.19 and its enabling statute, the National Forest Management Act, establishes Congress never intended to require the Forest Service to collect population data and make data-based population viability assessments as a precondi-

---

7. For example: although probable lynx tracks were recorded in the area in 1991, last confirmed lynx sighting was on Vail Ski Area during the winter of 1973–74; last reported lynx capture within Colorado occurred twenty-five years ago on the Vail Ski Area; lack of a verifiable lynx population in Colorado is attributable to a variety of natural conditions and historic factors; only two sets of lynx tracks were positively identified after transecting 190.5 miles on and around the Vail ski area in thirteen days in 1989; a single set of possible tracks identified after transecting 2,053 miles primarily within the boundaries of the White River National Forest in 1992; after intensive efforts using snowtracking (5,833.5 mi), hair snags (62 locations), remote cameras (110 locations) and snares (686 trap nights), only eleven sets of tracks that *appeared to have a high probability* of being lynx were found; the Colorado Division of Wildlife has offered a $500 reward for any positive information on lynx since 1993 and has not received any; there have been no road kills or accidental trapping or shooting of lynx since 1973.

tion to managing habitat if, despite good faith efforts to confirm the presence of lynx, no one has seen an actual lynx in the project area in over twenty-five years, and only a few sets of tracks have been documented in the past ten years. Under the circumstances, the best the Forest Service could do to comply with the Forest Plan mandate to develop additional skiing opportunities at existing resorts *and* provide for diversity of plant and animal communities within Category III, was to provide and distribute lynx habitat based on the best information available, on the remote chance a population of reproductive lynx might reoccupy the area in the future.

Our views on this issue are in complete accord with the Ninth Circuit's decision in *Inland Empire Pub. Lands Council v. United States Forest Serv.,* 88 F.3d 754 (9th Cir.1996). * * * To the extent other courts have read 36 C.F.R. § 219.19 to prohibit reliance on habitat analysis without hard population data, *see, e.g., Sierra Club v. Martin,* 168 F.3d 1 (11th Cir.1999) * * * those decisions are distinguishable from this case in at least two important ways: (1) they involved the application of § 219.19 under circumstances in which population data was available; and (2) they involved the provisions of § 219.19 applicable to the use of a Management Indicator Species as a proxy for determining the effects of management activities on other species. *See Martin,* 168 F.3d at 4–8. As discussed above, there simply is no lynx population data available to the Forest Service in this case. Moreover, when considering the Category III expansion, the Forest Service logically did not select the rare and elusive lynx as a Management Indicator Species. Thus, the population inventory requirements of § 219.19 that apply to Management Indicator Species are irrelevant to the issue before us.

It would be inappropriate to comment here on the soundness of those opinions requiring population inventories and data-based viability assessments under very different facts and forest planning contexts. We simply hold the regulatory language does not require the Forest Service, under the circumstances of this case, to collect actual lynx population data. It would be absurd to permit project opponents to utilize the population viability regulation to block consideration and approval of projects otherwise consistent with the applicable Forest Plan when no evidence shows a population of a given species is present within the relevant planning area, and when the viability of any individual members of that species can otherwise be protected by appropriate habitat preservation and distribution. Thus, in this case, where no viable population exists, we recognize habitat identification and preservation as a legitimate means of ensuring any future lynx viability.[9]

3.   Look closely at the Forest Service's regulation § 219.19, and how it defines "viability" of species. Do the regulations turn the concept of

---

9. Like the Ninth Circuit in *Inland Empire,* however, we encourage the Forest Service to analyze the viability of any species' population in terms of actual population size, trends, dynamics, and distribution when such data is available. *See Inland Empire,* 88 F.3d at 761 n. 8.

diversity in the statute into something like a duty to preserve self-sustaining populations of all or most species found in the national forests? Does that go beyond what the statute requires? How far beyond? How does it differ, if at all, from the sustained yield idea considered earlier?

4.   Is there a separation of powers consideration lurking here? The Forest Service has much to do–run campgrounds, rescue careless visitors, supervise ranchers and miners, etc. If it has to run wildlife surveys like the plaintiffs want in these cases, it may not be able to meet some of its other responsibilities. Should that be a relevant factor to a court addressing this issue?

5.   If the Forest Service regulations merely tracked the language of the statute, would the plaintiffs have a case? Could the Forest Service now moot all this litigation by changing the regulations? For more discussion, see Andrew Orlemann, Do the Proposed Forest Service Regulations Protect Biodiversity? An Analysis of the Continuing Viability of "Habitat Viability Analysis", 20 J. Land, Resources, and Envtl.L. 357 (2000). Orlemann points out that the draft version of the proposed new planning rules released by the Clinton Administration in 1999 (64 Fed. Reg. 54,074, 54,103) would combine several sections into a new set of provisions with the heading "ecological, social, and economic sustainability," using language quite different from the existing regulations. Orelemann concludes that the proposed regulations, if adopted, "are likely to give the Forest Service more discretion in its management of wildlife and other species, not less." They also explicitly adopt the *Inland Empire* rule, allowing the Forest Service to proceed in the "absence of data on the basis of expert opinion, and relying on habitat analysis for viability monitoring rather than collecting actual population data."

6.   On whether the proposed regulation should be adopted, Orlemann sums it up this way:

> If one views the Forest Service as an elite, efficient, conscientious agency seemingly fettered in its professional management by endless lawsuits, the proposed regulation is probably a reasonable one. It should provide the agency with more opportunities to apply its expertise to national forest management without the interference of public interest group generated injunctions. If, on the other hand, one views the Forest Service as an incompetent bureaucracy staffed by the proverbial timber beast, the proposed regulation is probably less than ideal. It does not provide very many specific requirements by which the Forest Service can be monitored by the interested public; much of the language is both ambiguous and permissive.

5.   ROTATION AGE AND CULMINATION OF MEAN ANNUAL INCREMENT (CMAI)

After the suitable inventory is established, the harvesting schedule must be set. Section 1604(m) prohibits cutting unless "stands of trees * * * generally have reached the culmination of mean annual increment of growth," with narrow exceptions. Is this a restatement, in modern technical language, of the requirement of the 1897 Organic Act, as interpreted in the *Monongahela* decision (see p. 714, supra) that only "dead, matured, or large growth of trees" can be harvested? That is, when trees reach biological maturity, rather than at the earlier point of economic maturity (except that this section speaks in terms of "stands" instead of individual trees)?

One writer described this section as setting out "a specific, enforceable maturity objective. * * * [C]ritics of Forest Service practices * * * now have a standard by which a court can judge the propriety of the sale." Timothy Pryor Mulhern, The National Forest Management Act of 1976: A Critical Examination, 7 B.C.Envt'l Aff.L.Rev. 99, 114 (1978). Its application is, however, complicated by the state of the forestry art: To take one example, the "rotation age for ponderosa pine on [on class of site] varies from 39 to 107 years, depending on the unit of measurement employed and the utilization standards assumed." Samuel Trask Dana & Sally Fairfax, FOREST AND RANGE POLICY 331 (2d ed. 1980). In Lamb v. Thompson, 265 F.3d 1038 (10th Cir.2001), the court held that a Forest Service decision to make an exception to CMAI must be subject to public participation. It went on to find that this requirement had not been met in the preparation of the forest plan before it, but was ultimately satisfied by a brief mention of the CMAI issue in an environmental assessment the Forest Service prepared on the particular timber sale being challenged.

6.   SUSTAINED YIELD AND THE CONCEPT OF NONDECLINING EVEN FLOW (NDEF)

In its broadest sense, sustained yield means only that the forest be managed so that timber can be produced in perpetuity. It does not tell us how much timber might be cut each year. Suppose, for example, a national forest has a managed, second-growth timber inventory of 100 million board feet, that the annual growth is 1 million board feet, and that the rotation cycle is 100 years. The "sustained yield" requirement could be met if all 100 million board feet were cut in 1990 and the ground were replanted, because the stand would regenerate and 100 million board feet would again be available for harvest in 2090. At that point, there could be another wholesale cut, and so on. The example is the extreme, but the same reasoning applies to a schedule of 50 million board feet twice a century, 10 million board feet every 10 years, and other variations. This has led some critics to describe "sustained yield" timber management as almost bereft of meaning. See, e.g., Richard Behan, Political Popularity and Conceptual Nonsense: The Strange Case of Sustained Yield Forestry, 8 Envt'l L. 309 (1978).

Nondeclining even flow is an awkward descriptor for the most conservative variant of sustained-yield management. It requires that the same level of harvest be maintained annually in perpetuity. Thus, in the example above, since annual growth is one million board feet and the rotation period is 100 years, the amount that can be removed annually forever is one million board feet per year.

Now suppose, instead of the hypothetical second-growth forest just described, a forest with a similar capacity for growth—with similar soil conditions, slopes, moisture, and exposure to sunlight—except that it is a virgin, old-growth forest. In the old-growth forest, with giant "overmature" trees, the timber inventory will be much greater and may approach, say, 500 million board feet on the same number of acres as the managed forest. Management of such old-growth stands in national forests in some areas of the Rocky Mountains and Pacific Northwest has been at the cutting edge of controversy between industry and environmentalists. If NDEF is *not* followed in this hypothetical old growth forest, and a conservative "conversion period" of 100 years is used to achieve a managed forest, then an accelerated harvest of 5 million board annually can be employed. Then, after 100 years, when the conversion period is completed and the old-growth is liquidated, the harvest must "fall down" to an average of 1 million board feet each year.

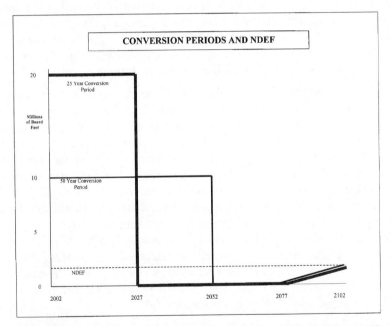

If NDEF is employed, the annual harvest of the old-growth stand cannot exceed the amount that can be produced annually in perpetuity, which cuts the annual yield to 1 mmbf. This conservative, level harvesting schedule means no fall-down in later years to disrupt local communities. But it also means that old-growth forests will be liquidated much more slowly. Indeed, in some cases, the numbers are such that there will always be a considerable amount of old growth in the forest. The computer modeling methods by which the formulae, economic projections, exceptions, and silvicultural assumptions are factored into the calculations are complex, and the method is less than an exact science. Almost everyone agrees, however, that application of NDEF results in significantly smaller present harvests of old-growth stands. On NDEF, see Marion Clawson, FORESTS; FOR WHOM AND FOR WHAT? 80–81 (1975); Samuel Trask Dana & Sally

Fairfax, FOREST AND RANGE POLICY 331–34 (2d ed. 1980); Symposium, Harvest Scheduling and the NFMA, 75 J. Forestry 699 (1977); Symposium, 8 Envt'l L. 239 (1978).

Using the above assumptions—an old-growth forest of 500 million board feet and annual growth of one million board feet—the following chart shows the difference between traditional harvests with 25 and 50–year "conversion periods" and NDEF. After the "fall downs" at 25 and 50 years, respectively, the forest will have been completely cleared, the annual harvest will be at zero, and local communities will likely be severely impacted. With NDEF, the annual harvest is far lower, but the forest will be essentially pristine and communities can depend on a low but reliable harvest.

The definition of "sustained yield" in the MUSY Act (which applies to all renewable resources, and not just timber) does not provide a crisp basis for choosing between these two extremes. It neatly straddles the issue by referring to "achievement and maintenance in perpetuity of a high-level *annual or regular periodic output * * *.*" 16 U.S.C. § 531(b). Congress set a considerably more rigorous standard as applied to timber in the NFMA, 16 U.S.C. § 1611, by codifying NDEF in this fashion:

> (a) The Secretary of Agriculture shall limit the sale of timber from each national forest to a quantity equal to or less than a quantity which can be removed from such forest annually in perpetuity on a sustained-yield basis: *Provided,* That, in order to meet overall multiple-use objectives, the Secretary may establish an allowable sale quantity for any decade which departs from the projected long-term average sale quantity that would otherwise be established: *Provided further,* That any such planned departure must be consistent with the multiple-use management objectives of the land management plan. * * * In addition, within any decade, the Secretary may sell a quantity in excess of the annual allowable sale quantity established pursuant to this section * * * [for] any national forest so long as the average sale quantities of timber from such national forest over the decade covered by the plan do not exceed such quantity limitation. * * *

> (b) Nothing in subsection (a) of this section shall prohibit the Secretary from salvage or sanitation harvesting of timber stands which are substantially damaged by fire, windthrow, or other catastrophe, or which are in imminent danger from insect or disease attack. The Secretary may either substitute such timber for timber that would otherwise be sold under the plan or, if not feasible, sell such timber over and above the plan volume.

Has Congress chosen NDEF in this language? The section begins with a pure NDEF formulation: The Forest Service cannot exceed a level of cut that can be removed "annually in perpetuity on a sustained-yield basis." But notice the qualifiers and exceptions. Do they swallow the rule set out before the first proviso? In the late 1970s, President Carter proposed a departure from NDEF for the 1980's to bring more lumber on the market to reduce housing costs as an inflation-fighting tool. Was that permitted under this language?

As of 2002, with the greatly reduced annual cut on the national forests, NDEF has much less significance than it did when the NFMA was enacted. Of course, if efforts are made to increase the harvest, NDEF will likely again play an important role.

7.   CLEARCUTTING

This harvesting practice, which triggered the *Monongahela* litigation that led to the National Forest Management Act, is one of three variants of what silviculturalists call "even-aged management." As applied to old growth forests, it aims at producing a new forest in which all of the trees in a given area will be of roughly the same age. The other two variants are the "seed tree" method, similar to clearcutting except that a few large trees per acre are left to provide seed for natural regeneration; and "shelterwood" or "shade tree" cutting, which leaves more trees per acre, usually to provide some filtered sunlight for the young trees. Seed tree and shelterwood cutting both eventually result in an even-aged forest because the veteran trees originally left standing are usually removed in an early second harvest. The "conversion period" is the period between the time when even-aged management in a given area begins and the time when harvesting of old-growth ends; at that point, the stand has been converted into a "managed forest."

Selective cutting, the other means of timber harvesting, differs from even-aged management in that it produces a diversified forest. Trees are removed individually or in small groups, and gradual harvesting continues over the entire rotation period.

Clearcutting often has economic advantages over selection harvesting. Yarding costs are lower; road engineering and construction costs are diminished (logging roads often must be improved or reconstructed after the passage of several years); and administrative costs of preparing sales are lower. Clearcutting also has some environmental advantages. Even-aged management can be conducted with a less extensive road system, thus causing less soil erosion. Further, large trees are subject to windthrow, or blowdown; selection cutting lessens protection and leaves the remaining trees vulnerable to wind damage. In addition, some animals such as deer, black bear, and ruffed grouse thrive on the sunlight and browse created by clearcuts. In some cases, clearcutting may prevent the spread of insects or disease. See generally CLEARCUTTING: A VIEW FROM THE TOP 126–48 (E. Horwitz, ed. 1974).

Moreover, some tree species in some climates cannot regenerate under a selection regime. The economically valuable Douglas fir, for example, is "shade-intolerant;" it cannot grow without direct sunlight. There are few young Douglas firs in old-growth forests. Without management, another species such as hemlock will become dominant; i.e., without clearcutting, no new Douglas fir forest will replace the old. Such forests may have depended upon cycles of fire to be reestablished under natural conditions.

Clearcutting also has prominent environmental disadvantages, some which remain long after the harvest. Beauty is subjective, but most agree that a clearcut area is an insult to the eye, an ugly practice that no amount of blending with the natural terrain can much change. The difference between a second-growth managed forest and a varied, virgin stand is, according to some, the difference between a tree farm and a cathedral. Beyond that, some argue that it is wrong to "prefer" one "valuable" species rather than letting the stand progress naturally to a climax stage. See generally Laurence Tribe, Ways Not to Think About Plastic Trees: New Foundations for Environmental Law, 83 Yale L.J. 1315 (1974).

Even-age management has serious impacts on wildlife and soil conditions. Species of birds, insects, bats, and small animals live in the old trees. Some forms of nitrogen-fixing bacteria, which provide essential nutrients for the soil, live only in dead or down timber. Ultimately, the productivity of the soil in old growth forests depends on the generations of trees that have rotted back into the earth. No forester can be certain of the long-range result if the process stops: it may take hundreds of years to learn the answer.

Clearcutting also has serious effects on water resources. The erosion can turn a pure mountain stream chocolate at the time of the cut and lesser erosion can continue in later years. Water temperature and runoff are affected: with no cover, snow will melt earlier in the season, increasing the spring flow and leaving unnaturally low and warm water in the summer and fall. Buffer zones and conservative clearcutting schedules can alleviate, though not eliminate, some of these conditions.

The drafters of the NFMA rejected a proposal that all clearcuts on national forest lands would be limited to 25 acres. Existing timber sale contracts calling for clearcutting were ratified, and 16 U.S.C. § 1604(g)(3)(F) provides that the regulations adopted by the Forest Service shall:

insure that [even-aged management shall be used] only where—

(i) for clearcutting, it is determined to be the optimum method, and for other such cuts it is determined to be appropriate, to meet the objectives and requirements of the relevant land management plan;

(ii) the interdisciplinary review as determined by the Secretary has been completed and the potential environmental, biological, esthetic, engineering, and economic impacts on each advertised sale area have been assessed, as well as the consistency of the sale with the multiple use of the general area;

(iii) cut blocks, patches, or strips are shaped and blended to the extent practicable with the natural terrain;

(iv) there are established according to geographic areas, forest types, or other suitable classifications the maximum size limits for areas to be cut in one harvest operation, including provision to exceed the established limits after appropriate public notice and review by the responsible Forest Service officer one level above the Forest Service officer who normally would approve the harvest proposal: *Provided,*

That such limits shall not apply to the size of areas harvested as a result of natural catastrophic conditions such as fire, insect and disease attack, or windstorm; and

(v) such cuts are carried out in a manner consistent with the protection of soil, watershed, fish, wildlife, recreation, and esthetic resources, and the regeneration of the timber resource.

Does this provision place significant limitations upon clearcutting? Are these limitations judicially enforceable? How might the agency go about showing that clearcutting is the "optimum" method of harvesting? Clearcuts must also comply with the provisions governing harvesting on all suitable lands. See § 1604(g)(3)(E), quoted supra at p. 723.

Since the adoption of the NFMA, the Forest Service has overhauled its clearcutting program. Many fewer clearcuts are used and, when they are, they are smaller and designed to eliminate the traditional square-cornered look in order to appear more natural (though even the most committed timber beast is likely to concede that a clearcut designed to look like a fire or a rock slide still looks mostly like a clearcut). In construing the "optimum method" NFMA language, the leading opinion on the subject found that Congress did not create a presumption against clearcutting. Sierra Club v. Espy, 38 F.3d 792 (5th Cir.1994), rejected arguments that clearcutting may be used only in "exceptional circumstances" and that clearcutting ought to be viewed as "an exception to the rule of uneven-aged management." While describing the Forest Service's discretion as "not unbridled," the court found that the agency's determination as to "the appropriate level of protection was not unreasonable."

See generally Federico Cheever, Four Failed Standards: What We Can Learn from the History of the National Forest Management Act's Substantive Timber Management Provisions, 77 Ore. L. Rev. 601 (1998); Jack Tuholske & Beth Brennan, The NFMA: Judicial Interpretation of a Substantive Environment Statute, 15 Pub.Lands L.Rev. 53 (1994); Kristen Potter, Judicial Review of Forest Service Decisions Made Pursuant to the National Forest Management Act's Substantive Requirements: Time for a Science Court?, 20 J.Natl. Assn. Of Admin.L.Judges 241 (2000); Susan Anderson et al., The National Forest Management Act: Law of the Forest in the Year 2000, 27 J.Land Res. & Envtl.L. 151 (2001).

8. The Binding Effect of Forest Plans

Neighbors of Cuddy Mountain v. United States Forest Service

United States Court of Appeals, Ninth Circuit, 1998.
137 F.3d 1372.

■ Fletcher, Circuit Judge:

* * * Plaintiffs seek to enjoin the Grade/Dukes timber sale in the Cuddy Mountain area of Payette National Forest (Payette) in Idaho. Plaintiffs are two not-for-profit groups, Neighbors of Cuddy Mountain and

Idaho Sporting Congress (collectively, Neighbors), who seek to protect the environment in the Cuddy Mountain area. Neighbors [contends, among other things,] * * * that the Forest Service failed to comply with the substantive requirements of the NFMA, and failed to comply with the procedural requirements of NEPA. The defendant is the Forest Service. Boise Cascade Corporation, the company that was awarded the Grade/Dukes timber contract, was allowed to intervene as a defendant.

The Forest Service began investigating the sale of timber from the Grade/Dukes area of Cuddy Mountain in the late 1980's. [An EIS was prepared in 1990 and a supplemental EIS was completed in 1994 in response to direction from the Deputy Regional Forester, acting on an administrative appeal from environmentalists. The final go-ahead to the sale was given in February 1994, administrative stays were denied, and 18.8 mmbf of timber was sold to Boise Cascade Corp. which began logging in August 1994. This suit was then commenced and the trial judge ruled for defendants.] * * *

The NFMA creates a statutory framework for the management of our national forests. It provides a two-step process for forest planning. The NFMA first requires the Forest Service to develop a Land Resource Management Plan (LRMP) and an EIS for the entire forest. Id.; 36 C.F.R. § 219.10(a), (b). A LRMP and EIS were prepared for Payette in May, 1988. Implementation of the LRMP occurs at the site-specific level. Thus, once the LRMP is in place, site-specific projects, such as the Grade/Dukes timber sale, are assessed by the Forest Service. Id.; 36 C.F.R. § 219.10(e). That assessment produced the two EIS's in the case at hand, as well as the supporting documents. * * * The NFMA imposes substantive requirements at both stages, such as the need to insure biological diversity.

A site-specific decision, such as one to sell timber, must be consistent with the LRMP for the larger area. 16 U.S.C. § 1604(i) ("Resource plans and permits, contracts, and other instruments for the use and occupancy of National Forest System lands shall be consistent with the land management plans."); 36 C.F.R. § 219.10(e).

* * * Neighbors is particularly concerned that the Grade/Dukes sale, alone and in combination with other timber sales in the Cuddy Mountain Roadless area, will greatly deplete the small amount of old growth habitat that remains in Payette. Old growth consists of the oldest trees in the forest, specifically, "mixed conifer, or grand-fir stand having: at least 15 trees/acre greater than 21 inches [Eds.: diameter at breast height], an average of .5 or more snags/acre greater than 21 DBH, two or more canopy levels, a canopy closure greater than 70 percent, and some trees with heart rot." Old growth is the exclusive habitat for a number of species within Payette.

Neighbors is also concerned with the impact of this sale on fisheries in the area. We agree that the Forest Service has violated the NFMA by failing to insure that the Grade/Dukes sale is consistent with the Payette LRMP * * *.

The Payette LRMP, developed in 1988, requires that a certain percentage of old growth habitat be retained in Payette. A number of species in Payette rely on old growth habitat, including the pileated woodpecker, flammulated owl, great gray owl, and northern goshawk. The pileated woodpecker is the "management indicator species" for old growth habitat. A management indicator species "is used as a bellwether ... for the other species that have the same special habitat needs or populations characteristics." Inland Empire, 88 F.3d at 762 n. 11. Thus, by studying the result of the sale on the habitat for the pileated woodpecker, the Forest Service can estimate the effect of the sale on other old growth-dependent species. See 36 C.F.R. § 219.19(a)(1).

With regard to the specific percentage of old growth that must be retained in Payette, the Payette LRMP states:

> Retain a minimum of 5 percent old growth or mature forest, of which 2.5 percent must be old growth habitat as defined by Thomas (1979), within each theoretical pileated woodpecker home range as described in the Forest planning documentation files. When insufficient old growth is provided from areas considered not appropriate or not suited for timber production, suited timber areas will be used to satisfy old growth habitat requirement. Old growth stands must be at least 30 acres in size.

Payette National Forest Land and Resource Management Plan (May 1988) (emphasis added).

Thus, to prove that the Grade/Dukes sale would be consistent with the Payette LRMP, the Forest Service should have shown that after the sale, there would be at least 5/2.5 percent of old growth "within each theoretical pileated woodpecker home range." The Forest Service has failed to do so. In fact, the Forest Service provides no information whatsoever regarding how many woodpecker home ranges there are within the sale area, or how many home ranges would be affected by the timber sale.[4] Having failed to do so, it certainly could not have demonstrated that after the sale, a sufficient percentage of old growth would remain in each affected pileated woodpecker home range. Instead, the Forest Service recited the results of a survey[5] to the effect that after the sale, there will be at least 5/2.5 percent of old growth in the Grade/Dukes sale area as a whole. In its final SEIS, the Forest Service stated:

> The proposed sale area contains 430 acres of forest meeting Forest Plan old-growth definitions, approximately 14% of the total timbered acres in the analysis area. The Forest Plan states that a minimum of

---

4. We do know from the Payette National Forest Eight–Year Monitoring Report (July, 1996), that there are 42 home ranges within the entire forest, and that each range is approximately 10 miles in diameter. The Eight–Year report was not part of the administrative record prepared for the Grade/Dukes sale as the report was prepared after the sale had been approved.

5. We note that the Forest Service provided only a cursory description of its survey of old growth in the sale area, and has at no time provided the actual survey results. It is impossible to determine the exact geographic scope of the survey, and whether the survey evaluated pileated woodpecker home ranges as it should have.

5% of the total timbered acres (in an analysis area) must be retained as old-growth with at least one-half meeting the Forest Plan definition of old-growth, with the other one-half being in a mature/overmature condition.

Following the harvest, the Proposed Alternative would retain 136 acres of forest in an old-growth condition; however, 57 acres of that is a partially fragmented vein which is not representative of a 30 acre block as suggested by the Forest Plan. Therefore, the actual old-growth remaining in the analysis area would be 79 acres, or slightly greater than the Forest Plan minimum of 75 acres.

1994 SEIS (internal references omitted) (emphasis added). The "analysis area" appears to be the Grade/Dukes sale area, and not the woodpecker home range(s), as required. Indeed, in quoting from the Payette LRMP, the Forest Service inexplicably deleted from that portion of the statement describing the percentage of old growth that must be retained, the phrase that specifies the geographic scope that must be analyzed, i.e., the pileated woodpecker home range. Thus, the Forest Service did not comply with the requirements of the LRMP in so far as the Forest Service evaluated the "analysis area" rather than the "home range" of the pileated woodpecker. As such, it did not demonstrate that the Grade/Dukes project would be consistent with the Payette LRMP, and thus it failed to comply with the NFMA. * * *

NOTES AND QUESTIONS

1. In Cronin v. U.S. Dept. of Agriculture, 919 F.2d 439 (7th Cir.1990), recreationists sought to stop a timber sale on a 660 acre tract in Shawnee National Forest in southern Illinois and argued, among other things, that the sale violated the applicable forest plan. Judge Posner's opinion contained the following:

[The applicable plan] authorizes "uneven-aged management" [in this area of the proposed sale] where necessary to achieve certain specified objectives, including "visual quality objectives," a euphemism for not too unsightly. Uneven-aged management can take the form of either cutting down individual trees or clearing small patches. The latter method is called "group selection"—a more informative name would be "clear-cutting at retail"—and has not been used before in the Shawnee National Forest.

* * * [The Forest Supervisor then approved group selection logging] on patches ranging from one-quarter acre to two acres in size scattered throughout the * * * area; added together the patches would come to 26 acres. * * * [The forest supervisor's written decision approving the project found the proposal consistent with the forest plan] because group selection is necessary to achieve the management plan's visual quality objectives. The decision does not say this in so many words, but the implication is unmistakable. Group selection is said to have been chosen because it "responds to public concerns about the effects of clearcutting on* * * forest services," and clear-cutting rejected be-

cause it "would not meet the established visual quality objectives of partial retention." * * * He could have said this more clearly, but a reviewing court may—without violating the rule of SEC v. Chenery Corp., 332 U.S. 194 (1947) against the court's supplying a rationale for the agency's decision—"uphold a decision of less than ideal clarity if the agency's path may reasonably be discerned." [citations omitted] That undemanding standard is satisfied here—especially when allowance is made for the fact that the decision is that of a local forest supervisor rather than of the members of a sophisticated agency in Washington. * * *

The plaintiffs read the plan to say that if the Service does not want to use clear-cutting it must demonstrate that group selection will make the forest look better than individual-tree selection or no logging at all. This of course would be an impossible burden, because a forest does not look better with bald patches than without. We read the plan differently, as did the forest supervisor * * *. We read it to say that clear-cutting is permissible throughout [the area in question] * * * *unless* the results would be too unsightly (fail to achieve "visual quality objectives"), in which event the Service can authorize a less unsightly form of logging, such as group selection. The plan authorizes clear-cutting * * * [and if] the Forest Service decides to authorize a less unsightly form of logging than the clear-cutting that it is allowed to authorize, this does not violate the plan. * * *

As for the plaintiffs' argument that [the plan] did not contemplate *widespread* use of group selection and that 26 acres out of 661 is widespread, the second half of this argument is a good deal more persuasive than the first. Depending on the precise scatter of the patches throughout the * * * area, they could well give it a scarred, ragged appearance that would justify calling the use of group selection "widespread" throughout the area. Since the patches are as small as a quarter of an acre, there could be dozens of them in what is after all little more than one square mile. But the management plan would have authorized the Forest Service to clear the whole area, and we find nothing in the plan to limit the amount of group selection that can be substituted for clear-cutting for the sake of visual quality, feebly as that quality may seem to be served by the substitution.

2. In Ecology Center, Inc. v. U.S. Forest Service, 192 F.3d 922 (9th Cir.1999), plaintiffs sought a court order requiring the Forest Service to comply with the requirements of the applicable forest plan to "produce annual, biannual and five-year reports containing monitoring data helpful for the Forest Service to make 'periodic determinations and evaluations of the effects of management practice.' " The Forest Service published reports on its monitoring activities, but did not do so every year. The court rejected the challenge, finding that the plaintiffs had not met either test of "final agency action" under the Administrative Procedure Act. 5 U.S.C. §§ 702, 704. Specifically, they had not showed that monitoring under the plan was an "action that marks the culmination of a decision making process;" instead, it was merely a step leading to an agency decision on management.

Second, "although the Forest Service's monitoring duty is mandatory under the Plan, legal consequences do not necessarily flow from that duty, nor do rights or obligations arise from it. See *Ohio Forestry* [supra p. 295]." Finally, the court rejected the argument that the Forest Service's alleged failure to carry out monitoring was "agency action unlawfully withheld or unreasonably delayed" under the APA, 5 U.S.C. § 706(1):

> The record demonstrates that the Forest Service performed extensive monitoring and provided detailed reports recounting its observations. The Forest Service merely failed to conduct its duty in strict conformance with the Plan and NFMA Regulations. Were we to hold the Forest Service liable under [the APA] for each oversight, we would discourage the Forest Service from producing ambitious forest plans.

3.   Are these plans, which are mostly written by generalists or Forest Service planners who are not lawyers, the equivalent of statutes or regulations? They do go through a notice and comment process, and typically are accompanied by NEPA compliance, in a manner similar to a regulation. Do the same principles of interpretation apply to them and their text, which is mostly written in narrative form? If so, would you advise agencies to have lawyers fly-speck the plans (which can run hundreds of pages) to qualify language appropriately to try to avoid being caught in "gotcha" litigation? (Typically, agency lawyers do not review plans before they are released.) Would that convert the planning process into something else, less useful? Or if plans are to be legally binding, is that the inevitable result?

9.   REVISION OF THE FOREST SERVICE PLANNING REGULATIONS

The Clinton Administration undertook two major rulemaking efforts involving the national forests—a revision of the Forest Service Planning Regulations, discussed here, and the roadless area initiative, which is taken up in the following section.

The planning regulations implement the NFMA and, as such, control or implicate a great amount of decisionmaking within the Forest Service. The agency produced its original regulations in 1979 with (as required by a distinctive provision of the NFMA) the advice of a Committee of Scientists. The 1979 regulations succeeded in breaking new ground in one major respect by including the diversity provisions (see pp. 726–29, supra) that laid the foundation for the long journey toward protection of the Northern spotted owl and the old-growth forests it inhabits.

By the late 1980s, there was widespread agreement that the Forest Service planning system needed to be overhauled. Planning had become too time-consuming and expensive, too dependent upon computer programming for setting the timber cut, too unresponsive to public input, and too-little-used—the plans, once all the effort to formulate them had been expended, mostly took up shelf space. Several efforts in the early and mid–1990s to amend the planning regulations bore no fruit. In 1997, Agriculture Secretary Glickman appointed a new Committee of Scientists to make recommendations. In 2000, the Forest Service issued new planning regulations based substantially on the Committee of Scientists report. See 36 C.F.R. Part 219 (2002).

The new planning regulations addressed a wide range of issues including public participation, increasing efficiency, relating to Indian tribes on a government-to-government basis, and collaborative decisionmaking. Probably the most important (and the most controversial) provisions involved the extensive use of scientific principles, including rigorous requirements of monitoring and evaluation; the incorporation of ecological principles, including acknowledging uncertainty and disturbances; restoration of degraded lands; and independent scientific review. The two most divisive issues involved ecological sustainability and species viability.

The Forest Service planning regulations go beyond other versions of sustainability, which is often defined as the objective of sustaining, for future generations, ecological, economic and social values. The regulations give primacy to one of the three components—ecological sustainability:

> The first priority for planning to guide management of the National Forest System is to maintain or restore ecological sustainability of national forests and grasslands to provide for a wide variety of uses, values, products, and services. The benefits sought from these lands depend upon long-term ecological sustainability. Considering increased human uses, it is essential that uses of today do not impair the functioning of ecological processes and the ability of these natural resources to contribute to sustainability in the future.

36 C.F.R. § 219.2. Giving primacy to ecological sustainability has received extensive criticism, centering on the belief that it departs from the Forest Service's multiple use statutory mandate and will deflate the production of commercial products from the national forests. See, e.g., Dan Quinn, The U.S. Forest Service at a Crossroads, 137 Resources 12 (Fall, 1999). Supporters of the ecological sustainability approach believe that healthy national forest ecosystems can and will produce many economic and social benefits—and that such benefits of necessity depend upon the integrity of the water, soil, vegetation, and air that healthy ecosystems provide. Refining the idea of sustainability in this way, they believe, gives an edge to the doctrine and offers guidance to land managers in a way that a policy like multiple use-sustained yield never can.

Species diversity is the driving force for measuring ecological sustainability, and national forest management, under the new regulations. Current scientific knowledge is not yet at the stage when it can accurately assess the integrity of whole ecosystems. More is known, however, about biological diversity. Of the different aspects of biological diversity—ecosystem, species, and genetic—the most is known about species diversity. Although the previous regulations already contained strict diversity provisions, see 36 C.F.R. secs 219.19 and 219.27 (1984), pp. 737–38, supra, the requirements of the current regulations are far more extensive. Section 219.20(b)(2), which is just one element of an elaborate five-page ecological sustainability section, begins as follows:

Plan decisions affecting species diversity must provide for ecological conditions that the responsible official determines provide a high likelihood that those conditions are capable of supporting over time the viability of native and desired non-native species well distributed throughout their ranges within the plan area. . . .

The Bush Administration considers the 2000 regulations to be burden-some or impossible to administer and that the emphasis on ecological sustainability is bad policy. In 2001, the administration announced that it intends to promulgate revised planning regulations; in the meantime, forest supervisors can do their planning according to either the 2000 regulations or those previously in force. See 66 Fed. Reg. 27552–01, 27555–01 (May 17, 2001). On the adoption of the 2000 regulations, see Charles Wilkinson, A Case Study in the Intersection of Law and Science: The 1999 Report of the Committee of Scientists, 42 Ariz L.Rev. 307 (2000).

QUESTIONS

1.   Does the Forest Service have the authority to promulgate regula-tions providing that ecological sustainability is the "first priority" in the national forests? The NFMA explicitly retains the multiple-use mandate, directing the agency to "provide for multiple use and sustained yield of the products and services obtained [from the national forests] in accordance with the Multiple–Use Sustained Yield Act of 1960." 16 U.S.C. § 1604(e)(1). Arguably, the 2000 regulations fly in the face of the MUSY Act, which at least in common usage has stood for a commitment to the extractive uses. On the other hand, MUSY itself is premised on a notion of sustainability and the NFMA states as a matter of policy that Forest Service management should "meet the requirements of our people in perpetuity." 16 U.S.C. § 1600(7). Further, the national forests must be managed according to many other statutes, including NEPA, the Clean Water Act, the Clean Air Act, and the ESA, all of which can be described as consistent with sustainability. In *Sierra Club v. Marita*, page 726, supra, the court ruled that existing law does not require the Forest Service to manage the National Forests in accordance with the science of conservation biology. The 2000 regulations, including the emphasis on species diversity, are rife with conservation biology. Does the *Marita* reasoning mean that the Forest Service exceeded its authority by relying so heavily on conserva-tion biology? Or are these matters left to the discretion of the Forest Service under the *Chevron* rule (see page 318, supra)?

2.   Should the national forests be managed according to ecological sustainability with a heavy emphasis on biodiversity, especially species diversity? Or do the 2000 regulations call for too much science? Should these decisions be left to Congress rather than the Forest Service?

10.   THE NATIONAL FOREST ROADLESS INITIATIVE

The Clinton Administration undertook a major initiative in national forest management which had implications for timber production. The concept was to do a national rule that would preempt (or effectively amend) all national forest plans and lay down a few general rules about how more than 58 million acres (or 30%) of the national forest system would be managed. The principal rules in such areas would be no roadbuilding and no timber harvesting. The rule was adopted through Administrative Procedure Act notice-and-comment rulemaking, accompanied by an environmental impact statement under NEPA (referred to as FEIS in the materials that follow). In examining this material, consider the following:

1.   What policy arguments are made for keeping roadless areas roadless? Is this purely an environmental issue? Spiritual? Economic?

2.   If the main focus is to stop further roadbuilding, why is timber harvesting also prohibited? Is that prohibition adequately justified in the preamble?

3.   Is the policy in this rule consistent with multiple use principles? Why or why not?

4.   A key question is whether such decisions should be made at the local level (by individual national forests) or at the national level. How well does the rule preamble make the case for action at the national level? What are the arguments for keeping it local?

Preamble and Final Roadless Area Rule (Excerpts)

66 Fed. Reg. 3244 (January 12, 2001).

SUMMARY: The Department of Agriculture is adopting this final rule to establish prohibitions on road construction, road reconstruction, and timber harvesting in inventoried roadless areas on National Forest System lands. The intent of this final rule is to provide lasting protection for inventoried roadless areas within the National Forest System in the context of multiple-use management. * * *

Purpose and Need for the Roadless Area Conservation Rule

The Department of Agriculture is responsible for managing National Forest System resources to sustain the health, diversity, and productivity of the nation's forests and grasslands to meet the needs of present and future generations. * * * In the future, expanding urban areas and increased fragmentation of private lands make it likely that the largest and most extensive tracts of undeveloped land will be those in public ownership.

This final rule prohibits road construction, reconstruction, and timber harvest in inventoried roadless areas because they have the greatest likelihood of altering and fragmenting landscapes, resulting in immediate, long-term loss of roadless area values and characteristics. Although other activities may also compromise roadless area values, they resist analysis at the national level and are best reviewed through local land management planning. Additionally, the size of the existing forest road system and attendant budget constraints prevent the agency from managing its road system to the safety and environmental standards to which it was built. Finally, national concern over roadless area management continues to generate controversy, including costly and time-consuming appeals and litigation. This final rule addresses these needs in the context of a national rulemaking.

Roadless Area Values and Characteristics

Inventoried roadless areas considered in this rule constitute roughly one-third of all National Forest System lands, or approximately 58.5 million acres. Although the inventoried roadless areas comprise only 2% of the land base in the continental United States, they are found within 661 of the over 2,000 major watersheds in the nation (FEIS Vol. 1, 3–50) and provide many social and ecological benefits.

As urban areas grow, undeveloped private lands continue to be converted to urban and developed areas, and rural infrastructure (such as roads, airports, and railways). An average of 3.2 million acres per year of forest, wetland, farmland, and open space were converted to more urban uses between 1992 and 1997. In comparison, 1.4 million acres per year were developed between 1982 and 1992. The rate of land development and urbanization between 1992 and 1997 was more than twice that of the previous decade, while the population growth rate remained fairly constant (FEIS Vol. 1, 3–12). In an increasingly developed landscape, large unfragmented tracts of land become more important. * * *

The following values or features often characterize inventoried roadless areas (FEIS Vol. 1, 3–3 to 3–7):

High quality or undisturbed soil, water, and air. These three key resources are the foundation upon which other resource values and outputs depend. Healthy watersheds catch, store, and safely release water over time, protecting downstream communities from flooding; providing clean water for domestic, agricultural, and industrial uses; helping maintain abundant and healthy fish and wildlife populations; and are the basis for many forms of outdoor recreation.

Sources of public drinking water. National Forest System lands contain watersheds that are important sources of public drinking water. Roadless areas within the National Forest System contain all or portions of 354 municipal watersheds contributing drinking water to millions of citizens. Maintaining these areas in a relatively undisturbed condition saves downstream communities millions of dollars in water filtration costs. Careful management of these watersheds is crucial in maintaining the flow and affordability of clean water to a growing population.

Diversity of plant and animal communities. Roadless areas are more likely than roaded areas to support greater ecosystem health, including the diversity of native and desired nonnative plant and animal communities due to the absence of disturbances caused by roads and accompanying activities. Inventoried roadless areas also conserve native biodiversity by serving as a bulwark against the spread of nonnative invasive species.

Habitat for threatened, endangered, proposed, candidate, and sensitive species and for those species dependent on large, undisturbed areas of land. Roadless areas function as biological strongholds and refuges for many species. Of the nation's species currently listed as threatened, endangered, or proposed for listing under the Endangered Species Act, approximately 25% of animal species and 13% of plant species are likely to have habitat within inventoried roadless areas on National Forest System lands. Roadless areas support a diversity of aquatic habitats and communities, providing or affecting habitat for more than 280 threatened, endangered, proposed, and sensitive species. More than 65% of all Forest Service sensitive species are directly or indirectly affected by inventoried roadless areas. This percentage is composed of birds (82%), amphibians (84%), mammals (81%), plants (72%), fish (56%), reptiles (49%), and invertebrates (36%).

Primitive, Semi–Primitive Non–Motorized, and Semi–Primitive Motorized classes of dispersed recreation. Roadless areas often provide outstanding dispersed recreation opportunities such as hiking, camping, picnicking, wildlife viewing, hunting, fishing, cross-country skiing, and canoeing. While they may have many Wilderness-like attributes, unlike Wilderness the use of mountain bikes, and other mechanized means of travel is often allowed. These areas can also take pressure off heavily used wilderness areas by providing solitude and quiet, and dispersed recreation opportunities.

Reference landscapes. The body of knowledge about the effects of management activities over long periods of time and on large landscapes is very limited. Reference landscapes of relatively undisturbed areas serve as a barometer to measure the effects of development on other parts of the landscape.

Natural appearing landscapes with high scenic quality. High quality scenery, especially scenery with natural-appearing landscapes, is a primary reason that people choose to recreate. In addition, quality scenery contributes directly to real estate values in nearby communities and residential areas.

Traditional cultural properties and sacred sites. * * *

Fiscal Considerations

The Department is also concerned about building new roads in inventoried roadless areas, when there presently exists a backlog of about $8.4 billion in deferred maintenance and reconstruction on the more than 386,000 miles of roads in the Forest Transportation System. * * * The agency receives less than 20% of the funds needed annually to maintain the existing road infrastructure. As funding needs remain unmet, the cost of fixing deteriorating roads increases exponentially every year. Failure to maintain existing roads can also lead to erosion and water quality degradation and other environmental problems and potential threats to human safety. It makes little fiscal or environmental sense to build additional roads in inventoried roadless areas that have irretrievable values at risk when the agency is struggling to maintain its existing extensive road system (FEIS Vol. 1, 1–5 and 3–22). The National Forest System was founded more than 100 years ago to protect drinking water supplies and furnish a sustainable supply of timber. Neither objective is fully achievable given the present condition of the existing road system. The risks inherent in building new roads in presently roadless areas threaten environmental, social, and economic values.

Development activities in inventoried roadless areas often cost more to plan and implement than on other National Forest System lands. Some planned timber sales in inventoried roadless areas are likely to cost more to prepare and sell than they realize in revenues received. Because of the level of public controversy and analytical complexity, projects in roadless areas often require development of costly environmental impact statements for most resource development activities, including timber harvesting, in inventoried roadless areas. In some cases, road construction costs are higher due to rugged terrain or sensitive ecological factors. Many development projects in inventoried roadless areas are appealed or litigated. These factors contribute to generally higher costs for the agency to plan and implement development activities in inventoried roadless areas.

National Direction vs. Local Decisionmaking

At the national level, Forest Service officials have the responsibility to consider the "whole picture" regarding the management of the National Forest System, including inventoried roadless areas. Local land management planning efforts may not always recognize the national significance of inventoried roadless areas and the values they represent in an increasingly developed landscape. If management decisions for these areas were made on a case-by-case basis at a forest or regional level, inventoried roadless areas and their ecological characteristics and social values could be incrementally reduced through road construction and certain forms of timber harvest. Added together, the nation-wide results of these reductions could be a substantial loss of quality and quantity of roadless area values and characteristics over time.

* * * [The Forest Service has twice conducted nationwide inventories and reviews of roadless areas] to determine their suitability for inclusion in the National Wilderness Preservation System. * * * Additional reviews have been conducted through the land management planning process and other large-scale assessments. The 58.5 million acres of inventoried roadless areas used as the basis for this analysis were identified from the most recent analysis for each national forest or grassland, including RARE II, land and resource management planning, or other large-scale assessments such as the Southern Appalachian Assessment.

Of the 58.5 million acres of inventoried roadless areas considered in the FEIS, approximately 34.3 million acres have prescriptions that allow road construction and reconstruction. The remaining 24.2 million acres are currently allocated to management prescriptions that prohibit road construction; however, protections in these existing plans may change after future forest plan amendments or revisions.

Over the past 20 years, roads have been constructed in an estimated 2.8 million of those 34.3 million acres of inventoried roadless areas. The agency anticipates that the trend of building roads in inventoried roadless areas will gradually decrease in the future even without this rule due to economic and ecological factors already discussed, changes in agency policy, increasing controversy and litigation, and potential listings under the Endangered Species Act. While these anticipated changes may reduce some of the impact to inventoried roadless areas, they would not eliminate the future threat to roadless area values (FEIS Vol. 1, 1–14 to 1–15).

On many national forests and grasslands, roadless area management has been a major point of conflict in land management planning. The controversy continues today, particularly on most proposals to harvest timber, build roads, or otherwise develop inventoried roadless areas. The large number of appeals and lawsuits, and the extensive amount of congressional debate over the last 20 years, illustrates the need for national direction and resolution and the importance many Americans attach to the remaining inventoried roadless areas on National Forest System lands (FEIS Vol. 1, 1–16). These disputes are costly in terms of both fiscal resources and agency relationships with communities of place and communities of interest. Based on these factors, the agency decided that the best means to reduce this conflict is through a national level rule. * * *

[The public comment process on the rule was described. It involved hundreds of public meetings and hundreds of thousands of responses, as well as more than 1 million postcards or other form letters. Some responses to comments follow.]

* * * These comments can be divided into two basic and very different perspectives (FEIS Vol. 1, 1–8 to 1–9). One perspective is that decisions concerning management of inventoried roadless areas should be left to the local responsible official, without national intervention. The other perspective is that national prohibitions on road construction, reconstruction, and timber harvest in inventoried roadless areas, along with a stop to other activities, must occur from a national level, as local decisionmaking does not always reflect the national significance of the issues involved. The agency considered and attempted to balance both perspectives throughout this rulemaking. * * *

Issues Raised by Those Opposed to Prohibitions. This group indicated that inventoried roadless areas should remain available for road construction and reconstruction to obtain resources, to provide increased motorized recreation opportunities, and for other uses. These individuals expressed the viewpoint that roadless areas, with active and prudent management, could support both intrinsic benefits and commodity uses, and that local responsible officials should make management decisions on inventoried roadless areas. This group also indicated that environmental concerns should not take precedence over human needs and desired uses, and that maintaining a healthy environment should not preclude resource production, motorized access, and developed recreation opportunities.

Many members of this group also stated that conservation requires active management, such as providing roads for: thinning forest vegetation, insect and disease treatment, commodity resource production, hazardous fuels reductions, and the development of recreation facilities. They stressed that the failure to actively manage forests and grasslands could result in insect infestations and uncharacteristic wildfire effects, and asserted that prudent management would benefit people and wildlife. They expressed concern for the impact this rule would have on future generations that would not be able to participate in a lifestyle that is dependent on resource use and production. They said that if future generations would not be able to access the land, they would not value the land.

Issues Raised by Those Who Favor Prohibitions. These respondents indicated that they viewed forestlands as whole ecosystems and that they thought roadless areas should be conserved for their intrinsic values and for esthetic benefits to humans. In their view, roadless areas should be allowed to evolve naturally through their own dynamic processes, although some proponents agreed with the need for limited stewardship activity. This second group stressed that human desire for commodity production should take second place to needs for a healthy environment (both locally and globally), for quiet natural places, for spiritual and psychological regeneration, and to meet the needs of other living things. They indicated that the social and economic needs of forest-dependent users could be met through job retraining, through development of alternative materials, and by designating already developed areas for motorized recreation and other ground-disturbing activities.

Most of the respondents in this second group maintained that the proposed rule did not prohibit enough development activities. They stated that the final rule should immediately ban timber harvest, other commodity production, and motorized recreation from roadless areas 1,000 acres or larger, and that the agency should not defer conservation of roadless areas to future land management planning processes. They also stressed that the Tongass National Forest should be included in this conservation effort, an issue that the agency specifically requested comment on in the DEIS. Many respondents in this group expressed a desire that future generations receive the benefits of clean air and water, habitat adequate to assure species diversity, and other social and ecological values provided by inventoried roadless areas.

Issues Raised by Federal, Tribal, State and Local Public Officials. * * * Many public officials from States and counties concerned about access to and across National Forest System lands and concerned about forest dependent communities expressed strong opposition to the proposed rule, citing negative economic impacts to these communities and commodity production industries, as well as negative impacts to rural lifestyles. Access to State-owned lands and impacts to statutory rights-of-way across public lands were major concerns as well. In general, those Western States with the greatest roadless acreage (for example, Idaho, Montana, Nevada, Utah, and Wyoming) tended to generate the greatest number of negative comments from Governors, agencies, and officials. Public officials from areas with larger urban populations generally supported the proposed rule because of their expressed desire for recreation opportunities, protection of water quality, and undisturbed landscapes. * * *

Comment on Multiple–Use. Some respondents commented that the proposed rule did not provide for multiple-use of inventoried roadless areas, since resources cannot always be accessed and developed without roads and, therefore, for example, forest health issues could not be addressed.

Response. The Multiple–Use Sustained–Yield Act of 1960 (MUSYA) provides the Forest Service authority to manage national forest and grasslands "for outdoor recreation, range, timber, watershed, and wildlife and fish purposes." The NFMA reaffirmed multiple-use and sustained-yield as the guiding principles for land management planning of National Forest System lands (16 U.S.C. 1600, 1604).

In defining "multiple use," the MUSYA, as amended, clearly provides that under multiple-use management some land will be used for less than all of the possible resource uses of the national forests and grasslands. The act also provides that even the establishment of wilderness areas is consistent with the purposes and provisions of the act. The Roadless Area Conservation rule, unlike the establishment of wilderness areas, will allow a multitude of activities including motorized uses, grazing, and oil and gas development that does not require new roads to continue in inventoried roadless areas.

Currently, a wide range of multiple uses is permitted in inventoried roadless areas subject to the management direction in forest plans. A wide range of multiple uses will still be allowable under the provisions of this rule. The National Forest System contains an extensive system of roads measuring approximately 386,000 miles. This final rule will not close or otherwise block access to any of those roads; the final rule merely prohibits the construction of new roads and the reconstruction of existing roads in inventoried roadless areas. * * *

Comments on Effect on Fire Suppression. Numerous respondents expressed concern with the effect of a road construction prohibition on fire fighter safety and access to suppress wildland fires.

Response. Proposed § 294.12(b)(1) allowed road construction and reconstruction in inventoried roadless areas when a road is needed to protect public health and safety in cases of an imminent threat of flood, fire, or other catastrophic event. In addition, using such suppression resources as smokejumpers and fire crews delivered by helicopters, the current fire suppression organization has been effective in suppressing at a small size approximately 98% of wildland fire starts in inventoried roadless areas. The agency also typically prioritizes fighting roadless and wilderness fires lower than fighting fires in more accessible and populated areas. The Agency has a long history of successfully suppressing fires in inventoried roadless areas and this high level of suppression performance is expected to continue. Furthermore, the agency rarely builds new roads to suppress fires. Building roads into inventoried roadless areas would likely increase the chance of human-caused fires due to the increased presence of people. Fire occurrence data indicates that prohibiting road construction and reconstruction in inventoried roadless areas would not cause an increase in the number of acres burned by wildland fires or in the number of large fires (FEIS Vol. 1, 3–115). * * *

[The following is part of the summary of proposed changes in final rule:] Final section 294.13. Prohibition on timber cutting, sale, or removal in inventoried roadless areas. The final rule adds a new prohibition on timber harvesting (the cutting, sale, or removal of timber): except for clearly defined, limited purposes; when incidental to the implementation of an activity not otherwise prohibited by this rule; for personal and administrative uses; or where roadless characteristics have been substantially altered in a portion of an inventoried roadless area due to the construction of a classified road and subsequent timber harvest. Both the road construction and subsequent timber harvest must have occurred after an area was designated an inventoried area. Even though this provision was not in the proposed rule, the DEIS analyzed timber harvesting prohibition alternatives for public comment and the FEIS identified a preferred alternative that included both timber harvesting and road construction prohibitions. Therefore, the public had sufficient opportunity to comment on this provision and there is adequate information to make a reasoned and informed decision. * * *

Forest Dependent Communities. Impacts to forest dependent communities were a major issue among those who commented on the proposed rule and DEIS. * * * [The rule] could reduce future timber harvest, mineral exploration and development, and other activities such as ski area development in inventoried roadless areas. Communities with significant economic activities in these sectors could be adversely impacted. However, the effects on national social and economic systems are minor. For example, the total timber volume affected by this rule is less than 0.5 percent of total United States production, and the total oil and gas production from all National Forest System lands is currently about 0.4 percent of the current national production. * * *

Some of [the areas the rule would make unavailable for new mineral leasing] are not currently available for leasing, as a result of leasing decisions or local forest * * * plan decisions. Moreover, current access restrictions would make many of these resources unavailable in the near future. In addition, the steep terrain that is typical of many inventoried roadless areas often makes these areas difficult to access for environmental and/or economic reasons. The likelihood of resources being recovered from inventoried roadless areas even in the absence of a final roadless rule is small, except where leases already exist. * * * To reduce the economic impacts of this decision, the Chief of the Forest Service will seek to implement one or more of the following provisions of an economic transition program for communities most affected by application of the prohibitions in inventoried roadless areas:

(1) Provide financial assistance to stimulate community-led transition programs and projects in communities most affected by application of the prohibitions in inventoried roadless areas;

(2) Through financial support and action plans, attract public and private interests, both financial and technical, to aid in successfully implementing local transition projects and plans by coordinating with other Federal and State agencies; and

(3) Assist local, State, Tribal and Federal partners in working with those communities most affected by the final roadless area decision. * * *

[Timber production impacts were treated as follows:] The prohibition on road construction, reconstruction, and timber harvest except for clearly defined, limited purposes would reduce development of roaded access to resources within inventoried roadless areas compared to the baseline. Roads are required for most timber sales to be economically feasible. For those sales that are financially profitable, the rule would reduce net revenues. In addition to lost revenue, there would be an estimated immediate impact of 461 fewer timber jobs and 841 total jobs, with an associated annual loss of $20.7 million in direct income and $36.2 million in total income. In the longer term, an additional 269 timber jobs and 431 total jobs could be affected from harvest reductions on the Tongass National Forest. The longer-term income effect was estimated at $12.4 million in direct income and $20.2 million in total income. A reduction in the timber program could also affect about 160 Forest Service jobs, with an additional 100 jobs affected on the Tongass in the longer term.

Jobs associated with road construction and reconstruction for timber harvest and other activities would also be fewer than under the baseline. Initially, between 43 and 51 direct jobs and between 88 and 104 total jobs could be affected by reduced road construction and reconstruction. An additional 39 direct jobs and 78 total jobs could be affected by harvest reductions on the Tongass National Forest in the longer term.* * *

New roads have the potential to reduce current operating costs for other users, for example grazing permittees and collectors of non-timber forest products, by allowing faster and easier access. These potential cost reductions would not be realized if road construction is prohibited. The agency, however, builds few roads for recreation, grazing, or collection of non-timber forest products, and this pattern is unlikely to change. New roads built for other purposes may provide additional access for recreationists, including hunters and anglers. Prohibiting construction of new roads would have minimal impacts on these groups, since all temporary roads and many of the other planned roads would be closed once the intended activity is concluded. Therefore, the number of additional road miles that would be available for recreational or other uses would be small.

Opportunities for some types of recreation special uses may be limited in the future. Developed recreation use and road-based recreation uses in general are more likely to occur at higher densities outside of inventoried roadless areas than under the baseline, since expansion into inventoried roadless areas would not occur. However, roads are rarely constructed into inventoried roadless areas for recreation purposes. The development of new ski areas within inventoried roadless areas would be unlikely. Other, new non-recreation special uses may be limited in the future as well. Such special uses include communication sites and energy-related transmission uses (such as ditches and pipelines, and electric transmission lines).

There could be a slight increase in the risk from uncharacteristic wildland fire or insect and disease as a result of reduced opportunities for forest health treatments. However, the Forest Service would likely treat few acres of inventoried roadless areas regardless of the issuance of the Roadless Rule, since moderate and high risk forests in inventoried roadless areas would be given a low priority for treatment, unless there was an imminent threat to public safety, private property, water quality, or threatened and endangered species. While overall fire hazard can still be reduced without roads, restricted road access would likely increase the cost of treatments, which would result in fewer acres treated. Some fuel treatment techniques available under the baseline would not be economically or logistically feasible. Of the 14 million acres in inventoried roadless areas identified as potentially requiring fuel treatment, 6.5 million could still be treated with prescribed fire without mechanical pretreatment. The use of timber harvest for fuel management would be limited to those activities that reduce uncharacteristic wildfire effects through the cutting, sale, or removal of small diameter timber that maintains or improves one or more of the roadless characteristics. For the next five years, about 22,000 acres could be treated by the limited timber harvest allowed under the final rule. Although this is a significant decline in treatment acres compared to acres that would have been harvested under the baseline, the total acreage affected is less than 1 percent of all inventoried roadless area that potentially require mechanical pretreatment. * * *

The effect of the final rulemaking on small governmental jurisdictions is tied to possible reductions in commodity outputs in cases where some portion of federal receipts is returned to the states for distribution to counties, and to changes in the jurisdiction's economic base from changes in employment and business opportunities related to National Forest System outputs and management. Payments to states from timber receipts will be unaffected by the final Roadless Rule through 2006 because the "Secure Rural Schools and Community Self–Determination Act of 2000" was signed into law on October 30 (Pub. L. 106–393). This legislation allows counties to select a payment based on historic payment levels rather than payments based on current receipts. However, this legislation does not affect revenue sharing of federal receipts from mineral leasing on national grasslands and from public domain lands of the national forests. Therefore, the final rule may result in a reduction in those receipts in the future, which would affect revenues shared with states and counties. The agency has also chosen to pursue funds to assist communities undergoing economic transition resulting from implementation of the final Roadless Rule. Such assistance could include financial assistance to stimulate community-led transition programs and projects, support to attract public and private interests in implementing local transition projects, coordination with other Federal and State agencies, and assisting local, State, Tribal, and Federal partners to work with the most affected communities. The Forest Service will pursue a six-year economic transition program. The Economic Adjustment Program will be used to fund or support projects that will be specific to the needs of individual communities and important to the national forest or grassland. The Forest Service anticipates requesting $72.5 million in support of these activities between fiscal years 2001 and 2006. * * *

[The regulations themselves were very short. Key provisions follow.]

§ 294.12 Prohibition on road construction and road reconstruction in inventoried roadless areas.

(a) A road may not be constructed or reconstructed in inventoried roadless areas of the National Forest System, except as provided in paragraph (b) of this section.

(b) Notwithstanding the prohibition in paragraph (a) of this section, a road may be constructed or reconstructed in an inventoried roadless area if the Responsible Official determines that one of the following circumstances exists:

(1) A road is needed to protect public health and safety in cases of an imminent threat of flood, fire, or other catastrophic event that, without intervention, would cause the loss of life or property;

(2) A road is needed to conduct a response action under the Comprehensive Environmental Response, Compensation, and Liability Act (CERCLA) or to conduct a natural resource restoration action under CERCLA, Section 311 of the Clean Water Act, or the Oil Pollution Act;

(3) A road is needed pursuant to reserved or outstanding rights, or as provided for by statute or treaty;

(4) Road realignment is needed to prevent irreparable resource damage that arises from the design, location, use, or deterioration of a classified road and that cannot be mitigated by road maintenance. Road realignment may occur under this paragraph only if the road is deemed essential for public or private access, natural resource management, or public health and safety;

(5) Road reconstruction is needed to implement a road safety improvement project on a classified road determined to be hazardous on the basis of accident experience or accident potential on that road;

(6) The Secretary of Agriculture determines that a Federal Aid Highway project, authorized pursuant to Title 23 of the United States Code, is in the public interest or is consistent with the purposes for which the land was reserved or acquired and no other reasonable and prudent alternative exists; or

(7) A road is needed in conjunction with the continuation, extension, or renewal of a mineral lease on lands that are under lease by the Secretary of the Interior as of January 12, 2001 or for a new lease issued immediately upon expiration of an existing lease. Such road construction or reconstruction must be conducted in a manner that minimizes effects on surface resources, prevents unnecessary or unreasonable surface disturbance, and complies with all applicable lease requirements, land and resource management plan direction, regulations, and laws. Roads constructed or reconstructed pursuant to this paragraph must be obliterated when no longer needed for the purposes of the lease or upon termination or expiration of the lease, whichever is sooner. * * *

§ 294.13 *Prohibition on timber cutting, sale, or removal in inventoried roadless areas.*

(a) Timber may not be cut, sold, or removed in inventoried roadless areas of the National Forest System, except as provided in paragraph (b) of this section.

(b) Notwithstanding the prohibition in paragraph (a) of this section, timber may be cut, sold, or removed in inventoried roadless areas if the Responsible Official determines that one of the following circumstances exists. The cutting, sale, or removal of timber in these areas is expected to be infrequent.

(1) The cutting, sale, or removal of generally small diameter timber is needed for one of the following purposes and will maintain or improve one or more of the roadless area characteristics as defined in § 294.11.

(i) To improve threatened, endangered, proposed, or sensitive species habitat; or

(ii) To maintain or restore the characteristics of ecosystem composition and structure, such as to reduce the risk of uncharacteristic wildfire effects, within the range of variability that would be expected to occur under natural disturbance regimes of the current climatic period; * * *

§ 294.14   Scope and applicability.

(a) This subpart does not revoke, suspend, or modify any permit, contract, or other legal instrument authorizing the occupancy and use of National Forest System land issued prior to January 12, 2001.

(b) This subpart does not compel the amendment or revision of any land and resource management plan. * * *

(e) The prohibitions and restrictions established in this subpart are not subject to reconsideration, revision, or rescission in subsequent project decisions or land and resource management plan amendments or revisions undertaken pursuant to 36 CFR part 219.

(f) If any provision of the rules in this subpart or its application to any person or to certain circumstances is held invalid, the remainder of the regulations in this subpart and their application remain in force.

The rule was scheduled to take effect on March 12, 2001, but upon taking office the Bush Administration promptly extended its effective date until May 12, 2001, to allow it time to review the rule. Some eight lawsuits were filed in various jurisdictions by a variety of opponents of the new rule. The first court to exercise review was Federal District Judge Lodge in Idaho. In April he stayed the effect of the rule, finding various procedural shortcomings. Kootenai Tribe v. Veneman, 142 F.Supp.2d 1231 (D.Idaho 2001), Idaho ex rel. Kempthorne v. U.S. Forest Service, 142 F.Supp.2d 1248 (D.Idaho 2001). The two decisions were virtually identical, and both focused primarily on NEPA compliance. The court first rejected the argument of environmentalist intervenors that no EIS was required for the Roadless Rule because it did not "commit resources to some affirmative human development of the environment, does not change existing environmental conditions, and does not alter the environmental status quo." The court concluded that the rule, "in changing or limiting existing active management in the national forest, drastically alters the current status quo * * * by preventing the enactment of land management techniques that provide for road construction, reconstruction or timber harvesting, despite recommendations of local officials * * *." The court also held that the plaintiffs had a likelihood of succeeding on their claim that the government had not considered a reasonable range of alternatives in its NEPA analysis, that the public comment process was inadequate, and that the EIS failed to adequately analyze the cumulative impacts of the proposal. A few weeks later the court enjoined implementation of the rule until the problems it found were cured. Kootenai Tribe v. Veneman, 31 Envtl.L.Rep. 20,617, 2001 WL 1141275 (D.Idaho 2001). Intervenor environmental groups, but not the United States, appealed to the Ninth Circuit, where it is pending as of this writing.

Instead, the Bush Administration reopened public comment on the policy and later issued additional directives and published them for public comment. See 66 Fed. Reg. 35918; 44111; 65796 (2001). The expectation is that the idea of a national rule of roadless area policy will continue to be a lively topic of political and legal debate for some time.

NOTES AND QUESTIONS

1.   Is it a misuse of NEPA for opponents of roadless area protection to argue that its procedures should be strictly followed, so as to throw out a rule that has stronger environmental protection as its goal?

2.   Strategically, was it wise for the environmentalist intervenors to argue that NEPA did not apply here at all, because the proposal did not change the status quo in roadless areas? Might it, if accepted, create a precedent undesirable for environmental interests in the long run? That is, usually environmentalists advocate expanding the coverage of NEPA; here they are arguing the opposite. Suppose a license for an environmentally destructive dam comes up for renewal. Can the dam operator argue that NEPA doesn't apply because renewal will not change the status quo?

3.   The Chief summarized the current state of affairs this way in the summer of 2001 (66 Fed. Reg. 35918):

> The Forest Service has been evaluating roadless areas for nearly 30 years. Decisions about how to manage inventoried roadless areas have been difficult and controversial. * * * The National Forest System is comprised of 192 million acres, which is 8.5 percent of the total land base of the United States. Within the National Forest System, there are currently 34.7 million acres of Wilderness, 58.5 million acres of inventoried roadless area, and 4.2 million acres of areas in Congressional designations other than Wilderness that are not included in the inventoried roadless areas, such as Wild and Scenic Rivers or National Recreation Areas. The remaining 94.9 million acres includes roaded and other non-inventoried unroaded areas. The January 12, 2001, roadless rule applies only to the inventoried roadless areas * * *. All of the 58.5 million acres of inventoried roadless areas were considered for

their potential as wilderness during the RARE II process. For a variety of reasons, most were not recommended for designation as Wilderness. For instance, other areas in comparison had greater wilderness values or more public support, or other resource potentials were believed to outweigh the area's contribution to the national wilderness system. Most of these areas still retain their natural characteristics and vary in importance for primitive types of recreation, pristine scenic quality, important fish and wildlife habitats, contributions to biological diversity, watershed protection, other natural values, and, in some cases, resource development options.

Approximately 2.8 million acres (4.8 percent) of inventoried roadless areas have undergone resource development in the form of road construction, timber harvest, mining, or recreational development during the last 30 years. Of the total inventoried roadless area acreage, current forest plans assign 24.2 million acres to roadless or non-development management prescriptions and 34.3 million acres are in prescriptions that allow road construction. In the latter category, there are about 9 million acres of productive timberland, and about 25 million acres are not suitable for timber production.

The [Final EIS] estimated that less than two-tenths of one percent of the total of inventoried roadless areas (94,600 acres of 58.5 million acres) might be developed between 2000 and 2004. * * *

4. Examine the overall statistics concerning how many acres of the national forest system are in what kind of roadless condition, and what their management status is. What does that suggest about how big an issue this whole roadless area controversy is? Might one say it's just about a relatively few acres in the overall system? The facts would suggest, for example, that many, perhaps most of the roadless acres will remain roadless for the foreseeable future, regardless of what policy is followed. (Only 5% of the areas inventoried as roadless in 1970 have been "developed" in some form in the last thirty years. Only 9 million of the 34 million roadless acres that were open to road construction have "productive" timberland.) Is this a tempest in a teapot? What are some arguments that it is not?

5. How much discretion does the Bush Administration have here in moving forward? Could it abandon the entire effort to craft a national policy, and go back to a forest-by-forest decisionmaking process on roadlessness? Do the supporters of more roadless area protection at the national level have any legal recourse at this point?

6. Does the Administration's call for more public comment on these various questions moot the appeal?

7. Where is Congress in all of this brouhaha over a national rule? Why hasn't it played more of a role? The issue of wilderness protection for these national forest and other roadless areas on the federal lands is discussed in Chapter 12, infra pp. 1131–40.

C. TIMBER MANAGEMENT ON BLM LANDS: THE O & C ACT

Most of the lands managed by the BLM do not support large holdings of commercial timber. BLM timber sales in fiscal 2000 totaled only about 73 million board feet producing revenues of about 14 million dollars. PUBLIC LANDS STATISTICS 2000, Table 3–12. Timber on these lands is managed by the BLM primarily pursuant to its multiple use/sustained yield mandate in FLPMA, although NEPA, the Endangered Species Act, and other environmental statutes apply. BLM is not, however, subject to the requirements of the NFMA or the RPA. See generally George Cameron Coggins and Robert Glicksman, PUBLIC NATURAL RESOURCES LAW § 20.46 (2001).

But BLM does manage some highly productive timber lands, retrieved by the United States after being conveyed for construction of the Oregon & California Railroad from near Sacramento to Portland. Delays in constructing the Oregon portion of the line and the failure of the railroad to abide by its obligation to sell the granted land to settlers led eventually to the forfeiture of the grant. Nearly 3 million acres of timber-rich lands were returned into federal ownership, to be managed by the BLM. In 1937, Congress enacted the O & C Lands Act (O & CLA) to govern their management, and until the last few years they have supported a large quantity of commercial timber production. As recently as fiscal 1990, about 1.1 billion board feet was harvested from them, producing about $370 million in revenue.

During the 1990s the O & C lands came under scrutiny as part of the reassessment of Pacific Northwest forest timber management triggered primarily by endangered species concerns, first the northern spotted owl and more recently, salmon. As a result of the Northwest Forest Plan, timber harvesting on O & C lands in FY 2000 totaled only about 61 million board feet, and about $12.5 million in revenue.

Because the applicable management standard in the 1937 O & CLA differs from that applicable on the national forests, a brief discussion is useful for comparison. The core governing statute, 43 U.S.C. § 1181a, is an interesting amalgam of resource management principles:

> [The O & C lands] shall be managed * * * for permanent forest production, and the timber thereon shall be sold, cut, and removed in conformity with the principal [sic] of sustained yield for the purpose of providing a permanent source of timber supply, protecting watersheds, regulating stream flow, and contributing to the economic stability of local communities and industries, and providing recreational facilties [sic] * * * Provided, That timber from said lands in an amount not less than one-half billion feet board measure, or not less than the annual sustained yield capacity when the same has been determined and declared, shall be sold annually, or so much thereof as can be sold at reasonable prices on a normal market.

Headwaters, Inc. v. BLM, Medford District

United States Court of Appeals, Ninth Circuit, 1990.
914 F.2d 1174.

■ WALLACE, CIRCUIT JUDGE.

[Environmental plaintiffs challenged a BLM timber sale, primarily on NEPA and FLPMA grounds. The court rejected the challenge. Part of the timber sold was on O & C lands, leading to the following discussion.]

* * * Headwaters contends that the O & C Act requires the BLM to manage these lands for multiple use, including wildlife conservation, rather than for the dominant use of timber production.

We have previously observed that "[t]he provisions of 43 U.S.C. § 1181a make it clear that the primary use of the [O & CLA] lands is for timber production to be managed in conformity with the provision of sustained yield." O'Neal v. United States, 814 F.2d 1285, 1287 (9th Cir.1987); see also Skoko v. Andrus, 638 F.2d 1154, 1156 (9th Cir.) (Skoko) (The O & C Act "provided that most of the O & C lands would henceforth be managed for sustained-yield timber production."), cert. denied, 444 U.S. 927 (1979).

While these statements are arguably dicta, we are convinced of their accuracy. * * *

* * * Headwaters argues that the phrase "forest production" in section 1181a encompasses not merely timber production, but also conservation values such as preserving the habitat of the northern spotted owl. However, Headwaters's proposed use—exempting certain timber resources from harvesting to serve as wildlife habitat—is inconsistent with the principle of sustained yield. As the statute clearly envisions sustained yield harvesting of O & C Act lands, we conclude that Headwaters's construction is untenable. There is no indication that Congress intended "forest" to mean anything beyond an aggregation of timber resources.

Nor does the legislative history support Headwaters's reading. The purposes of the O & C Act were twofold. First, the O & C Act was intended to provide the counties in which O & C Act land was located with the stream of revenue which had been promised but not delivered by the Chamberlain—Ferris Revestment Act, 39 Stat. 218 (1916). See Skoko, 638 F.2d at 1156. The counties had failed to derive appreciable revenue from the Chamberlain—Ferris Act primarily because the lands in question were not managed so as to provide a significant revenue stream; the O & C Act sought to change this. Id. Second, the O & C Act intended to halt previous practices of clear-cutting without reforestation, which was leading to a depletion of forest resources.

> All land classified as timber in character will continue in Federal ownership and be managed for permanent forest production on what is commonly known as a sustained-yield basis. Under such a plan the amount of timber which may be cut is limited to a volume not exceeding new growth, thereby avoiding depletion of the forest capital. This type of management will make for a more permanent type of

community, contribute to the economic stability of local dependent industries, protect watersheds, and aid in regulating streamflow.

H.R.Rep. No. 1119, 75th Cong., 1st Sess. 2 (1937). This report concludes that the O & C Act "establishes a vast, self-sustaining timber reservoir for the future." Id. at 4.

It is entirely consistent with these goals to conclude that the O & C Act envisions timber production as a dominant use, and that Congress intended to use "forest production" and "timber production" synonymously. Nowhere does the legislative history suggest that wildlife habitat conservation or conservation of old growth forest is a goal on a par with timber production, or indeed that it is a goal of the O & C Act at all. The BLM did not err in construing the O & C Act as establishing timber production as the dominant use. * * *

NOTES AND QUESTIONS

1.   Does the court correctly construe the O & CLA? May the BLM decide *not* to harvest some commercial timber on these lands in order to protect watersheds? Recreation? Wildlife? Note the first of these is stated in the Act; the second is mentioned (in the context of "recreational facil[i]ties"); and the third is not mentioned. Does the principal case here provide clear answers to these questions? Compare the construction of the similar but not identical 1897 Forest Service Organic Act in United States v. New Mexico, Chapter 6, supra p. 521.

2.   Although FLPMA's multiple use provisions apply to the O & C lands, a savings clause in FLPMA (§ 701(b)) provides that the O & CLA "shall prevail" to the extent there is any "conflict with or inconsistency between [FLPMA and the O & CLA] * * * insofar as [the O & CLA] relate[s] to management of timber resources * * *." Does the savings clause shed any light on the answers to the questions in note 1?

3.   *Headwaters* was not to be the last word on the subject. In Portland Audubon Society v. Lujan, 795 F.Supp. 149 (D.Or.1992), aff'd sub nom. Portland Audubon Society v. Babbitt, 998 F.2d 705 (9th Cir.1993) the court rejected BLM's argument that NEPA compliance would interfere with § 1181(a) of the O & CLA, which BLM interpreted to require it to sell a minimum of 500 million board feet annually. The court found that the Act did not mandate a minimum amount for annual sale, and did not exempt BLM from NEPA compliance. It also noted that BLM conceded that the Endangered Species Act "must be enforced despite any adverse effects upon the amount of timber available on O & C lands." In affirming, the Ninth Circuit found that the "plain language of the O & CLA supports the district court's conclusion that the Act has not deprived the BLM of all discretion with regard to either the volume requirements of the Act or the management of the lands entrusted to its care." 998 F.2d at 709. Then in Seattle Audubon Society v. Lyons, 871 F.Supp. 1291 (W.D.Wash.1994), aff'd sub nom Seattle Audubon Society v. Moseley, 80 F.3d 1401 (9th Cir.1996), Judge Dwyer had to address the O & CLA in the course of upholding the legality of the Northwest Forest Plan prepared by the Clinton Administra-

tion, because that Plan put a substantial amount of O & C lands off limits to timber harvesting. The court rejected the argument that the O & CLA was a constraint:

> [T]he Secretary of the Interior has, and for many years has exercised, broad authority to manage the O & CLA lands; the BLM is steward of these lands, not merely a regulator. Management under O & CLA must look not only to annual timber production but also to protecting watersheds, contributing to economic stability, and providing recreational facilities. * * *
>
> [The federal decision document on its Forest Plan noted that a] forward-looking land management policy would require that federal lands be managed in a way to minimize the need to list species under the ESA. Additional species listings could have the effect of further limiting the O & C Lands Act's goal of achieving and maintaining permanent forest production. This would contribute to the economic instability of local communities and industries, in contravention of a primary objective of Congress in enacting the O & C Lands Act. That Act does not limit the Secretary's ability to take steps now that would avoid future listings and additional disruptions. * * * The management decision made here in regard to the O & CLA lands was a lawful exercise of the Secretary's discretion.

The Ninth Circuit affirmed in a relatively brief opinion without addressing this issue. Neither here nor in the *Portland Audubon Society* case did the Ninth Circuit explain the different reading of the O & C Act from its earlier decision in *Headwaters*. Professor Michael Blumm and Jonathan Lovvorn conclude that

> BLM's management of the O & C lands enjoy[s] no special exemption from federal environmental laws. Despite the Headwaters court's interpretation of the O & C Act as a dominant-use statute, and regardless of any effects on the agency's ability to maintain a high level of timber production, the BLM must manage the O & C lands for non-timber uses when required to do so by federal environmental laws like NEPA and the ESA. Although the BLM's management of the O & C lands is still technically based on the O & C Act, the operation of the Northwest Forest Plan has almost completely preempted the application of the 1937 statute.

The Proposed Transfer of BLM Timber Lands to the State of Oregon: Environmental and Economic Questions, 32 Land & Water L.Rev. 353 (1997).

5. Various proposals have been made over the years to reconfigure federal landholdings in Western Oregon, including some that would divest the BLM of control of the O & C lands. The latest proposals were made by timber advocates as a result of the restrictions imposed by the Northwest Forest Plan. Blumm and Lovvorn review the history and the latest proposal, and conclude that it is "neither economically nor environmentally sound."

CHAPTER 9

THE RANGE RESOURCE

Livestock grazing has been a source of controversy over management of vast tracts of federal lands for a very long time. Early contests pitted cattlemen (and women) against sheepherders (see Omaechevarria v. Idaho, supra p. 130) and farmers (sodbusters) against ranchers. Early in the twentieth century, the young U.S. Forest Service took very modest steps to bring the livestock grazing industry on national forests under some regulation, leading to landmark legal opinions in *Grimaud* and *Light*, supra pp. 107–10. After the livestock industry acquiesced in the Taylor Grazing Act in 1934, western resentment toward federal regulation of livestock grazing led to a spirited (and to some observers, downright mean) attempt by Senator Pat McCarran of Nevada to starve the then-infant Bureau of Land Management into submission in the late 1940s, an episode recounted in E. Louise Peffer's masterly account, THE CLOSING OF THE PUBLIC DOMAIN, 247 et ff. (1951).

In modern times the disputes are between ranchers and recreationists or conservationists. Determining how many head of cattle or sheep will be allowed to graze where on the federal lands remains a volatile resource allocation issue, because livestock grazing can significantly impact other uses and values of the federal lands. Cattle ranching is at the core of the "western" self-image of rugged independence and self-reliance; an image burned on the national consciousness (it has a "great myth," one critic once wryly noted). The argument thus marks a great cultural and political divide, and was a major underlying cause of the Sagebrush Rebellion of the late 1970s and the County Supremacy movement of the 1990s.

Acre for acre, livestock grazing is in fact the most widespread extractive use of the federal lands, being found on more than a quarter of a *billion* acres, or a land area 2 ½ times that of the State of California. It is concentrated (and this chapter focuses primarily) on about 158 million acres of federal lands managed by the BLM, almost all in the eleven western states of the lower forty-eight. Some 18,000–19,000 ranchers and farmers hold BLM-issued grazing leases and permits; collectively, these authorized around 10 million "animal unit months" (AUMs)* of forage harvesting. Grazing is also an important use of some 100 million acres of the national forests, with about 12,000 ranchers and farmers authorized to use about four million AUM's on these lands. In total, then, some 25,000 ranchers and farmers use the federal lands (about 5000 hold permits to

---

* An AUM is the amount of forage eaten by one cow or five sheep or goats grazing for one month, or about 750–800 pounds of grass.

graze livestock on both BLM and Forest Service lands).**

While the number of acres involved is vast, the amount of meat produced is, compared to total national production, quite small. Federal land graziers comprise fewer than 10% of the total number of livestock producers in the western states, and about 2% of the cattle producers in the country. Federal lands grazing provides about 7% of beef cattle *forage* nationally, and about 2% of the total *feed* consumed by beef cattle in the Nation.

Exact numbers on total number of permittees, acres, animal unit months, and meat production traceable to federal lands grazing vary somewhat according to source. Part of the difficulty of making precise calculations is that many livestock forage on public lands only part of the year, or part of their lives; for example, about one-third of the beef cattle found in the western states graze at least part of the year on federal rangelands. A useful review of the various statistics, both historically and today, is found in Debra L. Donahue, THE WESTERN RANGE REVISITED 250–63 (1999). What all the statistics show, however, is clear: While federal rangelands can be important locally and even regionally, they play a small role in national meat production. In 1994, the Department of the Interior described the effects of eliminating grazing (the "No grazing" alternative) on all federal lands this way:

> No Grazing would affect about 8 percent of the beef cattle inventory in the 11 western states, and 2.4 percent of the beef cattle inventory in the 17 (including Texas) western states, and 0.8 percent of the sheep inventory in the 11 western states.

> Employment and income impacts would be minor relative to the total westwide economy. In agriculture, impacts would be relatively greater. But, in the long term, continued growth of employment and income in other industries would tend to offset [these impacts]. [Elsewhere, the EIS estimated a total loss of 18,300 jobs in agriculture and related industries, about 1 percent of total agricultural employment, and less than a tenth of one percent of total westwide employment.]

> The effect on beef prices of eliminating grazing on public lands would be slight. * * * In the long term, a 1 percent decrease in national cattle inventory could result in about a 1 percent increase in retail beef prices. But this price could be negated by an increase in the national cattle inventory.

Department of the Interior, Rangeland Reform (draft EIS, 1994), 4–118 to 4–121.

Range conditions in parts of the west are poor, and have long been so. Most of the lands now managed by the BLM were never very productive of vegetation, being mostly arid or semi-arid, with poor soil, and some with rugged terrain and some with short growing seasons. Those same factors

---

** Livestock grazing is permitted in some wildlife refuges (subject to the "compatibility" test discussed at pp. 873–87 infra). Previously established livestock grazing may be grandfathered in place in some wilderness areas (see pp. 116–17 infra) and some national park system areas.

make them even more vulnerable to overuse, and render restoration that much more difficult. As a result, over the decades, many public land grazing areas have suffered serious environmental insult. Erosion has depleted the sparse topsoil, streams have been scoured and fouled, deep arroyos have been created in some areas, "bad" plant species such as mesquite and sagebrush and exotic, non-native grasses have gained dominance, and the native grasses had declined in vigor and prevalence or simply disappeared. Regulation has in some cases stemmed the decline in the condition of the public lands, and, together with efforts of individual ranchers, has even promoted instances of local improvements. But long decades of heavy grazing use has taken its toll, so that today much of BLM's grazing lands bear little resemblance vegetatively to "potential natural, or climax" plant communities. See, e.g., PUBLIC LAND STATISTICS 2000, Table 2–1 (only 5% of lands surveyed have 76–100% similarity to such conditions; about half have less than 50% similarity, with 17% "unclassified"). BLM's surveys of riparian-wetland areas show similar results; i.e., only 40% of the areas surveyed are considered to be in "proper functioning condition." *Id.*, Table 2–2.

Meanwhile, demands for other uses and values of federal lands are increasing. Some ranchers are responding by working to make their operations more compatible with these new imperatives, but conflicts remain. Polarization remains all too common in range politics, as it has been for a century, with heated rhetoric overshadowing rational debate on preferred directions of public rangeland management. The following two excerpts— one from a cattlemen's association representative and the other from an outspoken gadfly—illustrate the diversity of views. First, from Ron Michieli, Response to "Role of Land Treatments on Public and Private Lands," in DEVELOPING STRATEGIES FOR RANGELAND MANAGEMENT 1421 (1984):

> In addition to cattle production, [the nation's cattlemen] are interested, as conservationists, in fish and wildlife, improved water quality, erosion control, and aesthetics. The cattlemen often do not get credit for the contributions they make to such benefits which accrue to the general public. The cost-benefit ratio of public range management programs considers only the animal production value. The non-livestock values—the side benefits, if you will—are not accounted for in the cost-benefit analysis of public range management programs. This is so even though these programs include requirements and restrictions intended to enhance nonlivestock benefits and these requirements and restrictions impose extra costs on the livestock users as well as on the government itself.
>
> * * * [T]he grazing of rangelands can have positive influences on the vegetative and soil resources, rather than all negative impacts in uncontrolled situations, which are occurring less today. Some positive impacts of grazing * * * include:
>
> • Grazed plants are often more productive than those ungrazed.
>
> • Grazing reduces excessive accumulation of dead vegetation and mulch that may inhibit new growth.

- Grazing tramples seed into the ground.

There are many examples that rangelands properly used can maintain or improve the plant communities. There are also examples which show that prolonged nonuse can result in range deterioration as surely as overuse will. I believe that today we now all realize there are many ways to improve rangelands other than reduction in cattle numbers.

The rangelands of this nation, public and private, are a valuable national resource. They must receive the appropriate consideration by the users of such resource, including the general public. As one of the prime users, the nation's cattlemen are hopeful that their story will be heard and fully considered.

The late Edward Abbey had a much different take on the subject, colorfully expressed in Even the Bad Guys Wear White Hats, HARPER'S (Jan. 1986), at 51:

There are some Western cattlemen who are nothing more than welfare parasites. They've been getting a free ride on the public lands for over a century, and I think it's time we phased it out. I'm in favor of putting the public lands livestock grazers out of business.

First of all, we don't need the public lands beef industry. Even beef lovers don't need it. According to most government reports (Bureau of Land Management, Forest Service), only about 2 percent of our beef, our red meat, comes from the eleven Western states. * * * More than twice as many beef cattle are raised in the state of Georgia than in the sagebrush empire of Nevada. And for a very good reason: back East, you can support a cow on maybe half an acre. Out here, it takes anywhere from twenty-five to fifty acres. In the red rock country of Utah, the rule of thumb is one section—a square mile—per cow.

Since such a small percentage of the cows are produced on public lands in the West, eliminating that industry should not raise supermarket beef prices very much. Furthermore, we'd save money in the taxes we now pay for various subsidies to these public lands cattlemen. Subsidies for things like "range improvement"—tree chaining, sagebrush clearing, mesquite poisoning, disease control, predator trapping, fencing, wells, stock ponds, roads. Then there are the salaries of those who work for government agencies like the BLM and the Forest Service. You could probably also count in a big part of the salaries of the overpaid professors engaged in range-management research at the Western land-grant colleges.

Moreover, the cattle have done, and are doing, intolerable damage to our public lands—our national forests, state lands, BLM-administered lands, wildlife preserves, even some of our national parks and monuments. * * *

Overgrazing is much too weak a term. Most of the public lands in the West, and especially in the Southwest, are what you might call "cowburnt." Almost anywhere and everywhere you go in the American West you find hordes of these ugly, clumsy, stupid, bawling, stinking, fly-covered, shit-smeared, disease-spreading brutes. They are a pest and a plague. They pollute our springs and streams and rivers. They infest our canyons, valleys, meadows, and forests. They graze off the native bluestem and grama and bunch grasses, leaving behind jungles of prickly pear. They trample down the native forbs and shrubs and cactus. They spread the exotic cheat grass, the Russian thistle, and the crested wheat grass. *Weeds*.

Even when the cattle are not physically present, you'll see the dung and the flies and the mud and the dust and the general destruction. If you don't see it, you'll smell it. The whole American West stinks of cattle. Along every flowing stream, around every seep and spring and water hole and well, you'll find acres and acres of what range-management specialists call "sacrifice areas"—another understatement. These are places denuded of forage, except for some cactus or a little tumbleweed or maybe a few mutilated trees like mesquite, juniper, or hackberry.

Considering the magnitude of the resource and the philosophical polarization, there was relatively little litigation or legislation directly aimed at livestock grazing on federal lands through the first three quarters of the twentieth century (other than the Taylor Grazing Act in 1934, discussed in Chapter 2, pp. 129–37 supra). This chapter examines federal rangeland management in two stages: before and after passage of the Federal Land Policy and Management Act in 1976.

A.   Pre–FLPMA Grazing: The Common Law and the Taylor Grazing Act

Until passage of the Taylor Grazing Act, ranchers could argue with considerable precedent and persuasiveness that they had permission, if not a "right," to run their herds on the public lands. Congress had never legislated otherwise, state law encouraged full and free use of the federal lands, and the U.S. Supreme Court had noted that congressional acquiescence in local practices conferred an implied license to graze that prevailed until federal legislation decreed otherwise.

Free grazing brought ranchers west, and they built their operations around it. The Homestead Act and other disposal statutes were used to obtain fee title to "base property" of 160, 320, or 640 acres, typically on bottom land on or near a creek, and water rights would be established for stockwatering, growing hay to see their livestock through the winters, and subsistence farming. In many sectors of the arid west, however, the grass is so scarce that a spread could not be profitable unless it encompassed several hundred or even several thousand acres. Some early settlers therefore selected their fee lands based on the availability of large tracts of nearby federal grazing land. In fact, the publicly owned grazing acres used by many western ranchers are many multiples of the land these ranchers own in fee. It is common in some parts of the west for a single ranch to have permits or leases to use BLM lands, state lands (often checkerboarded with BLM and, to a lesser extent, national forest lands), and national forest lands. Livestock may spend harsher winter months on lower elevation (often BLM) lands, and spend summer months foraging on higher elevation (often national forest) lands once the snow melts. Their use of (and dependency on access to) the federal lands led many ranchers to regard their permits or leases as giving them permanent, alienable, and inheritable property interests that could not, or at least should not, be diminished by governmental action.

The judiciary recognized that livestock owners had an implied license to use the public domain, extending so far as to give them a license to cross the lands of others to get there. In Buford v. Houtz, 133 U.S. 320 (1890), cattlemen owned 350,000 acres interspersed throughout an area of nearly one million acres, the rest of which was public land. They sought to enjoin sheepherders from trespassing on their own lands to reach the public lands. In holding that plaintiffs' bill failed for want of equity because the relief sought would allow plaintiffs to monopolize grazing on the public lands, the Court commented:

> We are of opinion that there is an implied license, growing out of the custom of nearly a hundred years, that the public lands of the United States, especially those in which the native grasses are adapted to the growth and fattening of domestic animals, shall be free to the people who seek to use them where they are left open and unenclosed, and no act of government forbids this use. For many years past a very large proportion of the beef which has been used by the people of the United States is the meat of cattle thus raised upon the public lands without charge, without let or hindrance or obstruction. The government of the United States, in all its branches, has known of this use, has never forbidden it, nor taken any steps to arrest it. No doubt it may be safely stated that this has been done with the consent of all branches of the government, and, as we shall attempt to show, with its direct encouragement. * * *

> The value of this privilege grew as the population increased, and it became a custom for persons to make a business or pursuit of gathering herds of cattle or sheep, and raising them and fattening them for market upon these unenclosed lands of the government of the United States. Of course the instances became numerous in which persons purchasing land from the United States put only a small part of it in cultivation, and permitted the balance to remain unenclosed and in no way separated from the lands owned by the United States. All the neighbors who had settled near one of these prairies or on it, and all the people who had cattle that they wished to graze upon the public lands, permitted them to run at large over the whole region, fattening upon the public lands of the United States, and upon the unenclosed lands of the private individual, without let or hindrance. The owner of a piece of land, who had built a house or enclosed twenty or forty acres of it, had the benefit of this universal custom, as well as the party who owned no land. Everybody used the open unenclosed country, which produced nutritious grasses, as a public common on which their horses, cattle, hogs and sheep could run and graze.

In that sparsely settled country, where the presence of government was minimal, abuses of and conflicts under the implied license were rampant. Judicial efforts to curb appropriation of the public lands for exclusive private use were largely unavailing. See Valerie Weeks Scott, The Range Cattle Industry: Its Effect on Western Land Law, 28 Mont.L.Rev. 155 (1967).

The open (if implied) invitation to use the forage on the public domain gave rise to a classic example of the "tragedy of the commons." As no controls or costs were imposed, it was in each rancher's private self-interest to run as many head as possible on the "free" range before somebody else did. The inevitable consequence was severe overgrazing and degradation of the forage-producing capacity of the land. In some areas, such as the arid southwest, dramatic, apparently permanent changes in entire ecosystems were wrought by livestock in a few years toward the end of the nineteenth century. Environmental historian Donald Worster has likened the "invasion" of the arid west by millions of introduced forage animals beginning in the late nineteenth century to the "explosive, shattering effect of all-out war." UNDER WESTERN SKIES: NATURE AND HISTORY IN THE AMERICAN WEST 45 (1992).

The unreserved public domain was carved up by the creation of national forest reserves in the 1890's and early 1900's. Grazing in national forests came under some primitive regulation (see United States v. Grimaud and Light v. United States, Chapter 2, supra pp. 107–10). Grazing on the unreserved public lands, however, remained free and unregulated. At least partly because of such regulation, national forest lands were far more productive by the mid–1930's than the public domain lands. See Thadis Box, The American Rangelands: Their Condition and Policy Implications for Management, in RANGELAND POLICIES FOR THE FUTURE 16 (1979).

State regulation provided the only controls on the public domain before 1934, but state law in this era was almost exclusively concerned with encouraging private grazing and keeping the peace, and not with regulation to protect the lands and resources. Compare Omaechevarria v. Idaho, 246 U.S. 343 (1918), Chapter 2, supra p. 130; Scott, supra. The failure or lack of state law to protect the range, coupled with drought conditions, led to the passage of the Taylor Grazing Act of 1934. See E. Louise Peffer, THE CLOSING OF THE PUBLIC DOMAIN (1951), excerpted at Chapter 2, supra pp. 133–35. The Grazing Service was created inside the Department of the Interior in 1936 to implement the Taylor Act. Ten years later, it was merged with the General Land Office to form the BLM.

THE TAYLOR GRAZING ACT

The background on the Taylor Grazing Act is set out in Chapter 2, supra pp. 129–37. Its approach was recently summarized by Justice Breyer in his opinion for a unanimous Supreme Court in Public Lands Council v. Babbitt, 529 U.S. 728, 733, 736 (2000), as follows (the main part of the opinion is set out further below):

The Taylor act seeks to "promote the highest use of the public lands." 43 U.S.C. § 315. Its specific goals are to "stop injury" to the lands from "overgrazing and soil deterioration," to "provide for their use, improvement and development," and "to stabilize the livestock industry dependent on the public range." 48 Stat. 1269. The Act grants the Secretary of the Interior authority to divide the public range lands into grazing districts, to specify the amount of grazing permitted in each district, to issue leases or permits "to graze livestock," and to charge "reasonable fees" for use of the land. 43 U.S.C. §§ 315, 315a, 315b. It specifies that preference in respect to grazing permits "shall be given . . . to those within or near" a grazing district "who are landowners engaged in the livestock business, bona fide occupants or settlers, or owners of water or water rights." § 315b. And, as particularly relevant here, it adds:

> "So far as consistent with the purposes and provisions of this subchapter, grazing privileges recognized and acknowledged shall be adequately safeguarded, but the creation of a grazing district or the issuance of a permit . . . shall not create any right, title, interest, or estate in or to the lands." *Ibid.*

The Taylor act delegated to the Interior Department an enormous administrative task. To administer the Act, the Department needed to determine the bounds of the public range, create grazing districts, determine their grazing capacity, and divide that capacity among applicants. It soon set bounds encompassing more than 140 million acres, and by 1936 the Department had created 37 grazing districts, see Department of Interior Ann. Rep. 15 (1935); W. Calef, Private Grazing and Public Lands 58–59 (1960). The Secretary then created district advisory boards made up of local ranchers and called on them for further help. See 2 App. 809–811 (Rules for Administration of Grazing Districts (Mar. 2, 1936)). Limited department resources and the enormity of the administrative task made the boards "the effective governing and administrative body of each grazing district." Calef, *supra*, at 60; accord, P. Foss, Politics and Grass 199–200 (1960).

By 1937 the Department had set the basic rules for allocation of grazing privileges. Those rules recognized that many ranchers had long maintained herds on their own private lands during part of the year, while allowing their herds to graze farther afield on public land at other times. The rules consequently gave a first preference to owners of stock who also owned "base property," *i.e.*, private land (or water rights) sufficient to support their herds, *and* who had grazed the public range during the five years just prior to the Taylor act's enactment. See 2 App. 818–819 (Rules for Administration of Grazing Districts (June 14, 1937)). They gave a second preference to other owners of nearby "base" property lacking prior use. *Ibid.* And they gave a third preference to stock owners without base property, like the nomadic sheep herder. *Ibid.* Since lower preference categories divided capacity left over after satisfaction of all higher preference claims, this system, in effect, awarded grazing privileges to owners of land or water. See

Foss, *supra,* at 63 (quoting Grazing Division Director F.R. Carpenter's remarks that grazing privileges are given to ranchers "not as individuals, nor as owners of livestock," but to "build up [the] lands and give them stability and value").

As grazing allocations were determined, the Department would issue a permit measuring grazing privileges in terms of "animal unit months" (AUMs), *i.e.,* the right to obtain the forage needed to sustain one cow (or five sheep) for one month. Permits were valid for up to 10 years and usually renewed, as suggested by the Act. See 43 U.S.C. § 315b; Public Land Law Review Commission, One Third of the Nation's Land 109 (1970). But the conditions placed on permits reflected the leasehold nature of grazing privileges; consistent with the fact that Congress had made the Secretary the landlord of the public range and basically made the grant of grazing privileges discretionary. The grazing regulations in effect from 1938 to the present day made clear that the Department retained the power to modify, fail to renew, or cancel a permit or lease for various reasons.

First, the Secretary could cancel permits if, for example, the permit holder persistently overgrazed the public lands, lost control of the base property, failed to use the permit, or failed to comply with the Range Code. * * * Second, the Secretary, consistent first with 43 U.S.C. § 315f, and later the land use planning mandated by 43 U.S.C. § 1712 * * * was authorized to reclassify and withdraw land from grazing altogether and devote it to a more valuable or suitable use. * * * Third, in the event of range depletion, the Secretary maintained a separate authority, not to take areas of land out of grazing use altogether as above, but to reduce the amount of grazing allowed on that land, by suspending AUMs of grazing privileges "in whole or in part," and "for such time as necessary." * * *

While the Taylor Act was aimed in part at "stabiliz[ing] the livestock industry dependent on the public range," it fell far short of being a sort of "Magna Carta" for grazing that the 1872 Mining Law came to be regarded for hardrock miners. Perhaps most important, as provided in § 315b quoted in excerpt above, the rancher's legal interest in the grazing permit does not rise to the status of a property interest akin to what can be obtained in a mining claim or a mineral lease or a timber sale contract.

Formally, the Taylor Act was a major shift: It ended the tradition of free uncontrolled use of public lands by any grazier, and substituted a new regimen of express allocation (which explicitly favored nearby landowners) of public land forage. But at least in the early days the on-the-ground change was less than the on-paper change. Ranchers remembering the open and bureaucracy-free grazing commons did not readily welcome what many saw as unjustifiable government interference into private affairs. Their strong interest combined with the brand-new federal Grazing Service's weak institutional status meant that implementation of the Act was through a system of semi-self-government. The holders of federal permits, through Stockmen's Advisory Boards and less formal means, dominated the administration of grazing districts for decades. BLM district officers often tended to act more as agents for the ranching industry than as regulators of it. See generally Debra L. Donahue, THE WESTERN RANGE REVISIT-ED, Chapter 4, pp. 67–113 (1999). Some of the 19,000 individuals and entities holding BLM grazing permits and leases* still believe that they are entitled, by law, equity or policy, to higher priority than any other resource use or consideration on federal lands. Their ranching structure is built upon federal land availability, and they have been quite successful in defending it. The materials that follow briefly examine the nature of the rancher's interest, grazing fees, and instances of attempted regulation under the Taylor Act.

THE GRAZIER'S LEGAL INTEREST IN THE PUBLIC LANDS

As we have seen a number of places in these materials, the nature and quantum of private rights (if any) in federal lands and resources varies with the mechanisms by which the Congress has allocated those lands and resources. Mining claims, oil and gas leases, and timber contracts all can give their holders some sort of property interest in federal minerals and timber. As shown in the excerpt of Justice Breyer's opinion in the *Public Lands Council* case, supra, Congress expressly addressed this issue in the Taylor Grazing Act, 43 U.S.C. § 315b: "[T]he issuance of a [grazing] permit * * * shall not create any right, title, interest, or estate in or to the lands."

Nevertheless, at least one court which addressed the interests of the grazing permittee soon after enactment of the Taylor Grazing Act seemed to hesitate to read this language literally, given the history of grazing on the public domain. In Red Canyon Sheep Company v. Ickes, 98 F.2d 308 (D.C.Cir.1938), the permittee had "long been grazing" sheep on public lands, and had been issued "interim permits, called licenses," shortly after the Taylor Act took effect. Under a special statute applying to the Lincoln National Forest, the Secretary of the Interior proposed to exchange the public lands it was grazing for fee land owned by another within the Forest. The permittee sued, arguing that the public lands it was grazing were not "unreserved and unappropriated" within the meaning of the exchange statute. The court addressed the nature of the rancher's claim on the land this way:

> Section 3 of the [Taylor Grazing] Act does not expressly speak of *rights* to permits; it uses the terms *authorized* and *entitled*. Nevertheless, looking at the Act in the light of its purpose and of its provisions as a whole, we think that the Congress intended that under it livestock owners, who, with their flocks, have been for a substantial period of time *bona fide* occupants of certain parts of the public domain, and

---

* The Taylor Act generally authorized the creation of grazing districts and the issuance of grazing *permits* in them. See 43 U.S.C. § 315b. The Act also authorized the issuance of grazing *leases* on isolated or disconnected public lands. 43 U.S.C. § 315m. Some cases and parts of the Taylor Act (e.g., 43 U.S.C. § 315m, proviso) refer also to federal grazing *licenses*. Generally speaking, the differences among these terms have no legal significance. This chapter uses grazing *permits* in a generic sense to cover grazing leases and grazing licenses as well.

who are able to make the most economic and beneficial use thereof because of their ownership of lands, water rights, and other necessary facilities, and who can thus bring themselves within a preferred class under the regulations by which the Secretary is authorized to implement in more detail the general policy of the Act, are entitled to grazing permits not exceeding ten years in duration, should the Secretary create a grazing district including that portion of the range which such livestock owners have been occupying. * * *

* * * We recognize that the rights under the Taylor Grazing Act do not fall within the conventional category of vested rights in property. Yet, whether they be called rights, privileges, or bare licenses, or by whatever name, while they exist they are something of real value to the possessors and something which have their source in an enactment of the Congress. The jurisdiction of equity is flexible and should not be confined to rigid categories so that the granting of an injunction will depend upon nomenclature rather than upon substance. * * *

[T]he right to hunt upon public waters bears a striking analogy to the right or privilege of grazing upon the public lands. Neither is an interest in the land itself, and both are subject to restriction or withdrawal, the one by game laws, and the other by laws in the interest of the protection of the public domain; yet both are of value to the persons possessing them.

We rule that the valuable nature of the privilege to graze which arises in a licensee whose license will in the ordinary course of administration of the Taylor Grazing Act ripen into a permit, makes that privilege a proper subject of equitable protection * * *.

Although *Red Canyon* was a victory for the rancher, the same circuit addressed the rancher's interest again a quarter century later, with a different result. LaRue v. Udall, 324 F.2d 428 (D.C.Cir.1963). The facts were similar—the Secretary of the Interior proposed to exchange public lands, on which LaRue grazed livestock under a Taylor Act permit, for lands owned by a defense contractor in Nevada. The exchange was proposed under § 8(b) of the Taylor Act itself, which authorized such exchanges when "public interests will be benefited thereby." 43 U.S.C. § 315g(b) (repealed 1976).* The court upheld the Secretary's view that the statutory standard "need not be related exclusively to conservation of Federal grazing resources nor need it be shown that a proposed exchange will promote range management." The court went on to reject other arguments of the rancher:

Appellants also assert that their grazing unit has been and is pledged as security for *bona fide* loans, and that therefore the Secretary may not terminate their grazing permit. As a basis for the assertion they rely upon the language we have italicized in the following portion of § 3 of the Taylor Grazing Act (43 U.S.C. § 315b): " * * * *no permittee*

---

* FLPMA now governs land exchanges of this type; see 43 U.S.C. § 1716. On the "public interest" standard for exchanges, compare National Audubon Society v. Hodel, Chapter 4, supra p. 369.

complying with the rules and regulations laid down by the Secretary of the Interior shall be denied the renewal of such permit, if such denial will impair the value of the grazing unit of the permittee, when such unit is pledged as security for any bona fide loan. * * * "

Their contention is that if the Secretary may not refuse to renew a permit when the permittee's grazing unit is pledged as security for a *bona fide* loan, "he can hardly bring about the same result indirectly by terminating a permit prior to the expiration of the term * * *." As the context shows[**], the provision relied upon by the appellants is one of the factors to be considered by the Secretary in establishing preferences between conflicting applications for permits on the federal range. By no means should it be construed as providing that, by maintaining a lien on his grazing unit, a permittee may also create and maintain a vested interest therein which will prevent the United States from exchanging it under § 8(b). * * *

Appellants' reliance on the Fifth Amendment disregards the provision of § 3 of the Act (43 U.S.C. § 315b) that

> * * * So far as consistent with the purposes and provisions of this chapter, grazing privileges recognized and acknowledged shall be adequately safeguarded, but the creation of a grazing district or the issuance of a permit pursuant to the provisions of this chapter shall not create any right, title, interest, or estate in or to the lands.

The command of Congress that grazing privileges shall be adequately safeguarded "so far as consistent with the purposes and provisions of this chapter" does not mean that a grazing permit is to prevent the Government's exercise of the right of exchange, which is "one of the provisions of this chapter."

Eventually the U.S. Supreme Court turned its authoritative gaze upon the question of property rights in grazing permits.

United States v. Fuller

Supreme Court of the United States, 1973.
409 U.S. 488.

■ MR. JUSTICE REHNQUIST delivered the opinion of the Court.

Respondents operated a large-scale "cow-calf" ranch near the confluence of the Big Sandy and Bill Williams Rivers in western Arizona. Their

---

** [Eds. The italicized quotation appears in the middle of 43 U.S.C. § 315b, three long sentences and some twenty-two lines before the section's concluding statement, that the issuance of a grazing permit "shall not create any right, title, interest, or estate in or to the lands." The reference to a grazing unit being pledged as security for a loan is stated as a second exception to a sentence that begins, "[p]reference shall be given in the issuance of grazing permits to" landowners, etc. The first exception is a transitional one, providing that "until July 1, 1935, no preference shall be given to" anyone acquiring property during calendar year 1934. The second exception, the one quoted by the court in *Larue*, immediately follows. The context of the italicized quotation, in other words, relates to the system of determining who gets preference should permits be issued, and not to the question of what interest the permit conveys.]

activities were conducted on lands consisting of 1,280 acres that they owned in fee simple (fee lands), 12,027 acres leased from the State of Arizona, and 31,461 acres of federal domain held under Taylor Grazing Act permits issued in accordance with § 3 of the Act, 43 U.S.C. § 315b. The Taylor Grazing Act authorizes the Secretary of the Interior to issue permits to livestock owners for grazing their stock on Federal Government lands. These permits are revocable by the Government. The Act provides, moreover, that its provisions "shall not create any right, title, interest, or estate in or to the lands." Ibid.

The United States, petitioner here, condemned 920 acres of respondents' fee lands. At the trial in the District Court for the purpose of fixing just compensation for the lands taken, the parties disagreed as to whether the jury might consider value accruing to the fee lands as a result of their actual or potential use in combination with the Taylor Grazing Act "permit" lands. The Government contended that such element of incremental value to the fee lands could neither be taken into consideration by the appraisers who testified for the parties nor considered by the jury. Respondents conceded that their permit lands could not themselves be assigned any value in view of the quoted provisions of the Taylor Grazing Act. They contended, however, that if on the open market the value of their fee lands was enhanced because of their actual or potential use in conjunction with permit lands, that element of value of the fee lands could be testified to by appraisers and considered by the jury. The District Court substantially adopted respondents' position, first in a pretrial order and then in its charge to the jury over appropriate objection by the Government. * * *

Our prior decisions have variously defined the "just compensation" that the Fifth Amendment requires to be made when the Government exercises its power of eminent domain. The owner is entitled to fair market value, United States v. Miller, 317 U.S. 369, 374 (1943), but that term is "not an absolute standard nor an exclusive method of valuation." * * *

The record shows that several appraiser witnesses for respondents testified that they included as an element of the value that they ascribed to respondents' fee lands the availability of respondents' Taylor Grazing Act permit lands to be used in conjunction with the fee lands. Under the District Court's charge to the jury, the jury was entitled to consider this element of value testified to by the appraisers. This Court has held that generally the highest and best use of a parcel may be found to be a use in conjunction with other parcels, and that any increment of value resulting from such combination may be taken into consideration in valuing the parcel taken. Olson v. United States, 292 U.S. 246, 256 (1934). The question presented by this case is whether there is an exception to that general rule where the parcels to be aggregated with the land taken are themselves owned by the condemnor and used by the condemnee only under revocable permit from the condemnor.

To say that this element of value would be considered by a potential buyer on the open market, and is therefore a component of "fair market value," is not the end of the inquiry. In United States v. Miller, supra, this Court held that the increment of fair market value represented by knowledge of the Government's plan to construct the project for which the land was taken was not included within the constitutional definition of "just compensation." * * *

* * * A long line of cases decided by this Court dealing with the Government's navigational servitude with respect to navigable waters evidences a continuing refusal to include, as an element of value in compensating for fast lands that are taken, any benefits conferred by access to such benefits as a potential portsite or a potential hydro-electric site. United States v. Twin City Power Co., 350 U.S. 222 (1956); United States v. Commodore Park, 324 U.S. 386 (1945).

These cases go far toward establishing the general principle that the Government as condemnor may not be required to compensate a condemnee for elements of value that the Government has created, or that it might have destroyed under the exercise of governmental authority other than the power of eminent domain. If * * * the Government need not pay for value that it could have acquired by exercise of a servitude arising under the commerce power, it would seem *a fortiori* that it need not compensate for value that it could remove by revocation of a permit for the use of lands that it owned outright.

We do not suggest that such a general principle can be pushed to its ultimate logical conclusion. In United States v. Miller, supra, the Court held that "just compensation" did include the increment of value resulting from the completed [federal] project to neighboring lands originally outside the project limits, but later brought within them. * * *

"Courts have had to adopt working rules in order to do substantial justice in eminent domain proceedings." United States v. Miller, supra, at 375. Seeking as best we may to extrapolate from these prior decisions such a "working rule," we believe that there is a significant difference between the value added to property by a completed public works project, for which the Government must pay, and the value added to fee lands by a revocable permit authorizing the use of neighboring lands that the Government owns. The Government may not demand that a jury be arbitrarily precluded from considering as an element of value the proximity of a parcel to a post office building, simply because the Government at one time built the post office. But here respondents rely on no mere proximity to a public building or to public lands dedicated to, and open to, the public at large. Their theory of valuation aggregates their parcel with land owned by the Government to form a privately controlled unit from which the public would be excluded. If * * * a person may not do this with respect to property interests subject to the Government's navigational servitude, he surely may not do it with respect to property owned outright by the Government. * * * We hold that the Fifth Amendment does not require the Government to pay for that element of value based on the use of respondents' fee lands in combination with the Government's permit lands.

* * * The provisions of the Taylor Grazing Act quoted supra make clear the congressional intent that no compensable property right be

created in the permit lands themselves as a result of the issuance of the permit. Given that intent, it would be unusual, we think, for Congress to have turned around and authorized compensation for the value added to fee lands by their potential use in connection with permit lands. We find no such authorization in the applicable congressional enactments.

Reversed.

■ Mr. Justice Powell, with whom Mr. Justice Douglas, Mr. Justice Brennan, and Mr. Justice Marshall join, dissenting.

I dissent from a decision which, in my view, dilutes the meaning of the just compensation required by the Fifth Amendment when property is condemned by the Government. * * *

The Government's role here is not an ambiguous one—it is simply a condemnor of private land which happens to adjoin public land. If the Government need not pay location value in this case, what are the limits upon the principle today announced? Will the Government be relieved from paying location value whenever it condemns private property adjacent to or favorably located with respect to Government property? Does the principle apply, for example, to the taking of a gasoline station at an interchange of a federal highway, or to the taking of a farm which in private hands could continue to be irrigated with water from a federal reservoir? * * *

NOTES AND QUESTIONS

1. What precisely is the legal interest a rancher has in a grazing permit? A protectable privilege? A license subject to administrative curtailment "in the public interest"? Compare United States v. Cox, 190 F.2d 293, 296 (10th Cir.1951), cert. denied, 342 U.S. 867 (1951): "Although the permits are available to the ranchers, they are not an interest protected by the Fifth Amendment against the taking by the Government who granted them with the understanding that they could be withdrawn at any time without the payment of compensation."

2. About three-fourths of the "base property" Fuller held in fee was condemned by the government, and as a result of this decision, Fuller was not allowed to recover the value that the permit lands might have added to that portion of the "base property." If Fuller had purchased the base property after enactment of the Taylor Grazing Act in 1934, what would a "willing buyer-willing seller" sale price have been based on? Phillip Foss's leading study confirmed what the appraisers said in their testimony in the *Fuller* case; namely, "grazing permits are ordinarily capitalized into the value of the ranch so that * * * a ranch buyer actually pays for both the private and public lands contained in the ranch unit." P. Foss, POLITICS AND GRASS 197 (1960); see also L. Allen Torell & Marc E. Kincaid, Public Land Policy and the Market Value of New Mexico Ranches, 1979–1994, 49 J. of Range Mgmnt. 270 (1996) (ranches with federal land grazing permits tend to sell for more than the base property is worth, and more than the earning potential of the livestock enterprise). The fact that the federal grazing permit may have a substantial value in the private marketplace,

even though it is not a compensable property right, helps account for the tenaciousness of ranchers in dealing with threats to their federal land grazing privileges.

3.   Dissenting Justice Powell compared the situation in *Fuller* with government condemnation of private land near a federal interstate highway interchange, where presumably the U.S. would have to pay for the value as enhanced by the interchange. Are the situations comparable? If compensation were provided here, would it violate the (arguably plain) intent of Congress as expressed in section 3 (43 U.S.C. § 315b) of the Taylor Grazing Act?

4.   There was a curious lineup of Justices here, with the majority comprised mostly of conservatives (normally thought to be more zealous in advocating and protecting property rights), and the dissent mostly of liberals (usually considered less zealous on the subject).

5.   Three years after *Fuller*, Congress enacted FLPMA, which contained this subsection:

> Whenever a permit or lease for grazing domestic livestock is canceled in whole or in part, in order to devote the lands covered by the permit or lease to another public purpose, including disposal, the permittee or lessee shall receive from the United States a reasonable compensation for the adjusted value, to be determined by the Secretary concerned, of his interest in authorized permanent improvements placed or constructed by the permittee or lessee on lands covered by such permit or lease, but not to exceed the fair market value of the terminated portion of the permittee's or lessee's interest therein. Except in cases of emergency, no permit or lease shall be canceled under this subsection without two years' prior notification.

43 U.S.C. 1752(g). Does this modify the principle or result of *Fuller?* Had it been in effect when Fuller's base property was condemned, could Fuller have recovered anything under it? What? See also the next subsection, § 1752(h), which provides that "[n]othing in this Act shall be construed as modifying in any way law existing on October 21, 1976, with respect to the creation of right, title, interest or estate in or to the public lands or lands in National Forests by issuance of grazing permits and leases."

6.   Arguments for some sort of protected property interest in grazing permits are still made but routinely rejected. See, e.g., Swim v. Bergland, 696 F.2d 712 (9th Cir.1983) (rejecting ranchers' claims that government could not revoke their grazing permits without compensation, the revocation in that case made in order to satisfy the terms of a treaty that gave Indians grazing rights on the federal land); Diamond Bar Cattle Co. v. United States, 168 F.3d 1209, 1215–16 (10th Cir.1999) (even more than a century of grazing use does not give any sort of prescriptive or appropriative rights to the land or to grazing privileges); Federal Lands Legal Consortium v. United States, 195 F.3d 1190 (10th Cir.1999) (ranchers have no property interests in the terms of prior permits sufficient to raise a Fifth Amendment taking question); Alves v. United States, 133 F.3d 1454 (Fed.Cir.1998)(neither grazing permit nor grazing preference is a property

interest compensable under the fifth amendment). In Hage v. United States, 51 Fed.Cl. 570 (2002), Judge Loren Smith, widely known for his vigorous defenses (and expansive interpretations) of property rights, conceded that while the permit may have value to the rancher, "value itself does not create a compensable property right, no matter how seemingly unjust the consequences * * * ". The plaintiff in that case, Wayne Hage, was a well-known firebrand rancher who wrote STORM OVER RANGELANDS: PRIVATE RIGHTS IN PUBLIC LANDS (1989), the title of which said it all.

7. If a rancher sells her "base property," she has some risk of losing the grazing privilege that has attached to it, even if the purchaser defaults and reconveys the property to the rancher. See Bischoff v. Glickman, 54 F.Supp.2d 1226 (D.Wyo.1999).

8. Permittee ranchers were in the vanguard of the 1970s Sagebrush Rebellion and the 1990s County Supremacy movement, partly as a protest to reductions in permitted numbers of grazing animals. For somewhat different reasons, a small but hardy band of free-market economists supports the ranchers' claims for federal divestiture and privatization, arguing that economic efficiency would thereby be promoted. One of these, Gary Libecap, concluded in LOCKING UP THE RANGE 102 (1981):

> * * * Assigning title to existing [BLM grazing] permittees is the least costly way of granting private property rights. Title can be subsequently traded at low cost to others (including conservation and wildlife groups). Limited areas of great amenity value, where exclusion is for some reason difficult, can be retained under state or federal control. However, most of the 174 million acres administered by the Bureau of Land Management are not affected by those strict conditions and are amenable to private ownership. Recognizing existing uses of the range in assigning title is consistent with U.S. and state policies which have historically recognized prior appropriation claims for water, farmland, and hard-rock minerals.

> Well-defined private rights capture individual incentive and initiative for using rangeland efficiently. Further, they insure response by profit-maximizing land owners to changing market demands for range use. Finally, they allow the U.S. to avoid socially costly scientific management programs advocated by the BLM. Private property rights are the necessary conditions for restoring and maintaining the productive value of a land area larger than New England and the Mid–Atlantic states combined which has been much maligned and fought over for one hundred years.

See also John Baden & Richard Stroup, Political Economy Perspectives on the Sagebrush Rebellion, 3 Pub.Land L.Rev. 103, 116 (1982).

NOTE: GRAZING FEES

The price for leasing public rangeland traditionally has been a political lightning rod, especially for ranchers, with two interrelated constants:

First, the fee has always been considerably lower than the going rate for comparable lands in private ownership, and second, raising the fee even to keep pace with inflation has proved stubbornly difficult. The Forest Service first charged a nominal fee for grazing on national forests in 1906, and it was upheld in United States v. Grimaud, Chapter 2, supra p. 107. Not until 1931 was a new formula employed on the national forests; fees then increased slowly but steadily up to $0.56 per animal-unit-month (AUM) by 1968, still well below market levels.

The BLM historically has charged even less than the Forest Service: Nothing was charged for grazing the public lands "common" until two years after the Taylor Act (which authorized the Secretary to charge "reasonable fees") was passed in 1934. This initial charge of a nickel an AUM* was in effect until 1946, and had risen to only $0.33 by 1968. In 1966 a joint fee study by the Secretaries of Agriculture and Interior (the Western Livestock Grazing Survey) concluded that the fee on BLM and national forest lands should be increased to $1.23 per AUM over ten years. The agencies adopted this schedule, and the first increase, to $0.44 an AUM in 1969, was upheld in Pankey Land & Cattle Company v. Hardin, 427 F.2d 43 (10th Cir.1970). This fee schedule was implemented, punctuated by four moratoria on annual increases during a nine year period.

FLPMA, enacted in 1976, contained a generic policy statement that the United States should "receive fair market value of the use of the public lands and their resources unless otherwise provided for by statute," 43 U.S.C. § 1701(a)(9). But in the same Act Congress mandated yet another grazing fee study by both agencies and put a one-year freeze on grazing fees pending the outcome of the report. 43 U.S.C. § 1751(a). The report concluded that the fee system should collect fair market value. See Secretary of Interior & Secretary of Agriculture, Study of Fees for Livestock Grazing on Federal Lands (1977).

The very next year, Congress essentially ignored this advice by adopting a new formula in the Public Rangelands Improvement Act of 1978, 43 U.S.C. § 1905(a), that simply redefined market value:

> For the grazing years 1979 through 1985, the Secretaries of Agriculture and Interior shall charge the fee for domestic livestock grazing on the public rangelands which Congress finds represents the economic value of the use of the land to the user, and under which Congress finds fair market value for public grazing equals the $1.23 base established by the 1966 Western Livestock Grazing Survey multiplied by the result of the Forage Value Index (computed annually from data supplied by the Economic Research Service) added to the Combined Index (Beef Cattle Price Index minus the Price Paid Index) and divided by 100: *Provided,* That the annual increase or decrease in such fee for any given year shall be limited to not more than plus or minus 25 per centum of the previous year's fee.

---

* The Supreme Court rejected a rancher's challenge to the initial BLM grazing fee in Brooks v. Dewar, 313 U.S. 354 (1941).

Being tied to the price ranchers received for cattle, this formula operated to keep fees substantially below fair market value. See S.Rep. No. 95–1237, 95th Cong., 2d Sess. 20–21, 58–59 (1978). By 1985, grazing fees had dropped below $1.40 per AUM, compared to a west-wide fair market value of between $6–15 per AUM for equivalent grazing on private lands. Congress still has not legislated a new fee formula, and the fee has remained in the $1.50 per AUM range. Secretary of the Interior Babbitt early on announced an intention to impose higher grazing fees, but succumbed to congressional opposition. See 35 Fed. Reg. 9894 (1995).

The low grazing fees have led some ranchers to "rent" all or part of their federal grazing permit allotments to other ranchers, at higher rates than the federal fee. See generally GRAZING LEASE ARRANGEMENTS OF BUREAU OF LAND MANAGEMENT PERMITTEES (General Accounting Office, 1986). The BLM's regulations generally prohibit "subleasing" the permit without also subleasing the base property. They define "subleasing" as where a grazing permittee allows grazing on the federal lands covered by his permit "by livestock that are not owned or controlled by the permittee * * *." 43 C.F.R. §§ 4140.1(a)(6); 4100.0–5 (2001). Some subleases are formalized by "livestock pasture agreements" that give the BLM permittee "control" over the livestock to meet the terms of the regulations. The practice has garnered the attention of some in Congress, but no legislation dealing with it has been enacted.

One of these editors has criticized many aspects of public rangeland management, including the subsidized fee. Its problem, he argues, is that the subsidy is capitalized into the purchase price and mortgage value of the base ranch, leading the subsidy recipients to resist fiercely any cuts in their permitted AUMs, even when the reductions would ultimately redound to the ranchers' economic benefit. See George C. Coggins & Margaret Lindeberg–Johnson, The Law of Public Rangeland Management II: The Commons and the Taylor Act, 13 Envtl.L. 1, 74–75 (1982). Other articles in the Public Rangeland Law series are at 12 Envtl.L. 535 (1982); 13 Envtl.L. 295 (1982); 14 Envtl.L. 1 (1983); and 14 Envtl.L. 497 (1984). A more recent comprehensive (and controversial, for it is unabashedly anti-grazing) survey of the law, economics, and politics of public land livestock grazing is Debra Donahue's THE WESTERN RANGE REVISITED (1999).

REGULATION UNDER THE TAYLOR ACT

Part of the impetus for what Phillip Foss has aptly called a "special private government" on the BLM public lands came from the nature of the Taylor Grazing Act itself, and especially how it was administered. The Act directed, for the very first time, that the government take its hand at supervising livestock grazing that had gone on for decades on public lands throughout the west. While henceforth all livestock grazing on the public lands had to be authorized by federal permit, the Congress did not leave the matter of who should get the permits entirely to the discretion of the Secretary of the Interior. Instead, § 3 of the Act provided, in pertinent part:

> The Secretary of the Interior is authorized to issue or cause to be issued permits to graze livestock on such grazing districts to such bona fide settlers, residents, and other stock owners as under his rules and regulations are entitled to participate in the use of the range * * *. Preference shall be given in the issuance of grazing permits to those within or near a district who are landowners engaged in the livestock business, bona fide occupants or settlers, or owners of water or water rights, as may be necessary to permit the proper use of lands, water or water rights owned, occupied, or leased by them * * *.

This "preference" was construed by the Secretary for the most part to displace those graziers who did not own "base property" or fee land in the vicinity of the public lands. See, e.g., Garcia v. Andrus, 692 F.2d 89, 93 (9th Cir.1982) (grazing lessee who loses a partial interest in his "base property" loses priority to renew his grazing lease "in a proportionate amount"). The statute also, one court held, restricted the Secretary's power to reallocate grazing privileges. That is, in McNeil v. Seaton, 281 F.2d 931 (D.C.Cir. 1960), the court concluded (over a dissent by retired Supreme Court Justice Burton, sitting as a Circuit Judge) that this "preference" language forbade the Secretary from reallocating public rangelands from one qualifying for the preference to another rancher who did not qualify:

> This appellant not only was engaged in stockraising when the Act was passed, but he qualified under the Range Code as and when first promulgated. He was entitled to rely upon the preference Congress had given him: to use the public range as dedicated to a special purpose in aid of Congressional policy. We deem his rights—whatever their exact nature—to have been "protected against tortious invasion" and to have been "founded on a statute which confers a privilege." Accordingly this appellant was entitled to invest his time, effort and capital and to develop his stockraising business, all subject, of course, to similar preferences to be accorded in the affected area to others comparably situated. We see no basis upon which, by a special rule adopted more than twenty years after appellant had embarked upon his venture, he may lawfully be deprived of his statutory privilege.

The court was careful, however, to limit its ruling:

> What particular *number* of stock a preference applicant might be entitled to graze must depend upon circumstances, having in mind the orderly use of the public lands, the possibility of overgrazing, the forage capacity of the base property, available water and other factors pertinent to such a complicated administrative problem. Subject to such considerations and others specified in the Code, the extent of the appellant's grazing privileges was to be determined.

In the end, McNeil's victory was Pyrrhic, as the BLM decision to restrict his grazing allocation was affirmed. McNeil v. Udall, 340 F.2d 801 (D.C.Cir. 1964). The cases arising from BLM efforts to implement and enforce the Taylor Act are concisely collected in Hugh E. Kingery, The Public Grazing Lands, 43 Denver L.J. 329 (1966).

The BLM administers the preference system through what has come to be rather formidably known as the Range Code, even though it is simply a set of ordinary federal regulations formulated shortly after passage of the Taylor Grazing Act, and now found, as amended, at 43 C.F.R. §§ 4110–4170 (2002). By all accounts, the BLM for many decades did very little to enforce the requirements of the Code. In the middle 1970s, the Department of the Interior suspended the grazing permit of a large ranch in Wyoming for two years for illegally spraying herbicide on public lands. On appeal, the rancher argued that the Department had no authority under applicable statutes and regulations to suspend grazing privileges as a penalty, and instead could only fine it a maximum of $500. In rejecting that argument, the Tenth Circuit Court of Appeals "treated this as a question of first impression," noting "a surprising dearth of prior prosecutions along this line." Diamond Ring Ranch, Inc. v. Morton, 531 F.2d 1397 (10th Cir.1976). Section 1752(a) of the Federal Land Policy and Management Act of 1976 confirmed the *Diamond Ring* result by giving the government express authority to cancel, suspend, or modify a grazing permit or lease for any violation of a grazing regulation or of any terms contained in a permit or lease. Section 1752(g), quoted at p. 792 supra, requires the Secretary to provide two years notice for permit cancellations necessitated by the agency's decision to manage the land for other public purposes, but this does not apply to actions taken under section 1752(a).*

Each grazing permit under the Taylor Act must specify the kind and number of livestock allowed to graze, and the time of year a particular allotment can be grazed. 43 U.S.C. § 315b; 43 C.F.R. subpart 4130 (2001). Trespass—referring both to grazing animals in excess of the permitted number, and permitting them to graze on federal lands where or when they are not supposed to graze—has historically been a common problem on public rangelands. Enforcement is, by most accounts, spotty. See, e.g., General Accounting Office, Rangeland Management: BLM Efforts to Prevent Unauthorized Livestock Grazing Need Strengthening (1991). Proof can be difficult because of intermingled land ownerships and the tradition of open rangeland still observed in parts of the west. BLM's attempts to deal with these problems have sometimes encountered difficulty, as the following case shows.

Holland Livestock Ranch v. United States

United States Court of Appeals, Ninth Circuit, 1983.
714 F.2d 90.

■ Canby, Circuit Judge.

The issue in this case is whether the government's "access trespass" presumption suffices to prove trespass. The district court held that the presumption was invalid and granted summary judgment for Holland. We affirm.

---

* The provisions of FLPMA that deal with grazing apply to national forest lands as well as BLM-managed public lands.

This is the latest in a series of cattle grazing disputes between appellees Holland Livestock Ranch and John Casey (together "Holland") and the Bureau of Land Management (BLM). The Holland ranch holds grazing permits for some public lands. The ranch also adjoins other public lands closed to grazing. The BLM believed that Holland's cattle were trespassing onto these forbidden public lands, and initiated administrative proceedings against Holland. The administrative law judge found that wilful trespass had been proved, assessed damages, and terminated Holland's grazing rights. The Interior Board of Land Appeals affirmed. 80 I.B.L.A. 516 (1981). Holland sought review in the district court, which vacated and remanded. 543 F.Supp. 158 (D.Nev.1982). The government's appeal brings the case to us.

Throughout these proceedings, the BLM offered no direct proof of trespass. Instead, it created and relied upon a new evidentiary presumption: that cattle with unrestricted access to public lands have in fact trespassed. To force reliance upon the presumption, the government stipulated that agents had sighted Holland's cattle "on public lands *or* on private lands with unrestricted access to public lands in an area closed to grazing." (Emphasis added.) The stipulated facts obviously furnish no proof that cattle were actually sighted on public lands. The government thus chose to rely solely on its "access trespass" presumption.

Administrative agencies are entitled to create evidentiary presumptions. Holland Livestock Ranch v. United States, 655 F.2d 1002, 1005 (9th Cir.1981). In reviewing the validity of a presumption, we must determine whether a "sound factual connection" exists between the facts giving rise to the presumption and the facts then presumed. The presumption, however, is entitled to "considerable deference."

The district judge found that the required factual connection was lacking:

> The probability that livestock grazing on unfenced private land will trespass on an adjoining public land taken in the abstract is speculative and questionable. That is, absent evidence of some actual trespass, the presumption fails to accommodate a myriad of equally likely possibilities which make it unreasonable to presume that livestock located on private land with unrestricted access to public land have in fact trespassed. Natural boundaries, herd regulation and supervision, as well as the difficulty of traveling a potentially vast distance in order to enter upon public land, are but a few possibilities. The presumption used here in order to find plaintiff liable was not an adequate substitute for definite proof.

543 F.Supp. at 160.

The government contends that the district court erred, that a sound factual connection does support the presumption. Counsel points out that unimpeded cattle are likely to trespass because "cows do not read plat books and are, accordingly, wholly indifferent to the law of trespass." This argument certainly carries some force. In addition, the government argues that we have already held the presumption reasonable in Holland Livestock

Ranch v. United States, 655 F.2d 1002 (9th Cir.1981) (*"Holland I"*). We consider first the effect of this case.

In *Holland I*, we considered the validity of the "access trespass" presumption in a slightly different context. We held that the access trespass presumption could be used to show damages once some actual trespass had been proved. The question whether unrestricted access will give rise to a presumption of trespass in the absence of such corroborative proof was expressly reserved. We face this question now.

Holland I establishes the existence of a sound factual connection underlying the presumption. Yet our inquiry there was not limited solely to the plausibility of the presumed fact. The usefulness of a presumption is also a factor to be considered in assessing its validity. In *Holland I* we observed that the presumption is necessary in measuring damages because demonstrating each individual trespass would be "extremely difficult, if not impossible." 655 F.2d at 1006. The law has long recognized that evidence showing amount of damage may be somewhat speculative once the existence of *some* damage is proved with certainty.

In contrast, the presumption is not necessary here. Proving that at least one animal has actually trespassed is not difficult, and imposes no undue burden on BLM resources. To make use of the presumption, agents would have to find some cattle on private lands with unrestricted access to public land. It will not add greatly to their labors to locate animals actually trespassing, if such trespasses are at all substantial.

Presumptions should not replace proof needlessly. The access trespass presumption is reasonable enough to apply where needed to measure damages. We hold, however, that the presumption cannot stand where it is not needed: as the sole evidence to establish a claim of trespass. The government must prove some actual trespass before relying upon the presumption. * * *

We conclude that the district court was correct in rejecting the presumption, and therefore do not address the other issues presented. The decision of the district court is affirmed.

NOTES

1.   In *Holland III*, the district court upheld revocation of the Holland grazing permit because of numerous and substantial trespass violations. Holland Livestock Ranch v. United States, 588 F.Supp. 943 (D.Nev.1984).

2.   The Forest Service trespass regulations, premised on its Organic Act, prohibit "[p]lacing or allowing unauthorized livestock to enter or be in" national forests. 36 C.F.R. § 261.7(a) (2001). The Eighth Circuit held that intent is not an element of the offense, United States v. Larson, 746 F.2d 455, 456 (8th Cir.1984), but the Ninth Circuit later held that the "Government must prove that the defendant willfully acted to allow his cattle to enter the National Forest, or willfully failed to prevent their entering when he had a clear opportunity to do so." United States v. Semenza, 835 F.2d 223, 225 (9th Cir.1987).

3. The BLM's alleged inability or lack of action to prevent trespass onto plaintiff's ranch by livestock from an adjacent permittee constitutes neither a compensable taking of property nor a breach of contract. Alves v. United States, 133 F.3d 1454 (Fed.Cir.1998).

B.   MODERN POST-FLPMA PUBLIC RANGELAND MANAGEMENT

As the foregoing materials indicate, BLM's control over private grazing operations on public lands has historically been considerably short of stellar, particularly from a resource protection standpoint. While the Taylor Act survived the onslaught of new federal lands statutes enacted in the1970's, other statutes adopted in that era have ushered in a new (and for some ranchers, a painful) era of public range management, the ultimate effects of which are still being played out. We have explored two of the most important statutes—NEPA and the ESA—earlier, in Chapter 5, supra pp. 390, 435.

NEPA's application is worth some mention here, for it was seized on by environmentalists in the early 1970s as the best hope of bringing more environmental sensitivity to livestock grazing on BLM lands. In Natural Resources Defense Council, Inc. v. Morton, 388 F.Supp. 829 (D.D.C.1974), aff'd per curiam, 527 F.2d 1386 (D.C.Cir.1976), cert. denied, 427 U.S. 913 (1976), the court said BLM had to do more than prepare a programmatic EIS on its entire livestock grazing program in order to comply with NEPA. The court noted that plaintiffs "do not ask that impact statements be filed for every license or permit issued or renewed by the BLM. Nor do they seek an immediate injunction of the licensing program which could admittedly have a most deleterious effect on the entire livestock industry." The court itself also did not answer the ultimate question of the appropriate level of EISs:

> The crucial point is that the specific environmental effects of the permits issued, and to be issued, in each district be assessed. It will be initially within the BLM's discretion to determine whether to make this specific assessment in a separate impact statement for each district, or several impact statements for each district, or one impact statement for several districts or portions thereof, or indeed by other means. So long as the actual environmental effects of particular permits or groups of permits in specific areas are assessed, questions of format are to be left to defendants.

Interestingly, while this case was pending before the district court, BLM released a report compiled by a team of BLM resource managers, examining the environmental effects of livestock grazing in Nevada on the public lands. The court summarized its results this way:

> "Uncontrolled, unregulated or unplanned livestock use is occurring in approximately 85 percent of the State and damage to wildlife habitat can be expressed only as extreme destruction." [Report] at 13. Over-grazing by livestock has caused invasion of sagebrush and rabbitbrush

on meadows and has decreased the amount of meadow habitat available for wildlife survival by at least 50 percent. The reduced meadow area has caused a decline in both game and non-game population. Id. at 26. In addition, there are 883 miles of streams with deteriorating and declining wildlife habitat, thus making it apparent, according to the report, that grazing systems do not protect and enhance wildlife values. Id. at 14, 29.[22]

NOTES AND QUESTIONS

1. If you were Director of BLM and you were asked to approve release of that report at that time, would you have done so (if you could have found an excuse to delay it)? Why or why not?

2. How should BLM go about complying with NEPA on a program involving some 18–19,000 permittees and 160 million acres of public land? Are individual EISs on individual permits out of the question? (By comparison, the entire federal government in recent years has prepared a roughly 400–500 EISs every year.)

3. Eventually BLM reached an agreement with NRDC, approved by the court, under which it committed to prepare well over one hundred site-specific EISs on its grazing program on a specific schedule over a several year period. With some delays and other bumps along the way, the EISs were eventually completed, and documented what many observers had understood all along; namely, much of the public grazing lands are in poor condition compared to their historic potential; one clear cause for this condition is overgrazing; and improvement in range condition depends largely upon reducing the number of grazing animals and limiting the areas available for grazing.

BLM was just getting its NEPA compliance underway when Congress enacted FLPMA. That statute gave BLM for the first time express, permanent authority to manage its lands for multiple use and sustained yield. See 43 U.S.C. § 1732, discussed in Chapter 8, supra pp. 707–08. Title IV of FLPMA (43 U.S.C. §§ 1751–53) also contained a number of provisions directly applicable to range management, one was quoted earlier in this chapter, p. 792, supra. All the rangeland provisions of FLPMA are expressly made applicable to livestock grazing on the national forests as well as on BLM lands.

In enacting FLPMA (and the Public Rangelands Improvement Act, or PRIA, two years later), Congress essentially found that the public rangelands are in bad condition, are deteriorating, and should be improved. In general, FLPMA did not remake the law of livestock grazing or the legal relationship between the permittee and the government. It left the Taylor

------

22. Whether the original deterioration occurred before or during BLM management is irrelevant since the crucial questions are whether it can be allowed to continue and whether it will be exacerbated by continued grazing.

Grazing Act's structure basically in place, and clarified and confirmed the government's authority in many important respects. It also expressly refused to modify the "grazing permits do not carry any right, title, interest or estate in public lands" language in the Taylor Grazing Act. (See 43 U.S.C. § 1752(h)) Finally, and perhaps most important, FLPMA also created a resource planning process for BLM lands, a subject generally addressed in Chapter 5, p. 431 supra, and addressed in the specific context of grazing further below, at pp. 829–35.

A subsection of FLPMA, 43 U.S.C. § 1752(a), sets ten years as the usual term for grazing permits or leases. A shorter term is allowed if the land is pending disposal, if it will be put to some other public purpose within ten years, or if it is "in the best interest of sound land management to specify a shorter term." Id. § 1752(b). The vast majority of permits are for ten year terms. FLPMA also addresses the renewal of grazing permits, this way (43 U.S.C. § 1752(c)):

> So long as (1) the lands for which the permit or lease is issued remain available for domestic livestock grazing in accordance with land use plans prepared pursuant to section 1712 of this title or section 1604 of Title 16, (2) the permittee or lessee is in compliance with the rules and regulations issued and the terms and conditions in the permit or lease specified by the Secretary concerned, and (3) the permittee or lessee accepts the terms and conditions to be included by the Secretary concerned in the new permit or lease, the holder of the expiring permit or lease shall be given first priority for receipt of the new permit or lease.

How much protection does this provision give to a rancher seeking renewal? A rancher-lawyer has offered policy arguments for priority renewals:

> Priority renewal does have advantages. A permittee becomes intimately familiar with the range. * * * [H]igh turnover of federal graziers does not permit them to get to know the range nearly as well. Only long use can teach an operator where the thicket is that hides the stubborn bull late in the fall. The seasonal pattern of drying up of the range and waterholes must be known to fully utilize the range resource. If the first areas to dry are not used early in the season, they will be wasted. The rancher who expects to use the same range for many years in the future will be careful not to hurt the resource. The range cattle themselves get to learn the range. An old range cow can find hidden waterholes and meadows that a new cow would not. And with the first snows of fall, the old cows will lead the herd back to the home ranch.

Marc Valens, FEDERAL GRAZING LANDS: OLD HISTORY, NEW DIRECTIONS (1978) (unpublished manuscript).

A basic tool for BLM grazing management is the Allotment Management Plan, or AMP. It is defined in FLPMA as a "document prepared in consultation with [permittees] * * * [which, among other things,] prescribes the manner in, and extent to, which livestock operations [on BLM or national forest lands] will be conducted in order to meet the multiple-use, sustained-yield, economic and other needs and objectives as determined for the lands by the [agency] * * *." 43 U.S.C. § 1702(k). An AMP may embrace several different ranches or allotments. Where AMPs exist, their terms are incorporated into the permit.

Professor Joseph Feller has described how grazing levels are determined by the BLM in actual practice:

> Although the permit or the AMP should prescribe the terms and conditions necessary to ensure proper management of livestock grazing on an allotment, in reality many management decisions are made on an annual basis. For example, although the permit specifies a number of livestock, the BLM annually determines how many livestock will actually graze on an allotment. The actual number allowed to graze may be less than the number in the permit either because the permittee has requested voluntary "non-use" of all or a part of the permitted number, or because the BLM has concluded that the allotment in its current condition cannot actually support the permitted number. On many allotments, the BLM also issues an annual grazing schedule specifying which pastures on an allotment will be grazed and which will be rested that year, and the dates of use and numbers of livestock for each of the pastures that will be grazed. Where an AMP is in place, this annual grazing schedule should be, but sometimes is not, consistent with the AMP.
>
> In principle, these annual decisions provide the flexibility needed to adapt the permitted numbers, and the terms and conditions of the permit or AMP, to changing and unpredictable circumstances, particularly variations in rainfall. In practice, these annual decisions sometimes supplant the permit and the AMP as the mechanisms for prescribing the management of an allotment. *The number of livestock specified in the permit often substantially exceeds the number that the permittee ever actually places on the allotment or that the allotment could accommodate without resource damage. In such a case, the permit acts as a blank check, allowing the permittee and the BLM to agree privately each year on how many livestock will actually graze.* Further, on many allotments without an AMP, the permit contains only the minimum specifications (number and kind of livestock and dates of use of the allotment), leaving all other management prescriptions to the annual grazing schedule.

Grazing Management on the Public Lands: Opening the Process to Public Participation, XXVI Land & Water L.Rev. 569, 575–76 (1991) (emphasis added).

ALLOTMENT MANAGEMENT PLANS AND GRAZING DECISIONMAKING—A SAMPLE CASE

Some indication of the nature of the issues posed and the depth of feeling engendered by the BLM's efforts, prodded by the courts, to get a regulatory grip on grazing can be gleaned from the following excerpts from the East Roswell (New Mexico) Grazing Environmental Statement (1979) (ES). In essence, after determining that available forage production was far less than grazing level that had been authorized (the methodology for such determination being hotly but not factually disputed), the BLM opted in the ES for a program of temporary grazing reductions coupled with widespread herbicide applications to destroy competing plant species such as mesquite and creosote bush which had invaded the area. The invasion had been caused largely by overgrazing, and the competing species in turn caused a decline in grass production. The BLM's preferred option was summarized this way in the ES:

> Livestock grazing would continue to be authorized on all 184 of the ES area's existing allotments (approximately 1,590,000 acres of public land) [Eds.: An area somewhat larger than the state of Delaware.] * * *
>
> The ES area's lands are presently classified as being suitable for grazing by cattle, sheep, goats, and/or horses. This classification would remain unchanged. The present grazing use of the public lands is primarily by cattle with some use authorized for domestic horses. Change from this present kind of use is not anticipated. * * *
>
> All allotments in the area are classified as being suitable for grazing yearlong and are presently authorized for such use. This classification and authorization would remain unchanged.
>
> There are approximately 175,167 AUMs (67,439 tons) of forage being produced on the ES area's public lands at the present time (this represents less than one half of the ES area's total vegetative production). The amount of forage being produced was determined by the 1977–78 range survey. * * *
>
> Of these 175,167 AUMs of forage, approximately 168,111 would initially be allocated to livestock use * * *. This allocation to livestock would be a reduction of approximately 65,774 AUMs from the present licensed use (233,885 AUMs).
>
> Allocations to livestock and big game would be expected to change as forage production changes. * * * It is anticipated that, by the year 2000, adequate forage would be produced to provide for an allocation of approximately 367,389 AUMs to livestock. This would be an increase of approximately 199,278 AUMs over the initial allocation. * * *
>
> Approximately 2,893 AUMs of forage would be initially allocated to meet the needs of big game animals. Allocations for wildlife would change in proportion to changes in big game populations, based on the amount of forage required to meet their needs (projected increases in big game populations within the next 20 years would result in a requirement for approximately 3,114 AUMs by the year 2000, an increase of 221 AUMs). * * *

The BLM proposal, even though it had not been translated into actual specific reductions through the Allotment Management Plan process, aroused considerable reaction, such as the following comment from an affected rancher:

> I have gone through the East Roswell Grazing Environment Statement, and as a rancher I have to say it looks like the BLM is trying to

put the rancher on the endangered species list! * * * This impact statement if passed in this form will do to part of the ranchers in this area what droughts, low cattle prices, hail and many other disasters have not been able to do, that is to put them out of ranching completely! These are men with an average age above 50 years. What are they going to do? Who is going to give them a job?

The BLM says the economic impact [on] the area will be negligible. How can you lose 1.5 million dollars per year out of the economy of Southeastern New Mexico and not feel it? I am tired of hearing people say the rancher is raping the land that we take our very existence, and for the most part a poor existence! I plan to spend the rest of my life on my ranch, so I am sure not going to rape it! I plan to leave this ranch to my children some day but in the meantime I will try to teach them to love it and take care of it as their dearest possession. Most ranchers I know hold these same ideas.

The Sierra Club representative, perhaps sensing that a doom-crying response was inappropriate in the circumstances, was more sanguine about the BLM environmental evaluation:

I have reviewed the East Roswell Draft Grazing Environmental Impact Statement for the Rio Grande Chapter of the Sierra Club. The data presented indicate that it is absolutely necessary that AUMs be reduced in the near-term to a level which the forage of the land can sustain. We strongly support that proposal. To do otherwise is to knowingly allow the continued deterioration of the range which would be in violation of your responsibility to manage the public lands on a sustained yield, multiple use basis. To do otherwise would allow the continued deterioration of the land to the point where grazing would be impossible, wildlife habitat would be all but destroyed, and soil erosion and water pollution from silt would be intolerable.

Politicians weighed in as well; here is the local Member of Congress, Harold Runnels:

The environmental impact of your proposed study is subject to considerable debate, both pro and con, but the economic impact of the BLM project can be described in one word, "disaster."

Recognizing that the Roswell BLM office has previously taken the position that cattle and other forms of livestock are foreign to the natural environment of these public lands of Eastern New Mexico, it appears that some within BLM have made the decision to eliminate this unwanted (apparently in the eyes of BLM) domestic livestock by making it economically unfeasible for any rancher to continue such operations on BLM lands.

I recognize also that the above suggestion will be rejected, but all the concern displayed about the role of antelope and now the lesser prairie chicken in recent months can only lead one to believe that perhaps the Roswell Daily Record was correct in suggesting that perhaps the ranchers are confronted either with a conspired effort to force them off public lands or are victims of colossal, unflinching stupidity.

I don't know how many lesser prairie chickens you've eaten in recent months, but most of us place a greater need on an adequate beef and lamb supply at the super market. The BLM proposal once again smacks of the all too popular image which the average citizen has of the federal government, that being that too many in the federal government think they always have the answer as to what's best for the average citizen. They seem to forget who is working for whom.

* * *

By BLM's own figures this proposal would mean a loss of 27 percent of the present livestock sales in the area and net returns to the ranchers would decrease by 61 percent. I wonder if the BLM employees would be as excited about a proposal that we reduce their levels by 27 percent and cut the salaries of those remaining by 61 percent during the same time span we expect the local ranchers to sit by while BLM implements this grandiose plan. * * *

The Bureau responded:

The facts which have been presented in this document indicate that an over-statement of forage production, perpetuated over many years, has been made. This purported production, in many cases, has never been used, perhaps because ranchers recognize that it is an over-statement. This recognition is reflected by the licensed use that has been made through the years. However, overuse on many acres of rangeland in the ES area is evident and the alignment of stocking rates with the forage production in these cases is a recognition of fact, rather than being a theoretical loss of livestock production. Unless these range-lands are restored to a productive level which approaches their potential, this loss will not be recovered, but would remain at the reduced level. A 40 percent loss in the area's production of beef would not occur. In fact, this loss would even be less than 28 percent for two reasons: 1) ranchers may have actually sold down because of dry conditions, and 2) much of the beef production comes from farms and ranches which do not have public lands. * * *

Robert H. Nelson, then an analyst in the Interior Department's Office of Policy Analysis, made the following comments in 1980 on BLM's efforts to comply with *NRDC v. Morton*:

Preparation of grazing EISs has in fact turned out to be very expensive. A BLM study of nine of the first EISs to be completed found that $5.7 million had been spent in direct preparation costs—an average of $630,000 per EIS. However, the direct preparation costs were only a fraction of the total EIS costs; for example, they did not include most of the inventories and land use planning required to lay the ground-work for writing the EIS. The same BLM study estimated that the direct preparation costs of the EIS were only about 10% of the total costs associated with completion of each grazing EIS. On this basis, the nine EISs could have cost as much as $50 million, or more than $5 million per statement. Seven million acres were covered by these grazing EISs, so the total cost per acre may well have been around $7 or $8 per acre.

There exists a limited market in grazing rights to public land in which one rancher may sell his rights to another rancher. In this market the rights to public land grazing might typically sell for anywhere from $30 to as much as $100 per AUM. Since the average AUM on BLM land requires about 12 acres, even using the highest purchase price of $100 an AUM, permanent grazing rights probably would be worth no more than $8 per acre. Hence, for the first nine grazing EISs, it appears that, if costs are completely accounted for, the total costs involved in grazing EISs approach the total value of the forage to ranchers for livestock grazing. To put the matter another way, if the government had instead used the EIS money to buy out grazing rights to public land, it might well have been able to buy out most of the grazing rights in the EIS areas for no more than the costs to prepare the EIS.

The costs of the first generation of EISs are likely higher than later ones and BLM's estimates of indirect or supporting costs for EISs may well be too high. But there is a strong case that the expenditures on grazing EISs far exceed what could be justified on any economically rational basis.

See also Robert H. Nelson, Economic Analysis in Public Rangeland Management, in WESTERN PUBLIC LANDS: THE MANAGEMENT OF NATURAL RESOURCES IN A TIME OF DECLINING FEDERALISM (1984).

Environmentalists have a few times asserted that NEPA requires a more particularized analysis of the environmental effects of grazing in particular areas. In the best known instance, National Wildlife Federation v. BLM, 140 IBLA 85 (1997) (the Comb Wash case), they challenged BLM's renewal of a grazing permit for an area in southern Utah that included Comb Wash, which drained streams from five scenic canyons. The BLM had prepared a Resource Management Plan (RMP) and accompanying EIS for the 1.8 million acre Resource Area of which the 72,000 acre Comb Wash was a part. The Board ruled that the record established "without doubt, that BLM failed to comply with NEPA." It noted the following findings made by the administrative law judge:

> The Proposed RMP/FEIS is simply devoid of any site-specific information or analysis regarding the impacts of grazing on the resource values of the particular allotment in question. At best, it contains some general information regarding the impacts of grazing on the entire San Juan Resource Area as a whole. The discussion focuses upon broad descriptions of the types of vegetative zones found in the Area and the general problems of grazing management. The "Affected Environment" and the "Preferred Alternative" of the document do not mention the Comb Wash allotment other than to list it in summary tables

showing such data as the number of acres, number of authorized AUM's, and number of acres in various ecological conditions.

Numerous BLM witnesses confirmed the following facts about the Proposed RMP/FEIS:

(1) That it is not useful or does not provide the detailed information necessary to determine whether to graze the canyons;

(2) That it does not contain an analysis of the 1990 proposed grazing plan or grazing system being implemented by issuance of the annual grazing authorizations nor does it contain information regarding the available forage, condition of the vegetation, or condition of the riparian areas in the canyons; and

(3) That it lacks any discussion of the relative values of the resources in the canyons and no balancing of the harms and benefits of grazing the canyons. * * *

The Board concluded that while BLM has wide discretion, NEPA requires an "adequate environmental review."

NOTES AND QUESTIONS

1. The lack of focused analysis in the Comb Wash case is quite common in BLM's administration of its grazing program. That is, the environmental evaluation contained in the broader resource management plans (covering several hundred thousand or even several million acres in a single document) is simply too broad-brush to be very informative at the level of an individual canyon or riparian area. This makes many grazing permit renewals vulnerable to similar attack, and leaves BLM in a difficult position: As Robert Nelson pointed out in the excerpt above, NEPA compliance is expensive, especially compared to the economic value of the resource at stake. The Congress has never been generous with BLM staffing, and the agency finds it difficult to obtain the money and staff to do the kind of extensive analysis required by the Comb Wash decision. Yet NEPA seems to require that kind of particularized, informed analysis. Moreover, increasingly, the Endangered Species Act is implicated in grazing permit renewals, particularly in desert areas where endangered tortoise, birds, and other riparian species are listed. (See Chapter 5, pp. 491–502, supra.)

2. In 1999, with a glut of permit renewals coming due and BLM's NEPA compliance in some disarray, Congress provided a little relief. It included a rider on the Interior Appropriations bill which directed that expiring grazing permits shall be renewed under the same terms and conditions, "until such time as the Secretary of the Interior completes processing" of such renewal "in compliance with all applicable laws and regulations, at which time such permit or lease may be canceled, suspended or modified, in whole or in part, to meet the requirements of such applicable laws and regulations." 113 Stat. 1501A–159–60.

THE CLINTON ADMINISTRATION AND RANGELAND REFORM

Soon after taking office, the Clinton Administration decided to reform grazing regulations and raise the grazing fee toward market levels. At first the idea was to adopt new regulations, but then an effort was made to adopt reforms by legislation. Congressional reformers eventually failed, after a struggle, to overcome a filibuster by rancher supporters in the Senate. The Administration backed off the idea of raising fees, but returned to the rulemaking process to adopt some procedural and structural reforms in grazing policy. The effort was completed in 1995. One of its key elements was abolition of the old rancher-dominated grazing advisory councils, and substitution of state-wide or area "resource advisory councils," or RACs (pronounced "racks"), which by regulation had to have a membership that was balanced by interest groups. Another was the preparation of fundamentals of rangeland health and standards and guides that would govern grazing in individual geographic areas. Still other elements are described in the next case. The livestock industry promptly challenged the regulations, and the case eventually reached the U.S. Supreme Court.

Public Lands Council v. Babbitt

United States Supreme Court, 2000.
529 U.S. 728.

■ Justice Breyer delivered the opinion of the Court.

This case requires us to interpret several provisions of the 1934 Taylor Grazing Act, 48 Stat. 1269, 43 U.S.C. § 315 *et seq*. The Petitioners claim that each of three grazing regulations [adopted as a part of Rangeland Reform] * * * exceeds the authority that this statute grants the Secretary of the Interior. We disagree and hold that the three regulations do not violate the Act. * * *

[Excerpts from Justice Breyer's introductory description of the Taylor Grazing Act are set out at pp. 783–85 supra. Those excerpts ended with the observation that the Secretary had long maintained authority under the TGA and its implementing regulations to suspend AUMs of grazing privileges "in whole or in part," and "for such time as necessary." The opinion continued:] Indeed, the Department so often reduced individual permit AUM allocations under this last authority that by 1964 the regulations had introduced the notion of "active AUMs," *i.e.*, the AUMs that a permit *initially* granted *minus* the AUMs that the department had "suspended" due to diminished range capacity. Thus, three ranchers who had initially received, say, 3,000, 2,000, and 1,000 AUMs respectively, might find that they could use only two-thirds of that number because a 33% reduction in the district's grazing capacity had led the Department to "suspend" one-third of each allocation. The "active/suspended" system assured each rancher, however, that any capacity-related reduction would take place proportionately among permit holders, see 43 CFR § 4111.4–2(a)(3) (1964), and that the Department would try to restore grazing privileges proportionately should the district's capacity later increase, see § 4111.4–1.

In practice, active grazing on the public range declined dramatically and steadily (from about 18 million to about 10 million AUMs between 1953 and 1998) * * *

Despite the reductions in grazing, and some improvements following the passage of the Taylor act, the range remained in what many considered an unsatisfactory condition. In 1962, a congressionally mandated survey found only 16.6% of the range in excellent or good condition, 53.1% in fair condition, and 30.3% in poor condition. Department of Interior Ann. Rep. 62 (1962). And in 1978 Congress itself determined that "vast segments of the public rangelands are ... in an unsatisfactory condition." [Public Rangeland Improvement Act, or PRIA, 43 U.S.C. § 1901(a)(1)]

In the 1960's, as the range failed to recover, the Secretary of the Interior increased grazing fees by more than 50% (from 19 cents to 30 cents per AUM/year), thereby helping to capture a little more of the economic costs that grazing imposed upon the land. And in 1976, Congress enacted a new law, the Federal Land Policy and Management Act of 1976 (FLPMA), which instructed the Interior Department to develop districtwide land use plans based upon concepts of "multiple use" (use for various purposes, such as recreation, range, timber, minerals, watershed, wildlife and fish, and natural and scenic, scientific, and historical usage), § 1702(c), and "sustained yield" (regular renewable resource output maintained in perpetuity), § 1702(h). The FLPMA strengthened the Department's existing authority to remove or add land from grazing use, allowing such modification pursuant to a land use plan, §§ 1712, 1714, while specifying that existing grazing permit holders would retain a "first priority" for renewal so long as the land use plan continued to make land "available for domestic livestock grazing." § 1752(c).

In 1978, the Department's grazing regulations were, in turn, substantially amended to comply with the new law. See 43 Fed.Reg. 29067. As relevant here, the 1978 regulations tied permit renewal and validity to the land use planning process, giving the Secretary the power to cancel, suspend, or modify grazing permits due to increases or decreases in grazing forage or acreage made available pursuant to land planning. * * *

That same year Congress again increased grazing fees for the period 1979 to 1986. See Public Rangelands Improvement Act of 1978, 43 U.S.C. § 1905. However neither [FLPMA nor PRIA] * * * significantly modified the particular provisions of the Taylor Act at issue in this case.

This case arises out of a 1995 set of Interior Department amendments to the federal grazing regulations. 60 Fed.Reg. 9894 (1995) (Final Rule). The amendments represent a stated effort to "accelerate restoration" of the rangeland, make the rangeland management program "more compatible with ecosystem management," "streamline certain administrative functions," and "obtain for the public fair and reasonable compensation for the grazing of livestock on public lands." 58 Fed.Reg. 43208 (1993) (Proposed Rule). The amendments in final form emphasize individual "stewardship" of the public land by increasing the accountability of grazing permit holders; broaden membership on the district advisory boards; change certain title rules; and change administrative rules and practice of the

Bureau of Land Management to bring them into closer conformity with related Forest Service management practices. See 60 Fed.Reg. 9900–9906 (1995).

Petitioners Public Lands Council and other nonprofit ranching-related organizations with members who hold grazing permits brought this lawsuit * * * challenging 10 of the new regulations. [The district court found 4 of 10 unlawful, but the court of appeals upheld three of the four, one judge partially dissenting.* The three regulations before the Supreme Court:] (1) change the definition of "grazing preference"; (2) permit those who are not "engaged in the livestock business" to qualify for grazing permits; and (3) grant the United States title to all future "permanent" range improvements. * * * [We] consider the ranchers' claim that these three regulatory changes exceed the authority that the Taylor act grants the Secretary.

The ranchers attack the new "grazing preference" regulations first and foremost. Their attack relies upon the provision in the Taylor act stating that "grazing privileges recognized and acknowledged shall be adequately safeguarded...." 43 U.S.C. § 315b. Before 1995 the regulations defined the term "grazing preference" in terms of the *AUM-denominated amount* of grazing privileges that a permit granted. The regulations then defined "grazing preference" as

> "the total number of animal unit months of livestock grazing on public lands apportioned and attached to base property owned or controlled by a permittee or lessee." 43 CFR § 4100.0–5 (1994).

The 1995 regulations changed this definition, however, so that it now no longer refers to grazing privileges "apportioned," nor does it speak in terms of AUMs. The new definition defines "grazing preference" as

> "a superior or priority position against others for the purpose of receiving a grazing permit or lease. This priority is attached to base property owned or controlled by the permittee or lessee." 43 CFR § 4100.0–5 (1995).

The new definition "omits reference to a specified quantity of forage." 60 Fed.Reg. 9921 (1995). It refers only to a priority, not to a specific number of AUMs attached to a base property. But at the same time the new regulations add a new term, "permitted use," which the Secretary defines as

> "the forage allocated by, or under the guidance of, an applicable land use plan for livestock grazing in an allotment under a permit or lease and is expressed in AUMs." 43 CFR § 4100.0–5 (1995).

This new "permitted use," like the old "grazing preference," is defined in terms of allocated rights, and it refers to AUMs. But this new term as defined refers, not to a rancher's forage priority, but to forage "allocated by, or under the guidance of *an applicable land use plan*." *Ibid.* (emphasis added). And therein lies the ranchers' concern.

---

* [Eds. The United States did not seek Supreme Court review of the one issue it lost in the court of appeals—the legality of issu-ing grazing permits for "conservation non-use." That issue is discussed on pp. 847–50 infra.]

The ranchers refer us to the administrative history of Taylor Act regulations, much of which we set forth in Part I. In the ranchers' view, history has created expectations in respect to the security of "grazing privileges"; they have relied upon those expectations; and the statute requires the Secretary to "safeguar[d]" that reliance. Supported by various farm credit associations, they argue that defining their privileges in relation to land use plans will undermine that security. They say that the content of land use plans is difficult to predict and easily changed. Fearing that the resulting uncertainty will discourage lenders from taking mortgages on ranches as security for their loans, they conclude that the new regulations threaten the stability, and possibly the economic viability, of their ranches, and thus fail to "safeguard" the "grazing privileges" that Department regulations previously "recognized and acknowledged." Brief for Petitioners 22–23.

We are not persuaded by the ranchers' argument for three basic reasons. First, the statute qualifies the duty to "safeguard" by referring directly to the Act's various goals and the Secretary's efforts to implement them. The full subsection says:

> *"So far as consistent with the purposes and provisions of this subchapter,* grazing privileges recognized and acknowledged shall be adequately safeguarded, *but* the creation of a grazing district or the issuance of a permit pursuant to the provisions of this subchapter shall *not* create any right, title, interest or estate in or to the lands." 43 U.S.C. § 315b (emphasis added).

The words "so far as consistent with the purposes . . . of this subchapter" and the warning that "issuance of a permit" creates no "right, title, interest or estate" make clear that the ranchers' interest in permit stability cannot be absolute; and that the Secretary is free reasonably to determine just how, and the extent to which, "grazing privileges" shall be safeguarded, in light of the Act's basic purposes. Of course, those purposes include "stabiliz[ing] the livestock industry," but they also include "stop[ping] injury to the public grazing lands by preventing overgrazing and soil deterioration," and "provid[ing] for th[e] orderly use, improvement, and development" of the public range. 48 Stat. 1269.

Moreover, Congress itself has directed development of land use plans, and their use in the allocation process, in order to preserve, improve, and develop the public rangelands. See 43 U.S.C. §§ 1701(a)(2), 1712. That being so, it is difficult to see how a definitional change that simply refers to the use of such plans could violate the Taylor Act by itself, without more. Given the broad discretionary powers that the Taylor Act grants the Secretary, we must read that Act as here granting the Secretary at least ordinary administrative leeway to assess "safeguard[ing]" in terms of the Act's other purposes and provisions. Cf. §§ 315, 315a (authorizing Secretary to establish grazing districts *"in his discretion"* (emphasis added), and to "make provision for protection, administration, regulation, and improvement of such grazing districts").

Second, the pre–1995 AUM system that the ranchers seek to "safeguard" did not offer them anything like absolute security—not even in respect to the proportionate shares of grazing land privileges that the "active/suspended" system suggested. As discussed above, the Secretary has long had the power to reduce an individual permit's AUMs or cancel the permit if the permit holder did not use the grazing privileges, did not use the base property, or violated the Range Code. And the Secretary has always had the statutory authority under the Taylor act and later FLMPA to reclassify and withdraw range land from grazing use, see 43 U.S.C. § 315f (authorizing Secretary, "in his discretion, to examine and classify any lands ... which are more valuable or suitable for the production of agricultural crops ... or any other use than [grazing]"); §§ 1712, 1752(c) (authorizing renewal of permits "so long as the lands ... remain available for domestic livestock grazing *in accordance with land use plans*" (emphasis added)). The Secretary has consistently reserved the authority to cancel or modify grazing permits accordingly. Given these well-established pre–1995 Secretarial powers to cancel, modify, or decline to review individual permits, *including the power to do so pursuant to the adoption of a land use plan,* the ranchers' diminishment-of-security point is at best a matter of degree.

Third, the new definitional regulations by themselves do not automatically bring about a self-executing change that would significantly diminish the security of granted grazing privileges. The Department has said that the new definitions do "not cancel preference," and that any change is "merely a clarification of terminology." 60 Fed.Reg. 9922 (1995). It now assures us through the Solicitor General that the definitional changes "preserve all elements of preference" and "merely clarify the regulations within the statutory framework." See Brief in Opposition 13, 14.

The Secretary did consider making a more sweeping change by eliminating the concept of "suspended use"; a change that might have more reasonably prompted the ranchers' concerns. But after receiving comments, he changed his mind. See 59 Fed.Reg. 14323 (1994). The Department has instead said that "suspended" AUMs will

> "continue to be recognized and have a priority for additional grazing use within the allotment. Suspended use provides an important accounting of past grazing use for the ranching community and is an insignificant administrative workload to the agency." Bureau of Land Management, Rangeland Reform '94: Final Environmental Impact Statement 144 (1994).

Of course, the new definitions seem to tie grazing privileges to land-use plans more explicitly than did the old. But, as we have pointed out, the Secretary has since 1976 had the authority to use land use plans to determine the amount of permissible grazing, 43 U.S.C. § 1712. The Secretary also points out that since development of land use plans began nearly 20 years ago, "all BLM lands in the lower 48 states are covered by land use plans," and "all grazing permits in those States have now been issued or renewed in accordance with such plans, or must now conform to them." Brief for United States 26. Yet the ranchers have not provided us with a single example in which interaction of plan and permit has jeopardized or might yet jeopardize permit security. An *amicus* brief filed by a group of Farm Credit Institutions says that the definitional change will "threate[n]" their "lending policies." Brief for Farm Credit Institutions as *Amicus Curiae* 3. But they do not explain *why* that is so, nor do they state that the new definitions will, in fact, lead them to stop lending to ranchers.

We recognize that a particular land use plan could change pre-existing grazing allocation in a particular district. And that change might arguably lead to a denial of grazing privileges that the pre–1995 regulations would have provided. But the affected permit holder remains free to challenge such an individual effect on grazing privileges, and the courts remain free to determine its lawfulness in context. We here consider only whether the changes in the definitions by themselves violate the Taylor act's requirement that recognized grazing privileges be "adequately safeguarded." Given the leeway that the statute confers upon the Secretary, the less-than-absolute pre–1995 security that permit holders enjoyed, and the relatively small differences that the new definitions create, we conclude that the new definitions do not violate that law.

The ranchers' second challenge focuses upon a provision of the Taylor act that limits issuance of permits to "settlers, residents, and other *stock owners....*" 43 U.S.C. § 315b (emphasis added). In 1936, the Secretary, following this requirement, issued a regulation that limited eligibility to those who "ow[n] livestock." 2 App. 808 (Rules for Administration of Grazing Districts (Mar. 2, 1936)). But in 1942, the Secretary changed the regulation's wording to limit eligibility to those "engaged in the livestock business," 1942 Range Code § 3(a), and so it remained until 1994. The new regulation eliminates the words "engaged in the livestock business," thereby seeming to make eligible otherwise qualified applicants even if they do not engage in the livestock business. See 43 CFR § 4110.1(a) (1995).

The new change is not as radical as the text of the new regulation suggests. The new rule deletes the entire phrase "engaged in the livestock business" from § 4110.1, and seems to require only that an applicant "own or control land or water base property...." *Ibid.* But the omission, standing alone, does not render the regulation facially invalid, for the regulation cannot change the statute, and a regulation promulgated to guide the Secretary's discretion in exercising his authority under the Act need not also restate all related statutory language. Ultimately it is *both* the Taylor act and the regulations promulgated thereunder that constrain the Secretary's discretion in issuing permits. The statute continues to limit the Secretary's authorization to issue permits to "bona fide settlers, residents, and *other stock owners.*" 43 U.S.C. § 315b (emphasis added).

Nor will the change necessarily lead to widespread issuance of grazing permits to "stock owners" who are not in the livestock business. Those in the business continue to enjoy a preference in the issuance of grazing permits. The same section of the Taylor act mandates that the Secretary accord a preference to "landowners engaged in the livestock business, bona fide occupants or settlers." *Ibid.* * * *

The ranchers' underlying concern is that the qualifications amendment is part of a scheme to end livestock grazing on the public lands. They say that "individuals or organizations owning small quantities of stock [will] acquire grazing permits, even though they intend not to graze at all or to graze only a nominal number of livestock—all the while excluding others from using the public range for grazing." Brief for Petitioners 47–48. The new regulations, they charge, will allow individuals to "acquire a few livestock, . . . obtain a permit for what amounts to a conservation purpose and then effectively mothball the permit."

But the regulations do not allow this. The regulations specify that regular grazing permits will be issued for livestock grazing, or suspended use. See 43 CFR §§ 4130.2(a), 4130.2(g) (1998). New regulations allowing issuance of permits for conservation use were held unlawful by the Court of Appeals, see 167 F.3d, at 1307–1308, and the Secretary did not seek review of that decision. * * *

The ranchers' final challenge focuses upon a change in the way the new rules allocate ownership of range improvements, such as fencing, well drilling, or spraying for weeds on the public lands. The Taylor Act provides that permit holders may undertake range improvements pursuant to (1) a cooperative agreement with the United States, or (2) a range improvement permit. 43 U.S.C. § 315c; see 43 CFR §§ 4120.3–2, 4120.3–3 (1998). The pre–1995 regulations applicable to cooperative agreements gave the United States full title to "nonstructural" improvements, such as spraying for weeds, and to "non-removable improvements," such as wells. 43 CFR § 4120.3–2 (1994). But for "structural or removable improvements," such as fencing, stock tanks, or pipelines, the regulations shared title between the permit holder and the United States "in proportion to the actual amount of the respective contribution to the initial construction." *Ibid.* And for range improvements made pursuant to permit, the pre–1995 regulations gave the permittee "title to removable range improvements." § 4120.3–3(b).

The 1995 regulations change the title rules for range improvements made pursuant to a cooperative agreement, but not the rules for improvements made pursuant to permit. For cooperative agreements, they specify that "title to permanent range improvements" (authorized in the future) "such as fences, wells, and pipelines . . . shall be in the name of the United States." 43 CFR § 4120.3–2(b) (1995).

The ranchers argue that this change violates 43 U.S.C. § 315c, which says:

> "No permit shall be issued which shall entitle the permittee to the use of such [range] improvements constructed *and owned* by a prior occupant until the applicant has paid to such prior occupant the reasonable value of such improvements. . . ." (Emphasis added.)

In their view, the word "owned" foresees ownership by a "prior occupant" of at least some such improvements, a possibility they say is denied by the new rule mandating blanket Government ownership of permanent range improvements.

The Secretary responds that, since the statute gives him the power to *authorize* range improvements pursuant to a cooperative agreement—a greater power, § 315c, he also has the power to set the terms of title ownership to such improvements—a lesser power—just like any landlord. See R. Schoshinski, American Law of Landlord and Tenant § 5:31 (1980) (ownership of tenant improvements is a matter open to negotiation with landlord); H. Bronson, A Treatise on the Law of Fixtures § 40 (1904); 2 J. Taylor, A Treatise on the American Law of Landlord and Tenant § 554, pp. 164–166 (1887). Under this reading, the subsequent statutory provision relating to "ownership" simply provides for compensation by some future permit holder *in the event* that the Secretary decides to grant title.

As detailed above, the Secretary did grant ownership rights to range improvements under certain circumstances prior to 1995. We see nothing in the statute that prevents him from changing his mind in respect to the future. And the Secretary has now changed his mind for reasons of administrative convenience and because what he takes as the original purpose of this provision (assuring that, in 1934, ranchers would pay compensation to nomadic sheep herders) is no longer important. In any event, the provision retains even the "contemplation of ownership" meaning stressed by the ranchers, for permit holders may still "own" removable range improvements, such as "corrals, creep feeders, and loading chutes, and temporary structural improvements such as troughs for hauled water," 43 CFR § 4120.3–3(b) (1995), which could be transferred to a new permit holder and thus compel compensation under § 315f.

In short, we find nothing in the statute that denies the Secretary authority reasonably to decide when or whether to grant title to those who make improvements. And any such person remains free to negotiate the terms upon which he will make those improvements irrespective of where title formally lies, including how he might be compensated in the future for the work he had done, either by the Government directly or by those to whom the Government later grants a permit. Cf. 43 U.S.C. § 1752(g) (requiring the United States to pay compensation to a permittee for his "interest" in range improvements if it cancels a permit).

The judgment of the Court of Appeals is *Affirmed.*

■ JUSTICE O'CONNOR*, with whom JUSTICE THOMAS joins, concurring.

I join the Court's opinion. I write separately * * * [to observe that a] permit holder may bring an as-applied challenge to the Secretary's action [on the ground that it failed to adequately safeguard the permit holder's grazing privileges, and that the agency rules as applied are arbitrary and capricious].

NOTES AND QUESTIONS

1. Look closely at the purposes of the TGA. The court of appeals had determined that the TGA's goal of stabilizing the livestock industry is "secondary" to the goals of safeguarding the rangeland and providing for its orderly use. 167 F.3d 1287, 1298 n. 5 (10th Cir.1999). Does the Supreme

---

* Justice O'Connor grew up on a ranch with public land grazing permits in southeastern Arizona and recently co-authored a book about the experience with her brother; Sandra Day O'Connor and H. Alan Day, LAZY B (2002).

Court endorse that view? Or are the goals of equal stature? Notice how this issue ties into the TGA's directive that grazing privileges be "adequately safeguarded."

2.   On the first issue (whether the grazing preference reforms adequately safeguard the grazing privileges), what is really at stake? The ranchers were not arguing that they had a property interest in the AUMs that had been allocated to them under their preference. And they were not denying the authority of the BLM to reduce their grazing privileges in order to protect rangeland health. So what were they arguing? What did they say they had, and how did it limit BLM's authority, if at all? Is this all about optics rather than substance? A tempest in a teapot?

3.   According to PUBLIC LANDS STATISTICS 2000, Table 3–10, BLM grazing permits in FY 2000 included about 2.1 million AUMS in the "suspended" category.

4.   Both Justice Breyer's opinion and Justice O'Connor's concurrence recognize that ranchers remain free to challenge individual BLM decisions to deny or reduce their grazing privileges, either through FLPMA's land use planning process or otherwise. If BLM decides that rangeland health requires reducing the number of livestock to be grazed in an area, what does the rancher have to show to sustain a successful challenge?

5.   In their second challenge, to the deletion of the requirement that permittees be "engaged in the livestock business," what are ranchers worried about? What is so bad, or threatening, about an organization like The Nature Conservancy buying a ranch and running a few cattle on the public lands while it works to restore rangeland health?

6.   On the third issue—title to certain range improvements being in the United States—note that the change was prospective, applying only to range improvements built in the future. Did this feature eliminate any fairness argument? On the title question, the policy issue here is similar to that raised in connection with ownership of water rights perfected to support grazing on the public lands. See Chapter 6, supra p. 552.

7.   The trial court in *Public Lands Council* upheld the core provisions of the 1995 range regulations, the Fundamentals of Rangeland Health, which it described as follows (929 F.Supp. at 1447):

> The Fundamentals allow the Bureau of Land Management to modify grazing practices to ensure that: (1) watersheds function properly or are making significant progress toward proper function; (2) ecological processes, including hydrologic cycles, nutrient cycles, and energy flow are maintained to support healthy biotic communities; (3) water quality complies with state standards and meets wildlife needs; and (4) certain endangered species habitats are maintained or restored. *Id.* The 1995 regulations also provide that the Bureau of Land Management will adopt state or regional standards and guidelines (Standards and Guidelines) to address these same concerns. 43 C.F.R. § 4180.2 (1995).
>
> If the Bureau of Land Management determines that grazing practices need to be modified, it "shall take appropriate action ... as soon as

practicable but not later than the start of the next grazing year." 43 C.F.R. § 4180.1 (1995). Available actions include reducing livestock, grazing, adjusting the grazing season, installing or moving range improvements, or developing alternative water sources.

The plaintiff ranching group conceded that the BLM had the authority to adopt the Fundamentals, and argued only that BLM failed to respond adequately to comments critical of them. The court tersely rejected the contention, pointing out that the final EIS contained ten pages acknowledging and responding to comments and criticism.

8. The grazing regulations require each state BLM office to prepare "standards and guidelines" (S & G) for rangeland health, in consultation with the local Resource Advisory Council, or RAC. These were subject to approval by the Secretary. In early 2001, the Interior Solicitor opined (and the Secretary concurred) that the proposed New Mexico S & Gs had to be rejected because they were inconsistent with the rangeland reform regulations and applicable law. ("Proposed New Mexico Standards and Guidelines for Grazing Administration; Evaluation and Recommendations," January 11, 2001.) The New Mexico S & Gs would have required BLM to consider socioeconomic impacts in determining whether federal rangeland is in a healthy condition. The Solicitor's Opinion pointed out that this could "dictate a BLM decision to put more livestock on public lands that are already in poor ecological condition, in order to serve short-term local economic needs." That, the Opinion continued, violates several laws, including FLPMA's definition of "multiple use" ("without permanent impairment of the productivity of the land and the quality of the environment"); and its mandate to avoid "unnecessary or undue degradation of the lands." The Opinion concluded that socioeconomic factors may inform the choice of options for improving rangeland health, but may not be used at the initial stage of assessing the condition of the range.

9. As implementation of Rangeland Reform moves forward, the courts are beginning to be asked to intervene. In Idaho Watersheds Project v. Hahn, 187 F.3d 1035 (9th Cir.1999), environmentalists complained that

> conditions in the Owyhee Resource Area violated the Bureau of Land Management's ("BLM") 1995 "fundamentals of rangeland health" regulations ("FRH regulations"), 43 C.F.R. § 4180 et seq., * * * and that in violation of the Administrative Procedure Act, 5 U.S.C. § 706(1), the BLM had unreasonably delayed in complying with the FRH regulations. The appellants sought a preliminary injunction: (1) barring "hot-season" grazing from July 15 to September 30, 1999, in riparian pastures in the Succor Creek and State Line allotments, and (2) ordering the BLM to implement changes in grazing management in the allotments no later than the start of the year 2000 grazing season. The district court denied the preliminary injunction * * *.

This regulation provides as follows:

> The authorized officer shall take appropriate action as soon as practicable but not later than the start of the next grazing year upon determining that existing grazing management practices or

levels of grazing use on public lands are significant factors in failing to achieve the standards and conform with the guidelines that are made effective under this section. Appropriate action means implementing actions pursuant to subparts 4110, 4120, 4130, and 4160 of this part that will result in significant progress toward fulfillment of the standards and significant progress toward conformance with the guidelines.

43 C.F.R. § 4180.2(c). 43 C.F.R. §§ 4110, 4120, 4130, and 4160 require the BLM to consult with affected parties, issue a proposed decision, consider any protests, and turn the proposed decision into a final decision.

The BLM made the triggering determination regarding grazing management practices in the Succor Creek and State Line allotments in October 1997. The next grazing year started in the spring of 1998, but the BLM has yet to issue its final decision modifying the relevant grazing permit and implementing changes in grazing management practices. The BLM contends that it is required only to begin the procedures by consulting with affected parties before the next grazing season begins.

We interpret 43 C.F.R. § 4180.2(c) to require the BLM not merely to begin the procedures set forth in 43 C.F.R. §§ 4110, 4120, 4130, and 4160, but rather to complete them and issue its final decision by the start of the next grazing year. The plain language of the regulation requires taking action that results in progress toward fulfillment of ecological standards and guidelines by the start of the next grazing year. * * * The BLM's instruction memorandum, issued by its Assistant Director for Renewable Resources and Planning on April 10, 1998, supports our interpretation in its statement that: "43 CFR subpart 4180 was written to achieve positive, on-the-ground changes in resource conditions.... Success will be measured in terms of concrete outcomes—*not* in terms of procedural actions." *See NRDC v. U.S. Department of Interior,* 113 F.3d 1121, 1124 (9th Cir.1997) (agency's interpretation of statute or regulation it is charged with administering is entitled to deference).

Accordingly, the district court erred in concluding that the appellants failed to establish a likelihood of success on the merits. We * * * [reverse and remand] for the district court to consider the possibility of irreparable injury and whether the balance of hardships tips in favor of the appellants.

10. The Rangeland Reform regulations are described in Todd M. Olinger, Public Rangeland Reform: New Prospects for Collaboration and Local Control Using the Resource Advisory Councils, 69 U.Colo.L.Rev. 633 (1998); Bruce M. Pendery, Reforming Livestock Grazing on the Public Domain: Ecosystem Management–Based Standards and Guidelines Blaze a New Path for Range Management, 27 Envtl. L. 513 (1997); Joseph Feller, "Til the Cows Come Home: The Fatal Flaw in the Clinton's Administration's Public Lands Grazing Policy," 25 Envt'l. L. 703 (1995) (the "fatal flaw," Feller argues, is that, in his view, the regulations fail to require a

determination that the lands at issue are suitable for any grazing at all, an issue considered further below).

REDUCING THE LEVEL OF AUTHORIZED GRAZING

Over the long term, the amount of authorized livestock grazing on federal lands has been rather steadily reduced. Some of this reduction has been voluntary, the result of ranchers going out of business or cutting back on their operations. Some has been the result of regulatory restrictions by federal land managers. Some of the legal issues involved in the latter are explored in the following excerpts from three cases from different areas. The first and third concern grazing on national forests, which presents largely the same legal, policy and environmental issues as grazing on the BLM public lands, although the Forest Service seems not as hampered by history and tradition as its counterpart. In each of the three cases the same basic statutory provision applies—FLPMA, 43 U.S.C.A. § 1752(e):

> The Secretary concerned shall also specify [in the permit] the number of animals to be grazed and the seasons of use and * * * he may reexamine the condition of the range at any time and, if he finds on reexamination that the condition of the range requires adjustment in the amount or other aspect of grazing use, [may require] that the permittee or lessee shall adjust his use to the extent the Secretary concerned deems necessary. Such readjustment shall be put into full force and effect on the date specified by the Secretary concerned.

Among the questions to consider in reading these excerpts is whether these cases interpret this statute the same way; whether they are consistent with each other in how much deference they give the agency, and to what extent differences in result are explainable by differences in the facts.

Perkins v. Bergland

United States Court of Appeals, Ninth Circuit, 1979.
608 F.2d 803.

■ GOODWIN, CIRCUIT JUDGE:

* * * Thomas and David Perkins hold permits entitling each of them to graze cattle within the Prescott National Forest. The permits are issued by the United States Forest Service, * * * [see] 16 U.S.C. § 580*l*. In 1972, the Forest Supervisor, on recommendation of the local District Ranger, reduced Thomas's permit from 517 to 250 head of cattle (subsequently corrected to 266). The following year, the Supervisor similarly reduced David's permit from 158 to 50 head (later corrected to 58).

The agency based the reduction decisions on its finding that the public land involved had been damaged by overgrazing. The decisions were finally upheld by the Secretary of Agriculture in 1977. After exhausting administrative remedies, Thomas and David [sued]. * * *

The district court correctly rejected the Perkins' first line of attack: that the reductions were so drastic as to constitute revocations of their grazing permits. The Perkins brothers argued that revocation requires application of the criteria found in the regulation governing revocation and suspension, 36 C.F.R. § 231.6 (1977).[1] The Forest Service admittedly did not apply those criteria here. However, the district court held, and we agree, that the permits were not in fact suspended or revoked.

The Forest Service reduced the allowable use of the lands for reasons unrelated to the punitive purpose of 36 C.F.R. § 231.6. That regulation allows revocation only in the case of misconduct by a grazing permittee, and in no way relates to allotment reductions necessitated by changed conditions of the range resulting from causes other than permittee misconduct. However drastic an effect on their livelihood the reductions here may have had, the permits were not revoked. Thus, the district court was right in rejecting the revocation theory.

The Perkins brothers argued, in the alternative, that the Secretary's decisions, if not "revocations," were nonetheless subject to judicial review. The government responded, and the district court agreed, that further review was unavailable because the decisions were "committed to agency discretion by law." 5 U.S.C. § 701(a)(2). This conclusion is challenged on two grounds: (1) the reduction decisions are not so committed; or (2), if so committed, the decisions are nevertheless subject to limited judicial review for clear arbitrariness, irrationality, or abuse of discretion.

Both sides purport to rely on the "law to apply" test established in Citizens to Preserve Overton Park v. Volpe, 401 U.S. 402 (1971), for determining when judicial review is precluded under section 701(a)(2). The Secretary also relies on a series of post-*Overton Park* cases in this circuit to support the district court's determination that the reduction decisions are immune from review. Neither party, however, appears to have called to the trial court's attention the new legislation enacted during the time this controversy was pending before the agency. Thus, the trial court never passed upon the effect of a comprehensive public lands statute [FLPMA] which now governs the reviewability issue.

FLPMA empowers the Secretaries of the Interior and Agriculture, each of whom grants grazing privileges on public lands within departmental jurisdictions, to incorporate in grazing permits and leases "such terms and conditions as [the Secretary] deems appropriate for management of the * * * lands." 43 U.S.C. § 1752(e). The same section further provides that the Secretary must specify in the agreement "the numbers of animals to be grazed * * * and that * * * [the Secretary] may reexamine the condition of the range at any time and, if he finds on reexamination that the condition of the range requires adjustment in the amount or other aspect of grazing use, that the permittee or lessee shall adjust his use to the extent the Secretary concerned deems necessary."

---

1. [Permits may be revoked or suspended if:] * * *

"(c) The permittee violates or does not comply with, Federal laws or regulations or State laws relating to protection of air, water, soil and vegetation, fish and wildlife, and other environmental values when exercising the grazing use authorized by the permit."

If we were confronted with the quoted language alone, we would have to consider the government's argument that the Secretary's discretion is so broad in determining grazing capacity—necessarily exercised in accord with expert judgments—as to preclude all judicial review under *Overton Park.* Elsewhere, however, FLPMA explicitly provides that "it is the policy of the United States that * * * judicial review of public land adjudication decisions be provided by law." 43 U.S.C. § 1701(a)(6). This declaration of policy at the outset of FLPMA removes any doubt Congress might otherwise have allowed to obscure the reviewability of grazing reduction decisions made subsequent to the law's enactment.* Since 1976, the Secretary's decision is reviewable.

The remaining issue thus requires us to define the scope of review appropriate to the Secretary's decisions here.

Appellants assert for the first time in this court that certain sections of the Multiple–Use Sustained–Yield Act of 1960 (MUSYA), 16 U.S.C. §§ 528 et seq., supply standards which a court can apply on judicial review to the highly technical assessment of the proper carrying capacity of grazing land. These statutory expressions give the appellants scant support. It must be presumed, at least initially, that those so-called standards were properly considered by the agency. These sections of MUSYA (16 U.S.C. §§ 528, 529, 531) contain the most general clauses and phrases. For example, the agency is "directed" in section 529 to administer the national forests "for multiple use and sustained yield of the several products and services obtained therefrom," with "due consideration [to] be given to the relative values of the various resources in particular areas." This language, partially defined in section 531 in such terms as "that [which] will best meet the needs of the American people" and "making the most judicious use of the land", can hardly be considered concrete limits upon agency discretion. Rather, it is language which "breathe[s] discretion at every pore." Strickland v. Morton, 519 F.2d 467, 469 (9th Cir.1975). What appellants really seem to be saying when they rely on the multiple-use legislation is that they do not agree with the Secretary on how best to administer the forest land on which their cattle graze. While this disagreement is understandable, the courts are not at liberty to break the tie by choosing one theory of range management as superior to another.

Thus, we conclude that only very narrow review is appropriate here. The district court should ascertain whether the agency's factual findings as to range conditions and carrying capacity are arbitrary and capricious. 5 U.S.C. § 706(2)(A).[10] If not, the matter ends there. In making that inquiry, the court may consider the Perkins brothers' contention that the methods

* [Eds. The court did not quote or refer to the concluding sentence in that introductory section of FLPMA, which provides: "The policies of this Act shall become effective only as specific statutory authority for their implementation is enacted by this Act or by subsequent legislation * * *." 43 U.S.C. § 1701(b).]

10. Although the Perkinses apparently received hearings within the agency's review process, there is no statutory requirement for a hearing. Thus, the substantial-evidence test of section 706(2)(E) does not apply. * * * Instead, section 706(2)(A) supplies the appropriate standard for the factual review. * * * [Eds. See Chapter 4, supra pp. 306–07 for the statutory language.]

utilized by the Forest Service in determining capacity were irrational.[12] But their charge that the agency decision was "unrelated to reality" sheds no light on the subject. We find nothing in the statutes authorizing courts to choose between battling experts on the definition of "reality." Consequently, the trial court must refrain from entering that fray if it turns out that the appellants' position would require a choice between experts.

The judgment is vacated and the case is remanded to the district court for the very limited factual review available under the "arbitrary and capricious" standard.

Hinsdale Livestock Co. v. United States

United States District Court, District of Montana, 1980.
501 F.Supp. 773.

■ Battin, Chief Judge.

[Plaintiffs are several ranchers in Valley County, Montana, who graze livestock on BLM land intermingled with private lands; the percentage of private lands on each grazing allotment ranges from 12% to 33%. Each plaintiff held BLM grazing permits which authorized grazing through late October or late November, 1980. About the end of August, 1980, BLM notified each plaintiff to remove its cattle from the public lands because drought conditions then prevailing created an emergency in which the range would suffer severe damage if grazing continued. Plaintiffs were told to remove their cattle by mid-September. Plaintiffs sued. The court's opinion included the following findings of fact and conclusions of law.]

19.   The data relied on by the defendant in reaching its decision that plaintiffs' cattle must be immediately removed from the public lands in order to prevent severe damage to the range land resource was based primarily on various written materials which defendant and authorized agent Terrence E. Wilson could not specify and on other principles that defendant Terrence E. Wilson testified to the effect that further grazing on the range resource in a year of drought is harmful to the range resource and makes it more difficult for the resource to recover from a year of drought.

20.   These reasons do not create an emergency such as was asserted by the defendant in its letters of eviction to plaintiff; the Court finds this on the basis of expert testimony. These experts are August Hormay, on behalf of the plaintiff, and Dr. Donald Ryerson, on behalf of the defendants. Both witnesses testified that continued grazing of the range resource throughout the balance of plaintiffs' permit seasons this year does not in any way create an emergency to the range land resource. * * *

22.   The range resource will not be severely damaged if livestock of plaintiffs continue to graze on it until the end of the permit seasons. There

---

12.   To prove that the agency employed "irrational" methods for calculating carrying capacity, a contesting party must show that there is virtually no evidence in the record to support the agency's methodology in gathering and evaluating the data.

is no emergency condition * * *. Such a finding is based on the testimony of experts * * * presented by both the plaintiffs and the defendants.

23.   The Court is of the opinion that plaintiffs would suffer severe and irreparable damage and harm if they were forced from the public lands before the expiration of their permit periods for 1980.

* * *

27.   The Court is of the opinion that the actions of the defendant as set forth above are arbitrary and capricious in that the decisions were not based on scientific evidence, nor based on any input from plaintiffs involved. The defendants' expert witness, Dr. Donald Ryerson, testified that all of the plaintiffs have been ranching their entire adult lives, were raised ranching, and that they have had extensive experience in conducting ranching operations on lands that include the public domain. * * *

28.   These ranchers have experienced many droughts in the areas that are the subject of this lawsuit. Evidence presented at hearing revealed they know how to judge the conditions of the range resource and have acted appropriately in managing their herds in accordance with the conditions of the range resources.

29.   The opinion of plaintiffs is that the range resources will not be severely damaged if the reduced number of livestock they now have on the range resources are allowed to remain there the balance of this permit season.

The Court adopts the opinion of Gus Hormay and these ranchers with respect to the condition of the range resource. Testimony has revealed that drought conditions never create an emergency with respect to the range resource, contrary to the opinion of defendant Bureau of Land Management. * * *

30.   The plaintiffs were deprived of any notion of due process of law with respect to the defendant's decision affecting the allotments plaintiffs lease. Significant portions of plaintiffs' privately owned and controlled land intermingle with the federal lands. Plaintiffs did not have an opportunity to participate in the decision to evict the livestock from the allotments plaintiffs lease. Tours the defendant conducted in conjunction with the plaintiffs were made subsequent to the Bureau's decision that evictions would be made.

31.   The Bureau failed to consider the fact that plaintiffs had all voluntarily reduced their use of the federal lands during this year * * * prior to any action taken by the Bureau. * * * [Hinsdale spent] approximately $34,000 * * * relocating cattle that normally would have remained on the allotments this year. As a result, plaintiffs will continue to incur costs of grazing and feeding relocated livestock.

32.   The Court finds the defendant is in violation of the contract[*] entered into with plaintiff Hinsdale Livestock Company. The allotment management plan provides for a rest rotation grazing system with two of seven pastures rested or unused each year. Plaintiffs have made substantial

---

* [Eds. The court apparently regarded the provisions of the Bureau's Allotment   Management Plan (AMP) that were incorporated into the plaintiff's grazing permit as a

investments related to the allotment plan covered by the seven pastures in the form of many miles of fence and construction of reservoirs. The allotment plan, on page 23, states:

> There is flexibility in management with this type of system. The rest pasture may be used in the event of * * * drought * * * but grazing will return to normal sequence immediately following the deviation. This flexibility is necessary in adjusting to short term climate and vegetative changes * * *.

33. The Court is of the opinion that the defendant is in violation of this agreement in that it is now denying plaintiff Hinsdale Livestock Company the opportunity to utilize the rest pastures in this year of proven drought. * * *

CONCLUSIONS OF LAW * * *

3. [BLM's actions] are not supported by the evidence and testimony heard by the Court.

4. Plaintiffs were deprived of due process of law by defendants' actions in evicting plaintiffs from the allotments in question, said allotments intermingling federal lands with private lands of plaintiffs.

5. Defendants have denied plaintiffs any meaningful opportunity for administrative appeal of the decision by the defendant evicting plaintiffs from the allotments in question during the balance of the grazing season for 1980.

6. The immediate effect of the defendant's decision to evict plaintiffs from the allotments in question for the balance of the 1980 grazing season is contrary to the policy of Congress expressed in 43 U.S.C. 1701(a)(6) which provides that it is the policy of the United States that judicial review of public land adjudication decisions be provided by law.

7. Plaintiffs will suffer irreparable harm if a preliminary injunction does not issue. Such an injunction should issue enjoining defendants from evicting plaintiffs from the allotments in question pending plaintiffs' pursuit of administrative remedies.

8. The evidence and testimony reveals there is no emergency condition on the range resource in question that requires the immediate removal of the livestock. The Court finds that the defendants will not be harmed by the issuance of a preliminary injunction enjoining defendant from implementing its decision to immediately evict plaintiffs' livestock from the range resource. * * *

McKinley v. United States

United States District Court, District of New Mexico, 1993.
828 F.Supp. 888.

■ HANSEN, DISTRICT JUDGE.

* * * This lawsuit seeks to set aside a decision by officials of the U.S. Forest Service which provided for a reduction in the number of cattle

contract. It noted in finding #34, omitted here, that the AMP was signed by a BLM manager and a Hinsdale official.]

permitted to graze on the 28,719 acre Barranca allotment located in the Cibola National Forest in the Manzano Mountains of central New Mexico. This allotment was formed in 1973 by consolidating three existing allotments because range evaluations from the 1950s and 1960s indicated the range was in generally poor condition and the Forest Service believed that the combination of the three allotments would provide an opportunity for improved management.

At the time of the consolidation, appellant Weldon McKinley was issued a Term Grazing Permit for 201 cattle on the Barranca allotment. Range evaluations indicated that a small portion of the allotment was in fair condition with an upward trend, but that the majority of the range was in unsatisfactory condition with a downward trend. Beginning in 1975, appellant elected to graze less than the number of cattle permitted. According to the Forest Service, average use between 1973 and 1988 was 50% of permitted numbers.

On July 7, 1988, McKinley was advised that a reduction in livestock numbers on the allotment had been recommended, based on Forest Service range studies. In August, 1988, and January, 1989, the Forest Service met with McKinley to discuss the allegedly unsatisfactory range conditions.

On July 21, 1989, defendant Cibola Forest Supervisor C. Phil Smith decided that grazing should be reduced to 100 cattle. On September 5, 1989, McKinley appealed that decision. On October 10, 1989, Smith modified his July 21 decision, based in part on the results of the Production/Utilization Study completed on September 28, 1989, and determined that the Barranca Allotment should be permitted 112 head of cattle. * * *

Appellant * * * argues that the Forest Service can modify the seasons of use, numbers, kinds and class of livestock allowed only because of resources condition or at the request of the permittee. 36 C.F.R. § 222.4. He contends that because he did not request a modification and because the Barranca allotment is in a stable or upward condition, the decision was not in accordance with the provisions of 36 C.F.R. § 222.4.

It is clear that the Forest Supervisor has the ability to reduce permitted numbers on the allotment. 36 C.F.R. § 222.5(a). The dispute in this case concerns the accuracy of the Forest Service studies which found that the range condition in the allotment was poor or very poor, indicating a need for a reduced stocking level on the allotment.

Range analysis of the allotment was performed in 1973, 1977–78, 1988 and 1989. The techniques utilized in this case included Parker Three Step Clusters, paced transects, and ocular estimates.[*]

Parker Three Step Cluster studies were conducted in 1973, 1977–78 and 1988. The purpose of these studies is to compare range conditions at

---

* [Eds. Another term for this is "ocular reconnaissance;" still another term is "eyeballing."]

the same spot over time. Permanent iron makers are placed in the grounds and metal tape is strung between the markers. Vegetative and soil conditions are examined and photographs taken to evaluate the current trend and these are compared with past data collected from the same location.

A paced transect was conducted by the Forest Service in June 1989 at the request of appellant's expert, Ralph Rainwater, who participated in the study. It involves walking a randomly selected line of 100 data points with soil and vegetation examined at a predetermined (i.e., every other pace) spacing.

Ocular estimates are merely visual observations of range conditions by range conservationists. They are conducted on an annual basis.

Production/utilization studies were also conducted by the Forest Service in 1982, 1983 and 1989. They measure the production of forage on the site and utilization or consumption of that forage by cattle.

Appellant's expert argues that the studies actually shows [sic] that the range condition is improving. Further, he contends that the sample size does not conform to the generally accepted sample size used by range experts.

The Forest Service argues that the evaluation of range trend is merely one factor to consider in the overall evaluation of range resources. Its findings demonstrate that in 1988, despite appellant's voluntary reduction in the number of grazing cattle on the property, only 8% of the allotment was in fair condition with 92% in poor or very poor condition and that the trend on 50% of the allotment was static, indicating that conditions were not improving, and a reduced stocking level was necessary.

The appellant's permit states that it "may be modified at any time during the term to conform with needed changes brought about * * * because of resource condition or other management needs." The Court agrees with the Forest Service that by the permit's own terms it is range condition, not trend, which is evaluated to determine grazing capacity.

* * * [The court rejected defendant's argument that the reduction raised a "takings" issue:] "It is safe to say that it has always been the intention and policy of the government to regard the use of its public lands for stock grazing, either under the original tacit consent or, as to national forests, under regulation through the permit system, as a privilege which is withdrawable at any time for any use by the sovereign without the payment of compensation." Swim v. Bergland, 696 F.2d 712, 719 (9th Cir.1983).

Appellant argues that the reduction in permitted numbers is a taking of private property because it affects the value of his associated base property which he holds in fee simple. He contends that reducing his grazing allowance by 44% will have the effect of rendering his entire operation, including his private property, useless. He cites a computer program model showing the relationship between the fixed costs of ranching operation, the number of livestock grazed on Forest Service managed lands, and the amount of money those animals would have to generate when sold on the market to make the ranching operation viable and submitted appraisal reports on the allotment and the base property in support of his argument.

While the Court does not doubt that the modification of appellant's permit has a negative effect on the value of his base property and the economic viability of his ranching operation, the value added to his property by his holding the permit * * * [does not require a takings analysis]. "Although the permits are valuable to ranchers, they are not an interest protected by the Fifth Amendment against taking by the government who granted them with the understanding that they could be withdrawn * * * without payment of compensation." Pankey Land and Cattle Co. v. Hardin, 427 F.2d 43, 44 (10th Cir.1970). No compensable taking was implicated by the Forest Service's actions in this case. * * *

NOTES AND QUESTIONS

1. *Perkins* holds that a court may review a permit reduction, but only to determine whether the agency's findings were arbitrary or its methods irrational. What realistic chance of reversal do those challenging agency grazing decisions have under this approach? Specifically, if there is conflicting testimony from the experts testifying for the government and for the ranchers, who wins?

2. Same result in *Perkins* if the Forest Service had decided to *increase* the number of allowable livestock in the area (and presented expert testimony in support of that decision), and environmentalists had sued?

3. What standard of review did the *Hinsdale* court apply? Did it give sufficient deference to the agency? In Valdez v. Applegate, 616 F.2d 570 (10th Cir.1980), the court stayed the implementation of BLM-ordered grazing reductions pending determination of the merits of the ranchers' complaint that the reductions were illegal, finding that while the public has an interest in protecting federal lands from overgrazing, it also has an interest in "economic stability of the area" affected.

4. Note the ranchers in *Hinsdale* had substantial amounts of private land intermingled with the federal land. How does that affect the issues here? If there are no fences separating private from federal land, how is the grazing reduction order to be carried out?

5. In Anchustegui v. Department of Agriculture, 257 F.3d 1124 (9th Cir.2001), the Forest Service cancelled a permit to graze sheep on an Idaho national forest on the ground that the permittee had violated the terms and conditions of the permit. The court held that the agency had failed to conform to a provision of the Administrative Procedure Act, 5 U.S.C. § 558(c), which provided that, "[e]xcept in cases of wilfulness or those in which the public health, interest, or safety requires otherwise," a permit or license may be revoked "only if, before the institution of agency proceedings therefor, the license has been given (1) notice by the agency in writing of the facts or conduct which may warrant the action; and (2) opportunity to demonstrate or achieve compliance * * *." The court said the agency's "show cause letter," which had stated that "permit action is warranted"

and proposed to cancel the permit, constituted the "institution of agency proceedings" without giving the rancher prior notice or an opportunity to achieve compliance. The court also said the record did not show wilful noncompliance. It did not consider whether the "public * * * interest" required waiver of the notice and opportunity to achieve compliance.

FLPMA PLANNING AND GRAZING REDUCTIONS

General background on BLM's planning process under FLPMA is set out in Chapter 5, supra p. 431. Because the great bulk of BLM land is devoted to livestock grazing, planning as it relates to the forage resource has remained the subject of considerable attention. The following case (sometimes called the Burns decision, after the judge who rendered it) is perhaps the most detailed examination of BLM's planning responsibilities in relation to grazing.

Natural Resources Defense Council, Inc. v. Hodel

United States District Court, District of Nevada, 1985.
624 F.Supp. 1045.

■ Burns, J.

This is a complex case of first impression, brought by environmental organizations seeking to overturn certain decisions made by the Bureau of Land Management (BLM) relating to livestock grazing on public lands in the Reno, Nevada area. The plaintiffs challenge the BLM's land use plan as being in conflict with Congressional statutory mandates, and as being arbitrary and capricious as a matter of administrative law. * * *

The BLM lands are divided for grazing purposes into districts, and subdivided into planning areas, such as the "Reno Planning Area" which is the subject of this action. The Reno Planning Area encompasses an overall area of just over 5 million acres, about 700,000 of which are under BLM supervision. The planning areas are further divided into grazing allotments, for which the BLM issues grazing permits or licenses. * * *

* * * [BLM began] in the late 1970s to lay the groundwork for a comprehensive grazing management plan and EIS for the Reno area. The agency began gathering inventory data, listing the available resources in portions of the planning area. Agency specialists then began preparation of the Management Framework Plan (MFP)*, which [took several months and was accompanied by NEPA compliance. The draft plan and EIS was published, and public comment taken, and then] * * * a final land use plan for grazing in the Reno planning area [was issued] on December 21, 1982. * * *

Plaintiffs first correctly point to the legislative histories of the Taylor Grazing Act, FLPMA, and PRIA, to demonstrate Congress' general concern

---

* [Eds.: The management framework plans were pre-FLPMA plans; BLM calls its post-FLPMA plans "resource management plans," or RMPs. MFPs remain in force until they are replaced by RMPs. See 43 U.S.C. § 1732(a).]

about overgrazing by livestock, and to indicate that reductions in livestock levels were one of the methods mentioned by Congress to prevent further deterioration of rangelands. Plaintiffs then cite portions of the record, including the DEIS, which indicate that there has been overuse of some portions of the Reno area by livestock. The conclusion plaintiffs say should then follow is that BLM has violated the law, and that the relatively modest improvements predicted from the MFP are insufficient to comply with the statutory mandates.

The facts established by the enormous record in this case do show that there has been overgrazing in the Reno area, but that in only four allotments could it be *conclusively* determined that the overgrazing was due to livestock use. On eight allotments the overuse could have resulted from a combination of livestock, deer, and wild horses; on the three remaining allotments there was no livestock grazing whatsoever. Thus, overgrazing due to livestock was not endemic to the entire Reno area.

A second important point to note in this context is that even where overgrazing is found to exist, the remedy is not necessarily the immediate removal of livestock. I give due weight to the proposition put forth by defendants' experts that other methods, such as vegetation manipulation and seeding, fencing, water development, or other range improvements or grazing systems may serve to address problems of selective overgrazing without a mandatory reduction in livestock use. * * * While reductions in AUMS for livestock may be one accepted method of addressing range deterioration, as recognized by Congress (see 43 U.S.C. § 1903(b)), it is not the only method.

A third important point here concerns the quality of data available to the BLM for making livestock management decisions. * * * [T]he BLM reached the decision that in order to defend its actions against attack from ranching interests it would need a solid data base upon which to ground livestock reduction orders. * * * Perkins v. Bergland, 608 F.2d 803, 807 (9th Cir.1979). As explained by defendants' experts, in order for the BLM to be certain of the proper livestock carrying capacity of a given allotment the agency must have: (1) actual use data (what kinds of animals grazed where and for how long), (2) how much vegetation has been consumed (utilization data), and (3) the overall effect of the specified grazing (trend). * * * The BLM said it lacked the first type of data for much of the Reno area and felt (at least after 1981) that in its absence it should refrain from immediate changes in livestock numbers, and concentrate its efforts on other techniques of range management.

Plaintiffs claim that the BLM is allowing overgrazing to continue. In reality, however, their complaint is with the *methods* selected by the BLM to allocate the resources within its control. Rather than immediate reductions in livestock numbers, the BLM chose to install range improvements and grazing systems on the areas ("I" allotments) that the BLM says are in need of the greatest attention. Moreover, the MFP does call for a significant reduction in livestock numbers, although this is to take place over a longer period of time than plaintiffs insist on. Finally, the MFP is predicted to bring about an overall improvement in the rated quality of many of the allotments. In sum, it is not entirely certain that the BLM has allowed continued overgrazing or deterioration of resources, in violation of statutory mandates.

The * * * MFP does result in limited improvements in overall ecological and forage conditions in the Reno area. Plaintiffs characterize the BLM's management as "do nothing", but in reality it appears that the real argument is that the BLM does not do what plaintiffs want, namely redress range conditions through immediate reduction or elimination of livestock grazing.

It must be noted that it is yet too early for a court to evaluate a claim that the BLM has not complied with its own plan, or that it has not taken the steps promised in the MFP. * * *

Plaintiffs argue that FLPMA and PRIA provide "standards" against which the court can determine whether the MFP is "arbitrary, capricious or contrary to law." The declarations of policy and goals in 43 U.S.C. §§ 1701(a), 1732, 1901, 1903 and ancillary provisions contain only broad expressions of concern and desire for improvement. They are general clauses and phrases which "can hardly be considered concrete limits upon agency discretion. Rather, it is language which 'breathes discretion at every pore.'" Perkins v. Bergland, 608 F.2d at 806. Although I might privately agree with plaintiffs that a more aggressive approach to range improvement would be environmentally preferable, or might even be closer to what Congress had in mind, the Ninth Circuit has made it plain that "the courts are not at liberty to break the tie choosing one theory of range management as superior to another." Perkins v. Bergland, 608 F.2d at 807. The modest plans adopted by the BLM for dealing with range conditions in the Reno area are not "irrational" and thus cannot be disturbed by the court.

The real question posed in this section of the case is what are BLM land use plans supposed to look like? That is, what kind of detail must the MFP contain to qualify as a legitimate land use plan required by Congress? FLPMA and PRIA refer to the importance of land use planning in several places. See 43 U.S.C. §§ 1701(a)(2), 1712, 1732(a), 1901(b). But nowhere in the statutes did Congress describe in detail what sort of information must be included in a land use plan. * * *

* * * It is therefore a reasonable assumption that Congress intended the BLM to continue its practice of setting grazing capacity at the permit-decision stage, and that land use planning (as required by 43 U.S.C. § 1712) deal with broader issues. These broader issues might include long-term resource conflicts, long-term range trends, planning of range improvements, and concentrating the BLM's limited resources on certain key areas.

This is the type of planning adopted by the BLM in this case. Clearly, the agency will continue to set grazing capacity on an on-going basis when it issues or renews grazing permits or licenses. A land use plan need not encompass every localized decision that must be made in the foreseeable future. Indeed, the legislative history indicates that Congress recognized "land use planning as dynamic and subject to change with changing conditions and values." [citing House Committee Report on what became FLPMA] * * *

The present BLM regulations cited by plaintiffs do not compel a contrary interpretation. * * * BLM district managers * * * know that after the first five years they must begin reducing livestock AUMs to meet the 30,618 level they have set as a long term goal, and that total consumption must not exceed 59,344 AUMs for all species. If they fail to take these long term limits into account in issuing grazing permits after the first five years of the plan then they may be liable to an enforcement action by plaintiffs, or others with a similarly deep concern for the environment.

* * * FLPMA and PRIA demand no more. The type of "planning" envisioned by plaintiffs, wherein the plan would effectively contain allotment management plans for each unit in the Reno area, allocating forage to each consumer species for each of the next ten years or more, is not a plan. It is an administrative straight-jacket which eliminates the room for any flexibility to meet changing conditions. In the absence of more directive legislation, or mandate from my appellate superiors, I will not command such a requirement. * * *

Defendant's * * * affidavits * * * are persuasive in refuting the notion that there is such a thing as an *a priori* "carrying capacity" or grazing capacity for any one piece of land. Consider a hypothetical allotment which could support 100 head of cattle in one year, and not show signs of downward trend. However, in the following year, depending on only one variable such as climate[,] the same allotment could perhaps support only 80 head. Cf. Hinsdale Livestock Co. v. United States, 501 F.Supp. 773, 777 (D.Mont.1980). Conversely, with the addition of certain range improvements that would improve dispersal of the livestock on the allotment, the same parcel could in the following year perhaps support 120 head without signs of deterioration. Each of these permutations could be further affected by other variables such as usage by wild horses, or mule deer, precipitation or temperature patterns, seeding, encroachment of inferior types of forage, changes in seasons of use, and so on. * * * Unrealistic, then, is plaintiffs' theory that there is a fixed and immutable level of acceptable livestock use that can be administratively determined for years into the future. * * *

Although the BLM had trend data for most of the area, such data alone is [sic] not useful for setting livestock grazing levels because a declining trend can be due to a wide number of factors, only one of which is overuse by livestock. Further, although the BLM had some utilization data (showing how much forage was consumed in a given plot) it was not able to conclusively determine actual use by livestock. The actual use by real numbers of cattle is not always the same as the authorized use contained in permits. [citing BLM affidavit] * * *

Because of these and other difficulties, the BLM decided to revamp its methodology of setting grazing levels, based primarily on continued monitoring over longer periods of time, and not based on one-point-in-time studies * * *. A new monitoring system for Nevada was developed by a joint task force and was adopted in 1981. It is a coincidence that this change in methodology took place around the time that Mr. Watt became

Secretary of the Interior, and the ultimate result of the decision was the continuation of existing grazing levels in the Reno area. But there is no direct evidence in this record that the change in methodology was primarily prompted by a political decision to postpone any adjustments in allocation that would adversely affect ranching interests. * * *

* * * If it were possible to glean more precise standards from the statutes or regulations, against which these policy decisions could be measured, then I might be more able to discern a pattern of illegal or arbitrary conduct, and to fashion appropriate relief. That is not the case before me. * * * The administrative record in this case does at least contain plausible support for defendants' position that existing monitoring data for the Reno area was [sic] not reliable for purposes of setting fixed grazing levels. While the BLM probably *could* have made defensible live-stock adjustments where their data showed overutilization, poor range condition, and downward trend, this court cannot say it was "irrational" for them to refrain from doing so without the sort of monitoring data they desired. At this point, judicial inquiry is at an end. * * *

CONCLUSION

* * * After considerable thought and deliberation, I have come to the conclusion that the role plaintiffs would have me play in this controversy is an unworkable one. Plaintiffs are understandably upset at what they view to be a lopsided and ecologically insensitive pattern of management of public lands at the hands of the BLM, a subject explored at length by many commentators. Congress attempted to remedy this situation through FLPMA, PRIA and other acts, but it has done so with only the broadest sorts of discretionary language, which does not provide helpful standards by which a court can readily adjudicate agency compliance.

Boiled down and stripped of legalese[8] this is a case in which plaintiffs ask me to become—and defendants urge me not to become—the rangemaster for about 700,000 acres of federal lands in western Nevada. For some reason, over the past 15 years or so, I and many of my [federal judicial] colleagues have become or have been implored to become forestmasters [eds. case citations are omitted in this list], roadmasters, schoolmasters, fishmasters, prisonmasters, watermasters, and the like. This trend has not escaped the notice and criticism of academic commentators.

That criticism has been based upon observations which include lack of training and expertise, lack of time, lack of staff assistance, and similar conditions. At bottom, however, the primary reason for the large scale intrusion of the judiciary into the governance of our society has been an inability or unwillingness of the first two branches of our governments—both state and federal—to fashion solutions for significant societal, environmental, and economic problems in America. Frankly, I see little likelihood that the legislative and executive branches will take the statutory (and occasional constitutional) steps which would at least slow, if not reverse,

---

8. This litigation has brought forth a confounding number of acronyms such as FLPMA, PRIA, SVIM, URA, AMP, and CRMP (pronounced either "cramp," "crimp," or "crump") and MFP (which I assure the reader is unpronounceable.)

this trend. Fortunately, for reasons set out in this opinion which (to me) are legally correct, I am able to resist the invitation to become western Nevada's rangemaster. * * *

NOTES AND QUESTIONS

1. The Ninth Circuit affirmed this decision with a brief opinion, noting:

> Reduced to its essence, the NRDC's challenge to the EIS and the final land use plan is a challenge to the BLM's policy decision to postpone livestock grazing adjustments until reliable data was [sic] available. While we sympathize with the NRDC's strong desire to preserve the environment, we agree with the district court that we cannot label this policy decision as either irrational, or contrary to law. Thus, "[a]t this point, judicial inquiry is at an end."

819 F.2d 927, 930 (9th Cir.1987). The opinion also contained this footnote (id. n.1):

> The NRDC complains that the district court incorrectly assumed that the BLM sets grazing capacity on an on-going basis when it issues or renews grazing permits or licenses. We agree with the BLM that this assumption was not essential to the district court's conclusion that [FLPMA and PRIA] "demand no more" than broad objective-oriented land use plans. * * *

2. Regarding the alleged lack of data, the district court referred in various places to BLM's claimed lack of data on such things as the actual (as opposed to authorized) level of livestock grazing, the amount of forage consumed, the environmental impacts of grazing on specific allotments or specific areas, and the environmental effects of adjustments in grazing levels. Does either court in this case *require* the BLM to *gather* that data? Does FLPMA (or NEPA) require gathering of relevant data? Is it lawful for a federal land management agency to put its head in the sand and ignore whatever problems might exist on its lands? So long as it does not have, and does not take steps to produce, reliable information to show that problems exist, is it immune from judicial interference? Is that good policy? On the other hand, if a federal land management agency may be said to have a legally enforceable duty to gather relevant data, how can that idea be cabined within reasonable bounds? Does it have a duty to commission studies to identify every species and the effect of proposed actions on them?

3. Suppose the BLM had, on the basis of the limited data it had here, gone ahead and provided in the final plan for reductions in the authorized level of livestock grazing. Would that have been arbitrary and capricious? Cf. *Perkins v. Bergland*, supra.

4. Recall that BLM is also under a mandate to achieve "sustained yield" of the forage resource here, defined in FLPMA as "the achievement and maintenance in perpetuity of a high-level annual or regular periodic output of the various renewable resources of the public lands consistent with multiple use." 43 U.S.C. § 1702(h). Did the BLM comply with this mandate on the facts of the principal case? Recall also the generic mandate of FLPMA, 43 U.S.C. § 1732(b), that "[i]n managing the public lands the

Secretary shall, by regulation or otherwise, take any action necessary to prevent unnecessary or undue degradation of the lands." (For other discussion of that statutory mandate, see Chapter 7, pp. 636–39.) Did the BLM comply with this mandate here in the Reno Planning Area?

5. One might question, after the Supreme Court's 1998 decision in Ohio Forestry Ass'n v. Sierra Club, supra p. 294, whether this challenge to the plan on its face would be ripe if brought today. If NRDC had to bring the challenge to the plan in the context of a renewal of a specific grazing permit, might that have made its case more appealing, by providing a real, on-the-ground factual context in which to judge BLM's action (or inaction)?

6. In that part of his opinion addressing plaintiffs' claim of inadequate compliance with NEPA, Judge Burns held that an alternative of completely banning grazing on BLM land in the Reno area was not reasonable and did not require consideration. He noted, among other things, that

> Livestock grazing has been going on in the Reno planning area, on public lands, for more than a century, [and it is] an important priority in the overall resource picture of this area. * * * NEPA does not require examination of alternatives that are so speculative, contrary to law, or economically catastrophic as to be beyond the realm of feasibility. The complete abandonment of grazing in the Reno planning area is practically unthinkable as a policy choice; it would involve monetary losses to the ranching community alone of nearly 4 million dollars and 290 jobs, not to mention unquantifiable social impacts. Of course, compared with the economy of the Reno area as a whole, ranching plays only a negligible role.[*] Nevertheless, eliminating all grazing would have extreme impacts on this small community.

7. Judge Burns is reluctant to become "rangemaster" of BLM lands in the Reno area. In Washington v. Washington State Commercial Passenger Fishing Vessel Ass'n, 443 U.S. 658 (1979), the Supreme Court held that the trial court was justified in assuming the role of "fishmaster" in the Columbia River basin to protect Indian treaty fishing rights, and "has the power to undertake the necessary remedial steps and to enlist the aid of the appropriate federal law enforcement agents in carrying out those steps." 443 U.S. at 696. Should the court's decision whether or not to become a "rangemaster" depend on whether the agency is implementing and complying with the law? On the seriousness of the abuses? On the complexity of the situation?

Central South Dakota Co-op. Grazing Dist. v. Secretary, U.S. Dept of Agriculture

United States Court of Appeals for the Eighth Circuit, 2001.
266 F.3d 889.

■ Before: MURPHY, HEANEY, and BEAM, CIRCUIT JUDGES.

---

* [Eds. Senator Harry Reid of Nevada, who has supported efforts to reform rangeland practices, has said that one large Las Vegas hotel employs more people than the entire agriculture industry in Nevada.]

■ BEAM, CIRCUIT JUDGE.

* * * [Under the National Forest Management Act,] a forest plan identifies suitable grazing lands, while permits to graze, if appropriate under that general plan, are issued pursuant to an appropriate site-specific project analysis. * * * Grazing permits "convey no right, title, or interest" in lands or resources, 36 C.F.R. § 222.3(b), and are subject to modification according to changes in management needs or resource conditions, 36 C.F.R. § 222.4(a)(7) & (8).

In this case, the Grazing District is an association that has a permit to graze cattle upon the Grasslands. In 1984, after completion of an EIS, the Forest Service adopted and approved the Nebraska National Forest Land and Resource Management Plan (Nebraska Forest Plan) to regulate use of the Grassland's resources. This plan emphasizes wildlife habitat, directing the Forest Service to "[a]lter grazing systems, season of use, and stocking levels to enhance wildlife habitat." It also requires the Forest Service to have developed residual cover[4] guidelines for the sharp-tailed grouse and greater prairie chicken "by [the] close of FY 1988." In 1985—prior to having considered all resource factors, seeking involvement of all interested parties, or conducting the requisite NEPA analysis—the Forest Service authorized the issuance of permits to graze cattle on the Grasslands at a maximum stocking rate of 70,436 Animal Unit Months (AUMs). Documentation incorporated into the Grazing District's grazing agreement indicated that proper range condition analyses needed to be conducted, that when residual cover requirements were established, the permits would be subject to them and that as monitoring and evaluation were conducted, the stocking levels could be revised.

After extensively studying[6] the impact of grazing on the wildlife habitat, the Forest Service ultimately determined that the 1985 stocking level made it impossible to satisfy the Nebraska Forest Plan's requirements for "long-term rangeland health and productivity, wildlife habitat, woody draw habitat, and soil and water protection." Therefore, in accordance with the NFMA and NEPA, the Forest Service prepared an Environmental Assessment in which it considered maximum grazing levels of 55,440 (an alternative considered at the request of the Grazing District), 45,211, 15,070, and 51,558 AUMs, along with a no-grazing alternative. In 1998, after giving public notice and receiving comments, the Forest Service issued a decision notice establishing the total maximum stocking level for the Grasslands at 51,558 AUMs and made a finding of no significant impact for the selected level.

---

4. "Residual cover" refers to the height and density of residual vegetation when measured in the fall after the grazing season has ended.

6. Specifically, the Forest Service collected data that:

include[d], but [was] not limited to, range analysis using the Natural Resource Conservation Service ... method-

ology, woody draw/riparian condition data, utilization measurements, and visual obstruction readings with the Robel pole to determine vegetation height and density. From 1985 through 1997, many monitoring techniques were used to monitor resource conditions on the [Grasslands] and specifically the effectiveness of the Interim Guidelines....

The Grazing District subsequently filed a complaint seeking judicial review of this agency action. Both the Grazing District and Forest Service filed simultaneous motions for summary judgment. The district court granted summary judgment in favor of the Forest Service. * * * [The court rejected plaintiff's NEPA challenge both for lack of standing and on the merits.]

The Grazing District also attacks the methodology the Forest Service employed to assess habitat suitability, which underpins the choice of stocking levels. The Grazing District's arguments are inspired, but unavailing. * * *

The Grazing District argues that the Forest Service's habitat suitability index was such an unreliable measure of sharp-tailed grouse nesting habitat that it rendered decisions stemming therefrom arbitrary and capricious. The index compares levels of residual cover that remained after grazing with levels of cover in ungrazed areas in order to assess whether habitat for management indicator species, such as the sharp-tailed grouse, achieved at least 40% of potential. * * * [T]he Grazing District's underlying assumption [was] that the Forest Service should have included the effect of visual obscurity on sharp-tailed grouse populations in its index. However, the Grazing District misapprehends the index, which was designed to assess the effect of grazing on the level of residual cover, not on the grouse population. The Forest Service obtained from other sources data regarding what constitutes habitat suitability and need not have included in chart-form what it knew from its other sources to be the case. For instance,

> Plains sharptail nesting cover tends to be more grassy and less shrubby than that of the prairie sharptail of the Great Lakes States. The lack of good quality nesting and brood-rearing cover generally is limiting for sharp-tailed grouse throughout their range. Plains sharp-tailed grouse are generally limited by intensive grazing and conversion of rangeland to cropland. Grazing reduces the quantity of residual vegetation. Residual herbaceous vegetation is important nesting cover because little current growth is available in early spring when most nests are constructed.

Bart L. Prose, *Habitat Suitability Index Models: Plains Sharp–Tailed Grouse*, U.S. Fish Wildl.Serv.Biol.Rep. 82(10.142), 9, (1987) (citing various authorities).[10] * * *

Furthermore, the Grazing District ignores the Forest Service's charge to protect the Grasslands habitat for fauna other than the sharp-tailed grouse, along with flora and other resources. As the Environmental Assessment points out:

10. Also, a 1988 study concluded that, "[f]or safe nesting, numerous clumps of similar, suitable vegetation must exist so that predators can not [sic] narrow their nest search. Hens need to be lost in a sea of potential nest sites to avoid predation." Other data demonstrated that high average residual cover is necessary for sufficient numbers of clumps of high, dense grass, and that as the visual obscurity reading increased, the number of clumps of cover increased.

Through visual observations, erosion and gullies were noticed due to a lack of vegetative cover and a lower range condition. If livestock continue to graze at this [initial] level, resource conditions will degrade. If intensive grazing continues during a prolonged drought, the vegetative composition will decrease to a lower level of condition and the overall rangeland health declines.

The Forest Service's habitat suitability index was not defective for the purpose it was used and does not undermine other data the Forest Service relied upon. Nor was the index the primary tool used in the Forest Service's decision-making, but was merely "one of many considerations ... along with many other pieces of information, both biological and social." The Forest Service accounted for discrepancies to which the Grazing District directs us and was entitled to rely upon its experts and data even though there may have been some conflicting data. * * * That the sharp-tailed grouse *can* nest in more heavily grazed areas misses the point since the Forest Service seeks to improve the habitat overall. The index was a reasonable tool among others employed and does not render the chosen stocking level arbitrary and capricious.

Also unpersuasive is the Grazing District's assertion that the Forest Service's reliance on a "one-point-in-time" range vegetation inventory violated the National Forest Management Act and rendered its choice of stocking levels arbitrary and capricious. The NFMA's general criteria require that, in developing and maintaining land management plans, the Forest Service use "a systematic interdisciplinary approach to achieve integrated consideration of physical, biological, economic, and other sciences." 16 U.S.C. § 1604(b).

The Grazing District claims that "inherent inadequacies of one point in time inventories as measures of overall stocking levels have been recognized by the scientific community and in court," citing *Hodel,* 624 F.Supp. at 1061. However, *Hodel* did not indicate that all one-point-in-time inventories were categorically unreliable, but that, there, the data obtained from a one-point-in-time study "was not ultimately used ... because it yielded inconsistent results." *Id.* Yet those inconsistencies were "due in part to an insufficient number of samples, errors in identifying plant species, and assumptions built into the model." *Id.* Furthermore, that conclusion was not reached by a court, but by the Bureau of Land Management, an agency to whose decision the trial court deferred. *Id.* * * *

The Grazing District refers us to the testimony of Dr. Jim Johnson of South Dakota State University to make its point that the Forest Service failed to consider the "best available information" regarding the relationship between the Grasslands' condition to stocking levels. Dr. Johnson testified:

> In order to perfectly [sic] [Eds.: correlate?] the range condition to stocking rates, we would also need grazing history, trend, and utilization data on a pasture by pasture basis. However, experiences of range scientists and producers in South Dakota strongly support the validity of using the Suggested Initial Stocking Guides as a good approximation

of where stocking levels should be to improve range or maintain high range conditions.

Our standard for agency action is not one of perfection, but whether the agency acted arbitrarily and capriciously. We find that the Forest Service has not.

The Grazing District also contends that the NFMA, 16 U.S.C. § 1610, required the Forest Service "to use information available from third parties." * * * Section 1610 states that, in carrying out her land management duties, "the Secretary of Agriculture shall utilize information and data available from other Federal, State, and private organizations and shall avoid duplication and overlap of resource assessment and program planning efforts of other Federal agencies." Although this is likely an efficiency provision, the Forest Service did look to available data from other agencies and private organizations. The statute does not require the Forest Service to adhere to the letter of each datum, which, judging from the various reports in this matter, would likely be virtually impossible. Furthermore, judging from Dr. Johnson's testimony, it appears that the Forest Service did rely on the best *available* data. The Forest Service did not contravene section 1610.

For the reasons we have outlined, we affirm the district court's grant of summary judgment in favor of the Forest Service.

NOTES AND QUESTIONS

1. In the NEPA portion of the opinion edited out of the above excerpt, the court noted that actual use of forage had not been above 52,400 AUMs since 1989, or about the level that the Forest Service set in the decision being challenged. Why, then, do you suppose the plaintiffs fought this new decision?

2. How can *Hodel* and *S.D. Co-op. Grazing Dist.* be reconciled? Both involved agency planning processes and grazing levels. Is it that the agency always (or usually) wins; i.e., that the deference principle is very strong? That the courts feel ill-equipped to delve into the details of federal land management? Especially when very large tracts of federal lands are involved? (The Reno planning area was considerably larger and more complex than the Fort Pierre National Grassland involved in the South Dakota case.)

3. Another way of comparing the two cases is to look at the quantity and type of information available to each agency. The Forest Service had the benefit of more than a dozen years of monitoring data that focused primarily on the relationship of grazing to a couple of species of wildlife. If BLM had had the same kind of focused information in the Reno planning area, might it have been able to reduce livestock grazing? Did, in other words, the Forest Service do its homework, and the BLM did not? Note that the Forest Service set the maximum stocking rate at 70,436 AUMs in 1985, in the court's words, "prior to having considered all resource factors, seeking involvement of all interested parties, or conducting the requisite NEPA analysis."

4. All told, does *Hodel* suggest that FLPMA's planning process has no or at best limited utility when it comes to addressing and setting appropriate levels of livestock grazing? Does the South Dakota case suggest otherwise about the Forest Service planning process? Is the issue the design and details of the planning process, or do factors of agency culture, history, and political will predominate regardless of process and facts? See generally Erik Schlenker–Goddrich, Moving Beyond Public Lands Council v. Babbitt: Land Use Planning and the Range Resource, 16 J.Envtl.L. & Litig. 139 (2001).

5. In Nevada Land Action Ass'n v. U.S. Forest Service, 8 F.3d 713 (9th Cir.1993), the court rejected ranchers' challenge to a Forest Service plan that they feared would result in a "drastic decrease" in grazing levels (even though the agency projected no significant decrease in grazing levels). The court found the plaintiffs had no standing to assert a NEPA claim because their alleged injury was economic, and rejected their arguments that, among other things, the Forest Service did not consider a sufficiently broad range of alternatives under the National Forest Management Act and did not adequately document its decisions.

6. The environmentalists' strategy in *NRDC v. Hodel* was step two in their effort to bring more environmental regulation to BLM's grazing program. Step one was for BLM to prepare NEPA documentation and plans in administering its grazing program. Step two was to try to force actions based on those EISs and plans. Both steps were conducted at a broadbrush level, and not at the level of individual permits or allotments. In substantial part this strategy was dictated by the sheer magnitude of the federal land grazing enterprise, involving many thousands of operations, and 258 million acres of land. This decision showed the limitations of that strategy.

7. After *Hodel*, environmental advocates began showing some interest in looking at the process from more of a micro, "bottom-up"—rather than a macro, "top-down"—perspective. To that end, a coalition of environmental groups led by the NRDC published HOW NOT TO BE COWED (1991) (subtitled "Livestock Grazing on the Public Lands: An Owner's Manual") showing in detail how BLM grazing decisions are made, and explaining the avenues and opportunities for the public to influence those decisions. See also Joseph Feller, Grazing Management on the Public Lands: Opening the Process to Public Participation, XXVI Land & Water L.Rev. 569 (1991). The *Comb Wash* decision discussed at pp. 807–08 supra, shows BLM's continuing vulnerability under NEPA in its grazing program. That decision also addressed whether BLM might have a duty under FLPMA simply to stop grazing on certain public lands altogether.

ELIMINATING GRAZING: WHEN MUST BLM SAY NO?

National Wildlife Federation v. BLM

Interior Board of Land Appeals, 1997.
140 IBLA 85.

[The facts are summarized on p. 807 supra.] * * * The next issue for resolution is whether Judge Rampton properly held that BLM violated

FLPMA. After citing section 302(a) of FLPMA, 43 U.S.C. § 1732(a) (1994), which requires the Secretary to "manage the public lands under principles of multiple use and sustained yield," Judge Rampton quoted the FLPMA definition of "multiple use." * * * He then cited a statement by the court in Sierra Club v. Butz [eds. supra p. 709] (9th Cir.1973), that the multiple-use principle "requires that the values in question be informedly and rationally taken into balance." He concluded that an agency is required to engage in such a balancing test in order to determine whether a proposed activity is in the public interest.

However, in applying those standards to the facts in this case, Judge Rampton held that "BLM violated FLPMA by failing to make a reasoned and informed decision that the benefits of grazing the canyons outweigh the costs." It is with this highlighted language that all Appellants disagree, asserting that FLPMA does not require an economic cost/benefits analysis.

It is not clear that Judge Rampton intended that BLM engage in an economic cost/benefits analysis. A reading of his Decision * * * discloses that the sentence quoted above is the only place in his Decision where he uses the word "costs," other than in the heading to the discussion. Later in his Decision when he is addressing the appropriate relief for the various violations, he describes the violation as the failure to make a reasoned and informed decision to graze the canyons in violation of FLPMA. He mentions neither costs nor benefits. He described the appropriate relief, as follows: "Because BLM may choose to prohibit grazing in the canyons in the future, BLM is not compelled to make a reasoned and informed decision that grazing the canyons is in the public interest. However, until a decision is made, BLM is prohibited from allowing grazing in the canyons." Again, no mention is made of benefits and costs.

Judge Rampton's analysis of the evidence relating to BLM's decision-making process is as follows:

> The Area Manager, Mr. Scherick, correctly believed that he had discretion under the RMP to allow or disallow grazing on the Comb Wash allotment. He testified that, in exercising this discretion, he had not considered the relative values of the resources in the canyons because consideration of those values would take place during the activity planning stage (formation of the new AMP). But a new AMP has not yet been developed * * *.

> Mr. Scherick also admitted that neither he nor any document, including the Proposed RMP/FEIS, weighs the benefits and harms of grazing the canyons. In authorizing grazing in the canyons, Mr. Scherick simply relied upon the information and recommendations provided to him by Mr. Curtis, the range conservationist responsible for the allotment.

> Contrary to the evidence and Mr. Scherick's belief, Mr. Curtis thought that the RMP had already considered the impacts of grazing on the allotment's resources and determined that the allotment should be grazed, regardless of the recognized conflict with recreational uses and the need for adjustment confirmed by monitoring. He therefore felt it

was not his responsibility to consider those impacts. Mr. Scherick's reliance upon Mr. Curtis, who believed that the decision to graze had already been made and was still binding, does not constitute a rational basis for determining whether the canyons should be grazed.

Furthermore, Mr. Curtis, an expert in range management only, does not have the expertise necessary to understand all the impacts of grazing in the canyons. Yet, he testified that he relied solely upon the utilization data, the Proposed RMP/FEIS, and ocular observations to determine the specific terms under which grazing would be allowed. There is some question whether he also sought and relied upon advice from experts in archaeology and other fields, but he provided no documentation and little evidence of the context or content of any discussions with those experts.

Mr. Curtis' reliance upon the Proposed RMP/FEIS is unavailing, as [everyone involved] admitted that the Proposed RMP/FEIS does not contain the detailed information necessary for determining whether or not to graze the canyons. * * *

In sum, BLM's decision to graze the canyons was not reasoned or informed, but rather based upon Mr. Curtis' misinterpretation of the RMP and a totally inadequate investigation and analysis of the condition of the canyons' varied resources and the impacts of grazing upon those resources.

We agree with that analysis. Even NWF does not argue that FLPMA requires an economic cost/benefits analysis. The NWF states: "To the extent the Judge's choice of words may be ambiguous, NWF has no objection to this Board clarifying that FLPMA does not require an economic cost-benefit analysis, but rather that BLM must informedly and rationally balance competing values."

To the extent Judge Rampton's Decision may be construed as requiring an economic cost/benefit analysis, it is modified to make it clear that no such analysis is required.

On appeal, BLM makes no argument that it satisfied FLPMA's multiple-use mandate in authorizing grazing in the canyons. Instead, it agrees that the actions it takes, including authorizing grazing on the public lands, are required to be "in the public interest," but it asserts that if Judge Rampton intended to impose a "specific public interest determination," such as is found in section 206(a) of FLPMA, 43 U.S.C. § 1716(a) (1994), dealing with exchanges, "he has clearly overstepped his authority." It contends that "FLPMA simply does not require a specific public interest finding in the grazing context."

We agree with BLM that FLPMA does not require a "specific" public interest determination for grazing. However, FLPMA's multiple-use mandate requires that BLM balance competing resource values to ensure that public lands are managed in the manner "that will best meet the present and future needs of the American people." 43 U.S.C. § 1702(c) (1994). Indeed, all parties agree that BLM must conduct some form of balancing of competing resource values in order to comply with the statute. Counsel for

BLM states that "we agree that all BLM decisions should be in the public interest as that interest is defined by Congress in law * * *." The [ranching interests also recognize] that "[c] learly, management for multiple use does require a balancing and review of the relative resource values," * * * that under FLPMA the BLM must give consideration to the relative values of the resources in the Comb Wash canyons. Moreover, we agree that those values must be rationally considered." And NWF concurs that "BLM must informedly and rationally balance competing values."

What is important in this case, and what we affirm, is Judge Rampton's finding that BLM violated FLPMA, because it failed to engage in any reasoned or informed decisionmaking process concerning grazing in the canyons in the allotment. That process must show that BLM has balanced competing resource values to ensure that the public lands in the canyons are managed in the manner that will best meet the present and future needs of the American people. * * *

NOTES AND QUESTIONS

1.   If you were representing the affected rancher here, what sort of reasoned decisionmaking analysis would you suggest BLM follow on remand if it wants to conclude that grazing should still be allowed in these canyons? Should it focus on the economic benefit to the rancher, and say that whatever environmental harm results is tolerable? Say that the area has already been so hammered by cows that things can't get worse? Is the Board saying anything more than that BLM must have *some* reason, and *some* factual basis, for going forward with the grazing permit renewal here?

2.   If Judge Burns had confronted this record in considering whether BLM should renew a specific grazing permit in part of the Reno Planning Area, might he have decided the same thing? That is, is how the Board of Land Appeals applied FLPMA here consistent or inconsistent with how Judge Burns applied FLPMA in *NRDC v. Hodel*?

3.   While this site-specific approach can be a tool to protect the health of federal rangeland, it has its limitations. Most prominently, bringing these specific challenges is labor and resource intensive, and the area involved in Comb Wash is a tiny fraction of the total area of BLM land that is grazed. Second, there is no guarantee of success, and a victory may only put the matter back in the agency's hands to come up with a better justification for renewal. Third, the livestock industry has enough friends in the Congress that a legislative "fix" is always a possibility.

4.   For whatever reasons, *Comb Wash* remains a rare if not unique case of using FLPMA to force BLM to take more steps to justify continued livestock grazing on its lands. But other laws have proved more promising as a way to restrict livestock grazing on environmental grounds. The Endangered Species Act and the Wild & Scenic Rivers Act have been so used. See, e.g., Chapter 5, supra p. 491; Chapter 12, infra pp. 1093–1102. The Clean Water has been tried, but so far without much success. See Oregon Natural Desert Ass'n v. Dombeck, 172 F.3d 1092 (9th Cir.1998), cert. denied, 528 U.S. 964 (1999) (cows, even cows that "discharge" directly

into streams, are not point sources under the Clean Water Act). Other parts of the Clean Water Act, in particular those that call for control of total maximum daily loads (TMDLs) of pollution, whether from point or nonpoint sources, have more promise. See, e.g., Debra L. Donahue, The Untapped Power of Clean Water Act Section 401, 23 Ecology L.Q. 201 (1996); Peter M. Lacy, Addressing Water Pollution From Livestock Grazing after ONDA v. Dombeck: Legal Strategies under the Clean Water Act, 30 Envtl.L. 617 (2000).

5. In recent years federal land management agencies have begun to pay more specific attention to riparian (stream-influenced) areas. These areas are usually rich wildlife habitat and the focus of recreation, especially in more arid regions. They are also a favorite of, and heavily impacted by, livestock. Pressure is building on the BLM and the U.S. Forest Service (from state fish and game agencies as well as environmentalists) to regulate grazing in riparian zones more heavily to protect other values. In this context, other resource-specific statutes such as the Endangered Species Act and the Clean Water Act may also become a much bigger factor than they have been. Richard H. Braun, Emerging Limits on Federal Land Management Discretion: Livestock, Riparian Ecosystems, and Clean Water Law, 17 Envt'l L. 43 (1986), usefully summarizes the science and the law applicable to riparian protection and grazing. Some ranchers are not persuaded that riparian rehabilitation seems to promise longer-term bene-fits to ranchers: "The Idaho Cattle Association accused environmentalists of suffering from 'ripariopsychorrhea,' a fictional mental disease with scatalogical overtones." Braun, id., at 50 n.16.

VOLUNTARY RETIREMENTS OF THE FEDERAL LANDS FROM GRAZING

As the wrangling between federal lands ranchers and environmental advocates continues, a promising non-regulatory solution to this long struggle has emerged—voluntary buyouts by conservation interests (in both the public and private nonprofit sectors), who purchase federal land grazing permits (with or without the accompanying "base property" held in fee simple), in order to retire the permits and retire the public lands subject to these permits from livestock grazing. These marketplace-based "pur-chases and retirements" appear to offer great benefits, environmental and otherwise. They lead to restoration of the health of riparian areas and wildlife populations. They give the government land managers more flexi-bility to cope with drought, fire, and insect outbreaks. They may achieve tangible, visible environmental improvements in a short time in a less contentious way than pitched battles over regulation.

Buyouts also often make sense for ranchers, who increasingly find themselves operating at the margin in many places. Sometimes, in fact, grazing allotments which have high biological or recreational value are the most marginal and troublesome to manage for livestock. Grasses may be sparse, access may be difficult, recreationists may leave gates open, regula-tions may be enforced more stringently, and controversy may be greater.

Ranchers sometimes find it simpler to cash out of such allotments, retire debts, and either retire from ranching altogether, or reorganize the ranch around less highly contested pastures.

There has been, in recent years, something of a boomlet in such efforts; for example:

The Grand Canyon Trust has reached agreements in a variety of transactions to remove cows from about 480,000 acres of National Monuments, Parks, Recreation Areas, and Wilderness Areas in southern Utah, including more than 200 miles of fragile desert stream canyons. Sometimes critical allotments have been totally retired (e.g., along 20 miles of the Paria River, and in the northern range in Capitol Reef National Park). In other cases, livestock are removed from ecologically critical portions of allotments that are bounded by topographic features, while leaving the stock on more appropriate parts of the range (e.g., along 67 miles of the Escalante River Canyon and in a system of five canyons added to Arches National Park in 1998).

In and around Great Basin National Park, the Conservation Fund, with the support of several private foundations, worked with ranchers and federal managers to retire permits on more than 100,000 acres of BLM, National Park, and National Forest lands, a transaction supported by the Nevada Cattleman's Association, Nevada Commission on Tourism, and the U.S. Fish and Wildlife Service.

In Idaho, the Bonneville Power Administration used fish restoration funds to buy and retire permits in a 49,000 acre Forest Service grazing allotment in the Elk Creek drainage, where there is prime habitat for salmon, steelhead, bull trout and westslope cutthroat trout. The price was $2.95/ acre. Retirement of the allotment by the U.S. Forest Service was supported by the Shoshone–Bannock Tribes and by the Idaho Department of Game and Fish.*

Four allotments within the Desolation Canyon Wilderness Study Area along the Green River in northeastern Utah were retired by BLM after sheep ranchers there were compensated by the Utah Division of Wildlife Resources. The area provides critical habitat for bighorn sheep. Sportsmen, worried about the condition of the range and about the danger of domestic sheep transmitting disease to the bighorns, ultimately provided Utah Wildlife Resources with the funds needed for the buyout on 125,000 acres.

In southern California, the National Park Service is implementing a buyout of livestock grazing through amendment of the Death Valley National Park's General Management Plan. BLM is amending a land use plan to retire grazing after a buyout in another part of the California Desert.

These examples show the wide variety of settings where permit purchase and retirement is an ecologically responsible, socially compassionate, and politically acceptable policy of enormous potential. Many observers believe that many more similar transactions are possible, with the promise of solving many contentious resource and value conflicts across the West, but for one major problem: Those committing funds for these deals have no assurance under current laws and policies that the federal lands on which the grazing permits are purchased and relinquished will be permanently retired from grazing. Except in National Park System Lands, where the grazing being retired has been grandfathered in, simple relinquishment of the permits leaves the federal land managers with discretion to reopen the federal lands involved for grazing by other operators. The federal land is, in other words, itself not permanently "retired" from grazing; only those particular permits are retired.

Usually, as part of these transactions, the public land managers have taken steps to amend the pertinent land use plan for the area involved, to provide that grazing shall not be restored on that area. These "grazing withdrawals by plan amendments" are, however, good only for the life of the plan. As we have seen, BLM and Forest Service plans may generally be amended at any time; in fact, the law requires the Forest Service to reexamine its plans at specific intervals. What one plan amendment accomplishes can be undone by another. The bottom line is that amending the plan to retire the area from grazing adds only a procedural hurdle should the federal land managers determine to make these public lands once again available for livestock. The underlying discretion to allow grazing remains intact, and with it a risk to those funding the buyouts.

Moreover, while these consensual transactions would seem to have something for everybody, making the prospect of future restoration to grazing dim, in fact the potential availability of the lands for future grazing can be a significant local issue. Neighboring ranchers may seek to expand their operations by introducing their livestock to the public lands being retired. Others in the local community (local businesses which depend on a viable local ranching industry, local governments who believe their tax revenues may be adversely affected by grazing retirements, and those who strongly identify with the ranching culture) may be strongly opposed to permanent retirements, which they may see as dooming a locally important economic sector as well as a treasured culture.

Although grazing retirements are usually dealt with under generic public land laws, the issue has not entirely escaped the attention of Congress, which has sometimes responded with *ad hoc* statutory enactments to solve immediate problems. At Great Basin National Park, for example, the Nevada delegation successfully sponsored a provision in 1996 to allow grazing permittees to donate or exchange their permits inside the Park, but the statute cautioned that exchanges should not be approved if it would "result in overgrazing of Federal lands." See 16 U.S.C. § 410mm–1(f). At Arches National Park two years later, Congress specially authorized retirement of a grazing allotment in a canyon that was being added to the Park. See 16 U.S.C. § 272b. In the California Desert legislation adopted in 1994, Congress directed that the Secretary give priority to acquiring base property from willing sellers, even as it grandfathered the "privilege of grazing domestic livestock on lands within the [new Mohave National Park and Preserve] at no more than the current level, subject to applicable laws and National Park Service regulations." 16 U.S.C. § 410aaa–5.

Insecurity over the permanence of such purchases and retirements casts a cloud on funding potential, and prevents the emergence of a much larger market for grazing permits. Funders of buyouts are concerned by the possibility that their objective—to restore health to tracts of public lands by permanently retiring grazing from them—may be later nullified by discretionary decisions by federal land managers.

The Solicitor addressed BLM's authority to act on requests for voluntary retirement of livestock grazing in an opinion issued January 19, 2001. It noted that both FLPMA and the Public Rangelands Improvement Act specifically provided for the possibility of retiring public land from grazing. FLPMA gives an existing permittee first priority for renewal "[s]o long as [among other things] the lands for which the permit or lease is issued remain available for * * * grazing in accordance with land use plans" prepared under FLPMA. 43 U.S.C. § 1752(c). PRIA has as its major goal improving conditions on the public range with an important exception: "Except where [FLPMA's] land use planning process * * * determines otherwise or the Secretary determines, and sets forth his reasons for this determination, that grazing uses should be discontinued (either temporarily or permanently) on certain lands * * *." 43 U.S.C. § 1903(b). The Solicitor opined that the decision to retire lands from grazing is a straightforward "multiple use/sustained yield" decision, and does not have to be based on a finding of "unnecessary or undue degradation," but rather may be made simply upon a determination that the public lands should be devoted to other uses.

NOTES AND QUESTIONS

1.   As a matter of policy, should such buyouts be preferred over more regulatory solutions?

2.   If you were a foundation interested in donating funds for such buyouts, what kind of security would you demand?

3.   Can the Secretary "withdraw" lands from grazing use through the FLPMA withdrawal procedure? Notice, however, that withdrawals are generally good only for twenty years, and can be revoked sooner (although they can also be renewed).

4.   If the local land use plan is amended to "retire" the federal lands in the area of the permits being relinquished from livestock grazing, can a neighboring rancher propose to amend the plan to open the area back up, and allow her to put her cows there? What does BLM need to show to retire the land from grazing? To open it back up again?

5.   Is this a problem that can be solved without legislation? One part of the Clinton Administration's Rangeland Reform was to authorize the issuance of grazing permits for what was called "conservation non-use." The purpose was to provide for the situation where a conservation group buys out a rancher's grazing permit and seeks to retire the land. The idea was to allow the buyer to BLM to put the grazing permit, which it would continue to hold, into "conservation non-use" status. The ranchers at-

tacked this provision in court, and the Tenth Circuit struck it down, and the United States did not seek review of this provision in the U.S. Supreme Court. Excerpts from the Tenth Circuit's discussion follow (Public Lands Council v. Babbitt, 167 F.3d 1287 (10th Cir.1999)):

> The 1995 regulations added "conservation use" as a permissible use of a grazing permit. See 43 C.F.R. § 4100.0–5 (1995) (defining "grazing permit" as a document that specifies "all authorized use [of public lands within a grazing district] including livestock grazing, suspended use, and conservation use"). "Conservation use" means "an activity, excluding livestock grazing, on all or a portion of an allotment" for the purpose of protecting the land and its resources, improving rangeland conditions, or enhancing resource values. Id. Conservation use may be approved for a period of up to ten years—i.e., for the entire duration of the permit. See id. § 4130.2(g)(1). According to the Secretary, conservation use will be initiated by request of the permittee and will not be forced on an unwilling permittee. See Final Rule, 60 Fed.Reg. at 9898. Allotments in conservation use will not be subject to grazing fees since no forage will be consumed by livestock. See id. BLM will not consider allowing another operator to use any resulting forage. See id. * * *

> Section three of the TGA authorizes the Secretary "to issue or cause to be issued permits to graze livestock" on the public lands. 43 U.S.C. § 315b. In the 1995 regulations, the Secretary has authorized the issuance of grazing permits or leases for "livestock grazing, suspended use, and conservation use." 43 C.F.R. § 4130.2(a) (1995). Conservation use, in turn, is defined as "an activity, excluding livestock grazing, on all or a portion of an allotment" for conservation purposes. 43 C.F.R. § 4100.0–5 (1995) (emphasis added). Thus, the Secretary has authorized the issuance of a grazing permit to an individual or group who will not graze livestock for the entire duration of a permit.

> The Secretary makes several arguments in support of the new regulation allowing "conservation use" permits. First, he points out (and PLC agrees) that resting land is a perfectly acceptable practice on the public range and is done with regularity in order to prevent permanent destruction of the lands. Indeed, under the pre–1995 regulations, active use could "be suspended in whole or in part on a temporary basis due to drought, fire, or other natural causes, or to facilitate installation, maintenance, or modification of range improvements." 43 C.F.R.§ 4110.3–2(a) (1994). The Secretary asserts that the issuance of grazing permits for conservation use merely reflects "a longstanding grazing management practice consistent with the resumption of grazing."

> The Secretary further argues that the issuance of permits for conservation use is authorized by the TGA, FLPMA, and PRIA. The Secretary points to section two of the TGA, which provides, "The Secretary shall ... do any and all things necessary to accomplish the purposes of this [Act]." 43 U.S.C. § 315a. One of the purposes of the TGA is "to preserve the land and its resources from destruction or unnecessary injury." Id. The Secretary asserts that issuance of permits authorizing

conservation use is fully consistent with this mandate. Moreover, FLPMA charges the Secretary with "manag[ing] the public lands under principles of multiple use and sustained yield." 43 U.S.C. § 1732(a). Multiple use requires that the Secretary consider, among other things, "the long-term needs of future generations for renewable and non-renewable resources." 43 U.S.C. § 1702(c). The Secretary argues that the issuance of conservation use permits helps achieve the goal of multiple use. Similarly, the Secretary contends that conservation use is a mechanism to achieving PRIA's goal of "manag[ing], maintain[ing], and improv[ing] the condition of the public rangelands so they become as feasible as possible for all rangeland values." 43 U.S.C. § 1901(b)(2).

Notwithstanding the reasonable arguments that the Secretary presents, we are not persuaded. The question before us is not whether the Secretary possesses general authority to take conservation measures—which clearly he does—but rather, whether he has authority to take the specific measure in question, i.e., issuing a "grazing permit" that excludes livestock grazing for the entire term of the permit. We conclude at the first step of the *Chevron* analysis that Congress has spoken directly to this precise question and answered it in the negative. Our decision rests on the plain language of the relevant statutes. The TGA provides the Secretary with authority to issue "permits to graze livestock on . . . grazing districts." 43 U.S.C. § 315b. That statute does not authorize permits for any other type of use of the lands in the grazing districts. FLPMA and PRIA confirm that grazing permits are intended for grazing purposes only. Both those statutes define "grazing permit and lease" as "any document authorizing use of public lands . . . for the purpose of grazing domestic livestock." 43 U.S.C. §§ 1702(p), 1902(c) (emphasis added). Thus, the TGA, FLPMA, and PRIA each unambiguously reflect Congress's intent that the Secretary's authority to issue "grazing permits" be limited to permits issued "for the purpose of grazing domestic livestock." None of these statutes authorizes permits intended exclusively for "conservation use." The Secretary's assertion that "grazing permits" for use of land in "grazing districts" need not involve an intent to graze is simply untenable.

The TGA authorizes the Secretary to establish grazing districts comprised of public lands "which in his opinion are chiefly valuable for grazing and raising forage crops." 43 U.S.C. § 315. When range conditions are such that reductions in grazing are necessary, temporary non-use is appropriate and furthers the preservation goals of the TGA, FLPMA, and PRIA, even when that temporary non-use happens to last the entire duration of the permit. BLM may impose temporary reductions, see 43 C.F.R. § 4110.3–2 (1994), or permittees may voluntarily reduce their grazing levels. The presumption is, however, that if and when range conditions improve and more forage becomes available, permissible grazing levels will rise. See, e.g., 43 C.F.R. § 4110.3–1(a) (1994) ("Additional forage temporarily available for livestock grazing use . . . may be apportioned on a nonrenewable basis."); id.

§ 4110.3–1(b) (providing that additional forage would first be apportioned "in satisfaction of grazing preferences" to permittees authorized to graze in the allotment containing the forage). The Secretary's new conservation use rule reverses that presumption. Rather than annually evaluating range conditions to determine whether grazing levels should increase or decrease, as is done with temporary non-use, the Secretary's conservation use rule authorizes placement of land in non-use for the entire duration of a permit. This is an impermissible exercise of the Secretary's authority under section three of the TGA because land that he has designated as "chiefly valuable for grazing livestock" will be completely excluded from grazing use even though range conditions could be good enough to support grazing. Congress intended that once the Secretary established a grazing district under the TGA, the primary use of that land should be grazing.

Thus, when the Secretary issues a permit under section three of the TGA, the primary purpose of the permit must be grazing. If range conditions indicate that some land needs to be rested, the Secretary may place that land in non-use on a temporary basis, in accordance with Congress's grants of authority that the Secretary manage the public lands "in a manner that will protect the quality of scientific, scenic, historical, ecological, environmental, [and other] values," 43 U.S.C. § 1701(a)(8), or he may reduce grazing on that land, see 43 C.F.R. § 4110.3–2 (1994) (providing that active use may be temporarily suspended in whole or in part for various reasons); id. § 4110.3–3 (describing procedures for implementing changes in active use). The Secretary may also employ other means to ensure that the resources of the public range are preserved. See, e.g., 43 U.S.C. § 1752(d) (stating that grazing permits may incorporate an allotment management plan); id. § 1702(k) (defining allotment management plan as a document which "prescribes the manner in, and extent to, which livestock operations will be conducted in order to meet the multiple-use, sustained-yield, and other needs and objectives" of the land).

In short, it is true that the TGA, FLPMA, and PRIA, give the Secretary very broad authority to manage the public lands, including the authority to ensure that range resources are preserved. Permissible ends such as conservation, however, do not justify unauthorized means. We hold that the Secretary lacks the statutory authority to issue grazing permits intended exclusively for conservation use. Because there is no set of circumstances under which the Secretary could issue such a permit, the new conservation use regulation is invalid on its face.

Is this analysis persuasive? Should the U.S. have appealed it to the U.S. Supreme Court?

7.   What might legislation look like that would "cure" this problem and allow voluntary buyouts to go forward? Simply create a mechanism providing for permanent withdrawal of federal lands from livestock grazing where a conservation group buys out a rancher? Might the general idea of a nonfederal entity "buying" a permanent management status on public

lands be objectionable? Should the federal land managing agency have the final say about how these lands are managed; i.e., whether they are permanently retired or not?

8. Should the government make efforts to mitigate so-called "third party effects" (for example, loss of business to local rancher-supply stores) when it retires public lands from grazing? Is the case for doing so stronger, weaker, or the same as the case for mitigating such effects when the government makes other changes in federal land use?

CHAPTER 10

THE WILDLIFE RESOURCE

The American public's attitude toward wildlife as a resource has gradually evolved from one of putting food on the table to one of recreational, scientific, and aesthetic interest. In the process, with population growth and the spread of civilization across the landscape, wildlife management and protection has more and more become controlled by law. The twentieth century saw the evolution of wildlife law from a set of relatively narrow hunting and fishing rules established under state law to a more comprehensive scheme which emphasizes maintenance and enhancement of quality habitat, with federal law playing a more prominent role. See generally Michael Bean & Melanie Rowland, THE EVOLUTION OF NATIONAL WILDLIFE LAW (3d ed. 1997). Despite the increasing prominence of federal law, state fish and game departments remain key actors in wildlife management.

The initial mission of state fish and game agencies was to protect the resource by curbing more pernicious abuses, but during most of the nineteenth century, the few rudimentary state wildlife statutes were ineffective for lack of wardens or other enforcement mechanisms. See Thomas Lund, Early American Wildlife Law, 51 N.Y.U.L.Rev. 703 (1976). The federal constitutional basis for pervasive state regulation was confirmed in by the U.S. Supreme Court in 1896 in Geer v. Connecticut, discussed in chapter 3, supra p. 192. The states used *Geer* to protect their sovereignty over wildlife, a particularly important matter because hunting and fishing license fees generate considerable revenues.

By the time *Geer* was decided, however, federal land policy had already begun to pay attention to wildlife management. The reservation of national forests and parks beginning in the late 19th century, while not motivated by a concern for protecting wildlife, did just that by providing large, relatively undisturbed regions of prime wildlife habitat. The irrepressible Teddy Roosevelt took a more direct step by asking Congress to create federal game refuges shortly after he became President in 1901. One Congressman described the proposal as "the fad of game preservation run stark raving mad." When the bill died, Roosevelt took matters into his own hands, asking: "Is there any law that will prevent me from declaring Pelican Island a Federal Bird Reservation?" When told not, he responded: "Very well, then I so declare it."* With his Pelican Island Bird Refuge Proclamation of March 14, 1903, a national program for protecting wildlife habitat was born. Congress then followed up, first by delegating express authority to the President to do what TR had already begun to do, and

---

* Henry Pringle, THEODORE ROOSEVELT: A BIOGRAPHY 469 (1931); Edmund Morris, THEODORE REX 519 (2001).

later by statutorily establishing specific refuges. It was not until 1966, however, that Congress consolidated the various wildlife and game areas into the National Wildlife Refuge System.

Federal wildlife law began to evolve in other contexts around the turn of the twentieth century. Congress legislated for wildlife conservation in the territories, and in 1900, it ventured into general wildlife regulation with passage of the Lacey Act, 16 U.S.C. §§ 701, 3371–3378, and 18 U.S.C. § 42. That Act backstopped state wildlife laws by forbidding transportation or sale in interstate commerce of animals taken illegally in the state of origin. The Migratory Bird Treaty Act of 1918 (MBTA), 16 U.S.C. §§ 703–711, took a much bolder step, creating a national program for managing migratory bird populations. Directly preempting state law, the MBTA set the Department of the Interior up as a national game agency, establishing hunting seasons and bag limits and regulating methods of taking. It was upheld by Justice Holmes' opinion in Missouri v. Holland, Chapter 3, supra p. 203.

For the next several decades, Congress only sporadically and rather haphazardly showed concern for national wildlife regulation. The Bald Eagle Act of 1940, 16 U.S.C. §§ 668–668d, flatly banned killing or molesting bald (and, since 1962, golden) eagles except with federal permission. (It authorized issuing permits to meet the religious needs of Indians and for the protection of domestic livestock against the depredations of golden eagles.) In 1958, in the Fish and Wildlife Coordination Act, 16 U.S.C. §§ 661–667e, Congress commanded federal agencies to ensure that "wildlife conservation" receives "equal consideration" and coordination with "other features of water-resource development programs," and required reports on plans for mitigation of wildlife habitat losses due to federal water projects. The Anadromous Fish Conservation Act of 1965, 16 U.S.C. §§ 757a–757f (anadromous fish being those, like salmon, that spawn in fresh water but live most of their lives in the oceans) simply directed the Secretary of the Interior to conduct studies and make appropriate recommendations "regarding the development and management of any stream or other body of water for the conservation and enhancement of anadromous fishery resources." Nevertheless, in one of the landmark judicial decisions in the early days of the modern environmental movement, the Supreme Court, speaking through Justice Douglas, relied on it to set aside a Federal Power Commission license to construct a dam. Udall v. FPC, 387 U.S. 428 (1967).

With the rise of the modern environmental movement, the legislative pace quickened dramatically. Primitive versions of an Endangered Species Act were enacted in 1966 and 1969. They were followed by the Wild and Free–Roaming Horses and Burros Act of 1971 (WF–RHBA), 16 U.S.C. §§ 1331–1340 (upheld in Kleppe v. New Mexico, Chapter 3, supra p. 184) and then the Marine Mammal Protection Act of 1972 (MMPA) 16 U.S.C.A. §§ 1361–1362, 1371–1384, 1401–1407. The latter declared a moratorium on all taking of or commerce in all marine mammals, with exceptions, such as incidental taking of porpoises by tuna fishermen. The next year saw a dramatic strengthening of the Endangered Species Act (ESA), 16 U.S.C. §§ 1531–1543, making it what some call the most stringent wildlife law ever enacted by any country. Since 1973, Congress has enacted the Sikes Act Extension of 1974, 16 U.S.C. §§ 667a–670f, the Fishery Conservation and Management Act of 1976, 16 U.S.C. §§ 1801–1882, the Fish and

Wildlife Conservation Act of 1980, 16 U.S.C. §§ 2901–2911, and the National Wildlife Refuge System Improvement Act (NWRSIA), 16 U.S.C. §§ 668dd-ee, as well as amending many of the older wildlife laws.

Missouri's challenge to the Migratory Bird Treaty Act that culminated in Missouri v. Holland was a typical state reaction to the growth of federal wildlife law. State fish and game departments, supported by hunting and fishing organizations, fiercely protect traditional state prerogatives, and their efforts have not been without some success. Federal law governing (or prohibiting) the take of wildlife applies to preempt state law only for certain species or in certain specific situations, or on certain land systems, such as the national park system. This has left states as the principal arbiters of most hunting, fishing, and trapping on the two largest systems of federal lands, the national forests and BLM-managed public lands. Even there, however, federal authority over wildlife remains important, because federal land managers now generally follow Aldo Leopold's premise that healthy wildlife populations are most effectively achieved by assuring healthy habitat; thus, the best wildlife management is in essence good land management. See A. Leopold, GAME MANAGEMENT (1933).

As in most areas of natural resources management, divergent viewpoints on wildlife management philosophy are common. For example, David S. Favre, in Wildlife Rights: The Ever–Widening Circle, 9 Envt'l L. 241 (1979), makes a case for according wildlife species certain legal rights:

> Arguably, a major stumbling block to recognizing wildlife rights is the problem of how humans can presume to know animals' best interests when animals cannot communicate with humans. With the possible exception of the most intelligent animals, it may be questionable whether humans can ever truly know what a particular animal or species desires or needs. However, the presumption that certain interests are so fundamental that all humans should be accorded legal rights to protect these interests, whether or not they individually ask for them, should be extended to wildlife. As humans have both a self-interest and a moral obligation to recognize the rights of other human beings, they have an equivalent interest and obligation to recognize the interests of wildlife since the stability and integrity of the ecosystem is at stake. Moreover, the moral burden demanding this recognition is particularly great when human activities cause serious intrusions upon the interests of the wildlife community. Given the reasonable presumption that humans should recognize the fundamental interests of wildlife, important questions remain: What are wildlife's interests? What rights should wildlife be accorded? After these rights are granted, how will conflicts between human rights and wildlife rights be resolved?
> * * *

Toward the other end of the spectrum, Susan M. Schectman, The "Bambi Syndrome:" How NEPA's Public Participation in Wildlife Management is Hurting the Environment, 8 Envt'l L. 611 (1978), concludes:

> * * * Non-native burros and native deer have increased in important scenic areas to the point where severe impacts are occurring to flora, fauna, and soil. Proper wildlife management requires reduction, and as a practical matter this can only be accomplished by shooting. * * * But attempts to reduce the herds have been delayed by NEPA actions and lengthy public involvement procedures. * * *

A common complaint was that the "Bambi Syndrome" subverted the involvement process. The public was concerned with individual animals and not their ecosystem as a whole, and seemed to respond more to emotional media presentations than technical assessments prepared by the managers. Skepticism towards the managers and emotionalism created by Walt Disney-like misconceptions of wildlife jeopardized the information function. The sentimental value of individual wildlife to the public became clear, but the decision-makers obtained few valuable comments or feasible alternatives; many suggested alternatives ranged from the emotional to the fanciful to the irrational. While the information function was partially served, managers felt that the public was often not interested in staff assessments and that the public input was simply not valuable enough to deserve a great deal of effort. In no case did the public suggest a feasible alternative that the staff had not previously considered. The public's "Bambi Syndrome" was simply incompatible with sound resource management. * * *

The constitutional underpinnings of federal law over wildlife were discussed in Chapter 3, pp. 203–07; and the Endangered Species Act was discussed in Chapter 5, supra pp. 434–508. Section A of this chapter addresses managerial priorities of the National Wildlife Refuge System, managed by the U.S. Fish & Wildlife Service (USFWS) in the Department of the Interior. Section B examines wildlife controversies in the national parks, national forests and on the BLM public lands. Sections C and D take brief looks at the Migratory Bird Treaty Act and the Wild, Free–Roaming Horses and Burros Act, respectively. An excellent introduction to these issues is found in Michael J. Bean & Melanie J. Rowland, THE EVOLUTION OF NATIONAL WILDLIFE LAW (3d ed. 1997). See also George Cameron Coggins & Robert Glicksman, 3 PUBLIC NATURAL RESOURCES LAW, ch. 18; Thomas Lund, AMERICAN WILDLIFE LAW (1980); for factual background on wildlife management, see WILDLIFE AND AMERICA (Howard P. Brokaw, ed. 1978).

A. THE NATIONAL WILDLIFE REFUGE SYSTEM

1. HISTORY AND ISSUES OF ADMINISTRATION

Michael J. Bean and Melanie J. Rowland, The Evolution of National Wildlife Law*

283–91 (3d ed. 1997).

The National Wildlife Refuge System is the only extensive system of federally owned lands managed chiefly for the conservation of wildlife.[**]

** [Eds. In 1997 Congress defined the "mission" of the National Wildlife Refuge System as "a national network of lands and waters for the conservation, management,

* * * The Refuge System comprises nearly 91 million acres, almost 76 million of which are in Alaska.

The origins of the Refuge System can be traced to the turn of the century, when presidential proclamation established the first federal wildlife refuges. Soon Congress also became involved in creating refuges, first by authorizing the President in 1905 and 1906 to designate certain areas as wildlife ranges. In 1908, Congress established a National Bison Range in Montana by its own action.

The Migratory Bird Treaty Act, passed in 1918, provided the stimulus for a systematic program of refuge acquisition. The Act's failure to authorize acquisition of migratory bird habitat came to be recognized as a serious shortcoming. To provide the needed authority, Congress passed the Migratory Bird Conservation Act (hereinafter Conservation Act) in 1929.

The Conservation Act established a Migratory Bird Conservation Commission to review and approve proposals of the Secretary of the Interior for the purchase or rental of areas under the Act. Although several subsequent statutes—including the Fish and Wildlife Coordination Act, the Fish and Wildlife Act of 1956, the Land and Water Conservation Fund Act, and the Endangered Species Acts of 1966, 1969, and 1973—contained acquisition authority, the Conservation Act continues to be a major source of authority for wildlife refuge acquisition.

The Migratory Bird Hunting Stamp Act, enacted in 1934, assured a steady source of funding for refuge acquisition under the Conservation Act. The Hunting Stamp Act, however, almost assured a refuge system keyed principally to the production of migratory waterfowl. * * * A 1958 amendment provided that funds derived from the Act could be used to acquire "waterfowl production areas," which are small wetland or pothole areas. * * *

Until 1966, there was no single law governing the administration of the many federal wildlife refuges. The numerous administrative units, known variously as "game ranges," "wildlife ranges," "wildlife management areas," "waterfowl production areas," and "wildlife refuges," were under the jurisdiction of the Fish and Wildlife Service, or, in a few cases, the joint jurisdiction of [FWS and BLM]. Each unit was, however, governed by the often vague standards of the law or executive order by which it was created.

The National Wildlife Refuge System Administration Act of 1966 introduced a measure of rationality into this system by consolidating the varied units into a single National Wildlife Refuge System. The Act, however, did little to spell out standards to guide System administration. It (1) placed restrictions on the transfer, exchange, or other disposal of lands

and where appropriate, restoration of the fish, wildlife, and plant resources and their habitats within the United States for the benefit of present and future generations of Americans." 16 U.S.C. § 668dd(a)(2).]

within the system, (2) clarified the Secretary's authority to accept donations of money to be used for land acquisition, and (3) most importantly, authorized the Secretary to "permit the use of any area within the System for any purpose, including but not limited to hunting, fishing, public recreation and accommodations, and access whenever he determines that such uses are compatible with the major purposes for which such areas were established."[34] This authorization of "compatible" uses thus made clear that the national wildlife refuges are not to be managed as "single-use" lands, but more properly as "dominant use" lands.

Similarly, although the Conservation Act provided that all refuges acquired pursuant to its authority be operated as "inviolate sanctuar[ies],"[36] later enactments rendered this language largely meaningless. Congress authorized the Secretary to permit public hunting on an ever-increasing proportion of the total area of any refuge, if "compatible with the major purposes for which such laws were established."**

The other major law governing refuge administration is the Refuge Recreation Act of 1962 [Eds.: which is addressed in the *Ruby Lake* decisions, further below]. * * *

Considerable controversy has arisen over refuge management. Conflicts have concerned FWS's jurisdiction over certain refuges, the Secretary's authority to transfer lands from the system, and, most frequently, his or her authority to permit or prohibit particular uses under the compatibility standard.

Consolidation of so many disparate units into a single National Wildlife Refuge System did not change the fact that many of the units were established for widely varying purposes. In particular, the System included units expressly established both for wildlife protection *and* for livestock grazing. Reflecting this duality of purpose, certain "game ranges" were jointly administered until 1975 by FWS and BLM. In that year, the Secretary of the Interior directed that BLM become sole manager of three game ranges. The prospect that FWS, whose paramount mission is wildlife conservation, would be divested of its authority in favor of the multiple-use-oriented BLM so alarmed wildlife proponents that they both filed a lawsuit

---

34. 16 U.S.C. § 668dd(d)(1). * * *

36. 16 U.S.C. § 715(d)(2).

** [Eds. In a later section, at pp. 295–96, Bean and Rowland point out:

Hunting was first permitted on a wildlife refuge in 1924. From then until 1949, hunting was permitted primarily on units where it was a traditional activity on the land in question before it became part of the refuge system. In 1949, Congress authorized the Secretary to permit public hunting on up to 25 percent of any unit acquired under the Conservation Act. The proportion was increased to 40 percent in 1958. Finally, the National

Wildlife Refuge System Administration Act of 1966 authorized the Secretary to permit "compatible" hunting on any unit of the National Wildlife Refuge System, retaining the 40 percent limitation only with respect to migratory waterfowl.

As a matter of politics, Congress tied the amount of hunting allowed on refuges to the cost of the federal duck stamp; i.e., the 1949 Act raised the cost of the duck stamp from $1 to $2 at the same time it permitted hunting on up to 25% of the land in a migratory bird refuge; the proportion went to a maximum of 40% when Congress raised the price of the stamp to $3 nine years later.]

and simultaneously introduced legislation to reverse the Secretary's decision.

Both the lawsuit and the legislative efforts were successful in 1976. In *Wilderness Society v. Hathaway*, the District Court for the District of Columbia enjoined the transfer of authority to the BLM on the ground that "the Secretary is required to exercise his discretion and authority with respect to the administration of game ranges and wildlife refuges through the Fish and Wildlife Service." One month later, Congress confirmed this result by amending the Refuge Administration Act to direct that all units of the System be administered through the FWS and that all units then within the System remain so except under certain limited conditions.

* * * [C]ourts have resolved jurisdictional conflicts under the Refuge Administration Act in favor of FWS. In *Trustees of Alaska v. Watt*, the Secretary of the Interior had delegated responsibilities pertaining to oil and gas exploration and development in the Arctic National Wildlife Refuge to the United States Geological Survey (USGS). The USGS was to develop initial guidelines for exploration, review and approve exploration plans, and, after a period of five years, recommend whether additional exploration or development was warranted. The USGS had the exclusive responsibility for the first and last of these. Its approval of exploration plans was subject to concurrent approval by FWS.

The court concluded that this arrangement violated the Refuge Administration Act's requirement that FWS administer all units of the Refuge System. To "administer" a refuge is to "manage" it, the court reasoned, and the Service's duty to manage required it "to control and direct the Refuge by regulating human access in order to conserve the entire spectrum of wildlife found in the Refuge." Even preparing a report to Congress that "supplies information essential to determining whether development activity will be permitted within the Refuge" was, in the court's view, "a Refuge administration function." As to the requirement that FWS concur in the approval of any exploration plan, the court concluded that this was the very sort of "joint administration" of a refuge that the 1976 amendments prohibited. The Ninth Circuit subsequently affirmed the district court's decision and embraced its opinion. [524 F. Supp. 1303 (D. Alaska 1981), aff'd, 690 F.2d 1279 (9th Cir.1982)].

NOTES AND QUESTIONS

1.   In 1997 Congress enacted an "organic" act for the USFWS which is discussed further below; pp. 882–87 infra. As of this writing, there are about 93 million acres in more than five hundred National Wildlife Refuges in all 50 states and several territories.

2.   Refuges may be created or added to in several ways: By executive withdrawal, by act of Congress, by transfers from other federal agencies, and by purchase, donation, or exchange under various authorities such as the Migratory Bird Conservation Act, the Endangered Species Act, or the Land and Water Conservation Fund. See generally Richard J. Fink, The National Wildlife Refuges: Theory, Practice, and Prospect, 18 Harv.

Envtl.L.Rev. 1 (1994). For a useful table showing the chronology of significant events surrounding the refuge system, see Kevin Gergely, J. Michael Scott & Dale Goble, A New Direction for the U.S. National Wildlife Refuges: The National Wildlife Refuge System Improvement Act of 1997, 20 Natural Areas J. 107 (2000).

3. Where do you suppose the first President Roosevelt found the authority to create wildlife refuges by executive order? Cf. United States v. Midwest Oil Co., Chapter 2, supra p. 119. The Secretary of the Interior retains the power to withdraw federal lands for wildlife protection purposes, whether or not he chooses to place the lands in the National Wildlife Refuge System under the jurisdiction of the USFWS. See Chapter 4, supra pp. 340–47. For example, in 1971 Secretary of the Interior Rogers Morton issued an order setting aside 26,000 acres of BLM-managed public lands in Idaho as the Snake River Birds of Prey Natural Area. To enhance protection for what was said to be the most dense nesting population of raptors in the world, in early 1980 the Carter Administration submitted a bill to Congress that would have enlarged the protected area and established it as a National Conservation Area. When Congress dragged its feet, and after the November 1980 election gave the Administration lame duck status, Secretary of the Interior (and past and future Idaho governor) Cecil Andrus used the Federal Land Policy and Management Act (FLPMA) to withdraw about 418,000 acres from disposal. This withdrawal was held to meet the procedural requirements of FLPMA in Sagebrush Rebellion, Inc. v. Hodel, 790 F.2d 760 (9th Cir.1986). In 1993, Congress finally got around to designating 483,000 acres as the Snake River Birds of Prey National Conservation Area, 16 U.S.C. § 460iii et seq., still managed by BLM.

4. Sometimes the President has used the Antiquities Act to set aside land to be managed for, among other things, wildlife, and sometimes given management authority over the area to the USFWS. President Carter's Alaska monuments included several large ones of this type, which Congress converted to national wildlife refuges in ANILCA. See p. 355 supra. In 2000, President Clinton proclaimed the Hanford Reach National Monument along the Columbia River, around the Hanford Nuclear reservation managed by the Department of Energy, and gave the USFWS primary management authority. See 65 Fed. Reg. 37,253 (Jan. 11, 2000).

5. The Bean and Rowland excerpt notes that some of the units of the Refuge system were originally established as "game ranges," with the dual and often conflicting purposes of grazing livestock and protecting wildlife. One such area was the Fort Peck Game Range (later redesignated the Charles M. Russell National Wildlife Range) in eastern Montana, created by executive order (No. 7509) by the second President Roosevelt in 1936. The order provided that the Range's "natural forage resources shall be first utilized for the purpose of sustaining in a healthy condition a maximum of" 400,000 sharptail grouse and 1500 antelope as "primary" species, and "such nonpredatory secondary species in such numbers as may be necessary to maintain a balanced wildlife population." It went on to say that "all" the Range's forage resources "shall be available, except as herein

otherwise provided with respect to wildlife, for domestic livestock" under secretarial regulation implementing the Taylor Grazing Act.

Does this language give wildlife a priority on the Game Range? All wildlife, or just the "primary" species? Or do cows have equal priority? Or does the Order basically leave it up to the Secretary to allocate the "natural forage resources" among these groups as she sees fit? In fact, the Secretary for a number of years gave cows and wildlife equal priority. See Schwenke v. Secretary of the Interior, 720 F.2d 571, 574 n. 4 (9th Cir.1983). In *Schwenke*, the Ninth Circuit construed the quoted language to give priority to the sharptail grouse and the antelope, up to the population numbers mentioned in the order; and after that, all wildlife and livestock had "equal priority in access to the forage resources of the Range."

Schwenke went on to consider the effect of Congress's decision in 1976 (briefly described in the Bean and Rowland excerpt, supra) to transfer exclusive control of game ranges to the Fish & Wildlife Service. Noting that the transfer statute "does not mention the relative priorities of livestock and wildlife in access to the forage resources" on these game ranges, the court opined, in *dictum*, that because the "primary mission" of the FWS is wildlife, the transfer of jurisdiction to that agency would ordinarily give wildlife priority in access. But because there was no mention of the 1936 Executive Order in either the 1976 Act or its legislative history, the court refused to find that the Order's scheme of priority had been repealed by implication. The court went on to hold that the 1976 transfer of jurisdiction meant that the FWS would administer livestock grazing on the Range not under the Taylor Grazing Act (as the 1936 Executive Order had provided), but rather under the Wildlife Refuge Act.

In the wake of this decision, what legal standards guide the manager of the Game Range in her decision to allocate forage between cows and wildlife? Prior to 1985, FWS followed BLM's prior practice and allocated about 60% of the forage to livestock. In that year, the FWS completed an EIS on livestock grazing on the Range, and decided to alter the allocation so that wildlife got 63% of the Range's forage and livestock 37%. NEPA compliance on the decision was upheld against attack in Schwenke v. Secretary of the Interior (II), 21 ELR 20542 (D.Mont.1990).

6. While wildlife professionals often speak of "wildlife management," frequently preceded by "the science of," a satisfactory definition is elusive. Its defenders maintain that it is a body of generally accepted principles derived from extensive research, but some suggest that modern practices of wildlife management are merely the residue of decades of one damn mistake after another. See generally J. Trefethan, AN AMERICAN CRUSADE FOR WILDLIFE (1975); D.Allen, OUR WILDLIFE LEGACY (rev. ed. 1962). One is tempted to say that "wildlife management," like "multiple use management," resembles obscenity: one may know it when one sees it, even though one admittedly cannot describe it in words. See Jacobellis v. Ohio, 378 U.S. 184, 197 (1964) (Stewart, J., concurring).

7. Comprehensive legal treatments of national wildlife refuge issues are found in Robert Fischman, The National Wildlife Refuge System and Hallmarks of Modern Organic Legislation, 29 Ecology L.Q. ___ (forthcom-

ing, 2002); Richard J. Fink, The National Wildlife Refuges: Theory, Practice, and Prospect, 18 Harv.Envtl.L.Rev. 1 (1994). See also Nathaniel Reed & Dennis Drabelle, THE FISH AND WILDLIFE SERVICE (1984). Reed, a longtime outstanding conservationist, was Assistant Secretary of the Interior for Fish, Wildlife & Parks in the early 1970s.

2. THE ROLE OF STATE LAW

State of Wyoming v. United States

United States Court of Appeals for the Tenth Circuit, 2002.
279 F.3d 1214.

■ Before LUCERO, POLITZ,* and BALDOCK, CIRCUIT JUDGES.

■ BALDOCK, CIRCUIT JUDGE.

Once again a federal court is called upon to unravel a congressionally-legislated Federal–State standoff. The National Elk Refuge (NER), a part of the National Wildlife Refuge System (NWRS), encompasses approximately 24,700 acres of wilderness north of Jackson Hole, Wyoming, in the greater Yellowstone area.[1] Brucellosis, a serious disease that causes miscarriage, is endemic to free-ranging elk in the greater Yellowstone area and a threat to Wyoming's domestic cattle industry. Plaintiff State of Wyoming and the United States Fish and Wildlife Service (FWS), a division of the United States Department of the Interior (USDI), disagree over how best to manage brucellosis on the NER. Specifically, the State challenges the FWS's refusal to permit the State to vaccinate elk on the NER with a brucellosis vaccine known as "Strain 19." According to the FWS, after several years of research and study, the biosafety and efficacy of Strain 19 vis-a-vis elk remain unproven. The State disagrees.

Resolution of this matter ultimately rests upon our construction of the National Wildlife Refuge System Improvement Act of 1997 (NWRSIA) (codified at 16 U.S.C. § § 668dd–668ee). Unfortunately, the NWRSIA does not (nor does any Federal law) directly address the problem of brucellosis in wildlife, or establish clear priority between wildlife and domestic livestock when interests involving the two conflict. In the jurisdictionally-fragmented Yellowstone area, however, one thing is certain: Wildlife management policies affecting the interests of multiple sovereigns demand a high degree of intergovernmental cooperation. Such cooperation is conspicuously absent in this case.

Brucellosis is a disease caused by Brucella abortus, a bacterial borne pathogen which infects the reproductive organs and lymphatic systems of

* The Honorable Henry A. Politz, United States Senior Circuit Judge for the Fifth Circuit Court of Appeals, sitting by designation.

1. * * * Congress established the NER in 1912, then 2,760 acres, to protect both human and elk interests in the Jackson Hole valley. See 16 U.S.C. § 673. The NER became a part of the NWRS in 1966. Numerous species make the NER their home during part or all of the year. In addition to elk, these species include birds, bison, mule deer, bighorn sheep, pronghorn antelope, moose, wolves, coyotes, badgers, and black and grizzly bears.

ungulates.[2] Brucellosis most often produces spontaneous abortion in female ungulates during the first pregnancy following infection. A small percentage of infected ungulates may develop inflamed joints resulting in arthritis and lameness. The disease also may produce sterility in infected males. Research has shown that female ungulates are largely responsible for the spread of brucellosis to other susceptible hosts. Aborted fetuses, vaginal fluids, newborn young, birth by-products, and milk from infected females all are contaminated with the Brucella bacteria. The disease spreads most commonly when ungulates consume infected tissue or contaminated feed or water. See B. Smith & T. Roffe, A Political Disease: Brucellosis, Bugle: The Quarterly Journal of the Rocky Mountain Elk Foundation, Summer 1992, at 71–74.[3]

Authorities first detected brucellosis in elk in the greater Yellowstone area around 1930. Today, brucellosis infects approximately thirty percent of the elk in western Wyoming. Thus, significant levels of brucellosis still occur in the feed ground elk population on the NER. See R. Keiter & P. Froelicher, Bison, Brucellosis, and Law in the Greater Yellowstone Ecosystem, 28 Land & Water L. Rev. 1, 18, 27 (1993). Experts estimate that the annual elk calf loss due to brucellosis-related abortions on the NER is seven percent of the calf crop.

The concentration of free-ranging elk herds on Wyoming and NER winter feed grounds appears to perpetuate brucellosis. The feed grounds, which host around 25,000 elk each winter, are prime locations for the transmission of brucellosis because the herds are in close contact during the critical birthing period. Because natural winter habitat in the region is not adequate to sustain the elk herds at their current numbers, closing the feed grounds would foster competition, which appears to increase the risk of brucellosis transmission. See Keiter & Froelicher, supra, at 60–61.

The primary significance of brucellosis-related abortions in Wyoming's elk herds is the potential for transmission of the disease to domestic cattle. Elk and other wildlife in the greater Yellowstone area do not respect jurisdictional boundaries. Instead, wildlife wanders freely across the region's public and private lands. Experts explain that the creation of artificial barriers to separate domestic cattle from wild elk is not feasible:

> Natural barriers to prevent commingling of wildlife and cattle do not exist, and artificial barriers, such as fences, have many drawbacks. Wildlife-proof fences, if effective, would interfere with traditional movement and migration routes of elk, bison and other species. The

---

2. An ungulate is defined as "a hoofed mammal." Random House Dictionary 2069 (2d ed. 1987).

3. Humans are susceptible to infection from the Brucella bacteria as well. The symptoms of undulant fever, as the disease is known in humans, are flu-like. Most cases of undulant fever, however, are caused by Brucella melitensis, which is found primarily in sheep and goats. The risk of human infection by elk or cattle is possible, but more remote.

But see Parker Land and Cattle Co. v. United States, 796 F. Supp. 477, 487 (D.Wyo.1992) (describing incident where ranch hand contracted undulant fever while assisting in the delivery of calves; "several courses of medication" proved effective in combating the disease). Cooked meat poses no threat of transmitting brucellosis and is considered safe for human consumption. See Smith & Roffe, supra, at 74, 76–77.

intensive and expensive maintenance required for such a program—and the fidelity of elk and bison to traditional ranges—ensure that this would fail.

Smith & Roffe, supra, at 78.

No documented cases of elk infecting domestic cattle with brucellosis under natural conditions exist. But see Parker Land and Cattle Co. v. United States, 796 F. Supp. 477, 488 (D.Wyo.1992) (concluding that a brucellosis outbreak in Wyoming cattle "was most likely caused by contact with infected elk or bison, as those are the only two known sources of the disease in the entire State of Wyoming"). Scientists at Texas A & M University, however, have transmitted brucellosis from elk to cattle in confined conditions. Thus, the impetus behind Wyoming's desire to eradicate brucellosis in elk is the potential for economic loss to its domestic cattle industry. Experts estimate that from 1951 to 1981, brucellosis cost the nation's cattle industry $1.6 billion. See Smith & Roffe, supra, at 72–76. Another estimate places that cost at $100 million annually. See Keiter & Froelicher, supra, at 9.

Despite disagreement over how effective the Strain 19 vaccine is in immunizing elk from brucellosis, experts agree that vaccinating cattle with Strain 19 plays an important role, together with test-and-removal of infected animals, in eradicating brucellosis from cattle herds. The vaccine, which has been in use in the cattle industry for several decades, provides approximately seventy percent protection against abortion in vaccinated cattle. Subject to the State's ongoing program of vaccination, and test-and-removal, the National Cooperative Brucellosis Eradication Program of the United States Department of Agriculture (USDA) certified the State of Wyoming's cattle industry as brucellosis-free in 1985. See Smith and Roffe, supra, at 74, 77.[4]

That same year, the State began vaccinating elk with Strain 19 on state feed grounds, apparently with some success. By the early 1990's, Wyoming reported that its vaccination program had resulted in a seventy percent calving success rate for vaccinated elk, as compared to a thirty percent calving success rate for unvaccinated elk. See Keiter & Froelicher, supra, at 30 n.199. By 1998, the State was vaccinating elk on twenty-one of twenty-two state feed grounds without notable adverse consequence. Since

4. For over half a century, federal and state officials have worked closely with the nation's domestic livestock industry to eradicate brucellosis in livestock. See generally Keiter & Froelicher, supra, at 21–27. Federal law authorizes the Secretary of the USDA "to control and eradicate any communicable diseases of livestock or poultry, including . . . brucellosis of domestic animals." 21 U.S.C. § 114a. Federal law also authorizes the Secretary to "seize, quarantine, and dispose of" infected livestock moving in interstate commerce. Id. § 134a. The USDA has promulgated regulations pursuant to 21 U.S.C. § 111, establishing a comprehensive brucellosis eradication program. See 9 C.F.R. Part 78. Notably, these regulations do not apply to wild elk. See id. § 78.1 (defining animals as "cattle, bison, and swine"). But see 7 U.S.C. § 426 (authorizing the Secretary of the USDA to "determine, demonstrate, and promulgate the best methods of eradication, suppression, or bringing under control on . . . areas of the public domain as well as on State, Territory, or privately owned lands . . . animal injurious to agriculture . . . [and] animal husbandry . . .").

1985, however, at least four documented incidents of brucellosis in Wyoming cattle have occurred. The source of the disease in these cases remains unidentified. See Smith and Roffe, supra, at 74; see also Parker Land and Cattle Co, 796 F. Supp. at 481–92 (describing 1988 brucellosis outbreak on the Parker ranch).

The USDA's revocation of Wyoming's brucellosis-free status would negatively impact the State's cattle industry by significantly (1) increasing costs to the State and its producers, and (2) limiting access to interstate and international markets. See * * * Fund for Animals, Inc., v. Lujan, 962 F.2d 1391, 1401–02 (9th Cir.1992) (loss of Montana's brucellosis-free status would require the State to spend over $2 million dollars per year testing cattle). Although Wyoming, for now, maintains its brucellosis-free certification, the continuing threat that the State's domestic cattle might contract the disease from free-ranging infected elk prompted several States in 1997 to threaten to restrict entry of Wyoming cattle into their borders.

In November 1997, the Governor of Wyoming wrote the Director of the FWS to request "immediate assistance and response to deal with our mutual concern with the brucellosis issue in the State of Wyoming." The Governor explained that to appease concerned States, Wyoming obtained a "station review" from the USDA's Animal Plant Health Inspection Service (APHIS). Among other things, APHIS dictated greater testing and control of Wyoming cattle at significant cost to the State. Meanwhile, according to the Governor, the FWS had proposed "an elaborate multi-year [vaccine] efficacy research study" to address the brucellosis problem on the NER. The Governor did "not support such a strategy, that under the guise of research, will defend the status quo for the next few years." Wyoming's Governor endorsed the vaccination of elk on the NER using Strain 19: "Our problem with brucellosis is now. We cannot wait for tomorrow's solutions, especially when we believe the Strain 19 vaccine to be effective based on experiences in vaccinating elk on state feed grounds."

When the FWS failed to respond, the Governor delivered a second letter to the Director of the FWS in January 1998 offering to undertake a vaccination program of elk on the NER at the State's own expense, and to "indemnify and hold harmless" the FWS from any claims arising out of the program. This time the Director responded, denying the State of Wyoming the authority to conduct a Strain 19 vaccination program on the NER:

> As you know, the Service disagrees that Wyoming has adequately demonstrated the effectiveness of the Strain 19 program. While we have no doubt that Wyoming has been successful at vaccinating elk [on state feed grounds], there are not adequate data to indicate whether or not the lowered seroprevalence is attributable to vaccination. Feed-line management on the Refuge, which minimizes the time that animals are concentrated on the feed line through the use of alfalfa pellets rather than hay also appears to have lowered seroprevalence according to Service data. However, in both cases (Wyoming vaccination and Refuge feed-line management), there are inadequate data to ensure that these particular management actions are solely responsible for or simply correlate with observed changes in seroprevalence. In the case

of the State's feed grounds, the Service would be far less skeptical of the vaccine's effect if rigorous clinical trials had demonstrated efficacy under controlled conditions....

The Service is willing to implement a vaccination program once adequate, scientifically sound data demonstrate that any proposed vaccine is both safe and effective. We believe such a vaccine does not exist at this time, but we continue to support its development....

Therefore, given the points raised in this letter outlining the Service's concerns for vaccination of elk with Strain 19, the Service does not authorize Wyoming to conduct a vaccination program on the Refuge at this time....

Aplt's App. at 35–36.

[Wyoming filed suit, claiming the state had a "sovereign right" to manage wildlife within its borders, including to vaccinate elk on the NER. The district court dismissed the case.] * * * The State asserts a concurrent, if not exclusive, right to manage wildlife on the NER, including a right to vaccinate elk on the NER with Strain 19, free from federal interference. The FWS counters by asserting exclusive unlimited discretion under the NWRSIA to manage wildlife on the NER in any manner the Secretary deems appropriate, free from state interference. Unfortunately, we do not believe this case is as clear cut and easily resolved as the parties urge.

[The court first addressed and rejected Wyoming's constitutional argument for control over wildlife on federal lands. See Chapter 3, supra pp. 183–94.] * * * [W]e believe the point painfully apparent that the Tenth Amendment does not reserve to the State of Wyoming the right to manage wildlife, or more specifically vaccinate elk, on the NER, regardless of the circumstances. * * * The remedy the State seeks must come, if at all, not from the Constitution but from Congress. To what extent Congress sought to exercise its power under the Property Clause in enacting the NWRSIA is the inquiry to which we turn next.

* * * According to the State, the NWRSIA reserves to the State the unencumbered right to manage wildlife on the NER. * * * The mission of the NWRS "is to administer a national network of lands and waters for the conservation, management, and where appropriate, restoration of the fish, wildlife, and plant resources and their habitats within the United States for the benefit of present and future generations of Americans." 16 U.S.C. § 668dd(a)(2). The NWRSIA directs the FWS to, among other things, "ensure that the biological integrity, diversity, and environmental health of the System are maintained." 16 U.S.C. § 668dd(a)(4)(B). * * *

While plainly vesting the FWS with authority to administer the Act and manage the NWRS,[11] the NWRSIA makes numerous mention of the need for cooperation between the FWS and the States to achieve the Act's

---

11. The NWRSIA does not define the term "administer." In its common usage, "administer" means to "manage," which in turn means to "direct govern or control in action or use." Random House Dictionary 26, 1166 (2d. ed. 1987). Manage is a lesser included term of administer.

objectives. At its outset, the NWRSIA directs that the FWS "shall" (1) "complement efforts of States and other Federal agencies to conserve fish and wildlife and their habitats;" (2) "ensure effective coordination, interaction, and cooperation with owners of land adjoining refuges and the fish and wildlife agency of the States in which the units of the System are located;" and (3) "ensure timely and effective cooperation and collaboration with Federal agencies and State fish and wildlife agencies during the course of acquiring and managing refuges." Id. § 668dd(a)(4)(C), (E), (M).

To that end, the NWRSIA directs the FWS to "issue a final conservation plan" for each refuge "consistent with the provisions of this Act and, to the extent practicable, consistent with the fish and wildlife conservation plans of the State in which the refuge is located." Id. at § 668dd(e)(1)(A)(iii). In preparing and periodically revising the plan, the FWS "shall, to the maximum extent practicable and consistent with this Act—(A) consult with adjoining Federal, State, local, and private landowners and affected State conservation agencies; and (B) coordinate the development of the conservation plan or revision with relevant State conservation plans for fish and wildlife and their habitats." Id. § 668dd(e)(3).

Notably for purposes of this case, the NWRSIA concludes with an opaque provision termed "State authority:"

> Nothing in this Act shall be construed as affecting the authority, jurisdiction, or responsibility of the several States to manage, control, or regulate fish and resident wildlife under State law or regulations in any area within the System. Regulations permitting hunting or fishing of fish and resident wildlife within the System shall be, to the extent practicable, consistent with State fish and wildlife laws, regulations, and management plans.

Id. § 668dd(m). The State of Wyoming primarily relies on the first sentence of this "saving clause" to support its claimed right to vaccinate elk on the NER with the Strain 19 brucellosis vaccine. According to the State, Congress specifically included the saving clause in the NWRSIA to "reserve[] to the States the right to manage wildlife on refuge lands within their borders." Consequently, the State opines the FWS exceeded its authority under the NWRSIA when it refused to permit the State to vaccinate elk on the NER. * * *

In Count I of its first amended complaint, the State of Wyoming does not seek "review" of the FWS decision to deny the State's request to vaccinate elk on the NER. Such review is available, if at all, through the APA. Instead, the State seeks to strike down a decision of the FWS (made on behalf of Defendants Secretary of the USDI and the United States), allegedly in excess of the powers Congress delegated to the agency in the NWRSIA. See Leedom v. Kyne, 358 U.S. 184, 188, 3 L. Ed. 2d 210, 79 S. Ct. 180 (1959). Whether the FWS's decision in this case was ultra vires as the State claims in Count I turns solely upon our legal construction of the NWRSIA and, in particular, its saving clause. We conclude the FWS's decision to deny the State's request to vaccinate elk on the NER was not ultra vires. * * *

Initially, we note that this is not a case in which the State of Wyoming seeks to invade "an area where the federal interest has been manifest since the beginning of our Republic." Compare United States v. Locke, 529 U.S. 89, 99 (2000) (recognizing the long-standing federal interest in the regulation of maritime commerce). Rather, as the Secretary of the USDI recognizes, wildlife management is a field which the States have traditionally occupied. Even today, the Secretary generally acknowledges that "State jurisdiction remains concurrent with Federal authority." 43 C.F.R. § 24.3(c); see also id. § 24.3(b) ("Despite the existence of constitutional power respecting fish and wildlife on Federally owned lands, Congress has, in fact, reaffirmed the basic responsibility and authority of the States to manage fish and resident wildlife on Federal lands."). According to the Secretary, "Federal authority exists for specified purposes while State authority regarding fish and resident wildlife remains the comprehensive backdrop applicable in the absence of specific, overriding Federal law." Id. § 24.1(a) * * *

The first sentence of the NWRSIA's saving clause, viewed in isolation, seems to support our assumption that even after the NWRSIA, the State retains the absolute right to manage wildlife on the NER free from federal intervention: "Nothing in this Act shall be construed as affecting the authority, jurisdiction, or responsibility of the several States to manage, control, or regulate fish and wildlife under State law or regulations in any area within the System." 16 U.S.C. § 668dd(m) (emphasis added). The State's sweeping interpretation of the first sentence in § 668dd(m) is not without force, and our assumption might be plausible if we interpreted the sentence in isolation. Such an interpretation of the saving clause, however, simply is not feasible in light of established rules of construction requiring us to consider the NWRSIA in its entirety, mindful of congressional purposes and objectives. But see Defenders of Wildlife v. Andrus, 627 F.2d 1238, 1248 (D.C.Cir.1980) (suggesting without analysis in dicta that the first sentence of § 668dd(m) reserves the authority to manage wildlife on federal lands to the States).

Unquestionably, the NWRSIA inspirits a "cooperative federalism," calling for, at a minimum, state involvement and participation in the management of the NWRS as that system affects surrounding state ecosystems. * * *

Still, the NWRSIA requires the FWS in developing conservation plans for a refuge to act in conformity with State objectives only "to the extent practical." Id. § 668dd(e)(1)(A)(iii); id. § 668dd(e)(3). The NWRSIA's legislative history confirms this, stating the Act requires that "to the extent practicable, the FWS should seek opportunities to coordinate the management of National Wildlife Refuges with the management of fish and wildlife resources generally by the State or States in which the refuges are located." H.R. Rep. No.105–106, at 8. Even the second and final sentence of the NWRSIA's saving clause, which appears to contradict its first sentence, requires only that "regulations permitting hunting or fishing of fish and resident wildlife within the system shall be, to the extent practicable, consistent with State fish and wildlife laws, regulations, and management plans." 16 U.S.C. § 668dd(m) * * *.

The legislative history behind § 668dd(m) lends little support to the State of Wyoming's claim that the saving clause unconditionally reserves to it the "sovereign" right to manage elk on the NER. * * * The discussion of the saving clause in the Senate Report together with the entire tone of the NWRSIA reveals that Congress was solicitous of state sensibilities and simply did not wish to face the Federal–State jurisdictional dilemma which the NWRSIA and its predecessor the NWRSAA created. Instead, Congress left the courts to resolve jurisdictional disputes on a case-by-case basis. As two commentators put it: "The main legislative theory seems to be on the order of 'let's just muddle through as best we can and let the courts handle the hard cases.' " [George Cameron] Coggins & [Patti] Ward, [The Law of Wildlife Management on Federal Public Lands, 60 Or.L.Rev. 59], at 84–85 [1981] (noting that "in the end, this jurisdictional imbroglio is more political than legal"); see also United States v. Vesterso, 828 F.2d 1234, 1240–41 & n. 5 (8th Cir.1987).

In the end, the proposition that the FWS lacks the power to make a decision regarding the health of wildlife on the NER when a State, for whatever reason, disagrees with that decision proves too much. * * * If we construed the NWRSIA to grant the State of Wyoming the sweeping power it claims, the State would be free to manage and regulate the NER in a manner the FWS deemed incompatible with the NER's purpose. But the Secretary alone is authorized, "under such regulations as he may prescribe," to "permit the use of any area within the System for any purpose . . . whenever he determines that such uses are compatible with the major purposes for which such areas were established. . . ." Id. § 668dd(d)(1)(A); see also id. § 668dd(d)(3)(A) (The Secretary shall not permit a use of a refuge "unless the Secretary has determined that the use is a compatible use.").

Yet, the NWRSIA's saving clause is not meaningless. Section 668dd(m) convinces us that Congress did not intend to displace entirely state regulation and management of wildlife on federal public lands, especially where such regulation and management bears directly upon the well being of state interests arising outside those public lands. In other words, Congress rejected complete preemption of state wildlife regulation within the NWRS. Rather, we believe Congress intended ordinary principles of conflict preemption to apply in cases such as this. * * *

Consistent with our construction of the NWRSIA, we hold that the FWS's decision to refuse to permit the State to vaccinate elk on the NER with Strain 19 based upon efficacy and biosafety concerns was not, in itself, beyond the agency's statutory authority or ultra vires. * * *

At the prompting of the district court, the State of Wyoming amended its original complaint and grudgingly added Count III to its first amended complaint seeking review of the FWS's decision under the APA, 5 U.S.C. § § 701–706. The State sought to overturn the FWS's decision under both § 706(2)(A) as "not in accordance with law," and § 706(2)(C) as "in excess of statutory jurisdiction." * * * We therefore focus on whether the FWS's decision was "arbitrary, capricious, an abuse of discretion, or otherwise not in accordance with law." 5 U.S.C. § 706(2)(A).

* * * We have seen that the FWS has the authority under the NWRSIA to make decisions binding on the State regarding wildlife management within the NWRS. But that authority is not unlimited as the district court seemed to suggest. Congress undoubtedly did not intend its call for "effective coordination, interaction, and cooperation with owners of land adjoining refuges and the fish and wildlife agencies of the State," 16 U.S.C. § 668dd(a)(4)(e), a theme running throughout the NWRSIA, to constitute merely a recommendation which the FWS might ignore with impunity.

Similarly, we reject any suggestion that Congress "committed to agency discretion by law" the FWS's decision to deny the State of Wyoming's request. * * * Congress throughout the NWRSIA has indicated an intent to circumscribe the FWS's discretion. The requirement that the FWS in developing a conservation plan for each refuge comply with State policies and objectives to the "extent" or "maximum extent practicable," id. § § 668dd(e), undoubtedly places limits on the agency's discretion. See Random House Dictionary 1517 (2d ed. 1987) (defining "practicable" as "capable of being done, effected, or put into practice, with the available means").

Additionally, in determining whether a proposed "use" of a refuge constitutes a "compatible use," i.e., a use that "will not materially interfere with or detract from the fulfillment of the mission of the System or the purposes of the refuge," the NWRSIA directs the Secretary to exercise "sound professional judgment." 16 U.S.C. § 668ee(1). The NWRSIA defines the phrase "sound professional judgment" as "a finding, determination, or decision that is consistent with principles of sound fish and wildlife management and administration, available science and resources, and adherence to the requirements of this Act and other applicable laws." Id. § 668ee(3). The legislative history of § 668ee reveals that Congress expected "the FWS to be energetic and creative in seeking such resources, including partnerships with the States, local communities and private and nonprofit groups." H.R. Rep. No. 105–106, at 6. Thus, Congress rejected the idea that the FWS's exercise of "sound professional judgment" under the NWRSIA is unreviewable.

* * * [W]e believe the FWS's decision may be subject to a "thorough, probing, in-depth review" under the traditional agency review principles set forth in § 706(2)(A) of the APA. * * * Our decision to construe Count III of the first amended complaint in this manner, despite the State's inartful pleading, rests upon the following factors-

(1) the long-standing and increasingly urgent nature of the brucellosis problem in elk on the NER and its threat to Wyoming's domestic cattle and resident elk populations;

(2) the FWS's inability after more than a decade to reach any real consensus regarding the efficacy and biosafety of the Strain 19 vaccine as applied to elk on the NER;

(3) the "Catch–22" in which the State of Wyoming finds itself in struggling with the apparently discordant views over brucellosis control and eradication between the USDA and the FWS;

(4) the Congress' ongoing reluctance to address the brucellosis problem in wildlife; and

(5) the State of Wyoming's and FWS's bipolar claims of absolute power to decide the fate of elk on the NER. * * *

The State alleges that extending its vaccination program to the NER will not adversely affect the refuge because Strain 19 is a safe and effective means of containing brucellosis, and thus "neither the ecosystem nor the elk herds will be negatively impacted." The State further alleges that the FWS's program to control brucellosis on the NER has proven ineffective.

> [The FWS] has continued with an ineffective disease program which has remained unchanged even though this [district] court previously found [the FWS's] actions to be negligent. The disease control methods used by [the FWS] today are the same methods used for the previous twenty years. [The Secretary] sets policy, supervises and directs the actions of the [FWS] in total disregard of the rights of Wyoming to control diseases and protect wildlife, livestock and its citizens in a health and safety matter.

Finally, the State alleges that the FWS has failed to conduct any independent studies on the efficacy and biosafety of Strain 19. Rather, according to the State, the FWS bases its criticism of Strain 19 solely on statistical analysis of limited depth and scope.

Accepting the foregoing allegation as true, we have little difficulty concluding that the State of Wyoming states a claim for relief in Count III of its first amendment complaint. If, as the State suggests, the Strain 19 vaccine is a safe and effective means of containing brucellosis in free-ranging elk, and the FWS has no viable alternative means of reducing the high rate of brucellosis-infected elk on the NER, then the FWS decision to deny the State's request to vaccinate elk on the NER with Strain 19 may very well be "arbitrary, capricious, an abuse of discretion, or otherwise not in accordance with law." 5 U.S.C. § 706(2)(A). Thus, we conclude that the district court erred in dismissing Count III for failure to state a claim upon which relief may be granted.

As we recently recognized, "habitat management is a delicate venture." Sierra Club–Black Hills Group v. United States Forest Serv., 259 F.3d 1281, 1286 (10th Cir.2001). To make matters worse, jurisdictional allocation regarding wildlife management within the NWRS is a legal quagmire. Unfortunately, the NWRSIA with its broad language and general directives is not particularly helpful in resolving any particular conflict, especially where resolution of that conflict, whether agreed upon or court ordered, will inevitably affect the interests of dual sovereigns. To that extent, wildlife management is inherently political. See Coggins & Ward, supra, at 70, 84. Thus, wildlife managers simply cannot view wildlife management in isolation, as the FWS appears to be doing in this instance. See id. at 70. The FWS's apparent indifference to the State of Wyoming's problem and the State's insistence of a "sovereign right" to manage wildlife on the NER do little to promote "cooperative federalism." Given the NWRSIA's repeated calls for a "cooperative federalism," we find inexcusable the parties' unwillingness in this case to even attempt to amicably resolve the brucellosis controversy or find any common ground on which to commence fruitful negotiations.

To be sure, deference to agency action is appropriate "where that action implicates scientific and technical judgments within the scope of agency expertise." Sierra Club–Black Hills Group, 259 F.3d at 1286. The problem is that after an extended period of time, the FWS still appears unable or unwilling to make any judgment regarding the biosafety and efficacy of Strain 19 as applied to free-ranging elk. But the law requires answers. For instance, the FWS has never explained why the State's proposal would "stand as an obstacle to the accomplishment and execution" of federal objectives. [citation omitted] Due to health and safety concerns, the FWS effectively pulled the plug on the State's vaccination of elk on the NER after a trial run from 1989–1991. That was over a decade ago and the FWS has yet to resolve these concerns.

* * * Given that the FWS effectively suspended the State's Strain 19 vaccination program on the NER over a decade ago due to health and safety concerns, the "temporary" nature of FWS's action has long since passed. Instead, in typical bureaucratic fashion, the FWS now claims that it needs an (1) elaborate efficacy study of Strain 19, (2) an environmental impact study, and (3) a comprehensive review of the State's proposed course of action as it affects the FWS's trust responsibilities to elk and other wildlife residing on the refuge. See Aplt's App. at 35–36. This proves too much too late in the day. If the executive and legislative branches of our Government will not act to resolve the brucellosis controversy in the State of Wyoming in what little time remains, the judicial branch may have to.

The State's apparent end purpose in pursuing this suit is to protect itself, its producer's domestic livestock, and its free-ranging elk from a threat arising out of the FWS's alleged lack of any meaningful program to combat brucellosis on the NER. Simplicity ends when we are faced with a situation where the program, or lack thereof, by one sovereign allegedly impairs the meaningful accomplishment of another sovereign's responsibilities. Unlike the district court, we do not read the NWRSIA as providing the FWS, through the Secretary of the USDI, with unlimited discretion to act or fail to act in a manner that threatens the well-being of a neighboring sovereign's livestock or game industry.

* * * We leave to the district court's discretion whether creation of that record requires a remand to the FWS. We also leave to the district court to determine in the first instance the appropriate level of deference, if any, to be given the FWS's position in this case. * * *

NOTES AND QUESTIONS

1. If brucellosis is such an insidious, infectious disease that threatens domestic livestock and the ranching industry, why does the USFWS resist

vaccinating the elk for brucellosis? If the scientific evidence on efficacy of such a course is ambiguous, is it better to be safe than sorry?

2.   The court seems to acknowledge that USFWS has the authority to prohibit the state from vaccinating the elk on the NER with Strain 19. Yet it remands the case for a reconsideration of the USFWS decision. What would you now advise the USFWS to do, assuming that the agency leadership has dug in, and continues to oppose vaccinating the elk, firmly believing that the risk of elk infecting domestic cattle with brucellosis is very small? Could the agency simply beef up the record to support its opposition? Could it say that it will entertain the State's vaccination proposal seriously, but will do so in the format of preparing an EIS under NEPA? While the court is showing impatience here, can the court enjoin the USFWS from preparing an EIS here?

3.   Is the court assuming that there is a meaningful risk of infected elk infecting cattle? Isn't that a key question on which the science is unclear? To the extent the science is unclear, and the State and the USFWS disagree about the risk, which has the ultimate authority to decide under the NWRSIA?

4.   Notice that the federal government wears several hats here. The U.S. Department of Agriculture has authority over whether to certify Wyoming's cattle industry as "brucellosis-free." See footnote 4 and accompanying text in the principal case. If the Department of Agriculture believes there is a significant risk of elk-cattle transmission, does that affect the authority of the USFWS regarding elk vaccination on the NER? Is the court saying that the USFWS has a duty to spend federal money to investigate the efficacy of Strain 19? For more on brucellosis and state-federal conflicts, see pp. 888–91, infra.

5.   Suppose USFWS responds by asking the Congress to fund a $10 million, ten-year study of the effectiveness of Strain 19. If Congress provides the funds, what does that do to the litigation? What effect on the litigation if Congress refuses to provide the funds?

6.   Could the State have vaccinated the elk without this litigation if it did so when the elk wandered off the Refuge to private land? Would it have made any difference whether the State knew the elk would likely wander back into the Refuge?

7.   Why did the State frame its lawsuit in the broadest possible terms, asserting that it had primacy as a matter of constitutional law over wildlife on federal lands? After the unanimous decision in *Kleppe v. New Mexico*, Chapter 3, supra p. 184, wasn't it clear that argument was a loser? Note that after "prompting" by the district court, the State "grudgingly" amended its complaint to challenge the USFWS decision as arbitrary and capricious under the APA.

8.   Look at the "State authority" clause in the NWRSIA. If the USFWS decides to allow public hunting or fishing on a national wildlife refuge (a matter discussed immediately below), must hunters or anglers have state licenses and conform to state seasons and bag limits? May the USFWS preempt such state laws? How?

3. National Wildlife Refuge Management and the Compatibility Test

As noted earlier, the national wildlife refuges do not offer "refuge" in one commonly accepted meaning of the word: hunting, fishing, and trapping have become normal activities on refuge lands, and other economically oriented practices, from haying to mineral leasing, may also occur. Like some other federal lands, some refuges are also threatened with degradation from human overuse, particularly recreational use. Until 1997, the basic legal standard for administration of the Refuge System was found in the National Wildlife Refuge Administration Act (16 U.S.C. § 668dd(d)(1)):

> The Secretary is authorized, under such regulations as he may prescribe, to—(A) permit the use of any area within the System for any purpose, including but not limited to hunting, fishing, public recreation and accommodations, and access whenever he determines that such uses are compatible with the major purposes for which such areas were established * * *.

(Changes introduced by the 1997 Act are discussed further below.) The Act went on to create certain exceptions and limitations on application of this generic "compatibility" standard, but it remained the principal management criterion. A prior statute, the Refuge Recreation Act of 1962 (considered in the next principal case), established a similar but not identical standard, and it was expressly preserved by the Refuge Administration Act (16 U.S.C. § 668dd(h)).

The compatibility test did not provoke litigation until the mid–1970s. (Udall v. Tallman, Chapter 4, supra p. 308, grew out of a controversy over the compatibility of oil and gas leasing in refuges, but no compatibility issues were involved in the case.) We have already seen one application of the "compatibility" standard, in National Audubon Society v. Hodel (St. Matthews Island exchange), Chapter 4, supra p. 369, which arose in connection with whether a proposed exchange of private inholdings inside Refuges for other federal lands elsewhere met a statutory "public interest" test. The following court opinions remain among the fullest explorations of the application of the compatibility standard.

Defenders of Wildlife v. Andrus (Ruby Lake Refuge I)

United States District Court, District of Columbia, 1978.
11 Envtl.Rptr.Cases 2098.

■ Pratt, J.

[In April 1978 the Fish & Wildlife Service adopted special regulations governing recreational boating in the Ruby Lake National Wildlife Refuge. Plaintiff filed this suit two months later, charging that the regulations violated the Refuge Recreation Act of 1962 (16 U.S.C. § 460k), and seeking injunctive relief against continued motorboat use in the Refuge.] * * *

Findings of Fact

I. *Ruby Lake National Wildlife Refuge.*

1.1   On July 2, 1938, by Executive Order No. 7923, President Franklin Roosevelt "reserved and set apart" the Refuge "as a refuge and breeding ground for migratory birds and other wildlife," in order to effectuate further the purposes of the Migratory Bird Conservation Act. The area so reserved and set apart * * * comprised all lands and waters within a described area of approximately 37,640 acres in Elko and White Pine Counties, Nevada. 3 Fed.Reg. 1639 (July 7, 1938).

1.2   Section 5 of the Migratory Bird Conservation Act, 15 U.S.C. § 715d, authorizes the United States to purchase, rent or otherwise reserve areas "for use as inviolate sanctuaries for migratory birds * * *." Section 6 of this Act, 16 U.S.C. § 715e, requires that easements and reservations retained by any grantor from whom the United States received title "shall be subject to rules and regulations prescribed by the Secretary of [Interior] for the occupation, use, operation, protection and administration of the areas as inviolate sanctuaries for migratory birds * * *."

1.3   The primary purpose for which the Refuge was established is for use as a refuge, breeding ground and inviolate sanctuary for migratory birds. * * *

1.6   The Refuge consists of 25,150 acres of wetlands and 12,468 acres of surrounding uplands. The wetlands portion of the Refuge consist of the 7,000–acre South Sump, which is the primary waterfowl nesting area, and the North and East Sumps, which are all maintained by a complex and intricate flowage of waters throughout the marsh basin. The average depth of water in the South Sump is approximately four feet, and in the North and East Sumps considerably less.

1.7   The management objectives of the Refuge are (1) to preserve, restore and enhance in their natural eco-systems all species of animals and plants that are endangered or threatened with becoming endangered on lands of the National Wildlife Refuge System; (2) to perpetuate the migratory bird resource for the benefit of people—to manage the refuge for an annual production of 5,000 canvasbacks and 5,000 redheads; (3) to preserve natural diversity and abundance of mammals and non-migratory birds on refuge land; and (4) to provide understanding and appreciation of fish and wildlife ecology and man's role in his environment, and to provide visitors with high quality, safe, wholesome, and enjoyable recreation which is fully compatible and consistent with, and which in no way harms or interferes with the area's primary purpose as a refuge and breeding ground for migratory birds and other wildlife.

1.8   All national wildlife refuges are maintained for the primary purpose of preserving, protecting and enhancing wildlife and other natural resources and of developing a national program of wildlife and ecological conservation and rehabilitation. These refuges are established for the restoration, preservation, development and management of wildlife and wildlands habitat; for the protection and preservation of endangered or threatened species and their habitat; and for the management of wildlife and wildlands to obtain the maximum benefits from these resources. 50 C.F.R. § 25.11(b).

II. *The Refuge Supports Canvasback and Redhead Ducks and a Diverse Population of Other Migratory Birds and Wildlife.*

2.1 The Refuge provides one of the most important habitats and nesting areas for over-water nesting waterfowl in the United States. The Refuge is particularly valuable to the canvasback and redhead duck, which use the area in approximately equal numbers for nesting and broodrearing during the spring, summer and early fall.

2.2 Continental populations of both the redhead and the canvasback duck are low and both species have suffered throughout their respective ranges from encroachment and habitat loss. In 1972, the annual winter waterfowl inventory conducted by the United States Fish and Wildlife Service showed an all time low of 179,000 canvasbacks. The redhead has faced intensive drainage programs in the prairie-parkland region of central North America, the major breeding area of this species. A more comprehensive program oriented towards habitat protection is necessary to conserve and protect these species.

2.3 The canvasback duck and the redhead duck have been listed as "migratory birds," as defined by Section 11 of the Migratory Bird Conservation Act, 16 U.S.C.A. § 715j, and are protected by the Migratory Bird Treaty Act, 16 U.S.C.A. §§ 703 to 711, and by [treaties between the U.S. and Great Britain (on behalf of Canada), Mexico, and Japan].

2.4 In addition to the canvasback and redhead duck, numerous species of waterfowl and other birds using the Refuge have been so designated as "migratory birds," including the prairie falcon, the peregrine falcon, the bald eagle, the golden eagle, the trumpeter swan, the white-faced ibis, the snowy egret, the great blue heron, the black-crowned night heron, the ruddy duck, the ringed-necked duck, the sandhill crane, the Canada goose, the coot and the cinnamon teal.

Conclusions of Law

III. *The Ruby Lake Special Regulations are Invalid in That They do not Include Appropriate Findings Necessary to Their Promulgation.*

3.1 On April 21, 1978, the Secretary of Interior promulgated the Ruby Lake Special Regulations, 50 C.F.R. § 25.34 (hereinafter referred to as "regulations").

3.2 These regulations permit year-round boating in an area designated as Zone 1 in the South Sump by boats without motors or boats with electric motors.

3.3 Beginning on July 1 on the east side and July 15 on the west side of an area designated as Zone 2 of the South Sump, and extending until December 31, boats without motors, boats with electric motors and boats with internal combustion motors of unlimited horsepower are permitted. No boat may exceed 20 miles per hour in any area or 5 miles per hour in areas so designated by the Refuge Manager.

3.4   Beginning on July 1 and extending until December 31, waterskiing is permitted on a designated area from 10 a.m. to 5 p.m. daily.

3.5   Beginning on August 1 and extending until December 31, boats without motors, boats with electric motors and boats with internal combustion motors of unlimited horsepower are permitted in an area designated as Zone 3 of the South Sump. No boat may exceed 20 miles per hour in any area or 5 miles per hour in areas so designated.

3.6   The Refuge Recreation Act of 1962 (16 U.S.C. § 460K) governs the Secretary's authority to permit recreation within the Ruby Lake National Wildlife Refuge and all other areas within the National Wildlife Refuge System, national fish hatcheries and other conservation areas administered by the Secretary for fish and wildlife purposes. The Refuge Recreation Act provides in pertinent part that:

> "In recognition of mounting public demands for recreational opportunities on areas within the National Wildlife Refuge System, * * * the Secretary of the Interior is authorized, as an appropriate incidental or secondary use, to administer such areas or parts thereof for public recreation when in his judgment public recreation can be an appropriate incidental or secondary use: Provided, That such public recreation use shall be permitted only to the extent that is practicable and not inconsistent with other previously authorized Federal operations or with the primary objectives for which each particular area is established: * * * And provided further, That none of the aforesaid refuges, hatcheries, game ranges, and other conservation areas shall be used during any fiscal year for those forms of recreation that are not directly related to the primary purposes and functions of the individual area *until the Secretary shall have determined—*
>
> (a) *that such recreational use will not interfere with the primary purposes for which the areas were established,* and
>
> (b) that funds are available for the development, operation, and maintenance of these permitted forms of recreation. This section shall not be construed to repeal or amend previous enactments relating to particular areas." (emphasis added)

3.7   In supporting enactment, Congressman Dingell stated on the floor of the House:

> "The Secretary must make certain findings before he throws these areas open to public use; the bill requires him to find, for example, that there is sufficient money available to administer and protect these areas, and *he must find that the utilization for recreational use will not be harmful to the basic purpose of the refuges.*" 108 Cong.Rec. 5548 (April 2, 1962) (Emphasis added).

3.8   In determining to permit recreational use of a National Wildlife Refuge, the burden of proof is necessarily on the Secretary to demonstrate that such use is incidental to, compatible with, and does not interfere with the primary purpose of the refuge as "an inviolate sanctuary for migratory birds."

3.9   The regulations violate the statutory standard because the Secretary failed to make the determination required by the statute that the permitted recreational use would not interfere with the Refuge's primary purpose as an "inviolate sanctuary for migratory birds."

3.10   The Refuge Recreation Act does not permit the Secretary to weigh or balance economic, political or recreational interests against the primary purpose of the Refuge.

3.11   When Congress has sought to authorize the weighing or balancing of competing interests it has done so explicitly.

3.12   Neither poor administration of the Refuge in the past, nor prior interferences with its primary purposes, nor past recreational uses, nor deterioration of its wildlife resource since its establishment, nor administrative custom or tradition alters the statutory standard. The Refuge Recreation Act permits recreational use only when it will not interfere with the primary purpose for which the Refuge "was established." The prior operation of the Refuge in a manner inconsistent with that purpose does not change the base point for applying the statute's standard. Past recreational use is irrelevant to the statutory standard except insofar as deterioration of the wildlife resource from prior recreational use serves to increase the need to protect, enhance and preserve the resource. Past recreational abuses may indeed require the Secretary to curtail recreational use to an even greater degree than mandated by the Refuge Recreation Act, in order to restore and rehabilitate the area promptly as required by the Secretary's existing regulations. 50 C.F.R. § 25.11(b).

IV.   *This Court Will Not Supply Findings to Support the Regulations on Behalf of the Secretary.* * * *

4.4   In adopting these regulations the Assistant Secretary balanced economic, political and recreational interests against the primary wildlife purpose of the refuge and reached a compromise.

4.5   The compromise reached by the Assistant Secretary in adopting these regulations was not supported by certain members of his staff. The former Refuge Manager, an expert in wildlife biology and management, testified in opposition to the regulation. The Deputy Associate Director for Wildlife refused to [endorse] the regulations because in his opinion the regulations were not in the best interest of the Refuge and the resources for which it was established. * * *

[The court enjoined the regulations and ordered the Secretary to promulgate, within five days, new regulations "which permit secondary uses of Ruby Lake only insofar as such usages are not inconsistent with the primary purpose for which the refuge was established," and to "take all appropriate and necessary steps to enforce the resulting regulations."]

Defenders of Wildlife v. Andrus (Ruby Lake Refuge II)

United States District Court, District of Columbia, 1978.
455 F.Supp. 446.

■ PRATT, J.

[The Secretary quickly issued new regulations that differed from the old ones only in setting lower speed (but not horsepower) limits for powerboats. On August 18, 1978, the court threw out the new version and ordered yet another round of rulemaking. The opinion noted that approximately 30,000 boaters annually used the 7000 acre South Sump that was the preferred nesting habitat for migratory birds. Boating was increasing dramatically; 19% per year in recent years. The opinion concluded:]

19.   If the regulations are permitted to continue in effect they will immediately and irreparably damage plaintiff's interests and the wildlife resources of the Refuge. The use of powerboats of unlimited horsepower on the Refuge (including for waterskiing) will directly and immediately harm the wildlife resources of the Refuge (i) by reducing submergent aquatic vegetation which is the principal food source for migratory waterfowl; (ii) by reducing macroinvertebrate populations which are the principal food sources for ducklings; (iii) by breaking up broods, by separating ducklings from their hen, by forcing broods out of brooding areas, and thereby reducing brood size; and (iv) by reducing the reproductive success of late nesting and re-nesting hens.

20.   Late nesting and re-nesting extends through September 1 of each season and occurs with sufficient frequency to be significant to the immediate and long-term productivity of the Refuge.

21(a).   The level of boating use permitted by these regulations is not incidental to or compatible with, and will interfere with the primary purpose of[,] the Refuge.

(b).   The suggestion that horsepower limitations would not be appropriate, and would not aid the primary purpose of the Refuge, is completely contrary to all reason and the facts of the record.

(c).   The proposed speed limitations to be used in conjunction with [unlimited] horsepower are so obviously unenforceable that to rely on a speed limitation, even as high as twenty miles an hour, is unrealistic because of its very unenforceability.

Conclusions of Law

22.   The regulations violate the statutory standard of the Refuge Recreation Act because the degree and manner of boating use which they would permit is not incidental or secondary use, is inconsistent, and would interfere with the Refuge's primary purpose.

23.   The regulations violate the statutory standard of the Refuge Recreation Act because the degree and manner of boating use which they would permit is not practicable because of their unenforceability.

24.   The Secretary's determination that the level of boating permitted by the regulations does not interfere with the Refuge's primary purpose is arbitrary and capricious.

25.   Based on the record in this action, the use of boats with unlimited horsepower in the South Sump of the Refuge is inconsistent and interferes

with its primary purpose as a refuge and breeding ground for migratory birds and wildlife.

NOTES AND QUESTIONS

1.   What legal restrictions did the Refuge Recreation Act place on the Secretary? A typical dictionary definition is that "compatible" means "capable of existing together in harmony." Does that support the court's ruling here?

2.   What recreational activities do you suppose occurred on the Refuge between the date of the Act (1962) and the first adoption of the regulations in 1978? As a matter of law, was unrestricted recreation allowed until the Secretary restricted or prohibited it? Or was it prohibited until the Secretary determined to allow it? Note that the Refuge Recreation Act said public recreation use "shall be permitted only to the extent that is * * * not inconsistent with * * * the primary objectives for which each particular area is established * * * [and] until the Secretary shall have determined (a) that such recreational use will not interfere with the primary purposes for which the areas were established."

3.   The 1966 National Wildlife Refuge Administration Act was worded somewhat differently, authorizing the Secretary to permit other uses "whenever he determines that such uses are compatible with the major purposes for which such areas were established." 16 U.S.C. § 668dd(d)(1). In Wilderness Society v. Babbitt, 5 F.3d 383 (9th Cir.1993), the court addressed whether the defendants' failure to examine the effects of cattle grazing in a wildlife refuge was "substantially justified" under the Equal Access to Justice Act, 28 U.S.C. § 2412(d)(1)(A). If it was not, the plaintiffs were eligible for attorneys fees under the Act after the government settled the lawsuit with the plaintiffs by agreeing to examine the compatibility of grazing with the Refuge's purposes. The court said:

> [T]he Service renewed annual grazing permits without regard to the incompatibility of grazing to the Refuge's purposes. As early as December 1989, the Service was aware that its grazing practices were damaging the Refuge. The Refuge Manager warned that "there is no question that current grazing practices causing this damage are negatively impacting fish and wildlife habitats and are (1.) in violation of the refuge's executive orders and (2.) currently not compatible with the uses for which the refuges were established."

> The Refuge Manager's report did not foreclose the possibility that the Service could formulate a grazing plan that would be compatible with purposes of the Refuge. Based upon this report, however, the Service had a duty to investigate the compatibility of grazing with the Refuge's purposes prior to permitting grazing on the Refuge. Nonetheless, the Service continued its same practices, issuing grazing permits for 1990 without any compatibility determination. It made little headway in formulating a new management plan prior to the initiation of the Wilderness Society lawsuit in 1991. In light of the Refuge Manager's

report, we cannot find that the Service's actions were substantially justified.

Absent the Refuge manager's December 1989 finding, was the Service's renewal of grazing permits without a finding of compatibility "substantially justified"? Judge Farris dissented from the court's ruling, construing the Refuge Act as "not specify[ing] that the Service has a duty to make a compatibility determination to permit the continuation of a preexisting use of the Refuge." Because grazing "had been permitted on the Refuge since 1936," Judge Farris opined that

> [w]ithout plain language or precedent to alert the Service to its "duty" under the Act, the Service was not unreasonable for continuing an age old practice while it formulated alternatives. * * * On the basis of a single memorandum, without benefit of trial, the majority confidently holds that the Service has breached its duty. I am troubled by the perverse incentives created by this holding and the adverse consequences it will have beyond this case. The majority tells all government agencies that if they discover a problem with one of their programs, they should never discuss it openly and frankly. If one member of an agency expresses an opinion, and the government does not immediately adopt his position, a court may later find that the agency illegally "disregarded" his advice. That is not and should not be the law.

4. In the 1997 organic act, Congress addressed the issue discussed in paragraphs 2–3 immediately above. It provided that the Secretary "shall not initiate or permit a new use of a refuge or expand, renew, or extend an existing use of a refuge, unless the Secretary has determined that the use is a compatible use * * *," except that "[c]ompatibility determinations in existence on [the date of enactment] shall remain in effect until and unless modified." 16 U.S.C. § 668dd(d)(3)(A)(i) and (iv). If this language had been applied by the court in the *Wilderness Society* case discussed in paragraph 3, what would have been the result?

5. Could nearby residents who, prior to 1978, bought high-powered boats for use on the Ruby Lake Wildlife Refuge maintain an estoppel argument against the government taking action to restrict their use? (Suppose there were no other places within hundreds of miles where such boats could be used.) Would they or should they have a credible claim that the regulations have unconstitutionally "taken" their property interests in their boats without compensation?

6. Did the court here show sufficient deference to agency expertise? Note some wildlife professionals in the Department thought the first regulations were too weak, and that the "former Refuge Manager, an expert in wildlife biology and management, testified in opposition to the regulation." Is this relevant to the court's determination of whether the regulations were lawful? Conclusive on the point? The Assistant Secretary of the Interior (a political appointee with supervisory power over the Fish & Wildlife Service) made the final decision and, according to Judge Pratt's first opinion, "balanced economic, political, and recreational interests against the primary wildlife purpose of the refuge and reached a compromise." Was this relevant? Unwise? Unlawful?

7.　An important part of applying the compatibility test is, of course, to determine the primary or major purposes of the Refuge. This is not always as simple as it may seem. What, for example, are the primary purposes of the Ruby Lake Refuge? Judge Pratt said (in finding 1.3 in his first opinion) that the primary purpose was as a "refuge, breeding ground and inviolate sanctuary for migratory birds." But Franklin Roosevelt's 1938 Executive Order established the Refuge "as a refuge and breeding ground for migratory birds *and other wildlife*." (Emphasis added) Suppose speedboats did not threaten migratory birds (at least in seasons when the birds were not present on the Refuge) but did threaten other forms of wildlife. Does the compatibility test require that speedboats be restricted?

8.　Also on this point of primary purposes, the court referred to the Migratory Bird Conservation Act (MBCA), which authorizes reservations "for use as inviolate sanctuaries for migratory birds." It was enacted in 1929, nine years before FDR reserved the Ruby Lake Refuge. Was FDR's order consistent with MBCA? Might FDR have reserved the area for "other wildlife" not under the MBCA, but under his more general withdrawal authority?

9.　This overlap of statute and orders, with somewhat different expressions of purposes, is more typical than not in the national wildlife refuge system. The 1997 legislation announces the "policy of the United States" to manage "each refuge * * * to fulfill the mission of the System, as well as the specific purposes for which that refuge was established." 16 U.S.C. § 668dd(a)(3)(A). It went on to say that "if a conflict exists between the purposes of a refuge and the mission of the System, the conflict shall be resolved in a manner that first protects the purposes of the refuge, and, to the extent practicable, that also achieves the mission of the System." Id., § 668dd(a)(4)(D). How would the hypothetical in paragraph 7, above (involving speedboat use that did not threaten migratory birds but did threaten other wildlife) be resolved under this language? See generally Robert Fischman, The National Wildlife Refuge System and Hallmarks of Modern Organic Legislation, 29 Ecology L.Q. ___ (forthcoming, 2002).

10.　The Humane Society and similar groups sought to stop sport and other hunting in wildlife refuges before 1997, relying primarily on the *Ruby Lake* rationale. They were unsuccessful. See, e.g., Humane Society v. Hodel, 840 F.2d 45 (D.C.Cir.1988); Humane Society v. Lujan, 768 F.Supp. 360 (D.D.C.1991); Bean & Rowland, at 294–97.

11.　In Animal Lovers Volunteer Ass'n v. Cheney, 795 F.Supp. 994 (C.D.Cal.1992), the court rejected plaintiffs' attempt to halt a program to trap red fox at a national wildlife refuge in order to protect two endangered bird species found there. One of plaintiffs' arguments (which the court described as "disjointed" and "couched in inflammatory rhetoric") was that oil production allowed in the refuge was more harmful to the birds than the foxes. The court concluded that Congress was aware that prior owners of a portion of the land acquired for the refuge had retained their oil and gas rights, and the legislative history of the act establishing the refuge acknowledged that oil production would continue. The court also found that USFWS had fulfilled its "compatibility" obligations because it had evidence that red foxes were playing a substantial enough role in "inhibiting" the two endangered bird species to justify the trapping program.

THE 1997 NATIONAL WILDLIFE REFUGE SYSTEM IMPROVEMENT ACT (NWRSIA) AND THE COMPATIBILITY TEST

In 1997, Congress enacted a long-sought organic act for the National Wildlife Refuge System. The NWRSIA restated the compatibility test this way: " 'compatible use' means a wildlife-dependent recreational use or any other use of a refuge that, in the sound professional judgment of the Director, will not materially interfere with or detract from the fulfillment of the mission of the System or the purposes of the refuge." 16 U.S.C. § 668ee(1). "Sound professional judgment" was defined as "a finding, determination, or decision that is consistent with principles of sound fish and wildlife management and administration, available science and resources, and adherence to the requirements of this Act and other applicable laws." Id., § 668ee(3).

One of the co-authors of this text opined that "[i]f this had been all that Congress chose to say on the question of compatibility, *Ruby Lake* would have been effectively overridden and the FWS would be free to do whatever it chose." George C. Coggins and Robert Glicksman, PUBLIC NATURAL RESOURCES LAW § 14A.02 (2001). Do you agree? Would a failure to impose limits on speedboats have satisfied this standard? Note that the statute, somewhat unusually, refers to the "sound professional judgment" not of the Secretary of the Interior, but of the Director of the U.S. Fish & Wildlife Service. Like the Secretary, the Director is a political appointee, appointed by the President and subject to Senate confirmation, but unlike the Secretary, the Director is also required by statute to be, "by reason of scientific education and experience, knowledgeable in the principles of fisheries and wildlife management." 16 U.S.C. § 742b(b). Should this make a difference in how the statute is interpreted?

Coggins and Glicksman continue:

But those definitions cannot be read in isolation. The NWRSIA not only dictates a hierarchy of use priorities, it also requires general use decisions to be made in the context of formal land use planning, and further requires particular use decisionmaking to observe elaborate procedural (and several substantive) requirements.* * * *

Like practically all legislation, the 1997 NWRSIA was the product of political compromise. In this case, the primary players were environmentalists who wanted strong protection for wildlife habitat and the ecological health of refuges, and sport hunters and anglers, who wanted to ensure that their interests would receive some priority consideration in refuge management. The broad architecture of the compromise, fashioned in a

---

* [Eds. Refuge planning under this Act is   432–33.] briefly described in Chapter 5, supra, pp.

series of meetings among the contending interests in Secretary of the Interior Babbitt's office, was rather elegant: The environmentalists got strong, bottom-line protection for the ecological health of refuges, and the sport hunters and anglers got priority attention through creation of a new category of "wildlife-dependent recreational uses," although this use had to be consistent with the ecological health standard. The losers in the process were non-wildlife-dependent recreational users (who were subjected to more stringent compatibility rules and processes that will make their uses increasingly fragile if not obsolete); and animal rights sympathizers (whose cause was set back by the priority positioning of hunting and angling on the refuges). Coggins and Glicksman summarize the results this way:

[1] The Hierarchy of Uses Under the NWRSIA

The NWRISA establishes three tiers of uses. At the top is the conservation of wildlife, plants, and their habitats.[5] Conservation is defined as sustaining, restoring, and enhancing healthy populations of wildlife using "methods and procedures associated with modern scientific resource programs," the latter including "regulated taking."[6] All human uses must be compatible with this overriding mission,[7] and no [new or renewal of permission for an existing] use may be allowed until such compatibility has been formally determined.[8]

Conservation of healthy wildlife populations for the benefit of future generations is a quasi-preservational standard. Refuges certainly are not to be "inviolate sanctuaries" under the NWRSIA, although no significant deterioration of the resource base may be allowed, at least theoretically.[9] The abstruseness of some of the congressional language will leave considerable room for argument in many situations. Phrases like "sound professional judgment," "principles of sound fish and wildlife management," "available science," and "modern scientific resource programs" are all more in the eye of the beholder than they are concrete rules or even principles. Refuge managers thus will have great latitude in resolving particular conflicts and in promulgating general policies. But that discretion remains bounded by the highest priority that Congress gave to the conservation mission. That mission in turn is subordinate to the purpose of individual refuge establishment.[11]

To the extent that any human use will be allowed in refuges, "wildlife-dependent recreational uses" are entitled to the highest priority.[12]

---

5. 16 U.S.C. § 668dd(a)(2). [The statute reads: "The mission of the System is to administer a national network of lands and waters for the conservation, management, and where appropriate, restoration of the fish, wildlife, and plant resources and their habitats within the United States for the benefit of present and future generations of Americans."]

6. *Id.* § 668ee(4).

7. *Id.* § 668dd(a)(3).

8. *Id.* § 668dd(d)(3)(A)(i). * * *

9. 16 U.S.C. § 668dd(a)(4)(B). [This section provides that the Secretary shall administer the System to, among other things, "ensure that the biological integrity, diversity, and environmental health of the System are maintained for the benefit of present and future generations of Americans."]

11. 16 U.S.C. § 668dd(a)(4)(D).

12. [Eds. The statute provides that "compatible wildlife-dependent recreational uses are the priority general public uses of the System and shall receive priority consid-

Those are "hunting, fishing, wildlife observation and photography, or environmental education and interpretation."[13] Congress found that these are "generally compatible uses"[14] and are "legitimate and appropriate public" System uses.[15] Priority general public uses are to receive "enhanced consideration over other general public uses."[16]

Wildlife observation, photography, and education are largely noncontroversial. The priority Congress accorded to hunting and fishing answers the question of compatibility so long debated and litigated. Those consumptive uses are generally compatible and of higher priority than all other commodity uses. They are to be "facilitated" where appropriate.[18] The first court to construe the NWRISA held that no compatibility determination was required for the decision to maintain an elk feeding program because it was not a "use" and because it was carried out by persons authorized to manage the refuge.[18.1] The court enjoined the proposed bison culling hunt, however, for lack of adequate environmental analysis.[18.2]

"All other uses" have the lowest priority. Thus, grazing, oil drilling, non-wildlife related recreation, water development, and timber harvesting are theoretically outlawed not only where they contradict the NWRS mission or the purposes for which individual refuges were established, but also where such uses would materially interfere with hunting, fishing, photography, and the other "wildlife-dependent recreational uses."

[2] Compatibility Standards and Procedures—Transition

By the year 2012, all national wildlife refuges are to be managed pursuant to a land use plan.[19] Those plans should prescribe and proscribe uses, at least generally, for each refuge. Until then, Congress specified several standards and procedures for determining compatibility. First, no new uses may be initiated until after a formal finding of compatibility (which may be issued during the planning process).[21] Second, for new land additions to the System, identified wildlife-dependent recreational uses may continue on an interim basis.[22] Third, uses previously deemed compatible may continue until "modified."[23]

Whether these provisions put in jeopardy all non-wildlife-dependent uses in existence in 1997 for which no formal consistency determina-

---

eration in refuge planning and management." 16 U.S.C. § 668dd(a)(3)(C).]

13. *Id.* § 668ee(2).

14. *Id.* § 668dd note.

15. § *Id.* § 668dd(a)(3)(B).

16. *Id.* § 668dd(a)(4)(J).

18. 16 U.S.C. § 668dd(a)(3)(D).

18.1 Fund for Animals v. Clark, 27 F.Supp.2d 8 (D.D.C.1998) (*Elk Refuge Bison*). [Eds. Specifically, the court suggested that "use" of the refuge is something that is to be

performed "by third parties or the public," not the government itself, an interpretation bolstered by the fact that the statute "specifically exempts from the compatibility requirement actions taken by 'persons authorized to manage' the refuge area. 16 U.S.C. § 668dd(c)." 27 F.Supp.2d at 11.]

18.2 *Id.* at 12–14.

19. 16U.S.C. § 668dd(e).

21. 16 U.S.C. § 668dd(d)(3)(A)(i).

22. *Id.* § 668dd(d)(3)(a)(ii).

23. *Id.* § 668d(d)(3)(A)(iv).

tion had been made is an open question. The Act says that "determinations" remain in effect, not that the uses may continue. Certainly, the legislation indicates a fairly strong bias against those other uses, a conclusion buttressed by the Act's consistency procedures.

The statute requires the Secretary, in implementing the compatibility provisions of the NWRSIA, among other things, to estimate the "timeframe, location, manner, and purpose of each use"; the "effects of each use;" and to provide for "the elimination or modification of any use as expeditiously as practicable after a determination is made that the use is not a compatible use." See 16 U.S.C. § 668dd(d)(3)(B)(i)–(ix).

NOTES AND QUESTIONS

1. In McGrail & Rowley v. Babbitt, 986 F.Supp. 1386 (S.D.Fla.1997), aff'd w/o opinion, 226 F.3d 646 (11th Cir.2000), the court upheld the USFWS's denial of a permit to operate a commercial boat tour on Boca Grande Key in the Key West National Wildlife Refuge because it was incompatible with refuge purposes. Among other things, the plaintiff argued that the FWS was being inconsistent because it allowed another company to operate tours on another key in the Refuge. The FWS distinguished the two because it found the permitted tours were "passive and education oriented" and its customers apparently obeyed admonitions not to enter into closed areas, whereas the tours conducted by the company being denied permission were recreational, involving picnicking, kayaking, and wading, and passengers were supplied with sports equipment like frisbees and paddleballs for use on the beach, and they had been observed entering closed areas. The court upheld the FWS, although it grumbled that it "might well have come to different conclusions" regarding the FWS decision to permit *any* commercial tours.

2. Where does recreational boating fit in? Might a speedboat operator on Ruby Lake claim that she is engaged in "wildlife-dependent recreational use" by occasionally fishing or observing wildlife (e.g., the panicked flight of migratory birds disturbed by the boat)?

3. Kevin Gergely, J. Michael Scott, & Dale Goble, A New Direction for the U.S. National Wildlife Refuges: The National Wildlife Refuge System Improvement Act of 1997, 20 Natural Areas J. 107, 115 (2000), describe the 1997 Act as establishing a

"hierarchy among * * * three categories of uses. Wildlife-based uses remain dominant, but "compatible wildlife-dependent recreational uses" are designated as "the priority general public uses of the system," are to receive "priority consideration in refuge planning and management" and "should be facilitated"; all other "compatible uses" are at the bottom of the hierarchy-they are to be permitted but not facilitated." * * *

"[The House Committee Report on the legislation] makes it clear that the use of the term "facilitated" with regard to wildlife-dependent recreation was carefully chosen. The phrase "should be facilitated" falls short of a definite requirement; in the language of the report, it is an "encouragement, but not a requirement." Read together, the report and the statute indicate that wildlife-dependent recreation is an important use of refuges—but "wildlife and wildlife conservation must come first." Thus, the Act reinforces and clarifies the "dominant use" concept that has historically characterized the system but shifts the emphasis toward conservation."

4.   The 1997 Act defines the "mission" of the National Wildlife Refuge System as "a national network of lands and waters for the conservation, management, and where appropriate, restoration of the fish, wildlife, and plant resources and their habitats within the United States for the benefit of present and future generations of Americans." 16 U.S.C. § 668dd(a)(2).

The mission statement raises a host of questions: Which plant and animal populations is the FWS to sustain, restore, or enhance? Those that might be expected to have occurred prior to the arrival of Euro– Americans? Those that were present when the particular refuge was established? Those that are now present on the refuge? The populations that we prefer because they are endangered or provide game for hunters or for some other reason? * * *

Although the [1997 Act] mandates that FWS administer refuges for "conservation," the Act is vague on the importance of preserving ecosystems and ecosystem functions. * * *

[There is a] need to provide flexibility for the managing agency, particularly given the diversity of individual refuges and the Refuge System's history. Although there is a growing concern for focusing conservation efforts at the ecosystem scale, individual refuges were established for a variety of different reasons. Many refuges were created primarily to provide breeding, feeding, and staging areas for migratory waterfowl; others were established to conserve endangered species or to protect large portions of ecosystems for multiple species. Congress chose to accommodate this historical variety through the RIA's mission statement and its definition of "conservation."*

Gergely, et al., 20 Natural Areas J. at 111–13 (2000).

5.   The 1997 Act directs the Secretary to administer the system of wildlife refuges to, among other things, "ensure that the biological integrity, diversity, and environmental health of the System are maintained for the benefit of present and future generations of Americans." 16 U.S.C. § 668dd(a)(4)(B). Gergely et al. discuss the challenge of applying these three goals as management standards, especially considering that many refuges were established for migratory bird habitat, and the production of waterfowl and other migratory game birds has long been an overriding objective of the System and the FWS. For example, a number of the wildlife refuges created for waterfowl are dependent upon water impoundments and other human measures to manipulate the hydrologic system to serve

---

* [Eds. The Act defines conservation in terms of "sustain[ing] and, where appropriate, restor[ing] and enhanc[ing] healthy pop- ulations of fish, wildlife, and plants." 16 U.S.C. § 668ee(4).]

the needs of the birds. "Such refuges almost certainly do not have the species composition, diversity, or functional organization that they would have in their unimpounded state. On the other hand, if they reproduce a now-missing composition, diversity, and functional organization, presumably the biodiversity goal of the [Act] is being advanced." 20 Natural Areas J. at 113. "Can the agency shift its focus beyond game species and adopt a more holistic, biodiversity conservation approach? Does this mean protecting the remaining components of drastically altered systems, or is there a mandate for restoration?" *Id.* at 117.

6.   Other commentary on the 1997 Act is beginning to emerge. See Cam Tredennick, The National Wildlife System Improvement Act of 1997: Defining the National Wildlife Refuge System for the Twenty–First Century, 12 Fordham Envtl.L.J. 41 (2000). Bean & Rowland discuss the pre–1997 compatibility litigation in THE EVOLUTION OF NATIONAL WILDLIFE LAW 293–98.

7.   Many decades ago a federal court of appeals acknowledged that federal power over migratory wildlife (under the Migratory Bird Treaty Act, see pp. 906–18 infra) authorizes the Secretary of the Interior to prohibit hunting of migratory waterfowl on nonfederal land adjacent to a national wildlife refuge "in order to make this refuge more effective." Bailey v. Holland, 126 F.2d 317 (4th Cir.1942).

B.   Wildlife Conservation and Management on Other Federal Lands

1.   The National Park System

Fishing, principally "catch and release," is generally permitted in many units of the national park system. Hunting, however, is generally prohibited (by regulation, rather than express statutory provision), although some units of the system are open to hunting by special legislative dispensation. For example, hunters and their allies in Alaska successfully sought in the Alaska National Interest Lands Conservation Act to designate some national park system lands in Alaska as "national park preserves" (where hunting would be allowed) instead of regular "national parks." See 16 U.S.C. § 3201.

The National Park Service sometimes licenses hunting to control park wildlife populations, and this has occasionally been controversial. See Davis v. Latschar, 202 F.3d 359 (D.C.Cir.2000) (deer harvest in military park upheld) (discussed at p. 1031 infra). Park Service wildlife management was attacked in Alston Chase, PLAYING GOD IN YELLOWSTONE (1986). See generally George Coggins, Protecting the Wildlife Resources of National Parks from External Threats, XXII Land & Water L.Rev. 1 (1987). Sometimes, as illustrated in the following case, the national park system and the wildlife found within its borders cannot be isolated from the surrounding lands, and in the process ranchers and other neighboring landowners, wildlife advocates and state and federal agencies can all be pitted against each other.

Intertribal Bison Co–op. v. Babbitt

United States District Court, District of Montana, 1998.
25 F.Supp.2d 1135, aff'd, 175 F.3d 1149 (9th Cir.1999).

■ LOVELL, DISTRICT JUDGE.

* * * The Yellowstone National Park ("YNP") bison herd of 2,500 or more animals is at or above YNP carrying capacity. *See Fund for Animals, Inc. v. Lujan,* 794 F.Supp. 1015, 1018 (D.Mont.1991) (Park capacity is approximately 2,400 bison). Particularly when the YNP bison herd exceeds Park capacity and when the Park experiences a harsh winter interfering with the herd's food supply within the Park, the herd tends to migrate north and west from the Park in search of additional forage. Uncontrolled migration of brucellosis-infected bison into Montana presents a danger to the Montana livestock industry and a health risk to humans. Migrating bison also present a significant risk of property damage outside the Park.

The YNP bison herd is genetically and numerically healthy and has recovered from the high mortality of the winter of 1996–97. The integrity and viability of the YNP herd is in no way threatened or endangered.

Genesis of 1996 Interim Plan

The size of the YNP bison herd has fluctuated repeatedly in this century. At the turn of the century the herd consisted of approximately 23 bison within the Park. The NPS imported domestic bison from Montana and Texas to enlarge the herd. The herd was managed as livestock, with YNP rangers cowboying the herd with the use of corrals and barns. By mid-century, the herd size was well over 1,000. The NPS reduced herd size to 397 animals in 1967. NPS then decided to discontinue its bison management program and allow the herd to roam free. In 1988 there were approximately 2,800 bison in the Park, and by 1995 the number reached approximately 3,900 bison.

As the YNP bison herd became larger, portions of the herd began to migrate out of the Park during harsh winters in search of food. As early as 1968, NPS embarked on a boundary protection program which involved NPS personnel shooting bison at the Park boundaries. NPS later discontinued this program, but eventually the State of Montana began a similar program on its side of the YNP boundary because of its concerns of private property damage, conflicts with humans, and disease transmission.

Montana has the right under its police powers to protect the health, safety, and welfare of its inhabitants by removing possibly infected YNP bison that migrate into Montana. *Fund for Animals, Inc. v. Lujan,* 794 F.Supp. 1015 (D.Mont.1991). In 1985 the Montana legislature authorized public hunting of migrating bison as a method of helping to control this problem. During the winter of 1988–89 large migrations of YNP bison resulted in the killing of 569 YNP bison within the State of Montana. Apparently because of negative publicity generated by these large-scale public hunts, Montana ended them and resumed control efforts of migrating bison through its agencies.

The State of Montana became increasingly dissatisfied with its boundary management role and the refusal of YNP to manage its bison. This culminated in suit against the federal government in 1995. *State of Montana v. United States*, [which] was settled with an agreement between Montana and the United States to prepare an interim bison management plan. After preparation of an Environmental Assessment, a Finding of No Significant Impact, and final agreement by the State of Montana and the federal agencies, the 1996 Interim Plan was implemented.

The 1996 Interim Plan called for increased cooperation between the two governments and for increased responsibilities for boundary management by the NPS. Important features of the 1996 Interim Plan were that the NPS agreed to prevent bison from migrating onto private land in the Reese Creek area by capturing such bison, if necessary, and shipping them to slaughter. The 1996 Interim Plan called for increased tolerance of migrating bison on federal lands adjacent to YNP, and a program of capture and testing in the West Yellowstone area, with bison testing seronegative for brucellosis to be marked and released.

The 1996 Interim Plan also contained procedures for emergency situations. Such contingency plans were put into effect during the winter of 1996–97 when, due to harsh winter conditions, more YNP bison were destroyed than was previously contemplated.

As a result of the experience of the parties with the 1996 Interim Plan during the unusually harsh winter of 1996–97, which resulted in some 1,100 bison being killed by government personnel and an additional number dying due to weather conditions, the 1996 Interim Plan was modified. After reevaluating the circumstances of YNP bison and the proposed modifications to the Plan, the parties agreed to implement the modified plan in December, 1997 (the "1997 Interim Plan").

[The court then addressed the claims of the plaintiff Great Yellowstone Coalition in one of the cases consolidated before the court.] * * * [The] National Park Service Organic Act, 16 U.S.C. § 1[,] * * * provides that the fundamental purpose of the National Park Service is to "conserve the scenery and the natural and historic objects and the wildlife therein . . ." of the national parks. 16 U.S.C. § 1. All parties agree that NPS must protect and conserve YNP bison.

Plaintiffs argue that NPS cannot destroy any YNP bison. NPS counters that part of its overall protection of the YNP bison herd may require it to destroy individual bison pursuant to the 1996 Interim Plan. NPS further argues that the alternative to the 1996 Plan is to return to indiscriminate destruction of bison as they leave the Park, as provided by the 1992 Interim Plan or as has occurred historically without the benefit of any federal-state cooperative agreement. NPS asserts that the Organic Act has provided it with broad discretion to manage and regulate the Park and its wildlife to best achieve the conservation mandate. NPS interprets its Congressional mandate to allow it to determine whether selective removal of individual bison protects and conserves the YNP bison herd. The court defers to reasonable agency interpretations of statute. *See Chevron, U.S.A.,*

Inc. v. Natural Resources Defense Council, Inc., 467 U.S. 837, 843–44 (1984).

[Another section of the Park Service Organic Act, 16 U.S.C. § 3,] states that the Secretary of the Interior "may also provide in his discretion for the destruction of such animals and of such plant life as may be detrimental to the use of any of said parks, monuments, or reservation." 16 U.S.C. § 3. Plaintiffs argue that because this is the sole statute providing for destruction of wildlife in the Park, a finding of detriment is necessary before Park wildlife can be destroyed. NPS disagrees, taking the position that the conservation mandate of 16 U.S.C. § 1 provides NPS with the requisite authority to destroy wildlife in the Park. The court also notes that one other statute authorizes NPS to "sell *or otherwise dispose* of the surplus buffalo of the Yellowstone National Park herd...." 16 U.S.C. § 36 (emphasis supplied). * * *

There is no statutory requirement that the Secretary make a finding of detriment to justify the destruction of wildlife. The court agrees with NPS that pursuant to § 3 of the Organic Act and NPS policy a finding of detriment is necessary to justify a controlled harvest, *see* 48 Fed.Reg. 30,264 (June 30, 1983), but an explicit finding of detriment is not otherwise necessary to justify destruction of wildlife, especially when serving the broader conservation goals of section one of the Organic Act. It is significant that section three, unlike section one, permits destruction of YNP wildlife to serve non-conservation goals. For example, section three would permit destruction of wildlife when wildlife causes detriment to the physical facilities or structures in YNP. In this sense, section three is a broader statute because it extends beyond the conservation mandate of section one.

Plaintiffs rely on § 26 of the Yellowstone Act, which provides that "[a]ll hunting, or the killing, wounding or capturing at any time of any bird or wild animal, except dangerous animals, when it is necessary to prevent them from destroying human life or inflicting an injury, is prohibited within the limits of said park...." 16 U.S.C. § 26. This statute criminalizes poaching by members of the general public. *Frost v. Garrison,* 201 F.Supp. 389, 390 (D.Wyo.1962). However, this anti-poaching statute does not limit the authority of NPS to destroy YNP wildlife pursuant to properly prepared wildlife management plans, and if this were not the case there could never be controlled harvests of wildlife. * * *

NOTES AND QUESTIONS

1. The court of appeals affirmed on the basis of the district court's opinion. Prior decisions in this dispute are Greater Yellowstone Coalition v. Babbitt, 952 F.Supp. 1435 (D.Mont.1996), aff'd w/o opinion,108 F.3d 1385 (9th Cir.1997); Fund for Animals, Inc. v. Lujan, 962 F.2d 1391 (9th Cir.1992). See also Fund for Animals v. Espy, 814 F.Supp. 142 (D.D.C.1993) (bison taking for brucellosis research program enjoined for lack of NEPA compliance); Peter Morrisette, Is There Room for Free–Roaming Bison in Greater Yellowstone?, 27 Ecology L.Q. 467 (2000).

2.   Is the Park responsible, legally or morally, for any damage caused by migrating bison outside the Park? Whether from brucellosis, or from trampling fences? Compare the "takings" litigation involving wild horses, Mountain States Legal Fdn. v. Hodel, Chapter 3, supra p. 246.

3.   Plaintiffs in National Rifle Ass'n v. Potter, 628 F.Supp. 903 (D.D.C. 1986), failed in their attempt to overturn a regulation that restricted hunting and trapping in the national park system to areas where it was plainly mandated by federal law. *Potter* was followed by the Sixth Circuit in a case challenging a Park Service regulation prohibiting trapping in two national lakeshores, where the statutes establishing the units expressly permitted hunting and fishing, but were silent on trapping. Michigan United Conservation Clubs v. Lujan, 949 F.2d 202 (6th Cir.1991). Similarly, a regulation ending commercial fishing in Everglades National Park was sustained in Organized Fishermen of Florida v. Hodel, 775 F.2d 1544 (11th Cir.1985), cert. denied, 476 U.S. 1169 (1986). The court in Alaska Wildlife v. Jensen, 108 F.3d 1065 (9th Cir.1997), ruled that the NPS could allow commercial fishing in Glacier Bay National Park except in those areas of the Park designated as wilderness.

4.   The National Park Service is largely unaffected by state law in managing national parks by virtue of its preservation mandate in 16 U.S.C. § 1, the enclave status of a number of parks, and the longstanding prohibition against hunting in the parks. See, e.g., New Mexico State Game Com'n v. Udall, 410 F.2d 1197 (10th Cir.1969), cert. denied, 396 U.S. 961 (1969). Its authority vis-a-vis state law may be somewhat more circumscribed on national monuments and other miscellaneous lands categories under its jurisdiction. See, e.g., The Cape Hatteras National Seashore Act, 16 U.S.C. § 459a–1.

5.   Sometimes the Park Service faces some truly exotic wildlife challenges. In recent years it has been trying, unsuccessfully, to eradicate oryx, imported by the state of New Mexico in the 1960s from southern Africa to enliven hunting, from the White Sands National Monument.

2.   NATIONAL FOREST AND BLM PUBLIC LANDS

Wildlife management on the vast majority of federal lands (outside the national wildlife refuges and the national park system) historically was characterized primarily by delegation of management responsibility to the informed discretion of professional managers and biologists. Grizzly bears don't vote, coyotes don't contribute to political campaigns, and all wildlife species are notoriously unresponsive to legal dictate. Hunters vote, pay the freight for fish and game agencies, and are politically powerful; consequently, wildlife regulation was primarily hunting and fishing regulation aimed at the satisfaction of participants in those sports. As a result, the law governing hunting and fishing on national forest and BLM-managed lands consists mostly of bodies of state administrative rules specifying who can shoot or angle for what species by what methods with what success at which times in what places. State wildlife agencies are financed by license fees and taxes paid directly and indirectly by sportsmen. State regulations have historically tended to favor encouragement of sport to the asserted detriment of "non-game" species and other values. This is changing, albeit slowly; stocking and artificial propagation of fish and wildlife are still usually undertaken primarily for the benefit of game species.

From its inception, the Forest Service has regarded wildlife as one of the major forest resources to be managed and protected like timber or watershed resources. Cf. United States v. New Mexico, Chapter 6, supra p. 521. This understanding was formalized in the 1960 Multiple–Use Sustained–Yield Act, declaring that fish and wildlife is one of the five resources to which "due consideration shall be given." 16 U.S.C. §§ 528–529. Section 528 also disclaims any intent to affect "the jurisdiction or responsibilities of the several States with respect to wildlife and fish on the national forests." There has long been no doubt, however, that the Forest Service need not comply with state law when it takes wildlife for federal management purposes on lands under its jurisdiction. In Hunt v. United States, 278 U.S. 96 (1928), for example, the Court summarily rejected Arizona's claim that the Secretary of Agriculture could not kill excess deer in violation of state law on the Kaibab National Forest and Game Reserve.

Until the enactment of the Federal Land Policy and Management Act (FLPMA) in 1976, BLM had no generic legal mandate with respect to wildlife, and state hunting and fishing laws generally applied. FLPMA generally gives BLM authority over wildlife comparable to that of the Forest Service, for wildlife is one of BLM's multiple uses. See 43 U.S.C. § 1702(c). (More detailed consideration of multiple use management is found in Chapter 8, infra pp. 706–12.)

The relationship between state and federal wildlife law on national forests and BLM lands is now set by FLPMA § 302(b), 43 U.S.C. § 1732(b). The tangled language and history of this provision is a measure of the states' concern with protecting their traditional authority over hunting and fishing on BLM and Forest Service "multiple use" lands. Indeed, the states' political power on this single issue nearly derailed, at the last minute, FLPMA itself, after six years of active congressional deliberation and compromise on a wide variety of issues. The following summary nicely illustrates how the legislative process can fail to yield crisp answers to politically controversial questions, especially those involving "states' rights."

a. *The statute.* After providing that the Secretary of the Interior "shall manage the public lands under principles of multiple use and sustained yield," and setting out other management prerogatives and restrictions, the statute continues, in 43 U.S.C. § 1732(b), by piling *proviso* upon *proviso*:

> *Provided further,* That nothing in this Act shall be construed as authorizing the Secretary [of the Interior or of Agriculture] * * * to require Federal permits to hunt and fish on public lands or on lands in the National Forest System and adjacent waters or as enlarging or diminishing the responsibility and authority of the States for management of fish and resident wildlife. However, the Secretary [of the Interior or of Agriculture] * * * may designate areas of public land and of lands in the National Forest System where, and establish periods

when, no hunting or fishing will be permitted for reasons of public safety, administration, or compliance with provisions of applicable law. Except in emergencies, any regulations of the Secretary concerned relating to hunting and fishing pursuant to this section shall be put into effect only after consultation with the appropriate State fish and game department.

b. *The House Committee Report.* The House-passed version of the bill permitted the secretary to close lands to hunting and fishing only for "reasons of public safety." The Committee report on that bill (H.Rep. No. 94–1163, 94th Cong., 2d Sess. 6 (1976)) explained that the bill

provides that hunting and fishing will be permitted in accordance with Federal and State laws and that no Federal permits for hunting or fishing are authorized by this section. It permits the Secretaries to close areas to hunting and fishing for reasons of public safety. The Secretaries are expected to use the authority granted by the bill to close areas only if essential to the public safety, and then only for the shortest periods needed to accomplish this purpose. Protection of the public safety includes prevention and avoidance of hazards to persons, animals, and property.

c. *The Senate Committee Report.* The Senate-passed version of the bill provided simply that nothing in the bill "shall be construed as authorizing the Secretary to require any Federal permit to hunt or fish on the [public lands]." The Committee Report (S.Rep. No. 94–583, 94th Cong., 1st Sess. 42 (1975)) explained:

" * * * [H]unting and fishing will continue under State control and State licenses or permits. Of course, this does not foreclose the Secretary's authority to limit access to [BLM and national forest] lands where necessary to protect the resources or users of the lands. This includes situations where there are fire hazards or where discharge of firearms would endanger human safety."

d. *The Conference Committee Report.* The Conference Committee's reconciliation of the differences between the House and Senate bills were explained in the Conference Committee Report (H.Rep. No. 94–1724, 94th Cong., 2d Sess. 60 (1976)) as follows:

The conferees authorize the two Bureaus to ban hunting and fishing for reasons of public safety, administration, and compliance with applicable law. The word "administration" authorizes exclusion of hunting and fishing from an area in order to maintain supervision. It does not authorize exclusions simply because hunting and fishing would interfere with resource-management goals.

e. *Floor Discussion.* Once the bill reported by the Conference Committee reached the floor of the House and the Senate, key legislators added some "spin" to the bill's impact on state-federal relations on hunting and fishing. Senator Lee Metcalf of Montana, Chairman of the Conference Committee, stated on the Senate floor (122 Cong.Rec. 34511 (1976)):

Mr. METCALF. * * * Unfortunately, in attempting to define the term "administration," the statement of managers confuses the issue and could be wrongly interpreted to prevent the Secretary from protecting the public lands.

Traditionally, the States have regulated fishing and hunting or resident species of wildlife. The BLM and the Forest Service have not attempted to manage resident species of wildlife, but have focused on management of their habitat. This bill does nothing to change that.

The language of the statement of the managers could be interpreted as so narrowing the definition of "administration" that the agency would be unable to close an area to hunting even where a number of species is drastically reduced. Carried further this language could be interpreted to mean that an area which was used for habitat research could not be closed to hunting or fishing "simply because hunting and fishing would interfere with resource management goals."

In this legislation for the first time we are giving BLM basic statutory authority to manage the public lands on a multiple-use basis. Two of those uses are hunting and fishing, but they should not take precedence over all other uses. Further, it makes no sense to give an agency authority and then to tie its hands.

When this matter was discussed by the conferees, the right—indeed the responsibility—of BLM and the Forest Service to manage wildlife habitat was agreed to by all. I believe the language in the statement of managers could be interpreted differently and thus does not accurately reflect the conferees' agreement on this issue.

On the House floor the next day, Representative John Melcher of Montana, Chairman of the Subcommittee of the House Interior Committee that handled the bill, engaged in the following colloquy with a key advocate for environmental interests, Representative John Seiberling of Ohio (122 Cong. Rec. 34217 (1976)):

Mr. SEIBERLING. * * * [I]n attempting to define the term "administration," the conference report language confuses the issues. * * * [T]he term "administration" * * * certainly would include the proprietary right of [federal] agencies as landlord to manage wildlife habitat, would it not?

Mr. MELCHER. Yes. The intent of the bill and the intent of the conference report is to assure that wildlife habitat management, and wildlife itself, are included in the management on our Federal lands.

We do not, however, intend to interfere with the States' prerogatives in setting the seasons for hunting of wildlife and wildfowl. On that score the Federal agencies go back to what has been left as State prerogatives, but the general management of wildlife habitat is expected, and also is a Federal responsibility.

Mr. SEIBERLING. I would certainly concur * * *. I would like to ask one further question. Would the gentleman agree that, consistent with the multiple-use policy of this legislation, management of wildlife habitat with that exception is a responsibility of the BLM and Forest Service on public lands?

Mr. MELCHER. Yes, we view wildlife as part of the resources on our Federal lands.

Mr. SEIBERLING. Therefore, I take it that the gentleman would agree that the BLM and the Forest Service could close lands under their jurisdiction to hunting and fishing for reasons related to the management of the wildlife habitat?

MR. MELCHER. Yes, I would agree to that, but we do expect to cooperate in all instances possible with the State Fish and Game Commissions to allow those authorities to set hunting seasons and to set requirements for hunting and fishing.

The meaning of this statutory section was quickly tested in court and ultimately led, after litigation that was, fittingly, as tangled as the legislative maneuvering that preceded it, to the next case. Two questions were raised in the litigation: (1) Did the Secretary of the Interior have authority under FLPMA § 302(b) to close federal BLM-managed lands in Alaska to a state wolf hunting program, and if so, (2) did NEPA apply to the Secretary's decision? The NEPA portion of Judge McGowan's opinion for the D.C.Circuit was discussed in Chapter 5, supra, p. 411. Reproduced here is that portion addressing the FLPMA issue.

Defenders of Wildlife v. Andrus (Alaska Wolf kill)

United States Court of Appeals, District of Columbia, 1980.
627 F.2d 1238.

■ McGOWAN, CIRCUIT JUDGE:

* * * On February 16, 1979, the Alaska Department of Fish and Game (ADFG) announced a program whose aim was to kill from aircraft 170 wolves (approximately sixty percent of the wolf population) in an area of 35,000 square miles in the interior part of the state. Many, perhaps most, of the wolves were to be killed on federal lands for which the Department of the Interior is responsible. On February 23, counsel for one of the appellees * * * asked the Department to prepare an environmental impact statement for Alaska's program before allowing it to begin. The Department, however, did not exercise whatever authority it may have to stop the program and did not prepare an impact statement. On March 12, appellees—organizations and individuals interested in the preservation of the environment in general and of wildlife in particular—filed a complaint asking for declaratory and injunctive relief against appellants—the Secretary and two other officials of the Department of the Interior.

The complaint predicted that, although the wolf hunt was proposed in order to increase the number of moose in the region by decreasing the numbers of their major predator, it would in fact weaken the moose herds by ending a "culling process [which] is natural selection in action, and [which] assures survival of the fittest moose * * *" and would devastate the wolf packs even beyond the ADFG's estimates. This interference with these two major species, the complaint continued, would disrupt the ecology of the entire area.

The complaint asserted that [FLPMA] authorizes the Secretary of the Interior to prevent the killing of wildlife on federal lands and requires him to evaluate whether he must intervene if he is fully to serve the environmental concerns of the Act. The complaint claimed as one of its "Violations of Law" that appellants failed to make that evaluation. * * *

On March 13, 1979, the United States District Court for the District of Columbia issued a temporary restraining order which enjoined appellants to "take all steps necessary to halt the aerial killing of wolves by agents of the State of Alaska" on the relevant federal lands. Although Alaska has apparently continued to kill wolves on its own lands, it has discontinued doing so on federal lands.

* * *

The District Court and appellees * * * reason that FLPMA imposes such supervisory duties on the Secretary that every failure to prohibit a state wildlife program which is carried out on Federal land and which may have significant environmental consequences must be accounted for with an impact statement. * * *

FLPMA * * * was enacted "to provide the first comprehensive, statutory statement of purposes, goals, and authority for the use and management of about 448 million acres of federally-owned lands administered by the Secretary of the Interior through the Bureau of Land Management." S.Rep. No. 94–583, 94th Cong., 1st Sess. 24 (1975). As such, it certainly imposes on the Secretary[, as the district court found,] a general duty "to plan for and manage federal land and resources." However, the District Court's reasoning seems to us to upset an allocation of functions Congress carefully and explicitly made in FLPMA, for Congress there assigned the states the primary responsibility for the management of wildlife programs within their boundaries.

It is unquestioned that "the States have broad trustee and police powers over wild animals within their jurisdictions," Kleppe v. New Mexico, 426 U.S. 529, 545 (1976). Neither is it questioned that * * * Congress may, if it wishes, pre-empt state management of wildlife on federal lands [pursuant to the Property Clause]. Despite its ability to take control into its own hands, Congress has traditionally allotted the authority to manage wildlife to the states. For instance, in the Multiple Use–Sustained Yield Act of 1960, Congress declared:

> It is the policy of the Congress that the national forests are established and shall be administered for outdoor recreation, range, timber, watershed, and wildlife and fish purposes. * * * Nothing herein shall be construed as affecting the jurisdiction or responsibilities of the several States with respect to wildlife and fish on the national forests. * * *

16 U.S.C. § 528.

Even in writing specifically "environmental" legislation, Congress has adhered to that allocation. Thus, Congress stated in the National Wildlife Refuge System Administration Act,

The provisions of this Act shall not be construed as affecting the authority, jurisdiction, or responsibility of the several States to manage, control, or regulate fish and resident wildlife under State law or regulations in any area within the System.

16 U.S.C. § 668dd(c). Similarly, the Wild and Scenic Rivers Act provides that "[n]othing in this chapter shall affect the jurisdiction or responsibilities of the States with respect to fish and wildlife."

16 U.S.C. § 1284(a).[7]

Far from attempting to alter the traditional division of authority over wildlife management, FLPMA broadly and explicitly reaffirms it. [The court then proceeded to quote the statutory section and parts of the legislative history set out in the text, supra pp. 892–95.]

The first quoted sentence of section 302(b) self-evidently places the "responsibility and authority" for state wildlife management precisely where Congress has traditionally placed it—in the hands of the states. The second quoted sentence of the section arguably permits ("may"), but certainly does not require ("shall"), the Secretary to supersede a state program,[9] and even when he does so, it must be after consulting state authorities. We are simply unable to read this cautious and limited permission to intervene in an area of state responsibility and authority as imposing such supervisory duties on the Secretary that each state action he

---

7. When Congress has wished to change this traditional allocation of tasks, it has done so self-consciously and precisely, as the Endangered Species Act of 1973, 16 U.S.C. § 1531 et seq., demonstrates. The House Committee responsible for the bill carefully noted that coherent national and international policies were needed adequately to protect endangered species. H.Rep. No. 93–412, 93d Cong., 2d Sess. 7 (1973). In the Act itself, Congress specifically provided:

> Any State law or regulation which applies with respect to the importation or exportation of, or interstate or foreign commerce in, endangered species or threatened species is void to the extent that it may effectively (1) permit what is prohibited by this chapter or by any regulation which implements this chapter, or (2) prohibit what is authorized pursuant to an exemption or permit provided for in this chapter or in any regulation which implements this chapter. This chapter shall not otherwise be construed to void any State law or regulation which is intended to conserve migratory, resident, or introduced fish or wildlife, or to permit or prohibit sale of such fish or wildlife.

16 U.S.C. § 1535(f). Even in this Act, however, the House Committee report continued the comments quoted above by reaffirming the importance of state management of wildlife:

> [T]he states are far better equipped to handle the problems of day-to-day management and enforcement of laws and regulations for the protection of endangered species than is the Federal government. It is true, and indeed desirable, that there are more fish and game enforcement agents in the state system than there are in the Federal government.

H.Rep. No. 93–412, 93d Cong., 1st Sess. 7 (1973).

9. Several parties in these "wolf hunt" cases have urged that the Secretary has no such power. At one point, the Secretary himself was among these, though he later withdrew that contention. The State of Alaska brought Alaska v. Andrus to establish that proposition, and in this court's first Defenders of Wildlife v. Andrus [decision], the International Association of Fish and Wildlife Agencies filed a brief *amicus* to the same effect. * * * Some of the legislative history * * * gives force to the argument of these parties * * *.

fails to prevent becomes a "Federal action." A state wildlife-management agency which must seek federal approval for each program it initiates can hardly be said to have "responsibility and authority" for its own affairs.

Appellees remind us that FLPMA directs the Secretary to "manage the public lands under principles of multiple use and sustained yield," 43 U.S.C. § 1732(a), and that

> "multiple use" means * * * a combination of balanced and diverse resource uses that takes into account the long-term needs of future generations for renewable and nonrenewable resources, including, but not limited to, recreation, range, timber, minerals, watershed, wildlife and fish, and natural scenic, scientific and historical values. * * *

43 U.S.C. § 1702(c). * * *

Nevertheless, * * * Section 302(b) * * * expressly commands that "nothing in this Act" enlarges or diminishes the state's responsibility for managing wildlife. We are therefore unable to conclude that appellees' citations to FLPMA should alter our understanding of the Secretary's obligation to prepare an environmental impact statement when he declines to exercise the power which FLPMA arguably gives him to preempt state wildlife-management programs.[10] * * *

NOTES AND QUESTIONS

1. Where does this decision leave matters; i.e., does the Secretary have authority under FLPMA to halt the wolf kill? Did the court decide the question? Did the court hold that FLPMA furnished the Secretary with no authority, or no duty, to close the lands to the hunt?

2. Same result if the plaintiffs had argued that the Secretary's failure to halt the wolf kill was a breach of his basic duty to protect the resources on the public lands and was thus arbitrary and capricious? See footnote 10. Is another part of FLPMA, § 302(b), relevant here? It provides: "In managing the public lands the Secretary shall, by regulation or otherwise, taken any action necessary to prevent unnecessary or undue degradation of the lands." Do the "lands" include the wolves? If Alaska proposed to shoot every wolf on the BLM lands, could the Secretary have found that "undue degradation"?

3. The district court had offered this view of FLPMA § 302(b):

> [T]he Act must be construed to mean that the Secretary does have the authority to close the federal lands to the instant wolf kill. By providing that the states' responsibility was not diminished by the Act, Congress intended to preserve to the states their traditional control

---

10. It is possible to read appellees' complaint as alleging that the Secretary has violated duties under FLPMA quite apart from FLPMA's effect on his obligation to prepare an environmental impact statement. However, we do not understand the District Court to have done more than instruct the Secretary to halt the killing of wolves until he has prepared an environmental impact statement. Therefore, although our discussion of FLPMA has necessarily touched on the limited nature of the Secretary's obligations under the Act, we do not otherwise reach the question of whether he has violated it.

over sport hunting and fishing seasons and the licensing of such hunting and fishing. However, by authorizing the Secretary to close the federal lands to hunting for public safety, administration and law enforcement reasons, Congress intended to vest defendants with some authority over the use of federal lands for hunting. The administration of the public lands includes their administration for multiple-use purposes, such as wildlife preservation, so that the Secretary can prevent, under certain circumstances, hunting on federal lands when a multiple use such as wildlife is seriously threatened. The court will not at this time delineate the exact parameters of the Secretary's authority to close federal lands to non-sport, state licensed hunting. The court determines only that the Secretary has the authority to prevent persons from coming on federal lands to hunt wildlife for purposes other than sport or subsistence where, as plaintiffs have shown to be true in the instant case, such hunting presents a serious threat to the existence of a form of wildlife on these lands, at least until BLM has the opportunity to assess and consider the impact of the proposed hunt and seek the cooperation of the state game officials.

Defenders of Wildlife v. Andrus, 9 ERC 2111 (D.D.C.1977) (Alaska Wolf III). Was the court of appeals just disagreeing with the district court here about whether the facts showed that the wolf hunt was, in the words of the district court, a "serious threat" to the continued existence of the wolves on federal land?

4.   The Ninth Circuit also published an opinion in this saga, declining to decide whether FLPMA gave the Secretary authority to close the lands to the Alaska hunt. Alaska v. Andrus, 591 F.2d 537 (9th Cir.1979). Notice that the Secretary himself waffled on the FLPMA authority issue. See footnote 9 in the principal case. For other related and inconclusive decisions, see National Rifle Ass'n of America, Inc. v. Kleppe, 425 F.Supp. 1101 (D.D.C.1976); Defenders of Wildlife v. Alaska Dept. of Fish and Game, 566 F.2d 1181 (9th Cir.1977).

5.   The statute gives the federal officials power to close federal lands to hunting and fishing for "reasons of public safety, administration, or compliance with provisions of applicable law." What might be examples of each of these reasons for prohibiting hunting and fishing on federal lands otherwise authorized under state law? For example, could the Secretary close lands to hunting because of a concern about endangered species? Fire danger? Disease spreading? What does "administration" mean in this context? Not enough personnel at hand to properly supervise and regulate activities on the ground?

6.   Is the statutory text dispositive? If not, does the legislative history clarify Congress's meaning? Or should the court resort to the history at all?

7.   The court reads the phrase "nothing in this Act shall be construed * * * as enlarging or diminishing the responsibility and authority of the States for management of fish and resident wildlife" as giving states "responsibility and authority for state wildlife management." Is that necessarily correct? Does it depend on what the prior jurisdictional relationships were? Is a program to increase moose or caribou populations by exterminat-

ing their predators more accurately characterized as hunting and fishing regulation or as general management of wildlife habitat (which is *not* mentioned in the quoted clause)?

8.   Suppose the Secretary of the Interior had proposed a BLM wolf kill program in order to promote caribou and moose populations or other values and uses of the public lands. Would he have to comply with state law? Cf. Hunt v. United States, noted supra p. 892.

9.   Aside from history and tradition, what justification is there for state wildlife management jurisdiction on federal lands? The need for local decisions to control local resources? More or better management or enforcement personnel? See John S. Gottschalk, The State–Federal Partnership in Wildlife Conservation, in WILDLIFE IN AMERICA 290 (H. Brokaw, ed., 1978).

10.   Wildlife habitat protection is an important part of the resource management planning process on both BLM and national forest land. For further discussion of these issues, see Chapter 5, supra pp. 427–34.

3.   PREDATOR CONTROL

Predator control to protect ranchers' livestock from depradation has had a long if not particularly illustrious history on federal lands and, as the following case illustrates, it introduces yet another governmental agency into the mix—the Department of Agriculture's Animal Damage Control unit.

Southern Utah Wilderness Alliance v. Thompson

United States District Court, District of Utah, 1993.
811 F.Supp. 635.

■ ALDON J. ANDERSON, SENIOR DISTRICT JUDGE.

* * * The Dixie and Fishlake National Forests support numerous types of wildlife and serve as grazing areas for livestock. Historically, Animal Damage Management ("ADM") decisions in these forests have led to conflicts between the supporters of the wildlife and of the domestic populations, especially because the ADMs authorize Animal Damage Control ("ADC"), which involves the control and reduction of predator species population, such as cougars and coyotes, through non-lethal and lethal control methods. Despite these conflicts, ADC programs have been conducted successfully since 1973, excluding 1991 and 1992.

Various statutes, regulations, and plans guide the implementation of ADC programs. Federal authority for ADM programs emanates from the Animal Damage Control Act of 1931, 7 U.S.C. §§ 426 to 426b (the "ADCA"), which directs the Secretary of Agriculture to "conduct campaigns for the destruction" of animals injurious to agriculture and livestock on the national forest and the public domain. Authority to conduct ADC programs currently resides with the Animal and Plant Health Inspection Service—Animal Damage Control ("APHIS—ADC").

The National Forest Management Act, 16 U.S.C. § 1604(i) (1988) ("NFMA"), authorizes the Forest Service to manage land designated as National Forests and assess the environmental impact of ADC programs. The Forest Service Manual ("FSM") * * * provides further guidance for implementation of ADM programs. In the FSM, the Forest Service recognizes the authority of the APHIS—ADC to conduct animal damage management services. The FSM requires both the Forest Service and the APHIS—ADC to reduce the damage done to wildlife by predation and to conduct ADM activities when predation causes or threatens to cause damage to livestock. FSM §§ 2650.3(9), 2650.1(4).

This shared responsibility and coordinated effort is memorialized in a Memorandum of Understanding ("MOU") prepared at the national level between the Forest Service and the APHIS—ADC. The MOU details the respective authority of each division. Generally, the APHIS—ADC is responsible for documenting predation loss and conducting the actual predation control pursuant to the ADCA, and the Forest Service is responsible for managing the land under its jurisdiction and for insuring compliance with environmental statutes.

Notwithstanding federal jurisdiction in this area, the states retain a significant amount of authority. State law authorizes ranchers with livestock on national forest allotments to protect their herds from predation. State law plays an important role in predator control in other ways. For example, federal statutes provide that state civil and criminal jurisdiction extends to forest reserves. 16 U.S.C. § 480 (1988). This jurisdiction includes the application of state wildlife and game laws to hunting, trapping, and fishing activities on the national forests. See also 16 U.S.C. § 528 (1988); 43 U.S.C. §§ 1701, 1732(b) (1988) (Federal Land Policy and Management Act of 1976).

* * * [B]ecause of this overlapping authority and of the possible conflict in state and federal predator control programs, both the Dixie and the Fishlake National Forest Plans call for cooperation between the state and federal agencies responsible for predator control.

In establishing an ADC program, the Forest Service is subject to other statutory constraints [found in the NFMA, and in NEPA, and it must not be arbitrary and capricious under the Administrative Procedure Act]. * * *

On April 25, 1991, Thompson, the supervisor of the Dixie National Forest, issued a [decision] * * * which authorized a full range of non-lethal and lethal control methods, including aerial gunning, a type of lethal predator control in which predators are tracked and shot from a helicopter. The decision requires ranchers to use a combination of the following non-lethal control measures: using of guard dogs; changing bed grounds daily; having the herder camp with the herd; disposing of dead sheep at least one-half mile away from the grazing band; using more than one herder with the band; avoiding areas where historically predation has been high; using experienced herders; and using more and better quality dogs. Under the [decision], the rancher must diligently apply non-lethal control measures before the Forest Service will authorize lethal control. When non-lethal measures prove ineffective, the forest supervisor then has available a full range of lethal control measures, including leghold traps and snares, hunting by calling and shooting, denning,[1] the use of hunting dogs, M–44s,[2] and the most objectionable measure, aerial gunning.[3] [Plaintiffs sought to enjoin the decision alleging numerous violations of law.] * * *

In establishing the need for injunctive relief, the court balances the last three requirements: (1) whether, in the absence of injunctive relief, Plaintiffs are threatened with irreparable injury; (2) whether Plaintiffs' potential injury outweighs any damage to Defendants; and (3) whether an injunction will be adverse to the public interest. Plaintiffs assert three types of irreparable harm: (1) that the ADCs threaten the viability of the coyote population; (2) that they lose enjoyment of recreational land and suffer psychological pain when lethal predator control is occurring; and (3) that the forest supervisors failed to follow NEPA * * *. Plaintiffs further contend that the permittees will suffer no further harm until spring because sheep predation ceases during the winter months. Contrariwise, the government asserts a long list of potential harms, including the threat to permittees' economic viability and the danger to wildlife from permit- tees' self-help efforts.

The court finds that the balance of harms does not "tip decidedly" in favor of Plaintiffs, but rather that it tips in favor of the permittees and the public. Injunctive relief would threaten permittees' interests in three ways. First, although predation loss varies from permittee to permittee, the record reveals a trend toward increased predation loss. This is evidenced by the fact that permittees are experiencing losses in allotments that have never suffered predation before. Second, actual losses to predation are much greater than confirmed losses. Various factors, including terrain and herd movement, make it impossible to assess the actual loss, but the court finds that predation loss is much greater than confirmed losses. Third, increased predation loss, the predominant reason why ranchers leave the sheep business, threatens the economic viability of the permittees.

Further, injunctive relief would not serve the public interest. The ADCA directs the Secretary of Agriculture to "conduct campaigns for the destruction" of animals injurious to agriculture and livestock on the national forest and the public domain. 7 U.S.C. §§ 426 to 426b (1988). By contrast, the State of Utah has protected two predators: (1) cougars and (2) black bears. The state, however, has not protected coyotes, but rather regulates coyotes as a predatory animal. Utah Code Ann. § 4–23–3 (1988). Coyote regulation extends to federal lands, including national forest land. Utah Code Ann. § 4–23–10 (1988). Because coyotes are a non-protected predatory animal, ranchers suffering predation loss may practice predatory control methods against them. Thus, even if the court were to grant the injunction, the permittees may, by law, exterminate predators in order to protect their livestock. Therefore, injunctive relief could become a two- edged sword cutting against the public interest: first, by restricting the

---

1. Denning involves the killing of coy- ote pups in the den.

2. M–44s eject a cloud of sodium cya- nide gas when activated by the coyote.

3. Aerial gunning is authorized only in the winter months and only in areas where other lethal methods have been unsuccessful.

government from achieving its statutory objective; and second, by transferring the authority to conduct predator control to those ill-suited to conduct it, the permittees. This self-help situation would create a substantial risk of irreparable harm to the public interest.

Finally, Plaintiffs will suffer no irreparable injury because, despite its contrary contention, even with the ADC programs, the coyote population will remain viable. * * *

Plaintiffs argue that the ADCs violate the APA because the Forest Service did not objectively address the economic damage to the permittees, but rather based its decision on the permittees' self-interested statements. Consequently, Plaintiffs contend that the ADCs violate the APA because they are not based on relevant factors. The court finds that Plaintiffs' APA arguments are without merit, and therefore, as fully set forth herein, concludes that Plaintiffs do not have a substantial likelihood of success on their APA claims. * * *

Plaintiffs argue that the EAs violate the APA because the respective forest supervisors have not established the need for the ADC program. Each forest supervisor must determine need based on studies conducted concerning that forest. Here, Plaintiffs contend, the forest supervisors have not assessed need beyond the word of the permittees.

Even then, Plaintiffs argue that the supervisors should establish some objective criteria for establishing need. For example, need for predator control might exist when the economic viability of the permittees is threatened by predation or when loss to predation reaches some percentage, such as five percent. Plaintiffs also assert that the ADCs have no rational basis because the need for the ADCs was never studied and is, therefore, uncertain, and because the effectiveness of the ADCs is open to dispute. In response, the government contends that the ADC programs are both necessary and effective.

Turning first to the need for the ADCs, the agency need not show that a certain level of damage is occurring before it implements an ADC program. In other words, it is not necessary to establish a criteria, such as economic viability of the permittees or percentage loss of a herd, to justify the need for an ADC. Chapter 2650.3 of the Forest Service Manual establishes a policy of animal damage management "when necessary to accomplish multiple-use objectives." Dixie Administrative Record at 000389 [hereinafter Dixie AR]. This policy allows for control activities in two circumstances: (1) when predators threaten "public health or safety"; and (2) when predators "cause or threaten to cause damage to threatened or endangered animals or plants, other wildlife, permitted livestock, or other resources, on National Forest System lands or private property." Id. "In evaluating the need for and in conducting animal damage management programs", the forest supervisor is instructed to "weigh the social, esthetic [sic], and other values of wildlife along with economic considerations." Id. at 000390. Hence, to establish need for an ADC, the forest supervisors need only show that damage from predators is threatened.

In this case, the record indicates that actual predation damage was occurring in both the Dixie and Fishlake National Forests. Consequently, the need for the ADC program is established. Moreover, the forest supervisors sought public comment and considered the competing social and economic values in evaluating the need for an ADC. Therefore, Plaintiffs have failed to show that the ADC was not needed.

Similarly, although disagreement exists concerning the effectiveness of predator control programs, the record establishes a rational basis for effectiveness. The supervisors have consulted numerous studies that establish the effectiveness of ADC programs. Further, they have discretion to decide when enough information has been gathered. Accordingly, this court will not second-guess the assessment of the forest supervisors concerning the effectiveness of the ADCs.

Finally, Plaintiffs argue that the ADCs violate the APA because they are contrary to the NFMA. 16 U.S.C. § 1604(i) (1988). Under the NFMA, the Forest Service must act in accordance with the forest plan promulgated for each forest. The respective forest plans permit predator control if needed. Plaintiffs assert that the ADCs violate the forest plans because they contain no objective analysis of the need for predator control. The court, however, has already found that the need for the ADCs was established because of actual and threatened damage to livestock. Therefore, Plaintiffs have failed to show that the ADCs are inconsistent with the respective forest plans or that the programs endanger the diversity of wildlife in the forests.

The record supports the hardiness of the coyote and attributes this hardiness to the coyotes['] adaptability and rapid reproductive capability. See, e.g., Davison, The Effect of Exploitation on Some Parameters of Coyote Population, pp. 110–125, Fishlake AR at 100499–100514, Dixie AR at 543 [hereinafter Davison Study]. To jeopardize the viability of the coyote population, seventy-five percent of that population would have to be eradicated yearly for fifty years. See Connolly & Longhurst, The Effects of Control on Coyote Population, Fishlake AR at 100588–100623, Dixie AR at 558 [hereinafter Connolly Study]. Under the worst case scenario, the cumulative impact on the coyote population will be no more than a forty percent loss. Id. Such losses will not endanger the coyote population. Therefore, the court finds that the ADCs as embodied in the EAs do not violate the APA. * * *

NOTES AND QUESTIONS

1. Could the court have demanded more evidence on the need for this program? More evidence that the program was effective?

2. Given the hardiness of the coyote, is the entire Animal Damage Control program a futile effort? Should the government give more respect to what used to be called the "balance of nature"? To protect livestock, wolves, mountain lions, coyotes, bobcats and eagles were largely eliminated around the Grand Canyon early in the 20th century, and the deer population exploded twenty-fold in fewer than two decades, leading to a govern-

ment program to kill large numbers of deer. See Hunt v. United States, 278 U.S. 96 (1928), and Joseph Wood Krutch, THE GRAND CANYON 215 (1957). The reintroduction of wolves into Yellowstone National Park caused the coyote population to diminish substantially. Is there a policy justification any more for eliminating predators on the federal lands in order to protect livestock?

3. See June C. Edvenson, Predator Control and Regulated Killing: A Biodiversity Analysis, 13 UCLA J. Envtl.L. & Policy 31 (1994).

NOTE: PROTECTING SUBSISTENCE USES OF WILDLIFE RESOURCES ON FEDERAL LANDS

In some situations, federal lands support wildlife taken by subsistence hunters, fishers, and trappers. Besides Indian hunting, fishing, and gathering rights that are sometimes preserved on federal lands (see Chapter 2, supra p. 46), an entire title of the Alaska National Interest Lands Conservation Act (ANILCA) is devoted to codifying a preference for rural Alaskans to engage in subsistence hunting and fishing on federal lands in Alaska. See 43 U.S.C. §§ 3111–3126; see also 50 C.F.R. § 100.4 (2002). The motivation was that a large number of rural Alaskans, mostly Native, rely on the subsistence take of fish, especially salmon, and big game. ANILCA not only establishes a preference for subsistence uses, id. § 3114, but also requires federal land management agencies to evaluate the effects on "subsistence uses and needs," and alternatives when "determining whether to withdraw, reserve, lease, or otherwise permit the use, occupancy, or disposition" of federal lands. Id. § 3120(a). Any such decision that would "significantly restrict subsistence uses" requires public notice and hearing and a determination that

> (A) such a significant restriction of subsistence uses is necessary, consistent with sound management principles for the utilization of the public lands, (B) the proposed activity will involve the minimal amount of public lands necessary to accomplish the purposes of such use, occupancy, or other disposition, and (C) reasonable steps will be taken to minimize adverse impacts upon subsistence uses and resources resulting from such actions.

In Hoonah Indian Ass'n v. Morrison, 170 F.3d 1223 (9th Cir.1999), the court upheld a Forest Service decision to go ahead with two timber sales despite objections from Native groups that subsistence resources would be significantly impaired. The Forest Service had estimated that the deer habitat capabilities in the area of the sales would decrease by 2% and 7%, respectively. It went on to assume (as did the parties) that these sales would, in combination with other sales involving timber on both federal lands and lands owned by Native corporations, "significantly restrict subsistence uses." The court agreed with the U.S. that the word "necessary" in the statute does not prohibit timber sales that are within the agency's discretion. Instead, it interpreted the statute to mean that a "significant restriction of subsistence uses might not be necessary to achieve compliance with law, yet necessary to conform to sound management principles for such 'utilization.' If so, the statutory language would make it 'necessary.' " Thus the Forest Service could find that the sale is necessary because the local economy was substantially dependent on a viable timber industry. The court also rejected the Natives' argument that the sales did not conform to the statutory requirement of involving the "minimal amounts of public lands necessary." The court said that the "measure of * * * what must be 'minimal' in the statutory language is 'the purposes of such ... disposition,' not minimization of impact on subsistence. The purpose of the disposition was to sell timber."

In Amoco Prod. Co. v. Village of Gambell, 480 U.S. 531 (1987), the Supreme Court held these subsistence provisions inapplicable to mineral activity on the outer continental shelf. See generally George C. Coggins & Robert Glicksman, 3 PUBLIC NATURAL RESOURCES LAW § 18.18–18.21 (2001); Joris Naiman, ANILCA Section 810: An Undervalued Protection for Alaskan Villagers' Subsistence, VII Ford. Envt'l. L.J. 211 (1996).

The program has been enmeshed in controversy for well over a decade. Consistent with its general tenderness toward state game and fish programs, Congress in ANILCA authorized the federal government to delegate responsibility for administering the preference to the state of Alaska, so long as it met the terms of the federal preference. The delegation was made shortly after ANILCA was enacted, but within a few years the Alaska Supreme Court ruled that the state constitution forbade the state from acknowledging a preference because it provided open access to fish and game. McDowell v. State, 785 P.2d 1 (Alaska 1989). The federal government then reassumed responsibility for administering the preference on federal lands, but initially took a narrow view of what constituted federal land to which the subsistence preference applied; specifically excluding most waters, which rendered the preference for subsistence fishing mostly meaningless. Alaska natives challenged the exclusion in federal court, and eventually the Clinton Administration reversed course, taking the position that reserved water rights were enough of a federal property interest to justify applying the subsistence preference to waters in or bordering federal conservation units (such as units of the national park, forest, and wildlife refuge systems) in the state. The Ninth Circuit eventually upheld this approach after tortuous litigation. See Katie John v. United States, 247 F.3d 1032 (9th Cir.2001) (en banc). See also David G. Shapiro, Jurisdiction and the Hunt: Subsistence Regulation, ANILCA, and Totemoff, 14 Alaska L. Rev. 115 (1997); Andrew Josephson, Katie John and Totemoff, 6 Dick. J.Env.L.Pol. 225 (1997).

C. THE MIGRATORY BIRD TREATY ACT (MBTA)

One of the earliest of the federal wildlife laws is the Migratory Bird Treaty Act of 1918, 16 U.S.C. §§ 703–711, the statute deemed constitutional in the landmark case of Missouri v. Holland, supra pp. 203–04. Its key provision reads, in pertinent part:

Unless and except as permitted by regulations made as hereinafter provided in this subchapter, *it shall be unlawful at any time, by any means or in any manner, to* pursue, hunt, *take*, capture, or kill, possess, offer for sale, sell, offer to barter, barter, offer to purchase, purchase, deliver for shipment, ship, export, import, cause to be shipped, exported, or imported, deliver for transportation, transport or cause to be transported, carry or cause to be carried, or receive for shipment, transportation, carriage, or export, *any migratory bird*, any part, nest, or egg of any such bird, or any product, whether or not manufactured, which consists, or is composed in whole or in part, of any such bird or any part, nest, or egg thereof, included in the terms of the [various treaties the U.S. has entered into with Great Britain (Canada), Mexico, Japan, and the former Soviet Union].

16 U.S.C. § 703 (emphasis added).

"A heady combination of strict liability, criminal penalty provision, and vague language * * * appeals to those seeking to control land use activity" and they have sought to extend its reach to 'activities that often result in bird death—such as farming, timber harvesting, and brush clearing.' " Benjamin Means, Prohibiting Conduct, Not Consequences: The Limited Reach of the Migratory Bird Treaty Act, 97 Mich.L.Rev. 823 (1998).

Sierra Club v. Martin

United States Court of Appeals for the Eleventh Circuit, 1997.
110 F.3d 1551.

■ Before Edmondson and Black, Circuit Judges, and Roney, Senior Circuit Judge.

■ Black, Circuit Judge:

The United States Forest Service (Forest Service) and a group of timber contractors, including Bert Thomas, Cook Brothers Lumber Company, Inc., Parton Lumber Company, Inc., and Thrift Brothers Lumber Company, Inc. (collectively Timber Contractors), appeal the issuance of a preliminary injunction on May 8, 1996, ordering the Forest Service to stop all timber cutting and road building activities in seven timber projects in the Chattahoochee and Oconee National Forests in Georgia (collectively Chattahoochee). We reverse.

* * * In 1991, pursuant to the Chattahoochee's land and resource management plan, the Forest Service proposed to sell the rights to cut timber on seven parcels of land * * * [which] encompass approximately 2,103 acres out of the 846,000 acres that comprise the Chattahoochee. * * *. [This lawsuit was filed in 1996 by a coalition of national and Georgia-based environmental organizations, alleging violations of several federal statutes.]

The Chattahoochee is home to numerous species of neotropical migratory birds, which typically winter in Mexico or the Caribbean and spend the nesting season in the Chattahoochee. These birds include species designated for protection under the MBTA. Sierra Club asserted that the Forest

Service's timber contracts violate the MBTA because they allowed timber cutting during the migratory bird nesting season and that tree cutting during nesting season would directly kill at least 2,000 to 9,000 neotropical migratory birds. The Forest Service did not dispute that cutting down a tree with an active nest directly killed migratory birds.[7] The district court held that the Forest Service's actions violated the MBTA because "thousands of migratory birds will be killed directly by cutting down trees with nests and juvenile birds in them." * * *

The MBTA, by its plain language, does not subject the federal government to its prohibitions. The MBTA makes it unlawful to "take" or "kill" birds. The penalties for violating its prohibitions are set forth in 16 U.S.C. § 707, which provides that a "person, association, partnership, or corporation" will be guilty of a misdemeanor or felony and subject to fine or imprisonment or both for violating the MBTA.[12] Sierra Club nonetheless asserts that because the prohibitions are stated broadly—that is, "it is unlawful" to "take" or "kill"—it should be unlawful for anybody, including federal agencies, to "take" or "kill" migratory birds. The MBTA, however, should be read as a whole to derive its plain meaning. The MBTA is a criminal statute making it unlawful *only* for persons, associations, partnerships, and corporations to "take" or "kill" migratory birds. Moreover, there is no expression of congressional intent which would warrant holding that "person" includes the federal government, thus enabling the United States to prosecute a federal agency, or a federal official acting in his official capacity, for taking or killing birds and destroying nests in violation of the MBTA. Congress has demonstrated that it knows how to subject federal agencies to substantive requirements when it chooses to do so. For example, the term "person" in the Endangered Species Act is defined to include "any officer, employee, agent, department, or instrumentality of the Federal Government." 16 U.S.C. § 1532(13).

The historical context of the MBTA's enactment further demonstrates that it does not apply to the federal government. In 1897, Congress established the National Forest System " '[t]o conserve the water flows, and to furnish a continuous supply of timber for the people.' " *United*

---

7. A Forest Service memorandum noted that tree cutting during nesting season would kill migratory birds: "The loss of individual nests and or birds is an un-avoidable cost of any type of land management activity, whether it be agricultural plowing, mowing, road maintenance, lawn maintenance, clearing land for construction, or cutting trees."

12. Section 707 provides, in relevant part:

(a) Except as otherwise provided in this section, any *person, association, partnership, or corporation* who shall violate any provisions of said conventions or of this subchapter, or who shall violate or fail to comply with any regulation made pursuant to this subchapter shall be deemed guilty of a misdemeanor and upon con-

viction thereof shall be fined not more than $500 or be imprisoned not more than six months, or both.

(b) Whoever, in violation of this subchapter, shall knowingly—

(1) take by any manner whatsoever any migratory bird with intent to sell, offer to sell, barter or offer to barter such bird, or

(2) sell, offer for sale, barter or offer to barter, any migratory bird shall be guilty of a felony and shall be fined not more than $2,000 or imprisoned not more than two years, or both.

16 U.S.C. § 707 (emphasis added).

States v. New Mexico, 438 U.S. 696, 707 (1978) (quoting 30 Cong.Rec. 967 (1897)). In light of that purpose, it is difficult to imagine that Congress enacted the MBTA barely twenty years later intending to prohibit the Forest Service from taking or killing a single migratory bird or nest "by any means or in any manner" given that the Forest Service's authorization of logging on federal lands inevitably results in the deaths of individual birds and destruction of nests. The application of the MBTA to the federal government would have severely impaired the Forest Service's ability to comply with the congressional directive to manage the national forests for timber production.

Congress's subsequent enactment of legislation relating to management of the National Forest System buttresses the conclusion that the MBTA does not apply to the federal government. In the NFMA, Congress expressed its intent that the Forest Service manage forests for multiple uses, including timber production. *See* 16 U.S.C. § 528 ("It is the policy of the Congress that the national forests are established and shall be administered for outdoor recreation, range, timber, watershed, and wildlife and fish purposes."). Through the NFMA, Congress has prescribed the procedures the Forest Service is to follow and the factors it is to consider in making land management decisions. *See* 16 U.S.C. § 1604. In the process of complying with the NFMA, NEPA, and their implementing regulations, the Forest Service ensures that the impact of land management on migratory bird populations is considered in the context of ensuring viability of native species. 36 C.F.R. § 219.19. The viability regulation requires that, in the context of multiple use planning, habitat be provided within the forest to support a minimum number of reproductive individuals in order to "maintain viable populations of existing native and desired non-native vertebrate species in the planning area." *Id.* The Forest Service's compliance with the viability regulation is subject to judicial review in actions challenging timber sales brought under the APA. *See, e.g., Inland Empire Public Lands Council v. United States Forest Service,* 88 F.3d 754, 759–63 (9th Cir.1996); *Seattle Audubon Soc'y v. Moseley,* 80 F.3d 1401, 1404 (9th Cir.1996). Congress intended that the Forest Service follow the NFMA's regulatory process, rather than the MBTA's criminal prohibitions, in addressing conservation of migratory birds.

The MBTA does not apply to the federal government. As no violation of the MBTA could occur by any formal action of the Forest Service, the Forest Service may not be enjoined under the APA.

Humane Society of the United States v. Glickman

United States Court of Appeals, District of Columbia Circuit, 2000.
217 F.3d 882.

■ Before: Edwards, Chief Judge, Randolph and Garland, Circuit Judges.

■ Randolph, Circuit Judge:

* * * At the center of the controversy is the Canada goose—*Branta canadensis.* With its black-stockinged neck and head and distinctive white

cheek patch, its loud resonant honking calls, and its V-shaped flight formations, the Canada goose is a familiar sight throughout most of North America. *See* FRANK C. BELLROSE, DUCKS, GEESE AND SWANS OF NORTH AMERICA 142 (3d ed.1980). The Mid–Atlantic population of Canada geese, one of eleven recognized races, winters in the coastal areas of Virginia, Maryland, Delaware, and New Jersey, and returns in the spring to the tundra zone of the Ungava Peninsula in Quebec, its traditional summer breeding grounds. In recent years, however, large flocks of Canada geese have stopped migrating, preferring to breed, nest and rear their young in the coastal states of the middle Atlantic region. The Commonwealth of Virginia has become a host to many of these full-time residents. In 1991, an estimated 66,169 Canada geese lived year round in Virginia. By 1998 Virginia's resident goose population had quadrupled to 254,000. *See* Wildlife Services, Animal and Plant Health Inspection Service, U.S. Dep't of Agriculture, *Environmental Assessment for the Management of conflicts associated with non-migratory (resident) Canada geese, migratory Canada geese, and urban/suburban ducks in the Commonwealth of Virginia* § 2.1, at 6 (Mar. 30, 1999) ("*Environmental Assessment*"). In the same year, only 70,000 migratory Canada geese wintered over in Virginia, *see id.* tbl.5, at 18, a number not much larger than the migratory population in the 1970s.

Residential owners, farmers, government officials and many others are deeply concerned about the exploding population of Canada geese. Browsing by Virginia's resident geese has reduced state-wide yields of cereal grains, peanuts, soybeans and corn. Goose droppings have spoiled water quality around beaches and wetlands, and interfered with the enjoyment of parks and ball fields. The geese have damaged gardens, lawns and golf courses. Their fecal deposits threaten to contaminate drinking water supplies. And they pose a hazard to aircraft. Resident geese are found at most of Virginia's airports and military bases. In 1995, a passenger jet hit ten Canada geese at Dulles International Airport, causing $1.7 million of wing and engine damage. *See id.* § 2.1.2.5, at 10. Collisions have also occurred at other Virginia airports. And "Langley Air Force Base and Norfolk Naval Air Station have altered, delayed, aborted, and ceased flight operations because of Canada geese on their field." *Id.*[2]

In response to these problems and others, the Department of Agriculture, through its Animal Health and Inspection Service's Wildlife Services division, instituted an "Integrated Goose Management Program" in conjunction with Virginia state agencies. The plan called for various measures such as harassment, biological control, habitat alteration, repellents, nest and egg destruction, and capture and killing. The killings were to take place during the "summer molt"—between mid-June and late-July—when the resident geese cannot fly (the migratory geese are in Canada at this time of year). An Environmental Assessment, issued on January 29, 1997,

---

2. Resident Canada geese and the problems they cause are not confined to the east coast. The Washington Post reported that the Agriculture Department, having obtained a permit from FWS, is rounding up resident Canada geese and killing them in twelve counties surrounding Puget Sound in Washington State. *See* Ben White, *Honk if You Hate Goose Droppings*, WASH. POST, June 29, 2000, at A29.

reflected the Interior Department's longstanding position that the Migratory Bird Treaty Act restricted not only private parties and states, but also federal agencies. Hence a "federal Migratory Bird Depredation Permit … would be required and obtained for the proposed action." Animal Damage Control, Animal and Plant Health Inspection Service, U.S. Dep't of Agriculture, *Environmental Assessment for the Management of conflicts associated with nonmigratory (resident) Canada geese and urban/suburban mallard ducks in the State of Virginia* 22 (Jan. 29, 1997). Interior's Fish and Wildlife Service (FWS) is authorized to issue such depredation permits for migratory birds that "bec[o]me seriously injurious to the agricultural or other interests in any particular community." International Convention for the Protection of Migratory Birds, art. VII, 39 Stat. 1702, 1704 (1916) ("International Convention"), *referenced in* 16 U.S.C. § 704; *see also* 50 C.F.R. pt. 21.

In 1997, the Director of FWS issued a memorandum to regional directors stating that federal agencies no longer needed to obtain a permit before taking or killing migratory birds. The Humane Society of the United States, Citizens for the Preservation of Wildlife, the Animal Protection Institute, and three individuals thereupon filed suit against the Secretaries of Agriculture and Interior and other officials in those departments seeking to enjoin implementation of the Goose Management Plan. The district court ruled that § 703 of the Migratory Bird Treaty Act restricted federal agencies * * * [and] enjoined the defendants "from conducting the Canada Goose Plan until such time as they shall obtain valid permits to do so pursuant to the" Act.

Although Virginia's Canada geese are year-long residents, they are members of a species that migrates and therefore fall within the category of "migratory birds" protected by the 1916 Treaty and the Act. *See* 50 C.F.R. § 10.13. Protected from whom? The district court thought § 703 of the Act gave the answer—from everyone in the United States, including federal agencies.

* * * As legislation goes, § 703 contains broad and unqualified language— "at any time," "by any means," "in any manner," "any migratory bird," "any part, nest, or egg of any such bird," "any product … comprised in whole or part, of any such bird." The one exception to the prohibition is in the opening clause—"Unless and except as permitted by regulations made as hereinafter provided in this subchapter…." For migratory game birds, of which the Canada goose is one, the exception gives the Interior Department authority to regulate hunting seasons and bag limits. Article II of the Treaty itself required a closed season—no hunting of these birds—between March 10 and September 1, the typical period when the birds breed, molt and raise their young. In addition to issuing hunting regulations, *see, e.g.,* 50 C.F.R. pt. 20; *id.* § 20.105, the Secretary of the Interior may issue permits for killing Canada geese and other migratory birds if this is shown to be "compatible with the terms of the [Migratory Bird] conventions." 16 U.S.C. § 704.[3] As we have said, Article VII of the Treaty contemplated that

---

3. "Subject to the provisions and in order to carry out the purposes of the convention … the Secretary of the Interior is authorized and directed, from time to time

permits allowing the killing of migratory birds would be available in "extraordinary conditions" when the birds have "become seriously injurious to the agricultural or other interests in any particular community," International Convention, art. VII, 39 Stat. 1704.

As § 703 is written, what matters is whether someone has killed or is attempting to kill or capture or take a protected bird, without a permit and outside of any designated hunting season. Nothing in § 703 turns on the identity of the perpetrator. There is no exemption in § 703 for farmers, or golf course superintendents, or ornithologists, or airport officials, or state officers, or federal agencies. In that respect, § 703 is rather like the statute in *United States v. Arizona*, 295 U.S. 174, 183–84 (1935), which also framed its prohibition in terms of the forbidden acts without mentioning the identity of the transgressor: there shall be no "construction of any bridge, dam, dike or causeway over or in any port, roadstead, haven, harbor, canal, navigable river or other navigable water of the United States until the consent of Congress shall have been obtained and until the plans shall have been submitted to and approved by the Chief of Engineers and by the Secretary of War." *Id.* at 184 (citing 33 U.S.C. § 401). The Court viewed the provision as restricting not only private parties, but also state and federal agencies, so that the Secretary of the Interior could not order the building of a dam without congressional authorization. "The plaintiff maintains that the restrictions so imposed apply only to work undertaken by private parties. But no such intention is expressed, and we are of opinion that none is implied. The measures adopted for the enforcement of the prescribed rule are in general terms and purport to be applicable to all. No valid reason has been or can be suggested why they should apply to private persons and not to federal and state officers." *Id.* at 184.

The defendants here, in order to promote their position that federal agencies are exempt from § 703, seek to introduce structural ambiguity into the Act, citing the criminal penalty provision of § 707(a):

> Except as otherwise provided in this section, any person, association, partnership, or corporation who shall violate any provisions of said conventions or of this subchapter, or who shall violate or fail to comply with any regulation made pursuant to this subchapter shall be deemed guilty of a misdemeanor and upon conviction thereof shall be fined not more than $15,000 or be imprisoned not more than six months, or both.

16 U.S.C. § 707(a). Federal agencies, they say, cannot be considered "persons" who may be held criminally liable for violating the Act or the Treaty. (They do not discuss whether federal officers carrying out the extermination of migratory birds could be considered "persons.") The defendants' reading of § 707(a) gains support from the canon that the term "person" does not ordinarily include the sovereign. *See United States v. Cooper Corp.*,

... to determine when, to what extent, if at all, and by what means, it is compatible with the terms of the conventions to allow hunting, taking, capture, [or] killing ... of any such bird ... and to adopt suitable regulations permitting and governing the same. . . ."

312 U.S. 600, 604 (1941).[4] And so we are willing to assume that the criminal enforcement provision could not be used against federal agencies. From this the defendants reason that Congress could not have intended to have § 703 restrict federal agencies because there would have been no means to enforce the restrictions; at the time of its enactment, they tell us, there was no provision in the Migratory Bird Treaty Act for injunctive relief. * * *

The argument goes nowhere. Even without a specific review provision, there still could have been a suit against the appropriate federal officer for injunctive relief to enforce § 703. *Missouri v. Holland,* for instance, was a "bill in equity brought by the State of Missouri to prevent a game warden of the United States from attempting to enforce the Migratory Bird Treaty Act." 252 U.S. at 430. * * * By 1903 the Court had determined that the "acts of all of [an agency's officers] must be justified by some law, and in case an official violates the law to the injury of an individual the courts generally have jurisdiction to grant relief." *American School of Magnetic Healing v. McAnnulty,* 187 U.S. 94, 108 (1902); *see also* U.S. DEP'T OF JUSTICE, ATTORNEY GENERAL'S MANUAL ON THE ADMINISTRATIVE PROCEDURE ACT 97 (1947); RICHARD H. FALLON ET AL., HART AND WECHSLER'S THE FEDERAL COURTS AND THE FEDERAL SYSTEM 1015–17 (4th ed.1996). Defendants are, in short, quite mistaken in supposing that § 703 could not be enforced against federal agencies except through the criminal provision contained in § 707(a).

Defendants' argument, and our assumption, that federal agencies are not "persons" within § 707(a)'s meaning therefore does not lead to the conclusion that Congress meant to exempt federal agencies from § 703. Indeed it would be odd if they were exempt. The Migratory Bird Treaty Act implements the Treaty of 1916. Treaties are undertakings between nations; the terms of a treaty bind the contracting powers. After ratification of the Treaty, President Woodrow Wilson affixed his signature to it and made it public, "to the end that the same and every article and clause thereof may be observed and fulfilled with good faith *by the United States* and the citizens thereof." 39 Stat. 1705 (italics added). If one year later, in 1917, Canadian authorities had started slaughtering eider ducks, no one would doubt that Canada would be guilty of violating Article IV of the Treaty, which protects these ducks. If some agency of the federal government did the same in Alaska, the United States too would be in violation of the Treaty. There is no reason to treat the Act differently from the Treaty since the legislation was meant to "give effect to the convention between the United States and Great Britain for the protection of migratory birds," ch. 128, 40 Stat. 755, 755 (1918). The Act incorporates the terms of the Treaty in determining, among other things, two critical issues: which birds are covered, *see* 16 U.S.C. § 703, and under what conditions the Interior Department may issue exemptions, *see id*. § 704. *See also id*. §§ 708, 709a,

---

4. The canon applies not only to the federal government but also to the States. *See Vermont Agency of Natural Resources v. United States ex rel. Stevens,* 529 U.S. 1858 (2000). Yet defendants maintain that States and state agencies are subject to the Act's restrictions.

712 (all referencing the conventions). In short, the fact that the Act enforced a treaty between our country and Canada reinforces our conclusion that the broad language of § 703 applies to actions of the federal government.

Canada too understood that legislation implementing the Treaty applied to the sovereign. If Canadian authorities kill migratory birds without a permit they violate not only the Treaty, but also Canada's Migratory Birds Convention Act. That Act "is binding on Her Majesty in right of Canada or a province." R.S.C., ch. 22, § 3 (1994). The Canadian Act, like its American counterpart, derives from Article VIII of the Treaty, which obligated both Contracting Powers to "propose to their respective appropriate law-making bodies the necessary measures for insuring the execution of the present Convention." International Convention, art. VIII, 39 Stat. 1704. That Canada treated this joint obligation to mean that implementing legislation would be binding on the sovereign indicates still further that § 703 restricts the actions of federal agencies in this country.

This too had been the longstanding conclusion of the Department of the Interior, which until 1997 had "historically interpreted the provisions of the MBTA as applying to actions of FWS employees themselves." Letter from Frank K. Richardson, Solicitor, U.S. Dep't of the Interior, to the Secretary of the Interior at 3 (May 31, 1985); *see also* 50 C.F.R. § 21.12. Although FWS has now changed its mind, neither Interior nor Agriculture asks us to defer to their interpretation of the Act, and for good reason. The Agriculture Department does not administer the Act and so its view of § 703's meaning is entitled to no special respect. For its part, the Interior Department conceded that the 1997 FWS change of heart, in a letter to regional offices, was not "a policy call on the part of the Service," nor "a 'filling in' of the 'gaps' in the" statute. Federal Defendants' Opposition to Plaintiff's Emergency Motion to Compel Defendants to File an Administrative Record at 2 (June 4, 1999). *Christensen v. Harris County*, 529 U.S. 576 (2000), holds that: "Interpretations such as those in opinion letters—like interpretations contained in policy statements, agency manuals, and enforcement guidelines, all of which lack the force of law—do not warrant *Chevron*-style deference."

For many of the reasons we have mentioned, we disagree with the * * * holding in *Sierra Club v. Martin*, 110 F.3d 1551, 1555 (11th Cir. 1997), that § 703 does not apply to federal agencies. * * * [It rests] on the mistaken idea that in 1918, § 703 could be enforced only through the criminal penalty provision in § 707(a). The *Martin* opinion adds the thought that Congress could not have wanted the Act to apply to the Forest Service in the early 1900s because whenever it cut trees it might be destroying migratory birds or their nests, in violation of the Act. *See* 110 F.3d at 1555. The *Martin* court's assumption that timber harvesting could violate the Migratory Bird Treaty Act is not shared by others. The Eighth Circuit in *Newton County,* following the lead of the Ninth Circuit in *Seattle Audubon Society v. Evans*, 952 F.2d 297, 302 (1991), held that § 703 does not prohibit "conduct, such as timber harvesting, that indirectly results in the death of migratory birds." 113 F.3d at 114. Even if the *Martin* court were correct about timber harvesting, its observation about the Forest Service ignores the facts that it was not until 1997 that the Interior Department asserted immunity for federal agencies; that before then the Fish and Wildlife Service interpreted the Act to apply to all federal agencies; that during the pre–1997 period the Forest Service, like other federal agencies, could obtain permits; and that—as the documents submitted in this case show—it was the *Martin* case and other pending litigation that "spurred" Interior to adopt the "new" interpretation.[7]

We conclude that because the Wildlife Services division of the Department of Agriculture did not obtain a permit from the Department of the Interior, its implementation of the Integrated Goose Management Plan by taking and killing Canada Geese violates § 703 of the Migratory Bird Treaty Act.

NOTES AND QUESTIONS

1. Note that two separate issues are raised here. One raised on the facts in *Martin* is whether the MBTA prohibits conduct like timber harvesting that indirectly or incidentally results in the death of migratory birds. It is addressed further below. The other is whether federal agencies are covered by the prohibition in the MBTA, which would seem to present a straightforward question of statutory construction. On that issue, the 11th Circuit and the D.C. Circuit take contrary positions. Which is more persuasive? The federal government took the position here that the MBTA did not apply to federal agencies but did apply to state and local governments. See footnote 4 in the *Humane Society* opinion. Is that a plausible position?

2. As a matter of policy, should the U.S. exempt itself from broad prohibitions it imposes on state or private actors? Should a court construing an ambiguous statute in these circumstances presume the federal agencies are covered (as a matter of fairness) or should it presume they are exempt (on the basis that waivers of sovereign immunity ought to be express)?

3. If federal agencies are not themselves constrained by the MBTA, are their permittees and licensees (such as those harvesting timber under Forest Service contract) nevertheless liable? Or should the permit or license provided by the federal agency be construed as permission to take migratory birds? Note that the Act provides for the federal government to give permission to take migratory birds under regulations, but the Act gives that authority to the Secretary of the Interior. See footnote 3 in *Humane Society*, supra p. 911. Thus the Secretary of Agriculture could not provide such permission (e.g., in a contract to harvest timber on national forest lands) without the concurrence of the Interior Secretary.

4. The scope of the MBTA has long caused conflicts among agencies within the executive branch. Wildlife advocates in the Interior Department

---

7. Nor did the *Martin* court acknowledge the Supreme Court's dictum in *Robertson v. Seattle Audubon Society*, 503 U.S. 429 (1992), that the Act applies to federal agencies.

have from time to time advocated fashioning a permit system under the MBTA that would allow the FWS to regulate all takes of migratory birds, by federal agencies or others. Other federal agencies resist the notion of seeking permission from another federal agency for conduct they otherwise have authority to pursue.

5.   In *Humane Society*, killing the geese was the object of the program. But in *Martin*, the timber harvesting only indirectly and unintentionally results in the death of migratory birds. Although *Martin* avoids answering the question because it holds federal agencies are not subject to the MBTA, some other courts have held that accidental killing of migratory birds violates the Act. See United States v. FMC Corp., 572 F.2d 902 (2d Cir.1978) (unintentional release of toxic substances by pesticide manufac-turer into a lagoon frequented by migratory waterfowl held actionable, reasoning by analogy from situations where strict liability is imposed on those engaging in "extrahazardous activities"); United States v. Moon Lake Electric Assn., 45 F.Supp.2d 1070 (D.Colo.1999) (rural electric cooperative may be held liable under MBTA for failing to install inexpensive equipment on 2,450 power poles located near eagle, hawk and owl habitat which has resulted in death or injury to birds). See Helen M. Kim, Chopping Down the Birds: Logging and the Migratory Bird Treaty Act, 31 Envtl. L. 125 (2001).

6.   In this connection, it is worth comparing the MBTA with the ESA. In Seattle Audubon Society v. Evans, 952 F.2d 297, 302 (9th Cir.1991), the court pointed out that the ESA defines "take" to include "harass" and "harm," while these expansive words do not appear in the MBTA. Finding the differences "distinct and purposeful," the court concluded "[h]abitat destruction causes 'harm' to the owls under the ESA but does not 'take' them within the meaning of the [MBTA]." Note, however, that the MBTA prohibits killing protected birds "at any time, by any means or in any manner" except as permitted by Interior Department regulations. 16 U.S.C. § 703. Does that suggest *Seattle Audubon Society* is wrong? Com-pare the discussion of habitat modification as ESA "take" in the various opinions in *Babbitt v. Sweet Home*, Chapter 5 supra, pp. 477–87.

7.   One way to think about this question is to focus on whether the MBTA is a "strict liability" statute, and to examine what kind of scienter is required to make out a violation. For an excellent review of this question, see Larry M. Corcoran, Migratory Bird Treaty Act: Strict Criminal Liability for Non–Hunting, Human Caused Bird Deaths, 77 Denv.U.L.Rev. 315 (1999). For recent court decisions wrestling with the issue not in the context of federal lands, see United States v. Lee, 217 F.3d 284 (5th Cir.2000); United States v. Pitrone, 115 F.3d 1 (1st Cir.1997). See generally Michael J. Bean & Melanie J. Rowland, THE EVOLUTION OF NATION-AL WILDLIFE LAW 72–82 (3d ed. 1997); see also Larry M. Corcoran and Elinor Colbourn, Shocked, Crushed and Poisoned: Criminal Enforcement in Non–Hunting Cases under the Migratory Bird Treaties, 77 Denv.U.L.Rev. 361 (2000).

8.   Benjamin Means, Prohibiting Conduct, Not Consequences: The Limited Reach of the Migratory Bird Treaty Act, 97 Mich.L.Rev. 823, 841–

42 (1998), argues that the Act should be read "only to criminalize activity directed against migratory birds":

> The MBTA's "plain meaning and legislative history" require a restrained interpretation. If interpreted broadly, the MBTA would resist principled limitation; prosecutorial discretion, extra-hazardous materials, and permit schemes all fail to provide a meaningful limit. Moreover, the fate of migratory birds does not depend upon such a strained interpretation of the MBTA. More recently minted environmental laws protect wildlife and seek to achieve a balance of various kinds of land use.

9. Millions of migratory birds are fated to die from incidental or non-directed take. Corcoran sketches out the dimensions of the migratory bird "take" problem: Domestic and feral cats kill hundreds of millions of migratory birds a year. Probably that many are killed by building window impacts. Rough estimates of annual mortality from other causes include motor vehicles (57 million); pesticide ingestion and other forms of water contamination from irrigation return flows, such as gave rise to a notorious case at the Kesterson National Wildlife Refuge in California's Central Valley in the 1980s[1] (67 million); communication towers (4–50 million); industrial spills and accidents (1.5 million or more; the Exxon Valdez oil spill killed several hundred thousand birds). Other significant causes include fishing bycatch (birds taken by nets, hooks, and longlines); electrocutions and power line impacts; wind generators, and aircraft bird strikes. Some of these causes are found on federal lands, while many others are not. Although there are hundreds of millions of migratory birds, Corcoran points out that 90 of an estimated 836 species of migratory birds found in the U.S. are listed as endangered (75) or threatened (15) under the ESA, and another 124 are on the FWS list of non-game species of management concern, and some populations are declining precipitously. As Corcoran notes, at least some of these unintended causes of bird death are avoidable by various measures, including more bird-friendly design and operation. See 77 Denv. U.L.J. at 346–55 (collecting sources).

10. The MBTA poses this practical dilemma: if its command is interpreted sweepingly, much conduct that is regarded as part of ordinary modern life is criminal. Who should bear the responsibility to try to accommodate its requirements to that reality? The courts, by narrow interpretations? The Department of Justice by the exercise of prosecutorial discretion? The Interior Department, by crafting a regulatory scheme to cover some or all of these multitude of acts and practices that kill migratory birds? The Congress, through legislation modifying the Act?

11. The MBTA does not itself define "migratory bird," but refers to the underlying treaties for definition. These "several aged" treaties themselves may not clearly answer the question, but in Hill v. Norton, 275 F.3d 98 (D.C.Cir.2001), the court held that the Secretary of the Interior's refusal

---

1. See Richard Wahl, MARKETS FOR FEDERAL WATER ch. 9 (1989) (documenting the problems at Kesterson and at other federally sponsored irrigation projects and suggesting possible solutions).

to include the mute swan on the list of protected birds was arbitrary and capricious.

NOTE: THE MBTA AS A NATIONAL HUNTING LAW

Under the MBTA, the FWS regulates hunting of migratory birds throughout the country through generic regulations governing such things as identification requirements, hunting methods, and the like. See 50 C.F.R. Part 20, subparts A–J and L, and Part 21 (2000). FWS also promulgates regulations annually prescribing season lengths, shooting hours, bag limits, and other such things, which are based on analysis of bird population data and recommendations of various interests, including states. 50 C.F.R. subpart K (2000). The Act preserves state regulation that is consistent with the treaties and the Act. 16 U.S.C. § 708.

Beyond these MBTA regulations, other federal laws like the Endangered Species Act may operate to restrict hunting opportunities on federal and non-federal lands. In the so-called "sunrise hunting case," Defenders of Wildlife v. Andrus, 428 F.Supp. 167 (D.D.C.1977), the court held that FWS regulations permitting waterfowl hunting from before sunrise until sunset were arbitrary, because the rulemaking proceedings "did not concern themselves with the amount, extent or nature" of the risk that hunters will misidentify their targets and mistakenly shoot endangered birds. The court said that the ESA does not necessarily require that "twilight shooting must be prohibited if protected species are subject to any killing by inadvertent action of hunters or otherwise," but the record must reflect that "hunting hours * * * are so fixed that such killing is kept to the minimum consistent with other obligations imposed on the Service by Congress." See also Connor v. Andrus, 453 F.Supp. 1037 (W.D.Tex.1978).

In 1991 the Fish & Wildlife Service completed a lengthy effort to ban the use of lead shot in hunting waterfowl. According to many studies, lead shot results in substantial mortality to protected bird species through lead poisoning by ingestion. Alternative non-toxic shot (typically steel) is less preferred by hunters because it is less accurate, more costly, and causes more barrel wear or safety concerns. Litigation in the long-running dispute resulted in rulings upholding federal limitations on lead shot. See, e.g., National Rifle Ass'n of America, Inc. v. Kleppe, 425 F.Supp. 1101 (D.D.C. 1976), aff'd mem., 571 F.2d 674 (D.C.Cir.1978). Congress delayed the inevitable with annual appropriations riders that for years prevented the Interior Department from enforcing the regulations except in states that agreed to them. But the phase-out of lead shot for waterfowl and coot hunting was completed in 1991. See Bean & Rowland, supra, at p. 82; Bruce B. Weyrauch, Waterfowl and Lead Shot, 16 Envtl.L. 883 (1986); U.S. Fish & Wildlife Service, FISH AND WILDLIFE '91 (1992) at 9.

D.   THE WILD, FREE–ROAMING HORSES AND BURROS ACT OF 1971

The focus of this section has already reared its head; see Kleppe v. New Mexico, Chapter 3, supra p. 184; and Mountain States Legal Foundation v.

Hodel, Chapter 3, supra p. 246. It is instructive that both cases grew out of conflicts between livestock graziers and wild horses and burros. Wild horses and burros are "in between" domesticated animals and true wildlife because they are feral, which means they are descended from domesticated animals that escaped from Spaniards, Indians, prospectors, and ranchers. Ranchers and others have long considered them pests that should be killed for dog food. This attitude resulted in a drop in wild horse population from perhaps 2 million in the early 1900s to about 20,000 in the 1950s. In an unreported 1968 lawsuit to protect the remnants of the once vast herds of horses, a judge was bemused over attempting to "define Constitutional due process for a herd of mustangs."[1] What the judge could not do, Congress did.

Passage of the Wild Free–Roaming Horses and Burros Act of 1971 (WF–RHBA), 16 U.S.C. §§ 1331–1340, was spurred by the efforts of thousands of school children appalled at the sometimes indiscriminate slaughter of these creatures, and the Act is often condemned as the product of mindless emotionalism. To the extent the Act was intended to increase populations of the feral ungulates, it is perhaps unique among wildlife statutes because it has been an unqualified, rapid success. As of September 30, 2000, the BLM estimated that its lands contained about 44,000 wild horses and 5000 burros; about 55% of the horses were in Nevada and nearly half the burros were in Arizona. PUBLIC LANDS STATISTICS 2000, Table 5–12.

Aside from Kleppe v. New Mexico, upholding the Act as it applied to federal lands, the implementation of the WF–RHBA and litigation under it have been concerned with coping with alleged surpluses. Most of the litigation has been by the plaintiff in the following case; the mainstream environmental protection organizations have not played a role. Much of the litigation has concerned NEPA, not the WF–RHBA. All in all, it has not been a pretty story.

American Horse Protection Ass'n, Inc. v. Watt

United States Court of Appeals, District of Columbia Circuit, 1982.
694 F.2d 1310.

■ [RUTH BADER] GINSBURG, CIRCUIT JUDGE.

The Bureau of Land Management ("BLM") manages a herd of wild horses that roams public lands near Challis, Idaho. In 1976 the district court permanently enjoined BLM from removing horses from the range without the court's approval. This is an appeal from the district court's November 19, 1981, order denying the Agency's motion to dissolve the 1976 injunction. We find no error in the district court's determination that BLM has not complied with instructions the district court supplied in its 1976 decree. But we hold that a 1978 change in the governing statute has

---

1. See Michael J. Bean, THE EVOLUTION OF NATIONAL WILDLIFE LAW 168–69 (1977); for a more recent discussion of the issues, see *id.*, (3d ed. 1997), by Michael J. Bean and Melanie J. Rowland, at 394–403.

superseded the court instructions at issue and compels a remand for prompt reconsideration of the Agency's motion.

I. BACKGROUND

In 1971 Congress enacted the Wild Free–Roaming Horses and Burros Act ("Wild Horse Act"), 16 U.S.C. §§ 1331–1340. The Act responded to the congressional concern that wild horses and burros, "living symbols of the historic and pioneer spirit of the West," were "fast disappearing from the American scene." 16 U.S.C. § 1331. The legislation extended federal protection to wild horses and empowered BLM to manage horses roaming public ranges as a part of the Agency's management of the public lands. At the time Congress passed the Act the Challis herd numbered 150.

The Challis public lands comprise 330,122 acres. Wild horses range on about 197,330 acres of that terrain; of that area, 146,214 acres make up the range accessible to horses in winter. The limited forage on the winter range determines the maximum number of wild horses that can survive on the Challis-area lands. In its current condition, with cattle competing for forage on the winter range in the summer, the winter range can, without significant deterioration * * *, support a stable herd of about 340 horses.[7]

In 1976 BLM proposed to reduce the Challis herd (numbering, according to a 1975 count, 407 horses) to the 1971 herd size of 150 animals. The American Horse Protection Association ("AHPA") challenged the Agency's plan. The district court enjoined the removal of horses by BLM, for the following reasons:

a) The Wild Horse Act's section 1333(a) mandate of "minimal feasible level[s]" of management by the Agency required BLM to consider "*all* alternative courses of action" that would affect the wild horse population less severely than would the proposed roundup and removal. Restricting cattle grazing on the horses' winter range—an option BLM had failed to consider closely—was a viable alternative that might achieve greater protection of the horses with less management by the Agency, and that therefore merited "full and careful consideration."

b) BLM's plan was based on inadequate data on horse population and other herd characteristics.

c) BLM failed adequately to consider means of population control that might reduce the need for periodic removal of horses, for example, concentrating roundup efforts on fertile mares.

---

7. [The BLM's Final Supplemental EIS noted, at pp. 8–14 to 8–15:]

* * * The present number of wild horses (586) is overstocking the winter range. [The data] indicate [ ] the wild horse range would be over grazed by * * * about 246 animals [if present horse population levels were maintained]. The quality and quantity of forage would de- crease due to overgrazing and the range would be severely damaged. * * * The damaged range would eventually produce malnutrition die-offs and migration of horses to other habitat[s] * * * Spring, winter and fall grazing by livestock at the present stocking level would remove forage needed for wild horses. * * *

d) BLM failed to provide for on-site veterinary assistance during the roundup, violating the Wild Horse Act's requirement that removal measures be humane. * * *

In the period 1976–78 BLM studied the management of the Challis lands and weighed alternative control strategies. BLM followed its "Management Framework Plan" ("MFP"). * * * BLM's "Final Supplemental Environmental Statement" ("FSES"), which analyzed alternatives and specified the Agency's "Proposed Action," was filed in November 1978; a "Summary Report" of BLM's final (revised) Range Management Program issued in March 1979.

By 1979 the herd had grown to 767 animals. BLM, under the district court's supervision, agreed with AHPA to remove only 167 horses that year, about half the number the Agency had planned to cull. Under a similar agreement BLM removed 307 horses in 1980. On both occasions the district court refused to dissolve the 1976 injunction.

In 1981 BLM proposed to cull a further 200 horses from the then 400–animal herd. The district court denied permission. It found that BLM had failed to comply with the court's 1976 decision instructing the Agency to give serious, detailed consideration to the possibility of protecting the horses' winter range by restricting cattle grazing. Further, the court rejected BLM's argument that 1978 amendments to the Wild Horse Act superseded the 1976 judicial stop order against removals pending careful study of a winter range management plan. Based upon these two determinations the court ordered that the 1976 injunction remain in full force and effect.

II. COMPLIANCE WITH THE 1976 INJUNCTION

BLM contends initially that it accorded sufficient consideration to protecting the wild horse winter range and thereby adequately complied with the 1976 decree. But the district court, after a hearing, found that the Agency "fail[ed] to give full consideration to alternatives involving the restriction of livestock grazing on the crucial winter range areas," and thus failed to fulfill the 1976 mandate. On the record before us, that finding is well supported.

We note at the outset that the question whether BLM gave "full and careful" consideration to restricting livestock grazing on the winter range is largely one of fact. District court adjudications of such questions should be reviewed under a "clearly erroneous" standard. * * * The district court heard the testimony of, and questioned BLM's experts; this court of review will not second-guess the trial court's skeptical assessment of testimony that court witnessed. Moreover, the documentary evidence abundantly supports the determination that BLM had not met the district court's command.

* * * The record securely indicates that BLM did not extensively consider eliminating or reducing livestock grazing on the winter range.

In MFP–Step 1 the Agency advanced two alternative strategies for protecting the winter range: eliminating cattle altogether from that range, and using fencing to segregate cattle and wild horses competing for the winter range's resources. Both approaches were rejected by BLM in MFP–Step 2, the first because it would have too great an impact on the local economy, the second because fencing was judged too expensive and likely to interfere with wildlife migration. The analysis and resulting rejection of both plans to protect the winter range occupied two pages of the agency record. The "Revised Range Management Program" and other alternatives presented in the FSES and the final RMP do not consider the possibility of fencing the winter range. BLM, the written record thus suggests, proceeded with dispatch in rejecting winter range strategies, and was reticent in explaining why it did so. * * *

The 1976 decision is clear in its insistence upon full consideration for the option of protecting the winter range by curtailing cattle grazing. BLM's efforts to fulfill that condition have been, at best, half-hearted. We therefore find unassailable the district court's rejection of BLM's claim that it has adequately complied with the directions given the Agency in the 1976 decree.

III.   THE 1978 AMENDMENTS TO THE WILD HORSE ACT

The Wild Horse Act was significantly amended in 1978. 92 Stat. 1803. The district court held, however, that the 1978 legislative alterations did not affect the 1976 decision. In the view of the district judge, the amended Act, just as the original 1971 measure, required detailed consideration of courses of action with an impact on the horse population less severe than removal. * * * We believe the district court misinterpreted the 1978 legislative design and failed to accord the Act, as revised, the effect Congress intended it to have.

In 1971 Congress announced the policy that "wild free-roaming horses and burros shall be protected * * * and to accomplish this they are to be considered in the area where presently found, as an integral part of the natural system of the public lands." 16 U.S.C. § 1331. The 1971 Wild Horse Act provided then, as it still does today, that "[a]ll management activities shall be at the minimal feasible level." 16 U.S.C. § 1333(a). By 1978, however, Congress recognized that circumstances had changed. On the Challis range, for example, a herd that numbered 150 horses in 1971 had grown to 586 in 1978. "In the case of wild horses and burros in the Western States, Congress acted in 1971 to curb abuses which posed a threat to their survival. The situation now appears to have reversed, and action is needed to prevent a successful program from exceeding its goals and causing animal habitat destruction." H.R.Rep. No. 95–1122, 95th Cong., 2d Sess. 23 (1978). Congress therefore found "certain amendments are necessary [to the Wild Horse Act] to avoid excessive costs in the administration of the Act, and to facilitate the humane adoption or disposal of excess wild free-roaming horses * * *." 92 Stat. 1803, 43 U.S.C. § 1901(a)(6).

The 1978 amendments embodied two substantive goals. First, Congress struck a new balance—or at least clarified the balance Congress intended to strike in 1971—between protecting wild horses and competing interests in the resources of the public ranges. Second, Congress judged that prompt action was needed to redress the imbalance that had developed; it directed that excess horses should be removed *expeditiously*. To facilitate BLM's implementation of these twin goals, the 1978 amendments specified both the circumstances under which BLM may determine that an overpopulation of wild horses exists and the means the Agency may use to control horse populations.

The main thrust of the 1978 amendments is to cut back on the protection the Act affords wild horses, and to reemphasize other uses of the natural resources wild horses consume. The amendments introduce a definition of "excess" horses: horses are in "excess" if they "must be removed from an area in order to preserve and maintain a thriving natural ecological balance and multiple-use relationship in that area." 16 U.S.C. § 1332(f). This definition makes explicit what was, at most, implicit in the 1971 Act: public ranges are to be managed for multiple uses, not merely for the maximum protection of wild horses. Other provisions of the 1978 legislation referring to domestic livestock grazing, multiple-use of the range, and other rangeland values,[32] 43 U.S.C. § 1901(a)(4), (6), reinforce this reading.

Next, the 1978 amendments made it clear that Congress expected prompt administrative action to deal with wild horse overpopulations that had developed in the period 1971–78. * * * Most importantly, the new section 1333(b)(2) specifies that excess horses "shall" be removed "immediately."

Congress gave BLM ancillary statutory tools to implement these complementary goals. First, the 1978 amendments direct the Secretary to maintain an inventory of wild horses roaming the public lands. 16 U.S.C.A. § 1333(b)(1). This inventory, the statute explains, is intended to assist the Secretary in determining where wild horse and burro overpopulations exist. Second, the 1978 amendments specify what information the Secretary must possess—or, more accurately, the information the Secretary need *not* possess—before removing wild horses deemed to be in excess. 16 U.S.C.A. § 1333(b)(2). Third, the 1978 amendments broaden the means the Secretary may employ in removing excess wild horses. The 1971 Act allowed the destruction of old or sick animals, or capture and private maintenance of healthy ones; the 1978 amendments allow, as a third and last resort, the destruction of healthy animals.

The most important 1978 amendment, for our purposes, is section 1333(b)(2). That section addresses in detail the information upon which BLM may rest its determination that a horse overpopulation exists in a particular area. The Agency is exhorted to consider (i) the inventory of federal public land, (ii) land use plans, (iii) information from environmental impact statements, [and] (iv) the inventory of wild horses. But the Agency

---

32. "Other rangeland values" include "fish, wildlife, recreation, water and soil conservation, [and] domestic livestock grazing." 43 U.S.C. § 1901(a)(6). One important objective of the final RMP for the Challis range is to preserve wildlife and protect the range from further deterioration and erosion. For example, the RMP allocates about three times as much forage to big game species as to wild horses. * * *

is explicitly authorized to proceed with the removal of horses "in the absence of the information contained in (i-iv)." Id. Clauses (i-iv) are therefore precatory; in the final analysis, the law directs that horses "shall" be removed "immediately" once the Secretary determines, *on the basis of whatever information he has at the time of his decision*, that an overpopulation exists. The statute thus clearly conveys Congress's view that BLM's findings of wild horse overpopulations should not be overturned quickly on the ground that they are predicated on insufficient information.

In light of the congressional purposes and the tenor of the 1978 provisions, BLM cannot be held to the prolonged pre-removal process "full and careful consideration" of *all* alternatives would entail. A study of the winter range adequate to satisfy the 1976 decree, AHPA concedes, might take a year, during which no removal of horses would be possible, absent agreement with AHPA. To insist upon such a delay pending further study at this juncture, at least in light of the time-consuming study of the Challis lands, the wild horses, and alternative management strategies that BLM *has* completed, is inconsistent with the amended Act's mandate to the Secretary "immediately" to remove excess horses once an overpopulation is determined to exist. We therefore hold that BLM's failure to study the "winter range" alternative in full detail no longer supplies a basis for enjoining the removal of horses from the Challis range.

IV. CONCLUSION

Although the injunction may not be maintained on the ground that BLM has not yet carefully considered restricting cattle grazing on the winter range, the Secretary's discretion remains bounded. His orders are subject to review and may be overturned if his action is arbitrary. Today we hold only that further consideration of the "winter range" alternative, on which the district court conditioned removal of horses in its 1976 injunction, is, in light of 1978 legislation, not required. It remains open to the district court to determine on remand whether, in light of the goals of the Act as it now stands, and on the basis of the information the Secretary now has, the Agency's current plan to reduce the size of the wild horse herd well below the 340 animals the winter range can support is rationally grounded.[42] * * *

■ ROBINSON, CHIEF JUDGE, dissenting in part.

* * * I cannot agree that [the 1978 amendment] entails that the Bureau need not give the winter range alternative suitable consideration.

---

42. We fully agree with our dissenting colleague that 16 U.S.C. § 1333(b)(2) does not license BLM to engage, with impunity, in an "arbitrary and capricious reasoning process." Dissenting Opinion, text accompanying note 18. We believe that BLM must rationally use all "information currently available" when it determines an overpopulation of wild horses exists. But we do not think that under the Wild Horse Act's specific guidance with respect to informational requirements the Agency acts arbitrarily or capriciously merely because it founds its decisions on the information at hand or an assessment of a reasonably limited number of alternative courses of action. * * *

I do not dispute the proposition that Section 1333(b)(2) precludes courts from formulating injunctions that would require the Bureau to engage in additional fact-investigation or factfinding on overpopulation. I submit, simply, that this provision is inapplicable here. The District Court denied the Bureau's motion to dissolve the injunction, not because the Bureau lacked information, but because the Bureau had not adequately considered an identified alternative—a course of action. On the face of its 1981 opinion, the District Court in no way required the Bureau to act on any data other than that already "currently available" to it. That the Bureau's superficial treatment of the winter range alternative was arbitrary represents a failure of reasoning and evaluation, not necessarily one of factfinding, and certainly not one of fact-investigation. In concluding that Section 1333(b)(2) dispenses with judicial review of the Bureau's reasoning as well as its factfinding and fact-investigation, the court resorts to an unnatural and uncommonly broad construction of the word "information." A process of reasoning is not "information" upon which the Bureau relies when it decides upon a course of action; it is the soul of the decision itself.

I am also troubled by my colleagues' failure to articulate a clear concept of the scope of judicial review under their interpretation of Section 1333(b)(2). Although they declare that the Bureau's discretion "remains bounded," it is difficult to delineate the intended constraints on this discretion in light of their holding in the case at bar. By overturning the District Court's decision not to dissolve the injunction, which was based on the Bureau's refusal to deal adequately with the winter range alternative, they apparently will allow the Bureau not only to limit fact-investigation and factfinding as it chooses, but also to indulge in any manner of reasoning based on the facts at hand without judicial reproach. * * *

NOTES AND QUESTIONS

1. In many situations like this one, the BLM must allocate existing forage among livestock, big game species of wildlife, and wild horses and burros. Does the Wild Horse & Burro Act provide any specific directions as to how to make that choice? Did it prior to the 1978 amendment discussed by the court?

2. Does FLPMA, adopted in 1976, provide any relevant direction? FLPMA's definition of multiple use does not refer to wild horses and burros, but does refer to "wildlife" and "natural scenic, scientific and historical values." 43 U.S.C. § 1702(c). Might these critters fit into this definition as an "historical value"? FLPMA also provides that nothing in it "shall be deemed to repeal any existing law by implication." § 701(e), 90 Stat. at 2786 (not codified).

3. Examine the 1978 amendment's definition of "excess" horses. Does that authorize the BLM to find *all* the wild horses and burros in a particular area as "excess"? How must the BLM go about deciding whether there are "excess" animals in a particular area? For some time after the amendment was adopted, the BLM regarded wild horse populations that

exceeded levels existing in 1971, when the Act was first adopted, as "excess." The Interior Board of Land Appeals has rejected that bright-line standard, reasoning that the determination of "excess" must be made on the basis of ecological balance, which cannot arbitrarily be fixed at a moment in time. Craig C. Downer, 111 IBLA 333 (1989). See also Dahl v. Clark, 600 F.Supp. 585 (D.Nev.1984), excerpted infra.

4. Why did the BLM so steadfastly refuse (over a period of several years) to consider seriously eliminating or removing livestock from the winter range? Who wins the debate between the majority and the dissent on whether the majority opinion effectively vests BLM with near-plenary discretion in this matter?

5. Did the court here effectively hold that the 1978 amendments have exempted wild horse removal decisions from NEPA? Should such exemptions (or partial repeals by implication) be lightly inferred, or should they require fairly explicit statements by Congress to be accomplished?

6. In the Howe Massacre litigation, AHPA v. U.S. Dept. of Interior, 551 F.2d 432 (D.C.Cir.1977), Idaho ranchers had conducted their own roundup, resulting in the death or mutilation of many of the animals. The court held that such lawlessness could not be validated by a state official's sham declaration that all of the horses were privately owned: the final decision on ownership, the court ruled, is vested in the federal agency. Compare Sheridan v. Andrus, 465 F.Supp. 662 (D.Colo.1979).

7. Fallini v. Hodel, 963 F.2d 275 (9th Cir.1992), adds an Alice-in-Wonderland touch to the wild horse chronicles. Over a vigorous dissent, the appellate court found that a guardrail was a gate and that wild horses were not wildlife within the meaning of a rancher's 1967 grazing permit and therefore the rancher did not violate its permit by failing to get BLM approval for guard rails intended to keep wild horses away from some of the rancher's wells.

The opinion in Dahl v. Clark, 600 F.Supp. 585 (D.Nev.1984), offers interesting insights into political realities and unrealities in public land management. Plaintiff ranchers sued to force the BLM to reduce the wild horse population in the area of their grazing allotments back to 1971 levels. They claimed that rapidly increasing horse populations (from 62 to 655 head in 13 years, they alleged) were harming range conditions. In the course of his decision, Judge Reed made these observations:

> * * * Defendants argue that the laws require them to remove wild horses only if actual ongoing substantial damage to the range is occurring because of an excess number of wild horses using it. Further, defendants argue that pursuant to his authority in 1981, Secretary of the Interior James Watt rejected prior BLM study methods and the conclusions reached from them as inaccurate, and directed the BLM officials in the field to maintain numbers of livestock and wild horses on the public lands at 1981 levels and to commence use of new

monitoring studies as to range utilization. Secretary Watt believed the new study methods utilized more modern scientific methods.[1] * * *

* * * BLM [initially] adopted a range survey approach, an inventory procedure, in order to estimate the carrying capacities of the ranges for the purposes of preparation of the EISs. The results of EISs based on the range survey approach were alarming[,] in many cases mandating drastic reductions in both livestock and wild horse use of the affected ranges. For example, in the Jersey Valley Allotments the applicable EIS would have required reduction of cattle use by 50–55% and reduction of wild horses to nothing in some areas.

It was at that time in 1981 that the directive came forth from Secretary Watt renouncing all the previous studies and requiring BLM to start afresh, using as a starting place the existing numbers of wild horses and livestock in each range area and to commence use of new scientific approaches to determine range carrying capacities. Defendants' Exhibit O, Letter from James Watt. The levels of then existing wild horse and livestock populations were to be continued and the animals were to continue to use their respective then existing ranges. Population levels were made subject to adjustment on the basis of intensive monitoring studies that were to continue. The effect of Secretary Watt's 1981 instructions was to reverse what appear [sic] to be the BLM's longtime orientation from one of looking for downward trends in range conditions to one of looking for upward trends or at least static range conditions. Until Secretary Watt's directive, the studies of the BLM and their management consistently found range conditions poor and on a downward trend calling for reduction in livestock numbers and removal of wild horses. Since the time Secretary Watt's letter was issued, the BLM has been making the opposite findings and recommendations. One has to admire the steadfast loyalty of the BLM officials in following the dictates of their superiors in the Department of Interior, no matter which way the wind blows at a particular time.

In this case, the BLM contends that all the data available to it in 1981 was [sic] outdated and unscientific. The evidence presented at trial, however, does not bear this out. It appears that the BLM had been conscientiously and efficiently studying the ranges on a continuing basis prior to and during the 1970s and early 1980s. Many of these studies (including those made on the subject allotments) were made on bases in conformity with the scientific approaches called for by Secretary Watt in his 1981 letter, rather than on the basis of the criticized "one point in time" observations. Such range investigations were frequent and continuous and cannot by any means be entirely discounted or discarded as inaccurate.

---

1. Although the reason for Secretary Watt's directive is not clear, it appears to the Court that it most likely resulted from the fact that the previous studies indicated that use of the public domain by livestock and by wild horses would have to be drastically reduced due to damage to the range caused by overutilization.

* * * While Secretary Watt specifically rejected one point in time observation studies as being inaccurate, the thrust of his 1981 directive is to reject all pre–1981 studies apparently because of his conclusion that then current numbers of animals should be maintained. The Watt directive places BLM in the position in this case of having to attack its previous studies, conclusions, decisions, and to some extent its own expert personnel. Previous BLM studies had indicated a downward trend in range condition and the necessity of reduction of numbers. Previous BLM studies included not only one point in time studies but studies which required repeated observations such as photo trend plots. Many of the pre–1981 studies appear to meet the criteria which are now supposed to be met to achieve accurate and reliable results. Despite Secretary Watt's rejection of them, the BLM nonetheless relies upon these pre–1981 studies * * * in attempting to show that the trend of the allotments is not downward and that the forage utilization is not excessive. * * *

It doesn't appear, therefore, that so far as these three allotments are concerned, the Secretary of the Interior is carrying out his mandate under the Wild Horse Act, as amended. The decision to maintain 1981 numbers has not been made after determining the optimum number of horses to be maintained on the area. It is simply an arbitrary decision to maintain 1981 numbers. While the BLM has attempted to support Secretary Watt's decision as best it could, the preponderance of the evidence is that the decision to maintain 1981 wild horse population levels is not based upon any evidence, analysis or studies but simply on the decision Secretary Watt made in order to avoid reductions in livestock and wild horse populations in 1981. * * *

The court found Secretary Watt's 1981 decision unsupportable and arbitrary, but refused to grant the requested relief because it could not find in the WF–RHBA any requirement that horse populations must be limited to 1971 levels.

NOTES

1.   Since the WF–RHBA became law, some 177,000 wild horses and burros rounded up as excess have been "adopted" into private ownership. See PUBLIC LAND STATISTICS 2000, Table 5–13. The adoption program has not been without problems. See, e.g, Animal Protection Institute of America v. Hodel, 860 F.2d 920 (9th Cir.1988) (a "qualified individual" who may adopt an animal under the Act does not include one whom the Secretary knows will use the animal for commercial purposes). See generally George Cameron Coggins & Robert Glicksman, 3 PUBLIC NATURAL RESOURCES LAW § 18.29 (2001).

2.   The Wild Horse & Burro Act applies only to "public lands," defined as BLM and Forest Service-managed lands. Thus it does not limit the ability of other federal land management agencies (such as the National Park Service) to rid their lands of these creatures. See Wilkins v. Secretary of Interior, 995 F.2d 850 (8th Cir.1993), cert. denied, 510 U.S. 1091 (1994),

upholding NPS plan to remove approximately 20 wild horses of unknown origin from the 71,000 acre Ozark National Scenic Riverways Park. The NPS decided to remove the horses for a variety of reasons, including that they were an exotic species whose presence conflicted with park purposes, competed with native wildlife, and caused environmental harm. A dissenting judge thought NPS "prejudged the issue" to suit its "convenience and preconceived notions of culture and history," and "translated statutes and policies that grant discretion to control exotic species into an absolute mandate for removal."

CHAPTER 11

THE RECREATION RESOURCE

Measured by total user days, the single greatest demand on the public lands is from persons seeking recreational opportunities. The burgeoning American penchant for refreshment of the spirit in the outdoors comes in varying forms, from motorized cross-country frolicking to quiet contemplation of nature. Exercised with varying degrees of intensity, it creates some of the most intractable land management problems of the modern era. Recreation is a resource like the more conventional ones: Congress has recognized that recreation is a valid and sometimes preferred land use and has encouraged and oftentimes subsidized it.

Recreation is one of the "multiple uses" to be provided for by the Forest Service and the BLM. The Fish and Wildlife Service may allow recreational use on refuges when it is compatible with wildlife purposes, and "wildlife-dependent recreation" is given "priority" status in the 1997 National Wildlife Refuge System Improvement Act. See 16 U.S.C. § 668dd(a)(3)(C); see Chapter 10, pp. 883–86 supra. Congress has charged the National Park Service with not only conserving the lands and other resources in the national park system but also providing for "the enjoyment of the same in such manner and by such means as will leave them unimpaired for future generations." National Park Organic Act of 1916, 16 U.S.C. § 1.

Increasingly in modern times Congress has applied relatively new overlaying statutory designations—such as national recreation area—to tracts of land managed by the NPS, the Forest Service, and the BLM. Each of these statutes varies in the extent to which it gives priority to recreation and excludes other multiple uses, but practically all are intended to elevate recreational use and management to a position of priority over other uses.

Like other activities, intensive recreation on federal lands can degrade the natural environment and pose conflicts with other resource uses. Access to hunting can be barred by mining claims and resisted by public lands ranchers; ski area proposals are fought by hikers, hunters, and birdwatchers; off-road vehicle enthusiasts are despised by many but may have no other large tracts of land available for their pursuit; increased sightseeing overwhelms parts of the "crown jewels" of the national park system; and so forth. As a general rule, the more mechanized or technologically advanced the form of recreation, the more potential for conflict and destruction it poses. Off-road vehicles, for example, are more dangerous to ecological stability than mountain bikes, but the latter may, in turn, have greater impact than hikers. Hunters tend to make more impact than birdwatchers; hotels cause more serious changes than tents. Quantity obviously is important as well: a horde of hikers can leave the terrain in worse condition than a single jeep. In one of the more worthwhile footnotes in legal literature, the late Professor Ralph Johnson captured the essence of the dilemma:

> Motorbikes are a particular bane in the wilderness. But, it is said, many people like to ride motorbikes on mountain trails. This led me to invite a number of friends to fill in the blank in the following sentence: Because people like to ride motorbikes on mountain trails they should be allowed to do so, is like saying that because they like to _____ on mountain trails they should be allowed to do so. Unfortunately, none of the entries were printable.

Ralph Johnson, Recreation, Fish, Wildlife and the Public Land Law Review Commission, 6 Land & Water L.Rev. 283, 289 n. 18 (1970).

Substantial economic interests are at stake in recreation management decisions made by federal land managers. The recreation industry includes, besides those operating concessions on federal lands, nearby resort operators, vehicle and equipment rental businesses, other supporting businesses, and manufacturers of motor homes, boats, off-road vehicles, skiing equipment, and other sporting goods. All have an interest in promoting recreational use of federal lands. Many settlements near the public lands are economically dependent on tourism; gateway communities like West Yellowstone, Montana would shrivel without the dollars brought in by recreation on nearby federal lands.

It should not be surprising that conflicts between recreation and other values or resources are finding their way to the courts. A number of cases in earlier chapters involve the recreation resource. In Leo Sheep Co. v. United States, supra at p. 147, the access rights at issue were intended for the benefit of fishermen. In the Burr Trail litigation (Sierra Club v. Hodel, supra p. 161), the conflict was between recreational access and preservation. The *Ruby Lake Refuge* cases, supra at pp. 873–82, show the conflict between recreation and wildlife, with the latter itself furnishing the basis for two large but very different recreational industries, sport hunting of migratory birds and birdwatching. Recreational access sometimes requires resolving fundamental questions of federal power and private rights, as in United States v. Curtis–Nevada Mines, Inc., supra at p. 622.

Jan G. Laitos & Thomas A. Carr, The Transformation on Public Lands

26 Ecology Law Q. 140, 178, 184 (1999).*

One of the major sociological and economic events in the twentieth century United States involves the dramatic increase in recreation, particularly outdoor recreation. By 1997, the Outdoor Recreation Coalition of America reported that more than 90% of Americans over the age of sixteen regularly participate in at least one outdoor recreational activity. Much of the increase has taken place on federal lands. For example, the BLM, whose lands were once thought to be conducive primarily to livestock and mining, recorded 72 million visits for recreation in 1990. The Interior Department's Assistant Secretary for Land and Minerals has acknowledged that the "BLM has changed to meet public needs," in part because "[w]e prize the public lands today for their scenic, recreational, environmental, and archeological significance."[224] The United States Forest Service, the original multiple-use federal agency, experienced a doubling of recreational use in national forests between the late 1960s (150 million visitors annually) and 1990 (almost 300 million visitors). As noted by the Agriculture Department's Under Secretary for Natural Resources: "Timber is not the agenda of the future. Recreation is." Public lands have become so popular for recreation that knowledgeable commentators have opined that "if aesthetic appreciation of nature is deemed a facet of recreation, then recreation is the most frequent, if not dominant, federal land use."[227]

But an overall increase in recreation does not explain why public lands have become recreation destinations. One needs to understand how traditional multiple-use public lands, such as Forest Service and BLM lands, have evolved from extractive uses to dominant, nonextractive, recreational uses. As discussed below, this change in use of public lands has been caused by psychological, sociological, economic, and legal factors.

1. Psychological and Sociological Factors

As the century comes to a close, one is left with the impression that the physical environments preferred at the beginning of the century have been replaced by a totally different vision of what constitutes an ideal community. One hundred years ago a prosperous setting was one in which extractive industries flourished—timber was being turned into pulp and paper; copper was being mined; cattle and sheep were grazing. Today, Americans are more aware that these economic activities impact other sources of well being. What is often far more desirable than a steel mill or paper factory is a pristine natural environment where recreation can flourish, health is protected, air and water are unpolluted, and wildlife is abundant. Americans increasingly judge an area's desirability not by the quantity of commodity goods produced there, but by the environmental and recreational amenities it offers.

Interest in recreation is being fueled by several factors related to how people feel about themselves and their world. Surveys reveal that outdoor recreation has become a significant part of the lives of over 75% of Americans. Reasons for the unprecedented popularity of recreation vary. People are increasingly aware of their health and their bodies. They also have more interest in the natural environment and the growing number of federally managed ecosystems and biologically diverse communities now subject to a preservation mandate.

224. Bob Armstrong, *Our Federal Public Lands*, 12 Nat. Resources & Env't 3, 7 (1997).

227. Coggins & Glicksman [PUBLIC NATURAL RESOURCES LAW] § 17.01.

Public perception of federal lands seems especially dependent on recreational potential. Over 95% of Americans surveyed believe that the federal government should preserve natural areas for the recreational use of future generations. This association between public lands and recreation is in part due to the feeling one has when traveling through these unfenced, unpopulated lands (particularly in the West). The impression that is gained is that "this belongs to me." Such an assumption creates citizen pressure for recreational noncommodity uses, such as backpacking, mountain biking, camping, and fishing.

Various sociological and demographic changes have also served to stimulate the public's desire to use public lands for recreational purposes. Recreation requires leisure time, and Americans enjoy an average of nearly 40 hours of leisure a week, up from 35 hours in 1965. This country's population is increasing, and much of it is concentrated in urban areas, whose dwellers comprise the fastest growing segment of the population using public lands for recreational purposes. America also enjoys a high level of disposable personal income and an interstate highway system that provides low cost-access to recreation areas far from home. Rising discretionary purchasing power and mobility combine to give recreation-minded urban residents access to public lands and nearby communities.

2.   Economic Factors Causing Increased Recreational Use of Public Lands

For many years, the economic health of states in the West was tied closely to the commodity resources found on public lands—hardrock minerals, coal, oil and gas, water, forage for crops and livestock, and timber. But with the decline of traditional commodity resource use on public lands has come a different economic reality, linked not to extractive industries, but to the emerging recreation value of public lands. Four factors help to explain the dominance of recreation use.

First, one can argue that the recreation resource on public lands is a public good. Public goods generally have two characteristics: (1) they are difficult to exclude persons from; and (2) as a consequence they tend to be over-used. Unlike most commodity resources such as a mining deposit or an oil reservoir, the recreation resource usually has no borders (other than the boundary line separating public and private property). Moreover, no administrative mechanism exists to easily restrict the flow of persons wishing to engage in public-lands recreation. As a result, once one person is allowed to use BLM or Forest Service lands for recreational purposes, it is quite difficult to exclude others from taking full advantage of similar recreational opportunities. Since it would be incredibly expensive to put impenetrable fences around all public lands not already devoted to recreation, and since it could be administratively burdensome and politically unpopular to collect fees at fixed entrance points to limit those who wish to gain access to these lands, BLM lands and national forests effectively become "commons." Visitors can hike, bike, camp, swim, ride horses, or drive their all-terrain vehicles without asking permission, making a reservation, or paying a fee. As a result, the recreation resource on public lands, as a public good or commons, becomes over used.

Second, recreation has economic worth. The economic value of recreation in part takes the form of dollars that flow into the outdoor recreation equipment market. In 1996, the Outdoor Recreation Coalition of America estimated that retail sales of such equipment (e.g., mountain bikes, hiking and walking shoes, outerwear, skis, kayaks) totaled almost $5 billion. The outdoor recreation industry provided nearly 800,000 full-time jobs, for a total of $13 billion in annual wages. Of course, since these are national figures, one cannot presume that the economic benefits of the recreation industry are directed at states in the West where most public lands are located. Still, one can assume that a significant portion of the retail sales for outdoor recreational equipment takes place in, and therefore benefits the economies of, the public lands states.

Third, apart from spending money on (and thereby employing those who manufacture) recreation equipment, outdoor enthusiasts who buy such equipment often use it on the public lands. During their visit to public lands, these individuals typically spend money in surrounding communities. Thus, nearby communities reap an economic benefit from the active participants who come to public lands to fish, hunt, camp, hike, snowboard, and raft, as well as the tourists whose recreation consists only of taking a few steps from an automobile to observe or photograph natural beauty. Both types of recreation create income for communities that are gateways to public lands, thereby boosting their economies. In virtually all population centers near public lands, recreational activities and tourism provide significantly greater employment than commodity resource extraction. Most interior West states now count on recreation and tourism as the first or second largest part of their economies.[244]

The important economic role played by recreation can be seen in two quite different classes of public lands—the national forests, which are subject to a multiple-use mandate, and the national parks, whose conflicting statutory purposes are recreation and preservation. The Chief of the United States Forest Service has estimated that by the year 2000, recreation will account for $97.8 billion of the total $130.7 billion generated by uses of the national forests, while fish and wildlife will generate another $12.9 billion. Most of these recreational dollars are spent in surrounding communities. By contrast, timber harvesting (traditionally the preferred use) is expected to yield only $3.5 billion. For the National Park Service, recreation has been increasingly favored over preservation. The sheer

---

244. See Atlas of the New West: Portrait of a Changing Region 125 (William E. Riebsame ed., 1997); see also [Thomas M.] Power, [Lost Landscapes and Failed Economies: The Search for a Value of Place (1996)], at 162 (noting that in eight of ten national forests in Montana, recreation provides three times as much employment as timber harvesting; in Wyoming's nonwestern national forestland, recreation provides nine jobs for every one associated with the timber harvest); [Christine] Bloomquist, [Tourism and Recreation Management: Strategies for Public Lands, Parks and Recreation, Sept. 1, 1996, at 2] (noting that communities near public lands have identified "nonextractive" methods, such as tourism, to capitalize on the decline of agricultural, mining, and forest uses of these lands); [Raymond] Rasker [A New Look at Old Vistas: The Economic Role of Environmental Quality in Western Public Lands (1994), 65 U.Colo. L.Rev. 369], at 375–78 (as the relative contribution of goods-producing industries to the economies of western states has declined, the economic role of tourism and recreation industries has grown).

number of visitors arriving at national parks annually has driven this choice. These visitors desire not only a wilderness experience, but also food, lodging, and travel services; amenities that are supplied by concessionaires, which have a tremendous influence on Park Service decisionmaking.

The "amenity resource value" of recreation is yet another type of economic benefit that flows from public lands. This value refers to the largely intangible, noncommercial benefits associated with unspoiled natural resources. One important amenity use of natural resources is recreational use. When public lands have recreational value, they become economic assets in much the same way that forage, water, timber, and mineral resources are. They help ensure that the existing people and businesses remain and they help lure potential employers and entrepreneurs. Finally, they provide a quality of life and a sense of place that has value both to people currently living there and to those who might want to move or travel there.

Amenity recreation resource values play an important role not so much in attracting short-term tourists and travelers to an area, but rather in encouraging the relocation of permanent residents and businesses. This, in turn, stimulates and supports diverse economic activity. The presence of such amenity values means that, in many areas near public lands, the use of the lands for recreation far exceeds the economic worth of the land for extraction of commodity resources. Also, communities closely tied to recreation tend to lead both metropolitan and nonmetropolitan areas in economic vitality. Some commentators have even concluded that "the amenity value of recreational opportunities in the intermountain West has been the dominant engine of population and economic growth in that region for decades."[258]

Recreation and American culture are intimately related. Preferred forms of recreation are influenced by available leisure time, prosperity, technology, and prevailing social mores. As recreation influences culture, so too does culture (and philosophy and morality) influence recreational policy—sometimes in unconventional fashion.* This chapter examines a melange of federal recreational policy topics. The first section briefly treats

---

258. Coggins & Glicksman, § 17.01.

*When in 1982 the Department of the Interior announced an intention to ban nudity on a beach in Assateague National Seashore, the Republican Study Committee described this initiative as "yet another move to protect the environment." When Secretary of the Interior James Watt announced a ban on the Beach Boys performing on the National Mall (managed by the Park Service) at the annual July 4th celebration (to be replaced by singer Wayne Newton), explaining the concerts were "attracting the wrong ele-

ment," Presidential assistant Michael Deaver retorted: "the Beach Boys are an American institution. Anyone who thinks they play hard rock thinks Mantovani plays jazz." The Secretary rescinded the ban the following day. In July 1999, the AP reported that U.S. Forest Service officials in Montana were trying to decide whether to grant a grant a permit for a concert—billed as a fundraiser to help convert Butte's old Dumas Brothel into a sex museum—to be held on U.S. Forest Service land.

federal acquisition of interests in land for recreational purposes. Section B examines recreation policy in the national park system (except for off-road vehicles, which are dealt with in Section E). Section C addresses management of an emerging important category of land management, the national recreation area and similar overlay legislative designations. Section D addresses a potpourri of federal land recreational management issues. Section E focuses on one particular kind of intensive recreational use with significant environmental impacts and associated controversy—off-road vehicles. Finally, Section F describes the basis of federal liability under the Federal Tort Claims Act for mishaps to recreational licensees.

A. ACQUISITION OF LANDS FOR RECREATION: THE LAND AND WATER CONSERVATION FUND

The Land and Water Conservation Fund, 16 U.S.C. §§ 460*l*–4 to 460*l*–11, is a keystone of federal recreational policy. The Fund is a paper account in the U.S. Treasury to which is credited federal receipts from oil and gas leasing and development on the Outer Continental Shelf. Since its inception in 1965, LWCF moneys have enabled federal agencies to purchase several million acres of land and interests in land for creation of new and enlargement of existing federal land recreational areas. LWCF grants to states have bought an additional several million acres for state and local government recreational land systems.

LWCF money cannot be spent absent an appropriation by Congress, and appropriations out of the Fund have never equaled receipts credited to it. Sometimes spending out of the Fund has come in for political criticism; for example, in 1981 Secretary of the Interior James Watt, decrying "park barrel politics," called for a moratorium on further LWCF acquisitions. See Dabney v. Reagan, 542 F.Supp. 756 (S.D.N.Y.1982); Robert Glicksman & George Cameron Coggins, Federal Recreational Land Policy: The Rise and Decline of the Land and Water Conservation Fund, 9 Colum.J.Envt'l L. 125 (1984). See generally Joseph Sax, Buying Scenery: Land Acquisitions for the National Park Service, 1980 Duke L.J. 709.

In more recent years, there has been growing interest in beefing up the Fund and spending more dollars on acquiring land into public ownership for recreational and related conservation uses. The Clinton Administration proposed a multi-billion dollar "Lands Legacy" initiative that called for full funding of the LWCF for the first time since it was enacted in 1965. It also proposed, starting in 2001, to provide a stream of money for the LWCF outside the annual appropriations process; that is, to make it a true revolving fund so that offshore oil receipts could be spent without annual appropriations by the Congress. Congress's traditional hostility to "revolving funds" beyond the control of appropriations committees seems to have defeated the latter idea (although it is still pending in Congress as of this writing). Nevertheless, unaccustomed (if short-lived) budget surpluses led to sharp increases in appropriations to the LWCF for land acquisitions at the turn of the century.

Not surprisingly, the federal money made available through the LWCF program for state and local recreational land acquisition come, as federal funds usually do, with strings attached. The primary string is, sensibly, to ensure that the money being made available will serve its statutory purpose.

Friends of Shawangunks, Inc. v. Clark

United States Court of Appeals, Second Circuit, 1985.
754 F.2d 446.

■ Oakes, Circuit Judge.

This case presents the novel question whether amendment of a conservation easement acquired in part with federal funds under the Land and Water Conservation Fund Act of 1965 so as to permit expansion of a golf course with limited access constitutes a conversion "to other than public outdoor recreation uses" under section 6(f)(3) of the Act, 16 U.S.C. § 460l–8(f)(3).[1] The Secretary of the Interior, acting through the National Park Service's Acting Regional Director, determined that a section 6(f)(3) conversion would not occur. * * *

The Shawangunk Range, located in Ulster County, New York, is noted for spectacular rock formations, sheer cliffs, windswept ledges with pine barrens, fast-flowing mountain streams and scenic waterfalls, as well as a series of five mountain lakes, the "Sky Lakes." Of these, Lake Minnewaska is one, with extremely steep banks and many magnificent cliffs rising as high as 150 feet along its northern and eastern shores. Lake Minnewaska is situated approximately in the center on a general north-south line of 22,000 acres of permanent open space extending for some sixteen miles along the crest of the Shawangunks. Large tracts of land within the overall area are owned, maintained, and made available to the public for hiking and other limited recreational activities by, among others, the Village of Ellenville, the Palisades Interstate Park Commission (PIPC), the Mohonk Preserve, Inc., Mohonk Mountain Houses, Inc., and the Nature Conservancy.

In 1971, the State of New York purchased about 7,000 acres of land bordering Lake Minnewaska to the south and west for the formation of Minnewaska State Park. The park is under the jurisdiction and management of the PIPC, an interstate park commission formed by compact between the State of New York and the State of New Jersey.

In 1977, the PIPC added 1,609 acres of land to the park and purchased an approximately 239–acre conservation easement over Lake Minnewaska

---

1. Section 6(f)(3) provides:

No property acquired or developed with assistance under this section shall, without the approval of the Secretary, be converted to other than public outdoor recreation uses. The Secretary shall approve such conversion only if he finds it to be in accord with the then existing comprehensive statewide outdoor recreation plan and only upon such conditions as he deems necessary to assure the substitution of other recreation properties of at least equal fair market value and of reasonably equivalent usefulness and location.

itself and certain land adjacent to it, all with the help of 50% federal matching funds from the Land and Water Conservation Fund. See 16 U.S.C. § 460*l*–8. The lands encumbered by the easement contain inter alia the lake itself, a nonoperating nine-hole golf course, a golf course pro shop, the water supply system for an adjacent resort building, and wooded land.

According to its terms, the easement is "for the purpose of, but not solely limited to, the conservation and preservation of unique and scenic areas; for the environmental and ecological protection of Lake Minnewaska and its watershed; and to prevent development and use in a manner inconsistent with the present use and operation of lands now owned and to be conveyed [to the PIPC] and to be part of Minnewaska State Park." It provides that the fee owner "shall not develop or erect new facilities within the described area; alter the landscape or terrain; or cut trees" but may

> operate, maintain and reconstruct existing facilities within the easement area, including, but not limited to buildings, roads, utilities and golf courses; provided that (a) Any reconstruction shall be in the same location and utilized for the same purpose as that which existed on the date hereof and that such reconstructed facilities shall be no larger in area than the facility being replaced.

In a limited exception to the prohibition against expanded or new construction, the PIPC agreed to the construction or reconstruction of several specific facilities, including "[t]he existing golf course pro shop and a golf course maintenance building" as well as "[a]n access road and parking lot for golf course patrons."

The Marriott Corporation, a national hotel and resort developer, acquired an option in 1980 to purchase approximately 590 acres, including the water and lands encumbered by the 239–acre easement. Marriott proposes to develop a resort facility, complete with a 400–room resort hotel and conference center, 300 condominium units, restaurants, ski facilities, and an expanded, professional grade 18–hole golf course. Eight golf course holes and related facilities, apparently with golf-cart roadways, would be constructed on property subject to the easement. * * *

Despite the Friends' arguments, the PIPC resolved on July 20, 1981, to amend the conservation easement to allow the Marriott Corporation to expand the golf course as proposed, drill wells within the easement area, increase the use of water from Lake Minnewaska, and utilize acreage encumbered by the easement for purposes of computing total average density of residential development. In consideration, Marriott agreed to extend the area covered by the easement, permit public access to footpaths through the easement area and adjacent lands owned by Marriott, maintain the lake level above an elevation of 1,646 feet, limit development on its other adjoining property, and open the golf course to the public twenty-five percent of the time. On October 20, 1981, [the Park Service notified] the PIPC that the contemplated amendment of the conservation easement did not constitute a section 6(f)(3) conversion and therefore did not require any federal authorization. This lawsuit followed.

* * * [The district court held] that the amendment did not constitute a conversion. The court reasoned that because the public had no access to the lands encumbered by the easement these lands "presently are not intended for outdoor, public, recreational use" within the meaning of the Land and Water Conservation Fund Act of 1965. Hence,

> [w]hatever limited public access is contemplated by the terms of the proposed amendment to that easement, therefore, must be viewed as nothing less than a bonus to the public, and not as a diminution in, or conversion of, the availability of public, outdoor, recreation facilities.

We agree with the Friends that the district court wrongly decided that the easement lands presently are "not intended for outdoor, public, or recreational use." Rather, in light of the policies of the Department of the Interior and the purposes of the statute, we interpret section 6(f)(3) "public outdoor recreation uses" broadly, to encompass uses not involving the public's actual physical presence on the property. After all, Webster's Third New International Dictionary (1971) defines "recreation" as "refreshment of the strength and spirits after toil," id. at 1899; surely by exposing scenic vistas and serving as a buffer zone between Minnewaska State Park and developed areas, the easement area provides such refreshment. * * *

It is after all a "conservation" fund act. Conservation may include, though it is by no means necessarily limited to, the protection of a present resource in its natural state. Indeed, the Act's stated purposes include "preserving" the "quality" of outdoor recreation resources. 16 U.S.C. § 460*l*–4. The focus on preservation reappears in section 460*l*–9(a)(1), which authorizes allocation of funds for federal acquisitions both to protect endangered and threatened species and also, by reference to section 460k–1, to protect "natural resources."

Thus, contrary to the district court's holding, the easement area presently *is* used for "public outdoor recreation uses," as that term of art was conceived by Congress and has been interpreted by the Interior Department. Having made this determination, we are next faced with the question whether the amendment at issue here constitutes a "conversion" of that easement to other than outdoor, public, recreation uses within the meaning of section 6(f)(3). Though the nature of a conservation easement makes the application of the concept of conversion somewhat elusive, we conclude that the proposed amendment does constitute such a conversion. The property acquired by PIPC through its purchase of the easement was the right to prevent further development of the land underlying the easement. By the proposed amendment, Marriott, the holder of the fee, would be permitted to engage in precisely such development, changing both the character of the land and the population having access to it. By the amendment, in effect, PIPC would convey away its right to prevent any change in the character of the land subject to the easement. The view that such a change constitutes a "conversion" is supported by the Department of the Interior's own practice. In a May 15, 1978 Memorandum, [the pertinent Interior official] defined "conversion" to include instances in which "property interests are *conveyed* for non-public outdoor recreation uses." (Emphasis added.) It is plain that there is a conversion from public enjoyment of an unspoiled area to private golfing.

What is the consequence of this determination? The Secretary, in the words of section 6(f)(3), must determine that the conversion is "in accord with the then existing comprehensive statewide outdoor recreation plan" and grant his approval "only upon such conditions as he deems necessary to assure the substitution of other recreation properties of at least equal fair market value and of reasonably equivalent usefulness and location." These findings may seem simple, but they nevertheless must be made. [The pertinent NPS official who determined that Marriott's plan was not a conversion] did look to these very criteria [but] we cannot assume that he gave them the attention outlined in the above-mentioned Memorandum of May 15, 1978, which instructs regional directors to determine, for example, that "all practical alternatives to the conversion have been evaluated and rejected on sound bases," and that the fair market values of the property to be converted and of the property to be substituted have been established and compared. Thus, though [the pertinent federal official] reviewed the [state's environmental documentation on the project, and] implicitly found that the amended easement was "reasonably equivalent" to the original easement * * * we cannot assume, for example, that he made sure that *all* practical alternatives were considered and rejected (*e.g.*, whether the new golf holes could be built elsewhere on Marriott land), or that he established and compared the fair market values of the original and amended easements. We assume, rather, that [he] would engage in more careful scrutiny before approving a conversion than before determining, as he did here, that his approval was unnecessary.

Here we hold that the amended easement constitutes a conversion to "other than public outdoor recreation uses," 16 U.S.C. § 460*l*–8(f)(3), requiring the Secretary's approval. However, we would require approval by the Secretary in this case even if the Marriott Corporation planned to build a completely public outdoor recreation facility, because such a plan would be inconsistent with the original easement's prohibition of new facilities. Our reasoning runs as follows. The Act requires the Secretary to approve all "planning, acquisition, or development projects" before allocating federal funds. Id. § 460*l*–8(f)(1). It envisions that these "projects" will affect the future of the area acquired, preserving outdoor recreation opportunities for "present and future generations." Id. § 460*l*–4. Consistent with Congress's concern for lasting recreation opportunities, the Secretary approved federal funding for the Minnewaska easement in part because of the plans for the easement area's future—specific constraints on development and guarantees of environmental protection. Consequently, any future change that contravenes these plans retroactively calls into question the basis for the original federal funding. Such a change necessarily requires the Secretary's approval, whether or not the change falls within the Act's definition of a "conversion." Otherwise, the Secretary's initial approval of a "project" extending into the future would be meaningless. Once again, it would not be enough for the Secretary to find that federal approval is unnecessary; while the statutory criteria for approval would not apply to a change from one public use to another, positive approval is still required.

We recognize with Marriott the rather cumbersome process involving a considerable amount of time and effort that undertaking this development has entailed. * * * Unfortunately, or fortunately perhaps, the courts do not control the process, let alone establish it. When one undertakes to develop for private purposes a project involving the use of lands encumbered by a government interest, one's expectations are, or should be, that a certain amount of process and expense will be involved; presumably the anticipated rewards offset the cost and hassle, though surely the ultimate consumer will pay the cost of the benefit the process achieves, or there will be a hole in the developer's pocket. A court is left with the thought that one challenge of the years ahead is to cut down the process, thus lowering the cost, even while preserving the benefit. Meanwhile, the court's duty remains to follow the law as written and intended. * * *

* * * The district court should enter judgment prohibiting amendment of the easement without an appropriate determination by the Secretary as to the effect of conversion.

NOTES AND QUESTIONS

1. Was the court correct in equating "preservation" with "recreation"? How do you define recreation? Are there any realistic limits to such a definition? In Idaho v. Hodel, 814 F.2d 1288 (9th Cir.1987), the Coeur D'Alene Tribe sought forfeiture of a tract of land that had formerly been part of its reservation but then conveyed to the State of Idaho in 1908 to be "held, used, and maintained solely as a public park." The Tribe contended that the State's issuing of leases to private parties for waterfront cottages and permits to maintain float homes on a lake within the park violated the terms of the grant. Rejecting the tribe's claim, the court found that both state and national park managers had historically issued leases for cottages, and noted that while the federal government generally no longer leases cottage sites on its lands, that change in policy does not affect how the 1908 statute should be construed. The court also found persuasive that state courts had traditionally accorded city park commissioners substantial discretion in the administration of public parks, and it emphasized that 99.67% of the land in the park was not encumbered by the contested leases. Judge Reinhardt dissented, arguing that the court should apply "modern day notions of proper public park uses" in interpreting the 1908 grant, and that Idaho's leasing practice "constitutes the privatizing of public lands" and violates the terms of the grant. He also found deference to state park administrators inappropriate because (a) enforcement of federal law is at stake; (b) turning park land over to "private individuals for their exclusive enjoyment and preclud[ing] all public access to prime public lakefront property constitutes a wholly different and far less benign use" of public parkland than was involved in the state cases cited by the majority, and (c) although masked by the small percentage of total park area involved, the state leases effectively denied public access to about half the usable shoreline of the lake.

2. The *Shawangunks* court concedes that the findings it requires of the Secretary "may seem simple." Are they; that is, is this litigation much ado about little? Note that § 6(f)(3) allows conversion only if the Secretary determines it is "in accord with the then existing comprehensive statewide outdoor recreation plan" and only upon "such conditions as [the Secretary] deems necessary to assure the substitution of other recreation properties of at least equal fair market value and of reasonably equivalent usefulness and location." Is the federal approval of the conversion the same as the NEPA process for considering a federal project? Does NEPA apply to the Secretary's determination?

3. What is suitable "mitigation land" here? What would be lost if the Marriott plan is implemented? How does one go about providing a scenic view of a value equal to one lost by development?

4. In the third paragraph from the end (beginning "Here we hold"), is Judge Oakes saying that the Secretary has a continuing responsibility to monitor and approve any changes in land use of any area acquired with Land & Water Conservation Fund moneys, whether or not they remove land from public outdoor recreation uses? 16 U.S.C. § 460l–8(f)(1) says that the Secretary may make LWCF moneys available to the states "only for those planning, acquisition, or development projects that are approved by him." The original "project" approved by Secretary was acquisition of the conservation easement in 1977. If the easement was broadly worded to protect the environment and scenery, does any adjustment of its terms require a new approval from the Secretary?

5. In Sierra Club v. Davies, 955 F.2d 1188 (8th Cir.1992), plaintiffs sought to enjoin test drilling proposed to determine whether commercial mining of diamonds was feasible in the Crater of Diamonds State Park in Arkansas. The parkland had been purchased by the state in 1972, and four years later, it received a LWCF grant to develop the park's recreational facilities, which mainly involved allowing the public to search a diamond-bearing geologic formation for diamonds. Therefore, the Secretary of the Interior had to approve any "conversion" of property developed with these funds to "other than public outdoor recreation uses." LWCF § 6(f)(3). The Park Service initially took the position (relying in part on *Friends of the Shawangunks*) that the test drilling was a "conversion" within the meaning of the Act, and disapproved it because it "could have the potential of progressing into a full-blown commercial diamond mining operation." Following intervention by the Departmental Solicitor's Office in Washington, the Park Service reversed itself and approved the testing as a "temporary non-conforming use," noting that any subsequent testing or mining activity would constitute a conversion. A divided court of appeals reversed a lower court decision and upheld the Department, deferring heavily to its application of the Act. The majority noted that the exploratory drilling would cause no permanent damage and "does not limit public uses of the park, except for the ten-to twelve-week period when a 5000 square foot region will be cordoned off." *Shawangunks* was distinguished because here "no change in the character of the land" would result. A vigorous dissent argued otherwise.

6. The Public Land Law Review Commission recommended that the federal government be "responsible for the preservation of scenic areas, natural wonders, primitive areas, and historic sites of *national significance.*" ONE THIRD OF THE NATION'S LAND, at 197 (1970) (emphasis in original). Is the federal government's role properly limited to areas of "national significance"? Who determines what is nationally significant?

7. The LWCF Act was preceded by the Recreation and Public Purposes Act of 1926, which authorizes the Secretary of the Interior to grant BLM land that lacks "national significance" to states, local governments, and nonprofit corporations "for any recreational or any other public purpose." 43 U.S.C. § 869(a). The Act, not repealed by FLPMA, is subject to several significant limitations; most important, the grant is conditional on the land being used for the purpose specified. If it is not, the grant may revert to the United States. 43 U.S.C. § 869–2. Such grants have been used for everything from landfills and golf courses to urban wilderness parks.

B. Recreation and the National Park System

Conflicts often arise between those desiring solitary, active, non-commercial activities and those preferring more "civilized," sedentary forms of entertainment. See, e.g., Edward Abbey, DESERT SOLITAIRE (1972). For some, just the existence of the federal lands is sufficient; they are content to enter on their own legs, carrying their basic requirements on their backs. They are a minority, perhaps a small minority. Most visitors desire more in the way of creature comforts and the means to let them pursue their more intensive interests. Casual visitors desire centers where someone explains the land's attractions, boaters require ramps, downhill skiers need lifts, motorized vehicles need gasoline, and most want soft beds, good food, and bathrooms with plumbing. The land management agencies often contract with private concessioners to provide such services when consistent with federal policy. This section discusses recreation management in the national park system, focusing substantially on the role and regulation of concessioners.

First, however, it is useful to examine the tension that exists between recreational enjoyment of resources and preservation of those resources for the future, a tension that is captured in the National Park Organic Act.

Joseph L. Sax, Fashioning a Recreation Policy for Our National Parklands: The Philosophy of Choice and the Choice of Philosophy*

12 Creighton L.R. 973 (1979).

A few years ago the National Park Service put forward a proposal for one of the less well-known areas that it manages. It recommended the construction of an aerial tramway to the top of Guadalupe Peak in Guadalupe Mountains National Park, the highest point of elevation in Texas. The plan seemed harmless enough. Guadalupe Peak is a place of considerable scenic merit, the park receives very few visitors, and it is located on the much-travelled road from El Paso to Carlsbad Caverns. Yet the tramway proposal elicited a surprisingly substantial and vehement opposition, and the Park Service soon shelved the plan.

The more one thinks about the Guadalupe incident, the more puzzling it becomes. For in one form or another it is repeated almost daily in the management of the public recreation lands. Should we permit the construction of a ski resort in a relatively pristine mountain valley? Should motor boats be permitted on the Colorado River in Grand Canyon? Should hotels be removed from the parks, or should they remain but without such facilities as swimming pools and tennis courts? These are all only particular instances of a general question that is a great deal more puzzling than it at first seems: What recreational policy ought we to want for the National Parks?

It is customary to believe that controversies of the sort just mentioned revolve around disputes over protection of the parks' natural resources, but a moment's reflection makes clear that environmental or scientific principles are rarely decisive. Every human use impairs the natural setting to some extent and whether a tramway impairs it "too much" is a question of policy, not of science. As with the question whether to build a road, to allow the noise of motorboats and snowmobiles, or even to establish a hiking trail, the issue we are really deciding is what kind of recreation we want to facilitate, and how much intrusion upon the untrammeled ecosystem we are prepared to tolerate for that purpose.

To be sure, some uses are far less disruptive than others, but to say that we want to minimize damage is to restate the problem rather than to solve it. Five hundred visitors a year on the river in Grand Canyon would put a great deal less pressure on the canyon ecosystem than 5,000 or the 15,000 whom we now permit to use it, and there is a great range of opinion on the point at which development, or use, becomes a spoiling factor. Some people don't want motors on wild river trips because they drown out the bird-song; others defend such trips as their only reasonable means of access to the place and find a good deal in the experience even at the expense of some quietude.

Just as these questions cannot be resolved as matters of science, neither can they be decided by economics. Should the Guadalupe Peak tramway have been built in response to public demand? The Park Service estimated that with the tramway, visitations to the Park would have increased from about 60,000 to some 500,000 persons per year. Demand is simply a measure of how people are willing to spend their time and money. No doubt many more people would be prepared to ride up Guadalupe Peak than can, or will, walk it. But just as clearly, there are many people who would patronize gambling casinos, race tracks, elegant restaurants or high rise condominia if we were willing to build them in the parks. There is demand, perfectly legitimate it may be assumed, for all these activities. Yet, at least so far, we have been unwilling to meet that demand in the parks.

Another common view is that parks should be reserved for activities that require the special resources parklands uniquely contain, or that cannot be provided by private enterprise. That position seems to explain why we have traditionally resisted building swimming pools, golf courses and tennis courts in the parks, but it does not adequately respond to the individual who aspires to play tennis in the grand setting of Yosemite Valley rather than to hike there. Nor does it explain whether those who like the solitude and silence of the parks should be preferred to those who find pleasure in a motorized, people-filled tramway or safari down the river. To assert that solitude is the essence of the park experience is to state a preference, not a fact. Each of these experiences is unique in its way, and unavailable in the private market.

Nor, finally, can we avoid the problem by asserting that government should simply hold parklands available and permit each of us to decide for ourselves how to enjoy them. This is another way of describing a policy of variety or diversity. But such a policy can only avoid preferences on the assumption of unlimited abundance. If there were many Yosemite Valleys, we could provide the Yosemite experience as everyone, in his own way, chose it. Of course there are not *many* Yosemites; and though the parks are varied enough to accommodate much diversity, someone—and not each visitor for him or herself—must decide what will happen in the one Yosemite Valley, and the one Grand Canyon, that we do have. It is at these special kinds of places that conflict is at its most intense.

Management decisions must perforce be made, and those decisions themselves imprint an agenda on the landscape. * * * To a significant extent, management decisions effectively determine who the visitors will be, what they will do, and in what numbers, by choices that *must* be made, one way or the other.

To say that none of these management theories is decisive is not to suggest any of them is irrelevant. It is only to say that before we can think usefully about how much natural impairment we should tolerate, or where we want to draw the line in meeting demand, we need to decide what we are trying to achieve by having a public recreation policy.

If it were evident to everyone that the National Parks should be used simply to accommodate a portion of the enormous quantity of leisure time that Americans have to spend, a proposal to build a tramway that could increase recreational opportunities nearly ten-fold with a rather modest impact on the land would not have produced anything like the vigorous outcry it actually elicited. Nor would the familiar controversies over motorized recreation, ski resorts and commercial facilities in the parks have anything like the intensity that is now so evident. Beneath the multitude of specific disputes is a much deeper battle over the question whether park policy should reflect a preference for certain kinds of recreational experiences.

Southern Utah Wilderness Alliance v. Dabney

United States Court of Appeals, Tenth Circuit.
222 F.3d 819.

■ Before SEYMOUR, CHIEF JUDGE, BRORBY and EBEL, CIRCUIT JUDGES.

■ EBEL, CIRCUIT JUDGE.

Plaintiff–Appellee Southern Utah Wilderness Alliance ("Wilderness Alliance") challenged portions of a National Park Service ("NPS") back-country management plan ("BMP") that affected access to areas of Canyonlands National Park in Utah. Wilderness Alliance alleged that the BMP violated * * * [among others] the National Park Service Organic Act ("the Organic Act" or "the Act"), 16 U.S.C. §§ 1–18(j); and the Canyonlands National Park Enabling Act, 16 U.S.C. § 271. Utah Shared Access Alliance ("Utah Shared Access"), a combination of groups supporting four-wheel drive vehicle recreation, intervened as defendants. On cross motions for summary judgment by Wilderness Alliance and the federal defendants, the district court * * * found in favor of Wilderness Alliance on its claim that the BMP's continued allowance of motorized vehicles on a ten-mile portion of the Salt Creek Jeep Road from Peekaboo Spring to Angel Arch was inconsistent with a clear legislative directive of Congress. See Southern Utah Wilderness Alliance v. Dabney, 7 F.Supp.2d 1205, 1211 (D.Utah 1998). * * * [The court] enjoined the NPS from allowing motorized vehicle travel in Salt Creek Canyon above Peekaboo Spring.

Utah Shared Access, the intervenor below, now appeals the district court's decision with respect to the ten-mile portion of the Salt Creek Road. Interestingly, the federal defendants did not appeal the district court's decision; however, they did submit a brief to this court "to advise the Court of the Department's views as to the proper legal construction of the [Organic] Act." In that brief, they take a position different from the position taken in the district court. * * *

In 1992, the NPS began developing a BMP for Canyonlands National Park and the Orange Cliffs Unit of Glen Canyon National Recreation Area in Utah. The goal of that plan as articulated by the NPS was "to develop backcountry management strategies to protect park resources, provide for high quality visitor experiences, and be flexible to deal with changing conditions." The plan was being developed in response to growing visitation to the areas, which had increased the impact on resources and diminished the quality of visitor experience.

One of the areas on which the plan was to focus was the area that is the subject of this appeal, a portion of Salt Creek Canyon. According to the NPS, the Salt Creek Road is a vehicle trail that runs in and out of Salt Creek, the only year-round, fresh water creek in Canyonlands National Park other than the Colorado and Green Rivers. There is no practical way to reroute the road to avoid the water course. To navigate this road safely, a high clearance four-wheel-drive vehicle and some experience in four-wheel driving, or the participation in a commercially guided tour, is necessary. The NPS found that it was receiving numerous requests every year for assistance in removing vehicles that broke down or became stuck on the Salt Creek Road. In addition, there were several instances every year of vehicles losing transmission, engine, or crankcase fluids in the water. The NPS became concerned with the adverse impacts inherent in the existence of a road and vehicle traffic in this narrow riparian corridor. A Notice of Intent to prepare a BMP was printed in the Federal Register. * * * The NPS solicited possible solutions to the problems in the area, and hosted public discussions in Utah and Colorado in late 1992 and early 1993.

* * * [Following publication of a draft environmental assessment, and numerous public meetings, NPS release a final BMP in early 1995 which] adopted an alternative that did not close the ten-mile portion of the Salt Creek Road; instead, it closed a one-half mile segment of the road and left the rest open to vehicles on a limited permit system.[3] Wilderness Alliance subsequently filed a complaint [claiming, among other things, that] * * * by approving the BMP and sanctioning continued vehicle-caused degradation in that area, the NPS violated the * * * the Organic Act, and the Canyonlands National Park Enabling Act. Wilderness Alliance sought declaratory and injunctive relief. Utah Shared Access intervened as defendants, opposing the closure of Salt Creek Canyon to vehicle access.

The * * * [district court] ruled in favor of Wilderness Alliance on its challenge to the portion of the BMP that left the ten-mile segment of the Salt Creek Road from Peekaboo Spring to Angel Arch open to vehicles[, holding] * * * that the Organic Act and the Canyonlands enabling legislation preclude the NPS from authorizing activities that permanently impair unique park resources. It then determined, based on the administrative record, that such a permanent impairment would occur from the continued use by motorized vehicles of this ten-mile segment[, and] * * * enjoined the federal defendants from permitting or otherwise allowing motorized vehicle travel in Salt Creek Canyon above Peekaboo Spring. * * *

* * * When the question before us involves an agency's interpretation of a statute it administers, we utilize the two-step approach announced in *Chevron U.S.A., Inc. v. Natural Resources Defense Council, Inc.,* 467 U.S. 837, 842–43 (1984). When Congress has spoken to the precise question at issue, we must give effect to the express intent of Congress. *See Chevron,* 467 U.S. at 842–43. If the statute is silent or ambiguous, however, we defer to the agency's interpretation, if it is a permissible one. *See id.* at 843–44.

The provision of the Organic Act relating to the creation of the NPS and the purpose of the national parks it oversees provides:

3. The relevant portion of the BMP stated as follows:

Salt Creek and Horse Canyon four-wheel drive roads in the Needles District will remain open to vehicular traffic, but travel will be by backcountry use permit only. A locked gate at the north end of the road (the location of the current gate) will control access. Day use permits for Salt Creek and Horse Canyon will be limited to ten (10) permits for private motor vehicles (one vehicle per permit), two (2) permits for commercial motor vehicle tours (one vehicle per permit), one (1) or more permits for up to seven (7) private or commercial bicyclists, one (1) or more permits for up to seven (7) pack or saddle stock.... All permits are available through the advance reservation system. Unreserved permits or cancellations will be available to walk-in visitors.

> The service thus established shall promote and regulate the use of the Federal areas known as national parks ... by such means and measures as conform to the fundamental purpose of the said parks ... which purpose is to conserve the scenery and the natural and historic objects and the wild life therein and to provide for the enjoyment of the same in such manner and by such means as will leave them unimpaired for the enjoyment of future generations.

16 U.S.C. § 1. Another provision of the Organic Act prohibits authorization of activities that derogate park values:

> The authorization of activities shall be construed and the protection, management, and administration of these areas shall be conducted in light of the high public value and integrity of the National Park System and shall not be exercised in derogation of the values and purposes for which these various areas have been established, except as may have been or shall be directly and specifically provided by Congress.

16 U.S.C. § 1a–1. The enabling legislation creating Canyonlands National Park provides: "In order to preserve an area in the State of Utah possessing superlative scenic, scientific, and archeologic features for the inspiration, benefit, and use of the public, there is hereby established the Canyonlands National Park ..." 16 U.S.C. § 271. That legislation also mandates that Canyonlands be administered, protected, and developed in accordance with the purposes of the Organic Act. *See* 16 U.S.C. § 271d.

In the district court, the NPS asserted that the Organic Act and the enabling legislation creating Canyonlands National Park authorized a balancing between competing mandates of resource conservation and visitor enjoyment, and that its BMP represented a reasonable accommodation of conflicting mandates that should be afforded considerable deference. The district court reviewed the agency's interpretation in accordance with the analysis set forth in *Chevron* * * *. According to the district court, the first *Chevron* inquiry was determinative on the issue of continued vehicle access to the ten-mile portion of the Salt Creek Road. The court stated:

> Congress has issued a clear answer to the question of whether the Park Service is authorized to permit activities within national parks that permanently impair unique park resources. The answer is no. As set out in the statutes discussed above, the Park Service's mandate is to permit forms of enjoyment and access that are *consistent* with preservation and *inconsistent* with significant, permanent impairment.

Southern Utah Wilderness Alliance, 7 F.Supp.2d at 1211. Finding that the evidence in the administrative record showed that "the riparian areas in Salt Creek Canyon are unique and that the effects of vehicular traffic beyond Peekaboo Spring are inherently and fundamentally inimical to their continued existence," the district court held that the BMP was inconsistent with the "clear legislative directive" of Congress. *Id.*

On appeal, Utah Shared Access argues that the district court erred in resolving the issue under the first *Chevron* inquiry. Utah Shared Access argues that the district court should have reached the second *Chevron* inquiry because of ambiguities inherent in the relevant statutes and their application to the issue of vehicular access.[6] We agree.

We first note that the district court erred in its framing of the question at issue for purposes of *Chevron* analysis. The district court characterized the question as whether the NPS is authorized to permit activities within national parks that permanently impair unique park resources. Stating the question that way predetermines the answer. We believe the precise question at issue is whether the BMP, in particular the portion of the BMP allowing vehicle use on the ten-mile segment of the Salt Creek Road from Peekaboo Spring to Angel Arch, is inconsistent with a clear intent of Congress expressed in the Organic Act and the Canyonlands enabling legislation. Framing the question in terms of "permanent impairment" might not necessarily be erroneous if the administrative record clearly showed that such permanent impairment would occur; however, we find that the record is not clear on that issue. *See* discussion *infra*.

The Organic Act mandates that the NPS provide for the conservation and enjoyment of the scenery and natural historic objects and the wildlife therein *"in such manner and by such means as will leave them unimpaired for the enjoyment of future generations."* 16 U.S.C. § 1 (emphasis added). Neither the word "unimpaired" nor the phrase "unimpaired for the enjoyment of future generations" is defined in the Act. It is unclear from the statute itself what constitutes impairment, and how both the duration and severity of the impairment are to be evaluated or weighed against the other value of public use of the park.

Although the Act and the Canyonlands enabling legislation place an overarching concern on preservation of resources, we read the Act as permitting the NPS to balance the sometimes conflicting policies of resource conservation and visitor enjoyment in determining what activities should be permitted or prohibited. *See* 16 U.S.C. § 1 ("to conserve ... and to provide for the enjoyment of...."); 16 U.S.C. § 271 ("to preserve ... for the inspiration, benefit, and use of the public....") [other citations omitted] * * * The test for whether the NPS has performed its balancing properly is whether the resulting action leaves the resources "unimpaired for the enjoyment of future generations." Because of the ambiguity inherent in that phrase, we cannot resolve the issue before us under step one of *Chevron;* instead we must reach step two.

---

6. Utah Shared Access also advances an argument that the Salt Creek Road was "grandfathered" in as a road and cannot be closed because it existed prior to the establishment of the park, and the park was established "subject to valid existing rights." 16 U.S.C. § 271. In support of its argument, Utah Shared Access cites language in the legislative history stating that road access to parts of Glen Canyon National Recreation Area is over jeep trails. *See* H.R.Rep. No. 92–1446, *reprinted in* 1972 U.S.C.C.A.N. 4915, 4916. We find this argument without merit. Utah Shared Access has not established that it had any legally cognizable right to use of this jeep trail at the time of the establishment of this park, or even that this particular portion of the jeep trail existed at that time. In any event, nothing in the statutory language indicates that a jeep trail cannot be closed if closure is deemed necessary for preservation. The legislative history is inconclusive at best on the issue, and thus carries little weight. [citation omitted]

The question for the court under step two of *Chevron* is "whether the agency's answer is based on a permissible construction of the statute." *Chevron*, 467 U.S. at 843. To resolve this question, we must first determine what the agency's position is. In its brief to this court and at oral argument, the NPS has advised us that the Department of the Interior "has conducted a substantive reassessment of the proper construction of the Organic Act." On the basis of that reassessment, the Department took the position in its brief to this court that the Act prohibits "permanent impairment of those resources whose conservation is essential to the fundamental purposes and values for which an individual park has been established." The Department also took the position that the NPS has discretion under the Act to determine what resources are essential to the values and purposes of a particular national park, and what constitutes the impairment of those resources. In supplemental authority provided to this court just prior to oral argument, the Department submitted Draft NPS Management Policies (the "Draft Policies"), which clarify its position further. The Draft Policies address impairment of resources in terms of the duration, extent, timing, and cumulative effect of various impacts on park resources and values. *See* Letter from Department of the Interior to U.S. Dep't of Justice, 1/13/00, at 2, Supplemental Authority of Federal Appellees. They also are based on a premise that the Organic Act forbids broader categories of impairment in addition to those considered as permanent. *See id.* In addition, the Draft Policies provide definitions for various terms in the Organic Act. *See* Draft NPS Management Policies, 1.4.2.

The Draft Policies propose to define "impairment of park resources and values" as "an adverse impact on one or more park resources or values that interferes with the integrity of the park's resources or values, or with the opportunities that otherwise would exist for the enjoyment of them by a present or future generation." *Id.* The Draft Policies also propose to define "park resources and values" as "all the resources and values of a park whose conservation is essential to the purposes for which the area was included in the national park system ... and any additional purposes stated in a park's establishing legislation or proclamation." *Id.*

The interpretation of the Act now offered by the Department and the NPS in this court and in the Draft Policies varies from the interpretation previously offered by the NPS in the district court.[8] We must determine what weight to give the new interpretation. We conclude that there is currently no valid agency position worthy of deference.

An agency is free to change the meaning it attaches to ambiguous statutory language, and the new interpretation may still be accorded *Chevron* deference. As the Supreme Court stated in *Chevron*:

> The fact that the agency has from time to time changed its interpretation of the term "source" does not, as respondents argue, lead us to conclude that no deference should be accorded the agency's interpreta-

---

8. The position adopted in the Draft Policies apparently supplants the former position of the NPS and the Department of the Interior. Thus, the former position is one to which the agency no longer subscribes.

tion of the statute. An initial agency interpretation is not instantly carved in stone. On the contrary, the agency, to engage in informed rulemaking, must consider varying interpretations and the wisdom of its policy on a continuing basis.

Chevron, 467 U.S. at 863–64. A position taken by an agency during litigation, however, is not sufficiently formal that it is deserving of *Chevron* deference. *See* 1 Kenneth Culp Davis & Richard J. Pierce, Jr., *Administrative Law Treatise* § 3.5, at 119–20 (3d ed.1994) (stating that *Chevron* should not be held to apply to agency pronouncements in less formal formats, such as litigating positions); *see also* Robert A. Anthony, *Which Agency Interpretations Should Bind Citizens and the Courts?,* 7 Yale J. on Reg. 1, 60–61 (1990) (stating that an agency's litigating position is not entitled to *Chevron* deference because "[i]t would exceed the bounds of fair play to allow an institutionally self-interested advocacy position, which may properly carry a bias, to control the judicial outcome") (quotations and citations omitted). The agency's litigation position in this court thus lacks the requisite formality for *Chevron* deference under step two.

Similarly, agency policy statements, like litigation positions, do not usually warrant deference under step two of *Chevron. See Christensen v. Harris County,* 529 U.S. 576 (2000) (stating that agency interpretations contained in policy statements, agency manuals, and enforcement guidelines do not warrant *Chevron*-style deference); 1 Davis & Pierce, *supra,* § 3.5, at 120 (stating that courts should not give binding effect under step two of *Chevron* to agency interpretative rules or statements of policy). Policy statements do not normally receive *Chevron* deference because they are usually expressed in an informal format and are not subject to rulemaking procedures. *See* 5 U.S.C. § 553(b) (exempting interpretative rules and general statements of policy from rulemaking procedures); Anthony, *supra,* at 43 (stating that "courts have recognized that an interpretation lacks power to command *Chevron* acceptance if it has been expressed only in an informal format-such as in interpretative rules and policy statements").

A notice of availability of the Draft Policies, however, was published in the Federal Register and the public was given an opportunity to comment on them. *See* Notice of Availability of Draft National Park Service Management Policies, 65 Fed.Reg. 2984 (2000). Thus, the Draft Policies are unlike typical informal agency policy manuals. The fact that a notice regarding the Draft Policies appeared in the Federal Register and that they were subjected to comment procedures does not, however, automatically make them deserving of *Chevron* deference. The comments must still be considered and a rule must be properly adopted with a statement of its basis and purpose to complete the notice and comment rulemaking procedures. *See* 5 U.S.C. § 553(c). If the Draft Policies are finalized and adopted pursuant to the requisite rulemaking procedures, and then construed as substantive or legislative rules, they should be accorded *Chevron* deference; however, if, when ultimately finalized, they lack the requisite formality and are construed merely as interpretative rules, they should be examined under a less deferential standard that asks whether the agency's interpretation is "well reasoned" and "has the power to persuade." *See Chrysler Corp. v. Brown,*

441 U.S. 281, 301–02 (1979) (distinguishing between substantive rules and interpretative rules) [other citations omitted].

At this time, the agency's Policies are still only in draft form and have not yet been finalized or adopted by the agency; therefore, we cannot accord either *Chevron* deference or the lesser deference applicable to interpretative rules to the agency's interpretation of the Act. Having no current interpretation in front of us that has been formally adopted by the agency, we examine the Act and the district court's disposition without giving deference to any agency interpretation. * * *

The district court's legal interpretation of the Act was that the NPS is prohibited from permitting activities that result in "significant, permanent impairment." *Southern Utah Wilderness Alliance,* 7 F.Supp.2d at 1211. We agree that permitting "significant, permanent impairment" would violate the Act's mandate that the NPS provide for the enjoyment of the parks "in such manner and by such means as will leave them unimpaired for the enjoyment of future generations." 16 U.S.C. § 1. Although "significant, permanent impairment" may not be coterminous with what is prohibited by the Act because other negative impacts may also be prohibited, we find that it is within the range of prohibitions contemplated by Congress.

The district court determined that the administrative record demonstrated that permanent impairment would occur; however, the parties continue to dispute whether the impairment caused by vehicles would be permanent and how serious it would be. The administrative record includes the NPS's FONSI, which stated that any impairment would be temporary and minor. In its discussion of the evidence in the administrative record on impairment, the district court did not mention that finding by the NPS, which should be reviewed under the standard set forth in § 706(2) of the APA. *See* 5 U.S.C. § 706(2). Given the conflicting views regarding the level of impairment that vehicles would cause to the ten-mile segment of the Salt Creek Road, we remand for the district court to re-examine the evidence in the record regarding impairment, applying the appropriate standard to the NPS finding of temporary impairment.

On remand, the district court should not limit its analysis under step two of *Chevron* to whether the evidence demonstrates significant, permanent impairment. Rather, it should assess whether the evidence demonstrates the level of impairment prohibited by the Act.[9] Moreover, by the time of trial, the Department of the Interior may have finalized and adopted its new NPS Management Policies. If the district court determines that those policies have been expressed in a binding format through the agency's congressionally delegated power, they should be considered legislative rules worthy of *Chevron* deference. If, however, the district court determines that they are merely interpretative rules, they should be evaluated pursuant to the less deferential standard articulated in * * * *Skidmore v. Swift & Co.,* 323 U.S. 134, 140 (1944).

---

9. As the NPS now acknowledges, the range of impairment prohibited by the Act may be broader than "significant, permanent impairment." *See* Letter from Department of the Interior to U.S. Dep't of Justice, 1/13/00, at 2, Supplemental Authority of Federal Appellees.

Because we find error in the district court's conclusion that the activity at issue is explicitly prohibited by the relevant statutes, we find the district court abused its discretion in granting an injunction. We therefore vacate the district court's order enjoining the BMP's allowance of continued motorized vehicle use on the Salt Creek Road in Salt Creek Canyon above Peekaboo Spring.

The district court erred in finding that step one of *Chevron* was determinative with respect to the issue of vehicle access on the ten-mile segment of the Salt Creek Road. The analysis must proceed under step two of *Chevron,* and, in conducting that analysis, the district court must re-examine the evidence in the record regarding impairment caused by vehicles in that area, applying the appropriate standard to the NPS finding of temporary impairment. The district court must also determine the weight to be given to the position of the NPS as to the standards set forth in the Organic Act. * * *

NOTES AND QUESTIONS

1. Look closely at the language in the Organic Act. Does it call for a balancing between recreational visitor use and preservation? Is one purpose dominant over the other? Or is it ambiguous? In Sierra Club v. Babbitt, 69 F.Supp.2d 1202, 1246–47 (E.D.Cal.1999), environmentalists challenged a Park Service decision to reconstruct a road providing one of the principal means of access into Yosemite National Park, arguing among other things that the project would permanently alter the Merced River canyon in the Park, and thus violate the Organic Act. The court found no violation:

> The Organic Act commits the NPS to the protection and furtherance of two fundamentally competing values; the preservation of natural and cultural resources and the facilitation of public use and enjoyment. These competing values of conservation and public use have been actively in conflict since before the establishment of the NPS. The Organic Act did not resolve the conflict in favor of one side or the other. See Nathan L. Scheg, Preservationists vs Recreationists in Our National Parks, Hastings W.-N.W.J.Envtl.L & Policy, 47 (1998). Rather, the Organic Act acknowledges the conflict and, saying nothing about how to achieve resolution, grants deference to NPS in balancing the competing and conflicting values. * * * The Organic Act would serve as a basis for a cause of action were the NPS to allow use of a national park in a way that was not in the interests of either conservation or public enjoyment or in a way that was clearly against the interests of future generations. The current action does not fall in either category. The current action concerns how best to preserve access to the park while at the same time preserving the values for which the Yosemite valley and the Merced River corridor were declared a national park.

See also Isle Royale Boaters Ass'n v. Norton, 154 F.Supp.2d 1098 (W.D.Mich.2001) (upholding the NPS's general management plan for Isle Royale National Park against a challenge by motorboaters, the court finding that the plan "equally emphasizes use and enjoyment and resource protection"). In Bicycle Trails Council v. Babbitt, 82 F.3d 1445, 1468 (9th Cir.1996), bicyclists sued the National Park Service challenging regulations that restricted the use of bicycles in certain parts of the Golden Gate National Recreation Area in the San Francisco Bay region. The court rejected the challenge, saying, in part:

> Courts have noted that the Organic Act is silent as to the specifics of park management and that "under such circumstances, the Park Service has broad discretion in determining which avenues best achieve the Organic Act's mandate. * * * Further, the Park Service is empowered with the authority to determine what sues of park resources are proper and what proportion of the park's resources are available for each use." [citations omitted] A decision to limit mountain bicycle use to trails affirmatively designated as appropriate for such use falls comfortably within this broad grant of discretion to the Secretary * * *.

2. Is the question what adjective to put in front of "impairment"? "Permanent" or "significant" versus "temporary" or "minor"? Does the Act literally prohibit "any" impairment? Is that a reasonable construction, if it would outlaw many uses visitors routinely make of national parks? Would a "permanent, significant impairment" standard prohibit the Park Service from ever authorizing any new road or building construction in a park? See Robin W. Winks, The National Park Service Act of 1916: "A Contradictory Mandate"?, 74 Denv.U.L.Rev. 575 (1997).

3. Here the district court cited evidence in the administrative record that the riparian areas in Salt Creek Canyon are "unique." Is that relevant? Might every area in every park be considered unique? (Recall the maxim of property law, justifying specific performance in contracts to convey land, that all parcels of land are unique; see 8A Thompson on Real Property, § 4479 (1963).) Does the Organic Act forbid the Park Service from building a road down to the bottom of the Grand Canyon from the South Rim in order to provide vehicular access to its depths?

4. Does the Act's reference to "future generations" provide a clue as to how it should be interpreted? Could, for example, the Park Service say that if a use causes some impairment, but that impairment can be erased within a generation (say, twenty-five years), it may be allowed? Would that be one permissible interpretation of the statute? The only permissible one?

5. If there is a line to draw here, is the court correct in its approach to the agency's rather inconsistent attempts to construe the statute? Might impairment have meant one thing in 1916, when the statute was enacted, and mean something else three quarters of a century later? If public opinion has shifted over that time about how "natural" it wants the parks kept, may the agency properly take that shift in values into account, or must the agency go back to Congress for more guidance? If the agency changes its interpretation of impairment over time, can it still receive the same amount of deference from the courts on its new interpretation as it would have with its original interpretation? If so, why doesn't it get deference here?

6.   Shortly before the Clinton Administration left office in early 2001, the draft policies discussed in the principal case were, after further modification, put in final form in "Director's Order #55: Interpreting the National Park Service Organic Act." The Order is, according the notice in 65 Fed. Reg. 56003 (2000), the Service's "official interpretation" of the 1916 Organic Act and the 1978 amendment, and "[a]ll NPS personnel must conduct their work activities and make decisions affecting the national park system in conformance with the interpretation in this Director's Order." The contents of the Order were published in NPS MANAGEMENT POLICIES 2001, Part 1.4, in December 2000. Excerpts follow:

1.4.2 "Impairment" and "Derogation": One Standard

Congress intended the language of the Redwood amendment to the General Authorities Act[1] to reiterate the provisions of the Organic Act, not create a substantively different management standard. [Legislative history discussion deleted.] * * * For simplicity, [these policies use] "impairment," not both statutory phrases, to refer to that single standard.

1.4.3 The NPS Obligation to Conserve and Provide for Enjoyment of Park Resources and Values

* * * [The Organic Act and the General Authorities Act] give the Service the management discretion to allow impacts to park resources and values when necessary and appropriate to fulfill the purposes of a park, so long as the impact does not constitute impairment of the affected resources and values. * * * The "enjoyment" that is contemplated by the statute is broad; it is the enjoyment of all the people of the United States, not just those who visit parks, and so includes enjoyment * * * by those who appreciate them from afar. Congress, recognizing that the enjoyment by future generations of the national parks can be ensured only if the superb quality of park resources and values is left unimpaired, has provided that when there is a conflict between conserving resources and values and providing for enjoyment of them, conservation is to be predominant. That is how courts have consistently interpreted the Organic Act * * *.

1.4.4 The Prohibition on Impairment of Park Resources and Values

While Congress has given the Service the management discretion to allow certain impacts within parks, that discretion is limited by the statutory requirement (enforceable by the federal courts) that the Park Service must leave park resources and values unimpaired, unless a particular law directly and specifically provides otherwise. This, the cornerstone of the Organic Act, establishes the primary responsibility of the National Park Service. It ensures that park resources and values will continue to exist in a condition that will allow the American people to have present and future opportunities for enjoyment of them.

---

1.   [Eds. The NPS refers to 16 U.S.C. § 1a–1, which contains the so-called Redwood amendment (see p. 387 supra) as part of the General Authorities Act.]

The impairment of park resources and values may not be allowed by the Service unless directly and specifically provided for by legislation or by the proclamation establishing the park * * * [which] must provide explicitly (not by implication or inference) for the activity, in terms that keep the Service from having the authority to manage the activity so as to avoid the impairment.

1.4.5 What Constitutes Impairment of Park Resources and Values

The impairment that is prohibited by [the statutes] is an impact that, in the professional judgment of the responsible NPS manager, would harm the integrity of park's resources or values, including the opportunities that otherwise would be present for the enjoyment of those resources or values. Whether an impact meets this definition depends on the particular resources and values that would be affected; the severity, duration, and timing of the impact; the direct and indirect effects of the impact; and the cumulative effects of the impact in question and other impacts.

An impact to any park resource or value * * * would be more likely to constitute an impairment to the extent that it affects a resource or value whose conservation is:

—Necessary to fulfill specific purposes identified in the establishing legislation or proclamation of the park;

—Key to the natural or cultural integrity of the park or to opportunities for enjoyment of the park; or

—Identified as a goal in the park's general management plan or other relevant NPS planning documents.

* * * Impairment may occur from visitor activities; NPS activities in the course of managing a park; or activities undertaken by concessioners, contractors, and others operating in the park.

1.4.6 What Constitutes Park Resources and Values

The "park resources and values" that are subject to the no-impairment standard include:

—The park's scenery, natural and historic objects, and wildlife; and the processes and conditions that sustain them, including, to the extent present in the park: the ecological, biological, and physical processes that created the park and continue to act upon it; scenic features; natural visibility; natural landscapes; natural soundscapes and smells; water and air resources; soils; geological resources; paleontological resources; archeological resources, cultural landscapes; ethnographic resources; historic and prehistoric sites, structures, and objects; museum collections; and native plants and animals;

—Opportunities to experience enjoyment of the above resources, to the extent that can be done without impairing any of them;

—The park's role in contributing to the national dignity, the high public value and integrity, and the superlative environmental quality of the national park system, and the benefit and inspiration provided to the American people by the national park system * * *

1.4.7 Decision-making Requirements to Avoid Impairments

Before approving a proposed action that could lead to an impairment * * * an NPS decisionmaker must consider the impacts of the proposed action and determine, in writing, that the activity will not lead to an impairment of park resources and values. If there would be an impairment, the action may not be approved. * * * [The] decision-maker must use his or professional judgment [and] consider * * * [NEPA documents] relevant scientific studies, and other sources of information; and public comments.

Whenever an NPS decision-maker becomes aware that an ongoing activity might have led or might be leading to an impairment of park resources or values, he or she must investigate and determine if there is, or will be, an impairment. Whenever practicable, such an investigation and determination will be made as part of an appropriate park planning process * * *. If it determined that there is, or will be, such an impairment, the Director must take appropriate action, to the extent possible within the Service's authorities and available resources, to eliminate the impairment.

NPS's responses to public comments it received on the draft policy included the following (see 65 Fed. Reg.56003–04):

Comment #2: It is virtually impossible to provide opportunities for enjoyment without causing at least some degree of impairment. The NPS should acknowledge this fact and not use the Organic Act as a pretext for curtailing the level of public use and enjoyment allowed in national parks.

Our response: The Organic Act and the General Authorities Act prohibit impairment of park resources and values, not all impacts to park resources and values. We have revised section 1.4 to make that distinction clearer. * * *

Comment #9: The new policy requirement for an "impairment review" by the NPS will be costly, contentious, and burdensome.

Our response: For the past 30 years the NPS has been complying with the requirement of the National Environmental Policy Act that we evaluate the environmental consequences of our proposed actions. We plan to integrate into the NEPA compliance process the new requirement for a determination that there would be no impairment of park resources and values from a proposed activity. We do not expect it to make the management decision-making process appreciably more costly, contentious, or burdensome.

7.   One section of the National Parks Omnibus Management Act of 1998 (which mostly dealt with concession reforms, discussed infra) provided:

The Secretary shall take such measures as are necessary to assure the full and proper utilization of the results of scientific study for park management decisions. In each case in which an action undertaken by the National Park Service may cause a significant adverse effect on a park resource, the administrative record shall reflect the manner in which unit resource studies have been considered.

16 U.S.C. § 5936. Are the Management Policies quoted in the preceding paragraph consistent with this statute? Does this statute reflect a congressional view that the Park Service has authority to take action that causes "a significant adverse effect on a park resource," as long as it does so with its eyes open?

8. Notice the interplay between the statute creating Canyonlands National Park and the generic National Park Organic Act. This kind of overlapping statutory guidance, with more general legislation supplemented by specific legislation applicable to the particular area or unit at issue, is typical in federal land law. Does the former add anything to the latter? On the issue generally, see Robert Fischman, The Problem of Statutory Detail in National Park Establishment Legislation, 74 Denver L.J. 779 (1997).

9. Since the principal case was decided, the pertinent local jurisdiction, San Juan County, Utah, has asserted an RS 2477 claim for the stream bottom. See discussion of that ancient statute in Chapter 2, pp. 161–67 supra.

Grand Canyon river trips are in some ways a microcosm of the challenge of managing recreation throughout the national park system. From John Wesley Powell's famous expedition down the River in 1869 until the mid–1960s, fewer than 1000 persons made the trip by water through the Grand Canyon. Improved technology, a dramatic increase in demand for outdoor adventure, and other factors combined in the mid–1960s to cause an explosion of interest. More than 1000 persons made the trip in the single year of 1966. Use exceeded 10,000 persons in 1971 and 16,000 in 1972, when the Park Service first placed limits on the number. The following case resulted.

Wilderness Public Rights Fund v. Kleppe

United States Court of Appeals, Ninth Circuit, 1979.
608 F.2d 1250, cert. denied, 446 U.S. 982 (1980).

■ MERRILL, CIRCUIT JUDGE:

These cases involve the manner in which use of the Colorado River for rafting and boating is apportioned between concessioners approved by the National Park Service and noncommercial users. Permits from the National Park Service are required for river use and the dispute here concerns the apportionment made in granting permits.

In December, 1972, the Secretary of the Interior found that the boating and rafting use of the Colorado River in the Grand Canyon National Park had experienced such an increase that it posed a threat to the ecology of the river. A study was initiated for the purpose of ascertaining river capacity and it was decided that until completion of the study use of the river should be frozen at the 1972 level. Accordingly, river use was limited to 96,600 user days per year (a user day being one day spent on the river by one person). This total use was apportioned between two user groups in the ratio of actual 1972 use by each group: 89,000 user days or 92 percent of the total use was allotted to commercial concessioners of the Park Service who, for a fee, make guided trips through the canyon; 7,600 user days or 8 percent of the total was allotted to noncommercial users who apply for permits as private groups. Noncommercial users for the most part are experienced in river running and furnish their own equipment and supplies. Expenses are shared, as is the performance of the necessary duties involved. Permits for river use and the apportionment thereof have remained frozen at the 1972 level.

Appellants are, or represent, noncommercial river runners who, on various grounds, challenge the apportionment between commercial and noncommercial users. They assert that they, or those they represent, have applied for permits from the Park Service which were denied, the Service instead having granted permits to persons who used them for commercial purposes. In January, 1975, a member of Wilderness Public Rights Fund petitioned the Secretary for a change in the allocation system for the issuance of permits. The request was denied. [Separate law suits were filed by two different plaintiffs in two different states challenging the Park Service's allocation between commercial and non-commercial permittees. In one, brought by the Wilderness Public Rights Fund in the Northern District of California, the plaintiff argued that noncommercial users are entitled to priority over commercial users. In the other, brought by individuals in the District of Arizona, the plaintiffs argued that noncommercial users should have equal access with commercial users. In both the Park Service was victorious in the lower courts, and the appeals were consolidated.] * * *

A number of statutes and regulations bear on the issues of these actions. 16 U.S.C. § 1 creates the National Park Service (hereinafter NPS) in the Department of the Interior and directs it to "promote and regulate the use of the Federal areas known as national parks, monuments and reservations * * * by such means and measures as conform to the fundamental purpose of said parks, monuments and reservations * * *." That purpose is stated to be "to conserve the scenery and the natural and historic objects and the wild life therein and to provide for the enjoyment of the same in such manner and by such means as will leave them unimpaired for the enjoyment of future generations."

16 U.S.C. § 3 provides in part:

"The Secretary of the Interior shall make and publish such rules and regulations as he may deem necessary or proper for the use and management of the parks, monuments, and reservations under the jurisdiction of the National Park Service * * *. He may also grant privileges, leases, and permits for the use of land for the accommodation of visitors in the various parks, monuments or other reservations [herein provided for] but for periods not exceeding thirty years; and no natural curiosities, wonders, or objects of interest shall be leased, rented, or granted to anyone on such terms as to interfere with free access to them by the public * * *.''

Pursuant to this authority the Secretary has promulgated 36 C.F.R. § 7.4(h)(3) as follows:

"(3) No person shall conduct, lead, or guide a river trip unless such person possesses a permit issued by the Superintendent, Grand Canyon National Park. The National Park Service reserves the right to limit the number of such permits issued, or the number of persons travelling on trips authorized by such permits when, in the opinion of the National Park Service, such limitations are necessary in the interest of public safety or protection of the ecological and environmental values of the area.''

The Concessions Policy Act, 16 U.S.C. § 20 provides in part: "It is the policy of the Congress that such development [concessions] shall be limited to those that are necessary and appropriate for public use and enjoyment of the national park area in which they are located * * *.''

* * * Appellants contend that allocation between commercial and noncommercial use of the river is not an acceptable method of accomplishing a limitation of river use. They propose that anyone wishing to run the river should apply for a permit, leaving to him, if his application be granted, the choice between joining a guided party or a noncommercial party; that permits then be granted by lottery or on a first-come-first-served basis. They assert that the record establishes that such a method is feasible. They contend that there is no justification for allocating between commercial and noncommercial use, and that to do so amounts to arbitrary action; that it denies them "free access" to the river contrary to 16 U.S.C. § 3 and permits development by concession to a degree in excess of that allowed by the Concessions Policy Act. We disagree.

The Secretary of the Interior, acting through the NPS, has the wide ranging responsibility of managing the national parks. 16 U.S.C. § 3. Pursuant to this authority, the NPS regulates use of the Colorado River through the permit requirement described in 36 C.F.R. § 7.4(h)(3), supra. In issuing permits, the Service has recognized that those who make recreational use of the river fall into two classes: those who have the skills and equipment to run the river without professional guidance and those who do not. The Service recognizes its obligation to protect the interests of both classes of users. It can hardly be faulted for doing so. If the overall use of the river must, for the river's protection, be limited, and if the rights of all are to be recognized, then the "free access" of any user must be limited to the extent necessary to accommodate the access rights of others. We must confine our review of the permit system to the question whether the NPS has acted within its authority and whether the action taken is arbitrary. Allocation of the limited use between the two groups is one method of assuring that the rights of each are recognized and, if fairly done pursuant to appropriate standards, is a reasonable method and cannot be said to be arbitrary. It is well within the area of administrative discretion granted to the NPS.

Throughout these proceedings Wilderness Public Rights Fund has persisted in viewing the dispute as one between the recreational users of the river and the commercial operators, whose use is for profit. It asserts that by giving a firm allocation to the commercial operators to the disadvantage of those who wish to run the river on their own the Service is commercializing the park. The Fund ignores the fact that the commercial operators, as concessioners of the Service, undertake a public function to provide services that the NPS deems desirable for those visiting the area. 16 U.S.C. § 20a. The basic face-off is not between the commercial operators and the noncommercial users, but between those who can make the run without professional assistance and those who cannot.

While the Concessions Policy Act, 16 U.S.C. § 20, supra, expresses the congressional intent that the granting of concessions shall be limited to "those that are necessary and appropriate for public use and enjoyment" of the park involved, the authority for the granting of concessions is given to the Secretary by 16 U.S.C. § 3, and there is no showing here of arbitrary action or abuse of that authority.

Appellants also complain that noncommercial applicants receive unfair and unequal treatment at the hands of the Service. They must apply to the Service for permits and thus must plan their trips well in advance. Deadlines must be met. The names of all in the proposed party (with signatures) must be set forth. Those who make the trip under guide may deal directly with the concessioners and make arrangements at the last minute. This comports with the NPS' right to regulate river trips in the interests of safety. 36 C.F.R. § 7.4(h)(3). We find nothing unreasonable in thus assuring, as matter of safety, that those who make the trip on their own without concessioners' supervision have undertaken the necessary preparation and possess the necessary skill to participate in the activities involved.

We conclude that allocation between the two classes of recreational users is not per se an arbitrary method of recognizing and accommodating the interests of the two classes. The question remaining is whether allocation has been fairly made pursuant to appropriate standards. * * *

Appellants challenge the method used by the Park Service in determining allocation between the classes of users for the reason that it is founded on 1972 data. It is asserted that since that year there has been a substantial increase in the demand for use by noncommercial users, and that to freeze allocation of use on the basis of seven-year-old data in the face of rapid change is arbitrary and unreasonable.

We are informed, however, that the study initiated by the National Park Service has now been completed and that the interim basis for allocation between the two classes of users—freezing at the 1972 level—is being abandoned. A proposed management plan for the river and a draft environmental impact statement have been completed and published. The allocation departs from the 1972 level of 92 percent user days for commercial operators and 8 percent user days for noncommercial river runners. Under the plan, 70 percent of the user days will be allocated for commercial trips and 30 percent for noncommercial trips. The period assigned for comment has expired and it is anticipated that a final plan will be forthcoming in a matter of weeks.

This renders moot challenges to the specifics of the interim management plan, now about to be superseded by a final plan. The basis for the claim of arbitrariness—that the freezing of use and allocation of use at the 1972 levels is, in 1979, unreasonable—falls from the case.

NOTES AND QUESTIONS

1. Examine 16 U.S.C. § 3, quoted in the opinion. Does this give the Park Service plenary authority to require permits and otherwise regulate visitor conduct? Where in 16 U.S.C. §§ 1 or 3 does the Park Service find authority either (a) to limit the total number of raft trips; or (b) to allocate trips between commercial and non-commercial users? By issuing concession contracts to rafting companies, and limiting others, is the agency making a grant of "natural curiosities on such terms as to interfere with free access * * * by the public" (expressly forbidden by 16 U.S.C. § 3)? Does "free" mean "free" in the same sense that the TAPS case read "50 feet" to mean "50 feet"? See Wilderness Society v. Morton, Chapter 4, supra p. 311.

2. The court did not rule on the split of 92% for commercial uses and 8% for non-commercial. Is that the kind of decision that should be left completely up to the agency? Or is this specific allocation so extreme that a court should require an especially strong administrative record and a compelling explanation in support of the decision?

3. Is allocation on the basis of "historical use" always rational? Are there other, better bases? Is the Park Service's legal obligation to ascertain and then meet the "public demand" for outdoor recreational experiences? Cf. Sax, supra p. 943. At least in areas of unique or scarce scenic or aesthetic resources like here, is some sort of rationing system inevitable?

4. What might be the Park Service's interest in encouraging commercial as opposed to non-commercial trips? Health and safety—risk management? Protecting the environment? Revenues? Could the Park Service ban *all* non-commercial trips? What would it need to show in order to do that? In Great American Houseboat Co. v. United States, 780 F.2d 741 (9th Cir.1986), the court rejected an equal protection attack on a Forest Service regulation banning commercial (under a time-sharing scheme) but not individual use of houseboats on a recreational lake: "The commercial/personal use distinction served the legitimate statutory purpose of allowing the Forest Service to regulate and accommodate multiple uses on Shasta Lake and to avoid overcrowding * * * and a degrading of the quality of the recreational experience there." 780 F.2d at 748. See also United States v. Garren, 893 F.2d 208 (9th Cir.1989).

5.   Many persons who travel through the Grand Canyon on the river do so on craft powered by small outboard motors. In the late 1970s, a controversy briefly raged when the Park Service considered banning motorized trips. Motor trips are about twice as fast through the entire Grand Canyon as oar-powered trips (8 versus 16 days, approximately) and are also about half as expensive (because the cost to the visitor is measured mostly by time on the river). Park Service studies have generally shown that, so long as the carrying capacity of the river corridor is not exceeded, the only environmental difference between the two kinds of trips is the (relatively modest) noise of the motors; i.e., all other impacts are basically the same. May the Park Service ban motors to provide a quieter river experience, even if that tends to put these trips beyond the reach of middle class people? Do the statutes provide any clue to answering that question, or is it a policy judgment for the agency that the courts should not interfere with? (The Park Service has established a "no-motors" period for a few weeks just after the peak summer season, but otherwise has not moved to ban motors.)

6.   Is it relevant to the "oars/motors" controversy, or to the "commercial/private" dispute, that the rafting experience in the Grand Canyon is not entirely "natural"? The Colorado River in the Grand Canyon has been much manipulated by the Glen Canyon Dam upstream. The dam captures much of the sediment that formerly gave the River its eponymous red color. The water is not only usually clear but cold, a uniform 48 degrees Fahrenheit as released from bowels of Lake Powell behind the dam, compared to pre-dam temperatures as high as the 70s or even 80s in low flow periods. (The temperature change has substantially altered aquatic life in the Canyon.) Finally, the dam has evened out the flows to a much more dependably uniform level, which has also facilitated the growth of the rafting industry. Mankind is increasingly manipulating nature practically everywhere federal lands are found, sometimes by design, sometimes inadvertently. How should that fact inform how those lands should be managed where the goal is to provide a "natural" recreational experience, or to preserve them (as addressed in the next chapter)?

RECREATION MANAGEMENT: YOSEMITE AND GRAND CANYON

The National Park Service's efforts to accommodate heavy visitor use demands while safeguarding the amenities of one of the Nation's flagship national parks has been much watched, debated, and, inevitably, litigated. The basis of the litigation has not, however, been the National Park Organic Act, but rather NEPA and the Wild & Scenic Rivers Act. The following are excerpts from Judge [Charles] Breyer's opinion in Sierra Club v. United States, 23 F.Supp.2d 1132 (N.D.Cal.1998) which lay out the facts and policy choices made by the NPS. The Wild & Scenic Rivers Act issues are discussed in the next chapter, see pp. 1081–1104, infra.

The National Park Service describes Yosemite as a "premiere masterwork of the natural world." Any change to this masterwork should only take place after there has been strict compliance with all applicable environmental laws. It is in this context that plaintiff Sierra Club asks the Court to halt implementation of Phase One of the Yosemite Lodge Area Development Plan in Yosemite National Park. * * *

In January 1997, the Merced River in Yosemite Valley overflowed its banks during a severe flood. This flooding caused substantial damage to buildings in the Yosemite Lodge area, located near the base of Yosemite Falls. Fifty percent of the public lodging facilities and one hundred percent of employee housing were damaged or destroyed.

In response to the flood damage, the National Park Service ("NPS") quickly developed a plan to construct new lodge facilities nearby so that it could continue to accommodate the same number of overnight visitors in the area. In addition to proposing the new facilities, the NPS set out to make other structural changes that it believed would improve the visitor experience in the Yosemite Lodge area.

The present layout of the lodge area is as follows: the accommodations that comprise Yosemite Lodge lie just to the north of the Merced River. Most of the cabins or buildings lie within the 100–year floodplain of the river, many of which were damaged in the January 1997 flood. Just north of Yosemite Lodge lies Northside Drive, which provides access to the area for both daytime and overnight visitors. Adjoining Northside Drive is a parking lot for cars and tour buses. Further north is the trailhead which begins the hike to Upper Yosemite Falls, approximately 3.5 miles away. Visitors have a view of the falls from the lodge area, although this view is impeded somewhat by the lodge facilities, parking lots, and cars proceeding along Northside Drive.

The lodge development plan crafted by NPS in the wake of the floods envisions substantial structural changes in the area. First, NPS seeks to remove the damaged lodging facilities from the floodplain. Rather than reconstruct the facilities in the same location, where they would remain exposed to potential flood damage, the Park Service seeks to construct new facilities—284 motel rooms, 96 cottage rooms, and 60 cabins—to the north of the current location of Northside Drive, which falls outside the floodplain. In turn, the plan calls for Northside Drive and its adjoining parking lots to be re-routed to the south, closer to Merced River. The Park Service's stated purpose for re-routing the road is to improve views of Yosemite Falls and move traffic further away from the new lodge facilities. Much of the new Northside Drive would be built in the area where the flood-damaged buildings currently rest.

NPS conceived the lodge development plan in the context of the ongoing park-wide planning process that has been in motion for almost 20 years. This process began with the adoption of the 1980 General Management Plan ("GMP"), which [was accompanied by an EIS and called, among other things, for removal of] * * * lodging facilities from the Merced River floodplain to avoid potential damage to those facilities. * * *

NPS adopted another major planning document in 1992—the Concession Services Plan ("CSP") [also accompanied by an EIS]. The CSP amended the GMP, reducing the number of overnight visitors that the GMP sought to accommodate in the park, and * * * [w]ith respect to the Yosemite Lodge Area, * * * reiterated that facilities would be removed from the floodplain and envisioned construction of new facilities elsewhere. However, the type, number, and location of these new facilities were not specified. * * *

In 1996, NPS initiated the Valley Implementation Plan ("VIP"), which seeks to implement the broad directives of the GMP and CSP by detailing, on a site-specific basis, the development projects with respect to visitor accommodations throughout the park. The Park Service decided that it was necessary to conceive these site-specific proposals in the course of one large, park-wide planning process in order to ensure that the overall impact of development within the park could be adequately monitored. The VIP has not yet been completed; the Park Service envisions that a draft will be submitted for public comment some time in the next few months. As with prior park-wide planning documents, the VIP will be accompanied by an Environmental Impact Statement.

Development activities pertaining to the Yosemite Lodge area were originally included in the VIP. However, in the wake of the flood, NPS determined that it needed to expedite the construction process in order to accommodate the number of visitors envisioned in the previous park-wide planning documents. Therefore, it separated the lodge area from the VIP process and crafted the Yosemite Lodge Area Development Plan on an individual basis.

In April 1997, less than four months after the flood, NPS drafted an Environmental Assessment, which set forth an initial version of the plan. In July 1997, NPS issued a Finding of No Significant Impact ("FONSI") which determined that an Environmental Impact Statement was not required for the project. In response to public comments, NPS issued a modified FONSI, which sets forth the lodge development plan as described above.

[The court later, in a footnote, discussed the lodge development plan in relation to the GMP and CSP, as follows:] It is by no means clear that the lodge development plan is wholly consistent with the GMP and CSP. * * * [W]hile there is no language in the GMP that explicitly precludes the lodge development plan at issue in this case, the document certainly did not contemplate any construction project in the area—or anywhere else in the park for that matter—with any degree of specificity. It merely discussed, in general terms, the kinds of services and accommodations, and the number of lodging facilities, that would be maintained in various areas throughout the park.

An examination of the CSP * * * also reveals that the type of project envisioned by the lodge development plan was not specifically contemplated. Unlike the GMP, the CSP does specify that new construction would take place in the Yosemite Lodge area * * * [but] also states, however, that "[c]reating new disturbance in the valley to relocate lodging structures is not acceptable." *CSP* at 73. Defendants explain that this statement indicates an unwillingness on the part of NPS to initiate construction on "undisturbed areas," and assert that much of the proposed development will take place on "previously disturbed and moderately degraded" woodland. However, defendants concede that the lodge development plan would cause 1.2 acres of previously undisturbed mixed conifer forest to be developed, and admit that this portion of the plan is inconsistent with the CSP. In light of this inconsistency, as well as the general terms in which the GMP and CSP addressed development in the Valley, it is not clear that the lodge development plan is consistent with prior park-wide planning documents. [end of footnote]

* * * The GMP and CSP lay out the goals of the Park Service with respect to the park in very broad terms. * * * However, neither document specifies how, when, or precisely where * * * construction [of facilities] would occur.

The court went on to issue a preliminary injunction to halt phase 1 of the lodge development plan, finding that plaintiffs had showed a substantial likelihood of success that they would succeed on their NEPA claims that the NPS had "failed to consider the cumulative impact of the lodge development plan, as well as several reasonable alternatives to that plan * * *."

NOTES AND QUESTIONS

1.   The NPS went back to fix its NEPA documentation and eventually produced a final master plan that has provoked continued controversy, this time mostly from people (including the local Member of Congress, who promptly introduced legislation to stop its implementation) who object to the removal of some visitor facilities from the Valley. The dimensions of the debate were captured in letters to the New York Times in January 2002. An opponent argued, among other things, that "[r]emoving a few hundred campsites, cabins and parking spaces would not result in a significant increase in the area available for nature," visitor demand for car-accessible Valley accommodations is very heavy, and that cabins "are the most affordable accommodation for middle-class families." A plan supporter argued that it would still leave 500 campsites in the Valley, and that visitors should "remember Yosemite for its waterfalls and vibrant meadows and not for its gridlock and asphalt."

2.   In Sierra Club v. Lujan, 716 F.Supp. 1289 (D.Ariz.1989), the court preliminarily enjoined the NPS from proceeding with construction of a hotel complex at the North Rim of the Grand Canyon. The proposal apparently violated both the master plan for the Park and NEPA, in that the decision was made before an EA was prepared, and sites outside of the Park were not considered. More than 99% of the Grand Canyon National Park is unroaded and has no developed visitor facilities. Nearly all the four million people who have visited the Park annually in recent years have

concentrated in a small area along the South Rim of the canyon. Much the same is true of Yosemite; the vast majority of visitors and visitor facilities are in the Yosemite Valley, which is a tiny fraction of the Park's 700,000 acres. About 95% of Yosemite Park is in wilderness. In these situations, should the Park Service attempt to diminish and disperse the crowds that congregate in these choice places by building or upgrading roads and providing new visitor facilities in what are now more remote regions of the Park? Or should the wilderness qualities of large areas of these parks be preserved? Is the answer to limit visitor use, a solution that is political anathema? Or is the problem in some of these places, as former Secretary of the Interior Babbitt was fond of saying, not too many people, but too many cars? If so, is the answer to require visitors to leave their cars (and provide lodging) at the periphery of the Parks, and use mass transit?

3. Does the Organic Act allow the Park Service to decide to provide *no* visitor facilities in some of its units? In the Gates of the Arctic National Park and Preserve, one of the largest park units at almost 8 million acres (about the size of Connecticut and Massachusetts combined), and located north of the Arctic Circle in northern Alaska, the Park Service has decided to provide no developed visitor facilities. Visitors may go there (and may hire private guides), but they are on their own.

4. Rationing recreational access at the other end of the use intensity spectrum also causes legal disputes. There are no roads to Alaska's spectacular Glacier Bay, and 80% of the park's visitors arrive on large, thousand-passenger cruise ships. The Park Service has for a couple of decades regulated the entry and activity of cruise ships and other vessels in Glacier Bay. The regulations are crafted in part to address endangered species concerns regarding humpback whales and Steller sea lions. NPS's 1984 Vessel Management Plan allowed 107 cruise ship entries per season. As demand continued to increase and cruise lines built ever more and larger ships, in the early and mid–1990s the NPS went through a public process of revising its VMP, accompanied by an environmental assessment that looked at alternatives including reducing as well as increasing entries, and ultimately decided in 1996 to increase the entry by 30% for the succeeding two years, with the possibility of further increases if certain conditions were met. Concluding that "Glacier Bay Park is too precious an ecosystem for the Parks Service to ignore significant risks to its diverse inhabitants and its fragile atmosphere," the court in National Parks & Conservation Ass'n v. Babbitt, 241 F.3d 722, 731, 739 (9th Cir.2001), held that a full EIS should have been prepared under NEPA because of "the high degree of uncertainty and the substantial controversy regarding the effects" of the increase on the environment, and enjoined any increase in cruise ship entry until one was completed. Should the NEPA threshold be lowered for proposals that could affect "precious ecosystems" like the "crown jewels" of the national park system?

5. Should there be hunting, fishing, and trapping in the national parks? National Rifle Ass'n v. Potter, 628 F.Supp. 903 (D.D.C.1986) upheld a Park Service regulation outlawing hunting and trapping in all units of the national park system except where specifically ordained by Congress.

The opinion reviewed the history of Park Service policy toward hunting and trapping, and concluded (628 F.Supp. at 912):

> The Secretary and the Park Service have been charged by Congress with the responsibility for achieving the sometimes conflicting goals of preserving the country's natural resources for future generations while ensuring their enjoyment by current users. Notwithstanding his recent predecessors may have permitted hunting and trapping in selected park areas of their choosing, the present Secretary has re-examined the subject in the light of recent amendments to the Organic Act and has concluded that his primary management function with respect to Park wildlife is its preservation unless Congress has declared otherwise. The regulation thus issues rationally from that conclusion, and if relief is to be forthcoming, plaintiff must look to Congress for it, not the courts.

6. A symposium on the National Park System containing several useful articles is found at 74 Denver U.L.Rev. 567–874 (1997).

C. NATIONAL RECREATION AREAS

With dramatic growth in recreation use on most federal lands in the last few decades, and with the rise of the modern environmental movement, increasing amounts of federal land, including much land formally subject to multiple use management (by the U.S. Forest Service and the BLM), are being managed primarily for recreation and conservation purposes. Congress has confirmed this trend by legislatively designating many areas of federal land primarily to serve recreational and conservation purposes. These statutes overlay and modify the underlying statutory management framework, whether it is multiple use or something else.

Congress has put a rather dizzying variety of different formal labels on such areas, such as national recreation areas, national conservation areas, special management areas, protection areas, scenic areas, and the like. The statutes are collected in various places, mostly in volume 16 of the U.S. Code. For convenience, we here lump them together under the generic heading of National Recreation Areas, or NRAs.

The areas covered by this category include ones that have varying proportions of federal ownership, and may be managed by the BLM, the Park Service, or the Forest Service. They may be small and urban or large and rural or many shades in between. All they basically have in common is that their management is primarily for conservation and recreation use, and to that end, use of the land and associated resources is subject to restrictions based on these area-specific federal statutes, as well as generic laws. Because conservation and recreation are so closely aligned in these statutes, the inclusion of the discussion in this chapter, rather than in the preservation chapter that follows, is somewhat arbitrary.

There is no overarching "organic act" for this category of federal land, but the individual area statutes tend strongly to have a number of features in common (with some differences as they are tailored to local conditions). They generally (a) require the area to be managed to serve dominant conservation and/or recreational uses; (b) withdraw the lands involved from the Mining Law and the mineral leasing acts; (c) ban or severely restrict timber harvesting; and (d) may place some restrictions on grazing. (Some other uses may be allowed to the extent the agency finds them consistent or compatible with these dominant purposes.) Often the legislation calls for the agency involved to set the details of the management through a formal planning process (which will include such standard features as public participation, NEPA compliance, and, if appropriate, ESA consultation). These statutes do not entirely displace the underlying generic laws that otherwise apply. Thus an NRA in a national forest is still subject to the National Forest Management Act; one in the national park system is still subject to the Park Service Organic Act, etc. But to the extent there is a conflict between the area-specific statute and the generic one, the specific one controls. Thus, for example, while livestock grazing may be subject to relatively broad U.S. Forest Service management discretion on ordinary national forest lands, the agency's discretion may be more sharply circumscribed in a national recreation area.

The largest chunk of lands in this category is found under the formal label of National Recreation Areas. The first NRA was created by Congress in 1964 around Lake Mead, formed by Hoover Dam on the lower Colorado River. Many of the other early NRAs were also established around large reservoirs constructed by the federal government both in the Colorado River Basin (e.g., Flaming Gorge NRA, 1968; Glen Canyon NRA, 1972); and elsewhere (e.g., Whiskeytown–Shasta–Trinity NRA, 1965; Bighorn Canyon NRA, 1966; Hells Canyon NRA, 1975). There are "gateway" recreation areas in the New York City and San Francisco Bay Areas, where scattered federal parcels (much of it formerly military land) have been cobbled together to provide urban open space, very heavily used, under National Park Service management. Golden Gate National Recreation Area Act, 16 U.S.C. §§ 460bb to 460bb–5; Gateway National Recreation Area, 16 U.S.C. §§ 460cc–2. The designation has proved popular enough to be extended, as of this writing, to more than three dozen areas, many of them not associated with reservoirs and some of them embracing mostly nonfederal land. (The statutes are collected beginning at 16 U.S.C. 460n.)

Other even more recent congressional inventions are the National Conservation Area (e.g., 16 U.S.C. § 460ccc—Red Rock Canyon in southern Nevada); the National Riparian Conservation Area (e.g., 16 U.S.C. § 460ddd—Gila Box in Arizona); and the Outstanding Natural Area (e.g., Yaquina Head in Oregon, 43 U.S.C. § 1783). Many of these are on BLM lands. In fact, the Nation's first NCA protected an area of BLM land, the King Range, along the northern California coast. See 84 Stat. 1067, codified at 16 U.S.C. § 4604. Adopted near the dawn of the modern environmental movement in 1970, the King Range NCA legislation contained an early expression of dominant use conservation management. Its history is also fairly typical: The area was first protected from disposal by an executive withdrawal, in 1929, and the congressional designation first encompasses about 25,000 acres, but has since been expanded to include 60,000 acres of isolated beaches and rugged mountains (rising to more than 4000 feet only three miles from the Pacific).

On national forest lands, Congress has used a variety of labels like special management areas (e.g., Greer Spring, Missouri, 16 U.S.C. § 539h), recreation management areas (e.g., Fossil Ridge, Colorado, 16 U.S.C. § 539i), protection areas (e.g., Bowen Gulch, Colorado, 16 U.S.C. § 539j), scenic areas (e.g., Columbia River Gorge, Oregon–Washington, 16 U.S.C. § 544–544m), scenic-research areas (e.g., Cascade Head, Oregon, 16 U.S.C. § 541); scenic recreation areas (e.g., Opal Creek, Oregon, 16 U.S.C. § 545b), national scenic areas (e.g., Mount Pleasant, Virginia, 16 U.S.C. § 545); national forest scenic areas (e.g., Mono Basin, California, 16 U.S.C. § 543); and national preserves (Valle Caldera, New Mexico, 16 U.S.C. § 698v).

Because all these areas have been individually established by Congress in legislation, they have relative permanence. Congress has also authorized executive branch agencies to put protective management (and a protective label) on areas of federal land. For example, the Federal Land Policy and Management Act of 1976 authorizes the Secretary of the Interior to designate areas of BLM-managed public land as "areas of critical environmental concern" and to give them "priority." See 43 U.S.C. §§ 1702(a); 1711(a). These are subject to modification or abolition without further action by Congress.

The general management standard for NRAs (albeit with some variation from statute to statute) resembles to some extent the "dominant but not exclusive use" idea behind the "compatibility" test applied on national wildlife refuges. A question emerging with increasing frequency, here as well as in the refuges, is how the test should be applied, and what process should be used to make compatibility decisions. The next case is one of the few judicial explorations of legal issues concerning NRAs. *Caveat*: While most statutes designating NRAs have some features in common, there is no "organic" or generic NRA Act, and at bottom the individual statutes are like snowflakes—no two seem to be identical.

Oregon Natural Resources Council v. Lyng

United States Court of Appeals, Ninth Circuit, 1989.
882 F.2d 1417.

■ TROTT, CIRCUIT JUDGE.

[Plaintiff environmental groups sued to enjoin a Forest Service timber sale in a portion of the Hells Canyon NRA (HCNRA) and also sought an order requiring the Forest Service to promulgate regulations under the HCNRA Act.]

The Hells Canyon National Recreation Area was established by Congress in 1975. It encompasses 652,488 acres of land in Eastern Oregon and Western Idaho, most of which had been managed under the National Forest System. This land, which includes the deepest gorge in North America and the seventy-one mile segment of the Snake River between the Hells Canyon Dam and the Oregon–Washington border, became the Hells Canyon National Recreation Area. The specified purpose of the HCNRA Act is "[t]o assure that the natural beauty, and historical and archeological values" of this area "are preserved for this and future generations, and that the recreational and ecologic values and public enjoyment of the area are thereby enhanced...."[1] 16 U.S.C. § 460gg(a).

The Act requires the Secretary to develop a "comprehensive management plan" ("CMP") that provides for a "broad range of land uses and recreation opportunities" in the HCNRA. 16 U.S.C. § 460gg–5. In accordance with NEPA, and after consulting with a large number of federal, state and local agencies, elected officials, and private organizations, the forest service prepared an Environmental Impact Statement ("EIS") to aid in formulating the CMP. The EIS, issued in May of 1981, identifies key issues and concerns pertinent to the management of the HCNRA and proposes seven alternative plans for managing the area. The CMP, finalized in 1984, designates "Alternative C" as the HCNRA management plan. This alternative allocates the HCNRA to seven land-use classifications. Twelve percent of HCNRA land, including the Duck Creek area at issue in this appeal, is designated as "dispersed recreation/timber management." This designation permits timber management but requires it to be consonant with providing "ample opportunities for dispersed recreation." Permissible timber management activities include salvage cutting and the harvest of between five and nine million board feet of timber each year.

In November of 1981 a violent storm toppled many trees in the HCNRA. During the following two summers bark beetles attacked storm-felled Engelmann Spruce trees in the Duck Creek area. By the summer of 1984, the bark beetle population had begun to attack standing green trees. The voracious beetles had infested virtually all large Engelmann Spruce trees in the Duck Creek area by the summer of 1987. Health and life

---

1. Section 7 of the HCNRA Act provides a more detailed description of the Act's objectives:

[T]he Secretary shall administer the recreation area in accordance with the laws, rules, and regulations applicable to national forests for public outdoor recreation in a manner compatible with the following objectives:

(1) the maintenance and protection of the freeflowing nature of the rivers within the recreation area;

(2) conservation of scenic, wilderness, cultural, scientific, and other values contributing to the public benefit;

(3) preservation, especially in the area generally known as Hells Canyon, of all features and peculiarities believed to be biologically unique including, but not limited to, rare and endemic plant species, rare combinations of aquatic, terrestrial, and atmospheric habitat, and the rare combinations of outstanding and diverse ecosystems and parts of ecosystems associated therewith;

(4) protection and maintenance of fish and wildlife habitat;

(5) protection of archeological and paleontologic sites and interpretation of these sites for the public benefit and knowledge insofar as it is compatible with protection;

(6) preservation and restoration of historic sites associated with and typifying the economic and social history of the region and the American West; and

(7) such management, utilization, and disposal of natural resources on federally owned lands, including, but not limited to, timber harvesting by selective cutting, mining, and grazing and the continuation of such existing uses and developments as are compatible with the provisions of section 460gg to 460gg–13 of this title.

16 U.S.C. § 460gg–4.

departed from the Duck Creek area, which held an estimated twenty million board feet of dead and dying Engelmann Spruce timber by early 1988. Because Engelmann Spruce is a soft white wood that deteriorates quickly, salvage value of this specie declines rapidly after the year of infestation.

The Forest Service responded to the bark beetle epidemic, which has spread to other areas of the HCNRA, by preparing a site-specific "Environmental Assessment" ("EA") for the Duck Creek area. This EA, issued in February of 1988, identifies issues and opportunities related to the beetle problem and considers six alternative methods of managing the Duck Creek area's beetle-infected spruce. These methods range from taking no action to harvesting fifteen million board feet of timber. The EA designates "Alternative F" as the preferred alternative. On April 3, 1988, Robert Richmond, Supervisor of the Wallowa–Whitman National Forest, approved this alternative and concluded that its implementation would not have a significant impact on the quality of the human environment.

Alternative F calls for the harvest of approximately six million board feet of beetle-threatened, beetle-infected and dead trees from the Duck Creek area. The harvest is to be accomplished by cable logging and helicopter systems in order to protect wet areas and soils on steep ground and to avoid having to build a road system in the large, "unroaded" section Duck Creek. The proposal leaves nearly sixty percent of the damaged timber unharvested in wildlife and visual areas and in riparian no-cut zones. The sawlog volume removed will postpone or defer cutting of an equal amount of volume on lower priority timber stands. Alternative F also requires that spruce "stringers" in a particular section of the Duck Creek area be left unharvested so as to protect elk habitat and migration.

[The timber was sold two days after this suit was filed. After initially granting a TRO against the logging, the trial court found for the defendants and dissolved the injunction, and the court of appeals refused to reinstate it pending appeal. In part II of the opinion, the court found that the agency had adequately complied with NEPA on the sale, and that the plaintiffs had not shown that the sale would violate the Clean Water Act or the state of Oregon's water quality standards.] * * *

Appellants allege that the timber sale violates the HCNRA Act in two respects. First, they state that section 8(f) of the Act limits timber harvesting to areas where such activity was occurring at the time of enactment. Second, they assert that section 10 of the Act compels the Secretary to promulgate regulations governing when, where, and how certain activities, including timber harvesting, may occur in the HCNRA.

[The district court had found plaintiffs barred from raising the § 8(f) claim by laches and failure to exhaust administrative remedies. It ruled against plaintiffs' § 10 claim on the merits. Without passing on the correctness of the first ruling, the court of appeals went directly to the merits on both claims.] * * *

* * * Section 8 is entitled "Management plan for recreation areas." 16 U.S.C. § 460gg–5. Section 8(f)[9] must thus be interpreted as part of a Congressional effort to describe the process by which the CMP is to be developed, the issues it must consider, and what may occur in the HCNRA while the CMP is under preparation. If section 8(f) is read in the context of section 8 as a whole, it becomes evident that section 8(f) addresses only that period of time between passage of the Act and development of the CMP and is not relevant to the Duck Creek Timber sale. Appellants argue that the legislative history of the Act supports their interpretation of section 8(f). Their arguments appear to have little force. Because the statute is clear on it[s] face, however, we need not be concerned with legislative history in interpreting its scope. * * *

We now turn to appellants' second contention, that section 10 of the Act directs the Secretary to promulgate regulations governing certain activities, including timber harvesting, in the HCNRA. In the almost fourteen years since enactment of the HCNRA Act, the Secretary has not promulgated any rules and regulations. This court has concluded that it would not be consistent with the overall purpose of the HCNRA Act, protection of the HCNRA, to interpret section 10 as stripping the Secretary of his general regulatory authority over the HCNRA, leaving him without power to act until he promulgates regulations under section 10. See United States v. Hells Canyon Guide Service, 660 F.2d 735, 737–38 (9th Cir.1981). If other regulations already apply to an activity in the HCNRA, we will not view section 10 as invalidating those regulations and requiring the Secretary "to take an additional, in fact, a redundant, affirmative step before he would be able to take *any* action to protect an area placed under his supervision." Id. at 738.

Thus, the question we must answer is whether section 10 compels the Secretary to promulgate the regulations it describes when those regulations would not be duplicative of other rules already in effect in the HCNRA. We respond to this question in the affirmative. The language and legislative history of section 10 clearly reveal an intent to create a mandatory duty to promulgate regulations in the specified categories.

Section 10 reads:

The Secretary shall promulgate, and may amend, such rules and regulations as he deems necessary to accomplish the purposes of section 460gg to 460gg–13 of this title. Such rules and regulations shall include, but are not limited to—

(a) standards for the use and development of privately owned property within the recreation area, which rules or regulations the

---

9. Section 8(f) reads:

(f) Continuation of ongoing activities[.] Such activities as are as compatible with the provisions of sections 460gg to 460gg–13 of this title, but not limited to, timber harvesting by selective cutting, mining, and grazing may continue during development of the comprehen-

sive management plan, at current levels of activity and in areas of such activity on December 31, 1975. Further, in development of the management plan, the Secretary shall give full consideration to continuation of these ongoing activities in their respective areas. 16 U.S.C. § 460gg–5.

Secretary may, to the extent he deems advisable, implement with the authorities delegated to him in section 460gg–6 of this title, and which may differ among the various parcels of land within the recreation area;

(b) standards and guidelines to insure the full protection and preservation of the historic, archeological, and paleontological resources in the recreation area;

(c) provision for the control of the use of motorized and mechanical equipment for transportation over, or alteration of, the surface of any Federal land within the recreation area;

(d) provision for the control of the use and number of motorized and nonmotorized river craft: *Provided*, That the use of such craft is hereby recognized as a valid use of the Snake River within the recreation area; and

(e) standards for such management, utilization, and disposal of natural resources on federally owned lands, including but not limited to, timber harvesting by selective cutting, mining, and grazing, and the continuation of such existing uses and developments as are compatible with the provisions of sections 460gg to 460gg–13 of this title.

16 U.S.C. § 460gg–7. Judge Panner perceived the phrase "as he deems necessary" to indicate that section 10 leaves the decision regarding whether to issue regulations to the Secretary's discretion. We do not believe that, read as a whole, the language of the section supports this view. The first sentence directs the Secretary to promulgate regulations but seems to limit that mandate to rules the Secretary decides are necessary to accomplish the purposes of the Act. The second sentence, however, extends that mandate beyond the confines of the Secretary's discretion to specific types of regulations. This interpretation makes grammatical sense. In both the first and second sentences of section 10 the predicate nominative of the word "shall" is "rules and regulations": "shall" describes the Secretary's relationship to the regulations. * * *

Such legislative history as exists supports our interpretation of section 10. The House Report on the HCNRA Act states that section 10 "directs the Secretary to promulgate regulations needed to accomplish the intent of the legislation. Specific regulation [sic] are to include...." House Committee on Interior and Insular Affairs, H.R.Rep. No. 94–607, 94th Cong., 1st Sess. 12, reprinted in 1975 *U.S.Code Cong. & Admin. News* 2281, 2286. And the Senate Report, which summarizes section 10 by subsection rather than as a whole, also states that the Act "directs" the Secretary to promulgate the specified types of regulation. See [Sen.] Rep. No. 94–153, 94th Cong., 1st Sess. 8 (1975).

We thus find that section 10 compels the Secretary to promulgate nonduplicative regulations of the sort described by subsections 10(a) through 10(e). In addition, the Secretary has discretion to issue additional regulations that he deems necessary to accomplish the purposes of the Act. Section 10(e) mandates regulations for timber harvesting by selective cutting on federally owned lands. We therefore reverse the district court's ruling on the regulation issue and remand for issuance of an order directing the Secretary to promulgate the regulations required by section 10.

It is conceivable that had the regulations been issued they would have affected the Duck Creek timber sale. This fact would ordinarily cause us to ask the district court to determine whether the Secretary's failure to issue the relevant regulations requires that the Duck Creek sale be enjoined. Given that timber harvesting in the Duck Creek area resumed in late April, however, such a request might be pointless. We therefore ask the district judge to consider the necessity of an injunction only if the Duck Creek harvest has not been completed on the date this opinion is filed. * * *

NOTES AND QUESTIONS

1. Is this a "recreation" area statute or a "conservation" area statute? Is the emphasis on both, or is conservation the dominant purpose? If yes, is the label in the statute a misnomer? A harmless one?

2. Is the same kind of compatibility judgment called for by § 7 of the HCNRA (reproduced in footnote 1 of the court's opinion) as is applied in wildlife refuges? See Chapter 10, pp. 873–87. Is determining what is compatible with recreation easier or more difficult than determining what is compatible with wildlife? Does each call for a scientific judgment or a policy or political one?

3. Apart from the order to prepare regulations, would the result have been any different here if this area had not been an NRA, but rather been subject to the multiple use/sustained yield standard that applies to most national forest land? Does § 7(7) of the Act give the Forest Service authority or direction to regulate hardrock mining activities more stringently than it does on ordinary national forest land? Could it, consistent with the Act, withdraw the entire NRA from the Mining Law? Prohibit all surface mining? Oust all livestock grazing? Sell no timber?

4. Did the court too quickly reject the plaintiffs' argument that section 8(f) of the HCNRA (quoted in footnote 9) prohibits expansion of timber harvesting into areas where it was not occurring when the HCNRA was enacted? The subsection allows continuation of timber harvesting (where compatible with the purposes of the HCNRA) *in areas of such activity* when the Act was passed, and directs the Secretary to give "full consideration" to allow them to continue *in their respective areas*. Doesn't that at least permit an inference that timber harvesting is not allowed outside such "areas"?

5. Why do you suppose the Secretary had not prepared the regulations required by § 10 of the Act in the fourteen years it had been on the books? Should that failure have been sufficient ground to enjoin this sale? If the sale had not been to salvage dead, rapidly deteriorating timber, should it have been enjoined? In a previous case noted in this opinion (see p. 986, infra, discussing United States v. Hells Canyon Guide Service, Inc.), the Ninth Circuit had upheld the Forest Service's application of its generic

regulations to a river guide service in Hells Canyon, notwithstanding the agency's failure to promulgate specific regulations dealing with the HCNRA. See also Hells Canyon Preservation Council v. United States Forest Service, 883 F.Supp. 534 (D.Or.1995) (relocation of road now in a wilderness area).

6. In October 1989, after the decision of the court of appeals here, the Forest Service adopted regulations governing Hells Canyon NRA. Among other things, they provide that timber shall be managed to "perpetuate healthy stands of diverse tree species and size and age classes and to emphasize stand condition, scenery, wildlife habitat, and recreation needs." Clearcutting is prohibited unless its use would "mitigate the situation" where timber has been "damaged by fire, insect, disease, or wind." 36 C.F.R. § 292.43(d) (2001). If these regulations had been in place when the principal case was litigated, what outcome?

7. Although mining is a prohibited or disfavored use in most if not all of these areas, mining issues occasionally arise. The statute creating the first NRA at Lake Mead provides that the area (which is managed by the Park Service) is to be administered generally for recreation, but that the Secretary may permit other specific uses (grazing, "mineral leasing," and vacation cabin sites) "to such extent as will not be inconsistent with * * * the recreational use" or with reservoir operation. 16 U.S.C.A. § 460n–3. The Act did not define the "minerals" that could be leased. The court in Sierra Club v. Watt, 566 F.Supp. 380 (D.Utah 1983), upheld as a reasonable interpretation of this statute an agency regulation allowing leasing of minerals in the NRA that would otherwise be locatable under the Mining Law. We have seen some other examples; for example, Swanson v. Babbit (p. 237, supra) both raised issues of the power of Congress to cut off patenting under the Mining Law of 1872 in national recreation area legislation.

8. In all of these great national land management systems, there is a tension between the value of having readily understood, uniform laws and policies that apply across the entire system, and the value of being able to tailor laws and policies to local conditions. The National Park System, for example, is now a sprawling empire that embraces many different kinds of units: the crown jewel national parks, national battlefields, seashores, monuments, historic sites, recreation areas, and the like. In 1970 and 1978 Congress enacted legislation that the Park Service took as a direction to bring more uniformity to the system. Its implications were explored in Bicycle Trails Council of Marin v. Babbitt, 82 F.3d 1445 (9th Cir.1996), where the court addressed plaintiffs' several challenges to the Park Service's limitation on the use of bicycles in the Golden Gate National Recreation Area in California's Bay Area. One of the arguments was that the Park Service had wrongfully decided to move toward a uniform policy throughout the national park system, that all lands were closed to bicycle use unless specifically opened. The court rejected the challenge, and in the process explained the old and new policies and the reasons behind the change:

In 1964, NPS at its own initiative implemented a management by categories scheme by which units of the National Park System would be classified "natural," "historical," or "recreational,"[1] and by which management policies would be formed so as to regulate these three types of units in conformity with their differing classifications. The effect of this scheme would be, *inter alia,* that recreational units would be managed in a less restrictive and less resource-protective manner than units classified natural or historical. Under this scheme, NPS in 1966 decided to alter its longstanding policy regarding bicycle use in park units from one wherein all trails were closed unless designated open to one in which the old rule generally applied except in units classified as recreational, in which trails would be presumed open to bicycle use unless designated closed by the local park superintendent.

By a series of amendments to the National Park Service Organic Act, 16 U.S.C. sections 1 et seq., Congress disapproved of this management by categories scheme and directed that all units of the national parks were to be treated consistently, with resource protection the primary goal, while retaining the flexibility for individual park units to approve particular uses consistent with their specific enabling legislation. Thus, NPS eliminated these management categories from its internal administration in 1978 and ultimately began promulgating regulations in the 1980's eliminating these categorical distinctions from the Code of Federal Regulations.[3]

---

1. The "recreational" management category was an internal administrative construction and was not necessarily coextensive with those units that Congress in enabling legislation had named "Recreation Areas." However, GGNRA was both named a "Recreation Area" in its enabling legislation, 16 U.S.C. section 460bb, and deemed a recreational unit under NPS's taxonomy.

3. For example, in 1982 NPS proposed regulations effecting substantial changes to the general Park Service regulations and noted:

A major effect of this rulemaking is the elimination of the management categories from Parts 1 through 3 of the Code of Federal Regulations. Secretary of the Interior Udall recognized, in a letter to the Director, that the National Park System was comprised of three broad categories—natural, historical and recreational, and that certain principles for guidance in resource management, resource use and physical developments of each category should be developed. Based upon these principles, the National Park Service developed a series of Administrative Policies for each category which served as guidelines for park management for a number of years.

One application of these guidelines was incorporation of the management categories in regulations established to control certain park uses. In general, these regulations reflected a feeling that public use could, in some instances, be less restricted in areas within the recreation category.... Since 1964, changes in the composition of the National Park System have been extensive. Each unit must now be given more individual attention in planning and management to ensure the legislative mandates and policy requirements are met. As a consequence, broad management categories are no longer effective tools to deal with many of these issues, and the National Park Service has determined that their use should be terminated.

47 Fed.Reg. 11598 (March 17, 1982).

When this change was adopted as a final rule, NPS repeated much of the above language, responded to comments regarding the elimination of these categories, and further noted that it was abolishing these categories in response to what it interpreted as a specific directive from Congress. 48 Fed.Reg. 30252, 30252–53 (June 30, 1983).

The 1987 regulation, adopted pursuant to notice and comment, established a uniform rule for national park units wherein all bicycle use of off-road areas would be prohibited unless local park superintendents designated particular trails to be open. (As noted, this had previously been the rule in all but the recreation units.) Local park officials determined that they would not enforce this rule in the GGNRA until it was determined which trails would be open and which closed to bicycle use. Thus, because of NPS's and the GGNRA Superintendent's exercise of prosecutorial discretion, the 1987 regulation was not enforced and bicyclists in fact retained access to all trails in the GGNRA pending the development of a trail use plan. Finally, after a long and contentious trail designation process, the 1992 trail plan was adopted (also pursuant to notice and comment) establishing which trails were to be open to bicycles and which trails were to be closed. * * *

Plaintiffs challenge the legality of the regulation on the theory that it is not based upon a permissible interpretation of the Organic Act. This challenge fails. A review of the Organic Act and the history of its amendments shows that NPS based its decision to eliminate the reference to management categories (and thus to eliminate the special "recreation" unit rule) in the 1987 regulation on a mandated and certainly permissible construction of the Organic Act and its amendments.

In response to congressional amendments to the Organic Act, NPS in 1978 began phasing out its usage of the "management categories" that had been earlier developed to allow for the different treatment of different classes of units in the National Park System. In the 1980's, NPS began eliminating such distinctions in its regulations. NPS interpreted Congress's amendments to the Organic Act to be clear in the message that NPS was not to single out a particular class of units of the park system (i.e. recreational units) for less protective treatment, but that instead NPS was to manage all units of the park system so as to effect the purpose of the Organic Act-primarily resource protection. *See* 48 Fed.Reg. 30252 (June 30, 1983); *Michigan United Conservation Clubs v. Lujan,* 949 F.2d 202 (6th Cir.1991); *National Rifle Assn. v. Potter,* 628 F.Supp. 903 (D.D.C.1986).

The 1987 amendment to section 4.30 was part of a rulemaking whose purposes included "to eliminate the remaining references to the management categories formerly used to classify park areas." 52 Fed.Reg. 10670. Formerly, regulations promulgated in 1966 had provided that in "historic" or "natural" park units, off-road trails and areas were "closed-unless-designated-open" for bicycle use, while in "recreational" units off-road trails and areas were "open-unless-designated-closed" for bicycle use. 36 C.F.R. section 2.30 (1967 ed.), moved to 36 C.F.R. section 4.3 (July 1, 1977 ed.). The new section 4.30 results in a "closed-unless-designated-open" status for off-road areas in all park units.

9.   Another example of a court integrating special legislation adopted for a particular area with general legislation applicable across an entire

land management system is Sierra Club–Black Hills Group v. U.S. Forest Service, 259 F.3d 1281 (10th Cir.2001). Congress created the Norbeck Wildlife Preserve in 1920, and the Forest Service manages, as part of the Black Hills National Forest, 28,000 of the Preserve's 35,000 acres. At issue were timber sales the Forest Service authorized in the Preserve, and how to mesh the National Forest Management Act's mandate regarding overall species diversity with the narrower statutory mandate of the Norbeck Preserve, "for the protection of game animals and birds and * * * as a breeding place thereof." 16 U.S.C. § 675. The court directed the Forest Service to reconsider the sales because the agency "cannot apply the NFMA mandate in a way that effectively abolishes the specific statutory mandates Congress has established" in the Norbeck Organic Act. Because the latter "requires the protection of game animals and bids, not the overall protection of all plant and animal species," the agency "must justify the proposed timber harvests not by showing that optimal diversity is served generally, but by showing specifically that game animals and birds are protected." Dissenting Judge Ebel would have found enough ambiguity in the Norbeck Act to justify deferring to the Forest Service's judgment. If there were a clearcut choice on the facts between promoting overall species diversity and promoting habitat for game, which side should environmental organizations be on?

D. MANAGING RECREATION ON FEDERAL LANDS: A POTPOURRI OF ISSUES

RECREATION FEES

In the Land and Water Conservation Fund Act, Congress limited the authority of federal land management agencies to charge fees for recreational access to many federal lands, 16 U.S.C. § 460*l*–6a. See, e.g., Wilkenson v. Department of the Interior, 634 F.Supp. 1265 (D.Colo.1986) (statute prohibits charging entrance fees for residents traveling roadway through national monument and not using it for recreational purposes); United States v. Maris, 987 F.Supp. 865 (D.Or.1997) (merely driving through national forest area was not recreational "use" subject to user fee).

The last few years have, however, seen a revolution in recreation fee policy on federal lands. Where federal land management agencies have had authority to charge entrance, campground, and other fees, they had little incentive to do so. Under longstanding federal law, any moneys collected had to be deposited into the federal treasury and could not be spent by the agencies directly, because the agencies could only spend money appropriated by Congress. In 1996, with support from the Clinton Administration (looking for ways to meet the management burdens associated with burgeoning growth in federal land recreation demand), the Congress adopted a recreational fee demonstration program. (Pub. L. 104–134, section 315) (amended and extended every year since, the latest being 115 Stat. 466 (2001)). Its key feature allows federal agencies to retain 100% of the recreation fees they generate, "without further appropriation," with 80% to stay at the particular unit where they are collected. The funds are to be used for "backlogged repair and maintenance projects (including projects relating to health and safety) and for interpretation, signage, habitat or facility enhancement, resource preservation, annual operation (including fee collection), maintenance, and law enforcement relating to public use." See 115 Stat. 466, § 312(c)(1); (c)(3). Congress also provided that the amounts collected "shall not be taken into account" in allocated revenues under various federal laws, including the Land & Water Conservation Fund Act. *Id.* § 312(d)(1). The idea is that the funds generated shall not be used to offset appropriations under other laws. Fees set under this demonstration program presumably must be set according to the general criteria under the Land & Water Conservation Fund Act, which provides that fees are to be

> fair and equitable, taking into consideration the direct and indirect cost to the Government, the benefits to the recipient, the public policy or interest served, the comparable recreation fees charged by non-Federal public agencies, the economic and administrative feasibility of fee collection and other pertinent factors. * * * It is the intent of this Act that comparable fees should be charged by the several Federal agencies for comparable services and facilities.

16 U.S.C. § 4601–6a(d). The latest authorization extends the Recreational Fee Demonstration Program through Fiscal Year 2003. *Id.* § 312(f).

The four principal land management agencies collected $180 million in recreation fees in fiscal year 1998, doubling the number collected before the program began two years earlier. The agencies are using the fees to reduce maintenance backlogs and provide enhanced public services. Visitor surveys show the vast majority believe the fee acceptable, especially when it was explained that most of the money was used at the site. Visitorship continued its steady increase, and, interestingly, vandalism decreased at many recreation areas once they began charging fees. Of course, the amount of fees collected varies widely with the popularity of the particular land management unit, and other factors. Grand Canyon National Park collected $21 million in fiscal 1998, and Yosemite $14 million; together they accounted for about 1/6 of the total collected at more than 300 demonstration sites. The money is being spent on things ranging from new signs and brochures to campgrounds and sanitation facilities. Grand Canyon had planned to use the revenues to help build a light rail system to relieve traffic congestion at the south rim, but this proposal was halted by Congress in late 2000.

QUESTIONS

1. Should recreationists "pay their own way" as a matter of principle? Some opponents of recreation fees argue they are a form of "dual taxation," because general tax revenues are also use to manage federal lands. Can miners or loggers or ranchers make the same argument about fees charged for their activities?

2.   Should fees be set at "fair market value"? Or should they be set high enough to cover all costs of land management? If less than the latter, why should recreation be subsidized? Is it because the market value is low or difficult to ascertain and the administrative burden of charging fees substantial? Because recreation may have a limited impact on the land-scape?

3.   Should fees be charged for activities that tend to cause more significant impact, such as camping, but not for activities of a more casual nature, such as hiking? Or for activities that cost more to maintain, like campgrounds with associated sanitation facilities or boat launch facilities?

4.   Some fear that over time, Congress will eventually reduce appropriated funds for federal land management agencies as they become more successful in generating revenue through fees. This would make agencies more reliant on visitors for funding, and the concern is expressed that this will give the agencies a powerful incentive to attract visitation (on the theme park model), even if it is at the expense of sound resource management. Is there any way to prevent that from happening, while still allowing agencies to charge fees and retain the revenues?

5.   Litigation is beginning to emerge about how to define "recreational activity" subject to the fee. See, e.g., United States v. Siart, 178 F.Supp.2d 1171 (D.Or.2001) (rejecting argument for nonpayment of fee that defendant visited the Oregon Dunes National Recreation Area not for recreation but for "professional reasons-i.e., to check on snowy plover habitat and the impact of a potential federal predator control project on that habitat").

RECREATION CONCESSIONS: THE NATIONAL PARK SERVICE

The legislation authorizing the world's first national park, Yellowstone, authorized the leasing of portions of the park for "the erection of buildings for the accommodation of visitors." 17 Stat. 33 (1872). Early leaders and promoters of the national park system sought to promote tourism to the parks as a way to build a constituency—public support—for the agency and its mission. Stephen Mather, first director of the National Park Service, said that "[s]cenery is a hollow enjoyment to a tourist who sets out in the morning after an indigestible breakfast and a fitful sleep in an impossible bed." Dennis J. Herman, Loving Them to Death: Legal Controls on the Type and Scale of Development in the National Parks, 11 Stan. Envtl. L. J. 3, 3 (1992). Roads, railroads, grand hotels, and other developments to facilitate visitation and provide creature comforts were encouraged, often in places and ways deemed unacceptable by today's tastes. See, e.g., Alfred Runte, NATIONAL PARKS: THE AMERICAN EXPERIENCE ch. 5 (1979).

The strategy worked; the agency's public support is wide and deep, but there has been a cost in terms of overuse of developed areas and deterioration of park facilities and in some cases the parks themselves. What are parks for—private profit, public use, or both? Is there an inherent conflict between the two? In National Parks & Conservation Ass'n v. Kleppe, 547 F.2d 673, 676 (D.C.Cir.1976) (addressing how much disclosure the Freedom of Information Act requires of financial data submitted to the Park Service by concessioners), the court observed:

> Concession activity in the national parks is a thriving business which is becoming increasingly dominated by large corporate concessioners. The relationship between the Park Service and the park concessioners is long-standing and has been fostered in large measure by various financial incentives aimed at maintaining the quality and continuity of goods and services available to park visitors.

Some concessions in federal recreation areas are indeed big business. The largest as of 1989 was the Yosemite Park & Curry Co., with gross receipts of nearly $83 million, followed by the Vail Corporation on the White River National Forest in Colorado and AMFAC Hotels & Resorts on the south rim of the Grand Canyon, at $53 million each. About half of the hundred largest federal recreation area concessions, measured by gross revenues, were ski areas (considered immediately below); many of the rest were in the crown jewel national parks. See General Accounting Office, Federal Lands: Improvements Needed in Managing Concessioners (June 1991), Appendix V. But there are also much smaller, mom and pop concessioners as well, including sole practitioner outfitters and guides. On the latter, see Arthur D.Smith, Outfitting on Public Lands: A Study of Federal and State Regulation, 26 Idaho L.Rev. 9 (1989). Some of the concessioners are effectively monopolies, and regulated by the federal agencies in a fashion similar to other "natural" monopolies like electrical utilities. Other concessioners are directly in competition with each other; e.g., nearly two dozen separate companies are licensed by the National Park Service to operate commercial river trips through the Grand Canyon.

Early on, the National Park Service offered "financial inducements to private contractors to convince them to provide and operate facilities in what were often remote locations." Amfac Resorts v. U.S. Dept. of the Interior, 282 F.3d 818 (D.C.Cir.2002). A preference for renewal, so long as "full and satisfactory service to the public had been given," was one of these inducements. *Id.* The 1965 National Park Service Concessions Policy Act wrote the preference into law, directing the Secretary to "give preference in the renewal of contracts * * * to the concessioners who have performed their obligations * * * to the satisfaction of the Secretary." 79 Stat. 969, 970. Over the years, this preferential right of renewal came to be seen as drastically limiting competition and entrenching existing concessioners in place regardless of performance. Following many years of effort, with strong bipartisan support, Congress in the fall of 1998 finally enacted a sweeping overhaul of the Concessions Policy Act of 1965. The changes were intended to further competition in the award of concession contracts and to ensure a better return to the government and better service for park visitors. For all but the smallest concessioners, this new Act ends, prospectively, the preferential right of renewal. In Amfac Resorts v. U.S. Dept. of the Interior, 282 F.3d 818 (D.C.Cir. 2002), the court rejected the concessioners' attempt to interpret the repeal as ineffective. See also Chapter 3, supra p. 282.

Capital improvements (such as hotels) constructed by park concessioners on federal land in the parks are the property of the United States. But concessioners have been recognized to have a monetary interest in facilities they construct pursuant to the concession contract, so that if the contract expires or is terminated, they are entitled to receive from their successor concessioner, or the government, the value of this so-called "leasehold surrender interest." Disagreement between key members of Congress over how much of a lease surrender interest to recognize in concession contracts (when an existing concessioner loses the bid for a new contract, how much of the loser's investment in facilities should the winner have to pay?) nearly doomed the 1998 Act, but a last minute compromise paved the way to enactment by providing more specificity in the administration of these interests. The National Park Service's regulations to implement these its changes were generally upheld against concessioner attack in *Amfac Resorts*, supra. The 1998 legislation, dubbed the National Parks Omnibus Management Act of 1998, 16 U.S.C. §§ 5901–6011, also makes a number of other important changes in concession policy, provides for science-based management of the system, sketches out a process for studying the addition of new units to the national park system, and authorizes a passport program for park visitors.

RECREATIONAL CONCESSIONS: THE U.S. FOREST SERVICE AND SKI AREAS

The most revenue-producing type of federal land recreational concession is downhill skiing. Nearly all of the major ski areas in the West, and many in the East, are located at least partially on national forest land. For general background, see Richard A. Lovett, The Role of the Forest Service in Ski Resort Development: An Economic Approach to Public Lands Management, 10 Ecology L.Q. 507 (1982). Until 1986, the Forest Service authorized these areas under an awkward "dual permit" arrangement.

The original 1897 Organic Act gave the Forest Service general authority to make rules and regulations governing occupancy and use of the forests. 16 U.S.C. § 551. The Forest Service often used this authority to regulate by permit such activities as livestock grazing (Light v. United States and United States v. Grimaud, supra pp. 107–10) and ancillary activities on mining claims (e.g., United States v. Rizzinelli, supra p. 619). In 1915 Congress enacted a separate law that specifically authorized the Forest Service to issue permits for recreational facilities. 16 U.S.C. § 497. This law capped permits at 80 acres in size and thirty years in duration, and did not provide for exclusive occupancy; i.e., it forbade "preclud[ing] the general public" from enjoying the forests. The legislative history of the 1915 Act suggested congressional awareness of the agency's authority to issue revocable permits for recreational developments under the 1897 Act.

Eventually, the Forest Service evolved a system it applied to most of the 200 ski areas found on the national forests—the operator would receive a base 80 acre permit for the lodge and related facilities, and a revocable permit under the 1897 Act for the other several hundred acres typically required. At the dawn of the modern environmental movement, one of the

Sierra Club's first uses of the courts challenged the legality of this arrangement in a highly publicized dispute over a proposal by Walt Disney Productions for development of the beautiful Mineral King valley in the southern Sierra Nevada range in California.

In Sierra Club v. Hickel, 433 F.2d 24 (9th Cir.1970), the court upheld the "dual permit" approach, rejecting the Club's argument that the acreage and term limits of the 1915 Act prevented the agency from using the 1897 Act. It found, among other things, that Congress had been made aware of the practice, and that its widespread use by the agency was "convincing proof of [its] legality."* The court's approach here might be contrasted with that of the D.C. Circuit in Wilderness Society v. Morton (TAPS), supra p. 312; and the Fourth Circuit in West Virginia Div. of Izaak Walton League v. Butz (Monogahela clearcutting), supra p. 713; both of which enforced antiquated statutory language, in effect remanding the issue to Congress. In fact, the D.C. Circuit in the TAPS case briefly addressed and distinguished the Ninth Circuit decision in the Mineral King case. See 479 F.2d at 869–870. The D.C. Circuit later followed the Ninth Circuit view on "dual permitting" for ski areas in Wilson v. Block, 708 F.2d 735 (D.C.Cir. 1983), distinguishing the TAPS case.

Even though no court had invalidated the "dual permit" scheme for ski areas, sufficient nervousness remained—especially given the ski industry's large investments undertaken on the shaky foundation of "revocable" permits—that Congress was eventually persuaded to enact the National Forest Ski Area Act of 1986, 16 U.S.C. § 497b. This Act removed the acreage limit on term permits for ski areas, extended the ordinary maximum term to 40 years, and allowed for renewal. But it also allowed permits to be cancelled by the Secretary of Agriculture on various grounds, such as upon a determination in forest plans "that the permitted area is needed for higher public purposes." Similarly, the Secretary can modify permits "from time to time * * * to accommodate changes in plans or operations in accordance with the provisions of applicable law." Permittees must also pay a fee "based on fair market value in accordance with applicable law." Existing "dual permit" facilities were given three years to decide whether to convert their permits to the new system. This posed somewhat of a dilemma for ski operators, who had to decide whether the increased security of their basic tenure was worth acknowledging the agency's more

---

* In the Mineral King case, the Ninth Circuit went on to reject the Club's other legal arguments. The case is better known as a landmark modern decision on standing to sue (under its caption in the U.S. Supreme Court, Sierra Club v. Morton, 405 U.S. 727 (1972)). See Chapter 4, supra p. 285. The Club lost the immediate legal battle but ultimately won the war. On remand from the Supreme Court, the district court allowed the Club to amend its complaint to obtain standing and add new claims, including one under NEPA. The Forest Service agreed to prepare an EIS, which further delayed matters. See Thomas Lundmark, Anne Mester, R.A. Cordes, & Barry S. Sandals, Mineral King Goes Downhill, 5 Ecology L.Q. 555 (1976). The project and the lawsuit were both eventually dropped; in 1978 the Valley was added to Sequoia National Park with this statutory explanation: "The Congress recognizes that the Mineral King Valley area has outstanding potential for certain year-round recreational opportunities, but the development of permanent facilities for downhill skiing within the area would be inconsistent with the preservation and enhancement of its ecological values." 16 U.S.C. 45(h).

explicit continuing regulatory authority and fair market value obligation in the new Act. The planning process for new ski areas can be quite involved, and is of course subject to NEPA. See Robertson v. Methow Valley Citizens Council, Chapter 5, supra p. 392. See also Wayne McKinzie, Ski Area Development After the NFSAPA of 1986: Still an Uphill Battle, 12 Va. Envtl.L.J. 299 (1993); James Briggs, Ski Resorts and National Forests: Rethinking Forest Service Management Practices for Recreational Use, 28 B.C.Envtl.Aff.L.Rev. 79 (2000) (concluding that the U.S. Forest Service does not "strike an adequate balance between the competing interests of conservationists, recreational users, and the Forest Service's [multiple use/sustained yield] mandate," and calling on the agency to provide ski areas with "incentives to develop new and innovative environmental policies" in the form of "regulatory flexibility and future expansion ability").

NOTE: NATIONAL TRAILS

National trails don't fit neatly into any particular category. They grew out of the National Trails System Act, 16 U.S.C. §§ 1241–1249, enacted in 1968, which begins with the statement (§ 1241(a)):

> In order to provide for the ever-increasing outdoor recreation needs of an expanding population and in order to promote presentation of, public access to, travel within, and enjoyment and appreciation of the open-air, outdoor areas and historic resources of the Nation, trails should be established (i) primarily, near the urban areas of the Nation, and (ii) secondarily, within scenic areas and along historic travel routes of the Nation, which are often more remotely located.

See John S. Davis, The National Trails System Act and the Use of Protective Federal Zoning, 10 Harv.Envtl.L.Rev. 189 (1986); George Cameron Coggins & Robert Glicksman, 3 PUBLIC NATURAL RESOURCES LAW § 17.41 (2001). The latter discusses the growing "rails-to-trails" movement seeking to implement Congress's direction in the National Trails System Act that federal agencies facilitate the conversion of unused railroad rights-of-way to trails. A section of the Trails Act provides that abandonment or discontinuance of a rail line should not be permitted if a "qualified" person wishes to operate a trail on the line, is willing to manage it, take legal responsibility for it and pay any taxes on it. See 16 U.S.C. § 1247(d). The Supreme Court considered, but ultimately ducked, the question of whether such conversion constituted a "taking" of the right of owners of abutting property who hold a reversionary interest in the railroad right of way. Preseault v. ICC, 494 U.S. 1 (1990). Eventually the court of appeals held that reversionary interest owners were not entitled to compensation because they purchased their interest in land subject to governmental approval of abandonment or discontinuance of the rail line. Preseault and 985 Associates, Ltd. v. United States, 66 F.3d 1167 (Fed.Cir. 1995).

RECREATIONAL PERMITTING ON NATIONAL FORESTS AND BLM–MANAGED PUBLIC LANDS

Recreation is of course one of the "multiple uses" for which national forests and BLM lands are managed. The MUSY mandate of FLPMA, along with the public land planning process the statute creates, constitutes the essential guidance for BLM recreation planning. The 1897 Organic Act, the 1915 recreational permitting statute (discussed above in connection with ski areas), the 1960 MUSY Act, and the 1975 RPA Act, as modified by the 1976 National Forest Management Act, form an equivalent, if much less tidy, legal structure for Forest Service recreation management. Except for ski areas, recreational permitting and regulation on national forests are still governed largely by the terms of the 1897 and 1915 Acts.

A number of cases have addressed the Forest Service's exercise of its authority over "occupancy and use" under the 1897 Organic Act in connection with recreational activities, primarily concerning outfitters who provide services such as horses and canoes to recreationists. The Forest Service regulation requires a permit in order to "conduct[] any kind of work activity or service" on the national forests, 36 C.F.R. § 261.10(e), and the courts generally sustain convictions for violating this provision. See, e.g., United States v. Richard, 636 F.2d 236 (8th Cir.1980), cert. denied 450 U.S. 1033 (1981) (hauling canoes to a U.S. Forest Service boat ramp, where the payment was allegedly for renting canoes on defendant's own property and he transported them to the boat ramp for no extra charge); United States v. Brown, 200 F.3d 710 (10th Cir.1999) (following *Richard* on similar facts, except snowmobiles were involved); United States v. Patzer, 15 F.3d 934 (10th Cir.1993) (outfitting and filming big game motion pictures on national forest lands, rejecting defendant's argument that he was not engaged in a commercial activity because he was merely leading a club—the Backcountry Sportsman's Club—he had organized, the court finding he actually received income for his activities); United States v. Peterson, 897 F.Supp. 499 (D.Colo.1995) (hauling horses and hay onto the national forest with no evidence of payment). On the other hand, the Ninth Circuit has held that the regulation prohibits the specified activities "only when they are engaged in for consideration." United States v. Strong, 79 F.3d 925 (9th Cir.1996) (relying on a provision of a USFS Special Uses Handbook). The federal agencies may enforce generic regulations promulgated under the Organic Act, even when the defendant is operating in an area subject to a special statute which authorizes protective regulations that the agency has not yet promulgated. See United States v. Hells Canyon Guide Service, Inc., 660 F.2d 735 (9th Cir.1981) (affirming a permanent injunction against a guide who persisted in operating jet and float boats in Hells Canyon National Recreation Area without obtaining a permit from the Forest Service). The court had this to say:

> The regulation of the use and occupancy of national parks, forests and waterways is a matter of great national importance. The strong national policy regarding the conservation of this country's natural resources dictates that we must view this legislation from a broad rather than a narrow perspective. * * * Appellants' argument [that the Forest Service must first promulgate regulations under the special statute] would necessarily run contrary to the well expressed intention of Congress to protect the Hells Canyon National Recreation Area, as well as national forests, parks and waterways in general. It would require the Secretary to take an additional, in fact, a redundant, affirmative step before he

would be able to take *any* action to protect an area placed under his direct supervision.

The question of how far either the U.S. Forest Service or the BLM can go in transferring what may effectively be a permanent or very long-term interest in federal lands under their supervision to a private recreational developer is not completely settled. Agency discretion may cut both ways; that is, courts have vested the agency with broad authority to revoke special land use permits for resort facilities; e.g., Ness Inv. Corp. v. United States Department of Agriculture, Forest Service, 512 F.2d 706 (9th Cir. 1975). In Mount Evans Co. v. Madigan, 14 F.3d 1444 (10th Cir.1994), the court upheld a Forest Service decision not to rebuild the "Crest House" at the summit of Mount Evans after it was destroyed by fire. The structure had been built by a private company under permit from the Forest Service. The court held the decision not to rebuild was not committed entirely to agency discretion and was subject to judicial review, but the agency had not acted arbitrarily. This was so even though the court found that the record did not support a Forest Service determination of traffic counts on the summit before and after the fire, "because the agency relied on a number of findings, not merely the number of visitors to Mount Evans' summit, to reach its decision." See also Yerger v. Robertson, 981 F.2d 460 (9th Cir.1992), where the court affirmed a Forest Service decision not to renew a use permit to operate a recreational facility and food concession because of lack of public need.

In general, special use permits do not create protected, compensable property rights. For example, in Paulina Lake Historic Cabin Owners Ass'n v. United States Department of Agriculture Forest Service, 577 F.Supp. 1188, 1193 n. 2 (D.Or.1983), the court noted that the plaintiffs, owners of recreational cabins built on national forest land pursuant to a special use permit from the Forest Service, did not claim a property right in the permit, "[n]or would such an allegation be well-taken. The law is settled that special use permits create no vested property rights." The court analogized the special use permit to a grazing permit, and cited United States v. Fuller, discussed in the grazing chapter, p. 788 supra.

Like private developers, the United States often has problems with its contractors. Is there anything to prevent the federal agency from itself building a ski area, a resort, or dock facilities? Should the federal agency prefer to (a) provide these facilities itself; (b) favor a few large developers or operators or (c) favor more numerous and potentially unruly small enterprises or individuals (such as individual dock owners)?

NOTE: HOLLYWOOD ON FEDERAL LANDS

First amendment issues were implicated in legislation adopted in 2000 that authorized the Secretaries of Agriculture and the Interior to "establish a reasonable fee for commercial filming activities or similar projects" on lands under their jurisdiction. The fee is to be set to provide a "fair return" to the U.S., and based on the length of the filming activity, the size of the film crew, the amount and type of equipment present, and such "other factors" as the "Secretary deems necessary." 16 U.S.C. § 460l–6d. The Park Service alone annually issues about 1500 film permits a year for both commercial and educational films. Parts of many memorable movies have been filmed on federal lands, including Star Wars (White Sands National Monument), Dances with Wolves (Badlands National Park), Raiders of the Lost Ark (Hanalei National Wildlife Refuge), Last of the Mohicans, The Deer Hunter, Thelma and Louise, and The River Wild. Often the unusual or unique nature of a federal land site attracts film-makers. The legislation also directs the Secretary not to permit filming and related activity if she determines there is a "likelihood of resource damage," there would be "unreasonable disruption of the public's use and enjoyment of the site," or the activity "poses health or safety risks to the public." Still photography is generally exempt, with some exceptions, such as where it "uses models or props which are not a part of the site's natural or cultural resources."

E.   OFF-ROAD VEHICLE REGULATION

The public may visit most federal lands for recreational purposes, but the "right" to do so is merely a license, revocable at the will of Congress or at the informed discretion of an authorized land management agency. The upsurge in recreational use has spurred the development of new kinds of controls on intensive recreation, including rationing of recreational experiences, to protect the most popular areas from overuse. Federal efforts to limit recreational access can provoke opposition inside as well as outside of land management agencies, for they can undermine public support for agency programs. Restrictions on the recreational license are usually regarded as the last resort. Congress has seldom directly addressed this volatile issue. Conflicts between restrictive policies and the traditional right of free access are most acute with respect to off-road vehicles (ORVs), including jeeps, motorcycles, 4 X 4s, snowmobiles, mountain bicycles, as well as their aquatic counterparts, jet skis and other personal watercraft.

From their introduction into the mass consumer market in the early 1960s, annual ORV sales quickly exploded to more than seven million vehicles in 1970, and ten million vehicles in 1979. See Jeffrey L. Bleich, Chrome on the Range: Off–Road Vehicles on Public Lands, 15 Ecology L.Q. 159, 161 (1988). ORVs pose a prominent danger to some federal lands, but regulating them is especially troublesome. As Jim Ruch, former BLM State Director for California, has said: "You can't understand true multiple-use management until you've stood on the top of a sand dune with the members of the Desert Lily Society coming up one side and, coming up the other, the Barstow Bombers." Enforcement of any regulatory system can be difficult because of the nature of the activity and the shortage of agency personnel in heavily used areas.

D. Sheridan, Off–Road Vehicles on Public Land

8–19 (1979).

From the standpoint of public land management, the initially important characteristic of the motorcycle, 4 x 4, and snowmobile boom was that it struck without warning. Recreational planners and economists who specialize in the use of natural resources for recreation did not anticipate the phenomenon; nor did they fully grasp its far-ranging significance once it was underway. * * *

In other words, the public land managers were ill prepared for the onslaught. This was particularly unfortunate because over half of all the off-road motorcycle, 4 x 4, and dune buggy driving in the nation takes place on federal land. Indeed, over half occurs on land managed by one federal agency—the Bureau of Land Management (BLM). * * *

ORV BENEFITS

Motorized recreation gives pleasure to millions of Americans. That is its greatest benefit. There are also certain economic benefits derived from ORV and snowmobile recreation. For the most part, these benefits accrue to the people and firms who make the equipment and those who sell [eds. or rent] them. In addition, communities in areas which attract riders enjoy a certain influx of dollars. For example, gas stations, restaurants, and motels in communities such as Gorman, California, or Webb, New York, benefit from money spent by people who visit those areas for motorized recreation. The overall economic benefits of this recreation have never been determined. * * *

In regard to recreation today, our society's principal concern is utilitarian: the greatest good for the greatest number. And as John Rawls has made clear, much more is involved in the application of this principle than crude arithmetic. Society must be concerned, for example, with the allocation of scarce resources, in terms of both efficiency and fairness. A major utilitarian concern with ORV recreation is the destruction of natural resources caused by these vehicles. Another is the infringement of other people's rights to recreate. Another is the alternatives available to ORV users. * * *

ENVIRONMENTAL COSTS

ORVs have damaged every kind of ecosystem found in the United States: sand dunes covered with American beach grass on Cape Cod; pine and cyprus woodlands in Florida; hardwood forests in Indiana; prairie grasslands in Montana; chaparral and sagebrush hills in Arizona; alpine meadows in Colorado; conifer forests in Washington; arctic tundra in Alaska. In some cases, the wounds will heal naturally; in others they will not, at least for millennia. * * *

CONFLICTS WITH OTHER USERS

Reports from public land managers in nine western states indicate that conflict occurs, upon occasion, between commercial users of the land, such as ranchers, and ORV recreationalists. The conflict with grazing, in fact, seems to be more common than with logging or mining. For example, New Mexico BLM director Arthur W. Zimmerman notes that complaints from ranchers have been received concerning trespass, cut fences, broken gates, polluted livestock water, new jeep roads, noise, gully erosion caused by hill climbs, and interference with their livestock operations. The less frequent complaints received from loggers and miners usually concern vandalism of their equipment and property by ORVers.

The most serious conflict arises between ORV operators and nonmotorized picnickers or campers, hikers, backpackers, sightseers, and so on—or between ORVers and persons using the land for educational purposes—students, teachers, researchers.

Nonmotorized recreationists do not enjoy their encounters with motorcycles, dune buggies, and four-wheel drive vehicles, numerous studies have shown. The ORV operator, on the other hand, is often quite tolerant, even oblivious of the person on foot or horseback.

ORVs, in other words, impair other people's enjoyment or understanding of the outdoors on public land. In terms of public policy, this is a problem equal in importance to ORV damage of the environment. * * *

* * * [A]s a BLM Environmental Impact Statement noted: "Silence is a resource. These sounds which man typically associates with the pristine natural environments are perceived by the senses as solitude. The solitude of the desert is one of its * * * valuable resources." Substitute the word forest or prairie or mountain or meadow for desert and the truth of this statement still stands. The noise of an ORV punctures that solitude. Hikers and campers, for example, do not trek miles into the wilds to hear a chorus of internal combustion engines, however polite the drivers, however well-tuned their engines, although certainly a good muffler and a courteous driver make the experience less unpleasant than it would be. Direct encounters with ORV machines simply are not compatible with the quality of outdoor experience being sought by a majority of Americans. * * *

The first major effort to regulate ORVs on federal lands started at the top: In February 1972, President Richard Nixon issued Executive Order No. 11644, which directed the federal land management agencies effectively to "zone" the federal lands with respect to ORV travel. The President directed each agency head to create a regulatory structure that would designate "specific areas and trails on public lands on which the use of off-road vehicles may be permitted, and areas in which the use of off-road vehicles may not be permitted," within a date certain. The Order contained general environmental criteria to be used in zoning the lands for ORV use, and required the agencies to carry out this task with full public participation. It recited that it was issued "by virtue of the authority vested in me as President of the United States by the Constitution of the United States and in furtherance of the purpose and policy of [NEPA]." 43 U.S.C. § 4321 note. See pp. 361–64 supra, regarding the President's authority to issue such orders.

Only the BLM implemented this order with regulations specific to ORV use. The other principal federal land agencies—the Park Service, Fish & Wildlife Service, and Forest Service—chose instead to make ad hoc determinations of the suitability of ORV use in particular areas or, in the case of the Forest Service, to issue ORV plans for specific national forests that generally codify existing management practices. In response to this tepid implementation, early in his administration President Carter issued an Executive Order, No. 11989 (1977), which required the federal land management agencies to ban ORVs from areas where the agency determines that continued use "will cause or is causing considerable adverse effects." This Order failed to produce any significant progress in the agencies. See Bleich, supra, 15 Ecology L.Q. at 165–67.

The BLM regulations implementing the 1972 Executive Order were promptly challenged by environmental groups. In National Wildlife Federation v. Morton, 393 F.Supp. 1286 (D.D.C.1975), the court found that the BLM had "significantly diluted the standards emphatically set forth in" the Order and not followed it in several other respects. For example, the court scored BLM's adding a new substantive criterion ("[t]he need for public use areas for recreation use") that was not specified, and implicitly not allowed, in the Executive Order. Perhaps the most important defect identified by the court was the following (393 F.Supp. at 1295):

> Instead of evaluating with regard to the environmental criteria mandated by Executive Order 11644 specific areas and trails to determine whether the use of ORV's should be permitted, BLM has engaged in a wholesale, blanket designation of "open" lands. By doing so, it has violated the express requirements of Executive Order 11644.

The BLM eventually responded with new regulations that contained criteria for the designation of ORV use and routes on public lands that rather closely tracked the 1972 Executive Order criteria. See 43 C.F.R. Part 8340 (1990). But BLM implementation of the Order and its regulations, particularly in the California Desert, continued to attract controversy.

David Sheridan (in OFF–ROAD VEHICLES ON PUBLIC LAND, supra) described part of the BLM's problem:

> The process of designating areas or trails open or closed to ORV use is a laborious undertaking for an agency such as the BLM, which administers [more than two hundred] million acres of public land. The task is compounded by the fact that almost no control over ORV uses was exercised prior to Executive Order 11644, and hence behavior patterns of millions of ORV recreationists had already become established. In addition, BLM has fewer men and women per acre than the other land management agencies.

Sheridan went on to describe the BLM's initial ORV regulation plan adopted in 1973 for the California Desert, the most intensively used ORV area in the nation:

> It designates 3 percent of the [BLM land in the California Desert] as "closed" to ORVs, 6 percent as "open," and the remainder as "restricted," which means that ORV drivers are supposed to stay on existing roads and trails.

> The major flaw in this scheme is that it does not take into account BLM's lack of presence in the field. A person can drive all day in the

desert on a motorcycle or in a four-wheel drive vehicle and never see a BLM sign or enforcement officer. Indeed, the BLM has only slightly more than a dozen rangers to patrol 12 million acres of land. * * *

As the BLM tried again to grapple with ORV use in the California Desert, it had in the meantime gained new management authority with passage of the Federal Land Policy and Management Act in 1976. § 601 of FLPMA created the California Desert Conservation Area (CDCA), and directed BLM to promulgate a plan for managing it. 43 U.S.C. § 1781.* Congress prefaced this section with special findings that, among other things, described the unique, "extremely fragile, easily scarred, and slowly healed" resources of the area, which were threatened by "pressures of increased use, particularly recreational use." It also found that

> (4) the use of all California desert resources can and should be provided for in a multiple use and sustained yield management plan to conserve these resources for future generations, and to provide present and future use and enjoyment, particularly outdoor recreational uses, including the use, where appropriate, of off-road recreational vehicles.

In American Motorcyclist Ass'n v. Watt, 543 F.Supp. 789 (C.D.Cal. 1982), the court addressed that portion of the BLM's plan for the CDCA specifying that in so-called "Class L" areas, motorized vehicles will be allowed only on "approved routes of travel." At issue were the specific criteria set out in the plan by which the approved routes were to be selected. The applicable BLM regulations (43 C.F.R. § 8342.1) provided (court's emphasis added):

> The authorized officer shall designate all public lands as either open, limited, or closed to off-road vehicles. All designations shall be based on the protection of the resources of the public lands, the promotion of the safety of all the users of the public lands, and the *minimization of conflicts* among various uses of the public lands; and in accordance with the following criteria:

> (a) Areas and trails shall be located to *minimize damage* to soil, watershed, vegetation, air, or other resources of the public lands, and to prevent impairment of wilderness suitability.

> (b) Areas and trails shall be located to *minimize harassment* of wildlife or significant disruption of wildlife habitats. Special attention will be given to protect endangered or threatened species and their habitats.

> (c) Areas and trails shall be located to *minimize conflicts between* off-road vehicle use and other existing or proposed recreational uses of the same or neighboring public lands, and to ensure the compatibility of

---

* The California Desert Conservation Area near the Los Angeles/San Diego megalopolis poses some of the toughest recreational management issues on the federal lands. The story of the movement to protect it (which included the 1976 designation of the CDCA in FLPMA and a second statute enacted in 1994, which designated the Mohave National Park and Preserve and millions of acres of wilderness, see 16 U.S.C. §§ 410aaa-aaa83), is well told by the late lawyer/conservationist Francis Wheat, in CALIFORNIA DESERT MIRACLE (1999).

such uses with existing conditions in populated areas, taking into account noise and other factors.

(d) Areas and trails shall not be located in officially designated wilderness areas or primitive areas. Areas and trails shall be located in natural areas only if the authorized officer determines that off-road vehicle use in such locations will not adversely affect their natural, esthetic, scenic, or other values for which such areas are established.

The BLM's California Desert Plan provided (at p. 91, court's emphasis added):

In Multiple–Use Class L areas, vehicle access is limited to only those routes "approved" and marked as vehicle access routes. Routes not "approved" for vehicle access in most instances will be obliterated, barricaded, signed, or shown "closed" on maps. "Approved" routes will be signed or otherwise marked or mapped so that those routes of travel which are clearly open will be readily identifiable.

Route Designation Factors—Multiple–Use Class L

Decisions on approval of vehicle routes for Class L *will be based* on an analysis of each situation, using the following decision criteria:

(1) Is the route new or existing?

(2) Does the route provide access for resource use or enjoyment?

(3) Are there alternate access opportunities?

(4) *Does the route cause considerable adverse impacts?*

(5) Are there alternate access routes which do not cause considerable adverse impacts?

The court concluded (543 F.Supp. at 797):

The route designation criteria, as shown above, are presented in such a manner so as to appear to be the exclusive standard pursuant to which route designation decisions are to be made. Concededly, the criteria are phrased in a neutral, interrogative form, such that they do not explicitly require that a route be approved if certain conditions are satisfied. At the same time, however, the criteria do not explicitly *prohibit* route designation in any defined situation. Thus, the Plan criteria would permit agency officials to make route designations without the minimization of environmental impacts and conflicts between uses expressly required by 43 C.F.R. § 8342.1. Furthermore, the criteria, even though neutrally phrased, will very likely lead BLM officials responsible for implementing the Plan to conclude that routes should be approved absent a finding of "considerable adverse impacts." The "considerable adverse impacts" standard is qualitatively different than the minimization criteria mandated by § 8342.1 and in practice is almost certain to skew route designation decision-making in favor of ORV use.

Defendants argue that various references in the Plan to E.O. 11,644, E.O. 11,989, and certain BLM regulations make it clear that the BLM does not intend to, or was not authorized to, apply the route selection criteria in a manner inconsistent with 43 C.F.R. § 8342.1. However, viewed in the context in which they appear, these references are not sufficient to counteract the impression, created in the presentation of the route designation criteria quoted above, that those criteria are to be the exclusive bases for route approval decisions. No mention of the executive orders or applicable BLM regulations is made in the text surrounding the criteria in the Plan. Furthermore, the Court has seen no language anywhere in the Plan which would alert a reader that the criteria presented in the Plan are inconsistent with 43 C.F.R. § 8342.1 or the executive orders. (If anything, the impression is given that the criteria faithfully implement these pre-existing directives.) Accordingly, I conclude that the Plan, viewed as a whole, is very likely to result in a route selection process which does not comply in significant respects with the express standards set forth in 43 C.F.R. § 8342.1.

The court enjoined BLM "from approving any route of travel in Class L areas, on either a one-time or permanent basis, without complying with the selection criteria set forth in 43 C.F.R. § 8342.1." That scarcely ended the matter, as the next case shows.

Sierra Club v. Clark

United States Court of Appeals, Ninth Circuit, 1985.
756 F.2d 686.

■ POOLE, CIRCUIT JUDGE:

* * * Dove Springs Canyon is located in the California Desert Conservation Area ("Desert Area"), established in 1976, 43 U.S.C. § 1781, under the Federal Land Policy Management Act ("the Act"), 43 U.S.C. § 1701 et seq. The Desert Area covers approximately 25 million acres in southeastern California, approximately 12.1 million of which are administered by the BLM. Dove Springs Canyon is comprised of approximately 5500 acres; 3000 acres are designated "open" for unrestricted use of ORVs.

Dove Springs Canyon possesses abundant and diverse flora and fauna. Over 250 species of plants, 24 species of reptiles, and 30 species of birds are found there. It also offers good habitat for the Mojave ground squirrel, the desert kit fox, and the burrowing owl. Because the rich and varied biota is unusual for an area of such low elevation in the Mojave Desert, the Canyon was once frequented by birdwatchers and naturalists, as well as hikers and fossil hunters.

Recreational ORV usage of Dove Springs Canyon began in 1965 and became progressively heavier in the ensuing years. By 1971, the Canyon was being used intensively by ORV enthusiasts. It became especially popular because the site's diverse terrain, coupled with relatively easy access, provides outstanding hill-climbing opportunities. By 1979, up to 200 vehicles used the Canyon on a typical weekend; over 500 vehicles used it on a holiday weekend. In 1973, the BLM adopted its Interim Critical Management Program for Recreational Vehicle Use on the California Desert ("Interim Program") which designated Dove Springs Canyon as an ORV

Open Area, permitting recreational vehicle travel in the area without restriction.

Extensive ORV usage has been accompanied by severe environmental damage in the form of major surface erosion, soil compaction, and heavy loss of vegetation. The visual aesthetics have markedly declined. The character of the Canyon has been so severely altered that the Canyon is now used almost exclusively for ORV activities.

In July of 1980 Sierra Club petitioned the Secretary of the Interior to close Dove Springs Canyon to ORV use under the authority of Executive Order No. 11644, as amended by Executive Order No. 11989, and 43 C.F.R. § 8341.2 because of "substantial adverse effects" on the vegetation, soil and wildlife in the Canyon. The Secretary responded that the matter would be addressed in the California Desert Conservation Plan and Final Environmental Impact Statement ("the Final Plan").

The Final Plan approved by the Secretary in December 1980 maintained unrestricted ORV use in Dove Springs of 3000 of the 5500 acres. Sierra Club filed this action on January 6, 1981, alleging that the Secretary's failure to close Dove Springs violated Executive Order No. 11644, as amended by Executive Order No. 11989, and 43 C.F.R. § 8341.2; 43 U.S.C. § 1732(b), which requires the Secretary to prevent "unnecessary or undue degradation of the lands;" and 43 U.S.C. §§ 1781(b) and (d), which require the Secretary to maintain and conserve resources of the Desert Area under principles of "multiple use and sustained yield." * * * [The cited regulation] provides:

> Notwithstanding the consultation provisions of § 8342.2(a), where the authorized officer determines that off-road vehicles are causing or will cause considerable adverse effects * * * the authorized officer shall immediately close the areas or trails affected. * * * Such closures will not prevent designation * * *, but these lands shall not be opened to the type(s) of off-road vehicle to which it was closed unless the authorized officer determines that the adverse effects have been eliminated and measures implemented to prevent recurrence.

43 C.F.R. § 8341.2(a). * * * [T]he closure standard of the Executive Orders and the Regulation applies independently of the designation of the land as open under the Act, the issue before us is whether the damage to Dove Springs Canyon amounts to "considerable adverse effects" which require the Canyon's closure. The parties agree that there is no genuine issue as to the extent of the damage to the Canyon, and therefore resolution of this issue depends upon whether the Secretary's interpretation of this phrase or that of the Sierra Club is to control. * * *

The Secretary interprets "considerable adverse effect" to require determining what is "considerable" in the context of the Desert Area as a whole, not merely on a parcel-by-parcel basis. The Secretary contends such a broad interpretation is necessary and is consistent with 43 U.S.C. § 1781(a)(4) which expresses a congressional judgment that ORV use is to be permitted "where appropriate."

Sierra Club argues against the Secretary's interpretation. Sierra Club contends that the interpretation of the Executive Orders set forth by the Council on Environmental Quality (CEQ) in its August 1, 1977 memorandum is entitled to great deference, and that the CEQ's interpretation requires the closure of the Canyon. This argument fails on two grounds.

First, the CEQ's interpretation of the Executive Order does not directly conflict with the Secretary's interpretation of the regulation. While it states that "the term 'considerable' should be liberally construed to provide the broadest possible protection reasonably required by this standard," it does not purport to decide whether the term "considerable adverse effects" should be analyzed in the context of the entire Desert Area, or on a site-specific basis. Moreover, the memorandum acknowledges that the responsibility for closing particular areas rests with "responsible federal officials in the field" "[b]ased on their practical experience in the management of the public lands, and their first-hand knowledge of conditions 'on-the-ground.' "

Second, the authority of the CEQ is to maintain a continuing review of the implementation of the Executive Order. Executive Order No. 11644, § 8(b). The authority of the Secretary, on the other hand, is to promulgate regulations to provide for "administrative designation of the specific areas and trails on public lands on which the use of off-road vehicles may be permitted, and areas in which the use of off-road vehicles may not be permitted." Id. at § 3(a). Discretion rests with the Secretary, therefore, to determine whether and to what extent specific areas should be closed to ORV use. Thus, it is the Secretary's interpretation which is entitled to our deference.

Sierra Club argues that even if the CEQ's interpretation of the closure standard is not controlling, the Secretary's interpretation should not be adopted because it is unreasonable. Sierra Club insists that the sacrifice of any area to permanent resource damage is not justified under the multiple use management mandate of 43 U.S.C. § 1702(c) that requires multiple use "without permanent impairment of the productivity of the land and the quality of the environment." In further support of its position Sierra Club adverts to the requirement in the Act that the Secretary prevent "unnecessary and undue degradation" of the public lands, 43 U.S.C. § 1732(b). In addition, Sierra Club contends, when Congress established the Desert Area it intended the Secretary to fashion a multiple use and sustained yield management plan "to conserve [the California desert] resources for future generations, and to provide present and future use and enjoyment, particularly outdoor recreational uses, including the use, where appropriate, of off-road recreational vehicles." 43 U.S.C. § 1781(a)(4). Sierra Club argues that it is unreasonable for the Secretary to find ORV use "appropriate" when that use violates principles of sustained yield, substantially impairs productivity of renewable resources and is inconsistent with maintenance of environmental quality.

We can appreciate the earnestness and force of Sierra Club's position, and if we could write on a clean slate, would prefer a view which would disallow the virtual sacrifice of a priceless natural area in order to accommodate a special recreational activity. But we are not free to ignore the mandate which Congress wrote into the Act. Sierra Club's interpretation of the regulation would inevitably result in the total prohibition of ORV use because it is doubtful that any discrete area could withstand unrestricted ORV use without considerable adverse effects. However appealing might be such a resolution of the environmental dilemma, Congress has found that ORV use, damaging as it may be, is to be provided "where appropriate." It left determination of appropriateness largely up to the Secretary in an area of sharp conflict. If there is to be a change it must come by way of Congressional reconsideration. The Secretary's interpretation that this legislative determination calls for accommodation of ORV usage in the administrative plan, we must conclude, is not unreasonable and we are constrained to let it stand.

The court must review agency action to determine if it complies with the Secretary's interpretation of the Regulation. In Perkins v. Bergland, 608 F.2d 803 (9th Cir.1979), we held that the scope of review of an agency's factual findings is very narrow where the Secretary has been vested with substantial discretion, as in the administration of public land. * * * We noted that the various goals of "multiple use," "sustained yield," and how "best [to] meet the needs of the American people," vested in the Secretary discretion to determine optimum means of administering forest and range land. We concluded that the agency's factual findings as to range conditions and carrying capacity would be overturned only if arbitrary and capricious.

Under the California Desert Conservation Area Plan, approximately 4 percent (485,000 acres) of the total acreage is now open to unrestricted ORV use. Dove Springs itself constitutes only 0.025 percent of BLM administered lands in the Desert Area. Although all parties recognize that the environmental impact of ORV use at Dove Springs is severe, the Secretary's determination that these effects were not "considerable" in the context of the Desert Area as a whole is not arbitrary, capricious, or an abuse of the broad discretion committed to him by an obliging Congress. * * *

NOTES AND QUESTIONS

1.   Does BLM's experience in implementing the executive orders here, and the federal courts' responses, show the toothlessness of presidential executive orders in the face of agency inertia or opposition? Who is entitled to deference in interpreting and applying the executive order, the CEQ or the BLM?

2.   How much deference should the BLM receive here? Would the result be the same if BLM *closed* Dove Springs Canyon to ORV use, while leaving other, less ecologically significant areas of the Desert open to unrestricted ORV use? Same result if BLM had left 25% of the Desert open to unrestricted ORV use? 50%? Is there a principled basis on which the BLM, or the courts, could draw a line?

3.   Congress's express purpose in creating the CDCA was to "provide for immediate and future protection and administration of the public lands

in the California desert within the framework of a program of multiple use and sustained yield, and the maintenance of environmental quality." 43 U.S.C. § 1781(b). Did the Congress really make a decision in FLPMA § 1781(a)(4) (quoted on at the bottom of p. 995 supra), that heavy, destructive use of portions of the California Desert by ORVs was proper? Does the phrase "where appropriate" in that subsection (a)(4) congressional finding mean that heavy ORV use had to be "appropriate" somewhere in the Desert? Is the court saying that if ORV traffic is to be banned here it must be banned everywhere in the Desert, and that can't be what Congress had in mind? But if the congressional intent is cloudy, should the court—given the damage being caused—err on the side of protection, enjoin ORV traffic, and in effect remand the matter to Congress to make its intentions more clear if it had something else in mind?

4.   Along the same lines, examine how the court deals with FLPMA's general statutory standards such as its mandate to prevent "unnecessary or undue degradation" (FLPMA § 302(b), 43 U.S.C. § 1732(b)). Is the court saying this mandate simply cannot meaningfully be applied merely to regulate (rather than prohibit) ORV use? (Cf. the discussion of this statutory standard in connection with hardrock mining; Chapter 7, supra pp. 636–39.) Note that the court's opinion here erroneously sometimes (but not consistently) quotes the standard as "unnecessary *and* undue." Is that a Freudian slip, or does the "or" make a difference? (And speaking of Freud, do you suppose the name of the Canyon influenced plaintiffs' decision to make a federal case out of BLM's decision?)

5.   Similarly, what about FLPMA's mandate (in the definition of multiple use) to prevent "permanent impairment of the productivity of the land and the quality of the environment." 43 U.S.C. § 1702(c). What about BLM's duty under FLPMA to provide "sustained yield" of the renewable resources of the public lands (see Chapter 8, supra pp. 706–07)? Why is the result in this case different from the Tongass logging case (Sierra Club v. Butz, Chapter 8, supra pp. 708–10), where the court of appeals vacated and remanded a lower court decision upholding a whole-hearted emphasis on logging? More generally, are all the grand statutory paeans to environmental quality and resource protection empty against the tide of massive amounts of mechanized recreation? Given those lofty goals, should the courts put the burden of legislative inertia on the side of the environment, or on the side of ORVs? That is, instead of allowing this kind of intensive, destructive, use until Congress expressly prohibits it, should the courts prohibit it until Congress expressly allows it?

6.   What about the "public trust" doctrine? See Chapter 5, supra pp. 382–89.

7.   Perhaps the pinnacle of ORV use of the federal lands was the annual Barstow to Las Vegas off-road motorcycle race. Attracting thousands of participants, it was run on Thanksgiving weekend from 1967 to 1974. At that point BLM decided not to issue permits for it because of adverse impacts to desert resources. ORV enthusiasts nevertheless held annual, unsanctioned "protest" races along the same course on succeeding Thanksgiving weekends. In 1983, BLM amended the CDCA Plan to allow

the race to resume with official sanction. The Plan amendment designated the 110–mile race course (covering some 2000 acres), and included mitigation measures. It was also accompanied by an EIS. When BLM followed up by issuing a permit for a 1983 race, the Sierra Club sued. The 1983 race was held before the court of appeals ruled, and in Sierra Club v. Clark, 774 F.2d 1406 (9th Cir.1985), the court followed the Dove Springs Canyon case and upheld the BLM. Among other things, the court seemed to accept a "if you can't lick 'em, join (and regulate) 'em" defense:

> While there is little doubt that negative impacts resulted from the 1983 race, so is there little doubt that harm would result if uncontrolled "protest rides" were to continue. The mitigation requirements seek to assure that impacts are minimized. These requirements are not static—they can be expanded to offer greater assurances of compliance and lessen the potential for harm. The challenged amendment * * * seems a reasoned approach to a difficult balancing act mandated by Congress.

Is it proper to permit the race simply because the agency recognizes that it cannot effectively prohibit a "protest" race? Could the BLM have allowed the race to resume on the sole ground that it had insufficient manpower to enforce its protective regulations? Could the court have overturned the BLM decision allowing the race, and ordered the BLM to divert personnel from other tasks in order to prevent a "protest" race from occurring? The Barstow—Las Vegas race was run annually through 1990. Recurring problems of enforcing the mitigation requirements, compounded by the listing of the Desert Tortoise as an endangered species, finally prompted the BLM to suspend it.

8.   Could the federal agencies look to private land and private markets to satisfy the demand for ORV use? Should (or could) the BLM sell off Dove Springs Canyon to ORV enthusiasts and take this problem off its plate? Is there any reason to keep the lands public if they are to be devoted to such a single narrow use? Would that rationale justify selling off grazing or mining or timber land?

Meanwhile, on a coast three thousand miles to the east, another federal agency, operating under a somewhat different statutory mandate, was grappling with ORV regulation.

Conservation Law Foundation of New England, Inc. v. Secretary of the Interior

United States Court of Appeals, First Circuit, 1989.
864 F.2d 954.

■ CAFFREY, SENIOR DISTRICT JUDGE.

The Conservation Law Foundation of New England, Inc. ("CLF") appeals from the district court's ruling upholding the validity of the National Park Service's 1985 Management Plan ("the 1985 Plan"). The

1985 Plan allows for the restricted use of off-road vehicles ("ORVs")[1] on the Cape Cod National Seashore ("the Seashore"). CLF contends that ORV use under the 1985 Plan violates the Cape Cod National Seashore Act, 16 U.S.C. §§ 459b et seq., and Executive Order 11644, which deals with ORV use on public lands. We affirm the district court's ruling.

Congress enacted the Cape Cod National Seashore Act ("the Seashore Act") in 1961, establishing the Seashore as part of the National Park System. The Seashore includes 48 miles of ocean front and bayside beaches, encompassing land and water within the towns of Chatham, Orleans, Eastham, Wellfleet, Truro, and Provincetown. The National Park Service maintains six Seashore beaches and provides facilities for a number of other recreational activities, including boating, fishing, bicycling, and horseback riding.

At the time the Seashore Act was enacted, limited ORV use existed on the Seashore. The National Park Service began to regulate such use in 1964, as the Seashore started to become one of the major ORV recreational areas in New England. By 1974, many miles of ORV trails covered the Seashore. [Eds.: According to the district court, ORV use on the beach escalated from 400 vehicles per year when the seashore was created in 1961 to almost 5000 vehicles per year in 1979. See 590 F.Supp. at 1471.] In that year, the Park Service contracted with the University of Massachusetts to conduct a study ("the U.Mass. Study") on the effects of ORV use on the Seashore's ecosystems. The results of the five-year study were published in thirteen volumes, and documented certain adverse ecological effects resulting from ORV travel on the Seashore.

In response to the findings of the U.Mass.Study, the National Park Service promulgated new regulations ("the 1981 Plan") restricting ORV use on the Seashore. Under the 1981 Plan, all tidal flats and salt marshes were closed to ORV travel. All upland areas and dune trails were also closed, except for an access route to be used by commercial dune taxis and cottage residents, and an emergency bypass route. Other significant restrictions were also created. Following adoption of the 1981 Plan, ORV travel on the Seashore decreased considerably.[5]

CLF filed this suit seeking to enjoin implementation of the 1981 Plan. * * * CLF argued that the 1981 Plan would cause significant damage to the coastal ecosystem and impermissible conflicts between ORV travel and other recreational activities on the Seashore, in violation of the Seashore Act and Executive Order 11644. The district court denied CLF's request for injunctive relief, but remanded the 1981 Plan to the Secretary for additional findings regarding whether[,] in relation to other protected uses of the Seashore[,] ORV use meets the definition of "appropriate public use" as set forth in the Act. * * *

---

1. The term "off-road vehicles" refers to vehicles that are capable of cross-country travel over natural terrain. These include jeeps, dune buggies, and other four-wheel drive vehicles.

5. ORV use permits issued by the National Park Service dropped 26% during the first year under the 1981 Plan, and dropped an additional 11% by 1984.

The National Park Service adopted an Amended Management Plan ("the 1985 Plan") in August of 1985 further restricting ORV use at the Seashore. CLF then amended its complaint to challenge the 1985 Plan, and [both sides] moved for summary judgment[.] * * *

The district court granted defendants' motion, ruling that the Secretary's decision to adopt the 1985 Plan * * * represents an appropriate public use of the Seashore in accordance with Section 7 of the Seashore Act. The court also found that the 1985 Plan "as implemented and enforced, effectively protect[s] the ecology of the Seashore and does not adversely affect the Seashore's natural, scenic and aesthetic values." CLF appeals from the district court ruling on both the appropriateness and ecological damage issues. * * *

Section 7 of the Seashore Act provides for the development of the Seashore in certain limited circumstances. The statute provides in pertinent part:

> *In order that the seashore shall be permanently preserved in its present state, no development or plan for the convenience of visitors shall be undertaken therein which would be incompatible with the preservation of the unique flora and fauna or the physiographic conditions now prevailing* or with the preservation of such historic sites and structures as the Secretary may designate: *Provided,* That the Secretary may provide for the public enjoyment and understanding of the unique natural, historic, and scientific features of Cape Code within the seashore by establishing such trails, observation points, and exhibits and providing such services as he may deem desirable for such public enjoyment and understanding: *Provided further, That the Secretary may develop for appropriate public uses such portions of the seashore as he deems especially adaptable for camping, swimming, boating, sailing, hunting, fishing, the appreciation of historic sites and structures and natural features of Cape Cod, and other activities of similar nature.*

16 U.S.C. § 459b–6(b)(1)(emphasis added). Under the express language of Section 7, development of the Seashore is permissible where it is ecologically compatible and where it is for an "appropriate" public use. It is crucial to observe, therefore, that despite the "preserved in its present state" language, the statute does not impose a ban on all development of the Seashore.

CLF argues that ORV use under the 1985 Plan violates Section 7 on the basis that such activity is not an "appropriate" public use of the Seashore. The district court held, however, that the Secretary's decision to adopt the 1985 Plan was not arbitrary, capricious or an abuse of discretion, and therefore must be upheld. We agree. After making substantial inquiry into the facts of this case, we conclude that a rational basis exists to support the Secretary's decision that ORV use under the 1985 Plan is an appropriate public use of the Seashore.

The 1985 Plan was adopted by the National Park Service after the district court remanded this case to the Secretary to consider more thoroughly the question of whether ORV use is an appropriate public use of the

Seashore. The district court instructed the Secretary to consider the general appropriateness of ORV use in light of the Seashore Act and Executive Order 11644, the nature and extent of user conflicts caused by ORVs, and the adequacy of allocation of the Seashore between ORV and non-ORV users. The defendants considered these and other factors on remand and amended the Management Plan to further restrict ORV use. Based on this analysis, and guided by the Regional Solicitor's opinion that ORV use at the Seashore is not an inappropriate public use *per se*, the Secretary found that limited ORV use under the 1985 Plan is consistent with the appropriateness requirement imposed by Section 7 for any development of the Seashore.

CLF argues that the defendants applied the wrong standard in determining whether ORV use is an appropriate public use of the Seashore under Section 7. CLF maintains that the crucial factor the agency must consider is whether the contemplated use would protect the traditional scenic value of the Seashore. Plaintiff seems to argue, moreover, that the "preserved in its present state" language of Section 7 means that the Secretary cannot authorize any development of the Seashore that would alter the scenery from its condition at the time the Seashore Act was enacted. According to this view, because parts of the Seashore may look different now than they did in 1961 due to ORV travel, the activity must be inappropriate *per se* as a public use. Nothing in the plain language of Section 7 or in the relevant legislative history persuades us that the Secretary should be constrained by this interpretation of the statute.

The district court explained in its June 28, 1988 Memorandum and Order granting defendants' motion for summary judgment that the Secretary on remand engaged in a meaningful analysis of the appropriateness issue. We agree, and need not repeat the thorough discussion provided by the district court. Before amending the Management Plan, the Secretary considered the factors that the court had set forth in its remand order. In addition and contrary to what plaintiff would have us believe, the Secretary considered the impact of ORV use on the aesthetic and scenic values of the Seashore. Upon consideration of all of these relevant factors, the Secretary determined that ORV use under the 1985 Plan is an appropriate public use of the Seashore. Given the Secretary's careful treatment of the issue on remand and the considerable restrictions placed on ORV use under the 1985 Plan, we cannot say that the Secretary's decision has no rational basis or represents an abuse of discretion.

Accordingly, we affirm the district court in granting defendants' motion for summary judgment on the appropriateness issue under Section 7 of the Seashore Act.

Executive Order No. 11644 * * * provides that ORV use on federal lands must be consistent with "the protection of the resources of the public lands, promotion of the safety of all users of those lands, and minimization of conflicts among the various uses of those lands." E.O. 11644 § 3(a). Section 3(a) of the Order requires that ORV trails be located in areas of the National Park System only "if the respective agency head determines that off-road vehicle use in such locations will not adversely affect their natural, aesthetic, or scenic values." Id. § 3(a)(4). Executive Order 11989, the 1977 amendment to Executive Order 11644, further provides that the agency head must,

> whenever he determines that the use of off-road vehicles will cause or is causing considerable adverse effects on the soil, vegetation, wildlife habitat or cultural or historic resources of particular areas or trails of the public lands, immediately close such areas or trails to the type of off-road vehicle causing such effects until such time as he determines that such adverse effects have been eliminated and that measures have been implemented to prevent future recurrence.

E.O. 11644 § 9(a). These provisions, then, restrict the Secretary's discretion regarding ORV use on the Seashore, along with Section 7 of the Seashore Act.[12]

CLF maintains that Executive Order 11644 requires the defendants to close the Seashore to ORV use because of alleged ecological damage and aesthetic degradation at the Seashore. CLF challenges the Secretary's finding that current regulations on ORV use effectively protect the ecology of the Seashore and that limited ORV use does not adversely affect natural or scenic values at the Seashore. The plaintiff argues in particular that numerous violations of the National Park Service regulations cause considerable damage to the Seashore ecology and aesthetics, and require that a ban be imposed on ORV travel, unless the violations can be prevented.

The Secretary determined that limited ORV use under the 1985 Plan does not adversely affect natural, aesthetic or scenic values at the Seashore. We agree with the district court that there is adequate support for this determination. The defendants considered the protection of natural values in arriving at the current regulations restricting ORV use on the Seashore. The extent and location of ORV trails were set under the 1985 Plan consistent with these values. Though unregulated ORV travel on the Seashore might well threaten the natural or scenic values of the Seashore, the restrictions imposed under the 1985 Plan are substantial and were designed specifically to protect those values that would otherwise be at risk.

The Secretary also determined that ORV use has caused no significant ecological damage at the Seashore since the adoption of the 1981 Plan. The district court correctly explained in its June 27, 1984 decision that an agency's technical conclusions are to be upheld by a reviewing court where they are "founded on supportable data and methodology, and meet minimum standards of rationality." We agree with the district court that the defendants' conclusion regarding effective protection of the Seashore ecology under the Management Plan is based on supportable data and methodology, and meets minimum standards of rationality. Accordingly, the defendants' finding as to adequate ecological protection should not be disturbed.

It may be true, as CLF points out, that ORVs caused certain adverse effects at the Seashore prior to the adoption of the 1981 Plan. Those effects

---

12. The district court determined that Executive Order 11644, as amended by Executive Order 11989, has the force and effect of law and is enforceable by CLF under APA review.

were addressed in the U.Mass.Study. What is at issue, however, is whether any significant ecological damage has occurred under the regulations that have been adopted and enforced since that time. Persuasive expert testimony submitted by the government supports its position that restrictions imposed originally under the 1981 Plan and then supplemented by the 1985 Plan have created effective protection of the Seashore ecology. The closure of the dune trails under the 1981 Plan, moreover, caused a significant decline in ORV use of the Seashore. In addition, the National Park Service has added a number of rangers to improve patrol of the Seashore. Finally, with the adoption of the 1985 Plan the government placed greater restrictions on ORV use of the Seashore. Though some ecological damage to the Seashore may have occurred prior to adoption of the 1981 Plan, we believe sufficient evidence exists to support defendants' conclusion that ORV use has caused no significant ecological damage at the Seashore since that time. We therefore affirm the district court on the issue of ecological protection under the 1981 and 1985 Plans. * * *

■ [STEPHEN] BREYER, CIRCUIT JUDGE (concurring).

I agree with the panel that, given the statute's *proviso*, one cannot reasonably read it as imposing an absolute ban on ORVs, particularly since many fishermen and campers like to use them. I also agree with the panel's opinion; we cannot now say that the Interior Department's regulations are "arbitrary, capricious" or an "abuse of discretion." 5 U.S.C. § 706(2)(A). I add only that this latter question is quite a close one. The Conservation Law Foundation, in its brief, notes that recreational "vehicles are used by less than 2.5 percent of the summertime visitors to the Seashore." The government, in its brief, says that it has set aside 8 miles, of 48 Cape Cod National Seashore beachfront miles, or 16 percent of the beach, for ORV use. Although it seems fairly obvious that those who use ORVs need a length of coastline in which to use them, it is also fairly obvious that their use is often incompatible with the quiet enjoyment of the seashore that the Cape Cod National Seashore Act contemplated the vast majority of visitors would seek. At some geographical point, reserving miles of coastline for ORVs would amount to taking too much from too many for the enjoyment of too few. We here hold only that, giving full and appropriate weight to the judgment of the administrators, we cannot say, on the basis of the record before us, that 16 percent actually crosses the line marked by the statutory word "arbitrary."

NOTES AND QUESTIONS

1. Did the Park Service and the courts correctly interpret the Seashore Act as permitting ORV use? Examine the proviso at the end of § 7 of that Act. Notice the illustrative list of "appropriate public uses" does not specifically include ORVs, but does say the Secretary may allow "other activities of similar nature." Should the agency or the courts have demanded a more express statement by Congress that ORV use was appropriate on the Seashore before allowing it? Or did the court properly defer to the agency's interpretation here, that ORV use is not *per se* inappropriate? Cf.

Judge Breyer's concurring opinion on this point, and compare the language of § 601 of FLPMA, dealing with the California Desert, which did refer specifically to ORV use, and which was heavily relied upon by the Ninth Circuit in the *Dove Springs Canyon* case (see pp. 994–98, supra).

2.   The plaintiff argued that there had been "numerous" violations of the Park Service regulations allowing limited ORV use, and therefore unless the agency could prevent such violations, all ORV use should be banned. Did the court adequately respond to that argument by noting that the NPS had "added a significant number of rangers to improve patrol of the Seashore"?

3.   How significant was the fact that the NPS had commissioned a study which documented the effects of ORV use here?

4.   Is a key question in this case—and in ORV regulation generally—whether most of the ORV damage occurred *before* or *after* regulatory efforts were undertaken? If the major damage has already occurred, is there much reason to ban or stringently regulate future ORV use? Does the answer depend upon how practicable it is to restore the area to its pre-ORV use condition? Recall that a similar issue is raised with respect to livestock grazing, where unregulated livestock use in the 1880s caused massive and seemingly irreversible change on some public rangelands; see pp. 130, 783 supra.

5.   Should the federal agencies distinguish between ORV use for access purposes (for fishing, hunting, hiking, etc.) as opposed to use purely for the thrill of riding? (Is Judge, now Justice, Breyer hinting in his concurring opinion that the NPS may be on stronger legal ground if it allows ORV use only for access for fishing and camping, but not otherwise? Would regulators be able to meaningfully distinguish the two kinds of ORV uses? On the Cape Cod National Seashore, should the Park Service institute a shuttle to provide access to remote areas as a substitute for ORV use? Should ORV use for thrill-seeking be banned on federal lands, leaving it to the private market, and private property owners, to satisfy that demand?) Cf. note 8 following the *Dove Springs Canyon* case, p. 999 supra.

6.   The U.S. Forest Service has also been caught up in these controversies. In Northwest Motorcycle Ass'n v. U.S. Dept. of Agriculture, 18 F.3d 1468 (9th Cir.1994), the court upheld a Forest Service decision in a forest plan to close areas of a national forest to ORV use. The agency was applying Executive Order 11644's directive to control ORVs in order to, among other things, minimize conflicts among various users. In meetings with various users, the Forest Service documented that, while ORV users did not perceive a conflict between their use and nonmotorized uses, nonmotorized users disagreed. The court ruled that the agency was "in the best position to determine the credibility of the comments offered by the public establishing the existence of 'user conflict,'" and need not await "actual physical altercations" in order to act. Furthermore, there was ample evidence that the closure was "for the protection of the resources on the land" as well as the safety of all land users.

7. The California and Cape Cod situations both illustrate the power and importance of the Endangered Species Act. In California, the listing of the Desert Tortoise and rare desert plants have helped curb ORV use; on the east coast, the listing of the piping plover, a shorebird that frequents areas popular for ORVs, and some endangered plants have had the same effect. NEPA has also sometimes helped; e.g., in Washington Trails Ass'n v. United States Forest Service, 935 F.Supp. 1117 (W.D.Wash.1996), the court, in a suit by hikers, halted proposed trail reconstructions which would make roadless areas more accessible to ORVs on the ground that the agency had violated NEPA by ignoring evidence indicating the possibility of significant environmental impacts.

8. Science columnist and author Jake Page put the ORV on his list of "Ten Mediocre 20th-Century Inventions," SCIENCE 84 (Nov. 1984), p. 28, explaining:

> Since its founding, this nation has spent billions and billions of dollars of local, state, and federal funds to construct an elaborate network of lanes, roads, streets, and highways. These have been produced in order that constantly improving vehicles can transport people to where they must go with ever decreasing difficulty. Yet this century has seen the deliberate creation of vehicles precisely designed *not* to use this helpful network but instead to career around in places explicitly avoided by roads and their accompanying pollutants and noise. Thus snowmobiles destroy the quiet of a snowy wood, dirt bikes scream through rural meadows like chainsaws gone mad, and fat-tired beach vehicles spray sand and noise into the eyes and ears of sunbathers. Except for rescuing people, the ORV should be universally recalled.

(Page's list also included the digital watch, the electric guitar, guilt, and the gassed tomato.) John Gatchell of the Montana Wilderness Association has groused that "you mix gasoline and testosterone, and you get an ATV [all-terrain vehicle] out of it."

9. Mountain bikes are another technological innovation that can damage public resources and pose management problems; see Scott Havlick, Mountain Bikes on Federal Lands: Over the River and Through Which Woods?, 75 J.Energy L. & Policy 123 (1986). In Bicycle Trails Council of Marin v. Babbitt, 82 F.3d 1445, 1454, 1455, 1464 (9th Cir.1996), the court upheld the Park Service's prohibition of mountain bicycle use of certain trails. Among other things, it said:

> A decision to limit mountain bicycle use to trails affirmatively designated as appropriate for such use falls comfortably within [the] broad grant of discretion to the Secretary under the Organic Act. The Organic Act is unquestionably silent on the precise issue of bicycle trail access. However, the Secretary is directed to conserve the natural elements of the parks for the future, 16 U.S.C. § 1, to "provide for the enjoyment" of the parks, to manage the parks "in light of the high public value and integrity of the National Park System," 16 U.S.C. § 1a–1, and to make such rules as "he may deem necessary or proper for the use and management of the parks." 16 U.S.C. § 3. In light of this language, an interpretation that the Organic Act allows for this

closed-unless-designated-open approach for bicycle trail access cannot be termed "manifestly contrary to the statute."

[The court also rejected plaintiffs' argument that the Park Service's reversal of its prior position that bicycle use was more favored in national recreation areas, noting that the NPS now] provides that the use of bicycles is allowed in park areas under the same basic conditions as are motor vehicles, i.e., on park roads, in parking areas, and on routes designated for their use. These provisions reflect the facts that the NPS generally considers bicycle use a very appropriate, low impact method for visitors to enjoy park areas, but that certain limitations on their use are necessary and appropriate in the interest of public safety, resource protection, and the avoidance of visitor conflicts.

[The court also found] ample evidence in the administrative record support[ing] the finding by NPS that bicycle access to all trails increases incidents of user conflict and compromises visitor safety.

NOTE: SNOWMOBILES AND JET SKIS

Technological innovations continue to lead to new recreational stresses and controversies on federal lands; in the last few years, attention has turned to the snowmobile and personal watercraft (or "jet-ski"). Both devices employ a noisy two-stroke engine that provides heretofore unavailable quick access to remote areas, but also shatters the tranquility many associate with the federal land recreation experience. The engine is also dirty: A coalition of environmental groups has calculated that in one hour a typical snowmobile produces more hydrocarbons than a typical automobile does in a year of average driving. Environmentalists also claim that, because of snowmobiles, the west entrance to Yellowstone National Park had the highest carbon monoxide levels in the nation in the winter of 1996, and that snowmobile engines spewed out 50,000 gallons of raw gasoline in the Park. At the same time, a thriving winter economy based upon snowmobiles has grown up at the Park, creating a strong economic interest opposed to snowmobile regulation. The Park Service is picking through this policy minefield.

In October 1997, the Interior Department settled a NEPA lawsuit brought by environmental groups by agreeing to complete an EIS process on winter use in the area. At the end of that process, in December 2000, the NPS decided to phase out snowmobile use in Yellowstone National Park by the winter of 2003–04. See 65 Fed. Reg. 79024; 80908 (2000). The decision allowed continued winter use of the parks by snowcoaches while eliminating the impacts on park resources and values from snowmobile use. Excerpts follow:

In the winter of 1999–2000, 76,571 visitor-days of snowmobile use occurred in Yellowstone, representing over 60 percent of all [winter] visitors. * * * This motorized, oversnow use of the parks is a relatively recent development, with virtually no such use present in the parks in the 1970s.

* * * [NOPS has recently] conducted a survey of [the 44 units of the national park system] in which snowmobile use is currently allowed. * * * We learned * * * that much of the snowmobile use that occurs in the national park system is not consistent with management objectives or the protection of park resources and values, and is not in compliance with the requirements of the two executive orders and the NPS general regulations on snowmobile use.* * *

NPS general regulations on snowmobile use, 36 CFR 2.18(c), state that:

> The use of snowmobiles is prohibited, except on designated routes and water surfaces that are used by motor vehicles or motorboats during other seasons. Routes and water surfaces designated for snowmobile use shall be promulgated as special regulations. Snowmobiles are prohibited except where designated and only when their use is consistent with the park's natural, cultural, scenic and aesthetic values, safety considerations, park management objectives, and will not disturb wildlife or damage park resources.

The NPS has determined that the snowmobile use occurring in [Yellowstone and other parks] * * * harms the integrity of the resources and values of the parks, and therefore constitutes an impairment. We have also determined that the snowmobile use * * * is inconsistent with the requirements of the Clean Air Act, Executive Orders 11644 and 11989, the NPS's general snowmobile regulations, and NPS management objectives for the parks. The types of impacts on which these determinations are based are summarized below.

Natural Soundscapes. * * * [Studies demonstrate that, i]n open terrain with a quiet background, the sound of a single snowmobile is audible for about 4,120 feet * * * [and] a group of four snowmobiles for 7,510 feet[.] * * * By comparison, an automobile in the same circumstances is audible for 2,330 feet. According to daytime audibility monitoring, in Yellowstone, snowmobile noise can be heard 95 percent of the time by visitors at Old Faithful and 87 percent of the time at the Grand Canyon of the Yellowstone[.] * * *

Wildlife. * * * Snowmobile use in the parks takes place during the season when animals are most stressed by high snow depths, extreme cold, and food shortages. Disturbance or harassment of wildlife during this sensitive time can adversely affect individual animals and, in some cases, populations as a whole. * * * Wildlife movements are * * * inhibited by traffic and snow berms created by plowing and grooming operations. * * *

Air Quality. * * * Even though snowmobiles are present in Yellowstone for only three months of the year and there are fewer of them than there are of other motor vehicles during the remainder of the year, the snowmobiles contribute more air pollution to the park than do other motor vehicles. The contribution from snowmobiles to total annual hydrocarbon emissions from all mobile sources can range from 68% to 90% at Yellowstone, depending on which emission factors are used to estimate emissions. Similarly, snowmobiles can contribute from 35% to 68% of total carbon monoxide annual emissions.* * * Employees at the entrance station have complained of adverse health effects from emissions from snowmobiles. * * * In 1993 and 1994, Yellowstone received over 1,200 complaint letters concerning employee and visitor health and excessive snowmobile pollution. * * * Snowmobiles can cause localized, perceptible decreases in visibility near the West Entrance and Old Faithful in Yellowstone[.] * * *

Water Quality. * * * Deposition of airborne pollutants from snowmobiles and snowplanes onto frozen lake surfaces and snowpack can lead to those pollutants entering groundwater and surface water when the snow and ice melts. * * * Concentrations of ammonium and sulfate at the sites in the snowpacked roadways between West Yellowstone and Old Faithful were greater than those observed at any of the 50 to 60 other snowpack-sampling sites in the Rocky Mountain region. * * *

Effects on Other Visitors. * * * Winter visitor surveys indicate that the most important factors for visitor enjoyment in the parks are opportunities to view scenery and wildlife, the safe behavior of others, and opportunities to experience clean air and solitude. * * * [S]nowmobiles can cause decreases in visibility and increased air pollution within the parks; disturb the natural presence and behavior of wildlife; interfere with the natural soundscapes of the parks, reducing a sense of solitude; and adversely affect public safety.

Safety Considerations. * * * In the last 10 years, eight fatalities in Yellowstone resulted from snowmobile accidents. In 1994, 44 percent of all park fatalities resulted from snowmobile accidents. During the past five winters, 92 percent of all incidents requiring response from an NPS ranger involved snowmobiles, which account for 61 percent of all winter users. During all of fiscal year 1998, snowmobilers, who represent two percent of all park visitors in the year, were involved in nine percent of Yellowstone's motor vehicle accidents. * * *

NPS Management Objectives. Prohibiting snowmobile use in Yellowstone * * * and providing instead for greater winter use of the parks by snowcoaches, is consistent with NPS's management objectives for these parks. Doing so would reduce adverse impacts on park resources and values, better provide for public safety, and provide for public enjoyment of the parks in winter.

Snowcoaches [larger vehicles, often converted passenger vans, that, like snowmobiles, operate over snow on belts, but more slowly] have lower impacts on park resources and values than snowmobiles. For example, a single newer snowcoach, capable of carrying eight or more passengers, emits much lower levels of air pollutants and much less noise than a single snowmobile, which carries one or two passengers. Also, snowcoaches, operated by professional, trained drivers operating under NPS concession contracts or permits, are much less likely to be operated in a way that disturbs wildlife than snowmobiles. As a result, expanding the use of snowcoaches and eliminating most use of snowmobiles will make it possible to accommodate large numbers of winter visitors to the parks, while still preserving an enjoyable experience for most visitors and avoiding substantial adverse impacts on park resources.

If the NPS were to continue to allow snowmobiles in the parks * * * it would be necessary to establish very strict limitations on that use to remain consistent with the NPS Organic, the relevant Executive Orders, the NPS general snowmobile regulations, and other applicable requirements. Even with strict user limitations, however, snowmobiles would continue to have substantial adverse impacts on natural soundscapes, wildlife, air quality, the experience of other park visitors, and other park resources and values. The remaining impacts would be substantial enough that it might be necessary to also limit the number of other types of users, at least including snowcoach users, to ensure that overall winter visitor impacts would not unlawfully or unacceptably affect park resources and values. Rather than establishing limitations on both snowmobile and snowcoach users, the NPS prefers to eliminate most snowmobile use in the parks and allow unlimited access to the parks by snowcoach users and other visitors.

Other Legal Requirements. The NPS has been unable to find any evidence that the Service, before now, made the determinations required by Executive Order 11644—that snowmobile use in particular areas and on particular trails in these parks will not adversely affect the park's natural, aesthetic, or scenic values of the parks—before deciding to allow snowmobile use in the parks. Further, until making this proposal for new rules, the NPS has not complied with the requirement of that Executive Order that the Service rescind or amend the designation or areas open to snowmobile use as necessary to avoid adverse effects on the park's natural, aesthetic, or scenic values.

Also, prior to proposing this rule, the NPS has not complied with the requirement of Executive Order 11989 that the Service, whenever it determines that the use of snowmobiles will cause or is causing considerable adverse effects on the natural resources of a park, take steps to prevent those effects, including immediately halting that use.

The regulations themselves were published at 66 Fed. Reg. 7260 (2001), along with responses to comments and other relevant information. Excerpts follow:

Some comments said we should not take away visitors' personal freedom to ride snowmobiles where and when they want to, leaving as their only option travel in snowcoaches driven by somebody else.

NPS Response—We understand that many people enjoy the freedom snowmobiles provide. However, we must comply with the applicable legal requirements. Snowmobilers will continue to be able to ride snowmobiles where and when they want to on other lands, including nearby national forest lands that are open to snowmobile use. In other parks, when necessary to protect their resources and values, we have prohibited travel by individual motor vehicles, providing mass transit instead. This has been widely acceptable to visitors to those parks. We

believe this change will be acceptable to visitors to these parks, too.
* * *

Numerous comments urged us to require the use of cleaner and quieter snowmobiles rather than prohibiting the use of all snowmobiles.

NPS Response—Some newer snowmobiles have promise for reducing some impacts, but not enough for the use of large numbers of those machines to be consistent with the applicable legal requirements. Cleaner, quieter snowmobiles would do little, if anything, to reduce the most serious impacts on wildlife, which are caused more by inappropriate use of snowmobiles than by the machines themselves. Quieter snowmobiles are still noisy, and are audible at a greater distance than 4-track conversion snowcoaches. Since snowcoaches carry many passengers and snowmobiles only one or two, snowcoaches can accommodate the same level of overall winter visitation with far fewer noise impacts on the natural soundscape and other visitors than even quieter snowmobiles. Also, the ultimate extent to which some new snowmobiles may produce less air pollution over their useful life is unclear in the absence of emission standards, testing, and certification. Under the Clean Air Act, the EPA has the authority to establish emission standards for snowmobiles, and it is at least two or three years away from setting any such standards, which then would not take effect for additional years. The need for us to comply with the applicable legal requirements does not allow for such a delay. * * *

Some comments said we are relying too much on snowcoaches, expressing concerns about their reliability, the comfort of passengers, their availability for purchase in sufficient numbers and at prices affordable for businesses, and their lack of speed.

NPS Response—Snowcoaches have been used successfully in national parks for over 45 years. We believe their mechanical reliability is satisfactory. They are fast enough for Yellowstone destinations to be within reach for a trip of reasonable duration. They are comfortable enough—for most passengers, more comfortable than snowmobiles. Businesses currently operate 45 snowcoaches in the parks, indicating their viability as a business option. Additional businesses have already expressed interest in new economic opportunities resulting from this rule, from producing them for sale to operating them in the parks.
* * *

[The Park Service also addressed economic impacts, and summarized a consultant's study it contracted for, which] estimates that the total adverse economic effect on businesses (mostly small businesses) will likely range from $4.8 million to $10 million annually. * * * Most affected will be 70 snowmobile rental businesses and 11 snowcoach tour companies, which could lose between $4.1 million to $4.4 million annually. Most are in West Yellowstone, Montana, with others in other gateway communities. Hotels, restaurants, gas stations, and retail establishments, again mostly in West Yellowstone but also in other gateway communities, will be less affected, and could lose between $700,000 to $5.6 million annually. One local government, the city of

West Yellowstone, will be an affected small entity, and could lose between $80,000 to $125,000 from reduced resort tax receipts. From a national perspective, these impacts do not constitute a significant impact to a substantial number of small entities. * * *

We have made several decisions on how to implement this action to mitigate any adverse economic impacts, especially those on small entities. To begin with, the elimination of snowmobiles will be phased over four winter seasons, allowing significant time for affected businesses to adjust to providing snowcoach service instead. Next, snowcoach access to the parks will require a concession permit from us. Permits will be awarded to numerous small businesses in the surrounding communities. We have already authorized existing snowmobile operators to add snowcoach service, and authorized existing snowcoach operators to add more coaches. Finally, we will join with the tourism offices of the affected states and counties, as well as destination marketing organizations, to market winter visitation to the parks under the new rules. We have committed $100,000 in fiscal year 2001 for this purpose.

NOTES AND QUESTIONS

1. How relevant is local and national public opinion to this decision? The Interior Department received about 5300 comments on its proposed rule, 4400 of which supported it. Should the Department take more account of public comments in the local area or elsewhere? More account of personal or reasoned responses than of preprinted postcards or form letters?

2. In December 2000 the International Snowmobile Manufacturers' Association filed suit challenging Interior's NEPA compliance and seeking to enjoin implementation of the decision. The State of Wyoming promptly intervened as a plaintiff. The Bush Administration settled the lawsuit in June 2001, and agreed to prepare a supplemental EIS and make a new decision in 18 months. Given the findings and conclusions expressed in the above excerpts, how would you advise the Bush Administration to go about reversing the ban on snowmobile use at Yellowstone? Is legislation necessary? Is repeal or revision of the Executive Orders dealing with off-road vehicles necessary in order to reverse the ban? Repeal or revision of Director's Order #55 interpreting the Organic Act? See pp. 955–58 supra. Is calling for new studies of the effects of snowmobiles a sufficient reason in and of itself to justify reversing the ban? Is it sufficient if the Administration decides it will await the development of four-stroke engines for snowmobiles, which would presumably be much quieter and less polluting? In the meantime, snowmobile technology continues to evolve in other ways, with the machines gaining power, losing weight, and being able to handle ever deeper snow.

3. In Voyageurs Region Nat'l Park Ass'n v. Lujan, 966 F.2d 424 (8th Cir.1992), the court upheld a NPS decision to allow snowmobile use of a roadless area in Voyageurs National Park, relying heavily on the fact that the statute designating that particular Park authorized the Secretary to

"include appropriate provisions for (1) winter sports, including the use of snowmobiles." 16 U.S.C. § 160h. Does that decision support or undercut a ban on snowmobiles at Yellowstone? See also note 3, p. 997, and note 1, p. 1004, supra.

4. The National Park Service in the Clinton Administration also adopted a new policy that limits personal watercraft (PWC) use to 25 national park system units (of the 32 where their use had been established before the policy was adopted) and prohibits it in the rest of the system. See 65 Fed. Reg. 15077 (2000), codified at 36 C.F.R. §§ 1.4, 3.24, 13.1 (2001). The preamble to the final rule noted:

> Over the years, NPS areas have been impacted with new, and what often prove to be controversial, recreational activities * * * [which] tend to gain a foothold in NPS areas in their infancy, before a full evaluation of the possible impacts and ramifications * * * can be initiated, completed and considered. PWC use fits this category.
>
> PWC use * * * has been observed in about 32 of the 87 areas of the National Park System that allow motorized boating. PWCs are high performance vessels designed for speed and maneuverability and are often used to perform stunt-like maneuvers. * * * Over 1.3 million PWCs are in use today with annual sales of approximately 150,000 units. * * *
>
> This rule takes a conservative approach to managing PWC use in areas of the National Park System based on consideration of the potential resource impacts, conflicts with other visitors' uses and enjoyment, and safety concerns. The rule prohibits PWC use in areas of the National Park System unless we determine that PWC use is appropriate for a specific area based on that area's enabling legislation, resources, values, other visitor uses, and overall management objectives. * * *
>
> [There are] 1,782 federally managed man-made lakes and reservoirs. The NPS manages 82 of these lakes (4.6%). A number of the NPS managed lakes will have continued PWC use. Therefore, well over 95% of the federally managed recreation lakes will be unaffected by this rulemaking.

See Karen D'Antuono, The NPS's Proposed Ban: A New Approach to Personal Watercraft Use in the National Parks, 27 B.C. Envt'l Aff. L. Rev. 243 (2000).

5. Is there an argument that snowmobiles and PWCs are legally forbidden in the park system by the terms of the National Park Organic Act? Or can they be allowed everywhere outside of wilderness (where motorized vehicles are generally forbidden, see p. 1115 infra)?

F. FEDERAL LIABILITY FOR RECREATIONAL MISHAPS

Mountain climbing, motorcycle racing, and white water rafting pose obvious risks; hiking and camping in an area inhabited by grizzly bears can unnerve even the stout-hearted. Even hiking in canyons prone to flash-flooding, swimming in unfamiliar places, or driving on primitive backcountry roads can be hazardous. People, especially those less experienced at such pursuits, have been killed or seriously injured when a recreational activity goes awry. Not infrequently, the United States as landowner and land manager is claimed to be liable.

The United States has sovereign immunity from tort liability, but has waived it in specified circumstances in the Federal Tort Claims Act, 28 U.S.C. §§ 1291, 1346, 1402, 2401, 2402, 2411, 2412, 2671–80 (FTCA). Specifically, the FTCA allows recovery for

> personal injury or death caused by the negligent or wrongful act or omission of any employee of the Government while acting within the scope of his office or employment, under circumstances where the United States, if a private person, would be liable to the claimant in accordance with the law of the place where the act or omission occurred.

Id. § 1346(b). The last-quoted clause makes federal liability somewhat dependent on state tort law. This has raised a number of issues. One is the extent to which the United States can be treated the same as a private party when it manages its lands for public recreational benefit. Another concerns the application and integration of state recreational use statutes which sharply limit private landowner liability. The next principal case grapples with these.

An important exception in the FTCA is that federal liability does not extend to performance of "discretionary functions." That is, the FTCA prohibits any claim against the United States "based upon the exercise or performance or the failure to exercise or perform a discretionary function or duty on the part of a federal agency or an employee of the Government, whether or not the discretion involved be abused." 28 U.S.C. § 2680(a). Application of this concept has long bedeviled the courts; see, e.g., Dalehite v. United States, 346 U.S. 15 (1953); United States v. S.A. Empresa de Viacao Aerea Rio Grandense (Varig Airlines), 467 U.S. 797 (1984); Berkovitz v. United States, 486 U.S. 531 (1988). Its application to federal land management is considered further below.

Otteson v. United States

United States Court of Appeals, Tenth Circuit, 1980.
622 F.2d 516.

■ SEYMOUR, CIRCUIT JUDGE.

* * * The tragic accident giving rise to this litigation occurred in San Juan National Forest in Colorado. The decedent Stacey Otteson was a passenger in a jeep returning from a pleasure trip. After traveling down a narrow dirt logging access road which reaches a dead end several miles beyond the point of the accident, the jeep was forced to return due to impassable snow and ice. On the way back, the jeep slid on an ice patch and rolled down an embankment. Stacey and the driver were killed, and two other passengers received minor injuries.

The estate of Stacey Otteson brought a wrongful death action against the United States under the Federal Tort Claims Act. It alleged that Stacey's death resulted from the government's negligent failure to maintain the road free from ice, to warn of hazards on the road, or to close it when it became unsafe. The government moved for summary judgment, contending it is immune from liability under the Tort Claims Act on two grounds: 1) it was performing a "discretionary function" in the design and maintenance of the road; and 2) a private individual would not be liable under the facts of the case and the law of the forum state. The trial court found the second contention dispositive and granted the government's motion. We affirm. * * *

The trial judge concluded that a private landowner is not liable for negligence to persons coming onto the land for recreational purposes under Colorado's "sightseer statute".[1] Therefore, he found as a matter of law * * * that the government had not waived its immunity from liability in accordance with the Tort Claims Act.

On appeal, plaintiff contends that the sightseer statute should not have been applied to bar its claim because the government is not in the same position as the private parties to whom the statute applies. The purpose of the statute is to encourage private landowners to open their land to the public for recreational purposes. However, plaintiff asserts that the government has an independent duty to maintain the national forests as public recreational areas. Therefore, plaintiff argues that the government has a corresponding duty to maintain the roads in the national forests for recreational use. Plaintiff would have us equate this duty with that which a political subdivision has to maintain public roads.

Plaintiff's argument misconceives the purposes of the national forests, as set forth in the National Forests Acts [sic], 16 U.S.C. §§ 471a et seq. The recent Supreme Court case of United States v. New Mexico, 438 U.S. 696 (1978) [eds., Chapter 6, supra p. 521], contains a thorough discussion of the legislative history and purposes of the national forest system. The Court there held that the Acts establishing the national forests had "only two purposes—'[t]o conserve the water flows and to furnish a continuous supply of timber for the people'. * * * National forests were not to be reserved for aesthetic, environmental, recreational, or wildlife-preservation

---

1. Sections 33–41–101 et seq. of the Colorado Revised Statutes (1973) provide that:

"33–41–101. Legislative declaration. The purpose of this article is to encourage owners of land within rural areas to make land and water areas available for recreational purposes by limiting their liability toward persons entering thereon for such purposes.

* * *

"33–41–103. Limitation on landowner's liability. (1) Subject to the provision of section 33–41–105, an owner of land who either directly or indirectly invites or permits, without charge, any person to use such property for recreational purposes does not thereby:

(a) Extend any assurance that the premises are safe for any purpose;

(b) Confer upon such person the legal status of any invitee or licensee to whom a duty of care is owed;

(c) Assume responsibility or incur liability for any injury to person or property or for the death of any person caused by an act or omission of such person."

purposes." Id. at 707, 708. While the Court noted that the Multiple–Use Sustained–Yield Act of 1960 broadened the purposes for which national forests are maintained to include recreation, the Court made clear that recreation was a secondary and supplemental purpose, and that a national forest could not be established for recreation alone. 438 U.S. at 713–715.

Bearing in mind the primary purposes for which national forests have been established, we now consider plaintiff's argument that the Forest Service has a duty to maintain roads in the national forests under the same standard imposed on a political subdivision. While it is true that Congress has stated recreation to be one of the uses for the national forest road system [16 U.S.C. § 532], the legislation and relevant regulations read as a whole clearly indicate that the roads are intended primarily to facilitate the harvesting, removal and management of timber. See 16 U.S.C. § 535 and 36 C.F.R. § 212.12 (1979). Although these provisions authorize the construction of roads of a higher standard than that needed for the harvesting and removal of timber, they do not require it. The road on which this accident occurred was constructed and maintained for logging.[5] We do not believe Congress intended to impose on the Forest Service the same standard of maintenance with respect to all logging roads that a political subdivision has regarding public thoroughfares. Therefore, we reject plaintiff's argument that the government should be treated as a political subdivision rather than a private landowner for purposes of the Tort Claims Act. * * *

Plaintiff's argument that the government should not be treated as a private party under the Colorado sightseer statute because it is somehow obligated to keep the national forests open to the public is unpersuasive. The Forest Service regulations allow each Forest Supervisor, among others, to close or restrict the use of forest areas and roads.[6] If liability were imposed upon the government in cases such as this one, the Forest Service might well choose to close the forests to public use rather than bear the heavy burden of maintaining logging roads as public thoroughfares. This result is precisely what the Colorado sightseer statute was enacted to prevent. Thus, we hold that the government is entitled to the protection of the Colorado sightseer statute and is therefore only liable "[f]or willful or malicious failure to guard or warn against a known dangerous condition * * *." Colo.Rev.Stat. § 33–41–104(a) (1973). * * * Accordingly, the trial court judgment is affirmed.

NOTES AND QUESTIONS

1. Is the court's reasoning consistent with the historical policy of keeping national forest lands open for recreation? Recall that the Multiple–

---

5. We need not decide what liability, if any, would be incurred by the Forest Service with respect to roads built to a standard higher than that required for logging. Thus this case is distinguishable from Miller v. United States, 597 F.2d 614 (7th Cir.1979), cited by plaintiff. In *Miller,* the area in which the accident occurred was maintained by the government and included bathroom facilities and a boat dock.

6. See 36 C.F.R. §§ 261.50, 261.53, and 261.54 (1979).

Use, Sustained Yield Act makes "outdoor recreation" one of the five co-equal authorized uses of the national forests, and that the National Forest Management Act requires forest plans to, *inter alia*, "provide for outdoor recreation," 16 U.S.C. § 1604(g)(3)(A). Do these statutes suggest the court's analysis in *Otteson* is wrong?

2.   A policy statement in FLPMA directs the BLM to manage federal lands under its care

> in a manner that will protect the quality of scientific, scenic, historical, ecological, environmental, air and atmospheric, water resource, and archeological values; that, where appropriate, will preserve and protect certain public lands in their natural condition; that will provide food and habitat for fish and wildlife and domestic animals; and that will provide for outdoor recreation and human occupancy and use.

43 U.S.C. § 1701(a)(8). What should be the result if a similar accident were to occur on BLM lands?

3.   Note that in the *Otteson* situation the federal land management agency has an incentive to argue against recreation management responsibility, in order to minimize its exposure under the FTCA. Here, in other words, the Forest Service argues that its roads are built for logging, while in other contexts the agency argues that part of the cost of the roads is properly accountable to recreation. See the discussion of "below-cost" timber sales in Chapter 8, pp. 724–26 supra. Can the agency have it both ways?

4.   Note the close interplay between federal and state law here. Under the FTCA, do the state legislatures and courts hold the keys to the federal treasury? What prevents them from adopting broad rules of liability to unlock the federal treasury on behalf of their injured citizens? (The court here did not explain why it examined plaintiff's argument that the Forest Service should be subject to the same standard of liability as a political subdivision of the state. The FTCA expressly equates federal agency liability with that of a "private person" under state law, not a political subdivision. 28 U.S.C. § 1346(b).)

5.   Before the advent of state recreational use statutes, federal liability for recreational accidents was more common. Earlier decisions are cited in George Cameron Coggins & Robert Glicksman, I, PUBLIC NATURAL RESOURCES LAW Ch. 10 (2001). Since 1960, nearly all states have responded to the collision between growth in outdoor recreation and expanding tort liability notions by adopting such statutes. See Paul A. Svoboda, Protecting Visitors to National Recreation Areas Under the FTCA, 84 Colum.L.Rev. 1792, 1798 (1984).

6.   The FTCA does not, however, incorporate state law in all cases. For example, in Bilderback v. United States, 558 F.Supp. 903 (D.Or.1982), Rocky, a "frisky but otherwise undistinguished Forest Service pack horse," got loose; while wandering on the road, Rocky was struck by plaintiffs' automobile, injuring them (and killing Rocky). The United States contended that it had no duty to keep its animals off the highways because the Oregon state "open range" law allows livestock to roam at large without

trespass liability. The court held that federal grazing regulations preempted that aspect of state law on the federal range. Then, finding in both federal law and analogous state law a duty to prevent animals from wandering where they ought not to be, the court adjudged the government negligent and awarded damages. The result is an interesting twist on federal preemption in the "open range" context; see the discussion in Chapter 2, pp. 97–98 supra.

7.   In some cases a state law other than the recreational use statute may apply. For example, in Miller v. United States, 597 F.2d 614 (7th Cir.1979), involving a diving accident at a National Wildlife Refuge, the court held the state recreational use statute inapplicable, and instead applied a separate state law that governed private recreational facilities open for more than "casual" recreational use.

NOTE: FEES AND THE SIGHTSEER STATUTES

In Ducey v. United States, 713 F.2d 504 (9th Cir.1983), the court considered the application of the Nevada recreational use statute in a suit against the United States seeking compensation for the deaths of three persons in a flash flood in Eldorado Canyon in the Lake Mead National Recreation Area. Decedents had been camping and boating. The Park Service had a ranger station, boat launching ramp, and comfort stations in the area, and a Park Service concessioner maintained and operated a cafe-store, boat slips, automobile fueling and boat service facilities, rental cabins, and trailer spaces. The decedents had paid no fees to the U.S.; two of them had paid rental fees to the concessioner for use of a boat slip, one had rented a trailer space, and all three had bought various goods at the concessioner's store. The concessioner was obligated to pay 1 1/4% of its gross receipts to the Park Service.

The Nevada statute was generally similar, but not identical, to the Colorado statute at issue in *Otteson*. It provided limited immunity for private property owners, except where permission to participate in recreational activities "was granted for a consideration * * *." Nev.Rev.Stat. § 41.510(3). The Park Service argued that it had not received consideration, both because no fee was charged to enter the area, and because the payments to the concessionaire were not "consideration" that should apply to the government. The court disagreed:

> First, the language of the consideration exception itself suggests a broad reading of section 41.510(3)(b). The exception is worded not in narrow terms of "fee" or "charge," but rather in the far more encompassing terms, "for a consideration." "Consideration" is a term of art, a word with a well-understood meaning in the law, embracing any "right, interest, profit or benefit." *Black's Law Dictionary* 277 (rev. 5th ed. 1979). Used in a statute, it should be accorded that meaning. The statutory exception, then, is itself literally applicable to situations well beyond those involving a strict charging of a "fee" for "permission" to recreate. * * *

The policy underlying the adoption of a consideration exception to the Nevada recreational use statute is to retain tort liability in actions involving recreational use of land where the use of the land for recreational purposes is granted not gratuitously but in return for an economic benefit. Since the potential for profit alone is thought sufficient to encourage those owners who wish to make commercial use of their recreational lands to open them to the public, the further stimulus of tort immunity is both unnecessary and improper. Furthermore, where a landowner derives an economic benefit from allowing others to use his land for recreational purposes, the landowner is in a position to post warnings, supervise activities, and otherwise seek to prevent injuries. Such a landowner also has the ability to purchase liability insurance or to self-insure, thereby spreading the cost of accidents over all users of the land.

The court also rejected the argument that the National Park Service was immune because the consideration was not paid to it:

Subsection 41.510(3)(b) does not specify to whom consideration must be tendered. We think it a fair reading of the provision, however, that consideration must be tendered directly or indirectly to a person who has the power to grant or deny permission to participate in recreational activities. Since the concession agreement did not give ECR the power to deny permission to recreate in Eldorado Canyon, the exception is applicable only if consideration was tendered, directly or indirectly, to the United States in return for permission to recreate in Eldorado Canyon. We conclude that this condition is met in this case.

Before entering its concession agreement with ECR, the United States certainly was free to deny permission to recreate in Eldorado Canyon. * * * Thereafter, however, it was not. The concession agreement required the concessioner to provide and maintain facilities, to offer services, and to pay to the government a fixed percentage of all revenues from operations. Implicit in the agreement was a commitment on the government's part that users would be allowed to enter the area to use the concession facilities. Under these circumstances, we conclude that the consideration tendered here by the users to ECR was in return for permission to participate in recreational activities in Eldorado Canyon in the sense of subsection 41.510(3)(b).

The court remanded for further proceedings on whether the United States was immune under the "discretionary function" exception. One judge dissented:

* * * I read the [Nevada] statute to mean quite clearly that the owner is exempt from liability unless he charges a *fee* for granting permission to participate in these recreational activities. Thus, I think that the attempt in the opinion to impose liability upon the owner in the event *any* transaction for consideration takes place while a person is on the property imposes a burden that is not intended by the statute. I cannot believe that the fact that the decedents may have bought coffee or a candy bar or paid a fee for a place to park a trailer should be allowed to negative the fact that they were given free access to the area. * * *

NOTES AND QUESTIONS

1. What is the underlying purpose of the "consideration" requirement? Is the majority applying it in accordance with that purpose? Did the United States open this area to recreation to make money? Did it charge for any of the activities mentioned in the statute? Did it allow use of its lands "gratuitously"? When plaintiffs bought candy bars at the cafe-store, what were they paying for?

2. What will be the consequences under the FTCA and state sightseer statutes of the fact that many federal land management agencies now charge fees for admission to federal recreation areas? See the note, pp. 979–81 supra, on recent developments in fees. While fees bring in useful revenue, if they result in less immunity for the United States, they may prove to be a mixed financial blessing. Of course, the discretionary function defense will still be available, as explored below, which could blunt the effect of the U.S. not being able to defend on the basis of state sightseer statutes.

3. Should Congress enact uniform standards defining federal liability for recreational accidents on the public lands, rather than leaving the questions substantially up to state law? What standards would be appropriate?

The Supreme Court has in recent decades expanded the scope of the FTCA's "discretionary function" exception, and this has had an impact in the federal lands context, as the following materials show.

Johnson v. United States

United States Court of Appeals, Tenth Circuit, 1991.
949 F.2d 332.

■ BRORBY, CIRCUIT JUDGE.

[Decedent and three companions hiked to the summit of Buck Mountain in Grand Teton National Park. The group descended in pairs in the late morning, and the two less experienced climbers, Feikin and the decedent Johnson, strayed from the trail and entered difficult terrain. Feikin became stuck on a ledge; the decedent continued on. Later that afternoon, the two experienced climbers (Macal and Wechner), who had descended without difficulty, decided to summon help. Macal went to the visitor's center where he reported to Park Ranger Springer at 4:30 P.M. that the other two climbers were off course. Springer radioed Ranger Harrington in the vicinity of Buck Mountain, who reported he had seen four climbers descending the mountain. Springer then told Macal to return to the trailhead to wait for his companions. At 8:45 P.M., Macal encountered Wechner, who reported that Feikin was still stuck on the ledge and the whereabouts of Johnson was unknown. It then became clear that the two other climbers Ranger Harrington had seen were not Feikin and Johnson. The Park

Service was informed, and after consultations, rangers were dispatched at 9:30 P.M. to search for the missing men. Feikin was found and rescued in the early morning. Johnson, who had fallen on a hard snowslope and sustained a serious head injury about 3:15 P.M. the previous day, was not located until a helicopter search was undertaken at first light. He had died of hypothermia several hours earlier.] * * *

Plaintiff alleges that Ben Johnson would not have died but for the Park Service's negligent failure to: (1) adequately regulate a recreational climbing activity in Grand Teton National Park; (2) initiate a rescue effort after Macal's initial report; and (3) conduct a reasonable rescue effort after Macal's second report. In response to these allegations, Defendant filed a motion to dismiss, or, in the alternative, for summary judgment, asserting as a matter of law: (1) Plaintiff's action is jurisdictionally barred by the discretionary function exception to the FTCA, 28 U.S.C. 2680(a); and (2) the United States had no legal duty to rescue Ben Johnson. * * * Because we conclude the discretionary function exception deprived the district court of jurisdiction, we do not address the propriety of the district court's summary judgment rulings regarding legal duty, breach of duty or proximate cause.

* * * [The FTCA's] broad waiver of sovereign immunity is limited, however, by the discretionary function exception, which prohibits any claim against the United States "based upon the exercise or performance or the failure to exercise or perform a discretionary function or duty on the part of a federal agency or an employee of the Government, *whether or not the discretion involved be abused.*" Id. § 2680(a) (emphasis added). The discretionary function exception "marks the boundary between Congress' willingness to impose tort liability upon the United States and its desire to protect certain governmental activities from exposure to suit by private individuals." United States v. S.A. Empresa de Viacao Aerea Rio Grandense (Varig Airlines), 467 U.S. 797, 808 (1984). Application of this exception is therefore a threshold issue—a jurisdictional issue which precedes any negligence analysis. * * *

* * * [T]he principles set forth in Berkovitz v. United States, 486 U.S. 531 (1988) * * * guide * * * application of the discretionary function exception. * * * We first consider whether the challenged action "is a matter of choice for the acting employee." Berkovitz, 486 U.S. at 536. If a statute, regulation, or policy prescribes a specific course of conduct, then an employee must "adhere to the directive" and no discretion is involved. Id. If, however, the challenged action is discretionary, we must then determine whether it is of the kind Congress intended to shield through the exception. Id. The Court concluded that Congress intended to shield only those "governmental ... decisions based on considerations of public policy"—decisions " 'grounded in social, economic and political policy.' " Id. at 537 (quoting *Varig,* 467 U.S. at 814). Accordingly, the discretionary function exception will not bar a negligence claim if the government's "policy leaves no room for an official to exercise policy judgment in performing a given act, or if the act simply does not involve the exercise of such judgment." Id. at 546–47.

Interestingly, no federal court has been asked to apply the discretionary function exception to circumstances similar to those presented here. Therefore, the issue of whether the National Park Service's climbing regulation and rescue decisions in Grand Teton National Park are shielded from liability is one of first impression.[4] We do not approach this issue lightly—"exceptions to the FTCA are to be narrowly construed." *Miller*, 710 F.2d at 662. For that reason, we must carefully apply the *Berkovitz* analysis to the unique facts of this case, examining separately Plaintiff's claims regarding (1) regulating climbing activity, and (2) initiating and conducting rescue efforts. We examine the regulation claim first.

Plaintiff challenges, inter alia, Park Service decisions not to require additional warnings regarding the potential danger of mountain climbing, not to require safety equipment use, not to test the competency of each mountain climber, and not to "clear" the mountains of all climbers before dark. They assert that these decisions regarding the nature and extent of mountain climbing regulations in Grand Teton National Park do not invoke the discretionary function exception * * *. We disagree.

* * * [N]o federal statutes or regulations apply to the National Park Service or to Grand Teton National Park which specify how mountain climbing should be regulated. The Park Service has never promulgated a formal mountain climbing policy or climbing regulations. The Park does, however, require climbers to obtain a permit before departing on a climb. The purpose of the permit system is to educate climbers via face-to-face ranger contact. When a permit is requested, rangers attempt to evaluate the climbers' capabilities, and suggest alternative climbs if appropriate. Rangers have no authority, however, to prohibit climbers from taking a particular route.

Within this broad statutory/regulatory framework, we first examine Plaintiff's assertion that Park Service decisions regarding climbing regulation are not insulated from liability. Plaintiff concedes these decisions involve an exercise of judgment or choice, and thereby satisfy the first *Berkovitz* prong. No statute, regulation, or policy specifically prescribes a course of action for the National Park Service to follow. Decisions as to the extent or nature of mountain climbing regulation are truly the product of the Park Service's independent judgment—they are discretionary.

Plaintiff argues, however, that these regulatory decisions fail the second prong of *Berkovitz*—they do not implicate social, economic, or political policy considerations. To the contrary, Superintendent Stark asserts that each of Plaintiff's contentions have been considered, but were rejected for the following social and economic policy reasons: (1) the inherent dangers of mountain climbing are patently obvious; (2) both

---

4. A review of case law addressing the scope of the discretionary function exception reveals that the cases typically fall into one of two broad categories: alleged negligence in program design/construction (technical decisions requiring economic, social, or political judgments such that the exception is applicable) or alleged negligence in failure to warn of a hazardous condition (safety considerations under an established policy such that the exception is not applicable). * * * This case does not fall squarely within either category.

manpower and economic resources should be conserved to preserve availability during emergency situations; (3) it would be impractical if not impossible to test competency, monitor equipment use, or "clear" the mountain given the limited available manpower and economic resources; and (4) many Park visitors value backcountry climbing as one of the few experiences free from government regulation or interference. Plaintiff has presented no evidence to dispute Superintendent Stark's assertions. We conclude that decisions if, when and how to regulate mountain climbing in Grand Teton National Park go to the essence of the Park Service's judgment in maintaining the Park according to the broad statutory directive. By their very nature, these decisions involve balancing competing policy considerations pertaining to visitor safety, resource availability, and the appropriate degree of governmental interference in recreational activity. The Park Service's actions, insofar as they relate to the regulation of mountain climbing in Grand Teton National Park, are therefore shielded from judicial review by the discretionary function exception.

Plaintiff's failure to warn claim[7] should be analyzed separately from the alleged failure to adequately regulate mountain climbing. * * * "[A] decision not to warn 'still may be a policy decision *or part of a policy decision* protected by the discretionary function exception.'" [quoting Zumwalt v. United States, 928 F.2d 951, 955 (10th Cir.1991).]

* * * [T]he record here indicates the Park Service's decision not to place additional warnings in the Teton Range, whether explicit or implicit, was part of the overall policy decision to limit governmental regulation of climbing, educate climbers via the permit system, and preserve the Park in accordance with the statutory directive. This decision cannot be divorced from the overall policy not to engage in strict regulation of climbing activity in the Park. "A decision that is a component of an overall policy decision protected by the discretionary function exception also is protected by this exception." *Zumwalt*, 928 F.2d at 955. * * * In the absence of facts indicating the failure to post additional warnings was a distinct, nonpolicy decision, we conclude that Plaintiff's failure to warn claim is barred by the discretionary function exception.

We now turn to the issue of whether Park Service decisions if, when and how to conduct rescue operations are shielded by the discretionary function exception. Fundamentally, Plaintiff alleges that the National Park Service was negligent in its response to Ben Johnson's plight. However, the dispositive threshold issue is not whether the Park Service was negligent, but rather what was the nature of the Park Service's decisions. In response to this issue, Plaintiff baldly asserts that "the rangers [sic] negligent actions in responding to Macal and Wechner 'simply did not involve the exercise of [social, economic and political] judgment,'" and, therefore, do

---

7. Try as he might, Plaintiff cannot legitimately characterize this case as a * * * "failure to warn" case. The record makes it abundantly clear that the basis of Plaintiff's suit is the alleged negligent failure to rescue. In fact, the record indicates that a warning was posted at the Buck Mountain trailhead informing climbers of the dangers of snowslopes—the specific danger encountered by Ben Johnson.

not invoke the discretionary function exception. A closer analysis is in order.

Again, we must first determine whether the challenged action "is a matter of choice for the acting employee." *Berkovitz*, 486 U.S. at 536. In addition to the general statutory directive quoted above, the Secretary of the Interior is authorized, not mandated, to assist National Park visitors in emergencies. 16 U.S.C. 12 (1988). No statute imposes a duty to rescue, nor are there regulations or formal Park Service policies which prescribe a specific course of conduct for search or rescue efforts. Instead, the decision if, when or how to initiate a search or rescue is left to the discretion of the SAR [search and rescue] team. Therefore, the rangers must act without reliance upon fixed or readily ascertainable standards when making a search or rescue decision in the field. Plaintiff wisely concedes that these decisions are discretionary and therefore satisfy the first prong of *Berkovitz*.

Plaintiff contends, however, that Park Service rescue responses do not involve the kind of discretionary judgment protected by the discretionary function exception. We therefore focus our attention on the second prong of the *Berkovitz* analysis—whether the decision if, when or how to initiate a search or rescue is the kind of decision the discretionary function exception was designed to shield. *Berkovitz*, 486 U.S. at 536. Congress intended that this exception protect from judicial second-guessing only those governmental actions and decisions based on public policy considerations. Id. at 536–37. The key to a proper construction of the discretionary function exception thus lies in the determination of whether a governmental decision is "*grounded* in social, economic, and political policy." *Varig*, 467 U.S. at 814 (emphasis added).

Governmental actions outside the regulatory context may be protected by the discretionary function exception. *Varig*, 467 U.S. at 810–14. Furthermore, "the nature of the conduct, rather than the status of the actor * * * governs whether the discretionary function exception applies in a given case." *Varig*, 467 U.S. at 813. The fact that the rangers, as employees, make nonregulatory search and rescue decisions is therefore inconsequential to our determination of whether those decisions are policy judgments. The nature of the rescue decision process is the critical inquiry: Do Park Service search and rescue decisions simply involve weighing safety considerations under an established program or do they involve the balancing of competing policy considerations?

Park Service search and rescue decisions are not guided by formal standards. Yet, these decisions are not arbitrary. The record demonstrates that Park rangers make individual search and rescue decisions based on the following considerations:

(1) Safety—It is a primary objective of the Park Service to protect the safety of both the visitors and the rangers. For this reason the rangers consider a variety of factors, including but not limited to, the nature of the situation reported (e.g., lost, overdue, off route, injured),[8] the weather, the

---

8. Because it is not uncommon for climbers to be overdue, unaccounted for, or off route, it is not Park policy to initiate a search or rescue effort based on a report that

nature and difficulty of the terrain, the number of climbers, and the presence or absence of a leader at the scene.

(2) Human resources—The Park Service has limited manpower resources which it must allocate and deploy carefully. In June 1987, Grand Teton National Park had 17,197 visitors per day. Hikers and climbers accounted for 1,009 of these daily visitors. During this same period, forty seasonal and twelve permanent rangers (including the eighteen search and rescue rangers in the Jenny Lake Subdistrict) patrolled 332,331 acres— over 519 square miles of extremely rugged terrain.

(3) Economic resources—The Park Service has limited economic resources which it must use wisely. Search and rescue efforts are expensive. For example, a helicopter search costs $750 per hour.

(4) Governmental interference—The climbing community appreciates the inherent danger of the sport and is perceived to value the individual freedom of a backcountry experience.

We need not find evidence in the record that the rangers in this instance considered each of the identified policy factors. The discretionary function exception may apply in the absence of a conscious decision, so long as the Park Service's search and rescue program allowed room for the rangers to make independent policy judgments. See *Berkovitz*, 486 U.S. at 546 * * * The record before us adequately supports our conclusion that the rangers' decision if, when or how to rescue inherently involves the balancing of safety objectives[9] against such practical considerations as staffing, funding and minimizing government intrusion. As such, these decisions are grounded in social and economic policy, and thus are shielded from liability under the FTCA discretionary function exception. * * *

After careful examination of the record, we find nothing to contradict the government's evidence that Park Service search and rescue decisions are discretionary decisions requiring rangers to balance competing policy considerations. * * *

We recognize that in Plaintiff's view this is a harsh end. However, Plaintiff's entire case rests on the assertion that Park Service personnel could have communicated more accurately and responded more quickly. While this assertion may be true (i.e., the rangers' interview and response may have deviated from standards against which liability is measured where liability is available) it is not sufficient to establish FTCA liability. * * * Factual issues concerning negligence are irrelevant to the threshold issue whether the officials' actions are shielded from liability by the discretionary function exception. * * * The Park Service's conduct involved the permissible exercise of policy judgment, therefore governmental immu-

---

a climber is overdue, unaccounted for, or off route, or simply because another climber demands one.

9. Contrary to Plaintiff's argument, the fact that visitor safety is a primary Park Service objective does not make search and rescue decisions any less discretionary, or remove them from the discretionary function exception.

nity is preserved under 28 U.S.C. 2680(a) "whether or not the discretion involved be abused."

NOTES AND QUESTIONS

1. Should the Congress enact a statute (or should the federal land agencies adopt regulations) addressing such adventurous recreational activities as mountain climbing, river running, etc.? Do agencies like the Park Service already have statutory authority to do so? Did the Park Service here in fact regulate by requiring a permit, and "face-to-face ranger contact," before undertaking a climb?

2. Same result if the Park Service had been notified of a climbing accident, and the rangers had decided not to mount an immediate rescue because they wanted to attend a dinner honoring the retiring Park superintendent, or meet with a visiting dignitary (such as the chair of a congressional committee with jurisdiction over the Park Service)? Would that be a decision "grounded in social, economic, and political policy" protected by the "discretionary function" exception?

3. Does the result in this case suggest that federal land management agencies have broad immunity, even from negligence in regulating or failing to regulate, under the "discretionary function" exception? If the plaintiff in *Otteson* had shown that the government's conduct would have made it liable under the Colorado "sightseer" statute, would the government have still won under that exception?

4. Do federal agencies owe a duty to warn recreationists on federal lands that they might face dangerous conditions? See footnote 7 and accompanying text, supra. In a later phase of the *Ducey* litigation discussed at pp. 1018–19 supra, the district court ruled that the flood was not foreseeable and that the U.S. had no duty to warn the decedents and dismissed the case. In *Ducey II*, 830 F.2d 1071 (9th Cir.1987), the appeals court reversed again. It found that the Park Service was "aware that a life-threatening, 100–year flood was long overdue," relying on statements of concern about flash flood danger made at public meetings by Park Service officials. Citing Nevada state law decisions, it found that the agency did have a duty to warn of a 100–year flood. It remanded the matter to the district court to determine whether the Park Service had given reasonable warnings, and if not, whether the warnings would have prevented the deaths. One judge dissented.

5. In Tippett v. United States, 108 F.3d 1194 (10th Cir.1997), the court applied the discretionary function exception to shield a decision by a park ranger not to move a moose that had been threatening snowmobilers on a winter day, in a suit by a snowmobiler injured when the moose charged him. See also Autery v. United States, 992 F.2d 1523 (11th Cir.1993), cert. denied, 511 U.S. 1081 (1994) (NPS decision on how to handle dead trees protected by discretionary function exception, in suit by the estate of a park visitor killed by a falling tree).

Reed v. U.S. Department of the Interior

United States Court of Appeals for the Ninth Circuit, 2000.
231 F.3d 501.

■ Before: WOOD, JR.,[1] KLEINFELD, and GRABER, CIRCUIT JUDGES.

■ WOOD, CIRCUIT JUDGE:

Plaintiff-appellant Daniel Reed was severely injured in the early morning hours of September 2, 1996, when a car ran over the tent in which he was sleeping. At the time of the accident, Reed was attending an event known as the Burning Man Festival, which was held on the desolate Black Rock Desert playa[2] in Nevada. The playa is federally owned land managed by the Bureau of Land Management ("BLM"). [Reed sued under the FTCA; the district court granted summary judgment to the U.S., finding the discretionary function exception applied.] * * *

It may be helpful in viewing plaintiff's injuries in context to explain the Burning Man event. According to its promoters, the event began on a beach in San Francisco in 1986, but in 1990 was moved to the "vast and oceanic space" of the Black Rock Desert of Nevada near Gerlach. The San Francisco Examiner described the event as "based loosely on European pagan straw man festivals at which people gather to erect and burn a large human effigy as dedication to the earth's fertility." The Journal of the Burning Man describes the event as "ritualistic . . . anarchic . . . primal . . . a radical communal experiment . . . art . . . the death of art . . . dream-like . . . surreal . . . creative . . . destructive . . . absurd . . . spiritual" and "real." The Journal tells us:

> Think of Burning Man as Disneyland turned inside out. But unlike an escapist fantasy produced by others, Burning Man is not vicarious. At Burning Man *you* are the fantasy. People do not come to this event to be distracted from themselves, they come here to discover and distill what they uniquely are. We will not tell you what it means, for Burning Man is based on your immediate experience.

(Emphasis in original.) The Journal advises attendees to "[c]ome prepared to camp here and confront your own survival." In answer to the question, "What is Burning Man?", the Journal states, "It's what you make it." Participants enter the event through the "Gate of Hell" on which is inscribed the admonition, "ABANDON HOPE YOU WHO ENTER HERE." The Burning Man 1996 Survival Guide handout warns: "All participants must take personal responsibility for their own survival, safety and comfort" and cautions participants to bring common sense as "the desert is notoriously unkind to fools." The Survival Guide also warns that "[t]here are no roads, signs or street lights" on the playa. The Pershing County Sheriff's Office issued a report on the 1996 festival, estimating that

---

1. The Honorable Harlington Wood, Jr., United States Circuit Judge for the Seventh Circuit, sitting by designation.

2. A playa is "the flat-floored bottom of an undrained desert basin that becomes at times a shallow lake which on evaporation may leave a deposit of salt or gypsum." Webster's Third New Int'l Dictionary 1737 (1981).

participants numbered approximately 7,000, with an additional 3,000 to 4,000 onlookers.[6]

Reed, age 21, * * * pitched his tent near a few other tents on the playa several miles from the main camp. September 1, 1996, appears to be the day the event concluded, although the following day was designated as "clean-up day." Early on the morning of September 2, the car of another attendee, traveling across the playa, ran over Reed in his tent. Reed alleges that he suffered severe, permanent brain damage and was left permanently disabled. * * *

Reed contends that the following four actions by the BLM fall outside the scope of the discretionary function exception: (1) failing to warn, or to require Burning Man organizers to warn, of the hazard of camping in an area subject to unrestricted night-time vehicular travel; (2) approving a site plan that failed to segregate cars from tents; (3) failing to monitor the event as prescribed by regulation and policy; and (4) failing to suspend the permit once public safety was in jeopardy.

With respect to the first two challenged actions, the first prong of the discretionary function test clearly is met. The BLM was granted discretion to determine whether to issue the permit or not and, if issued, to decide the restrictions to be applied. The agency is given specific authority to include in a recreation permit "such stipulations as the authorized officer considers necessary to protect the lands and resources involved and the public interest in general." 43 C.F.R. § 8372.5(b). As a practical matter, it could be no other way than by the exercise of discretion. No federal statute, regulation, or policy requires a particular course of action. * * * Even if the permit had been granted without any conscious policy decision (contrary to the facts of this case), the discretionary exception function would still apply. * * * The BLM, in its exercise of discretion, balanced competing public policy concerns, including concerns about public access, safety, resource allocation, and the environment * * *.

The record reveals that the government exercised its discretion in granting Burning Man the event permit. Even if the exercise of that governmental discretion was ill-advised, it does not make the discretionary function exception inapplicable. Even if the particular provisions included in the permit itself were not well-conceived or sufficient, that exercise of discretion is also beyond Reed's reach. After the BLM received the event application * * * [it] sent out letters to interested parties * * * seeking comments related to the proposed event. The comments received expressed concerns about safety, morality, and the environmental impact of the event.

---

6. Time magazine published an article with pictures of the most recent burning man event. Joel Stein, *The Man Behind Burning Man,* Time, Sept. 18, 2000, at 76. The event was referred to as a "punk-pagan celebration." *Id.* Two readers responded to the article in the "letters to the editor" column in a following issue. *Letters,* Time, Oct. 9, 2000, at 20, 22. One respondent had recently worked with Indians in Nevada and took exception to the "pagan" reference, stating that "the puerile horde that invades the desert on Labor Day has no clue about the earth or true spirituality." The other reader wrote that he had attended the festival for the first time this year. He characterized it as "an example of how everyone should live." This court passes no judgment on the event.

Following consideration of those comments, the BLM prepared an Environmental Assessment, which considered the possible impact of the event on the environment, but found that there would be no significant environmental impact. It noted that the area to be used was believed to be one of the largest, flattest dry lake beds in the world.[7] In its judgment, BLM considered that the Burning Man event had had no prior significant safety problems from 1992 through 1995. Even though the event was growing in size each year, the record shows that it also had a good compliance record with BLM licensing requirements. As part of the process, the promoters were required to submit a "site plan" with some indication of the physical layout for the event, bearing in mind the openness, vastness, and flatness of the area. The BLM reviewed the site plan submitted and, in its discretion, considered it adequate for the short-term recreational event.

The BLM also considered Congressional directives, as stated in the Federal Land Policy and Management Act of 1976, ("FLPMA"), to manage the land for multiple uses in a manner that would help meet the present and future needs of the citizens, including recreational uses. * * * According to a BLM district manager, the government land use plan in effect at the time Burning Man applied for its 1996 permit dictated that "as many recreational opportunities as possible" be provided, "without undue environmental degradation." And, of course, under the Constitution's First Amendment, the agency's discretion could not be used to abridge the legitimate rights of expression or association of the participants. The BLM was aware that many event participants pursued and encouraged an "alternative lifestyle," but it believed that the actions taken in the exercise of its discretion should not be affected by the personal philosophies of the participants. The BLM believed that the proposed policing strategies would be sufficient to handle any illegal activity that might occur. According to the record, there had been some use of alcohol and illegal drugs in the past but, in the BLM's judgment, there had been no serious problems. The provisions for policing were expected to be adequate. The BLM also took into consideration planned coordination with local law enforcement officials, in addition to the event's own acceptance of responsibility for the safety of its participants. There is no need to further explore all the details involved in the BLM's exercise of its discretion. Some would disagree with the manner of the agency's exercise of its discretion, but that is irrelevant.

Reed argues that, even though the BLM may have had discretion to issue the permit, "the decision to approve an event involving thousands of campers and cars without segregating them, or requiring Burning Man to do so, was not the kind protected by the discretionary jurisdiction exception, it violated standard, elementary objective, technical standards for events of this size." Reed is mistaken. This issue is the type of judgment the discretionary function exception was designed to shield. * * * There was one discretionary license issued for this event, and what its terms were and how those terms might be enforced were all discretionary. Reed's own

---

7. According to the BLM district manager during the period of these events, because the playa was so vast and flat, the area had been used in 1981 and 1997 to set new land speed records.

argument shows the need for agency discretion. He disagrees with the way discretion was exercised, but the discretionary function exception makes that objection irrelevant.

Reed next argues that the BLM was required by regulation and policy to monitor the event and that its failure to do so falls outside the discretionary function exception. Under 43 C.F.R. § 2920.9–2, the BLM was required to "inspect and monitor . . . to assure compliance with the plan of management and protection of the resources, the environment and the public health, safety and welfare." Although Reed asserts that BLM agents chose not to monitor the event, in fact, they did monitor it. Rather, his real argument is that, because the agents left the site by 10:00 p.m. each evening, the agents failed to monitor in a reasonable manner. However, * * * the discretionary decisions made as to the precise *manner* in which the BLM should monitor events also fall within the exception. No regulation required twenty-four hour monitoring; in fact, the BLM Manual H–8372–1–Special Recreation Permit for Commercial Use, VIIA, states that the amount of monitoring should be "commensurate with the resource values at risk, the permittee's past record of compliance, the ability to obtain monitoring services through other means such as local police, other permittees, the public, and other factors." The decision as to the nature and extent of monitoring clearly involves both discretion on the part of BLM employees and a balancing of public policy concerns.

Finally, Reed contends the BLM had a duty to suspend the permit once public safety was in jeopardy, but failed to do so. * * * Both the regulations and the BLM Manual require not only a finding of a violation, but also a finding that the violation affects public health or safety. There were no set standards in place outlining what types of permit violations would be sufficient to justify permit suspension; the BLM Manual, H–8372–1, VIIC, states only that "[a]n example could be the lack of a required local license for food service." The decision to suspend the permit would necessarily include a discretionary balancing of policy considerations. * * * Therefore, again, the discretionary function exception applies.

This was a tragic accident. However, under the circumstances, the government is not liable for any of Reed's damages.

NOTES AND QUESTIONS

1. Did BLM do all it should have done here in connection with this event? What if plaintiff could show there had been a history of safety problems at past Burning Man events, but BLM decided to go ahead and permit it anyway on the same terms as the past? Would that have changed the outcome?

2. Should BLM have required, as a condition of the permit, that the event sponsors purchase liability insurance to cover accidents like the one that injured Reed, to back up what the court called "the event's own acceptance of responsibility for the safety of its participants"? Does it have the authority to do that, under FLPMA? Even if that arguably might have

a limiting effect on what the court called "the legitimate [first amendment] rights of expression or association of the participants"?

3.   The January 22, 2002 Wall Street Journal reported that the Nevada Commission on Tourism is running a nationwide ad campaign touting Nevada as a "primal playground with more * * * tear-yourself-to-shreds terrain than any other place in this great nation," which can provide a "nice quiet place to get in touch with your inner masochist," and asked, "Ready to get medieval?"

4.   Occasionally public lands users have sought relief under the FTCA for non-recreational injuries. Nearly all such attempts have been unsuccessful. For example, the discretionary function exception was applied in Barton v. United States, 609 F.2d 977 (10th Cir.1979) to prevent recovery under the FTCA when plaintiffs sold their livestock after their public lands grazing privileges were reduced in a drought. See also Parker Land & Cattle Co. v. United States, 796 F.Supp. 477 (D.Wyo.1992) (government not liable for brucellosis infections). See generally George Cameron Coggins & Robert Glicksman, PUBLIC NATURAL RESOURCES LAW § 10:5 (2001).

CHAPTER 12

THE PRESERVATION RESOURCE

Preservation is as much a resource of the federal lands as the more traditional ones surveyed elsewhere in this book. A natural area is nonrenewable, at least for generations, if its essential qualities are destroyed. Preserving artifacts and other items of historical and scientific value are essential to pursuit of a civilized life. While the "outputs" or values of preservation are less susceptible of measurement in economic terms, contemporary society has, by a variety of mechanisms explored in this chapter, assigned preservation considerable, sometimes surpassing, importance.

Still, the preservation resource escapes easy definition. To many, it connotes leaving well enough alone; they emphasize the need to protect natural areas and certain objects and values from human manipulation, profit-seekers and wrecking balls. To others, the concept is simply a means by which elitists lock up resources and put them off-limits to "productive" use and the reach and discipline of the marketplace. No prosaic definition will do. For present purposes, the description in the Wilderness Act is an appropriate starting point: wilderness is "an area where the earth and its community of life are untrammeled by man, where man himself is a visitor who does not remain." 16 U.S.C. § 1131(c).

The urge to preserve tangible things and areas of historic significance preceded the desire to set aside tracts of scenic, aesthetic, or ecological value. Famous battlegrounds, for instance, have long been of great popular interest; e.g., United States v. Gettysburg Electric R. Co., 160 U.S. 668 (1896), p. 103 supra. Yellowstone National Park in 1872 became the first significant reservation of public land for scenic purposes, but it was initially to be a "pleasuring ground" rather than a strict preserve. And in fact Yellowstone and some other units of the National Park System were, over the years, festooned with roads, lodges, shops, sanitary facilities, and other amenities that many claim are antithetical to a "true wilderness experience." Nevertheless, that system still encompasses some of the most spectacularly pristine country in the Nation; large amounts of land within it have been formally declared as wilderness and much of the remainder is managed primarily for maintenance of an essentially wilderness character.

Although the basic thrust of preservation of much federal lands and resources is to "leave nature alone," that is often not possible. Man's activities inside and outside protected areas can have significant effects. Federal land managers sometimes conclude that human intervention is necessary if the preservation purpose is to be carried out. In Davis v. Latschar, 202 F.3d 359 (D.C.Cir.2000), for example, animal rights groups and nearby residents sought to enjoin a Park Service "controlled harvest" of deer at Gettysburg National Military Park. The National Park Organic

Act authorizes the Secretary to "provide in his discretion for the destruction of such animals and of such plant life as may be detrimental to the use of" a park unit. 16 U.S.C. § 3. The court of appeals approved the district court's conclusion that the NPS had made a sufficient finding that over-browsing by deer was detrimental to the purposes of the parks, because it thwarted the objective of "preserving the historic appearance of woodlots and cropfields, components of the landscape critical to the understanding and interpretation of the historic events that took place" in the Park. Plaintiffs did not vigorously contest the purpose of the harvest, but argued that the NPS should have paid more attention to other means to protect the Park purposes. The court upheld the NPS, rejecting NEPA and other claims.

Two important federal preservation laws have already been addressed in these materials: The Endangered Species Act, addressed in Chapter 5, has become perhaps the most famous "preservation" law of all, but will not be considered further here. Chapter 4 covered the Antiquities Act of 1906, by which presidents of both political parties have acted to preserve of some of our best-loved natural areas and historic and scientific resources. The "Organic Acts" for the four principal federal land management agencies all contain preservationist elements and tools. In this final chapter we will cover some important preservation laws and issues not yet addressed. The first section briefly examines protection of cultural, archaeological and historic resources, and also examines related First Amendment issues. Section B addresses the authority of federal land managers, particularly those in the National Park Service, to combat external threats to the scenic and ecological integrity of federal lands managed primarily for preservation and recreation. Section C deals briefly with issues of science, profit, and preservation. Section D sketches some highlights of river preservation, a matter of intense popular concern since before Justice Holmes noted that a river "is more than an amenity, it is a treasure," New Jersey v. New York, 283 U.S. 336, 342 (1931). The final and largest section in this chapter examines the designation and management of official wilderness areas under the Wilderness Act of 1964, 16 U.S.C. §§ 1131–1136, which established the growing National Wilderness Preservation System, the flagship of the movement for strict legal preservation of natural areas in not only the United States but the world.

What Roderick Nash said about the wilderness movement applies to resource preservation across the board:

> While the American conception of wilderness has almost always been a compound of attraction and repulsion, the relative strengths of these attitudes, both in single minds and in the national opinion, have not remained constant. Appreciation * * * [has grown] from an esoteric and eccentric notion into a broad public sentiment capable of influencing national policy and securing statutory protection for wild country.

R. Nash, WILDERNESS AND THE AMERICAN MIND (3d ed. 1982). The quickening of the trend toward preservation raises fundamental questions. Is "preservation" of a "natural" world even possible, given emerging notions of the constant of change and disequilibrium in the natural world, the spread of exotic species, and man's unwitting manipulation of the global climate? Can and must preservation be justified by weighing costs and benefits? Should costs and benefits be measured over a longer time than the conventional marketplace tends to measure these things? Should preservation be pursued for ecological reasons alone, or should it be premised on anthropocentric considerations, since wilderness can be, in the words of the late Supreme Court Justice William O. Douglas, "one pledge to freedom"? See generally Joseph Sax, MOUNTAINS WITHOUT HAND-RAILS (1981).

A.   Preservation of Archaeological and Historical Artifacts and First Amendment Issues

America's historical and archaeological sites, many found on federal lands, constitute a resource that Congress has deemed important for nearly a century. In 1906, Congress enacted the Antiquities Act, 16 U.S.C. §§ 431–433. The first section authorized the withdrawal and reservation of lands containing objects or values of historic, scientific, or scenic significance as national monuments. See Chapter 4, supra pp. 353–60. The second section was intended to halt commercial exploitation of cultural and historic objects on the public lands:

> * * * Since the 1890's there had been great public interest in the art and history of the Indians of the southwestern United States, and this interest had created a great demand for authentic prehistoric artifacts. As a result, ruins and cliff dwellings, such as Casa Grande, Mesa Verde, and Chaco Canyon, were indiscriminately excavated and vandalized. There were no state and federal laws that provided for the protection of prehistoric sites, and there were few professional archaeologists. Thus, the need for protective legislation was particularly acute when the Antiquities Act was passed in 1906.

> The act * * * prohibited the appropriating, excavating, injuring, or destroying of any "historic or prehistoric ruin or monument" or "object of antiquity" found on government-owned or-controlled land, without the permission of the secretary of the department of the government having jurisdiction over the land. * * *

Robert Bruce Collins & Dee F. Green, A Proposal to Modernize the American Antiquities Act, 202 Science 1055 (Dec.1978). A variety of problems hobbled the effectiveness of the Antiquities Act. The maximum fine of $500 was not a sufficient deterrent, and the Act imposed penalties only on appropriators, not on dealers or other purchasers. Worse yet, one federal appellate court struck down the Act's definition of "object of antiquity" as unconstitutionally vague. United States v. Diaz, 499 F.2d 113 (9th Cir. 1974); contra, United States v. Smyer, 596 F.2d 939 (10th Cir.1979).

These difficulties were each overcome by passage of the Archaeological Resources Protection Act of 1979 (ARPA), 16 U.S.C. §§ 470aa–470ll. It prohibits excavation, removal, or damaging archaeological resources on federal or Indian lands without a permit, and also prohibits trafficking in illegally acquired artifacts.

ARPA offers greater protection for archaeological resources on public lands than did prior federal law. ARPA's definition of "archaeological resource" includes a wide range of artifactual, contextual, and environmental information and can expand as archaeologists begin to use new types of information. ARPA's enforcement provisions give federal land managers the tools necessary to curtail commercial looting of archaeological sites and trading in illegally obtained archaeological resources.

In addition to providing increased protection, ARPA clarifies federal policy concerning the development of archaeological resources and establishes, in conjunction with other federal laws, a comprehensive program for the management of the remaining archaeological resources on public lands and Indian lands. ARPA gives the federal land managers considerable discretion to deny permits if development is inconsistent with land management plans or if conservation is more appropriate. ARPA leaves the resolution of conflicts with natural resource development to other federal laws; implicitly, ARPA says that the public interest in such cases requires preservation only of "archaeologically significant" resources. ARPA also contains the first statutory recognition of Indian religious and cultural interests in archaeological resources and offers them a greater role in archaeological resource management, particularly on Indian lands. * * *

Congress' desire to protect treasure hunters and recreational users of public lands from unreasonable civil or criminal penalties has also resulted in several significant exceptions to ARPA. For example, the exemption provided to collectors of arrowheads found on the ground surface unduly restricts the Act's protection. There is no reason to give collectors of arrowheads greater protection than persons who destroy other resources, such as shell mounds, that are less clearly of archaeological interest. * * *

Archaeological resources are valuable, vanishing, and nonrenewable. ARPA is a significant step toward halting unnecessary destruction of these resources and ensuring their rational development. The effort must not end here, however. * * * Environmentalists and other citizens can, of course, contribute by reporting any illegal removal, damage, or destruction of archaeological resources on public lands and Indian lands. With such efforts, archaeological resources can be preserved for both the present and the future.

Lorrie D. Northey, The Archaeological Resources Protection Act of 1979: Protecting Prehistory for the Future, 6 Harv.Envtl.L.Rev. 61, 113 (1982). See generally Symposium, Legal Protection of America's Archaeological Heritage, 22 Ariz.L.Rev. 675 (1980)

The key sections provide:

No person may excavate, remove, damage, or otherwise alter or deface, or attempt to excavate, remove, damage, or otherwise alter or deface any archaeological resource located on public lands or Indian lands unless such activity is pursuant to a permit ... [or] exemption. [16 U.S.C. § 470ee(a)].

The term "archaeological resource" means any material remains of past human life or activities which are of archeological interest, as determined under uniform regulations promulgated pursuant to this chapter. Such regulations containing such determinations shall include, but not be limited to: pottery, basketry, bottles, weapons, weapon projectiles, tools, structures or portions of structures, pit houses, rock paintings, rock carvings, intaglios, graves, human skeletal materials, or any portion or piece of any of the foregoing items. Nonfossilized and fossilized paleonotological specimens, or any portion or piece thereof, shall not be considered archaeological resources, under the regulations under this paragraph, unless found in an archaeological context. No item shall be treated as an archaeological resource under regulations under this paragraph unless such item is at least 100 years of age. [16 U.S.C. § 470bb(1).]

The Act defines "public lands" to include lands in all BLM-managed lands, lands in the national park, national forest, and national wildlife refuge systems, and all other lands where the United States owns fee title, other than lands on the Outer Continental Shelf and lands under the jurisdiction of the Smithsonian Institution. *Id.*, § 470bb(3). It does not "affect the lawful recovery, collection, or sale of archaeological resources from land other than public land or Indian land," 16 U.S.C. § 470kk(c).

United States v. Shivers

United States Court of Appeals, Fifth Circuit, 1996.
96 F.3d 120.

■ EDITH H. JONES, CIRCUIT JUDGE:

Billy Ray Shivers found buried treasure at the site of an abandoned lumber mill company town. Unfortunately for Shivers, the site is located in the Angelina National Forest, and the federal government claimed ownership of and seized from Shivers some 50–70 metal tokens he uncovered with a metal detector. The district court denied his Fed.Rule Crim.Proc. 41(e) motion seeking return of the tokens, as it concluded Shivers did not own them pursuant to either the Archeological Resources Protection Act ("ARPA"), 16 U.S.C. § 470ee, or the common law of finds. This court approves the district court's conclusion and therefore affirms.

The tokens that Shivers excavated from the Aldridge Lumber Company mill site were used by the saw mill as payment for workers 50–100 years ago. The tokens and other items were seized pursuant to a search warrant from Shivers's home when the government came to believe he had obtained them in violation of ARPA, which forbids the un-permitted excavation of archeological resources from federal lands.

When the government chose not to pursue criminal charges against Shivers, it eventually gave back the rest of the seized property, but refused to return the tokens to him. The district court's rebuff of Shivers's

Fed.R.Crim.Proc. 41(e) motion for return of seized property gives rise to this appeal. * * *

Shivers argues that the plain language of ARPA § 470kk vests him with ownership of the Aldridge tokens because he is a private collector of coins and other artifacts not defined by the ARPA as archaeological resources.

ARPA was enacted by Congress to protect "archaeological resources" found on public lands and to promote study and evaluation of these resources. See 16 U.S.C. § 470aa(b). An "archaeological resource" is statutorily defined as

> any material remains of past human life or activities which are of archeological interest, as determined under uniform regulations promulgated pursuant to this chapter.... No item shall be treated as an archaeological resource under regulations under this paragraph *unless such item is at least 100 years of age.*

16 U.S.C. § 470bb(1) (emphasis added). "Archaeological resources" so defined remain property of the United States if removed from public lands. See 16 U.S.C. § 470cc(b)(3); 36 C.F.R. § 296.6(b)(5); H.R.Rep. No. 311, 96th Cong., 1st Session, 7, 1979 U.S.Code Cong. & Admin.News pp. 1709, 1710. Since the Aldridge tokens are between 50 and 100 years old, however, they are not "archaeological resources" for purposes of the ARPA.

Shivers's principal argument rests on a facile premise: because the tokens are not "archaeological resources," § 470kk of the ARPA conveys an ownership interest to him as a private collector of coins. Section 470kk provides that

> [n]othing in this chapter applies to, or requires a permit for, the collection for private purposes of any rock, coin, bullet, or mineral which is not an archaeological resource, as determined under uniform regulations promulgated under section 470bb(1) of this title.

16 U.S.C. § 470kk(b). From this provision, Shivers infers that private individuals are authorized by ARPA to remove coins less than 100 years old from public land and to retain ownership.

Shivers also suggests that the purpose and policy of the ARPA support his conclusion. By encouraging private collection of non-"archaeological resources", the ARPA may actually help safeguard these resources, protecting them from further dislocation caused by either human or natural disturbances. To achieve such protection, Congress did not explicitly retain an ownership interest in non-"archaeological resources" found on public lands, though it did prevent private ownership of statutorily covered artifacts. Shivers urges that the asserted failure to retain ownership over non-"archaeological resources" evinces congressional intent to cede their ownership to private collectors.

But the premise on which Shivers's argument rests is a faulty one, belied by the very passage on which he relies. Section 470kk(b) provides that "[n]othing in this chapter applies to ... the collection for private purposes of any rock, coin, bullet, or mineral which is not an archaeological resource...." (emphasis added). Because the ARPA does not apply to artifacts less than 100 years old, it does not regulate the private collection of such non-"archaeological resources". This statute cannot vest Shivers with an ownership interest in the tokens because it neither divests ownership interest from the United States or, indeed, says anything at all about "archaeological resources" it does not cover.

Even assuming arguendo that the ARPA regulates private collection of non-"archaeological resources," however, Section 470kk(b) does not transfer to or vest ownership of the Aldridge tokens in Shivers. The statute merely provides that private collectors need not obtain a permit for the collection of certain artifacts. Shivers implies a transfer of property rights from this provision, arguing that since the statute allows for the private collection of non-"archaeological resources," it necessarily entitles the collector to retain or own what he has collected. This conclusion, however, is neither supported by the text of the statute nor is it a necessary implication of the right to collect non-"archaeological resources." Admittedly, the express statutory authorization to collect non-"archaeological resources" without a permit is much less valuable to a private collector if he may not retain what he collects; unless the collector enjoys collection for its own sake, ARPA furnishes little incentive to discover and gather non-"archaeological resources." But it would not be absurd to conclude that Congress dispensed with the cumbersome process of requiring permits for gathering non-"archaeological resources," even though it refused to transfer ownership of these less ancient artifacts.

Further, the ARPA is concerned with protecting the integrity of archaeological sites, presumably even more so if they are located in national forests. See, e.g., 16 U.S.C. § 470cc(b)(1)-(b)(2) (requiring that those who apply for a permit to excavate archaeological resources be "qualified to carry out the permitted activity."); 36 C.F.R. § 296.8(a)(1); 1979 U.S.C.C.A.N. 1709, 1712 (recognizing the importance of protecting the unaltered integrity of archaeological sites). The record suggests that several hundred shovel holes found at the Aldridge site were attributed to Shivers's excavation activities. Considering the resulting landscape alteration, Congress's intent to regulate digging or excavating on public archaeological sites is easy to understand, while Shivers's contrary position in favor of encouraging unregulated amateur collection is virtually incomprehensible.

Finally, the "arrowhead exception" to the ARPA discussed by Shivers is inapposite and irrelevant. This exception is not intended to encourage removal of arrowheads from public lands, but rather to exempt such removal from the civil and criminal penalty provisions of the ARPA. See 16 U.S.C. § 470ff(a)(3); 36 C.F.R. § 296.3(a)(3)(iii). Unlike the tokens excavated by Shivers, the arrowhead exception is limited to those found on the surface of public lands. See 16 U.S.C. § 470ff(a)(3) ("[n]o penalty shall be assessed ... for the removal of arrowheads located on the surface of the ground."). Also, the ARPA expressly provides that the removal of arrowheads can be penalized under other regulations or statutes. See, e.g., 49 Fed.Reg. 1016, 1018 ("regulations under other authority which penalize [the removal of surface arrowheads] remain effective.") No inferences or implications helpful to Shivers are found in these provisions.

Because the ARPA does not vest Shivers with an ownership interest in the tokens, we need not discuss the Forest Service regulations, relied upon by the government, which go beyond ARPA and attempt to define as "archaeological resources," prohibited from excavation, artifacts that are at least 50 years old. See 36 C.F.R. §§ 261.2, 261.9(g). The asserted conflict between the Forest Service regulations and the ARPA does not need to be resolved in this case.

The district court concluded not only that the ARPA did not convey to Shivers an ownership interest in the Aldridge tokens, but also that in the absence of express or statutory title transfer, the federal common law of finds dictates that the United States, not Shivers, owns the tokens.

The federal common law of finds, including certain critical exceptions, is pertinent to this case. As the Eleventh Circuit explained,

> [t]he common law of finds generally assigns ownership of the abandoned property without regard to where the property is found. Two exceptions to the rule are recognized: First, when the abandoned property is embedded in the soil, it belongs to the owner of the soil; Second, when the owner of the land where the property is found (whether on or embedded in the soil) has constructive possession of the property such that the property is not "lost," it belongs to the owner of the land.

Klein v. Unidentified Wrecked & Abandoned Sailing Vessel, 758 F.2d 1511, 1514 (11th Cir.1985) (emphasis added). In Klein, a vessel submerged beneath the waters of Biscayne National Park, Florida, had been rediscovered and salvaged by a private diver. Holding that the wreck was property of the government, not the diver, the court emphasized that the "ship is buried in the soil. The soil belongs to the United States as part of its national park system.... When the United States acquired title to the land from Florida in 1973, it also acquired title to the shipwrecks embedded in that soil.... Thus the United States has never legally lost the subject shipwreck and, as the owner of the land on and/or water in which the shipwreck is located, it owns the shipwreck." Id. at 1514 (emphasis added). Similarly, the Aldridge tokens excavated by Shivers were buried in the soil of the Angelina National Forest. As in Klein, this soil belongs to the United States, and with it the embedded tokens under the first exception to the federal common law of finds discussed in Klein.[2]

Shivers does not challenge this interpretation of the federal common law of finds. Indeed, his only retort is that the common law of finds is inapplicable because Congress expressly provided in § 470kk(b) of the ARPA that private collectors enjoy ownership of the non-archaeological resources that they discover on public lands. As already discussed, this

---

2. Analyzing the ARPA, Judge Posner has also explained that "there is no right to go upon another person's land, without his permission, to look for valuable objects buried in the land and take them if you find them." United States v. Gerber, 999 F.2d 1112, 1114–15 (7th Cir.1993), cert. denied, 510 U.S. 1071 (1994).

contention is indefensible. The district court correctly held that the United States owns the tokens that Shivers discovered.

For the foregoing reasons, the judgment of the district court denying Shivers's 41(e) motion for the return of the Aldridge tokens is AFFIRMED.

NOTES AND QUESTIONS

1.   Does ARPA fully cure the problems of vagueness the Ninth Circuit found in its predecessor? As the *Shivers* opinion points out, the metal tokens he found on federal land were not covered by ARPA because they were less than 100 years old. Could a criminal prosecution be brought against a person for removing, say, pottery shards from federal lands without an ARPA permit when their age could not be determined without sophisticated testing? Cf. the related issue of the scienter required for determining whether someone has taken a protected endangered species or migratory bird; see Chapter 10, p. 916, para. 7, supra.

2.   Significant problems remain of detection and proof that artifacts in one's possession came from federal or Indian land. Particularly in the southwest, where estimates of undiscovered archeological resource sites run into the millions, and federal lands extend over vast areas, enforcement remains a huge problem. For some perspective on the magnitude of the task, see James Conaway, THE KINGDOM IN THE COUNTRY 146–67 (1987). See generally Kristine Olson Rogers, Visigoths Revisited: Prosecution of Archaeological Resource Thieves, Traffickers, and Vandals, 2 J. Envtl.L. & Lit. 47 (1987). ARPA was amended in 1988 to criminalize attempts to take as well as actual takings; to strengthen the penalties for violation; and to require federal agencies to establish programs to "increase public awareness" of the significance of and need to protect archaeological resources, and to undertake surveys and formulate plans to protect these resources. 102 Stat. 2983.

3.   In United States v. Austin, 902 F.2d 743 (9th Cir.1990), the government indicted Austin on eight counts of violating ARPA and five counts of theft of government property after seizing 2,800 Native American artifacts, excavation implements, photographs, and documents on his property after a lengthy investigation. The parties eventually stipulated to a bench trial on one count, charging him with violating ARPA by excavating "archaeological resources in an archaeological site, including obsidian weapon projectile points and tools such a scrapers." In upholding his conviction, the court tersely rejected his argument that ARPA was unconstitutionally vague, finding "no doubt nor lack of fair notice that the scrapers and arrow points for which he was convicted are indeed weapons and tools. The statute provided fair notice that it prohibited the activities for which Austin was convicted." The court also rejected his "creative" argument that "because curiosity motivated him, his activity was academic * * *," noting that he "has not demonstrated that he is affiliated with any academic institution, nor has he posited how his own curiosity is otherwise academic."

4. In Attakai v. United States, 746 F.Supp. 1395 (D.Ariz.1990), Navajo tribal members resisting relocation from land belonging to the Hopi tribe claimed that the construction of fences and livestock water facilities violated ARPA. The court rejected the argument on a variety of grounds: (a) the statute exempts excavations by an Indian Tribe on its land, 16 U.S.C. § 470cc(g)(1); (b) its implementing regulations exempt general earth moving excavations pursuant to other authorization, and activities carried out under the direction of the federal land manager (43 C.F.R. § 7.5 (2002)); and (c) the statute "is clearly intended to apply specifically to purposeful excavation and removal of archeological resources, not excavations which may, or in fact inadvertently do, uncover such resources." 746 F.Supp. at 1410–11.

5. In another portion of her article excerpted above, Northey writes: "Congress did not want to subject mineral resource development, reclamation, and other multiple uses of public lands and Indian lands to additional permit requirements and therefore exempted these activities from ARPA." 6 Harv. Envtl.L.Rev. at 114. The matter is not so simple. The Act provides that it shall not be "construed to repeal, modify, or impose additional restrictions on the activities permitted under existing laws and authorities relating to mining, mineral leasing, reclamation, and other multiple uses of the public lands." 16 U.S.C. § 470kk(a). Could the Secretary of the Interior include in a mineral lease (or in an approval of a plan of operations for a mining claim), a specific stipulation or condition requiring protection of archaeological resources encountered in mining? Where would the Secretary find legal authority to include such a provision; in ARPA or somewhere else? Compare the discussion of the Secretary's authority to include protective stipulations in mineral leases in Chapter 3, supra pp. 211–13 (in connection with the Ventura County decision) and Chapter 7, pp. 657–67, supra. Is such a condition forbidden by § 470kk(a)? See generally 43 C.F.R. § 7.5(b)(1) (2002).

6. A number of states have adopted regulations similar to ARPA, although the extent to which they apply to private lands varies. Controversies have flared in some areas over "pothunting" and "grave plundering" on private land. Interesting preemption questions might be raised if states adopt more protective laws than ARPA and try to apply them to federal lands; e.g., suppose a state outlawed the collection of archaeological resources older than 50 years of age (as compared to the 100–year age limit in ARPA) anywhere in the state. Could that expanded prohibition be applied to federal lands? ARPA speaks in several places of "uniform regulations;" e.g., 16 U.S.C. § 470bb(1); and outlaws trafficking in interstate commerce of any archaeological resource held in violation of State or local law, id. § 470ee(c); but does not directly address the application of state law to federal lands. Cf. California Coastal Com'n v. Granite Rock Co., Chapter 3, supra p. 213. In United States v. Gerber, 999 F.2d 1112 (7th Cir.1993), cited in footnote 2 of Shivers, the court upheld an ARPA conviction for transporting in interstate commerce Indian artifacts taken from private lands without the consent of the owner (and thus committing criminal trespass and conversion in violation of state law, even though the state's theft statute was not specifically directed at archaeological resources).

Judge Posner's opinion found federal law sufficient to cover situations where the state law violated is "related to the protection of archaeological sites or objects" even if the law is not "limited to that protection."

7.   Regarding the law of finds and the problem of protecting shipwrecks found on submerged lands offshore, see Treasure Salvors, Inc. v. Unidentified Wrecked and Abandoned Sailing Vessel, 569 F.2d 330 (5th Cir.1978); California and State Lands Commission v. Deep Sea Research, Inc., 523 U.S. 491 (1998); the Abandoned Shipwreck Act of 1987, 43 U.S.C. §§ 2101–2106; Jeffrey T. Scrimo, Raising the Dead: Improving the Recovery and Management of Historic Shipwrecks, 5 Ocean & Coastal L.J. 271 (2000); Christopher R. Bryant, The Archaeological Duty of Care: The Legal, Professional, and Cultural Struggle over Salvaging Historic Shipwrecks, 65 Albany L.Rev. 97 (2001).

8.   Fossils, too, have generated litigation in recent years. Ownership of a well-preserved Tyrannosaurus Rex skeleton (named "Sue") discovered on Indian allotted land in South Dakota, held in trust by the United States for an individual Indian, generated several judicial opinions. See Black Hills Inst. v. South Dakota School of Mines, 12 F.3d 737 (8th Cir.1993), cert. denied, 513 U.S. 810 (1994); see generally Gretchen Lundgren, Protecting Federal Fossils From Extinction, 26 B.C. Envtl. Aff. 225 (1998); David J. Lazerwitz, Bones of Contention: The Regulation of Paleontological Resources on the Federal Public Lands, 69 Ind. L.J. 601 (1994).

PROTECTION OF SITES SACRED TO NATIVE AMERICANS AND ASSOCIATED FIRST AMENDMENT ISSUES

Lyng v. Northwest Indian Cemetery Protective Ass'n

Supreme Court of the United States, 1988.
485 U.S. 439.

■ JUSTICE O'CONNOR delivered the opinion of the Court.

This case requires us to consider whether the First Amendment's Free Exercise Clause prohibits the Government from permitting timber harvesting in, or constructing a road through, a portion of a National Forest that has traditionally been used for religious purposes by members of three American Indian tribes in northwestern California. We conclude that it does not.

As part of a project to create a paved 75–mile road linking two California towns, Gasquet and Orleans, the United States Forest Service has upgraded 49 miles of previously unpaved roads on federal land. In order to complete this project (the G–O road), the Forest Service must build a 6–mile paved segment through the Chimney Rock section of the Six Rivers National Forest. That section of the forest is situated between two other portions of the road that are already complete.

In 1977, the Forest Service issued a draft environmental impact statement that discussed proposals for upgrading an existing unpaved road that runs through the Chimney Rock area. In response to comments on the draft statement, the Forest Service commissioned a study of American Indian cultural and religious sites in the area. The Hoopa Valley Indian Reservation adjoins the Six Rivers National Forest, and the Chimney Rock area has historically been used for religious purposes by Yurok, Karok, and Tolowa Indians. The commissioned study, which was completed in 1979, found that the entire area "is significant as an integral and indispensible part of Indian religious conceptualization and practice." Specific sites are used for certain rituals, and "successful use of the [area] is dependent upon and facilitated by certain qualities of the physical environment, the most important of which are privacy, silence, and an undisturbed natural setting." The study concluded that constructing a road along any of the available routes "would cause serious and irreparable damage to the sacred areas which are an integral and necessary part of the belief systems and lifeway of Northwest California Indian peoples." Accordingly, the report recommended that the G–O road not be completed.

In 1982, the Forest Service decided not to adopt this recommendation, and it prepared a final environmental impact statement for construction of the road. The Regional Forester selected a route that avoided archeological sites and was removed as far as possible from the sites used by contemporary Indians for specific spiritual activities. Alternative routes that would have avoided the Chimney Rock area altogether were rejected because they would have required the acquisition of private land, had serious soil stability problems, and would in any event have traversed areas having ritualistic value to American Indians. At about the same time, the Forest Service adopted a management plan allowing for the harvesting of significant amounts of timber in this area of the forest. The management plan provided for one-half mile protective zones around all the religious sites identified in the report that had been commissioned in connection with the G–O road.

The Free Exercise Clause of the First Amendment provides that "Congress shall make no law ... prohibiting the free exercise [of religion]." It is undisputed that the Indian respondents' beliefs are sincere and that the Government's proposed actions will have severe adverse effects on the practice of their religion. Those respondents contend that the burden on their religious practices is heavy enough to violate the Free Exercise Clause unless the Government can demonstrate a compelling need to complete the G–O road or to engage in timber harvesting in the Chimney Rock area. We disagree.

In *Bowen v. Roy,* 476 U.S. 693 (1986), [the Court rejected a challenge to a federal requirement that applicants to certain welfare programs use their Social Security numbers, the challengers arguing that it violated their religious beliefs.] * * * Similarly, in this case, it is said that disruption of the natural environment caused by the G–O road will diminish the sacredness of the area in question and create distractions that will interfere with "training and ongoing religious experience of individuals using [sites within] the area for personal medicine and growth ... and as integrated parts of a system of religious belief and practice which correlates ascending degrees of personal power with a geographic hierarchy of power." ("Scarred hills and mountains, and disturbed rocks destroy the purity of the sacred areas, and [Indian] consultants repeatedly stressed the need of a training doctor to be undistracted by such disturbance"). The Court rejected this kind of challenge in *Roy:*

> "The Free Exercise Clause simply cannot be understood to require the Government to conduct its own internal affairs in ways that comport with the religious beliefs of particular citizens. Just as the Government may not insist that [the Roys] engage in any set form of religious observance, so [they] may not demand that the Government join in their chosen religious practices by refraining from using a number to identify their daughter.... ... The Free Exercise Clause affords an individual protection from certain forms of governmental compulsion; it does not afford an individual a right to dictate the conduct of the Government's internal procedures." 476 U.S., at 699–700.

The building of a road or the harvesting of timber on publicly owned land cannot meaningfully be distinguished from the use of a Social Security number in *Roy.* In both cases, the challenged Government action would interfere significantly with private persons' ability to pursue spiritual fulfillment according to their own religious beliefs. In neither case, however, would the affected individuals be coerced by the Government's action into violating their religious beliefs; nor would either governmental action penalize religious activity by denying any person an equal share of the rights, benefits, and privileges enjoyed by other citizens.

We are asked to distinguish this case from *Roy* on the ground that the infringement on religious liberty here is "significantly greater," or on the ground that the Government practice in *Roy* was "purely mechanical" whereas this case involves "a case-by-case substantive determination as to how a particular unit of land will be managed." Brief for Indian Respondents 33–34. Similarly, we are told that this case can be distinguished from *Roy* because "the government action is not at some physically removed location where it places no restriction on what a practitioner may do." Brief for Respondent State of California 18. * * * In this case, * * * it is said that the proposed road will "physically destro[y] the environmental conditions and the privacy without which the [religious] practices cannot be conducted." *Ibid.*

These efforts to distinguish *Roy* are unavailing. This Court cannot determine the truth of the underlying beliefs that led to the religious objections here or in *Roy* * * * and accordingly cannot weigh the adverse effects on the appellees in *Roy* and compare them with the adverse effects on the Indian respondents. Without the ability to make such comparisons, we cannot say that the one form of incidental interference with an individual's spiritual activities should be subjected to a different constitutional analysis than the other. * * *

Whatever may be the exact line between unconstitutional prohibitions on the free exercise of religion and the legitimate conduct by government of its own affairs, the location of the line cannot depend on measuring the effects of a governmental action on a religious objector's spiritual development. The Government does not dispute, and we have no reason to doubt, that the logging and road-building projects at issue in this case could have devastating effects on traditional Indian religious practices. Those practices are intimately and inextricably bound up with the unique features of the Chimney Rock area, which is known to the Indians as the "high country." Individual practitioners use this area for personal spiritual development; some of their activities are believed to be critically important in advancing the welfare of the Tribe, and indeed, of mankind itself. The Indians use this area, as they have used it for a very long time, to conduct a wide variety of specific rituals that aim to accomplish their religious goals. According to their beliefs, the rituals would not be efficacious if conducted at other sites than the ones traditionally used, and too much disturbance of the area's natural state would clearly render any meaningful continuation of traditional practices impossible. To be sure, the Indians themselves were far from unanimous in opposing the G–O road, and it seems less than certain that construction of the road will be so disruptive that it will doom their religion. Nevertheless, we can assume that the threat to the efficacy of at least some religious practices is extremely grave.

Even if we assume that we should accept the Ninth Circuit's prediction, according to which the G–O road will "virtually destroy the ... Indians' ability to practice their religion," 795 F.2d, at 693 (opinion below), the Constitution simply does not provide a principle that could justify upholding respondents' legal claims. However much we might wish that it were otherwise, government simply could not operate if it were required to satisfy every citizen's religious needs and desires. A broad range of government activities—from social welfare programs to foreign aid to conservation projects—will always be considered essential to the spiritual well-being of some citizens, often on the basis of sincerely held religious beliefs. Others will find the very same activities deeply offensive, and perhaps incompatible with their own search for spiritual fulfillment and with the tenets of their religion. The First Amendment must apply to all citizens alike, and it can give to none of them a veto over public programs that do not prohibit the free exercise of religion. The Constitution does not, and courts cannot, offer to reconcile the various competing demands on government, many of them rooted in sincere religious belief, that inevitably arise in so diverse a society as ours. That task, to the extent that it is feasible, is for the legislatures and other institutions. Cf. The Federalist No. 10 (suggesting that the effects of religious factionalism are best restrained through competition among a multiplicity of religious sects).

* * * Respondents attempt to stress the limits of the religious servitude that they are now seeking to impose on the Chimney Rock area of the Six Rivers National Forest. While defending an injunction against logging operations and the construction of a road, they apparently do not *at present* object to the area's being used by recreational visitors, other Indians, or forest rangers. Nothing in the principle for which they contend, however, would distinguish this case from another lawsuit in which they (or similarly situated religious objectors) might seek to exclude all human activity but their own from sacred areas of the public lands. The Indian respondents insist that "*[p]rivacy* during the power quests is required for the practitioners to maintain the purity needed for a successful journey." Brief for Indian Respondents 8 (emphasis added; citation to record omitted). Similarly: "The practices conducted in the high country entail intense meditation and require the practitioner to achieve a profound awareness of the natural environment. Prayer seats are oriented so there is an unobstructed view, and the practitioner must be surrounded by *undisturbed* naturalness." *Id.*, at 8, n. 4 (emphasis added; citations to record omitted). No disrespect for these practices is implied when one notes that such beliefs could easily require *de facto* beneficial ownership of some rather spacious tracts of public property. Even without anticipating future cases, the diminution of the Government's property rights, and the concomitant subsidy of the Indian religion, would in this case be far from trivial: the District Court's order permanently forbade commercial timber harvesting, or the construction of a two-lane road, anywhere within an area covering a full 27 sections (*i.e.* more than 17,000 acres) of public land.

The Constitution does not permit government to discriminate against religions that treat particular physical sites as sacred, and a law prohibiting the Indian respondents from visiting the Chimney Rock area would raise a different set of constitutional questions. Whatever rights the Indians may have to the use of the area, however, those rights do not divest the Government of its right to use what is, after all, *its* land. * * *

Nothing in our opinion should be read to encourage governmental insensitivity to the religious needs of any citizen. The Government's rights to the use of its own land, for example, need not and should not discourage it from accommodating religious practices like those engaged in by the Indian respondents. It is worth emphasizing, therefore, that the Government has taken numerous steps in this very case to minimize the impact that construction of the G–O road will have on the Indians' religious activities. * * * In fact, a major factor in choosing among alternative routes for the road was the relation of the various routes to religious sites: the route selected by the Regional Forester is, he noted, "the farthest removed from contemporary spiritual sites; thus, the adverse audible intrusions associated with the road would be less than all other alternatives." * * *

Except for abandoning its project entirely, and thereby leaving the two existing segments of road to dead-end in the middle of a National Forest, it is difficult to see how the Government could have been more solicitous. * * *

The dissent proposes an approach to the First Amendment that is fundamentally inconsistent with the principles on which our decision rests. Notwithstanding the sympathy that we all must feel for the plight of the Indian respondents, it is plain that the approach taken by the dissent cannot withstand analysis. On the contrary, the path towards which it points us is incompatible with the text of the Constitution, with the precedents of this Court, and with a responsible sense of our own institutional role. * * *

■ JUSTICE KENNEDY took no part in the consideration or decision of this case.

■ Justice Brennan, with whom Justice Marshall and Justice Blaackmun join, dissenting.

* * * [The majority] concludes that even where the Government uses federal land in a manner that threatens the very existence of a Native American religion, the Government is simply not *"doing"* anything to the practitioners of that faith. Instead, the Court believes that Native Americans who request that the Government refrain from destroying their religion effectively seek to exact from the Government *de facto* beneficial ownership of federal property. * * * The constitutional guarantee we interpret today, however, * * * is directed against any form of governmental action that frustrates or inhibits religious practice. * * *

* * * [F]or Native Americans religion is not a discrete sphere of activity separate from all others, and any attempt to isolate the religious aspects of Indian life "is in reality an exercise which forces Indian concepts into non-Indian categories." D. Theodoratus, Cultural Resources of the Chimney Rock Section, Gasquet–Orleans Road, Six Rivers National Forest (1979). * * * A pervasive feature of this lifestyle is the individual's relationship with the natural world; this relationship, which can accurately though somewhat incompletely be characterized as one of stewardship, forms the core of what might be called, for want of a better nomenclature, the Indian religious experience. While traditional Western religions view creation as the work of a deity "who institutes natural laws which then govern the operation of physical nature," tribal religions regard creation as an on-going process in which they are morally and religiously obligated to participate. U.S. Federal Agencies Task Force, American Indian Religious Freedom Act Report 11 (1979) (Task Force Report). Native Americans fulfill this duty through ceremonies and rituals designed to preserve and stabilize the earth and to protect humankind from disease and other catastrophes. Failure to conduct these ceremonies in the manner and place specified, adherents believe, will result in great harm to the earth and to the people whose welfare depends upon it. *Id.,* at 10. * * *

* * * [T]oday's ruling sacrifices a religion at least as old as the Nation itself, along with the spiritual well-being of its approximately 5,000 adherents, so that the Forest Service can build a 6–mile segment of road that two lower courts found had only the most marginal and speculative utility, both to the Government itself and to the private lumber interests that might conceivably use it.

Similarly, the Court's concern that the claims of Native Americans will place "religious servitudes" upon vast tracts of federal property cannot justify its refusal to recognize the constitutional injury respondents will suffer here. It is true, as the Court notes, that respondents' religious use of the high country requires privacy and solitude. The fact remains, however, that respondents have never asked the Forest Service to exclude others from the area. Should respondents or any other group seek to force the Government to protect their religious practices from the interference of private parties, such a demand would implicate not only the concerns of the Free Exercise Clause, but also those of the Establishment Clause as well. That case, however, is most assuredly not before us today * * *.

Today, the Court holds that a federal land-use decision that promises to destroy an entire religion does not burden the practice of that faith in a manner recognized by the Free Exercise Clause. Having thus stripped respondents and all other Native Americans of any constitutional protection against perhaps the most serious threat to their age-old religious practices, and indeed to their entire way of life, the Court assures us that nothing in its decision "should be read to encourage governmental insensitivity to the religious needs of any citizen." I find it difficult, however, to imagine conduct more insensitive to religious needs than the Government's determination to build a marginally useful road in the face of uncontradicted evidence that the road will render the practice of respondents' religion impossible. Nor do I believe that respondents will derive any solace from the knowledge that although the practice of their religion will become "more difficult" as a result of the Government's actions, they remain free to maintain their religious beliefs. Given today's ruling, that freedom amounts to nothing more than the right to believe that their religion will be destroyed. The safeguarding of such a hollow freedom * * * fails utterly to accord with the dictates of the First Amendment.

NOTES AND QUESTIONS

1.   Does the majority deny that the U.S. has any constitutional obligation to use its vast tracts of federal land in any way that accommodates religious practices? Can any argument be made that Indians ought to have some special access or consideration regarding federal land use given the special character of their beliefs, as discussed in Brennan's dissent? Is it relevant that Indian Tribes are mentioned in the Constitution (e.g., Art. I, § 8, cl. 3 authorizes Congress to "regulate commerce * * * with the Indian tribes")?

2.   Could Congress reverse this decision by statute, and adopt a general policy requiring the federal land managing agencies to give priority to protection of Native American cultural and religious interests? Cf. City of Boerne v. Flores, 521 U.S. 507 (1997) (holding that Congress could not command states to refrain from burdening religions except to serve a compelling state interest, leaving open the question whether Congress could command federal agencies to do so). On the specific ground at stake in *Lyng*, ten years later Congress designated part of the national forest area consider sacred by the Indians as wilderness, and the road has not been built. See 104 Stat. 3209 (1990).

3.   Post-*Lyng* cases on the subject have included United States v. Means, 858 F.2d 404 (8th Cir.1988), cert. denied, 492 U.S. 910 (1989) (upholding Forest Service's denial of special use permit to an Indian group seeking to erect a "permanent camp" encompassing 800 acres in the Black Hills National Forest, finding no burden on the free exercise of their religion); Havasupai Tribe v. United States, 752 F.Supp. 1471 (D.Ariz. 1990), aff'd on other grounds sub nom. Havasupai Tribe v. Robertson, 943 F.2d 32 (9th Cir.1991), cert. denied, 503 U.S. 959 (1992) (Forest Service approval of plan of operations for uranium mine on national forest land did

not violate Tribe's free exercise right); Miccosukee Tribe v. United States, 980 F.Supp. 448 (S.D.Fla.1997), aff'd w/o opinion, 163 F.3d 1359 (11th Cir.1998), cert. denied, 528 U.S. 810 (1999) (federal government's failure to alleviate flooding of tribal land did not infringe on Tribe's free exercise of religion).

4. In 1996 President Clinton signed an Executive Order on Indian sacred sites that directed every federal land managing agency (including the military) to "(1) accommodate access to and ceremonial use of Indian sacred sites by Indian religious practitioners and (2) avoid adversely affecting the physical integrity of such sacred sites." E.O. No. 13007, § 1. The directive was qualified: "To the extent practicable, permitted by law, and not clearly inconsistent with essential agency functions, * * * " *Id*. A sacred site was defined as "any specific, discrete, narrowly delineated location on Federal land that is identified ... as sacred by virtue of its established religious significance to, or ceremonial use by, an Indian religion." *Id*. § 1(b)(iii). The Order also provided that it was for internal housekeeping purposes only, and did not create any right of action against the U.S. *Id*. § 4.

5. Armed with this Order, on the facts of *Lyng v. Northwest Indian Cemetery Protective Ass'n, supra*, could the Forest Service have decided not to authorize road construction and timber harvesting in the area sacred to the Indians? Could it have decided to issue the special use permit to the Indians on the facts of *United States v. Means, supra* para. 1? Stop the uranium mine on the facts of *Havasupai*?

6. Justice Brennan's dissent notes that, should the government act to protect religious practices from interference by others, it "would implicate not only the concerns of the Free Exercise Clause, but also those of the Establishment Clause as well." If the government were to fence off federal lands to protect Indian religious practices or concerns, would it violated the Establishment Clause? So far courts have not squarely answered that question. See Bear Lodge Multiple Use Ass'n v. Babbitt, 2 F.Supp.2d 1448 (D.Wyo.1998), aff'd, 175 F.3d 814 (10th Cir.1999), cert. denied, 529 U.S. 1037 (2000) (Establishment Clause challenge to National Park Service's promotion of a voluntary cessation of recreational climbing during the month of June in order to protect Native American religious ceremonies failed for lack of standing); Wyoming Sawmills, Inc. v. U.S. Forest Service, 179 F.Supp.2d 1279 (D.Wyo.2001) (similar result in establishment clause challenge to a Forest Service Historic Preservation Plan for the Medicine Wheel National Historic Landmark, a prehistoric feature consisting of a circular structure of rocks 80 feet in diameter, where the plan led to cancellation of a timber sale, closed several roads previously open to commercial logging, and led to the expenditure of tax dollars to educate tourists about Indian religion).

7. See generally Walter E. Stern & Lynn H. Slade, Effects of Historic and Cultural Resources and Indian Religious Freedom on Public Lands Development: A Practical Primer, 35 Nat. Res. J. 133 (1995). An interesting discussion of the history of interactions between Indians and the national parks is found in Philip Burnham, INDIAN COUNTRY, GOD'S

COUNTRY (2000). In January 2001, the Park Service invited comment on a proposal to allow Hopi Indians to take eagles from Wupatki National Monument for ceremonial use. See 66 Fed. Reg. 6516 (2001).

8. In 1990, Congress adopted the Native American Graves Protection and Repatriation Act (NAGPRA), codified at 25 U.S.C. §§ 3001–3013. It establishes, among other things, a protocol for the protection and return to Native Americans of cultural items (broadly defined to include not only human remains and associated funerary objects, but also sacred objects and objects of cultural patrimony) found on federal land (broadly defined to include all land "controlled or owned by" the United States). See Jack F. Trope and Walter Echohawk, The Native American Graves Protection and Repatriation Act: Background and Legislative History, 24 Ariz. St.L.J. 35 (1992); Francis McManamon and Larry Nordby, Implementing the Native American Graves Protection and Repatriation Act, 24 Ariz. St.L.J. 217 (1992) (both part of a general symposium issue on the Act). Its most controversial application so far has to do with the so-called "Kennewick Man," a 9000 year old skeleton discovered on land managed by the Corps of Engineers along the Columbia River in 1996. See Bonnichsen v. United States, 969 F.Supp. 628 (D.Or.1997). See also United States v. Corrow, 119 F.3d 796 (10th Cir.1997), cert. denied, 522 U.S. 1133 (1998) (discussing the statutory definition of "objects of cultural patrimony" and rejecting arguments that it is void for vagueness)

NOTE: THE CONSTITUTION AND FREE SPEECH ON FEDERAL LANDS

Here the leading case is Clark v. Community for Creative Non–Violence, 468 U.S. 288 (1984), upholding Park Service regulations prohibiting demonstrators seeking to call attention to the plight of the homeless from sleeping in District of Columbia national park system units. The majority concluded that the Court's First Amendment decisions do not "assign to the judiciary the authority to replace the Park Service as the manager of the Nation's parks or endow the judiciary with the competence to judge how much protection of Park lands is wise and how that level of conservation is to be attained." Since then a variety of cases have sustained federal agency regulation of recreational activities against first amendment challenges. See, e.g., Craft v. Hodel, 683 F.Supp. 289 (D.Mass.1988) (no constitutional right to nude sunbathing on federal lands). The National Mall in Washington D.C., sometimes called the "nation's front yard" and managed by the National Park Service, is the scene of frequent public demonstrations and litigation over first amendment issues.

Perhaps the most extensive consideration of the collision between free expression and use and occupancy of federal lands can be found in United States v. Rainbow Family, 695 F.Supp. 294 (E.D.Tex.1988). There the United States sought to enjoin a gathering of several thousand "Rainbow Family" members on a national forest in Texas, on the ground that they had failed to apply for and obtain a "special use" permit from the Forest Service. The "Family" is, according to the district court, a "loosely-knit but identifiable group of persons" who use their annual gatherings to exchange views on many subjects, including political topics (such as peace and ecological concerns), as well as educational seminars and various forms of worship. In the first decision, the court found that the regulations embodied a decision by the agency to treat "expressive" activity differently from other forms of group activity on the forests, and thus implicated the First Amendment. Like public streets and parks, the public lands are, said the court, "the type of forum in which expressive activity has historically occurred, and in which public expression of views must be tolerated to a maximal extent." Regulation of such activity "must therefore be narrowly tailored as to time, place and manner, and serve substantial governmental interests, as well as leave open ample alternative channels of communication. Any prior restraint on expressive activity in such a context is particularly suspect." The regulations were struck down because they left "virtually unfettered discretion" to the agency, with no requirement to "justify or explain any denial of a permit."

Shortly after this decision, the court issued another opinion acknowledging that "where there is some * * * genuine interest to protect or defend, such as preserving public health and safety, the federal government may justifiably seek equitable intervention of the courts to forestall irreparable damage or some other public nuisance." 695 F.Supp. 314 at 326. Acting on the agency's evidence that a previous Family gathering had caused outbreaks of bacterial infections, and that the Family's failure to observe proper sanitary conditions were "substantial contributory conditions" to the outbreak; and also that a prior gathering had left garbage and other debris, the court issued an order limiting the number of persons on any one site to 5000, imposed basic sanitary standards and required the Family to comply with "reasonable requirements for cleaning and rehabilitating any gathering site." 695 F.Supp. at 327–32.

Litigation between the Rainbow Family and the Forest Service has become practically an annual event, with the Rainbow Family usually losing. See, e.g., United States v. Kalb, 234 F.3d 827 (3d Cir.2000) (upholding convictions of organizers of Rainbow Family gathering for using Forest Service land without permission, rejecting various challenges); Black v. Arthur, 201 F.3d 1120 (9th Cir.2000) (rejecting, among other arguments, that Forest Service regulation governing "group use" of national forests should not apply to the Rainbow Family gathering because it "does not have an internal governing structure that would make it a 'group' "); United States v. Linick, 195 F.3d 538 (9th Cir.1999) (upholding the Forest Service regulation, as explained and narrowed in an interpretive rule, against constitutional attack, but affirming dismissal of the prosecution because the interpretive rule was promulgated after the prosecution commenced; hence defendants did not have adequate notice). Cf. United States v. Beam, 686 F.2d 252 (5th Cir.1982), where the court reversed the conviction of the Grand Dragon of the Texas Ku Klux Klan for conducting military maneuvers on national forest land without a permit. The court found the agency regulation requiring a written permit for "public meetings, assemblies and special events" not applicable because the KKK activities were decidedly not open to the public. And see United States v.

Griefen, 200 F.3d 1256 (9th Cir.2000), where the court rejected a First Amendment defense in upholding the convictions of protestors against logging on federal lands who violated a Forest Service "closure order" that prohibited persons from entering the area of the logging operation without permission. The court found the closure order embodied reasonable time, place, and manner restrictions, served a significant governmental interest, and was narrowly tailored to protect health, safety and property. The court also sustained a conviction for violating a Forest Service regulation that required a permit for maintaining structures on national forest land.

NOTE: HISTORIC PRESERVATION

By the Historic Sites Act of 1935, 16 U.S.C. §§ 461–470t, the Secretary of the Interior was given the responsibility to implement "a national policy to preserve for public use historic sites, buildings, and objects of national significance for the inspiration and benefit of the people of the United States." Id. § 461. The Act requires salvage operations, at a minimum, whenever qualifying historical and archaeological resources are threatened by federal dams or by any alteration resulting from any federal construction project or federally licensed activity or program. Id. § 469. Sections 469a–1 and 469a–2 extend the survey-evaluation-recovery program to all federal activities but impose few substantive constraints. See, e.g., Paulina Lake Historic Cabin Owners Ass'n v. United States Department of Agriculture Forest Service, 577 F.Supp. 1188 (D.Or.1983).

In 1966, Congress extended federal protection to historic resources of other than "national significance" by adopting the National Historic Preservation Act (NHPA). 16 U.S.C. §§ 470–470w–6. Under it the Secretary of the Interior maintains the National Register of Historic Places. The Act creates a NEPA-like process under which federal agencies must consider the effect on any property listed on the Register before it authorizes or funds any project. Like NEPA, section 106 of the NHPA demands only consideration, not substantive protection. The key section requires federal agencies to "take into account the effect of [any federal action] on any [property listed or eligible for listing on the National Register]. 16 U.S.C. § 470f. See Davis v. Latschar, 202 F.3d 359 (D.C.Cir.2000) ("Section 106 only requires that the Park Service consult the SHPO [State Historic Preservation Officer, pronounced 'Ship–O'] and the ACHP [Advisory Council on Historic Preservation, no pronunciation available] and consider the impacts of its undertaking").

In National Mining Ass'n v. Slater, 167 F.Supp.2d 265 (D.D.C.2001), the court struck down two regulations adopted by the Advisory Council on Historic Preservation under the NHPA. The court found that the Council was authorized to issue procedural regulations that are binding on federal agencies in going through the section 106 process, and went on to find many of the challenged regulations (such as those requiring documentation during the § 106 process) procedural and valid. It did, however, strike down regulations that required an agency to continue the § 106 process at the Council's request if the Council disagreed with the agency's determinations, and which granted the Council authority to review an agency finding of no adverse effect if other interested parties disagreed with the finding. These were held to be beyond the ACHP's authority because "they require the agency to proceed with the § 106 process in the face of that agency's own determination to the contrary." Often NHPA and NEPA counts are married in both complaints and judicial opinions. Court decisions finding a failure to adequately consult under the NHPA are rare. Other NHPA decisions involving federal lands include Yerger v. Robertson, 981 F.2d 460 (9th Cir.1992), and Hoonah Indian Ass'n v. Morrison, 170 F.3d 1223 (9th Cir.1999), the latter discussing, among other things, how precisely located a historical "site" must be. See generally George Cameron Coggins and Robert Glicksman, PUBLIC NATURAL RESOURCES LAW § 15B.8–10 (2001).

Historic preservation concerns led to a sustained effort to protect Bodie, California—by most accounts the largest, best-preserved ghost town in the western United States—from a modern gold mining operation proposed to be conducted on patented and unpatented mining claims adjacent to the town. In its heyday Bodie—listed on the National Register and made a State Park in 1962—was, ironically, a mining town. In 1994, Congress ended the controversy by enacting the Bodie Protection Act, which withdrew the federal lands in and around the town from the Mining Law, subject to valid existing rights. 108 Stat. 4509 (1994).

Another controversy still alive as of 2002 has involved efforts by Glamis Gold, Inc., to open a large open-pit gold mine on its mining claims on federal land in the California desert west of Yuma, Arizona, on a site that contains a historic trail considered sacred by the local Quechan Indians. The Advisory Council on Historic Preservation issued a report on the question that recommended that the Department of the Interior deny approval of the company's plan of operations if it had the legal authority to do so. The Interior Solicitor opined in 1999 that the legal authority existed, but a new Solicitor overruled that opinion in 2001. See Chapter 7, pp. 637–39 supra. The matter is still in litigation.

B. External Threats

In previous chapters, a variety of what might be called "internal" threats to the "naturalness" of federal land areas were considered; e.g., off road vehicles in Chapter 11, supra pp. 988–1013. The federal land management agencies generally have adequate legal authority to deal with such internal threats, if they can muster the political will to do so and valid existing rights do not intervene. Sometimes, however, equally serious threats to federal land units which are managed to preserve natural, historic, and aesthetic values are posed by activities conducted outside their boundaries. These questions can, of course, arise with respect to all federal land management agencies, but because the Park Service is generally acknowledged to manage the "crown jewels" of the federal landholdings, the external threat problem is most acute there, and the discussion that follows concentrates on that context.

Robert B. Keiter, On Protecting the National Parks From the External Threats Dilemma*

XX Land & Water L.Rev. 355 (1985).

The 1980 report to Congress entitled the *State of the Parks* identified myriad "threats" that endangered the natural and cultural resources of the parks. While the report covered both internal and external threats to park resources, over fifty percent of the threats were traced to sources located outside of the parks. * * *

In the face of these threats, the national parks are not entirely defenseless. * * * The Organic Act provides the Park Service with the legal authority to deal with problems internal to the parks, such as overcrowding, resource destruction, and vehicle use. The Act apparently also imposes the legal responsibility on the Park Service to protect the parks from threatening external activities.

The Park Service, however, is generally unable to regulate or to control effectively activities or developments originating on federal, state or private lands located outside park boundaries. The Park Service cannot claim jurisdiction over these adjacent lands since they are not part of the parks. Nevertheless, the Park Service cannot ignore developments outside the parks in view of the threat posed to park resources and the preservation mandate of the Organic Act. Although park officials can rely upon existing federal and state environmental control legislation to challenge external activities or to influence the decision-making processes of coordinate federal agencies and local governments, these statutes often fail to protect park resources meaningfully. Most of them only establish general standards governing environmental quality and land use decisions without regard for the unique status of the national parks. Moreover, much of the federal legislation only applies when external threats originate on public lands; it has no application when these threats are traced to activities on private lands. * * *

By the mid-twentieth century, with increased population growth and expanded resource and energy demands, it was inevitable that the parks would begin to feel the pressure of incompatible external activities. At about the same time that visitor use of parks surged dramatically, the Park Service also began experiencing added problems traceable to human activity outside park boundaries. Early external threats which attracted national attention included upstream logging activities on lands adjacent to Redwood National Park [eds.: addressed in the next cases, immediately below] and the construction and operation of large coal-fired power plants near several southwestern parks. The more recent energy crises have slowed visitor pressures on the parks, but ironically the energy crises have also been responsible for even more external pressures. For example, the search for coal, oil and gas reserves has led to exploratory seismic and drilling activities on the borders of Glacier National Park and a proposed open pit mine next to Bryce Canyon National Park. Plans have also been prepared

* Reprinted with permission of the Land
& Water Law Review.

to develop geothermal energy sources on the border of Yellowstone National Park, and the lands immediately adjacent to Canyonlands National Park are being considered as a site for the long term storage of nuclear waste materials. * * *

* * * The studies reveal that park managers are widely concerned about non-park activities which threaten air and water quality, wildlife and fish resources, and the general aesthetic quality of the parklands. The surveys also indicate that the parks are most usually threatened by adjacent activities such as: residential, commercial, industrial, and road development; logging, mining, and agriculture; energy extraction and production; and recreation. Both reports conclude that existing laws do not adequately protect park resources against continued degradation from external threats.

* * *

* * * Park administrators reported a systemwide average of 13.6 threats per park. Among the large national parks exceeding 30,000 acres in size, an average of 24.5 threats per park were reported. * * *

* * * The national parks are amazingly diverse, and the nature and degree of external threats vary widely from park to park. The large, wilderness-like parks with ecosystems substantially intact generally face problems similar to those experienced by Glacier National Park. While external developments on nearby public and private lands threaten specific park resources, the cumulative effect of these activities severely threatens these parks' ecosystems. On the other hand, the smaller, non-wilderness parks, such as the national monuments and historic sites, are much less likely to be defined by ecosystem characteristics, and their concern usually is with controlling external activities that threaten to degrade the park's particular attractions. Congress can reasonably take some account of these and other notable differences among the parks in framing a response to the external threats problem. * * *

There also is another approach to the external threats problem that would substantially protect selected parks, and that might be adopted alone or in conjunction with one of the proposed statutory schemes. Under this approach Congress should create a national resource area land management program to administer federal lands located adjacent to designated national parks and encompassed within the park's ecosystem boundaries. This would protect selected parks against incompatible activities traceable to these federal lands. Congress also should combine the national resource area approach with meaningful federal spending limitations keyed to insuring consistency in federal policy respecting the encompassed state and private lands. In particular, Congress should condition grants to the states under the Land and Water Conservation Fund Act upon a state's willingness to establish land-use policies protective of national park resources. Although this approach does not present a plausible systemwide solution for the parks' problems, it provides meaningful protection once Congress has been persuaded to act, and it does so without administrative restructuring or drastic displacement of state prerogatives.

The materials that follow in this section consider two different kinds of "external" threats: First, those emanating from non-federal lands; and second, those emanating from federal lands or projects under the jurisdiction of other federal agencies.

1. EXTERNAL THREATS FROM NON-FEDERAL LANDS

In the continuing absence of generic legislation dealing with external threats, Congress, the Park Service, and the courts have occasionally addressed such issues in specific contexts. The Redwoods National Park litigation that follows raises a variety of interesting questions on this emerging dilemma.

Sierra Club v. Department of Interior I

United States District Court, Northern District of California, 1974.
376 F.Supp. 90.

■ SWEIGERT, DISTRICT JUDGE.

This is an action by plaintiff, Sierra Club, against the Department of the Interior, and officials of the Department, to obtain judgment of this court directing defendants to use certain of their powers to protect Redwood National Park from damage allegedly caused or threatened by certain logging operations on peripheral privately-owned lands. * * *

[Congress created the Redwood National Park by statute in 1968. Little of the 58,000 acres Congress included in the Park was then in federal ownership; most of it was acquired by exchange and purchase. At an initial authorized cost of $92 million, the Park was the most expensive (in terms of federal outlay of funds) in history. The coastal redwoods, *Sequoia Sempervirens* (to be distinguished from the *Sequoia Gigantea* in the Sierra Nevada foothills) are the tallest living things in the world, some reaching more than 350' in height. They are also old—some were alive at the time of Christ. The wood is a highly prized building material—straight, clear-grained, light, strong, and rot-resistant. Much of the land in the area of the Park was being logged, providing jobs for the chronically depressed economy along California's north coast.

Because of the expense and other political considerations, the boundaries of the Park drawn by Congress were quite gerrymandered. As the Park bill was making its way through Congress, a grove of redwoods outside the boundaries as then drawn was discovered to contain several of the very tallest of these tall trees. The bill was then changed to include a narrow eight-mile strip of land along Redwood Creek to ensure that this "tall trees grove" was included within the Park. The upland part of the Redwood Creek watershed outside this "worm" area remained in private hands, and logging of it continued after establishment of the Park. Indeed, it was said that the crowd assembled to hear First Lady Lady Bird Johnson dedicate the Park could not hear her remarks because of the noise of chainsaws operating just outside the nearby Park boundary.

The court was ruling on the government's motion to dismiss or, in the alternative, for summary judgment. The plaintiff's complaint contained the following allegations:]

That subsequent to the establishment of the Redwood National Park in 1968 plaintiff learned that logging operations on slopes surrounding and upstream from the park were seriously endangering the park's resources, and that these dangers were reported to defendants and were offered in testimony at United States Senate hearings in Washington, D.C., on May 10, 1971;

That on September 24, 1971, plaintiff formally petitioned the Secretary of the Interior to take immediate action pursuant to his authority under the Redwood National Park Act to prevent further harm to the park's resources, and that a task force was then created by the Department of the Interior to make intensive field investigations of the threatened and actual damage to the Redwood National Park and to prepare a report of its findings;

That defendants have taken no action to prevent damage to the park from the consequences of logging on lands surrounding or upstream from the park, except to request the voluntary cooperation of timber companies to reform their operations on minor portions upstream and upslope from the park; that the timber companies have not effectively cooperated with this request and that defendants manifest no intent to protect the park from further damage to the park's trees, soil, scenery and streams;

That past and present logging operations on privately-owned steep slopes on the periphery of the park leave the park vulnerable to high winds, landslides, mudslides and siltation in the streams which endangers tree roots and aquatic life.

Plaintiff, citing 16 U.S.C. § 1 (hereinafter referred to as the National Park System Act) and 16 U.S.C. § 79a et seq., particularly § 79b(a), 79c(c), 79c(d) (hereinafter referred to as the Redwood National Park Act) contends that defendants have a judicially-enforceable duty to exercise certain powers granted by these provisions to prevent or to mitigate such actual or potential damage to the park and its redwoods as is alleged in the complaint. * * *

The National Park System Act, 16 U.S.C. Sec. 1, provides [that] the National Park Service * * * shall:

> promote and regulate the use of Federal areas known as national parks, monuments, and reservations * * * by such means and measures as conform to the fundamental purpose of said parks, monuments, and reservations, which purpose is to conserve the scenery and the natural and historic objects and the wild life therein and to provide for the enjoyment of the same in such manner and by such means as will leave them unimpaired for the enjoyment of future generations.

The responsibilities of the Secretary of the Interior concerning public lands have been stated in Knight v. United Land Association * * * as follows:

> The secretary [of the Department of the Interior] is the guardian of the people of United States over the public lands. The obligations of his oath of office oblige him to see that the law is carried out, and that none of the public domain is wasted or is disposed of to a party not entitled to it. 142 U.S. 161 at 181 (1891). * * *.

In addition to these general fiduciary obligations of the Secretary of the Interior, the Secretary has been invested with certain specific powers and obligations in connection with the unique situation of the Redwood National Park.

The Redwood National Park was created on October 2, 1968 by the Redwood National Park Act, 16 U.S.C. Secs. 79a–79j,

> to preserve significant examples of the primeval coastal redwood (Sequoia sempervirens) forests and the streams and seashores with which they are associated for purposes of public inspiration, enjoyment, and scientific study * * *. 16 U.S.C. Sec. 79a.

Congress limited the park to an area of 58,000 acres; appropriated 92 million dollars to implement the Act, of which, according to the Second Claim of the Amended Complaint, 20 million dollars remain unspent; and conferred upon the Secretary specific powers expressly designed to prevent damage to the park by logging on peripheral areas.

Title 16 U.S.C. Sec. 79c(e) provides:

> In order to afford as full protection as is reasonably possible to the timber, soil, and streams within the boundaries of the park, the Secretary is authorized, by any of the means set out in subsection (a) and (c) of this section, to acquire interests in land from, and to enter into contracts and cooperative agreements with, the owners of land on the periphery of the park and on watershed tributary to streams within the park designed to assure that the consequences of forestry management, timbering, land use, and soil conservation practices conducted thereon, or of the lack of such practices, will not adversely affect the timber, soil, and streams within the park as aforesaid.

The question presented is whether on the allegations of the amended complaint, considered in the light of these statutory provisions, this court can direct the Secretary to exercise the powers granted under 16 U.S.C. Secs. 79c(e), 79b(a), 79c(d).

Under the Administrative Procedure Act agency action becomes nonreviewable only upon a clear and convincing showing that Congress intended to preclude judicial review. Abbott Laboratories v. Gardner, 387 U.S. 136 at 141 (1967).

The mere fact that the statute is couched in terms of a grant of discretion to the agency does not necessarily indicate an intent to preclude judicial review of the exercise of such discretion; judicial non-reviewability must be determined by an analysis of the entire statutory scheme.

Good sense suggests that the existence, nature and extent of potentially damaging conditions on neighboring lands and the effect thereof on the park, and the need for action to prevent such damage are matters that rest, primarily at least, within the judgment of the Secretary. However, neither the terms nor the legislative history of the Redwood National Park Act are such as to preclude judicial review of the Secretary's action or inaction.

In Rockbridge v. Lincoln, 449 F.2d 567 (9th Cir.1971) our Circuit * * * held that, in view of the trust relationship of the Secretary toward the Indians * * * such discretion as was vested in the Secretary was not an unbridled discretion * * * and, therefore, a cause for judicial relief under the Administrative Procedure Act was stated * * *.

In view of the analogous trust responsibility of the Secretary of the Interior with respect to public lands as stated in Knight v. United Land, supra, and the analogous legislative history indicating a specific set of objectives which the provisions of the Redwood National Park Act were designed to accomplish, we consider Rockbridge, supra, to be strongly persuasive to the point that a case for judicial relief has been made out by plaintiff. * * *

We are of the opinion that the terms of the statute, especially § 79c(e), authorizing the Secretary "in order to afford as full protection as is reasonably possible to the timber, soil, and streams within the boundaries of the park"—"to acquire interests in land from, and to enter into contracts and cooperative agreements with, the owners of land on the periphery of the park and on the watersheds tributary to streams within the park"—impose a legal duty on the Secretary to utilize the specific powers given to him whenever reasonably necessary for the protection of the park and that any discretion vested in the Secretary concerning time, place and specifics of the exercise of such powers is subordinate to his paramount legal duty imposed, not only under his trust obligation but by the statute itself, to protect the park. * * *

* * * Although the inquiry into the facts is to be searching and careful, the ultimate standard of review is a narrow one that stops short of substitution of the court's judgment for that of the Secretary. * * *

Accordingly, defendants' motion to dismiss and defendants' motion for summary judgment should be, and hereby are, denied.

Sierra Club v. Department of Interior II

United States District Court, Northern District of California, 1975.
398 F.Supp. 284.

■ Sweigert, District Judge.

* * * [T]he issue for decision is whether the Secretary, since the establishment of the Park, has taken reasonable steps to protect the resources of the Park and, if not, whether his failure to do so has been under the circumstances arbitrary, capricious, or an abuse of discretion. * * *

In the pending case the conduct of the Secretary must be considered in the light of a very [sic] unique statute—a statute which did more than establish a national park; it also expressly vested the Secretary with authority to take certain specifically stated steps designed to protect the Park from damage caused by logging operations on the surrounding privately owned lands.

As the legislative history shows, these specific provisions were put into the statute because the Park boundaries authorized by Congress represented a compromise and did not include certain lands within the Redwood Creek Watershed upslope and upstream from the southernmost portion of the Park. Out of its concern that continued logging operations on those privately owned lands could cause damage within the Park, the Congress expressly invested the Secretary with these specific powers to take administrative action designed to protect it * * * [including:]

(1) power to modify the boundaries of the Park with particular attention to minimizing siltation of the streams, damage to the timber and preservation of the scenery, 16 U.S.C. § 79b(a).[*]

(2) power to acquire interests in land from and to enter into contracts and cooperative agreements with the owners of land on the periphery of the Park and on watersheds tributary to streams within the Park designed to assure that the consequences of forestry management, timbering, land use and soil conservation practices conducted thereon, or the lack of such practices, would not adversely affect the timber, soil and streams within the Park, 16 U.S.C. § 79c(e).

(3) power to acquire lands and interests in land bordering both sides of the highway near the town of Orick to a depth sufficient to maintain a corridor—a screen of trees between the highway and the land behind the screen and the activities conducted thereon, 16 U.S.C. § 79c(d).

As pointed out in this court's previous decision, there is, in addition to these specific powers, a general trust duty imposed upon the National Park Service, Department of the Interior, by the National Park System Act, 16 U.S.C. § 1 et seq., to conserve scenery and natural and historic objects and wildlife [in the National Parks, Monuments and reservations] and to provide for the enjoyment of the same in such manner and by such means as will leave them unimpaired for the enjoyment of future generations * * *.

The evidence in the pending case shows that, beginning in April of 1969, the Secretary has conducted a series of five consecutive studies of damage and threats of damage to the Park caused by the logging operations of certain timber companies on adjacent lands. These studies have resulted in many specific recommendations for steps to be taken by the Secretary,

* [Eds. The authority given to the Secretary in this section to modify the boundaries of the Park did not on its face authorize the Secretary to acquire nonfederal lands in order to expand the boundaries and the protection of the Park resources, and it did not make any appropriations of funds for this purpose.]

pursuant to his various powers set forth in the statute, to prevent or minimize such damage.

[The opinion discusses each of the five reports at length. The reports analyzed the factual setting; emphasized the destructive effects of nearby logging on the Park; and urged that the Park Service develop a master plan and otherwise take action to protect the Park from the logging. The following excerpt from one of the reports is illustrative.]

The Curry Task Force Report—1973

In February, 1973, the defendants released a document prepared by Dr. Richard Curry, an official within the Department of the Interior. The Curry Task Force Report * * * set forth in detail the damage and threats of damage to the Park resources posed by logging practices on the lands adjacent to the Park. * * * The Curry Task Force Report found, as did the earlier reports, that, while landslides, erosion, and consequent high sediment loads in Redwood Creek are naturally occurring phenomena within the Redwood Creek watershed, man's timber harvesting activities within the watershed accelerate and aggravate these natural processes. In this regard, the Curry Task Force Report specifically identified such timber harvesting practices as clearcutting, the use of bulldozers within unstable areas to yard logs, and the construction of layouts and road systems over steep and unstable terrain.

The Curry Task Force Report made five specific recommendations for actions to be taken by the Secretary:

"1. Since the greatest threat to the Park emanates from man-induced acceleration of natural erosion processes, it is imperative that present land use practices be revised. The Secretary must secure the cooperation of the companies * * * to use harvesting techniques that minimize the degree of ground surface and vegetation disruption and to perform maintenance management on the harvested land in an effort to reduce the rate of erosion in these areas.

"These actions might include but are not limited to:

"a. Cable logging or such other system that minimizes ground disruption.

"b. More sensitive placement of the road net so as to minimize land slippage.

"c. A high performance road maintenance system which would include an effective erosion control program. * * *

"d. Application of stabilization procedures in active slide areas.

"e. Minimize the burning of slash.

"f. Planting of areas where regeneration from seeding and/or sprouting may be difficult.

"2. The Secretary should seek by cooperative agreement with the companies at least a two-year cutting moratorium extending at least 75 feet from the bank of all second order and higher tributary streams that are upslope from the Corridor. The purpose is to permit the accumulation of baseline data for these streams. At the end of the period, the companies would be permitted to continue with their operations as long as the integrity of the stream is maintained.

"3. The acquisition in fee of a management zone around the 'worm' portion of the Redwood Creek unit that would be contoured to deal with specific impact and terrain conditions. The buffer would average 800 feet in width or encompass approximately 1,650 acres. * * * "

The evidence shows, and the court finds, that to date the Secretary has not implemented any of the recommendations made by or on behalf of his own agency in the above mentioned studies except (1) to enter into so-called "cooperative agreements" with the timber companies who own and operate on the lands surrounding the Park and (2) to conduct further studies.

The Secretary contends that these cooperative agreements amount to reasonable compliance with the intent of the statute and with his trust duties, pointing out that the timber companies voluntarily abstained from logging operations within an 800–foot zone of the Park until 1973 when they resumed logging under the so-called cooperative agreements; that their operations since 1973 have conformed to these agreements and that the agreements have restrained the harvesting practices of the timber companies and have thus mitigated damage to the Park.

The Secretary further points out that he is presently conducting another study through the U.S. Geological Survey of the Redwood Creek watershed and that this study, headed by a Dr. Richard Janda, is expected to be completed by the fall of 1975, at which time the Secretary will be in a position to further consider the Park situation.

The Secretary also contends that his failure to thus far implement other recommendations made by his own agency has been reasonable because of lack of sufficient scientific data to justify some of the recommendations already received and because of lack of the funds that would be required for the adoption of others. * * *

On the other hand, plaintiff Sierra Club contends that the Secretary has complied with neither the intent of the statute nor with his general fiduciary duty to protect the Park * * *.

Plaintiff contends and the Court finds that the so-called cooperative agreements with the three timber companies are in fact not contracts or cooperative agreements within the meaning of Section 79c(e) because only one has been signed by one of the timber companies, and none of them has been signed by the Secretary; that they are, therefore, not legally binding contracts enforceable against the timber operators; also that, even if the so-called cooperative agreements were enforceable, their language is so general and so full of qualifications as to render them practically meaningless and unenforceable for that reason as well; also, that in any event the so-called cooperative agreements do not purport to carry out any of the recommendations of the defendants' studies with the arguable exception of Recommendation Number One of the Curry Task Force Report and, indeed, are contrary to other specific recommendations. * * *

The Court further finds that the cooperative agreements do not fully implement even Curry Task Force Recommendation Number One in that the agreements set up an arbitrary 800 foot area surrounding the corridor portion of the Park while the recommendations do not so limit the harvesting restrictions.

The Court also finds that, even assuming none of the above deficiencies existed, the restraints placed upon the companies by the so-called cooperative agreements are unreasonably inadequate to prevent or reasonably minimize damage to the resources of the Park resulting from timber harvesting operations; that there is substantial on-going damage presently occurring to the timber, soil, streams, and aesthetics within the Park downslope from and as a result of clearcutting within the so-called buffer zone, even as such clearcutting is done in conformity with the so-called cooperative agreements.

With respect to the defendants' contentions concerning unavailability of funds, the Court further finds that it is the Congress which must make the ultimate determination whether additional sums should be authorized or appropriated and also the ultimate determinations concerning the items to which such funds should be applied; that the Secretary has never yet gone to the Congress * * * either to request the appropriation of the balance of money authorized by the statute, or to obtain whatever additional sums of money may be necessary to implement the specific powers of the statute designed for the protection of the Park.[6]

Finally, the Court finds that in light of the emphasis in each of the Secretary's own studies that time is of the essence, the Secretary has taken (to the detriment of the Park) an unreasonably long period of time to negotiate the proposed cooperative agreements. * * *

The foregoing findings must be considered in the light of what might be called an implied recognition by the defendants of some degree of fault on their part. This recognition is evidenced by the fact that, prior to the time the Curry Report was released to the public (which was not until after and as a result of legal steps taken in this action by the Sierra Club under the Freedom of Information Act), the Department of Interior had intentionally removed from the Report the last two pages which contained the five recommendations for action to be taken by the Secretary of the Interior. The existence of these last two pages was thereafter discovered only in the course of subsequent discovery proceedings which were initiated by the Sierra Club in the instant action.

With all due respect for the narrow limits of judicial intervention in matters entrusted primarily to executive agencies, the Court concludes that, in light of the foregoing findings, the defendants unreasonably, arbitrarily and in abuse of discretion have failed, refused and neglected to take steps to exercise and perform duties imposed upon them by the

---

6. The only step taken by the Secretary in this direction was to consult, not the Congress, but only the Executive Office of Management of the Budget (OMB) concerning the recommendation of the Curry Report that certain property be acquired in fee; the OMB evidently advised against such acquisition.

National Park System Act, 16 U.S.C. § 1, and the Redwood National Park Act, 16 U.S.C. § 79a, and duties otherwise imposed upon them by law; and/or that defendants have unreasonably and unlawfully delayed taking such steps.

Therefore * * * it is hereby ordered:

That defendants Secretary of the Interior and Assistant Secretary for Fish, Wildlife and Parks, take reasonable steps within a reasonable time to exercise the powers vested in them by law (particularly 16 U.S.C. § 79c(e), 79c(d) and 79b(a)), and to perform the duties imposed upon them by law (particularly 16 U.S.C. § 1), in order to afford as full protection as is reasonably possible to the timber, soil and streams within the boundaries of the Redwood National Park from adverse consequences of timbering and land use practices on lands located in the periphery of the Park and on watershed tributaries to streams which flow into the Park; that such action shall include, if reasonably necessary, acquisition of interests in land and/or execution of contracts or cooperative agreements with the owners of land on the periphery or watershed, as authorized in 16 U.S.C. § 79c(e); that such action shall include, if reasonably necessary, modification of the boundaries of the Park, as authorized in 16 U.S.C. § 79b(a); and that such action shall include, if reasonably necessary, resort to the Congress for a determination whether further authorization and/or appropriation of funds will be made for the taking of the foregoing steps, and whether the powers and duties of defendants, as herein found, are to remain or should be modified.

Defendants are further ordered to file herein, and serve upon plaintiff [within a specified time] * * * a progress report upon their compliance with the foregoing order, or, in lieu of compliance, a report, showing cause why compliance has not been made, is not being or will not be made with the foregoing order. * * *

NOTES AND QUESTIONS

1. Is there any doubt about the constitutional power of Congress to authorize the Secretary to regulate logging on private lands around the Park? The National Park Service for a long time expressed doubt about the constitutional power of the federal government to regulate lands near and within the parks, see Joseph Sax, Helpless Giants: The National Parks and the Regulation of Private Lands, 75 Mich.L.Rev. 239 (1976), but the general issue would seem to have been laid to rest by decisions like Kleppe v. New Mexico and Minnesota v. Block; see Chapter 3, supra pp. 184–203. The more vexing questions are usually whether, in any particular instance, Congress has delegated authority to the federal land managing agency to abate the threats from non-federal development—and if so, whether the agency has the will to exercise it.

2. Look closely at what Congress has authorized the National Park Service to do. For example, note that the National Park Organic Act, 16 U.S.C. § 1, directs the Secretary to "regulate the use of *Federal areas* known as national parks * * *"(emphasis added). Does the italicized

language allow an inference against regulating non-federal areas? Does it allow an inference that the Park Service can regulate activities on non-federal inholdings (entirely surrounded by federal Park land), but not activities on adjacent land outside park boundaries?

3. To what extent has Congress authorized the Secretary to address logging on adjacent private lands in the specific statute creating Redwood National Park, 16 U.S.C. § 79c(e)? Does the statutory reference to "cooperative agreements" (presumably referring to agreements reached by mutual consent) negate any argument that Congress intended to authorize the Secretary to regulate logging around the Park without the companies' consent? For a discussion of the relationship of provisions in specific statutes creating national parks to generic national park legislation, see Robert L. Fischman, The Problem of Statutory Detail in National Park Establishment Legislation and Its Relationship to Pollution Control Law, 74 Denver L.J. 779 (1997).

4. On the reviewability in court of the Secretary's inaction, one part of the Administrative Procedure Act authorizes courts to "compel agency action unlawfully withheld or unreasonably delayed." 5 U.S.C. § 706(1). Does that apply here? Is Judge Sweigert's decision here consistent with the Supreme Court's subsequent decision in Heckler v. Chaney, Chapter 4, p. 305 supra?

5. Could the Secretary take actions other than those listed in § 79c(e)? For example, could the United States bring a common law public nuisance action against the timber companies, arguing that their logging practices unreasonably interfered with the Park? Under federal or state common law? Cf. Camfield v. United States, Chapter 2, supra p. 92. In 1979 the Secretary of the Interior was unsuccessful in attempting to stop construction of four office towers and a hotel that allegedly interfered with visual enjoyment of the Washington D.C. national capital park units. United States v. County Bd. of Arlington County, 487 F.Supp. 137 (E.D.Va. 1979). The court ruled the Attorney General could bring suit on federal public nuisance grounds without express statutory authority in order to protect the federal property but held, on the merits, that the United States had not made a case that the construction was a nuisance. Another court granted a request by the Park Service to enjoin pesticide spraying by the State of West Virginia on federal and private land within the boundaries of New River Gorge National River without permission from the Park Service, citing general grants of authority from the Congress to the Secretary to make necessary and proper regulation of national park system units. United States v. Moore, 640 F.Supp. 164 (S.D.W.Va.1986).

7. Unsuccessful efforts have been made by third parties to protect national parks from private developments, using state law. See, e.g., Commonwealth v. National Gettysburg Battlefield Tower, Inc., 454 Pa. 193, 311 A.2d 588 (1973). There the State of Pennsylvania sought, on public nuisance grounds, to stop construction of a large, Seattle-space-needle type observation tower on an inholding in Gettysburg National Battlefield Park. The National Park Service stood on the sidelines in the litigation because it had, reluctantly, negotiated an agreement with the tower developer to

relocate the tower on a site a little more removed from the heart of the battlefield. The litigation failed, the tower was built and loomed as an eyesore over one of America's most historic places for a quarter of a century, before the Clinton Administration worked with Congress to find several million dollars to condemn, demolish, and remove it.

8.   What role did the public trust doctrine play in this case? See Chapter 5, supra pp. 382–89; and specifically Sierra Club v. Andrus, 487 F.Supp. 443 (D.D.C.1980), aff'd on other grounds, 659 F.2d 203 (D.C.Cir. 1981), supra p. 387.

9.   Examine closely the court's order at the end of the second opinion. The court here professes to apply a "narrow" standard of review. Is the order broad or narrow? Does it have any teeth? What *must* the Secretary do to comply with it? Does anything in the order give the timber companies an incentive to negotiate and execute cooperative agreements with the Secretary that meaningfully restrict their actions?

Pursuant to the District Court's order, the Department of the Interior undertook a series of efforts without beneficial results: (A) Interior requested permission from the Office of Management and Budget (OMB) in the White House (which must approve agency requests to Congress for funding and legislation), to seek additional statutory authority for the regulation of off-park timber operations; the OMB disapproved the request. (B) Interior requested the timber companies to comply voluntarily with timber harvesting guidelines; the companies declined. (C) Interior asked the Governor of California to review an earlier rejection by the State Board of Forestry of the same proposed guidelines; the Governor did not respond. (D) Interior asked the Justice Department to commence litigation against the timber companies to restrain timber practices imminently endangering the Park; the Justice Department took it under consideration (but did not act). (The Justice Department makes an independent determination whether to bring suit in such cases; at other times it has been more amenable; see, e.g., Cappaert v. United States, Chapter 6, supra p. 516.) In addition to these rebuffs, the Department determined that it lacked sufficient appropriations to embark on acquisitions beyond those already made.

In the third Redwoods decision, Sierra Club v. Department of the Interior, 424 F.Supp. 172 (N.D.Cal.1976), the district court found that the Department had made a good faith attempt to perform its statutory duties as ordered, that it was therefore "purged" of its previously-found failure to do so, and that "in order adequately to exercise its powers and perform its duties in a manner adequately to protect the Park, Interior * * * stands in need of new Congressional legislation and/or new Congressional appropriations."

Those appropriations were subsequently provided by Congress in the Redwood Park Expansion Act of 1978, 92 Stat. 163 (1978), which authorized the purchase of an additional 48,000 acres for the Park (including much of the upland in Redwood Creek, a substantial amount of it already logged). The total cost of the expansion was about $350 million, the largest expenditure ever made for the National Park System. Among other things the 1978 Act provided economic benefits to certain forest industry workers who lost their jobs due to the decrease in timber harvesting. See, e.g., Hoehn v. Donovan, 711 F.2d 899 (9th Cir.1983); Patterson v. Donovan, 707 F.2d 1011 (9th Cir.1983).

NOTES AND QUESTIONS

1. Could the court have ordered Congress to appropriate funds to enlarge the Park? Why or why not? Could it have ordered the President's Office of Management & Budget to send Interior's request for more money to the Congress? Consider U.S. Constitution, Art. I, § 9, cl. 7, "No Money shall be drawn from the Treasury, but in Consequence of Appropriations made by Law." In its third opinion in this case, the Court refused the Club's request to add OMB as a party and hold it in contempt for blocking Interior's request, explaining (424 F.Supp. at 175):

> Such decisions of the Congress and/or the Executive concerning further, future, additional legislation, funds or litigation, involve new policy-making which is the exclusive function of the Congress and the Executive under the doctrine of separation of powers.
>
> It is beyond the province of this court to say whether and, if so, to what extent the Congress or Executive should act—much less to order such action. All that this court can do, and now has done, is to make sure that Interior has taken all reasonable steps toward the exercise of its statutory powers and performance of its duties within the limits of existing law and available funds.
>
> Any further orders of this court, designed to mandate the Congress or the Executive to act to provide new legislation, new funds or new litigation, no matter how well intended by the court or how desirable for the protection of the Park, would be an extra-judicial and, therefore, futile injection of this court into the prerogatives of the Congress and the Executive.

2. On a few occasions Congress has directly authorized the regulation of a class of activities that threaten a number of Parks. In 1987, for example, in response to numerous complaints about noise and safety in connection with the growing popularity of commercial sightseeing flights over such Parks as the Grand Canyon, Congress enacted legislation directing the Secretary of the Interior to conduct a study of the problem, and in the meantime to take specific action to control overflights over the Grand Canyon, on the basis of a congressional finding that the noise associated with such flights "is causing a significant adverse effect on the natural quiet and experience of the park." See 101 Stat. 674; 16 U.S.C. § 1a–1 note. In Grand Canyon Air Tour Coalition v. FAA, 154 F.3d 455 (D.C.Cir. 1998), cert. denied, 526 U.S. 1158 (1999), the court upheld the FAA's plan to reduce aircraft noise in response to the act, against attack by a variety of interests claiming the rule was too lenient or too strict. The court deferred to the agency's reasonable exercise of its judgment and technical expertise,

but noted that many of the challenges failed on ripeness grounds because of the FAA's proposed solution was to be implemented in phases. See generally Brenton Alexander, The National Park Service and the Regulation of the Air Tour Industry at Grand Canyon National Park, 38 Nat. Res. J. 277 (1998).

3. The Clean Air Act contains some mechanisms for protecting air quality over national park system and national wilderness preservation system lands from external sources. See 42 U.S.C. §§ 7470–7492, noted briefly on p. 1128 infra. In the fall of 1991, conservationists and electrical utilities reached a landmark agreement to install scrubbers on a large power plant just outside Page, Arizona, to protect visibility over the Grand Canyon. The Clean Water Act has been used, along with the Endangered Species Act, as principal levers to obtain agreement on a multi-billion dollar plan to restore a semblance of natural flows to protect Everglades National Park and other federally protected areas in southern Florida while still making fresh water and flood control available for the several million residents of southeast Florida. See Mary Doyle & Don Jodrey, Everglades Restoration: Forging New Law in Allocating Water for the Environment, 8 Envtl. Lawyer 255 (2002). Projected to cost at least $8 billion (shared by the federal government and the State of Florida), it is one of the most ambitious environmental restoration initiative ever undertaken.

4. As discussed in Chapter 10, supra pp. 861–72; 888–91, ranchers and the States of Wyoming and Montana have been greatly concerned about the health of the livestock industry because of a possible risk of brucellosis from infected bison or elk that wander onto private land from their sanctuaries on federal lands. Could the federal government adopt regulations under the National Park Organic Act preventing the State of Montana from killing bison on private land outside Yellowstone National Park? Does the fact that the context is wildlife (as opposed to air, water, or vegetation) make any difference? See generally Robert Keiter, Bison, Brucellosis, and Law in the Greater Yellowstone Ecosystem, 28 Land & Water L. Rev. 1 (1993).

2.   EXTERNAL THREATS FROM OTHER FEDERAL LANDS

As Professor Keiter observes, supra p. 1054, some external threats originate on nearby federal land, or from federal projects authorized by other agencies. And some external threats stem from both federal and non-federal sources. For example, the geothermal resources that originally inspired the creation of the world's first national park at Yellowstone might be impaired by geothermal development on both nearby private and Forest Service lands. As discussed further below, Congress has been considering legislation in recent years to strengthen federal protection.

Where the threats originate from nearby federal land under the jurisdiction of another federal agency, the legal framework may be different. Sometimes Congress provides specific guidance in a site-specific context. For example, in Friends of the Earth v. Armstrong, 485 F.2d 1 (10th Cir.1973), cert. denied, 414 U.S. 1171 (1974), the plaintiffs sought to require the Secretary of the Interior to prevent the water being impounded in Lake Powell behind Glen Canyon Dam on the Colorado River from spreading into Rainbow Bridge National Monument. Rainbow Bridge, reserved by President Taft under the Antiquities Act in 1910, is a huge natural sandstone arch extending across a creek tributary to the Colorado River upstream from the dam. The dam was authorized in 1956 in the Colorado River Storage Project Act and completed in 1963; when filled to capacity its reservoir, Lake Powell, would back water up the creek to a depth of about 48 feet below Rainbow Bridge (with the water surface reaching within 25 feet of the base of the arch itself). The 1956 Act declared the "intention of Congress that no dam or reservoir constructed under * * * this Act shall be within any national park or monument." 43 U.S.C. § 620b.

Despite the seeming clarity of this phrase, the Tenth Circuit, sitting en banc, reversed a lower court ruling and held that subsequent acts of Congress appropriating funds for construction of the dam had implicitly repealed this section, and denied relief. These subsequent appropriations acts specifically prohibited federal funds from being spent "for construction or operation of facilities to prevent waters of Lake Powell from entering any National Monument." This "specific prohibition," said the court, "has overridden the expression of intent in [the 1956 dam authorization]." Two judges dissented. On this issue of "legislation by appropriation," compare the snail darter case, TVA v. Hill, Chapter 5, supra p. 435. See also Jay D. Christensen, Friends of the Earth v. Armstrong—Water Under the Bridge, 1973 Utah L.Rev. 808.

Remarkably, after reaching this conclusion, the Tenth Circuit nevertheless went on to direct the trial court to retain jurisdiction for ten years to permit the plaintiffs to apply for further relief if "some unexpected structural damage to the Arch might become evident." 485 F.2d at 12. This order seems wholly inconsistent with the holding that Congress had decided not to prevent the reservoir from entering the national monument. Even if the Congress had been persuaded that the reservoir would not damage the Arch, can the courts supply a remedy if that assumption proved false? Perhaps the Tenth Circuit's order is explainable, if at all, by some unarticulated notion that the Secretary remains some sort of "trustee" for Rainbow Bridge despite Congress's determination to permit Lake Powell to invade it.

The Park Service was not a separate party to this case; the defendants were the Secretary of the Interior and the Commissioner of the Bureau of Reclamation. Any difference of opinion in this kind of situation between the Bureau and the Park Service would normally be resolved by the Secretary of the Interior. Where the disagreeing federal agencies are in separate departments, the Justice Department ordinarily resolves the dispute in formulating the federal government's litigation position. See generally 28 U.S.C. §§ 516–519. On rare occasions, the Department of Justice has advocated the position of one agency but advised the court of the views of the dissenting agency by means of a "split brief." See note 1 following TVA v. Hill, Chapter 5, supra p. 445.

The kinds of legal issues that can arise in coordinating management policies of different federal land agencies are illustrated by the following hypothetical, which also provides a useful review of material in some earlier chapters: As noted in Chapter 7, supra pp. 676–77, the Secretary of the Interior has discretionary authority to lease geothermal resources on BLM and Forest Service land when he determines the "public interest" will be served. Suppose that geothermal resource developers apply for geothermal leases on national forest land adjacent to Yellowstone.

(1) May the Secretary consider the effect of leasing on the Park? *Must* she do so?

(2) Suppose the Secretary considers the effect, and the evidence is not clear whether Old Faithful and the other geothermal resources inside the Park will be harmed because of possible "plumbing" interconnections with the geothermal resources targeted for leasing outside the Park. May the Secretary issue the leases?

(3) What law applies to this secretarial decision, the Geothermal Leasing Act or the National Park Service Organic Act, or both?

(4) Does NEPA help address this kind of problem? How? Cf. the "worst-case analysis" issue in the *Methow Valley* case, Chapter 5, supra p. 392.

(5) Would the analysis be any different if, instead of geothermal leases, the Forest Service proposes to sell timber on a national forest outside the Park, which might adversely affect the migration route of an elk herd that spends part of each year inside the Park, and is a prime tourist attraction? Does the National Forest Management Act or the Multiple–Use, Sustained Yield Act help answer these questions?

(6) Would the analysis be different if the proposal were to develop an open pit gold mine under the Mining Law of 1872 on BLM land just outside the Park, which could cause noise, odors, water quality deterioration, and other impacts that could interfere with wildlife and visitor enjoyment in the Park? Would FLPMA come into play here? How?

In recent years pressure has grown on the federal land management agencies to pay more attention to what happens across jurisdictional boundaries. Some of this pressure has been exerted by a new kind of environmental advocacy organization that is to some extent positioned between national groups (like the Sierra Club and NRDC) and local groups. The Greater Yellowstone Coalition and the Grand Canyon Trust, for example, both seek to address a range of environmental management issues across a relatively distinct bioregion (the greater Yellowstone ecosystem and the Colorado Plateau, respectively) which contains mostly federal land, but divided among the federal agencies rather than in unitary management.

These larger areas often have economic and well as ecological unities, but coordinating the activities of these different agencies, with different legal mandates for management, has proved a challenge, especially given some of the traditional rivalries that exist among the agencies. The Forest Service and the Park Service worked for some years to prepare a common "vision" for management of the federal lands in the Greater Yellowstone region, but that vision caused concern from some local residents and politicians who were concerned that it was too preservationist in orientation.

As the questions listed above hint, the laws now in place contain some mechanisms that allow, and to some extent direct, federal land management agencies to consult with their brethren. The Forest Service and BLM planning mandates, for example, generally require consultation with interested federal and state and local agencies, as well as the general public. NEPA contains a similar consultation process. On their face, however, none of these *mandate* that the land manager follow the recommendations of another agency managing land nearby, and the courts have rarely been asked to intervene in this consultation process.

The hypothetical regarding geothermal development around Yellowstone National Park is based upon genuine proposals for such development. Congress responded in 1984 with an appropriations act rider flatly banning federal geothermal leasing on national forest land in the Island Park area west of the Park, 98 Stat. at 1874. Then in 1988 it amended the geothermal leasing act to require that "all leases or drilling permits issued, extended, renewed or modified" contain stipulations "necessary to protect significant thermal features" within national park system units whenever the Secretary determines, "based on scientific evidence," that geothermal development is "reasonably likely to adversely affect [such a feature]." 30 U.S.C. § 1026. Another part of the same act directed the Secretary of the Interior to conduct a special study of geothermal developments outside of the Park to the north and report the results to Congress. 102 Stat. 1771 (1988). At the same time, a moratorium was placed on any federally licensed geothermal activity, and geothermal developers on private land voluntarily honored it as well, pending the results of the study.

The Interior Solicitor issued an opinion in 1998 addressing the Secretary's responsibility under the National Park Organic Act in making discretionary decisions on proposals outside units of the national park system that could have adverse effects on those units. See Options Regarding Applications for Hardrock Mineral Prospecting Permits on Acquired Lands Near a Unit of the National Park System, M #36993 (April 16, 1998) (known colloquially as the Doe Run opinion, after the mining company involved). At issue was whether to grant prospecting permits for mineral activity on the Mark Twain National Forest in Missouri, in the face of concern that mining could disrupt and degrade water flows in the nearby Ozark National Scenic Riverway. (Under the law applicable to this acquired federal land, the Secretary of the Interior has final decisionmaking authority, although the Forest Service has a veto over the issuance of any permits.)

After reviewing the Act (including the 1978 amendment), the legislative history, case law and commentary, the Solicitor concluded that the Secretary's discretionary decisions in such circumstances must be "infuse[d] ... with a concern for park values and purposes, and [he must exercise] caution where [they] ... could be threatened." The Opinion says that the 1978 amendment does not require the Secretary "to overhaul the Department's decisionmaking apparatus to make park protection the paramount concern," nor does it require the Secretary to "give credence to every imaginable threat that a proposed Secretarial action may have" on the parks. It does mean, however, that the Secretary has a duty to "ensure that potential impacts on park units have been thoroughly examined in the Department's decisionmaking process" which would ordinarily be done through the NEPA process, properly implemented.

In one of the more celebrated resolutions of an external threat in modern times, the Clinton Administration in 1996 announced a buyout of the site for the proposed New World Mine a couple of miles from the northeast border of Yellowstone National Park. It ended a proposal to build a large underground gold mine in an area that had seen relatively low level mining many decades ago, and that was still causing acid mine drainage. The mine would have put a tailings pile in a wetland and created concern about eventual contamination of Soda Butte Creek, which flowed into the Park. Much of the mine site was private, having been patented under the Mining Law many decades ago, but the company still needed Forest Service approval (because a piece of the mine was on a national forest), as well as a wetlands permit from the Corps of Engineers. The mining company was, ironically, subject to potential liability under the federal Superfund Law because it had bought the contaminated property. The deal struck by the Administration, and eventually funded by Congress, paid the company $65 million for the property; the company in turn devoted about half that to clean up the existing contamination.

QUESTION

What are the policy advantages and disadvantages of pursuing negotiated settlements of such controversies that involve compensation to the proponents of such developments? For commentary on this and other federal lands controversies (focusing primarily on the Yellowstone region) by the Assistant Attorney General for Environment and Natural Resources in the Clinton Administration, see Lois J. Schiffer and Sylvia Quast, Public Lands Litigation in the Geography of Hope, 1 Wyo. L.Rev. 413 (2001)

These "external threat" issues remain at the cutting edge of federal natural resource law and policy. One solution to such problems—redrawing agency boundaries—may be politically difficult to obtain, but is sometimes achieved. The boundaries of Grand Canyon National Park were, for example, significantly expanded in 1975 partly to ameliorate "external threat" problems. Park units located in urban or urbanizing areas, such as some of the Civil War battlefield parks around Washington D.C., have been the scene of significant conflict with local zoning authorities. On occasion Congress has created a kind of over-arching federal umbrella to govern management of large tracts of private and state as well as federal land deemed of national significance. See the examples (e.g., New Jersey Pine Barrens, Columbia Gorge) discussed in connection with delegation of federal management authority, in Chapter 4, supra pp. 335–37.

In short, the wisdom of John Muir's *dictum* that everything "is hitched to everything else in the universe" (MY FIRST SUMMER IN THE SIERRA

157 (1917)) is increasingly influencing how Congress and the federal land managers operate, but no uniform policy response has emerged. There is much commentary on the topic; e.g., Joseph L. Sax & Robert Keiter, Glacier National Park and Its Neighbors: A Study of Federal Interagency Relations, 14 Ecology L.Q. 207 (1987); Robert Keiter, Taking Account of the Ecosystem on the Public Domain: Law and Ecology in the Greater Yellowstone Region, 60 U.Colo.L.Rev. 923 (1989); George Cameron Coggins, Protecting the Wildlife Resources of the National Parks from External Threats, XXII Land & Water L.Rev. 1 (1986).

C. SCIENCE, PROFIT, AND THE PARKS

Edmonds Institute v. Babbitt

United States District Court, District of Columbia, 2000.
93 F.Supp.2d 63.

■ LAMBERTH, DISTRICT JUDGE.

This matter comes before the court on the parties cross-motions for partial summary judgment. Plaintiffs, three environmental advocacy organizations and a frequent visitor to Yellowstone National Park ("Yellowstone" or "Park"), challenge as arbitrary and capricious the Department of the Interior's ("Interior") entry into a research agreement with a private biotechnology company for the "bioprospecting" of microbial organisms from geysers and other thermal features in Yellowstone. * * *

Yellowstone is the nation's oldest national park. To commemorate its 125th anniversary, defendants hosted a ceremony on August 17, 1997, * * * [at which] it was announced that the federal government had entered into a novel contract with San Diego-based Diversa Corporation, by which Diversa would obtain a nonexclusive right to "bioprospect"[1] microbial organisms in Yellowstone, in exchange for an agreement to share with Yellowstone a portion of any financial returns generated by commercial applications or products developed from these research materials.

This novel agreement, officially termed a Cooperative Research and Development Agreement ("CRADA"), was the first of its kind to involve a national park. The Statement of Work in the CRADA explains how Yellowstone and Diversa will cooperate in researching and cataloguing the Park's biological diversity, primarily in the Park's thermal features such as geysers, hot springs, fumaroles, and mud pots, as well as in Yellowstone's "alpine tundra ecosystems, subalpine forests; riparian habitats, sedge marshes, bogs, swamps, streams and lakes." CRADA, Statement of Work at 2. Following an initial survey, sites will be "prioritized and systematically

---

1. * * * [B]ioprospecting refers to a relatively new method of natural resource utilization that targets microscopic resources, such as the genetic and biochemical information found in wild plants. Bioprospecting is an extension of the field of biotechnology, which uses biological resources like genes and enzymes to develop beneficial pharmaceutical and industrial products and applications.

sampled by [Diversa] scientists,'' using techniques to be ''jointly selected by YNP and [Diversa] to ensure that there is no significant impact to park resources or other appropriate park uses.'' *Id.* Once raw samples have been extracted from the selected sites, nucleic acids will be isolated, purified and used to create a library of genetic information. *Id.* at 2–3. The resulting gene libraries will be the starting point for the discovery and cloning of biocatalytic and bioactive compounds, which will be evaluated for potential commercial applications. *Id.* These libraries of genetic information will also be available to Park scientists for their own research. The CRADA and Statement of Work explicitly state that all activity carried on under the agreement will be in accordance with applicable law, including Yellowstone's management policy. According, to conduct the research under the CRADA, Diversa applied for and was issued a Research Authorization/Collection Permit, which authorized the Collection of certain biological materials from Yellowstone. Since 1994, prior to its entry into the CRADA, Diversa, under its previous name Recombinant Biocatalysis, Inc., had already been conducting the same sort of sampling from Yellowstone, pursuant to permits issued in accordance with Park regulations. The main difference, however, is that prior to the CRADA, the company was under no obligation to share any of the economic or other benefits that might result from its research on Park resources.

Thus, perhaps the most notable feature of the CRADA is the consideration that Yellowstone stands to receive in exchange for access to its biodiversity. Defendants have disclosed that Diversa will make annual payments of around $20,000 to the defendants, as well as provide research equipment and other support for Yellowstone's use and benefit. More importantly, however, Diversa will pay royalties to Yellowstone on any future commercial use or product derived from the company's bioprospecting activities in the Park. Although the specifics are not public, Yellowstone has indicated that it will receive royalties of between .5% and 10% depending upon the nature of the raw material and the final product. By virtue of the CRADA, Yellowstone will share in any revenues generated by future beneficial applications or products developed from Diversa's research at Yellowstone.

Notwithstanding the novelty of the Yellowstone–Diversa CRADA itself, this agreement is not the first time that the National Park Service has permitted scientific research and collection of microbial specimens from Yellowstone's thermal features. To the contrary, the earliest research permit authorizing collection of microbial samples from Yellowstone was in 1898. Indeed, in recent years, the number of annual requests by researchers for access to Yellowstone has averaged 1,500, with some 250–300 research permits issued each year (between 40 and 50 of which are for microbial research projects). Declaration of Michael Soukoup (''Soukoup Decl.''), at ¶ 8 Exhibit 1 to Defendants' Motion to Dismiss and for Summary Judgment. National Park Service regulations govern this permit system and ensure that research activities are consistent with the Yellowstone and Interior's overall goals.

Prior to the CRADA, Diversa or other researchers were free to remove any specimen within the purview of their permit and develop it as they wished. If such development led to commercial uses, the Park Service never saw any proceeds from the derivative products. Thus, recognizing that resources yielding potentially valuable properties were being removed from Yellowstone with no remuneration to Yellowstone or the American people, *see* Soukup Decl. ¶ 9, officials at Interior began to consider a resource management scheme, patterned on the successes of Costa Rica and other nations, which would use bioprospecting to provide funds and incentives for the conservation of biological diversity. To that end, the defendants opened negotiations in 1995 with the Diversa Corporation and other biotechnology companies to explore possible bioprospecting contracts. These potential agreements would be drafted as cooperative research and development agreements (CRADA) under the Federal Technology Transfer Act of 1986, which authorizes federal laboratories to enter into CRADAs with nonfederal entities to facilitate the sharing of research developed in conjunction with government scientists. By the fall of 1996, Diversa and the defendants had begun drafting a CRADA that would permit the collection of raw environmental materials from Yellowstone. The final version of the CRADA was signed by National Park Service Director Robert Stanton and Yellowstone Superintendent Mike Finley on May 4, 1998.

[Plaintiffs are a group of nonprofit organizations who advocate regulation of biotechnology, the maintenance and protection of biodiversity, and one individual who recreates in Yellowstone. They sued, alleging violations of, among others, the public trust doctrine, the Technology Transfer Act of 1986, 15 U.S.C. § 3701 et seq., the National Park Service Organic Act of 1916, 16 U.S.C. § 1 et seq., and Yellowstone National Park Organic Act, 16 U.S.C. § 21, et seq.] * * *

The validity of this CRADA under the FTTA turns upon whether Yellowstone falls within the meaning of "laboratory" as that term is defined in the statute. By its terms, the FTTA defines "laboratory" as "a facility or group of facilities owned, leased, or otherwise used by a Federal agency, a substantial purpose of which is the performance of research, development, or engineering by employees of the Federal Government." 15 U.S.C. § 3710a(d)(2)(A). Plaintiffs object to the application of the FTTA to the Yellowstone CRADA because they assert that the plain meaning of "laboratory" forecloses application of that term to the research facilities in Yellowstone. Specifically, plaintiffs argue that Yellowstone is not a "facility" because Yellowstone's organic statute describes the Park only as a "tract of land." 16 U.S.C. § 21.

While the court agrees that a national park does not immediately conjure the term "laboratory," the court finds that defendants have provided a reasoned basis for concluding that the broad, statutorily-assigned definition encompasses Yellowstone's extensive research facilities. * * * S.Rep. No. 283, 99th Cong.2d Sess. 1, 11 (1986) (stating that statutory definition of "laboratory" in FTTA was "a broad definition which is intended to include the *widest possible range of research institutions operated by the Federal Government*") (emphasis added). * * *

Yellowstone's research facilities fall within the definition of laboratory under the FTTA as a "facility owned ... or otherwise used by a Federal agency," a "substantial purpose of which is the performance of research." While the term "laboratory" is defined in the statute, "facility" is not. Thus, the court must look to the ordinary meaning of that word. "Facility" is broadly defined as "*something* (as a hospital, machinery, plumbing) that is built, constructed, installed *or established* to perform some particular function or *to serve or facilitate some particular end*". WEBSTER'S THIRD NEW INTERNATIONAL DICTIONARY 812 (1961) (emphasis added). The extensive array of research facilities at Yellowstone plainly satisfy this definition. To begin with, as defendants correctly note, the statute makes no requirement that the entire facility be used exclusively for research. To the contrary, the only statutory restriction is that a "substantial purpose" of the facility be for "the performance of research, development or engineering by employees of the Federal government." 15 U.S.C. § 3710a(d)(2)(A). Defendants have adequately demonstrated that a substantial purpose of the facilities at Yellowstone is scientific research. *See* Affidavit of John Varley * * *. Specifically, Yellowstone employs approximately 43 individuals engaged in scientific activities. * * * Moreover, the plethora of scientific and research structures and equipment at Yellowstone plainly fall within the FTTA definition. * * * Thus, in light of these extensive scientific research facilities, the court finds that Yellowstone falls within the meaning of "laboratory" under the FTTA.

Legislation enacted subsequent to the Yellowstone–Diversa CRADA also reinforces the conclusion that application of the FTTA to this CRADA is consistent with Congressional intent regarding cooperative scientific research agreements with units of the National Park System. Notably, in 1998, Congress enacted the National Parks Omnibus Management Act ("Parks Management Act"), 16 U.S.C. §§ 5901–6011, for the purpose of "enhanc[ing] management and protection of national park resources by providing clear legal authority and direction for the conduct of scientific study in the National Park System and to use information gathered for management purposes" and "to encourage others to use the National Park System for study to the benefit of park management as well as broader scientific value." 16 U.S.C. § 5931. To achieve this end, the statute specifically authorizes the Secretary of the Interior to "solicit, receive and consider requests from Federal or non-Federal public or private agencies, organizations, individuals, or other entities for the use of any unit of the National Park System for purposes of scientific study." *Id.* at § 5935(a). Moreover, the statute further empowers the Secretary to "enter into negotiations with the research community and private industry for equitable, efficient benefits-sharing arrangements." *Id.* at § 5935(d). Under these broad terms, the CRADA at issue here plainly constitutes an "equitable, efficient benefits-sharing arrangement" with a private entity for the purposes of scientific study. *Id.* Had Congress wished to foreclose units of the National Park System from entering into cooperative scientific research agreements with private industry in the wake of the Yellowstone–Diversa CRADA, its subsequent enactment displays a contrary intent. Instead, the far-reaching terms of the Parks Management Act reinforce the conclusion that the Yellowstone–Diversa CRADA is proper.

Having concluded that defendants have provided a rational basis for their determination that the FTTA definition of laboratory encompasses Yellowstone's myriad scientific research facilities, the court must next consider whether the CRADA is consistent with the relevant Park Service statutes and regulations. Plaintiffs contend that the CRADA conflicts with defendants' statutory mandates under the relevant organic statutes, the National Park Service Organic Act ("NPS Act"), 16 U.S.C. § 1, et seq., and the Yellowstone National Park Organic Act ("YNP Act"), 16 U.S.C. § 21, et seq. Specifically, plaintiffs maintain that the CRADA constitutes a "consumptive use," and hence, is contrary to the conservation emphasis of the NPS Act and the YNP Act. * * * Plaintiffs further argue that the CRADA violates the Park Service's own regulations, which prohibit the "[s]ale or commercial use of natural products." 36 C.F.R. § 2.1(c)(3)(v). As explained below, this court disagrees with plaintiffs' contentions and finds that defendants have offered a reasoned basis explaining how the CRADA is consistent with the organic statutes and regulations.

Review of plaintiffs' challenges under the Park Service authorizing statutes, like plaintiffs' FTTA claim, is governed by the APA. Thus, as Congress has delegated the administration and preservation of national park resources to Interior and the Park Service, these agencies enjoy broad discretion in implementing their statutory responsibilities under the authorizing statutes. * * *

As its name indicates the National Park Service Organic Act ("NPS Act") is the general authorizing statute for the National Park Service. [Here the court quotes 16 U.S.C. § 1.] The Yellowstone National Park Organic Act ("YNP Act") established Yellowstone as a unit of the National Park service, by providing that

> The tract of land in the States of Montana and Wyoming [within specified boundaries] is reserved and withdrawn from settlement, occupancy, or sale under the laws of the United States, and dedicated and set apart as a public park or pleasuring ground for the benefit and enjoyment of the people; and all persons who locate, or settle upon, or occupy any part of the land thus set apart as a public park, except as provided in section 22 of this title, shall be considered trespassers and removed therefrom.

16 U.S.C. § 21.

The court finds that defendants reasonably determined that the Yellowstone–Diversa CRADA is consistent with the above-quoted statutory authority and is not an impermissible "consumptive use" of park resources. Specifically, defendants concluded that the CRADA does not authorize consumptive use of natural resources because it does not grant Diversa the authority to sell any living material taken from the Park. Valley Aff., ¶ 37. In fact, as Yellowstone's Research Permitting Policy makes clear, Diversa never actually owns the specimens its collects, and thus has no right to transfer ownership of them. A.R. I.1, at 3 ("All specimens collected within the park are the property of the National Park Service and, regardless of where the collections are housed, must be properly accessioned and catalogued into the National Park Service's cataloguing system."); *see also* Varley Aff., ¶ 75 ("A sale of [Yellowstone's] resources will *not* occur pursuant to a CRADA.").

More fundamentally, however, the CRADA does not conflict with the conservation mandate of the organic statutes because it does not grant Diversa the right to collect any research specimens at all. Indeed, contrary to plaintiffs' assertion, neither the CRADA nor its Scope of Work authorizes Diversa to take any natural materials from Yellowstone. Rather, the CRADA outlines the rights and responsibilities of Yellowstone and Diversa with respect to information and inventions developed *after* the conclusion of research specimen collection and analysis. Thus, the legal force and scope of the CRADA covers the use, ownership, development and allocation of revenues from useful discoveries or potential proprietary information developed from the research activities. By contrast, to conduct its research activities at Yellowstone, Diversa—like all other researchers in the Park— must apply for and obtain a research permit, which prescribes the terms and conditions of on-site research activities. 36 C.F.R. § 2.5; *see also* A.R. § II.20, ¶ 2.18 (noting that "[t]he term 'Research Specimen' means those items [Diversa] has the authority to collect under the collection permit or permits issued by [Yellowstone]"). Thus, while in certain respects the CRADA may impose restrictions on Diversa's research activities over and above those provided by a permit alone,[2] the research permit, not the CRADA, provides the legal basis for Diversa to collect specimens.

In mounting a frontal attack on the CRADA, plaintiffs fail to recognize this critical legal distinction. While they challenge the CRADA, they do not in any way contend that the research permit issued to Diversa is improper or is otherwise invalid. Indeed, plaintiffs' misconception of the legal force of the CRADA reveals the fundamental flaws in their challenge. If the court were to find that the CRADA was improper under the relevant statutes, Diversa could still collect specimens under a research permit, as it has since 1994. The only—albeit critical—difference would be that Yellowstone could not share in any of the potential benefits from Diversa's research. Instead, the positive gains from the research would go exclusively to Diversa. Plaintiffs' challenge is further undermined by the fact that finding the CRADA to be an impermissible "consumptive use" of Park resources would necessarily imply that every other scientific research permit issued over the past century was equally invalid. Soukoup Decl., at ¶ 8 (stating that the earliest research permit allowing the collection of microbial samples was issued in 1898 and the Park currently issues approximately 250–300 research permits per year). But plaintiffs have offered no argument, evidence or suggestion that Diversa's research permit or the research permit

---

2. For example, the CRADA may give Park officials greater control over specimen extraction, as it expressly provides that "the specific sampling techniques and strategies will be jointly selected by [Yellowstone] and Diversa to ensure that there is no significant impact to park resources or to other appropriate uses." A.R. § II.20, Statement of Work, at 2; *see also* Varley Aff., at ¶ 66.

program at Yellowstone are improper. Thus, in light of the longstanding policy and practice of allowing specimen collection at the Park, and because they are not properly before the court, the court need not reach the questions of the validity of the permit or the permit program.

Finally, the court finds that defendants properly determined that the CRADA was consistent with the governing statutes because it would produce direct, concrete benefits to the Park's conservation efforts by affording greater scientific understanding of Yellowstone's wildlife, as well as monetary support for Park programs. As early as 1994, defendants recognized that cooperation between Park officials and private researchers would be mutually beneficial. *See* A.R. § II.211; Varley Aff., at ¶ 44. Defendants determined that the potential scientific and economic benefits resulting from collaboration with private industry would support and strengthen the Park Service's primary mission of resource conservation. Varley Aff., at ¶ 46–47. Agreements like the Yellowstone–Diversa CRADA would allow the Park to share in revenues generated by beneficial developments, and thus, provide a valuable source of funding to support the Park Service's ongoing wildlife preservation, protection, and study initiatives. Equally critical to the Park's conservation efforts as adequate funding, improved scientific knowledge and understanding of Yellowstone's habitat generated by these types of joint research projects would be shared with the Park and used to support its efforts to preserve the environment.

In addition to their challenges under the organic statutes, plaintiffs also contend that the CRADA violates a Park Service regulation that bars the "sale or commercial use" of natural materials from the Park. 36 C.F.R. § 2.1(c)(3)(v) ("Section 2.1"). Specifically, plaintiffs advance that Park Service officials proceeded with the CRADA despite their awareness that such action was "illegal" under Park regulations. * * *

The court finds that the Park Service reasonably determined that the Yellowstone–Diversa CRADA does not involve the "sale or commercial use" of park resources within the meaning of Section 2.1. The record discloses that defendants have provided a thoughtful and rational approach to research conducted on Park resources. In concluding that the regulations did not foreclose the CRADA, the Park Service determined that there was a critical distinction between researchers profiting from the sale of the actual specimens themselves, which is prohibited by Section 2.1, and profiting from a future development based on scientific discoveries resulting from research on those resources, which is permitted. *See* A.R. II.40, Memorandum from Director of Yellowstone Center for Resources to Yellowstone Superintendent (May 21, 1997), at 3; *see also* A.R. II.20, CRADA (distinguishing between "research specimens" collected under the agreement (§ 2.18) and "products" derived from research involving those specimens (§ 2.14)). In reaching this conclusion, the Park Service considered several critical factors. First, it recognized that permit holders, such as Diversa, do not, by virtue of either the permit or the CRADA, acquire title to the specimens or the right to transfer them to third parties. A.R. II.1, Yellowstone Permitting Policy, at 3 (stating that "[a]ll specimens collected within the park are the property of the National Park Service and regardless of

where the collections are housed, must be properly accessioned and catalogued in the National Park Service's cataloging system"); *id.* at 5 (noting
that the "[s]ale of collected research specimens and other transfer to third
parties is prohibited"). Second, the Park Service determined that permittees like Diversa, who later develop useful products, information or applications, are making "commercial use" of scientific discoveries, not Park
resources. A.R. II. 45.m, at 3 (noting that "to date no firm has asked
Yellowstone for a permit to collect research specimens for the purpose of
replication and subsequent commercialization"). This interpretation accords with the fact that patent rights derive from human ingenuity brought
to bear on scientific specimens, not the specimens themselves. *See Diamond
v. Chakrabarty,* 447 U.S. 303, 313 (1980) (stating that "the relevant
distinction was not between living and inanimate things, but between
products of nature, whether living or not, and human-made inventions, . . .
the result of human ingenuity and research"); *see also* Varley Aff. at ¶ 39.

Plaintiffs do not persuade the court that the defendants' interpretation
of the regulation is unreasonable. Plaintiffs aver that because patent law
allows scientists to obtain intellectual property rights over natural organisms, the CRADA at issue in this case necessarily involves the prohibited
sale of natural materials. But this view of the scope of patent law ignores
relevant precedent, which instructs that a substance occurring in nature
may not be patented in that form. Instead, to obtain a patent rights, a
researcher must bring to a naturally-occurring substance a contribution
that is non-obvious, novel and demonstrably useful. *See* 35 U.S.C. §§ 101–
103. Thus, in accord with these fundamental principles, the Park Service
has interpreted its regulations only to allow researchers to study, not sell,
Park resources. The CRADA, in turn, accords with the regulations because
any "commercial use" flowing from such research is limited to applications
or products generated from the scientific study of the resources, not the
resources themselves. Accordingly, the court finds that defendants reasonably construed Park regulations and concluded that the CRADA was
consistent with their requirements.

For the reasons set forth above, the court hereby GRANTS defendants'
motion for partial summary judgment and DENIES plaintiffs' motion for
partial summary judgment.

NOTES AND QUESTIONS

1. How real is the risk that arrangements like these will commercialize the Parks? Does the judge give too short a shrift to the long term policy
implications of giving the federal land managing agency a financial interest,
something akin to a "profit motive," in allowing scientific research in the
parks that may have commercial value? Compare the discussion of recreation fees, where the land managing agencies are given a financial incentive
to charge recreational visitors a fee, Chapter 11, supra pp. 979–81. Is this
an issue that might be addressed through the public trust doctrine (the
plaintiffs alleged that doctrine was implicated, but the court essentially
ignored it in its opinion)? See Chapter 5, pp. 382–89 supra.

2.   Or is this a tempest in a teapot? The plaintiffs did not question that scientific research was a legitimate purpose of the parks, and in fact the National Park Service (and other federal land managing agencies) issue thousands of research permits every year. If that is the case, what is the harm in reserving to the land managers (and, by implication, the general public who "own" these resources) a financial interest in the results of the research?

3.   The National Park Omnibus Management Act of 1998, quoted in Judge Lamberth's opinion, also directs the Secretary of the Interior to "undertake a program of inventory and monitoring of National Park System resources to establish baseline information and to provide information on the long-term trends in the condition of National Park System resources." 16 U.S.C. § 5934.

4.   For commentary, see Sandra Bourgasser–Ketterling, Bioprospecting on Public Lands: Should Private Companies Compensate the Government for their Use of Public Land Resources?, 8 J.L. & Policy 481 (2000); Holly Doremus, Nature, Knowledge and Profit: The Yellowstone Bioprospecting Controversy and the Core Purposes of America's National Parks, 26 Ecology L.Q., 401 (1999).

D.   RIVER PRESERVATION

Over time, reflecting what Holmes called the "felt necessities of the times," Congress has changed its perception of the primary value of rivers. For many decades the touchstone was navigability; from the beginning, the federal government has asserted a strong interest in maintaining the navigable capacity of waterways in order to assist the commerce of the Nation. Gibbons v. Ogden, 22 U.S. (9 Wheat.) 1 (1824). Flood control was another early (and constant) impetus for river development by means of dams, diversions, dredging, and channelization. 33 U.S.C. § 701 et seq. See, e.g., John Barry, RISING TIDE (1997), an excellent account of the corruption of science by the Corps of Engineers in advancing its agenda (with sometimes disastrous effects) to build flood control facilities on the Mississippi River in the late nineteenth and early twentieth centuries. As advancing settlement crossed the one hundredth meridian and encountered the arid and semiarid areas of the west, the focus shifted to using rivers for irrigation, culminating in the Reclamation Act of 1902. 43 U.S.C. §§ 371–376; see pp. 98–101 supra. Within a few years, the potential of rivers for hydroelectric power generation led to the Federal Power Act of 1920. 16 U.S.C. § 791 et seq. See Chapter 6, supra pp. 560–82.

All this emphasis on controlling and manipulating river systems led to a vast network of dams and other works which in the aggregate dwarf the Interstate Highway System as the engineering marvel of this hemisphere. A 1982 survey by the National Park Service counted some 300,000 dams in the United States, and found only about 2% of the river mileage in the country was in relatively natural, undeveloped condition. Another estimate is that there are 75,000 dams in the U.S. over six feet tall, one built for every day since George Washington was President.

These water resource developments have costs as well as benefits, and many costs were not reflected in the traditional cost/benefit calculations used to justify more dams and storage projects. One of the first major political conservation battles in this century was fought over whether a river in Yosemite National Park should be dammed to provide a water supply for San Francisco. Some of the Hetch Hetchy story is recounted in Wood, supra at pp. 114–17; see also Gray Brechin, IMPERIAL SAN FRANCISCO 71–117 (1999). Later, many others came to believe that the sacrifice of the natural values of the Nation's dwindling supply of free-flowing rivers was ultimately counterproductive. What is usually marked as the first major conservation fight in the modern era was sparked by the Bureau of Reclamation's proposal to build the Echo Park Dam in Dinosaur National Monument on the Colorado River in the early 1950's. This battle was won by dam opponents, but at a significant cost—the tradeoff was to build another, even larger dam (Glen Canyon) that flooded the heart of southern Utah's canyon country with Lake Powell. See Russell Martin, A STORY THAT STANDS LIKE A DAM 43–74 (1989). It did not take long before battles over whether particular river segments should be preserved in free-flowing condition were occurring in many areas of the United States.

Concomitantly, support began to grow to establish a system that would make informed judgments on which river segments were worthy of preservation before crises were reached. In 1960, the National Park Service recommended to the Senate Select Committee on National Water Resources that some remaining free-flowing streams be preserved. The need for such preservation was documented in a 1962 Outdoor Recreation Review Commission Report, later endorsed by President Johnson. The concept of a river-based, parklike reservation reached initial fruition when Congress created in 1964 the Ozark National Scenic Riverways, 16 U.S.C. § 460m to 460m–7, under which the Current and Jack's Fork Rivers in Missouri became "National Rivers." (The Buffalo River in Arkansas was also made a national river (sort of a ribbon national park administered by NPS) in 1972. See Buffalo National River Act, 16 U.S.C. § 460m–8 to 460m–14.) Then in 1968, Congress enacted the Wild and Scenic Rivers Act (WRSA), 16 U.S.C. §§ 1271–1287, described in the following excerpt. For more detail on the Act and its implementation, see generally George C. Coggins and Robert Glicksman, PUBLIC NATURAL RESOURCES LAW § 15.02 (2001).

Sally K. Fairfax, Barbara T. Andrews & Andrew P. Buchsbaum, Federalism and the Wild and Scenic Rivers Act: Now You See It, Now You Don't*

59 Wash.L.Rev. 417 (1984).

* * * The WSRA was essentially a reform measure. It was specifically designed to blend with not always compatible missions of established

---

* Reprinted with permission of the Washington Law Review.

agencies while remedying inadequacies in long-established state and federal approaches to land and water management programs. As with any entrant into a crowded policy arena, the Wild and Scenic Rivers Act was a compromise, sculpted to blend new interests with old. The final wording is ambiguous at precisely the points where advocates seek clarity. As a result, it is extremely difficult to identify "the" federal position on wild and scenic rivers specifically, or on water more generally. * * *

In passing a national WSRA, Congress was responding to three major concerns. The first was the apparent inadequacy of state systems for preserving and protecting rivers, especially in the West. More Western States have historically followed the water rights doctrine of prior appropriation which evolved to encourage private development of water. Traditionally, water left in place was not a "beneficial use" of water and, hence, was not protected under state law. Even though several state legislatures have moved to include instream uses within their appropriation systems, states still have the reputation of being poor guardians of these uses. A major goal of WSRA was to enhance both state and federal attention to protection of instream values.

Congress' second concern was to control federal water development. Section I of the Act declares that

> the established national policy of dam and other construction at appropriate sections of the rivers of the United States needs to be complemented by a policy that would preserve other selected rivers or sections thereof in their free-flowing condition to protect the water quality of such rivers and to fulfill other vital national conservation purposes.

The federal presence in developing water, spread among numerous agencies, was piecemeal and poorly integrated, yet powerful. As the country's "environmental consciousness" evolved, it became highly controversial. In passing WSRA, Congress sought balance in the federal program.

A third congressional goal behind WSRA was to increase congressional control over the federal land management agencies. In the 1960's and 1970's, "Congress took unprecedented steps in giving the land managing agencies specific directions for managing designated areas of the public lands" for environmental purposes. The WSRA was part of this trend toward specialized, environmentally protective legislation. It affected the activities of the National Park Service, the Bureau of the Land Management, the Fish and Wildlife Service, and the United States Forest Service. Whether these agencies were preservation or multiple-use entities made little difference; Congress intended to control federal agency activities affecting land along designated wild and scenic river corridors. * * *

B. *Basic Provisions of the National Wild and Scenic Rivers Act*

The WSRA is a special-purpose statute designed to preserve "selected rivers," along with their "immediate environments," that possess one or more "outstandingly remarkable scenic, recreational, geologic, fish and wildlife, historic, cultural, or other similar values."[52] The rivers are to be protected for their "free-flowing" characteristics, which specifically include water quality.[53] These values are imprecise, frequently sounding more hortatory than implementable.

The Act is more concrete in defining classifications of rivers, methods of including them in the system, and responsibilities for federal and state agencies involved in the intricate management process. Pristine *wild* rivers, relatively undisturbed *scenic* rivers, or developed *recreational* rivers may be included in the federal system. Congress also established a phased approach to river inclusion: in addition to *included*, fully protected rivers, it identified *potential additions* and administrative study rivers in order to protect rivers under consideration. * * *

---

1.   DESIGNATING WILD & SCENIC RIVERS

a.   *By Congress.* Usually Congress designates individual river segments as part of the Wild & Scenic Rivers System by statute. The political process in Congress tends to dictate, with rare exceptions, that any such designation have the support of the entire (or at least most) of the state's congressional delegation before it will be enacted. At last count about 165 river segments in 35 states, comprising thousands of miles, have been designated. See 16 U.S.C. § 1274(a).

b.   *By the Secretary.* The Act contains a mechanism to bypass Congress, for the Secretary of the Interior is given authority, upon request of a state's governor, to include rivers in the federal system that have been designated as wild, scenic or recreational rivers by an "act of the [state] legislature." 16 U.S.C. § 1273(a)(ii). If the Secretary agrees, and the rivers are designated for inclusion in the federal system, they are basically managed the same as other rivers designated by Congress, although they are administered by the state or its political subdivision. The federal lands in the included segment, however, remain under federal control; see *Wilderness Society v. Tyrrel*, infra this section.

In June 1980, Governor Jerry Brown of California requested Interior Secretary Cecil Andrus to designate five river segments in northern California which had been protected under state law as part of the national system. An expedited EIS process ensued, during which counties in California and Oregon obtained preliminary orders enjoining the Secretary from acting. On the last day of the Carter Administration, however, the Ninth Circuit vacated the injunctions. Secretary Andrus had been optimistic enough to anticipate the decision: When President Carter had sent a routine memo to all cabinet officers requesting their resignations as of 5:00 p.m. on January 19th, Andrus asked permission to delay his resignation. Carter (a devotee of wild rivers who had been one of the first persons to raft the Chatooga River in his native Georgia, and who had while President

---

52.   16 U.S.C. § 1271 (1982).   **53.**   Id.

spent several days rafting the Middle Fork of the Salmon River with Secretary Andrus) agreed. The Secretary was attending a reception at the White House on the evening of January 19th when an aide phoned to say that the injunction had been lifted. Andrus returned to his office to sign the North Coast river proclamations, his last official act in office. In Del Norte County v. United States, 732 F.2d 1462 (9th Cir.1984), the court upheld the Department's accelerated NEPA compliance.

In City of Klamath Falls v. Babbitt, 947 F.Supp. 1 (D.D.C.1996), the plaintiff city wanted to construct a dam on a scenic river segment added to the national system by the Secretary after it had been put into the state wild & scenic river system by the Oregon voters in an initiative. (Congress had not acted on a proposal to legislate its inclusion.) The court determined that the popular vote was an "act of the legislature" within the meaning of the WSRA.

c. *Study Rivers.* Congress has also from time to time passed legislation requiring federal agencies to study particular river segments for possible inclusion in the system, and to report their findings to Congress for possible action. As of 2001, more than 100 studies had been ordered; see 16 U.S.C. § 1276(b). In the meantime, federal land in a quarter-mile corridor on each side is withdrawn from "entry, sale, or other disposition" and from the Mining Law (but not the Mineral Leasing Act). Id. §§ 1279(b), 1280(b). Furthermore, the Federal Energy Regulatory Commission (FERC, formerly the Federal Power Commission, or FPC) may not license hydroelectric dams on any so-called "study" river for a period of time to allow for the study and congressional consideration. Id. § 1278(a). But such protection against the FERC apparently does not extend to rivers that a state has studied and applied to the Secretary for inclusion. See North Carolina v. FPC, 533 F.2d 702 (D.C.Cir.1976), remanded, 429 U.S. 891 (1976). Thus the FERC could license a dam on the river anytime before the Secretary designated it for inclusion. But see Appalachian Power Co. v. United States, 607 F.2d 935 (Ct.Cl.1979), cert. denied, 446 U.S. 935 (1980) (no compensation for loss of opportunity to build the dam because no property interest vested in the FERC license until judicial review of the FERC action was completed).

d. *Determining the Boundaries of Designated River Segments.* The Act contemplates that the Congress, in designated a river segment for inclusion in the system, will not specify how much land along the river should be included. Instead, it directs the administering Secretary to select detailed boundaries within one year of designation, which "shall include an average of not more than 320 acres of land per mile measured from the ordinary high water mark on both sides of the river." 16 U.S.C. § 1274(b). In Sokol v. Kennedy, 210 F.3d 876 (8th Cir.2000), the court rejected the Park Service's argument that it had complete discretion (other than the acreage limitation) regarding its selection of land for inclusion in the Niobrara River Scenic Area. Instead, the court opined, the selection process should be governed by a determination that the land has "outstandingly remarkable scenic, recreational, geologic, fish and wildlife, historic, cultural, or other similar values," since that standard was found in Congress's introductory statement of policy in the Act, 16 U.S.C. § 1271, which was incorporated into the general management standard of 16 U.S.C. § 1281(a). This meant, according to the court, that the agency was not prohibited from including

> unremarkable land; indeed, the Act could require such inclusion where necessary to protect outstandingly remarkable resources, e.g., because of the need for buffer zones around resources or because of discontinuities in a resource's locations. Equally, the Act does not require that the boundaries encompass all the outstandingly remarkable resources; this might be impossible given the acreage limitation. * * * The Act allows the administering agency discretion to decide which boundaries would best protect and enhance the outstandingly remarkable values in the river area, but it must identify and seek to protect those values, and not some broader category.

The court therefore struck down the agency's boundary-setting, which had used the standard of including "significant" or "important" resources rather than "outstandingly remarkable."

2. MANAGING WILD & SCENIC RIVERS

The Act directs that, upon designation, every river "shall be classified, designated, and administered" as either

> (1) *wild*; that is, "generally inaccessible except by trail, with watershed or shorelines essentially primitive and waters unpolluted * * * represent[ing] vestiges of primitive America;"

> (2) *scenic*; whose shorelines and watershed are "still largely primitive and * * * undeveloped, but accessible in places by roads;" or

> (3) *recreational*; that is, "readily accessible by road or railroad," with some development along their shorelines, and that "may have undergone some impoundment or diversion in the past."

See 16 U.S.C. § 1272(b)(1–3). These definitions have been further refined by "guidelines" adopted by the agencies; see 41 Fed.Reg. 39,454 (1982), discussed at p. 1102, note 4, infra.

Classification of the river segments according to these criteria presumably should influence how they are managed to serve the goals of the Act. Some, however, have expressed doubt about this; e.g.: "One might suppose that the degree of protection afforded a river would be based on the river's classification. However, one would be wrong: the Act specifies protections based on river classification *only* with regard to mining." Fairfax, Andrews & Buchsbaum, supra, 59 Wash.L.Rev. at 429 (emphasis in original). While it is true that the Act expressly differentiates among the categories of rivers only with respect to mining, the commentators' conclusion may be overstated. As shown in the next principal case, the controlling management directive is to protect rivers "in accordance with the purposes of" the Act. Because the Act itself creates these different categories, presumably Congress intended them to serve somewhat different purposes and their management should be affected accordingly.

Dams. The W & SRA designation forbids dams and other interferences with the free-flowing condition of the designated river segment, regardless of whether it is classified as wild, scenic, or recreational. The pertinent statutory section,16 U.S.C. § 1278(a), is not a paragon of clarity. It begins by prohibiting FERC from licensing any project works "on or directly affecting" a designated river. The same sentence goes on to prohibit *all* federal agencies (including FERC) from assisting any water project that would have a "direct and adverse effect on the values for which such river was established, as determined by the Secretary charged with its administration." The next sentence says that these limitations shall "not preclude licensing of, or assistance, to developments below or above [the designated reach] or on any stream tributary thereto which will not invade the area or unreasonably diminish the scenic, recreational, and fish and wildlife values present in the area" when it was designated. It is not clear whether the second sentence establishes an independent standard or is merely an elaboration of the "direct and adverse effect" standard in the first sentence. For discussion of these provisions, see High Country Resources and Glacier Energy Co. v. FERC, 255 F.3d 741 (9th Cir.2001) (including concurring and dissenting opinions); see also Swanson Mining Co. v. FERC, 790 F.2d 96 (D.C.Cir.1986). This section does not, however, apply to a congressionally authorized dam, so that the consent of the agencies administering a designated W & S River is not required. See Oregon Natural Resources Council v. Harrell, 52 F.3d 1499 (9th Cir.1995).

Mining. 16 U.S.C. § 1280 covers mining. Generally speaking, it provides that designation permanently withdraws federally owned minerals within one-quarter mile of the bank of a designated river that is classified as *wild* from development under either the Mining Law or the leasing acts. All mining activity in all designated river corridors, regardless of how they are classified, is to be regulated "to effectuate the purposes of" the Act, including to provide "safeguards against pollution of the river involved and unnecessary impairment of the scenery within the component in question." Mining patents shall convey the right to the minerals only. All these restrictions are "subject to valid existing rights."

Other Management Activities. The Act is not so clear on what other management restrictions apply, or even where or how they apply. Three of the key provisions are as follows:

> For rivers designated on or after January 1, 1986, the Federal agency charged with the administration of each component of the National Wild and Scenic Rivers System shall prepare [within three years of the date of designation] a comprehensive management plan for such river segment to provide for the protection of the river values. The plan shall address resource protection, development of lands and facilities, user capacities, and other management practices necessary or desirable to achieve the purposes of this chapter. The plan shall be coordinated with and may be incorporated into resource management planning for affected adjacent Federal lands.

16 U.S.C. § 1274(d)(1). For rivers designated before January 1, 1986, the agency is directed to review "all boundaries, classifications and plans * * *

for conformity within the requirements of this subsection within ten years through regular agency planning processes." 16 U.S.C. § 1274(d)(2). The provisions were added by amendment in 1986; previously, the Act mandated management plans only for rivers designated by Congress.

> Each component of the national wild and scenic rivers system shall be administered in such manner as to protect and enhance the values which caused it to be included in said system without, insofar as is consistent therewith, limiting other uses that do not substantially interfere with public use and enjoyment of these values. In such administration primary emphasis shall be given to protecting its esthetic, scenic, historic, archeologic, and scientific features. Management plans for any such component may establish varying degrees of intensity for its protection and development, based on the special attributes of the area.

16 U.S.C. § 1281(a).

> (a) The Secretary of the Interior, the Secretary of Agriculture, and the head of any other Federal department or agency having jurisdiction over any lands which include, border upon, or are adjacent to, any river included within the National Wild and Scenic Rivers System or under consideration for such inclusion * * * shall take such action respecting management policies, regulations, contracts, plans, affecting such lands * * * as may be necessary to protect such rivers in accordance with the purposes of this chapter. * * * Particular attention shall be given to scheduled timber harvesting, road construction, and similar activities which might be contrary to the purposes of this chapter.
>
> (b) Nothing in this section shall be construed to abrogate any existing rights, privileges, or contracts affecting Federal lands held by any private party without the consent of said party.
>
> (c) The head of any agency administering a component of the [WSR System] shall cooperate with the Administrator, Environmental Protection Agency and with the appropriate State water pollution control agencies for the purpose of eliminating or diminishing the pollution of waters of the river.

16 U.S.C. § 1283. The courts have in recent years begun to answer some of the interpretive questions posed.

Newton County Wildlife Ass'n v. U.S. Forest Service

United States Court of Appeals for the Eighth Circuit, 1997.
113 F.3d 110.

■ Before FAGG, FLOYD R. GIBSON, and LOKEN, CIRCUIT JUDGES.

■ LOKEN, CIRCUIT JUDGE.

Newton County Wildlife Association, the Sierra Club, and certain individuals (collectively "the Wildlife Association") sued the United States Forest Service and four of its employees (collectively the "Forest Service") seeking judicial review of four timber sales in the Ozark National Forest.

Parties favoring timber harvesting intervened to support the Forest Service. The Wildlife Association filed sequential motions to preliminarily enjoin the sales as violative of the Wild and Scenic Rivers Act ("WSRA"), 16 U.S.C. §§ 1271 *et seq.*[*] * * *

Enacted in 1968, WSRA authorizes Congress or a responsible federal agency to designate river segments that possess "outstandingly remarkable" environmental or cultural values as "components of the national wild and scenic rivers system." 16 U.S.C. §§ 1271, 1274. The responsible federal agency, here the Forest Service, must establish detailed boundaries for each designated segment, including an average of not more than 320 acres of land per mile along both sides of the river. § 1274(b). * * *

In 1992, Congress designated segments of six rivers within the Ozark National Forest. The Forest Service's three-year deadline for completing comprehensive management plans for these segments (the "Plans") was September 30, 1995. It is undisputed that the Plans were not completed on time. Therefore, the Wildlife Association argues that logging under the four timber sales must be preliminarily enjoined until the agency complies with this statutory mandate.

The Forest Service issued final agency actions approving the four timber sales between August 23, 1994, and September 12, 1995, before the agency's WSRA planning deadline. The Wildlife Association fails to relate this subsequent planning delinquency to judicial review of the timber sales. It relies upon cases in which plans or studies were a statutory precondition to the agency actions under review. *See Kleppe v. Sierra Club,* 427 U.S. 390, 398–402 (1976) (National Environmental Policy Act), * * * and *Thomas v. Peterson,* 753 F.2d 754, 763–64 (9th Cir.1985) (Endangered Species Act). But WSRA does not mandate completion of § 1274(d)(1) plans before timber sales may be approved. Therefore, the Forest Service did not violate WSRA by approving timber sales during the planning process. That being so, the agency was not required to suspend on-going implementation of the timber sales when it later failed to complete the Plans on time. Absent specific statutory direction, an agency's failure to meet a mandatory time limit does not void subsequent agency action. * * *

Moreover, because the preparation of WSRA Plans was not a precondition to approving the timber sales, a reviewing court may not enjoin or set aside the sales based upon the failure to prepare the Plans. Although the Forest Service may well have WSRA compliance obligations in approving timber sales (an issue not before us), the agency has substantial discretion in deciding procedurally how it will meet those obligations. The Forest Service maintains land and resource management plans for each national forest. Those plans "provide for multiple use and sustained yield of [forest] products and services ... [and] coordination of outdoor recreation, range, timber, watershed, wildlife and fish, and wilderness." 16 U.S.C. § 1604(e)(1); *see* 36 C.F.R. Part 219. In 1994, the Forest Service amended

* [Eds. The plaintiff also alleged violation of the Migratory Bird Treaty Act; that issue   is discussed in Chapter 10, supra pp. 906–18.]

its management plan for the Ozark National Forest to take into account the 1992 WSRA designations. In addition, the agency prepared an environmental assessment before approving each of the timber sales in question. Had the Forest Service relied on WSRA Plans as evidencing its compliance with WSRA in approving the timber sales, then we would carefully examine that rationale. But absent a specific statutory directive, we would usurp the agency's procedural autonomy if we compelled it to channel its compliance efforts into a particular planning format.[2]

Finally, a preliminary injunction would be inappropriate in this case because the Forest Service contends that the four timber sales lie outside the boundaries of the WSRA-designated river segments, and the Wildlife Association has not refuted that contention. The district court avoided this issue by ruling that WSRA plans must encompass federally controlled areas that lie outside but *may affect* a designated river segment. On appeal, the Forest Service argues that WSRA plans need only encompass lands lying within a designated segment and therefore its failure to timely prepare the Plans cannot affect the timber sales in question. We agree.

Under WSRA, each designated river segment becomes a "component" of the national system. § 1274(a). Following designation, the responsible agency defines the boundaries of "each component," determining how much land adjacent to the river is included in the designation. § 1274(b). At that point, the agency "charged with the administration of each component . . . shall prepare a comprehensive management plan for such river segment to provide for the protection of the river values." § 1274(d)(1). In our view, the plain meaning of that provision limits the planning requirement to the boundaries of the designated river segment, because it is the designated "segment" that becomes a "component" of the national system. This reading is confirmed by § 1281(a) of the Act, which links agency planning and administration to the designated component.[4] Because the Forest Service may limit WSRA plans to lands lying within designated river segments, failure to timely prepare the Plans cannot be a basis for enjoining timber sales on lands lying outside any designated area.

NOTES AND QUESTIONS

1. Other courts have agreed that the requirement to prepare a management plan under § 1274(d) is independent of whatever duties 16 U.S.C. § 1283(a) places on federal land management agencies, and that a

---

2. Of course, a party aggrieved by an agency's failure to meet a statutory planning deadline may seek a court order compelling the agency to complete the required plan. *See Brock v. Pierce County*, 476 U.S. 253, 260 n. 7 (1986). However, the Wildlife Association has not separately challenged the Forest Service's failure to prepare WSRA Plans.

4. WSRA § 1283(a) imposes a general obligation on agencies having jurisdiction over lands "which include, border upon, or are adjacent to" a designated river segment to protect the river in accordance with WSRA. But in our view, § 1283(a) does not require agencies managing adjacent federal land to prepare or join in a WSRA plan. It merely instructs their managers to take actions that protect designated rivers. Whether that standard has been met in a particular case is a question of fact. *See Wilderness Soc'y v. Tyrrel*, 918 F.2d 813, 820 (9th Cir. 1990).

failure to prepare a management plan within the statutory deadline is not in itself grounds for enjoining timber sales or other activities being conducted within the designated river corridor. Wilderness Society v. Tyrrel, 918 F.2d 813 (9th Cir.1990) ("A requirement to consider river values protected under the Act in the course of undertaking any independent project or plan differs from a procedural requirement that federal agencies prepare a plan under the Act itself"); Sierra Club v. United States, 23 F.Supp.2d 1132 (N.D.Cal.1998) ("The WSRA provides no indication that a court may enjoin an agency's land management activities with respect to a wild and scenic river area merely because the agency has failed to timely adopt a comprehensive management plan"); Sierra Club v. Babbitt, 69 F.Supp.2d 1202, 1251 (E.D.Cal.1999) (however, the agency's failure to develop the required plan may be "highly material in the analysis of the agency's compliance with the substantive requirements of the WSRA"). The latter court went on to find the Park Service's program to reconstruct one of the major access roads in Yosemite National Park violated the substantive requirements of the Act in part because it was planned and executed "without reference to the required comprehensive management plan or any other pre-existing plan that would have adequately informed the decision whether the construction activities * * * were an allowable degradation of the values for which the Merced River was included in the [NWRS] System." For criticism of *Newton County*, see Douglas McHoney, The Wild and Scenic River Act's Comprehensive Management Plans: Are They Really Mandatory?, 5 Mo. Envtl.L. & Policy Rev. 155 (1998).

2.   What kind of evidence would have been persuasive in showing that the proposed timber sales conflicted with the W & SR Act? What governing standard does that Act contain? Look at §§ 1281 and 1283, pertinent parts set out before the principal case. Is it whether the timber sale "substantially interfere[s] with public use and enjoyment of the[ ] values" which caused this river to be designated a W & S River? (§ 1281) Does the same section's reference to giving "primary emphasis" to esthetic, scenic, archaeologic, and scientific features create a "compatibility" principle applicable to managing wildlife refuges and many national recreation areas (see Chapter 10, supra pp. 873–87 and Chapter 11, supra pp. 968–79), or something else? What kind of standard is created for a reviewing court in § 1283(a)'s direction to federal administering agencies to "take such action * * * as may be necessary to protect such rivers in accordance with the purposes of this chapter"? Does the Forest Service here have the burden of showing that the proposed timber sale is consistent with the W & S Act, or do the opponents have the burden of showing the opposite? In Sierra Club v. United States, 23 F.Supp.2d 1132 (N.D.Cal.1998), the court characterized the substantive management requirements of the WSRA as "very broad and vest[ing] the relevant agency with substantial discretion in its management of protected river areas." Do you agree?

3.   In the original version of the Act, § 1283(a) required federal agencies simply to "review" their activities in or near river segments being *studied* for possible inclusion in the system "in order to determine what actions shall be taken to protect such rivers" while they were being considered for inclusion. In 1978 the section was amended to its current

form. The amendment thus both strengthens the agencies' duty to protect, and extends it to designated rivers as well as study rivers. Is this legislative background relevant to the questions in the preceding paragraph? For a discussion of the obligations of federal land managers regarding study rivers, see Solicitor's Opinion #M–36989, Managing Areas Eligible for Protection under the W & SR Act (Nov. 12, 1997).

4. What does the Forest Service need to show to demonstrate that it has "cooperated" with federal and state water quality authorities regarding water pollution control as required by § 1283(c)? If responsible federal and state authorities object to the proposed sale on water quality grounds, can the Forest Service override their objections? Upon what kind of showing? Should a reviewing court defer to the expertise of the Forest Service, or the expertise of the water quality agencies, when there is a conflict between the two? Can this section be interpreted to give state water quality authorities a veto over federal land management where necessary to protect water quality? Cf. the preemption discussion in Chapter 3, supra pp. 206–26.

5. On remand of the principal case, the district court upheld the Forest Service's determination that the timber sales would not adversely effect WSR values, and in Newton County Wildlife Ass'n v. Rogers, 141 F.3d 803 (8th Cir.1998), the court of appeals affirmed in a terse opinion. After noting that the Act "requires federal agencies responsible for land adjacent to designated river components to protect designated rivers", with "[p]articular attention" paid to "scheduled timber harvesting, road construction, and similar activities which might be contrary to the purposes of this chapter," see 16 U.S.C. § 1283(a), it said the "plaintiff points to nothing in the administrative record establishing that the Forest Service acted arbitrarily and capriciously in finding that logging and road work will have an insignificant effect on WSRA-designated river components. The EAs [prepared on the sales] thoroughly discuss the impact of the sales on water quality of the Buffalo River and Richland Creek and call for mitigation measures designed to protect affected waters. We reject the Wildlife Association's contention that the Forest Service failed to cooperate with state water pollution control agencies simply because the Arkansas Department of Pollution Control and Ecology and the Arkansas Natural and Scenic Rivers Commission opposed the sales. The record reflects that the Forest Service considered the State's objections even though they were not expressed until after the comment period ended."

6. In Sierra Club v. United States, 23 F.Supp.2d 1132 (N.D.Cal.1998), the court upheld the National Park Service's decision to move some lodge facilities out of the WSR corridor, in a tradeoff that placed a road within the corridor, but overall restored seven acres of riparian area in the corridor, with the agency finding that the changes "will enhance the overall visitor experience in the Merced River area." The court rejected plaintiff's argument that § 1283(a) suggests that road construction in a scenic river area is prohibited by the WSRA.

> The agency has discretion to categorize a protected area as "wild", "scenic" or "recreational." Although NPS had previously categorized the Merced River area as "recreational" in light of the substantial

human intrusion, the Environmental Assessment for the lodge plan reclassified it as "scenic" in light of its proposal to remove most lodging facilities from the river corridor. A scenic river area is one that is "free of impoundments, with shorelines or watersheds still largely primitive and shorelines largely undeveloped, *but accessible in places by roads.*" Section 1273(b) (emphasis added). The statute therefore does not preclude, in all circumstances, the existence of a road in a river corridor. Rather, the controlling principle is that the agency has substantial discretion to manage the river area, in light of its special attributes, to further the purposes of the WSRA.

7.   In Wilderness Watch v. U.S. Forest Service, 143 F.Supp.2d 1186 (D.Mont.2000), the court held that the Forest Service's issuance of special use permits to construct permanent resort lodges in a "wild river" corridor violated the provision in the Wild & Scenic Rivers Act that such corridors should be have "watersheds or shorelines essentially primitive." 16 U.S.C. § 1273(b)(1).

Oregon Natural Desert Association v. Green

United States District Court, District of Oregon, 1997.
953 F.Supp. 1133.

■ HAGGERTY, DISTRICT JUDGE:

Plaintiffs, various named environmental groups (collectively referred to as "ONDA"), filed this action * * * [alleging, among other things, that] the river management plan BLM prepared for the Donner und Blitzen Wild and Scenic River [designated by Congress in 1988] violates the Wild and Scenic Rivers Act, 16 U.S.C. §§ 1271–1287 * * * [and seeking] to enjoin BLM from any further implementation of the activities authorized in the river management plan. * * *

The river area includes outstandingly remarkable vegetation, fisheries, wildlife, scenery, recreation, geology and cultural values. Of the 74.8 miles of streambed, 63 miles are publicly-owned and 11.8 miles are privately-owned. The river area is comprised of a total of 22,265 acres of land; 19,353 acres are publicly-owned and 3,312 acres are privately-owned.

In 1991, BLM hired five scientists from the Nature Conservancy to survey and report on sensitive native plants and unique natural areas in the river area. The scientists reported that the river area possesses an extraordinary number and diversity of native plant species. They also reported that the river area possesses plant communities that are rare in the Great Basin region. According to ONDA, the scientists determined that cattle grazing has had a broad scale adverse effect on native plants and plant communities. BLM and intervenors dispute this assertion and submit that the scientists actually stated that "[g]razing has had a broad scale effect upon the riparian and upland vegetation in the Blitzen River system." Harney County submits that the report also noted the "overall high quality condition of the natural communities found within the river corridor." The scientists expressed specific concern about the lack of reproduction in woody plant species in riparian areas.

The scientists unanimously recommended that BLM remove grazing from the entire river corridor and prevent any trespass cattle. BLM points out, however, that the Nature Conservancy biologist who authored the sensitive plants report subsequently advised BLM in comments on the River Plan that, while grazing should be banned "in the canyons of the river," grazing in the South Fork of the Blitzen was "recognized as not being as easily controlled as the river does not flow through steep canyons," and that a "well crafted" allotment management plan should be adopted to protect that part of the river.

[BLM issued its river plan, accompanied by an environmental assessment, in 1993, and] * * * has issued at least two other site-specific decisions that tier to and implement the River Plan.

ONDA maintains that cattle grazing has degraded and continues to degrade native plants and plant communities in part of the river area. BLM and intervenors agree that, in the past, cattle grazing has degraded native plants and plant communities in part of the river area. They dispute, however, ONDA's statement that the cattle grazing continues to degrade the native plants and communities. Rather, BLM insists that the trend in condition of riparian habitat, which includes vegetation, is stable or upward in all publicly-owned parts of the river area. According to BLM, changes in grazing management that it is implementing this year, including reduced stocking levels, changes in season of use and pasture rotation and periodic rest, will produce an upward trend in areas that are currently stable and will accelerate the improvement in areas that already show an upward trend. * * *

The River Plan does not require the exclusion of cattle from any new part of the river area. ONDA contends that removal of cattle from parts of the river area and the prevention of any trespassing cattle is necessary so that certain native plants and plant communities may be restored to a natural function and may thereafter be protected and enhanced. BLM agrees that cattle should be removed from the high-elevation gorges of the river corridor; namely, Little Indian Gorge, Big Indian Gorge and Little Blitzen Gorge, where a number of sensitive plant communities are located. In fact, BLM represents that is has already excluded livestock from the Little Blitzen and Big Indian Gorges. Further, steep terrain allows only few livestock to reach Little Indian Gorge. BLM disagrees that livestock should be removed from other parts of the river because research has shown that, if livestock are carefully managed, riparian plant communities can be restored without completely eliminating grazing. * * *

To address the impact of cattle on river values, the River Plan states as a management "objective" improving "trend in riparian condition." ONDA states that the trend standard fails to restore, protect or enhance certain native plants and plant communities in the river area. BLM and intervenors take exception to this assessment because the affidavit cited in support of this assertion is stated in general, hypothetical terms and does not identify any particular plant species or plant community that is native to the Donner und Blitzen River area that is located in parts of the river where livestock normally graze and that would not be likely to improve under a "trend" standard.

BLM defines "trend in range condition" as meaning a movement toward or away from the "climax or potential natural community." BLM considers the indicators of trend in riparian condition to include: 1) increase in ground cover; 2) composition changes in herbaceous species; 3) establishment or increase in woody species; 4) changes in streambank stability; and 5) changes in stream depth and width. BLM classifies riparian condition as "poor," "fair," "good," or "excellent," depending on several criteria, including: 1) percent of the stream that is shaded; 2) vegetation species composition, vigor and abundance; and stability of streambanks.

The River Plan states as a management "action" that grazing will not exceed in riparian areas 45 percent utilization of herbaceous plants and 20 percent utilization of woody plants. ONDA asserts that certain herbaceous plants that are components of the vegetation value of the river area may not thrive or reproduce under the utilization standard. Similarly, ONDA claims that certain woody plants in riparian areas cannot thrive or reproduce well under the utilization standard. BLM and intervenors dispute these two assertions and argue that the extent to which any particular utilization standard may permit vegetation to thrive cannot be assessed independently of other components of a grazing system, such as rest periods and season of use. BLM explains that the River Plan does not purport to detail the grazing systems for the allotments around the Donner und Blitzen River; rather, this subject is left to the management plans for individual allotments. Further, the South Steens Allotment Management Plan provides for an early season of use for the pasture surrounding the South Fork of the Blitzen, with a year of rest every four years.

The river area provides habitat for certain resident fish species that rely on cold and clean water, including wild redband trout. ONDA informs that the health of fish is linked to water quality and the health of riparian vegetation, especially woody species. Although BLM agrees with this statement, Harney County disputes that statement and offers that the Nature Conservancy report stated instead that "[c]loser monitoring of the redband trout fishery is recommended on a species basis as it is a valuable indicator of the health of the system as well as being a rare species." In 1991 and 1992, BLM conducted an "aquatic habitat survey" of 40 of the river area's 74.8 miles. Forty-five percent of the surveyed habitat was in "poor" or "fair" condition. BLM agrees with this statement, but Harney County presents that the aquatic habitat surveys in 1991 and 1992 found thirty-six percent of the surveyed habitat was in "poor" or "fair" condition and that sixty-four percent was in "good" or "excellent" condition.

Water quality is also degraded in the river area. ONDA submits that the Oregon Department of Environmental Quality found that the Little Blitzen River is "water quality limited," because it exceeds the state temperature standard. BLM presents that the Oregon Department of Environmental Quality has not found that the Little Blitzen River is "water quality limited." Rather, the Oregon Department of Environmental Quality has proposed listing the Little Blitzen River as "water quality limited" for temperature, in a draft list that has been issued for public comment.

ONDA maintains that the River Plan states no management standard for fish based on instream conditions. Rather, it iterates the forage utilization and condition trend standards. BLM agrees, but adds that improvement in riparian conditions, including vegetation, shading and streambank stability, should improve instream conditions, such as pool frequency and depth, sedimentation and temperature. BLM adds that its analysis of monitoring data on instream conditions, collected in 1994 and 1995, indicates that the condition of stream habitat on the South Fork of the Blitzen had improved along 7.3 miles, or seventy percent, of that river segment, compared with conditions in 1991. According to BLM, this improvement occurred in the parts of the South Fork that were in the worst condition in 1991. * * *

The River Plan will allow motorized vehicles to operate in more than seven miles inside the river area. ONDA informs that BLM plans to improve two primitive secondary access roads not usually frequented by the general public and make them high standard gravel roads. BLM responds that the River Plan calls for improvement of only one primitive road: The access road that leads from the Steens Mountain Loop Road to the Riddle Brothers Ranch. That access road is approximately two miles long and about half of it is outside the river corridor. BLM also plans to construct two new parking lots in the river area. ONDA claims access by and use of motorized vehicles in the river area will harm its recreational and scenic values, particularly its aesthetic beauty and solitude. BLM challenges that assertion on the basis that the River Plan will allow motor vehicle access only in some parts of the river area where motor vehicles had access prior to designation of the river under the WSRA. The River Plan closes one mile of existing road within the river corridor to motor vehicles and closes 17 miles of the river corridor to mountain bikes and other mechanized equipment. * * *

In 1988, the Donner und Blitzen was designated by Congress as a component of the System [in the Omnibus Oregon Wild and Scenic Rivers Act of 1988 ("OOWSRA") 16 U.S.C.] § 1274(a)(74). Significantly, when Congress designated the Donner und Blitzen it classified the river, including its major tributaries, as a "wild" river. *Id.* Under the WSRA, a "wild" river is defined as "[t]hose rivers free of impoundments and generally inaccessible except by trail, with watersheds or shorelines essentially primitive and waters unpolluted. These represent vestiges or primitive America." *Id.* at § 1273(b)(1). The classification "wild" is the most restrictive of the three possible classifications. *Id.* at § 1273(b) * * *.

ONDA argues that BLM violated the WSRA by adopting, without any rational basis, a management plan for the river that fails to protect and enhance native plants, plant communities and fisheries. Specifically, ONDA insists there are four aspects of the River Plan that violate the WSRA. Namely, the River Plan improperly authorizes the: 1) continued grazing of cattle, 2) construction of new parking lots, 3) the improvement of a secondary access road, and 4) implementation of a water resource project to divert water to irrigate hay fields.

ONDA submits that BLM had an affirmative duty under the WSRA and NEPA to fully consider, disclose and analyze whether excluding cattle grazing from all or part of the public lands in the river area was necessary to restore, protect and enhance the values of the Donner und Blitzen River. According to ONDA, BLM failed to meet this duty in preparing the River Plan and the EA because it: 1) erroneously concluded that it did not have authority under the WSRA to exclude cattle from public lands in the river area, and 2) erroneously concluded that the River Plan could not affect activities allowed under pre-existing programmatic plans for the river area.

BLM does not dispute that it had authority to exclude cattle grazing from the river area. Further, it insists that the River Plan does not presume that BLM lacked authority to exclude livestock from the river area. In fact, BLM refers the court to the following portion of the River Plan: "Grazing management changes will be implemented to protect and enhance the outstandingly remarkable values of the Wild and Scenic River System. This will require fencing, development and protection of alternative water sources, or elimination of livestock grazing." The River Plan also describes the segments of the river totaling 40 miles of the 74.8 mile river corridor that already have been excluded from grazing.

[The intervening local county and affected ranchers] * * * maintain, however, that Congress intended existing livestock grazing, as well as other commercial uses, to continue in designated wild and scenic river areas. Specifically, they argue that the OOWSRA was designed to "maintain the status quo and specifically recognized that existing uses and facilities were 'grandfathered' under the [OOWSRA] and were not required to be extracted from the river corridor." Harney County relies extensively on the legislative history of both the WSRA and the OOWSRA to argue that those statutes are intended to preserve and protect the outstandingly remarkable features of the designated rivers by maintaining the existing character and status quo of the rivers at the time of designation.

The court agrees with ONDA and the BLM that the BLM had authority to exclude cattle grazing from the river area. The plain language of the statute mandates that the federal agency administer the river in such a manner as "to protect and enhance the values which caused it to be included in said system without, insofar as is consistent therewith, limiting other uses that do not substantially interfere with public use and enjoyment of these values." 16 U.S.C. § 1281(a). Absent ambiguity or an absurd result, the plain meaning of the statute must control. In addition, the court is able to discern from other federal statutes that Congress is cognizant of its ability to grandfather specific commercial uses of a wild and scenic river that might otherwise be prohibited by the WSRA. *See, e.g.,* 16 U.S.C. §§ 1274(a)(17), (a)(18), (a)(22), (a)(24) and (a)(53).

Moreover, the legislative history relied on by the intervenors is unpersuasive. The legislative history consists primarily of statements made by individual legislators during the hearings on the OOWSRA. The OOWSRA simply designated the Donner und Blitzen, classified it as "wild" and established its length by river mile. The OOWSRA did not alter any substantive provision of the WSRA. This does not mean, however, that cattle grazing must be excluded from the river area. Rather, cattle grazing may continue, but only in accordance within the strictures of the WSRA to protect and enhance.

Here, BLM contends that it was required to restrict grazing only where grazing would "substantially interfere" with the public's enjoyment of river values. According to BLM, because the WSRA does not define "substantially interfere," it is left to its judgment to determine whether grazing is compatible with protection and enhancement of river values. BLM determined that livestock should be excluded from some parts of the river, but that grazing in other parts of the river would not "substantially interfere" with the public's enjoyment of river values. BLM determined that it is possible to protect and enhance river values and allow grazing to continue in some areas on a managed schedule. As such, BLM insists that the court must defer to its judgment.

The court disagrees with BLM's assertion that the River Plan strikes the appropriate balance between continued grazing and protecting and enhancing the river values. The River Plan identifies seven outstandingly remarkable values: scenic, geologic, recreational, fish and wildlife, vegetation, cultural—traditional practices/prehistoric, cultural—historic. The record in this case establishes that several of these values are being degraded by continued cattle grazing in the river area.

The *Final Report* prepared by the five botanists in cooperation with BLM, included the following Management Recommendation for grazing in the river area:

> Grazing has had a broad scale affect upon the riparian and upland vegetation in the Blitzen River System. Nearly every reach of every river segment had been grazed this year, some of which was obvious trespass. The South Fork Blitzen River was so heavily grazed that the riparian [area] had been essentially destroyed over a significant part of the segment. In contrast, in most of the upper reaches of the glacial canyons of the Blitzen River system * * * [it] was essentially intact and in good condition. The detrimental effects of grazing in riparian systems is well documented and the Blitzen River system exhibits the usual effects. Of greatest concern to the surveyors was the general lack of reproduction in black cottonwood and willow stands. *Our unanimous recommendation is to remove grazing from the entire river corridor and to effectively prevent trespass from nearby allotments.*
>
> *Final Report Donner Und Blitzen Wild & Scenic River Sensitive Plants And Unique Natural Areas Inventory* (emphasis added).

In addition, nearly half of the surveyed aquatic habitat remains in a "poor" or "fair" condition due to poor water quality and riparian vegetation. It is undisputed that the health of the coldwater fish in the river area is linked to the vitality of water and vegetation. Further evidence of the declining water quality was delivered on June 26, 1996. The Environmental

Protection Agency issued a final decision approving the State of Oregon's finding that two of the major streams in the river area are "water quality limited" under the federal Clean Water Act, on the ground that the water temperature exceeds the allowable maximum standard established for the protection of the native fish. The BLM does not challenge ONDA's assertion that the primary cause of the overheated water and siltation in the river is "denuded and collapsed streambanks due to grazing." * * *

It also appears from the record that at the time BLM prepared the River Plan it did not believe it had authority to exclude cattle grazing entirely from the river area. Further, it appears from the record that BLM relied on the Andrews Management Framework Plan, written well before the Donner und Blitzen was designated a part of the System as a "wild" river, to determine the impact of cattle grazing in the river area for purposes of the River Plan. While BLM was permitted to coordinate and incorporate the River Plan into other resource management plans for affected adjacent Federal lands, 16 U.S.C. § 1274(d)(1), those existing plans do not simply excuse the agency's duties under the WSRA. * * *

ONDA also challenges the River Plan on the ground it illegally allows motorized vehicles to operate in more than seven miles inside the river area. In addition, BLM plans to build two "high standard gravel roads" along "primitive secondary access roads not usually frequented by the general public." BLM also plans to build two new parking lots in the river area. ONDA insists that these BLM decisions that improve and increase vehicle access within the river area violates the WSRA and NEPA.

As stated above, Congress defined "wild" rivers as "free of impoundments and generally inaccessible except by trail." 16 U.S.C. § 1273(b)(1). Section 1283(a) directs that the agency charged with managing the river pay "particular attention ... to ... road construction." In fact, federal regulations authorize BLM to close roads, if necessary, to comply with the WSRA. *See* 43 C.F.R. § 8351.2–1(a).

In spite of its express duties under the WSRA, BLM authorized the construction of new parking lots and the improvement of primitive roads within the river area [and] * * * it appears BLM failed to consider, much less analyze, whether such new development would violate the WSRA. * * *

NOTES AND QUESTIONS

1.   In Oregon Natural Desert Ass'n v. Singleton, 75 F.Supp.2d 1139 (D.Or.1999), the same judge ordered livestock grazing to be eliminated permanently from specific areas of the Owyhee River WSRA, 120 miles of which were designated by Congress in 1984 and additional 66 miles of tributaries were designated in 1988, with all segments classified as "wild." Cattle are grazed on 67 miles of the 186–mile river system. Livestock had been grazing the river corridor for many years. When it prepared its management plan in 1991, BLM found that 18 of these miles constituted "areas of livestock concern," *i.e.,* showed noticeable negative effects created by grazing. The areas most affected by livestock grazing were trail cross-

ings and "water gaps," the places where livestock come to the river to drink. The court was rather harsh in its assessment of the BLM's failure to control livestock grazing.

[The United States and the intervenor Oregon Cattleman's Association] have consistently taken the position that a total prohibition on grazing in the river corridor is scientifically unnecessary and would be economically catastrophic for the permittees. However, they have also insisted on the practical and financial impossibility of any exclusionary options other than a prohibition on grazing, such as building fences, developing alternate sources of water, or using riders to contain herds. And despite several invitations from the court, neither the defendants nor the intervenor has proffered evidence on, or seriously discussed, the feasibility of an injunction limited to the areas of concern. Instead, the defendants and the intervenor have treated the possibility of an injunction as an "all-or-nothing" proposition, and have vehemently opposed any change in the status quo.

The court might be more inclined to maintain the status quo if it were persuaded that continuation of the BLM's current grazing management practices could lead to restoration of the areas of concern. However, the BLM has not demonstrated that its current practices have led to any significant improvement in the areas of concern over the past seven years, and the court concludes that the continued degradation of the areas of concern can be remedied only by closing these areas entirely to cattle grazing.

The BLM has previously closed certain areas to grazing but then allowed the affected permittees to add their herds to those grazing in other areas. The court therefore concludes that only the complete elimination of permits for a certain number of animal unit months ("AUMs") will prevent the possibility that cattle will be removed from one degraded area only to increase grazing pressure elsewhere.

The court now permanently enjoins cattle grazing in the "areas of concern" identified by the BLM, including the Deary Pasture area, which is currently closed. The permits for those AUMs are to be eliminated, rather than shifted to more lightly grazed areas. * * *

Although the BLM asserts that its grazing management practices have generated improvements in the areas of concern first identified in 1993, the court concludes that the assertion is unsubstantiated by objective evidence except for the closure of Deary Pasture. Perhaps the most troubling evidence is Mr. Taylor's testimony that the numbers of animals and the seasons of use have remained completely unchanged since implementation of the Plan, except when grazing permits have been increased to exploit good water years.

The Plan provided that restrictions on levels and seasons of use would be implemented where necessary to ensure that utilization standards were met, riparian vegetation was in a properly functioning condition, and livestock impacts on vegetation and soils within the river corridor, at water gaps and trail crossings were minimized so that vegetative cover would not decrease and, if possible, would increase. None of this has been done. Mr. Taylor testified that the BLM has neither made changes to seasons of use nor reduced the number of AUMs permitted for any of the allotments since the Plan was implemented. In fact, Mr. Taylor admitted that the BLM has actually *increased* the number of AUMs in some allotments, because greater than anticipated rainfall had yielded more vegetation. The court is troubled by this indication that the BLM regards beneficial natural events as justifications for increased grazing, rather than as opportunities for recovery and enhancement of natural resources. * * *

It has been almost seven years since the BLM recognized that cattle grazing was creating noticeable negative effects on the rivers' values in some parts of the corridor. The BLM found that grazing conflicted with recreational values where livestock congregated, grazed and defecated around campsites; that the visual impact of livestock trailing and grazing affected scenic and recreation values; and that the ecological condition of upland and riparian areas was being degraded by livestock grazing, trampling and defecation. The BLM designated specific areas of concern in 1993, and stated its goal of managing those areas so as to maintain or improve the vegetative cover of key species and the visual aspect of native perennial plants, ensure proper utilization of key species, minimize livestock impact on vegetation and soils, and reduce livestock/recreation conflicts. * * *

The court also considered the economic impact, noting that closing the areas of concern would represent a loss of 26,976 AUMs, or about 26% of the total in the river corridor. The court found that eliminating these AUMs would cause a maximum loss of personal income in the county of approximately $700,000, against a total personal income in the county of $491 million. The court concluded that the "reduction in subsidized grazing privileges will have an adverse economic effect on some of the individual permit holders, its overall effect on the county's economy is negligible."

2. In National Wildlife Federation v. Cosgriffe, 21 F.Supp.2d 1211 (D.Or.1998), a different judge ruled that the BLM had violated the WSRA by failing to produce a management plan for the John Day River component of the WSR System, which included 194.5 miles of the main stem and a tributary, designated by Congress in the 1988 OOWSR Act as a "recreational" river. BLM managed only about 42% of the lands on the main stem and about 29% of the tributary. BLM had categorized some of the lands in the corridor that were subject to livestock grazing as in poor or fair condition. The court rejected plaintiffs' request to halt grazing on lands so identified. It distinguished *ONDA v. Green* on the ground that here there was no expert scientific report recommending a halt to grazing; here many of the facts relied on by plaintiffs here "fail to link the BLM's *current* grazing practices to the health of the John Day WSRs." Also, "BLM only manages a relatively small amount of public land within the John Day WSRs interim river areas, making it likely that management practices on private land may have more affect on the overall health of the rivers." Further, "[b]ecause private land makes up the majority of the John Day

WSRs, the shifting of grazing onto unregulated private land could well cause the overall health of the John Day WSRs to suffer as an unintended and unfortunate effect of plaintiffs' requested injunction.''

3.   For commentary, see Charlton H. Bonham, The Wild and Scenic Rivers Act and the Oregon Trilogy, 21 Pub.L. & Resources L. Rev. 109 (2000).

4.   In 1970, "guidelines" (never published as formal regulations) were prepared to govern the study of candidates for designation, and the management of designated wild and scenic rivers. They were updated in 1982. Fairfax, Andrews & Buchsbaum described the guidelines this way (59 Wash.L.Rev. at 450):

> The Reagan guidelines rejected the Carter Administration's * * * [draft that contained s]pecific water quality standards, mining prohibitions, restrictions on dams, and controls on federal appropriation of land and water * * *. The Carter language also allowed "selective timber harvest" in scenic river areas, while the final allows "timber harvest." Although the regulations [sic] are ostensibly a joint product of the Departments of Agriculture and the Interior, it would be a serious error to assume that the guidelines presage a uniform federal approach to the program. The provisions are suggestive rather than binding, and offer ample room for exercise of discretion by diverse agencies operating under significantly different mandates.

5.   The W & SR Act is not very precise on how far away from the designated river segment its special management obligations extend. 16 U.S.C. § 1283(a) applies them to "any [federal] lands which include, border upon, or are adjacent to, any river" designated or under consideration for designation. Does this include any federal land anywhere in the affected watershed? Might a Forest Service timber sale outside the designated river corridor be subject to management restrictions flowing from the Act? (If so, how far does this extend; e.g., what about a timber sale twenty miles upstream, on a tributary of the designated river segment?) The courts have not spoken entirely consistently on the point. In Wilderness Society v. Tyrrel, 918 F.2d 813, 819 (9th Cir.1990), the court said that the WSRA would apply to a proposed sale of timber outside of but "adjacent to" what the court called the designated river "system" or river "area," to the extent it "impact[ed] protected values." This was questioned in Sierra Club v. United States, 23 F.Supp.2d 1132, 1139 n.3 (N.D.Cal.1998), which emphasized that the statute speaks of lands adjacent to the indicated "river" rather than the river "area" or "system." The court in *Sierra Club* said a broader interpretation seemed to depart not only from the statute's plain meaning, but was also "inconsistent with the entire thrust of the WSRA, which requires the agency to manage rivers and land falling within the boundary that the agency has determined will define the river corridor." Cf. footnote 4 in *Newton County,* supra. Who is right here? Is it relevant that another part of the Act, § 1274(d)(1), directs that WSR management plans "be coordinated with and may be incorporated into resource management planning for affected adjacent federal lands"?

6. Management problems along W & S Rivers are usually more complex than management problems in areas of the National Wilderness Preservation System (considered in the next and final section of this chapter). Areas designated as wilderness are usually entirely or almost entirely federal land. By contrast (primarily because settlers tended to concentrate along rivers), much of the land along many of the designated W & S Rivers is privately owned, as the *Singleton* case shows. (Recall the facts of *NPCA v. Stanton*, involving the Niobrara National Scenic River, in Chapter 4, p. 322 supra.) The Act contains a number of features that seek to deal with this situation, including provisions for land acquisition (16 U.S.C. § 1277) and cooperative agreements with state and local governments (id. § 1281(e)). But the extent to which the Act authorizes federal regulation of non-federal lands in these river corridors, and preempts state and local land use regulation, is nowhere plainly answered. Cf. United States v. Lindsey, 595 F.2d 5 (9th Cir.1979), noted in Chapter 3, supra p. 201.

7. The Act allows the United States to acquire "scenic easements," defined as the "right to control the use of land (including the air space above such land) within the authorized boundaries of [a designated river segment] for the purpose of protecting the natural qualities of a designated * * * river area," but it goes on to caution that "such control shall not affect, without the owner's consent, any regular use exercised prior to the acquisition of the easement." 16 U.S.C. § 1286(c). In condemnation proceedings, a district court held that the Interior Department was entitled to obtain an easement prohibiting logging, since one previous harvest, in 1958, was not a "regular" use; the defendants did, however, establish the regular use of a "salmon board"—a temporary fishing platform—and the court ruled that the defendant was entitled to continue the use. United States v. Hanten, 500 F.Supp. 188 (D.Or.1980). See also United States v. 55.0 Acres of Land, 524 F.Supp. 320 (W.D.Mo.1981) (ruling on various regular uses); Kiernat v. Chisago County, 564 F.Supp. 1089 (D.Minn.1983) (purchase of scenic easement does not limit more stringent land zoning by county). To some extent the threat of condemnation may be a useful check on controlling intensive development of private land, although the Act does limit the exercise of the condemnation power in various ways; see 16 U.S.C. § 1277; as does the availability of funds for land purchase.

8. Wild & Scenic River corridor management can be complicated in other ways too. For one thing, there is always the delicate matter of state-federal relations in water rights. The federal reserved water rights doctrine applies to rivers designated wild or scenic under the Act, see Chapter 6, supra p. 536. For another, the state may have an ownership interest in the bed of the designated river if the river was "navigable" at statehood. See Chapter 2, supra pp. 52–58. The Act provides that it shall not "affect existing rights of any State, including the right of access, with respect to the beds of navigable streams * * *" in the designated area. 16 U.S.C. § 1284(f). Could a state authorize, over federal objection, oil drilling in the bed of a federally designated wild river that was navigable at statehood? Could it allow private parties to travel by off-road vehicle below the highwater mark of a federally designated wild river, over the managing

federal agency's objection that this would interfere with the wild character of the river? Cf. Chapter 3, pp. 198–204 supra.

9. The BLM has faced an interesting management dilemma on the Fortymile Wild & Scenic River in Alaska, the scene of the first gold rush in the State a century ago. On a portion of the river that is conceded to be navigable, the state of Alaska has issued permits for suction drudges to take gold from the river bottom. Initially, BLM refused to issue permits to these miners to camp on BLM land, above the highwater mark. The miners then camped on gravel bars below the highwater mark, on state land. This has posed some danger to the miners because of the potential of floods, created eyesores for recreational users of the river, and threatened pollution from gasoline caches. Should BLM issue permits for miners to camp on the uplands away from the river? In the "wild" as well as the "scenic" portions of the River? Note that the Act withdraws a quarter mile on each side of the "wild" portion from the Mining Law. Does the Act give BLM the authority to prohibit mining altogether; i.e., by preempting state permitting authority below the highwater mark?

10. President Clinton launched an American Heritage Rivers Initiative by Executive Order in September 1997, E.O. #13,061, 62 Fed. Reg. 48,445. It called for federal agencies to establish partnerships with local areas wishing to "spur economic revitalization, protect natural resources and the environment, and preserve our historic and cultural heritage" in waterways. The program was voluntary and not regulatory. Any designated River was to be assigned a "River Navigator," a federal employee appointed to help implement each river-community's management and development plans and to serve as a liaison with federal agencies. An interagency team of federal officials was also assigned to work with river-communities to identify technical and funding needs and to help facilitate delivery of appropriate federal services. For a debate on the initiative's pros and cons, see Ray Clark, George C. Landrith III, and Roger Marzulla, THE AMERICAN HERITAGE RIVERS INITIATIVE: A MAGNIFICENT IDEA OR THE GREAT LAND/POWER GRAB (1998). The program was controversial with some members of Congress, whose effort to block it foundered because they were deemed not to have standing. Chenoweth v. Clinton, 181 F.3d 112 (D.C.Cir.1999), cert. denied 529 U.S. 1012 (2000).

E. WILDERNESS PRESERVATION

1. THE EVOLUTION OF OFFICIAL WILDERNESS

America pioneered an international preservation movement when it established Yellowstone National Park in 1872; there are now thousands of parks in nearly every country around the globe. Roderick Nash, The American Invention of National Parks, 22 Am.Quart. 726 (1970). The concept of preservation was taken a step further when, first by administrative fiat in 1924 and then by legislative action in 1964, the United States became the first nation to set aside areas in their pristine state as wilderness. In a world where natural places are becoming ever scarcer, future generations may count the preservation of wild lands as one of America's great contributions to civilization. See generally Roderick Nash, WILDERNESS AND THE AMERICAN MIND (3rd ed. 1982); see also Hans Huth, NATURE AND THE AMERICAN (1957). A definition of wilderness is advanced in a remarkable Forest Service book that encompasses philosophical, historical, legal, economic, and management issues, John C. Hendee, George H. Stankey, & Robert L. Lucas,WILDERNESS MANAGEMENT 9 (1978) (2d ed., 1990):

> What is wilderness? This is the crucial question for both allocation and management—the issue to which all allocation and management decisions must be related. At one extreme, wilderness can be defined in a narrow legal perspective as an area possessing qualities outlined in Section 2(c) of the Wilderness Act. At the other extreme, it is whatever people think it is; potentially, the entire universe, the *terra incognita* of people's minds. We can call these two extreme definitions legal wilderness and sociological wilderness.
>
> There is little possibility of deriving a universally accepted definition of sociological wilderness because perceptions of wilderness vary widely. For some urbanites with scant knowledge of, or experience in, the natural environment, wilderness might be perceived in any undeveloped wildland, uncut forest, or woodlot.
>
> On the other hand, legal wilderness as defined by the Wilderness Act of 1964 (Sec. 2c) is much more precise. "A wilderness, in contrast with those areas where man and his own works dominate the landscape, is hereby recognized as an area where the earth and its community of life are untrammeled by man, where man himself is a visitor who does not remain." This legal definition places wilderness on the "untrammeled" pole of the environmental modification continuum. Furthermore, the concept of legal wilderness in the Act is sanctioned by the tradition of this particular kind of land use in America and rests on ideas espoused decades ago.
>
> For example, Aldo Leopold envisioned wilderness as "a continuous stretch of country preserved in its natural state, open to lawful hunting and fishing, big enough to absorb a 2 weeks' pack trip, and kept devoid of roads, artificial trails, cottages, or other works of man." Robert Marshall offered a similar definition:
>
>> * * * [I] shall use the word *wilderness* to denote a region which contains no permanent inhabitants, possesses no possibility of conveyance by any mechanical means and is sufficiently spacious that a person in crossing it must have the experience of sleeping out. The dominant attributes of such an area are: First, that it requires any one who exists in it to depend exclusively on his own effort for survival; and second, that it preserves as nearly as possible the primitive environment. This means that all roads, power transportation and settlements are barred. But trails and

temporary shelters, which were common long before the advent of the white race, are entirely permissible. * * *

Some of the reasons for preserving wilderness were catalogued by Michael McCloskey, former Executive Director of the Sierra Club:

Michael McCloskey, The Wilderness Act of 1964: Its Background and Meaning*

45 Ore.L.Rev. 288 (1966).

What attitudes in America's cultural history produced national leadership that was finally able to persuade its citizens to value wilderness? The inquiry is an important prelude to understanding why the Wilderness Act was passed and what is expected of it.

An agglomeration of accumulating attitudes toward nature explains why today's leaders value wilderness and how they perceive it. Little in America's European intellectual heritage, however, stressed the value of nature in unsullied form. * * *

* * * From the time of the earliest settlements, there is a thread of interest in wild nature which continues throughout America's intellectual history and finally flourishes in the twentieth century. The thread's early strands were formed in response to historical situations and political and religious values. The later strands assert values which are a contemporary rationale for having wilderness.

Early Valuations. One. Though the wilderness of a new continent was a challenge to those who explored it and settled it, from the beginning some valued that setting. The wilderness held a fascination for them on which they built their reputations. This attitude is reflected in the chronicles of exploration and settlement and in the accounts of early travelers. Moreover, wilderness was a gauge of capacity to triumph over adversity, and it was a setting for self-discovery. Wilderness allowed the frontier trappers and mountain men to build their legends. Even later transitory visitors, like Theodore Roosevelt, could use their experience in the West to build legends.

Two. The powerful presence of nature in the wilderness of a new continent also served as an aid to religion and as a setting for religious experience. Puritan preachers such as Jonathan Edwards used the omnipresent plan of nature as evidence of the planning of the God of his revealed religion. Deists, such as Thomas Jefferson, could look to nature's plan as the chief support of the cosmological proof of God's existence. * * *

Three. Wilderness has also been viewed as a setting for political reform. It was the environment of Rousseau's "noble savage"—for untaint-

ed children of nature, and presumably a pre-condition of the good society.
* * *

Four. For those not interested in reforming society or who had been
alienated by it, wilderness served as a refuge or sanctuary. * * *

Five. Beginning with George Perkins Marsh in the latter part of the
nineteenth century, a literary tradition began of describing threats to
nature. Alarms were sounded about depletion of natural resources and
massive wastage. In the writings of John Muir and others, the need to
protect wild country was stressed. * * *

Contemporary Valuations. Six. Today, as a result of the foregoing
history, wilderness is regarded as a cultural heritage. In his association
with the wilderness he spent three centuries taming, the American grew
accustomed to being close to nature. Now that he has tamed so much of it,
he misses it. Clearing the wilderness was a hardening experience that
promoted self-reliance and self-respect. Wilderness has become a symbol
imbedded in our national consciousness—a nostalgia for a lost opportunity.
The wilderness that remains is a reassuring referent for a symbolic idea
that is valued in itself. Actual contact with wilderness today is primarily
valued as an aesthetic experience. * * *

With wilderness users tending to come from higher educational levels
than other outdoor recreationists, a certain elitism surrounds discussions of
this encounter. * * *

But the elitism may reflect primarily the greater ability of educated
wilderness users to articulate their reactions to experience with wilderness,
rather than lack of capacity to have such an experience on the part of less
educated users. * * *

Seven. In addition to being a setting for an aesthetic experience,
wilderness is now regarded as an important setting for scientific research
in the biological sciences. * * * Finally, the complex ecosystems that
develop in undisturbed areas support a genetic diversity that maximizes the
possibilities of the evolutionary process. Wilderness, in effect, becomes a
"gene bank" that evolution can draw upon to offset man's influence in
narrowing the number of species on the planet. * * *

Eight. For some, maintenance of wilderness is evidence of serious
intent to meet newly conceived ethical obligations. Moving beyond a mere
humanistic "reverence for life," Aldo Leopold and others have advocated a
new "land ethic" which substitutes a biocentric view of nature for the
traditional anthropocentric view. Modern biological knowledge, they feel,
should instill an "ecological conscience" in man that will cause him to live
in harmony with the other living things of the earth. In response to that
conscience, man should exercise self-restraint in the extent to which he
disturbs the rest of nature.

Nine. Wilderness today is valued, particularly, as an opportunity for an
educational experience. It provides the setting in which to learn the
cultural, scientific, and ethical values associated with untrammeled nature.
* * *

Ten. Highly urbanized wilderness users value wilderness for therapeutic reasons. Writers like Sigurd Olson have reminded Americans that exertion in wilderness can be a tonic for regaining vigor and serve as an aid to physical recuperation. * * *

Eleven. Finally, wilderness is regarded as the optimum setting for many sport forms of highest quality. These are sports such as mountain climbing, fly fishing, trophy hunting, cross-country backpacking, ski mountaineering, cave exploration, and amateur nature study. All require uncommon natural settings that cannot be duplicated by man.

Resource development is generally prohibited in wilderness areas; for that reason, timber companies, miners, utilities, power companies, and ranchers frequently oppose official wilderness, sometimes bitterly. Their objections are directed not only at the designation of wilderness per se, but also at studies by federal agencies of large tracts of lands for possible inclusion in the wilderness system. During those often lengthy study periods, the land is for the most part "locked up" to avoid destruction of its wilderness characteristics, and the economic ramifications of these choices cannot be ignored. On wilderness and economics, see Glen O. Robinson, Wilderness: The Last Frontier, 59 Minn.L.Rev. 1 (1974); Richard G.Walsh, John B. Loomis, & Richard A. Gillman, Valuing Option, Existence and Bequest Demands for Wilderness, Land Economics 14 (Feb. 1984); Mark Sagoff, On Preserving the Natural Environment, 84 Yale L.J. 205 (1974); Lloyd C. Irland, The Economics of Wilderness Preservation, 7 Envt'l L. 51 (1976).

Institutional wilderness is generally considered to date back to 1924 when Aldo Leopold of the Forest Service succeeded in convincing the agency to set aside as wilderness 700,000 acres in the Gila National Forest in New Mexico, and Arthur Carhart did the same for an area in Colorado. Leopold's writings, including A SAND COUNTY ALMANAC (1949), formed an important part of the philosophical basis for later wilderness proposals. By the mid–1930's several dozen such areas had been established but—true to a Forest Service tradition of decentralized administration—considerable discretion was left to the field officials, who in some cases allowed logging, grazing, and road building. Bob Marshall, a vigorous outdoorsman and founder of the Wilderness Society, became chief of the Forest Service's Division of Recreation in 1937. Among his many contributions to the wilderness movement during his brief two years in office (and his short life; he died at 38) were the so-called U Regulations, tightening the restrictions on uses in wilderness areas.

In a few instances prior to 1964, Congress had adopted acts requiring specific areas of federal lands to be managed as roadless and primitive; e.g., the Shipstead–Nolan Act in 1930 contained what may have been the first express congressional recognition of the wilderness idea by mandating (subject to certain exceptions) that a certain area of the Superior National Forest in Minnesota remain "in an unmodified state of nature." 16 U.S.C.

§ 577b. But in the absence of a generic statutory foundation for formal wilderness areas in the forests, litigation was occasionally brought to challenge restrictions on use of such areas. It was uniformly unsuccessful. For example, in McMichael v. United States, 355 F.2d 283 (9th Cir.1965) (decided after enactment of the Wilderness Act but arising from an incident occurring before passage), the court upheld misdemeanor convictions of persons riding motorcycles in a "Primitive Area" of a national forest where motorized vehicles were prohibited. Authority to designate such an area was found in several sources, including the administrative practice of regulating recreation under the 1897 Organic Act, congressional appropriations for such purpose, and the Multiple Use/Sustained Yield Act of 1960. See also United States v. Perko, 108 F.Supp. 315 (D.Minn.1952), aff'd, 204 F.2d 446 (8th Cir.1953), cert. denied, 346 U.S. 832 (1953) (upholding the Secretary of Agriculture's authority to keep other areas of the Superior National Forest as roadless, and the President's authority to reserve and regulate use of air space over such areas).

2.   THE WILDERNESS ACT OF 1964: MANAGEMENT OF WILDERNESS AREAS

Wilderness received little attention during World War II but the movement revived in the late 1940's and early 1950's, spearheaded by Howard Zahniser, Executive Director of the Wilderness Society. In 1956 Senator Hubert Humphrey introduced the first wilderness bill into Congress. Wilderness legislation was spurred by events proving the central thesis of Zahniser and other advocates: that congressional designation was essential because administrative wilderness could be administratively revoked at any time. In Oregon, the old-growth French Pete Valley was returned to general forest designation for potential logging. In New Mexico, the Gila Wilderness itself was partially opened. Other intrusions on wilderness areas drew regional and national attention. Controversy over the proposal to build the Echo Park Dam in Dinosaur National Monument along the Utah–Colorado border—perhaps the single largest environmental controversy of the first two decades after World War II—demonstrated the emerging strength of the preservationists.

As Professor Nash explained (WILDERNESS AND THE AMERICAN MIND 222 (3d ed. 1982)):

> The concept of a wilderness system marked an innovation in the history of the American preservation movement. It expressed, in the first place, a determination to take the offensive. Previous friends of the wilderness had been largely concerned with defending it against various forms of development. But the post-Echo Park mood was confident, encouraging a bold, positive gesture. Second, the system meant support of wilderness in general rather than of a particular wild region. As a result, debate focused on the theoretical value of wilderness in the abstract, not on a local economic situation. Finally, a national wilderness preservation system [created by congressional, rather than administrative, action] would give an unprecedented degree of protection to wild country.

The Forest Service initially opposed wilderness bills, arguing that statutory wilderness was contrary to multiple use, sustained yield management. Passage of the Multiple–Use, Sustained–Yield Act of 1960 not only codified the agency's multiple use authority, but included a provision that "the establishment and maintenance of areas of wilderness are consistent with the purposes * * * [of this Act]," 16 U.S.C. § 529, and after that Forest Service opposition abated. An even more serious threat to wilderness legislation was the opposition of Congressman Wayne Aspinall of Colorado, Chairman of the Interior Committee, who refused to let any wilderness legislation out of committee until conservationists agreed to support his pet proposal, the creation of the Public Land Law Review Commission. Once that was done, and after concessions were made to miners, ranchers, and other economic interests in amendments, the Wilderness Act—still one of the most idealistic pieces of federal legislation ever enacted—became law on September 3, 1964.

The Forest Service previously had designated 54 areas as "wilderness," "wild," or "canoe." The Wilderness Act, 16 U.S.C. § 1131–36, made them the initial units in the National Wilderness Preservation System. 16 U.S.C. § 1132(a). These "instant wilderness areas" totalled 9.1 million acres. The Act also required the Forest Service to study an additional 5.4 million acres of designated "primitive areas" and to report to the President within 10 years on their suitability as wilderness. In turn, the President was to report his findings on the primitive areas to Congress. 16 U.S.C. § 1132(b). In the Department of Interior, ten-year studies for wilderness suitability were also required on all roadless areas over 5000 acres (and roadless islands of any size) in the National Wildlife Refuge System and on all roadless areas of more than 5000 acres in the National Park System. 16 U.S.C. § 1132(c). These mechanisms for adding to the system are considered more fully in the final section of this chapter, infra pp. 1128–62.

While Congress did not disturb federal land agency authority to use existing law to manage areas in a roadless or primitive status, it took care in the Wilderness Act to provide that "no Federal lands shall be designated as 'wilderness areas' except as provided for in [the Wilderness Act] or by a subsequent Act [of Congress]." 16 U.S.C. § 1131(a). To quell longstanding interagency rivalries, the Act provided that any area included in the wilderness system would continue to be managed by the same agency that administered it before wilderness designation. 16 U.S.C. § 1131(b). To prove that neither conservationists nor Congress had yet learned all of the lessons of history, the Act did not expressly deal with the single largest block of federal lands, those managed by the BLM.

The definition of wilderness in 16 U.S.C. § 1131(c) reads precious little like an ordinary federal statute:

> A wilderness, in contrast with those areas where man and his own works dominate the landscape, is hereby recognized as an area where the earth and its community of life are untrammeled by man, where man himself is a visitor who does not remain. An area of wilderness is further defined to mean in this chapter an area of undeveloped Federal land retaining its primeval character and influence, without permanent improvements or human habitation, which is protected and managed

so as to preserve its natural conditions and which (1) generally appears to have been affected primarily by the forces of nature, with the imprint of man's work substantially unnoticeable; (2) has outstanding opportunities for solitude or a primitive and unconfined type of recreation; (3) has at least five thousand acres of land or is of sufficient size as to make practicable its preservation and use in an unimpaired condition; and (4) may also contain ecological, geological, or other features of scientific, educational, scenic, or historical value.

The first sentence of the section defines wilderness in an ideal sense. It is similar to the definition offered by David Brower, happily mixing metaphors, that wilderness is an area "where the hand of man has never set foot." VOICES FOR THE WILDERNESS xi (W. Schwartz ed. 1969). The remainder of the section defines wilderness for legal purposes, and it is replete with qualifying phrases that depart from the ideal. The definition remains important as the guiding objective for wilderness management. 16 U.S.C. § 133(b) generally mandates that, except where otherwise specified:

> each agency administering any area designated as wilderness shall be responsible for preserving the wilderness character of the area and shall so administer such area for such other purposes for which it may have been established as also to preserve its wilderness character. Except as otherwise provided in this chapter, wilderness areas shall be devoted to the public purposes of recreational, scenic, scientific, educational, conservation, and historical use.

The definition is also important in guiding subsequent additions to the system, because they presumably qualify under it. In the end, however, wilderness designations are political judgments, and nothing except self-restraint prohibits Congress from following what former House Interior Committee Chair Morris Udall once described as former Secretary of the Interior James Watt's definition of wilderness: "a parking lot without stripes."

NOTES AND QUESTIONS

1. Is the concept of wilderness, as defined in the Act, consistent with the "multiple use" concept? Note that Congress said it was even before the Wilderness Act was adopted; see 16 U.S.C. § 529, quoted above, part of the 1960 MUSY Act. Is that a correct interpretation of "multiple use"?

2. Does the definition of wilderness by itself outlaw mining, timber harvesting, or grazing? Does an area in the eastern U.S. that was logged fifty years ago, but which has now revegetated to such an extent that only a trained eye could distinguish it from virgin forest, qualify as wilderness under this definition? Do the wild upper slopes of a mountain near an urban area, which is within sight and earshot of urban civilization, qualify? This question of "purity" is considered further below, at p. 1130.

COMPROMISES ON WILDERNESS MANAGEMENT

Key restrictions and guidance on wilderness management are found in sections 1133(c) and (d). Here are reflected the political accommodations that had to be made to pass the Act. These protect some existing uses, and allow for limited commercial use and resource development in wilderness areas. The federal land agencies have adopted generic regulations governing wilderness area management that sometimes provide helpful guidance on answering some of the issues posed in this section. See, e.g., 36 C.F.R. Part 293 (2001) (national forests); 36 C.F.R. § 228.15 (2001) (mining in national forest wilderness); 43 C.F.R. Part 6300 (2001) (BLM); 43 C.F.R. Part 3802 (2001) (mineral activities in BLM wilderness study areas).

Some of the exceptions and special provisions in this part of the Wilderness Act apply to "wilderness areas designated by this chapter," (e.g., subsection (d)(1)); while others apply to "wilderness areas in the national forests designated by this chapter" (e.g., subsections (d)(3) and (4)); and still others apply to "national forest wilderness areas" (e.g., subsection (d)(2)). Furthermore, every area added to the National Wilderness Preservation System is done so by statute. In these individual statutes Congress sometimes incorporates, and sometimes varies, the generic management guidelines contained in the Wilderness Act. Thus some care is required to determine exactly what restrictions apply where.

The following addresses the compromises that were made in the Wilderness Act itself on specific issues. For general commentary, see Symposium: Wilderness Act of 1964: Reflections, Applications, and Prediction, 76 Denv.U.L.Rev. 331–679 (1999); George Cameron Coggins and Robert Glicksman, PUBLIC NATURAL RESOURCES LAW § 14.04 (2001). On wilderness in the general context of national forest management and planning, see Charles Wilkinson and Michael Anderson, Land and Resource Planning in the National Forests, 64 Oregon L.Rev. 1, 334–70 (1985).

A.   *Mining*. The Wilderness Act, 16 U.S.C. § 1133(d):

> (2) Nothing in this chapter shall prevent within national forest wilderness areas any activity, including prospecting, for the purpose of gathering information about mineral or other resources, if such activity is carried on in a manner compatible with the preservation of the wilderness environment. * * *

Subsection (d)(3) created a twenty-year window for the mining industry to operate in national forest wilderness areas designated by the Wilderness Act that had not already been withdrawn. See Brown v. U.S. Dept. of Interior, 679 F.2d 747 (8th Cir.1982). Specifically, it said that, "[n]otwithstanding any other provisions of [the Wilderness Act]," federal mining and mineral leasing laws should apply in these areas "to the same extent" they applied prior to passage of the Wilderness Act. Any mining activity proposed in such areas was, however, to be subject to (and the specificity of this section tells you the mining industry lawyers were hard at work here):

> reasonable regulations governing ingress and egress as may be prescribed by the Secretary of Agriculture consistent with the use of the land for mineral location and development and exploration, drilling, and production, and use of land for transmission lines, waterlines, telephone lines, or facilities necessary for transmission lines, waterlines, telephone lines, or facilities necessary in exploring, drilling,

producing, mining, and processing operations, including where essential the use of mechanized ground or air equipment and restoration as near as practicable of the surface of the land disturbed * * *.

16 U.S.C. § 1134(b) covers some of the same ground in a somewhat different way, providing in part that the Secretary of Agriculture "shall, by reasonable regulations consistent with the preservation of the area as wilderness, permit ingress and egress [to valid mining claims] by means which have been or are being customarily enjoyed with respect to other such areas similarly situated."

The limited "window of opportunity" for the mining industry in certain wilderness areas expired of its own terms on January 1, 1984, at which point the minerals in wilderness areas were "withdrawn from all forms of appropriation under the mining laws and from disposition under all laws pertaining to mineral leasing and all amendments thereto." Congress has occasionally made some exceptions; e.g., it withdrew the Boundary Water Canoe Area Wilderness from mining in 1978 and the Sawtooth and Hell's Canyon Wilderness Areas in Idaho in 1982. On the other hand, Congress provided that withdrawal of the Gospel Hump Wilderness in Idaho would not occur until January 1, 1988, and a "special management zone" in The River of No Return Wilderness in Idaho remains open to locations for cobalt indefinitely.

There has been little hardrock mining in wilderness areas. See, e.g., Kathryn Toffenetti, Valid Mining Rights and Wilderness Areas, 20 Land & Water L.Rev. 31 n. 1 (1985) (estimating as many as 10,000 potential claims in wilderness areas but little extraction). See also Kenneth D. Hubbard, Marily Nixon, Jeffrey A. Smith, The Wilderness Act's Impact on Mining Activities: Policy vs. Practice, 76 Denver U.L.Rev. 591 (1999); Robert L. Glicksman & George Cameron Coggins, Wilderness in Context, 76 Denver U.L.Rev. 383 (1999). The lack of activity may be partially due to stricter Forest Service mining regulations for wilderness areas. 36 C.F.R. § 228.15 (2001). In Clouser v. Espy. 42 F.3d 1522 (9th Cir.1994), the court found "no doubt whatever that the Forest Service enjoys the authority to regulate means of access," and upheld the Forest Service's policy of refusing to approved motorized access to mining claims "unless and until claim validity is established." It also found Forest Service regulations limiting access to those means "customarily used with respect to other such claims," and limiting mechanized transport and motorized equipment to situations where they were "essential" to mining activities were drawn "nearly verbatim from the statute" so there is "no question" about their validity. Finally, it upheld the Forest Service's application of its regulations to require the use of pack animals for access, upon its finding that motorized access was not "essential" for the miner to use a small dredge in a proposed mining operation four miles into the wilderness, and was not "customary" because the access trails in question had been closed to traffic for a decade.

The Interior Solicitor, noting the limited extent of mining activities in wilderness areas, has surmised that "possible causes include poor mineral prospects, stringent regulation of proposed mineral operations, and the reluctance of the mining industry to risk adverse public reaction by opening major mining operations in wilderness areas." 86 I.D. 89, 110 n. 50 (1979). Costs associated with accessibility to remote areas in rugged terrain doubtless also played a role.

16 U.S.C. § 1133(d)(3) also provides that, subject to valid existing rights, all patents issued under the Mining Law should convey title only to the mineral deposits, not the surface, and no patent should issue after December 31, 1983, again subject to valid existing rights. Such restrictions on patenting have been deemed not a taking, see Swanson v. Babbitt, supra p. 237, but remarkably, for many years thereafter the Interior Department issued patents to surface and minerals in wilderness areas, on the theory that the right to the land surface was a valid existing right. The Interior Solicitor ruled otherwise in 1998, M #36994, Patenting of Mining Claims and Mill Sites in Wilderness Areas. On the Mining Law and wilderness, see generally John Leshy, THE MINING LAW: A STUDY IN PERPETUAL MOTION 229–242 (1987).

Almost no mineral leases were ever issued in statutory wilderness areas despite this twenty-year window. Successive Secretaries of the Interior, in other words, exercised their discretion under the mineral leasing acts against leasing. Secretary James Watt refused to honor that tradition, and in 1981 announced plans to issue mineral leases in several wilderness areas. This provoked the House Interior Committee to request an "emergency withdrawal" under FLPMA, which he reluctantly issued. See Pacific Legal Foundation v. Watt, Chapter 4, supra p. 349. In 1982, Congress used the appropriations process to ban expenditure of federal funds for processing leases in wilderness areas through September 30, 1983, the end of the fiscal year. This left a three-month "window" from September 30 through December 31, 1983, when all wilderness lands were to be withdrawn from mineral leasing pursuant to the Wilderness Act. In late 1982, Secretary Watt capitulated, declaring that he would issue no new oil and gas leases in wilderness.

The Geothermal Steam Act excludes from leasing national parks, recreation areas, and wildlife refuges, but does not mention wilderness areas. 30 U.S.C. § 1014(c). The Wilderness Act itself was enacted six years before the Geothermal Act, and therefore is silent on geothermal leasing. Whether leasing is allowed in congressionally–designated wilderness areas is not an idle inquiry: there are known geothermal resources in wilderness areas and developers have applied, unsuccessfully, for leases. The question of compatibility is examined in Jan D. Sokol, Geothermal Leasing in Wilderness Areas, 6 Envt'l L. 489 (1975). Because other mineral leasing is now generally prohibited in wilderness areas, geothermal leasing would seem to be politically if not legally untenable in such areas.

Overall, then, there has been very little mineral activity in wilderness areas. Mineral potential of roadless areas that are candidates for congressional designation frequently remains, of course, a key political issue when Congress deliberates over adding new areas to the system, and Congress has frequently gerrymandered the boundaries of designated wilderness to avoid areas that have mineral potential. See John Leshy, supra, at 232–33.

B. *Motorized Equipment and Vehicles.* Section 1133(c) is a general prohibition:

> Except as specifically provided for in this chapter, and subject to existing private rights, there shall be no commercial enterprise and no permanent road within any wilderness area designated by this chapter and, except as necessary to meet minimum requirements for the administration of the area for the purpose of this chapter (including measures required in emergencies involving the health and safety of persons within the area), there shall be no temporary road, no use of motor vehicles, motorized equipment or motorboats, no landing of aircraft, no other form of mechanical transport, and no structure or installation within any such area.

The provision, which protects "existing private rights," is then qualified in several respects by section 1133(d). For example, § 1133(d)(1) says that within statutory wilderness, "the use of aircraft or motorboats, where these uses have already become established, may be permitted to continue subject to such restrictions as the [managing agency] deems desirable." "May" does not mean "shall" in this context, as the pilot in United States v. Gregg, 290 F.Supp. 706 (W.D.Wash.1968), discovered to his chagrin. He was fined for landing an airplane in a wilderness area contrary to Forest Service regulations, the court rejecting his argument that because he had an established use, the Forest Service could not prohibit him from landing. The Forest Service policy is found at 36 C.F.R. § 293.6 (2001). Congress can ban motorized vehicles from state or private land within the boundaries of a federally designated wilderness; see Minnesota v. Block, Chapter 3 supra p. 200. After a two-day trial, former race car driver Bobby Unser was fined $75 when he drove his snowmobile into a wilderness area in New Mexico and garnered considerable publicity in the late 1990s. Unser's defense that he was lost was rejected, the court holding that the unlawful possession and operation of a motorized vehicle in national forest wilderness is an offense without a *mens rea* requirement. United States v. Unser, 165 F.3d 755 (10th Cir.), cert. denied, 528 U.S. 809 (1999).

The agencies managing wilderness have some discretion to use motorized equipment for the "purpose" of the Act, including rescue missions, section 1133(c), and for controlling "fire, insects, and disease," section 1133(d)(1). This latter provision is explored under subsection D, below, dealing with logging. The Forest Service uses chain saws and other equipment to clear trails and construct some rough bridges; it fights some but not all fires; and it uses motorized equipment for rescue operations, but not to bring out dead bodies where no "emergency" exists. For policy questions raised by such issues, see A Colloquy Between Congressman [Jim] Weaver and Assistant Secretary [of Agriculture Rupert] Cutler, 75 J. Forestry 392 (1977).

What about the installation, with battery-powered motorized drills, of permanent climbing bolts in wilderness areas? Is a drill "motorized equipment"? Federal agencies generally believe so. Are the climbing bolts a "structure or installation"? Here the agencies have sometimes split, although the current view seems to be that they are not prohibited across the board, although they may be regulated and even prohibited by local land managers. See Timothy Dolan, Fixed Anchors and the Wilderness Act: Is the Adventure Over?, 34 U.S.F.L.Rev. 355 (2000). Courts have recognized that commercial outfitters in wilderness may be allowed to install facilities such as hitching posts and to store lumber that may be used for temporary corrals in wilderness areas. Wilderness Watch v. Robertson, 978 F.2d 1484 (9th Cir.1992). And see Jennie Bricker, Wheelchair Accessibility in Wilderness Areas: The Nexus Between the ADA and the Wilderness Act, 25 Envtl.L. 1243 (1995).

C.   *Grazing*. Under 16 U.S.C. § 1133(d)(4), "the grazing of livestock, where established prior to September 3, 1964, *shall* be permitted to continue subject to such reasonable regulations as are deemed necessary." (emphasis added) Does this provision, unlike the discretionary language used for aircraft and motorboats, create a right where none existed before? Michael McCloskey argued no, in The Wilderness Act of 1964: Its Background and Meaning, 45 Ore.L.Rev. 288, 311–12 (1966):

> * * * Traditionally, under the law grazing permits are held not as a matter of right but merely as a matter of privilege, with the administering agency having the right to discontinue permits on their expiration. Does this provision establish any statutory rights in existing permittees? The fact that the continuance of grazing is made subject to reasonable regulation by the secretary implies there was no intent to establish definite rights. Indeed, if there had been any intent to change the basic law on this point, there would have been considerable debate. There was none. Under the "reasonable regulations" that the Forest Service has prepared for its manual, continuance of grazing will be contingent on being consistent with wilderness values and maintenance of soil values. What the draftsmen of this section probably intended, then, was merely to make it clear that the existence of the Wilderness Act *per se* would not preclude continuance of grazing. The Forest Service would still have the authority to decide whether grazing on a given site was desirable and at what levels of stocking.

Are you persuaded by this argument? Can the managing federal agency restrict or prohibit livestock grazing in a wilderness area in order to preserve wilderness character? Can it do so for reasons *unrelated* to wilderness? See generally Michael P. McLaran, Livestock in Wilderness: A Review and Forecast, 20 Envtl.L. 857 (1990).

In the Colorado Wilderness Act of 1980, Congress declared that, "without amending the Wilderness Act of 1964, with respect to livestock grazing in wilderness areas," the Act's provisions on livestock grazing "shall be interpreted and administered in accordance with the guidelines contained in" the House Report (No. 96–617) accompanying the Act. 94 Stat. 3271, § 108 (1980). The Report basically said that existing grazing uses may continue in wilderness areas, but reductions in grazing intensity may be made through agency planning processes to improve poor range conditions. Reductions may not be made, however, solely because the area in which grazing is permitted has been designated as wilderness.

Subsection 1133(d)(4) speaks of grazing established *prior to* enactment of the Wilderness Act. Can the federal land management agency allow grazing in wilderness where the use was *not* established prior to the Act? Is grazing of domesticated livestock *per se* incompatible with the statutory definition of wilderness? On grazing in BLM wilderness and wilderness study areas, see Harold Shepard, Livestock Grazing in BLM Wilderness and Wilderness Study Areas, 5 J.Envtl.L. & Litig. 61 (1990).

D. *Logging.* Somewhat curiously, the Wilderness Act does not expressly refer to timber harvesting even though it was a major issue leading up to enactment. The legislative history, the general provisions of the act, and the ban on roads and motorized equipment all make clear, however, that commercial logging is a prohibited activity. See Lyng v. Northwest Indian Cemetery Protective Ass'n, 485 U.S. 439, 443 (1988) (wilderness "means commercial activities such as timber harvesting are forbidden"). Several courts have enjoined timber harvests in areas being considered for wilderness designation on the ground that wilderness suitability would be destroyed by logging. See, e.g., Parker v. United States and California v. Block, pp. 1130–34 infra.

E. *Control of Fire, Insects and Disease.* Section 4(d)(1) of the Wilderness Act of 1964 allows the federal managing agency to take "such measures * * * as may be necessary in the control of fire, insects, and diseases, subject to such conditions as the Secretary deems desirable." 16 U.S.C. § 1133(d)(1). This section, in conjunction with the Department of Agriculture's effort to control the infestation of the southern pine beetle, has led to the following opinions, which together comprise what is probably the most complete judicial discussion of agency management obligations in designated wilderness.

Sierra Club v. Lyng I

United States District Court, District of Columbia, 1987.
662 F.Supp. 40.

■ GESELL, DISTRICT JUDGE.

By a complaint filed July 12, 1985, Sierra Club and the Wilderness Society have challenged the legality of a program initiated by the United States Forest Service under direction of the Secretary of Agriculture to control infestations of the Southern Pine Beetle in federally designated Wilderness Areas located in Arkansas, Louisiana and Mississippi.

[Plaintiffs alleged that the "extensive tree-cutting and chemical-spraying campaign involved" violated NEPA, the Endangered Species Act (because of the presence of the red-cockaded woodpecker in the areas), and the Wilderness Act. The district court had earlier enjoined much of the program pending preparation of an EIS. 614 F.Supp. 488 (D.D.C.1985). In this opinion the court addressed the application of 16 U.S.C. § 1133(d)(1), quoted above.]

* * * Plaintiffs' primary contention is that the Secretary is not authorized to undertake an insect control program in a designated Wilderness

Area unless the Secretary can demonstrate that the program is necessary in the sense that it is effective, and that the program for the Southern Pine Beetle infestations which are under attack here must be restrained since the program is ineffective. They argue that the Wilderness Areas were being destroyed by extensive and continuing spot cutting of infestations pursuant to the Secretary's program without any appreciable success in curbing the pest and that wilderness values Congress sought to preserve as a matter of affirmative national policy were, as a consequence, being permanently injured. The complex life cycle of the Southern Pine Beetle, an indigenous, well-known pest, has been elaborately studied and plaintiffs offered considerable data indicating the program's dubious effectiveness.

The Secretary presents both a legal and factual opposition. First, he asserts that the Court has no authority to consider the motion since Section 4(d)(1) leaves all management decisions affecting Wilderness Areas to his nonreviewable discretion. It is further suggested that since a different program may emerge with the eventual publication of the EIS the Court is being asked to issue an advisory opinion. Factually, the Secretary contends the program is effective in the sense that although continued cutting of spot infestations would be required, the program has somewhat slowed the appearance of new infestations as more and more mature pine trees are cut down and destroyed.

The Wilderness Act, as the Secretary urges, clearly places broad discretion in the Secretary to manage designated Wilderness Areas. Each area differs. There are no standards indicated for control of fire, insects or disease. Technical information and research must in the end guide the Secretary in the sensitive task of keeping nature's precarious balance within each area stable. Resolution of these decisions through litigation is surely counterindicated except upon the most explicit showing of arbitrary irresponsibility.

However, a further circumstance overhangs this particular dispute which must be considered. The Southern Pine Beetle program is not limited to Wilderness Areas and indeed the purpose and effect of the program is solely to protect commercial timber interests and private property, including, of course, national forests in which more draconian steps can be taken to eliminate the beetle. The extensive cutting in the Wilderness Areas that was being carried out under the program until preliminarily enjoined was conducted solely to aid outside adjacent property interests, not to further wilderness interests or to further national wilderness policy.[1]

Both plaintiffs and the Secretary agree that Congress also intended by Section 4(d)(1) to authorize the Secretary to take actions within Wilderness Areas where necessary to control fire, insects, or disease from spreading beyond the areas and harming adjacent or neighboring private or commercial interests. The legislative history sustains this view. Plaintiffs' case

---

1. To the extent any cutting may have been desirable to prevent undue harm to the red-cockaded woodpecker such cutting would be minor due to the very few woodpecker habitats in these areas. This issue could be addressed in specific terms along the lines suggested by the Court's preliminary injunction if the program were abandoned.

therefore poses the declared national policy to preserve pristine wilderness ecology and values into sharp juxtaposition with the program's effectiveness, or lack of effectiveness, in controlling the harm being caused by pine beetles on adjacent property. Management of wilderness areas as such is not involved and the program could not be approved as a wilderness-management program.

Unfortunately, the material submitted on the motion provides no clear answers to the dilemma suggested. Pine beetles have a considerable range of flight and studies leave in doubt the extent to which they may migrate to or from adjacent pine land. There is no way the Court can determine from the material submitted to what extent beetle migration out of these particular Wilderness Areas into commercial timber properties may be adequately controlled under the program. Nor is it clear whether adjacent properties can be equally well controlled against beetle infestation by measures taken outside of the Wilderness Areas that would be wholly inappropriate within the Wilderness Areas.

Thus this case does not involve the management of Wilderness Areas as such. Rather, it presents a different question, one that is not fully addressed by the Act itself. That question is whether the Secretary has been given the same Section 4(d)(1) broad management discretion previously noted when he takes actions within the Wilderness Areas for the benefit of outside commercial and other private interests. This question must be answered in the negative because in a situation like this the Secretary is not managing the wilderness but acting contrary to wilderness policy for the benefit of outsiders.

A fair reading of the Wilderness Act places a burden on the Secretary affirmatively to justify his actions under these circumstances. Where such actions are shown to contravene wilderness values guaranteed by the Wilderness Act, as they do here, then the Secretary must, when challenged, justify them by demonstrating they are necessary to effectively control the threatened outside harm that prompts the action being taken. Here the Secretary has not addressed this affirmative burden.

Plaintiffs have amply demonstrated that the Southern Pine Beetle program as carried out in these three Wilderness Areas was wholly antithetical to the wilderness policy established by Congress.

The destruction of many acres of pine trees by chain sawing, and chemical spraying accompanied by noise and personnel in a continuing process unlimited in scope, is hardly consonant with preservation and protection of these areas in their natural state. These are delicate, sensitive places where the often mysterious and unpredictable process of nature were [sic] to be preserved for the study and enjoyment of mankind. Congress directed that man must tread lightly in these areas, in awe and with respect. Ruthless intrusion in disregard for these values was condemned as a matter of national policy. While many facts remain unclear, the record before the Court suggests that within Wilderness Areas, as mature pines are destroyed by the beetle there will be less and less possibility of outbreaks infecting neighboring areas. Only a clear necessity for upsetting the equilibrium of the ecology could justify this highly injurious, semi-experimental venture of limited effectiveness.

The Secretary has failed to demonstrate that the Southern Pine Beetle program as carried out in the three Wilderness Areas is necessary to control the presence of that pest in neighboring pine forests or that it has in any way been more than marginally effective in doing so. There is little evidence relating to the effect of the program on the beetle's tendency, if any, to move out of the Wilderness Areas. Conversely, the Court has not received any material indicating whether adjacent pine land, which has been already infected by the beetle, could be managed with less effective controls in the absence of the accompanying Wilderness authority. Nor is the Secretary's weighing of alternatives apparent. The record strongly suggests that the beetle cannot be eradicated and the solution of the problem is long-term, dependent for its ultimate efficacy upon further research and scientific study.

While the Secretary's program covers the South, this particular case only concerns a limited aspect. Serious problems exist in other southern regions and indeed the United States District Court for the Eastern District of Texas has before it a challenge to the Southern Pine Beetle program as it affects five Wilderness Areas in Texas, *see Sierra Club v. Lyng*, No. L–85–69–CA (E.D.Tex.). That Court has also been awaiting the EIS. The problems in different regions in all probability vary and what may be a necessity in one Wilderness Area, or effective there, may not be so in another. The very generality of the Secretary's approach suggests inadequate sensitivity to his wilderness duties.

Because this Court's analysis raises issues not fully addressed in the papers and because it suggests a need to particularize any approach to the Southern Pine Beetle program in terms of each Wilderness Area, area by area, the Court has concluded that final resolution of the motion can most appropriately await the EIS. * * *

A little less than two months later, the Forest Service published a three-volume Final Programmatic EIS on "short-term beetle control" on national forest units in fourteen southern states (which included fifteen designated wilderness areas); and a "Record of Decision" (ROD) setting out the agency's final decision. The court then took up the Wilderness Act issues again.

Sierra Club v. Lyng II

United States District Court, District of Columbia, 1987.
663 F.Supp. 556.

■ GESELL, DISTRICT JUDGE.

* * * The Secretary's ROD greatly narrows the scope of the beetle control program in the Wilderness Areas from that in effect when this

litigation began. The Forest Service previously authorized the cutting of thousands of acres of wilderness pineland in an attempt, among other things, to create "buffer" areas against the spread of beetles—a process seriously unsettling to the values underlying the Wilderness Act. * * *

The Forest Service ultimately adopted the fourth of nine alternatives considered in detailing the FEIS, relating to beetle-control action within the Wilderness Areas.[4] Control efforts will be made under the program only: (1) to protect established woodpecker colony sites in immediate foraging areas; and (2) to protect "State and private lands, and high value Federal forest resources," excluding federal land being used for commercial timber operations. This alternative contemplates "spot-control" techniques confining cutting in the Wilderness Areas to edges contiguous to neighboring property. Cutting will be allowed only if a spot infestation of beetles is located within one-quarter mile of bordering non-wilderness lands, and a biological evaluation predicts the spot will expand into neighboring lands to be protected and cause unacceptable damage. A number of other cautionary factors must be considered in each site-by-site specific analysis prior to cutting. ROD, at 6–7.

The Forest Service emphasizes that under this selective approach, beetle control will be the exception; natural forces will be allowed "to play their role in the wilderness ecosystem," and "[i]t is only when these natural forces are predicted to threaten an essential [woodpecker] colony or cause unacceptable damage to specific resources adjacent to the wilderness that control in wilderness may be taken." ROD, at 1. It is emphasized that control efforts will be made only after detailed site-specific analysis.

Decisions on boundary cutting will take into account both the value of adjacent land and of the wilderness qualities damaged by control methods, and must be premised on a reasonable prediction that control will be effective. The Court has been assured, at argument on the motions, that no control efforts will be initiated in a Wilderness Area unless the owner of adjacent land to be protected has taken reasonable steps on the adjacent land to combat spread of the beetle and will continue such efforts. The public will be kept informed of control efforts and may object to site-specific control decisions. ROD, at 12–13.

Plaintiffs * * * persist in urging that the Secretary has not demonstrated that any boundary cutting of Wilderness Areas for the benefit of adjacent state and private timberland is "necessary" within the meaning of the Section.

Plaintiffs argue that no action by the Secretary can be deemed "necessary" unless the Secretary has first proven by scientific evidence that the contemplated spot-control cutting will be further effective in accomplishing the desired objectives. They seize on a dictionary definition of "necessary,"

4. Less intrusive options considered were those of allowing no cutting, and of allowing cutting only for the benefit of essential woodpecker colony sites. The more intrusive options considered were to allow cutting in the one-quarter mile boundary area also to benefit Federal commercial timberland, and to allowing cutting throughout the wilderness. See ROD at 5–8.

arguing that it can only mean "essential to a desirable . . . end," and urge that if control measures intruding on wilderness values have not been scientifically proven effective, by definition they cannot be necessary—i.e., essential—to control beetles.

Plaintiffs suggest the Secretary has little or no basis for concluding that the various spot-control methods that may be employed in the program will have any significant effect in controlling the spread of beetles to contiguous areas, and they attack past studies of control methods as scientifically unsophisticated, emphasizing that only area-wide control efforts can check the beetles. They note that in the regions of the country where spot control is contemplated under the program, beetles are generally present in both wilderness and non-wilderness areas, in varying degrees. Thus, the beetle does not present a natural hazard present only in Wilderness Areas that uniquely threatens uninfested adjacent lands; rather, it is indigenous to pineland areas generally, with beetles spreading back and forth between wilderness and non-wilderness land. Plaintiffs conclude that if control methods are adopted at all, they must be designed to check spread of the beetle in an entire area of pineland, because there is no other way of scientifically ensuring that even successful spot control applied in the border of a Wilderness Area will have lasting protective benefit to adjacent lands.

The degree of effectiveness of the spot-control methods to be employed under the program does remain in doubt. The record establishes considerable differences of opinion among biologists and other scientists studying the problem. The Secretary stresses the narrowness of the control allowed under the program, and the fact that a site-specific analysis must be employed before each control effort is undertaken. He cites numerous prior control efforts as supporting his view that the methods of spot control employed in the program have efficacy, and has concluded that the program will minimize significant harm from the spread of beetles.

Whether the Secretary has met his burden, on this record, of justifying intrusion on wilderness values for the benefit of adjacent landowners depends initially upon how Section 4(d)(1)'s allowance of "necessary" measures is interpreted. If plaintiffs are correct that only measures which are proven to be fully successful in effectively preventing the spread of beetles in an entire area are to be allowed, then the Secretary has failed to meet his burden; he admits that effective area-wide control measures have not yet been identified. If the statute incorporates a less stringent necessity standard, however, the record will support the Secretary's judgment.

Plaintiffs read the Act too broadly. First, there is no ground for concluding the Congress used the term "necessary" in the absolute sense urged by plaintiffs. Under the statute, various measures are authorized to the extent that they "may be necessary in the control . . . of insects. . . ." The most natural reading of the Section focuses on the phrase "necessary in the control." In this context "necessary" simply embraces measures "needed to achieve a certain result or effect," *American Heritage Dictionary of the English Language* 877 (1981)—that is, measures that are needed as part of a program designed to control, in the sense of restrain or curb, beetle infestations. Cf. McCulloch v. Maryland, 17 U.S. (4 Wheat.) 316, 421 (1819) (construing the necessary and proper clause of art. I, § 8, cl. 18, as sanctioning "all means which are appropriate, which are plainly adapted to [the desired] end").

The pertinent section of the statute is therefore most reasonably construed as allowing the Secretary to use measures that fall short of full effectiveness so long as they are reasonably designed to restrain or limit the threatened spread of beetle infestations from wilderness land onto the neighboring property, to its detriment.

The degree of efficacy of various control methods is not to be debated between various scientists and resolved before this Court. The Secretary's judgment that the control measures authorized are reasonably efficacious is entitled to respect under Section 10 of the Administrative Procedure Act, 5 U.S.C. § 706(2)(A) (1982), unless shown to be "arbitrary, capricious, an abuse of discretion, or otherwise not in accordance with law." Although the Secretary has not conducted the most elaborate studies of the proposed measures that are scientifically possible, and perhaps would have welcomed funds enabling him to do so,[9] the Court is satisfied that his judgment is reasonable given the information now available from the past actual experience of the Forest Service in combating the beetle threat, and available scientific opinion. Of great importance is the fact that the effectiveness of these measures will ultimately be determined by specific study of each potential spot-control site, and a decision to cut does not rest upon the promulgation of the Secretary's underlying policy decision alone.

One further point must also be stressed. The Secretary's burden under Section 4(d)(1) affirmatively to justify control actions taken for the benefit of adjacent landowners is grounded on the need to ensure that wilderness values are not unnecessarily sacrificed to promote the interests of adjacent landowners which Congress authorized the Secretary to protect. The Secretary has now made clear that unless adjacent landowners and federal authorities responsible for neighboring lands are following all reasonable means for combating beetles, the well-settled policies governing preservation of Wilderness Areas will not be compromised. Vigorous control efforts along the borders of wilderness land will be undertaken, therefore, only when met by equally vigorous efforts on adjacent land, ensuring that the burden of beetle control will not fall disproportionately on the Wilderness Areas. Those who seek protection of their lands must demonstrate to the Forest Service a willingness to share the burden of acting in a manner that will minimize any necessary intrusions upon wilderness values.

There are no material facts in dispute. The Secretary has met his burden. The Secretary's action is rational and not arbitrary. It constitutes a proper exercise of his discretion and contemplates action consistent with the requirements of the Wilderness Act as interpreted by the Court. [Defendants' motion for summary judgment granted.]

---

9. The lack of such studies was accounted for on the grounds of scientific feasi- bility and cost in the FEIS, at 2–20 to 2–21.

NOTES AND QUESTIONS

1.   The judicial intervention here seemed to have a significant impact on the agency's policy; e.g., the court noted at one point in the second opinion that the Secretary's ultimate decision "pays close attention to the Court's specification [in its first opinion] of the Secretary's burden." 663 F.Supp. at 560 n.10. The court's interpretation of the Wilderness Act was followed in a Texas case raising nearly identical issues. Sierra Club v. Lyng, 694 F.Supp. 1260, 1274 (E.D.Tex.1988), aff'd in part, vacated in part on other grounds sub nom. Sierra Club v. Yeutter, 926 F.2d 429 (5th Cir. 1991). See generally John Shurts, Resource Integration: Wilderness Management and the Southern Pine Beetle, 17 Envtl. L. 671 (1987).

2.   What is or should be the obligation of the federal managing agency where natural forces operating within wilderness areas may have impacts beyond their borders? (In a sense, this is the reverse of the "external threats" problem discussed in section B of this chapter, supra p. 1053.) Is Judge Gesell correct in saying that the agency has less discretion, and the courts should give closer scrutiny, to management actions that are undertaken not to promote wilderness values, but instead to protect "outside commercial and other private interests"? Is it fair to reverse the burden of proof as a counterweight to pressure agencies will usually feel from outside commercial interests?

3.   Would the result have been the same if the Forest Service had not required rigorous control measures on the adjacent land outside the wilderness?

4.   Would it make a difference if the southern pine beetle were an exotic pest, imported from abroad, and thus poses an "unnatural" threat to wilderness?

5.   Should the federal agencies fight fires in wilderness areas? Only those caused by human activity as opposed to natural forces (lightning)? Only those that could conceivably threaten persons and property outside the boundaries of the area? See, e.g., J. Hendee, G. Stankey & R. Lucas, WILDERNESS MANAGEMENT 263–78 (1978) (2d ed. 1990).

6.   Proposals are occasionally made to seed clouds over wilderness areas in order to enhance precipitation to benefit water users downstream from wilderness areas. If the best scientific evidence is that such man-induced precipitation would generally not exceed variations in precipitation that could naturally occur, is such cloud-seeding lawful? Might it be lawful if it were done from airplanes, but not if it were done from ground-based generators inside the wilderness areas?

E.   *Access to Non–Federal Inholdings.*   16 U.S.C. § 1134(a) requires the Secretary of Agriculture to give a non-federal property owner (state or private) whose land is "completely surrounded" by national forest wilderness, "such rights as may be necessary to assure adequate access" to the land, "or the [inholding] * * * shall be exchanged for" federal land of "approximately equal value" elsewhere in the state. Somewhat curiously, the latter clause is not clear on whether the choice to provide access or an exchange is the Forest Service's or the inholder's. The Attorney General has opined that the choice is the federal agency's, Op. Atty.Gen. (June 23, 1980), and the Ninth Circuit has agreed that "the Secretary has the option of exchanging land of equal value so that the wilderness may be preserved." Montana Wilderness Ass'n v. U.S. Forest Service, 655 F.2d 951, 957 n. 12 (9th Cir.1981), cert. denied, 455 U.S. 989 (1982).

Subsection (b) of this section requires the Secretary of Agriculture to "permit ingress and egress * * * by means which have been or are being customarily enjoyed with respect to other such areas similarly situated" to "valid mining claims or other valid occupancies * * * wholly within a designated national forest wilderness area * * *." But it also says that the Secretary shall impose "reasonable regulations consistent with the preservation of the area as wilderness." No published litigation has tested the implementation of this subsection.

F. *Water Resources.* In the deliberations leading up to enactment of the Wilderness Act, traditional water resource development interests in the west (sometimes known as "water buffaloes") fought for the opportunity to build water projects inside wilderness areas. Wilderness advocates resisted, and the congressional compromise left the President (rather than the agency head or Cabinet officer) with the discretion, "under such regulations as he may deem desirable, [to] authorize" water resource development projects and ancillary facilities, included roads, "upon his determination that such use or uses in the specific area will better serve the interests of the United States and the people thereof than will its denial." 16 U.S.C. § 1133(d)(4). The authority has never been exercised, although former President Gerald Ford reportedly had to lobby his successor Ronald Reagan not to invoke the provision to thwart a proposed water project in a wilderness area near Vail, Colorado. The legislative history suggests this provision was intended to allow only small scale water projects. Also on water, section 1133(d)(6) provides that "nothing in this chapter shall constitute an express or implied claim or denial on the part of the Federal Government as to exemption from state water laws." On the Presidential exemption and the general question of federal reserved water rights in wilderness (the latter discussed in Chapter 6, supra pp. 535–36), see John Leshy, Water and Wilderness/Law and Politics, XXIII Land & Water L.Rev. 389, 402–04 (1988).

G. *Commercial Enterprises and Services.* Section 1133(c) contains a general ban, "subject to existing private rights," on any "commercial enterprise * * * within any wilderness area." It also prohibits, among other things, any "structure or installation" within any such area "except as necessary to meet minimum requirements for the administration of the area." Section 1133(d)(5) provides that "[c]ommercial services may be performed" within wilderness areas "to the extent necessary for activities which are proper for realizing the recreational or other wilderness purposes of the areas." This applies to services provided by outfitters, guides, river-runners and the like. In Wilderness Watch v. Robertson, 978 F.2d 1484 (9th

Cir.1992), the court upheld the Forest Service's allowance of certain permanent installations by commercial outfitters in designated wilderness. The court found the agency should manage the wilderness "with an eye not only toward strict conservation, but also to ensure the 'use and enjoyment of the American people.'" and the installations were appropriate to "make the Wilderness accessible to those Americans who wish to use it." Is this consistent with the definition of wilderness in the Act, supra p. 1110? Cf. Zumwalt v. United States, 928 F.2d 951, 953 n. 3 (10th Cir.1991), holding that the discretionary function exception of the Federal Tort Claims Act barred a suit to recover for injuries sustained in a fall in a cave in a national park wilderness area, quoted from the Park Service's relevant management policies:

> The visitor must accept wilderness largely on its own terms. Modern conveniences are not provided for the comfort of the visitor; and the risks of wilderness travel, of possible danger from accidents, wildlife, and natural phenomena must be accepted as part of the wilderness experience.

See also High Sierra Hikers Ass'n v. Powell, 150 F.Supp.2d 1023 (N.D.Cal. 2001) (despite the court's "serious concerns" about evidence of environmental degradation, held, the Forest Service did not abuse "its broad discretion under the very general requirements of the Wilderness Act" by allowing large pack groups with stock to use wilderness areas); Isle Royale Boaters Ass'n v. Norton, 154 F.Supp.2d 1098 (W.D.Mich.2001) (a campground is neither a "structure" nor an "installation" within the meaning of the Wilderness Act).

All sorts of nice questions can be raised. A state project took eggs from salmon in Lake Tustumena in designated wilderness in the Kenai National Wildlife Refuge in Alaska, raised the fry in a hatchery outside the wilderness, and released them back into the Lake. When the fry grew into mature salmon, they were harvested commercially outside the wilderness area. (The state activity was ongoing when Congress designated the wilderness area, but the designation legislation was silent on the subject.) Is this a "commercial enterprise * * * within [a] wilderness area" prohibited by § 1133(c)?

H. *Hunting and Fishing.* Section 1133(d)(7) provides that "nothing in this Chapter shall be construed as affecting the jurisdiction or responsibilities of the several States with respect to wildlife and fish in the national forests;" thus hunting and fishing are generally allowed in most wilderness areas. Does the Forest Service have authority to set seasons or bag limits? To order closures of specified areas in order to protect wilderness values? Does FLPMA help answer this last question? Recall the Alaska Wolf Kill litigation, Chapter 10, supra p. 895. In O'Brien v. State, 711 P.2d 1144 (Wyo.1986), the court relied on this section in holding that the Wilderness Act did not preempt a state law requiring non-resident hunters to employ guides when hunting in federal wilderness areas.

Should managing agencies be under a legal obligation to reintroduce native species of flora and fauna that have been extirpated from wilderness areas; even those (like the wolf and the grizzly bear) that could pose a threat to persons or property inside or outside the wilderness? Should agencies have a duty to eliminate non-native species that have been introduced into such areas, even those (like certain species of sport fish) that attract substantial recreational use? See, e.g., Dan Rohlf & Doug Honnold, Managing the Balances of Nature: The Legal Framework of Wilderness Management, 15 Ecology L.Q. 249 (1988).

I. *Exceptions and Variations.* Of course, Congress can make exceptions to any of these rules, or draw entirely different rules if it wants, in designating particular areas as part of the National Wilderness Preservation System. For example, a special provision in the Wilderness Act itself authorized logging in one specific wilderness area, the Boundary Waters Canoe Area in northern Minnesota. See Minnesota Public Interest Research Group v. Butz, 541 F.2d 1292 (8th Cir.1976). This exception provoked enough controversy for Congress to revisit it in 1978, resulting in the designation of the 1,075,500–acre Boundary Water Canoe Area Wilderness, consisting of the BWCA plus additions to it. The Act repealed the provision allowing logging, and provided for the termination of all timber contracts within one year after passage. Among other things, the Act also directed the Secretary to "expedite the intensification of resource management including emphasis on softwood timber production and hardwood utilization on the national forest lands in Minnesota outside the wilderness to offset" the reduction in harvest from the wilderness. The BWCAW Act is highly specific and includes many compromise provisions as to the use of motorboats and snowmobiles in specified areas. Section 11 of the 1978 Amendment established a mouthful entitled the Boundary Waters Canoe Area Mining Protection Area, an adjacent buffer zone of 222,000 acres where mining is prohibited so that adverse impacts from mining will not infringe on the wilderness area. See generally Minnesota v. Block, Chapter 3, supra p. 199. It also included a specific provision which directed the Secretary of Agriculture to terminate certain previously allowed motorized portages between certain lakes unless she "determines that there is no feasible nonmotorized means of transporting boats across the portages." 92 Stat. 1649. In Friends of Boundary Waters Wilderness v. Robertson, 978 F.2d 1484 (8th Cir.1992), cert. denied sub nom City of Ely v. Friends of the Boundary Waters Wilderness, 508 U.S. 972 (1993), the court, over a dissent, disagreed with the Secretary's interpretation of "feasible" as meaning "reasonable," "practicable," or "likely," and held that the purposes of the Wilderness Act were best served by interpreting "feasible" to mean "physically possible."

J. *Buffer Zones.* A number of statutes designating particular wilderness areas disclaim any intent on the part of Congress to create "protective perimeters or buffer zones around each wilderness area." See, e.g., Arkansas Wilderness Act, § 7, 98 Stat. at 2352 (1984). In Newton County Wildlife Ass'n v. Rogers, 141 F.3d 803 (8th Cir.1998), the court relied on this language to reject a challenge to Forest Service timber sales outside of and upstream from designated wilderness areas, on the ground that the logging would degrade the quality of water in streams flowing through the designated wilderness. If the Forest Service prohibited an activity outside a wilderness areas "solely because of its potential effect" on the area, it would violate the "no buffer zone" idea. The court went on, however, to conclude that the agency had "thoroughly considered the effect of logging and road construction on the water quality" of the streams in question, and concluded that it would be "insignificant," and the court found this not arbitrary or capricious. A similar interpretation was made in Northwest Motorcycle Ass'n v. U.S. Dept. of Agriculture, 18 F.3d 1468, 1480 (9th Cir.1994), where the court upheld a Forest Service decision to eliminate ORV use in an area adjacent to a designated wilderness area, because it did so for numerous resource management reasons, including user conflicts, and not solely to create a buffer zone around the wilderness, even though the proximity to the wilderness was one factor in the agency's decision.

Most wilderness areas are not simply left alone after designation. Inevitably, some degree of human regulation or management is required. As demand for "wilderness experiences" grows, some areas may be "loved to death." Philosophical questions of purity become concrete when officials are faced with fires, insect attacks, rescue operations, trail maintenance, hunting, sanitation, and pack trains. Activities on adjacent lands also pose management problems. See J. Hendee, G. Stankey, & R. Lucas, WILDERNESS MANAGEMENT 137–46 (1978); Roderick Nash, WILDERNESS AND THE AMERICAN MIND 316–41 (3rd ed. 1982).

Congress has recognized that preservation of the wilderness resource requires protection of the quality of its air as well as preservation of land and the living things on it. One part of the Clean Air Act, 42 U.S.C. §§ 7470–7492, restricts construction of major emitting facilities that will cause significant deterioration of air quality in areas zoned as "Class I;" which includes designated wilderness areas over 5,000 acres (as well as national parks over 6,000 acres) in existence on August 7, 1977; id., § 7472. Wilderness areas over 10,000 acres designated after that date may be redesignated as Class I under id., § 7474; see Kerr–McGee Chemical Corp. v. U.S. Department of Interior, 709 F.2d 597 (9th Cir.1983).

The stereotypical wilderness user is a "yuppie;" young, urban, professional. Several studies show, however, that while wilderness visitors tend to be slightly younger than average, all age classes are fairly well represented. Also, users are only moderately above-average in income, and as much rural as urban. Characteristics of wilderness users are skewed in only one respect: they tend to be relatively well educated. Thus "the stereotype is largely a myth * * * and should be discarded once and for all." J. Hendee, et al., supra, at 304–06. And contrary to the arguments often heard that wilderness designation has a dampening effect on economic activity, studies have shown a positive correlation between the proportion of land in a county that is designated as wilderness and county per capita income.

3.   EXPANDING THE WILDERNESS SYSTEM

Most of the wilderness areas designated in the Wilderness Act or shortly thereafter were so-called "rocks and ice" areas—high altitude, remote, relatively inaccessible and with few known resources of demand in the marketplace like timber and minerals. From passage of the Act, however, wilderness advocates have pushed for more and more designations, which have become more controversial over time. Since 1964, the wilderness study and designation process has proceeded apace.

Scrutiny of candidate areas for addition to the National Wilderness Preservation System has been conducted under several different processes, varying mostly by agency, with somewhat differing legal consequences. The first of these wilderness study programs was initiated by the Wilderness Act itself. In addition to creating "instant wilderness," it called for studies of three different categories of land for wilderness suitability, each to be completed within ten years: (a) Forest Service lands then administratively designated as primitive areas; (b) all roadless areas over 5000 acres and roadless islands of any size in the National Wildlife Refuge System; and (c) all National Park Service roadless areas of more than 5000 acres. 16 U.S.C. § 1133. Beyond this, in 1967 the Forest Service embarked on a voluntary study—beyond the requirements of the Wilderness Act itself—of all of its roadless lands—well over fifty million acres—for possible designation as wilderness. In 1976, FLPMA required a study of the wilderness potential of all roadless areas over 5000 acres on BLM lands, some 25 million acres. These last two major wilderness study efforts are treated in some detail further below.

Congress has enacted dozens of statutes designating new wilderness areas. Each added area is governed generally by the provisions in the 1964 Act, although the legislation designating specific areas may vary these generic requirements in local settings. Usually (though nothing requires this) Congress has found it easier to consider wilderness bills on a state-wide basis, by individual federal managing agency. The Alaska National Interest Lands Conservation Act of 1980, 16 U.S.C. § 3101–3233, was easily the largest wilderness legislation; it designated 56.4 million Alaskan acres as wilderness, nearly two-thirds of the entire system. All wilderness areas are listed in the Historical Note after 16 U.S.C. § 1132. The following charts show the size of the National Wilderness Preservation System as of 1999 (including and excluding Alaska):

Agency	Units	Acres (in millions)	% of Total
Forest Service	400	34.77	33.2%
National Park Service	44	44.05	42.1%
U.S. Fish & Wildlife Service	71	20.69	19.8%
BLM	133	5.24	5.0%
	628	104.74	

Excluding Alaska			
Agency	Units	Acres (in millions)	% of Total
Forest Service	381	29.01	62.3%
National Park Service	36	10.30	22.1%
U.S. Fish & Wildlife Service	50	2.01	4.3%
BLM	133	5.24	11.3%
	600	46.56	

Source: Peter Landres and Shannon Meyer, A National Wilderness Preservation System Database: Key Attributes and Trends, 1964–99 (USDA Forest Service General Technical Report, 2000).

One of the issues raised in many wilderness studies is how "purely natural" an area has to be to receive wilderness consideration. For quite some time, for example, the Forest Service was very reluctant to recommend wilderness designation for areas in the eastern United States. Many of these areas, almost all of which had been acquired under the Weeks Act, had been logged or otherwise developed decades earlier. Others argued that this was too narrow a construction on the definition of wilderness in the Act. That definition seemed to offer something to each side of this "purity" debate, speaking as it did of areas "untrammeled by man" and "retaining * * * primeval character and influence," but also speaking of areas "generally *appear[ing]* to have been affected *primarily* by the forces of nature, with the imprint of man's work *substantially* unnoticeable." 16 U.S.C. § 1131(c) (emphasis added). Eventually the Forest Service adopted a more liberal view of wilderness for study purposes, and Congress has itself not hesitated to embrace wilderness that was less than pristine. For example, in its report on the Endangered American Wilderness Act of 1978, 92 Stat. 40, the House Interior Committee disapproved of the view that an area could be disqualified where "any trace of man's activity" was present, and where the "sights and sounds" of cities (often many miles away) could be perceived from anywhere in candidate areas. It welcomed consideration of areas not necessarily "entirely free of the marks of mankind, but [which are] fully capable of providing in the long term, wilderness benefits to many people." H.R.Rep. No. 540 (95th Cong., 1st Sess. 4–6 (1977)). Two years earlier, finding that areas in "the more populous eastern half of the United States are increasingly threatened by the pressures of a growing and more mobile population, [and] large-scale industrial and economic growth," Congress designated as wilderness 15 national forest areas totaling 206,988 acres in Alabama, Arkansas, Florida, Georgia, Kentucky, North Carolina, New Hampshire, South Carolina, Tennessee, Virginia, Vermont, West Virginia, and Wisconsin. Pub.L. No. 93–622, 88 Stat. 2096. Many more eastern areas have been designated since then.

In the national park and national wildlife refuge systems, wilderness tends to be handled in a relatively low-key manner. These areas are generally not subject to uses such as timber harvesting and mining, and roadbuilding is carefully controlled and limited. De facto wilderness in these areas is not, therefore, subject to much development pressure. A rare bit of litigation led to Voyageurs Region National Park Ass'n v. Lujan, 966 F.2d 424 (8th Cir.1992), where the court reviewed a Park Service decision to establish a snowmobile trail in a wilderness study area. The applicable NPS regulation said that potential wilderness areas shall be managed "in such manner as will leave them unimpaired for future use and enjoyment as wilderness, with inconsistent uses held to a minimum." 43 C.F.R. § 19.6. The Department waived this policy by memorandum after the litigation was filed, relying on the fact that (a) the Voyageurs Park enabling legislation authorized the Secretary, "when planning for development of the park, [to] include appropriate provisions for * * * winter sports, including the use of snowmobiles;" (b) the trail would not be artificially hardened and would require only minimal clearing and signing, and would not "preclude future designation as wilderness if snowmobile use were discontinued," and (c) widely dispersed snowmobile use had occurred in the area before the Park was designated, and confining the use to a corridor would be preferable. The court upheld the Park Service.

Wilderness advocates have not, in general, focused all that much attention on securing legislation to designate Park and Refuge wilderness areas, and Congress has generally moved at a leisurely pace in making such designations. In both agencies, the acreage designated is heavily skewed toward Alaska. Eight Park Service designated wilderness areas in that state comprise more than 80% of the total park system wilderness acreage; just three of them—Gates of the Arctic Wilderness (over 7 million acres); Noatak Wilderness (5.8 million acres); and Wrangell–Saint Elias Wilderness (8.7 million acres)—together comprise over one-half of all National Park wilderness acres. Twenty-one of the Fish & Wildlife Service's 71 designated wilderness areas are in Alaska, and they contain more than 90% of the total acreage. General Interior Department wilderness management regulations are found at 43 C.F.R. Part 19 (2001).

De facto wilderness study and management in the U.S. Forest Service and the BLM have commanded the most attention and raised the most controversy. These are examined in turn.

A. The National Forest System

As noted above, the Wilderness Act itself required the Secretary of Agriculture to study all Forest Service lands administratively designated as "primitive areas" and recommend to the President, and the President to recommend to the Congress, whether such areas should be designated as wilderness. This gave rise to the first major court decision to address wilderness study issues, and the decision established a practice of strict scrutiny of agency decisions that could affect wilderness values that has largely been followed since. In Parker v. United States, 448 F.2d 793 (10th Cir.1971), cert. denied, 405 U.S. 989 (1972), the question was whether the Forest Service could sell timber in a national forest area that was adjacent to, but not within, such a "primitive area." The section of the Wilderness Act that called for a study and report to Congress on whether such "primitive areas" were suitable for designation as wilderness also provided that it should not "limit the President in * * * recommending the addition of any contiguous area of national forest lands predominantly of wilderness value." 16 U.S.C. § 1132(b). This seemed to leave it up to the executive branch to decide what to do with these adjacent areas, but the court didn't see it that way. The court began by describing the general purpose of the wilderness study provision this way:

> It is simply a congressional acknowledgment of the necessity of pre-
> serving one factor of our natural environment from the progressive,
> destructive and hasty inroads of man, usually commercial in nature,
> and the enactment of a "proceed slowly" order until it can be deter-
> mined wherein the balance between proper multiple uses of the wilder-

ness lies and the most desirable and highest use established for the present and future. A concerned Congress, reflecting the wishes of a concerned public, did by statutory definition choose terminology that would seem to indicate its ultimate mandate.

The court then held that the Forest Service and the timber company to whom it had sold timber in the area adjacent to the "primitive area" could not proceed to harvest the timber:

> Should we, in the case at bar, concede to federal appellants the discretionary right to destroy the wilderness value of the subject area, one contiguous to a designated wilderness, we would render meaningless the clear intent of Congress expressed in 16 U.S.C. § 1132(b) that both the President and the Congress shall have a meaningful opportunity to add contiguous areas predominantly of wilderness value to existing primitive areas for final wilderness designation. This statutory limitation on agency discretion is, of course, a narrow one dictated by necessity as contained in the definition of wilderness and by the specifics of the statutory words creating the limitation.

The court also ordered the Forest Service to include its study of the adjacent area in its report to the President and Congress, although it conceded that this did not limit the Secretary or the President in decided what to recommend to Congress about the future of the area.

Parker may have taken some liberties with the narrow statutory language, but its general thrust of limiting the discretion of federal land managing agencies to take wilderness-destroying actions in advance of congressional decision has endured.

The Wilderness Act made no mention of the largest category of roadless areas in the national land estate—those wild lands in the National Forest System not already classified as wilderness or primitive areas or adjacent thereto. In a momentous step, the Forest Service voluntarily undertook, in 1967, a comprehensive wilderness study process of its roadless lands. This first Roadless Area Review and Evaluation (RARE I) evaluated all such areas for their wilderness potential, as a complement to the congressionally mandated study of primitive areas. The RARE I inventory was released in 1972. It included 1449 areas totaling 56 million acres. Because this massive wilderness study was not mandated by the Wilderness Act, that statute provided no basis for judicial review. By this time, however, NEPA had been enacted, and it did give wilderness advocates a tool they have used frequently since.

When the Forest Service offered timber for sale in some of these inventoried roadless areas, the Sierra Club promptly filed suit under NEPA, and a district court in San Francisco preliminarily enjoined any new timber sales on RARE lands across the country until NEPA compliance was achieved. Sierra Club v. Butz, 3 ELR 20071 (N.D.Cal.1972). Soon thereafter the Tenth Circuit dropped a second shoe, by enjoining timber harvesting under some *existing* contracts in roadless areas because NEPA had not been complied with. Wyoming Outdoor Coordinating Council v. Butz, 484 F.2d 1244 (10th Cir.1973). The court, echoing its earlier decision in *Parker*, found "there is an overriding public interest in preservation of the undeveloped character of the area."

The final national EIS on RARE I lands was released in October 1973. It dropped most roadless areas from the inventory and selected 274 areas totalling 12.3 million acres for detailed study for wilderness suitability. On RARE I, see J. Hendee, G. Stankey, & R. Lucas, WILDERNESS MANAGEMENT 99–105 (1978). The RARE I study lagged after the 1973 EIS. With the advent of a new Administration in 1977, the Forest Service essentially started over by developing a new roadless area inventory and a new study process, which naturally became known as RARE II. The new inventory included 2918 units (more than twice as many as RARE I) comprising slightly more than 62 million acres—six million more acres than RARE I and one-third of all land within the national forest system. The Final RARE II EIS was released in early 1979. It recommended Congress designate 15 million acres of RARE II lands as Wilderness, called for further assessment of 10.8 million acres, and allocated the remaining 36 million acres to Nonwilderness.

Once again wilderness advocates returned to court, challenging the adequacy of the agency's NEPA compliance, and once again the courts responded. In California v. Block, 690 F.2d 753 (9th Cir.1982), the court sent the agency back to the drawing boards. The court described the "fundamental issue" as whether the Forest Service had made a critical decision with respect to lands it designated for nonwilderness uses.

> The Forest Service argues that the district court erred in concluding that Nonwilderness designation is tantamount to a decision to permit development. It emphasizes that the RARE II process is only the first step in a multi-stage planning process to allocate roadless areas to competing social uses. At this step, the Service contends, a RARE II Nonwilderness designation means only that the areas will not be considered for inclusion in the NWPS during the first generation of forest management plans under the NFMA, a period lasting between ten to fifteen years. In the meantime the Forest Service will entertain specific development proposals concerning these areas, but will prepare separate EIS's if federal action is contemplated and will consider wilderness values in devising forest plans for these areas. Given the limited impact of the Nonwilderness designation, the Forest Service urges that it is permissible to limit the scope of the EIS to a generalized discussion of the designations' overall impact.

> California argues, and the district court agreed, that the Forest Service unfairly minimizes the consequences of the Nonwilderness designation. California and the district court decision focus upon the following Forest Service regulation pertaining to Nonwilderness designated areas:

>> Lands reviewed for Wilderness designation under the review and evaluation of roadless areas conducted by the Secretary of Agriculture but not designated as wilderness or designated for further planning * * * will be managed for uses other than wilderness in accordance with this subpart. No such area will be considered for

designation as wilderness until a revision of the forest plan under § 219.11(f) * * *.

36 C.F.R. § 219.12(e) (1981).

California and the district court decision interpret this regulation to mean that the Forest Service will not consider a Nonwilderness area's *wilderness features* for *any* purpose during the area's forest plan life. Thus, while an EIS on specific development proposals will consider substantial pollution effects, California argues that the Forest Service will be precluded from considering the desirability of utilizing the proposed site as a wilderness area, and will not consider wilderness features (e.g., solitude, primitive character and wilderness recreation) in assessing the environmental consequences. They conclude that if the wilderness features and values of each Nonwilderness area are ever to be individually evaluated, they must be evaluated now.

On balance, we conclude that California's description of the effect of Nonwilderness designation is more accurate and therefore affirm the district court. We agree with the Forest Service that the *last* sentence in the above quoted regulation only restricts the Forest Service from considering Nonwilderness areas for Wilderness designation, and does not explicitly forbid the Forest Service from considering Nonwilderness areas' wilderness features or values in devising forest plans. The sentence that *precedes* this clause, however, explicitly mandates that Nonwilderness areas "will be managed for uses other than wilderness." This command is not subject to any ambiguity. At least during the first generation of forest plans, Nonwilderness designated areas will be managed for purposes other than wilderness preservation. This command is repeated in the text of the Final EIS itself, which indicates that "[a]reas allocated to nonwilderness *will* become available on April 15, 1979, for multiple resource use activities *other than wilderness.*"

Future decisions concerning these areas will be constrained by this choice. While the regulations technically permit consideration of wilderness values and features in forest planning, such consideration is pointless in the absence of the discretion to manage a Nonwilderness area in a manner consistent with wilderness preservation. Similarly, the promise of site-specific EIS's in the future is meaningless if later analysis cannot consider wilderness preservation as an alternative to development. The "critical decision" to commit these areas for nonwilderness uses, at least for the next ten to fifteen years, is "irreversible and irretrievable." The site-specific impact of this decisive allocative decision must therefore be carefully scrutinized now and not when specific development proposals are made. * * *

[The court went on to conclude that the final RARE II EIS was woefully lacking in site-specific consideration of the areas it recommended for nonwilderness uses.] Under Forest Service regulations, Nonwilderness areas may be reconsidered for Wilderness System inclusion in devising the second generation of forest plans ten to fifteen years hence. In the interim, however, these areas will be managed for uses other than wilderness. The foreclosing of the wilderness management option requires a careful assessment of how this new management strategy will affect each area's benchmark characteristics as identified in the Wilderness Act.

* * * While the EIS carefully identifies the economic benefit attributable to development in each area, no effort is made to weigh this benefit against the wilderness loss each area will suffer from development. This evaluation need not be in the form of a formal cost benefit analysis, but it should reflect that the Forest Service has compared for each area the potential benefits of Nonwilderness management against the potential adverse environmental consequences. * * *

We concede that conducting a detailed site-specific analysis of the RARE II decision will be no simple task and will be laden with empirical uncertainty. The scope of the undertaking here, however, was the Forest Service's choice and not the courts'. NEPA contains no exemptions for projects of national scope. Having decided to allocate simultaneously millions of acres of land to nonwilderness use, the Forest Service may not rely upon forecasting difficulties or the task's magnitude to excuse the absence of a reasonably thorough site-specific analysis of the decision's environmental consequences.

NOTES AND QUESTIONS

1.   On the EIS's lack of specificity in commenting upon individual roadless areas, the district court opinion noted (483 F.Supp. at 486 n. 22):

> The comments are of a brief, and very general nature. For example, one comment under the "opportunity for solitude" attribute merely stated "good topographical variation." The type of land features or vegetation present in this area is undisclosed. Major features of an area are reduced to highly generalized description such as "mountain" or "river." One can hypothesize how the Grand Canyon might be rated: "Canyon with river, little vegetation."

2.   Does the decision in this case suggest that the RARE process—representing a systematic, nation-wide, comprehensive single process to evaluate wilderness suitability—was a mistake? If the agency had not embarked on the RARE II process, it would still have had to consider impacts on possible wilderness designation each time it undertook to sell timber or build roads or otherwise take actions in de facto wilderness that threatened the area's potential for designation as wilderness. But it would have arguably been easier, and less controversial, to take such action individually and locally, than in a high visibility effort. Compare the Clinton Administration's undertaking of its "roadless area initiative" recounted in Chapter 8, supra pp. 758–72.

3.   The injunction entered in *California v. Block* covered only roadless areas recommended for non-wilderness in California, but it was still a major blow to the Forest Service wilderness review program, because it effectively called into question the entire RARE II process. Shortly thereafter the Reagan Administration announced plans to scrap RARE II and start over with a new program dubbed (surprise) "RARE III," but soon Congress

itself stepped into the breach, substantially short-circuiting the RARE III process in many states by passing nineteen separate wilderness bills in 1984 alone, adding nearly nine million acres (nearly all of it national forest land studied in the RARE II process) to the NWPS. This outburst included individual state bills for Arizona (1 million acres), Arkansas, California (3.2 million acres), Florida, Georgia, Mississippi, New Hampshire, New Mexico, North Carolina, Oregon (850,000 acres), Pennsylvania, Tennessee, Texas, Utah (750,000 acres), Vermont, Virginia, Washington (1 million acres), Wisconsin, and Wyoming (883,000 acres). Congress failed to reach agreement on bills for national forest land in Colorado, Idaho, Montana, and several states with smaller amounts of potential wilderness. RARE II bills were enacted in Nevada in 1989, and Colorado in 1993.

4. As explained in the following discussion of "release," the courts continue to hold agencies to a standard of strict accountability under NEPA when they propose to take actions on roadless lands that have the effect of removing an area from consideration for designation as wilderness.

THE FUTURE OF WILDERNESS CONSIDERATION: THE "RELEASE" ISSUE

For a long time a major point of contention in Forest Service (and BLM) wilderness legislation was the extent to which a congressional decision *not* to designate particular roadless tracts as statutory wilderness "released" them from further wilderness consideration in individual forest (or BLM) land use plans and NEPA decisionmaking. The timber and minerals industries and other wilderness opponents generally advocated what came to be known as "hard" release; namely, that once Congress has decided not to designate a particular area as wilderness in a piece of wilderness legislation, it should be fully and permanently made available for non-wilderness uses without the need for further restrictions or evaluation. Wilderness advocates, on the other hand, argued for no release; they wanted the agency to continue to consider the wilderness option in plans and EISs on development proposals so long as the area in question remained roadless.

The chasm between "hard" and no release stymied legislative action on wilderness for some time. In 1984 Congress adopted a compromise formula that came to be known as (surprise) "soft" release, and thereafter included it in individual bills. "Soft" release means that roadless areas not designated by Congress as wilderness in a bill are "released" from further consideration until the next generation of land use plans is prepared by the agency. The 1984 Washington State Wilderness Act (WSWA), 98 Stat. 299, contained typical "soft release" language, which came in two parts: One part provided that, with respect to lands reviewed in the RARE II process, and roadless lands less than 5000 acres in size, "the Department of Agriculture shall not be required to review the wilderness option prior to the revisions of the [NFMA] plans, but shall review the wilderness option when the plans are revised, which revisions will ordinarily occur on a ten-year cycles, or at least every fifteen years * * *." In the meantime, such areas "shall be managed for multiple use: in accordance with applicable plans." 98 Stat. 272 (1984) (WSWA § 5). The other part aimed at preventing further environmental challenges to its decision to release roadless lands in the Washington National Forest System. The Act directed that RARE II be deemed adequate consideration of the suitability of inventoried land for classification as wilderness. WSWA § 5(b)(2), 98 Stat. at 303. Specifically, it said, "without passing on the question of the legal and factual sufficiency of the RARE II [EIS] * * * with respect to * * * [national forest] lands in states other than Washington, such [EIS] shall not be subject to judicial review with respect to [national forest] lands in the State of Washington." 98 Stat. 303, § 5(b)(1).

The net effect was that the WSWA provided general immunity for the Forest Service from wilderness-based judicial review for the time being with one exception: It was required to consider the wilderness option prior to authorizing development in a roadless area if (1) the area had not been inventoried pursuant to RARE II; *and* (2) the area is larger than 5,000 acres in size. The implications of this "soft release" language were explored in Smith v. United States Forest Service, 33 F.3d 1072 (9th Cir.1994), where plaintiff wilderness advocates claimed that the Forest Service had failed in NEPA documents to address the impact of a timber sale on a roadless area of more than 6000 acres. The tract in question consisted of 4200 acres of uninventoried land and 2000 acres of inventoried land. The court concluded that under § 5(b) of the WSWA, it could "not review the adequacy of the agency's consideration of the wilderness option for this land because a portion of the land was inventoried pursuant to RARE II and the remainder is smaller than 5,000 acres."

Plaintiff then argued that even if the agency does not have to consider the "wilderness option," it still had a legal duty to consider the effect on the area's roadless character before deciding to sell timber in the area, and the court should enforce that duty. The Forest Service countered that the

> sole significance of the fact that a parcel of land is roadless is that the parcel is potentially eligible for wilderness designation. Because Congress has, in the WSWA, precluded judicial review of the suitability of inventoried lands for inclusion into the wilderness system, the appellees argue, the fact that a parcel of released land is roadless is, in itself, immaterial and need not be addressed in NEPA documents.

The court rejected the Forest Service's argument. It relied on an earlier decision, National Audubon Society v. U.S. Forest Service, 4 F.3d 832 (9th Cir.1993), which construed identical language in the 1984 Oregon Wilderness Act not to preclude judicial review of the agency's decision not to consider the effect of the proposed sale on roadless parcels of inventoried land. The language prohibiting judicial review, the court said in *National Audubon*, "applies not to *roadless or roaded* determinations, but to the Act's *wilderness or non-wilderness* designations. * * * Further, the Act provides that review of the *wilderness* option, and not of the *roadless* option," is not required prior to plan revision. 4 F.3d at 837 (emphasis in original). The court in *Smith* continued:

The distinction we drew in *National Audubon* between wilderness designations and roadless determinations would be meaningless if, as the appellees suggest, an area's roadless character has no environmental significance. As we stated in that case, "the decision to harvest timber on a previously undeveloped tract of land is 'an irreversible and irretrievable decision' which could have 'serious environmental consequences.'" Id. at 842 (quoting the lower court opinion). That the land has been released by Congress for nonwilderness use does not excuse the agency from complying with its NEPA obligations when implementing a land-use program.

There is, moreover, an additional significance, beyond the effect on "roadlessness," to the agency's decision to approve a logging sale on a 5,000 acre roadless area. Judicial review of the wilderness option is not foreclosed forever by the WSWA. Under that Act, the wilderness option for inventoried lands may be revisited in second-generation Forest Plans. WSWA § 5(b)(2), 98 Stat. at 303; National Audubon, 4 F.3d at 837. Accordingly, when the agency is considering the development of a 5,000 acre roadless area, selection of a no-action alternative, which the agency is required to consider [under NEPA], would preserve the possibility that the area might some day be designated as wilderness. Clearly, under the WSWA, the agency is not required to preserve any released roadless area for wilderness consideration in second-generation Forest Plans. WSWA § 5(b)(3), 98 Stat. at 303. But the possibility of future wilderness classification triggers, at the very least, an obligation on the part of the agency to disclose the fact that development will affect a 5,000 acre roadless area.

The Forest Service argues that even if the fact that an area is roadless is environmentally significant, the documents it prepared in this case—the Colville Forest Plan EIS and the Gatorson EA—are adequate under NEPA. "Roadless character," the Forest Service asserts, is merely a synonym for specific environmental resources, including soil quality, water quality, vegetation, wildlife and fishery resources, recreational value, and scenic quality. All of these resources were addressed explicitly in the Gatorson EA, and the Forest Supervisor's finding that the Gatorson Sale will have no significant impact on these resources has not, itself, been challenged by Smith. In addition, the Gatorson EA specifically discussed the effect of the sale on "unroaded solitude."

Nevertheless, we must conclude that the agency's NEPA documents are inadequate. * * * The agency has never, in its NEPA documents, taken into account the fact that the sale will affect a 5,000 acre roadless area. In both the Colville Forest EIS and the Gatorson EA, the agency recognized that a portion of the Twin Sisters RARE II Area contains no roads, but dismissed the fact as irrelevant for wilderness consideration purposes because that portion would not stand alone as a 5,000 acre roadless area. Similarly, in both documents, the agency concluded that the Conn Merkel Area cannot stand alone as a 5,000 acre roadless area because of Thompson Ridge Road. But nowhere has the agency disclosed that the inventoried and uninventoried lands together comprise one 5,000 acre roadless area. * * * [T]he decision to harvest timber in a 5,000 acre roadless area is environmentally significant. We held in *National Audubon* that the agency must, under NEPA, consider the effect of a logging project on such a resource. We now therefore must hold that the agency's obligation to take a "hard look" at the environmental consequences of the proposed sale and consider a no-action alternative require it, at the very least, to acknowledge the existence of the 5,000 acre roadless area.

The courts have construed the "release" immunity from judicial review narrowly in other contexts as well. For example, in City of Tenakee Springs v. Block, 778 F.2d 1402 (9th Cir.1985), wilderness advocates brought a NEPA challenge to a Forest Service decision to construct a road in an area RARE II had classified for nonwilderness. The RARE II EIS had relied, in making this classification, upon the EIS for the Tongass Forest Plan that had been prepared nearly simultaneously. The Alaska National Interest Lands Conservation Act (ANILCA) had provided that the "legal and factual sufficiency" of the RARE II EIS with respect to Alaska National Forests was "not * * * subject to judicial review." See 94 Stat. 2371, 2421 (1980). The court held that this provision did not immunize the Tongass Forest Plan EIS from judicial review, and held, on the record before it, that NEPA compliance had not been achieved with respect to this particular road, and directed the entry of injunction against the road pending further proceedings.

A number of these statewide acts also direct that some specific roadless areas be put in a "further planning" category. This idea was also used by the Forest Service itself, as the Ninth Circuit opinion in California v. Block shows (RARE II put more than 10 million acres in this category). Congress has sometimes agreed to put some lands in this form of limbo—not designating them as wilderness per se, but directing in statute that they be managed to preserve their wilderness characteristics until Congress revisits the question of whether to include them in the NWPS at some future time. Congress has, in other words, forbidden the agency from "releasing" these lands to nonwilderness uses.

The upshot of all this activity and controversy is a decidedly mixed legal picture for wilderness evaluation and planning on the national forests, varying from place to place, depending upon whether Congress has enacted a wilderness bill following on the RARE II process, and the specific terms of that bill. Where Congress has not acted, Forest Service proposals to develop areas that it has recommended against wilderness will presumably be subject to NEPA obligations (such as those spelled out in California v. Block), as well as possible challenge under other statutes such as the NFMA or the ESA. Even where Congress has acted, areas not designated as wilderness that are subject to "soft release," and that have retained their wilderness characteristics, will be subject to further consideration for wilderness designation in the next generation of NFMA land use plans. Finally, the courts will likely continue their historic pattern of holding the Forest Service strictly accountable for full compliance with NEPA on any decision to develop roadless lands in a way that takes the wilderness designation option off the table.

WHAT IS A ROAD?

One important question raised by many wilderness inventories is how to define a "road," because a key characteristic of wilderness is that it is "roadless." Many federal lands are traversed by jeep tracks or other ways created solely by use by vehicles, often 4x4s. Interestingly, the Wilderness Act itself does not define "road," even though it uses the term "roadless." Thus each agency has evolved its own definition of "road." See, e.g., 43 C.F.R. § 19.2(e) (2001) (Fish and Wildlife Service and Park Service definition "roadless area" to mean, among other things, where there is "no improved road that is suitable for public travel by means of four-wheeled, motorized vehicles intended primarily for highway use").

BLM's definition comes straight from the legislative history of its governing statute, FLPMA. That is, the House Committee Report defined "road" narrowly, to include only those vehicle tracks "which have been improved and maintained by mechanical means to insure relatively regular and continuous use. A way maintained solely by the passage of vehicles does not constitute a road." H.R.Rep.No. 1163, 94th Cong., 2d Sess. 17 (1976).

The Forest Service's definition was discussed in Smith v. U.S. Forest Service, 33 F.3d 1072 (9th Cir.1994), as follows:

> Since RARE II, the agency has defined "roadless area" as an area "within which there are no improved roads maintained for travel by means of motorized vehicles intended for highway use." 1977 Roadless Area Inventory Criteria[.] * * * Smith challenges the agency's interpretation of the phrase "intended for highway use" as irrational, apparently because of his opinion that a road must be navigable by ordinary passenger vehicles before it can disqualify an area from being classified as roadless.

> The identification of "roads" in the National Forest System is a task legislatively delegated to the Department of Agriculture, and the agency is in far better position than we are to make these fact-specific determinations. In response to the district court's directive, Forest Service agents drove the length of Thompson Ridge Road in two four-wheel drive vehicles that were suitable for travel on U.S. interstates. The agency also conducted an historical evaluation and determined that Thompson Ridge Road had been created by bulldozer equipment in the early 1960s, and, periodically, had been maintained by the Forest Service. The agency concluded that the road was maintained for vehicles intended for highway use. After a careful review of the record, which includes photographs of Thompson Ridge Road, we find that the agency's conclusion, that the Conn Merkel Area is not a roadless area of more than 5,000 acres under the appropriate criteria, is not arbitrary and capricious.[2] Accordingly, we are without jurisdiction to

---

2. Smith contends that the agency's classification of Thompson Ridge Road as a road is arbitrary because the agency has classified as roadless other areas containing simi-

consider Smith's challenge to the agency's failure to consider the wilderness option in its NEPA documents. * * *

Forest Service transportation regulations define "road," "classified road," "unclassified road," and "temporary road," see 36 C.F.R. § 212.1, with "road" defined as a "motor vehicle travelway over 50 inches wide * * *."

MINERAL LEASING IN WILDERNESS STUDY AREAS

Because the Forest Service roadless area review was not driven by statute (other than respecting so-called "primitive areas"), mineral leasing was still possible in national forest roadless areas for many years (assuming NEPA would have been complied with). When Congress directed a wilderness review for BLM lands in the Federal Land Policy and Management Act (FLPMA) (discussed further below), it did address mineral leasing. Specifically, § 603(c) provided generally that wilderness study areas should be managed to preserve their suitability for designation as wilderness until Congress decides upon their future, and then provided, somewhat awkwardly, for "the continuation [in wilderness study areas] of * * * mineral leasing in the manner and degree in which the same was being conducted on October 21, 1976." In a 1978 opinion, the Interior Solicitor concluded that the reference to "existing * * * mineral leasing" in the grandfather clause referred to actual, on-the-ground activities being conducted under mineral leases in force on that date. BLM could continue to issue mineral leases in WSAs, but only if it included in the leases themselves a standard "wilderness protection stipulation" that put lessees on notice that any activity they might wish to undertake on the lease was subject to the "nonimpairment" standard.

The oil and gas industry promptly challenged the Solicitor's interpretation of the grandfather clause, but the Tenth Circuit upheld the Solicitor. Rocky Mountain Oil & Gas Ass'n (RMOGA) v. Watt, 696 F.2d 734 (10th Cir.1982). Closely analyzing the statute and its legislative history, the court concluded:

> One of the prime concerns of Congress in enacting the FLPMA was that BLM lands suitable for wilderness preservation at the date of the Act's passage be given a chance for consideration as wilderness. Under Interior's policy, the wilderness review period will result in only a brief hiatus from potential mineral development for most of the lands concerned. Lands containing oil and gas, and of no wilderness value, will be released from the review unharmed and fully suitable for mineral development. Under RMOGA's interpretation, however, lands suitable for wilderness could be irrevocably altered by development and

---

lar trails. Even assuming that these other roads are, as a factual matter, identical to Thompson Ridge Road, we find, after reviewing the record, that the alleged dissimilar treatment is as likely the result of misidentification or of different circumstances in these other regions as it is the result of a deliberate disregard by the agency of its own regulations in classifying Thompson Ridge Road. In the absence of any other evidence of a nefarious motive in connection with the allegedly inconsistent treatment, we presume that the agency has acted with regularity.

their wilderness values destroyed. It would be [inconsistent with the statute to] give disruptive mineral leasing activities carte blanche.

In light of the language of section 603(c) and its legislative history, we hold that Interior's interpretation of the section's effect on mineral leasing activities, as expressed in the Solicitor's Opinion of September 5, 1978, is reasonable and entitled to deference. Indeed, under our analysis it is compelling. We hold that mineral leasing is subject to the nonimpairment standard of section 603(c), and that the grandfather clause affords protection only to activities on mineral leases in the manner and degree actually occurring on October 21, 1976. * * *

Eventually, in the wake of strenuous efforts by Secretary of the Interior James Watt to open both designated wilderness and wilderness study areas to mineral leasing (see Chapter 4, supra pp. 349–51), the Congress confirmed and expanded upon the result in the *RMOGA* case by calling a nearly complete halt to mineral leasing in wilderness study areas on both BLM and national forest land. A moratorium on mineral leasing (including geothermal leasing) was first adopted annually as an appropriations rider, and was made permanent in the Federal Onshore Oil & Gas Leasing Reform Act in 1987; see 30 U.S.C. § 226–3. The only exception is "where oil and gas leasing is specifically allowed to continue by the statute designating the study area." Congress left intact the Secretary's authority to issue permits for mineral exploration under the mineral leasing laws "by means not requiring construction of roads or improvement of existing roads if such activity is conducted in a manner compatible with the preservation of the wilderness environment." Id. § 226–3(b).

While there generally can be no new mineral leasing in such areas until Congress acts, some of these study areas on both Forest Service and BLM lands are encumbered with mineral leases issued prior to the moratorium. On BLM land, *RMOGA* affirmed the conclusion in the 1978 Solicitor's Opinion that the FLPMA grandfather clause protects only actual physical activities being conducted on those leases from the non-impairment standard. Mineral lessees who were not conducting any such activities when FLPMA was enacted might have had a takings or a rescission argument if they were prevented from developing their leases by the non-impairment standard. But this risk has diminished over time as leases in wilderness study areas have expired. On Forest Service land, where no statute addresses the handling of existing mineral leases, the matter is less clear. See Getty Oil Co. v. Clark, 614 F.Supp. 904 (D.Wyo.1985), aff'd sub nom., Texaco Producing, Inc. v. Hodel, 840 F.2d 776 (10th Cir.1988), where the court held that the Secretary of the Interior could add new, wilderness-protective conditions to an oil and gas lease which had been issued in a national forest area before it was designated by Congress as wilderness. The court left open key questions whether the lessee had a vested right to develop that survived wilderness designation, and whether all oil and gas activity was incompatible with wilderness.

B. Bureau of Land Management Lands

Considered strictly from a legal standpoint, Congress happily avoided many of the knotty problems involved in wilderness review on national forest lands when it came to create a wilderness review process for the BLM lands in 1976. Specifically, section 603(a) of FLPMA, 43 U.S.C. § 1782, established an unambiguous directive that within fifteen years the Secretary of the Interior

> review those roadless areas [of the public lands] of five thousand acres or more * * * identified * * * as having wilderness characteristics described in the Wilderness Act "and give the President" his recommendation as to the suitability or nonsuitability of each such area * * * for preservation as wilderness.

The President in turn was to forward his own recommendations to the Congress within two years of receiving those of the Secretary, § 603(b).* As with other agencies, the executive's recommendations for wilderness "shall become effective only if so provided by an Act of Congress." Id.

From a practical standpoint, however, the BLM wilderness review process has not been free from difficulty. BLM manages considerably more land than the Forest Service, with considerably fewer employees. In addition, BLM roadless areas tend to be more arid, at lower elevation, and tend to attract more competing uses in the form of hardrock mining, mineral leasing, and grazing. Congress provided specific guidance on how the BLM lands identified as candidates for wilderness designation were to be managed during the study process, until Congress made final decisions. This so-called "interim management policy" is set out in § 603(c) of FLPMA. It generally requires that these lands must be managed "so as not to impair the[ir] suitability * * * for preservation as wilderness, subject, however, to the continuation of existing mining and grazing uses and mineral leasing in the manner and degree in which the same was being conducted on October 21, 1976 * * *." The BLM review is comprehensively analyzed in John Leshy, Wilderness and its Discontents—Wilderness Review Comes to the Public Lands, 1981 Ariz.St.L.J. 361.

The key questions that have emerged in the BLM wilderness review may be subdivided into two categories: First, questions about the inventory process, of identifying public lands that are "roadless * * * with wilderness characteristics" for intensive study of their suitability for wilderness designation; and second, questions about "interim management" under § 603(c)—how these identified lands are to be managed pending final decisions by Congress on whether to add them to the NWPS. These will be addressed in turn.

i. THE INVENTORY PROCESS

The process by which the Secretary of the Interior was to identify BLM lands that were "roadless * * * with wilderness characteristics" was, according to FLPMA, to be the "inventory" of the "values and resources" of the public lands that § 201(a) of FLPMA required to be maintained on a continuous basis. 43 U.S.C. § 1711(a). Partly for speed, administrative

---

* BLM had, prior to FLPMA, designated a few small tracts as "natural" or "primitive" areas; the statute directed that recommendations on the suitability of these areas for preservation as wilderness be given to the President by 1980.

convenience, and efficiency, and partly to avoid disabling litigation over proposals to develop roadless areas that had not yet been formally inventoried, the Secretary decided to conduct a generic, one-time review of all BLM lands to identify these so-called "wilderness study areas," or WSAs. The review was conducted pursuant to a "Wilderness Inventory Handbook" (WIH), which identified the criteria for selecting wilderness study areas (emphasis in original):

1. Size. At least 5,000 contiguous roadless acres of public land.

2. Naturalness. The imprint of man's work must be substantially unnoticeable.

3. Either:

    a. An *outstanding* opportunity for solitude, or

    b. An *outstanding* opportunity for a primitive and unconfined type of recreation.

To qualify for wilderness study identification an area of public land must be shown to meet both factors 2 and 3.

The Handbook also directed that areas with fewer than 5000 acres but which met factors 2 and 3 should also be identified as WSAs if they were contiguous with land managed by another agency which either had been formally determined to have potential wilderness values (e.g., Forest Service RARE II lands) or when combined with adjacent lands managed by another agency totaled 5000 acres or more. Finally, the Handbook also called for BLM voluntarily (that is, outside the scope of the section 603 inventory, which applied only to tracts of 5000 acres or more) to identify tracts fewer than 5000 acres which had "strong public support" for wilderness study status, and which were "clearly and obviously of sufficient size as to make practicable [their] preservation and use in an unimpaired condition, and of a size suitable for wilderness management."

The initial inventory, completed in November 1980, reviewed nearly 174 million acres, and identified 919 WSAs totaling nearly 24 million acres. The balance of land was found to be without the requisite wilderness characteristics. 45 Fed.Reg. 77,574 (November 14, 1980). It was not without controversy. For one thing, in December 1982 Secretary of the Interior James Watt ordered that three categories of land be deleted from WSA status: (1) lands in which the United States does not own the subsurface mineral rights (split-estate lands); (2) lands that had been found to have wilderness characteristics only in conjunction with lands administered by another agency; and (3) lands with fewer than 5000 total acres. All told, about 1.5 million acres were stripped of WSA status by Watt's order. His order relied on a Solicitor's Opinion that relied in turn on some Interior Board of Land Appeals (IBLA) opinions.

The Sierra Club promptly challenged these exclusions, and the court rejected Watt's order in Sierra Club v. Watt, 608 F.Supp. 305 (E.D.Cal. 1985). On the exclusion of "split-estate" lands, the court noted that FLPMA required wilderness review of "public lands," and that FLPMA defined public lands as including "any land and interest in land owned by the United States" with certain exceptions. 43 U.S.C. § 1702(e). It continued:

> To say that the language is straightforward is to state the obvious. To apply the statute to the split-estates over 5,000 acres seems equally straightforward. In such lands, the United States holds the interest in the surface estate while private parties hold the interest in the subsurface estate. Since the interest in the surface estate is an "interest in land owned by the United States," it appears clearly to fall within the definition of public land provided by the statute. Nor does the fact that private parties have an interest in the minerals below the surface appear to preclude their inclusion as WSAs because such a condition is incompatible with the status of wilderness. The definition of wilderness, incorporated into section 603(a), is directed at the surface attributes of public lands. Indeed, this conclusion is wholly consonant with the Wilderness Act, 16 U.S.C. §§ 1131–1136, which section 603(a) of FLPMA specifies is the guide for the wilderness review process of FLPMA. The Wilderness Act expressly allows for the preservation and exploitation of mining claims and interests in wilderness areas. * * *

> The IBLA found and the defendants argue that such an interpretation is too rigid. The defendants suggest that the statute must be read in conjunction with other responsibilities of the Secretary. * * * [T]hey note that section 603(c) requires that management of areas as wilderness during the study period is nonetheless subject to existing mining rights and that section 701(h), 43 U.S.C. § 1701 n. (h), requires the Secretary's conduct be subject to all valid existing rights. From these two provisions, defendants argue that it is incorrect to interpret the statute to include split-estate lands as subject to wilderness evaluation. I consider each statute in turn.

> Section 603(c) provides that the "Secretary shall continue to manage such lands * * * so as not to impair the suitability of such areas for preservation as wilderness, subject, however, to the continuation of existing mining and grazing uses and mineral leasing * * * ".

> Two things seem directly contemplated by this provision; one, the mere fact that mining rights exist does not preclude management as, much less consideration for wilderness status, but two, that under such circumstances, some adjustment of the management practices might be required. * * *

> Nor do the provisions of section 701(h) require a different conclusion. There the statute requires that "all actions by the Secretary concerned under this Act shall be subject to valid existing rights." 43 U.S.C. § 1701, n. (h). Defendants argue that the subsurface estate carries with it implied easements for development and that the possible extraction of minerals is inconsistent with the protection of wilderness qualities. * * *

> * * * The fact that Congress specifically provided for mining activities to continue in WSA's under the provisions of section 603(c), 43 U.S.C. § 1782(c), directly demonstrates that defendants' position is untenable.

If Congress had intended that the split-estate lands be excluded from the inventory it would not have expressly provided for the continuance of existing mining activities during the period of review. * * *

The IBLA * * * nevertheless found that the ownership of the subsurface estate constitutes a "vested right" which could not be denied or extinguished by exercise of Secretarial discretion. Whatever validity the IBLA's premise has, it does not follow that such estates may not be studied for wilderness. The flaw in the IBLA majority's reasoning is that the placement of these areas into wilderness review and even eventually into wilderness designation does not deny or extinguish the owner's property right in the subsurface estate. The land may still be mined subject to certain controls under the Wilderness Act or Congress may choose to recompense the owner through exchange or payment. Finally, as the dissent in [the IBLA case] notes, placing the land in WSA status may not have any adverse consequences to the owner of the subsurface rights since the Secretary's final recommendations may exclude such lands.

A final basis for the IBLA's decision was that placement of the split-estate lands into the wilderness study under section 603 would be a futile exercise as the lands could never be placed in permanent wilderness status. * * * It appears to the court that the IBLA simply misconstrues the statutory scheme and the nature of the wilderness review process. * * * The statutory scheme contemplated executive study but congressional disposition of wilderness issues. Clearly, if Congress elects to include within the wilderness preservation system split-estate lands, it may authorize the purchase or condemnation of the reserved mineral rights in the subsurface estate, or the exchange of reserved mineral rights for other federal lands or mineral interests.

The court went to hold that the other parts of Secretary Watt's order were likewise invalid, on the ground that it rested on the mistaken determination that Secretary Watt had no legal authority to classify tracts of BLM-managed land smaller than 5000 acres as wilderness study lands. The court acknowledged that the Secretary had concluded, correctly, that sub–5000 acre areas were exempt from the § 603 wilderness review process. But the Secretary overlooked the fact that he retained authority to classify these smaller tracts as wilderness study areas under FLPMA's general land use planning authority in § 202. Because of that, until the Secretary decided to overrule his predecessor and exclude the areas from wilderness consideration (a decision to which NEPA attaches), the court directed that the lands be managed to preserve their suitability for possible preservation as wilderness.

NOTES AND QUESTIONS

1. What about deference to the agency? Is this another example of searching judicial review to preserve wilderness status for congressional decision? Why should the courts be so aggressive about preserving the possibility of permanent protection of federal lands as wilderness? Is it

because "they aren't making any more" of it? Or is this a simple case of overzealous administrative lawmaking?

2. The "split-estate" lands here were mostly the legacy of railroad land grants that the United States had eventually reacquired in a complex series of transactions in which the railroad had retained the mineral rights. Does the wilderness study process mandated by this opinion prevent the railroad from developing its private mineral interests, even if that is inconsistent with the preservation of these lands as wilderness? May BLM regulate the railroad's exercise of these rights? To what degree, and to what end? May it regulate them in order to protect the wilderness characteristics of the surface? For example, may it require the railroad to conduct mineral exploration by pack mule or helicopter in order to avoid road-building that would disqualify the area from wilderness consideration? Compare the discussion of access across public lands to private inholdings; Chapter 2, supra p. 160, and the "split-estate" problems discussed in Chapter 7, supra pp. 695–703.

3. The Interior Department chose not to appeal the decision. The questions raised in paragraph 2 were mooted for a considerable portion of the lands in question when the railroad conveyed its mineral rights in a number of these areas for BLM lands of equivalent value elsewhere. Following the exchange, in the first major BLM wilderness bill enacted by Congress, a number of these formerly split-estate areas (as well as several other tracts of BLM land in Arizona) were designated as wilderness. See 104 Stat. 4469 (1990).

4. Given the long tradition of many BLM lands being open to mining, mineral leasing, grazing, and many other laws allowing exploitation and disposition, it was perhaps not entirely surprising that BLM's initial inventory of "wilderness study areas" yielded only about 24 million acres, or only about 13% of the roughly 180 million acres it manages in the lower 48 states (compared with somewhere between 30 and 40% of the national forest system being roadless). The rest were "released" from further study. Wilderness advocates and their allies in Congress did, however, produce considerable evidence that BLM inventory decisions in some regions, especially in the canyonlands of southern Utah, had wrongfully excluded roadless areas because of their potential for mineral or other uses. As the court pointed out in Sierra Club v. Watt, under FLPMA such a balancing of competing uses was to be made by BLM only at the second stage of the process—the determination whether to WSA was "suitable" for preservation as wilderness. And even then BLM's decision was only a recommendation, for Congress carefully reserved for itself, rather than the executive, the final decision on wilderness suitability.

5. A number of the BLM inventory decisions were appealed to the IBLA, where wilderness advocates met with mixed success. In the most important such case, covering nearly one million acres of Utah lands that BLM had not designated as WSAs, the IBLA reversed and remanded many of the individual areas to the BLM in a lengthy decision. Utah Wilderness Coalition, 72 IBLA 125 (1983). BLM ultimately reclassified about half this land as WSAs. In 1984 and 1985, the House Public Lands Subcommittee

under Congressman John Seiberling held a series of oversight hearings to investigate problems with the BLM inventory, and requested the Secretary of the Interior to reexamine a number of specific areas in Utah, but the request was rebuffed. For a long time wilderness advocates adopted a rallying cry that BLM lands in Utah contained 5.2, then 5.4, then 5.9, and eventually something like 9 million acres of wilderness, even though BLM's official inventory includes only about 3.25 million acres. In the late 1990s, Secretary Bruce Babbitt ordered BLM to undertake another review of BLM lands in Utah to try to settle the question of how much roadless land existed under BLM's management there. An initial survey suggested that well over 5 million acres could be classified as roadless with wilderness characteristics, but the formal inventory process and designation process has not been completed as of this writing. Anti-wilderness advocates attempted to stop the reinventory, but after gaining an injunction from the district court, were thrown out on appeal on standing grounds. Utah v. Babbitt, 137 F.3d 1193 (10th Cir.1998). See H. Michael Anderson & Aliki Moncrief, America's Unprotected Wilderness, 76 Denv. U.L. Rev. 413 (1999).

6.   FLPMA called for the BLM lands to be reviewed and recommendations made to Congress regarding their wilderness suitability within fifteen years of enactment, or by October 1991. While that process has expired, the Interior Solicitor and the BLM have taken the position that the BLM has continuing authority to evaluate wilderness suitability of its lands. This stems from BLM's responsibility under Section 202 of FLPMA to maintain and revise as appropriate land use plans guiding use of the public lands. 43 U.S.C. § 1712. Roadless areas that may be identified as wilderness study areas under this Section 202 authority are not governed by the interim management provisions of section 603(c), discussed in the next section. But they may, as a matter of administrative discretion (though not statutory command), be managed to preserve their suitability for wilderness. And, of course, NEPA would apply to any proposed action that would disqualify them from further consideration for wilderness. The courts would, presumably, apply the same heightened scrutiny to BLM actions in this regard as they apply to the Forest Service.

7.   Westwide, about 5.3 million acres of BLM land have been designated by Congress as wilderness through September 2000 (3.6 million acres in California, and most of the rest in Arizona). About 18 million acres are in 618 wilderness study areas. Nevada (5.1 million acres), Utah (3.26), and Oregon (2.8) account for more than half of the WSA acreage. PUBLIC LAND STATISTICS 2000, Tables 5–4, 5–5. Although § 603 originally applied to BLM lands in Alaska, in the ANILCA enacted in 1980, Congress exempted Alaskan BLM lands from further mandatory wilderness study, although it allowed the Secretary to identify areas in Alaska that he believes "are suitable as wilderness" and to recommend that Congress designate them. 94 Stat. 2487 (1980); adding 43 U.S.C. § 1784. Secretary Watt promptly ordered BLM not to consider wilderness any further in Alaska; Secretary Babbitt reversed that order. As of September 2000, about 800,000 acres in Alaska were in BLM WSAs. PUBLIC LAND STATISTICS 2000, table 5–5.

ii.   INTERIM MANAGEMENT: FLPMA § 603(C)

The issues posed in the following case illuminate the interim management standards for WSAs under FLPMA. They also provide a useful lens through which may be examined (and memories refreshed of) a host of issues addressed in this book, including statutory interpretation and deference to agencies; states' rights in common school grants; rights of access to inholdings and regulation of those rights; property rights/takings issues; regulation of mining claims; and preservation versus development.

State of Utah v. Andrus

United States District Court, District of Utah, 1979.
486 F.Supp. 995.

■ ALDON J. ANDERSON, CHIEF JUDGE.

[Cotter Corporation (Cotter), a uranium mining subsidiary of Commonwealth Edison, an electrical utility in northern Illinois, acquired mining claims on federal land and a mineral lease on a state school section in an area of Utah, and began exploration for uranium deposits. Cotter constructed some access roads across BLM land without notifying the agency. BLM was in the meantime engaged in its wilderness inventory under FLPMA, and preliminarily identified land in the vicinity of the Cotter exploration as a wilderness study area. When BLM became aware of Cotter's road construction, it requested that it be halted. Cotter agreed for a period of time, but then decided to resume construction, and BLM brought suit. The state of Utah intervened as a defendant.]

At stake here are three very important and conflicting interests. The state of Utah has a clear interest in protecting its rights under the grant of school trust lands and in being able to use those lands so as to maximize the funds available for the public schools. Cotter, of course, has an interest in developing its claims in the most economical way possible. Finally, the United States has an interest in preserving for future generations the opportunity to experience the solitude and peace that only an undisturbed natural setting can provide. As noted herein, these public interests conflict. This is reflected in the more narrow questions of statutory interpretation and reconciliation posed for decision. In order to resolve the issues and effect a balance of interests, it is important to examine each interest and its statutory base.

I.   State School Trust Land

* * * [T]he state school land grants were not unilateral gifts made by the United States Congress. Rather, they were in the nature of a bilateral compact entered into between two sovereigns. In return for receiving the federal lands Utah disclaimed all interest in the remainder of the public domain, agreed to forever hold federal lands immune from taxation, and agreed to hold the granted lands, or the proceeds therefrom, in trust as a common school fund. Thus, the land grants involved here were in the nature of a contract, with a bargained-for consideration exchanged between the two governments. See Utah v. Kleppe, 586 F.2d 756, 758 (10th

Cir.1978), cert. granted 442 U.S. 928 (1979) [eds.: subsequently rev'd sub nom. Andrus v. Utah, p. 62 supra].

Recognition of the special nature of the school land grants is important both in determining the Congressional intent behind the grant and in understanding judicial treatment of similar grants. Generally, land grants by the federal government are construed strictly, and nothing is held to pass to the grantee except that which is specifically delineated in the instrument of conveyance. E.g., United States v. Union Pacific Railroad Co., 353 U.S. 112, 116 (1957). But the legislation dealing with school trust land has always been liberally construed. Wyoming v. United States, 255 U.S. 489, 508 (1921); Utah v. Kleppe, supra at 761. Further, it is clear that one of Congress' primary purposes in enacting the legislation was to place the new states on an "equal footing" with the original thirteen colonies and to enable the state to "produce a fund, accumulated by sale and use of the trust lands, with which the State could support the [common schools]". Lassen v. Arizona Highway Dept., 385 U.S. 458, 463 (1967).

Given the rule of liberal construction and the Congressional intent of enabling the state to use the school lands as a means of generating revenue, the court must conclude that Congress intended that Utah (or its lessees) have access to the school lands. Unless a right of access is inferred, the very purpose of the school trust lands would fail. Without access the state could not develop the trust lands in any fashion and they would become economically worthless. This Congress did not intend.

Further, traditional property law concepts support Utah's claimed right of access. Under the common law it was assumed that a grantor intended to include in the conveyance whatever was necessary for the use and enjoyment of the land in question. * * * When a grantor conveys only a portion of his land, and the land received by the grantee is surrounded by what the grantor has retained, it is generally held that the grantee has an easement of access, either by implication or necessity, across the grantor's land. * * * Although this common law presumption might not ordinarily apply in the context of a federal land grant, the liberal rules of construction applied to school trust land allow for the consideration of this common law principle and justify its application here.[11]

Therefore, the court holds that the state of Utah and Cotter Corporation, as Utah's lessee, do have the right to cross federal land to reach section 36, which is a portion of the school trust lands. The extent and nature of that right, however, remain to be determined. In order to reach that decision the court must examine the character and extent of BLM's authority under the Federal Land Policy and Management Act.

*II. Federal Land Policy and Management Act * * ***

Under section 603(c) [43 U.S.C. § 1782(c)], BLM is required, during the period of wilderness review, to manage the public land

---

11. The case of Leo Sheep Co. v. United States, 440 U.S. 668 (1979) is not apposite. In that case the United States Supreme Court held that the government had not reserved an access easement in a particular land grant because the government had the power to condemn the land in question. The defendants in this case have no such power.

in a manner so as *not to impair the suitability of such areas for preservation as wilderness, subject,* however, to the continuation of *existing mining * * * uses * * * in the manner and degree* in which the same *was being conducted* on October 21, 1976: *Provided,* That, in managing the public lands [BLM] shall by regulation or otherwise *take any action required to prevent unnecessary or undue degradation* of the lands and their resources or to afford environmental protection.

(Emphasis added in part.)

Cotter argues that this language authorizes only one management standard: preventing undue or unnecessary degradation of the environment. It is Cotter's position that the use of the word "impair" "merely gives direction to the existing authority of [BLM] to manage with a view toward environmental protection."

The United States, on the other hand, argues that under section 603(c) there are two management standards: one that applies to uses of the land existing on October 21, 1976, and one that applies to uses coming into existence after that date. Under this interpretation, existing uses are to be regulated only to the degree required to prevent unnecessary and undue degradation. New uses, however, may be (indeed, must be) regulated to the extent necessary to prevent impairment of wilderness characteristics. Obviously, the latter standard is more strict.

The Solicitor of the Department of Interior has issued an opinion dated September 5, 1978, (hereinafter referred to as "Solicitor's Opinion") which interprets the effect of section 603(c). Under this interpretation, section 603(c) does indeed mandate two standards, the first of which governs regulation of uses not in existence on October 21, 1976, and the second of which governs uses existing on that date. Generally, the interpretation of a statute by those charged with its execution is entitled to great deference. E.g., Udall v. Tallman, 380 U.S. 1, 16 (1965). The court can find no reason not to give such deference in this case.

Further, the Solicitor's interpretation finds support in the Act's legislative history. In the Report [H.Rep. No. 94–1163, 94th Cong.2d Sess. 17 (1976), U.S.Code Cong. & Admin.News 1976, p. 6175] accompanying the House version of what was to become FLPMA, the language of section 603(c) was described as follows:

While tracts are under review, they are to be managed in a manner to preserve their wilderness character, *subject to continuation of existing grazing and mineral uses and appropriation under the mining laws.* The Secretary *will continue* to have authority to prevent unnecessary and undue degradation of the lands, including installation of minimum improvements, such as wildlife habitat and livestock control improvements, where needed for the protection or maintenance of the lands and their resources * * *. (Emphasis added.)

It appears to the court that the above passage indicates that the authority to manage lands so as to prevent impairment of wilderness characteristics was meant to be a new addition to the Secretary's continuing authority to regulate all uses so as to prevent undue degradation. Other parts of the legislative history confirm this view. * * *

* * * It appears that the Senate and the House were concerned about devising a way to protect both existing uses and wilderness values present on tracts not subject to existing uses. As interpreted by the Solicitor, section 603(c) reflects that concern. The Secretary's authority to preserve wilderness is subject to existing uses which may not be arbitrarily terminated, nor regulated solely with a view to preserving wilderness characteristics. But the Secretary may continue to regulate such uses in order to prevent unnecessary or undue degradation. On the other hand, activity on lands with potential wilderness value which are not subject to existing uses may be regulated more stringently so as to preserve wilderness characteristics. The Solicitor's interpretation is consistent with the Act's legislative history and reflects the full measure of Congressional intent in the adoption of 603(c). Cotter's interpretation reflects only one of Congress' concerns, i.e., protection of existing uses.

Finally, the Solicitor's interpretation is supported by the language and structure of the statute itself. The word "impair" would prevent many activities that would not be prevented by the language of "unnecessary or undue degradation." For example, commercial timber harvesting, if conducted carefully, would not result in unnecessary or undue degradation of the environment. But the same activity might well impair wilderness characteristics as those are defined in 16 U.S.C. § 1131. * * * Further, if Congress had not intended to mandate two standards, it would merely have indicated that the Secretary was to continue to manage all lands so as to prevent unnecessary degradation. If one takes the position that this is what Congress intended, then the language of impairment must be mere surplusage. Statutory rules of construction are against such a finding.[14] Wilderness Society v. Morton, 479 F.2d 842, 856 (D.C.Cir.1973), cert. den., 411 U.S. 917 (1978).

Moreover, legislative history confirms that the language of impairment was not surplusage. * * *

Therefore, the court holds that under the terms of FLPMA the BLM has the authority to manage public lands so as to prevent impairment of wilderness characteristics, unless those lands are subject to an existing use.

---

14. There is further indication within FLPMA itself that the Congress intended two management standards. Section 302(b) provides:

> Except as provided in 1744, 1781(f) and 1782[section 603] of this title *and in the last sentence of this paragraph,* no provision * * * shall in any way amend the Mining Law of 1872 * * *.

The last sentence of 302(b) is as follows:

In managing the public lands the Secretary shall, by regulation or otherwise, take any action necessary to prevent unnecessary or undue degradation of the lands.

If the standard of undue degradation were not separate and distinct from the impairment standard contained in section 603(c), there would have been no need to include both the last sentence and reference to section 603(c) in section 302(b). By making distinct reference to both standards in 302(b), Congress indicated its intent to formulate two different approaches to management of the public lands.

In the latter case BLM may regulate so as to prevent unnecessary or undue degradation of the environment. * * *

Given that there are two standards by which BLM can manage the public lands, it remains to be determined what standards apply to Cotter's activity. Cotter argues that its activity falls within the existing use provision of 603(c). The main thrust of Cotter's argument is as follows:

(1) under the Mining Law of 1872, Cotter has a right of access to its unpatented claims;

(2) Cotter, as Utah's lessee, also has a right of access to state school land;

(3) these rights, even though not exercised prior to October, 1976, constitute existing uses under FLPMA.

Section 603(c) mandates that existing uses may continue in the "same manner and degree" as being conducted on October 21, 1976. Unless the statute is referring to activity that was actually taking place on that date, there is no way to give meaningful context to the "manner and degree" language. In order to determine whether or not a given operation is being conducted in the same manner and degree as it was formerly being conducted, there must be *some* former activity against which the extent of the present operation can be measured. Presumably, when the statute refers to existing uses being carried out in the same manner and degree it is referring to *actual* uses, not merely a statutory right to use.

Cotter next points to section 302(b) as an indication that its rights of access cannot be denied under FLPMA. Cotter's emphasis in quoting 302(b) is, however, selective. Section 302(b) provides in pertinent part:

> *Except as provided in* 1744, 1781(f) and *1782* [*section 603*] of this title and in the last sentence of this paragraph no provision of this section or any other section of this Act shall in any way amend the Mining Law of 1872 or impair the rights of any locators of claims under that Act, including, but not limited to, rights of ingress and egress. (Emphasis added.)

Cotter emphasizes only the latter portion of this section and from this argues that no provision of FLPMA can be taken to amend the Mining Law of 1872. On its face, however, this section makes clear that section 603 *does* amend the Mining Law of 1872. Rights under that law, including rights of ingress and egress, can be impaired by virtue of section 603. Moreover, the Mining Law itself makes clear that rights of access to mining claims are not absolute. Such rights are subject to regulation under 30 U.S.C. § 22. * * *

It is clear that the Congress intended to provide a balanced solution to the problem of land management during the inventory process. While Congress did not intend the use of public lands to be frozen pending the outcome of the inventory process, neither did it want future uses to be foreclosed by the impact of present activity. Further, the Congress recognized that it might not be possible to both allow present uses and prevent foreclosure of certain other future uses.

This is consistent with the decision in Parker v. United States, supra. In that case, involving the Wilderness Act, the court held that the Department of Agriculture could not take any action that would foreclose Congressional consideration of an area's potential for wilderness designation. In this case, if BLM could not prevent activity that would permanently impair wilderness characteristics, then those characteristics could be destroyed before either BLM or the Congress had the chance to evaluate an area's potential uses. This Congress did not intend.

Therefore, the court holds that (1) BLM may regulate activity on federal land so as to prevent impairment of potential wilderness characteristics; (2) the authority to so regulate is subject to uses actually existing on October 21, 1976; (3) section 603 does amend the Mining Law of 1872 and subjects rights thereunder to BLM's authority to regulate so as to prevent wilderness impairment; (4) section 201 does not mandate that BLM allow all potential uses to take place on a particular portion of land regardless of wilderness characteristics.

BLM's authority is, however, limited to preventing *permanent* impairment of potential wilderness values. Although it is not explicitly provided for in FLPMA, it is consistent with Congress' attempt to balance competing interests and with the Wilderness Act which provides the legislative backdrop for section 603 to find that if a given activity will have only a temporary effect on wilderness characteristics and will not foreclose potential wilderness designation then that activity should be allowed to proceed.

The definition of wilderness provided for in the Wilderness Act (16 U.S.C. § 1131[c]) and incorporated by reference into FLPMA in section 603(a) contemplates that some human activity can take place in wilderness areas as long as the area *"generally* appears to have been affected *primarily* by the forces of nature, with the imprint of man's work *substantially* unnoticeable * * *."

Further, the draft statement of BLM's Interim Management Policy and Guidelines for Wilderness Study Areas (January 12, 1979, at 9) recognizes that temporary activities, the negative impacts of which could be substantially reversed through appropriate reclamation procedures, would not impair wilderness characteristics under the terms of 603(c).

There has been a great deal of argument in this case over whether or not the effects of Cotter's proposed road and drilling operations can be successfully reclaimed. Unfortunately the factual matters inherent in such an argument have not been sufficiently addressed. At the July 12 hearing on the motion for permanent injunction, Cotter proffered, for the first time, its reclamation plan. BLM has not had the opportunity to review the plan nor to make a comparison of the costs and feasibility of reclamation of a land access route over the cost and effect of other forms of access.

In view of the court's findings and conclusions of law, the BLM must be given the opportunity to review and respond to Cotter's reclamation plan. BLM has no formal regulations for review of proposed activity within potential WSAs. But BLM is authorized under FLPMA to manage the public lands "by regulation or otherwise * * *." See sections 302(b) and

603(c). Thus, the agency's authority is not dependent on the issuance of formal regulations. Further, in a lawsuit involving issues of the magnitude and importance as those involved here, it is imperative that all parties have the opportunity to respond to critical factual issues. Moreover, the question of the adequacy of a reclamation plan is precisely the kind of question to which the expertise of an administrative agency is most relevant. The court is ill-equipped at this stage of the litigation to make a factual determination on the complex question of the comparative costs and feasibility of reclamation efforts over other forms of access. Thus, the court orders that BLM must be given the opportunity to expeditiously review Cotter's reclamation plan with a view to determining whether or not the impact of the proposed road will be temporary or permanent and with a view toward comparing the cost and feasibility of reclamation with the cost and feasibility of alternative forms of access.

If BLM should decide that the effects of the road will, indeed, be permanent, then the parties (and probably this court) may be required to confront this and other disputed issues. * * * [I]n light of the possibility that further litigation will be necessary, and in light of the fact that throughout the litigation BLM has assumed that the effects of the road would be permanent and thus has put the questions of regulation of access to federal and state land at issue, the court will address the questions remaining in the lawsuit.

III. FLPMA and the State School Lands

The state must be allowed access to the state school trust lands so that those lands can be developed in a manner that will provide funds for the common schools. Further, because it was the intent of Congress to provide these lands to the state so that the state could use them to raise revenue, Lassen v. Arizona Highway Dept., supra, the access rights of the state cannot be so restricted as to destroy the lands' economic value. That is, the state must be allowed access which is not so narrowly restrictive as to render the lands incapable of their full economic development. * * *

Thus, the court finds that (1) BLM can regulate the method and route of access to state school trust lands; (2) this regulation may be done with a view toward preventing impairment of wilderness characteristics (assuming no existing use); (3) the regulation may not, however, prevent the state or its lessee from gaining access to its land, nor may it be so prohibitively restrictive as to render the land incapable of full economic development.

IV. FLPMA and Access Rights Over Federal Land

Section 701(h) [codified at 43 U.S.C. § 1701 note (Supp.1979)] of FLPMA provides:

All actions by the Secretary concerned under this Act shall be subject to valid existing rights.

The Solicitor has interpreted this section to mean that valid existing rights cannot be taken pursuant to section 603. The court agrees with this interpretation. The court has also found, however, that Cotter's right of access to both its federal and state claims can be regulated.

The parties have stipulated that "Cotter's proposed road appears to be the only feasible and least environmentally disruptive *land access* for Cotter to its targeted drilling sites *and* for entry into state section 36 * * *." Thus, in this case, regulation to prevent wilderness impairment could result in total prohibition of land access. BLM has contended that helicopter access is available, feasible and acceptable to the agency. Cotter contends that such access would be prohibitively expensive and would not result in any substantial saving of the environment. This issue was not, however, the subject of live testimony with full cross-examination. The court is not, therefore, provided with sufficient information on which to base a ruling. To further complicate the case, it is not clear that the entire proposed road is necessary for Cotter to gain access to section 36. This is important because different criteria may be applied to judge the propriety of regulation of state, as opposed to federal, access rights. It may be that requiring helicopter access to section 36 would be sufficiently expensive so as to render minerals on that section incapable of economic development. Therefore, requiring such access and denying land access would violate the intent of the school trust grant. It may be, however, that requiring such access to federal claims would not be so expensive as to constitute a taking under 701(h). If the entire road is not necessary to gain access to section 36, then it could be that substantial parts of it could be prohibited, while other parts could not. Unfortunately, on the record as it now stands, this matter is far from clear.

Finally, the record contains very little factual information relevant to the taking issue. The court recognizes that a government can regulate without engaging in a taking. The court also recognizes, however, that when regulation reaches the point of seriously impinging on "investment-backed expectations," it can constitute a taking. Pennsylvania Coal Co. v. Mahon, 260 U.S. 393 (1922) * * *. Given its current information, the court feels that there is a substantial question of a taking in this case if access to federal claims are indefinitely prohibited or if alternative access is unreasonably expensive. The facts in this case are not, however, sufficiently clear at this time for the formulation of a ruling on this matter.

In sum, the court holds that Utah does have a right of access to state school trust lands. That right is subject to federal regulation when its exercise requires the crossing of federal property. Such regulation cannot, however, prohibit access or be so restrictive as to make economic development competitively unprofitable. Further, the court holds that BLM may regulate federal public land so as to prevent impairment of wilderness characteristics. Such authority is, however, subject to uses which were existing on October 21, 1976. These uses must have been actually existing on that date. Cotter's right to gain access was not an existing use on October 21, 1976. Therefore, Cotter's activity may be regulated so as to prevent wilderness impairment. But such regulation cannot be so restrictive as to constitute a taking. * * *

NOTES AND QUESTIONS

1. *Mining claimant's right of access.* On these facts, does Cotter Corp. have valid rights against the federal government under the Mining Law?

Do its claims give it the right to build a road across federal lands to its claims? Might, instead, the BLM require Cotter to use helicopter or pack mule access to its claims? Is Cotter protected by the "grandfather" clause of § 603 of FLPMA?

2. *State's right of access.* What right of access does the state of Utah have to cross federal land to reach the isolated common school grant sections of land it owns? Notice that this case was decided before Congress added a general access provision in the Alaska National Interest Lands Conservation Act in 1980. See the discussion of this statute in Chapter 2, pp. 167–71 supra. If this case arose today, would the BLM access section of that legislation apply? Would it change the outcome? Assuming the state has some right of access to its inholding, to what extent can the access rights be regulated by the United States? Is the state protected by the "grandfather" clause of § 603?

3. Is the state's right of access to its inholding stronger, weaker, or the same as Cotter Corp.'s right of access to its federal mining claims?

4. What standards does the court set out for determining whether a "taking" of either Cotter's, or the State's, property rights has occurred? Could the United States rely on the "nuisance" exception to conventional takings analysis (see Chapter 3, pp. 240–42 supra) to justify protecting the wilderness qualities of this area without being obliged to compensate either Cotter or the State?

5. What is the difference, if any, between regulating against a standard of "non-impairment" of suitability for preservation as wilderness, and regulating against a standard of preventing "unnecessary or undue degradation of the lands"? Section 302(b) of FLPMA already contains a generic directive to the Secretary to prevent "unnecessary or undue degradation" of public lands everywhere. 43 U.S.C. § 1732(b), discussed in Chapter 7, supra pp. 636–38. Section 603(c) of FLPMA repeats this language as a standard for regulating grandfathered "existing mining and grazing uses and mineral leasing" in WSAs, and then adds the directive that the Secretary shall "afford environmental protection." What do those last three words add, if anything, to the Secretary's authority to regulate the State or Cotter here?

6. Another part of § 603(c) provides that the Secretary shall not withdraw BLM wilderness study areas from operation of the Mining Law *except* "for reasons other than preservation of their wilderness character." Could the Secretary withdraw the area involved in *Utah v. Andrus* from the Mining Law in order to protect its wildlife values or its scenery? Assuming the Secretary did so, and the withdrawal was valid, what effect, if any, would it have on Cotter Corp.'s rights to develop its uranium claims?

The district court's opinion in *Utah v. Andrus* was not appealed. Shortly after it was issued, the BLM determined that the specific area in question did not have "wilderness characteristics" and it was not classified as a wilderness study area under § 603. Years later, however, the Tenth Circuit in effect affirmed much of the district court's view of § 603 in its decision in the Burr Trail litigation. Sierra Club v. Hodel, 848 F.2d 1068 (10th Cir.1988) (portions of which were reproduced in Chapter 2, supra p. 161). There, having determined that the county in that case had a valid existing right of way under R.S. 2477, the court proceeded to mesh that right with the interim management scheme of § 603(c).

In the meantime, shortly after the Reagan Administration had taken office, its new Solicitor issued an opinion modifying the 1978 opinion discussed in Utah v. Andrus; see 88 I.D. 909 (1981). The new opinion focused on the "savings clause" in FLPMA that made "[a]ll actions by the Secretary * * * under this Act * * * subject to valid existing rights." § 701(h); 43 U.S.C. § 1701 note. In conformity with this opinion, BLM modified its Interim Management Policy to provide, in pertinent part (quoted at 848 F.2d at 1086):

> Valid existing rights limit the nonimpairment standard. Although the nonimpairment standard remains the norm, valid existing rights that include the right to develop may not be restricted to the point where the restriction unreasonably interferes with the enjoyment of the benefit of the right. Resolution of specific cases will depend upon the nature of the rights conveyed and the site-specific conditions involved. When it is determined that the rights conveyed can be exercised only through activities that will impair wilderness suitability, the activities will be regulated to prevent unnecessary or undue degradation. Nevertheless, even if such activities impair the area's wilderness suitability, they will be allowed to proceed.

The Tenth Circuit approved this approach (848 F.2d at 1087–88):

> Sierra Club * * * contends that "valid existing rights," including rights-of-way, are subject to the nonimpairment standard regardless of how they are exercised. This argument perhaps is supported by the plain language of § 603(c). * * * We nevertheless uphold the district court's determination that valid existing rights are exempt from the nonimpairment standard. * * *
>
> The conflict between FLPMA's savings provisions [protecting "valid existing rights"] and the nonimpairment standard of § 603(c) constitutes a latent ambiguity in the statute. * * * BLM * * * [has] reconciled FLPMA's express protection of valid existing rights with the conservation duties under § 603(c) by analogizing the valid existing rights to the grandfathered uses and affording them the same protections. We uphold this interpretation as a reasonable one.

The Tenth Circuit went on to affirm the district court order that the county apply for a right-of-way permit under FLPMA in order to move the road in question from an area known as The Gulch to another location on an adjacent bench. The lower court had made this order based on its finding that, while the county had a "valid existing right" to the existing road in the Gulch area, a significant upgrading of that road in that location would "unreasonably or unduly degrade the adjacent WSA * * *." The

Tenth Circuit approved the trial judge's fine-tuned accommodation of "valid existing rights" with protection of wilderness values (848 F.2d at 1088):

> Although the district court ordered the County to apply to BLM for a permit to move the road, we do not construe that order to mean that BLM may deny the permit, or impose conditions it might [impose] on ordinary right-of-way requests under FLPMA which would keep the County from improving the road. Rather, the effect of the order is to require BLM to specify where on the bench the road should be located in order that it make the least degrading impact on the WSA, the court having already determined that location on the bench would be less degrading than in the Gulch. * * * [W]e are satisfied that BLM * * * must allow the road improvement in one place or the other. So construed, we have no problems with the [lower] court's order. This did not end the matter, however, because the court then addressed whether NEPA applied to the BLM's regulatory decision in applying the "unnecessary or undue degradation" standard to the county's valid existing right. Here it agreed with the Sierra Club that the BLM's duty to regulate injects an element of federal control for required action that elevates this situation to one of major federal action [subject to NEPA]. * * * [A]s to improvement on rights-of-way affecting WSAs, while BLM may not deny improvements because they impair WSAs, it retains a duty to see that they do not unduly degrade. * * * Thus, when a proposed road improvement will impact a WSA the agency has a duty under FLPMA § 603(c) * * * to determine whether there are less degrading alternatives, and it has the responsibility to impose an alternative it deems less degrading upon the nonfederal actor. While this obligation is limited by BLM's inability to deny the improvement altogether, it is sufficient, we hold, to invoke NEPA requirements.

848 F.2d at 1090–91. The court rejected BLM's argument, based on the *Alaska Wolf Kill* cases (see Chapter 5, supra p. 411), that BLM's "inaction" in letting the county road improvement go forward does not trigger NEPA. The Alaska cases, said the court, involved a decision by the Secretary "not to exercise its permissive authority under FLPMA § 302(b) * * * to regulate a state-sponsored wolf kill on federal land." Here, "[i]n contrast, the Secretary's nondegradation duty toward WSAs is mandatory." Id.

In Colorado Envt'l Coalition v. Bureau of Land Management, 932 F.Supp. 1247 (D.Colo.1996), the court rejected plaintiffs' request to enjoin construction of a .4 mile spur from an existing right of way and the drilling of two wells on a portion of a federal oil and gas lease located within a BLM WSA. The lease had been issued 6 years before FLPMA, and a well on the lease (but outside the WSA) had been producing gas since 1977. The court followed *Sierra Club v. Hodel* and found that the lease and road spur (located entirely on the leased land) were valid existing rights exempt from the "non-impairment" standard of § 603. The court noted that BLM did have an obligation under § 302(b) to regulate to protect against unnecessary or undue degradation, and held that the record, which included an environmental assessment and several pages of mitigation requirements, showed BLM had adequately exercised its authority.

The Solicitor's Opinion cited in *Utah v. Andrus* dealt with a broad range of legal issues arising out of § 603. It was subjected to harsh criticism in some quarters; e.g., Pamela A. Ray & Craig Carver, Section 603 of the Federal Land Policy and Management Act: An Analysis of the BLM's Wilderness Study Policy, 21 Ariz.L.Rev. 373 (1979); a reply by one of the Opinion's authors is found at John Leshy, Wilderness and Its Discontents: Wilderness Review Comes to the Public Lands, 1981 Ariz.St.L.J. 361.

Shortly after the district court opinion in *Utah v. Andrus*, and with guidance from the Solicitor, BLM promulgated its so-called IMP, or "Interim Management Policy and Guidelines for Lands Under Wilderness Review." Among other things, the IMP said that activities may be deemed nonimpairing if they are "temporary." It defined "temporary" as where the impacts are "capable of being reclaimed to a condition of being substantially unnoticeable in the wilderness study area * * * as a whole by the time the Secretary is scheduled to send his recommendations on that area to the President." The objective was, according to the IMP, to avoid "significantly constrain[ing] the Secretary's recommendation with respect to the area's suitability or nonsuitability for preservation as wilderness."

In Sierra Club v. Clark, 774 F.2d 1406 (9th Cir.1985), challenging the Barstow to Las Vegas motorcycle race (see Chapter 11, pp. 998–99 supra), the plaintiffs attacked the BLM's decision to allow the race despite its adverse impacts on a WSA. The court conceded the adverse impacts, but upheld BLM's determination that they were not "sufficiently egregious" to violate the IMP standard. It permitted the race to proceed because its impacts would be substantially unnoticeable "in the context of the WSA as a whole—not on a parcel-by-parcel basis." Does the BLM's interpretation, which the Court allowed to stand, mean that the larger the wilderness study area, the greater the impact allowed on any one part of it?

Numerous questions remain regarding the IMP. For example, may the BLM open up a previously ungrazed WSA to livestock grazing, arguing that this does not impair its suitability for preservation as wilderness because livestock grazing is itself allowed in designated wilderness? See Committee for Idaho's High Desert, 108 IBLA 277 (1989). The Interior Board of Land Appeals has decided numerous other challenges to BLM decisions implementing its IMP in a wide variety of contexts; see, e.g., Wilderness Soc., 90 IBLA 221 (1986); Mesa Wind Developers, 113 IBLA 61 (1990).

The BLM wilderness bill enacted by Congress for Arizona contains "release" language that provides, with a couple of specific exceptions, that all the WSAs in Arizona not designated as wilderness by that bill "are no longer subject to" the non-impairment standard of § 603(c). 104 Stat. 4469 (1990). Congress followed the same model (generic release except for about 300,000 acres in 7 specified units) in section 104 of the big California Desert legislation enacted in 1994, which designated 3.6 million acres of BLM land as wilderness. See 108 Stat. 4482–83. While this approach releases BLM from any mandatory obligation to protect the wilderness qualities of these areas, it does not prevent BLM from managing these areas as *de facto* wilderness or reconsidering whether to recommend that any of them be designated as wilderness in future BLM land use planning. It remains to be seen whether the Congress will follow these precedents in future BLM wilderness bills.

The BLM's regulations for management of designated wilderness areas under its jurisdiction are found at 43 C.F.R. Part 6300 (2001).

THE FUTURE

How many wilderness areas does the nation need? When asked this question long ago, Bob Marshall, one of the founders of the Wilderness Society, countered: "How many Brahms symphonies do we need?" But some oppose any wilderness at all, or say enough has already been designated. While the future, as the wag says, lies ahead, it seems likely that most future controversies over management of federal lands will not involve controversies between the traditional adversaries—ranchers, loggers, miners pitted against recreationists and environmentalists.

Jan G. Laitos & Thomas A. Carr, The Transformation on Public Lands*

26 Ecology L.Q. 140, 214–216.

* * * [C]onsumptive use of public lands is falling. While timber, mining, oil and gas, and grazing operations will continue on federal lands, their dwindling impact should elicit less interest from both public land managers and environmental organizations. Multiple-use agencies, as well as the environmental proponents that have traditionally sued them, should find their attention being drawn to a different kind of controversy. Future public lands battles are likely to be a consequence of the emerging dominant use reality of recreation and preservation uses. Advocates for each are now discovering that these two nonconsumptive uses are in fact largely incompatible. These interests formerly were allies in the fight against commodity users. When asked to referee and resolve this conflict, the two major multiple-use agencies, BLM and the Forest Service, will have little experience, and even less statutory guidance.

Recreation and preservation intersect at several points along the spectrum of public land uses. By far the most disturbing is when outdoor recreation disrupts wildlife. Studies have suggested that recreational activities, such as skiing, mountain biking, off-road vehicle use, and even hiking, contribute more to species endangerment and habitat destruction than resource extractive activities. This concern about recreational impacts on wildlife becomes evident when ski resorts seek to expand their boundaries within Forest Service lands. For example, after the Colorado ski resorts of Vail and Loveland proposed an expansion of their skiing areas, opposition

---

* Reprinted with permission.

to these proposals came mainly from the state wildlife division, which feared the changes would be detrimental to prime lynx and wolverine habitat. Apart from wildlife issues, the Forest Service has also become alarmed at the growing number of whitewater rafters and rock climbers in national forests. As a result, it has called for dramatic cuts in river tourism and outfitters on certain rivers, as well as a ban on fixed anchors for climbers in certain wilderness areas. When federal agencies fail to rein in use of motorized recreational vehicles, they may be subject to litigation initiated by preservationist organizations.

Future conflicts about nonconsumptive uses of public lands will not be limited to the recreation versus preservation issue. Within the class of recreational users, there is a sharp division between recreation that is soft-impact (non-motorized) and hard-impact (motorized). Off-road vehicles, snowmobiles, jet skis, and tour planes are increasingly being challenged by non-motorized recreational users—hikers, swimmers, cross country skiers, and tourists using horses and llamas. The focal point of this challenge is often a federal lands agency that must choose, with virtually no statutory guidance other than a vague multiple-use standard, between these incompatible recreational uses of public lands. These agencies must also decide when the lands under their jurisdiction have exceeded their carrying capacity—when the influx of visitors and competition among concessionaires and outfitters endangers both the visitor experience and the ecological health of the area.

INDEX

†